Frommer's®
Caribbean 2003

The Baths, Virgin Gorda, where giant boulders form a series of pools and caves. A great spot for swimming and snorkeling. © M. Timothy O'Keefe Photography.

Beach on the laid-back island of Cayman Brac. See chapter 9. © Stephen Frink/Waterhouse.

Aerial view of Little Bay on the small, secluded island of Anguilla. See chapter 3.
© Susan Pierres Photography.

The sheltered harbor of Gustavia, the capital of St. Barthélemy. See chapter 19.
© Susan Pierres Photography.

The Anse Chastanet reef off St. Lucia (see chapter 22). Other great dive sites are Bonaire (chapter 7), Virgin Gorda (chapter 8), Grand Cayman (chapter 9), Saba (chapter 18), and St. Croix (chapter 26). © *M. Timothy O'Keefe Photography.*

Grand Anse Beach in Grenada, with its clear, calm waters and pure white sand, is two miles of heaven. See chapter 13. © M. Timothy O'Keefe Photography.

The Buccaneer Golf Course in St. Croix offers scenic views and challenging play. See chapter 26. © M. Timothy O'Keefe Photography.

For a different side of Grenada, visit the market in St. George, especially lively on Saturday mornings, with everything from spices to sandals for sale. See chapter 13. © M. Timothy O'Keefe Photography.

Carnival transforms Port-of-Spain, Trinidad, into one big colorful party, complete with dazzling costumes, calypso, and dancing. See chapter 25. © Robert Holmes Photography.

The lush rain forest in Morne Trois Pitons National Park, Dominica, is dotted with hot springs and waterfalls. See chapter 11. © Markham Johnson/Robert Holmes Photography.

A view of Antigua's historic English Harbour from Shirley Heights. The harbor is known for its sailing facilities. See chapter 4. © Susan Pierres Photography.

Nevis's reef-protected Pinney's Beach, a 3-mile strip of golden sand that culminates in a sleepy lagoon. See chapter 21. © Susan Pierres Photography.

A New Star-Rating System & Other Exciting News from Frommer's!

In our continuing effort to publish the savviest, most up-to-date, and most appealing travel guides available, we've added some great new features.

Frommer's guides now include a new **star-rating system.** Every hotel, restaurant, and attraction is rated from 0 to 3 stars to help you set priorities and organize your time.

We've also added **seven brand-new features** that point you to the great deals, in-the-know advice, and unique experiences that separate travelers from tourists. Throughout the guide, look for:

Finds	Special finds—those places only insiders know about
Fun Fact	Fun facts—details that make travelers more informed and their trips more fun
Kids	Best bets for kids—advice for the whole family
Moments	Special moments—those experiences that memories are made of
Overrated	Places or experiences not worth your time or money
Tips	Insider tips—some great ways to save time and money
Value	Great values—where to get the best deals

We've also added a **"What's New"** section in every guide—a timely crash course in what's hot and what's not in every destination we cover.

Here's what the critics say about Frommer's:

Frommer's®

Caribbean

2003

by Darwin Porter & Danforth Prince

Wiley Publishing, Inc.

About the Authors

A native of North Carolina, **Darwin Porter** was a bureau chief for the *Miami Herald* when he was 21, and later worked in television advertising. A veteran travel writer, he is the author of numerous best-selling Frommer's guides, including those to the Bahamas and Bermuda. He is assisted by **Danforth Prince,** formerly of the Paris Bureau of the *New York Times.* They have been frequent travelers to the Caribbean for years, and are intimately familiar with what's good there and what isn't. They have also written *Frommer's Caribbean from $70 a Day,* the most candid and up-to-date guide to budget vacations on the market. In this guide they share their secrets and discoveries with you.

Published by:

Wiley Publishing, Inc.

909 Third Ave.
New York, NY 10022

ISBN 0-7645-6652-0
ISSN 1044-2375

Editor: Amy Lyons
Production Editor: Donna Wright
Cartographer: John Decamillis
Photo Editor: Richard Fox
Production by Wiley Indianapolis Composition Services

Special Sales

For information on our other products and services or to obtain technical support, please contact our Customer Care Department within the U.S. at 800-762-2974, outside the U.S. at 317-572-3993 or fax 317-572-4002.

Wiley also publishes its books in a variety of electronic formats. Some content that appears in print may not be available in electronic formats.

Manufactured in the United States of America

5   4   3

Contents

List of Maps

The Disappearance of Claudia Kirschhoch

Claudia Kirschhoch, an assistant editor for Frommer's Travel Guides, went on a Sandals Resort press trip with a group of journalists on May 24, 2000. The itinerary was originally New York City to Cuba by way of Montego Bay, Jamaica. The American journalists were unexpectedly denied entry into Cuba. Because all return flights to New York were full, Claudia stayed on in Jamaica, at Sandals' Beaches Negril, expecting to depart on her scheduled return flight to New York on June 1, 2000.

The last confirmed sighting of Claudia was at the resort on Saturday, May 27, 2000. Her luggage, purse, passport, cash, credit cards, and camera were found in her room. Claudia was 29 years old at the time of her disappearance. She is 5'2" tall and 105 pounds, with long dark brown hair, brown eyes, and fair skin. If you have any information, please contact the police department in Jamaica at © **888/991-4000** or the information hot line in the U.S. at © **888/967-9300.** For more information about Claudia and the latest media coverage of her disappearance, please visit the "Find Claudia" website at http://find claudia.homestead.com.

Frommer's is fully supportive of the ongoing investigation. Because we do not know the full story of Claudia's disappearance, Frommer's is not currently advising travelers against visiting Jamaica. According to the Bureau of Consular Affairs, however, crime is a serious problem in Jamaica. Thus, we encourage you to consult the bureau's website (http://travel.state.gov) for Consular Information Sheets, travel advisories, and safety tips. Our readers' safety is important to us, and we will continue to provide you with pertinent information to assist your safe and happy travel experiences.

An Invitation to the Reader

In researching this book, we discovered many wonderful places—hotels, restaurants, shops, and more. We're sure you'll find others. Please tell us about them, so we can share the information with your fellow travelers in upcoming editions. If you were disappointed with a recommendation, we'd love to know that, too. Please write to:

Frommer's Caribbean 2003
Wiley Publishing, Inc. • 909 Third Avenue • New York, NY 10022

An Additional Note

Please be advised that travel information is subject to change at any time—and this is especially true of prices. We therefore suggest that you write or call ahead for confirmation when making your travel plans. The authors, editors, and publisher cannot be held responsible for the experiences of readers while traveling. Your safety is important to us, however, so we encourage you to stay alert and be aware of your surroundings. Keep a close eye on cameras, purses, and wallets, all favorite targets of thieves and pickpockets.

New! Frommer's Star Ratings & Icons

Every hotel, restaurant, and attraction listing in this guide has been ranked for quality, value, service, amenities, and special features using a star-rating scale. In country, state, and regional guides, we also rate towns and regions to help you narrow down your choices and budget your time accordingly. Hotels and restaurants in the Very Expensive and Expensive categories are rated on a scale of one (highly recommended) to three stars (exceptional). Those in the Moderate and Inexpensive categories rate from zero (recommended) to two stars (very highly recommended). Attractions, towns, and regions are rated according to the following scale: zero stars (recommended), one star (highly recommended), two stars (very highly recommended), and three stars (must-see).

In addition to the rating system, we also use seven icons to highlight insider information, useful tips, special bargains, hidden gems, memorable experiences, kid-friendly venues, places to avoid, and other useful information:

Finds   *Fun Fact*   *Kids*   *Moments*   *Overrated*   *Tips*   *Value*

The following abbreviations are used for credit cards:

AE American Express	DISC Discover	V Visa
DC Diners Club	MC MasterCard	

FROMMERS.COM

Now that you have the guidebook to a great trip, visit our website at **www.frommers.com** for travel information on nearly 2,500 destinations. With features updated regularly, we give you instant access to the most current trip-planning information available. At Frommers.com, you'll also find the best prices on airfares, accommodations, and car rentals—and you can even book travel online through our travel booking partners. At Frommers.com, you'll also find the following:

- Online updates to our most popular guidebooks
- Vacation sweepstakes and contest giveaways
- Newsletters highlighting the hottest travel trends
- Online travel message boards with featured travel discussions

What's New in the Caribbean

ANGUILLA One of the most enduringly popular hotels on island, Cinnamon Reef Resort, flies new colors as the restored **Enclave at Cinnamon Reef** (© 800/223-1108 or 264/497-2727), under new management. It's still intimate and luxurious, but with better rooms and a finer cuisine, and, as such, hopes to retain its habitués of the past and gain new admirers in its stylish new dress. See chapter 3.

ANTIGUA B&B aficionados are flocking to Antigua to check into **Ocean Inn** (© 268/463-7950), the first world-class B&B ever to open on this island. Cozy and homelike in decor, its rooms overlook the marina at English Harbour, where Lord Nelson used to arrive with his fleet of ships. Either in the main building or in cottages on site, guests are housed in comfort in one of the island's most atmospheric places to stay.

On the culinary front, **HQ** (© 268/562-2563), has also opened at Nelson's Dockyard at English Harbour. This invasion comes from an Aussie who has imported a fusion cuisine, with lots of Pacific Rim dishes, to these once-staid shores. Darryn Pitman now challenges all independent chefs for island supremacy in the kitchen. See chapter 4.

ARUBA More changes and openings are occurring on this island than anywhere else in the southern Caribbean. For the upmarket, the number one hotel choice for golfers is now the **Tierra del Sol Aruba Resort & Country Club** (© 297/8-67800), which features luxurious villa living with a world-class fitness center and spa on 600 landscaped acres (40 hectares) with a Robert Trent Jones, Jr. designed golf course. You live in two- or three-bedroom luxury condos or else in free-standing villas.

Local eateries are opening to lure guests away from the megaresorts along the beach. Chief among these is **Cuba's Cookin'** (© 297/8-80627), in Oranjestad. Pre-Castro Cuba lives on here and the food is really savory. Seafood just caught by the owner is featured at the new **Driftwood** (© 297/8-32515), also in Oranjestad. In an antique Aruban house, you can feast on the day's catch such as wahoo or mahi-mahi. See chapter 5.

BARBADOS The biggest hotel news in all the southern Caribbean involves the opening of the completely rebuilt **Sandy Lane Hotel & Golf Club** (© 246/444-2000), the single most luxurious hotel in this part of the world. Bouncing back and better than ever, the new Sandy Lane is almost identical in appearance to its original incarnation, but with the addition of a mammoth spa, better restaurants, and a trio of world-class golf courses. It's been an instant success in its reincarnated form. See chapter 6.

BONAIRE A pocket of posh has opened to attract the discerning traveler—often a diver—who might normally have checked into the *luxe* Harbour Village Beach Resort, which has closed to go condo. The aptly named **Deep Blue View** (© 599/ 717-8073), houses its guests in beautifully furnished private villas with a large patio and swimming pool, ideal for honeymooners or other romantically inclined couples. It's personalized, luxurious, and oh, so private. See chapter 7.

GRAND CAYMAN This has always been known as a pricey island, relieved somewhat by **Sleep Inn** with its affordable prices. The 121-unit resort is still there, except that it's now reincarnated as **The Cayman Inn and Resort** (© 345/949-9111), lying 250 feet from the sands, and the closest hotel along Seven Mile Beach to the center of George Town, capital of the Cayman Islands. See chapter 9.

CURAÇAO The tired old Princess Beach Resort is fresh and new again in its reincarnation as **Breezes Curaçao** (© 599/9-7367888), the first major all-inclusive hotel to open on this Dutch island. Boasting the largest on-island casino, it lies adjacent to the Undersea National Park, and is a high-energy hotel with restored rooms and an upgraded cuisine. See chapter 10.

GRENADA The biggest development—and the latest—on this southern Caribbean island is the opening of **Laluna** (© 473/439-001) on the extreme southern tip of Grenada. It evokes a resort you'd encounter in Bali. Covered in thatch, a cluster of 16 cottages are beautifully furnished and

lie within a 2-minute walk from a beach of golden sand. See chapter 13.

ST. LUCIA Just as he swept Jamaica with its all-inclusive, couples-only resorts, hotelier Butch Stewart is also making inroads with the same style properties on this island. In a development that caught local competitors by surprise, **Sandals** (© 800/SANDALS) took over one of the island's most prestigious hotels, the Hyatt Regency St. Lucia, and transformed it into the new **Sandals Grand St. Lucian Beach Resort,** opening for business in the summer of 2002. This makes a total of three Sandals footprints on St. Lucian beachfronts, since Stewart also operates two other all-inclusives on that island. This big new acquisition lies at the northern tip of St. Lucia on Pigeon Island.

ST. MAARTEN/ST MARTIN On the Dutch side of this Dutch-French island, **La Vista** (© 599/54-43005), a new hotel, is creating a stir. This is a small West Indian–style complex at the foot of Pelican Cay, offering a huge diversity of bedrooms ranging from junior suites to one-bedroom Antillean cottages with front porches housing up to four guests.

Some of the island's best food is found at the new **Turtle Bar Pier & Restaurant** (© 599/54-52562), opening onto Simpson Bay. American dishes are prominently featured, but it's the fresh seafood that keeps them coming. Wednesday is lobster night. See chapter 23.

Choosing the Perfect Island: The Best of the Caribbean

In the Caribbean, you can hike through national parks and scuba dive along underwater mountains. But perhaps your idea of the perfect island vacation is to plunk yourself down on the sands with a frosted drink in hand. Whether you want a veranda with a view of the sea or a plantation house set in a field of sugarcane, this chapter will help you choose the lodgings that best suit your needs. Whether you're looking for a rum-and-reggae cruise or an utterly quiet evening, read on.

For a thumbnail portrait of each island, see "The Islands in Brief," in chapter 2.

1 The Best Beaches

Good beaches with soul-warming sun, crystal-clear waters, and fragrant sea air can be found on virtually every island of the Caribbean, with the possible exceptions of Saba (which has rocky shores) and Dominica (where the few beaches have dramatically black sands that reflect the hot sun).

- **Shoal Bay** (Anguilla): This luscious stretch of silvery sand helped put Anguilla on the world tourism map. Snorkelers are drawn to the schools of iridescent fish that dart among the coral gardens offshore. You can also take the trail walk from Old Ta to little-known Katouche Beach, which offers perfect snorkeling and is also a prime site for a beach picnic under shade trees. See chapter 3.
- **The Beaches of Antigua:** Legend has it that there is a beach here for every day of the year, though we haven't bothered to count them. Antiguans claim, with justifiable pride, that their two best beaches are Dickenson Bay, in the northwest corner of the island, and Half

Moon Bay, which stretches for a white sandy mile along the eastern coast. Chances are your hotel will be built directly on or near a strip of white sand, as nearly all major hotels open onto a good beach. See chapter 4.

- **Palm Beach** (Aruba): This superb strip of white sand is what put Aruba on the tourist map in the first place. Several publications, including *Condé Nast,* have hailed it as 1 of the 12 best beaches in the *world.* It's likely to be crowded in winter, but for swimming, sailing, or fishing, it's idyllic. See chapter 5.
- **The Gold Coast** (Barbados): Some of the finest beaches in the Caribbean lie along the so-called Gold Coast of Barbados, site of some of the swankiest deluxe hotels in the northern hemisphere. Our favorites include Paynes Bay, Brandon's Beach, Paradise Beach, and Brighton Beach, all open to the public. See chapter 6.
- **Cane Garden Bay** (Tortola, British Virgin Islands): One of the

The Caribbean Islands

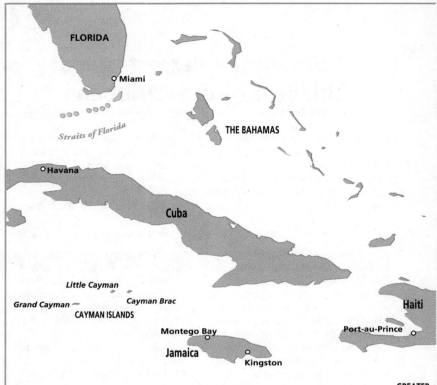

FLORIDA

Miami

Straits of Florida

THE BAHAMAS

Havana

Cuba

Little Cayman

Grand Cayman — Cayman Brac

CAYMAN ISLANDS

Haiti

Port-au-Prince

Montego Bay

Jamaica   Kingston

GREATER

Caribbean Sea

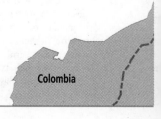

Colombia

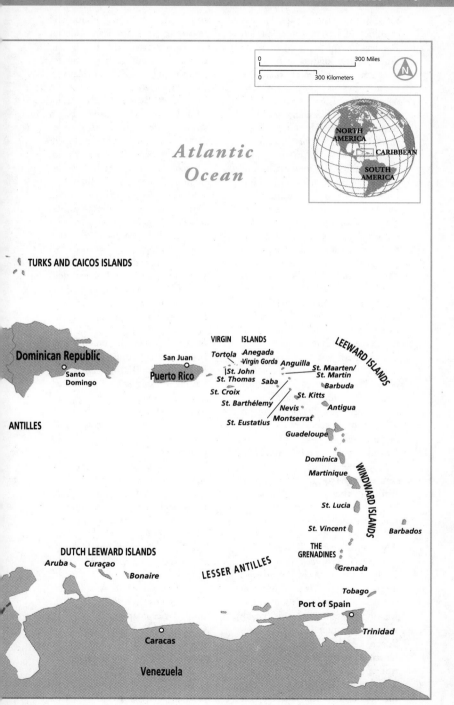

Atlantic Ocean

NORTH AMERICA
CARIBBEAN
SOUTH AMERICA

0   300 Miles
0   300 Kilometers

TURKS AND CAICOS ISLANDS

Dominican Republic

Santo Domingo

ANTILLES

San Juan

Puerto Rico

VIRGIN   ISLANDS

Tortola   Anegada
           Virgin Gorda   Anguilla
St. John   St. Maarten/
St. Thomas   Saba   St. Martin
St. Croix   Barbuda
St. Barthélemy   St. Kitts
              Nevis   Antigua
St. Eustatius   Montserrat

LEEWARD ISLANDS

Guadeloupe

Dominica
Martinique

WINDWARD ISLANDS

St. Lucia

St. Vincent   Barbados

THE GRENADINES

DUTCH LEEWARD ISLANDS
Aruba   Curaçao   Grenada
              Bonaire

LESSER ANTILLES

Tobago

Port of Spain

Trinidad

Caracas

Venezuela

Caribbean's most spectacular stretches of beach, Cane Garden Bay has 1½ miles (2km) of white sand and is a jogger's favorite. It's a much better choice than the more obvious (and crowded) Magens Bay beach on neighboring St. Thomas. See chapter 8.

- **Seven Mile Beach** (Grand Cayman, Cayman Islands): It's really about 5½ miles (9km) long, but who's counting? Lined with condos and plush resorts, this beach is known for its array of watersports and its translucent aquamarine waters. Australian pines dot the background, and the average winter temperature of the water is a perfect 80°F. See chapter 9.

- **The Beaches of the Dominican Republic:** There are two great beach options here: the beaches of resort-riddled Punta Cana at the easternmost tip of the island or the beaches at Playa Dorada along the northern coast, which fronts the Atlantic. Punta Cana is a 20-mile (32km) strip of oyster-white sands set against a backdrop of palm trees, and Playa Dorada is filled with beaches of white or beige sands. See chapter 12.

- **Grand Anse Beach** (Grenada): This 2-mile (3km) beach is reason enough to go to Grenada. Although the island has some 45 beaches, most with white sand, this is the fabled one, and rightly so. There's enough space and so few visitors that you'll likely find a spot just for yourself. The sugary sands of Grand Anse extend into deep waters far offshore. Most of the island's best hotels are within walking distance of this beach strip. See chapter 13.

- **Seven Mile Beach** (Negril, Jamaica): In the northwestern section of the island, this beach stretches for 7 miles (11km) along the sea, and in the backdrop lie

some of the most hedonistic resorts in the Caribbean. Not for the conservative, the beach also contains some nudist patches along with bare-all Booby Cay offshore. See chapter 15.

- **Diamond Beach** (Martinique): This bright, white sandy beach stretches for about 6½ miles (10km) , much of it undeveloped. It faces a rocky offshore island, Diamond Rock, which has uninhabited shores. See chapter 16.

- **Luquillo Beach** (Puerto Rico): This crescent-shaped public beach, 30 miles (48km) east of San Juan, is the local favorite. Much photographed because of its white sands and coconut palms, it also has tent sites and picnic facilities. The often-fierce waters of the Atlantic are subdued by the coral reefs protecting the crystal-clear lagoon. See chapter 17.

- **St-Jean Beach** (St. Barthélemy): A somewhat narrow, golden sandy beach, St. Jean is the gem of the island, reminiscent of the French Riviera (though you're supposed to keep your top on). The beach strip is protected by reefs, which makes it ideal for swimming. See chapter 19.

- **The Beaches of St. Maarten/St. Martin:** Take your pick. This island, divided about equally between France and the Netherlands, has 36 white sandy beaches. Our favorites include Dawn Beach, Mullet Bay Beach, Maho Bay Beach, and Great Bay Beach on the Dutch side. Orient Beach is another standout—not because of its sands but because of the nudists. See chapter 23.

- **Canouan** (the Grenadines): Most of the other beaches recommended in this section have been discovered and may be crowded in winter. But if you're looking for an idyllic, secluded stretch of perfect white sand, head for the remote and tiny island of Canouan, one of the pearls of the Grenadines, a string of islands lying south of its parent, St. Vincent. You'll have the beaches and the crystal-clear waters to yourself, even in winter. See chapter 24.

- **The Beaches of Tobago** (Tobago): For your Robinson Crusoe holiday in the southern Caribbean, head for the little island of Tobago. Even Trinidadians fly over here on weekends to enjoy the beach life. It doesn't get any better than a long coral beach called Pigeon Point on the northwestern coast. Other

good beaches on Tobago include Back Bay (site of an old coconut plantation) and Man-O-War Bay, known for its beautiful natural harbor and long stretch of sand. See chapter 25.

- **Trunk Bay** (St. John): Protected by the U.S. National Park Service, this beach is one of the Caribbean's most popular. A favorite with cruise-ship passengers, it's known for its underwater snorkeling trail, where markers guide you along the reef just off the white sands; you're sure to see a gorgeous rainbow of tropical fish. See chapter 26.

2 The Best Snorkeling

The Virgin Islands offer some particularly outstanding sites, but there are many other great places for snorkeling in the Caribbean.

- **Antigua:** This island is a snorkeler's dream. Most of its lovely beaches open onto clear, calm waters that are populated by rainbow-hued tropical fish. The marine life offshore is particularly dense, including gentle manta rays and colorful sea anemones. The rich types of different elk and brain coral make snorkeling a particularly rewarding adventure. See chapter 4.
- **Bonaire Marine Park** (Bonaire): All the attributes that make Bonaire a world-class diving destination apply to its snorkeling, too. Snorkelers can wade from the shores off their hotels to the reefs and view an array of coral and a range of colorful fish. The reefs just off Klein Bonaire and Washington/Slagbaai Park receive especially rave reviews. See chapter 7.
- **Stingray City** (Grand Cayman): Stingray City is an easy 12-foot (4m) diving site that can also be seen while snorkeling. It's an

extraordinary experience to meet the dozens of tame, gentle stingrays that glide around you in the warm, crystal-clear waters. See chapter 9.

- **Curaçao Underwater Marine Park** (Curaçao): In contrast to Curaçao's arid terrain, the marine life that rings the island is rich and spectacular. The best-known snorkeling sites, in the Curaçao Underwater Marine Park, stretch for 12½ miles (20km) along Curaçao's southern coastline, and there are many other highly desirable sites as well. Sunken ships, gardens of hard and soft coral, and millions of fish are a snorkeler's treat. See chapter 10.
- **St. Martin:** The best snorkeling on the island lies on the French side, where the government religiously protects the calm waters, which are populated with schools of brilliantly colored fish. Find a tiny cove and explore the shallow reefs along its shores, especially in the northeastern underwater nature reserve, which is ideal for snorkelers. See chapter 23.
- **The Grenadines:** Every island offers great snorkeling possibilities

right off of magnificent white sandy beaches. In most places you'll have the waters to yourself. A reef stretching for a mile along white sands on the island of Canouan invites snorkelers, and the waters are filled with beautiful brain coral and rainbow-hued fish. The snorkeling is also good at Palm Island and Petit St. Vincent. See chapter 24.

- **Tobago:** The shallow, sun-dappled waters off the Latin American coastline boast enormous colonies of marine life. Buccoo Reef on Tobago is especially noteworthy, and many local entrepreneurs offer snorkeling cruises. See chapter 25.
- **Coki Point Beach** (St. Thomas): On the north shore of St. Thomas, this beach offers year-round snorkeling, especially around the coral ledges near Coral World's underwater tower, a favorite with cruise-ship passengers. See chapter 26.
- **Buck Island** (St. Croix): More than 250 species of fish, as well as a variety of sponges, corals, and crustaceans, have been found at this 850-acre (340-hectare) island and reef system, 2 miles (3km) off St. Croix's north shore. The reef is strictly protected by the National Park Service. See chapter 26.

- **Cane Bay** (St. Croix): One of the best diving and snorkeling sites on St. Croix is off this breezy north-shore beach. On a clear day, you can swim out 150 yards (137m) and see the Cane Bay Wall that drops off dramatically to deep waters below. Multicolored fish and elkhorn and brain coral are in abundance here. See chapter 26.
- **Trunk Bay** (St. John): Trunk Bay's self-guided 225-yard-long (205m) trail has large underwater signs that identify species of coral and other items of interest. The beach offers showers, changing rooms, equipment rentals, and a lifeguard. See chapter 26.
- **Leinster Bay** (St. John): With easy access from land and sea, Leinster Bay is filled with calm, clear, and uncrowded waters, with an abundance of sea life. See chapter 26.
- **Haulover Bay** (St. John): A favorite with locals, this small bay is rougher than Leinster and is often deserted. The snorkeling is dramatic, with ledges, walls, nooks, and sandy areas set close together. At this spot, only about 200 yards (182m) separate the Atlantic Ocean from the Caribbean Sea. See chapter 26.

3 The Best Diving

All the major islands offer diving trips, lessons, and equipment, but here are the top picks.

- **Bonaire:** The highly accessible reefs that surround Bonaire have never suffered from poaching or pollution, and the island's environmentally conscious diving industry will ensure that they never do. Created from volcanic eruptions, the island is an underwater mountain, with fringe reefs right off the beach of every hotel

on any part of the island. See chapter 7.
- **Virgin Gorda:** Many divers plan their entire vacations around exploring the famed wreck of the HMS *Rhone,* off Salt Island. This royal mail steamer, which went down in 1867, is the most celebrated diving site in the Caribbean. See chapter 8.
- **Grand Cayman:** This is a world-class diving destination. There are 34 dive operators on Grand

Cayman (with 5 more on Little Cayman, plus 3 on Cayman Brac). A full range of professional diving services is available, including equipment sales, rentals, and repairs; instruction at all levels; underwater photography; and video schools. See chapter 9.

- **Saba:** Islanders can't brag about its beaches, but Saba is blessed with some of the Caribbean's richest marine life. It's one of the premier diving locations in the Caribbean, with 38 official diving sites. The unusual setting includes underwater lava flows, black sand, large strands of black coral, millions of fish, and underwater mountaintops submerged under 90 feet (27m) of water. See chapter 18.

- **St. Croix:** Increasingly known as a top diving destination, St. Croix hasn't overtaken Grand Cayman yet, but it has a lot going for it. Beach dives, reef dives, wreck dives, nighttime dives, wall dives—they're all here. But the highlight is the underwater trails of the national park at Buck Island, off St. Croix's mainland. Other desirable sites include the drop-offs and coral canyons at Cane Bay and Salt River. Davis Bay is the location of the 12,000-foot-deep (3,600m) Puerto Rico Trench, the fifth-deepest body of water on earth. See chapter 26.

4 The Best Sailing

Virtually every large-scale hotel in the Caribbean provides small sailboats (especially Sunfish, Sailfish, and small, one-masted catamarans) for its guests. If you're looking for larger craft, the Virgin Islands and the Grenadines come instantly to mind for their almost-ideal sailing conditions. These two regions offer many options for dropping anchor at secluded coves surrounded by relatively calm waters. Both areas are spectacular, but whereas the Virgin Islands offer more dramatic, mountainous terrain, the Grenadines offer insights into island cultures little touched by the modern world.

Other places to sail in the Caribbean include Antigua, Barbados, St. Martin, and the French-speaking islands. But if you plan on doing a lot of sailing, know in advance that the strongest currents and biggest waves are usually on the northern and eastern sides of most islands—the Atlantic (as opposed to the Caribbean) side.

- **The Grenadines:** Boating is a way of life in the Grenadines, partly because access to many of the tiny remote islands is difficult or impossible by airplane. One of the most prominent local charter agents is **Nicholson Yacht Charters** (© **800/662-6066** in the U.S., or 617/661-0555), headquartered in nearby St. Vincent. On Bequia, Mustique, Petit St. Vincent, and Union Island, all the hotels can put you in touch with local entrepreneurs who rent sailing craft. See chapters 2 and 24 for more details.

- **The Virgin Islands:** Perhaps because of their well-developed marina facilities (and those of the nearby United States), the Virgin Islands receive the lion's share of really devoted yachties. The reigning capital for sailing is Tortola, the largest island of the British Virgins. On-site are about 300 well-maintained sailing craft available for bareboat rentals and perhaps 100 charter yachts.

  The largest of the Caribbean's yacht chartering services is **The Moorings** (© **284/494-2332**). This yachting charter center is described more fully in chapter 8, as are the other outfits in this paragraph. If you'd like sailing lessons, consider Tortola's **Treasure Isle Hotel** (© **284/494-2501**), which offers courses in seamanship year-round. (One of Treasure Isle's programs is exclusively on how to sail catamarans.) On the island of Virgin Gorda, in the British Virgin Islands (B.V.I), the best bet for both boat rentals and accommodations, as well as for a range of instruction, is the **Bitter End Yacht Club** (© **800/872-2392** in the U.S., or 284/494-2746).

Some of the biggest charter business in the Caribbean is conducted on St. Thomas, especially at **American Yacht Harbor,** Red Hook (© **340/775-6454**), which offers bareboat and fully crewed charters. Other reliable rental agents include **Charteryacht League,** at Flagship (© **800/524-2061** in the U.S., or 340/774-3944). The U.S. Virgin Islands are covered in chapter 26; look there for more information.

On St. Croix, boating is less a factor in the local economy than it is on St. Thomas or in the British Virgins, so if you're planning a Virgin Islands sailing trip, plan accordingly.

5 The Best Golf Courses

Some of the world's most famous golf architects, including Robert Trent Jones (both Junior and Senior), Pete Dye, and Gary Player, have designed challenging courses in the Caribbean.

- **Tierra del Sol Golf Course** (Aruba; © **297/8-67800**): Robert Trent Jones, Jr. has designed an 18-hole, par-71, 6,811-yard (6,198m) course that is one of the grandest in the southern Caribbean. On the northwest coast of this arid, cactus-studded island, the course takes in Aruba's indigenous flora, including the divi-divi tree. See p. 126.
- **Teeth of the Dog** and **The Links,** both at Casa de Campo (Dominican Republic; © **809/523-3333**): Teeth of the Dog is one of designer Pete Dye's masterpieces. Seven holes are set adjacent to the sea, whereas the other 11 are confoundedly labyrinthine. The resort also has a second golf course, The Links, which some claim is even more difficult. See chapter 12.
- **Golf de St-François** (Guadeloupe; © **590/88-41-87**): Six of its 18 holes are ringed with water traps, the winds are devilishly unpredictable, and the par is a sweat-inducing 71. This fearsome course displays the wit and skill of its designer, Robert Trent Jones, Sr. Most of the staff is multilingual, and because it's owned by the local municipality, it's a lot less snobby than you might expect. See chapter 14.
- **Tryall Club Jamaica** (Montego Bay, Jamaica; © **876/956-5660**): This is the finest golf course on an island known for its tricky breezes. The site occupied by the Tryall Club was once the home of one of Jamaica's best-known sugar plantations, the only remnant of which is a ruined waterwheel. The promoters of Johnnie Walker Scotch, who know a lot about golfing, selected this place for their most prestigious competition. In winter, the course is usually open only to guests of the Tryall Club. See p. 392.
- **Wyndham Rose Hall Golf & Beach Resort** (Rose Hill, Jamaica; © **876/953-2650**): This is one of the top five courses in the world, even though it faces other tough

competition in Montego Bay. The signature hole is number 8, which doglegs onto a promontory and a green that thrusts about 200 yards (182m) into the sea. The back nine, however, is the most scenic and most challenging, rising into steep slopes and deep ravines on Mount Zion. See p. 392.

- **Hyatt Dorado Beach Resort & Casino** (Puerto Rico; ✆ **787/ 796-1234**): This resort maintains two golf courses, both set on what were originally citrus and coconut plantations. Both courses were designed by Robert Trent Jones, Sr. No one can agree on which of the two courses is the more inter- esting, but the elegance of both is breathtaking. If you're an absolute golf glutton, the Hyatt's compan- ion resort, the Cerromar, a short drive down the coastal road, offers an additional pair of golf courses. See p. 504.

- **Doral Palmas del Mar Resort** (Puerto Rico; ✆ **787/852-6000**): Designed by Gary Player, this par- 72 golf course near Humacao is one of the most noteworthy any- where. Its botanical highlights include thousands of mature palm trees and carefully maintained sec- tions of tropical rain forest. The course is so good that many golf- playing retirees have bought homes adjacent to the fairways. The most challenging holes are numbers 11 through 16, although many beginners have lost their tempers over 18 as well. Lessons are offered to players of all levels. See p. 518.

- **Four Seasons Resort Nevis** (Nevis; ✆ **869/469-1111**): We consider this our personal favorite in all of the Caribbean, and so do readers of *Caribbean Travel & Life*. It was carved out of a coconut plantation and tropical rain forest in the 1980s, and its undulating beauty is virtually unequaled. Designed by Robert Trent Jones, Jr., the course begins at sea level, rises to a point midway up the slopes of Mount Nevis, and then slants gracefully back down near the beachfront clubhouse. Electric carts carry golfers through a labyrinth of well-groomed paths, some of which skirt steep ravines. See p. 583.

6 The Best Tennis Facilities

- **Curtain Bluff** (Antigua; ✆ **212/ 289-8888** in New York, or 268/ 462-8400): It's small, select, and carefully run by people who love tennis, and it's also the annual site of a well-known spring tour- nament. The courts are set in a low-lying valley. See p. 94.

- **Casa de Campo** (Dominican Republic; ✆ **809/523-3333**): The facilities here include 13 clay courts (half are lit, and 2 are ringed with stadium seating), 4 all- weather Laykold courts, a resident pro, ball machines, and tennis pros who are usually available to play with guests. During midwinter, residents and clients of Casa de Campo have first crack at court times. See p. 289.

- **Half Moon Golf, Tennis, & Beach Club** (Montego Bay, Jamaica; ✆ **876/953-2211**): This resort sprawls over hundreds of acres, with about a dozen tennis courts and at least four squash and/or racquetball courts. Jamaica has a strong, British-based affinity for tennis, and Half Moon keeps the tradition alive. See p. 393.

- **Wyndham El Conquistador Resort & Country Club** (Puerto Rico; ✆ **787/863-1000**): Facili- ties at this megaresort include seven Har-Tru tennis courts, a resident pro, and a clubhouse with its own bar. If you're looking for a partner, the hotel will find one for you. Only guests of the hotel can use the courts, some of which are illuminated for night play. See p. 516.

- **Hyatt Regency Cerromar Beach/Hyatt Dorado Beach** (Puerto Rico; ✆ **787/796-1234**): These twin beachfront resorts are within a 15-minute walk of each other. There are 15 Laykold tennis courts, some lit, some ringed with stadium seats; all are administered by a tennis pro who gives lessons. If you want pointers on improving your serve or strokes, someone will be on hand to videotape you. These facilities are open only to resort guests. See p. 503.

- **Wyndham Sugar Bay Beach Club** (St. Thomas; ✆ **340/777-7100**): The resort offers the first stadium tennis court in the U.S. Virgin Islands, with a capacity of 220 spectators. In addition, it has about half a dozen Laykold courts, each of which is lit for night play. There's an on-site pro shop, and lessons are available. See p. 722.

- **The Buccaneer** (St. Croix; ✆ **340/773-2100**): Hailed as having the best tennis facilities in the Virgin Islands, this resort hosts several tournaments every year. There are eight all-weather Laykold courts, two of which are illuminated at night; there's also a pro shop. Nonguests can play here for a fee. See p. 744.

7 The Best Honeymoons

More and more couples are exchanging their vows in the Caribbean. Many resorts will arrange everything from the preacher to the flowers, so we've included in the following list some outfits that provide wedding services. For more information about the various options and the legal requirements for marriages on some of the more popular Caribbean islands, see chapter 2.

- **Cap Juluca** (Anguilla; ✆ **888/858-5822** in the U.S., or 264/497-6779): This resort boasts a unique postmodern design, multimillion-dollar decor, and a thrillingly beautiful beach. The result: something like a Saharan Casbah whose domed villas seem to float against the scrubland and azure sky. It's an extremely stylish setting for romance. More than any other resort on Anguilla, Cap Juluca affords the most privacy on its 179 acres (72 hectares). In a private villa, honeymooners enjoy private pools and huge tubs

for two. You can join in dining and sports with other guests or else retreat into total seclusion. See p. 63.

- **St. James's Club** (Antigua; ✆ **800/345-0271** in the U.S., or 954/481-8787): There are enough diversions available at this very posh, British-style resort to keep a honeymoon couple up and about for weeks. Breakfast, lunch, and dinner are included, along with unlimited drinks. Among the perks is a private, candlelit dinner for two in a romantic setting. Honeymooners are offered a choice of private villas, suites, or, for complete seclusion, a hillside home. Honeymooners are greeted with a bottle of champagne and freshly cut bougainvillea in their rooms. Unlike Cap Juluca, which is more into seclusion, this is for honeymooners who prefer an active lifestyle, gambling at the casino, taking in the beach, or enjoying the widest array of dining and drinking options of any hotel on the island. See p. 84.

- **Biras Creek Estate** (Virgin Gorda, B.V.I.; © **800/608-9661** in the U.S., or 284/494-3555): If you're eager to escape your in-laws and bridesmaids after a wedding ceremony, this is the place. It's a quintessential mariner's hideaway that can be reached only via a several-mile boat ride across the open sea. Perched on a narrow promontory jutting into the Caribbean, it's an intensely private retreat set on 150 acres (60 hectares) with a crisscrossing network of signposted nature trails. A couple can get better acquainted in the spacious, open-air, walled showers that are provided in each bathroom. Honeymooners come here not to be pampered, but to be left alone to do their thing. Entertainment and dancing enliven some evenings, but for the most part there is utter tranquility here. Its king-sized beds are the best on the island. *Warning:* Don't come here for a lot of activities. "Honeymooners are into indoor sports here," a hip staffer told us. See p. 202.

- **Peter Island Resort** (Peter Island, B.V.I.; © **800/346-4451** or 284/ 495-2000): Romantics appreciate the isolation of this resort, on a 1,800-acre (720-hectare) private island south of Tortola and east of St. John. Reaching it requires a 30-minute waterborne transfer, which many urban refugees consider part of the fun. It's very laid-back—bring your new spouse and a good book, and enjoy the comings and goings of yachts at the island's private marina while you recover from the stress of your wedding. See p. 213.

- **Hyatt Regency Grand Cayman** (Grand Cayman; © **800/233-1234** or 345/949-1234): Hands down, this is the most glamorous and best-landscaped resort in the Cayman Islands. Honeymooners can buy a package that includes champagne and wine, a room with an oversize bed, a 1-day Jeep rental, a romantic sundowner sail on a 65-foot (12m) catamaran, and discounts at clothing stores, the resort's restaurants, and a golf course. They'll even present you with a honeymoon memento for your home. See p. 220.

- **Sutton Place Hotel** (Dominica; © **767/449-8700**): If you want something completely different, head for the remote island of Dominica. It's an inexpensive destination, with a lush, tropical setting, although the beaches aren't great (there is river swimming instead). Start off your married life at this romantic old place, where Princess Margaret and Noël Coward retreated in days of yore (not together). Opt for one of the top-floor suites for a real romantic getaway, and relax in your four-poster bed. See p. 270.

- **Sandals** (Jamaica; © **800/ SANDALS** in the U.S.): There are a handful of members of this resort chain in Jamaica alone (plus two others on St. Lucia, another luxe one at Cable Beach outside Nassau, and yet another one on the island of Antigua that is far less grand). Each one prides itself on providing an all-inclusive (cash-free) environment where meals are provided in abundance. Enthusiastic members of the staff bring heroic amounts of community spirit to ceremonies celebrated on site. Sandals provides everything from a preacher to petunias (as well as champagne, a cake, and all the legalities) for you to get hitched here. Any of these resorts can provide a suitable setting, but one of the most appealing is **Sandals Royal Caribbean,** outside Montego Bay, Jamaica. See p. 383.

- **The SuperClubs of Jamaica** (© **800/GO-SUPER** in the U.S.): These all-inclusive properties, including the Breezes and the Grand Lido hotels, are for upscale honeymooners who can afford a little more elegance and luxury. They operate somewhat like Sandals, but have far more style and a higher price tag. Prices are high in winter, but when mid-April arrives, rates plummet. SuperClubs, such as Grand Lido and Grand Lido Sans Souci, are scattered between Ocho Rios and Negril. If you pay for the food and room packages, the hotel chain will throw in the wedding for free—it'll provide the license, the witnesses, the minister, and even a two-tier wedding cake. You can be married in the garden or on a white sandy beach. See chapter 15.

- **Wyndham El Conquistador Resort & Country Club** (Puerto Rico; © **800/468-5228** in the U.S., or 787/863-1000): A complex of hotels set on a forested bluff overlooking the sea, this is one of the most lavish resorts ever built in the Caribbean. The architecture incorporates Moorish gardens and Andalusian fortresses. You'll find hammocks for two on the resort's offshore private island, as well as about a dozen private Jacuzzis artfully concealed by vegetation throughout the grounds. See p. 516.

- **Horned Dorset Primavera** (Puerto Rico; © **800/633-1857** in the U.S., or 787/823-4030): This resort, on the western side of Puerto Rico, has a main clubhouse that's reminiscent of an Iberian villa. Great care is lavished on the sophisticated continental and California cuisine, and drinks are

served in a well-stocked library. The comfortable, dignified accommodations contain oversize mahogany beds and large private verandas, with views of lushly planted hillsides sloping down to a narrow sandy beach. See p. 505.

- **Golden Lemon Inn & Villas** (St. Kitts; © **800/633-7411** in the US, or 869/465-7260): It started its life as a French manor house during the 17th century, but by the time its present owners began restoring it, the Golden Lemon was decidedly less glamorous. It required the refined tastes of Arthur Leaman, a former editor at *House & Garden,* to bring it to its full potential. Today the Golden Lemon is an authentic Antillean retreat—luxurious, laid-back, and romantic—set in an isolated fishing village loaded with charm. See p. 562.

- **Four Seasons Resort Nevis** (Nevis; © **800/332-3442** in the U.S., 800/268-6282 in Canada, or 869/469-1111): Though not as historic as some of the island's plantation-style inns, the Four Seasons rules without peer as the most deluxe hotel on the island, with the most extensive facilities. Set in a palm grove adjacent to the island's finest beach, it has the atmosphere of a supremely indulgent country club. The Four Seasons offers a 4-day wedding package with a choice of ceremony styles (in a church or on a beach, with a judge or with a civil magistrate). Each wedding cake is individually designed by the resort's pastry chef, and music, photographs, flowers, legalities, and virtually anything else you want can be arranged by the staff. See p. 575.

- **Anse Chastanet** (St. Lucia; © **800/223-1108** in the U.S., or 758/459-7000): Offering panoramic views of mountains and jungle, this intimate hotel is a winner with romantics. With its small size, it offers a lot of privacy and rustic charm. See p. 591.

- **Petit St. Vincent Resort** (The Grenadines; ✆ **800/654-9326** in the U.S., or 784/458-8801): If your idea of a honeymoon is to run away from everybody except your new spouse, this is the place. It takes about three planes and a boat to reach it, but the effort to get here is worth it, if you want total isolation and privacy. Even the staff doesn't bother you unless you raise a flag for room service. If the honeymoon's going well, you may never have to leave your stone cottage by the beach. The artfully built clubhouses and bungalows were crafted from tropical woods and local stone. The results are simultaneously rustic and lavish. See p. 669.
- **The Cotton House** (The Grenadines; ✆ **800/826-2809** in the U.S., or 784/456-4777): Cosmopolitan and stylish, this hotel was built as a cotton warehouse on the tiny island of Mustique during the 18th century. It's intimate, exclusive, and full of undeniable charm and romance. See p. 664.
- **Le Grand Courlan Resort & Spa** (Tobago; ✆ **800/223-6510** in the U.S., or 868/639-9667): This is the favorite honeymoon retreat on Tobago. If you want to be fussed over, you and your new spouse can attend the spa for "release massages," or you can be left entirely alone to enjoy the bay outside your window or the sandy beach at your doorstep. From Guyanan hardwood to Italian porcelain, the decor is refined elegance. See p. 689.
- **The Buccaneer** (St. Croix; ✆ **800/255-3881** in the U.S., or 340/773-2100): Posh and discreet, this resort boasts some of the most extensive vacation facilities on St. Croix—3 beaches, 8 tennis courts, a spa and fitness center, an 18-hole golf course, and 2 miles (3km) of carefully maintained jogging trails. The accommodations include beachside rooms with fieldstone terraces leading toward the sea. The resort's stone sugar mill (originally built in 1658) is one of the most popular sites for weddings and visiting honeymooners on the island. See p. 733.
- **Hilty House** (St. Croix; ✆ **340/773-2594**): So you don't want a big, expensive resort? Try this romantic little B&B hideaway. As you pass through iron gates into a well-manicured garden, you'll know you've arrived at a special place. That vision is reinforced when you're shown a four-poster bed and a sunken shower. It's a quiet retreat of charm and grace—and the price is right, too. See p. 735.

8 The Best Places to Get Away from It All

In addition to the choices below, see also the listings under "The Best Honeymoons" for additional information on Biras Creek Estate and Peter Island Resort, both in the British Virgin Islands, and the Petit St. Vincent Resort and the Cotton House, both in the Grenadines.

- **Biras Creek Estate** (Virgin Gorda, B.V.I.; ✆ **800/608-9661** in the U.S., or 284/494-3555): The only access to this resort is by private launch. The sea air and the views over islets, cays, and deep blue waters will relax you in your charming guest room. The nautical atmosphere will quickly remove all thoughts of the 9-to-5 job you left behind. See p. 202.

- **Guana Island Club** (Guana Island, B.V.I.; ✆ **800/544-8262** in the U.S., or 284/494-2354): One of the most secluded hideaways in the entire Caribbean, this resort occupies a privately owned 850-acre (340-hectare) bird sanctuary with nature trails. Head here for views of rare plant and animal life and for several excellent uncrowded beaches. See p. 214.

- **Little Cayman Beach Resort** (Cayman Islands; ✆ **800/327-3835** in the U.S. and Canada, or 345/948-1033): The only practical way to reach the 10-square-mile (26 sq. km) island where this resort is located is by airplane. Snorkelers will marvel at some of the most spectacular and colorful marine life in the Caribbean. The resort has the most complete watersports facilities on the island, and bikes are available for exploring. See p. 238.

- **Rawlins Plantation** (St. Kitts; ✆ **800/346-5358** in the U.S., or 869/465-6221): Surrounded by 25 acres (10 hectares) of carefully manicured lawns and tropical shrubbery, and set on a panoramic hillock about 350 feet (105m) above sea level, this hotel evokes a 19th-century plantation with its rugs of locally woven rushes and carved four-poster beds. You'll be separated from the rest of the island by hundreds of acres of sugarcane, and there are few phones and no televisions. See p. 564.

9 The Best Family Vacations

- **Hyatt Regency Aruba Resort & Casino** (Aruba; ✆ **800/233-1234** in the U.S. and Canada, or 297/8-61234): Designed like a luxurious hacienda, with award-winning gardens, this resort is the most upscale on Aruba. Supervised activities for children age 3 to 12 include games and contests such as crab races and hula-hoop competitions. See p. 113.

- **Almond Beach Village** (Barbados; ✆ **246/422-4900**): One of the best programs for kids in the southern Caribbean is found at this hotel set on the site of a 19th-century sugar plantation. There's a nursery, along with children's programs that encompass everything from lessons in Bajan culture to pool activities to computer games, even instruction in reggae. Family suites are available, and babysitting can be arranged at night. See p. 140.

- **Sandy Beach Hotel** (Barbados; ✆ **246/435-8000**): Set amid lots of fast-food and family-style restaurants on the southwest coast, this family-oriented hotel offers one- and two-bedroom suites. Each unit has a kitchen, so you can cook for yourself and save money. The beach is a few steps away, and the ambience is informal. If you bring the kids, they'll have plenty of playmates. See p. 147.

- **Hyatt Regency Grand Cayman** (Grand Cayman Island; ✆ **800/233-1234** in the U.S., or 345/949-1234): Safe and serene, Grand Cayman Island, with its 7-mile (11km) sandy beach, seems designed for families with children. No one coddles children as much as the Hyatt people, who offer not only babysitting but also Camp Hyatt, with an activity-filled agenda, for children age 3 to 12. See p. 220.

- **Negril Cabins Resort** (Negril, Jamaica; ✆ **800/382-3444** in the U.S., or 876/957-5350): Rising on stilts, these wooden cottages with private decks add a sense of adventure to a beach vacation. Surrounded by tropical vegetation, families are only steps from the beach. Features for kids include a playground, computer games, arts and crafts lessons, and even storytelling sessions. Children under age 16 stay free if they share a room with their parents. See p. 402.

- **FDR Pebbles** (Runaway Bay, Jamaica; ✆ **888/FDR-KIDS** in the U.S. or 876/617-2495): FDR gives you a suite with its own kitchen, and a "Vacation Nanny" whose duties include babysitting. Neither its beach nor its pool is the most appealing on Jamaica, but the price is right, and the babysitting is part of the all-inclusive price. Programs for children include dress-up parties, donkey rides, basketball, tennis, and snorkeling. See p. 385.
- **Hyatt Regency Cerromar Beach Hotel** (Puerto Rico; ✆ **800/233-1234** in the U.S. or 787/796-1234): This is the best place for kids in all of Puerto Rico. The big attraction is a water playground that contains the world's longest freshwater swimming pool: It's a 1,776-foot (533m) fantasy pool with 5 different depths, 5 interconnected free-form pools, and 14 waterfalls with tropical landscaping. As if that weren't enough, Hyatt also offers Camp Hyatt, a day camp for kids age 3 to 12. See p. 503.
- **Wyndham El Conquistador** (Puerto Rico; ✆ **800/468-5228**

in the U.S., or 787/863-1000): Children aren't forgotten amid the glamour and hoopla of this fabulous resort. Camp Coquí provides day care daily from 9am to 3pm for children age 3 to 12, at a price of $40 per child per day. Activities include fishing, sailing, arts and crafts, and nature treks. Babysitting services are available, and children age 15 and under stay free in a room with their parents. See p. 516.

- **Four Seasons Resort Nevis** (Nevis; ✆ **800/332-3442** in the U.S., 800/268-6282 in Canada, or 869/469-1111): The staff of the Kids for All Seasons day camp are kindly, matronly souls who work well with children. During the adult cocktail hour, when parents might opt for a romantic sundowner, kids attend a supervised children's hour that resembles a really good birthday bash. Other kid-friendly activities include tennis lessons, water sports, and storytelling. See p. 575.
- **The Buccaneer** (St. Croix; ✆ **800/255-3881** in the U.S., or 340/773-2100): Posh, upscale, and offering extremely good service, this hotel is a longtime favorite that occupies a 240-acre (96-hectare) former sugar estate. Its kids' programs (ages 2–12) include a half-day sailing excursion to Buck Island Reef and guided nature walks that let kids touch, smell, and taste tropical fruit. See p. 733.

10 The Best Inns

- **The Admiral's Inn** (Antigua; ✆ **800/223-5695** in the U.S., or 268/460-1027): The most historically evocative corner of Antigua is Nelson's Dockyard, which was originally built in the 1700s to repair His Majesty's ships. The

brick-and-stone inn that flourishes here today was once a warehouse for turpentine and pitch. In the late 1960s it was transformed into a well-designed and very charming hotel. (But note that if you're sensitive to noise, you might be bothered by the some-times raucous scene in the hotel's bar and restaurant.) See p. 87.

- **Avila Beach Hotel** (Curaçao; © **599/9-4614377**): This hotel's historic core, built in 1780 as the "country house" of the island's governor, retains its dignity and simplicity. Although it's been a hotel since the end of World War II, a new owner added 40 bed-rooms in motel-like outbuildings and upgraded the sports and din-ing facilities in the early 1990s. Today the Avila provides a sandy beach and easy access to the shops and distractions of nearby Willemstad. See p. 247.
- **Spice Island Inn** (Grenada; © 473/444-4258): Each of this hotel's 56 units is a suite (with Jacuzzi) either beside the beach (one of Grenada's best) or near a swimming pool. Friday nights fea-ture live music from the island's most popular bands. See p. 322.
- **François Plantation** (St. Barthél-emy; © **590/29-80-22**): At this inn, about a dozen pastel-colored bungalows are scattered among the lushest gardens on St. Barts. The mood is discreet, permissive, and fun. The food is French inspired and served on a wide veranda decorated in a whimsical colonial style. See p. 536.
- **Ottley's Plantation Inn** (St. Kitts; © **800/772-3039** in the U.S., or 869/465-7234): As you approach, the inn's dignified verandas appear majestically at the crest of 35 acres (14 hectares) of impeccably maintained lawns and gardens. It's one of the most charming plantation-house inns anywhere in the world, main-tained with style and humor by its expatriate U.S. owners. The food is the best on the island, and the setting will soothe your tired

nerves within a few hours after your arrival. See p. 563.
- **Montpelier Plantation Inn & Beach Club** (Nevis; © **869/ 469-3462**): Style and grace are the hallmarks of this former 18th-century plantation, now con-verted to an inn and set on a 100-acre (40-hectare) estate. Guests have included the late Princess of Wales. Cottage rooms are spread across 10 acres (4 hectares) of ornamental gardens. Swimming, horseback riding, windsurfing, a private beach, and "eco-rambles" fill the agenda. See p. 576.
- **Hermitage Plantation** (Nevis; © **800/682-4025** in the U.S., or 869/469-3477): Guests stay in clapboard-sided cottages separated by carefully maintained bougain-villea and grasslands. The beach is a short drive away, but this slice of 19th-century plantation life (com-plete candlelit dinners amid the antiques and polished silver of the main house) is decidedly romantic. See p. 576.
- **Frangipani Hotel** (Bequia, the Grenadines; © **784/458-3255**): This is the century-old homestead of the Mitchell family, whose most famous scion later became prime minister of St. Vincent. Today it's a small, very relaxed inn. It's fun to watch the yachts setting out to sea from the nearby marina. See p. 658.
- **Villa Madeleine** (St. Croix; © **800/496-7379** in the U.S., or 340/778-8782): This recently built, almost perfect re-creation of a 19th-century great house occu-pies the summit of a scrub-covered ridge. The food is among the best on St. Croix. Accommodations include richly furnished hideaway suites with sweeping views over the coastline. See p. 734.

11 The Best Destinations for Serious Shoppers

Because the U.S. government allows its citizens to take (or send) home more duty-free goods from the U.S. Virgins than from other ports of call, the U.S. Virgin Islands remain the shopping bazaar of the Caribbean. U.S. citizens may carry home $1,200 worth of goods untaxed, as opposed to only $400 worth of goods from most other islands in the Caribbean. (The only exception to this rule is Puerto Rico, where any purchase, regardless of the amount, can be carried tax free back to the U.S. mainland.) Although it is not a U.S. possession, St. Maarten/St. Martin, which is ruled jointly by France and the Netherlands, gives the Virgins some serious shopping competition. It is virtually a shopper's mall, especially on the Dutch side. Although the U.S. doesn't grant the generous customs allowances on St. Maarten/St. Martin that it does to its own islands, the island doesn't have duty so you still can find some lovely bargains.

- **Aruba:** The wisest shoppers on Aruba are cost-conscious souls who have carefully checked the prices of comparable goods before leaving home. Duty is relatively low (only 3.3%). Much of the European china, jewelry, perfumes, watches, and crystal has a disconcerting habit of reappearing in every shopping mall and hotel boutique on the island, so after you determine exactly which brand of watch or china you want, you can comparison-shop. See chapter 5.
- **Barbados:** Local shops seem to specialize in all things English. Merchandise includes bone china from British and Irish manufacturers, watches, jewelry, and perfumes. Bridgetown's Broad Street is the shopping headquarters of the island, although some of the stores here maintain boutiques (with similar prices but a less extensive range of merchandise) at many of the island's hotels and in malls along the congested southwestern coast. Except for cigarettes and tobacco, duty-free items can be hauled off by any buyer as soon as they're paid for. Duty-free status is extended to anyone showing a passport or ID and an airline ticket with a date of departure from Barbados. See chapter 6.

- **The Cayman Islands:** Goods are sold tax free from a daunting collection of malls and minimalls throughout Grand Cayman. Most of these are along the highway that parallels Seven Mile Beach; you'll need a car to shop around. There are also lots of stores in George Town, which you can explore on foot, poking in and out of some large emporiums in your search for bargains. See chapter 9.
- **Curaçao:** In the island's capital, tidy and prosperous Willemstad, hundreds of merchants will be only too happy to cater to your needs. A handful of malls lie on Willemstad's outskirts, but most shops are clustered within a few blocks of the center of town. During seasonal sales, goods might be up to 50% less than comparable prices in the United States; most of the year, you'll find luxury items (porcelain, crystal, watches, and gemstones) priced at about 25% less than in the U.S. Technically, you'll pay import duties on virtually everything you buy, but rates are so low you may not even notice. See chapter 10.
- **The Dominican Republic:** The island's best buys include handcrafts, amber from Dominican mines, and the distinctive pale-blue semiprecious gemstone known as *larimar*. The amber sold by street vendors may be nothing

more than orange-colored, transparent plastic; buy only from well-established shops if your investment is a large one. Other charming souvenirs might include a Dominican rocking chair (remember the one JFK used to sit in?), which is sold boxed, in ready-to-assemble pieces. Malls and souvenir stands abound in Santo Domingo, in Puerto Plata, and along the country's northern coast. See chapter 12.

- **Jamaica:** The shopping was better in the good old days, before new taxes added a 10% surcharge. Despite that, Jamaica offers a wealth of desirable goods, including flavored rums, Jamaican coffees, handcrafts (such as wood carvings, woven baskets, and sandals), original paintings and sculpture, and cameras, watches, and VCRs. Unless you're a glutton for handmade souvenirs (which are available on virtually every beach and street corner), you'd be wise to limit most of your purchases to bona fide merchants and stores. See chapter 15.

- **Puerto Rico:** For U.S. citizens, there's no duty on anything (yes, anything) you buy in Puerto Rico. That doesn't guarantee that prices will be particularly low, however. Jewelry and watches abound, often at competitive prices, especially in the island's best-stocked area, Old San Juan. Also of great interest are such Puerto Rican handcrafts as charming folkloric papier-mâché carnival masks and *santos,* carved wooden figures depicting saints. See chapter 17.

- **St. Maarten/St. Martin:** Because of the massive influx of cruise ships, shopping in Dutch St. Maarten is now about the finest in the Caribbean, though you may have to fight the crowds. Because there's no duty, prices can be 30% to 50% lower than in the U.S. Forget about local crafts and concentrate on leather goods, electronics, cameras, designer fashions, watches, and crystal, along with linens and jewelry. Philipsburg, capital of the island's Dutch side, is the best place to shop. Although it can't compete effectively with Dutch St. Maarten, French St. Martin has been rising rapidly as a shopping destination, especially for goods such as fashion or perfumes imported from motherland France. See chapter 23.

- **St. Thomas:** Many of its busiest shops are in restored warehouses that were originally built in the 1700s. Charlotte Amalie, the capital, is a shopper's town, with a staggering number of stores stocked with more merchandise than anywhere else in the entire Caribbean. However, despite all the fanfare, real bargains are hard to come by. Regardless, the island attracts hordes of cruise-ship passengers on a sometimes frantic hunt for bargains, real or imagined. Look for two local publications, *This Week* and *Best Buys;* either might steer you to the type of merchandise you're seeking. If at all possible, try to avoid shopping when more than one cruise ship is in port—the shopping district is a madhouse on those days. See chapter 26.

- **St. Croix:** This island doesn't have the massive shopping development of St. Thomas, but merchandise there has never been more wide-ranging than it is today. Even though most cruise ships call at Frederiksted, with its urban mall, our favorite shops are in Christiansted, which boasts many one-of-a-kind boutiques and a lot of special finds. Prices are about the same here as on St. Thomas. See chapter 26.

12 The Best Nightlife

Nighttime is sleepy time on the British Virgins, Montserrat, Nevis, Anguilla, St. Eustatius, Saba, St. Barts, Dominica, Bonaire, St. Vincent, and all of the Grenadines. The serious partyer will probably want to choose the following destinations.

- **Aruba:** This island has 10 casinos, each with its own unique decor and each with a following of devoted gamblers. Some offer their own cabarets and comedy shows, dance floors with live or recorded music, restaurants of all degrees of formality, and bars. The casinos are big, splashy, colorful, and, yes, people even occasionally win. Drinks are usually free while you play. Conveniently, the legal tender in most of Aruba's casinos is the U.S. dollar. See chapter 5.
- **Barbados:** Bridgetown is home to at least two boats (the *Bajan Queen* and the *Jolly Roger*) that embark at sundown for rum-and-reggae cruises, as well as oversized music bars like Harbour Lights. Otherwise, a host of bars, British-style pubs, dozens of restaurants, and discos (both within and outside large hotels) beckon from St. Lawrence Gap or the crowded southwest coast. See chapter 6.
- **Curaçao:** At least a dozen casinos beckon from strategic points throughout the island. See chapter 10.
- **The Dominican Republic:** Large resort hotels in the Dominican Republic evoke a Latino version of Las Vegas. If cabaret shows aren't your thing, there are enough discos in the major towns and resorts to keep a *soca*, or hip-hop fan, busy for weeks. The tourist areas of Puerto Plata and Santo Domingo are sprinkled with casinos, and the island's ever-developing north shore

contains its share of jingle-jangle, too. Our favorite is the casino in the Renaissance Jaragua Hotel & Casino in Santo Domingo, which offers floor shows, live merengue concerts, a wraparound bar, and at least five different restaurants. See chapter 12.
- **Jamaica:** Many visitors are drawn here by a love for the island's distinct musical forms. Foremost among these are reggae and *soca,* both of which are performed at hotels, resorts, and raffish dives throughout the island. Hotels often stage folkloric shows that include entertainers who sing, dance, swallow torches, and walk on broken glass. There are also plenty of indoor/outdoor bars where you might actually be able to talk to people. Local tourist boards in Negril and Montego Bay sometimes organize weekly beach parties called "Boonoonoonoos." See chapter 15.
- **Puerto Rico:** Puerto Rico contains all the raw ingredients for great nightlife, including casinos, endless rows of bars and bodegas, cabaret shows with girls and glitter, and discos that feature everything from New York imports to some of the best salsa and merengue anywhere. The country's gaming headquarters lies along the Condado in San Juan, although there are also casinos in megaresorts scattered throughout the island. The casinos here are the most fun in the Caribbean, and they're also some of the most spectacular. Each contains lots of sideshows (restaurants, merengue bars, art galleries, piano bars, shops) that can distract you from the roulette and slots. Puerto Ricans take pride in dressing well at their local casinos, which

enhances an evening's glamour. (Note that you can't drink at the tables.) If you're a really serious partyer, you'll have lots of company in Puerto Rico. Be prepared to stay out very late; you can recover from your Bacardi hangover on a palm-fringed beach the next day. See chapter 17.

- **St. Maarten/St. Martin:** This island has a rather cosmopolitan nightlife and contains the densest concentration of restaurants in the Caribbean, each with its own bar. Discos are often indoor/outdoor affairs. Hotel casinos abound on the Dutch side, and if you're addicted to the jingle of slot machines and roulette wheels, you won't lack for company. The casinos tend to be low key, which might appeal to you if you dislike high-stakes tables with lots of intensity. See chapter 23.

- **St. Thomas:** The Virgin Islands' most active nightlife is found here. Don't expect glitzy shows like those in San Juan's Condado area, and don't expect any kind of casino. But you'll find plenty of fun at the beach bars, restaurants, concerts, clubs, and folklore and reggae shows. See chapter 26.

2

Planning Your Trip to the Caribbean

Golden beaches shaded by palm trees and crystalline waters teeming with colorful tropical fish—it's all just a few hours' flight from the east coast of the United States. Dubbed the "Eighth Continent of the World," the Caribbean islands have an amazing variety of terrain that ranges from thick rain forests to haunting volcanoes, from white- to black-sand beaches. Spicy food, spicier music, and the gentle, leisurely lifestyle of the islands draw millions of visitors each year, all hoping to find the perfect place in the sun. In this chapter, we'll help you choose the right destination, the right time to go, and the best strategies for getting a good package deal or airfare.

1 The Islands in Brief

ANGUILLA Although it's developing rapidly as vacationers discover its 12 miles (19km) of arid but spectacular beaches, Anguilla (rhymes with *vanilla*) is still quiet, sleepy, and relatively free of racial tensions. A flat, coral island, it maintains a maritime tradition of proud fisherfolk, many of whom still make a living from the sea, catching lobsters and selling them at high prices to expensive resorts and restaurants. Although there's a handful of moderately priced accommodations, Anguilla is a very expensive destination, with small and rather exclusive resorts. It's as posh as St. Barts, but without all the snobbery. There are no casinos (and that's the way most of the locals want it). There's not much to do here except lie in the sun, bask in luxury, and enjoy fine dining.

ANTIGUA Antigua is famous for having a different beach for each day of the year, but it lacks the lushness of such islands as Dominica and Jamaica. Some British traditions

(including a passion for cricket) linger, even though the nation became independent in 1981. The island has a population of 80,000, mostly descended from the African slaves of plantation owners. Antigua's resorts are isolated and conservative but very glamorous; its highways are horribly maintained; and its historic naval sites are interesting. Antigua is politically linked to the sparsely inhabited and largely undeveloped island of Barbuda, about 30 miles (48km) north. In spite of its small size, Barbuda has two posh, pricey resorts.

ARUBA Until its beaches were "discovered" in the late 1970s, Aruba, with its desertlike terrain and almost lunar interior landscapes, was an almost-forgotten outpost of Holland, valued mostly for its oil refineries and salt factories. Today vacationers come for the dependable sunshine (it rains less here than virtually anywhere else in the Caribbean), the spectacular beaches, and an almost total lack of racial tensions despite an amazingly culturally diverse population. The high-rise hotels of Aruba are within walking distance of each other along a strip of fabulous beach. You don't stay in old, converted, family-run sugar mills here, and you don't come for history. You come here if you're interested in gambling and splashy high-rise resorts.

BARBADOS Originally founded on a plantation economy that made its aristocracy rich (on the backs of slave laborers), this Atlantic outpost was a staunchly loyal member of the British Commonwealth for generations. Barbados is the Caribbean's easternmost island, floating in the mid-Atlantic like a great coral reef and ringed with glorious beige-sand beaches. Cosmopolitan Barbados has the densest population of any island in the Caribbean, with few racial tensions despite its history of slavery. A loyal group of return visitors appreciate its many stylish, medium-size hotels (many of which carry a hefty price tag). Service is usually extremely good, a by-product of its British mores, which have flourished for a century. Topography varies from rolling hills and savage waves on the eastern (Atlantic) coast to densely populated flatlands, rows of hotels and apartments, and sheltered beaches in the southwest. If you're looking for a Las Vegas–type atmosphere and fine beaches, go to Aruba. If you want history (there are lots of great houses and old churches to explore), a quiet and conservative atmosphere, and fine beaches, come here.

BONAIRE Its strongest historical and cultural links are to Holland, and although it has always been a poor relation of nearby Curaçao, Bonaire boasts better scuba diving and better bird life than any of its larger and richer neighbors. The terrain is as dry and inhospitable as anything you'll find in the Caribbean, a sparse desert landscape offset by a wealth of marine life that thrives along miles of offshore reefs. Except for its scuba diving and snorkeling, the island isn't overly blessed with natural resources. But those coral reefs around most of the island attract divers from all over the world. The casino and party crowd should head for Aruba.

THE BRITISH VIRGIN ISLANDS (B.V.I.) Still a British Crown Colony, this lushly forested chain consists of about 50 small, mountainous islands (depending on how many rocks, cays, and uninhabited islets you want to include). Superb for sailors, the B.V.I. are less populated, less developed, and have fewer social problems than the U.S. Virgin Islands. **Tortola** is the main island, followed by **Virgin Gorda,** which boasts some of the poshest hotels in the West Indies. **Anegada,** a coral atoll geologically different from the other members of the B.V.I., mainly attracts the yachting set. Come here for the laid-back lifestyle, the lovely sandy beaches, the friendly people, and the small, intimate inns.

THE CAYMAN ISLANDS This is a trio of islands set near the southern coast of Cuba. This prosperous, tiny nation depends on Britain for its economic survival and attracts millionaire expatriates from all over because of its lenient tax and banking laws. Relatively flat and unattractive, these islands are covered with scrubland and swamp, but they boast more than their share of expensive private homes and condominiums. Until recently, **Grand Cayman** enjoyed one of the most closely knit societies in the Caribbean, although with recent prosperity, some of that is beginning to unravel. The warm, crystal-clear waters and the colorful marine life in the offshore reefs surrounding the island attract scuba divers and snorkelers. Many hotels line the luscious sands of Seven Mile Beach.

CURAÇAO Because much of the island's surface is an arid desert that grows only cactus, its canny Dutch settlers ruled out farming and developed Curaçao into one of the Dutch Empire's busiest trading posts. Until the post–World War II collapse of the oil refineries, Curaçao was a thriving mercantile society with a capital (Willemstad) that somewhat resembled Amsterdam and a population with a curious mixture of bloodlines, including African, Dutch, Venezuelan, and Pakistani. The main language here is Papiamento, a mixture of African and European dialects, though Dutch, Spanish, and English are spoken as well. Tourism began to develop during the 1980s, and many new hotels have been built since then. The island has a few interesting historic sights, and Willemstad is one of the most charming towns in the Caribbean. Go to Aruba for beaches and gambling, Bonaire for scuba diving, and Curaçao for little cove beaches, shopping, history, and its distinctive "Dutch-in-the-Caribbean" culture.

DOMINICA An English-speaking island set midway between Guadeloupe and Martinique, Dominica (*doh-mi-NEE-kah*), the largest and most mountainous island of the Windwards, is not to be confused with the Dominican Republic (see below). A mysterious, little-visited land of waterfalls, rushing streams, and rain forests, it has only a few beaches, which are mainly lined with black volcanic sand. But if you like the offbeat and unusual, you may find this the lushest and most fascinating island in the Caribbean. Some 82,000 people live here, including 2,000 descendants of the once-fierce Carib Indians. The capital is Roseau. Dominica is one of the poorest islands

in the Caribbean, and it has the misfortune of lying directly in the hurricane belt.

THE DOMINICAN REPUBLIC Occupying the eastern two-thirds of Hispaniola, the island it shares with Haiti, the mountainous Dominican Republic is the second-largest country of the Caribbean. Longtime victim of an endless series of military dictatorships, it now has a more favorable political climate and is one of the most affordable destinations in the entire Caribbean. Its crowded capital is Santo Domingo, with a population of two million. The island offers lots of Latin color, zesty merengue music, and many opportunities to dance, drink, and party. Unfortunately, the contrast between the wealth of foreign tourists and the poverty of locals is especially obvious here, and it's not the safest of the islands. The Dominican Republic was hard-hit by Hurricane Georges in 1998, but it's bounced back. For fun in the sun and good beaches, too, head for La Romana in the southeast, Punta Cana on the easternmost shore, Puerto Plata in the northwest, or any resorts along the Amber Coast in the north.

GRENADA The southernmost nation of the Windward Islands, Grenada (*gre-NAY-dah*) is one of the lushest islands in the Caribbean. With its gentle climate and extravagantly fertile volcanic soil, it's one of the largest producers of spices in the western hemisphere. There's a lot of very appealing local color on Grenada, particularly since the political troubles of the 1980s seem, at least for the moment, to have ended. There are beautiful white-sand beaches, and the populace (a mixture of English expatriates and islanders of African descent) is friendly. Once a British Crown Colony but now independent, the island nation also incorporates two smaller islands: Carriacou and Petit

Martinique, neither of which has many tourist facilities. Grenada's capital, St. George's, is one of the most charming towns in the Caribbean.

GUADELOUPE   It isn't as sophisticated or cosmopolitan as the two outlying islands over which it holds administrative authority, St. Barthélemy and the French section of St. Martin. Despite that, there's a lot of natural beauty in this *département* of mainland France. With a relatively low population density (only 340,000 people live here, mostly along the coast), butterfly-shaped Guadeloupe is actually two distinctly different volcanic islands separated by a narrow saltwater strait, the Riviére Salée. It's ideal for scenic drives and Creole color, offering an unusual insight into the French colonial world. The island has a lot of good beaches, each one different, and a vast national park (a huge tropical forest with everything from wild orchids to coffee and vanilla plants). It's life *a la française* in the tropics, but we'd still give the nod to Martinique (see below) if you can visit only one island.

JAMAICA   A favorite of North American honeymooners, Jamaica is a mountainous island that rises abruptly from the sea 90 miles (145km) south of Cuba and about 100 miles (161km) west of Haiti. One of the most densely populated nations in the Caribbean, with a vivid sense of its own identity, Jamaica has a history rooted in the plantation economy and some of the most turbulent and impassioned politics in the western hemisphere. In spite of its economic and social problems, Jamaica is one of the most successful black democracies in the world. The island is large enough to allow the more or less peaceful coexistence of all kinds of people within its beach-lined borders, including everyone from expatriate English aristocrats to dyed-in-the-wool Rastafarians. Its

tourist industry has been plagued by the island's reputation for aggressive vendors and racial tension, but it is taking steps to improve the situation. Overall, and despite its long history of social unrest, increasing crime, and poverty, Jamaica is a fascinating island. It offers excellent beaches, golf, ecotourism adventures, and fine hotels in all price brackets, making it one of the most popular destinations in the Caribbean, especially since you can find package deals galore.

MARTINIQUE   One of the most exotic French-speaking destinations in the Caribbean, Martinique was the site of a settlement demolished by volcanic activity (St. Pierre, now only a pale shadow of a once-thriving city). Like Guadeloupe and St. Barts, Martinique is legally and culturally French (certainly many islanders drive with a Gallic panache—read: very badly), although many Creole customs and traditions continue to flourish. The beaches are beautiful, the Creole cuisine is full of flavor and flair, and the island has lots of tropical charm. Even more than Guadeloupe, this is the social and cultural center of the French Antilles. If you'd like the chance of speaking French on a charmingly beautiful island with elegant people, the Martiniquaise are waiting to wish you *bonjour.*

NEVIS & ST. KITTS   Now forging its own road to independence from St. Kitts, from which it is separated by 2 miles (3km) of water, Nevis was spotted by Columbus in 1493 on his second voyage to the New World. He called it *Nieves*—Spanish for snows—when he saw the cloud-crowned volcanic isle that evoked for him the snow-capped peaks of the Pyrenees. Known for its long beaches of both black and white sand, Nevis, more than any other island in the Caribbean, has turned its former great houses, built during the plantation era, into some of the most charming and atmospheric inns in the West Indies. It also boasts the Four Seasons Resort for those who want world-class elegance and service. The capital city of Charlestown looks like a real Caribbean backwater, though it is home to hundreds of worldwide businesses that are drawn to Nevis for its tax laws and bank secrecy.

The first English settlement in the Leeward Islands, St. Kitts has a rich sense of British maritime history. With 68 square miles (176 sq. km) of land, St. Kitts (also known as St. Christopher) enjoyed one of the richest sugarcane economies of the plantation age. This island lies somewhat off the beaten tourist track and has a very appealing, intimate charm. A lush, fertile mountain island with a rain forest and waterfalls, it is crowned by the 3,792-foot (1,138m) Mount Liamuiga—a crater that thankfully has remained dormant (unlike the one at Montserrat). St. Kitts is home to some 35,000 people and Brimstone Hill, the Caribbean's most impressive fortress. Come here for the beaches and the history, for lush natural scenery, and to stay at a restored plantation home that's been turned into a charming inn. Lots of sporting activities, ranging from mountain climbing to horseback riding, are also available.

PUERTO RICO   Home to 3.3 million people whose primary language is Spanish (though English is widely spoken, too), the Commonwealth of Puerto Rico is under the jurisdiction of the United States and has a more-or-less comfortable mix of Latin culture with imports from the U.S. mainland. It's the most urban island of the Caribbean, with lots of traffic and relatively high crime, though it compensates with great beaches, glittering casinos, a range of hotels in all price brackets, sports and ecotourism offerings, good hearty food, and sizzling

salsa clubs. The island's interior is filled with rain forest and ancient volcanic mountains; the coastline is ringed with gorgeous sandy beaches. The commonwealth also includes a trio of small offshore islands: Culebra, Mona, and Vieques (the last has the most tourist facilities). San Juan, the island's 16th-century capital, has some of the most extensive and best-preserved Spanish colonial neighborhoods in the New World, with historic sites and lots of things to see and do, and a steady flow of cruise-ship passengers who keep the stores and casinos filled throughout much of the year. You can usually find great package deals offered by Puerto Rico's hotels and resorts.

SABA   Saba is a cone-shaped extinct volcano that rises abruptly and steeply from the watery depths of the Caribbean. There are no beaches to speak of, but the local Dutch- and English-speaking populace has traditionally made a living from fishing, trade, and needlework, rather than tourism. Hotel choices are limited. Saba's thrifty, seafaring folk can offer insights into the old-fashioned lifestyle of the Antilles. There's only one road on the island, and unless you opt to hike away from its edges, you'll have to follow the traffic along its narrow, winding route. Basically, you come here if you want to hang out at your hotel pool, climb up to a rainforest, go diving, and perhaps make a day trip to one of the nearby islands. It's a place to visit if you like to collect untouristy islands. You may want to come only for an afternoon—you can do this by plane or trimaran. You don't come for fabulous white-sand beaches and ocean swimming or for historic sights.

ST.   BARTHÉLEMY   (ALSO CALLED   ST.   BARTS   OR   ST. BARTHS)   Part of the French *département* of Guadeloupe, lying 15 miles (24km) from St. Martin,

St. Barts is a small, hilly island with a population of 3,500 people who live on 13 square miles (34 sq. km) of verdant terrain ringed by pleasant white-sand beaches. A small number of African descendants live harmoniously on this chic Caribbean island with descendants of Norman and Breton mariners and a colony of more recent expatriates from Europe. An expensive and exclusive stamping ground of the rich and famous, with a distinctive seafaring tradition and a decidedly French flavor, St. Barts has a lovely "storybook" capital in Gustavia. For sophistication and luxury living, St. Barts is equaled in the Caribbean only by Anguilla, and the price tag isn't cheap. If your name is Rockefeller or Rothschild, you'll fit in well here. It's a place to come to if you want to wind down from a stressful life.

ST. EUSTATIUS (ALSO CALLED STATIA) Statia is part of the Netherlands Antilles and the Leeward Islands, lying to the west of Dutch Sint Maarten. During the 1700s, this Dutch-controlled island ("The Golden Rock") was one of the most important trading posts in the Caribbean. During the U.S. War of Independence, a brisk arms trade helped to bolster the local economy, but the glamour ended in 1781, when British Admiral Romney sacked the port, hauled off most of the island's wealth, and propelled St. Eustatius onto a path of obscurity—where it remained for almost 200 years, until the advent of tourism. Today the island is among the poorest in the Caribbean, with 8 square miles (21 sq. km) of arid landscape, beaches with strong and sometimes dangerous undertows, a population of around 1,700 people, and a sleepy capital named Oranjestad. Out of desperation, the island is very committed to maintaining its political and fiscal links to the Netherlands. This is a destination for people who are interested in revolutionary-era history and who like hanging out around a pool at a friendly, informal local inn. Most people will want to make a day trip to see the historic sites, have lunch, and leave.

ST. LUCIA St. Lucia (*LOO-sha*), 24 miles (39km) south of Martinique, is the second largest of the Windward Islands, with a population of around 150,000. Although in 1803 Britain eventually won control of the island, French influence is still evident in the Creole dialect spoken here. A volcanic island with lots of rainfall and great natural beauty, it has both white- and black-sand beaches, bubbling sulfur springs, and beautiful mountain scenery. Most tourism is concentrated on the island's northwestern tip, near the capital (Castries), but the arrival of up to 200,000 visitors a year has definitely altered the old agrarian lifestyle throughout the island. Come here for the posh resorts and the gorgeous beaches, the rain forests, and the lush tropical foliage.

ST. MAARTEN/ST. MARTIN Lying 144 miles (232km) east of Puerto Rico, this scrub-covered island has been divided between the Dutch (Sint Maarten) and the French (Saint Martin) since 1648. Regardless of how you spell its name, it's the same island on both sides of the unguarded border—though the two halves are quite different. The Dutch side contains the island's more important airport, more shops, and more tourist facilities, and the French side has some of the poshest hotels and superior food. Both sides are modern, urbanized, and cosmopolitan. And both suffer from traffic jams, a lack of parking space in the capitals, tourist-industry burnout (especially on the Dutch side), and a disturbing increase in crime. In spite of the drawbacks, there's a lot to attract you here—great beaches, the shopping (some of the Caribbean's best), the gambling, the self-contained resorts, the nonstop flights from the U.S., nightlife, and some of the best restaurants in the Caribbean. From here, you can fly over for a day trip to St. Eustatius or Saba.

ST. VINCENT & THE GRENADINES Despite its natural beauty, visitors have only recently discovered this mini-archipelago, though it has always been known to divers and the yachting set, who consider its north-to-south string of cays and coral islets one of the most beautiful sailing regions in the world. The nation's population is only about 105,000 people (of mostly African descent). **St. Vincent,** 18-miles (29km) long and 11-miles (18km) wide, is by far the largest and most fertile island in the country. Its capital is the sleepy, somewhat dilapidated town of Kingstown (not to be confused with Kingston, Jamaica). **The Grenadines,** some 32 neighboring islands, stretch like a pearl necklace to the south of St. Vincent. These include the charming boatbuilding communities of **Bequia** and **Mustique,** where Princess Margaret has a home. Less densely populated islands in the chain include the tiny outposts of **Mayreau, Canouan, Palm Island,** and **Petit St. Vincent,** which was mostly covered with scrub until hotel owners planted much-needed groves of palm and hardwood trees and opened resorts.

TRINIDAD & TOBAGO The southernmost of the West Indies, this 2-island nation lies just 7 miles (11km) off the coast of Venezuela. Both islands once had sugar-plantation economies and enjoyed fantastic wealth during the 18th century. **Trinidad** is the most industrialized island in the Caribbean, with oil deposits and a polyglot population derived from India, Pakistan, Venezuela, Africa, and Europe. Known for its calypso music and carnival celebrations, Trinidad is one of the most

culturally distinctive nations in the Caribbean, with a landmass of more than 1,800 square miles (4,662 sq. km), a rich artistic tradition, a bustling capital (Port-of-Spain), and an impressive variety of exotic flora and fauna. You don't come to Trinidad for the beach; it has some excellent beaches but they are far removed from the capital of Port-of-Spain and hard to locate. For beach life, head for Tobago and just pass through Trinidad, which makes a worthy stopover if you're visiting one of its wildlife sanctuaries.

About 20 miles (32km) northeast of Trinidad, tiny **Tobago** (9 miles/14km wide and 26 miles/42km long) is calmer and less heavily forested, with a rather dull capital (Scarborough) and an impressive array of white-sand beaches. While Trinidad seems to consider tourism only one of many viable industries, Tobago is absolutely dependent on it. Life is sleepy on Tobago, unlike bustling Trinidad. Until the developers ruin it, there are coral reefs ideal for scuba diving, rain forests, luscious sands, shoreline drives, lanes of coconut palms, and a soothing get-away-from-it-all atmosphere.

THE U.S. VIRGIN ISLANDS Formerly Danish possessions, these islands became part of the United States in 1917. Originally based on a plantation economy, **St. Croix** is the largest and flattest of the U.S. Virgins, and St. Thomas and St. John are more mountainous. St. Thomas and, to a lesser degree, St. Croix have lots of diversions, facilities, bars, restaurants, and modern resort hotels. **St. Thomas,** which is overbuilt, is sometimes referred to as the shopping mall of the Caribbean, and cruise-ship passengers constantly pass through. Much of the surface of **St. John** is devoted to a national park, a gift from Laurance Rockefeller to the national park system. Crime is on the increase, however—an unfortunate fly in the ointment of this otherwise soothing U.S.-owned corner of paradise. If you want a somewhat commercial ambience and better shopping, head for St. Thomas. St. Croix is more laid-back, a better place to escape for peace and quiet. St. John is most often visited on a day trip from St. Thomas. All three islands offer stunning beaches, great snorkeling, sailing, and lovely scenery, but they are, unfortunately, rather expensive destinations.

2 Visitor Information

All the major islands have tourist representatives who will supply information before you go; we list each one in the "Fast Facts" section of the individual island chapters.

The **Caribbean Tourism Organization,** 80 Broad St., 32nd Floor, New York, NY 10004 (© **212/635-9530;** www.doitcaribbean.com), can also provide general information.

SIGHTSEEING: INFO ON THE WEB The Internet is a great source of current travel information. **"Planning Your Trip Online,"** at the end of this chapter, is a detailed guide that will help you use the Web to its best advantage to research and perhaps even book your trip.

Whenever possible throughout this book, we've included Web addresses along with phone numbers and addresses for hotels, outfitters, and other companies. We've also given each hotel and resort's website, so you can see pictures of a property before you make your reservation.

TRAVEL AGENTS Travel agents can save you time and money by steering you toward the best package deals, hunting down the best airfares, and arranging cruises and rental cars. Most travel agents still charge nothing for their services—they're paid through commissions from the airlines and other agencies they book for you. However, airlines have begun to cut commissions, and increasingly agents are finding they have to charge a fee to hold the bottom line. In the worst instances, unscrupulous agents will only offer you travel options that bag them the juiciest commissions. Shop around and ask questions, and use this book to become an informed consumer. Don't be pushed into booking a vacation that's not right for you.

If you decide to use a travel agent, make sure the agent is a member of the **American Society of Travel Agents (ASTA),** 1101 King St., Alexandria, VA 22314 (© **703/739-8739;** www.astanet.com). If you send a self-addressed, stamped envelope, ASTA will mail you the free booklet *Avoiding Travel Problems.*

3 Entry Requirements & Customs

ENTRY REQUIREMENTS

Even though most of the Caribbean islands are independent nations and, therefore, are classified as international destinations, passports may not be strictly required of Americans. We recommend carrying them nevertheless. You'll certainly need identification at some point, and a passport is the best form of ID for speeding through Customs and Immigration. Driver's licenses are not acceptable as a sole form of ID. Visas are usually not required, but some countries may require you to fill out a tourist card (see the individual island chapters for details).

Before leaving home, make two copies of your documents—including your passport and your driver's license, your airline ticket, and any hotel vouchers—and leave them home with someone.

CUSTOMS

Each island has specific guidelines on what you can bring in with you; these are detailed in the destination chapters that follow. Generally, you're permitted to bring in items intended for your personal use, including tobacco, cameras, film, and a limited supply of liquor—usually 40 ounces.

Just before you leave home, check with your country's Customs or Foreign Affairs department for the latest guidelines—including information on items that are not allowed to be brought in to your home country, since the rules are subject to change and often contain some surprising oddities.

U.S. Customs allows $1,200 worth of duty-free imports every 30 days from the U.S. Virgin Islands; if you go over this amount, you're taxed at 5% rather than the usual 10%. The duty-free limit is $400 for such international destinations as the French islands of Guadeloupe and Martinique, and $600 for many other islands. If you visit only Puerto Rico, you don't have to go through Customs at all, since the island is a U.S. commonwealth.

Joint Customs declarations are possible for members of a family traveling together. For instance, if you are a husband and wife with two children, your purchases in the U.S. Virgin Islands become duty free up to $4,800! Unsolicited gifts can be sent to friends and relatives at the rate of $100 per day from the U.S. Virgin Islands and $50 a day from the other islands. U.S. citizens, or returning residents at least 21 years of age, traveling directly or indirectly from the U.S. Virgin Islands, are allowed to bring in free of duty 1,000 cigarettes, 5 liters of alcohol, and 100 cigars (but not Cuban cigars). Duty-free limitations on articles from other countries are generally 1 liter of alcohol, 200 cigarettes, and 200 cigars.

You should collect receipts for all purchases made abroad. You must also declare on your Customs form the nature and value of all gifts received during your stay abroad. It's prudent to carry proof that you purchased expensive cameras or jewelry on the U.S. mainland. If you purchased such an item during an earlier trip abroad, you should carry proof that you have previously paid Customs duty on the item.

Sometimes merchants suggest a false receipt to undervalue your purchase. But beware: You could be involved in a sting operation—the merchant might be an informer to U.S. Customs.

If you use any medication that contains controlled substances or requires injection, carry an original prescription or note from your doctor.

For more specifics, contact the **U.S. Customs Service,** 1301 Constitution Ave., P.O. Box 7407, Washington, D.C. 20044 (© 202/354-1000; www. customs.ustreas.gov), and request the free pamphlet *Know Before You Go.* It's also available on the Web at **www. customs.ustreas.gov.**

U.K. citizens should contact **HM Customs & Excise Passenger Enquiries** (© 0845/010-9000) or visit **www.hmce.gov.uk.**

For a clear summary of **Canadian** rules, call © 506/636-5064, or visit the comprehensive website of the **Canada Customs and Revenue Agency** at **www.ccra-adrc.gc.ca.**

Citizens of **Australia** should request the helpful Australian Customs brochure *Know Before You Go,* available by calling © 02/921/32-000 from within Australia. For additional information, go to **www.customs. gov.au** and click on International Travel.

For **New Zealand** customs information, contact the **New Zealand Customs Service** at © 09/359-6655, or go to **www.customs.govt.nz.**

4 Money

CASH/CURRENCY Widely accepted on many of the islands, the U.S. dollar is the legal currency of the U.S. Virgin Islands, the British Virgin Islands, and Puerto Rico. Many islands use the Eastern Caribbean dollar, even though your hotel bill will most likely be presented in U.S. dollars. For details, see "Fast Facts" in the individual island chapters.

TRAVELER'S CHECKS Traveler's checks are something of an anachronism from the days before the ATM made cash accessible at any time. These days, traveler's checks seem unnecessary. However, if you want to avoid ATM service charges, if you're staying in a remote place, or if you just want the security of knowing you can get a refund in the event that your wallet is stolen, you may want to purchase traveler's checks—provided that you don't mind showing identification every time you want to cash one.

You can get traveler's checks at almost any bank. **American Express** offers checks that usually incur a service charge ranging from 1% to 4%. You can buy American Express traveler's checks over the phone by calling ℂ **800/221-7282** or 800/721-9768; you can also purchase checks online at **www.americanexpress.com**. American Express gold or platinum cardholders can avoid paying the fee by ordering over the telephone; platinum cardholders can also purchase checks fee-free in person at Amex Travel Service locations (check the website for the office nearest you). **American Automobile Association** members can obtain checks fee-free at most AAA offices.

Visa offers traveler's checks at Citibank branches and other financial institutions nationwide; call ℂ **800/221-2426** (www.visa.com) to find a purchase location near you. **MasterCard** (ℂ **800/223-9920;** www.

mastercard.com) also offers traveler's checks through **Thomas Cook Currency Services;** call ℂ **800/223-7373** in the U.S. and Canada, or 813/937-7300 for a location near you.

If you carry traveler's checks, be sure to keep a record of their serial numbers (separately from the checks, of course), so you're ensured a refund in case they're lost or stolen.

ATMs ATMs are linked to a huge network that most likely includes your bank at home. **Cirrus** (ℂ **800/424-7787;** www.mastercard.com) and **Plus** (ℂ **800/843-7587;** www.visa. com) are the two most popular networks; check the back of your ATM card to see which network your bank belongs to. Use the toll-free numbers to locate ATMs in your destination; most islands now have ATMs, though they may be hard to find outside the main towns.

If you're traveling abroad, ask your bank for a list of overseas ATMs. Be sure to check the daily withdrawal limit before you depart, and ask whether you need a new personal ID number (PIN).

CREDIT CARDS Credit cards are invaluable when traveling. They are a safe way to carry money and provide a convenient record of all your expenses.

You can also withdraw cash advances from your credit cards at any bank (though you'll start paying hefty interest on the advance the moment you receive the cash, and you won't receive frequent-flyer miles for cash advances on an airline credit card). At most banks, you don't even need to go to a teller; you can get a cash advance at the ATM if you know your PIN.

Almost every credit-card company has an emergency toll-free number that you can call if your wallet or purse is stolen. Credit-card companies may be able to wire cash advances immediately, and in many places, they

The U.S. Dollar, the British Pound, the Canadian Dollar, and the Euro

At the time of this writing, 1 British Pound traded at an average of U.S.$1.50, 1 Canadian dollar traded at an average of U.S.$1=$1.59 Canadian, and the Euro traded at about 1.12 Eurocents to each U.S. dollar. The chart below gives a rough approximation of the conversion equivalents you're likely to find throughout the Caribbean. Rates fluctuate, so be sure to confirm the exchange rate that's in effect before you make any serious transactions.

U.S.$	U.K.£	Can$	Euro€
1	0.67	1.59	1.12
2	1.34	3.18	2.24
3	2.01	4.77	3.36
4	2.68	6.36	4.48
5	3.35	7.95	5.60
6	4.02	9.54	6.72
7	4.69	11.13	7.84
8	5.36	12.72	8.96
9	6.03	14.31	10.08
10	6.70	15.90	11.20
15	10.05	23.85	16.80
20	13.40	31.80	22.40
25	16.75	39.75	28.00
50	33.50	79.50	56.00
75	50.25	119.25	84.00
100	67.00	159.00	112.00
125	83.75	198.75	140.00
150	100.50	238.50	168.00
175	117.25	278.25	196.00
200	134.00	318.00	224.00
225	150.75	357.75	252.00
250	167.50	397.50	280.00
275	184.25	437.25	308.00
300	201.00	477.00	336.00
350	234.50	556.50	392.00
400	268.00	636.00	448.00
500	335.00	795.00	560.00
1,000	670.00	1,590.00	1,120.00

can deliver an emergency credit card in a day or two. **Citicorp Visa**'s U.S. emergency number is © **800/336-8472. American Express** cardholders and traveler's check holders should call © **800/221-7282** for all money emergencies. **MasterCard** holders should call © **800/307-7309. Diners**

Card users should call ℂ **800/234-6377,** and **Discover Card** users should call ℂ **800/347-2683.**

Odds are that if your wallet is gone, the police won't be able to recover it for you. However, after you realize that it's gone and you cancel your credit cards, it is still worth informing them. Your credit-card company or insurer may require a police report number.

CASH It's always a good idea to carry around some cash for small expenses, like cab rides, or for that rare occasion when a restaurant or small shop doesn't take plastic, which can happen if you're dining at a neighborhood joint or buying from a small vendor. U.S. dollars are accepted nearly everywhere, and in some countries, such as Jamaica, most locals prefer their tips to be in U.S. dollars. Perhaps $100 in cash (small bills) will see you through.

5 When to Go

THE WEATHER

The temperature variations in the Caribbean are surprisingly slight, averaging between 75° and 85° Fahrenheit in both winter and summer. It can get really chilly, however, especially in the early morning and at night. The Caribbean winter is usually like a perpetual May. Overall, the mid-80s prevail throughout most of the region, and trade winds make for comfortable days and nights, even without air-conditioning.

The humidity and bugs can be a problem here year-round. However, more mosquitoes come out during the rainy season, which traditionally occurs in the autumn.

If you come in the summer, be prepared for really broiling sun in the midafternoon.

Brochures make people feel that it's virtually always sunny in the Caribbean and that isn't always so. Different islands get different amounts of rain. On Aruba it hardly ever rains; on other islands, you can have overcast skies your entire vacation. Winter is generally the driest season, but even then, it can be wet in mountainous areas, and you can expect brief afternoon showers, especially in December and January, on Martinique, Guadeloupe, Dominica, St. Lucia, on the north coast of the Dominican Republic, and in northeast Jamaica.

If you want to know how to pack just before you go, check the Weather Channel's online 5-day forecast at **www.weather.com,** or, for 95¢ per minute, you can call ℂ **900-WEATHER** for the latest information.

HURRICANES The curse of Caribbean weather, the hurricane season lasts—officially, at least—from June 1 to November 30. But there's no cause for panic: Satellite forecasts give enough warning that precautions can be taken.

To get a weather report before you go, call the nearest branch of the **National Weather Service,** listed in your phone directory under the "U.S. Department of Commerce." You can also check the **Weather Channel** on the Web at **www.weather.com.**

THE HIGH SEASON & THE OFF-SEASON

The Caribbean has become a year-round destination. The "season" runs roughly from mid-December to mid-April, which is generally the driest time of year in the Caribbean and the most miserable time of year in the U.S. Northeast and Midwest and in Canada. Hotels charge their highest prices during the peak winter period, and you'll have to make your reservations well in advance—months in advance if you want to travel over Christmas or in the depths of

February, especially around U.S. President's Day weekend.

The off-season in the Caribbean—roughly from mid-April to mid-December (although this varies from hotel to hotel)—is one big summer sale, though it's become more popular in recent years. In most cases, hotels, inns, and condos slash 20% to 50% off their winter rates.

Dollar for dollar, you'll spend less money by renting a summer house or self-sufficient unit in the Caribbean than you would on Cape Cod, Fire Island, or Laguna Beach. You just have to be able to tolerate strong sun if you're considering coming in the summer.

Off-season the beaches are less crowded and you can get good deals, but restaurants close, hotels offer fewer facilities, and hotels use the off-season for construction—so make sure you ask what work is going on and if you decide to go anyway, make sure your room is far away from the noise. If you're single and going off-season, ask for the hotel's occupancy rate. You want crowds!

Because there's such a drastic difference in high-season and low-season rates at most hotels, we've included both on every property we review. You'll see the incredible savings you can enjoy if your schedule allows you to wait a couple of months for your fun in the sun.

6 Health & Insurance

STAYING HEALTHY

Keep the following suggestions in mind:

- It's best to drink bottled water during your trip.
- If you experience diarrhea, moderate your eating habits and drink only bottled water until you recover. If symptoms persist, consult a doctor.
- The Caribbean sun can be brutal. Wear sunglasses and a hat and use sunscreen liberally. Limit your time on the beach the first day. If you do overexpose yourself, stay out of the sun until you recover. If your exposure is followed by fever or chills, a headache, or a feeling of nausea or dizziness, see a doctor.
- One of the biggest menaces is the "no-see-ums," which appear mainly in the early evening. You can't see these gnats, but you sure can "feel-um." Window screens can't keep these critters out, so carry bug repellent.
- Mosquitoes are a nuisance. Malaria-carrying mosquitoes in the Caribbean are confined largely to Haiti and the Dominican Republic. If you're visiting either, consult your doctor for preventive medicine at least 8 weeks before you leave.
- Dengue fever is prevalent in the islands, most prominently on Antigua, St. Kitts, Dominica, and the Dominican Republic. To date, no satisfactory treatment has been developed; visitors are advised to avoid mosquito bites—as if that were possible. Infectious hepatitis has been reported on islands such as Dominica and Haiti. Unless you have been immunized for both hepatitis A and B, consult your doctor about the advisability of getting a gamma-globulin shot before you leave. The **U.S. Centers for Disease Control and Prevention** (CDC; © **800/311-3435** or 404/639-3534; www.cdc. gov) provides up-to-date information on necessary vaccines and health hazards by region or country. The CDC provides an informational booklet ($25 by mail; free on the Internet).

- Pack prescription medications in your carry-on luggage. Carry written prescriptions in generic, not brand-name, form, and dispense all prescription medications from their original labeled vials. Many people try to slip drugs such as cocaine into the Caribbean (or pick them up there). Drugs are often placed into a container for prescription medication after the legal medications have been removed. Customs officials are well aware of this type of smuggling and often check medications if they suspect a passenger is bringing illegal drugs into or out of a country.
- If you wear contact lenses, pack an extra pair in case you lose one.

WHAT TO DO IF YOU GET SICK AWAY FROM HOME

Finding a good doctor in the Caribbean is not a problem, and most speak English. See the "Fast Facts" section in each chapter for specific names and addresses on each individual island.

If you worry about getting sick away from home, you might want to consider medical travel insurance (see the section on travel insurance below). In most cases, however, your existing health plan will provide all the coverage you need. Be sure to carry your identification card in your wallet.

If you suffer from a chronic illness, consult your doctor before your departure. For conditions such as epilepsy, diabetes, or heart problems, wear a **Medic Alert** identification tag (© **800/825-3785;** www.medicalert. org), which will immediately alert doctors to your condition and give them access to your records through Medic Alert's 24-hour hot line.

Contact the **International Association for Medical Assistance to Travelers** (IAMAT; © **585/754-4883** in the U.S. or 519/836-0102 in Canada; www.sentex.net/~iamat) for tips on travel and health concerns in the countries you'll be visiting, plus lists of local English-speaking doctors.

INSURANCE

There are three kinds of travel insurance: trip-cancellation, medical, and lost-luggage coverage. Rule number one: Check your existing medical and homeowner's policies before you buy any additional coverage, and don't pay for more insurance than you really need.

Trip-cancellation insurance is a good idea if you have paid a large portion of your vacation expenses up front, say, by purchasing a package or a cruise. Trip-cancellation insurance should cost approximately 6% to 8% of the total value of your vacation. (Don't buy it from the same company from which you've purchased your vacation—talk about putting all your eggs in one basket!) Trip-cancellation insurance will protect you in case you need to cancel your trip because of sickness or a death in the family.

Medical contingencies may be covered by your existing policies; check them carefully to see if this is true. In many cases existing health coverage does not include emergency evacuation, and Medicare often doesn't cover all medical expenses overseas (note that **Medicare** only covers U.S. citizens traveling in Mexico and Canada). For example, if you need to be flown off a cruise ship, you can spend a fortune.

If you need hospital treatment, most health insurance plans and HMOs will cover out-of-country hospital visits and procedures, at least to some extent. Most make you pay the bills up front at the time of care, however, and you'll get a refund only after you've returned home and filed all the necessary paperwork. Members of **Blue Cross/Blue Shield** can now use their cards at select hospitals in most major cities worldwide. Call

© 800/810-BLUE or visit www.blue cares.com for a list of hospitals.

The differences between **travel assistance** and **insurance** are often blurred, but in general, the former offers on-the-spot assistance and 24-hour hot lines (mostly oriented toward medical problems), and the latter reimburses you for travel problems (medical, travel, or otherwise) after you have filed the paperwork.

Your homeowner's insurance should cover stolen luggage. The airlines are responsible for $1,250 if they lose your luggage on domestic flights; if you plan to carry anything more valuable than that, keep it in your carry-on bag.

Among the reputable issuers of travel insurance are **Access America** (© 800/284-8300; www.access america.com); **Travel Guard International** (© 800/826-1300; www.travel guard.com) and **Travelex Insurance Services** (© 800/228-9792; www. travelex-insurance.com). For medical coverage, try **MEDEX International** (© 888/MEDEX-00 or 410/453-6301; www.medexassist.com) or **Travel Assistance International** (Worldwide Assistance Services, Inc.; © 800/821-2828 or 317/575-2652; www.travelassistance.com). The **Divers Alert Network** (© 800/446-2671 or 919/684-8111; www.diversalert network.org) insures scuba divers.

7 Tips for Travelers with Special Needs

FOR TRAVELERS WITH DISABILITIES

A disability shouldn't stop anyone from traveling. There are more resources out there today than ever before.

Moss Rehab ResourceNet (© 215/456-5995; www.mossresourcenet. org) is a great source for information, tips, and resources related to accessible travel. You'll find links to a number of travel agents who specialize in planning trips for disabled travelers here and through **Access-Able Travel Source** (www.access-able. com), another excellent online source. You'll also find relay and voice numbers for hotels, airlines, and car-rental companies on Access-Able's user-friendly site, as well as links to accessible accommodations, attractions, transportation, tours, local medical resources and equipment repairers, and much more.

You can join **The Society for Accessible Travel & Hospitality (SATH),** 347 Fifth Ave. Suite 610, New York, NY 10016 (© 212/447-7285; www.sath.org), to gain access to SATH's vast network of connections in the travel industry. SATH provides information sheets on destinations and referrals to tour operators that specialize in traveling with disabilities. Its quarterly magazine, *Open World,* is full of good information and resources.

A World of Options, a massive book of resources for disabled travelers, covers everything from biking trips to scuba outfitters. It costs $45 ($35 for members) and is available from **Mobility International USA** (© 888/241-3366 or 541/343-1284, voice and TDD; www.miusa.org). Annual membership for Mobility International is $35, which includes the quarterly newsletter *Over the Rainbow.*

Travelers with disabilities may also want to consider joining a tour that caters specifically to them. One of the best operators is **Flying Wheels Travel** (© 800/535-6790 or 507/451-5005; www.flyingwheelstravel. com). It offers various escorted tours and cruises, with an emphasis on sports, as well as private tours in minivans with lifts. Other reputable specialized tour operators include **Access Adventures** (© 716/889-9096), which offers sports-related vacations;

Accessible Journeys (© 800/ TINGLES or 610/521-0339), for slow walkers and wheelchair travelers; The Guided Tour, Inc. (© 800/ 783-5841 or 215/782-1370; www. guidedtour.com); Wilderness Inquiry (© 800/728-0719 or 612/676-9400; www.wildernessinquiry.org).

Vision-impaired travelers should contact the American Foundation for the Blind, 11 Penn Plaza, Suite 300, New York, NY 10001 (© 800/ 232-5463; www.afb.org), for information on traveling with Seeing Eye dogs.

You can obtain a free copy of *Air Transportation of Handicapped Persons,* published by the U.S. Department of Transportation. Write for Free Advisory Circular No. AC12032, Distribution Unit, U.S. Department of Transportation, Publications Division, 3341Q 75 Ave., Landover, MD 20785 (© 301/322-4961; fax 301/386-5394; http://isddc.dot. gov). Only written requests are accepted.

FOR BRITISH TRAVELERS The Royal Association for Disability and Rehabilitation (RADAR), Unit 12, City Forum, 250 City Rd., London, ECIV 8AF (© 020/7250-3222; fax 020/7250-0212; www.radar.org.uk), publishes holiday "Fact Packs," three in all, which sell for £2 each or all three for £5. The first one provides general information, including planning and booking a holiday, insurance, finances, and useful organization and holiday providers. The second outlines transportation available when going abroad and equipment for rent. The third deals with specialized accommodations.

FOR GAY & LESBIAN TRAVELERS

Some Caribbean islands are more gay friendly than others. The most gay-friendly islands are the U.S. possessions, and most notably Puerto Rico, which is hailed as the "gay capital of the Caribbean" and offers gay guesthouses, nightclubs, bars, and discos. To a lesser extent, the U.S. Virgin Islands are welcoming, too.

The French islands—St. Barts, St. Martin, Guadeloupe, and Martinique—are technically an extension of mainland France, and the French have always regarded homosexuality with a certain blasé tolerance.

The Dutch islands of Aruba, Bonaire, and Curaçao are quite conservative, so discretion is suggested.

Gay life is fairly secretive in many of the sleepy islands of the Caribbean. Some islands even have repressive antihomosexual laws. Homosexuality is actively discouraged in places like the Cayman Islands. Gay travelers might also note that the Cayman Islands refused to allow an all-gay cruise ship to dock on Grand Cayman, and several gay advocacy groups have even called for a boycott on travel to the Caymans in response. In Barbados, homosexuality is illegal, and there is often a lack of tolerance in spite of the large number of gay residents and visitors on the island.

Jamaica is the most homophobic island in the Caribbean, with harsh antigay laws, even though there is a large local gay population. Many all-inclusive resorts, notably the famous Sandals of Jamaica, have discriminatory policies, allowing only male-female couples; gay men and lesbians are definitely excluded from their love nests. However, not all the all-inclusives practice such blatant discrimination. Hedonism II, a rival of Sandals in Negril, is not a "couples-only" resort, though it will help you find a roommate so that you can travel on the lower double-occupancy rate. The Grand Lido, a more upscale all-inclusive in Negril, welcomes whatever combinations show up (even singles, for that matter). For more information on all these resorts, see chapter 15.

If you want help planning your trip, **The International Gay & Lesbian Travel Association** (IGLTA; ✆ **800/448-8550** or 954/776-2626; www.iglta.org), can link you up with the appropriate gay-friendly service organization or tour specialist.

Many travel agencies are affiliated with the **International Gay Travel Association,** based in Key West, Florida. Any of these agencies can work with you to choose gay-friendly destinations and accommodations. General gay and lesbian travel agencies include **Above and Beyond Tours** (✆ **800/397-2681;** www.abovebeyond tours.com for mainly gay men); and **Kennedy Travel** (✆ **800/988-1181** or 516/352-4888; www.kennedy travel.com). There are many others, all over the United States; you'll find a list of gay-friendly travel agencies across the U.S. on the RSVP Vacations and Out & About websites mentioned below.

Several companies now assemble gay travel packages. **RSVP Vacations** (✆ **800/328-RSVP** or 612/729-1113; www.rsvp.vacations.com) offers gay cruises on ships both large and small in the Caribbean. **Atlantis Events** (✆ **800/628-5268** or 310/281-5450; www.atlantisevents.com) books Club Med resorts for all-gay,

all-inclusive vacations; it also does all-gay cruises, often in the Caribbean.

Out & About (✆ **800/929-2268** or 415/644-8044; www.outandabout. com) offers a monthly newsletter packed with good information on the global gay and lesbian scene. Out & About's guides are available at most major bookstores.

FOR SENIORS

One of the benefits of age is that travel often costs less. Don't be shy about asking for discounts, but always carry some kind of ID, such as a driver's license, if you've kept your youthful glow. Also, mention the fact that you're a senior citizen when you first make your travel reservations; many hotels and most airlines and cruise lines offer senior discounts.

Members of the **AARP,** 601 E St. NW, Washington, D.C. 20049 (✆ **800/424-3410** or 202/434-AARP; www.aarp.org), get discounts on hotels, airfares, and car rentals, plus *Modern Maturity* magazine and a monthly newsletter.

Grand Circle Travel, based in Boston (✆ **800/221-2610** or 617/350-7500; www.gct.com), is one of the hundreds of travel agencies that specialize in vacations for seniors. Ask for Grand Circle's helpful publication *101 Tips for the Mature Traveler.*

8 Package Deals

For value-conscious travelers, packages are often the smart way to go because they can save you a ton of money. Especially in the Caribbean, package tours are *not* the same thing as escorted tours. You'll be on your own, but in most cases, a package to the Caribbean will include airfare, hotel, and transportation to and from the airport—and it'll cost you less than just the hotel alone if you booked it yourself. A package deal might not be for you if you want to stay in a more intimate inn or guesthouse, but if you like resorts, read on.

You'll find an amazing array of packages to popular Caribbean destinations. Some packages offer a better class of hotels than others. Some offer the same hotels for lower prices. Some offer flights on scheduled airlines, and others book charters. Remember to comparison shop among at least three different operators, and always compare apples to apples.

Many land-and-sea packages include meals, and you might find yourself locked into your hotel dining room every night if your meals are prepaid. If you're seeking a more varied dining experience, avoid **AP (American Plan)**, which means full board, and opt for **MAP (Modified American Plan)**, meaning breakfast and either lunch or dinner. That way, you'll at least be free for one main meal of the day and can sample a variety of an island's regional fare.

The best place to start your search is the travel section of your local Sunday newspaper. Also check the ads in national travel magazines like *Arthur Frommer's Budget Travel, National Geographic Traveler,* and *Travel Holiday.*

Liberty Travel (© **888/271-1584** to be connected with the agent closest to you; www.libertytravel.com) is one of the biggest packagers in the Northeast, and it usually boasts a full-page ad in Sunday papers. **Certified Vacations** (© **800/241-1700;** www.deltavacations.com) is another option.

Another good resource is the airlines themselves, which often package their flights together with accommodations. Among the airline packagers, your options include **American Airlines Vacations** (© **800/321-2121;** www.aavacations.com), **Delta Dream Vacations** (© **800/872-7786;** www.deltavacations.com), and **US Airways Vacations** (© **800/455-0123;** www.usairwaysvacations.com). American usually has the widest variety of offerings since it's the major carrier to the region.

The biggest hotel chains, casinos, and resorts also offer package deals. If you already know where you want to stay, call the resort itself and ask if it offers land/air packages.

To save time comparing the prices and value of all the package tours out there, contact **TourScan, Inc.**

(© **800/962-2080** or 203/655-8091; www.tourscan.com). Every season, the company computerizes the contents of travel brochures that contain about 10,000 different vacations at 1,600 hotels in the Caribbean, the Bahamas, and Bermuda. TourScan selects the best-value vacation at each hotel and condo. Two catalogs are printed each year, which list a choice of hotels on most of the Caribbean islands in all price ranges. The price of a catalog ($4) is credited toward any TourScan vacation.

Another source for one-stop shopping on the Web is **VacationPackager** (www.vacationpackager.com), a search engine that will link you to many different package-tour operators offering Caribbean vacations.

Other tour operators include the following:

- **Horizon Tours** (© **877/TRIPSAI** or 202/393-8390; www.horizontours.com) specializes in good deals for all-inclusive resorts in the Bahamas, Jamaica, Aruba, Puerto Rico, Antigua, and St. Lucia.
- **Club Med** (© **800/258-2633;** www.clubmed.com) has various all-inclusive options throughout the Caribbean and the Bahamas, as does **Sandals** (© **800/SANDALS;** www.sandals.com). **SuperClubs** (© **800/859-7873;** www.superclubs.com) has a wide variety of all-inclusive resorts in Jamaica.
- **Globus & Cosmos Tours** (© **800/338-7092;** www.globusandcosmos.com) gives escorted island-hopping expeditions to three or four islands, focusing on the history and culture of the West Indies.

9 Finding the Best Airfare

American Airlines (© 800/433-7300; www.aa.com) is the major carrier throughout the region. Other airlines

serving the islands include **Air Canada** (© 888/247-2262 in the U.S.; 800/268-7240 Canada;

www.aircanada.ca), **Air Jamaica** (© 800/523-5585; www.airjamaica. com), **British Airways** (© 0845/ 773-3377 in the U.K.; www.british-airways.com), **BWIA** (© 888/853-8560; www.bwee.com), **Continental** (© 800/231-0856; www.continental. com), **Delta** (© 800/241-4141; www. delta.com), **LIAT** (© 800/468-0482; www.liatairline.com), **Northwest** (© 800/447-4747; www.nwa.com), **United** (© 800/241-6522; www.ual. com), and **US Airways** (© 800/428-4322; www.usairways.com), plus some smaller regional carriers. In each of the island chapters that follow, we'll list details on which airlines fly the various routes.

Before you do anything else, read the section "Package Deals," earlier in this chapter. But if a package isn't for you, and you need to book your airfare on your own, keep in mind these money-saving tips:

- **When you fly makes all the difference.** If you fly in spring, summer, and fall, you're guaranteed substantial reductions on airfares to the Caribbean. You can also ask if it's cheaper to fly Monday through Thursday or to stay an extra day. (Many airlines won't volunteer this information, so ask lots of questions and be persistent.)
- **Keep an eye out for sales.** Check the newspaper for advertised discounts or call the airlines directly and ask if any promotional rates or special fares are available. You'll almost never see a sale during the peak winter vacation months of February and March, or during the Thanksgiving or Christmas seasons; but in periods of low-volume travel, you should find a discounted fare. If you already hold a ticket when a sale breaks, it may even pay to exchange your ticket, which usually incurs a $50 to $75 charge. Note, however,

that the lowest-priced fares are often nonrefundable, require advance purchase of 1 to 3 weeks and a certain length of stay, and carry penalties for changing dates of travel.

- **Consolidators, also known as bucket shops, are sometimes a good place to find low fares.** Consolidators buy seats in bulk from the airlines and then sell them back to the public at prices below even the airlines' discounted rates. But go carefully here. Make sure you know the airlines' current fares before buying from a consolidator. Before you pay, ask for a record locator number and confirm your seat with the airline itself. Also be aware that bucket-shop tickets are usually nonrefundable or rigged with stiff cancellation penalties, often as high as 50% to 75% of the ticket price.

Our staff has gotten great deals on many occasions from **Cheap Tickets** (© 800/377-1000; www. cheaptickets.com). **Council Travel** (© 800/2COUNCIL; www. counciltravel.com) and **STA Travel** (© 800/781-4040; www. statravel.com) cater especially to young travelers, but their bargain-basement prices are available to people of all ages. Other reliable consolidators include **Lowestfare. com** (© 888/278-8830; www. lowestfare.com); **1-800-AIRFARE** (www.1800airfare.com); **Cheap Seats** (© 800/451-7200; www. cheapseatstravel.com); and **1-800-FLY-CHEAP** (www.flycheap.com).

- **Search the Internet for cheap fares.** Although it's still best to compare your findings with the research of a dedicated travel agent if you're lucky enough to have one, especially when you're booking more than just a flight, the Internet can be a good resource too. A few of the better-respected virtual travel agents are **Travelocity** (**www. travelocity.com**) and **Microsoft Expedia** (**www.expedia.com**). **Smarter Living** (**www.smarterliving.com**) is a good source for great last-minute deals. See "Planning Your Trip Online," at the end of this chapter, for further discussion on this topic and other recommendable sites.

10 Organized Adventure Trips

BIKING   The Dominican Republic is the best mountain bike destination in the Caribbean. *Bicycling Magazine* said the island "with its towering mountains and miles of single track, defy all stereotype." The best organized trips are offered by **Iguana Mama Mountain Bike,** Cabarete (© **800/ 849-4720** in the U.S., or 809/571-0908; www.iguanamama.com).

BIRD-WATCHING   Victor **Emanuel Nature Tours** (© **800/ 328-8368;** www.ventbird.com) offers weeklong bird-watching trips led by a biologist in Trinidad and Tobago. Each trip costs approximately $2,300 per person, and trips are based at the **Asa Wright Nature Center** (© **868/ 622-7480;** www.asawright.org) which has 150 of the more than 400 species of birds found in Trinidad. Discussion sessions on the symbiosis between plant and bird life are offered, along with field trips.

The company also operates weeklong birding trips to Jamaica (home to some 30 species of birds found nowhere else in the world), and these trips cost from $2,750 per person. A Jamaican ornithologist conducts the trips.

ECOTOURS   Some of the best wildlife cruises are packaged by **Oceanic Society Expeditions** (© **800/326-7491** in the U.S., or 415/441-1106; www.oceanic-society. org). Whale-watching jaunts and some research-oriented trips are also featured. You can swim with humpback whales in the Dominican Republic, or be part of the research swim with dolphins in the Bahamas.

Puerto Rico's varied and often hard-to-reach natural treasures have been conveniently packaged into a series of affordable ecotours. **Hillbilly Tours,** Route 181, km. 13.4, San Juan (© **787/760-5618**), specializes in nature-based and countryside tours in Puerto Rico's rain forest. **Adventours,** Luquillo (© **787/530-8311;** www. angelfire.com/f12/adventours), features customized private tours that include such activities as bird-watching, hiking, camping, visits to coffee plantations, and kayaking. **Aventuras Tierra Adentro,** 268 Piñero Avenue, San Juan (© **787/766-0470;** www.aventurastierraadentro.com), specializes in rock climbing, body rafting, caving, and canyoning in Puerto Rico. **Eco Xcursion Aquatica,** Route 191, km. 1.7, Rio Grande, Fajardo (© **787/ 888-2887**), offers some of the best rain forest hikes and mountain bike tours.

Machias Adventures (© **888/427-3497;** www.machiasadventures.com) offers adventure tours to St. Vincent, including hiking up a volcano, a day's sailing with a crew, seeking out the huge variety of bird life, and hiking up a river canyon to a dramatic water pool, a perfect pool for swimming. The cost of these 7-day jaunts is $2,800 per person, based on double occupancy.

The best ecotours in lush Trinidad and Tobago are offered by **Wildways,** Ariapita Rd., St. Ann's, Port-of-Spain (© **868/623-7332;** www.wildways. org). The most exciting is the 8-day Trinidad "Trek & Tour," following Amerindian trails through rain forests to watching turtle laying and other adventures.

> **Tips Websites for Divers**
>
> For useful information on scuba diving in the Caribbean, check out the website of the **Professional Association of Diving Instructors (PADI)** at **www.padi.com**. This site provides descriptions of dive destinations throughout the Caribbean and a directory of PADI-certified dive operators. *Rodale's Scuba Diving Magazine* also has a helpful website at **www. scubadiving.com**. Both sites list dive package specials and display gorgeous color photos of some of the most beautiful dive spots in the world.

You might also inquire about Caribbean offerings from **Ecosummer Expeditions** (© **800/465-8884** or 250/674-0102; www.ecosummer.com).

HIKING   Unlike many of its neighboring islands, Jamaica offers mountain peaks of up to 7,400 feet (2,220m). The flora, fauna, waterfalls, and panoramas of those peaks have attracted increasing numbers of hikers, each determined to experience the natural beauty of the island firsthand. Because of possible dangers involved, it's often best to go on an organized tour, the best of which are offered by **Sunventure Tours,** 30 Balmoral Ave., Kingston 10, Jamaica W.I. (© **876/ 960-6685;** www.sunventuretours. com). For more information, refer to the section "The Blue Mountains," in chapter 15.

SCUBA TRIPS   A number of outfitters offer scuba packages and cruises. **Travelon** (© **800/203-2539;** www. allscuba.com) offers 3-day trips to St. Kitts and Nevis. **Into the Blue** (© **800/6-GETWET** or 610/642-1920; www.intotheblue.com) is a travel company specializing in diving trips throughout the Caribbean, for individuals, couples, and families. Their destinations range from the British Virgin Islands all the way to Bonaire. **Island Dreams Tours & Travel** (© **800/346-6116** or 713/ 973-9300; www.islanddream.com) also offers trips, including itineraries in the Cayman Islands and Bonaire.

Explorer Ventures (© **800/322- 3577** or 903/887-8521; www.explorer ventures.com) takes divers on its *Caribbean Explorer* to excursions in the waters of St. Kitts and Saba. Trips usually last a week.

Another specialist in this field is **Tropical Adventures** (© **800/621- 1270;** www.caribbeans.com/1advent. htm) which offers adventurous scuba-cruise packages to Bonaire, St. Croix, and St. Kitts.

SEA KAYAKING   The only outfitter in the Virgin Islands that offers sea-kayaking/island-camping excursions is **Arawak Expeditions,** based in Cruz Bay, St. John (© **800/238-8687** in the U.S., or 340/693-8312; www. arawakexp.com). It provides kayaking gear, healthy meals, camping equipment, and two experienced guides. Multiday excursions range in price from $999 to $1,500.

11 Getting Married in the Caribbean

See also "The Best Honeymoons," in chapter 1, for information on specific resorts that offer wedding and honeymoon packages. **Club Med** (© **800/ CLUB-MED**), **Sandals** (© **800/ SANDALS**), and **SuperClubs** (© **800/** 859-7873) are three chains that have helped many couples tie the knot.

If you yearn to take the plunge on a sun-dappled island, you need to know a bit about the requirements on the different islands.

ANGUILLA Couples need to file a license application on Anguilla, which takes approximately 48 hours to process. You'll need to present a passport, and, if applicable, you'll have to show proof of divorce or the death certificate of a deceased spouse. The fee for the license and stamp duty is $284. For further information, contact the **Registrar of Births, Deaths, and Marriages,** Judicial Department, The Valley, Anguilla, B.W.I. (© **264/ 497-2377**). A local wedding service, **Sunshine Lady Productions,** P.O. Box 85, The Valley, Anguilla, Leeward Islands, B.W.I. (© **264/497-2911;** fax 264/497-3884), can make all the needed arrangements for you.

ANTIGUA There's a 24-hour waiting period for marriages on Antigua. A couple appears at the Ministry of Justice in the capital of St. John to complete and sign a declaration before a marriage coordinator and pays a $190 license fee. The coordinator will arrange for a marriage officer to perform a civil ceremony at any of Antigua's hotels or another place the couple selects. The fee for the marriage officer is $50. Several hotels and resorts offer wedding/honeymoon packages. For more information on civil or religious wedding ceremonies, contact the **Antigua Department of Tourism,** 610 Fifth Ave., Suite 311, New York, NY 10020 (© **888/268- 4227,** or 212/541-4117).

ARUBA Civil weddings are possible on Aruba only if one of the partners is an Aruban resident, which obviously rules out most people. Consider it for your honeymoon instead.

BARBADOS Couples can now marry the same day they arrive on Barbados, but they must first obtain a marriage license from the **Ministry of Home Affairs** (© **246/228-8950**). Bring either a passport or a birth certificate and photo ID, $88 (U.S.) in fees, $25 for the revenue stamp which

you can obtain at the local post office, a letter from the authorized officiant who will perform the service, plus proof, if applicable, of pertinent deaths or divorces from any former spouse(s). A Roman Catholic wedding on Barbados carries additional requirements. For more information, contact the **Barbados Tourism Authority,** 800 Second Ave., New York, NY 10017 (© **800/221-9831** in the U.S., or 212/986-6516).

BONAIRE The bride and/or groom must have a temporary residency permit, obtained by writing a letter to the governor of the **Island Territory of Bonaire,** Wilhelminaplein 1, Kralendijk, Bonaire, N.A. (© **599/717- 5330**). The letter, submitted within 2 months of departure for Bonaire, should request permission to marry on Bonaire and to apply for temporary residency. You'll also need to inform the governor of your arrival and departure dates and the date you wish to marry. The partner who applies for residency must be on the island for 7 days before the wedding. A special dispensation must be issued by the governor if there is less than a 10-day time period between the announcement of the marriage and the ceremony. In addition, send three passport photos, copies of the bride's and groom's passports, birth certificates, and proof of divorce or, in the case of widows and widowers, the death certificate of the deceased spouse.

If you desire, you can arrange your wedding on Bonaire through **Multro Travel and Tours,** Attn: Mrs. Marvel Tromp, Light House Beach Resort #22 (P.O. Box 237), Bonaire, N.A. (© **599/717-8834;** fax 599/717- 8334), or check with the hotel where you're planning to stay. Some hotels arrange weddings on special request. For further information, contact the **Bonaire Tourist Office** (© **800/ BONAIRE** or 212/956-5911).

THE BRITISH VIRGIN ISLANDS

Island residency is not required, but a couple must apply for a marriage license at the attorney general's office and must stay in the B.V.I. for 3 days while the application is processed. Present a passport or original birth certificate and photo identification, plus certified proof of your marital status and any divorce or death certificates that apply to any former spouse(s). Two witnesses must be present. The fee is $110. Marriages can be performed by the local registrar or by the officiant of your choice. Contact the **Registrar's Office,** P.O. Box 418, Road Town, Tortola, B.V.I. (© **284/494-3134** or 284/468-3701).

THE CAYMAN ISLANDS

Visitors have to call ahead and arrange for an authorized person to marry them. The name of the "marriage officer," as it is called, has to appear on the application for a marriage license. The application for a special marriage license costs $200 and can be obtained from the **Deputy Secretary's Office,** 3rd Floor, Government Administration Building, George Town (© **345/949-7900**). There is no waiting period. Present a birth certificate, the embarkation/disembarkation cards issued by the island's immigration authorities, and, if applicable, divorce decrees or proof of a spouse's death. Complete wedding services and packages are offered by **Cayman Weddings of Grand Cayman,** which is owned and operated by Caymanian marriage officers Vernon and Francine Jackson. For more information, contact them at P.O. Box 678, Grand Cayman (© **345/949-8677;** fax 345/949-8237). A brochure, *Getting Married in the Cayman Islands,* is available from **Government Information Services,** Broadcasting House, Grand Cayman (© **345/949-8092;** fax 345/949-5936).

CURAÇAO

Couples must be on-island 2 days before applying for a marriage license, for which there is a 14-day waiting period. Passport, birth certificate, return ticket, and divorce papers (if applicable) are required. The $167 fee is subject to change, so check in advance. For further information, call the **Curaçao Tourist Board,** 475 Park Ave. S., Suite 2000, New York, NY 10016 (© **800/328-7222;** fax 212/683-9337).

JAMAICA

In high season, some Jamaican resorts witness several weddings a day. Many of the larger resorts have wedding coordinators on staff who can arrange for an officiant, a photographer, and even the wedding cake and champagne. Some resorts even throw in your wedding with the cost of your honeymoon at the hotel. Both the Jamaican Tourist Board and your hotel will assist you with the paperwork. Participants must reside on Jamaica for 24 hours before the ceremony. Bring birth certificates and affidavits saying you've never been married before. If you've been divorced or widowed, bring copies of your divorce papers or a copy of the deceased spouse's death certificate. The license and stamp duty costs J$2,000 (US$46.50). Or you can apply in person at the **Ministry of National Security and Justice,** 12 Ocean Blvd., Kingston, Jamaica (© **876/906-4909**).

PUERTO RICO

There are no residency requirements for getting married in Puerto Rico. For U.S. citizens, blood tests are required, although a test conducted on the U.S. mainland within 10 days of the ceremony will suffice. A doctor in Puerto Rico must sign the license after conducting an examination of the bride and groom. For complete details, contact the **Commonwealth of Puerto Rico Health Department,** Demographic

Register, 171 Quisaueya St., Hato Rey, PR 00917 (© **787/767-9120**).

ST. LUCIA   Both parties must be on the island for 48 hours before the ceremony. Present your passport or birth certificate, plus (if either participant has been widowed or divorced) proof of death or divorce from the former spouse(s). It usually takes about 2 days before the ceremony to process all the paperwork. Fees run around $200 for a lawyer (one is usually needed for the application to the governor-general), $40 for the registrar to perform the ceremony, and $150 for the stamp duty, notary, certificates, and the license. Some resorts and vacation properties also offer wedding packages that include all the necessary arrangements for a single fee. For more information, contact the **St. Lucia Tourist Board,** 800 Second Ave., 9th Floor, New York, NY 10017 (© **212/ 867-2950;** fax 212/867-2795).

THE U.S. VIRGIN ISLANDS   No blood tests or physical examinations are necessary, but there is a $50 notarized application and license, and an 8-day waiting period, which is sometimes waived depending on circumstances. Civil ceremonies before a judge of the territorial court cost $250 each; religious ceremonies performed by clergy are equally valid. Fees and schedules for church weddings must be negotiated directly with the officiant. More information is available from the **U.S. Virgin Islands Division of Tourism,** 1270 Ave. of the Americas, New York, NY 10020 (© **212/332-2222**).

The U.S. Virgin Islands tourism offices distribute the guide *Getting Married in the U.S. Virgin Islands,* which gives information on all three islands, including wedding planners, places of worship, florists, and limousine services. The guide also provides a listing of island accommodations that offer in-house wedding services.

Couples can apply for a marriage license for **St. Thomas** or **St. John** by contacting the **Territorial Court of the Virgin Islands,** P.O. Box 70, St. Thomas, U.S.V.I. 00804 (© **340/ 774-6680**). You can apply for weddings on **St. Croix** by contacting the **Territorial Court of the Virgin Islands,** Family Division, P.O. Box 929, Christiansted, St. Croix, U.S.V.I. 00821 (© **340/778-9750**).

12 Cruises

Here's a brief rundown of some of the major cruise lines that serve the Caribbean. For more detailed information, pick up a copy of *Frommer's Caribbean Cruises & Ports of Call 2003.*

BOOKING A CRUISE

If you've developed a relationship with a favorite travel agency, then by all means, leave the details to the tried-and-true specialists. Many agents will propose a package deal that includes airfare to your port of embarkation. It's possible to purchase your air ticket on your own and book your cruise ticket separately, but in most cases you'll save big bucks by combining the fares into a package deal.

You're also likely to save money—sometimes *lots* of money—by contacting a specialist who focuses on cruise bookings. He or she will be likely to match you with a cruise line whose style suits you, and can also steer you toward any special sales or promotions.

Here are some travel agencies to consider: **Cruises, Inc.** (© 800/854-0500 or 954/958-3700), **Cruise Masters** (© 800/242-9000 or 310/555-2925), **The Cruise Company** (© 800/289-5505 or 402/339-6800), **Kelly Cruises** (© 800/837-7447 or 630/990-1111), **Hartford Holidays Travel** (© 800/828-4813 or 516/746-6670), and **Mann Travel and Cruises** (© 800/849-2301 or 704/556-8311).

These companies stay tuned to last-minute price wars; cruise lines don't profit if their megaships don't fill up near peak capacity, so sales pop up all the time.

You're likely to sail from Miami, which has become the cruise capital of the world. Other departure ports in Florida include Port Everglades (at Fort Lauderdale), Port Canaveral, and Tampa. Additionally, some cruises depart from San Juan (PR), New Orleans, and Los Angeles (reaching the Caribbean via the Panama Canal).

CRUISE LINES

- **American Canadian Caribbean** (© **800/556-7450** or 401/247-0955; www.accl-smallships.com): These tiny, 80- to 100-passenger coastal cruisers make 11-day excursions through the Caribbean and offer an experience that's quiet and completely unpretentious. The line's two almost identical ships are as plain as can be, like a roadside motel that floats, but the itineraries they offer are the big drawing card. They visit small, out-of-the-way ports that you'll never see on one of the big cruise ships. At least one of the line's vessels spends part of the winter cruising around The Bahamas, the Virgin Islands, the Grenadines and the coasts of Central America.

- **Carnival Cruise Lines** (© **800/ 327-9501** or 305/599-2200; www.carnival.com): Offering affordable vacations on some of the biggest and most brightly decorated ships afloat, Carnival is the brashest and most successful mass-market cruise line in the world. More than 12 of its vessels depart for the Caribbean from Miami, Tampa, New Orleans, Port Canaveral, and San Juan (including *Paradise,* one of the very few totally non-smoking ships in the

world), and 8 of them specialize in 7-day or longer tours that feature stopovers at selected ports throughout the eastern, western, and southern Caribbean, including St. Lucia, San Juan, Guadeloupe, Grenada, Grand Cayman, and Jamaica; 4 others offer 3- to 5-day itineraries visiting such ports as Nassau, Key West, Grand Cayman, and Playa del Carmen/Cozumel. The cruises offer good value and feature nonstop activities of the theme park variety (with brightly colored drinks added). Lots of single passengers opt for this line, as do families attracted by the well-run children's program. The average onboard age is a relatively youthful 42, although ages range from 3 to 95.

- **Celebrity Cruises** (© **800/ 327-6700** or 305/539-6000; www.celebrity-cruises.com): Celebrity maintains 8 newly built, stylish, medium to large ships offering cruises that last between 7 and 10 nights and visit ports such as Key West, San Juan, Grand Cayman, St. Thomas, Ocho Rios, Antigua, and Cozumel, Mexico, to name a few. The ships themselves are works of art—gorgeously designed, with a penchant toward clean lines and modern materials—and the onboard atmosphere is classy without being at all stuffy. Accommodations are roomy and well equipped, cuisine is the most refined of any of its competitors, and its service is impeccable. It's the thinking man's mainstream cruise line—and you get it all for a competitive price, to boot.

- **Clipper Cruise Line** (© **800/ 325-0010** or 314/727-2929; www.clippercruise.com): Clipper has two 102- and 138-passenger ships on Caribbean itineraries every winter. Like the vessels of the American Canadian Caribbean line, the Clipper ships are small, conservative, and lacking the flashy amenities of the megaships, though between the two lines, Clipper's ships are much, much more comfortable (and cruises aboard them cost commensurately more), resembling tiny versions of Holland America's or Princess's ships—albeit without all the activities and profusion of public rooms. Clipper's itineraries are all about the ports, and onboard naturalists and historians give frequent lectures throughout the trips to make the experience even more enlightening. Itineraries visit small, out-of-the-way ports in the Virgin Islands, plus such southern Caribbean ports as Dominica, Bequia, Union Island, and Petit St. Vincent. Other stops include Bonaire, Isla Margarita (Venezuela), Tobago and Trinidad, and destinations along the banks of Venezuela's Orinoco River. Vessels also make transits of the Panama Canal (many of which are sold out months in advance) and stop in more frequently visited ports of call like St. Thomas, St. Kitts and/or Nevis, and St. Lucia.

- **Costa Cruise Lines** (© 800/462-6782 or 305/358-7325; www.costacruises.com): Costa sails the 2,112-passenger *CostaAtlantica* and the 1,928-passenger *CostaVictoria* on western and eastern Caribbean cruises on alternate weeks, departing from Fort Lauderdale. Ports of call during the eastern Caribbean itineraries include stopovers in San Juan, St. Thomas, and Nassau. Itineraries through the western Caribbean include stopovers at Grand Cayman, Ocho Rios or Montego Bay (Jamaica), Key West, and Cozumel. There's an Italian flavor and lots of Italian design on board here, and an atmosphere of relaxed indulgence.

- **Cunard Line** (© 800/5-CUNARD or 305/463-3000; www.cunardline.com): Cunard, one of the most legendary names in shipping, offers a series of Caribbean and Caribbean/South American voyages aboard its classic *Caronia*. Built in 1973 and formerly named *Vistafjord,* the vessel was renamed in late 1999 after extensive renovations, and is a true classic, a ship that looks like a ship rather than a hotel on water. Carrying only 665 guests, it boasts comfortable, spacious cabins; enough public areas and entertainment options to keep things varied (though not so many that it becomes overwhelming); and a great nautical feel, from the wide promenades to the gorgeously tiered aft decks, where the pool and several bars and cafes are located. *Caronia* sails 12- to 16-night Caribbean itineraries, sailing round-trip from Fort Lauderdale and visiting such ports as St. Croix, Antigua, Barbados, San Juan, the British Virgin Islands, Dominica, St. Maarten, St. Thomas, Grenada, and others.

- **Disney Cruise Line** (© 800/951-3532 or 407/566-7000; www.Disney.go.com/disneycruise): The *Disney Magic* and *Disney Wonder* are the famous company's first foray into cruising, and boast a handful of innovative, Disney-style features including a rotating series of restaurants on every cruise, cabins designed for families, monumental Disney entertainment, and the biggest kids' facilities at sea. In many ways, the experience is more Disney than it is cruise—there's no casino or library, for instance, and fewer adult activities in general. On the other hand, the ships are beautifully designed. Disney's cruises can usually be combined with a visit to Disney World (though you can book the cruise segment on its own). The *Disney Magic* offers 7-day itineraries through the eastern Caribbean year-round. The upside: The ships have the best kids' facilities at sea, and practically the only cabins designed with families in mind.

- **Holland America Line–Westours** (© **800/426-0327** or 206/281-3535; www.hollandamerica.com): Holland America offers the most old-world-style cruise experience of the mainstream lines, aboard a fleet of respectably hefty and good-looking ships. They offer solid value, with few jolts or surprises, and attract a solid, well-grounded clientele of primarily older travelers (so late-night revelers and serious partiers might want to book cruises on other lines, such as Carnival). Seven- and 10-day cruises stop at deep-water mainstream ports throughout the Caribbean, visiting such ports as Key West, Grand Cayman, St. Maarten, St. Lucia, Curaçao, Barbados, and St. Thomas.

- **Norwegian Cruise Line (NCL)** (© **800/327-7030** or 305/436-4000; www.ncl.com): Norwegian operates a diverse fleet ranging from the medium-sized *Norwegian Majesty* to the megaship *Norwegian Sky,* carrying 2,002 passengers. On board ship, NCL administers a snappy, high-energy array of activities and sometimes brings aboard international sports figures for game tips and lectures (this goes along with NCL's very spectator sports-oriented approach, which also means the ships have great sports bars with giant-screen TVs). All in all, the experience is very mainstream, in the same class as Carnival though perhaps not as well executed. Ships are based in Miami and San Juan, and sail 3-and 7-night cruises, visiting such eastern Caribbean posts as Aruba, Curaçao, Tortola, Virgin Gorda, St. Thomas, St. Lucia, Antigua, St. Kitts, St. Croix, and the company's private island, Great Stirrup Cay, and ports in the western Caribbean such as Cancun, Cozumel, and Honduras's Roatan Bay.

- **Princess Cruises** (© **800/421-0522** or 661/753-0000; www.princess.com): Currently operating 8 megavessels that cruise through Caribbean and Bahamian waters, Princess offers a cruise experience that's part Carnival- or Royal Caribbean–style party-time fun and part Celebrity-style classy enjoyment. The *Ocean Princess, Dawn Princess,* and *Sea Princess,* almost identical vessels all built in the late 1990s, offer the bulk of Princess's Caribbean itineraries, with the *Dawn* and *Ocean* running two alternating 7-night southern Caribbean itineraries round-trip from San Juan, while the *Sea* sails 7-night western Caribbean runs round-trip from Fort Lauderdale. Depending on the exact itinerary, ports on the southern Caribbean runs include Curaçao, Isla Margarita (Venezuela), La Guaira/Caracas (Venezuela), Grenada, Dominica, St. Vincent, St. Kitts, St. Thomas, Trinidad, Barbados, Antigua, Martinique, St. Lucia, and St. Maarten. Western Caribbean itineraries visit Ocho Rios (Jamaica), Grand Cayman, Cozumel, and Princess Cays, the line's private island. The huge, beautiful *Grand Princess,* second largest passenger ship in the world, sails 7-night eastern Caribbean itineraries round-trip from Fort Lauderdale, visiting St. Thomas, St. Maarten, and Princess Cays. All of the line's ships are stylish and comfortable, though the *Grand* ups it a notch in the style department, offering amazing open deck areas and some really beautiful indoor public areas.

- **Royal Caribbean International (RCI)** (© 800/327-6700 or 305/539-6000; www.royalcaribbean.com). RCI leads the industry in the development of megaships. Most of this company's dozen or so vessels weigh in at around 73,000 tons. In November 1999 RCI launched what was to that point the biggest cruise ship, the 142,000-ton, 3,114-passenger *Voyager of the Seas*, with a year-round itinerary taking in such Caribbean ports as Jamaica's Ocho Rios and Mexico's Cozumel. In October 2000, RCI launched yet another megaship, the 142,000-ton, 3,838-passenger *Explorer of the Sea*. This vessel has a year-round Caribbean itinerary; it leaves from Miami and makes stops at ports such as Nassau, St. Thomas, and San Juan. One of the line's latest ships—a megaship masterpiece—is the 2,100-passenger *Radiance of the Seas*, with the largest cabins of any of its sibling vessels. If you'd like to sail the newest and the best, you can float along 7-night eastern Caribbean trips leaving from Miami September to May, visiting Antigua, St. Thomas, Dutch Sint Maarten, St. Lucia, and Barbados.

  RCI's ships offer such cruise ship firsts as an ice-skating rink and a rock-climbing wall. A mass-market company that has everything down to a science, RCI encourages a house-party theme that's just a little less frenetic than the mood aboard Carnival.

- **Seabourn Cruise Line** (© 800/929-9595; www.seabourn.com): Seabourn is deservedly legendary for the unabashed luxury aboard its elegant, small-scale ships. The

Seabourn Pride conducts 3- to 16-day October-to-April cruises in the Caribbean. Its identical twin, the *Seabourn Legend,* spends the entire winter from home ports of San Juan and Fort Lauderdale. Ports of call for both ships include Jamaica, St. Barts, St. Martin, St. Lucia, Bequia, Tobago, Barbados, St. Croix, and Virgin Gorda, some of which are visited before or after transits of the Panama Canal. There are more activities than you'd expect aboard such a relatively small ship (each carries only 204 passengers), and there's an amazing amount of onboard space per passenger. Cuisine is superb, served in a dining room that's unapologetically formal. Other small ships in the fleet include the 4,250-ton, 116-passenger *Seabourn Goddess I & II,* usually sailing between St. Thomas and Barbados on 4-, 5-, and 7-night jaunts from November to May. On all the line's ships the emphasis is on top-notch service, luxury, discretion, and impeccably good taste. All in all, you get what you pay for—and you pay *a lot.*

- **Star Clippers** (© 800/442-0553 or 305/442-0550; www.starclippers.com): Star Clippers's two replica 19th-century clipper ships were built in 1992 as the hobby of a Swedish industrialist, and are among the fastest sailing vessels ever constructed. Though based on the best shipbuilding principles of the 19th century, the ships are thoroughly modern, utilizing space-age materials and all the latest computerized equipment—for instance, just 10 deckhands are needed to hoist sails that would have required 4 dozen hands on the original clippers. From November to April, the *Star Clipper* sails round-trip from Sint Maarten, visiting St. Barts, Nevis,

Guadeloupe, Dominica, Iles des Saintes, and Antigua for the first week. For the second week, it leaves Sint Maarten, visiting St. Barts, St. Kitts, and Anguilla, with stopovers at tiny islands in the British Virgins. The line's latest ship, launched in 2000, is the grandest: the 228-passenger *Royal Clipper,* fully rigged at 439 feet (132m). This is one of the largest sailing vessels ever constructed, with 5 masts and 42 sails. In winter it will sail on 7-night Caribbean jaunts from Barbados.

- **Windjammer Barefoot Cruises** (© **800/327-2601** or 305/672-6453; www.windjammer.com): Windjammer operates six sailing ships, all faithful renovations of antique schooners or sail-driven private yachts, plus one motored vessel that's part cargo ship and part passenger vessel. True to the line's name, many passengers really do forego footgear for the

majority of their vacation, and few ever pack more than shorts, T-shirts, and sunscreen. From bases like San Juan, St. Martin, Grenada, Tortola, Antigua, and Grenada, the ships sail 5- and 13-night itineraries, visiting small, rarely visited outposts in the eastern and southern Caribbean. Port calls often mean just anchoring off a small beach and shuttling passengers ashore, and the ships often stay in port late into the evening, giving passengers an opportunity to enjoy nightlife ashore. The *Amazing Grace,* the line's only ship without sails, acts as a supply vessel for all the others, sailing 13-night itineraries that visit an amazing range of islands, albeit slowly. The line's website offers e-mail updates of last-minute bargains, so if you're able to travel at short notice, you can often get a weeklong cruise at a very low rate.

13 Chartering Your Own Boat

Experienced sailors and navigators can charter "bareboat," a fully equipped rental boat with no captain or crew. You're on your own, and you'll have to prove your qualifications before you're allowed to rent one. Even an experienced skipper may want to take along someone familiar with local waters, which may be tricky in some places.

You can also charter a boat with a skipper and crew. Charter yachts, ranging from 50 to more than 100 feet (30m), can accommodate 4 to 12 people.

Most yachts are rented on a weekly basis, with a fully stocked bar and equipment for fishing and watersports. The average charter carries 4 to 6 passengers, and usually is reserved for 1 week.

The Moorings (© **800/535-7289** in the U.S. and Canada; fax 727/530-9747; www.moorings.com) operates

the largest charter yacht fleet in the Caribbean. Its main branch is located in the British Virgin Islands, but it has outposts in St. Martin, Guadeloupe, Martinique, St. Lucia, and Grenada, to name a few. Each location has a regatta of yachts available for chartering. Depending on their size, yachts are rented to as many as four couples at a time. You can arrange to rent bareboat (for qualified sailors only) or rent yachts with a full crew and cook. Depending on circumstances, the vessels come equipped with a barbecue, snorkeling gear, a dinghy, and linens. The boats are serviced by an experienced staff of mechanics, electricians, riggers, and cleaners. If you're going out on your own, you'll get a thorough briefing on Caribbean waters, reefs, and anchorages. Seven-night combined hotel-and-crewed-yacht packages can run $1,100 to $1,500 per person in Tortola, $900 to $1,500 in St. Lucia, and $870 to $1,500 in Grenada.

Nicholson Yacht Charters (© **800/662-6066** in the U.S., or 617/661-0555; fax 617/661-0554; www.yachtvacations.com) is one of the best in the business, handling charter yachts for use throughout the Caribbean basin, particularly the route between Dutch St. Maarten and Grenada and the routes around the U.S. Virgin Islands and British Virgin Islands and Puerto Rico. Featuring boats of all sizes, the company rents motorized vessels or sailing yachts up to 298 feet (89m) long. Sometimes groups of friends rent two or more yachts (each sleeping eight guests in four double cabins) to race each other from island to island during the day and anchor near each other in secluded coves at night. The price for renting a yacht depends on the number in your party, the size of the vessel, and the time of the year. Weekly rates range from $3,575 up to $85,000 plus or so. You can get a nice, comfortable vessel for $6,000 to $12,000 weekly for your whole group.

Sunsail (© **800/327-2276** in the U.S., or 410/280-2553; fax 410/280-2406; www.sunsail.com) specializes in yacht chartering from its bases in the British Virgin Islands, Antigua, St. Vincent, and the French West Indies. More than 60 bareboat and crewed yachts, between 30 and 52 feet (9 and 16m), are available for cruising these waters. Programs include Caribbean racing and regattas, flotilla sailing, skippered sailing, and one-way or stay-and-sail bareboat cruises. The company usually requires a deposit of 25% of the total rental fee; arrangements should be made months in advance. Sunsail also offers charter flights from the United States to the Virgin Islands.

14 Tips on Accommodations

WATCH OUT FOR THOSE EXTRAS! Nearly all islands charge a government tax on hotel rooms, usually 7½%, but that rate varies from island to island. When booking a room, make sure you understand whether the price you've been quoted includes the tax. That will avoid an unpleasant surprise when it comes time to pay the bill. Sometimes the room tax depends on the quality of the hotel—it might be relatively low for a guesthouse but steeper for a first-class resort.

Furthermore, most hotels routinely add 10% to 12% for "service," even if you didn't see much evidence of it. That means that with tax and service, some bills are 17% or even 25% higher than the price that was originally quoted to you! Naturally, you need to determine just how much the hotel, guest house, or inn plans to add to your bill at the end of your stay, and whether it's included in the initial price.

That's not all. Some hotels slip in little hidden extras that mount quickly. For example, it's common for many places to quote rates that include a continental breakfast. Should you prefer ham and eggs, you will pay extra charges. If you request special privileges, like extra towels for the beach or laundry done in a hurry, surcharges may mount. It pays to watch those extras and to ask questions before you commit.

WHAT THE ABBREVIATIONS MEAN Rate sheets often have these classifications:

• **MAP (Modified American Plan)** usually means room, breakfast, and dinner, unless the room rate has been quoted separately, and then it means only breakfast and dinner.

- **CP (Continental Plan)** includes room and a light breakfast.
- **EP (European Plan)** means room only.
- **AP (American Plan)** includes your room plus three meals a day.

HOTELS & RESORTS Many budget travelers assume they can't afford the big hotels and resorts. But there are so many packages out there (see the section "Package Deals," earlier in this chapter) and so many frequent sales, even in winter, that you might be pleasantly surprised.

The rates given in this book are only "rack rates"—that is, the officially posted rate that you'd be given if you just walked in off the street. Almost no one actually pays them. Always ask about packages and discounts. Think of the rates in this book as guidelines to help you comparison shop.

A good travel agent can help save you serious money. Some hotels are often quite flexible about their rates, and many offer discounts and upgrades whenever they have a big block of rooms to fill and few reservations. The smaller hotels and inns are not as likely to be generous with discounts, much less upgrades.

ALL-INCLUSIVE RESORTS The promises are persuasive: "Forget your cash, put your plastic away." Presumably, everything's all paid for in advance at an "all-inclusive" resort. But is it?

The all-inclusives have a reputation for being expensive, and many of them are, especially the giant **Super-Clubs** of Jamaica or even the **Sandals** properties (unless you book in a slow period or off-season).

In the 1990s, so many competitors entered the all-inclusive game that the term now means different things to the various resorts that use this marketing strategy. The ideal all-inclusive is just that—a place where everything, even drinks and watersports, is included. But in the most narrow sense, it means a room and three meals a day, with extra charges for drinks, sports, whatever. When you book, it's important to ask and to understand exactly what's included in your so-called all-inclusive. Watersports programs vary greatly at the various resorts. Extras might include horseback riding or sightseeing.

The all-inclusive market is geared to the active traveler who likes organized entertainment, a lot of sports, and workouts at fitness centers, and who also likes a lot of food and drink.

If you're single or gay, avoid Sandals. If you have young children, stay away from Hedonism II in Negril, Jamaica, which lives up to its name. Even some Club Meds are targeted more for singles and couples, although many now aggressively pursue the family market. Some Club Meds have Mini Clubs, Baby Clubs, and Teen Clubs at some of their properties, at least during holiday and summer seasons.

The trick is to look for that special deal and to travel in off-peak periods, which doesn't always mean just from mid-April to mid-December. Discounts are often granted for hotels during certain slow periods, called "windows," most often after the New Year's holiday. If you want a winter vacation at an all-inclusive, choose the month of January—not February or the Christmas holidays, when prices are at their all-year high.

One good deal might be **Club Med's "Wild Card,"** geared to singles and couples. You must be 18 or over. Reservations must be made 2 or more weeks before departure. One week before departure, Club Med tells you which "village" on which island you're going to visit. If this uncertainty doesn't bother you, you can save $150 to $300 per weekly package. Deals like this can change constantly, so check to see exactly how "wild" this card is to play. Each package includes round-trip air transportation from New York, double-occupancy accommodations, all meals with complimentary wine and beer, use of all sports facilities except scuba gear (extra charges), nightly entertainment, and other recreational activities such as boat rides, snorkeling expeditions, and picnics. For more information, call *(C)* **800/CLUB-MED.**

GUEST HOUSES An entirely different type of accommodation is the guesthouse, where most of the Antilleans themselves stay when they travel. In the Caribbean, the term *guesthouse* can mean anything. Sometimes so-called guesthouses are really like simple motels built around swimming pools. Others are small individual cottages, with their own kitchenettes, constructed around a main building in which you'll often find a bar and a restaurant that serves local food. Some are surprisingly comfortable, often with private baths and swimming pools. You may or may not have air-conditioning.

For value, the guesthouse can't be topped. You can always journey over to a big beach resort and use its seaside facilities for only a small charge, perhaps no more than $5. Although they don't have any frills, the guesthouses we've recommended are clean and safe for families or single women. The cheapest ones are not places where you'd want to spend a lot of time, because of their simple, modest furnishings.

RENTING A CONDO, VILLA, OR COTTAGE Particularly if you're a family or a group of friends, a "housekeeping holiday" can be one of the least expensive ways to vacation in the Caribbean, and if you like privacy and independence, it's a good way to go. Accommodations with kitchens are now available on nearly all the islands. Some are individual cottages, others are condo complexes with swimming

pools, and some are private homes that owners rent out while they're away. Many (though not all) places include maid service, and you're given fresh linen as well.

In the simpler rentals, doing your own cooking and laundry or even your own maid service may not be your idea of a good time in the sun, but it saves money—a lot of money. The savings, especially for a family of three to six people, or two or three couples, can range from 50% to 60% of what a hotel would cost. Groceries are sometimes priced 35% to 60% higher than on the U.S. mainland, as nearly all foodstuffs have to be imported, but even so, preparing your own food will be a lot cheaper than dining at restaurants.

There are also quite lavish homes for rent, where you can spend a lot and stay in the lap of luxury in a prime beachfront setting.

Many villas have a staff, or at least a maid who comes in a few days a week, and they also provide the essentials for home life, including linens and housewares. Condos usually come with a reception desk and are often comparable to a suite in a big resort hotel. Nearly all condo complexes have pools (some more than one). Like condos, villas range widely in price and may begin at $500 per week for a modest one and go up to $35,000 a week for a luxurious one. More likely, the prices will be somewhere in between.

You'll have to approach these rental properties with a certain sense of independence. There may or may not be a front desk to answer your questions, and you'll have to plan your own watersports.

For a list of agencies that arrange rentals, refer to the hotel sections of the individual island chapters. You can also ask each island's tourist office for good suggestions. Make your reservations well in advance.

Here are a few agencies renting throughout the Caribbean:

- **Villas of Distinction** (✆ **800/ 289-0900** in the U.S., or 914/ 273-3331; www.villasofdistinction.com) offers upscale private villas with one to six bedrooms and a pool. Domestic help is often included. They have offerings on St. Martin, Anguilla, Mustique, Barbados, the U.S. and British Virgins, the Cayman Islands, St. Lucia, St. Barts, and Jamaica. Descriptions, rates, and photos are available online.
- **Home Abroad** (✆ **212/421- 9165;** fax 212/752-1591) has private upscale homes for rent on Barbados, Jamaica, Mustique, St. John, St. Lucia, St. Martin, St. Thomas, Tortola, and Virgin Gorda, most with maid service included.
- **Caribbean Connection Plus Ltd.** (✆ **800/893-1100** or 203/261-8603, fax 203/261- 8295; www.islandhoppingexpert. com) offers many apartments, cottages, and villas in the Caribbean, especially on St. Kitts, Nevis, and Montserrat, but also on some of the more obscure islands such as St. Eustatius, Tobago, St. Vincent, Dominica, and Nevis. Caribbean Connection specializes in island hopping with InterIsland Air, and offers especially attractive deals for U.S. West Coast travelers. This is one of the few reservations services staffed by people who have

actually been on the islands, so members can talk to people who really know the Caribbean.

- **Hideaways International** (✆ **888/843-4433** in the U.S. or 603/430-4433; www.hideaways. com) publishes *Hideaways Guide,* a pictorial directory of home rentals throughout the world, including the Caribbean, especially the British Virgin Islands, the Cayman Islands, Jamaica, and St. Lucia, with full descriptions so you know what you're renting. Rentals range from cottages to staffed villas to whole islands! Other services include yacht charters, cruises, airline ticketing, or car rentals, and hotel reservations. Annual membership is $129; a 4-month trial membership is $49. Membership information, listings, and photos are available online.
- **Heart of the Caribbean Ltd.** (✆ **800/231-5303** or 262/783- 5303; www.hotcarib.com) is a villa wholesale company offering travelers a wide range of private villas and condos on several islands, including St. Maarten/St. Martin, Barbados, and St. Lucia. Accommodations range from one to six bedrooms, and from modest villas and condos to palatial estates. Homes have complete kitchens and maid service. Catering and car rentals can also be provided. Rates, listings, and photos are available online.

15 Planning Your Trip Online

With a mouse, a modem, and a little do-it-yourself determination, Internet users can tap into the same travel-planning databases that were once accessible only to travel agents. Sites such as **Travelocity, Expedia,** and **Orbitz** allow consumers to comparison shop for airfares, book flights,

learn of last-minute bargains, and reserve rooms and rental cars.

But don't fire your travel agent just yet. Although online booking sites offer tips and data to help you bargain shop, they cannot endow you with the hard-earned experience that makes a seasoned, reliable travel agent an invaluable resource, even in the Internet age. And for consumers with a complex itinerary, a trusty travel agent is still the best way to arrange the most direct flights to and from the best airports.

Still, there's no denying the Internet's emergence as a powerful tool in researching and plotting travel time. The benefits of researching your trip online can be well worth the effort:

- **Last-minute specials,** known as **E-Savers,** such as weekend deals or Internet-only fares, are offered by airlines to fill empty seats. Most of these are announced on Tuesday or Wednesday and must be purchased online. They are only valid for travel that weekend, but some can be booked weeks or months in advance. Sign up for weekly e-mail alerts at airline websites or check mega-sites that compile comprehensive lists of E-savers, such as **Smarter Living** (www.smarter living.com) or **WebFlyer** (www. webflyer.com).
- Some sites will send you **e-mail notification** when a cheap fare to your favorite destination becomes available. Some will also tell you when fares to a particular destination are lowest.
- The best of the travel planning sites are now **highly personalized;** they track your frequent-flier miles, and store your seating and meal preferences, tentative itineraries, and credit-card information, letting you plan trips or check agendas quickly.
- All major airlines offer **incentives**—bonus frequent-flier miles, Internet-only discounts, sometimes even free cell phone rentals—when you purchase online or buy an e-ticket.
- Advances in mobile technology provide business travelers and other frequent travelers with **the ability to check flight status, change plans, or get specific directions** from handheld computing devices, mobile phones, and pagers. Some sites will e-mail or page a passenger if a flight is delayed.

TRAVEL PLANNING & BOOKING SITES

The best travel planning and booking sites cast a wide net, offering domestic and international flights, hotel and

Frommers.com: The Complete Travel Resource

For an excellent travel planning resource, we highly recommend **Arthur Frommer's Budget Travel Online** (www.frommers.com). We're a little biased, of course, but we guarantee you'll find the travel tips, reviews, monthly vacation giveaways, and online-booking capabilities thoroughly indispensable. Among the special features are: **"Ask the Expert"** bulletin boards, where Frommer's authors answer your questions via online postings; **Arthur Frommer's Daily Newsletter,** for the latest travel bargains and inside travel secrets; and **Frommer's Destinations archive,** where you'll get expert travel tips, hotel and dining recommendations, and advice on the sights to see for more than 200 destinations around the globe Once your research is done, the **Online Reservation System** (http://frommers.travelocity.com) takes you to Frommer's favorite sites for booking your vacation at affordable prices.

rental-car bookings, plus news, destination information, and deals on cruises and vacation packages. Keep in mind that free (one-time) registration is often required for booking. Because several airlines are no longer willing to pay commissions on tickets sold by online travel agencies, be aware that these online agencies will either charge a $10 surcharge if you book a ticket on that carrier—or neglect to offer those air carriers' offerings.

The sites in this section are not intended to be a comprehensive list, but rather a discriminating selection to get you started. Recognition is given to sites based on their content value and ease of use and is not paid for—unlike some website rankings, which are based on payment. Remember: This is a press-time snapshot of leading websites—some undoubtedly will have evolved or moved by the time you read this.

- **Travelocity** (www.travelocity.com or http://frommers.travelocity. com) and **Expedia** (www.expedia. com) are the most longstanding and reputable sites, each offering excellent selections and searches for complete vacation packages. Travelers search by destination and dates coupled with how much they are willing to spend.
- There's a good buzz in the online travel world about **Orbitz** (www.orbitz.com), a site launched by United, Delta, Northwest, American, and Continental airlines. It shows all possible fares for your desired trip, offering fares lower than those available through travel agents. (Stay tuned: At press time, travel-agency associations were waging an antitrust battle against this site.)
- **Qixo** (www.qixo.com) is another powerful search engine that allows you to search for flights and hotel rooms on 20 other travel-planning sites (such as Travelocity) at once. Qixo sorts results by price, after which you can book your travel directly through the site.

SMART E-SHOPPING

The savvy traveler is one who is armed with good information. Here are a few tips to help you navigate the Internet successfully and safely:

- **Know when sales start.** Last-minute deals may vanish in minutes. If you have a favorite booking site or airline, find out when last-minute deals are released to the public. (For example, Southwest's specials are posted every Tuesday at 12:01am central time.)
- **Shop around.** Compare results from different sites and airlines—and against a travel agent's best fare, if you can. If possible, try a range of times and alternate airports before you make a purchase.
- **Follow the rules of the trade.** Book in advance, and choose an off-peak time and date if possible. Some sites will tell you when fares to a particular destination tend to be cheapest.
- **Stay secure.** Book only through secure sites (some airline sites are not secure). Look for a key icon (Netscape) or a padlock (Internet Explorer) at the bottom of your web browser before you enter credit card information or other personal data.
- **Avoid online auctions.** Sites that auction airline tickets and frequent-flier miles are the number-one perpetrators of Internet fraud, according to the National Consumers League.
- **Maintain a paper trail.** If you book an e-ticket, print out a confirmation, or write down your confirmation number, and keep it safe and accessible—or your trip could be a virtual one!

ONLINE TRAVELER'S TOOLBOX

Veteran travelers usually carry some essential items to make their trips easier. Following is a selection of online tools to bookmark and use:

- **Visa ATM Locator** (www.visa. com) or **MasterCard ATM Locator** (www.mastercard.com). Find ATMs in hundreds of cities in the U.S. and around the world.
- **Foreign Languages for Travelers** (http://dictionaries.travlang.com). Here you can learn basic terms in more than 70 languages and click on any underlined phrase to hear what it sounds like. *Note:* To use this site, you must have speakers and downloadable free audio software.
- **Intellicast** (www.intellicast.com). Get weather forecasts for all 50 states and cities around the world. *Note:* Temperatures are in Celsius for many international destinations.
- **Mapquest** (www.mapquest.com). This best of the mapping sites lets you choose a specific address or destination, and in seconds, it returns a map and detailed directions.
- **Cybercafes.com** (www.cybercafes. com). Locate Internet cafes at hundreds of locations around the globe. Catch up on your e-mail and log onto the Web for a few dollars per hour.
- **Universal Currency Converter** (www.xe.com). See what your dollar or pound is worth in more than 100 other countries.
- **U.S. State Department Travel Warnings** (www.travel.state.gov). Reports on places where health concerns or unrest might threaten U.S. travelers. It also lists the locations of U.S. embassies around the world.

3

Anguilla

If you want a small, serene, secluded, and exclusive island, this is the place for you. Instead of high rises, one local commented, you get "low-rise dreams" here, referring to the posh inns. Anguilla used to tout itself as the Caribbean's best-kept secret. Those days are gone: The news is out. But you still get tranquility here. Exclusive St. Barts is a prettier island and just as luxurious as Anguilla. Anguilla's interior offers no waterfalls, rivers, or lush tropical foliage. Its scant rainfall makes for unproductive soil that supports mainly low foliage and sparse scrub vegetation. But its white-sand beaches are among the finest in the Caribbean; more than 30 of them dot the coastline, shaded by sea-grape trees. Come here to rest, unwind, and be pampered on the gorgeous sands or by your hotel pool.

Since Anguilla is just a short hop from St. Maarten/St. Martin, you can enjoy the privacy of a small-island experience and still be close to St. Maarten/St. Martin, with its gambling, shopping, and nightlife. You can also take a number of day trips if you get bored with the beach, including visits to Dutch-held St. Eustatius and Saba.

The northernmost of the British Leeward Islands in the eastern Caribbean, 5 miles north of St. Maarten, Anguilla (rhymes with *vanilla*) is only 16 miles (26km) long, with 35 square miles (91 sq. km) in land area. The little island has a population of approximately 9,000 people. Most are of African descent, though many are European, predominantly Irish. The locals work primarily in the tourist industry or fish for lobster.

Once part of the federation with St. Kitts and Nevis, Anguilla gained its independence in 1980 and has since been a self-governing British possession. In 1996, however, London issued a policy statement that locals have viewed as a move to push them toward independence. Many Anguillians believe that Britain has now reduced its global ambitions and wants to relinquish colonies that have become too expensive to maintain. Many islanders fear going it alone as a nation just yet. They know, however, that to retain Britain's protection, they would also have to abide by British laws—including its liberal position on gay rights. For the most part, islanders remain archly conservative and often homophobic.

With the opening of some super-deluxe (and super-expensive) hotels in the 1990s, Anguilla has become one of the Caribbean's most chic destinations, rivaling even St. Barts. Recently more moderately priced hotels have opened, too. Operations tend to be small and informal, though, as Anguilla has tried to control development and conserve natural beauty and resources.

1 Essentials

VISITOR INFORMATION

The **Anguilla Department of Tourism,** Old Factory Plaza, P.O. Box 1388, The Valley, Anguilla, B.W.I. (© 264/497-2759), is open Monday to Friday from 8am to 5pm. They're on the Web at **www.anguillavacation.com**.

In the United Kingdom, contact the **Anguilla Tourism Office,** Oakwood House, 414 Hackney Rd., London E27SY (© 020/7729-8003).

GETTING THERE

BY PLANE More than 50 flights into Anguilla are scheduled each week, not counting various charter flights. There are no nonstop flights from mainland North America, however, so visitors usually transfer through San Juan, Puerto Rico, or nearby St. Maarten. Some visitors also come in from St. Kitts, Antigua, and St. Thomas.

Anguilla's most reliable carrier, **American Eagle** (© 800/433-7300 in the U.S.), the commuter partner of American Airlines, has one nonstop daily to Anguilla from American's hub in San Juan. Flights leave at different times based on the seasons and carry 44 to 46 passengers. Schedules are subject to change, so check with the airline or your travel agent.

From Dutch St. Maarten, **Winair** (Windward Islands Airways International; © 800/634-4907) has three daily flights to Anguilla.

LIAT (© 800/468-0482 in the U.S. and Canada, or 869/465-2286) offers two flights daily to Anguilla from Antigua via St. Kitts. It's not the most reliable airline for leaving on time.

Tyden Air (© 264/497-2719) offers daily flights between St. Maarten and Anguilla, and a charter service between San Juan and Anguilla. It maintains a kiosk at the St. Maarten airport.

Flights from St. Maarten to Anguilla take 7 minutes; from San Juan and Antigua, 50 minutes; from St. Thomas, 40 minutes; and from St. Kitts, 1½ hours.

BY FERRY Ferries run between the ports of Marigot Bay, French St. Martin, and Blowing Point, Anguilla, at approximately 45- to 60-minute intervals daily. The trip takes 20 minutes, making it easy for visitors on one island to do a day trip to the other. The first ferry leaves St. Martin at 8am and the last at 7pm; from Blowing Point, the first ferry leaves at 7:30am and the last at 6:15pm. The daytime one-way fare is $10, which rises to $12 in the early evening. There's a $2 departure tax for those leaving by boat. No reservations are necessary; schedules and fares, of course, are always subject to change. Ferries are small, and none take vehicles.

Fun Fact **A Special Celebration**

Anguilla's most colorful annual festival is **Carnival,** held jointly under the auspices of the Ministries of Culture and Tourism. Boat races are Anguilla's national sport, and they form 60% of the Carnival celebration. The festival begins on Friday before the first Monday in August and lasts a week. Carnival harks back to Emancipation Day, or "August Monday," in 1834, when all enslaved Africans were freed.

Anguilla Great House
  Beach Resort **13**
Arawak Beach Inn **1**
Blue Waters Beach Apartment **9**
Cap Juluca **11**
Cove Castles **10**
CusinArt Resort & Spa **12**
Easy Corner Villas **3**
Enclave at Cinnamon Reef **15**
Fountain Beach Hotel **2**
Frangipani Beach Club **6**
La Sirena **7**
Malliouhana **5**
Mariners Cliffside Beach Resort **4**
Skiffles Villas **8**
Sonesta Beach
  Resort & Villas Anguilla **14**

GETTING AROUND

BY RENTAL CAR   To explore the island in any depth, it's best to rent a car, though be prepared for badly paved roads. Several rental agencies on the island can issue the mandatory Anguillian driver's license, which is valid for 3 months. You can also get a license at police headquarters in the island's administrative center, The Valley, and at ports of entry. You'll need to present a valid driver's license from your home country and pay a one-time fee of $6. Remember to *drive on the left side of the road!*

Most visitors take a taxi from the airport to their hotel and arrange, at no extra charge, for a rental agency to deliver a car there the following day. All the rental companies offer slight discounts for rentals of 7 days or more.

There's a branch of **Avis** at The Quarter (© **800/331-1084** in the U.S., or 264/497-2642 in Anguilla; www.avis.com), which offers regular cars and some four-wheel drive vehicles. Local firms include **Connor's Car Rental,** c/o Maurice Connor, South Hill (© **264/497-6433**), and **Triple K Car Rental,** Airport Road (© **264/497-5934**).

BY TAXI   Typical taxi fares are $20 from the airport to Cap Juluca; $14 to the Fountain Beach Hotel; and $16 to the Malliouhana hotel. Most rides take 15 to 20 minutes. For a cab company, call © **264/497-5054** or 264/497-4238.

FAST FACTS: **Anguilla**

Banking Hours Banks are open Monday to Thursday from 8am to 3pm, Friday from 8am to 5pm. You'll find a couple of bank branches in The Valley with ATMs.

Currency The Eastern Caribbean dollar (EC$) is the official currency of Anguilla, although U.S. dollars are the actual "coin of the realm." The official exchange rate is about EC$2.70 to each US$1 (EC$1 = 37¢). (Just before you leave home, you can check the current exchange rates on the Web at **www.x-rates.com**.)

Customs Even for tourists, duties are levied on imported goods at varying rates: from 5% on foodstuffs to 30% on luxury goods, wines, and liquors.

Documents All visitors must have an onward or return ticket. For U.S. and Canadian citizens, the preferred form of ID is a passport, even if it has expired within the past 5 years. In place of a passport, a photo ID with an original birth certificate is required (play it safe and bring a passport anyway). Citizens from the United Kingdom or other countries must have a valid passport.

Electricity The electricity is 110-volt AC (60 cycles), so no transformers or adapters are necessary to use U.S. appliances.

Hospitals For medical services, consult the **Princess Alexandra Hospital,** Stoney Ground (© **264/497-2551**), or one of several district clinics.

Language English is spoken here, often with a West Indian accent.

Liquor Laws Beer, wine, and liquor are sold 7 days a week during regular business hours. It's legal to have an open container on the beach.

Pharmacies Go to the **Government Pharmacy** at the Princess Alexandra Hospital, Stoney Ground (© **264/497-2551**), open Monday to Friday from 8am to 4pm; on Saturday from 10am to noon. In addition, **Paramount Pharmacy,** Water Swamp (© **264/497-2366**), is open Monday through Saturday 8:30am to 7pm and Sunday 2 to 5pm.

Police You can reach the police at their headquarters in The Valley (© **264/497-2333**) or the substation at Sandy Ground (© **264/497-6354**). In an emergency, dial © **911.**

Post Office The main post office is in The Valley (© **264/497-2528**). Collectors consider Anguilla's stamps valuable, and the post office also operates a philatelic bureau, open Monday to Friday from 8am to 3:30pm. Airmail postcards and letters cost $1.50 to the U.S. and Canada, $1.90 to the United Kingdom.

Safety Although crime is rare here, secure your valuables; never leave them in a parked car or unguarded on the beach. Anguilla is one of the safest destinations in the Caribbean, but you should still take standard precautions.

Taxes The government collects an 8% tax on rooms and a departure tax of US$10 if you leave the island by air, $2 if you leave by boat.

Telephone Telephone, cable, and telex services are offered by **Cable & Wireless Ltd.,** Wallblake Road, The Valley (© **264/497-3100**), open Monday to Friday from 8am to 5pm. To call the United States from Anguilla,

dial **1**, the area code, and the 7-digit number. You can call **MCI** by dialing
℗ **800/888-8000.**

Time Anguilla is on Atlantic standard time year-round, which means it's
usually 1 hour ahead of the U.S. east coast—except during daylight saving
time, when the clocks are the same.

Weather The hottest months in Anguilla are July to October; the coolest,
December to February. The mean monthly temperature is about 80°F.

2 Accommodations

Instead of staying at a hotel, you might want to consider renting a private villa.
Several rental agencies list villas in a vast range of prices. One of the best is
Anguilla Connection (℗ 800/916-3336 in the U.S., or 264/497-4403; fax
264/497-4402; www.luxuryvillas.com). Choices range from luxurious, secluded
houses to condos.

Don't forget that the government adds an 8% tax to your hotel bill, and you'll
pay 10% for service. Be sure to read the section "Package Deals" in chapter 2
before you book your hotel on your own!

VERY EXPENSIVE

Cap Juluca ✿✿✿ This is one of the most boldly conceived, luxurious oases
in the Caribbean, fronting one of the island's best white sandy beaches. On a
rolling 179-acre (72-hectare) site, Cap Juluca caters to Hollywood stars and
financial barons and offers serious pampering. This is the only resort on the
island to match the classy Malliouhana. Cap Juluca is more fun-loving and has
a party atmosphere, whereas Malliouhana is more subdued—take your pick.
Malliouhana has superior dining and service, but Cap Juluca fronts a better
beach, and its accommodations are plusher.

Most of the villa-style accommodations have soaring domes, walled courtyards, labyrinthine staircases, and concealed swimming pools ringed with thick
walls where you can take it all off. Inside, a mixture of elegantly comfortable
wicker furniture is offset with Moroccan accessories. Rooms are spacious, with
luxurious beds, and floors are made from Italian tile. All units are fully accessorized, but if money is no object, opt for the extravagant suites with their own
plunge pools. Large marble and mirrored baths are luxuriously appointed, with
shower/tub combinations. The cuisine at this hotel has never been better—the
chefs have been called "the dream team." But as hard as it tries, it still can't equal
Malliouhana. The elegant Pimms (℗ **264/497-6666** for reservations) is one of
the island's finest restaurants, with fresh and exotic ingredients flown in regularly. Count on imaginative seafood-based dishes with Asian accents.

Maunday's Bay (P.O. Box 240), Anguilla, B.W.I. ℗ **888/858-5822** in the U.S., 264/497-6779, or 305/466-0916
in Miami. Fax 264/497-6340. www.capjuluca.com. 98 units. Winter/spring $420–$735 double; from $905
suite. Off-season $325–$395 double; from $500 suite. MAP (breakfast and dinner) $85 per person extra. AE,
MC, V. **Amenities:** 3 restaurants; 2 bars; pool; 3 tennis courts; fitness center; watersports; business center;
room service; massage; babysitting; children's programs; laundry. *In room:* A/C, minibar, hair dryer, safe.

CoveCastles ✿✿ A cross between a collection of private homes and a monumental yet minimalist resort on a white sandy beach, this is a wonderful (if shockingly expensive) small resort, with an attentive staff. Designed by award-winning
architect Myron Goldfinger in 1985 and enlarged in 1998, the structure combines

elements from North Africa, the Caribbean, and the futuristic theories of Le Cor-busier. Don't call the staff at *Architectural Digest*—they've already visited here. The units include an interconnected row of town house–style beach structures that accommodate two to four persons, and a handful of larger, fully detached villas that house up to six. Large bedrooms have twin- or king-size beds with hand-embroidered linens and deluxe mattresses, and bathrooms are large and stylish with shower/tub combinations. This place offers even more privacy than Cap Juluca.

Each building has optimal views of the sea, amid the dunes and scrublands of the southwestern coast. Guest rooms have louvered doors and windows crafted from Brazilian walnut, terra-cotta tiles, comfortably oversized rattan furniture, a fully equipped, state-of-the-art kitchen, and a hammock. The most spectacular place to stay is the four-bedroom grand villa that opens directly on the beach; this is one of the most fabulous accommodations in the Caribbean.

The resort's French chef pampers guests with candlelit dinners of impeccable quality, in an intimate private dining room that overlooks the beach or en suite.

Shoal Bay West (P.O. Box 248), Anguilla, B.W.I. Ⓒ **800/223-1108** in the U.S., or 264/497-6801. Fax 264/497-6051. www.covecastles.com. 14 units. Winter $795–$1,195 beach house; $1,095–$2,995 villa. Off-season $525–$625 beach house; $625–$1,495 villa. AE, MC, V. Closed Sept–mid-Oct. **Amenities:** Restaurant; tennis court; aerobics; Sunfish sailboats, kayaks, snorkeling, deep-sea fishing, scuba, windsurfing, glass-bottom boat excursions; bicycles; car rental; massage; secretarial service; room service; babysitting; laundry. *In room:* ceiling fan, TV, hair dryer.

CuisinArt Resort & Spa ★★★ Yes, it's owned by Cuisinart, and, yes, it fronts a powdery beach of white sand (assuming that this is your next question). Evoking the architecture of nearby Cap Juluca, this is Anguilla's latest word in luxury. For privacy and seclusion, this "new kid on the block" provides the most competition to CoveCastles, of which it is an equal in a head-to-head race for supremacy. A complex of whitewashed villas crowned by blue domes and surrounded by lush tropical foliage, it seems straight out of Mykonos. The resort offers the first-ever hydroponic farm and the only full-service resort spa in Anguilla (their milk-and-honey almond scrub is the most fantastic we've ever known). The resort also features an herb garden, an orchid solarium, and a rare plant house. Italian fabrics, Haitian cottons, and furniture and large shower/tub combination bathrooms in soft-toned Italian marble characterize the well-furnished accommodations.

The Hydroponic Café's daily lunch features the freshest vegetables, grown in the $1 million hydroponic 1½-acre (.6-hectare) farm for salads and other light fare. The Santorini Restaurant is the fine-dining choice, with a French rotisserie on-site. Brawny, lusty dishes are served infused with the flamboyant flavors and spices of the Caribbean.

Rendezvous Bay (P.O. Box 2000), Anguilla, B.W.I. Ⓒ **800/943-3210** or 264/498-2000. Fax 264/498-2010. www.cuisinartresort.com. 93 units. Winter $730 double; from $790 suite. Off-season $295 double; from $350 suite. AE, MC, V. **Amenities:** 2 restaurants, bar; 3 tennis courts; fitness center; salon and spa; Jacuzzi; snorkeling, windsurfing, deep-sea fishing; babysitting; laundry. *In room:* A/C, TV, minibar, hair dryer, safe.

Enclave at Cinnamon Reef ★ Stay here if you're seeking first-class comfort in a club-like atmosphere without the flash and glitz of Cap Juluca or Malliouhana, but know in advance that its beach is only fair, with cloudy water. Under new management and with a name change, the resort has been totally refurbished. Five miles west of the airport on the southern coast, this intimate, luxurious hotel sits astride a circular cove with calm waters. The resort's

Mediterranean-inspired buildings are surrounded by acres of rolling lush greenery. The limited size of the resort makes it feel like a pleasantly informal private estate. Accommodations are in individual white stucco villas and garden suites; each unit contains well-appointed bedrooms and dressing areas, plus ceiling fans. Each of the spacious units has oversized four-poster beds, a sunken living room with leather couches, and a private patio. Most desirable are villa suites with private dressing rooms, opulent bathrooms with step-down showers, hammocks, and gorgeous views. Lovers of peace and quiet will request rooms at the far point from the main clubhouse. Noise is rarely a problem here, however, because of the thick concrete walls—not merely soundproof but bombproof and virtually hurricane resistant.

The Palm Court Restaurant and the bar area are the focal points of the resort. The cuisine has improved here in recent years; it doesn't rival the food served at Cap Juluca and Malliouhana, but it is first rate and offers better value. The veranda offers lovely harbor views. Some entertainment and occasional dancing are offered at night.

Little Harbour (5 miles west of the airport on the southern coast), Anguilla, B.W.I. ⓒ 800/223-1108 in the U.S. or 264/497-2727. Fax 264/497-3727. www.cinnamon-reef.com. 22 units. Winter $400–$525 suite; $475 villa suite. Off-season $200–$300 suite; $325 villa suite. Rates include continental breakfast. MAP (breakfast and dinner) $60 per person extra. Extra person $75. All-inclusive packages available. AE, MC, V. Closed Sept–Oct. **Amenities:** Restaurant, bar; pool; 2 tennis courts; Jacuzzi; sailboats, paddleboats, windsurfers, kayaks, snorkeling, fishing equipment, scuba diving; room service; laundry. *In room:* A/C, TV, minibar, coffeemaker, hair dryer.

Malliouhana ★★★ The ultra-chic hotel of the Caribbean, this cliff-side retreat conjures up images of Positano in the tropics. It looks even more spectacular than Cap Juluca—opulent and lavishly decorated, and situated on a rocky bluff between two white-sand beaches. It out-dazzles Cap Juluca in every way except for that resort's fabulous beach and glitzier digs. Malliouhana's 25 acres (10 hectares) are lushly landscaped with terraces, banks of flowers, pools, and fountains. Thick walls and shrubbery provide seclusion. A 224-member staff attends to 56 units; their motto is "Your wish is my command."

Haitian art and decorations are so splendid that you might not spot Gwyneth Paltrow sitting among the palms. Spacious bedrooms and suites are distributed among the main buildings and outlying villas. Each room has tropical furnishings and wide private verandas; each villa can be rented as a single unit or subdivided into three. Most of the rooms are air-conditioned. Three of the suites have private Jacuzzis, and one unit has a private pool. Some accommodations open onto garden views, and others front Mead's Bay Beach or Turtle Cove. Many rooms have luxurious four-poster beds, plus spacious Italian marble bathrooms with tubs and shower stalls.

Meads Bay (P.O. Box 173; 8 miles west of the airport), Anguilla, B.W.I. ⓒ 800/835-0796 in the U.S., or 264/497-6111. Fax 264/497-6011. www.malliouhana.com. 56 units. Winter $555–$735 double; from $910 suite. Off-season $369–$480 double; from $590 suite. No credit cards. Closed Sept–Oct. **Amenities:** Restaurant, bar; 3 pools; 4 tennis courts; exercise room; watersports center; children's playground; TV room; salon; library; room service (7am–10pm); massage; laundry. *In room:* A/C, minibar, hair dryer, safe.

Sonesta Beach Resort & Villas Anguilla ★ On the edge of a 3-mile strip of beachfront, this garishly designed hotel offers views of St. Martin's nearby mountains. In the 1980s, Arab investors commissioned architects to emulate a Moroccan palace beside an oasis. Moroccan artisans spent months on marble floors, intricate geometric mosaics, and imperial green tile roofs. It was designed to compete with the hyper-expensive hotels such as Cap Juluca and Malliouhana-that was too big an ambition, but it is still top rate. Its chief advantage over the stellar properties reviewed above is that it is a midprice luxury leader, and no one asks for your secret Swiss bank account number when you check in.

Frankly, less money should have been spent on the scalloped arches, elaborate mosaics, minarets, and fantastic Moorish/Arabesque public decor and more on the bedrooms, which, although fine in every way, come as a bit of a letdown after the poshness outside. Accommodations are scattered among a complex of buildings set either beside the beach or in a lush garden, the latter units renting for less money. Each room features Italian marble, a private patio, and high ceilings with fans. Beds are plush, with excellent mattresses and fine linens. Bathrooms have large circular tubs, stall showers, and marble counters.

A respectable Italian cuisine is served in the Il Mare Restaurant. The food here isn't in the same league as that in the resorts reviewed above, but it's prepared with quality ingredients, and many low-fat options are available. The resort has one of the most exotic-looking swimming pools on Anguilla, plus a health club overlooking the sea.

Rendezvous Bay West, Anguilla, B.W.I. © **800/SONESTA** or 264/497-6999. Fax 264/497-6899. www. sonesta.com. 97 units. Winter $370–$555 double; $945 suite. Off-season $205–$355 double; $650 suite. MAP (breakfast) $20 per person extra. AE, MC, V. **Amenities:** 2 restaurants, bar; pool; 2 tennis courts; health club; watersports; salon; room service (7am–midnight); massage; babysitting; laundry; valet. *In room:* A/C, TV, mini-bar, hair dryer, safe.

EXPENSIVE

Frangipani Beach Club ☆   Set on a mile of luscious white sand, this condo complex feels like a villa complex along the Spanish Mediterranean, with wrought-iron railings and red-tile roofs. Its major competitor is La Sirena, but La Sirena is more of a resort, with better facilities, including dining, whereas Frangipani attracts more self-catering types who want to have their own condos in Anguilla. Accommodations are light and airy, done in soft pastels with natural rattan furnishings; they're very comfortable, with king-size beds. All units also have tiled or marble bathrooms with shower/tub combinations, along with private terraces or balconies. Many of the more expensive rooms have full kitchens, and two- or three-bedroom units work for families or friends traveling together.

On-site is one of the island's finest hotel dining rooms, Frangipani Restaurant (see "Dining," below).

Meads Bay (P.O. Box 98), Anguilla, B.W.I. © **800/892-4564** in the U.S., or 264/497-6442. Fax 264/497-6440. www.frangipani.ai. 23 units. Winter $300–$400 double; from $650 suite. Off-season $185–$215 double; from $270 suite. AE, MC, V. **Amenities:** Restaurant, 2 bars; room service; laundry. *In room:* TV, hair dryer.

La Sirena ☆   Built in 1989 on 3 acres (1 hectares) of sandy soil, a 4-minute walk from a clean white beach, this Swiss-owned resort is inviting, intimate, and low key. At least 80% of its clientele comes from Switzerland or Germany. Accommodations, arranged in two-story bougainvillea-draped wings, are large and airy, with fine rattan and wicker furnishings. Some have air-conditioning; all have ceiling fans. Rooms have large double-, queen-, or king-size beds with fine linens. Bathrooms are spacious, with shower/tub combinations. To reach the beach, guests walk down through the garden and a sandy footpath. Beach hats, umbrellas, and lounge chairs await you on the sand. If possible, request rooms away from the second-floor Top of the Palms restaurant, thereby avoiding the noise and kitchen fumes.

The Top of the Palms restaurant, open only for dinner, is open to cool ocean breezes and offers views over Meads Bay and the surrounding treetops. A well-trained local chef prepares specialties ranging from alpine fondues to West Indian favorites, and there's also a less formal cafe.

Meads Bay (P.O. Box 200), Anguilla, B.W.I. **800/331-9358** in the U.S., 800/223-9815 in Canada, or 264/497-6827. Fax 264/497-6829. www.la-sirena.com. 29 units. Winter $260–$330 double; $400–$560 villa. Off-season $145–$190 double; $230–$360 villa. MAP (breakfast and dinner) $48 per person extra. AE, MC, V. **Amenities:** Restaurant, bar; 2 pools; tennis court; dive center; room service; babysitting; laundry. *In room:* Ceiling fan, minibar, hair dryer, safe.

MODERATE

Anguilla Great House Beach Resort   On Rendezvous Bay, with its 2½ miles of white sand, this is not really a "great house," but a bungalow colony, the type you often see on the fringes of Los Angeles. These cottages with their gingerbread trim sit in landscaped gardens. Each bungalow contains a number of well-furnished bedrooms, which can be rented in various configurations depending on your needs. You get an offering of different beds here, including both king- and queen-sized, or else two double beds. We particularly like the private porches opening onto water views. Cooled by ceiling fans, rooms can also be opened to capture the trade winds unless you prefer to chill out with air-conditioning. Bathrooms are small, tidily kept, and contain showers. The beachside amenities are good here, including lounge chairs, umbrellas, kayaks, Sunfish, windsurfers, and both snorkeling and fishing gear.

Rendezvous Bay, Anguilla, B.W.I. **264/497-6061.** Fax 264/497-6019. www.anguillagreathouse.com. 35 units. Winter $250 double. Off-season $140 double. AE, DISC, MC, V. **Amenities:** Restaurant, bar; pool; watersports; laundry. *In room:* A/C, iron and ironing board, hair dryer.

Arawak Beach Resort *Value*   Built on the site of an ancient Arawak village and only minutes from beautiful Shoal Bay Beach, this comfortable and inviting family-run hotel is a good value (for pricey Anguilla, anyway), especially during the summer months. It opens onto views of Scilly Cay and Captains Ridge. The property has been greatly improved. Today it offers studios and one-bedroom suites in octagonal-shaped buildings. Beachfront units are built in the style of a re-created Amerindian village and are equipped with wet bars and coffeemakers, plus large balconies or terraces. Furnishings are comfortable and include king-size beds, plus small bathrooms with a tub and shower.

A good continental and West Indian menu is a feature of the rather formal restaurant.

Island Harbour (P.O. Box 1403, The Valley), Anguilla, B.W.I. **800/451-3734** or 264/497-4888. Fax 264/497-4889. www.arawakresort.com/html/home1.shtml. 17 units. Winter $175–$210 double. Off-season $110–$160 double. AE, MC, V. **Amenities:** Restaurant, beach bar, cafe; windsurfing, canoeing; bicycle rental; car rental; babysitting; laundry. *In room:* Ceiling fan, no phone.

Blue Waters Beach Apartments   Fronting a half mile of white sandy beachfront, this tranquil resort has a vaguely Moorish look. It offers well-designed and immaculately kept one-bedroom units and two-bedroom apartments, each opening directly on the beach and cooled by a ceiling fan. Family friendly, it's really a do-it-yourself kind of place, so plan to be self-sufficient; units have their own kitchens so you can do your own cooking. You'll find ample closets and comfortable furnishing such as king-size beds. Bathrooms are immaculately white, very Calvin Klein, each with a shower stall. Rooms have terraces down below or balconies if on the second floor.

Shoal Bay West (P.O. Box 69), Anguilla, B.W.I. ✆ **264/497-6292**. Fax 264/497-6982. www.caribbean concepts.com/bwb/Default.htm. 9 units. Winter $250 1-bedroom apt., $360 2-bedroom apt. Off-season $125 1-bedroom apt., $175 2-bedroom apt. AE, MC, V. **Amenities:** Nearby dive shop; babysitting; breakfast terrace. *In room:* TV, ceiling fans, kitchen, coffeemaker.

Fountain Beach Hotel ✦   Built right on a gorgeous stretch of golden sand in 1989, this coral-colored resort was inspired by Mediterranean architecture, and it's more like a B&B or a small inn than a hotel. After the fantasy resorts described above, this inn is like a reality check. Surrounded by 5 acres (2 hectares) of sloping and forested land on the island's underpopulated north coast, it's simple, with few facilities, but lots of peace and quiet. The bedrooms are large and airy, with ceramic-tile floors and sliding glass windows. Each unit has an unstocked refrigerator, and some have kitchenettes. Accommodations range from a junior suite (the smallest) to a roomy two-bedroom cottage with full kitchen and two bathrooms. Each has a marble shower-only bathroom, and a sitting area; some also offer private balconies, and none have TV.

Shoal Bay Beach, Anguilla, B.W.I. ✆ **264/497-3491**. Fax 264/497-3493. www.fountainbeach.com. 12 units, 2 cottages. $245–$280 double; $365 2-bedroom unit. AE, DISC, MC, V. *In room:* Coffeemaker, no phone.

Skiffles Villas   Overlooking Road Bay but a 10-minute drive from a beach, this hotel is for independent types. It offers well-furnished one-, two-, and three-bedroom apartments, each equipped with a full kitchen and a porch. Accommodations are comfortable and decently maintained, opening onto water views. If you want isolation, opt for Sea Grapes, a single-story villa set away from the other units. The Flamboyant and Bougainvillea units are upper-story villas that have the best views. The most luxurious unit is Peppertree, a three-bedroom villa with its own lap pool, cable TV, phone, and stereo system.

Lower South Hill, Meads Bay (P.O. Box 82), Anguilla, B.W.I. ✆ **219/642-4445** in the U.S., or 264/497-6110. www.skiffles.com. 5 units. Winter $240 double; $280–$525 for 4. Off-season $168–$190 double; $230–$470 for 4. No credit cards. **Amenities:** Pool. *In room:* Ceiling fan, no phone.

INEXPENSIVE

Easy Corner Villas   On a bluff overlooking Road Bay, this modest villa complex lies a 5-minute walk from a good beach. On the main road west of the airport, Easy Corner Villas is owned by Maurice E. Connor, the same entrepreneur who rents many of the cars on the island. His one-, two-, and three-bedroom apartments are simply furnished and set on landscaped grounds with views of a good beach from their private porches. Each comes equipped with a kitchen, combination living and dining room, a ceiling fan and air-conditioning, good beds, and large, airy living areas, plus small bathrooms with shower stalls. Daily maid service is available for an extra charge.

South Hill (P.O. Box 65), Anguilla, B.W.I. ✆ **264/497-6433**. Fax 264/497-6410. www.caribbean-inns.com. 12 units. Winter $160–$195 apt.; off-season $125–$155 apt. AE, MC, V. No children under age 2. *In room:* A/C, TV, kitchen.

3 Dining

VERY EXPENSIVE

Blanchards ✦✦ INTERNATIONAL   Bob and Melinda Blanchard are the masterminds behind this elegantly casual, intensely fashionable restaurant on a garden-swathed pavilion beside the sea, next to the Hotel Malliouhana's beach. The cuisine is among the most creative and interesting on the island,

and Blanchards has attracted a sprinkling of celebs (say hi to Robert de Niro or Janet Jackson if you see them).

Behind tall teal shutters (which can be opened to the sea breezes), you'll enjoy sophisticated food with a Caribbean flair, enhanced with spices from Spain, Asia, California, and the American Southwest. Dishes change according to the inspiration of chef Melinda but are likely to include Cajun grouper on a bed of onion marmalade; swordfish stuffed with toasted corn dressing; and jerk Jamaican-style chicken, with bananas grilled and glazed with molasses and rum.

Meads Bay. *C* **264/497-6100.** Reservations recommended. Main courses $24–$47. AE, MC, V. Mon–Sat 6:30–9pm.

Cedar Grove ★ CARIBBEAN   In the olden days, if you wanted to be fed at this beachfront, you had to dine out with chickens in someone's backyard. No more. Cedar Grove continues the volcanic restaurant explosion on Anguilla. It's one of the newest, latest, and hottest dining tickets. In a setting evocative of *Casablanca,* you can enjoy a series of ever-changing specialties, based on the best and freshest ingredients. Signature dishes likely to be on the menu include lobster cakes given added zest by the use of slivers of fresh ginger, with a final dash of curry cream sauce for good measure. The shrimp in coconut curry is fairly routine, but the coriander-crusted red snapper is one of the finest dishes we sampled on our latest Anguilla culinary round-up.

Rendezvous Bay. *C* **264/497-6549.** Main courses $16–$28. AE, MC, V. Daily 7am–11pm. Closed Sept–Oct.

Hibernia ★ FRENCH/INDOCHINESE   Just a shade under the superb viands of Blanchards, this is another little stunner of creativity in the kitchen. Chef Raoul Rodriguez and his wife, hostess Mary Pat O'Hanlon, have converted a lovely West Indian cottage into a charming restaurant, with a French- and Indonesian-inspired decor that's a nice change of pace. When you taste some of the delectable and creative cuisine of Chef Raoul, you'll know why he was voted chef of the year in 1997. His cuisine is as good now as it was back then—maybe even better. Start off with a Caribbean vegetable and lentil soup flavored with cumin, or a selection of finely sliced West Indian fish smoked in their own kitchen. Main courses are likely to include Caribbean fish fillets cooked and served in a spicy Thai broth, accompanied by wild rice, or grilled breast of chicken roasted with pineapple and goat cheese. It's a strange marriage, but it works divinely. French duck magret is a stunning choice; its light glaze of honey is the perfect touch.

Island Harbour. *C* **264/497-4290.** Reservations recommended. Main courses $23.50–$35.50. AE, MC, V. Tues–Sat noon–2pm; Tues–Sun 7–9pm.

KoalKeel Restaurant ★ CONTINENTAL/CARIBBEAN   When you tire of the beachfront eateries (if such a thing is possible), make a hasty retreat here, where character, charm, and island atmosphere await you. Housed in a dignified coral stone-and-clapboard manor built in 1790, this restaurant is set on a hillside that overlooks The Valley. The two-story dining area has an airy decor and sea views from its outdoor patio and second story. Some of the menu items (slow-cooked lamb and rock-oven chicken with locally grown herbs) are cooked in the stone-sided, wood- and charcoal-burning oven (the KoalKeel) that was part of the original building. Grilled snapper with Creole sauce, lobster crepes, and smoked grouper on a bed of leeks are deservedly popular. We like how the chef makes use of local ingredients when they are available.

On the premises, **Le Dôme** (a wine cellar and retail wine shop) stocks thousands of bottles, and the antique-filled **Old Rum Shop** sells "designer" rums (some of them vintage and very old). A tearoom upstairs (**Le Petit Patissier**) serves steaming pots of tea and deliciously fattening, freshly made Viennese and French pastries.

The Valley. ℂ **264/497-2930.** Reservations recommended for dinner. Main courses $24–$48. AE, MC, V. Tues–Sun 7am–11pm. Closed Sept–mid-Oct.

Malliouhana Restaurant ★★★ FRENCH/CARIBBEAN   Even better than the restaurant at Cap Juluca, Malliouhana Restaurant, with the Caribbean's most ambitious French menu, offers fluidly choreographed service, fine food, a 25,000-bottle wine cellar, and a glamorous clientele. Michel Rostang, the successful son of the legendary Jo Rostang, one of the most acclaimed chefs of southern France, is often in charge. You'll dine in an open-sided pavilion on a rocky promontory over the sea. At night your candlelit table will be set with French crystal, Limoges china, and Christofle silver. There are well-spaced tables, an ocean view, and a splashing fountain.

The hors d'oeuvres selection is the finest on the island, including warm lobster medallions with celery pancake and curry sauce; a fabulous smoked-salmon purse filled with yogurt, cucumber, and mint; and a delectable beef carpaccio with fresh tomato and basil. Main courses are likely to range from a perfectly prepared braised fillet of mahi-mahi served with a sweet potato purée to roasted whole lobster with a basil butter sauce.

Meads Bay (8 miles west of the airport). ℂ **264/497-6111.** Reservations required. Main courses $28–$44. AE, MC, V. Daily 12:30–3pm and 7:30–10:30pm.

Straw Hat ★ ECLECTIC/INTERNATIONAL   Winning rave reviews from such magazines as *Bon Appétit,* chef Bryan Malcarney lives up to his hype. Even if the cuisine weren't as good as it is, you might want to visit anyway to enjoy the panoramic setting by the sea and the distant vistas of French St. Martin. Malcarney features exceptional meats, seafood, and produce, handling them with a finely honed technique. We revel in his appetizers, such as conch spring rolls with pickled ginger and delightful steamed mussels with herb-flavored broth. For a main dish, the chef prepares one of the best versions of Anguillian spiny lobster we've had (sautéed and topped with a Pernod cream sauce). Other delights include grilled loin of tuna with mango chutney for real island flavor and flair, a saffron-laced seafood stew made with fresh local fish, and shrimp and mussels given an extra meaty flavor by spicy chorizo.

Forest Bay. ℂ **264/497-8300.** Reservations recommended. Main courses $19–$35. AE, MC, V. Mon–Sat 6:30–9pm. Closed Sept–Oct.

Trattoria Tramonto ★ NORTHERN ITALIAN   One of our latest discoveries, and one of the island's best, this breeze-swept restaurant lies between Blue Waters beach apartments and CoveCastle. The chef, Valter Belli, hails from Emilia Romanga in central Italy, often called the gastronomic center of that country. The tables lie near the water with distant views of the hills of French-controlled St. Martin, the neighboring island. The "sundowners" here are the best on island, including a peachy Bellini, as good as that served at Harry's Bar in Venice. Other champagne drinks are mixed with such fruits as mango, passion fruit, and guava, and called names like the Puccini or the Michelangelo. The chef takes special care with his appetizers, including a *zuppa di pesce* (fish soup with porcini mushrooms) and spicy hot penne with a garlic, tomato, and red-pepper sauce. All the ingredients for the main courses are superb and treated with care, including a delectable red snapper with a caper-laced fresh tomato sauce or, our favorite and the house specialty, lobster-filled ravioli in a truffle cream sauce. "It's of the Gods," we heard a diner at the next table say. Anguillian lobster also appears in medallions in a savory seafood sauce.

Shoal Bay West. (© 264/497-8819. Reservations required. Main courses $8–$22 lunch, $22–$38 dinner. MC, V. Tues–Sun noon–3pm and 6:30–9:30pm. Closed Sept–Oct.

MODERATE

Bistro Phil ✦ FRENCH/ITALIAN   Perched on a cliff 50 feet (15m) above the sea, this restaurant is a showcase for the talents of French-born Philippe Kim, the owner and chef, who draws a stylish crowd of diners to his restaurant. Many of them request a table on the terrace with its view of the sea. Kim is a master at flavoring, and he cooks with zest and spice, importing excellent ingredients into Anguilla. He also makes the best pizza on island, and sometimes guests order a small one at the start of their meal. Our favorite is the savory pie made with lobster, calamari, and shrimp. You can also order such continental appetizers as delectable slices of Parma ham with melon, or else sautéed shrimp salad in a garlic and lemon buttery sauce. It's impossible to resist the fresh Anguilla lobster that appears in the fettuccine, served in a sauce of sun-dried tomatoes, mushrooms, and crayfish. His pan-seared tuna steak arrives in a warm vinaigrette with a selection of fresh vegetables, and he takes the old-fashioned veal Parmigiana recipe and jives up its flavor with a marinara sauce, sprinkling it for a finish with fresh Parmesan cheese. His tiramisu flavored with orange zest is the island's finest.

South Hill. (© 264/497-6810. Reservations recommended. Main courses $10–$28 lunch, $20–$36 dinner. AE, DC, MC, V. Mon–Sat noon–2:30pm (mid-Dec–Apr only) and 6:30–9:30pm. Closed mid-Aug to mid-Oct.

Frangipani Restaurant FRENCH/CARIBBEAN/MEDITERRANEAN With its 12-foot (4m) wall of wine bottles, elegantly designed interior, panoramic views, and superb cuisine, this restaurant is becoming better known every season. The chef's mastery of various cuisines is reflected in such dishes as cold creamy zucchini soup and steamed crayfish flan flavored with tamarind and coconut milk. The truffle and scallop ravioli is a delight, as is the Anguillian red mullet, flavored with fennel and served with red wine–rosemary sauce. Although meats are imported, they don't taste that way, especially the stuffed lamb fillet with tomatoes and basil in a crust of bacon and rosemary sauce. A skilled pastry chef prepares exotic desserts such as chocolate sushi and frozen soufflé of tropical fruits. Except for a few pricey items, most dishes are moderate in cost. Boaters are especially fond of showing up here in the early morning hours, when big breakfasts are served.

In the Frangipani Beach Club, Meads Bay. (© 264/497-6442. Reservations required. Lunch main courses $16–$24; dinner main courses $23–$37. AE, MC, V. Daily 7:30–10:30am, noon–2:30pm, and 7–9:30pm. Closed for dinner on Wed.

Mango's ✦ AMERICAN/CARIBBEAN   In a pavilion a few steps from the edge of the sea, on the northwestern part of the island, Mango's is a great choice, with healthier cuisine than any of the island's other top restaurants. Mango's serves very fresh fish, meat, and produce, cooked on the grill with an absolute minimum of added fats or calories. All the breads and desserts, including the ice cream and sorbet, are made fresh daily on the premises. You might start with delectable lobster cakes and homemade tartar sauce or creamy conch chowder.

Grilled local lobster and spicy whole snapper are featured main courses, but the best main dish is simply grilled fish with lemon-and-herb butter.

Seaside Grill, Barnes Bay. © 264/497-6479. Reservations required for dinner, as far in advance as possible. Main courses $21–$36. AE, MC, V. Wed–Mon 6:30–9pm. Closed Aug–Oct.

Zara's Restaurant ★ ITALIAN/CARIBBEAN   Award-winning master chef Shamsh presides at this casually elegant place, which opened in 1996. Since then it has won many fans who visit every time they return to Anguilla. The chef uses excellent ingredients, which are prepared to order. He's known island-wide for his pasta dishes, especially his Rasta Pasta. You will also delight in his fish dishes, especially the crusted snapper, although he does veal, chicken, and steak dishes equally well. Try his Bahamian cracked conch, and look for various daily specials. A few items are costly, but most dishes are in the moderate range.

Allamanda Beach Club, Upper Shoal Bay East. © 264/497-3229. Reservations required. Main courses $16–$38. AE, MC, V. Daily 6:30–9pm.

INEXPENSIVE

Good, affordable food is served in a festive atmosphere at **Johnno's,** Road Bay (© 264/497-2728), and at **The Pumphouse Bar & Grill** (© 264/497-5154). See "Anguilla After Dark" later in this chapter for details. Johnno's is open for lunch and dinner; the Pumphouse is open only for dinner.

Cora's Pepperpot ★ *Finds* WEST INDIAN   This is one of the most charming and authentic restaurants in Anguilla, run by Ms. Cora Richardson, a former local police officer. Find the concrete-sided building adjacent to the island's secondary school, and prepare to sample Cora's lip-smacking fare like spare ribs. Forget the fancy restaurants when you dig into Cora's fare. She cooks the way people used to eat before all the glamour people arrived. That means Anguillan pea soup and red snapper grilled just as you like it. When it's available, she offers grilled Anguillan lobster, but at a higher price than the main courses indicated below. Her most local dish (try it at least once) is curried goat meat, an island favorite.

The Valley. © 264/497-2328. Reservations recommended for dinner, not necessary at lunch. Main courses $5–$16. MC, V. Mon–Sat 7am–10pm, Sun noon–3pm.

Ferryboat Inn *Value* CARIBBEAN/FRENCH   Established by English-born John McClean and his Anguillian wife, Marjorie, this place is one of the best values on the island. On the beach, a short walk from the Blowing Point ferry pier, it features French onion soup, black bean soup, some of the best lobster Thermidor on the island, and scallop of veal Savoyard. Unless you order expensive shellfish, most dishes are reasonable in price.

The McCleans also rent six one-bedroom apartments and one two-bedroom beach house. In winter, apartments cost $165 to $190, and the beach house is $230. Off-season, an apartment is $85 to $95, and the beach house is $130.

Cul de Sac Rd., Blowing Point. © 264/497-6613. Reservations recommended. Main courses $8–$32. AE, MC, V. Mon–Sat noon–3pm; daily 7:30–10pm. Closed Tues Apr–mid-Dec. Turn right just before the Blowing Point Ferry Terminal and travel 150 yards (137m) before making a left turn.

Ripples CARIBBEAN/INTERNATIONAL   This restaurant is earthier and more British than most of the other restaurants in Sandy Ground, which has the biggest cluster of bars and restaurants on Anguilla. Its cheerful staff and long, busy bar will make you feel like you're on the set of *Cheers*. Set in a restored clapboard house, it has a raised deck, a casual West Indian decor, and a crowd of regulars. Local fish is served here—mahi-mahi, snapper, tuna, and grouper, prepared any way you'd like but always zesty. The coconut shrimp, puffy Brie in beer batter, and Creole-style conch are our favorites and the reason we keep coming back. Only a few dishes are at the high end of the price scale.

Sandy Ground. ⓒ 264/497-3380. Reservations recommended. Main courses $11–$23. AE, DISC, MC, V. Daily noon–midnight.

4 Beaches

Superb beaches put Anguilla on the tourist map. There are dozens of them, plus another handful on the outer cays. The island's interior may be barren, but there's no denying the beauty of its shores. Miles and miles of pristine, powdery-soft sands open onto crystal-clear waters. Many of the beaches are reached via bone-jarring dirt paths that ultimately give way to sand and sea. All the beaches are open to the public, and you may have to walk through the lobby of a deluxe hotel to reach one.

The best beaches are on the west end of the island, site of the most expensive hotels. **Rendezvous Bay** is the island's most famous, a long curving ribbon of pale gold sand that stretches along the bay for 2½ miles (4km). It's calmer, warmer, and shallower than Shoal Bay, which is on the Atlantic side. With an alfresco beach bar, it attracts all kinds, from families to romantic couples.

Our favorite is 2-mile (3km) **Shoal Bay** ✦✦ in the northeast, one of the best beaches in the Caribbean. With silver-white, powder-soft sands, it also boasts some of Anguilla's best coral gardens, the habitat of hundreds of tiny iridescent fish, making it great for snorkeling. Umbrellas, beach chairs, and other equipment are available here so you can enjoy the backdrop of coconut palms and sea-grape trees. This beach is often called "Shoal Bay East" to distinguish it from "Shoal Bay West" (see below). The waters are usually luminous, transparent, and brilliant blue. At noon the sands are so white they almost blind you, but at sunrise or sunset, they turn so pink they could rival any beach in Bermuda. Music graces the shores from the terraces of the Hard Broke Café and Uncle Ernie's. The Upper Shoal Bar serves first-rate tropical drinks. On the beach, souvenir shops hawk T-shirts and suntan lotion. For a little more tranquility, you can also take the trail walk from Old Ta to little-known **Katouche Beach,** which offers perfect snorkeling and is also a prime site for a beach picnic under shade trees.

Shoal Bay West, next to Maunday's Bay, has pristine white sands opening onto the southwest coast. You'll find some deluxe accommodations rising from these shores, including CoveCastles.

Adjoining Shoal Bay West, and site of Cap Juluca, is mile-long, white-sand **Maunday's Bay Beach,** justifiably one of the island's most popular shorelines, with good snorkeling and swimming. Though the waters are luminescent and usually calm, sometimes the wind blows enough to attract windsurfers and sailboats. On a clear day you can see St. Martin across the way.

Sandy Isle, on the northwest coast, is a tiny islet with a few palms surrounded by a coral reef. It lies offshore from Road Bay. Once here, you'll find a beach bar and restaurant, and a place to rent snorkeling gear and buy underwater cameras. **Sandy Island Enterprises** (ⓒ 264/497-5643) has daily trips from the pier by Johnno's Beach Bar at Sandy Ground. The cost of a round-trip ticket is $8, and the first boat leaves at 10am. The last boat back usually departs at 4pm. You can also go farther out, to Prickly Pear Cay, which stretches like a sweeping arc all the way to a sand spit populated by sea birds and pelicans.

Moments Grilled Lobster on a Remote Cay

At Island Harbor, just wave your arms, and a boatman will pick you up and transport you across the water to **Scilly Cay,** pronounced "silly key." You wouldn't really call this place an island. It's more like a spit of sand 170 yards (155m) off the coast of the main island's northeastern shoreline. At a little cafe and bar here, you can select a fabulous fresh lobster. Grilled while you wait, the lobster is marinated in a sauce of honey-laced orange juice, orange marmalade, roasted peanuts, virgin olive oil, curry, and tarragon. Chicken is prepared here the same way. Lunch is daily Tuesday to Sunday from noon to 3pm.

The northwest coast has a number of other beaches worth seeking out, notably **Barnes Bay Beach,** filled with powdery white sand and opening onto clear blue waters. You can relax in the shade of the chalky hillside or a beach umbrella or join the windsurfers and snorkelers who come here. It's usually less crowded after lunch.

Almost never crowded, **Little Bay Beach** is also one of the most dramatic in Anguilla, set against steep cliffs. Here the sands are grayish, but snorkelers and scuba divers don't seem to mind. The beach also attracts bird-watchers and picnickers. Local weddings are sometimes performed here.

Road Bay Beach, also on the northwest coast, is known for spectacular sunsets and clear blue waters, often filled with yachts coming from St. Martin. A watersports center here on the beach will set you up with gear. You can also watch fishermen set out in their boats to pursue the elusive, valuable Anguillian lobster.

The beaches along the northeast coast are the stuff of fantasies—especially if you've got a four-wheel drive. Calm and tranquil, the incredibly blue waters of **Island Harbour Beach** attract both locals and the odd visitor or two. For centuries Anguillians have set out from these shores to haul in Anguillian lobster. There are a few beach bars and alfresco dining rooms here, so you can make a day of it—or take a 3-minute boat ride over to Scilly Cay.

Chances are you'll have **Captain's Bay's beach** all to yourself. Near Junk's Hole, it's better for enjoying the sun and sand than it is for swimming. The undertow is dangerous, though the setting is dramatic and appealing.

5 Sports & Other Outdoor Pursuits

CRUISES & BOATING A great way to have fun on Anguilla is to cruise to a secluded beach on an offshore cay for a picnic and some snorkeling, whether on your own or with a group. Several outfitters on the island rent vessels, including the **Anguillian Divers** (© 264/497-4750), offering a 30-foot (9m) motorboat, and the **Island Yacht Charter Company** (© 264/497-3743), who offers 35-foot (11m) motorboats.

FISHING Your hotel can arrange for you to cast your line with a local guide, but you should bring your own tackle. Agree on the cost before setting out, however, to avoid the "misunderstandings" that have been reported.

Malliouhana, Meads Bay (© 264/497-6111), has a 34-foot (10m) fishing cruiser, *Kyra,* which holds up to 8 passengers at a time. You can charter it for fishing parties for $400 for up to 4 hours, with a $100 surcharge for each additional hour. All fishing gear is included, and they can pack you a boxed lunch for an additional charge.

SCUBA DIVING & SNORKELING   Most of the coastline of Anguilla is fringed by coral reefs, and the island's waters are rich in marine life, with sunken coral gardens, brilliantly colored fish, caves, and stingrays offshore. Conditions for scuba diving and snorkeling on the island are ideal. In addition, the government of Anguilla has artificially enlarged the existing reef system, a first for the Caribbean. Battered and outmoded ships, deliberately sunk in carefully designated places, act as nurseries for fish and lobster populations and provide new dive sites. **Stoney Bay Marine Park** off the northeast coast is a place to explore the ruins of a Spanish ship that sank in the 1700s.

The **Dive Shop,** Sandy Ground (© 264/497-2100), is a five-star PADI international training center and offers a complete line of PADI certification courses. It carries several lines of scuba equipment for sale or rental. A two-tank dive costs $100, and night dives go for $60.

It's easy to find places to rent snorkeling gear on the island's most popular beaches, if your hotel doesn't provide it. The snorkeling's great at Shoal Bay, Maunday's Bay, Barnes Bay, Little Bay, and Road Bay.

TENNIS   Most of the resorts have their own tennis courts (see "Accommodations," earlier in this chapter). **Malliouhana,** Meads Bay (© 264/497-6111), has a pro shop and four championship Laykold tennis courts with a year-round professional coach, Peter Burwash. Three courts are lit for night games. There are also two courts at **Enclave at Cinnamon Reef,** Little Harbour (© 264/497-2727).

6 Anguilla After Dark

Nightlife on Anguilla centers mainly on the various hotels, especially in winter, when they host barbecues, West Indian parties, and singers and other musicians. The hotels hire calypso combo groups and other bands, both local and imported.

Open-air **Johnno's Beach Bar,** Road Bay, Sandy Ground (© 264/497-2728), is a favorite of Hollywood types when they visit Anguilla. The club offers Beck's beer on the beach, barbecued spareribs, grilled chicken, and fresh fish for lunch and dinner. Live entertainment takes place Wednesday, Friday, Saturday, and Sunday from 8pm to 1am. A weekly Sunday barbecue begins at 11am, with live music starting mid-afternoon in winter. John Edwards, the Anguilla-born owner, should probably run for office. Try the Johnno special (similar to a piña colada, but made with rum and guava berries).

A restaurant-cum-beach bar, **Palm Grove Bar & Grill,** Junk's Hole Bay (© 264/497-4224), offers a long stretch of uncrowded curving white sand and offshore reefs full of eels, squid, and manta rays. Nat Richardson, the owner, is

---

Tips **Island Tours**

The best way to get an overview of the island is on a **taxi tour.** In about 2½ hours, a local driver (all of them are guides) will show you everything for $50. The driver will also arrange to let you off at your favorite beach after a look around, and then pick you up and return you to your hotel or the airport.

waiting to boil or grill fresh-caught lobster, crayfish, or shrimp for you. *Bon Appétit* liked his johnnycakes so much it stole the recipe and published it. On Friday nights, partygoers rock the sands to live music.

Pumphouse Bar & Grill, Sandy Ground (© **264/497-5154**), is the island's latest hotspot, boasting 30 different rums. The food is good, too, served in a funky dining room with an uneven concrete slab floor that was originally designed as a repair station for heavy trucks. Standard but satisfying menu items include grilled half-chickens, 8-ounce beef burgers, pizzas, and a Caesar salad with slices of jerk chicken. Go any time from 7pm to 2am, except Sunday, when it's closed. Reggae lovers should show up on Wednesday, Friday, and Saturday nights, and Thursday nights are often devoted to merengue.

There are some other little nighttime joints on island that seem to close with irritating irregularity. Most of these dives are active only on the weekend, including **Dune Preserve** at Rendezvous Bay (© **264/497-2660**), where the best-known singer on island, "Bankie" Banx, performs. You might also check out another weekend hot spot, **Rafe's Back Street** at Sandy Ground (© **264/ 497-3918**), offering live music for dancing on Friday and Saturday nights, which are also the nights to hit **Red Dragon**, The Valley (© **264/497-2687**), a dance club where a DJ provides the music.

Antigua

Antiguans boast that they have a different beach for every day of the year. That may be an exaggeration, but the beaches here are certainly spectacular: Most are protected by coral reefs, and the sand is often sugar white.

Antigua, Barbuda, and Redonda form the independent nation of Antigua and Barbuda, within the Commonwealth of Nations. Redonda is an uninhabited rocky islet of less than a square mile, located 20 miles (32km) southwest of Antigua. Barbuda, which lies 26 miles (42km) to the north of Antigua, is covered at the end of this chapter.

Antigua (*an-TEE-gah*) is an independent nation, but it is still British in many of its traditions. Economically, it has transformed itself from a poverty-stricken island of sugar plantations to a modern-day vacation haven. The landscape of rolling, rustic Antigua is dotted with stone towers that were once sugar mills.

The inland scenery isn't as dramatic as what you'll find on St. Kitts, but, oh, those beaches! If you want high rises and glittering gambling and nightlife, head elsewhere, perhaps to Puerto Rico. Antigua does have some casinos, but they're hardly a reason to visit, and most of its hotels are intimate one- or two-story inns rather than glitzy, sprawling resorts. In general, the dining and shopping of Antigua are comparable to those of St. Kitts but don't hold up to those of St. Maarten or the U.S. Virgin Islands.

Most locals will treat you with respect if you show them respect, but Antigua is hardly the friendliest of islands in the Caribbean—too much unemployment, too great a gap between rich and poor.

Most hotels, restaurants, beach bars, and watersports facilities lie north of the capital of **St. John's,** in the northwest. St. John's is a large, neatly laid-out town 6 miles (10km) from the airport and less than a mile from Deep Water Harbour Terminal. This port city is the focal point of commerce and industry and the seat of government and shopping. Protected within a narrow bay, St. John's is charming, with cobblestone sidewalks and weather-beaten wooden houses with corrugated iron roofs and louvered Caribbean verandas. Trade winds keep the wide streets cool. Since all the major resorts are on good beaches, most visitors tend to stay put, going into St. John's for a day's shopping jaunt or to English Harbour for some history.

Before volcanic ash covered much of Antigua's neighbor, **Montserrat,** the little island was a destination in its own right. It was once a haven for many American expatriates, mostly retired couples, and at one time was the Caribbean island of choice for many music stars, including Paul McCartney, who came here to write songs and record them.

Unless Montserrat is hit by another volcanic eruption, it is slowly bouncing back, hoping to recapture the tourism it once enjoyed. Until the dust settles, Montserrat is most often visited as a day trip from Antigua, mainly by curiosity or adventure seekers.

1 Essentials

VISITOR INFORMATION

Before you leave, you can contact the **Antigua and Barbuda Department of Tourism,** 610 Fifth Ave., Suite 311, New York, NY 10020 (© **212/541-4117**); or 25 SE Second Ave., Suite 300, Miami, FL 33131 (© **305/381-6762**). A new toll-free number also provides information: © **888/268-4227.** Live operators are available Monday to Friday 9am to 5pm eastern standard time. You can also look up the department's website, at **www.antigua-barbuda.org.**

In Canada, contact the **Antigua and Barbuda Department of Tourism & Trade,** 60 St. Clair Ave. E., Suite 304, Toronto, ON, M4T 1N5 (© **416/961-3085**).

In the United Kingdom, information is available at **Antigua House,** 15 Thayer St., London, England W1M 5LD (© **020/7486-7073**).

On the island, the **Antigua and Barbuda Department of Tourism,** on Friendly Alley, in St. John's (© **268/462-0480**), is open Monday to Thursday from 8am to 4:30pm and on Friday from 8am to 3pm.

GETTING THERE

Before you book your airline ticket on your own, refer to the section "Package Deals" in chapter 2. Even if you don't buy a package, you should still look over our tips on how to get the best airfare.

The major airline that flies to Antigua's V. C. Bird Airport is **American Airlines** (© **800/433-7300** in the U.S.; www.aa.com), which offers four daily nonstop flights to Antigua from its hub in San Juan, Puerto Rico. A flight takes about 1½ hours, and each of them departs late enough in the day to allow easy transfers from other flights.

Continental (© **800/231-0856;** www.flycontinental.com) has daily flights out of Newark, New Jersey.

British Airways (© **800/247-9297** in the U.S.; www.british-airways.com) offers flights four times a week from London's Gatwick Airport.

Air Canada (© **888/247-2262;** www.aircanada.ca) has regularly scheduled flights from Toronto to Antigua on Saturday only.

BWIA (© **800/538-2942** in the U.S.; www.bwee.com) is increasingly popular. Each week, three flights depart for Antigua from Miami; one from Toronto; five from Kingston, Jamaica; and five from London.

GETTING AROUND

BY TAXI   Taxis meet every airplane, and drivers wait outside the major hotels. If you're going to spend a few days here, a particular driver may try to "adopt" you. The typical one-way fare from the airport to St. John's is $12, but to English Harbour it's $25 and up. The government of Antigua fixes rates, and taxis are meterless.

Fun Fact Special Events

The week before the first Tuesday in August, summer **Carnival** envelops the streets in exotic costumes that recall Antiguans' African heritage. Festivities include a beauty competition and calypso and steel-band competitions. The big event in spring is Antigua's annual **Sailing Week** in late April or early May.

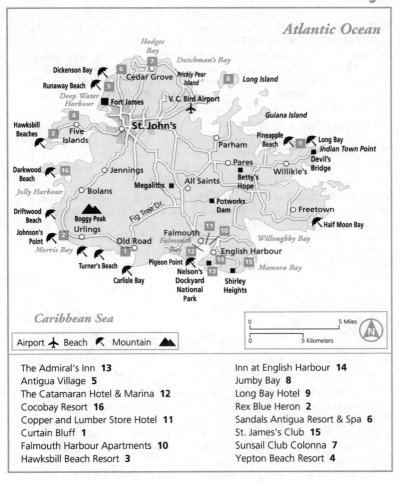

Airport ✈ Beach 🏖 Mountain ▲▲

The Admiral's Inn **13**
Antigua Village **5**
The Catamaran Hotel & Marina **12**
Cocobay Resort **16**
Copper and Lumber Store Hotel **11**
Curtain Bluff **1**
Falmouth Harbour Apartments **10**
Hawksbill Beach Resort **3**

Inn at English Harbour **14**
Jumby Bay **8**
Long Bay Hotel **9**
Rex Blue Heron **2**
Sandals Antigua Resort & Spa **6**
St. James's Club **15**
Sunsail Club Colonna **7**
Yepton Beach Resort **4**

Taxis aren't cheap, but they're the best way to see Antigua, as the drivers also act as guides. Most taxi tours go from the St. John's area to English Harbour. Drivers generally charge $40 for 3 or 4 passengers and often wait 30 minutes or more while you sightsee around English Harbour. If you split the cost with another couple, these tours become more affordable.

To call a taxi in St. John's, dial ✆ **268/462-0711;** after 6pm, dial ✆ **268/ 462-5190.**

BY RENTAL CAR   Renting a car on Antigua is not advisable. Newly arrived drivers quickly learn that the island's roads are terribly potholed and poorly sign-posted.

If you want to drive despite these caveats, you must obtain an Antiguan license, which costs $20 and requires a valid driver's license from home. Most car-rental firms can issue you an Antiguan license, which they usually do without a surcharge. Remember to *drive on the left.*

It's best to stick with the major U.S. rental companies rather than use a local agency. **Avis** (ⓒ **800/331-1212** in the U.S., or 268/462-2840 in Antigua; www.avis.com) and **Hertz** (ⓒ **800/654-3131** in the U.S., or 268/462-6450 in Antigua; www.hertz.com) offer pickup service at the airport. Another agency to try is **Dollar** on Nevis St., St. John's (ⓒ **800/800-4000** in the U.S., or 268/462-0362 in Antigua; www.dollarcar.com). **Budget** is also represented on Antigua with a kiosk at the airport (ⓒ **800/472-3325** in the U.S., or 268/462-3009 in Antigua; www.budgetrentacar.com).

BY MOTORCYCLE & SCOOTER   For the cheapest wheels on the island, rent a motorcycle or scooter from **Shipwreck,** English Harbour (ⓒ **268/464-7771**). Yamaha and Honda motorcycles rent for about $35 per day or $150 per week; scooters cost $25 per day or $85 per week. You'll save so much by renting one of these that you may not even mind the bumpy ride.

BY BUS   We don't recommend buses for the average visitor, though they are an inexpensive option. Service is erratic and undependable, and roads are impossibly bumpy. Buses are supposed to operate between St. John's and the villages daily from 5:30am to 6pm, but don't count on it. In St. John's, buses leave from two different "stations"—on Market Street, near the Central Market, and on Independence Avenue, adjacent to the Botanical Gardens. Most fares are $1.

 FAST FACTS: **Antigua**

Banks   Banks are usually open Monday to Thursday from 8am to 1pm and on Friday from 8am to 1pm and 3 to 5pm. The best bank for visitors is Royal Bank at High and Market streets in St. John's. You'll find an ATM here and one at the airport.

Currency   These islands use the Eastern Caribbean dollar (EC$). Nearly all hotels bill in U.S. dollars, however, and only certain tiny restaurants present their prices in EC$. When you inquire about a price, make sure you know the type of dollars quoted. The EC dollar is worth about 37¢ in U.S. currency (EC$2.70 = US$1). *Unless otherwise specified, rates in this chapter are quoted in U.S. dollars.*

Customs   Arriving visitors are allowed to bring in 200 cigarettes, 1 quart of liquor, and 6 ounces of perfume.

Documents   A valid passport is preferred from U.S., British, and Canadian nationals. An original birth certificate accompanied by a photo ID that's issued by a government agency is also acceptable, but we recommend that you carry a passport when visiting a foreign country. All arriving visitors must have a departing ticket.

Electricity   Most of the island's electricity is 220-volt AC (60 cycles), which means that U.S. appliances require transformers. The Hodges Bay area and some hotels, however, are supplied with 110-volt AC (60 cycles).

Emergencies   In an emergency, contact the police (ⓒ **268/462-0125**), the fire department (ⓒ **268/462-0044**), or an ambulance (ⓒ **268/462-0251**). You can also call ⓒ **911** or ⓒ **999** for any type of emergency.

Hospital   The principal medical facility on Antigua is **Holberton Hospital,** on Hospital Road, St. John's (ⓒ **268/462-0251**).

Language The official language is English.

Liquor Laws Beer and liquor are sold in many stores, 7 days a week. It's legal to have an open container on the beach.

Safety Antigua is generally safe, but that doesn't mean you should wander alone at night on St. John's near-deserted streets. Don't leave valuables unguarded on the beach, either.

Taxes & Service Charges Visitors must pay a departure tax of US$20 and an 8.5% government tax on hotel bills. Most hotels also add a service charge of between 10% and 15%.

Telephone Telephone calls can be made from hotels or the office of Cable & Wireless, on Long Street., in St. John's (© 268/462-0840). You can also send faxes and telegrams from here. To call Antigua from the United States, dial 1, 268, and the number. To call the United States from Antigua, dial 1, the area code, and the number. You might want to purchase a phone card, which you can use to connect with an American long-distance company. You can access AT&T Direct from some pay phones and some hotels by dialing © **800/872-2881**. You can reach MCI at © **800/888-8000** and Sprint at © **800/366-4643**.

Time Antigua is on Atlantic standard time year-round, so it's 1 hour ahead of U.S. eastern standard time. When daylight saving time takes over in the U.S., then Antigua's time is the same as in the eastern United States.

Water Tap water is generally safe to drink here, but many visitors prefer to drink only bottled water.

Weather The average year-round temperature ranges from 75° to 85°F.

2 Accommodations

Antigua's hotels are generally small, and many are closed during the summer. Owners may decide to shut down early if business isn't good. Air-conditioning is uncommon except in first-class hotels, so be duly warned, since Antigua at midday can be quite steamy and uncomfortable.

An 8.5% government tax and a service charge of between 10% and 15%, depending on your hotel, are added to your hotel bill, which makes quite a difference in your final tab.

Antigua has lots of shockingly expensive hotels and resorts, but there are ways you can bring down the prices. Consider booking a package if you're interested in one of those pricey places. Refer to the section "Package Deals," in chapter 2.

Because getting around the island is difficult, your choice of where to stay is crucial (the hotels are all plotted on the island map at the beginning of this chapter). Those who prefer high winds, breaking waves, and dramatic scenery should stay on the northwest side, north of the capital of St. John's. This is an area of middle-bracket resorts such as Sandals. If you want to spend most of your vacation at one resort, venturing out only occasionally, and can afford it, try one of the super exclusives such as Curtain Bluff or St. James's Club in the remote southern coast. History buffs who like atmospheric B&Bs should try either Admiral's Inn or the Inn at English Harbour, unless a good beach is crucial. If it is, then head for one of the big resorts, all of which are built on sandy beaches.

VERY EXPENSIVE

Curtain Bluff ★★★   This serene oasis on two beautiful beaches is the island's premier resort, with a price tag to match. The place has such ambience and class it makes St. James's Club look like a glorified Holiday Inn. Fifteen miles (24km) from the airport on the southwest shore, the hotel occupies the most lushly tropical section of the island, in the village of Old Road, and sits on two beautiful beaches (one turbulent, the other calm as can be). This place is for a mature old-money crowd, who like the clubby feel and the good service. Curtain Bluff hosts Sailing Week each year and has good sports facilities.

The beautifully furnished accommodations include deluxe units with king-size beds; a terrace room with a king-size, four-poster bed; and spacious suites with two balconies. The roomy bathrooms have beautiful tiles, deluxe toiletries, tubs and showers, dual vanities, and bidets. Accommodations in the newer units are more spacious, with upgraded furnishings and two double beds each. The two-story suites are among the most luxurious in all the Caribbean. Although at times in the heat of midday you may wish for air-conditioning, ceiling fans and trade winds generally keep the accommodations cool. Some guests come primarily for the superb food. French-born Christophe Blatz keeps his continental menu limited, so he can freshly prepare and artistically arrange everything. Curtain Bluff restaurant boasts the Caribbean's most extensive wine selection. Although it's not a formal requirement, men are encouraged to wear jackets during the dinner hour in high season.

Morris Bay (P.O. Box 288), Antigua, W.I. © 212/289-8888 in New York, or 268/462-8400. Fax 268/462-8409. www.curtainbluff.com. 73 units. Dec 19–Apr 14 $750–$1,045 double; from $995 suite. Apr 15–May 14 and Oct 12–Dec 18 $555–$795 double; from $755 suite. Rates are all-inclusive. AE, MC, V. Closed mid-May–late Oct. **Amenities:** 2 restaurants, bar; pool; 4 tennis courts; squash; putting green; fitness center, aerobics; sailing, waterskiing, snorkeling, deep-sea fishing, dive shop, scuba diving, windsurfing; room service (8am–11pm); babysitting; access to computer facilities *In room:* Ceiling fan, safe.

Hawksbill Beach Resort ★   Named after an offshore rock that resembles a hawksbill turtle, this 37-acre (15-hectare) resort is 10 miles (16km) west of the airport and 4 miles (6km) southwest of St. John's. Set on four beaches (one reserved for those who want to go home sans tan lines), it caters to active types and is popular for weddings and honeymoons. This is your classic midrange resort, catering to families and happy couples who like its informality and might feel uncomfortable in the atmosphere of pretension and social climbing that you get at Curtain Bluff. The hotel revolves around an open-air, breezy central core. Bedrooms are small and comfortably furnished, with tubs and showers. The least expensive accommodations open onto a garden; there are more secluded beachfront units available as well. The West Indian great house has three bedrooms for three to six occupants, with king-size beds and kitchenettes. Note that rooms have neither TVs nor air-conditioning.

Although the chefs use quality ingredients and the food is fine, it isn't the real reason to stay here. It's usually lively at this resort, with limbo dancers and calypso singers 4 nights a week in season.

Five Islands Village (P.O. Box 108), St. John's, Antigua, W.I. © 800/223-6510 in the U.S., or 268/462-0301. Fax 268/462-1515. www.hawksbill.com. 111 units. Winter $300–$380 double; $1,500 great house. Off-season $210–$250 double; $1,330 great house. AE, MC, V. **Amenities:** 2 restaurants, 2 bars; pool; tennis court; sunfish sailing, windsurfing, snorkeling, waterskiing; babysitting; laundry. *In room:* Ceiling fan, coffeemaker.

The Inn at English Harbour ★   This small inn occupies one of the finest sites on Antigua, 10 acres (4 hectares) that directly flank a beach, with views over Nelson's Dockyard and English Harbour. It's tranquil and informal, very unpretentious. And it's also better run that its closest competitor, the Copper and Lumber Store Hotel, and more elegant than the nearby Admiral's Inn. "We don't put on airs here," one staffer said, "unlike those other posh places." This is the quintessential charming old-fashioned resort, with a historic feel that maintains its appeal even though more glamorous places have popped up elsewhere on the island. The late actor Richard Burton liked it so well he spent two of his honeymoons here. You can take a free water taxi to finer beaches along English Harbour. White-tile floors, screened plantation shutters, balconies, and excellent beds invite you to linger. The least expensive units are farthest from the beach, on a hillside. In 2002, management added an additional six accommodations, each of them a suite decorated with a scattering of British and Caribbean antiques.

The inn is known for high-quality cooking. Lunch is served both at the beach house and in the main dining room. Have a drink before dinner in the old-style English Bar with stonewalls and low overhead beams. Live entertainment is provided in winter.

English Harbour (P.O. Box 187), St. John's, Antigua, W.I. © 268/460-1014. Fax 268/460-1603. www.theinn.ag. 34 units. Winter $224–$440 double; from $410 suite. Off-season $175–$224 double; from $270 suite. MAP (breakfast and dinner) $85 per person extra. AE, DC, MC, V. Closed Sept–Oct. From St. John's, head south, through All Saints and Liberta, until you reach the south coast. **Amenities:** 2 restaurants, 2 bars; pool; golf; tennis courts nearby; health club; horseback riding; waterskiing, day sailing, deep-sea fishing; scuba diving; bike rental; water taxi to Nelson's Dockyard; car rental; room service (7am–10pm); babysitting; laundry. *In room:* Ceiling fan, minibar, fridge, coffeemaker, hair dryer, safe.

Jumby Bay ✿✿✿   On secluded beaches, this is a sybaritic retreat of the rich and famous, with a celebrities-and-CEOs crowd that can afford the expensive rates. Taken over during the late 1990s by the prestigious Half Moon Golf, Tennis & Beach Club of Jamaica, it occupies a 330-acre (132-hectare) offshore island. Boats depart from the Antiguan "mainland" every hour from 10am to 10pm daily. You can pre-register for the 2-mile (3km) ride on the Antiguan side. With white sandy beaches along a coastline protected by coral reefs, the grounds have been handsomely planted with loblolly and white cedar.

Guests are coddled and pampered in luxury. Only Curtain Bluff tops this place. A haven for naturalists, the resort features Pasture Bay Beach on the island's windward side, home to endangered species of turtles, rare birds, and sheep. All the accommodations are recently refurbished, including a 12-unit Mediterranean-style complex, 2- and 3-bedroom luxury villas, and several spacious private manor houses. Beds are luxurious, as are the spacious marble and tile bathrooms with tubs. Note that there are no TVs in the rooms, and only the bedrooms within the suites are air-conditioned. In light of the constant trade winds, no one seems to mind.

For breakfast and lunch, it's casual fare at the open-air Beach Pavilion. Dinner 6 nights a week is at the historic Estate House, the signature restaurant in the 230-year-old English plantation manor. Dinner every Wednesday night is configured as an upscale beachfront barbecue. Imaginative and well-prepared dishes take their inspiration from Europe, America, and the Caribbean.

Long Island (P.O. Box 243), St. Johns, Antigua, W.I. © 800/421-9016 or 268/462-6000. Fax 268/462-6020. www.elegantresorts.com. 51 units. Winter $950–$1,150 junior suite; $1,250 suite; $2,500 2-bedroom villa; $3,750 3-bedroom villa. Off-season $650–$750 junior suite; $850 suite; $1,500 2-bedroom villa; $2,250 3-bedroom villa. Children age 12 and under stay free in parents' room in summer only. AE, DC, MC, V. **Amenities:** 2 restaurants, 2 bars; golf arranged; 3 tennis courts; watersports; fitness center; room service (7am–10pm). *In room:* A/C, ceiling fan, minibar, hair dryer, safe.

Long Bay Hotel ★★   On a remote spit of land between the open sea and a sheltered lagoon, Long Bay is on the eastern shore, a mile (2km) northeast of the hamlet of Willikie's. It faces one of the island's best beaches and a lagoon that's safe for watersports. Owned and operated by the Lafaurie family since 1966, it's more of an inn than a resort, with breezy rooms and six furnished cottages for extra privacy. Come here for the complete remoteness and peace, to escape all the glitter of places like the St. James's Club, and to experience one of the last intimate family-run resorts on the island. The spacious rooms, in motel-like wings along the lagoon, have ceiling fans and firm mattresses, plus half tubs with showers. Instead of TV, you get the sound of waves crashing on the beach. The best units are on the upper floors.

The resort centers on a clubhouse within the stone-walled Turtle Restaurant, which provides perfectly good, if not gourmet, food. There's a special dinner seating for children.

Long Bay (P.O. Box 442), St. John's, Antigua, W.I. © **800/291-2005** in the U.S., or 268/463-2005. Fax 268/463-2439. www.longbayhotel.com. 24 units. Winter $355–$400 double; $400–$474 cottage for 2. Off-season $267–$297 double; $297–$350 cottage for 2. Rates include MAP (breakfast and dinner). Extra person $101. AE, MC, V. Closed Sept–Oct. **Amenities:** Restaurant, bar; golf nearby; tennis court; scuba facilities, sailboats, windsurfers, snorkeling, fishing, waterskiing, boat trips; library; game room; room service (breakfast only); babysitting; laundry. *In room:* Ceiling fan, no phone.

St. James's Club ★★   This remote, 100-acre (40-hectare) resort on Mamora Bay on 2 sand beaches tries for glamour, but it falls far behind Curtain Bluff and Jumby Bay, and it doesn't have the state-of-the-art maintenance of those properties, either. (To be fair, although it's very expensive, at least it hasn't jacked up its prices to the shocking levels of those two places.) Mid-range package tours from Britain and America continue to fill many of the rooms on occasions. The sports facilities are among the Caribbean's best.

Some of the rooms are standard and medium in size, but others are spacious. The resort has never been able to escape the architectural curse of its former role as a standard and somewhat banal-looking Holiday Inn. Despite that, all units have excellent beds, combination bathrooms (tub and shower), commodious vanities, dual basins, and sliding-glass doors that open onto private balconies or patios. Pricey two-bedroom villas and hillside homes are also available.

If you're looking into a package all-inclusive deal, know that the cuisine here is merely average. You can relax in the Rainbow Garden Dining Room, or dine alfresco by candlelight at the Docksider Restaurant overlooking Mamora Bay. Piccolo Mondo serves Italian and international food, and simple lunches are the venue at the Coco Beach Barbecue. Sometimes the setting is more exciting than the cuisine, although the finest of ingredients are imported. Guests can top off the evening at the Jacaranda nightclub. Many enjoy gambling in the glamorous but small European-style casino.

Mamora Bay (P.O. Box 63), St. John's, Antigua, W.I. © **800/345-0271** in the U.S., or 268/481-8787. Fax 268/481-1661. www.antigua-resorts.com. 105 units, 73 villas. Winter $320–$370 double; $470 suite; from $660 villa for 2. Off-season $250–$300 double; $400 suite; from $502 villa for 2. Children age 5 and under stay free in parents' room. AE, DC, MC, V. **Amenities:** 4 restaurants, 4 bars; 3 pools; 7 tennis courts; casino; disco; spa facilities, exercise room; hairdresser; Jacuzzi; playground and playhouse for children; croquet court; marina, watersports, sailboards, aqua bikes, deep-sea fishing, waterskiing, snorkeling, scuba diving; salon; room service; massage; babysitting; laundry. *In room:* A/C, ceiling fan, TV, hair dryer, safe.

EXPENSIVE

Antigua Village ★   On a peninsula that stretches into turquoise waters 2 miles (3km) from St. John's, Antigua Village is like a self-contained condo community, with a freshwater pool and mini-market on the premises. It has a great location on one of the most tranquil and best sandy beaches on island, next to the Siboney Beach Club. Don't expect grand resort service, as the whole place is geared toward time-share sales. Come here if you are a self-sufficient type who wants a fantastic beach. Each studio apartment and villa has a kitchenette, a patio, a balcony, twin beds with firm mattresses, and a sofa bed in the living room. The units are generally spacious, and a tropical decor brightens things considerably; expect standard motel-style bathrooms with shower stalls. Most accommodations open onto views of the water.

Dickenson Bay (P.O. Box 649), St. John's, Antigua, W.I. © **268/462-2930.** Fax 268/462-0375. www.antiguavillage.net. 54 units. Winter $190–$215 studio; $230–$270 suite; $450–$570 house. Off-season $110–$130 studio; $130–$155 suite; $260–$330 house. AE, DISC, V. **Amenities:** 4 restaurants, 4 bars; pool; watersports; mini-mart. *In room:* A/C, ceiling fan, TV.

CocoBay Resort ⭐ Set near 4 beaches, this compound of colorful wood-sided, tin-roofed cottages lies on 10 headland acres (4 hectares). Cocobay opened in 2000 as Antigua's newest all-inclusive resort, giving Sandals some real competition. Understated elegance and West Indian charm combine in this cliff-side setting on the "sunset side" of the island.

Accommodations are simple and unpretentious, modeled on local architecture raised on stilts, with hand-carved furnishings and island art providing both comfort and color. It attracts a hip clientele who'd never patronize some of the stuffier resorts such as Curtain Bluff. Guests stay in the above-mentioned cottages or in one of four "plantation houses," suitable for up to four occupants, on the hill. Each cottage has a four-poster king-size bed, a private porch, and wooden louvered windows, plus a bathroom with a shower. Bathrooms in the plantation house offer full-size tubs.

Valley Church (P.O. Box 431), St. John's, Antigua, W.I. © **800/816-7587** in the U.S., or 268/562-2400. Fax 268/562-2424. www.cocobayresort.com. 47 units. $160–$190 per person double; $820 cottage for 4. Off-season $100–$130 per person double; $600 cottage for 4. Rates include all meals, drinks, watersports. AE, MC, V. **Amenities:** Restaurant, bar; pool; snorkeling, kayaking; massage and beauty treatments; laundry. *In room:* Coffeemaker, hair dryer, fridge, ceiling fan, safe, no phone.

The Copper and Lumber Store Hotel ⭐ Forget a pool. Forget a beach. This is the "museum hotel" of English Harbour, with more atmosphere than even The Inn at English Harbour and Admiral's Inn nearby. As its name suggests, this charming, 18th-century building was originally a store that sold wood and copper for repairing British sailing ships. The store and its adjacent harbor structures are built of brick that once was used as ships' ballast. Each of the period units is brick-lined, uniquely designed, and filled with fine Chippendale and Queen Anne reproductions, antiques, brass chandeliers, hardwood paneling, and hand-stenciled floors. The showers look as if they belong in a sailing vessel, with thick mahogany panels and polished brass fittings. All suites have kitchens with aging equipment, private bathrooms (with showers only), and ceiling fans. Request a room with a half-tester bed and mosquito netting. All the mattresses are first rate. The downside of this place is that you might be bothered by rubbernecks who view the place as the museum we said it was and not as an inn. Although the place was founded, with great imagination and flair, by English expatriates in the 1980s, in 1999, it was taken over by the Antiguan government, and is run today with less personalized flair by a government bureaucracy.

A traditional English pub serves standard food daily, and the Wardroom serves a stolid continental dinner nightly. You may want to skip both of these for fish and chips and Bass on tap at the jumping **Mainbrace Pub,** next door.

Nelson's Dockyard, English Harbour (P.O. Box 184), St. John's, Antigua, W.I. ℂ **268/460-1058.** Fax 268/460-1529. www.antiguanice.com. 14 units. Winter $195–$275 double; $325 suite. Off-season $135 double; $145–$275 suite. AE, MC, V. From St. John's, follow the signs southeast to English Harbour. **Amenities:** Restaurant, pub; ferry service to Galleon Beach; babysitting; laundry. *In room:* Kitchen, coffeemaker, hair dryer, iron and ironing board.

Rex Blue Heron ★

On the most beautiful beach on Antigua, 15 miles (24km) south of St. John's, this hotel offers peace and quiet and tends to appeal to couples and honeymooners. Casually comfortable, with a staff that's sometimes a wee bit too casual and easy-going, it crowns Johnson's Point with two-story white-stone buildings with rooms that overlook either well-kept gardens, the pool, or the beach. The beachfront units have air-conditioning, ceiling fans, and TVs; the standard rooms offer only ceiling fans. Each room has a patio or balcony. Standard rooms have only one double bed, whereas most of the others contain twins.

An intimate on-site restaurant serves good-tasting West Indian meals, although many guests quickly tire of eating all their holiday meals in the same dining room and from the same kitchen every night.

Johnson's Point Beach (P.O. Box 1715), St. John's, Antigua, W.I. ℂ **800/255-5859** or 305/471-6170 in the U.S., or 268/462-8564. Fax 305/471-9547 in the U.S., or 268/462-8005. www.rexcaribbean.com. 64 units. Winter $280–$360 double. Off-season $260–$340 double. Rates are all-inclusive. AE, DC, DISC, MC, V. **Amenities:** Restaurant, 2 bars; watersports; babysitting; laundry. *In room:* Ceiling fan, no phone.

Sandals Antigua Resort & Spa ★

For straight couples—all others are denied admittance—this is the best all-inclusive on the island, dwarfing the previously recommended Rex Blue Heron all-inclusive. If you like a resort where everything's paid in advance and you virtually live in a walled compound with lots of organized activities, this might be for you, providing you meet the sexual orientation criterion. On one of the island's best beaches, the resort offers eight different room categories, most of which are medium in size and some of the more romantic ones with four-poster beds and ocean views. The usual amenities include small patios and plush mattresses. If you want honeymoon privacy, opt for a cottage suite (because of its octagonal shape, the staff calls it a rondavel) that opens directly onto Dickenson Beach.

A quintet of bars and restaurants are available, serving everything from Tex-Mex fare to Japanese sushi. Il Palio is especially good, serving an array of antipasti and Italian specialties. A beachfront restaurant is also an excellent rendezvous for meals.

Dickenson Bay (P.O. Box 147), St. John's, Antigua, W.I. ℂ **888-SANDALS** or 268/462-0267. Fax 268/462-4135. www.sandals.com. 193 units. All-inclusive rates: winter $650–$750 double; from $815 rondavel suite. Off-season $580–$720 double; from $760 rondavel suite. AE, DC, MC, V. **Amenities:** 5 restaurants, 5 bars; 5 pools; tennis courts; fitness center; spa (spa services not included in all-inclusive rate); 5 whirlpools; watersports. *In room:* A/C, TV, coffeemaker, hair dryer.

Siboney Beach Club ★

Owned by Australia-born Tony Johnson and his wife, Ann, the Siboney Beach Club is named after the Amerindian tribe who predated the Arawaks. Set north of St. John's on a thickly foliated acre of land fronting the mile-long white-sand beach of Dickenson Bay, the resort is shielded on the inland side by a tall, verdant hedge. The club's social center is the Coconut Grove restaurant (see "Dining," below). The comfortable suites are in a three-story balconied building draped with bougainvillea and other vines. The suites have louvered windows for natural ventilation, and TVs are available. All units have separate bedrooms, living rooms, and balconies or patios, plus tiny kitchens behind moveable shutters. Each comes with a small, immaculately kept private bathroom with shower. There's also a tree house: a single room with a king-size bed and jungle decor perched high in a *Ficus benjamina* tree.

Dickenson Bay (P.O. Box 222), St. John's, Antigua, W.I. © 800/533-0234 in the U.S., or 268/462-0806. Fax 268/462-3356. www.siboneybeachclub.com. Winter $190–$310 double. Off-season $130–$180. AE, MC, V. **Amenities:** Restaurant, bar; pool; room service; laundry. *In room:* A/C.

Yepton Beach Resort ⭐   At one edge of Hog John Beach, this small, middle-bracket resort, set on 37 acres (15 hectares) of beachfront, was built in the late 1980s. Relatively basic and straightforward, it is hardly the choice of demanding visitors seeking lavish amenities. The neo-Hispanic, three-story white-walled building has a red terra-cotta roof and a verdant lawn that extends to the sandy beach on the Five Islands Peninsula. There's nothing glitzy here; the resort is full of laid-back, unpretentious charm and intimacy. Bedrooms have beige-tile floors and streamlined modern furniture, including firm mattresses; bathrooms are rather routine, motel-style affairs, with shower stalls. Ground-floor bedrooms have direct beach access. Cable television is available in the lounge.

There's a decent restaurant and bar on the premises, with live reggae or calypso music 3 nights a week.

Hog John Beach (P.O. Box 1427), St. John's, Antigua, W.I. © 800/361-4621 in the U.S., or 268/462-2520. Fax 268/462-3239. www.yepton.com. 38 units. Winter $200–$290 double; $390 suite with kitchen for up to 4; $580 suite with kitchen for up to 6. Mid-Apr–mid-Dec $130–$200 double; $270 suite with kitchen for up to 4; $390 suite with kitchen for up to 6. AE, MC, V. **Amenities:** Restaurant, bar; pool; horseback riding; 2 tennis courts; windsurfing, snorkeling, scuba diving; bike rental; car rental; babysitting; laundry. *In room:* A/C, ceiling fan.

MODERATE

The Admiral's Inn ⭐⭐   Though way down in third position when stacked against its nearby competitors, The Inn at English Harbour and the Copper and Lumber Store Hotel, this place is full of character and atmosphere. Designed in 1785, the year Nelson sailed into the harbor as captain of the HMS *Boreas,* and completed in 1788, the building here once used to house British officers stationed at the dockyards, with its ground floor devoted to the storage of tar and boat-repair supplies. Loaded with West Indian charm, this place in the heart of Nelson's Dockyard is constructed of weathered brick that was brought from England to be used as ships' ballast. You stay here if you want to recapture a sense of old Caribbean history, especially if you're an Anglophile and don't mind the commute to the beach.

There are three types of character-filled accommodations. The most expensive are the ground-floor rooms of a tiny brick building across the courtyard from the main structure. Each of these spacious units has a little patio, a garden entry, and air-conditioning. The front rooms on the first floor of the main building, with views of the lawn and harbor, are also more expensive. The back rooms on this floor are less pricey, and all have air-conditioning. With dormer-window views over the yacht-filled harbor, the least expensive rooms on the top floor are smaller and quiet, but they may get warm on summer afternoons. Some rooms have air-conditioning, but not all.

For details on the inn's restaurant, see "Dining," below.

English Harbour (P.O. Box 713), St. John's, Antigua, W.I. © 800/223-5695 in the U.S., or 268/460-1027. Fax 268/460-1534. www.antiguanice.com. 14 units. Winter $130–$160 double, $400 apt. for 4. Off-season $100–$120 double, $240 apt. for 4. $25 per extra person. MAP (breakfast and dinner) $48 per person. AE, MC, V. Closed Sept–mid-Oct. Take the road southeast from St. John's, following the signs to English Harbour. **Amenities:** Restaurant, bar; free transport to beaches; snorkeling; room service (7:30am–9pm); babysitting; laundry. *In room:* Ceiling fan, safe, hair dryer upon request.

Falmouth Harbour Apartments If you'd like to be near historic English Harbour, this relatively simple, casual place, set on a hillside above the Antigua Yacht Club, within a 10-minute walk downhill to the beach, may be for you, even though it has none of the charm or character of the 3 properties just recommended at English Harbour. Each studio apartment has twin beds, a ceiling fan, an electric stove, a fridge, an oven, and a terrace overlooking the water. The rooms don't, however, have air-conditioning, phones, or TVs.

Nearby you'll find restaurants, a supermarket, a bank, a post office, boutiques, and galleries. Next door, Temo Sports offers tennis and squash facilities. A dive operation in the dockyard arranges sailing and fishing boat charters. Bus service runs daily to and from St. John's, so you don't need a car if you can deal with the erratic bus service.

English Harbour Village, Yacht Club Rd. (P.O. Box 713), St. John's, Antigua, W.I. © **268/460-1027.** Fax 268/460-1534. 6 units. Winter $135 double; $160 triple. Off-season $100 double; $125 triple. Children age 15 and under stay for $15 when sharing their parents' studio. AE, MC, V. Free parking. Take the road southeast from St. John's and follow the signs to English Harbour. *In room:* Ceiling fan, kitchenette, fridge, no phone.

Sunsail Club Colonna Operated by Italians, at the northern tip of Antigua, this resort is like something along the coast of Sardinia, and attracts those interested in reasonably priced windsurfing and sailing. The first venture of Sunsail into the Caribbean, the resort has some disadvantages, including a human-made beach (nothing special), public spaces that aren't exactly state of the art, and some accommodations that were badly positioned outside the path of the trade winds; but there are compensations, including the reasonable prices. Bathrooms are tiled and contain only showers. Built on the site of an old sugar plantation, the hotel has the largest swimming pool in Antigua, plus a friendly, efficient staff. Guest rooms are well cared for and have decent furnishings. Many of the doubles are just standard, but others are in rather smart villas and have two or three bedrooms. A Mediterranean feeling is evoked by the pastel walls, colonnaded facades, and red-slate roofs.

Hodges Bay (P.O. Box 591), St. John's, Antigua, W.I. © **800/327-2276** or 268/462-6263. Fax 268/462-6430. www.sunsail.com. 100 units, 15 villas. Winter $120 double; from $250 villa. Off-season $110 double; $230 villa. Rates include breakfast. AE, MC, V. **Amenities:** 2 restaurants; watersports; babysitting; laundry. *In room:* A/C, TV, minibar, fridge, hair dryer.

INEXPENSIVE

The Catamaran Hotel & Marina A longtime favorite on Antigua since the 1970s, the Catamaran opens onto a palm-lined beach at Falmouth Harbour, a 2-mile (3km) drive from English Harbour. When we first discovered the property years ago, a film crew had taken it over to make a movie about pirates of the West Indies. The management had to post a sign: TODAY'S "PIRATES" MUST WEAR BATHING SUITS ON THE BEACH. It's not as wild around here anymore, and peace, tranquility, and lots of bougainvillea plants prevail.

On the second floor, each of eight self-contained, motel-style rooms has a comfortable bed (in many cases, a four-poster), a queen-size mattress, and a balcony overlooking the water. The Captain's Cabin is the most luxurious. The ground-floor rooms are small but comfortable. Additional units are within a waterside annex. All but two of the units have kitchens, and each is furnished with a tiled, shower-only bathroom.

Boaters will like the hotel's location at the 30-slip Catamaran Marina. You can purchase supplies at a nearby grocery store.

Falmouth Harbour (P.O. Box 958), St. John's, Antigua, W.I. © **268/460-1036.** Fax 268/460-1339. www. catamaran-antigua.com. 17 units. Winter $90–$165 double. Off-season $80–$135 double. Extra person $25;

children under age 10 stay free in parents' room. AE, MC, V. Closed May–Oct. **Amenities:** Restaurant, bar; sport-fishing, diving, boat rentals. *In room:* Ceiling fan, no phone.

Ocean Inn ★★ *Finds*   This is Antigua's premier B&B, just a 10-minute walk from some golden sandy beaches. This is a special place, with the coziest and most homelike decor on the island, the ambience created by its friendly owners, Sandra and Eustace Potter, who are on-site to welcome you. Accommodations are divided between units in the main building or in one of the cottages on the grounds, each coming with a little deck opening onto the marina. Each room is equipped with a small, tiled bathroom with shower, and everything is beautifully kept. The garden of the hotel overlooks the historic Dockyard. Guests share the communal swimming pool, or else meet each other for drinks in the Tree Trunk Bar. The most popular night here is Thursday, when there's an open-air barbecue. We think this is a delightful way to stay in Antigua if you prefer the B&B route when you travel.

P.O. Box 838, English Harbour, Antigua W.I. ✆ 268/463-7950. Fax 268/463-7950. www.theoceaninn.com. 12 units. Winter $75–$120 double. Off-season $55–$90 double. AE, MC, V. **Amenities:** Grill, bar; pool. *In room:* A/C, TV, no phone.

3 Dining

Although the Eastern Caribbean dollar (EC$) is used on these islands, only certain tiny restaurants present their prices in the local currency. When you inquire about a price, make sure you know which type of dollars is being quoted. Unless otherwise specified, rates quoted in this section are given in U.S. dollars.

IN ST. JOHN'S

Big Banana Holding Company ★ PIZZA/BURGERS/SALADS   In former slave quarters, this place serves up some of the best pizza and grilled chicken sandwiches in the eastern Caribbean. It stands amid the most stylish shopping and dining emporiums in town, a few steps from the Heritage Quay Jetty. The frothy libations, coconut or banana crush, are practically desserts. You can also order overstuffed baked potatoes, fresh-fruit salad, or conch salad. On Thursday a reggae band entertains from 9pm to 1am.

Redcliffe Quay, St. John's. ✆ 268/480-6986. Pizzas, sandwiches, and salads $4–$14. AE, DC, MC, V. Mon–Sat 8am–11:30pm.

Redcliffe Tavern CARIBBEAN/INTERNATIONAL   If you don't want pizza (see above), this is one of your best bets along the water at Redcliffe Quay, especially at lunch. This waterside restaurant was originally a warehouse constructed by the British in the 18th century. The place displays plantation-era water pumps and other Antiguan artifacts from that time. Don't expect a quiet and romantic evening here, however; the place is usually crowded. The menu features zesty creations such as plantain-stuffed chicken breasts in tomato or basil sauce, Brie wrapped in phyllo with a tomato-raspberry vinaigrette, and steaks with mushrooms or peppercorn sauce. The Normandy-style apple tart is superb.

Redcliffe Quay. ✆ 268/461-4557. Reservations recommended. Main courses $8–$28. AE, DISC, MC, V. Mon–Sat 8am–11pm.

ELSEWHERE AROUND THE ISLAND

The Admiral's Inn ★ AMERICAN/CREOLE   Partake of lobster, seafood, and steaks in this 17th-century hotel (see "Accommodations," above). Our favorite appetizer is pumpkin soup. Four or five main courses are served daily, including local red snapper, a perfectly grilled steak, or lobster. The service is agreeable, and sometimes the atmosphere is more exciting than the cuisine. But the chefs use good-quality ingredients that are generally deftly handled in the kitchen. Before dinner, drink up in the bar and read where sailors carved their names in wood 100 years ago.

In Nelson's Dockyard, English Harbour. ⓒ 268/460-1027. Reservations recommended, especially for dinner in high season. Lunch main courses $10–$16.65; dinner main courses $19.25–$27.75. AE, MC, V. Daily. 7:30am–9:30pm. Closed Sept–mid-Oct.

Alberto's ✿ INTERNATIONAL   One of the most stylish and cosmopolitan restaurants on Antigua is Alberto's, the creative statement of Venice-born Alberto Ravanello and his English wife, Vanessa, who prepares much of the food herself. You'll find it close to the edge of the sea, near the St. James's Club, in an open-sided pavilion lavishly draped with bougainvillea. The owners' frequent travels have inspired the menu's satisfying medley of Italian, French, and continental dishes. The best examples include ravioli stuffed either with pulverized asparagus and shrimp, or with mascarpone cheese and sage-flavored butter; a zesty pasta with fresh local clams; savory stuffed crabs; and one of our favorites, fresh wahoo steak with a wasabi, ginger, and soy sauce. Lobster, a favorite here, is boiled in seawater, then grilled and served simply, usually with garlic-flavored butter. It's lip-smacking good, but pricey.

Willoughby Bay. ⓒ 268/460-3007. Reservations recommended. Main courses $20–$30. AE, DC, MC, V. Tues–Sun 7–10pm. Closed May–Nov.

Chez Pascal ★ FRENCH   This small but well-groomed corner of France blooms with tropical vegetation and well-prepared cuisine on the west coast. On a plateau near the Royal Antiguan and the Galley Bay Hotels, it centers on a terrace with an illuminated swimming pool.

French colonial trappings include copper pots, rough-textured ceramics, dark-stained wicker and rattan, and tropically inspired fabric designs. The chef, Pascal Milliat, inherited generations of cooking skills in his former home, Lyon. Assisted by his Brittany-born wife, Florence, he prepares and serves classic French dishes with sublime sauces and seasonings. Fine cookery showcases a chicken liver mousse with basil-flavored butter sauce, lobster bisque en croute, sea scallops on a bed of leeks, roasted rack of lamb with herbes de Provence (prepared for only two diners at a time), and grouper with beurre blanc sauce.

On the premises are four very large bedrooms, none with TV or phone. (Friends and fans of the Milliats have urged them never to add these modern "inconveniences.") Each unit has a whirlpool tub, air-conditioning, fridge, rattan furniture, sea views, and color schemes influenced by the sand and sky. With breakfast included, singles or doubles range from $90 to $105 in low season, from $135 to $165 in winter.

Galley Bay Hill, Five Islands. ⓒ 268/462-3232. Reservations recommended. Main courses $20–$74. AE, DC, MC, V. Daily 11:30am–3pm and 6:30–9:30pm. Closed Sept.

Coconut Grove ★ INTERNATIONAL/SEAFOOD   North of St. John's in a coconut grove right on the beach, simple tables on a flagstone floor beneath a thatch roof are cooled by sea breezes. This is every visitor's dream of what a Caribbean restaurant should be. And it's one of the island's best. Soup is prepared fresh daily from local ingredients like ginger, carrot, and pumpkin. Appetizers include a seafood delight: scallops, shrimp, crab, lobster, and local fish with a mango-and-lime dressing. Lobster and shrimp dishes figure prominently, along with a catch of the day and a daily vegetarian special. Lunch fare is lighter. During happy hour at the bar (4–7pm), all drinks are half price.

In the Siboney Beach Club, Dickenson Bay. ℂ **268/462-1538.** Reservations required for dinner. Lunch main courses $12–$23; dinner main courses $21–$31. AE, DC, MC, V. Daily 7:30am–10pm.

Colombo's Restaurant ★ ITALIAN   Colombo's serves the island's best Italian food on a Polynesian-style, open-air terrace sheltered by a woven palm-frond ceiling. It's only a few steps across the flat sands to the water. Lunches might include spaghetti marinara, lobster salad, and sandwiches. Dinners are more elaborate, with daily specials from a classic Italian inventory of veal scaloppine, veal pizzaiola, and lobster Mornay. Some dishes lack polish, but most selections are brimming with flavor. You can choose from a wide assortment of French or Italian wines. Live reggae, rock, jazz, and calypso music is offered on Monday and Wednesday night. (There's no cover, but there is a two-drink minimum.)

In the Galleon Beach Club, English Harbour. ℂ **268/460-1452.** Reservations required. Lunch main courses $10–$23. Dinner main courses $16–$23. AE, DC, DISC, MC, V. Daily noon–2:30pm and 7–9:30pm. Closed Sept–Oct 5.

HQ ★★★ PACIFIC RIM/FRENCH   Aussie-born Darryn Pitman, a resident of Asia for 5 years, creates some of the most sophisticated cuisine on-island. There's a lot of emphasis on sushi, chutneys, relishes, and spices evocative of the lands where he has lived, including tamarind, lemongrass, and star anise. His signature dishes—each of them superb in texture and flavor—include a pan-seared game fish, wahoo, which is served with a lime and ginger-flavored dressing. His tender roast pork comes with an amazingly good chutney made with such fruits as bitter orange and apple. And wait until you taste his desserts. They are the finest and most imaginative on the island, including a first for us—a cake that's made with fresh beets and gobs of chocolate. His other signature dessert, for which he has been praised by food critics, is a passion-fruit crème brûlée made with white Swiss chocolate. His restaurant occupies three storefronts, plus most of the veranda, of the 18th-century stone-and-brick monument in Nelson's Dockyard known as Officers' Quarters. At lunch, you can dine informally on the veranda, soaking up rum-based cocktails and eating salads, sandwiches, and snacks. Emphasis is on high-turnover, affordable prices, and dishes that are relatively uncomplicated.

Dinners are more elaborate, served in a dining room that's outfitted with international flags, ropes, antique maritime hardware, and a venue inspired by an antique officers' mess in the days of Lord Nelson.

Nelson's Dockyard, English Harbour. ℂ **268/562-2563.** Reservations required. Lunch main courses $7.40–$27.75; dinner main courses $12.95–$27.75. AE, DC, MC, V. Wed–Mon 11:30am–5pm and 6:30–10pm.

Le Bistro ★ FRENCH   A ½ mile (.8km) inland from the coast of Hodges Bay, this restaurant occupies a stone-sided structure that was built as a clubhouse for a now-defunct golf course. Sporting informal charm, it's the oldest continuously operated restaurant in Antigua (since 1981). The owners are English-born Philippa Esposito and her husband, Raffaele, from Capri. Together, they concoct a mostly French menu that includes succulent lobster with creamy basil sauce; lightly blackened fresh salmon with raspberry/lime butter sauce; and your choice of either medallions of veal or duckling, both of them grilled with an aromatic passion fruit and pink peppercorn sauce, There's also an innovative version of roasted snapper in pumpkin-thyme sauce, very full of island flavor. A favorite dessert is apple crepes in spiced honey sauce.

Hodges Bay. ℂ **268/462-3881.** Reservations recommended. Main courses $24–$38. AE, MC, V. Tues–Sun 6:30–10:30pm.

Shirley Heights Lookout ✦ AMERICAN/SEAFOOD Good food and an even greater view make this an enduring favorite directly east of English Harbour on the southern coast. In the 1790s, this was a lookout station for unfriendly ships heading toward English Harbour, site of a powder magazine constructed to strengthen Britain's position in this strategic location. Today this panoramic spot serves up burgers and sandwiches, as well as pumpkin soup, grilled lobster in lime butter, garlic-flavored shrimp, and good desserts, such as pecan pie flambé. It's not the world's grandest cuisine—overcooking is the most frequent flaw—but it's a fun crowd-pleaser, and who can argue with that view? There's live music every Thursday from 4 to 8pm. Also, one of the most popular Sunday afternoon parties in Antigua takes place here every Sunday from 4 to 10pm, when live music (a steel band followed by a reggae band) performs to crowds that spill out into the garden. On Sunday, a cover charge of $3.70 includes the first drink.

Shirley Heights. ⓒ **268/460-1785.** Reservations recommended. Main courses $8.50–$25. AE, DC, MC, V. Mon–Thurs 9am–8pm, Fri–Sun 9am–10pm.

4 Beaches

There's a lovely white-sand beach on **Pigeon Point** at Falmouth Harbour, about a 4-minute drive from Admiral's Inn (see earlier in this chapter). With calm waters and pristine sands, this is the best beach near English Harbour, but it's likely to be crowded, especially when a cruise ship is in port. It's ideal for snorkelers and swimmers of most ages and abilities.

Dickenson Bay ✦✦ in the northwest, directly north of St. John's, is one of the island's finest beaches, with its wide strip of powder-soft sand and blissfully calm turquoise waters. This safe beach often attracts families with small children in tow. The center point here is the **Halcyon Cove Hotel,** where you can rent watersports equipment. You can visit the hotel for refreshments, or mosey over to the casual bars and restaurants nearby.

On the north side of Dickenson Bay, you'll find more secluded beaches and some ideal snorkeling areas along the fan-shaped northern crown of Antigua. For a fee, locals will sometimes take beachcombers to one of the uninhabited offshore islets, such as **Prickly Pear Island,** enveloped by beautiful coral gardens. Glass-bottom excursion boats often visit one of the island's best snorkeling spots, **Paradise Reef,** a mile-long (2km) coral garden of stunning beauty north of Dickenson Bay (see "Scuba Diving, Snorkeling & Other Water Sports," in "Sports & Other Outdoor Pursuits," below).

If you want to escape from everybody, flee to **Johnson's Point.** Between the hamlets of Johnson's Point and Urlings at Antigua's southwestern tip below Jolly Harbour, it opens onto the tranquil Caribbean Sea. There are no facilities, but the sand is dazzling white, and the waters, usually clear and calm, are populated with schools of rainbow-hued tropical fish.

Near Johnson's Point on the southwest coast, **Turner's Beach** is idyllic. This is one of the best places to lie out in the tropical sun, cooled by trade winds. The beach has fine white sand and gin-clear waters. If the day is clear (as it usually is), you can see the volcanic island of Montserrat.

If you head east of Urlings and go past the hamlet of Old Road, you'll reach **Carlisle Bay,** site of one of the island's most celebrated shores. Against a backdrop of coconut groves, two long beaches extend from the spot where Curtain Bluff, the island's most deluxe hotel, sits atop a bluff. The waters are impossibly blue here, where the calm Caribbean Sea meets the more turbulent Atlantic.

South of Jolly Harbour, **Driftwood Beach** is directly north of Johnson's Point, in the southwest. The white sands and calm, clear waters are delightful. It is close to all the villas at Jolly Harbour Beach Resort Marina, however, and may be overcrowded.

In the same vicinity is **Darkwood Beach,** a 5-minute drive south of Jolly Harbour Marina and the Jolly Harbour Golf Club. Here the shimmering waters are almost crystal blue. The snorkeling is great, and you can bet that gentle trade winds will keep you cool. Located in a tourist zone, it is likely to be crowded— almost impossibly so when cruise ships are in port.

If you continue north toward St. John's and cut west at the turnoff for Five Islands, you'll reach the four secluded **Hawksbill Beaches** on the Five Islands peninsula. The beaches here have white sands, dazzling blue-and-green waters, and coral reefs ideal for snorkeling. On one of them, you can sunbathe and swim in the buff. The Five Islands peninsula is the site of major hotel developments. Though it's secluded, the beaches are sometimes crowded.

Perhaps Antigua's most beautiful beach, **Half Moon Bay** ★★ stretches for nearly a mile (2km) on the southeastern coast, a 5-minute drive from Freetown village. The Atlantic surf is liable to be rough, but that doesn't stop a never-ending stream of windsurfers, who head out beyond the reef, which shelters protected waters for snorkeling. Half Moon is now a public park and is an ideal choice for a family outing. Half Moon Bay lies east of English Harbour near Mill Reef.

Directly north of Half Moon Bay, east of Willikie's, **Long Bay** fronts the Atlantic on the far eastern coast of Antigua. Guests of the Long Bay Hotel and the Pineapple Beach Club are likely to populate this sandy strip. The shallow waters here are home to stunning coral reefs and offer great snorkeling.

In the same vicinity, **Pineapple Beach** is a 5-minute drive heading northeast from the village of Willikie's. It opens onto **Long Bay** and the west coast (Atlantic side) of Antigua. Crystal blue waters make it ideal for snorkeling. Most beach buffs come here just to sun on nearly perfect white sands.

5 Sports & Other Outdoor Pursuits

BOATING & YACHT CHARTERS   If you're contemplating serious yachting around Antigua, as many well-heeled visitors do, make arrangements through **Nicholson Yacht Charters** (© **800/662-6066**) well in advance of your trip. They offer boats of all sizes.

Once on Antigua, if you plan only minor sailing such as in a Sunfish or small catamaran (i.e., Hobie Waves), or windsurfing, contact **Sea Sports,** on the beach in front of the Halcyon Cove Hotel at Dickenson Bay (© **268/462-3355**).

CRUISES   All the major hotel desks can book a day cruise on the 108-foot "pirate ship," the *Jolly Roger,* Redcliffe Quay. For information and reservations, call **Tropical Adventures** (© **268/462-2064**). Outfitted like a Disney-inspired version of an early 18th-century schooner, it's the largest sailing ship in Antiguan waters. For $60 for adults and $30 for children under age 12, you get a fun-filled day of sightseeing, with drinks and barbecued steak, chicken, or lobster. Lunch is combined with a snorkeling trip. On the poop deck, members of the crew teach passengers how to dance calypso. Cruises last 4 hours and sail every Saturday morning. A Thursday-night dinner cruise costs $65, leaving Heritage Quay in St. John's at 7pm and returning at 11pm. The same organization also offers day trips to remote Barbuda aboard a motorized catamaran, the

Excellence, that's suitable for up to 70 passengers at a time. Departures are every Friday and Sunday at 9:30am, returning the same day around 4:30pm. No children under age 8 are allowed. The price for everyone else is $100 per person, which includes lunch, use of snorkeling equipment, and a visit to Barbuda's bird sanctuary. **Barbuda-bound cruises** depart from Tony's Water Sports at Dickenson Bay. For information and reservations, call *C* **268/480-1225.**

FISHING   Many anglers visit Antigua just for the big-game fishing offshore, where wahoo, tuna, and marlin abound. The *Obsession* (*C* **268/462-2824**) is a 50-foot Hatteras Sportfisherman with excellent equipment. You can battle the big ones in a featured "fighting chair." For the day, the *Obsession* charges from $1,300, a fee that is shared by all the passengers (usually at least a dozen). A competitor of similar size, the *Nimrod* (*C* **268/463-8744**) is captained by Terry Bowen, who knows where the best catches are. You can arrange for the *Nimrod* to circle the island or go on sunset cruises. A full around-the-island tour costs $1,600, with a half day going for $1,300. This price is usually divided among at least 12 passengers.

GOLF   Antigua's golf facilities are not on par with some of the other islands', but its premier course is good. The 18-hole, par-69 **Cedar Valley Golf Club,** Friar's Hill Road (*C* **268/462-0161**), is 3 miles (5km) east of St. John's, near the airport. With panoramic views of Antigua's northern coast, the island's most popular and largest course was designed by the late Richard Aldridge to fit the contours of the area. Daily greens fees are $35 for 18 holes. Cart rentals cost $35 for 18 holes, and club rentals cost $15 to $20, depending on how many holes you play.

HIKING   The best hiking tours in Antigua are offered by **Tropikelly Trails** (*C* **268/461-0383**). The trail leads from the hamlet of Wallens, in the tropical rain forest on the south side of Antigua, and climbs to the top of Signal Hill. Tours cost $40 per person, and last for about 3 hours each, but they're only conducted when a minimum of 6 participants can be assembled.

PARASAILING   Parasailing is gaining popularity on Antigua. Facilities are available during the day, Monday to Saturday, on the beach at Dickenson Bay.

SCUBA DIVING, SNORKELING & OTHER WATERSPORTS   The reefs that fringe Antigua are home to beautiful, brilliantly colored fish. Many of the island's beaches (see "Beaches," above) have clear, pure, calm waters that make for great snorkeling, and the most popular beaches, like Dickenson Bay, have concessions where you can rent snorkel gear and other equipment if it isn't available from your hotel.

Scuba diving is best arranged through **Dive Antigua,** at the Rex Halcyon Cove, Dickenson Bay (*C* **268/462-3483**), Antigua's most experienced dive operation. A resort course is $88, and a 2-tank dive costs $73. A 5-dive package goes for $310, and open-water certification costs $492. Prices do not include equipment, an additional $20.

Splish Splash (*C* **268-462-3483**) regularly offers 2-hour snorkeling jaunts over to Paradise Reef.

TENNIS   True tennis buffs—well-heeled ones, that is—check into **Curtain Bluff** (see "Accommodations," earlier in this chapter). Its courts are the finest on the island. Most of the major hotels have courts as well, and some are lit for night games. (We don't recommend playing tennis at noon—it's just too hot!) Guests of a hotel usually play for free; if you're not a guest, you'll have to book a court and pay charges that vary from place to place. You might also try the **Temo Sports Complex** at Falmouth Bay (© **268/463-1781**), which offers two floodlit tennis courts.

WINDSURFING   Located at the Lord Nelson Beach Hotel, on Dutchman's Bay, **Windsurfing Antigua** (© **268/461-9463**) offers windsurfing for the absolute beginner, the intermediate sailor, and the hard-core windsurfer. The outfit guarantees beginners will enjoy the sport after a 2-hour introductory lesson for $60. A 1-hour rental costs $20; a half day, $50.

6 Exploring the Island
IN ST. JOHN'S
If you're staying outside St. John's (which is highly likely), take a local bus into the city on **market day** on Saturday morning. Many of the locals with stuff to sell get right on the bus with whatever they'll be peddling in town at the market: chickens, birds, luscious fruit, beautiful flowers, and certainly plenty of handcrafts. They'll probably start bargaining with you before you even get to the market. In the southern part of St. John's, the semi-open-air market, on the lower end of Market Street, is colorful and interesting, especially from 8am to noon.

St. John's Cathedral, the Anglican church between Long Street and Newgate Street at Church Lane (© **268/461-0082**), has resurrected itself time and again—it's been destroyed by earthquakes and rebuilt on the same site at least three times since the original structure was constructed in 1683. The present structure dates from 1845.

Exhibits at the **Museum of Antigua & Barbuda,** at Market and Long streets (© **268/462-1469**), is set within one of Antigua's oldest buildings, built by English colonials in 1750 as a courthouse. The museum covers the island's history, from its prehistoric days up to its independence from Britain in 1981. Exhibitions include examples of each of the semiprecious stones (especially jade) you can find on Antigua, as well as models of sugar plantations, paintings, and historical prints. It's open Monday through Friday from 8:30am to 4pm and on Saturday from 10am to 2pm; admission is by donation; $2 is suggested.

AROUND THE ISLAND
Eleven miles (18km) southeast of St. John's is **Nelson's Dockyard National Park** ★★★ (© **268/460-1379**), one of the eastern Caribbean's biggest attractions. English ships took refuge from the hurricanes in this harbor as early as 1671. The park's centerpiece is the restored Georgian naval dockyard, which was used by admirals Nelson, Rodney, and Hood, and was the home of the British fleet during the Napoleonic Wars. From 1784 to 1787, Nelson commanded the British navy in the Leeward Islands and made his headquarters at English Harbour. The dockyard museum recaptures the 18th-century era of privateers, pirates, and battles at sea. A sort of Caribbean Williamsburg, its colonial naval buildings stand as they did when Nelson was here. Although Nelson never lived at **Admiral House** (© **268/460-8181**)—it was built in 1855—his telescope and tea caddy are displayed here, along with other nautical memorabilia.

The park itself has sandy beaches and tropical vegetation, with various species of cactus and mangroves. A migrating colony of African cattle egrets shelters in the mangroves. Archaeological sites here predate Christ. Nature trails, with coastal views, lead you through the flora. Tours of the dockyard last 15 to 20

⌒ **Tips**   **Forts and Photo Ops**

Once, in the 1700s, the coastline of Antigua was ringed with British forts, though they're all in ruins today. Even if there isn't much left to see, the views from these former military strongholds are among the most panoramic in the Caribbean—and you can visit them for free. You can begin at St. John's harbor (the capital), which was once guarded by **Fort Barrington** on the south and **Fort James** on the north. Later you can head down to **Fort James Bay,** where you'll find a couple of bars right on the sand, including **Russell's Beach Bar,** which is most active on Sunday afternoon. It's an ideal place to unwind with a beer. In the south, near English Harbour, check out the view from **Shirley Heights.**

---

minutes; nature walks along the trails can last anywhere from 30 minutes to 5 hours. The dockyard and all the buildings noted in this section are open daily from 9am to 5pm. Children age 12 and under are admitted free. The admission price of $5 includes admission to Admiral House, Clarence House, and Dow's Hill Interpretation Center (see below).

The best **nature trail** on Antigua, a well-tended footpath, goes up the hill from English Harbour to **Shirley Heights** ✿, beginning at the Galleon Beach Hotel. Follow the sign that points "TO THE LOOKOUT." The trail is marked with tape on the branches of trees. Eventually you reach a summit of nearly 500 feet (150m) where you're rewarded with a panoramic view. If you'd like to get more information about the walk, you can pick up a free brochure at the dockyard at the office of the National Parks Authority. This walk is easy; it takes less than an hour to reach the peak.

Another major attraction is the **Dow's Hill Interpretation Center** (© 268/ 481-5045), just 2½ miles (4km) south of the dockyard. The only one of its kind in the Caribbean, it offers multimedia presentations that cover six periods of the island's history, including the era of Amerindian hunters, the era of the British military, and the struggles connected with slavery. A belvedere opens onto a panoramic view of the park. Admission to the center, including the multimedia show, is included in the price of admission to the dockyards. Hours are daily from 9am to 5pm.

On a low hill overlooking Nelson's Dockyard, **Clarence House** (© 268/ 463-1026) was built by English stonemasons to accommodate Prince William Henry, later known as the Duke of Clarence—and even later known as William IV. The future king stayed here when he was in command of the *Pegasus* in 1787. At present it's the country home of the governor of Antigua and Barbuda. At the time of publication, it was temporarily closed for renovation, but in theory, it's open to visitors whenever His Excellency is not in residence. A caretaker will show you through (it's customary to tip), and you'll see many pieces of furniture on loan from the National Trust. Princess Margaret and Lord Snowdon stayed here on their honeymoon.

On the way back, take **Fig Tree Drive** ✿, a 20-some-mile (32km) circular drive across the main mountain range. It passes through lush tropical hills and fishing villages along the southern coast. You can pick up the road just outside Liberta, north of Falmouth. Winding through a rain forest, it passes thatched villages, every one with a church and lots of goats and children running about. But don't expect fig trees: *Fig* is an Antiguan name for bananas.

Betty's Hope (© 268/462-1469), a picturesque ruin just outside the village of Pares on the eastbound route to Long Bay, was Antigua's first sugar plantation (from 1650). You can tour it Tuesday to Saturday from 10am to 4pm ($2 for adults, free for children). Exhibits in the visitor's center trace the sugar era, and you can also see the full restoration of one of the original plantation's two windmills. At press-time, a team of local masons had begun the partial restoration of the curing and boiling plant, where sugarcane used to be processed into sugar, rum, and molasses.

Indian Town is one of Antigua's national parks, on the island's northeastern point. Over the centuries, Atlantic breakers have lashed the rocks and carved a natural bridge known as Devil's Bridge. It's surrounded by numerous blowholes spouting surf, a dramatic sight. An environmentally protected area, Indian Town Point lies at the tip of a deep cove, Indian Town Creek. The park fronts the Atlantic at Long Bay, just west of Indian Town Creek at the eastern side of Antigua. Birders flock here to see some 36 different species. The park is blanketed mainly by the acacia tree, a dry shrub locally known as "cassie." A large, meadowy headland around Devil's Bridge makes a great spot for a picnic. Arm yourself with directions and a good map before you start out. The main highway ends at Long Bay, but several hiking trails lead to the coastline. Our favorite hike is to Indian Town Point at a distance of 1½ miles (2km) . This is the most scenic walk in the park, passing through a protected area of great natural beauty. Long Bay is also great for snorkeling, if you bring along your gear.

7 Shopping

Most of Antigua's shops are clustered on **St. Mary's Street** or **High Street** in St. John's. Some stores are open Monday to Saturday from 8:30am to noon and 1 to 4pm, but this rule varies greatly from place to place—Antiguan shopkeepers are an independent lot. Many of them close at noon on Thursday.

Duty-free items include English woolens and linens. You can also purchase Antiguan goods: local pottery, straw work, rum, floppy foldable hats, shell curios, and hand-printed fabrics.

If you're in St. John's on a Saturday morning, visit the **fruit and vegetable market.** The juicy Antiguan black pineapple alone is worth the trip.

One prime hunting ground in St. John's is the **Redcliffe Quay** waterfront on the southern edge of town, where nearly three dozen boutiques are housed in former warehouses set around tree-shaded, landscaped courtyards. Our favorite is **A Thousand Flowers** (© 268/462-4264), which sells Indonesian batiks crafted on Antigua into sundresses, knock-'em-dead shirts, sarongs, and rompers.

At the **Gazebo** (© 268/460-2776), expect a little bit of everything, a mass of south-of-the-border pottery to Indonesian wood items, and (our favorite) stunning blue-glaze plates. **West Indies Oil Co.** (© 268/462-0141) is a big hit with kids, offering British toys, beach games, island crafts, and more. Additional Redcliffe Quay shops include **Isis** (© 268/462-4602) for unique Egyptian jewelry, leather, finely woven cotton, and handcrafts; and **The Goldsmitty** (© 268/462-4601), where precious stones are set in unique, exquisite creations of 14- and 18-karat gold.

Noreen Phillips, Redcliffe Quay (© 268/462-3127), is one of the island's major fashion outlets. Cruise-ship passengers beeline here for both casual wear and beaded glitzy dress clothes. **Island Hopper,** Jardine Court, St. Mary's Street (© 268/462-2972), specializes in Caribbean-made gifts and clothing, including T-shirts and casual wear, spices, coffees, and handcrafts.

The Scent Shop, Lower High Street (© 268/462-0303), is the oldest and best perfume shop on the island, and also stocks an array of crystal. **Shoul's Chief Store,** St. Mary's Street at Market Street (© 268/462-1140), is an all-purpose department store selling fabric, appliances, souvenirs (more than 300 kinds), and general merchandise.

Heritage Quay, Antigua's first shopping-and-entertainment complex, features some 40 duty-free shops and an arcade for local artists and craftspeople. Its restaurants and food court offer a range of cuisines and views of St. John's Harbour. Many shops are open all day, Monday through Saturday.

At the foot of St. Mary's Street, stop in at **Benjies Photo Centre** (© 268/462-3619), a Kodak distributor and photofinisher, selling film and brand-name cameras. **Fashiondock** (© 268/462-9672) is known for its duty-free Gianni Versace jeans and accessories, plus other Italian styles. **Sunseekers** (© 268/462-4523) carries the largest collection of duty-free swimwear in the Caribbean. **Colombian Emeralds** (© 268/462-3462) is the world's largest retailer of these gemstones. **Albert's Jewelry** (© 268/462-3108) sells the best selection of watches on Antigua, plus china and crystal. **Island Arts,** upstairs at Heritage Quay (© 268/462-2787), was founded by Nick Maley, a makeup artist who worked on *Star Wars* and *The Empire Strikes Back.* You can purchase his own fine-art reproductions or browse through everything from low-cost prints to works by artists exhibited at the Museum of Modern Art in New York. You can also visit **Nick's home and studio** at Aiton Place, on Sandy Lane directly behind the Hodges Bay Club, 4 miles (6km) from St. John's. The residence is open Monday to Wednesday and on Friday, but call first (© 268/461-6324).

Other worthwhile specialty stores include **Caribelle Batik,** St. Mary's Street (© 268/462-2972), a reasonably priced outlet for the Romney Manor workshop on St. Kitts. The Caribelle label consists of batik and tie-dye beach wraps, scarves, and casual wear for women and men.

Rain Boutique, Lower St. Mary's (© 268/462-0118), offers casual clothes, formal wear, hats, scarves, shoes, jewelry, and handbags.

At Falmouth Harbour, **Seahorse Studios & Gift Shop** (© 268/460-1457) specializes in batiks, T-shirts, and table linens. Their affiliated branch at English Harbour, **Seahorse Art Gallery** (© 268/460-1485), sells paintings, engravings, and watercolors, with lots of emphasis on seascapes.

The best for last: Head for **Harmony Hall** ✪, in Brown's Bay Mill, near Freetown (© 268/460-4120), following the signs along the road to Freetown and Half Moon Bay. This restored 1843 plantation house and sugar mill overlooking Nonsuch Bay is ideal for a lunch stopover or a shopping expedition. It displays an excellent selection of Caribbean arts and crafts. Lunch is served daily from noon to 4pm, featuring Green Island lobster, flying fish, and other specialties. Sunday is barbecue day.

8 Antigua After Dark

Antigua has some of the best steel bands in the Caribbean. Most nightlife revolves around the hotels. If you want to roam Antigua at night looking for that hot local club, arrange to have a taxi pick you up, so you're not stranded in the wilds somewhere.

The **Royal Casino,** in the Royal Antiguan Hotel, Deep Bay (© 268/462-3733), has blackjack, baccarat, roulette, craps, and slot machines. It's open daily from 2pm until around 1am, and there's no cover. Far better and the most glamorous place to go if you have time for only one casino is the **St. James's Club** at Mamora Bay (© **268/463-1113**), which has the island's most flamboyant gambling palace. Other action is found at **King's Casino** on Heritage Quay (© **268/462-1727**), the only casino in St. John's proper.

Steel bands, limbo dancers, calypso singers, folkloric groups—there's always something happening by night on Antigua. Your hotel can probably tell you where to go on any given night. The following clubs are reliable hot spots.

Eighteen Carats, Long Street at Market Street, St. Johns (no phone), opened in 2002, and rose instantly to the status of most popular and sought-after dance club and night bar on the island. Expect a cover charge of less than $3 per person, an indoor-outdoor format that's open to a view of the night air of downtown St. John's, and a barrage of music that includes lots of reggae and soca. It's open Friday to Sunday from around 8pm to 1am.

Stop in at the **Bay House,** Tradewinds Hotel, Marble Hill (© **268/462-1223**), for the island's best mix of singles (both straight and—to a much lesser degree—gay). A guitarist performs every Monday and a local reggae band performs every Wednesday night at **Colombo's,** a previously recommended restaurant in the Galleon Beach Club in English Harbour (© **268/460-1452**).

Live nightly entertainment takes place right on the beach at **Millers by the Sea,** at Runaway Beach (© **268/462-9414**). Spilling over onto the sands, its happy hour is the best in town.

At English Harbour, action centers around the **Admiral's Inn** (© **268/460-1027**), a barefoot-friendly kind of place. In the British style, you can always play a game of darts. Thursday and Saturday nights feature live music, most often a local 14-piece steel band. Try one of Norman's daiquiris (the island's best), and ask the bartender about the famous guests he's served, from Richard Burton to Prince Charles. Also at English Harbour, two other much-frequented watering holes include **Hype,** Nelson's Dockyard (© **268/562-2353**), the most popular spot for visitors arriving aboard yachts. We like its real nautical atmosphere, the action centering on a wooden pier. At certain times, it's West Indian party time, with live groups performing. The most authentic British pub at Nelson's Dockyard is **Mainbrace** (© **268/460-1058**), with darts, of course, beer on tap, fish 'n chips, and on some nights the jazz is live. The pub is part of the Copper and Lumber Store hotel (see previous recommendation).

9 Barbuda

Barbuda is part of the independent nation of Antigua and Barbuda. It's the Caribbean's last frontier, even though it is home to two of the region's most expensive and exclusive resorts. (See below for a review of the K-Club. The other property is the Coco Point Beach Resort, which we don't recommend because we think it has an exclusive, snobbish, private club atmosphere.) Charted by Columbus in 1493, the island is 26 miles (42km) north of Antigua. Fifteen miles (24km) long by 5 miles (8km) wide, it has a population of only 1,200 hardy souls, most of whom live around the unattractive village of Codrington. There's no lush tropical scenery, no paved roads, few hotels, and only a handful of restaurants.

So what's the attraction? The island's 17 miles (27km) of pink- and white-sand beaches—almost like those of Bermuda. (We prefer the sands north of Palmetto Point.) Barrier reefs protect the island and keep most of the waters tranquil. Beaches on the southwestern shore stretch uninterrupted for 10 miles (16km);

these are the best for swimming. Fronting the Atlantic, the beaches on the island's eastern shore are somewhat rougher, but they're suitable for beachcombing and shell-collecting. The temperature seldom falls below an average of 75°F.

Hunters, anglers, and beachcombers gravitate to Barbuda to see fallow deer, guinea fowl, pigeons, and wild pigs. You can also negotiate with small-boat owners to fish for bonefish and tarpon.

Day visitors usually head for **Wa'Omoni Beach Park** ✿, to visit the frigate bird sanctuary, snorkel for lobster, and eat barbecue. A most impressive sight, the frigate bird sanctuary is one of the world's largest. Visitors can see the birds, *Fregata magnificens,* sitting on their eggs in the mangrove bushes, which stretch for miles in a long lagoon accessible only by small motorboat. At various hotels and resorts on Antigua, you can arrange tours to the sanctuary. The island attracts about 150 other species of birds, including pelicans, herons, and tropical mockingbirds.

While you're here, look into the **"Dividing Wall,"** which once separated the imperial Codrington family from the African islanders. Also visit the **Martello Tower,** which predates the known history of the island. Purportedly the Spanish erected it before the British occupied the island. Several tours explore interesting **underground caves** on Barbuda. Stamp collectors might want to stop in at the **Philatelic Bureau** in Codrington.

ESSENTIALS

GETTING THERE   The island is a 15-minute flight from Antigua's V. C. Bird Airport. Barbuda has two airfields: one at Codrington, the other a private facility, the Coco Point Airstrip, which lies some 8 miles (13km) from Codrington at the Coco Point Lodge.

To reach Barbuda from Antigua, you can contact **Carib Aviation** (© 268/462-3147), a carrier that's loosely associated the LIAT, the national airline of Antigua and Barbuda. It operates two daily flights from Antigua's Byrd airport to Barbuda's Codrington Airport. Planes hold 19 passengers each for a ride that takes between 15 and 20 minutes, each way. Round-trip passage costs from EC$183 to EC$193 (US$67.70–US$71.40) per person, depending on restrictions.

GETTING AROUND   Many locals rent small four-wheel-drive Suzukis, which are the best way to get around the island. They meet incoming flights at Codrington Airport, and prices are negotiable. You'll need an Antiguan driver's license (see "Getting Around," in "Essentials," earlier in this chapter) if you plan to drive.

ACCOMMODATIONS & DINING

K-Club ✿✿   The most interesting, and super-expensive, hotel to open in the Caribbean in recent years, the beachfront K-Club brings a chic Italian panache to one of the most far-flung backwaters of the Antilles. The resort opened in 1990, when a planeload of glitterati, spearheaded by Giorgio Armani, headed for Barbuda en masse. The K-Club is the creative statement of Italy's Krizia Mariuccia Mandelli, whose sports and eveningwear empire has grossed a spectacular fortune. The resort is set on more than 200 acres (80 hectares), adjacent to the island's only other major hotel, a private club. Conceived by Italian architect Gianni Gamondi, the cottages and main clubhouse have roofs supported by a forest of white columns. Accommodations come in a huge range of styles and shapes; a hip island vibe predominates throughout. The furnishings include Hamptons-style wicker and sumptuous beds. Bathrooms have two sinks, a bidet

Airport ✈ Beach ✵ Reef |||

Goat Point
Atlantic Ocean
Cobb Cove
Hog Point
Cedar Tree
Point
Wa' Omoni
Beach Park
Two Foot Bay
Codrington Lagoon
Low Bay
○ Codrington
✈
Martello Tower
Palmetto Beach
Hotel ■
Palmetto
Point
■ K-Club
Pelican
Bay
Coco Point ✵
Caribbean Sea
Gravener Spanish
Bay Point

0   3 Miles
0   3 Kilometers

and adjacent shower, and a basket of deluxe toiletries. Rooms also have plenty of space for luggage.

The all-inclusive rates provide for all meals (but no drinks or wine). The cuisine is Mediterranean, with an emphasis on Italian specialties and fresh pasta. The chef passionately believes in fresh ingredients, and his food is not only the finest on Barbuda but also tops anything on Antigua.

Barbuda, Antigua, W.I. ✆ **268/460-0304.** Fax 268/460-0305. 47 units. Winter $1,050–$1,200 cottage for 2; $1,700 suite; $2,800 villa. Off-season $650–$800 cottage for 2; $1,150 suite; $2,000 villa. Rates include all meals, but no drinks. AE, DC, MC, V. Closed Sept–Nov 15. No children under age 12. **Amenities:** Restaurant, bar; 2 tennis courts; pool; waterskiing, snorkeling, Sunfish sailing, windsurfing, deep-sea fishing; transportation from Codrington Airport. *In room:* A/C, minibar, hair dryer, safe, ceiling fan.

Palmetto Beach Hotel ⭐ *Finds*   This is the only really affordable hotel on Barbuda, although to some its prices may seem outrageous, too. Run by an Italian company, the resort doesn't have the style or world class of K-Club, but then how many places do? The hotel opens onto 35 miles (56km) of white sand, and on any given day you'll have at least a mile (2km) of beachfront all to yourself. The intimate size makes for one giant house party, with guests occupying stylishly decorated living accommodations with natural wood tables and chairs. Further grace notes are the original silk paintings and the beautiful fabrics used throughout. All rooms are junior suites, and a private veranda with deck chairs opens onto a view from each unit. Bathrooms are well equipped, with two sinks, shower, tub, and amenities such as deluxe toiletries.

Palmetto Point, Barbuda, Antigua, W.I. ℂ **800/537-8483** in the U.S., or 268/460-0442. Fax 268/460-0440. www.palmettohotel.com. 22 suites. Winter $460–$560 double; off-season $360–$460 double. Children under age 12 stay free with parents. Rates include all meals. AE, DISC, MC, V. Closed Sept–Nov. **Amenities:** Restaurant, bar; pool; tennis court; volleyball; mountain bikes; watersports; library. *In room:* A/C, minibar, safe.

10 Montserrat

Ever so slowly, adventurous visitors are returning to the partially destroyed island of Montserrat. Known as "the Emerald Isle of the Caribbean" because of its verdant vegetation and because of its historic links to Ireland, Montserrat is 12 miles (19km) long and 7 miles (11km) wide, about the size of Manhattan. Two-thirds of the population of 12,000 had to be evacuated in 1995 and 1996 after the island's volcano, Chance's Peak, blew its top, smothering the southern two-thirds of the island with pyroclastic flows of hot gases and boiling hot ash, sometimes traveling at hurricane velocity. In the aftermath, much of the island's southern tier—including the airport—was burnt, buried, or rendered uninhabitable.

Even though the biggest blast occurred on June 25, 1997, Mount Chance and other peaks in the Soufrière Hills had been rumbling for generations. Since the explosions, only about one-third of the island's original population remained on-island, the others having been evacuated, or emigrating of their own volition, to the U.K. or, less frequently, to such neighboring islands as Antigua. Today, the path of future pyroclastic flows can more or less be predicted. That has allowed tourism to return, to a limited degree, to the island, albeit in very small volumes. In fact, the volcano has led to the promotion of Montserrat as one of the most haunting natural and geological spectacles in the Caribbean.

Since the destruction of Plymouth, the island's capital, Montserrat's new commercial center and jerrymandered capital is Little Bay, on the island's north coast. Overall, you'll get the sense of a small community galvanized into new forms of self-reliance and cooperation, with lots of emphasis on somewhat gritty business-related visits from construction crews and British and International relief agencies.

Pear-shaped and mountainous, and most definitely volcanic in origin, Montserrat lies 27 miles (43km) southwest of Antigua, about midway between Nevis and Guadeloupe. Ironically, before the volcanic eruptions, most of the world heard of this island for the first time when such musical luminaries as Elton John, Paul McCartney, Sting, and Stevie Wonder opened studios here. They, along with much of the rest of Montserrat's glitterati, moved long ago to safer, and more convenient, sites.

English is the island's official language, although it's spoken with a faint Irish brogue, a cultural holdover from the island's early Irish settlers. The Eastern Caribbean dollar is the official unit of currency, although U.S. dollars are widely accepted. By international agreement each EC dollar is permanently fixed—at the time of this writing—at 37¢. The on-island agent for American Express is **Travel World International,** Davey Hill (ℂ **664/491-2713**).

Proof of citizenship is required. A valid passport is recommended for all visitors; however, U.S., Canadian, and British citizens may present a driver's license or official ID card with photo as proof of citizenship in lieu of a passport.

Information is available from the **Montserrat Tourist Board,** P.O. Box 7, Salem Main Road, Salem, Montserrat, B.W.I. (ℂ **664/491-2230**).

ESSENTIALS

GETTING THERE   Montserrat is most easily reached from Antigua, but because its airport was destroyed by the volcano, it's accessible only by boat and by helicopter.

Twice-daily helicopter service departs from Antigua's Byrd airport for Montserrat's newly built heliport in Gerald's, a hamlet on the still-intact north side of the island. Containing room for about 11 passengers, each helicopter charges $300 round-trip for a ride that takes about 15 minutes each way.

Less expensively, ferryboats depart twice daily from Heritage Quay in Antigua's capital of St. John's, landing about an hour later at Montserrat's Little Bay. Round-trip ferryboat passage, depending on which day of the week you travel, costs from EC$120 to EC$200 (US$44.40–US$74). Whereas reservations are required aboard the helicopter, ferryboat seats don't require advance bookings.

For information about departures for either mode of transport, contact **Montserrat Aviation** (© **664/491-2533**). There's no helicopter service to Montserrat on Wednesday, and no ferryboat service on Sunday.

GETTING AROUND   By Taxi & Bus   Although the island has about 15 miles (24km) of surfaced roads, only those within the island's northern tier are currently accessible, and most of the island's vehicular traffic is limited to the route between the island's heliport and the designated "safe zone" in the northern tier. The typical taxi fare from the heliport to any of the hotels in the northern tier, including Vue Pointe, is EC$49 (US$18.15). Sightseeing tours in a local taxi, when viable, cost between EC$80 and EC$120 (US$29.60 and US$44.40) per hour, depending on how many hours you want to spend touring.

The only regular bus service remaining on the island since the volcanic explosions are those that run from Salem and Lookout, site of a newly built, government-funded residential community on the island's northern tip. Fares cost EC$2 (75¢) for transit between any two points along this route. Don't expect conventional buses like you'd find in large cities of North America. Vehicles along the ride are usually 15-seater minivans, each painted according to the tastes of the owner/drivers. If you want the bus to make a reasonable detour away from the designated route described above, the driver will usually do it for an additional fee you'll negotiate, pending the approval of the other passengers.

By Rental Car   None of the major U.S.-based car-rental companies offers an outlet on Montserrat, although you'll find a handful of privately owned agencies. Before you rent, you'll be warned that volcanic ash, when spread in a fine layer over any of the island's roads, contributes to slippery driving conditions. You'll also be required to buy a local Montserrat driver's license for EC$50 (US$18.50), which should accompany your valid U.S., British, Canadian, or other driver's license. These are sometimes (i.e., very rarely) available directly from the rental agency. More frequently, they're available from the immigration offices at both the heliport or the ferryboat terminal, and from the island's **police headquarters** in Salem (© **664/491-2555**), which is open 24 hours a day. *Drive on the left* in Montserrat, and know in advance that many of the winding, steeply inclined roads are treacherous.

Most island car-rental agencies stock a battered roster of Toyota Corollas, Toyota RAV4s, Suzuki Jeeps, or Mazdas, which rent—depending on the model—for $35 and up a day, depending on their make, model, and the duration of your rental. A collision-damage waiver costs from $9 to $11 per day.

Even if you buy it, you'll still be liable for the cost of some of the repairs to your vehicle if you damage it, for any reason, during your tenure. Two of the island's leading car-rental agencies include **Be-Beeps Car Rentals** (© 664/491-3787), in the hamlet of Olveston, near Salem, across the road from the Vue Pointe Hôtel. An agency with equivalent cars and prices that's closer to the ferryboat terminal is **Carib World Travel,** Davy Hill (© 664/491-2713).

Before you begin driving here, be warned that there's only one gasoline station on Montserrat, barely enough to serve all of the gas-related needs of an island that made do with five gas stations before the shutdown of Plymouth. Plan your refill stops accordingly, and remember the location of the **A&F Service Center,** St. John's main road, in the hamlet of Sweeney.

On Montserrat, accommodations are extremely limited, but if you want to spend the night, book into either of the island's two best hotels, **Vue Pointe Lodge** (© 664/491-5210; see below), or **Tropical Mansions,** (© 664/491-8273). Located within the hamlet of Sweeney's, it has its own pool and restaurant. When Emmanual Galloway, the owner, built the hotel, his wife thought he was crazy. But this contractor and hardware store owner pressed on and opened this $2 million 18-room inn. Double rooms, with breakfast included, cost $143 to $155 per night, although packages, with breakfast, lunch or dinner, and transfers from either the heliport or the ferryboat dock, are $99 per person, double occupancy, per night. MasterCard and Visa are accepted.

Vue Pointe Hotel, P.O. Box 65, Old Towne, Montserrat, B.W.I. (© 664/491-5210), is the best on island, with 22 units, perhaps rising to 40 during the life of this guide. Year-round, cottages with kitchenettes cost $150 double, and cottages and rooms without kitchenettes rent for $125 double, with MasterCard and Visa accepted. Each unit comes with a TV and phone. This is a family-run cottage colony consisting of a cluster of hexagonal, shingle-roofed villas, plus some interconnected rooms. They're set on 5 acres (2 hectares) of sloping land near a black-sand beach, within a 30-minute drive from both the heliport and the ferryboat landing dock. Most of the accommodations are built with natural lumber, open-beamed ceilings, and they're furnished with a comfortable blend of bamboo and modern pieces. Each has a private bath, a small refrigerator, a sitting-room area, and either two twin beds or one king-size bed. A natural breeze sweeps through accommodations in lieu of air-conditioning, assisted by ceiling fans. About a dozen of the units have kitchenettes of their own, and everywhere, the Caribbean's most-talked-about piece of geology (Mount Chance) seems to loom upward in panoramic beauty.

Although at press-time, no meals were served here other than breakfast, we expect the owners, Cedric and Carol Osborne, to resume their restaurant services—the best on the island prior to the volcanic catastrophe—during the life of this edition. On the premises is a freshwater swimming pool, dive shop, and two tennis courts. Many different watersports, including fishing, sailing, and snorkeling, can be arranged.

DINING

Additional restaurants are likely to crop up soon. Currently many of the island's eateries are simple takeaway stands. Two noteworthy exceptions, in addition to the well-recommended restaurant that's within the above-recommended Tropical Mansions Hotel, are the following.

Tina's Restaurant (Brades Main Rd.; (© 664/491-3538), where reservations are recommended, is set within a green-and-white Antillean house, less than a

5-minute drive uphill from the ferryboat terminal. This restaurant was established in 1998 by Tina Farrell, after she was evacuated from her home on Montserrat's southern tier. Expect a cozy, down-home Caribbean feel, with savory portions of chicken or beef, as well as grilled chicken salads or lobster salads, and whatever type of fresh fish that was hauled in by local fishermen that day. Open Monday to Saturday from 8am to midnight, it charges EC$10 to EC$25 (US$3.70–US$9.25) for main courses at lunch; EC$25 (US$9.25) for a set menu at lunch, and EC$45 to EC$65 (US$16.65–US$24.05) for set menus at dinner. No credit cards are accepted.

JJ's Cuisine (Sweeney's Center, St. John's Main Rd.; ✆ 664/491-9024), with reservations recommended, is owned and operated by Dominica-born Zephrina Jnofinn. This popular restaurant lies within a building that's within a 5-minute drive from the heliport. Inside the simple dining room you can order lobster, a worthy version of mountain chicken (frog's legs) sautéed in butter with garlic, sandwiches, and excellent burgers that Zephrina concocts herself with one or two secret flavorings. Open Monday to Saturday from 8am to midnight. Burgers and sandwiches cost EC$8 to EC$20 (US$2.95–US$7.40); platters go for EC$16 to EC$65 (US$5.90–US$24.05). No credit cards are accepted.

AROUND THE ISLAND

SCUBA DIVING   Montserrat offers 30 excellent dive sites, each with a rich assortment of marine life, including spotted drums and copper sweepers, and perhaps a large sea turtle. At the rim of the island's marine shelf, where relatively shallow waters suddenly drop off to great depths, divers can plunge into 70-feet-deep (21m) waters to see mammoth sponges along with large star and brain coral reefs. The experts on the island's marine botany and zoology are found at the **Sea Wolf Diving School,** Woodlands (✆ 664/491-7807), where one-tank dives cost $60, and two-tank dives cost $80. Snorkeling equipment can be rented for $10.

SIGHTS   Visiting an island with an active volcano is an attraction in itself. Consider Mount Etna on Sicily. The **Soufrière Hills Volcano** in the still-restricted southern part of the island holds fascination for visitors. It's legally forbidden for anyone to remain within the southern two-thirds of the island from 6pm till 6am the following morning. The government's motivation for this involves the lack of electricity and running water in that zone, and the wish to prevent squatters from settling on land abandoned after the exodus of many homeowners from the island. (Regrettably, the only deaths suffered during the island's volcanic explosions occurred on June 25, 1997, when 19 people were

---

Tips BEACHES

Montserrat isn't known for its white sandy beaches. Most of its beaches are of volcanic black sand, and they lie on the northern (unspoiled) rim of the island, the part not threatened by volcanic activity. The best beach on the island—and the only one whose sands are heat-reflective white—is **Rendezvous Bay.** Less popular, and hotter on bare feet, are the dark-sand (a slate-gray color) beaches at **Carr's Bay, Woodlands Beach, Lime Kiln Bay,** and **Bunkum Bay.** The staff at the Vue Pointe Hotel can arrange day sails to these beaches.

farming in an area that had been declared an Exclusion Zone, but since it was their livelihood, they took a terrible chance, and paid the ultimate price.)

Armed with clear instructions from geologists about where and where *not* to visit, taxi drivers and tour operators (see below) know where to take you on the island's southern tier, always in relative safety, for views of mud slides, layers of volcanic ash, and ghost-like tours of the partially destroyed former capital of Plymouth.

A good place to first learn about the volcanic catastrophe is the **Montserrat Volcano Observatory** (© **664/491-2230**) on Mongo Hill in the north coast, near the village of St. John's. The observatory is about a 60-minute drive from the ferry terminal, and about a 5-minute drive from the heliport. Visitors can stop by for a 3:30pm tour given Monday to Saturday. Tours cost EC$10 (US$3.70) for adults and EC$5 (US$1.85) for children aged 7 to 12. Children under 7 enter free, and no advance appointments are necessary. The tour consists of a 30-minute talk about the observatory's goals and objectives, and an introduction to its activity over the past few years. There's an opportunity to look at a number of informative exhibits, including the instruments that constantly monitor the volcano's pulse and power. Observatory souvenirs are sold in the site's gift shop.

TOURS   By no means should any novice visitor to Montserrat venture into the island's southern tiers without a trained guide, or as part of a guided tour. One of the best of the lot, and especially appealing if you're based in Antigua, is **Jenny's Montserrat Day Tours,** P.O. Box W471, Antigua (© **268/461-9361** in Antigua; no local phone in Montserrat; advance reservations are necessary; no tours on Sunday). Operated by Montserrat-born Jennifer Burke from a base in Antigua, it charges between $130 and $150 per person, depending on the day of the week you select. Tours begin and end at the Heritage Quay at St. John's in Antigua. The price includes ferryboat transit to Montserrat, breakfast and lunch, and a detailed tour of between 6 and 7 hours, with guided English-language commentary from a trained guide and driver. Highlights include close-up views of the volcano from a panoramic aerie known as "Jack Boy" Hill.

SHOPPING   Your best bet for some island products is the **Oriole Gift Store,** Salem (© **664/491-3086**), which sells Montserratian souvenirs that include preserves made from local fruits (try their mango chutney), polo shirts embroidered with the black Montserratian oriole (the national bird), necklaces made from conch shells, and relics of the sputtering volcano, such as souvenir bottles filled with gray volcanic ash.

Aruba

Aruba has a growing number of fans, from honeymooners and sun worshippers to snorkelers, sailors, and weekend gamblers. When you lie back along the 7-mile (11km) stretch of white-sand beach, you'll enjoy an average 82°F daytime temperature, trade winds, and very low humidity. Moreover, you won't be harassed by peddlers on the beach, you'll find it relatively safe, and you won't feel racial tensions.

Don't come for local culture and history—just for the good times, the gambling, and that fantastic sandy beach. The main resort area is a row of comfortable but familiar high-rise hotels along a gorgeous beach, like a beach strip out of Florida. The island's Palm Beach, one of the best beaches in the world, draws droves of tourists, as do its glittering casinos. Aruba is for vacationers who think that sun-drenched flesh is best complemented by a night out gambling, drinking, dining, or strolling along a moonlit beach. There are daily nonstop flights from the U.S.; you can leave New York in the morning and still get in some beach time before sunset.

The smallest of the ABC Islands (Aruba, Bonaire, and Curaçao), Aruba is 20 miles (32km) long and 6 miles (10km) wide, with a landmass of 115 square miles (298 sq. km). Its coastline on the leeward side is smooth and serene, with white-sand beaches; but on the eastern coast, the windward Atlantic side, it looks rugged and wild. Dry and sunny almost year-round, Aruba has clean, exhilarating air, like in the desert of Palm Springs, California. Forget lush vegetation here. Aruba lies outside the hurricane belt and gets less rain than virtually any other popular island in the Caribbean.

Though it is still a Dutch protectorate, Aruba became a nation unto itself in 1986. With more than a dozen resort hotels populating its once-uninhabited beaches, it is now one of the Caribbean's most popular destinations. A recent moratorium on hotel construction, however, has halted the building of new resorts—so for now, Aruba remains safe from rampant overdevelopment.

1 Essentials

VISITOR INFORMATION

Before you leave home, contact the **Aruba Tourism Authority** at the following locations: 1000 Harbor Blvd., **Weehawken, NJ** 07087 (© **201/330-0800;** fax 201/330-8757; newjersey@taruba.com); One Financial Plaza, Suite 136, **Fort Lauderdale, FL** 33394 (© **954/767-6477;** fax 954/767-0432; ata.florida@ taruba.com); 3455 Peachtree Rd., N.E., 5th Floor, **Atlanta, GA** 30326 (© **404/ 892-7822;** fax 404/873-2193; ata.atlanta@taruba.com); 10655 Six Pines Dr., Suite 145 **Houston, TX** 77060 (© **281/362-1616;** fax 281/362-1644; ata.houston@taruba.com); and Suite 201, Business Centre 5875, Highway 7,

Vaughan, **Ontario,** L4L 8Z7 (© **905/264-3434**). (There is no Aruba information office in the U.K.)

Information is available on the Web at **www.aruba.com**.

Once on the island, you can go to the **Aruba Tourism Authority** at L. G. Smith Blvd. 172, Oranjestad (© **297/8-23777**) for information.

GETTING THERE

Before you book your airline tickets, read the section "Package Deals" in chapter 2—it could save you a bundle. Even if you don't book a package, you should see that chapter's tips on finding the best airfare.

On **American Airlines** (© **800/433-7300;** www.aa.com), Aruba-bound passengers can catch a daily nonstop 4½-hour flight from New York's JFK airport. American also offers daily nonstop flights from Boston, Miami, and San Juan, Puerto Rico. American offers lots of great-value packages to Aruba, including a selection of several resorts. Ask for the tour department, or talk to a travel agent.

ALM (© **800/327-7230;** www.airalm.com) has good connections into Aruba from certain parts of the United States, but it offers no direct flights—all flights stop first in Curaçao.

US Airways (© **800/428-4322;** www.usairways.com) offers daily nonstop flights from Charlotte, NC, Philadelphia, and Pittsburgh. **Delta** (© **800/241-4141;** www.delta.com) operates flights from Kennedy Airport in New York with a quick stop in Atlanta.

Continental Airlines (© **800/231-0856;** www.continental.com) flies to Aruba via nonstop flights from Newark on Monday, Wednesday, and Friday.

United Airlines (© **800/241-6522;** www.ual.com) has weekend service from Chicago, but only in winter.

Air Canada (© **888/247-2262** in the U.S., or 888/247-2262 in Canada; www.aircanada.ca) has good connections from Toronto and Québec to Miami. Once in Miami, Canadians and other passengers can fly Air Aruba to the island.

GETTING AROUND

BY RENTAL CAR   It's easy to rent a car in Aruba. Excellent roads connect major tourist attractions, and all the major rental companies accept valid U.S. or Canadian driver's licenses. Major U.S. car-rental companies maintain offices on Aruba at the airport and at major hotels. No taxes are imposed on car rentals on Aruba, but insurance can be tricky. Even when you purchase a collision-damage waiver, you are still responsible for the first $300 to $500 worth of damage. (Avis doesn't even offer this waiver. In the event of an accident, you would be liable for up to the full value of damage to your car unless you have private insurance.) Rental rates range between $50 and $70 per day.

Try **Budget Rent-a-Car,** at Divi Aruba Beach Resort, L. G. Smith Blvd. 93 (© **800/472-3325** in the U.S., or 297/8-24150 ext. 429 in Aruba; www.budget rentacar.com); **Hertz,** Sabana Blanca 35 142 (© **800/654-3001** in the U.S., or

---

(Fun Fact   **Carnival**

Many visitors come here for the annual pre-Lenten Carnival, a month-long festival held in February or March, with events day and night. With music, dancing, parades, costumes, and "jump-ups" (Caribbean hoe-downs), Carnival is the highlight of Aruba's winter season.

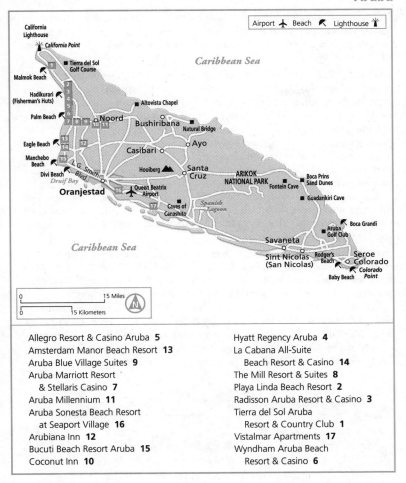

Airport ✈ Beach ᐟ Lighthouse ⵣ

Caribbean Sea

California Lighthouse
California Point
Tierra del Sol Golf Course
Malmok Beach
Hadikurari (Fisherman's Huts)
Palm Beach
Noord
Altovista Chapel
Bushiribana
Natural Bridge
Eagle Beach
Casibari
Ayo
Manchebo Beach
Hooiberg
Santa Cruz
ARIKOK NATIONAL PARK
Boca Prins Sand Dunes
Divi Beach
L.G. Smith Blvd.
Druif Bay
Fontein Cave
Guadarikiri Cave
Oranjestad
Queen Beatrix Airport
Caves of Canashito
Spanish Lagoon
Boca Grandi
Aruba Golf Club
Savaneta
Caribbean Sea
Sint Nicolas (San Nicolas)
Rodger's Beach
Seroe Colorado
Colorado Point
Baby Beach

0 — 15 Miles
0 — 15 Kilometers
N

Allegro Resort & Casino Aruba **5**
Amsterdam Manor Beach Resort **13**
Aruba Blue Village Suites **9**
Aruba Marriott Resort
& Stellaris Casino **7**
Aruba Millennium **11**
Aruba Sonesta Beach Resort
at Seaport Village **16**
Arubiana Inn **12**
Bucuti Beach Resort Aruba **15**
Coconut Inn **10**

Hyatt Regency Aruba **4**
La Cabana All-Suite
Beach Resort & Casino **14**
The Mill Resort & Suites **8**
Playa Linda Beach Resort **2**
Radisson Aruba Resort & Casino **3**
Tierra del Sol Aruba
Resort & Country Club **1**
Vistalmar Apartments **17**
Wyndham Aruba Beach
Resort & Casino **6**

297/8-21845 in Aruba; www.hertz.com), and **Avis,** Kolibristraat 14 (© **800/331-1212** in the U.S., or 297/8-25496 in Aruba; www.avis.com). Car rentals are also available at **Dollar Rent-a-Car** (© **800/800-4000** in the U.S.; www.dollarcar.com), whose branch is at the Queen Beatrix Airport (© **297/8-25651**). **National** (© **800/CAR-RENT** in the U.S.; www.nationalcar.com) has branches at Tanki Leendert 170 (© **297/8-71967**), and at the Queen Beatrix Airport (© **297/8-25451**).

For a better deal, consider **Hedwina Car Rental,** Bubali 93A (© **297/8-76442,** or 297/8-30880 at the airport). If you rent for a week, you sometimes pay for only 5 days. Also consider **Thrifty Car Rental,** Balashi 65 (© **297/8-55300,** or 297/8-35335 at the airport), which offers rentals starting from $35 per day. You can also rent Jeeps starting at $65 per day.

BY BUS Aruba has excellent bus service, with regular daily service from 6am to midnight. Round-trip fare between the beach hotels and Oranjestad is $2.

Bus schedules are available at the Arubus Office at the central bus station on Zoutmanstraat. Your hotel reception desk will know when the buses pass by. Try to have the exact change. For bus schedules and information, call **Arubus Co.** (© **297/8-27089**).

BY TAXI   Taxis are unmetered but rates are fixed, so tell the driver your destination and ask the fare before you get in. The main office is on Sands Street between the bowling center and Taco Bell. A dispatch office is located at the Bosabao (© **297/8-22116**). A ride from the airport to most of the hotels, including those at Palm Beach, costs about $16 to $18 per car, with a four-passenger maximum. Some locals don't tip, but we suggest you do, especially if the driver has helped you with luggage. On some parts of the island, it's next to impossible to locate a taxi and you'll have to call. If you're going to a remote location, it's a good idea to ask the driver to return for you at a certain time.

The English-speaking drivers are usually willing tour guides. Most seem well informed and eager to share their knowledge with you. A 1-hour tour (you don't need much more than that) costs from $30 for a maximum of four passengers.

BY MOTORCYCLE & MOPED   Because Aruba's roads are good, and the terrain is flat, many visitors like to rent mopeds and motorcycles. They're available at **George's Scooter Rental,** L. G. Smith Blvd. 136 D (© **297/8-25975**), and **Nelson Motorcycle Rental,** Gasparito 10A, Noord (© **297/8-66801**). Scooters rent for $30 per day and motorcycles for $45 to $100.

Melcor Cycle Rental, Bubali 106B (© **297/8-75203**), in front of Adventure Golf Club, rents scooters for $32 per day. You can also rent dirt bikes and street bikes, beginning at $45 per day. These are cash prices; a 4% handling charge is assessed if you use a credit or charge card. You can also find rentals at **Semver Cycle Rental,** Noord 22 (© **297/8-66851**), where bikes begin at $25 per day.

 FAST FACTS: Aruba

Banks   Banks are open Monday to Friday from 8am to 4pm. The most centrally located bank is **Aruba Bank** at Caya Betico Croes 41 (© **297/8-21550**). It's not hard to find an ATM (including one at the airport).

Currency   The currency is the **Aruba florin (AFl),** which is divided into 100 cents. Silver coins are in denominations of 5¢, 10¢, 25¢, and 50¢, and 1 and 2½ florins. The 50-cent piece, the square *yotin,* is Aruba's best-known coin. The current exchange rate is 1.77 AFl to US$1 (1 AFl is worth about 56¢). (Just before you leave home, you can check the current exchange rates on the Web at **www.x-rates.com**.) U.S. dollars, traveler's checks, and major credit and charge cards are widely accepted throughout the island. *Unless otherwise stated, prices are quoted in U.S. dollars in this chapter.*

Documents   To enter Aruba, U.S. and Canadian citizens and British subjects may submit a valid passport or a birth certificate along with photo ID. We always recommend carrying your passport whenever you visit a foreign country.

Electricity   The electricity is 110-volt AC (60 cycles), the same as in the United States.

Emergencies   For the police, dial © **11100**. For a medical emergency, dial © **8/74300** For the fire department, call © **115**.

Hospital For medical care, go to the **Horacio Oduber Hospital** on L. G. Smith Boulevard (📞 **297/8-74300**; also the number to call in case of a medical emergency). This modern building near Eagle Beach has excellent medical facilities. Hotels also have medical doctors on call, and there are good dental facilities as well (appointments can be made through your hotel).

Language The official language is Dutch, but nearly everybody speaks English. Spanish is also widely spoken, as is the local dialect, Papiamento.

Liquor Laws Liquor is sold on any day of the week throughout the island in most stores, including grocery stores and delis. By law (which doesn't seem to be heavily enforced), you can have an open container on the beach, but only if the liquor is purchased at one of the bars of the resort hotels lining the beachfront.

Safety Aruba is one of the Caribbean's safest destinations, in spite of its numerous hotels and casinos. Pickpockets and purse-snatchers are around, of course, but they're rare. Still, it's wise to guard your valuables. Never leave them unattended on the beach or even in a locked car.

Taxes & Service Charges The government of Aruba imposes a 6% room tax and a $34.25 airport departure tax. Your hotel will add a 15% to 20% service charge for room, food, and beverages.

Telephone To call Aruba from the United States, dial **011** (the international access code), then **297** (the country code for Aruba), then **8** (the area code) and the five-digit local number. Once you're in Aruba, dial only the five-digit local number for locations on the island. AT&T customers can dial 📞 **800-8000** from special phones at the cruise docks and at the airport to get service; from other phones, dial 📞 **121** to place a collect or AT&T calling card call. You can reach **MCI** at 📞 **800/888-8000.**

Time Aruba is on Atlantic standard time year-round, so most of the year, Aruba is 1 hour ahead of eastern standard time (when it's 10am on Aruba, it's 9am in New York). When daylight saving time is in effect in the United States, clocks in New York and Aruba show the same time.

Water The water, which comes from the world's second-largest desalination plant, is pure.

2 Accommodations

Most of Aruba's hotels are bustling, self-contained resorts. There's a tremendous dearth of family or budget hotels. Guesthouses are also few and tend to fill up early in winter with faithful return visitors.

In season, it's imperative to make reservations well in advance; don't ever arrive expecting to find a room on the spot. You must give Immigration the address where you'll be staying when you arrive.

Don't forget to ask if the 6% room tax (see above) and service charge are included in the rates quoted when you make your reservation.

Before you try to book your hotel on your own, read the section "Package Deals" in chapter 2. Lots of the big resorts in Aruba are frequently featured in packages, which can bring their rates down dramatically.

In lieu of renting an actual house or villa, which you can do on some islands, your best bet here is to rent an apartment or condo. Amsterdam Manor Beach Resort is a good place for such rentals.

VERY EXPENSIVE

Allegro Resort Aruba ✿   Rising high above Palm Beach, this hotel underwent a $25 million renovation in 1998. Today, the ambience is that of an ongoing, all-inclusive house party with a lot of action and organized activities. Guests have direct access to one of the island's prime beachfronts. The hotel was designed as a pair of nine-story interconnected towers in a landscaped garden with a lagoon-shaped swimming pool in the center. Bedrooms have carpeting, rattan furniture, comfortable beds, tub showers, and very small balconies overlooking the beach. Well managed, the resort attracts families, repeat guests, and international tour groups.

The Caruso is the most upscale and formal restaurant, with sophisticated cuisine, and requires advance reservations. Otherwise, the food is fine but unremarkable.

L. G. Smith Blvd., Oranjestad, Aruba. ✆ **800/858-2258** in the U.S., or 297/8-64500. Fax 297/8-63191. www. arubatourism.com/stay/h-allegro.html. 419 units. Winter $2,758–$3,374 double per week; off-season $2,240–$3,178 double per week. Rates are all-inclusive. AE, MC, V. **Amenities:** 3 restaurants, 4 bars; casino; pool; 2 tennis courts; drugstore; deli; fitness center; salon; Jacuzzis; dive shop, snorkeling, windsurfing, boating; children's programs; room service (breakfast only); massage; babysitting; laundry. *In room:* A/C, hair dryer, safe.

Aruba Marriott Resort & Stellaris Casino ✿   Although it's no Hyatt, this eight-story luxury high-rise lies at a far extension of Palm Beach, forming a U around a large courtyard with lush landscaping. When you walk in, all the waterfalls, streams, and fountains evoke a tropical garden. Known also for its casino and health spa, the hotel offers spacious and vividly decorated bedrooms, with large balconies opening onto prime views of the ocean. Each room is loaded with amenities, including a walk-in closet, dual sinks, and in-room movies. Some units are nonsmoking; others are wheelchair accessible.

Lunch can be poolside or else at Waves on the beach. La Vista offers continental fare in a casual atmosphere. For more elegant dining, head for Tuscany's Ristorante, which has a northern Italian menu. Spa lovers should give this hotel top priority, as it is state-of-the-art, with a re-creation of a Java rainforest with Balinese music, great massages and body wraps evocative of Indonesia, and everything from aromatic masks to beachside cabana treatment.

L. G. Smith Blvd. 101, Palm Beach, Aruba. ✆ **800/223-6388** in the U.S., or 297/8-69000. Fax 297/8-60649. www.marriott.com. 433 units. Winter $415–$485 double; from $655 suite. Off-season $235–$285 double; from $340 suite. AE, DC, MC, V. **Amenities:** 4 restaurants, 3 bars; casino; pool; health club and deluxe Mandara Spa; Jacuzzi; saunas; watersports; 2 tennis courts; children's program; game room; room service; babysitting; massage; laundry. *In room:* A/C, TV, minibar, hair dryer, iron, safe.

Aruba Sonesta Beach at Seaport Village ✿✿   What you don't get here that you do get at the properties just reviewed, is Palm Beach. But Sonesta has a lot of other attractions to make up for that. This sprawling, bustling place is two resorts in one, located in the Seaport Village Complex (the island's largest shopping and entertainment facility). Next to two marinas and a recreational park, it's the only major resort at Oranjestad Harbor and the only resort on Aruba that boasts a 40-acre (16-hectare) private island, 6 beaches, and a round-the-clock casino. The first resort, Aruba Sonesta Resort & Casino (with 300 units), is adjacent to the Seaport Mall and has an outdoor pool and terrace. The Aruba Sonesta Suites & Casino (with 250 1-bedroom suites) is a time-share resort that caters to yachties; rooms are rented out when time-share owners are not present. Each of the one-bedroom suites opens onto the beach. Each unit has a kitchenette, blond rattan furniture with floral pastel prints, and a small balcony, plush carpeting, and either a king- or two queen-size beds. Bathrooms offer deluxe toiletries and a combination tub and shower.

The top restaurant, L'Escale, is reviewed later (see "Dining"); it's connected to Aruba's only 24-hour casino.

L. G. Smith Blvd. 9, Oranjestad, Aruba. © 800/SONESTA in the U.S. and Canada, or 297/8-36000. Fax 297/8-25317. www.arubasonesta.com. 550 units in 2 resorts. Winter $215 double; $265–$450 suite. Off-season $140–$200 double; $270–$385 suite; extra person $40. Children age 12 and under stay free in parents' room. Breakfast and dinner $45 per person. AE, MC, V. **Amenities:** 4 restaurants; 5 bars; 2 casinos; 3 pools; tennis courts; exercise room; spa; watersports; children's programs; room service; babysitting; laundry. *In room:* A/C, TV, minibar, hair dryer, iron, safe.

Hyatt Regency Aruba Resort & Casino ★★★   The most glamorous resort on Aruba—even more so than the Radisson—lies on 12 landscaped beachfront acres (5 hectares) 2 miles (3km) north of Oranjestad. Built in the early 1990s for more than $57 million, the nine-story resort offers a series of public rooms reminiscent of a large-scale Latin American hacienda. Its gardens, Aruba's finest, are dotted with waterfalls and reflecting pools. The bedrooms are luxurious, with many extras, including original artworks commissioned from around the Americas. They are not as large, however, as those at the Marriott. Room extras include a king or two double beds, and big bathrooms with combination tubs and showers and tile floors. Guests in the hotel's 29 Regency Club rooms enjoy a private concierge, upgraded linens, and other amenities.

In general, the Hyatt has better restaurants than any other hotel in Aruba. You can choose among four restaurants and lounges, including the lovely indoor/outdoor Ruinas del Mar restaurant, with Mediterranean food. The Casino Copacabana offers entertainment and gaming tables.

A $2.5 million multilevel pool complex and lagoon (with waterfalls, tropical gardens, and slides) is the showcase of the resort.

J. E. Irausquin Blvd. 85, Palm Beach, Aruba. © 800/233-1234 in the U.S. and Canada, or 297/8-61234. Fax 297/8-61682. www.hyatt.com. 354 units. Winter $400–$550 double; from $895–$2,150 suite. Off-season $240–$365 double; from $550–$1,750 suite. MAP (breakfast and dinner) $70 per person extra. AE, DC, DISC, MC, V. **Amenities:** 4 restaurants; 4 bars; ice cream and coffee shop; casino; pool; 2 tennis courts; health club and spa; horseback riding; fitness center; Jacuzzi; watersports; children's programs and center; game room; car rental; salon; 24-hr. room service; babysitting; laundry/dry cleaning. *In room:* A/C, TV, minibar, coffeemaker, hair dryer, iron, safe.

Radisson Aruba Resort & Casino ★★★   One of the 10 most luxurious resorts in the Southern Caribbean, this 8-floor hotel grabs up 14 choice acres (6 hectares) along Palm Beach. The restored property, Radisson's premier flagship, shows what $55 million in renovation money can do, even though it still doesn't achieve the lofty Hyatt pinnacle. Its dramatic high points are cascading waterfalls and the Aruba Tower, from whose rooms guests enjoy panoramic views of the Caribbean. Pampering sets the tone—everything from spacious balconies with teak patio furniture, full-size marble bathrooms with shower-tub combinations, to the most elaborate package of toiletries in the Caribbean. Spacious guest rooms are in a Colonial/West Indian style, with mahogany four-poster beds, oversized mirrors, and plantation shutters. The private accommodations here are even more stylishly inviting than those at Hyatt and Marriott. For the best steaks and seafood in Aruba, see The Sunset Grille recommendation under "Dining," below.

J. E. Irausquin Blvd. 81, Palm Beach, Aruba. © **800/333-3333** in the U.S., or 297/8-66555. Fax 297/8-63260. www.radisson.com 358 units. Winter $425–$445 double; from $650 suite. Off-season $210–$230 double; from $425 suite. AE, DC, MC, V. **Amenities:** 3 restaurants, 2 bars; casino; 2 pools; golf privileges; 2 tennis courts; fitness center; spa; watersports, dive shop; children's center; room service; babysitting; laundry. *In room:* A/C, TV, minibar, hair dryer, iron, safe.

Tierra del Sol Aruba Resort & Country Club ✿

The number one choice for golfers in the Southern Caribbean is this resort, which offers a unique stay in Aruba. Luxurious villa living is combined with a state-of-the-art fitness center and spa on 600 acres (240 hectares) of landscaping that includes one of the Caribbean's best 18-hole golf courses, the creation of Robert Trent Jones, Jr. The vast complex sprawls across a cactus-studded landscape on the north coast, evocative of parts of Arizona. Your choice is 2- or 3-bedroom condos or free-standing villas—your own home in Aruba—that also come with 2 or 3 bedrooms, ideal for families or friends traveling together. A great deal of Aruba's "only planned community" is owned by "second homers," so expect a widely varied décor. We have, however, found the furnishings tasteful and tropical, very Caribbean in their breezy motif. Each unit opens onto a view of the golf course or ocean, and bedrooms come with queens or twins, each with private tiled bathrooms with tubs and showers. Accommodations open onto covered terraces with tables and chairs. You're not on the beach, but a free hotel shuttle will take you to the white sands of Arashi.

The complex is the site of one of Aruba's best restaurants, Ventanas del Mar (see "Dining," below).

Malmokweg, Oranjestad, Aruba. © **297/8-67800.** Fax 297/8-64970. www.tierradelsol.com. 114 units. Winter $450 2-bedroom condo; $550 2-bedroom villa; $600 3-bedroom condo; $655 3-bedroom villa. Off-season $225 2-bedroom condo; $375 2-bedroom villa; $375 3-bedroom condo; $455 3-bedroom villa. $50 extra per day for villas with pool. AE, DISC, MC, V. **Amenities:** 2 restaurants, 2 bars; pool; 2 tennis courts; golf. *In room:* A/C, TV, kitchen, iron, washer, dryer.

Wyndham Aruba Beach Resort & Casino ✿✿

This 18-story "skyscraper" rises beside a white-sand beach in a cluster of other high-rise hotels north of Oranjestad; it's rather straightforward, though it does have good facilities, and it tends to host a lot of conventions and tour groups, which makes it lag behind the Hyatt and Radisson in ambience. It recently underwent a renovation worth millions, and the bustling lobby is now sheathed in layers of stucco tinted in desert-inspired colors of terra cotta and cerulean blue. Each of the spacious bedrooms has a balcony, an ocean view, comfortable furniture, and fresh draperies. Bathrooms are small but well organized, with adequate shelf space and combination tubs and showers.

The Casablanca Casino occupies a large room near the lobby. Rick's Cabaret Lounge and the Baci Café serve Italian cuisine, and Pago Pago (see review later in this chapter) features Polynesian cuisine.

J. E. Irausquin Blvd. 77, Palm Beach, Aruba. © **800/WYNDHAM** or 297/8-64466. Fax 297/8-68217. www.arubawyndham.com. 480 units. Winter $305–$385 double; from $420 suite. Off-season $215–$285 double; from $285 suite. AE, DISC, MC, V. **Amenities:** 6 restaurants, 4 bars; pool; 2 tennis courts; health club and spa; Jacuzzi; sauna; watersports; car rental; room service (7am–12:30am); massage; babysitting; laundry/dry cleaning. *In room:* A/C, TV, fridge, coffeemaker, hair dryer, safe.

EXPENSIVE

Bucuti Beach Resort Aruba ✿✿ *Finds*

At the little 3-story Bucuti, you get personal service, European charm, and lush landscaping on a lovely 14-acre (6-hectare) stretch of one of the Caribbean's best beaches, the most secluded part of Eagle Beach. What this hotel has that those just described don't is intimacy, a personal approach to innkeeping, and a sense of seclusion, making it a top choice of honeymooners. Each spacious, well-furnished, bright bedroom is on the beach and has two queen-size beds or one king-size bed and sleeper sofa. The most expensive units have two queen-size beds and an oceanfront balcony or terrace. All rooms have well-maintained bathrooms with shower-tub combinations.

Across from the Alhambra Bazaar and Casino, the hotel operates the oceanfront Pirates' Nest Restaurant, a replica of a 17th-century Dutch galleon that specializes in good steaks, fresh seafood, and theme nights.

Eagle Beach, Aruba. ☎ 297/8-31100. Fax 297/8-25272. www.bucuti.com. 63 units. Winter $240–$270 double; $320 bungalow or junior suite. Off-season $140–$160 double; $200 bungalow suite or junior suite. Breakfast and dinner $43 per person extra. AE, DC, DISC, MC, V. **Amenities:** Restaurant, bar; pool; health club; library; tour desk; business center; laundromat; room service; babysitting; laundry/dry cleaning. *In room:* A/C, TV, minibar, fridge, microwave, coffeemaker, hair dryer, iron, safe.

MODERATE

Amsterdam Manor Beach Resort ★★ *Kids*   Inspired by the canal-front row houses in Amsterdam, this hotel sports one of the most interesting facades on the island. In an arid landscape across the street from Eagle Beach, where there's good snorkeling and swimming, it has a series of inner courtyards.

Even the accommodations are Dutch colonial in style, done with pine furniture, country-rustic blues, soft reds, and greens. In some cases, high ceilings lead to gable-capped peaks. Both studios and one- or two-bedroom apartments have fully equipped kitchens. This is an especially good choice for families, with babysitting, use of washer/dryers, and a children's playground. Units are small but well maintained and inviting, with ceiling fans, balconies or terraces (often with a sea view), white tile floors, and textured walls. The rather small bathrooms have tubs and showers.

J. E. Irausquin Blvd. 252 (P.O. Box 1302), Oranjestad, Aruba. ☎ 800/932-6509 in the U.S., or 297/8-71492. Fax 297/8-71463. www.amsterdammanor.com. 72 units. Winter $185–$195 studio; from $255 suite. Off-season $130–$140 studio; from $165 suite. AE, DC, MC, V. **Amenities:** Restaurant, 2 bars; playground; outdoor pool; kiddie pool; minimarket; laundry/dry cleaning. *In room:* A/C, TV, kitchenette, fridge, coffeemaker, hair dryer, iron, safe.

Aruba Blue Village Suites *Kids*   If you stay here, you'll have to forego a beachfront location, but the prices are reasonable (for Aruba) at this single-story complex in a residential area removed from the hotel strip. Although winter rates have been rising in the last couple years, families can still economize here if four people share a junior suite or six guests occupy a two-bedroom suite. The typical resort-style accommodations are plain but comfortable. Features include a separate bathroom with shower/tub combination and a fully equipped kitchenette. The rooms don't normally have phones, but you can request one. Twenty-six suites contain pull-out sofas. You're 5 minutes from the beach (free bus service will haul you there) and close to casinos and nightlife.

Cunucu Abao 37, Aruba. ☎ 297/8-78618. Fax 297/8-70081. www.arubabluevillage.com. 56 units. Winter $111–$140 suite. Off-season $88–$105 suite. AE, MC, V. **Amenities:** Restaurant, poolside bar; 2 pools; 2 sun terraces; table tennis; children's playground; room service; babysitting; laundry/dry cleaning. *In room:* A/C, TV, minibar, safe.

Caribbean Palm Village Resort   One of the major drawbacks of the timeshare Caribbean Palm Village is that it doesn't have a beachfront. It has pools for all ages, however, and public beaches at Palm Beach are within a 15- to 20-minute walk. The Spanish mission–style resort is located in the village of Noord in the Palm Beach district, a ½ mile from the beach and 7 miles (11km) from the airport. In the Spanish style, the resort offers handsomely decorated and streamlined bedrooms, plus one- and two-bedroom suites in a tropical garden setting. Suites include full kitchen facilities. Each room has air-conditioning and a ceiling fan, two queen- or one king-size bed, and a pull-out sofa. Roomy bathrooms have combination tubs and showers and adequate shelf space.

The upscale Valentino's restaurant, described in "Dining," below, is Aruba's most elegant Italian restaurant.

Noord 43-E, Aruba. **(** **800/992-2015** in the U.S., or 297/8-62700. Fax 297/8-62380. 228 units. Winter $160–$170 double; $215–$225 1-bedroom suite; $280–$295 2-bedroom suite. Off-season $90–$100 double; $115–$125 1-bedroom suite; $155–$165 2-bedroom suite. AE, DC, DISC, MC, V. **Amenities:** Restaurant; 2 pools; tennis court; shuttle to beach. *In room:* A/C, TV, kitchenette, safe.

Coconut Inn (Value)

Set inland from the sea, within a 7-minute walk from the village of Noord and a 20-minute walk to Palm Beach, this affordable hotel was built in five yellow-and-white sections between 1975 and 1996. Its rates are a steal. Though you won't be near the beach, the location is convenient to supermarkets and a public bus stop. The conventional rooms and one-bedroom suites contain almost the same amount of floor space; the studios are relatively cramped. All motel-style accommodations have a neatly-kept bathroom with a shower unit, a balcony or patio, and either a kitchenette or a microwave and refrigerator. There's no maid service on Sunday.

Noord 31, Aruba. **(** **297/8-66288.** Fax 297/8-65433. www.coconutinn.com 40 units. Winter $80 studio for 2; $95 double or 1-bedroom suite for 2. Off-season $65 studio for 2; $75 double or 1-bedroom suite for 2. Rates include breakfast. Extra person $20 in winter, $15 in off-season. MC, V. **Amenities:** Restaurant, bar; pool; laundry. *In room:* A/C, TV, hair dryer, kitchenette or fridge and microwave.

La Cabana All-Suite Beach Resort & Casino ★★ (Kids)

This is megaresort city, one of the Caribbean's largest hotel complexes that dwarfs anything else on island. If an intimate West Indian inn is in your dreams, flee the premises. Otherwise join in the communal fun, which has been ongoing here since 1991. Couples of all ages and persuasions, honeymooners, and families with very active kids live harmoniously on acres of landscaped grounds in self-contained "villages" across the street from Eagle Beach. Spacious, well-furnished suites come in widely varied combinations, and range from studios for one or two adults, to one-, two-, or three-bedroom suites. Ground-floor rooms afford less privacy. Suites come with well-equipped kitchens, patios, or verandas.

J. E. Irausquin Blvd. 250, Oranjestad, Aruba. **(** **800/835-7193** in the U.S. or Canada, or 298/8-79000. Fax 297/8-75474. www.lacabana.com/resort. 803 units. Winter $220–$302 studio; $260–$380 1-bedroom; $520–$745 2-bedroom; $765–$980 3-bedroom. Off-season $135–$175 studio; $175–$235 1-bedroom; $332–$470 2-bedroom; $500–$580 3 bedroom. Children age 11 and under stay free in parents' room. Various packages offered. **Amenities:** 3 restaurants, 4 bars; casino; 3 outdoor pools; 5 tennis courts; health club and spa; children's center; business center; babysitting; laundry/dry cleaning. *In room:* A/C, TV, hair dryer, kitchenette, iron and ironing board, safe.

The Mill Resort & Suites ★ (Finds)

This complex of two-story concrete buildings with red roofs is set in an arid, rather dusty location near the Wyndham. It's adjacent to a large, modern re-creation of a Dutch windmill, a kitschy Aruban landmark. Units ring a large swimming pool, and glorious Palm Beach (which is used by the megahotels) lies across the highway, a 5-minute walk away. The room decor is tropical, with white rattan furniture and carpeting or white floor tiles; many units have king-size beds and Jacuzzi-style tubs. This hotel is best for independent travelers who don't mind venturing out to find their own dining and fun.

Book your air, hotel, and transportation all in one place.

Hotel or hostel? Cruise or canoe? Car? Plane? Camel? Wherever you're going, visit Yahoo! Travel and get total control over your arrangements. Even choose your seat assignment. So. One hump or two? travel.yahoo.com

powered by
COMPAQ

YAHOO!
Travel

L. G. Smith Blvd. 330, Palm Beach, Aruba. ✆ **297/8-67700.** Fax 297/8-67271. www.arubaaccess.com/themill. 200 units. Winter $160–$256 double; $290–$360 suite. Off-season $102–$145 double; $175–$245 suite. AE, DC, MC, V. **Amenities:** Restaurant, bar; pool; fitness center; sauna; 2 tennis courts; children's programs; babysitting; salon; massage; laundry. *In room:* A/C, TV, hair dryer, iron, safe.

Playa Linda Beach Resort ⛱   Designed in an **M** shape of receding balconies, this salmon-colored time-share, nine-story complex sits amid tropical foliage on a desirable stretch of Palm Beach, 6 miles (10km) northwest of the airport. The units offer private verandas and foldaway sofa beds suitable for children. Accommodations are generally roomy, with attractive tropical decor, rattan furniture, ceiling fans, bathrooms with shower units, and fully equipped kitchens. The simplest rentals are the studios with kitchenettes, with the one-bedroom accommodations having better kitchens and more living and planning space. The one-bedroom lanais offer private patios opening onto the pool, with large wooden decks. There are also some two-bedroom accommodations opening onto the sea with spacious master suites and two-sink bathrooms with kitchens. Before booking, discuss carefully the type of accommodations here, since they vary so much.

J. E. Irausquin Blvd. 87, Palm Beach (P.O. Box 1010), Oranjestad, Aruba. ✆ **297/8-61000.** Fax 297/8-63479. www.playalinda.com. 194 units. Winter $265 studio for 1–4; $375 1-bedroom suite; $700 2-bedroom suite. Off-season $175 studio for 1–4; $245 1-bedroom suite; $345 2-bedroom suite. Rates include continental breakfast. Extra person $20. AE, DC, DISC, MC, V. **Amenities:** 2 restaurants, 2 bars; pool, children's pool; 3 tennis courts; health club; Jacuzzi; car rental; room service; babysitting; laundry/dry cleaning. *In room:* A/C, TV, kitchenette, minibar, hair dryer, coffeemaker, safe.

INEXPENSIVE

Aruba Millennium *(Value)*   This is a roadside motel evocative of Florida that is similar in appeal to the Arubiana Inn (below), except it rises two stories and is a short walk from the white sands of Palm Beach and six casinos. Many of the island's best restaurants are also within a walk of the complex. Accommodations are sold as studios or one-bedroom suites, the latter with complete kitchen and dining facilities and a private balcony. Furnishings are very Caribbean, with pastel fabrics and walls and white wicker and bamboo furnishings. Rooms are coated in white tile, each with a small but efficiently organized private bathroom with shower. Breakfast is taken by the pool where you can also order drinks throughout the day.

Palm Beach 33, Palm Beach, Aruba. ✆ **297/8-63700.** Fax 297/8-62506. www.arubamillenniumresort.com. 22 units. Winter $130–$172 double. Off-season $60–$95 double. Children age 11 and under stay free in parents' room. **Amenities:** Bar, snack bar; pool. *In room:* A/C, TV, coffeemaker, kitchenette in some.

Arubiana Inn *(Value)*   Lying only a 12-minute stroll over to Eagle Beach, one of the island's finest, this small and intimate inn is for those who shun the mega-resorts along the beachfront strip. The place is really like a motel you might encounter along the Florida Keys, not dramatic or spectacular in any way, but offering good, decent, and well-maintained accommodations. The cacti-studded landscape may cause you to think you've landed in Scottsdale. Built of coral stone with much use of a russet-brown terracotta, the complex encloses a communal section with a pool and chaise longues. Rooms are comfortable but rather basic, very West Indian in motif with light pastels, tiles, wicker, and rattan, along with tiny bathrooms with shower only. Each unit also comes with a small living room area.

Bubali 74, Noord, Aruba. ✆ **297/8-77700.** Fax 297/8-71700. www.arubianainn.com. 16 units. Winter $85 double. Off-season $55 double. Children age 11 and under stay free in parents' room. AE, MC, V. **Amenities:** Pool; minimarket; babysitting; massage. *In room:* A/C, TV, microwave, fridge.

Vistalmar Apartments *Value* An affordable and intimate place to stay on Aruba, this property doesn't have access to the celebrated beaches, but it lies across from the water in a residential section near the airport. It's quite a bargain, however, for in addition to your accommodations you will have complimentary use of boats, bikes, picnic coolers, snorkeling equipment, beach towels, and an outdoor grill. The complex of apartments is in two similar buildings, each with a balcony or courtyard offering water views. A little more stylish than some of the more barebones apartment units rented on the island, the accommodations here are spacious and furnished for comfort. Your hosts, among the island's more personable, are known for having a wealth of island information. They even stock your refrigerator with food for your first night here.

Each apartment has a king-size bed with a good mattress, a well-maintained bathroom with a tub and shower, a separate dressing area, a fully equipped kitchen, and a living room with a sleeper sofa. There's also a second sleeping room and a sun porch.

Bucutiweg 28, Aruba. © **297/8-28579.** Fax 297/8-22200. 8 units. Winter $100 apt. Off-season $50 apt. No credit cards. **Amenities:** Laundry service. *In room:* A/C, fridge and complimentary food upon arrival, no phone.

3 Dining

Sometimes—at least on off-season package deals—visitors on the MAP plan (breakfast and dinner) are allowed to dine around on an exchange plan with other hotels. Ask your hotel for details.

IN ORANJESTAD
EXPENSIVE

Chez Mathilde ★★ FRENCH Oranjestad's French restaurant is expensive, but most satisfied customers agree that it's worth the price. The chef's savory kettle of bouillabaisse contains more than a dozen different sea creatures. We also recommend rack of lamb chops with fine French herbs, juicy veal sirloin cooked in a raspberry liqueur and lime sauce and topped with melted Brie, and filet of red snapper prepared with a lightly peppered crust and lemon dressing. You get not only distinguished food and service but an elegant setting as well. In this carefully preserved 19th-century building, dining rooms are intimate, tables are beautifully set, and the decor is restrained but romantic. Live piano music enhances the total experience. The restaurant is near the Sonesta hotel complex, a 5-minute drive north of the airport.

Havenstraat 23. © **297/8-34968.** Reservations recommended. Main courses $22–$36. AE, DC, DISC, MC, V. Mon–Sat noon–2:30pm; daily 6–11pm.

Gasparito ★ ARUBAN/INTERNATIONAL This bright, upbeat restaurant is set in a traditional Aruban-style house, with yellow walls and local artwork. The atmosphere is lively and the food varied. With zest, flair, and consummate skill, the chef uses only top-quality ingredients. Diners can enjoy baked chicken stuffed with a peach, filet mignon served with either sautéed mushrooms or black-pepper sauce, or *keshi yena*—Dutch cheese stuffed with a choice of beef, chicken, or seafood. The menu also features an array of fresh seafood, including lobster served with a garlic-butter sauce or sautéed with onions, green peppers, tomatoes, and a multitude of spices.

Gasparito 3. © **297/8-67144.** Reservations recommended. Main courses $15–$33. AE, DISC, MC, V. Mon–Sat 5–11pm.

Le Petit Cafe ✦ STEAKS/SEAFOOD   Come here for two-fisted portions of steak and seafood—some of it grilled in the churrasco style you might expect on the Argentinean pampas. You can dine either inside, where it's air-conditioned, or on an outdoor terrace with views of potted palms, busy downtown streets, and boats bobbing at anchor in the harbor. A wide selection of cuisine may include filet mignon, zesty barbecued ribs, or a mixed grill with various sausages and cuts of meat. The latter dish is a bit heavy for the tropics. Seafood crêpes, shrimp in garlic sauce, and various preparations of grouper and snapper will please most seafood lovers.

In the Royal Plaza Mall, L. G. Smith Blvd. ✆ 297/8-38471. Reservations recommended. Main courses $17–$30. AE, MC, V. Mon–Sat 11am–11pm, Sun 6–11pm.

L'Escale ✦✦ CARIBBEAN/INTERNATIONAL   Some savvy locals prefer this to Chez Mathilde (see above) and claim that l'Escale is Aruba's best restaurant. We think it's a toss-up between the two. L'Escale offers direct access to Oranjestad's bustling Crystal Casino, but remains calm and elegant, thanks to a raised bar area that separates it from the action nearby. Designed in French Empire style, it offers panoramic views of the harbor, formal service, and well-prepared cuisine. The service here is formal, although formal attire is not required. The Hungarian string quartet plays every night except Monday.

The meals rely on imported foodstuffs, but they are perfectly cooked. The chefs skillfully handle only the best ingredients. Try *vol-au-vent*—chicken with island spices served in puff pastry—or an award-winning lobster bisque. A 5-ounce portion of tenderloin steak transforms the seafood pasta into the Caribbean's most elegant surf-and-turf ("seafood mignon").

In the Aruba Sonesta Resort & Casino at Seaport Village, L. G. Smith Blvd. 82. ✆ 297/8-36000. Reservations recommended in winter. Main courses $29–$50; Sun brunch $32.15. AE, DC, DISC, MC, V. Daily 6:30–11pm; Sun brunch 10am–2pm.

MODERATE

Kowloon CHINESE/INDONESIAN   This elegant Asian restaurant offers two red-and-black dining rooms, accented with varnished hardwoods and Chinese lamps, that overlook one of the capital's thoroughfares. Skilled at preparing Hunan, Szechuan, and Shanghai cuisine, chefs here also offer Indonesian staples such as the classic *nasi goreng* and *bami goreng*, made with rice or noodles and tidbits of pork, vegetables, and shrimp. The elaborate *rijsttafel* combines dozens of small curried vegetables in one impressive display, and the house special seafood combines fish, scallops, lobster, shrimp, and Szechuan-style black-bean sauce.

Emmastraat 11, Oranjestad. ✆ 297/8-24950. Reservations recommended. Main courses $13–$24.30. Set-price *rijsttafel* (rice table), $36–$56 for 2 diners. AE, MC, V. Daily 11am–10pm.

La Dolce Vita ✦ NORTHERN ITALIAN   This restaurant is the most acclaimed Italian dining spot on Aruba, recognized by the food and wine critics at *Gourmet* magazine. It may not be as elegant as Valentino's, but its food is even better. In an arid neighborhood inland from the sea, this rustic restaurant is ringed with a cactus garden. The creative Italian menu includes most of the usual favorites and a few unusual dishes. A meal might include slices of veal served either Parmesan style, cordon bleu style, with Marsala sauce, à la Florio (with artichokes), or à la Bartolucci (with ricotta, spinach, and mozzarella). Snapper comes four ways: simmered with clams and mussels, broiled with lemon or with wine, or stuffed with pulverized shrimp. We salivate over the stewpot of fish, which comes with linguine in either red or white clam sauce.

Italia straat 46, Eagle Beach. ⓒ 297/8-85592. Reservations recommended, especially in winter. Main courses $13–$39. AE, MC, V. Daily 6–11pm.

Le Dôme ⭐ BELGIAN/FRENCH   On Eagle Beach, this elegant restaurant is run and owned in part by Belgian Peter Ballière. Some 12,000 bricks were shipped from Belgium to create an "Antwerp atmosphere." The menu is sumptuous and excellently prepared, including such appetizers as goose liver pâté imported from France and, a most unusual dish for the Caribbean, creamy endive soup. From escargots to frog legs, you can proceed to such tempting dishes as filet of lamb or Dover sole, or even salmon with asparagus. The Sunday brunch is an island tradition. You can order wine, of course, or else wash it down with the island's best selection of Belgian beer. And, of course, don't forget the Belgian chocolates for dessert. The terrace, La Galerie, offers a view of Eagle Beach.

J. E. Irausquin Blvd. 224, Oranjestad. ⓒ 297/8-71517. Reservations recommended. Main courses $12–$33; $60 7-course set menu. AE, DC, MC, V. Daily noon–3pm and 5:30–11:30pm.

The Waterfront Crabhouse *Kids* SEAFOOD/STEAK   This restaurant overlooks a manicured lawn at the most desirable end of a shopping mall in downtown Oranjestad. With painted murals of underwater life, rattan furniture, and dining indoors and outdoors on a garden terrace, it evokes a restaurant on the California coast. Menu items include stuffed clams and fried squid with a marinara sauce and linguine with white or red clam sauce. The chef lists "crabs, crabs, crabs" as his specialty, including garlic crabs, Alaska crab legs, and (in season) softshell crabs. Over an open fire, he grills a wide range of fish, including yellowfin tuna and swordfish. He also serves stuffed Maine lobster and Cajun grilled shrimp. All fish are caught by hook-and-line, never from drift nets. The restaurant's steak menu includes a delectable 10-ounce Black Angus filet mignon, as well as a less expensive chopped sirloin smothered in onions.

In the Seaport Market, L. G. Smith Blvd., Oranjestad. ⓒ 297/8-35858. Reservations recommended. Main courses $19–$40; lunch $7–$22. Children's menu $3.95–$8.95. AE, DISC, MC, V. Daily 8am–11pm.

INEXPENSIVE

Cuba's Cookin' ⭐ *Finds* CUBAN   One of the oldest buildings on Aruba, constructed as a private home in 1877, in a downtown Oranjestad location across from the police station, is the setting for a restaurant where Batista-era Havana seems to come back to life. The most popular drink at its bar is a mint, rum, and sugar-laced *mojito*, which although high in calories, seems to produce an effect akin to a mild psychedelic. There's a main dining room plus three smaller areas, each lined with paintings inspired by the urban life in the tropics and in some cases, imported from Cuba. Menu items at lunch include simple recipes, usually configured as heaping platters of fish, chicken, or steak, each garnished with salad and vegetables. Dinners are more elaborate, and more representative of old-time Cuban cuisine. The best examples include *ropa vieja* (shredded skirt steak fried with green peppers, tomatoes, and onions) and a succulent version of *picadillo de res* (ground beef garnished with olives and raisins). Dessert might be a portion of coconut-flavored *flan*, and Cuban or Dominican cigars are available for anyone who wants one at the end of a meal. Every Wednesday and Saturday night this place gets mobbed with islanders coming for the live merengue, salsa, and Cuban jazz that's produced by live bands, who play on those evenings from 10:30pm until at least 1am.

Wilhelminastraat 27, Oranjestad. ⓒ 297/8-80627. Reservations recommended. Lunch main courses $10 each; dinner main courses $15–$20. AE, DC, MC, V. Mon–Sat noon–3pm and 5:30–11pm.

Driftwood ★ *Finds* SEAFOOD   The married partners who run this restaurant have an unusual setup: He (Herbert Merryweather) spends the day on the high seas catching the fish served that night in the restaurant, while she (Francine Merryweather) stays on-site, directing the sometimes busy traffic in the dining room. The setting is an antique Aruban house in the center of Oranjestad, with interior walls whose every surface is covered with (guess what) irregular pieces of driftwood. There's a list of menu items always available that includes Argentinian filet mignon served with a bacon-flavored mushroom sauce, boneless breast of chicken with parmesan and linguine, stewed conch, and shrimp in Creole sauce. But the composition of the fish menu varies according to the day's catch. It might include mahi-mahi, wahoo, kingfish, grouper, and lobster. These will be prepared in ways that you'll discuss with a staff member, usually Francine, who will propose any of several methods of preparation, either blackened, meuniere, fried, or baked, along with appropriate garnishes and sauces.

Klipstraat 12, Oranjestad. © 287/8-32515. Reservations recommended. Main courses $15–$33. AE, MC, V. Wed–Mon 5:30–10:30pm (last order).

The Paddock INTERNATIONAL   In the heart of Oranjestad, this cafe and bistro overlooks the harbor, a short walk from virtually every shop in town. Much of the staff is hip, and European. No one will mind whether you opt for a drink, a cup of tea or coffee, a snack of sliced sausage and Gouda cheese, or a full-fledged meal. The menu offers crab, salmon, shrimp, and tuna sandwiches; salads; pita-bread sandwiches stuffed with sliced beef and an herb sauce with plenty of tang; fresh poached or sautéed fish; and a glazed tenderloin of pork. Happy hours change frequently, but whenever they're offered, this place becomes packed with a festive crowd.

L. G. Smith Blvd. 13, Oranjestad. © 297/8-32334. Sandwiches, snacks, and salads $3.75–$6; main courses $10–$16.50. AE, MC, V. Mon–Thurs 10:30am–2am, Fri–Sun 10:30am–3am.

NEAR PALM BEACH
EXPENSIVE

Pago Pago ★★ POLYNESIAN   With their flaming torches and drinks crowned by pastel-colored umbrellas, many so-called Polynesian restaurants are more show than flavor. Not this one, whose chefs secure exotic ingredients and then shape them into luscious dishes to tempt the palate. You can begin with a South of Pago Pago drink while taking in nighttime views of the waters washing up on Palm Beach, a romantic setting with tables set on different levels. Piano music and a small combo put you in the mood for some of the most tempting dishes you'll find in Aruba. While waiting for your main course, you can dip huge plantain chips in a chili-laced sauce created with fresh ginger and bitter orange before being sweetened with honey. A large shrimp cocktail comes with a mango relish instead of all that red stuff, and the lobster spring roll tastes like it should and rarely does. From fresh seafood to the finest meats, you dine in style here. The chef's signature dishes include grouper under a crust of macadamia nuts served with a coriander sauce made with fresh lime and papaya. That or the twice-cooked pork, bathed with a citrus-enhanced honey glaze, will set the night on fire. For desserts the pastry chef is a whiz at making mousse, either chocolate or coconut.

In the Wyndham Aruba Beach Resort and Casino, J. E. Irausquin Blvd. 77, Palm Beach. © 297/8-64466. Reservations required. Main courses $21–$36. Fixed price menu $31.50. AE, DISC, MC, V. Mon–Sat 6–10:30pm.

The Sunset Grille ✰✰ STEAK/SEAFOOD If you'd like the type of cuisine that amused former Rat Packers like Sinatra and Martin, head here for some of Aruba's top quality seafood and its best steaks. Either is succulent, although everything is imported at this Art Deco restaurant with a terrace open to the breezes. The salmon filets come from Norway and taste of the fjords and are perfectly grilled, as are the filet mignon or the New York strip sirloin. For variety you can also order sushi, along with the best of shellfish such as shrimp and crab legs. We recently heard some Japanese visitors raving over the pan-seared tuna with a peppercorn crust and a "wake-up" soy sauce with ginger. Even the side dishes are perfectly prepared; all our favorites from broccoli to asparagus.

In the Radisson Aruba Resort & Casino, J. E. Irausquin Blvd. 81, Palm Beach. ✆ **297/8-66555.** Reservations required. Main courses $20–$49. AE, DISC, MC, V. Tue–Sun 5–10pm, Sun 11am–2:30pm.

MODERATE

Chalet Suisse ✰ SWISS/INTERNATIONAL Set beside the highway near La Cabana Hotel, this alpine-chalet restaurant feels like an old-fashioned Swiss dining room. In deliberate contrast to the arid scrublands that surround it, the restaurant is an air-conditioned refuge of thick plaster walls, pinewood panels, and a sense of *gemutlichkeit* (well-being). Tempting menu items include a lobster bisque, Dutch pea soup, beef Stroganoff, a pasta of the day, wiener schnitzel, roast duckling with orange sauce, red snapper with Creole sauce, and an array of high-calorie desserts. The hearty Swiss fare is good, if a bit heavy for the tropics. Most dishes are at the lower end of the price scale.

J. E. Irausquin Blvd. 246, Oranjestad. ✆ **297/8-75054.** Reservations recommended. Main courses $16–$42. AE, DC, MC, V. Mon–Sat 6–10:30pm.

De Olde Molen (The Old Mill) ✰ INTERNATIONAL This landmark is just across the street from the Wyndham and within walking distance of a number of other Palm Beach hotels. A gift from the queen of Holland, the windmill housing the restaurant was built in the Netherlands in 1804 and was torn down, shipped to Aruba, and reconstructed piece by piece. Since 1960 it has been a restaurant, albeit mostly for tourists. International and regional cuisine are served, including thick Dutch split-pea soup, chateaubriand for two, veal cordon bleu, shrimp Provençal, and red snapper arubiano (with Creole sauce). Most dishes are moderate in price. Although the windmill setting may seem gimmicky, the cuisine is actually pretty good—although we've found some dishes too heavy for a hot night. Don't come here expecting anything adventurous; everything's tried and true.

L. G. Smith Blvd. 330, Palm Beach. ✆ **297/8-62060.** Reservations recommended. Main courses $15–$30. AE, DC, DISC, MC, V. Daily 6–10:30pm.

The Old Cunucu House ✰ ARUBAN/INTERNATIONAL When it was originally constructed as a private house in the 1920s, this was the only building in the neighborhood. Today it retains its original decor of very thick, plaster-coated walls, ultrasimple furniture, and tile floors. Many visitors start with a cocktail under a shed-style roof in front, where chairs and tables overlook a well-kept garden studded with desert plants. The restaurant maintains a warm, traditional feeling, and focuses on local and international recipes including fish soup, fried squid, coconut fried shrimp, and broiled swordfish. Several dishes are served with *funchi* (made of cornmeal) and *pan bati* (a local pancake). The skilled chef knows how to embroider a traditional repertoire with first-class ingredients. Mariachi bands provide entertainment every Saturday night.

Palm Beach 150, Noord. (?) **297/8-61666.** Reservations recommended. Main courses $16–$22. AE, DISC, MC, V. Mon–Sat 5–10pm.

IN OR NEAR NOORD

The Buccaneer ✿ SEAFOOD/INTERNATIONAL   In a rustic-looking building near the hamlet of Noord, close to many of the island's biggest high-rise hotels, The Buccaneer is one of Aruba's most popular seafood restaurants. Inside, you'll find a nautical decor and bubbling aquariums. A number of dishes will tempt your palate as an opener—perhaps a crabmeat cocktail or a savory plate of escargots with an infusion of Pernod. Lobster Thermidor appears on the menu, and you can always order a land-and-sea platter with fresh fish, shrimp, and tender beef tenderloin. The food is hearty and delicious. A spacious bar area is a good place to linger over drinks.

Gasparito 11-C, Noord. (?) **297/8-66172.** Reservations not accepted. Main courses $12–$20. AE, DC, DISC, MC, V. Mon–Sat 5:30–10pm.

Lekker Brasserie CHINESE/DUTCH   Set within a 10-minute drive north of Oranjestad, this is one of Aruba's newest restaurants, with an unusual combination of Dutch and Chinese food. (*Lekker,* in Dutch, means "tasty.") There's a semicircular bar area, and a dining room filled with rattan and bamboo furniture. The chefs prepare many of the Chinese favorites, along with the kind of dishes that evoke nostalgia in Dutch visitors on holiday in Aruba.

Noord 39. (?) **297/8-62770.** Reservations recommended. Main courses $15–$25. No credit cards. Mon–Fri 4pm–2am, Sat–Sun noon–2am.

Valentino's ✿ NORTHERN ITALIAN   This is the most elegant Italian restaurant on Aruba, even if La Dolce Vita's food is somewhat better. Perhaps if you're on the island long enough, you'll give both of them a try. In the central courtyard of an upscale condominium complex, guests enjoy cocktails near the entrance, and then climb a flight of stairs to the peak-ceilinged dining room. Here you can check out the glassed-in, well-designed kitchen, and enjoy views over the palms and pools of the condominium complex and the attentions of the young but well-trained international staff. The prices are a bit high, but they're forgivable once you taste the food. It's a cozy, comfortable place. Best on the menu are chicken Parmesan, veal scaloppine, tenderloin pepper steak, rack of lamb in rosemary sauce with mint jelly, and a selection of fish dishes. The latter offering is likely to be your best bet.

In the Caribbean Palm Village, Noord 43-E. (?) **297/8-62700.** Reservations recommended. Main courses $19–$50. AE, DC, MC, V. Mon–Sat 6–11pm.

AT TIERRA DEL SOL/NORTH ARUBA

La Trattoria "El Faro Blanco" ✿ ITALIAN   Charming and authentically Italian, this restaurant, built in 1914, was originally the local lighthouse keeper's home. It's now managed by the same people who maintain the nearby golf course. The staff is mostly European, and the head chef studied in Italy. Views sweep out over the sea, the island's northern coastline, and the island's largest golf course. The menu covers a full range of Italian cuisine, with a heavy dose of aromatic Neapolitan specialties. The best examples include heaping platters of fish and vegetable antipasti; linguine with shrimp, octopus, scallops, clams, and tomatoes (wins our vote for the island's best pasta); red snapper cooked in a potato crust with olive oil and rosemary; and veal shank (*osso buco*) served with Parmesan-laced risotto Milanese. The desserts are excellent; we recommend tiramisu or pears poached in red wine served with ice cream. The bar is a favorite stopover for golfers.

At the California Lighthouse, North Aruba. © 297/8-60787. Reservations required. Main courses $18–$32. AE, DC, DISC, MC, V. Daily noon–3pm and 6–11pm.

Ventanas del Mar ✿ SEAFOOD/INTERNATIONAL   Surrounded by an emerald golf green, this restaurant offers sweeping views of the coastline and a comfortably contemporary decor. Lunch is less formal than dinner, with sandwiches and salads in addition to the steaks and grilled fish offered at dinner. Evening meals focus instead on Caribbean lobster, seafood pasta, conch ceviche, grilled garlic shrimp, and sautéed grouper. One of the best dishes and a personal favorite is fried whole red snapper served in ginger-soy sauce. A bar on the premises, decorated with golf memorabilia, remains open throughout the afternoon.

In the Clubhouse of the Tierra del Sol Golf Course, Malmokweg. © 297/8-67800. Reservations recommended for dinner. Main courses $15 at lunch, $18–$39 at dinner. AE, DC, DISC, MC, V. Tues–Sun 11am–3pm and 6–10:30pm.

EAST OF ORANJESTAD

Brisas del Mar ✿ *Finds* SEAFOOD/ARUBA   A 15-minute drive east of Oranjestad, near the police station, Brisas del Mar, in very simple surroundings right at the water's edge, is a little hut with an air-conditioned bar where locals gather to drink the day away. The place is often jammed on weekends with many of the same locals, who come here to drink and dance. In back the tables are open to sea breezes, and nearby you can see the catch of the day, perhaps wahoo, being sliced and sold to local buyers. Specialties include a mixed seafood platter, baby shark, and broiled lobster; you can order meat and poultry dishes as well, including tenderloin steak and broiled chicken. It's all solid, traditional fare, nothing too subtle or fancy.

Savaneta 222A. © 297/8-47718. Reservations required. Main courses $14–$26. AE, MC, V. Tues–Sun noon–2:30pm; daily 6–9:30pm.

Charlie's Bar and Restaurant SEAFOOD/ARUBAN   Charlie's is the best reason to visit San Nicolas. The bar dates from 1941 and is the most overly decorated joint in the West Indies, sporting an array of memorabilia and local souvenirs. Where roustabouts and roughnecks once brawled, you'll now find tables filled with contented visitors admiring thousands of pennants, banners, and trophies dangling from the high ceiling. Two-fisted drinks are still served, but the menu has improved since the good old days, when San Nicolas was one of the toughest towns in the Caribbean. You can now enjoy freshly made soup, grilled scampi, Creole-style squid, and churrasco. Sirloin steak and red snapper are usually featured. Come here for the good times and the brew, not necessarily for the food, although it isn't bad.

Main St., San Nicolas (a 25-min. drive east of Oranjestad). © 297/8-45086. Daily soup $6; main courses $19–$31. AE, DISC, MC, V. Mon–Sat noon–9:30pm (bar open until 10pm).

4 Beaches

The western and southern shores of Aruba are called the Turquoise Coast. Along this stretch, Palm Beach and Eagle Beach (the latter closer to Oranjestad) are the best. No hotel along the strip owns these beaches, all of which are open to the public (if you use any of the hotel's facilities, however, you'll be charged).

The major resort hotels are built on the southwestern and more tranquil strip of Aruba. These beaches open onto calm waters, ideal for swimming. The

Moments *Sunset at Bubali Pond*

The **Bubali Pond** bird sanctuary lies on the north side of Eagle Beach at Post Chikito, south of De Olde Molen (a 19th-century windmill-turned-restaurant, Aruba's most famous landmark). Flocks of birds cluster at this freshwater pond, particularly at sunset, which makes for a memorable sight. You can see pelicans galore, black olivaceous cormorants, the black-crowned night herons, great egrets with long, black legs and yellow bills, and spotted sandpipers. Even the large wood stork and the glossy scarlet ibis sometimes fly in from Venezuela.

beaches on the northern side of Aruba, although quite beautiful, face choppy waters with stronger waves.

Palm Beach ★★★ is a superb stretch of wide white sand that fronts hotels such as the Allegro Resort. It's great for swimming, sunbathing, sailing, fishing, and snorkeling. Unfortunately, it's crowded in the winter. The waters off this beach are incredibly blue and teeming with neon-yellow fish and flame-bright coral reefs. Billowing rainbow-colored sails complete the picture. Along Palm Beach, all the resorts are set in flowering gardens. Of course, a river of water keeps these gardens blooming in this otherwise arid landscape, but the gardens take on a special beauty precisely because the island is so dry. As you walk along the beach, you can wander through garden after garden, watching the native bird life. The tropical mockingbird feeds on juicy local fruits, and the black-faced grass quit or the green-throated carib hover around the flowers and flowering shrubs. If you stop to have a drink at one of the hotels' open-air bars, chances are you'll be joined by a bananaquit hoping to steal some sugar from you.

Also worth seeking out is **Hadikurari** (Fisherman's Huts), where swimming conditions, in very shallow water, are excellent. The only drawback to this white powder-sand beach is some pebbles and stones at the water's edge. This beach is known for some of the finest windsurfing on island. It is, in fact, the site of the annual **Hi-Winds Pro-Am Windsurfing Competition.** Facilities include picnic tables.

Quite similar to Palm Beach, **Eagle Beach** ★ is next door on the west coast, fronting a number of time-share units. With gentle surf along miles of white-powder sand, swimming conditions here are excellent. Hotels along the strip organize watersports and beach activities.

The white-powder sands of **Punta Brabo,** also called **Manchebo Beach,** are a favorite among topless sunbathers. Actually Manchebo is part of the greater Eagle Beach (see above), and the Manchebo Beach Resort is a good place to stop, as it offers a dive shop and rents snorkeling gear. It's also set amid 100 acres (40 hectares) of gardens, filled with everything from cacti to bougainvillea.

Practically every visitor winds up on Eagle Beach and Palm Beach. If you'd like something more private, head for **Baby Beach** ★ on the eastern end of Aruba. The beach has white-powder sand and tranquil, shallow waters, making this an ideal place for swimming and snorkeling. There are no facilities other than a refreshment stand and shaded areas. You'll spot the Arubans themselves here on weekends. (Our local friends love this beach and may be furious at us for telling you about it!) Baby Beach opens onto a vast lagoon shielded by coral rocks that rise from the water. Bring your own towels and snorkeling gear.

Next to Baby Beach on the eastern tip of the island, **Rodger's Beach** also has white-powder sand and excellent swimming conditions. The backdrop, however, is an oil refinery at the far side of the bay. But the waters remain unpolluted, and you can admire large and small multicolored fish here and strange coral formations. The trade winds will keep you cool.

5 Sports & Other Outdoor Pursuits

CRUISES   For a boat ride and a few hours of snorkeling, contact **De Palm Tours,** which has offices in eight of the island's hotels. Its main office is at L. G. Smith Blvd. 142, in Oranjestad (© **800/766-6016** or 297/8-24400). De Palm Tours offers a 1½-hour glass-bottom-boat cruise that visits two coral reefs and the German shipwreck *Antilla* on Thursday and Friday. The cost is $25 per person.

DEEP-SEA FISHING   In the deep waters off the coast of Aruba you can test your skill and wits against the big ones—wahoo, marlin, tuna, bonito, and sailfish. **De Palm Tours,** L. G. Smith Blvd. 142, in Oranjestad (© **297/8-24400**), takes a maximum of six people (four can fish at the same time) on one of its four boats, which range in length from 27 to 41 feet (8–12m). Half-day tours, with all equipment included, begin at $270 for up to four people. The price for a full-day trip is $500. Boats leave from the docks in Oranjestad. De Palm maintains 11 branches, most of which are located in Aruba's major hotels.

GOLF   Aruba's **Tierra del Sol Golf Course** (© 297/8-67800), designed by Robert Trent Jones, Jr., is on the northwest coast near the California Lighthouse. The 18-hole, par-71, 6,811-yard (6,198m) course was designed to combine lush greens with the beauty of the island's indigenous flora, such as the swaying divi-divi tree. Facilities include a restaurant and lounge in the clubhouse, plus a swimming pool. Golf Hyatt manages the course. In winter greens fees are a whopping $133, including golf cart, or $78 after 3pm. Off-season greens fees are $88, or $68 after 2pm. The course is open daily from 7am to 7pm.

A less pricey alternative is the **Aruba Golf Club,** Golfweg 82 (© **297/8-42006**), near San Nicolas on the southeastern end of the island. Although it has only 10 greens, you play them from different tees to simulate 18-hole play. Twenty-five different sand traps add an extra challenge. Greens fees are $20 for 9 holes. The course is open daily from 7am to 5pm. You can rent golf carts and clubs in the on-site pro shop. On the premises, you'll find an air-conditioned restaurant and changing rooms with showers.

HORSEBACK RIDING   De Palm Tours, L. G. Smith Blvd. 142 (© 297/8-24400), will make arrangements for you to ride at **Rancho Del Campo** (© 297/8-50290). Two daily rides last 3 hours each and cut through a park to a natural pool, where you can dismount and cool off with a swim. The price is $50 to $75 per person, and the minimum age is 10 years.

TENNIS   Most of the island's beachfront hotels have tennis courts, often swept by trade winds, and some have top pros on hand to give instruction. Many of the courts can also be lit for night games. We don't advise playing in Aruba's hot noonday sun. Some hotels allow only guests on their courts.

The best tennis is at the **Aruba Racket Club** (© **297/8-60215**), the island's first world-class tennis facility, which has eight courts, an exhibition center court, a swimming pool, a bar, a small restaurant, an aerobics center, and a fitness center. The club is open Monday through Saturday from 8am to 11pm and on Sunday from 3 to 8pm. Rates are $10 per hour per court, and lessons are $20 for a half hour or $40 per hour. The location is part of the Tierra del Sol complex on Aruba's northwest coast, near the California Lighthouse.

WATERSPORTS   You can snorkel in shallow waters, and scuba divers find stunning marine life with endless varieties of coral and tropical fish in myriad hues; at some points visibility extends up to 90 feet (27m). Most divers set out for the German freighter *Antilla,* which was scuttled in the early years of World War II off the northwestern tip of Aruba, not too far from Palm Beach.

Red Sails Sports, Palm Beach (© **297/8-61603**), is the island's best watersports center. The extensive range of activities here includes sailing, water-skiing, and scuba diving. Red Sail dive packages include shipwreck dives and marine-reef explorations. Guests first receive a poolside dive-safety course from Red Sail's certified instructors. Those who wish to become certified can achieve full PADI certification in 4 days for $350. One-tank dives cost $40, and two-tank dives are $65.

Divi Winds Center, J. E. Irausquin Blvd. 41 (© **297/8-37841**), near the Tamarind Aruba Beach Resort, is the island's windsurfing headquarters. Equipment, made by Fanatic, rents for $15 to $20 per hour, $35 per half day, or $45 for a full day. The resort is on the tranquil (southern) side of the island, safe from fierce northern waves. A private Sunfish lesson is $50; group instruction is $30. You can also rent snorkeling gear.

6 Seeing the Sights

IN ORANJESTAD ⊛
Aruba's capital, Oranjestad, attracts more shoppers than sightseers. The bustling city has a very Caribbean flavor, with part-Spanish, part-Dutch architecture. The main thoroughfare, Lloyd G. Smith Boulevard, cuts in from the airport along the waterfront and on to Palm Beach, changing its name along the way to J. E. Irausquin Boulevard. Most visitors cross it to head for **Caya G. F. Betico Croes** and the best duty-free shopping.

After a shopping trip, you might return to the harbor where fishing boats and schooners, many from Venezuela, are moored. Nearly all newcomers to Aruba like to photograph the **Schooner Harbor.** Colorful boats dock along the quay, and boat people display their wares in open stalls. The local patois predominates. A little farther along, at the **fish market,** fresh fish is sold directly from the boats. **Wilhelmina Park,** named after Queen Wilhelmina of the Netherlands, is also on the sea side of Oranjestad. The park features a tropical garden along the water and a sculpture of the Queen Mother.

AN UNDERWATER JOURNEY
One of the island's most fun activities is an underwater journey on one of the world's few passenger submarines, operated by **Atlantis Submarines** ⊛, Seaport Village Marina (opposite the Sonesta), Oranjestad (© **800/253-0493** or 297/8-36090). Even nondivers can witness a coral reef firsthand without risking the obstacles and dangers of a scuba expedition. Carrying 46 passengers to a depth of up to 150 feet (45m), the ride provides all the thrills of an underwater dive—but keeps you dry. In 1995 an old Danish fishing vessel was sunk to create a fascinating view for divers and submariners.

There are four departures from the Oranjestad harbor front every hour on the hour, Monday to Sunday from 10am to 12:30pm. Each tour includes a 30-minute catamaran ride to Barcadera Reef, 2 miles (3km) southeast of

Aruba—a site chosen for the huge variety of its underwater flora and fauna. At the reef, participants are transferred to the submarine for a 1-hour underwater lecture and tour.

Allow 2 hours for the complete experience. The cost is $74 for adults and $35 for children age 2 to 16 (children under age 2 are not admitted). Advance reservations are essential. A staff member will ask for a credit card number (and give you a confirmation number) to hold the booking for you.

IN THE COUNTRYSIDE

If you can lift yourself from the sands for an afternoon, you might like to drive into the *cunucu*, which in Papiamento means "the countryside." Here Arubans live in modest, colorful, pastel-washed houses, decorated with tropical plants that require expensive desalinated water. Visitors who venture into the center of Aruba will want to see the strange **divi-divi tree,** with its trade-wind-blown coiffure.

You probably will want to visit Aruba's most outstanding landmark, **Hooiberg,** affectionately known as "The Haystack." From Oranjestad, take Caya G. F. Croes (7A) toward Santa Cruz. Anybody with the stamina can climb steps to the top of this 541-foot-high (162m) hill. On a clear day, you can see Venezuela from here.

Aruba is studded with massive boulders. You'll find the most impressive ones at **Ayo** and **Casibari,** northeast of Hooiberg. Diorite boulders stack up as high as urban buildings. The rocks weigh several thousand tons and puzzle geologists. Ancient Amerindian drawings appear on the rocks at Ayo. At Casibari, you can climb to the top for a panoramic view of the island or a close look at rocks that nature has carved into seats or prehistoric birds and animals. Pay special attention to the island's unusual species of lizards and cacti. Casibari is open daily from 9am to 5pm, with no admission charge. There's a lodge at Casibari where you can buy souvenirs, snacks, soft drinks, and beer.

Guides can also point out drawings on the walls and ceiling of the **Caves of Canashito,** south of Hooiberg. You may get to see some giant green parakeets here as well.

On the jagged, windswept northern coast of Aruba, the unrelenting surf carved the **Natural Bridge** out of coral rock. You can order snacks in a little cafe overlooking the coast. You'll also find a souvenir shop with trinkets, T-shirts, and wall hangings for reasonable prices.

NEAR SAN NICOLAS

As you drive along the highway toward the island's southernmost section, you may want to stop at the **Spaans Lagoen** (Spanish Lagoon), where pirates hid and waited to plunder rich cargo ships in the Caribbean. Today it's an ideal place for snorkeling, and you can picnic at tables under the mangrove trees.

To the east, you'll pass an area called **Savaneta,** where some of the most ancient traces of human habitation on Aruba have been unearthed. You'll see here the first oil tanks that marked the position of the **Lago Oil & Transport Company,** the Exxon subsidiary around which the town of San Nicolas developed. San Nicolas was a company town until 1985, when the refinery curtailed operations. Twelve miles (19km) from Oranjestad, it is now called the Aruba Sunrise Side, and tourism has become its main economic engine.

Boca Grandi, on the windward side of the island, is a favorite windsurfing location; if you prefer quieter waters, you'll find them at Baby Beach and Rodgers Beach, on Aruba's leeward side. Baby Beach offers the island's best beach-based snorkeling. Seroe Colorado (Colorado Point) overlooks the two beaches. From here, you can see the Venezuelan coastline and the pounding surf on the windward side. If you climb down the cliffs, you're likely to spot an iguana; protected by law, the once-endangered saurians now proliferate in peace.

You can see cave wall drawings at the **Guadarikiri Cave** and **Fontein Cave.** At the **Huliba** and **Tunnel of Love** caves, guides and refreshment stands await visitors. In spite of its name, the Tunnel of Love cave requires some physical stamina to explore. It is filled with steep climbs, and its steps are illuminated only by hand-held lamps. Wear sturdy shoes and watch your step.

7 Shopping

Aruba manages to offer goods from six continents along the ½-mile-long (.8km) **Caya G. F. Betico Croes,** Oranjestad's main shopping street. Technically this is not a free port, but the duty is so low (3.3%) that prices are attractive—and Aruba has no sales tax. You'll find the usual array of Swiss watches; German and Japanese cameras; jewelry; liquor; English bone china and porcelain; Dutch, Swedish, and Danish silver and pewter; French perfume; British woolens; Indonesian specialties; and Madeira embroidery. Delft blue pottery is an especially good buy. Other good buys include Dutch cheese (Edam and Gouda), Dutch chocolate, and English cigarettes in the airport departure area.

8 Aruba After Dark

CASINOS: LET THE GOOD TIMES ROLL ★★

The casinos of the big hotels along Palm Beach are the liveliest nighttime destinations. They stay open as long as business demands, often into the wee hours. In plush gaming parlors, guests try their luck at roulette, craps, blackjack, and, of course, the one-armed bandits. Limits and odds are about the same as in the United States.

Excelsior Casino, J. E. Irausquin Blvd. 230 (© **297/8-67777**), wins the prize for all-around action. Its casino doors are open from 8am to 4am. The **Aruba Grand,** J. E. Irausquin Blvd. 79 (© **297/8-63900**), opens its games at 10am; it stays open until 1:30am. **Casino Masquerade,** at the Radisson Aruba Caribbean Resort & Casino, J. E. Irausquin Blvd. 81, Palm Beach (© **297/ 8-66555**), is one of the newest casinos on Aruba. On the lower-level lobby of the hotel, it's open from noon to 4am daily. It offers blackjack, single deck, roulette, Caribbean stud, craps, and Let It Ride.

One of the island's best is the **Crystal Casino** at the Aruba Sonesta Resort & Casino at Seaport Village (© **297/8-36000**), open daily 24 hours. The 14,000-square-foot (1,260m) casino offers 11 blackjack tables, 270 slot machines, 4 roulette tables, 3 Caribbean stud-poker tables, 2 craps tables, 1 mini-baccarat table, and 3 baccarat tables. This place has luxurious furnishings, ornate moldings, marble, and crystal chandeliers.

Visitors have a tendency to flock to the newest casinos on the island, like the one at the **Wyndham Hotel and Resort,** J. E. Irausquin Blvd. 77 (© **297/ 8-64466**), or the **Hyatt Regency Aruba,** J. E. Irausquin Blvd. 85 (© **297/8-61234**). The **Royal Cabana Casino,** at the **La Cabana All Suite Beach Resort & Casino,** J. E. Irausquin Blvd. 250 (© **297/8-74665**), outdraws them all. It's known for its multitheme three-in-one restaurant and its showcase cabaret theater and nightclub, with Las Vegas–style revues, female impersonators, and comedy series on the weekend. The largest casino on Aruba, it offers 33 tables and games, plus 320 slot machines.

Alhambra, J. E. Irausquin Blvd. 47 (℃ **297/8-35000**), is a complex of buildings and courtyards designed like an 18th-century Dutch village. About a dozen shops here sell souvenirs, leather goods, jewelry, and beachwear. From the outside, the complex looks Moorish, with serpentine mahogany columns, arches, and domes. A busy casino operates on the premises (open from 10am until very early in the morning, usually 3am). In addition to the casino, there is also the Kismet-like **Aladdin Theatre** adjoining it. Here routine shows feature gymnasts, dancers, singers, and impersonators, but don't have the professionalism and appeal of the big hotel revues recommended below.

At the Allegro Resort & Casino Aruba, the **Royal Palm Casino,** J. E. Irausquin Blvd. 83, (℃ **297/8-69039**), is known for its Caribbean stud poker at the tables, and also for games of blackjack, roulette, baccarat, and craps. Its slot machines open for action at noon. Another choice, the **Stellaris Casino,** at Marriott's Aruba Ocean Club, L. G. Smith Blvd. 1012, Palm Beach (℃ **297/ 8-69000**), is a large casino that starts to get busy daily at 4pm, when gamblers arrive to play super seven, craps, Caribbean stud poker, and something called "Wild Aruba Stud."

BIG STAGE REVUES

Aruba stages more spectacles a la Las Vegas than any other island in the Caribbean. These shows are most often at hotels but are open to nonguests who reserve a table. Some of the best shows are staged at the **Seaport's Crystal Theatre,** in the Aruba Sonesta Beach Resort, L. G. Smith Blvd. 82, in Oranjestad (℃ **297/8-36000**). "Let's Go Latin," its current and long-running revue, has been attracting audiences from Oregon to Venezuela, with its lavish costumes, nearly 200 in all, and some two dozen performers. Exquisite bods strut the stage in this Ooh Lah-Lah extravaganza. The talent comes from Cuba where, as one performer told us, "rhythm is in our blood." To catch the future Gloria Estefan, Jennifer Lopez, or Marc Anthony of tomorrow, head there.

Tickets cost $37 or $17 for children under age 12, which is only for the show. A dinner show package costs $64 per person. Show times are Monday to Saturday at 9pm.

The biggest stage shows in Aruba are at **Las Palmas Showroom,** in the Allegro Resort & Casino Aruba, J. E. Irausquin Blvd. 83, Palm Beach (℃ **297/ 8-64500**). Six different spectacles a week are offered every Monday to Saturday, starting at 8:30pm. The cost is $42.50 per person, including dinner and one show. The show is different every night—a revue of Latino rhythms one night, Broadway tunes the next night, or a "fantasy" on another night.

If you're not planning to slip into Havana illegally on your trip to the Caribbean, you'll think you've arrived when you attend performances at the **Cabaret Royal Showroom,** Wyndham Aruba Beach Resort & Casino, J. E. Irausquin Blvd. 77, Palm Beach (℃ **297/8-64466**). It stages hot Cuban revues, with dancing and salsa music. Nearly all of the performers—music makers, dancers, and singers—come from Cuba. It's a high-energy revue with Latino and American classic songs, ballads, and Broadway favorites. The dinner show includes a 3-course menu for $46 per person, but for only $28 you can enjoy the "cocktail show." Dinner show seatings are at 7:15pm, with cocktail show seatings at 8:30pm, and the revue beginning at 9pm. There is no show on Wednesday and Sunday.

The best female impersonator shows on island are at the **Tropicana Show-room,** Royal Cabana Casino, J. E. Irausquin Blvd. 250 (© **2977/8-79000**). You meet all the saucy ladies here from Joan Rivers, Bette Midler, and Madonna, to Celine Dion, and, of course, Tina Turner. If drag divas are your thing, this is the place to see them. On Wednesday and Friday shows start at 10pm; on Monday, Tuesday, Thursday, and Saturday at 9pm.

THE CLUB & BAR SCENE

We like to begin our Aruban nights at **Salt 'n Pepper,** J. E. Irausquin Blvd. 368A (© **297/8-633301**), where we can order the island's best tapas. Three or four of these appetizers are large enough to make a main course. If you bring in a set of original salt and pepper shakers for the owners to keep, you get your first glass of wine free with your dinner. (Note that sets can't be "borrowed" from local restaurants and hotels.) Sangria, consumed in an alfresco courtyard, is the usual drink of choice, and the bar stays open until 1 am.

Mumbo Jumbo, in the Royal Plaza Mall, L. G. Smith Boulevard (© **297/8-33632**), is sultry and relaxing. Expect a cosmopolitan blend of Dutch and Latino visitors, and lots of Latin rhythms. The volume is kept at a tolerable level for wallflowers and anyone who wants to have a conversation. There's an array of specialty drinks; imagine coconut shells, very colorful straws, and large fruit. Hours are from sunset until between 2 and 3am, depending on the night of the week.

Havana Beach Club, L. G. Smith Blvd. 2 (© **297/8-23380**), rents chairs and umbrellas during the day and has a swimming pool. After 8pm, it trans-forms into one of the island's busiest nightclubs, with recorded or live salsa music and lots of high-energy exhibitionism on the dance floor. It's open every night until 5am. The cover ranges from $6 to $10.

Iguana Joe's Caribbean Bar & Grill, Royal Plaza Mall, L. G. Smith Blvd. (© **297/8-39373**), enjoys an equal vogue among visitors and islanders. It's known for its huge array of specialty drinks, including "Pink Iguana," "Grandma Joe's Pink Lemonade," and the aptly named "Lethal Lizard," the lat-ter packing four shots of liquor served in a half-liter carafe. Patrons come here to drink and have a good time, and they can also eat here, ordering fresh salads, pastas, fresh mahi-mahi, sizzling fajitas, and rich homemade desserts.

Another hot spot worth checking out is **Café Bahia,** Westraat 7 in Oranjes-tad (© **297/8-89982**), which is both a bar and a dance club. Some of the best island bands show up here.

6

Barbados

Bajans like to think of their island as "England in the tropics," but endless pink- and white-sand beaches are what really put Barbados on the map. Rich in tradition, Barbados is easily reached from the United States and has a grand array of hotels (many of them super-expensive). Although it doesn't offer casinos, it has more than just beach life. It's a rich destination for travelers interested in learning about West Indian culture, and it offers more sightseeing attractions than most Caribbean islands.

After morning mists burn off to expose panoramas of valley and ocean, the Bajan landscape is one of the most majestic in the southern Caribbean. It's an ideal place to go on lovely driving tours to take in all the little seaside villages, plantations, gardens, and English country churches, some dating from the 17th century.

Afternoon tea remains a tradition in many places, cricket is still the national sport, and many Bajans speak with a British accent. Despite Barbados being called "Little England" in the Caribbean, many islanders are weighing the possibility of a divorce from the mother country.

Don't rule out Barbados if you're seeking a peaceful island getaway. Although the south coast is known for its nightlife and the west-coast beach strip is completely built up, some of the island remains undeveloped. The east coast is fairly tranquil, and you can often be alone here (but because it faces the Atlantic, the waters aren't as calm as they are on the Caribbean side). Many escapists, especially Canadians seeking a low-cost place to stay in winter, don't seem to mind the Atlantic waters at all.

A lot of visitors actually prefer the more remote life on the Atlantic coast, which not only has Bathsheba Beach going for it, but some of the most visited attractions on the island, including Andromeda Botanical Garden, Farley Hill National Park, Barbados Wildlife Reserve, and Harrison's Cave.

Although crime has been on the rise in recent years, Barbados is still a relatively safe destination. The difference between the haves and the have-nots doesn't cause the sometimes violent clash here that it does on other islands, such as Jamaica. Bajans have a long history of welcoming foreign visitors, and that tradition of hospitality is still ingrained in most locals.

1 Essentials

VISITOR INFORMATION

In the United States, you can contact the following offices of the **Barbados Tourism Authority:** 800 Second Ave., New York, NY 10017 (© **800/221-9831**); 3440 Wilshire Blvd., Suite 1215, Los Angeles, CA 90010 (© **213/380-2198**); or 158 Alhambra Circle, Suite 1270, Miami, FL 33134 (© **305/442-7471**).

The Canadian office is located at 105 Adelaide St. West, Suite 1010, Toronto, Ontario M5H 1P9 (© **416/214-9880**). In the United Kingdom, contact the

Barbados Tourism Authority at 263 Tottenham Court Rd., London W1P 0LA (© 020/7636-9448).

On the Internet, go to www.barbados.org. The tourism office may be able to help you track down condo and villa rentals.

On the island, the local Barbados Tourism Authority office is located on Harbour Road (P.O. Box 242), Bridgetown (© 246/427-2623).

GETTING THERE

Before you book your flight, be sure to read the section "Package Tours" in chapter 2; it can save you a bundle. Even if you don't book a package, see that chapter's tips on finding the best airfare.

More than 20 flights arrive on Barbados from all over the world every day. Grantley Adams International Airport is on Highway 7, on the southern tip of the island at Long Bay, between Oistins and a village called The Crane. From North America, the four major gateways to Barbados are New York, Miami, Toronto, and San Juan. Flying time to Barbados is 4½ hours from New York, 3½ hours from Miami, 5 hours from Toronto, and 1½ hours from San Juan.

American Airlines (© 800/433-7300; www.aa.com) has dozens of connections passing through San Juan, plus daily nonstop flights to Barbados from New York and Miami. BWIA (© 800/538-2942; www.bwee.com), the national airline of Trinidad and Tobago, also offers daily flights from New York and Miami, plus many flights from Trinidad.

Canadians may opt for nonstop flights to Barbados from Toronto. Air Canada (© 888/247-2262 in the U.S., or 800/268-7240 in Canada; www.aircanada.ca) has three flights per week from Toronto in winter, plus one Sunday flight from Montréal year-round. In summer, when demand wanes, there are fewer flights from Toronto.

Barbados is a major hub of the Caribbean-based airline LIAT (© 800/468-0482 in the U.S. and Canada, 246/434-5428 for reservations, or 246/428-0986 at the Barbados airport), which provides generally poor service to Barbados from a handful of neighboring islands, including St. Vincent & the Grenadines, Antigua, and Dominica.

Air Jamaica (© 800/523-5585; www.airjamaica.com) offers daily flights that link Barbados to Atlanta, Baltimore, and Miami through the airline's Montego Bay hub. Air Jamaica offers service between Los Angeles and Barbados on Friday and Sunday, (but it requires an overnight stay in Montego Bay). Nonstop flights from New York to Barbados are available 5 days a week.

Cayman Airways and Air Jamaica have joined forces to provide an air link from Grand Cayman to Barbados and Trinidad, going via Kingston in Jamaica. Flights wing out of Grand Cayman on Monday, Wednesday, and Friday, linking up in Kingston with continuing flights to Barbados and Port-of-Spain, with return flights scheduled for Thursday, Friday, and Sunday. For reservations and information, call Air Jamaica at © 800/523-5585.

British Airways (© 800/AIRWAYS; www.british-airways.com) flies nonstop service to Barbados from London's Gatwick Airport. Virgin Atlantic (© 800/862-8621 in the U.S., or 1293/747-747 in the U.K.; www.virgin-atlantic.com) also has one daily direct flight from London to Barbados.

GETTING AROUND

BY RENTAL CAR   If you don't mind *driving on the left*, you may find a rental car ideal on Barbados. You'll need a temporary permit if you don't have an

Barbados

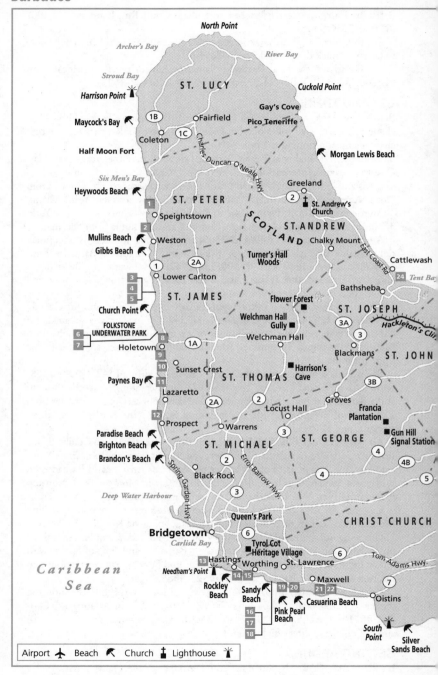

North Point
Archer's Bay
River Bay
Stroud Bay
Harrison Point
ST. LUCY
Cuckold Point
Maycock's Bay
1B
Fairfield
Gay's Cove
Coleton
1C
Pico Teneriffe
Half Moon Fort
Morgan Lewis Beach
Six Men's Bay
Heywoods Beach
Greeland
2
ST. PETER
St. Andrew's Church
1 Speightstown
SCOTLAND
ST. ANDREW
2 Mullins Beach
Weston
Chalky Mount
Gibbs Beach
Cattlewash
1 2A
Turner's Hall Woods
3 Lower Carlton
Bathsheba
4 ST. JAMES
Flower Forest
ST. JOSEPH
5
24 Tent Bay
Church Point
Welchman Hall Gully
3A
FOLKSTONE UNDERWATER PARK
3
6 8
Welchman Hall
7 Holetown 1A
Blackmans
ST. JOHN
9
10 Sunset Crest
Harrison's Cave
11 Paynes Bay
ST. THOMAS
3B
Lazaretto
Groves
2A 2
Locust Hall
Francia Plantation
12 Prospect
Warrens
Gun Hill Signal Station
Paradise Beach
3
ST. GEORGE
Brighton Beach
ST. MICHAEL
4
Brandon's Beach
2
4B
Black Rock
Errol Barrow Hwy
4
5
3
Deep Water Harbour
Queen's Park
CHRIST CHURCH
Bridgetown
6
Carlisle Bay
Tyrol Cot Heritage Village
6
Caribbean Sea
Tom Adams Hwy.
St. Lawrence
13 Hastings
Worthing
Needham's Point
14 15
Maxwell
7
Rockley Beach
19 20
Sandy Beach
21 22
Casuarina Beach
Oistins
16
Pink Pearl Beach
17
South Point
18
Silver Sands Beach

Airport ✈ Beach 🏖 Church ✝ Lighthouse 🗼

134

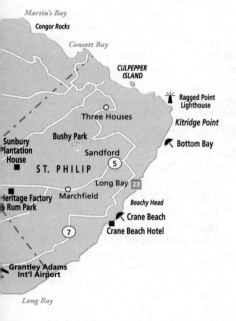

Atlantic Ocean

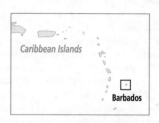

Caribbean Islands

Barbados

Accra Beach Hotel & Resort **14**
Almond Beach Village **1**
Bagshot House Hotel **15**
Bougainvillea Beach Resort **21**
Cobblers Cove Hotel **2**
Coconut Creek Hotel **3**
Coral Reef Club **5**
Divi Southwinds Beach Resort **19**
The Edgewater Inn **23**
Fairholme **20**
Glitter Bay **3**
Grand Barbados Beach Resort **12**
Mango Bay Hotel & Beach Club **7**
Royal Pavillion **4**
Sam Lord's Castle Resort **22**
Sandpiper **6**
Sandy Beach Hotel **16**
Sandy Lane Hotel & Golf Club **9**
Southern Palms **17**
Tamarind Cove **10**
Traveller's Palm **8**
Treasure Beach **11**
Turtle Beach Resort **18**
Woodville Beach Hotel **13**

Martin's Bay
Congor Rocks
Consett Bay
CULPEPPER ISLAND

Ragged Point Lighthouse

Three Houses

Kitridge Point

Bushy Park

Bottom Bay

Sunbury Plantation House

Sandford

ST. PHILIP

5

Long Bay 23

Heritage Factory & Rum Park

Marchfield

Beachy Head

Crane Beach
Crane Beach Hotel

7

Grantley Adams Int'l Airport

Long Bay

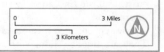

0   3 Miles
0   3 Kilometers

international driver's license. The rental agencies listed below can all issue this visitor's permit, or you can go to the police desk upon your arrival at the airport. You must have a license from home and pay a registration fee of BD$10 (US$5). The speed limit is 20 miles per hour (.02kmph) inside city limits, 45 miles per hour (.05kmph) elsewhere on the island. Due to frequent delays at airport counters, we suggest taking a taxi from the airport to your hotel, and then calling to have your rental car delivered. No taxes apply to car rentals on Barbados.

None of the major U.S.-based car-rental agencies operate on Barbados, but a host of local companies rent vehicles. Except in the peak midwinter season, cars are usually readily available without prior reservations. Be forewarned that many local companies continue to draw serious complaints from readers, both for overcharging and for the poor conditions of their vehicles. Proceed very carefully with rentals on this island. Check the insurance and liability issues carefully when you rent.

The island's most frequently recommended agency is **National Car Rentals,** Lower Carlton, St. James (© **246/426-0603**), which offers a wide selection of Japanese cars (note that it's *not* affiliated with the U.S. chain of the same name). National is 10 miles (16km) north of Bridgetown, near the main highway (Highway 1); it delivers cars to almost any location on the island upon request, and the driver who delivers it will carry the necessary forms for the Bajan driver's license, which may be purchased for $5.

Other comparable companies include **Sunny Isle Motors,** Dayton, Worthing Main Road, Christ Church (© **246/435-7979**), and **P&S Car Rentals,** Pleasant View, Cave Hill, St. Michael (© **246/424-2052**). One company conveniently close to hotels on the remote southeastern end of Barbados is **Stoutes Car Rentals,** Kirtons, St. Philip (© **246/435-4456**). Because it's closer to the airport than its competitors, it can theoretically deliver a car there within 10 minutes of a call placed when you arrive.

BY TAXI   Taxis aren't metered, but rates are fixed by the government; one cab can carry up to five passengers for the same fare. Taxis are plentiful and easily identifiable by the letter Z on their license plates. Drivers will produce a list of standard rates ($20 per hour, subject to change). To call a taxi, contact one of the following services: **Paramount Taxi Service** (© **246/429-3718**), **Royal Pavilion Taxi Service** (© **246/422-5555**), or **Lyndhurst Taxi Service** (© **246/ 436-2639**). A typical taxi ride from the airport to Bridgetown costs $30; to Holetown along the western Gold Coast, $35 to $40; and to St. Lawrence Gap, site of many of the less expensive hotels, $15 to $20.

BY BUS   Barbados has a reliable bus system fanning out from Bridgetown to almost every part of the island. The nationally owned **buses** of Barbados are blue with yellow stripes. They're not numbered, but their destinations are marked on the front. On most major routes, buses run every 20 minutes or so. Wherever you go, the fare is BD$1.50 (75¢), exact Bajan change required. Departures are from Bridgetown, leaving from Fairchild Street for the south and east; from Lower Green and the Princess Alice Highway for the north going along the west coast. Call the **Barbados Tourist Board** (© **246/427-2623**) for schedules and information.

Privately operated **minibuses** run shorter distances and travel more frequently. They are bright yellow, with their destinations displayed on the bottom-left corner of the windshield. Minibuses in Bridgetown are boarded at River Road, Temple Yard, and Probyn Street. The fare is BD$1.50 (75¢).

Finds **Special Events**

One of the hottest "cool" jazz festivals in the Caribbean takes place at the **Barbados Jazz Festival.** The festival is called "Paint It Jazz" and is scheduled for mid-January in 2003. International artists appear, along with the best in local jazz talent. For tickets and further details, contact festival organizers at **bdosjazz@caribsurf.com**.

In mid-February, the **Holetown Festival** at St. James is a week-long event commemorating the landing of the first European settlers at Holetown in 1627. Highlights include street fairs, police band concerts, a music festival in the parish church, and a road race.

In the last week of March, the **Oistins Fish Festival** commemorates the signing of the charter of Barbados with fishing, boat racing, fish-boning competitions, a Coast Guard exhibition, food stalls, arts and crafts, dancing, singing, and road races.

Beginning in mid-July and lasting until the first week of August, the **Crop Over Festival** is the island's major national festival, celebrating the completion of the sugarcane harvest and recognizing the hardworking men and women in the sugar industry. Communities all over the island participate in fairs, concerts, calypso competitions, car parades, and other cultural events. The climax of the festival occurs at Kadooment Day, a national holiday on the first Monday in August which becomes the biggest party of the year in Barbados.

 FAST FACTS: **Barbados**

American Express The island's affiliate is **Barbados International Travel Services,** Horizon House, McGregor Street (© **246/431-2423**), in the heart of Bridgetown.

Banks Most banks are open Monday through Thursday from 9am to 3pm, Friday from 9am to 1pm and 3 to 5pm. The major banks of Barbados, all with ATMs, are found along Broad Street in Bridgetown, including branches of Barclays, the Barbados National Bank, and the Bank of Nova Scotia. These banks also have branch offices in Holetown, Speightstown, and along the St. Lawrence Gap south of Bridgetown. There are ATMs at the airport as well, plus at bank branches throughout the island.

Consulates & High Commissions The **U.S. Consulate** is found in the ALICO Building, Cheapside, Bridgetown (© **246/436-4950**); the **Canadian High Commission** is located at Bishop Court Hill, Pine Road (© **246/429-3550**); and the **British High Commission** is found at Lower Collymore Rock, St. Michael (© **246/436-6694**).

Currency The Barbados dollar **(BD$)** is the official currency, available in $5, $10, $20, and $100 notes, as well as 10¢, 25¢, and $1 silver coins, plus 1¢ and 5¢ copper coins. The Bajan dollar is worth 50¢ in U.S. currency. *Currency quotations in this chapter are in U.S. dollars unless otherwise specified.* Most stores take traveler's checks or U.S. dollars. However, it's best to convert your money at banks and pay in Bajan dollars. (Just before you leave home, you can check the current exchange rates on the Web at **www.x-rates.com.**)

Customs Most items for personal use (within reason, of course) are allowed into Barbados, except agricultural products and firearms. You can bring in perfume for your use if it's not for sale. You're also allowed a carton of cigarettes and a liter of liquor.

Dentists **Dr. Derek Golding,** with two other colleagues, maintains one of the busiest practices on Barbados, at 5 Stafford House, The Garrison, St. Michael (© **246/228-2201**). They will accept any emergency (they treat most of the cruise-ship passengers' emergencies) and often stay open late. Otherwise, hours are Monday through Friday from 8:30am to 3:30pm.

Doctors Your hotel may have a list of doctors on call; some of the best recommended are **Dr. J. D. Gibling** (© **246/432-1772**), and **Dr. Adrian Lorde** or his colleague **Dr. Ahmed Mohamad** (© **246/424-8236**). All will pay house calls to patients who are unable or unwilling to leave their hotel rooms.

Documents U.S. or Canadian citizens coming directly from North America to Barbados for a period not exceeding 3 months must have proof of identity and national status, such as a passport, which we always recommend carrying. However, a birth certificate (either an original or a certified copy) is also acceptable, provided it's backed up with photo ID. For stays longer than 3 months, a passport is required. An ongoing or return ticket is also necessary. British subjects need a valid passport.

Electricity The electricity is 110-volt AC (50 cycles), so at most places you can use your U.S.-made appliances.

Emergencies In an emergency, dial the **police** at © **211,** the **fire department** at © **311,** and an **ambulance** at © **511.**

Hospitals The **Queen Elizabeth Hospital** is located on Martinsdale Road in St. Michael (© **246/436-6450**). Of the several private clinics, one of the most expensive and best recommended is the **Bayview Hospital,** St. Paul's Avenue, Bayville, St. Michael (© **246/436-5446**).

Language The Bajans speak English, but with their own island lilt.

Liquor Laws Liquor, beer, and wine are sold throughout the island at every outlet from grocery stores to convenience stores on any day the stores are open. Be discreet with open containers on the beach, as legally they are not allowed.

Safety Crimes against tourists used to be rare, but the U.S. State Department reports rising crime, such as purse snatching, pick-pocketing, armed robbery, and even sexual assault. Avoid leaving cash or valuables in your hotel room, beware of purse-snatchers when walking, exercise caution on the beach or at tourist attractions, and be wary of driving in isolated areas.

Taxes A 7½% government sales tax is tacked on to hotel bills. A 15% VAT (value-added tax) is levied on all meals. (For example, if your hotel costs $200 per night, and you are charged $50 per person for a MAP, you'll have to pay a 7½% government tax plus the 10% additional service charge for the $200 room rate, then an additional 15% VAT on the MAP rate.) Some visitors view these additional charges as "larcenous." They certainly won't make you happy when you go to pay your final bill. There's also a BD$25 (US$12.50) departure tax.

Telephone   To call Barbados from the United States, dial **1**, then **246** (the area code for Barbados) and the local number. Once on Barbados, to call another number on the island, only the local number is necessary. You can reach **AT&T Direct** by dialing © **800/872-2881** or **MCI** at © **800/888-8000.**

Time   Barbados is on Atlantic standard time year-round, placing it 1 hour ahead of New York. However, when the United States is on daylight saving time, Barbados matches the clocks of the U.S. east coast.

Tipping   Most hotels and restaurants add at least a 10% service charge to your bill. If service is extremely good, you may want to supplement that. If it has not been included, you may want to tip your waiter 10% to 15%. Taxi drivers expect a 10% tip.

Water   Barbados has a pure water supply. It's pumped from underground sources in the coral rock that covers most of the island, and it's safe to drink.

Weather   Daytime temperatures are in the 75° to 85°F range throughout the year.

2 Accommodations

Barbados has some of the best hotels in the Caribbean, many of which are small and personally run.

Most of our recommendations are on fashionable St. James Beach, which is the entire strip of beachfront bordering the parish of St. James. Although hotels are scattered around Barbados, most of them lie on the tranquil west coast as opposed to opening onto the turbulent Atlantic in the east. If you're into the grand life, head for one of the fashionable resorts north of Bridgetown, all opening onto sandy beaches. If you're in Barbados on business, you may want a hotel in Bridgetown, the capital. Otherwise, if you like more informality and cheaper prices, go to the lower south coast, especially around the busy strip of St. Lawrence Gap, where you'll find the most reasonably priced nightlife, restaurants, and local bars. This area also has beaches, although they're not as fabulous as those claimed by the pricey resorts north of Bridgetown.

Because Barbados is so popular with charter groups, hotels are often extremely expensive in high season. Many also insist that you take their meal plans if you're there in the winter.

But Barbados does have some bargains, and we've surveyed the best of these as well. You'll have to head south from Bridgetown to such places as Hastings and Worthing for the best buys, which are often self-contained efficiencies or studio apartments where you can do your own cooking. See also the section "Package Deals," in chapter 2. You can often get a steal in the off-season, which lasts from April until mid-December.

Prices cited in this section, unless otherwise indicated, are in U.S. dollars. See "Taxes" in "Fast Facts: Barbados" above, for additional information.

To rent your own villa, cottage, or house on Barbados, contact **Property Management Services Ltd.,** The Cays, Greenridge Dr., Paynes Bay, St. James (© **246/432-6562;** fax 246/432-5616; property@sunbeach.net), which has properties in a wide range of prices.

ON THE WEST COAST
VERY EXPENSIVE

Almond Beach Village ⭐⭐ *Kids* This is our favorite of the island's all-inclusive resorts, and it's a good choice for (wealthy) families. Set near a string of even more expensive hotels (referred to as the island's Gold Coast), the Almond Beach Village occupies the site of a 19th-century sugarcane plantation. In 1994, it was acquired by Barbados Shipping and Trading and underwent a $13 million renovation. All meals, drinks, and most sports are included in one net price.

One section of the hotel is specifically set aside for families with kids (separate from all the honeymooning couples); it comes complete with a Kids' Club and lots of family suites.

The resort stands on 30 acres (12 hectares) of tropically landscaped gardens and a mile (2km) of prime beachfront. Accommodations are clustered into seven different compounds to create something akin to a miniature, self-contained village. Rooms, though not large, are well appointed, with ceiling fans, well-upholstered chairs, and small bathrooms with combination tub/showers. Exchange privileges are available with the hotel's all-inclusive twin, the Almond Beach Club.

La Smaritta, the most formal of the restaurants, serves excellent seafood pastas. Horizons, the main dining room, offers standard fare. The Reef focuses on fresh seafood. Least formal is Enid's, for spicy Bajan food.

Speightstown (15 miles/24km north of Bridgetown along Hwy. 2A), St. Peter, Barbados, W.I. © **800/4-ALMOND** in the U.S., or 246/422-4900. Fax 246/422-1581. www.almondresorts.com. 330 units. Winter $600–$820 double. Off-season $500–$710 double. Rates are all-inclusive. AE, MC, V. **Amenities:** 4 restaurants, 5 bars; dance club; 10 pools; 9-hole golf course; 4 tennis courts; 2 squash courts; fitness center; windsurfing, boating, water-skiing; children's program; room service; babysitting; laundry. *In room:* A/C, TV, hair dryer, safe.

Cobblers Cove Hotel ⭐⭐⭐ This former mansion on a white-sand beach is built in a mock-medieval style over the site of a former British fort. Now a member of Relais & Châteaux, the hotel is a favorite honeymoon retreat. Elegant suites are housed in 10 Iberian-style villas, situated throughout lush gardens. Each unit has a spacious living room, a private balcony or patio, and a kitchenette. Each year nine bedrooms are completely redecorated, so the property is always in top-notch condition. The spacious bathrooms come with combination shower/tubs. Two of the most exclusive accommodations on the entire island are the Camelot and Colleton suites, on the rooftop of the original mansion; they're beautifully decorated and offer panoramic views of both the beach and the garden. The Colleton suite even has its own pool.

The award-winning cuisine served at Genners is generally lighter and more refined than the heavier French food offered at some of its competitors along the Gold Coast. The open-air dining room overlooks the sea.

Road View, St. Peter, Barbados, W.I. © **800/890-6060** in the U.S., 020/8350-1000 in London, or 246/422-2291. Fax 246/422-1460. www.cobblerscove.com. 40 units. Winter $776–$1,090 double; from $1,925 suite. Off-season $306–$459 double; from $893 suite. Rates include breakfast. AE, MC, V. Closed late Sept–mid-Oct. **Amenities:** Restaurant, bar; pool; tennis courts; watersports; tour desk; car rental; babysitting; laundry. *In room:* A/C, minibar, safe.

Coconut Creek Hotel ⭐ Small, intimate, and known as an escape for publicity-shy European celebrities, this is an elegantly informal and beautifully landscaped retreat, about a mile (2km) south of Holetown. Completely renovated in 1995, it resembles a country house hotel you might find in Devonshire,

England. About half of the accommodations lie atop a low bluff overlooking the two most secluded beaches on the island's west coast. Many of the rooms are built on the low cliff edge overlooking the ocean, whereas others open onto the pool or the garden. Each tropically decorated room has whitewashed wooden ceilings, a veranda or balcony (where breakfast can be served), a small fridge, and rattan furnishings, including a king-size bed or twins. Bathrooms, though small, are well equipped and have shower/tub combinations.

The restaurant, Cricketers, is modeled after an upscale English pub. Bajan buffets and barbecues are served on the vine-covered open pergola, overlooking the gardens and the sea. The inn's food has been praised by *Gourmet* magazine, and we agree. There's dancing to the music of West Indian calypso and steel bands almost every night. Clients on the MAP are encouraged to dine at the restaurants connected to this chain's three other properties (the Crystal Cove Hotel, the Tamarind Cove Hotel, and the Colony Club) for no additional charge.

Derricks, St. James, Barbados, W.I. © 800/326-6898 in the U.S., or 246/432-0803. Fax 246/432-0272. www. eleganthotels.com 53 units. Winter $418–$496 double; from $576 suite. Off-season $312–$376 double; $418 suite. Rates are all-inclusive. AE, MC, V. **Amenities:** Dining room, bar; pool; golf privileges; watersports; car rentals; babysitting; laundry; public TV in lounge. *In room:* A/C, hair dryer, safe.

Coral Reef Club ★★ This family-owned and -managed luxury hotel is one of the best and most respected establishments on the island, set on elegantly landscaped grounds beside a white-sand beach that's ideal for swimming. A collection of veranda-fronted private units is scattered about the main building and clubhouse on a dozen landscaped acres (5 hectares), fronting the ocean. Rental units, housed in cottages, the main building, or in small, coral-stone wings in the gardens, can vary greatly, but each has a luxurious bed (a king, twins, or a four-poster) and a tiled bathroom, with a combination shower/tub. All units have private patios, and some have separate dressing rooms.

You can lunch in an open-air area, take afternoon tea, and then enjoy a first-rate dinner in a room with three sides open to ocean views. There's a folklore show and barbecue every Thursday, plus a Monday Bajan buffet featuring an array of food (including whole baked fish) and local entertainment.

St. James Beach (a 5-min. drive north of Holetown), Barbados, W.I. © 800/223-1108 or 246/422-2372. Fax 246/422-1776. www.coralreefbarbados.com. 88 units. Winter $600 double; from $740 suite. Off-season $290 double; from $320 suite. AE, MC, V. No children under age 12 in Feb. **Amenities:** Restaurant, bar; 2 pools; tennis court; dive shop; watersports; salon; room service; massage; laundry. *In room:* A/C, hair dryer, safe.

Glitter Bay ★★★ This carefully maintained resort near a sandy beachfront offers low-key charm and Mediterranean style. It isn't as formal or as elegant as its next-door sibling, the Royal Pavilion (see below). With its cottagelike suites with kitchenettes, plus a wide array of sports facilities, it's a favored choice for families (well-to-do families, that is). The resort was created in 1981 from the estate of shipping mogul Sir Edward Cunard, who'd constructed it in the 1930s to resemble his palazzo in Venice. The accommodations, in an Iberian-style mini-village with thick beams and terra-cotta tiles, surround a garden with a pool, an artificial waterfall, and a simulated lagoon. Most units contain art, built-in furniture, louvered doors, and spacious outdoor patios or balconies ringed with shrubbery. The larger units have small kitchenettes, and some of the most spacious suites can accommodate four to six people. Each bedroom has a small, well-appointed bathroom with a shower/tub combination and bidet.

The Piperade Restaurant serves excellent American and international cuisine and has its own bar. The food here is first rate and prepared with a fine technique. The Sunset Beach Bar is a popular rendezvous spot. Guests can dance on an outdoor patio and enjoy local entertainment, such as a steel-drum band or calypso.

Porters (a mile/2km north of Holetown), St. James, Barbados, W.I. ℂ **246/422-5555**. Fax 246/422-3940. www.fairmont.com. 83 units. Winter $529 double; $679 1-bedroom suite; from $1,199 2-bedroom suite. Off-season $259 double; $279 1-bedroom suite; from $539 2-bedroom suite. MAP (breakfast and dinner) $79 per person extra. AE, DC, DISC, MC, V. **Amenities:** Restaurant, bar; 2 pools; golf privileges; 2 tennis courts; health club, aerobics; horseback riding; watersports; bike rental; car rental; business services; 24-hr. room service; babysitting; laundry/dry cleaning. In room: A/C, TV, kitchenette, minibar, coffeemaker, hair dryer, safe.

Mango Bay Hotel & Beach Club ✿   This all-inclusive resort offers barefoot elegance on a white-sand beach. The complex's several whitewashed buildings are set in tropical gardens. You get a lot for your money here: accommodations; three meals a day; afternoon tea; all drinks, including house wine with meals; watersports such as Sunfish sailing, kayaking, snorkeling, and windsurfing; tennis; one catamaran cruise; one in-pool scuba lesson; glass-bottom boat rides; nightly entertainment; and walking tours.

Guest rooms range from standard to pool view to beachfront. Most units don't face the beach but open onto the gardens instead. Rooms are sold as standard, pool view, and beachfront. Decorated in tropical pastels, each accommodation has one king or two double beds, wicker furnishings, and a private terrace or balcony. Bathrooms are a bit small, and they contain shower/tub combinations.

Tasty grilled steaks, fresh seafood (including flying fish), and island fruits are just some of the delightful offerings in the resort's beachside restaurant. Nightly entertainment is presented in the piano lounge.

Holetown, Barbados, W.I. ℂ **877/MANGO-4-U** or 246/432-1384. www.mangobaybarbados.com. 64 units. Winter $381–$488 double. Off-season $310–$405 double. Extra person $110. Children age 3 and under stay free in parents' room. Rates are all-inclusive. AE, MC, V. **Amenities:** Restaurant, bar; 2 pools; 2 tennis courts; watersports. In room: A/C, TV, hair dryer, safe.

Royal Pavilion ✿✿✿   British grace and Bajan hospitality meet at the Royal Pavilion. It sits on the white-sand beach, next door to Glitter Bay (part of the same chain, whose gardens it shares) and was built in a lush setting of lily ponds and splashing fountains. A celebrity and CEO crowd checks in. You'll be coddled in comfort in grand surroundings, with grand service, enjoying the tranquility of a romantic oasis (no kids yelling on the beach). In spite of its grandeur, the place is not at all stuffy.

The architects applied a California-hacienda style to the waterfront deluxe rooms and the villa, which houses three suites. Guest rooms are spacious and airy, with marble floors and beautiful rattan furnishings, including comfortable beds. The full-size bathrooms have marble vanities and shower/tub combinations.

Both the oceanfront Café Taboras and the more formal Palm Terrace, set below the seaside columns of an open-air *loggia* on the water, serve Caribbean and international fare, and they do so with exceptional flair.

Porters (a mile/2km north of Holetown), St. James, Barbados, W.I. ℂ **800/441-1414** in the U.S., 246/422-5555. Fax 246/422-3940. www.fairmont.com. 75 units. Winter $789 suite for 2; $1,419 villa for 4; $2,009 villa for 6. Off-season $289 suite for 2; $479–$750 villa for 4; $699–$1,070 villa for 6. MAP (breakfast and dinner) $79 per person extra. AE, DC, MC, V. Children age 11 and under not accepted in winter. **Amenities:** 2 restaurants, 2 bars; pool; golf privileges; 2 tennis courts; fitness center; watersports; salon; 24-hr. room service; massage; laundry. In room: A/C, TV, minibar, hair dryer, safe.

Sandpiper ✿   The Coral Reef Club (see above) does it better but may be full, so consider this South Seas resort on a white-sand beach instead. It's a self-contained, intimate resort, set in a small grove of coconut palms and flowering trees. A cluster of rustic-chic units surrounds the pool; some have fine sea views. The rooms, some of which show wear and tear, open onto little terraces that stretch along the second story, where you can order drinks or have breakfast. Accommodations are generous in size, consisting of superior rooms and one- or two-bedroom suites that are beautifully furnished with tropical pieces. Each has a private terrace, luxurious bed, and small fridge. The medium-size bathrooms are equipped with combination tub/showers.

The refined cuisine is both continental and West Indian; weekly buffets are offered in winter. The menu is varied and based on the best of seasonal products, so you can dine here every night without boring your palate.

Holetown (a 3-min. walk north of town), St. James, Barbados, W.I. © 800/223-1108 in the U.S., 800/567-5327 in Canada, or 246/422-2251. Fax 246/422-1776. www.sandpiperbarbados.com. 45 units. Winter $585–$660 double; $760–$865 suite. Off-season $240–$325 double; $430 suite. Rates include breakfast and dinner. AE, MC, V. Children not accepted in Feb. **Amenities:** Restaurant, 2 bars; pool; 2 tennis courts; fitness center; room service (7am–10:30pm); babysitting; laundry. *In room:* A/C, fridge, coffeemaker, hair dryer.

Sandy Lane Hotel & Golf Club ★★★ Long closed for a total demolition and rebuilding, the island's most famous hotel—set on 380 acres (152 hectares) of prime beachfront—has bounced back better than ever. Its prices are as horrifying as ever, but you get the ultimate in luxury in all of the southern Caribbean. Sandy Lane enjoyed a celebrity-haunted heyday in the 1960s when it was constructed by Ronald Tree, an heir to the Marshall Field's department store fortune. After falling into neglect, it was rescued by Irish investors in 1997 who poured $350 million into its reconstruction.

The new Sandy Lane is practically identical to its first version, with the addition of a mammoth spa, better restaurants, and a trio of golf courses. You'll feel like royalty when checking in—especially when your butler unpacks your suitcase. All guests arrive in style—you'll be picked up at the airport in the hotel's Rolls-Royce. Fortunately, its pristine beach set against a backdrop of swaying palms is still there and still in great shape.

The rooms are furnished with grand comfort, with lots of extras not found at any of its competitors—such as a motion-sensor alarm to alert maids you're in the room, and a marble shower with seven adjustable nozzles. Accommodations are decorated mostly with redwood furnishings, each with a king-sized bed for lovers or else two twins for others. The bathrooms are the most luxurious on the island, and in addition to the shower, also contain the most oversized tubs and a bidet.

A trio of on-site restaurants offer the finest hotel dining on Barbados and serve mostly a French or Mediterranean cuisine. There's also a new Spa Café for figure-watchers (or those who'd like their figures watched).

Highway 1, Paynes Bay, St. James. © 246/444-2000. Fax 246/444-2222. www.sandylane.com. Winter $800–$1,400 double, $1,200–$3,700 suite. Off-season $600–$900 double, $800–$3,000 suite. AE, DC, MC, V. **Amenities:** 3 restaurants; 4 bars; 24-hr. room service; pool; 3 golf courses; health spa; fitness center; massages; beauty salon; 9 tennis courts; children's center; watersports center. *In room:* A/C, TV, minibar, hair dryer, safe.

Tamarind Cove ★ On 800 feet (240m) of prime beachfront, this flagship of a British-based hotel chain (St. James Properties) is a major challenger to the Coral Reef Club/Sandpiper properties, attracting the same upscale clientele. An $8 million restoration in the 1990s made this one of the most noteworthy hotels on Barbados. In 1995 a freshwater swimming pool with a beachfront terrace was added, as well as a new south wing with more than 40 luxurious rooms and suites, some with private plunge pools.

Designed in an Iberian style, with pale-pink walls and red terra-cotta roofs, the hotel occupies a desirable location on St. James Beach, 1½ miles (2km) south of Holetown. The chic and comfortable rooms are in a series of hacienda-style buildings interspersed with vegetation. Each unit has a patio or balcony over-looking the gardens or ocean. The well-appointed bathrooms boast dual basins, spacious Roman tubs, stall showers, and long marble counters.

The cuisine here is among the finest of the glittering resorts along the Gold Coast. There's some kind of musical entertainment every night.

Paynes Bay, St. James Beach (P.O. Box 429), Bridgetown, Barbados, W.I. ℂ 800/326-6898 in the U.S., 800/561-1366 in Canada, or 246/432-1332. Fax 246/432-6317. www.eleganthotels.com. 152 units. Winter $454–$600 double; $486–$786 suite. Off-season $238–$266 double; $299–$384 suite. Half-board $75 per person extra. AE, DC, MC, V. **Amenities:** 3 restaurants, 3 bars; pool; golf privileges; 2 tennis courts; fitness center; watersports; children's programs; horseback riding; massage; laundry. *In room:* A/C, TV, minibar, hair dryer, safe.

Treasure Beach ⭐   This small but choice property with a loyal following is set on an acre (.4 hectares) of white sandy beachfront. It's known for its well-prepared food and the comfort and style of its amenities. The atmosphere is intimate, quiet, and relaxed, with personalized service a mark of the well-trained staff. This mini-village of two-story buildings is arranged in a horseshoe pattern around a pool and garden. The accommodations, furnished in a tropical motif, open onto private balconies or patios. Bedrooms have king-size beds or twins, and a small, well-maintained bathroom with combination tub/showers. The clientele is about evenly divided between North Americans and Brits.

Even if you aren't staying here, try to sample some of the excellent culinary specialties at the Treasure Beach Restaurant, including freshly caught seafood and favorites of Bajan cuisine.

Paynes Bay (about a ½ mile/.8km south of Holetown), St. James, Barbados, W.I. (ℂ 800/223-6510 in the U.S. and Canada, or 246/432-1346. Fax 246/432-1094. www.barbados.org/hotels/h64.htm. 29 units. Winter $495–$905 1-bedroom suite; $1,800 superior luxury suite. Off-season $240–$355 1-bedroom suite; $700 superior luxury suite. MAP (breakfast and dinner) $45 per person extra. AE, DC, DISC, MC, V. Children age 11 and under accepted only by special request. **Amenities:** Restaurant, bar; snorkeling; sailboat rental; car rental; room service (7:30am–9:30pm); laundry. *In room:* A/C, safe.

INEXPENSIVE

Traveller's Palm   Within a 10-minute walk of a good beach, this is for self-sufficient types who are not too demanding and who like to save money. There's a choice of simply furnished, one-bedroom apartments with fully equipped kitchens and well-maintained bathrooms with shower units. They're simple, slightly worn apartments, with bright but fading colors, but they're quite a deal in this high-rent district. The apartments have living and dining areas, as well as patios where you can have breakfast or a candlelit dinner you've prepared your-self (no meals are served here).

265 Palm Ave., Sunset Crest, St. James, Barbados, W.I. ℂ 246/432-6750. www.barbadostraveler.com. 16 units. Winter $100 apt. for 2. Off-season $75 apt. for 2. MC, V. **Amenities:** Pool. *In room:* A/C.

SOUTH OF BRIDGETOWN/THE SOUTH COAST
VERY EXPENSIVE

Turtle Beach Resort ⭐⭐   Opening onto 1,500 feet (450m) of white-sand beach, this is the only real "pocket of posh" on the south coast. Most deluxe hotels don't lie south of Bridgetown, but this one breaks the rule. A member of the Elegant Hotels Group, a swanky group of Bajan hotels, the resort opened in 1998 and was named after the turtles who sometimes nest on the nearby sands. It's an all-inclusive property, drawing families, couples, and honeymooners. An open-air lobby opens onto the beach. All mid-size rooms have ocean views, wicker furniture, ceiling fans, and voice mail. Beds have fine linens, and each one-bedroom suite offers both a king-size bed and a sofa bed. If needed, free rollaway beds are provided. Bathrooms are luxurious, with tubs and showers.

The open-air restaurant, Chelonia, serves a fine creative cuisine. The casually elegant Waterfront offers informal food such as design-your-own pizzas. The equally casual Asiago offers pleasant Italian fare. For diversity, Turtle Beach offers a dine-around program with its other tony properties, including Crystal Cove and Coconut Creek. There's also nightly entertainment—calypso, jazz, cabaret, and more.

Dover, near St. Lawrence Gap, Barbados, W.I. ℂ 800/326-6898 in the U.S., or 246/438-4680. Fax 246/428-6089. 166 units. Winter $576–$758 suite for 2. Off-season $390–$496 suite for 2. Rates are all-inclusive. AE, DC, MC, V. **Amenities:** 3 restaurants, 3 bars; 3 pools; golf privileges; 2 tennis courts; fitness center; watersports; children's playground; room service; laundry. *In room:* A/C, TV, minibar, hair dryer, safe.

EXPENSIVE

Accra Beach Hotel & Resort ⭐   This hotel, totally rebuilt in 1996, lies on the prettiest beach on the south coast. On manicured grounds, you are in the center of the south strip, only 10 minutes from the airport, with Bridgetown lying about 2 miles (3km) to the west.

In a West Indian "mega style," the 3-story property is tastefully laid out, and it offers spacious rooms opening onto a view of the pool or ocean. The units have large balconies and wooden shutters, plus full-size bathrooms with showers and tubs. The look is a bit sterile, more like a business person's hotel than a resort inn. Steer clear of units marked "island view," as the panorama is of the parking lot. This is one of the best hotels on Barbados for those with disabilities. One drawback: Much of the hotel is open air, and the man- (or woman-) eating mosquitoes appreciate that fact.

Accra Beach, Rockley, Christ Church, Barbados. ℂ 246/435-8920. Fax 246/435-6794. www.accrabeachhotel. com. 128 units. Winter $175–$220 for double, from $230 suite. Off-season $140–$170 double, from $190 suite. AE, MC, V. **Amenities:** 3 restaurants, 2 bars; open-air dance floor; fitness center; business center; room service; babysitting; laundry. *In room:* A/C, TV, hair dryer.

Bougainvillea Beach Resort ⭐ *Kids* *Value*   This resort, which lies on a broad sandy beach, is one of the best south-coast deals. A family favorite, it is a low-rise time-share with an assortment of studios and suites. It features all-suite first-class rooms and studios with one-, two-, or three-bedroom suites, each with a private balcony opening onto a seafront view. Bedrooms are furnished along modern lines, a medley of pastels, comfortable and tasteful without being too exciting. Each unit has a small bathroom containing a shower unit.

Maxwell Coast Rd., Christ Church. ℂ 800/988-6904 in the U.S. and Canada, or 246/418-0990. Fax 246/428-2524. www.bargainvillearesort.com. 100 units. Winter $240–$345 double, from $450 suite. Off-season $138–$250 double, from $280 suite. Extra person $30. AE, MC, V. **Amenities:** 2 restaurants, bar; 2 pools; tennis court; small exercise room; kayaks; sunfish; snorkeling; business services; room service; babysitting; laundry. *In room:* A/C, TV, kitchenette, hair dryer, safe.

Divi Southwinds Beach Resort ⭐ *Kids*   Midway between Bridgetown and the village of Oistins, this resort was created when two distinctly different complexes were combined. The present resort consists of buildings scattered over 20 or so acres (8 hectares) of sandy flatlands. The showpiece is the newer (inland) complex, housing one- and two-bedroom suites with full kitchens—perfect for small families. These units look like a connected series of town houses, with wooden balconies and views of a large L-shaped pool. From here, you need only cross through two groves of palm trees and a narrow lane to reach the beach. The older units, more modestly furnished but fully renovated, lie directly on the beachfront, ringed with palm trees, near an oval pool. Each unit contains a full-size bathroom with tub and shower.

The Aquarius Restaurant serves decent food, and there's another casual spot for drinks and snacks by the beach.

St. Lawrence Gap, Christ Church, Barbados, W.I. © **800/367-3484** or 246/428-7181. Fax 246/428-4674. www.divibarbados.com. 166 units. Winter $240–$255 studio double; $310–$340 suite. Off-season $165–$210 studio double; $210–$230 suite. MAP (breakfast and dinner) $45 per person extra. AE, DC, MC, V. **Amenities:** Restaurant, beach snack bar, 2 bars; 2 pools; 2 tennis courts; sailboat rentals, diving shop, snorkeling; salon. *In room:* A/C, TV, safe.

Grand Barbados Beach Resort ✦ About a mile (2km) south of Bridgetown, this well-designed eight-story resort is on scenic Carlisle Bay. It opens onto a good white-sand beach, although it's close to an oil refinery whose smell sometimes drifts over. Set on 4 acres (2 hectares), the resort offers well-furnished but often small bedrooms with many extras, including eight-channel satellite TV and excellent beds; the storage space for luggage, however, is inadequate. Rooms open onto furnished balconies with views of the water and of Bridgetown. The spacious bathrooms have vanity areas, combination baths, and dual basins. The two top floors are devoted to executive rooms, including a lounge where a complimentary continental breakfast is served.

The Schooner Restaurant, at the end of a 260-foot (78m) historic pier, specializes in seafood and buffet lunches. Pier One is an informal alfresco dining area, and it's also the hotel's entertainment center, where live shows are often presented. In general, the cuisine is well prepared if not that imaginative.

Aquatic Gap, Bay St. (P.O. Box 639), Bridgetown, St. Michael, Barbados, W.I. © **800/814-2235** in the U.S., or 246/426-4000. Fax 246/429-2400. 134 units. Winter $155–$240 double; $375–$475 suite. Off-season $145–$210 double; $350 suite. MAP (breakfast and dinner) $54 per person extra. AE, DISC, MC, V. **Amenities:** 2 restaurants, bar; pool; golf privileges; tennis court; fitness center; Jacuzzi; sauna; watersports including Sunfish sailing, glass-bottom boat rides; room service (7am–11pm); laundry. *In room:* A/C, TV, hair dryer, safe.

MODERATE

Southern Palms A seafront club with a distinct personality, Southern Palms lies on the Pink Pearl Beach of Barbados, midway between the airport and Bridgetown. The core of the resort is a pink-and-white manor house built in the Dutch style, with a garden-level colonnade of arches. Spread along the sands are arched two- and three-story buildings, with Italian fountains and statues adding to the Mediterranean feel. In its more modern block, an eclectic mixture of rooms includes some with kitchenettes, some facing the ocean, others opening onto the garden, and some with penthouse luxury. The suites have small kitchenettes. Each unit has a small bathroom containing a shower stall. A cluster of straw-roofed buildings, housing the drinking and dining facilities, link the accommodations together.

The Khus-Khus Bar and Restaurant serves both West Indian and continental cuisine. In general, the local Bajan dishes are the best. A local band often entertains with merengue and steel-band music.

St. Lawrence, Christ Church, Barbados, W.I. © **800/223-6510** in the U.S., or 246/428-7171. Fax 246/428-7175. www.southernpalms.net. 92 units. Winter $200–$236 double; $287 suite. Off-season $125–$154 double; $182 suite. MAP (breakfast and dinner) $40 per person extra. AE, DC, DISC, MC, V. **Amenities:** Restaurant, bar; 2 pools; 2 tennis courts; scuba lessons, windsurfing; room service; babysitting; laundry/dry cleaning. *In room:* A/C, TV, hair dryer, safe.

INEXPENSIVE

Bagshot House Hotel ✦ Completely renovated in 1996, this small, family-managed hotel sits on a white-sand beach and has been painted pink since the

1940s. The Bagshot has flowering vines tumbling over the railing of the balconies and an old-fashioned, unhurried charm. The hotel was named after the early-19th-century manor house that once stood on this site. Some of the well-kept guest rooms boast views of the water and the beach. Each unit has a small tiled bathroom that contains a shower stall.

A sunbathing deck, which doubles as a kind of living room for the resort, is perched at the edge of a lagoon. Also on site are the Sand Dollar restaurant (see "Dining," below) and a deck-side lounge, decorated with paintings by local artists.

St. Lawrence Coast Rd., St. Lawrence, Christ Church, Barbados, W.I. ⓒ 246/435-6956. Fax 246/435-9000. www.funbarbados.com. 16 units. Winter $120 double; off-season $80 double. Extra person $20. Rates include breakfast. AE, CB, DC, DISC, MC, V. **Amenities:** Restaurant; car rental; room service (7am–10pm); laundry/dry cleaning. *In room:* A/C.

Fairholme   Lying a 5-minute walk from a good beach, this converted plantation house has been enlarged over the past 20 years or so with a handful of connected annexes. The main house and its original gardens are just off a major road, 6 miles (10km) southeast of Bridgetown. The older section has 11 double rooms, each with a living-room area and a patio overlooking an orchard and a pool. The best units are the 20 Spanish-style studio apartments, fairly recently added, which have cathedral ceilings, dark beams, traditional furnishings, and balconies or patios. All units have neatly kept bathrooms with shower units. Air-conditioning is available only in the studios: The reception desk sells $3 brass tokens that you insert into your air-conditioning unit in exchange for around 8 hours of cooling-off time.

The restaurant here has a reputation for home cooking—wholesome and nothing fancy, but the ingredients are fresh. Guests may also use the waterfront cafe and bar at Fairholme's neighbor, the Sea Breeze.

Maxwell, Christ Church, Barbados, W.I. ⓒ **246/428-9425.** Fax 246/420-2389. 31 units. Winter $35 double; $65 studio apt. Off-season $32 double; $45 studio apt. MC, V. **Amenities:** Restaurant; pool. *In room:* Ceiling fan, no phone.

Sandy Beach Hotel ★★ *Kids*   Definitely not to be confused with Sandy Lane, this hotel, originally established in 1980 and renovated in 1994, is a simple but thoroughly reliable choice, resting on 2 acres (.8 hectares) of beach-front land, 4 miles (6km) southeast of Bridgetown. The Bajan-owned property rises around its architectural centerpiece, a soaring, cone-shaped structure known as a *palapa*. Great for families, the resort contains standard motel-like double rooms, 1- and 2-bedroom suites, and 16 honeymoon suites. All the simply decorated and spacious units have fully equipped kitchenettes, private balconies or patios, and locally made furniture, plus small bathrooms containing shower units. Facilities for travelers with disabilities are available in some of the ground-floor suites.

Kolors, specializing in average seafood and steaks, is situated under the *palapa* and opens onto a view of the sea and pool. Every Monday, when nonguests are welcome, the resort sponsors a rum-punch party and a Bajan buffet. Entertainment is offered 3 nights a week.

Worthing, Christ Church, Barbados, W.I. ⓒ **800/448-8355** in the U.S., or 246/435-8000. Fax 246/435-8053. www.sandybeachbarbados.com. 129 units. Winter $130 double; $231 1-bedroom suite; $335 2-bedroom suite. Off-season $91–$96 double; $138–$177 1-bedroom suite; $187–$249 2-bedroom suite. MAP (breakfast and dinner) $45 per adult extra. Extra person $25. Children age 11 and under stay free in parents' room. AE, MC, V. **Amenities:** Restaurant, bar; pool; snorkeling, windsurfing, boating, sailfish, scuba lessons; children's play area. *In room:* A/C, TV, hair dryer, safe.

Woodville Beach Hotel *Value*   These apartments, last renovated in 1995, are one of the best bargains on Barbados and are ideal for families. Directly on a rocky shoreline 2½ miles (4km) southeast of Bridgetown, the hotel is in the heart of the village of Hastings. The U-shaped complex is built around a pool terrace overlooking the sea. Functional and minimalist in decor, the apartments are clean and comfortable, with tiny but fully equipped kitchenettes. All have balconies or decks, and some units have air-conditioning. Each unit has a small bathroom with a shower stall.

Although some athletic guests attempt to swim off the nearby rocks, most walk 5 minutes to the white sands of nearby Rockley (Accra) Beach. A small restaurant on the property serves very average American and Bajan fare.

Hastings, Christ Church, Barbados, W.I. © **246/435-6694.** Fax 246/435-9211. www.allamandabeach.com. 48 units. Winter $125–$130 studio apt.; $165 1-bedroom apt.; $215 2-bedroom apt. Off-season $90–$95 studio apt.; $112 1-bedroom apt.; $135 2-bedroom apt. Extra person $25. AE, MC, V. **Amenities:** Restaurant; pool; bike rentals; babysitting. *In room:* Ceiling fan, kitchen, fridge, hair dryer.

ON THE EAST COAST
VERY EXPENSIVE

Sam Lord's Castle Resort ★ *Overrated*   A bit overhyped and overpriced, this is the second most famous hotel in Barbados (Sandy Lane is the best known), opening onto an Atlantic coast beach. The resort is far removed from the west coast scene, a drawback to many. In spite of its name, this is a collection of motel units that happens to have a great house as its reception area. It was built in 1820 by one of Barbados's most notorious scoundrels. According to legend, Samuel Hall Lord (the "Regency Rascal") constructed the estate with money acquired by luring ships to wreck on the jagged but hard-to-detect rocks of Cobbler's Reef. The house, near the easternmost end of the island, was built in the pirate's more mellow "golden years." Craftspeople were brought from England to reproduce sections of the queen's castle at Windsor. The decor includes the dubiously acquired but nonetheless beautiful art of Reynolds, Raeburn, and Chippendale.

Set on 72 landscaped acres (29 hectares), the estate has a wide, lengthy private beach edged by tall coconut trees. Guest rooms have private balconies or patios, well-kept bathrooms with shower/tub combinations, and most have king-size beds. The main house contains only seven rooms, stylishly decorated with antique furnishings; three have canopied beds. The rest of the accommodations are in cottages and wings, either two or four floors high; there are some rather tacky motel rooms with a faux-castle theme. (Some of these units evoke southwest Miami in the 1950s—no great compliment.) For privacy's sake and to get more light, try to avoid the ground-floor units. The best (and most expensive) accommodations are in structures 7, 8, and 9.

The Wanderer Restaurant serves all three meals; you can order a hamburger at the Oceanus Café, right on the beach. The cuisine is pretty standard, yet satisfying to many palates. For a more formal atmosphere (and much better food) head to the Sea Grill for fresh seafood. The hotel also has an Italian restaurant, Emma's.

Long Bay, St. Philip, Barbados, W.I. © **246/423-7350.** Fax 246/423-6361. www.samlordscastle.com. 248 units. Winter $350–$395 double; $455–$500 triple. Off-season $275–$330 double; $350–$430 triple. Rates include all meals and afternoon tea. AE, DC, DISC, MC, V. The hotel is a 15-min. drive northeast of the airport. **Amenities:** 3 restaurants, 3 bars, beach cafe; 3 pools; fitness center; horseback riding; sailing, snorkeling, fishing; room service; laundry. *In room:* A/C, TV, safe.

MODERATE

The Edgewater Inn   Built as a dramatically isolated private home and converted into a hotel in 1947, this inn is set directly on the Atlantic coast, a short drive southeast of the island's Scotland district. The beach closest to the hotel can be treacherous, but the staff will direct you to a 9-mile (14km) coral sand beach to the north. You will also be directed to Joe's River, the only free-flowing river in Barbados. Located in an 85-acre (34-hectare) tropical rain forest atop a low cliff, the property opens onto ocean views, and a nearby wildlife sanctuary invites exploration. Cozy and intimate, the small inn is decorated with beveled leaded-glass windows from Asia; furnishings reflect an island motif, with mahogany pieces handcrafted by local artisans. If they're available, request rooms 215 or 216 for their upgraded furnishings and panoramic views. Bathrooms are small, and each has a shower/tub combination.

The freshwater pool, shaped like the island of Barbados, is the focal point of the resort. Surfers and nonguests often drop by, either for a drink or a meal. The restaurant serves excellent West Indian and continental cuisine.

Bathsheba (13 miles/21km northeast of Bridgetown on Hwy. 3), St. Joseph, Barbados, W.I. © **246/433-9900.** Fax 246/433-9902. www.edgewaterinn.com. 20 units. Winter $105–$199 double; off-season $85–$145 double. Breakfast and dinner $35 per person. AE, MC, V. **Amenities:** Restaurant, bar; pool; room service; laundry. *In room:* A/C in some units; no phone.

3 Dining

ON THE WEST COAST
EXPENSIVE

Bagatelle Restaurant ★★ FRENCH/CARIBBEAN   Built in 1645, Bagatelle is located in what was originally the residence of the island's first governor (Lord Willoughby). This sylvan retreat, one of the island's finest and most elegant choices for French cuisine with Caribbean flair, is in the cool uplands, just south of the island's center and a 15-minute drive north of Bridgetown. Only The Cliff equals it. Candles and lanterns illuminate the old archways and the ancient trees. The service is the best we've found on Barbados. Try the homemade duck-liver pâté, succulent deviled Caribbean crab backs, or a wake-up-the-tastebuds smoked flying-fish mousse with horseradish mayonnaise. The beef Wellington Bagatelle-style with a chasseur sauce is a favorite, as is the crisp roast duckling with orange-and-brandy sauce. The local catch of the day can be prepared grilled, barbecued, or in the style of Baxters Road (spicily seasoned and sautéed in deep oil). Cruise-ship passengers can take advantage of Bagatelle's light lunches before their ships sail at sunset.

Hwy. 2A, St. Thomas. © **246/421-6767.** Reservations recommended. Lunch main courses $14–$21; dinner main courses $18–$35. MC, V. Daily 11am–2:30pm and 7–10pm. Cut inland near Paynes Bay north of Bridgetown, 3 miles (5km) from both Sunset Crest and the Sandy Lane Hotel.

Carambola ★★ FRENCH/CARIBBEAN/ASIAN   Built beside the road that runs along the island's western coastline, this restaurant sits atop a 20-foot (6m) seaside cliff and offers one of the most panoramic dining terraces in the Caribbean. But you'll have to go early for dinner to see the view because lunch isn't served. This is the only restaurant in Barbados in the same league as The Cliff and Bagatelle, but what makes Carambola different is its Asian offerings. For sheer romance in dining, however, Carambola has all competitors beat. The prize-winning cuisine is creative, with modern, French-nouvelle touches. The dishes may sound continental, but they definitely have Caribbean flair and flavor, as exemplified by the filet of swordfish or dolphin (mahi-mahi). Try the chef's rich, frothy lobster cappuccino, or his stir fry of shrimp and scallops in roasted peanut sauce. Another spectacular dish is rack of lamb cooked under a honey-mustard crust. Save room for one of the luscious desserts, such as lime mousse. The impressive wine list features mostly French vintages.

Derricks (1½ miles/2km south of Holetown), St. James. ℂ **246/432-0832.** Reservations recommended. Main courses $24–$55. AE, MC, V. Mon–Sat 6:30–9pm. Closed Aug.

The Cliff ★★ INTERNATIONAL/CARIBBEAN   Built atop a 10-foot (3m) coral cliff adjacent to the Coconut Creek Hotel, this open-air restaurant features a four-level dining room crafted with terra-cotta tiles and coral stone. Though it's not exclusive or even particularly formal, it has attracted Prince Andrew and other titled and bejeweled guests of the nearby upscale hotels. No one will mind, however, if you wear well-tailored shorts; it's surprisingly low-key. The culinary technique is impeccably sharp, and the chefs here select only the finest cuts of beef, the freshest seafood, and the choicest vegetables, such as juicy tomatoes. The best items on the menu are grilled snapper drizzled with three types of coriander sauce (cream-based, oil-based, and vinaigrette style), accompanied with garlic mashed potatoes and Thai-style curried shrimp. For sheer innovation, dishes such as this put The Cliff ahead of Bagatelle. Fresh sushi comes complete with wasabi. As you dine, watch for manta rays, which glide through the illuminated waters below; a sighting is considered a sign of good luck.

Hwy. 1, Derrick, St. James. ℂ **246/432-1922.** Reservations required in winter. Set-menu $65. AE, MC, V. Mon–Sat 6:30–10pm.

The Emerald Palm ★ INTERNATIONAL   This stucco-and-tile house is 2 miles (3km) north of Holetown in a tropical garden dotted with a trio of gazebos. After passing under an arbor, you'll be invited to order a drink, served on one of the flowered banquettes that fill various parts of the restaurant. You can then enjoy a candlelit meal on the rear terrace, alfresco style. Come here for zesty dishes packed with international and island flavors. Begin, perhaps, with a spicy cucumber soup or a succulent version of Caribbean fish soup with fresh peppers. Move on to roast red snapper in coconut juice with local baby spinach (a specialty), or go for a classic dish like medallions of beef tenderloin in mustard sauce. For a real taste of Barbados and a real wakeup, try the charcoal-grilled scallops and baby squid, seasoned with chile-pepper dressing.

Porters, St. James. ℂ **246/422-4116.** Reservations required. Main courses $21–$35. AE, MC, V. Tues–Sun 6:30–9:30pm (last seating). Closed Sept.

Ile de France ★ FRENCH   Located north of Holetown and 8 miles (13km) north of Bridgetown, this restaurant offers classic French cuisine in a charming, traditional atmosphere. Place yourself in the capable hands of Michel and Martine

---

⌒Finds The Island's Freshest Fish

Savvy locals can guide you to the **Oistins Fish Market,** a historic fish market southeast of Bridgetown and past the settlements of Hastings and Worthing. This is where Bajan fishermen unload their catch of the day and sell it directly to the customer. This is ideal if you have an accommodation with a kitchen. If not, you'll find nearly a dozen rundown shacks selling fried fish you know is fresh: Flying fish is in the fryer and fish steaks such as wahoo are on the grill. Buy a beer or a soft drink, and the day is yours.

Gramaglia, two French-born expatriates who handle their kitchen and dining room with grace and style. Ingredients are obtained fresh on Barbados, or flown in from France or Martinique. Specialties might include *escargots de Bourgogne,* a flavor-filled version of fish soup with lobster, or—our favorite—a marinade of three fish, based on the catch of the day. Other classic dishes include tournedos with a béarnaise sauce, rack of lamb, shrimp, and roast lobster. Although hardly innovative, each of these time-tested favorites is prepared with exactitude and refinement. For dessert, try the tart tatin, crème brûlée, or banana terrine.

In the Settlers' Beach Hotel, Holetown, St. James. (C) 246/422-3245. Reservations recommended. Main courses $22.50–$37.50. AE, MC, V. Daily 8am–11pm (last order).

LaTerra ★★ BAJAN/INTERNATIONAL   Overlooking Baki Beach in Hole-town, this kitchen offers an exciting medley of flavors that roam the world for inspiration but contain hints of Caribbean spicing. Chef Larry Rogers and his wife, Michelle, who created the famous Olives, did it again when they opened this charmer on New Year's Day in 1999. It's a romantic setting—an orchid spray on each of the 24 tables, fireflies lighting the garden, the sounds of taped jazz from New Orleans competing with the tree-frog symphony, and the soothing surf.

We've enjoyed not only the decor, but all the dishes sampled here. Larry uses quality ingredients and searches for local produce whenever available. A kind of harmonious simplicity is achieved in every dish: True flavors are allowed to surface and aren't buried in too-heavy sauces. Our appetizer of risotto primavera with white truffle oil set the tone of the meal. That was followed by baked barracuda, flavored with tarragon, and served with caper-studded red wine sauce on a bed of fettuccine with fresh greens. Many of the meat dishes are made with imported frozen meat but don't taste that way, as exemplified by the grilled black angus tenderloin on baked polenta with a zesty touch of roasted shallots and béarnaise sauce.

After 10pm diners can head downstairs to the Casbah Nightclub.

Baku Beach, Holetown. (C) 246/432-1099. Reservations required. Main courses $29–$40. AE, MC, V. Daily 6:30–10pm.

Lone Star Garage ★ *Finds* INTERNATIONAL. Owned and operated by a trend-conscious British-based hotel-and-restaurant chain (the WOW group), this is a hip and stylish restaurant set directly on the beach, on the island's relatively calm Caribbean side. It consists of a very large awning-covered deck, a 1970sapartment building that was reincarnated as a four-suite hotel, and a battered-looking cement bungalow (site of the kitchens and toilets) that functioned as a gas station during the 1940s. Most of its traffic derives from its restaurant, where shellfish on ice, caviar, and less glamorous fare such as seafood-stuffed ravioli and grilled fish contribute to succulent dinners. Crab cakes are always a good bet, as are the grilled tenderloin, various preparations of lobsters, grilled soft-shell crabs, fast-seared tuna steaks, salads, chowders, and a fish sandwich known as a "flying fish cutter." The house drink is a Lone Star Punch, ($7.50), a quasi-psychedelic concoction made from coconut rum, banana rum, and more.

Four hotel suites have attracted a clientele that has included a mostly British roster of VIPs including the Spice Girls, Joan Collins and her entourage, John Cleese, various rock-music and soccer stars, and composer Sir Tim Rice. Suites have full-grained (and very beautiful) floors crafted from rot-resistant Guyanan purpleheart; lots of mirrors, A/C, TV, VCRs, safes, internet connections, comfortable airy furniture that's usually crafted from local mahogany, and tiled shower stalls that are big enough for a dozen partygoers to cram into simultaneously

(This phenomenon, the staff broadly hints, has happened here more than once.) Suites, double occupancy, rent for $325 a night in off season, and $575 a night in winter.

Hwy 1, Mont Standfast, St. James. © **246/419-0598.** Fax 246/419-0597. www.thelonestar.com. Lunch main courses $10–$37; dinner main courses $24–$40. AE, MC, V. Daily 11:30am–4:30pm and 6:30–10pm.

Olives Bar & Bistro ⭐ MEDITERRANEAN/CARIBBEAN   Olive oil is used to prepare almost all the dishes here, and olives are the only snack served in the bar, where there's a welcome rowdiness. The street-level, air-conditioned dining room (where no smoking is permitted) spills out from its original coral-stone walls and scrubbed-pine floorboards into a pleasant garden. The cuisine celebrates the warm climates of southern Europe and the Antilles, and does so exceedingly well. Even some local chefs like to dine here on their nights off. The best items include yellowfin tuna, marinated and seared rare and served on a bed of roasted-garlic mashed potatoes with grilled ratatouille. You can also order roast lamb, flavored with honey, garlic, and fresh herbs; or, for something more Caribbean, jerk tenderloin of pork. Next door is a sandwich bar that serves light lunch fare, Monday through Friday from 8am to 4pm.

Second St. at the corner of Hwy. 1, Holetown. © **246/432-2112.** Reservations required in winter. Main courses $15–$33. AE, MC, V. Daily 6:30–10pm.

MODERATE

Angry Annie's Restaurant & Bar ⭐ (Value) INTERNATIONAL   Don't ask Annie why she's angry—she might tell you! Annie and Paul Matthews, both from the United Kingdom, run this friendly, cozy, 34-seat joint. It's decorated in tropical colors with a circular bar, and rock-and-roll classics play on the excellent sound system. The dishes are tasty with lots of local flavor. The place is known for its ribs, the most savory on the island. We like the garlic-cream potatoes and the use of local vegetables whenever possible. Annie also turns out fresh fish and excellent pasta dishes. Take advantage of the take-out service if you'd like to dine back in your room.

First St., Holetown, St. James. © **246/432-2119.** Main courses $19–$38.50. AE, MC, V. Daily 6–10pm (sometimes until midnight).

Mango's by the Sea ⭐ INTERNATIONAL   This restaurant and bar overlooking the water is best known for its seafood: The owners, Montréal natives Gail and Pierre Spenard, buy the catch of the day directly from the fishermen's boats. The food is exceedingly good, and the seasonings aren't too overpowering, as they are at many Bajan restaurants. Market-fresh ingredients are used to good advantage. Appetizers might be anything from an intriguing green peppercorn pâté to pumpkin soup. If you don't want fish, opt for the 8-ounce U.S. tenderloin steak cooked to perfection or the fall-off-the-bone barbecued baby back ribs. Top off your meal with passion-fruit cheesecake or star fruit torte. There's live entertainment on some nights. Next door is an art gallery under the same management which features the silk screen prints of artist Michael Adams.

2 West End, Queen St., Speightstown, St. Peter. © **246/422-0704.** Reservations recommended. Main courses $16–$32.50 MC, V. Daily 6–9:30pm. Also open Sat 6–9:30 pm Dec–Apr.

Nico's Champagne Wine Bar & Restaurant ⭐ (Value) INTERNATIONAL Set on the landward side of a road that bisects some of the most expensive residential real estate on Barbados, Nico's is a great value, an informal bistro inspired by the wine bars of London. In a 19th-century building originally constructed as the headquarters for a plantation, it does a thriving business from its air-conditioned bar area. Meals are served at tables under a shed-style roof in the back garden. About a dozen wines are sold by the glass; the flavor-filled food is designed to accompany the wine. The finest plates include deep-fried Camembert with passion-fruit sauce, chicken breasts stuffed with crab, and some of the best lobster (grilled simply and served with garlic butter) on Barbados.

Derricks, St. James. ✆ 246/432-6386. Reservations recommended. Main courses $14–$23 lunch, $22.50–$32.50 dinner. AE, MC, V. Mon–Sat 11:30am–10pm.

Ragamuffin's ★ Value CARIBBEAN This is a real discovery: an affordable, lively place that serves authentic island cuisine. The broiled T-bones are juicy and perfectly flavored; there's always an offering of fresh fish; and vegetarians aren't ignored either, as the cooks are always willing to stir-fry some vegetables with noodles. Highlights on the menu include blackened fish, the local version of a spicy West Indian curry, and a zesty jerk chicken salad.

First St., Holetown, St. James. ✆ 246/432-1295. Main courses $15–$28. AE, MC, V. Sun–Fri 6:30–9:30pm.

BRIDGETOWN

Waterfront Café INTERNATIONAL/BAJAN This is your best bet if you're in Bridgetown shopping or sightseeing. In a turn-of-the-century warehouse originally built to store bananas and freeze fish, this cafe serves international fare with a strong emphasis on Bajan specialties. Try the fresh catch of the day prepared Creole style, peppered steak, or the fish burger made with kingfish or dolphin. For vegetarians, the menu features such dishes as pasta primavera, vegetable soup, and usually a special of the day. Both diners and drinkers are welcome here for Creole food, beer, and pastel-colored drinks. Tuesday nights bring live steel-band music and a Bajan buffet. To see the Thursday night Dixieland bands, reserve about a week in advance. There's jazz on Friday and Saturday.

The Careenage, Bridgetown. ✆ 246/427-0093. Reservations required. Main courses $16–$26.50. AE, DC, MC, V. Mon–Sat 10am–10pm.

SOUTH OF BRIDGETOWN

Brown Sugar ★ BAJAN Brown Sugar serves the tastiest Bajan specialties on the island. The alfresco restaurant is hidden behind lush foliage in a turn-of-the-century coral limestone bungalow. The ceiling is latticed, with slow-turning fans, and there's an open veranda for dining by candlelight beneath hanging plants. We suggest starting with gungo-peak soup (pigeon peas cooked in chicken broth and zested with fresh coconut milk, herbs, and a touch of white wine). Among the main dishes we like, Creole orange chicken is the best, or you might like stuffed crab backs. A selection of locally grown vegetables is also offered. Only the lobster is expensive; most of the other dishes are reasonably priced. For dessert, we recommend walnut-rum pie with rum sauce. The restaurant is known for its buffet-style lunches, popular with local businesspeople for its good value.

Aquatic Gap, St. Michael. ✆ 246/426-7684. Reservations recommended. Main courses $15–$33; fixed-price buffet lunch $19 or $20 Sun. AE, DC, DISC, MC, V. Sun–Fri noon–2:30pm and 6–9:30pm (last order), Sat 6–9:30pm (last order).

ON THE SOUTH COAST
MODERATE

Bellini's Trattoria ★ NORTHERN ITALIAN South of Bridgetown, this trattoria evokes the Mediterranean. The restaurant lies on the main floor of this hotel, in a beautiful setting that opens onto a veranda overlooking the water. The menu has a changing array of freshly made antipasti, plus well-prepared seafood

Moments Going Native at the Market

Every vendor at the major markets in the centers of Bridgetown, Oistins, and Speightstown seems to offer something delightful. Start off with a glass of *mauby,* a refreshing but slightly bitter iced tea made from tree bark. Move on to pumpkin fritters, formed into a ball and fried in butter, or pepper pot, meat stew preserved in cassava juice. On our recent rounds, we discovered a mango-based variation on gazpacho—it's addictive. For dessert, seek out a hawker pushing an oversized cart filled with coconuts; he'll take his machete to a green coconut, then offer you a cool drink followed by "the jelly," that soft essence that slithers sweetly down your throat.

dishes. The pasta menu is extensive and most often includes a succulent sauce. After an appetizer, perhaps a small pizza, you can order tender and well-flavored beef tenderloin, chicken parmigiana, or jumbo shrimp in white wine, lemon, and garlic sauce. The Italian desserts, such as tiramisu, are velvety smooth.

Little Bay Hotel, St. Lawrence Gap, Christ Church. ✆ **246/435-7246.** Reservations required. Main courses $17–$26.50. AE, MC, V. Daily 6–10pm.

David's Place ✿ BAJAN   Owner/operators David and Darla Trotman promise you'll sample "Barbadian dining at its best"—and they deliver on that promise, at reasonable prices, too. The cuisine may not be as exotic as that at Brown Sugar, but it's delectable nonetheless. The restaurant is south of Bridgetown between Rockley Beach and Worthing, in an old-fashioned seaside house on St. Lawrence Bay. The tables are positioned so that diners enjoy a view of the Caribbean. Pumpkin or cucumber soup might get you going, or you can try the pickled chicken wings. Try the Baxters Road chicken, seasoned the Bajan way—marinated in lime, salt, and herbs, then deep-fried. Pepper pot is a hot-and-spicy dish with beef, salt pork, chicken, and lamb. Fish steak, the best choice on the menu, might be mahi-mahi, kingfish, barracuda, shark, or red snapper, served in a white-wine sauce or deep-fried Bajan style. Order one of the old-fashioned desserts: a banana split, coconut cream pie, or carrot cake in rum sauce.

St. Lawrence Main Rd., Worthing, Christ Church. ✆ **246/435-9755.** Reservations recommended. Main courses $20–$43. AE, DISC, MC, V. Tues–Sun 6–10pm.

Luigi's Restaurant ✿ ITALIAN   This restaurant serves those old favorites beloved by the late Frank Sinatra. The menu might be 1950s retro, but it's still dependable. This open-air Italian trattoria has been around since 1963. The atmosphere is contemporary, airy, and comfortable. Appetizers include pizzas, classic choices such as escargots and Caesar salad, and half orders of many pastas. The baked pastas, such as creamy lasagna, are delectable, or you can go for the fresh fish or veal special of the day. For dessert, try the zabaglione and one of the wide selection of coffees, ranging from Italian to Russian to Turkish.

Dover Woods, St. Lawrence Gap, Christ Church. ✆ **246/428-9218.** Reservations recommended. Main courses $15–$30. MC, V. Mon–Sat 6:30–10:30pm (last order).

Pisces ✿ BAJAN/SEAFOOD   This beautiful restaurant with a tropical decor offers alfresco dining at the water's edge. Begin with one of the soups, perhaps split pea or pumpkin, or a savory appetizer like flying fish Florentine. Seafood lovers enjoy the Pisces platter—charcoal-broiled dolphin (mahi-mahi), fried flying fish, broiled kingfish, and butter-fried prawns. You might also be drawn to the seasonal Caribbean fish, which can be broiled, blackened, or pan-fried, and then served with lime-herb butter. A limited but good selection of poultry and meat is offered, including roast pork Barbados with a traditional Bajan stuffing.

St. Lawrence Gap, Christ Church. © **246/435-6564.** Reservations recommended. Main courses $17–$34. AE, DC, MC, V. Daily 6–10pm (last order). From Bridgetown, take Hwy. 7 south about 4 miles (6km); turn right at the sign toward St. Lawrence Gap.

Sand Dollar ✰ INTERNATIONAL   Since the early 1940s one restaurant after another on this spot has lured south-coast-beach lovers here. The name has changed several times, but the spot remains a staple in the minds of frequent visitors to Barbados. Opening onto a masonry terrace extending to the edge of the water, the restaurant's latest incarnation, as Sand Dollar, is less formal than ever. Diners show up in shorts, but not bathing attire, please. The cuisine is more reliable than innovative. At lunch you can get the usual sandwiches and salads, but at night the chefs work harder. Their brochettes of jerk shrimp might be a little overcooked, but not the chicken in honey-and-rum sauce. Expect different preparations of lobster and steak, along with some zesty ribs and a well-seasoned pepper steak.

In Bagshot House Hotel, St. Lawrence Coast Rd., Christ Church. © **246/435-6956.** Reservations recommended. Main courses $11–$17 at lunch, $14–$26 at dinner. AE, DC, DISC, MC, V. Daily 7am–10pm.

INEXPENSIVE

The Ship Inn ENGLISH PUB/BAJAN   South of Bridgetown between Rockley Beach and Worthing, The Ship Inn is a traditional English-style pub with an attractive, rustic nautical decor. You can also enjoy a drink in the garden bar's tropical atmosphere. Many guests come to play darts, to meet friends, and especially to listen to top local bands (see "Barbados After Dark," later in this chapter). The Ship Inn serves substantial bar food, such as homemade steak-and-kidney pie, shepherd's pie, and chicken, shrimp, and fish dishes. For more formal dining, visit the Captain's Carvery, where you can have your fill of succulent cuts from prime roasts from the buffet, plus an array of traditional Bajan food, like filets of flying fish.

St. Lawrence Gap, Christ Church. © **246/435-6961.** Reservations recommended for the Captain's Carvery only. Main courses $10–$20; all-you-can-eat carvery meal $15 at lunch, $21 (plus $7.50 for appetizer and dessert) at dinner. DC, MC, V. Daily noon–3pm and 6–10:30pm (last order).

ON THE EAST COAST

Atlantis Hotel ✰ *Finds* BAJAN   Harking back to the Barbados of many years ago, the slightly run-down Atlantis Hotel is often filled with both Bajans and visitors. It's located between Cattlewash-on-Sea and Tent Bay on the east (Atlantic) coast. From the sunny, breeze-filled restaurant, with a sweeping view of the turbulent ocean, this staple of local cuisine has been welcoming visitors through its doors since 1945. The copious buffets are one of the best values on the island. From loaded tables, you can sample such Bajan foods as pumpkin fritters, peas and rice, macaroni and cheese, chow mein, *souse* (pigs' feet marinated in lime juice), and Bajan pepper pot. No one ever leaves here hungry.

Bathsheba, St. Joseph. © **246/433-9445.** Reservations required for Sun buffet and 7pm dinner, recommended at all other times. 2-course fixed-price lunch $16.50; fixed-price dinner $17.50; Sun buffet $22.50. AE, MC, V. Daily 9am–8pm.

4 Beaches

The island's beaches are all open to the public—even those in front of the big resort hotels and private homes—and the government requires that there be access to all beaches, via roads along the property line or through hotel entrances. The beaches on the west coast, the **Gold Coast** ★★, are the most popular.

ON THE WEST COAST   The waters are calm here. Major beaches include **Paynes Bay,** which is accessed from the Coach House, south of Holetown, and has a parking area. This is a good choice for watersports, especially snorkeling. The beach can get rather crowded, but the beautiful bay is worth the effort. Directly south of Payne's Bay, at Fresh Water Bay, are three of the best west-coast beaches: **Brighton Beach, Brandon's Beach,** and **Paradise Beach.**

We also recommend **Mullins Beach,** where the glassy blue waters attract snorkelers. There's parking on the main road and some shady areas. At the Mullins Beach Bar, you can order that rum drink you've been craving.

ON THE SOUTH COAST   **Casuarina Beach** is accessed from Maxwell Coast Road, going across the property of the Casuarina Beach Hotel. This is one of the wider beaches of Barbados, and we've noticed that it's swept by trade winds even on the hottest days of August. Windsurfers are especially fond of this one. Food and drinks can be ordered at the hotel.

Silver Sands Beach, to the east of Oistins, is near the southernmost point of Barbados, directly east of South Point Lighthouse and near the Silver Rock Hotel. This white-sand beach is a favorite with many Bajans (who probably want to keep it a secret from as many tourists as possible). Drinks are sold at the Silver Rock Bar.

Sandy Beach, reached from the parking lot on the Worthing main road, has tranquil waters opening onto a lagoon, the epitome of Caribbean charm. This is a favorite of families, and is especially boisterous on weekends. Food and drinks are sold here.

ON THE SOUTHEAST COAST   The southeast coast is the site of the big waves, especially at **Crane Beach,** the white-sand strip set against a backdrop of palms that you've probably seen in all the travel magazines. The beach is spectacular, as Prince Andrew, who has a house overlooking it, might agree. It offers excellent bodysurfing, but at times the waters may be too rough for all but the strongest swimmers. The beach is set against cliffs, with the Crane Beach Hotel towering above it. This is ocean swimming, not the calm Caribbean, so take precautions.

Bottom Bay ★, north of Sam Lord's Castle Resort, is one of our all-time Bajan favorites. Park on the top of a cliff, then walk down the steps to this much-photographed tropical beach with its grove of coconut palms; there's even a cave. The sand is brilliantly white against the aquamarine sea, a picture-postcard perfect beach paradise.

ON THE EAST (ATLANTIC) COAST   There are miles and miles of uncrowded beaches along the east coast, but this is the Atlantic side, thus swimming here is potentially dangerous. Many travelers like to visit the beaches here, especially those in the **Bathsheba/Cattlewash** areas, for their rugged grandeur. Waves are extremely high on these beaches, and the bottom tends to be rocky. The currents are also unpredictable. But the beaches are ideal for strolling, if not for going into the water.

5 Sports & Other Outdoor Pursuits

DEEP-SEA FISHING   The fishing is first-rate in the waters around Barbados, where anglers pursue dolphin (mahi-mahi), marlin, wahoo, barracuda, and sailfish, to name only the most popular catches. There's also an occasional cobia. The **Dive Shop,** Pebbles Beach, Aquatic Gap, St. Michael (© **800/693-3483** or 246/426-9947), can arrange half-day charters for one to six people, costing $350 per boat (including all equipment and drinks). A whole-day jaunt goes for $700.

GOLF   Open to all are the trio of 18-hole championship golf courses of the **Sandy Lane Hotel,** St. James (© **246/444-2000**), on the west coast. Greens fees are $220 in winter and $200 in summer for 18 holes, or $60 year-round for 9 holes. Carts and caddies are available.

Another option, the **Royal Westmoreland Golf & Country Club,** Westmoreland, St. James (© **246/422-4653**), is one of the island's premier golf courses. Designed by Robert Trent Jones, Jr., this $30 million, 27-hole course is spread across 500 acres (200 hectares) overlooking the Gold Coast. It is part of a private residential community and can be played only by guests of the Royal Pavilion, Glitter Bay, Colony Club, Tamarind Cove, Coral Reef, Crystal Cove, Cobblers Cove, Sandpiper Inn, and Sandy Lane. It costs $75 for 9 holes, or $165 for 18 holes, including a cart.

HIKING   The **Barbados National Trust** (© **246/426-2421**) offers Sunday morning hikes throughout the year, often attracting more than 300 participants. Led by young Bajans and members of the National Trust, the hikes cover a different area of the island each week, giving you an opportunity to learn about the natural beauty of Barbados. The guides give brief talks on subjects such as geography, history, geology, and agriculture. The hikes, free and open to participants of all ages, are divided into fast, medium, and slow categories, with groups of no more than 10. All hikes leave promptly at 6am, are about 5 miles (8km) long, and take about 3 hours to complete. There are also hikes at 3:30 and 5:30pm, the latter conducted only on moonlit nights. For more information, contact the Barbados National Trust.

In 1998, Barbados created a nature trail that explores the natural history and heritage of Speightstown, once a major sugar port and even today a fishing town with old houses and a bustling waterfront. The **Arbib Nature & Heritage Trail** takes you through town, the mysterious gully known as "the Whim," and the surrounding districts. The first marked trail is a 4.7-mile (8km) trek which begins outside St. Peter's Church in Speightstown, traverses the Whim, crosses one of the last working plantations in Barbados (Warleight), and leads to the historic 18th-century Dover Fort, following along white-sand beaches at Heywoods before ending up back in town. Guided hikes are offered on Wednesday, Thursday, and Saturday. For information and reservations, call the Barbados National Trust, and ask for a trail map at the tourist office.

The rugged, dramatic **east coast** stretches about 16 miles (26km) from the lighthouse at Ragged Point, the easternmost point of Barbados, north along the Atlantic coast to Bathsheba and Pico Teneriffe. This is the island's most panoramic hiking area. Some hardy souls do the entire coast; if your time is limited, hike our favorite walk, the 4-mile (6km) stretch from Ragged Point to Consett Bay, along a rough, stony trail that requires only moderate endurance. Allow at least 2½ hours. A small picnic facility just north of Bathsheba is a popular spot for Bajan families, especially on Sundays. As for information, you're pretty much on your own, although if you stick to the coastline, you won't get lost.

HORSEBACK RIDING   A different view of Barbados is offered by the **Caribbean International Riding Centre,** St. Andrew, Sarely Hill (© **246/ 422-7433**). With nearly 40 horses, Mrs. Roachford and her daughters offer a variety of trail rides for all levels of experience, ranging from a 1½-hour jaunt for $60 to a 2½-hour trek for $90. You'll ride through some of the most panoramic parts of Barbados, including the hilly terrain of the Scotland district. Along the way, you can see wild ducks and water lilies, with the rhythm of the Atlantic as background music.

SCUBA DIVING & SNORKELING   The clear waters off Barbados have a visibility of more than 100 feet (30m) most of the year. More than 50 varieties of fish are found on the shallow inside reefs, and there's an unusually high concentration of hawksbill turtles. On night dives, you can spot sleeping fish, night anemones, lobsters, moray eels, and octopuses. Diving is concentrated on the leeward west and south coasts, where hard corals grow thick along the crest of the reef, and orange elephant ear, barrel sponge, and rope sponge cascade down the drop-off of the outer reef.

On a mile-long (2km) coral reef 2 minutes by boat from **Sandy Beach,** sea fans, corals, gorgonias, and reef fish are plentiful. *J.R.,* a dredge barge sunk as an artificial reef in 1983, is popular with beginners for its coral, fish life, and 20-foot (6m) depth. The *Berwyn,* a coral-encrusted tugboat that sank in Carlisle Bay in 1916, attracts photographers for its variety of reef fish, shallow depth, good light, and visibility.

Asta Reef, with a drop of 80 feet (24m), has coral, sea fans, and reef fish in abundance. It's the site of a Barbados wreck that was sunk in 1986 as an artificial reef. **Dottins,** the most beautiful reef on the west coast, stretches 5 miles (8km) from Holetown to Bridgetown and has numerous dive sites at an average depth of 40 feet (12m) and drop-offs of 100 feet (30m). The *SS Stavronikita,* a Greek freighter, is a popular site for advanced divers. Crippled by fire in 1976, the 360-foot (108m) freighter was sunk a ¼ mile (.4km) off the west coast to become an artificial reef in **Folkestone Underwater Park,** north of Holetown. The mast is at 40 feet (12m), the deck at 80 feet (24m), and the keel at 140 feet (36m). While you explore the site, you might spot barracuda, moray eels, and a vibrant coat of bright yellow tube sponge, delicate pink rope sponge, and crimson encrusting sponge. The park has an underwater snorkel trail, plus glass-bottom boat rides, making it a family favorite.

The **Dive Shop,** Pebbles Beach, Aquatic Gap, St. Michael (© **800/693-3483** or 246/426-9947), offers some of the best scuba diving on Barbados, charging $55 for a one-tank dive and $80 for a two-tank dive. Every day, three dive trips go out to the nearby reefs and wrecks; snorkeling trips and equipment rentals are also available. Visitors with reasonable swimming skills who have never dived before can sign up for a resort course. Priced at $70, it includes pool training, safety instructions, and a one-tank open-water dive. The establishment is NAUI- and PADI-certified, and is open Sunday to Friday from 9am to 5pm. Some other dive shops in Barbados that rent or sell snorkeling equipment include the following: **Carib Ocean Divers,** St. James (© **246/422-4414**); **Hazel's Water World,** Bridgetown, St. Michael (© **246/426-4043**); and **Explore Sub,** Christ Church, near Bridgetown (© **246/435-6542**).

Several companies also operate snorkeling cruises that take you to particularly picturesque areas; see "Tours & Cruises" under "Seeing the Sights," below.

TENNIS   The big hotels have tennis courts that can be reserved even if you're not a guest. In Barbados, most tennis players still wear traditional whites.

Folkestone Park, Holetown (© **246/422-2314**), is a public tennis court available for free. Courts at the **Barbados Squash Club,** Marine House, Christ Church (© **246/427-7913**), can be reserved for $12.75 for 45 minutes.

WINDSURFING   Experts say the windsurfing off Barbados is as good as any this side of Hawaii. Judging from the crowds that flock here, they're right. Windsurfing on Barbados has turned into a very big business between November and April, attracting thousands of windsurfers from as far away as Finland, Argentina, and Japan. The shifting of the trade winds between November and May and the shallow offshore reef of **Silver Sands** create unique conditions of wind and wave swells. This allows windsurfers to reach speeds of up to 50 knots and do complete loops off the waves. Silver Sands is rated the best spot in the Caribbean for advanced windsurfing (skill rating of five to six), so you've gotta be good.

The **Barbados Windsurfing Club,** with two branches on the island, can get you started. Beginners and intermediates usually opt for the branch in Oistins (© **246/428-7277**), where winds are constant but the sea is generally flat and calm. Advanced intermediates and experts usually go to the branch adjacent to the Silver Sands Hotel, in Christ Church (© **246/428-6001**), where stronger winds and higher waves allow surfers to combine aspects of windsurfing and conventional Hawaiian-style surfing. Both branches use boards and equipment provided by the Germany-based Club Mistral. Lessons at either branch cost between $40 and $65 per hour, depending on how many people are in your class. Equipment rents for $25 per hour, or $55 to $65 per half day, depending on where and what you rent; rates are less expensive at the Oistins branch.

6 Seeing the Sights
TOURS & CRUISES

Barbados is worth exploring, either in a rental car or with a taxi-driver guide. Unlike so many islands of the Caribbean, Barbados has fair roads. They are, however, poorly signposted, and newcomers invariably get lost—not only once, but several times. If you lose your way, you'll find the people in the countryside generally helpful.

ORGANIZED TOURS   Bajan Tours, Erin Ct., Bishop Ct., St. Michael (© **246/437-9389**), is a locally owned and operated company. The best bet for the first-timer is the Exclusive Island Tour, departing daily between 8:30 and 9am and returning between 3:30 and 4pm. It covers all the highlights of the island, including the Barbados Wildlife Reserve, the Chalky Mount Potteries, and the rugged east coast. On Friday, the Heritage Tour takes in mainly the island's major plantations and museums. Monday through Friday, the Eco Tour explores the natural beauty of the island. All tours cost $60 per person and include a full buffet lunch.

CRUISES   Most popular and fun are the **Jolly Roger "Pirate" Cruises** run by Jolly Roger Cruises (© **246/436-6424**), operating out of Bridgetown Harbour.

Tips **Heading for the Hills**

Be sure to check out the "Seeing the Inland Sights" section under "Seeing the Sights," later in this chapter, for details on hikes, hill climbs, and horseback rides through the lush interior of Barbados.

Passengers can rope swing, swim, snorkel, and suntan on the top deck. Even mock weddings are staged. A buffet lunch with rum punch is presented Thursday and Saturday from 10am to 2pm. Lunch cruises cost $61.50 per person. You can also sail on a catamaran lunch cruise, a 4-hour cruise offered daily from 10am to 3pm, costing $65 per person. Children age 12 and under sail for half price.

Part cruise ship, part nightclub, the *M/V Harbour Master* (© **246/430-0900**) is a 100-foot (30m), 4-story vessel with theme decks, a modern gallery, and 3 bars. It boasts a dance floor and a sit-down restaurant, and also offers formal buffets on its Calypso Deck. On the Harbour Master Deck, there's a bank of TVs for sports buffs. The showpiece of the vessel is an onboard semi-submersible, which is lowered hydraulically to 6 feet (2m) beneath the ship. This is, in effect, a "boat in a boat," with 30 seats. Lunch and dinner cruises cost $61.50 and $65 per person; the semi-submersible experience costs another $10.

SUBMERGED SIGHTSEEING   You no longer have to be an experienced diver to see what lives 150 feet (45m) below the surface of the sea. Now anybody can view the sea's wonders on sightseeing submarines. The air-conditioned submersibles seat 28 to 48 passengers and make several dives daily from 9am to 4pm. Passengers are transported aboard a ferryboat from the Careenage in downtown Bridgetown to the submarine site, about a mile (2km) from the west coast of Barbados. The ride offers a view of the west coast of the island.

The submarines, *Atlantic I* and *III,* have viewing ports that allow you to see a rainbow of colors, tropical fish, plants, and even a shipwreck that lies upright and intact below the surface. The cost is $80 for adults, $40 for children. For reservations, contact **Atlantis Submarines (Barbados),** Shallow Draught, Bridgetown (© **246/436-8929**).

It's also possible to go cruising over one of the shore reefs to observe marine life. You sit in air-conditioned comfort aboard the *Atlantis Seatrec,* a semi-submersible boat, which gives you a chance to get a snorkeler's view of the reef through large viewing windows. You can also relax on deck as you take in the scenic coastline. A second *Seatrec* tour explores wreckage sites. Divers go down with video cameras to three different wrecks on Carlisle Bay, and the video is transmitted to TV monitors aboard the vessel. Both tours cost $35 for adults, half for children age 4 to 12 (not suitable for kids age 3 and under). For reservations, call the number above.

EXPLORING BRIDGETOWN

Often hot and clogged with traffic, the capital, Bridgetown, merits a morning's shopping jaunt (see "Shopping," later in this chapter), plus a visit to some of its major sights.

Since about half a million visitors arrive on Barbados by cruise ship each year, the government has opened a $6 million **cruise-ship terminal** with 20 duty-free shops, 13 local retail stores, and scads of vendors. Cruise passengers can choose from a range of products, including the arts and crafts of Barbados, jewelry, liquor, china, crystal, electronics, perfume, and leather goods. The interior was designed to re-create an island street scene; some storefronts appear as traditional chattel houses in brilliant island colors, complete with streetlights, tropical landscaping, benches, and pushcarts.

Begin your tour at the waterfront, called **the Careenage** (French for "turning vessels on their side for cleaning"). This was a haven for clipper ships, and even though today it doesn't have the color of yesteryear, it's still worth exploring.

Bridgetown

BARBADOS

○ Bridgetown

American Express **2**
Barbados Gallery of Art **5**
Barbados Museum **10**
Careenage **6**
Garrison Savannah **8**
Public Buildings **3**
St. Ann's Fort **9**
St. Michael's Cathedral **4**
Synagogue **1**
Trafalgar Square **7**

At **Trafalgar Square,** the long tradition of British colonization is immortalized. The monument here, honoring Lord Nelson, was executed by Sir Richard Westmacott and erected in 1813. The great gray Victorian/Gothic **Public Buildings** on the square look like those you might expect to find in London. The east wing contains the meeting halls of the Senate and the House of Assembly, with some stained-glass windows representing the sovereigns of England. Look for the "Great Protector" himself, Oliver Cromwell.

Behind the Financial Building, **St. Michael's Cathedral,** east of Trafalgar Square, is the symbol of the Church of England. This Anglican church was built in 1655 but was completely destroyed in a 1780 hurricane. Reconstructed in 1789, it was again damaged by a hurricane in 1831. George Washington supposedly worshipped here on his visit to Barbados.

The **Synagogue,** Synagogue Lane (no phone), is one of the oldest synagogues in the western hemisphere and is surrounded by a burial ground of early Jewish settlers. The present building dates from 1833. It was constructed on the site of an even older synagogue, erected by Jews from Brazil in 1654. It's now part of the National Trust of Barbados—and a synagogue once again. It's open Monday to Friday from 9am to 4pm; a donation is requested for admission.

First made popular in 1870, **cricket** is the national pastime on Barbados. Matches can last from 1 to 5 days. If you'd like to see a local match, watch for announcements in the newspapers or ask at the **Tourist Board,** on Harbour Road (① 246/427-2623). From Bridgetown, you can take a taxi to **Garrison Savannah,** just south of the capital, a venue for frequent cricket matches and horse races.

Barbados Gallery of Art, Bush Hill (① 246/228-0149), in a restored old building in the historic Garrison district, displays the very best Bajan and Caribbean visual art. The gallery also pays tribute to the memory of the late actress Claudette Colbert, longtime resident of Barbados. She is memorialized in a beautiful garden here, and the gallery even owns one of her own paintings. Hours are Tuesday through Saturday from 10am to 5pm. Admission is $3 for adults, free for children.

Barbados Museum, St. Ann's Garrison, St. Michael (① 246/427-0201), is housed in a former military prison. Extensive collections show the island's development from prehistoric to modern times, as well as fascinating glimpses into the natural environment and fine examples of West Indian maps and decorative arts. The museum sells a variety of quality publications, reproductions, and handcrafts. Its cafe is a good place for a snack or light lunch. Hours are Monday to Saturday from 9am to 5pm, Sunday from 2 to 6pm. Admission is $6 for adults, $3 for children.

Nearby, the russet-red **St. Ann's Fort,** on the fringe of the savanna, garrisoned British soldiers in 1694. The fort wasn't completed until 1703. The Clock House survived the hurricane of 1831.

A GREAT HOUSE OUTSIDE BRIDGETOWN

Tyrol Cot Heritage Village ⋆ If you arrived at the airport, you'll recognize the name of Sir Grantley Adams, the leader of the Bajan movement for independence from Britain. This was once his home, and his wife, Lady Adams, lived in the house until her death in 1990. Once you had to wrangle a highly prized invitation to visit, but the home is now open to all. It was built sometime in the mid-1850s from coral stone, in a Palladian style. The grounds have been turned into a museum of Bajan life, including small chattel houses where potters and artists work. The museum attracts mainly those with a genuine interest in Bajan culture; it may not be for the average visitor intent on getting to the beach on time. The Old Stables Restaurant is located in the former stables and serves meals until 4pm.

Codrington Hill, St. Michael. © 246/424-2074. Admission $6 adults, $3 children. Mon–Fri 9am–5pm.

SEEING THE INLAND SIGHTS
IN THE CENTER OF THE ISLAND ★★

Many visitors stay on those fabulous west-coast beaches, but the island's true beauty is its lush interior. If you have the time, we highly recommend a hike, drive, or tour through such rarely visited parishes as St. Thomas and St. George (both of which are landlocked) and the wild Atlantic coast parishes of St. Andrews and St. John.

Flower Forest ★   This old sugar plantation stands 850 feet (255m) above sea level near the western edge of the Scotland district, a mile (2km) from Harrison's Cave. Set in one of the most scenic parts of Barbados, it's more than just a botanical garden; it's where people and nature came together to create something beautiful. After viewing the grounds, visitors can purchase handcrafts at Best of Barbados (see "Shopping," below).

Richmond Plantation, St. Joseph. © 246/433-8152. Admission $7 adults, $3.50 children age 5–16, free for children age 4 and under. Daily 9am–5pm.

Harrison's Cave ★★ *Kids*   The underground world here, the number-one tourist attraction of Barbados, is viewed from aboard an electric tram and trailer. On the tour, you'll see bubbling streams, tumbling cascades, and subtly lit deep pools, while all around stalactites hang overhead like icicles, and stalagmites rise from the floor. Visitors may disembark and get a closer look at this natural phenomenon at the Rotunda Room and the Cascade Pool. Although it's interesting, it may not impress Americans who have been to the far more spectacular Carlsbad or Luray Caverns.

Welchman Hall, St. Thomas. © 246/438-6640. Tour reservations recommended. Admission $12.50 adults, $5 children 16 and under. Daily 9am–4pm. Closed Good Friday, Easter Sunday, and Christmas.

Morgan Lewis Sugar Mill   Created in 1727 when Barbados was one of Britain's major sugar colonies, this mill is now restored, one of only two intact sugar mills in the Caribbean (the other is in Antigua). It is maintained by the Barbados National Trust. The mill includes an exhibit of the equipment, including horse-driven machinery, once used to make sugar. The on-site plantation house has seen better days, but makes a picturesque ruin with its rubble walls. The mill lies on a scenic mount in the northeast of the island, offering panoramic views of the east coast. Before its restoration, this mill appeared on a list of the 100 most endangered historical sites in the world.

Signposted near the Barbados Wildlife Reserve, St. Andrew. © 246/422-7429. Admission $5 adults, $2.50 children. Mon–Sat 9am–5pm.

Welchman Hall Gully ★   This lush tropical garden is owned by the Barbados National Trust. You'll see some specimens of plants that were here when the English settlers landed in 1627. Many of the plants are labeled—clove, nutmeg, tree fern, and cocoa, among others—and occasionally you'll spot a wild monkey. You can also see breadfruit trees that are supposedly descendants of the seedlings brought ashore by Captain Bligh, of *Bounty* fame.

Welchman Hall, St. Thomas. © 246/438-6671. Admission $5.75 adults, $3 children age 6–12, free for children age 5 and under. Daily 9am–5pm. Take Hwy. 2 from Bridgetown.

Francia Plantation ⟨★⟩   A fine family home, the Francia Plantation stands on a wooded hillside overlooking the St. George Valley and is still owned and occupied by descendants of the original owner. Built in 1913, the house blends West Indian and European architectural influences. You can explore several rooms, including the dining room with its family silver and an 18th-century James McCabe bracket clock. On the walls are antique maps and prints, including a map of the West Indies printed in 1522.

St. George, Barbados. ✆ **246/429-0474**. Admission $5. Mon–Fri 10am–4pm. On the ABC Hwy., turn east onto Hwy. 4 at the Norman Niles Roundabout (follow the signs to Gun Hill); after going a ½ mile (.8km), turn left onto Hwy. X (follow the signs to Gun Hill); after another mile (2km), turn right at the Shell gas station and follow Hwy. X past St. George's Parish Church and up the hill for a mile, turning left at the sign to Francia.

Gun Hill Signal Station   One of two such stations owned and operated by the Barbados National Trust, the Gun Hill Signal Station is strategically placed on the highland of St. George and commands a panoramic view from the east to the west. Built in 1818, it was the finest of a chain of signal stations and was also used as an outpost for the British army. The restored military cookhouse houses a snack bar and gift shop.

Hwy. 4. ✆ **246/429-1358**. Admission $4.60 adults, $2.30 children age 12 and under. Mon–Sat 9am–5pm. Take Hwy. 3 from Bridgetown, then go inland from Hwy. 4 toward St. George Church.

IN THE SOUTHEAST (ST. PHILIP)

While you're driving around this part of the island, you might like to stop off at the **Crane Beach Hotel,** on Crane Bay, St. Philip (✆ **246/423-6220**). We don't recommend staying here, but nonguests can buy a day pass for $2.50. It's a great place to have a relaxing drink at the bar and enjoy the views over the Atlantic.

Heritage Park & Rum Factory   After driving through cane fields, you'll arrive at the first rum distillery to be launched on the island since the 19th century. Inaugurated in 1996, this factory is located on a former molasses and sugar plantation dating back some 350 years. Produced on site is ESA Field, a white rum praised by connoisseurs. Adjacent is an admission-free park where Barbadian handcrafts are displayed in the Art Foundry (see "Shopping," below). You'll also find an array of shops and carts selling global foods, handcrafts, and products.

Foursquare Plantation, St. Philip. ✆ **246/420-1977**. Admission $7.50. Mon–Fri 9am–5pm.

Sunbury Plantation House ⟨★⟩   If you have time to visit only one plantation or great house in Barbados, make it this one. It's the only great house on Barbados where all the rooms are open for viewing. The 300-year-old plantation house is steeped in history, featuring mahogany antiques, old prints, and a unique collection of horse-drawn carriages. Take the informative tour, then stop in the Courtyard Restaurant and Bar for a meal or drinks; there's also a gift shop.

⟨ *Tips* **The Great Tour**

From mid-January through the first week of April, you can tour a different great house every Wednesday afternoon. Houses include those rarely seen by the public, as well as major attractions such as Bleak House. You'll see a great array of plantation antiques and get a feeling for the elegant colonial lifestyle once commonplace on Barbados. For more information, call ✆ **246/426-2421**.

Moments   A Beautiful Picnic Spot

Farley Hill National Park surrounds what used to be one of the greatest houses of Barbados, Farley Hill, a mansion in ruins. The park lies to the north of the parish of St. Peter, directly across the road leading into the Barbados Wildlife Reserve. You can bring in a picnic and wander in the park, over-looking the turbulent waters of the Atlantic. You can enter the park for free if you're walking, but it costs $2 to bring a car in. Hours are daily 8:30am to 6pm.

A candlelight dinner is offered at least once a week; this five-course meal, served at a 200-year-old mahogany table, costs $75 per person.

6 Cross Rd., St. Philip. © **246/423-6270.** Admission $7.50 adults, $3.75 children. Daily 9:30am–4pm (last tour).

IN THE NORTHEAST

Andromeda Botanic Gardens ⭐ On a cliff overlooking the town of Bathsheba on the rugged east coast, limestone boulders make for a natural 8-acre (3-hectare) rock-garden setting. Thousands of orchids, hundreds of hibiscus and heliconia, and many varieties of ferns, begonias, palms, and other species grow here in splendid profusion. You'll occasionally see frogs, herons, lizards, hum-mingbirds, and sometimes a mongoose or a monkey.

Bathsheba, St. Joseph. © **246/433-9384.** Admission $6 adults, $3 children; free for kids age 5 and under. Daily 9am–5pm.

St. Nicholas Abbey Surrounded by sugarcane fields, this Jacobean planta-tion great house has been around since about 1650. It was never actually an abbey—around 1820 an ambitious owner simply christened it as such. More than 200 acres (80 hectares) are still cultivated each year. The house, character-ized by its curved gables, is believed to be one of three Jacobean houses in the western hemisphere. At least the ground floor of the structure is open to the public. You can have lunch or afternoon tea at the cafe, and perhaps catch an intriguing home movie from the 1930s.

On Cherry Tree Hill, Hwy. 1. © **246/422-8725.** Admission $5 adults; free for children age 11 and under. Mon–Fri 10am–3:30pm.

Barbados Wildlife Reserve Across the road from Farley Hill National Park, in northern St. Peter Parish, the reserve is set in a mahogany forest that's maintained by the Barbados Primate Research Center. Visitors can stroll through what is primarily a monkey sanctuary and an arboretum. Aside from the uncaged monkeys, you can see wild hares, deer, tortoises, otters, wallabies (which were brought into Barbados), and a variety of tropical birds.

Farley Hill, St. Peter. © **246/422-8826.** Admission $11.50 adults, $5.75 for children age 12 and under. Daily 10am–5pm.

7 Shopping

You may find duty-free merchandise here at prices 20% to 40% lower than in the United States and Canada—but you've got to be a smart shopper to spot bargains, and you should be familiar with prices back in your hometown. Duty-free shops have two prices listed on items of merchandise: the local retail price and the local retail price less the government-imposed tax.

Some of the best duty-free buys include cameras, watches, crystal, gold jewelry, bone china, cosmetics and perfumes, and liquor (including locally produced Barbados rum and liqueurs), along with tobacco products and cashmere sweaters, tweeds, and sportswear from Britain. If you purchase items made on Barbados, you don't have to pay duty.

The outstanding item in Barbados handcrafts is black-coral jewelry. Another Bajan craft, clay pottery, originated at **Chalky Mount Potteries** (no phone), which is worth a visit. Potters turn out different products, some based on designs that are centuries old. The potteries (which are signposted) are north of Bathsheba on the east coast, in St. Joseph Parish near Barclay's Park. In shops across the island, you'll also find a selection of locally made vases, pots, pottery mugs, glazed plates, and ornaments.

Wall hangings are woven from local grasses and dried flowers, and island craftspeople also turn out straw mats, baskets, and bags with raffia embroidery. Still in its infant stage, leather work is also found on Barbados, particularly handbags, belts, and sandals.

IN BRIDGETOWN Cruise passengers generally head for the **cruise-ship terminal** at Bridgetown Harbour, which has some 20 duty-free shops, 13 local shops, and many vendors (see "Exploring Bridgetown" under "Seeing the Sights," earlier in this chapter).

At **Articrafts,** Broad Street (© 246/427-5767), John and Roslyn Watson have assembled an impressive display of Bajan arts and crafts. Roslyn's distinctive wall hangings are decorated with objects from the island, including sea fans and coral. The unique **Colours of De Caribbean,** the Waterfront Marina (next to the Waterfront Café, on the Careenage; © 246/436-8522), carries a limited selection of original hand-painted and batik clothing, all made in the West Indies, plus jewelry and decorative objects.

Cave Shepherd, Broad Street (© 246/431-2121), is the largest department store on the island and the best place for duty-free merchandise. There are branches at Sunset Crest in Holetown, Da Costas Mall, Grantley Adams Airport, and the Bridgetown cruise-ship terminal, but if your time is limited, try this outlet, as it has the widest selection. The store sells perfumes, cosmetics, fine crystal and bone china, cameras, jewelry, swimwear, leather goods, men's designer clothing, handcrafts, liquor, and souvenirs. You can take a break in the cool comfort of the Balcony, overlooking Broad Street, which serves vegetarian dishes and has a salad bar and beer garden.

Harrison's, 1 Broad St. (© 246/431-5500), has 14 branch stores, all selling a wide variety of duty-free merchandise, including china, crystal, jewelry, leather goods, and perfumes—all at fair prices. Also for sale are some fine leather products handcrafted in Colombia. Harrison's is the major competitor to Cave Shepherd on the island, but we'd give the edge to Cave Shepherd.

Little Switzerland, in the Da Costas Mall, Broad Street (© 246/431-0030), offers a wide selection of fragrances and cosmetics, watches, fine jewelry, Mont Blanc pens, and an array of goodies from Waterford, Lalique, Swarovski, Baccarat, and others. Also on Broad Street, at Mall 34, is a branch of **Best of Barbados** (© 246/436-1416); see "Elsewhere Around the Island," below.

About a ½ hour drive north of Bridgetown, **Luna Jewelers,** Queen St., Spice Town, St. Peter (© 246/419-5862), sells diamonds and precious stones, watches, and gift items. What makes Luna unusual is its emphasis on art-nouveau and art-deco designs set into gold and silver, crafted on Barbados in alluring designs.

Fossilized Bajan coral is carefully polished and set into gold or silver settings, and in some cases, intricate mosaic-style inlays.

Pelican Crafts Center, Harbour Road (© 246/426-4391), offers bargains from Bajan artisans. In Bridgetown, go down Princess Alice Highway to the city's Deep Water Harbour, where you'll find this tiny colony of thatch-roofed shops. Some of the shops here are gimmicky, but interesting items can be found. Sometimes you can see craftspeople at work.

ELSEWHERE AROUND THE ISLAND   The best shop on the island for local products is **Best of Barbados,** in the Southern Palms, St. Lawrence Gap, Christ Church, on the south coast (© 246/420-8040). Part of an island-wide chain of eight stores, this tasteful shop sells only products designed or made on Barbados, such as prints, coasters, T-shirts, pottery, dolls, games, and cookbooks. Also in the town of St. Lawrence Gap is **Walker's Caribbean World** (© 246/428-1183), near the Southern Palms, which offers many locally made items for sale, as well as handcrafts from the Caribbean Basin and the famous Jill Walker prints.

One of the most interesting shopping jaunts in Barbados is to the previously recommended **Tyrol Cot Heritage Village** (see p. 162), the former home of the Bajan national hero, Sir Grantley Adams. On the grounds of the former prime minister's estate is a colony of artisans and craftspeople who turn out an array of articles for sale that range from paintings to pottery, from baskets to handmade figurines.

Earthworks Pottery/The Potter's House Gallery, Edgehill Heights 2, St. Thomas (© 246/425-0223), is one of the artistic highlights of Barbados. Deep in the island's central highlands, Canadian-born Goldie Spieler and her son, David, create whimsical ceramics in the colors of the sea and sky; many objects are decorated with Antillean-inspired swirls and zigzags. On the premises are a studio and a showroom that sells the output of at least half a dozen other island potters. Purchases can be shipped.

The **Shell Gallery,** Carlton House, St. James (© 246/422-2593), has the best collection of shells in the West Indies and features the art of Maureen Edghill, the finest artist in this field and the founder of this unique gallery. Also offered are hand-painted china, shell jewelry, local pottery and ceramics, and batik and papier-mâché artwork. **Greenwich House Antiques,** Greenwich Village, Trents Hill, St. James (© 246/432-1169), a 25-minute drive from Bridgetown, feels like a genteel private home where the objects for sale seem to have come from the attic of your favorite slightly dotty great aunt. Dozens of objects fill every available inch of tabletop or display space.

8 Barbados After Dark

ON THE WEST COAST   A lot of the evening entertainment around here revolves around the big resorts, all of which have lovely bars and many of which host bands and beach parties in the evening. See "Accommodations," earlier in this chapter.

Some say the green-and-white **Coach House,** Paynes Bay (on the main Bridgetown-Holetown road, just south of Sandy Lane, about 6 miles (10km) north of Bridgetown), St. James (© 246/432-1163), is 200 years old. Attracting mostly visitors, this is a Bajan version of an English pub, with an outdoor garden bar. From 6 to 10:30pm you can order bar meals, including flying-fish burgers, priced at $9 and up. Most nights, there's live music—everything from steel bands to jazz, pop, and rock, attracting an attentive crowd from 9pm on. The lunchtime buffet, offered Monday through Friday ($15.50), is popular.

John Moore Bar, on the waterfront, Weston, St. James (© **246/422-2258**), is the most atmospheric and least pretentious bar on Barbados. It's the nerve center of this waterfront town, filled throughout the day and night with a congenial group of neighborhood residents, with a scattering of foreigners. Most visitors opt for a rum punch or beer, but you can order up a platter of local fish as long as you don't mind waiting.

Head for **Upstairs at Olives,** Holetown, St. James (© **246/432-2112**), where you can order excellent drinks while seated in an atmosphere of potted palms and old-fashioned ceiling fans that's straight out of *Casablanca.*

IN BRIDGETOWN For the most authentic Bajan evening possible, head for **Baxters Road** in Bridgetown, where there's always something cooking on Friday and Saturday after 11pm. In fact, if you stick around until dawn, the party's still going strong. Some old-time visitors have compared Baxters Road to the back streets of New Orleans in the 1930s. If you fall in love with the place, you can "caf crawl" up and down the street, where nearly every bar is run by a Bajan mama.

The most popular "caf" on Baxters Road is **Enid's** (she has a phone, "but it doesn't work"), a little ramshackle establishment where Bajans come to devour fried chicken at 3 in the morning. This place is open daily from 8:30pm to 8:30am, when the last satisfied customer departs into the blazing morning sun and the employees go home to get some sleep before the new night begins. Stop in for a Banks beer.

The Rusty Pelican, The Careenage (© **246/436-7778**), is an atmospheric choice if you're in Bridgetown at night. It's right on the waterfront, and in addition to the good drinks, the club often has a musician (or musicians) to entertain. **The Boatyard,** Bay Street, Bridgetown (© **246/436-2622**), has a pubby atmosphere, with a DJ and occasional live bands.

Harbour Lights, Marine's Villa, Lower Bay Street, about a mile (2km) southeast of Bridgetown (© **246/436-7225**), is the most popular weekend spot for dancing, drinking, and flirting on all of Barbados. In a modern seafront building with an oceanfront patio (which gives dancers a chance to cool off), the place plays reggae, soca, and whatever else is popular until the wee hours every night. The barbecue pit/kiosk serves up grilled meats and hamburgers. Monday is beach party night; the $49 charge includes transportation to and from your hotel, a barbecue buffet, drinks, and a live band. On Wednesday and Friday, there's a cover of $12.50 to $17.50. The place attracts a large following among locals, with a few foreign visitors showing up.

ON THE SOUTH COAST **Cafe Sol,** St. Lawrence Gap, Christ Church (© **246/435-9531**), has an encircling veranda opening onto a view of the water. A very convivial crowd gathers here to enjoy the bustling activity. As a specialty of the house, the bartender rubs the margarita glasses with Bajan sugar instead of the usual salt.

Plantation Restaurant and Garden Theatre, Main Road (Hwy. 7), St. Lawrence, Christ Church (© **246/428-5048**), is the island's main showcase for evening dinner theater and Caribbean cabaret. It's completely touristy, but despite that, most people enjoy it. Every Wednesday and Friday, dinner is served at 6:30pm, followed by a show, *Plantation Tropical Spectacular II,* at 8pm. Expect elaborate costumes and lots of reggae, calypso, and limbo. For $67.50, you get dinner, the show, and transportation to and from your hotel; the show alone costs $37.50. Reserve in advance.

The Ship Inn, St. Lawrence Gap, Christ Church (© **246/435-6961**), recommended earlier in this chapter as a restaurant, is now among the leading entertainment centers on the south coast. The pub is the hot spot: Top local bands perform nightly, offering reggae, calypso, and pop music. The entrance fee, which changes daily, is redeemable for food or drink at any of the other bars or restaurants in The Ship Inn complex, so you're actually paying only a small fee for the live entertainment. The place draws an equal mixture of visitors and locals.

One of our favorite bars in Barbados, **Olives Bar & Bistro,** Second St. at the corner of Hwy. 1, in Holetown (© **246/432-2112**), is not only a fine restaurant (see previous recommendation) but a good place to spend 2 or 3 hours before or after dinner—maybe both. Found on the second floor in a *Casablanca*-like setting of potted palms and whirling fans, it draws a convivial international crowd, mostly ex-pats, Americans, and English visitors in their 30s and 40s.

Bert's Bar, at the Abbeville Hotel in Worthing, on the Main Road in Christ Church (© **246/435-7924**), is known for making the best daiquiris on the island. Sports fans head for **Bubba's Sports Bar,** Rockley Main Road, Christ Church (© **246/435-6217**), which offers a couple of satellite dishes, a 10-foot (3m) video screen, and a dozen TVs. Wash a Bubba burger down with a Banks beer here. The longest bar on the island is at **After Dark,** St. Lawrence Gap, Christ Church (© **246/435-6547**), where you can often hear live reggae, soca, Bajan calypso, and jazz.

7

Bonaire

Unspoiled Bonaire is only gently touched by development. Although your options here range from bird-watching to doing nothing, Bonaire is foremost a scuba diver's delight and also offers some of the Caribbean's best snorkeling. This sleepy island doesn't attract crowds and has none of Aruba's glitzy diversions. Instead, turquoise waters beckon travelers to discover colorful clouds of tropical fish.

Bonaire is a bird-watcher's haven, where flamingos nearly outnumber the sparse human population. There are more than 190 different species of birds—not only the flamingo, but also the big-billed pelican, parrots, snipes, terns, parakeets, herons, and hummingbirds. A pair of binoculars is an absolute necessity.

Bonaireans zealously protect their precious environment. Even though they eagerly seek tourism, they aren't interested in creating another Aruba, with its high-rise hotel blocks. Spearfishing isn't allowed in its waters, nor is the taking or destruction of any coral or other living animal from the sea. Unlike some islands, Bonaire isn't just surrounded by coral reefs—it *is* the reef, sitting on the dry, sunny top of an underwater mountain. Its shores are thick with rainbow-hued fish.

Boomerang-shaped Bonaire is close to the coast of Latin America, just 50 miles (81km) north of Venezuela. Part of the Netherlands Antilles (an autonomous part of the Netherlands), Bonaire has a population of about 10,000 and an area of about 112 square miles (290 sq. km). The capital is **Kralendijk** (*KROLL-en-dike*). It's most often reached from its neighbor island of Curaçao, 30 miles (48km) to the west; like Curaçao, Bonaire is desertlike, with a dry and brilliant atmosphere. Often it's visited by day-trippers, who rush through here in pursuit of the shy, elusive flamingo. Its northern sector is hilly, tapering up to Mount Brandaris, all of 788 feet (236m). However, the southern half, flat as a pancake, is given over to bays, reefs, beaches, and a salt lake that attracts the flamingos.

1 Essentials

VISITOR INFORMATION

Before you go, you can contact the **Bonaire Government Tourist Office** at Adams Unlimited, 10 Rockefeller Plaza, Suite 900, New York, NY 10020 (© **800/-BONAIR** or 212/956-5911). There's also information on the Web at **www.bonaire.org**.

On the island, you can go to the **Bonaire Government Tourist Bureau,** Kaya Libertad Simón Bolivar 12, Kralendijk (© **599/717-8322**), open Monday to Friday from 8am to noon and 1:30 to 5pm.

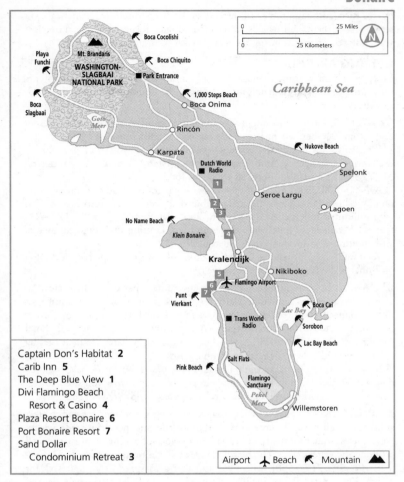

Captain Don's Habitat **2**
Carib Inn **5**
The Deep Blue View **1**
Divi Flamingo Beach
    Resort & Casino **4**
Plaza Resort Bonaire **6**
Port Bonaire Resort **7**
Sand Dollar
    Condominium Retreat **3**

Airport ✈ Beach 🗻 Mountain ▲▲

GETTING THERE

Before you book your flight, be sure to read the section "Package Tours" in chapter 2; it can save you a bundle. Even if you don't book a package, see that chapter's tips on finding the best airfare.

ALM (© **800/327-7230;** www.alm-airlines.com) is one of your best bets for flying to Bonaire. It offers daily flights from both Miami and Atlanta.

American Airlines (© 800/433-7300; www.aa.com) offers one daily nonstop flight to Curaçao from its hub in Miami. These depart late enough in the day (11am) to allow easy connections from cities all over the northeast, and they reach Curaçao early enough to allow immediate transfers to Bonaire. American Airlines can book (but not ticket) your connecting flight to Bonaire on Bonaire Airways.

Other routes to Bonaire are possible on any of American's daily nonstop flights to Aruba through American's hubs in New York, Miami, and San Juan,

Puerto Rico. Although these transfers are somewhat complicated, American will set up any of them, and will also offer reduced rates at some Bonairean hotels if you book your reservation simultaneously with your air passage.

GETTING AROUND

Even though most of the island is flat and renting a moped or motor scooter is fun, you'll have to be prepared for sections of the island with unpaved, pitted, and rocky roads.

BY RENTAL CAR   You might want to rent a four-wheel-drive vehicle, especially from October to January, which can be a muddy season.

It pays to shop around: Sometimes—but not always—you can make a better deal with a local agency. Among local agencies, **Island Rentals,** Kaya Industria 31 (© 599/717-2100), offers soft-top Jeeps for $50 a day.

Avis (© 800/331-1212 in the U.S.; www.avis.com) is also at Flamingo Airport. Weekly arrangements are cheaper, but daily rates range from $48 to $73, with unlimited mileage. At the airport, **Total Car Rental** (© 599/717-7424) rents such vehicles as four-wheel drives and Suzuki minivans. Some automatic, air-conditioned four-door sedans are available.

Your valid U.S., British, or Canadian driver's license is acceptable for driving on Bonaire. *Driving on Bonaire is on the right.*

BY TAXI   Taxis are unmetered, but the government has established rates. All taxis carry a license plate with the letters *TX*. Each driver should have a price list to be produced upon request. As many as four passengers can go along for the ride, unless there's too much luggage. A trip from the airport to your hotel should cost about $12 to $15. From 8pm to midnight, fares are increased by 25%; from midnight to 6am, they go up by 50%.

Most taxi drivers can take you on a tour of the island, but you'll have to negotiate a price according to how long a trip you want and what you want to see. For more information, call **Taxi Central Dispatch** (© 599/717-8100).

BY BICYCLE   If you're in good shape, you might consider renting a bike, although you'll have to contend with the hot sun and powerful trade winds. Nevertheless, much of the island is flat, and if you follow the main road, you'll go along the water's edge. The best deals are at **Cycle Bonaire,** Kaya L. D. Gerjharts (© 599/717-7558), where you can rent a 21-speed or an 830 Trek for $15 to $20 per day. Rental includes a water bottle, lock, helmet, repair kit, and pump. A map is provided for free.

 FAST FACTS: **Bonaire**

Banks Banks are usually open Monday to Friday from 8am to noon and 2 to 3:30pm. **ABM Bank,** Caya Corona 15 (© 599/717-8417), is the most convenient facility for visitors, and it has an ATM. There's also an ATM at the airport.

Currency Bonaire's coin of the realm is the Netherlands Antillean florin (NAf), sometimes called a guilder. The official rate is 1.77 NAf to US$1. However, U.S. dollars are widely accepted. *Unless otherwise specified, rates in this chapter are quoted in U.S. dollars.*

Customs There are no Customs requirements for Bonaire.

Documents U.S. and Canadian citizens don't need a passport to enter Bonaire, although an original birth or naturalization certificate or an alien registration card is required, plus a return ticket and photo ID. (We suggest just carrying your passport anyway.) British subjects may carry a British Visitor's Passport, obtainable at post offices on Bonaire, although a valid passport issued in the United Kingdom is preferred, especially if you plan to visit other countries in the area. We recommend that all travelers carry a valid passport.

Electricity The electricity on Bonaire is slightly different from that used in North America (110–130 volts/50 cycles), as opposed to U.S. and Canadian voltages of 110 volts (60 cycles). Adapters and transformers are necessary for North American appliances, but because of the erratic current, you should still proceed with caution when using any appliance and try to avoid usage if at all possible. Be warned, further, that electrical current used to feed or recharge finely calibrated diving equipment should be stabilized with a specially engineered electrical stabilizer. Every diving operation on the island has one of these as part of its standard equipment for visiting divers.

Emergencies In an emergency, call © **110** for the police or ambulance service.

Hospital The **St. Franciscus Hospital** is located at Kaya Soeur Bartola 2 in Kralendijk (© **599/717-8900**). A plane on standby at the airport takes seriously ill patients to Curaçao for treatment.

Language English is widely spoken, but you'll hear Dutch, Spanish, and Papiamento, the local dialect, as well.

Liquor Laws Beer, wine, and liquor are sold in all kinds of stores 7 days a week. It's legal to have an open container on the beach.

Safety Bonaire is quite a safe haven in this crime-infested world. But remember, any place that attracts tourists also attracts people who prey on them. Safeguard your valuables.

Taxes The government requires a $6.50-per-person daily room tax on all hotel rooms. Upon leaving Bonaire, you'll be charged an airport departure tax of $10, so don't spend every penny. There's also an inter-island departure tax of $5.75 if you are flying to Curaçao.

Telephone To call Bonaire from the United States, dial **011** (the international access code), then **599** (the country code for Bonaire), and then **7** (the area code) and the four-digit local number. Once on Bonaire, to call another number on the island, only the four-digit local number is necessary. You can access **AT&T Direct** on the island by dialing © **001-800/ 872-2881**. It's often difficult to make international calls from Bonaire; phone service here lags far behind that on Aruba and Curaçao. Once you're connected to your party, the line isn't always crystal clear. Many hotel rooms don't have private phones. If you want to place an important international call, it's better to go to **TELBO,** the central phone company for the island. It's found at Kaya Libertador Simon Bolivar, next to the tourist office.

Time Bonaire is on Atlantic standard time year-round, 1 hour ahead of eastern standard time (when it's noon on Bonaire, it's 11am in Miami).

When daylight saving time is in effect in the United States, clocks in Miami and Bonaire show the same time.

Tipping Most hotels and guest houses add a 10% service charge in lieu of tipping. Restaurants generally add a service charge of 15% to the bill. Taxi drivers expect a 10% tip.

Water Drinking water comes from distilled seawater and is pure and safe.

Weather Bonaire is known for its warm climate, with temperatures hovering around 82°F. The water temperature averages 80°F. It's warmest in August and September, coolest in January and February. The average rainfall is 22 inches, and December to March are the rainiest months. Like all the Dutch ABC islands, Bonaire lies outside the hurricane belt, which comes as a relief to many visitors planning to visit the Caribbean during the hurricane season.

2 Accommodations

Hotels, all facing the sea, are low-key, personally run operations where everybody gets to know everybody else in no time. Hotels, opening onto beaches, are concentrated on the west coast of the island immediately north or immediately south of the capital of Kralendijk.

Remember that taxes and service charges are seldom included in the prices you're quoted, so ask about them when making your reservations. Be sure to read the section "Package Deals" in chapter 2 before you book a hotel on your own.

EXPENSIVE

Captain Don's Habitat ⋆ Built on a coral bluff overlooking the sea and a tiny beach about 5 minutes north of Kralendijk, this divers' resort, with an air of congenial informality, is for those whose souls belong to the sea. Habitat and its accompanying dive shop are the creation of Captain Don Stewart, Caribbean pioneer and "caretaker of the reefs," a former Californian who sailed his schooner from San Francisco through the Panama Canal, arriving on a reef in Bonaire in 1962—and he's been here ever since. Called the "godfather of diving" on the island, Captain Don was instrumental in the formation of the Bonaire Marine Park, whereby the entire island became a protected reef.

More than 90% of the guests here opt for one of the packages, which incorporate a variable number of dives with accommodations in settings ranging from standard double rooms to oceanfront villas, each with a bathroom with shower/tub combinations. The most popular arrangement is the 8-day/7-night package. Recent expansions have added on more upscale junior suites, plus villas with full kitchens and ocean-view verandas.

This resort has an oceanfront restaurant and two seaside bars. A casual, laid-back crowd gathers for good meals at Rum Runners, the social hub. Theme nights are staged weekly, which divert guests from the rather standard fare served here.

Kaya Gobernador N. Debrot 103, Pier 7, Bonaire, N.A. © **599/717-8290.** Fax 599/717-8240. For all reservations and business arrangements, contact Captain Don's Habitat, 903 South America Way, Miami, FL 33132 (© **800/327-6709;** fax 305/371-2337). www.habitatdiveresorts.com/BonaireHome.html. 84 units. Winter $1,566–$2,293 per person. Off-season $934–$1,373 per person. Rates are for 8-day/7-night stays and include breakfast, airport transfers, tax, service, equipment, 6 boat dives, and unlimited 24-hr. shore dives. AE, MC, V. **Amenities:** Restaurant, 2 bars; pool; dive program; babysitting; laundry. *In room:* A/C, TV, phone (in most units) kitchenette in some, hair dryer, safe.

The Deep Blue View ★★ *Finds*   A stay here is like having your own private villa. Small and intimate, it offers informal luxury and privacy, and is our favorite retreat on the island. Ideal if you want to sneak away with Julia Roberts (or Brad Pitt, if you're so inclined). In the Santa Barbara Heights district, each of the beautifully furnished guest rooms, with bathrooms with a tub and shower, comes with a large patio and pool area. Luxuriant foliage envelops the villa, which attracts honeymooners, families, and romantic couples, among others. All accommodations rest under vaulted ceilings and contain tiled floors and excellent bedding. The little extras count a lot here. The staff will even "brown bag" your breakfast if you've got an early flight, and when you head to the beach they give you thick towels, packed lunches, and cold drinks in coolers. From the villa's tiled patio, you experience an 180° vista of the Caribbean, whose color—deep blue—led to the name of the villa. As the sun goes down, you can enjoy your own happy hour or barbecue on the patio. Menneo de Bree, a dive instructor, will give you valuable tips on diving off the coast of Bonaire.

Santa Barbara Heights, Kaya Diamanta 50. © **599/717-8073.** Fax 599/717-7826. www.deepblueview.com. 4 units. Winter $1,050–1,365 per week double; $1,750 per week for 3 or 4. Off-season $1,260 per week double; $1,650 per week for 3 or 4. AE, DC, DISC, MC, V. **Amenities:** Pool; laundry. *In room:* A/C, ceiling fan, no phone.

Plaza Resort Bonaire ★   This luxury resort lies a short drive from the airport, on a strip of land midway between a saltwater lagoon and a sandy stretch of Caribbean beachfront. Designed in 1995 by a team of Italian architects, it resembles a white-sided village along the coast of southern Portugal, thanks to terra-cotta roofs and a pair of bridges that traverse the lagoon for easy access to the 12 acres (5 hectares) of grounds. It's an extremely large property for Bonaire, where most hotels are more intimate. Some units are privately owned. Rooms are quite large, though be aware that what management here refers to as suites are actually very large bedrooms, without interior dividers. Each contains a kitchenette, ceiling fans, and simple, summery furnishings. Most units are large and airy, with private balconies, and queen-sized beds. Bathrooms are roomy and luxurious, with showers and deep tubs.

Three on-site restaurants serve some of the island's best hotel food (see "Dining," below). The casino (see "Bonaire After Dark," later in this chapter) is the larger of two on the island. Some evenings, there's live entertainment.

J. A. Abraham Blvd. 80, Bonaire, N.A. © **800/766-6016** in the U.S., or 599/717-2500. Fax 599/717-7133. www.plazaresortbonaire.com. 200 units. Winter $205–$245 suite; $270–$290 1-bedroom apt.; $340–$370 2-bedroom apt. Off-season $155–$195 suite; $210–$230 1-bedroom apt.; $280–$310 2-bedroom apt. Extra person $30. AE, DC, MC, V. **Amenities:** 3 restaurants; 3 bars; pool; 4 tennis courts; casino; health club and spa; bikes; dive shop, windsurfing, boats, sailing, marina; children's programs. *In room:* A/C, TV, fridge, hair dryer, safe.

Port Bonaire Resort ★   Set within a short walk of the Plaza Resort Bonaire (see above) and operating under the same management, this small, upscale apartment complex is adjacent to the airport and not on a beach. Most of the luxurious units are rented out when their owners are away for at least part of the year, so they all have individual decor; they have sweeping views over the sea, fully equipped kitchens, washer/dryers, excellent bathrooms with shower/tub combinations, and maid service. A small, low-rise resort of three floors, this is a lovely complex, but it lags way behind the style and comfort of Plaza Resort Bonaire and Harbour Village Beach Resort. Guests can use any of the facilities at the Plaza Resort Bonaire.

J. A. Abraham Blvd. 80, Bonaire, N.A. © **800/766-6016** in the U.S., or 599/717-2500. Fax 599/717-7133. www.netcarib.com/bonaire/resort-bonaire.html. 24 units. Winter $210–$320 apt. (sleeps up to 4). Off-season $180–$280 apt. AE, DC, MC, V. **Amenities:** Pool; sundeck; private dock; parking. *In room:* A/C, TV, safe.

MODERATE

Divi Flamingo Beach Resort & Casino Divi is the comeback kid, having reinvented itself after a massive restoration. New furnishings, paint, tiles, and rejuvenated air-conditioning have made this once-tired old waterfront hostelry more comfortable than it's been in years. It began as a gone-to-seed hotel with a cluster of flimsy wooden bungalows used to intern German prisoners in World War II. With foresight and taste, the owners turned it into a resort, offering individual cottages and seafront rooms with private balconies resting on piers above the surf, so you can stand on your balcony and watch rainbow-hued tropical fish in the waters below.

The resort's original rooms were supplemented in 1986 with the addition of time-share units, forming Club Flamingo. These are the newest and best rooms, and each of the units is rentable by the day or the week. The accommodations in both sections are spacious and sunny, with ceiling fans and Mexican accents. The newer units are clustered into a green-and-white neo-Victorian pavilion facing its own curving pool. Each contains a kitchenette with carved cupboards and cabinets of pickled hardwoods. All units have well-kept bathrooms with shower/tub combinations.

A pair of restaurants, Chibi-Chibi and Calabase, provide satisfying, straightforward meals, nothing special.

J. A. Abraham Blvd., Bonaire, N.A. ℂ **800/367-3484** in the U.S., 919/419-3484 in Chapel Hill, NC, or 599/717-8285. Fax 599/717-8238. www.diviresorts.com. 129 units. Winter $130–$170 double; from $190 studio. Off-season $110–$120 double; from $140 studio. Rates about 10% higher between Christmas and New Year's. MAP (breakfast and dinner) $42 per person extra. Several inclusive packages offered. AE, DC, MC, V. **Amenities:** 2 restaurants, 3 bars; pool; casino; dive shop, snorkeling; laundry. *In room:* A/C, TV, no phone.

Sand Dollar Condominium Retreat ⭐ On a tiny beach, just 1½ miles (2km) north of Kralendijk and 3 miles (5km) north of the airport, this time share, with its festive, upbeat atmosphere, offers spacious studios and apartments with all the style, comfort, and convenience of a full-service hotel, although some units don't have a phone. All the accommodations are equipped with full kitchens, custom cabinets, and modern furnishings, including good beds, plus decks or balconies facing the ocean. Bathrooms with shower/tub combinations are average but well maintained. The beach is engulfed at high tide.

On the grounds is the Sand Dollar Terrace and Bar (see "Dining," below).

Kaya Gobernador N. Debrot 79, N.A. ℂ **800/288-4773** in the U.S., or 599/717-8738. Fax 599/717-8760. www.sandollarbonaire.com. 85 units. Winter $189 studio for 2; $228 1-bedroom apt.; $268 2-bedroom apt.; $402 3-bedroom apt. Off-season $167 studio; $195 1-bedroom apt.; $224 2-bedroom apt.; $336 3-bedroom apt. AE, DISC, MC, V. **Amenities:** Restaurant, bar; pool; 2 lighted tennis courts; dive shop. *In room:* A/C, TV, kitchen, no phone.

INEXPENSIVE

Carib Inn *Value* On a sliver of a beach, this inn, owned and managed by the American diver Bruce Bowker, is occupied by dedicated scuba divers drawn to its five-star PADI dive facility. This is the most intimate little diving resort on Bonaire and remains one of the island's best values. Eight rooms have kitchens, all units are equipped with fridges, and maid service is provided daily. The accommodations are furnished with tropical rattan pieces, and the bathrooms have been enlarged and refurbished, each with a shower stall. Repeat guests are likely to book this place far in advance in winter.

J. A. Abraham Blvd. (P.O. Box 68), Kralendijk, Bonaire, N.A. ℂ **599/717-8819.** Fax 599/717-5295. www.caribinn.com. 10 apts. Year-round $119 studio efficiency apt.; $139 1-bedroom apt.; $150 2-bedroom apt.; $169 3-bedroom house. Extra person $10. DISC, MC, V. *In room:* A/C, TV, kitchenette, no phone.

3 Dining

EXPENSIVE

Capriccio ✪ NORTHERN ITALIAN   One of the most charming (and most consistently booked) restaurants on Bonaire is run by Andrea Scandeletti and his wife, Lola, experienced Italian restaurateurs whose efforts were well-received before their exodus from Italy to Bonaire. In a small, pink-and-green dining room that has room for 50 diners, they prepare skillful interpretations of modern Italian cuisine based largely on olive oil, and only rarely on cream and butter. Pizzas emerge from a brick oven in at least 10 different variations, and can make a light meal for two with a salad. More fulfilling is the set-price menu, which includes carpaccio, seafood pasta, filet mignon, and tiramisu. A la carte items include a platter of smoked fish, savory pastas, prosciutto with hearts-of-palm salad, and pumpkin ravioli with Parmesan cheese and sage. The wine list is mostly Italian, with a few French choices. Dining options include an alfresco area, set across the coastal road from the sea (it can get very hot in midsummer), and a more comfortable air-conditioned interior studded with flickering candles in the evening.

Kaya Isla Riba 1, Kralendijk. ✆ **599/717-7230.** Reservations required. Pizzas and pastas $8–$21; main courses $20–$23; fixed-price menu $40. AE, MC, V. Mon and Wed–Sat noon–2pm; Wed–Mon 6:30–10:30pm.

Den Laman Restaurant ✪ SEAFOOD   Located between the Sunset Beach Hotel and the Sand Dollar Condominium Retreat, Den Laman serves the best seafood on Bonaire. An excellent beginning is the fish soup (the chef's special). You might move on to conch Flamingo, a local favorite, or lobster from the tank. The best dishes are grouper Creole and a tender, perfectly cooked New York sirloin steak. When it's featured, we always go for the red snapper meunière. Meals are served on a breezy seaside terrace, and a 6,000-gallon aquarium complements the decor.

Kaya Gobernador N. Debrot 77. ✆ **599/717-8955.** Reservations required. Main courses $18–$35. AE, MC, V. Wed–Mon 6–10pm. Closed Sept 1–22.

MODERATE

Beefeater Garden Restaurant CARIBBEAN/SEAFOOD   The name may lead you to believe that this is just a steak-and-ale joint. It isn't. In fact, it offers more vegetarian choices (at least five) than any other restaurant on Bonaire. It was established in the mid-1970s by an English expatriate ("Beefeater" Richard Dove) who was joined later by his German-born wife, Brigitte Kley, and the Venezuelan-born manager, Nelson France. Together, they maintain three indoor dining rooms and an artfully lit garden. Outside, near a convivial bar area, you can enjoy spinach or seafood crepes; seafood pasta; Curaçaon goat-meat stew; the catch of the day garnished with crabmeat, mussels, and fruit sauce; and a well-seasoned array of curry dishes (pork, shrimp, fish, and lamb). What should you do if you accidentally stumble in thinking the place is just a steakhouse? Order the filet steak—it's very good.

Kaya Grandi 12. ✆ **599/717-7776.** Main courses $8–$22. AE, DISC, MC, V. Thurs–Tues 11am–10:30pm.

Blue Moon INTERNATIONAL   This seafront bistro near the Divi Flamingo is in one of the island's oldest houses. Intimate tables and candlelight create a romantic ambience in the main restaurant, although you can dine less formally outside on the terrace overlooking the harbor. The menu always features the catch of the day as well as steak dishes. Sample a delectable stuffed chicken breast with mango, or jumbo shrimp hollandaise, followed by one of the home-made desserts. Finish off with one of their rich, Cuban-style coffees. Flavors are precisely defined, although nearly all ingredients have to be imported. Specials change daily.

Kaya Hellmund 5. ⓒ 599/717-8617. Reservations recommended. Main courses $12–$28. AE, MC, V. Tues–Sun 6–10pm.

The Caribbean Point *Value* INTERNATIONAL   This is the island's best deal. Everything is buffet style and all you can eat from breakfast to dinner, and you can drop in virtually any time. The food is kept fresh. The dinner menu is changed daily. Monday, for example, is Caribbean night, Wednesday is Italian night, and on Thursday there's an array of seafood. Other nights might be devoted to a French buffet or even a Pacific Rim buffet. On one night we attended the buffet was filled with the zesty flavors of Indonesia. Tuesday and Saturdays are beach barbecue nights at the hotel's Coconut Crash Bar.

Plaza Resort Bonaire, J. A. Abraham Blvd. 80. ⓒ 599/717-2500. Reservations recommended. Breakfast $12, lunch $19, dinner $27.50. AE, DC, MC, V. Daily 7am–10pm.

Mona Lisa ⭐ FRENCH/INTERNATIONAL   A local favorite on the main street of town, this is one of the best places for food that tastes homemade. The prices are more than reasonable, considering the quality of the food and the generous portions. Although many regulars come just to patronize the Dutch bar and catch up on the latest gossip, the old-fashioned dining room deserves serious attention. Guests enjoy the fresh fish of the day (often wahoo) or such meat dishes as a leg of lamb filet, tournedos, and sirloin steak. The most popular appetizers are onion soup, smoked fish, and shrimp cocktail. Mona Lisa is known for serving the freshest vegetables on an island where nearly everything is imported.

Kaya Grandi 15. ⓒ 599/717-8718. Reservations recommended. Main courses $15–$27; fixed-price menu $32.50. AE, MC, V. Mon–Fri 6–10pm.

Richard's Waterfront Dining ⭐⭐ STEAK/SEAFOOD   On a recent visit, we had our best meal on Bonaire here. On the airport side of Kralendijk, within walking distance of the Divi Flamingo Beach Resort, this restaurant, with its large covered terrace, was once a private home. Reasonable in price, it's the favorite of many locals who have sampled every restaurant on the island. Boston-born Richard Beady and his Aruban partner, Mario, operate a welcoming oasis with a happy hour at 5:30pm. Gathered around the coral bar, guests consider the chalkboard menu listing the offerings for the night: grilled wahoo or the fresh catch of the day, filet mignon béarnaise, U.S. sirloin with green-peppercorn sauce, scampi, or pasta. If it's on the menu, start with the fish soup. The menu is wisely kept small so that each night's entrees can be given the attention they deserve. The kitchen focuses on bringing out the natural flavors of a dish without overwhelming it with sauces or too many seasonings. You'll be welcomed with warm hospitality.

J. A. Abraham Blvd. 60. ⓒ 599/717-5263. Reservations recommended for groups of 6 or more. Main courses $15–$24. AE, MC, V. Tues–Sun 6:30–10:30pm.

Sand Dollar Terrace INTERNATIONAL   Along the poolside of a resort complex that's a 15-minute drive from the airport, this restaurant serves burgers, pasta, sandwiches, and seafood dishes. You can relax over a frozen tropical-fruit drink and watch the sunset. The food consistently ranks as some of the island's best, especially the charcoal-grilled fish (based on the catch of the day). You might also try the barbecued chicken and ribs, various U.S. beef cuts (from T-bone to filet mignon), garlic shrimp, or the highly flavored onion strings (like an onion loaf). Saturday nights bring a barbecue buffet with live entertainment. Come here for fun and good times.

In the Sand Dollar Condominium Retreat, Kaya Gobernador N. Debrot 79. ✆ **599/717-3985.** Reservations recommended. Main courses $12.50–$30; lunch $7–$10. AE, MC, V. Daily 7:30am–10:30pm.

Zeezicht Restaurant INTERNATIONAL   This is the best place in the capital to go for a sunset. Join the old salts or the people who live on boats to watch the sun go down, and try to see the "green flash" that Hemingway wrote about. Zeezicht (pronounced *ZAY-zict* and meaning "sea view") has long been popular for its excellent local cooking. It serves a small Indonesian *rijsttafel,* as well as fresh fish from the nearby fish market, plus lobster and steak.

Kaya Corsow 10. ✆ **599/717-8434.** Main courses $19–$35. AE, MC, V. Daily 8am–11pm.

4 Beaches

Come to Bonaire for the diving (see below), not the beaches. For the most part, the beaches are full of coral and feel gritty to bare feet. Those on the leeward side (the more tranquil side of the island) are often narrow strips. To compensate, some hotels have shipped in extra sand for their guests.

Pink Beach, south of Kralendijk, out past Salt Pier, is the best, despite its narrow strip of sand, shallow water, and lack of shade. It's aptly named: The beach really is a deep pink color, from the corals that have been pulverized into sand by the waves. Bring your own cooler and towels, as there are no refreshment stands or equipment rentals to mar the panoramic setting. It's also wise to bring along some sun protection, as the few palm trees bordering the dunes offer little shade. Enter the water at the southern end of this beach, as the northern tier has some exposed rock. Many Bonaireans flock here on weekends, but during the week you'll have the beach to yourself.

Bonaire's offshore island, tiny, uninhabited **Klein Bonaire,** just three-quarters of a mile (2km) offshore, has some of the most pristine beaches. Popular for snorkeling, scuba diving, and picnicking, **No Name Beach,** on the north side of Klein Bonaire, features a 300-yard (273m) white-sand beach. Snorkelers can see a rainbow of colorful fish darting through stunning formations of elkhorn coral. Accessible only by boat, Klein Bonaire is home to sea turtles and other indigenous wildlife. Ask at your hotel to see if arrangements can be made for reaching the island. **Playa Funchi,** within Washington-Slagbaai National Park, is good for snorkeling. Regrettably, it has almost no sand, there are no facilities, and the area surrounding the beach is a bit smelly. On one side of the beach, there's a lagoon where flamingos nest; snorkelers find the water most desirable on the other side. Also within the park, the more desirable **Boca Slagbaai** draws snorkelers and picnickers. You can spot flamingos nearby. A 19th-century building houses decent toilets and showers; drinks and snacks are also available. Don't venture into the waters barefoot, as the coral beach can be quite rough. A final beach at the national park is **Boca Cocolishi,** a black-sand strip on the northern coast. This is the windiest beach on Bonaire; you'll certainly stay cool as the trade winds whip the surf up. The waters are too rough for swimming, but it's a good picnic spot.

Many of Bonaire's beaches are situated along the east coast. The best spot for windsurfers is **Lac Bay Beach,** on the southern shore of Lac Bay. There are mangroves at the north end of the bay. A couple of windsurfing concessions usually operate here, and food and drink are available. One of the more unusual is **Nukove Beach,** a minicave in a limestone cliff with a small white-sand channel, which cuts through the dense wall of elkhorn coral near the shore, giving divers and snorkelers easy access to the water. Further north is **1,000 Steps Beach,** where 67 steps (although it can feel like 1,000 on the way back up) carved out of the limestone cliff lead to the white-sand beach. This beach offers good snorkeling and diving, a unique location and view, and nearly perfect solitude.

5 Diving & Snorkeling ✶✶✶

The true beauty on Bonaire is under the sea, where visibility is 100 feet (30m), 365 days of the year, and the water temperatures range from 78° to 82°F. One of the richest reef communities in the entire West Indies, Bonaire has plunging walls that descend to a sand bottom at 130 or so feet (39m). The reefs are home to various coral formations that grow at different depths, ranging from the knobby brain coral at 3 feet to staghorn and elkhorn up to about 10 feet (3m) deeper, and gorgonians, giant brain, and others. Swarms of rainbow-hued tropical fish inhabit the reefs, and the deep reef slope is home to a range of basket sponges, groupers, and moray eels. Most of the diving is done on the leeward side, where the ocean is lake flat. There are more than 40 dive sites on sharply sloping reefs.

The **Bonaire Marine Park** ✶✶ was created to protect the coral-reef ecosystem off Bonaire. The park incorporates the entire coastline of Bonaire and neighboring **Klein Bonaire.** The park is policed, and services and facilities include a Visitor Information Center at the **Karpata Ecological Center,** lectures, slide presentations, films, and permanent dive-site moorings.

Visitors are asked to respect the marine environment and to refrain from activities that may damage it, including sitting or walking on the coral. All marine life is completely protected. This means there's no fishing or collecting fish, shells, or corals—dead or alive. Spearfishing is forbidden, as is anchoring; all craft must use permanent moorings, except for emergency stops (boats shorter than 12 ft./4m may use a stone anchor). Most recreational activity in the marine park takes place on the island's leeward side and among the reefs surrounding Klein Bonaire.

Bonaire has a unique program for divers: The major hotels offer personalized, close-up encounters with the island's fish and other marine life under the expertise of Bonaire's dive guides.

Dive II, on the beachfront of the Divi Flamingo Beach Resort & Casino, J. A. Abraham Boulevard (© **599/717-8285**), north of Kralendijk, is among the island's most complete scuba facilities. It's open daily from 8am to 12:30pm and

---

Fun Fact The *Hooker*

The waters off the coast of Bonaire received an additional attraction in 1984. A rust-bottomed general cargo ship, 80 feet long (24m), was confiscated by the police, along with its contraband cargo, about 25,000 pounds of marijuana. Known as the *Hilma Hooker* (familiarly dubbed "The Hooker" by everyone on the island), it sank unclaimed (obviously) and without fanfare one calm day, in 90 feet (27m) of water. Lying just off the southern shore near the capital, its wreck is now a popular dive site.

1:30 to 5pm. It operates out of a well-stocked beachfront building, renting div-ing equipment and offering expeditions. A resort course for first-time divers costs $99; for experienced divers, a one-tank dive goes for $38.50, a two-tank dive for $55.

Captain Don's Habitat Dive Shop, Kaya Gobernador N. Debrot 103 (© **599/717-8290**), is a PADI five-star training facility. The open-air, full-service dive shop includes a classroom, photo/video lab, camera-rental facility, equipment repair, and compressor rooms. Habitat's slogan is "Diving Freedom": Divers can take their tanks and dive anywhere, day or night. Most head for "The Pike," a ½ mile of protected reef right in front of the property. The highly qual-ified staff is here to assist and advise, but not to police or dictate dive plans. Diving packages include boat dives, unlimited offshore diving (24 hr. a day), unlimited air, tanks, weights, and belts. Some dive packages also include accom-modations and meals (see "Accommodations," earlier in this chapter). If you're not staying at the hotel as part of a dive package, you can visit for a beach dive, costing $21. If you want to rent snorkeling equipment, the charge is $8.50 a day. A half day of diving, with all equipment, goes for $40.

Sand Dollar Dive and Photo, at the Sand Dollar Condominium Retreat, Kaya Gobernador N. Debrot (© **599/717-5252**), is open daily from 8:30am to 5:30pm. It offers dive packages, PADI and NAUI (National Association of Underwater Instructors) instruction, and equipment rental and repairs; boat and shore trips with an instructor are available by appointment. A beginning course, including two dives, costs $95 per person. The photo shop offers underwater photo and video shoots, PADI specialty courses by appointment, E-6 slide pro-cessing, print developing, and equipment rental and repair.

Bonaire's coral reefs are also an underwater paradise for snorkelers. They start in just inches of water and therefore have dense coral formations in very shallow surf. Most snorkeling on the island is conducted in 15 feet (5m) of water or less, and there's plenty to see even at this depth. As you travel around the island, par-ticularly in the northern area, you'll see evidence of prehistoric reefs now 30 to 40 feet (12m) above sea level, having lived submerged for hundreds of thousands of years and then uplifted as the island slowly rose.

Snorkeling equipment can be rented at the **Carib Inn,** J. A. Abraham Boule-vard (© **599/717-8819**); **Sand Dollar Dive and Photo,** Kaya Gobernador N. Debrot (© **599/717-5252**); and **Captain Don's Habitat Dive Shop,** Kaya Governador N. Debrot (© **599/717-8290**).

6 Sports & Other Outdoor Pursuits

The true beauty on Bonaire is under the sea, but sailing and birding are great, too.

BIRD-WATCHING   Bonaire is home to 190 species of birds, 80 of which are indigenous to the island. But most famous are its flamingos, which can number 10,000 during the mating season. For great places to bring your binoculars, see "Exploring the Island," below.

FISHING   The island's offshore fishing grounds offer some of the best fishing in the Caribbean. A good day's catch might include mackerel, tuna, wahoo, dol-phin (mahi-mahi), blue marlin, amberjack, grouper, sailfish, or snapper. Bonaire is also one of the best-kept secrets of bonefishing enthusiasts.

Your best bet is Chris Morkos of **Piscatur Fishing Supplies,** Kaya Herman 4, Playa Pabao (© **599/717-8774**). A native Bonairean, he has been fishing all his life. A maximum of 6 people are taken out on a 42-foot (13m) boat with a guide and captain, at a cost of $375 for a half day or $525 for a whole day, including all tackle and bait. Reef fishing is another popular sport, in boats averaging 15 and 19 feet (5 and 6m). A maximum of two people can go out for a half day at $250 or a whole day at $425. For the same price, a maximum of two people can fish for bonefish and tarpon on the island's large salt flats.

HIKING **Washington-Slagbaai National Park** (see "Exploring the Island," below) has a varied terrain; those ambitious enough to climb some of its steep hills are rewarded with panoramic views. The hiking possibilities are seemingly endless. Small hidden beaches with crashing waters by the cliffs provide an ideal place for a picnic.

MOUNTAIN BIKING Biking is an ideal way to see Bonaire's hidden beauty; you can explore more than 186 miles (299km) of trails and dirt roads, venturing off the beaten path to enjoy the scenery. Ask at the tourist office for a trail map that outlines the most scenic routes. You can check with your hotel about arranging a trip, or call **Cycle Bonaire,** Kaya L. D. Gerharts 11D (© **599/ 717-7558**), which rents 21-speed mountain bikes and arranges half- and full-day excursions. The cost is $55 and $80, respectively, in addition to the bike-rental charges.

SEA KAYAKING Paddle the protected waters of Lac Bay, or head for the miles of flats and mangroves in the south (the island's nursery), where you can see baby fish and wildlife. Kayak rentals are available at **Jibe City,** Lac Bay (© **599/717-5233**), for $25 per half day or $35 for a full day.

TENNIS There are two courts, lit for night play, at the **Sand Dollar Condominium Retreat,** Kaya Governador N. Debrot 79 (© **800/288-4773**).

WINDSURFING Consistent conditions, enjoyed by windsurfers with a wide range of skill levels, make the shallow, calm waters of Lac Bay the island's home to the sport. Call **Bonaire Windsurfing** (© **599/717-2288**) for details. A half day costs $40.

7 Exploring the Island

Bonaire Sightseeing Tours (© **599/717-8778**) will show you the island, both north and south, taking in the flamingos, slave huts, conch shells, Goto Lake, the Amerindian inscriptions, and other sights. Each of these tours lasts 2 hours and costs $18 per person. You can also take a half-day City and Country Tour, lasting 3 hours and costing from $25.50 per person, which allows you to see the entire northern section and the southern part as far as the slave huts.

KRALENDIJK

Kralendijk is often referred to by locals as *Playa,* Spanish for "beach." A dollhouse town of some 2,500 residents, Kralendijk is small, neat, pretty, Dutch-clean, and just a bit dull. Its stucco buildings are painted pink and orange, with an occasional lime green. The capital's jetty is lined with island sloops and fishing boats.

Kralendijk nestles in a bay on the west coast, opposite **Klein Bonaire,** or Little Bonaire, an uninhabited, low-lying islet that's a 10-minute boat ride away.

The main street of town leads along the beachfront on the harbor. A Protestant church was built in 1834, and **St. Bernard's Roman Catholic Church** has some interesting stained-glass windows.

At **Fort Oranje,** you'll see a lone cannon dating from the days of Napoleon. If possible, try to get up early to visit the **Fish Market** on the waterfront, where you'll see a variety of strange and brilliantly colored fish.

THE TOUR NORTH

The road north is one of the most beautiful stretches in the Antilles, with turquoise waters on your left and coral cliffs on your right. You can stop at several points along this road, where there are paved paths for strolling or bicycling.

After leaving Kralendijk and passing the Sunset Beach Hotel and the desalination plant, you'll come to **Radio Nederland Wereld Omroep (Dutch World Radio).** It's a 13-tower, 300,000-watter. Opposite the transmitting station is a lovers' promenade, built by nature; it's an ideal spot for a picnic.

Continuing, you'll pass the storage tanks of the Bonaire Petroleum Corporation, the road heading to **Goto Meer,** the island's inland sector, with a saltwater lake. Several flamingos prefer this spot to the salt flats in the south.

Down the hill, the road leads to a section called **Dos Pos** ("two wells"); the palm trees and vegetation here are a contrast to the rest of the island, where only the drought-resistant kibraacha and divi-divi trees, tilted before the constant wind, can grow, along with forests of cacti.

Bonaire's oldest village is **Rincón.** Slaves who used to work in the salt flats in the south once lived here. The Rincón Ice Cream Parlour makes homemade ice cream in a variety of interesting flavors; there are also a couple of bars here. Above the bright roofs of the village is the crest of a hill called Para Mira, which means "stop and look."

A side path outside Rincón takes you to some **Arawak inscriptions** supposedly 500 years old. The petroglyph designs are in pink-red dye. At nearby **Boca Onima,** you'll find grotesque grottoes of coral.

Before going back to the capital, you might take a short bypass to **Seroe Largu,** which has a good view of Kralendijk and the sea. Lovers frequent the spot at night.

THE NATIONAL PARK

Washington-Slagbaai National Park ★★ (© 599/717-8444) has a varied terrain that includes desertlike areas, secluded beaches, caverns, and a bird sanctuary. Occupying 15,000 acres (6,000 hectares) of Bonaire's northwesternmost territory, the park was once plantation land, producing divi-divi, aloe, and charcoal, and now it exists as a wildlife preserve.

You can see the park in a few hours, although it takes days to appreciate it fully. If you want to drive through the park, you must use a four-wheel-drive vehicle. Even so, if it's rained recently, consider not going—even with a four-wheel drive—as the roads quickly become deeply mired in mud and difficult to navigate. There are two routes: a 15-mile (24km) "short" route, marked by green arrows, and a 22-mile (35km) "long" route, marked by yellow arrows. The roads are well marked and safe, but somewhat rugged, although they're gradually being improved. For those wanting a closer look, the hiking possibilities are nearly endless. The entrance fee is $10 for adults and $2 for children age 11 and under. The park is open daily except holidays from 8am to 5pm. You must enter before 3pm.

Whichever route you take, there are a few important stops you shouldn't miss. Just past the gate is **Salina Mathijs,** a salt flat that's home to flamingos during the rainy season. Beyond the salt flat on the road to the right is **Boca Chiquito,** a white-sand beach and bay. A few miles up the beach lies **Boca Cocolishi,** a two-part black-sand beach. Many a couple has raved about their romantic memories of this beach, perfect for a secluded picnic. Its deep, rough seaward side and calm, shallow basin are separated by a ridge of calcareous algae. The basin and the beach were formed by small pieces of coral and mollusk shells (*cocolishi* means "shells"), thus the black sand. The basin itself has no current, so it's perfect for snorkeling close to shore.

The main road leads to **Boca Bartol,** a bay full of living and dead elkhorn coral, sea fans, and reef fish. A popular watering hole good for bird-watching is **Poosdi Mangel. Wajaca** is a remote reef, perfect for divers and home to the island's most exciting sea creatures, including turtles, octopuses, and triggerfish. Immediately inland towers 788-foot (236m) **Mount Brandaris,** Bonaire's highest peak, at whose foot is **Bronswinkel Well,** a watering spot for pigeons and parakeets. Some 130 species of birds live in the park, many with such exotic names as bananaquit and black-faced grassquit. Bonaire has few mammals, but you'll see goats and donkeys, perhaps even a wild bull.

HEADING SOUTH

Leaving the capital again, you pass the **Trans World Radio antennae,** towering 500 feet (150m) in the air, transmitting with 810,000 watts. This is one of the hemisphere's most powerful medium-wave radio stations, the loudest voice in Christendom, and the most powerful nongovernmental broadcast station in the world. It sends out interdenominational Gospel messages and hymns in 20 languages to places as far away as Eastern Europe and the Middle East.

You then come to the **salt flats** ⚐, where the brilliantly colored pink flamingos live. Bonaire shelters the largest accessible nesting and breeding grounds in the world. The flamingos build high mud mounds to hold their eggs. The best time to see the birds is in spring, when they're usually nesting and tending their young. The salt flats were once worked by slaves, and the government has rebuilt some primitive stone huts, bare shelters little more than waist high. The slaves slept in these huts, and returned to their homes in Rincon in the north on weekends. The centuries-old salt pans have been reactivated by the International Salt Company. Near the salt pans, you'll see some 30-foot (9m) obelisks in white, blue, and orange, built in 1838 to help mariners locate their proper anchorages.

Farther down the coast is the island's oldest lighthouse, **Willemstoren,** built in 1837. Still farther along, **Sorobon Beach, Lac Bay Beach,** and **Boca Cai** come into view. They're at landlocked Lac Bay, which is ideal for swimming and snorkeling. Conch shells are stacked up on the beach. The water here is so vivid and clear, you can see coral 65 to 120 feet (20–36m) down in the reef-protected waters.

8 Shopping

Walk along Kaya Grandi in Kralendijk to see an assortment of goods, including gemstone jewelry, wood, leather, sterling, ceramics, liquors, and tobacco, priced 25% to 50% less than in the United States and Canada. Prices are often quoted in U.S. dollars, and major credit cards and traveler's checks are usually accepted.

Benetton, Kaya Grandi 49 (© **599/717-5107**), has invaded the island and offers its brightly colored merchandise at prices about one-quarter less than most U.S. outlets, or so it is said.

Littman Jewelers, Kaya Grandi 33 (© **599/717-8160**), sells Tag Heuer dive watches and also carries Daum French crystal and Lladró Spanish porcelain.

Next door is **Littman's Gifts,** selling standard and hand-painted T-shirts, plus sandals, hats, Gottex swimsuits, gift items, costume jewelry, and toys.

Although hardly great, there are some other stores you might want to visit, including **Best Buddies,** Kaya Grandi 32 (© 599/717-7570), which is known for its *pareos* or beach wraps and its batiks from Indonesia. Nearby at **Island Fashions,** Kaya Grandi 5 (© 599/717-7565), you can pick up the latest swimwear.

9 Bonaire After Dark

Underwater **slide shows** provide entertainment for both divers and nondivers. The best shows are at **Captain Don's Habitat** (© 599/717-8290; see "Diving & Snorkeling," earlier in this chapter). Shows are presented in the hotel bar, Rum-Runner, Thursday night from 7 to 8:30pm.

Divi Flamingo Beach Resort & Casino, J. A. Abraham Boulevard (© 599/717-8285), promoted as "The World's First Barefoot Casino," offers blackjack, roulette, poker, wheel of fortune, video games, and slot machines. Gambling on the island is regulated by the government. Entrance is free; hours are Monday to Saturday from 8pm to 2am.

Plaza Resort Bonaire Casino, J. A. Abraham Blvd. 80 (© 599/717-2500), is the larger of Bonaire's two casinos—and usually the noisier and more animated. It glitters, vibrates, and jangles with the sound of slot machines that cover entire walls, plus gaming tables that purvey all the games of chance you might want. It's open daily from 8pm to 4am. Jackets and ties aren't required, but shorts after dark are frowned upon.

Karel's Beach Bar, on the waterfront (© 599/717-8434), is almost Tahitian in its high-ceilinged, Tiki hut design. This popular place is perched above the sea on stilts. You can sit at the long rectangular bar with many of the island's dive and boating professionals, or select a table near the balustrades overlooking the illuminated surf. Local bands entertain on weekends. Drink prices are reduced during happy hour, from 5:30 to 7pm. Because Bonaire is a Dutch island, Heineken is the beer of choice, but you might also sample Polar from nearby Venezuela or else Amstel from the fraternal island of Curaçao.

We nominate the **City Cafe,** Kaya Grandi 7 (© 599/717-8286), as the island's funkiest bar. Painted in screaming shades of electric blue, scarlet magenta, and banana, this bar is a popular local hangout with a no-holds-barred vibe.

The island's leading disco is **The Fantasy,** Kaya L. D. Gerharts 11 (© 599/717-6345). A DJ spins the latest tunes from the U.S. and spices it up with some Jamaican reggae, popular with locals. On rare occasions some live group of island musicians comes in to entertain. There's also a wide-screened television to keep you amused when you can't find a dancing partner.

8

The British Virgin Islands

With their small bays and hidden coves, the British Virgin Islands are among the world's loveliest sailing grounds. Strung over the northeastern corner of the Caribbean, about 60 miles (97 miles) east of Puerto Rico, are some 40 islands (although that's including some small, uninhabited cays or spits of land). Only three of the British Virgins are of any significant size: Tortola (which means "Dove of Peace"), Virgin Gorda ("Fat Virgin"), and Jost Van Dyke. Remote Norman Island is said to have been the inspiration for Robert Louis Stevenson's *Treasure Island*. On Deadman Bay, a rocky cay, Blackbeard marooned 15 pirates and a bottle of rum, which gave rise to the ditty.

Columbus came this way in 1493, but the British Virgins apparently made little impression on him. Although the Spanish and Dutch contested it, Tortola was officially annexed by the English in 1672. Today these islands are a British colony, with their own elected government and a population of about 17,000.

The vegetation is varied and depends on the rainfall. In some parts, palms and mangos grow in profusion, whereas other places are arid and studded with cactus.

There are predictions that mass tourism is on the way, but so far the British Virgins are still a paradise for those who want to get away from it all in a peaceful, stunningly beautiful setting.

1 British Virgin Islands Essentials

VISITOR INFORMATION

Before you go, contact the **British Virgin Islands Tourist Board,** 370 Lexington Ave., Suite 313, New York, NY 10017 (© **212/696-0400**). Other branches of the **British Virgin Islands Information Office** are located at Culver City, Los Angeles, CA 90231 (© **310/287-2200**); and 3390 Peachtree Rd. NE, Suite 1000, Lenox Towers, Atlanta, GA 30326 (© **404/240-8018**).

In the United Kingdom, contact the **B.V.I. Information Office,** 54 Baker St., London WIM 1DJ (© **020/7240-4259**).

The tourist board's official website is **www.bviwelcome.com.**

GETTING THERE

BY PLANE There are no direct flights from New York to the British Virgin Islands (B.V.I.), but you can make connections from San Juan and St. Thomas to Beef Island/Tortola (see chapters 17 and 26 for information on flying to these islands).

Your best bet to reach Beef Island/Tortola is to take **American Eagle** (© **800/433-7300** in the U.S.; www.aa.com), which has dozens of flights to its hub in San Juan, and then at least four daily trips from San Juan to Beef Island/Tortola.

The British Virgin Islands

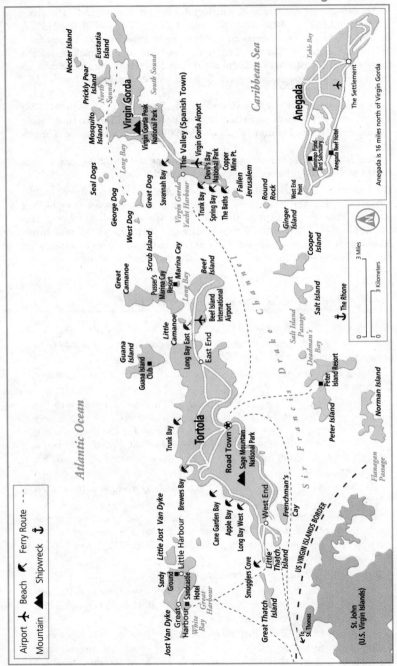

Airport ✈ Beach ⌐ Ferry Route ---
Mountain ▲ Shipwreck ⚓

Atlantic Ocean

Caribbean Sea

Anegada

Table Bay

The Settlement

Flamingo Pond Bird Sanctuary
Anegada Reef Hotel

West End Point

Anegada is 16 miles north of Virgin Gorda

Necker Island

Eustatia Island

Prickly Pear Island

Mosquito Island

North Sound

South Sound

Virgin Gorda

Virgin Gorda Peak National Park

The Valley (Spanish Town)

Virgin Gorda Airport

Devil's Bay National Park

Copper Mine Pt.

Fallen Jerusalem

Round Rock

Long Bay

Seal Dogs

George Dog

West Dog

Great Dog

Savannah Bay

Virgin Gorda Yacht Harbour

Trunk Bay

Spring Bay

The Baths

Ginger Island

Cooper Island

Great Camanoe

Scrub Island

Pusser's Marina Cay Resort

Marina Cay

Long Bay

Beef Island

Beef Island International Airport

Guana Island

Guana Island Club

Little Camanoe

Long Bay East

East End

Salt Island

The Rhone ⚓

Salt Island Passage

Deadman's Bay

Peter Island Resort

Peter Island

Norman Island

D r a k e   C h a n n e l

S i r   F r a n c i s

Trunk Bay

Tortola

Road Town ✈

Sage Mountain National Park

West End

Frenchman's Cay

Little Thatch Island

US VIRGIN ISLANDS BORDER

Flanagan Passage

Brewers Bay

Cane Garden Bay

Apple Bay

Long Bay West

Smugglers Cove

Great Thatch Island

Little Harbour

Little Jost Van Dyke

Sandy Ground

Jost Van Dyke

Great Harbour

White Bay

Sandcastle Hotel

St. John (U.S. Virgin Islands)

To St. Thomas

St. Thomas

3 Miles

3 Kilometers

187

Another choice, if you're on one of Tortola's neighboring islands, is the much less reliable **LIAT** (© **800/468-0482** in the U.S. and Canada, 284/495-2577, or 284/495-1187). This Caribbean carrier makes the short hop to Tortola from St. Kitts, Antigua, St. Maarten, St. Thomas, and San Juan in small planes not known for their frequency or careful scheduling. Reservations are made through travel agents or through the larger U.S.-based airlines that connect with LIAT hubs.

Two minor airlines winging in include **Air Sunshine** (© **284/495-1122**) flying between San Juan or St. Thomas to Beef Island (Tortola) and Virgin Gorda, and **Air St. Thomas** (© **284/495-8900**), going between St. Thomas and Virgin Gorda.

Beef Island, the site of the major airport serving the British Virgins, is connected to Tortola by the one-lane **Queen Elizabeth Bridge.**

BY FERRY You can travel from Charlotte Amalie (St. Thomas) by public ferry to West End and Road Town on Tortola, a 45-minute voyage along Drake's Channel through the islands. Boats making this run include **Native Son** (© **284/495-4617**), **Smith's Ferry Service** (© **284/495-4495**), and **Inter-Island Boat Services** (© **284/495-4166**). The latter specializes in a somewhat obscure routing—that is, from St. John to the West End on Tortola.

 FAST FACTS: The British Virgin Islands

American Express There are local representatives on Tortola.

Banking Hours Banks are generally open Monday through Thursday from 9am to 3pm, Friday from 9am to 5pm.

Currency The U.S. dollar is the legal currency, much to the surprise of British travelers.

Customs You can bring items intended for your personal use into the British Virgin Islands. For U.S. residents, the duty-free allowance is only $400, providing you have been out of the country for 48 hours. You can send unsolicited gifts home if they total less than $50 per day to any single address. You don't have to pay duty on items classified as handcrafts, art, or antiques.

Electricity The electrical current is 110-volt AC (60 cycles), as in the United States.

Entry Requirements U.S. citizens and Canadians need a valid passport or a birth certificate with a raised seal along with a government-issued photo ID (we recommend that you carry a passport). U.K. residents need a valid passport.

Language The official language is English.

Liquor Laws Alcoholic beverages can be sold any day of the week, including Sunday. You can have an open container on the beach, but be careful not to litter, or you might be fined.

Mail Postal rates in the British Virgin Islands are 30¢ for a postcard (airmail) to the United States or Canada, 50¢ for a first-class airmail letter (½ oz) to the United States or Canada, or 35¢ for a second-class letter (½ oz) to the United States or Canada.

Maps The best map of the British Virgin Islands is published by Vigilate and is sold at most bookstores in Road Town.

Medical Assistance The B.V.I.'s major hospital is on Tortola; the island has more than a dozen doctors. There's only one doctor practicing on Virgin Gorda. If you need medical help, your hotel will put you in touch with the islands' medical staff.

Newspapers & Magazines The B.V.I. has no daily newspaper, but the *Island Sun*, published Wednesday and Friday, is a good source of information on local entertainment, as is the *Beacon*, published on Thursday.

Safety Crime is rare here; in fact, the British Virgin Islands are among the safest places in the Caribbean. Still, you should take all the usual precautions you would anywhere, and don't leave items unattended on the beach.

Taxes There is no sales tax. A government tax of 7% is imposed on all hotel rooms. A $10 departure tax is collected from everyone leaving by air, $5 for those departing by sea.

Telephone You can call the British Virgins from the United States by just dialing **1**, the area code **284**, and the number. From all public phones and from some hotels, you can access **AT&T Direct** by dialing ✆ **800/872-2881**. You can reach **MCI** at ✆ **800/999-9000** and **Sprint** at ✆ **800/877-8000**.

Time The islands operate on Atlantic standard time year-round. In the peak winter season, when it's 10am in the British Virgins, it's 9am in Florida. However, when Florida and the rest of the U.S. east coast go on daylight saving time, the clocks do not change here.

Tipping & Service Charges Most hotels add on a 5% to 15% service charge; ask if it's already included when you're initially quoted a price. A 10% service charge is often (but not always) added on to restaurant bills; you can leave another 5% if you thought the service was unusually good. You usually don't need to tip taxi drivers, since most own their own cabs, but you can tip 10% if they've been unusually helpful.

Water The tap water in the British Virgin Islands is safe to drink.

2 Tortola ★★

Most visitors head to Virgin Gorda if they want to check into one of the posh, secluded inns and stay there, and they barely leave the grounds. Tortola, on the other hand, offers a larger selection of accommodations, many at more moderate prices. Here you'll sample more of the local life, ranging from visiting colorful markets to sailing. Tortola has more shopping, restaurants, attractions, nightlife, and diversions than Virgin Gorda. It also boasts one of the great beaches of the Caribbean, Cane Garden Bay.

On the southern shore of this 24-square-mile (62 sq. km) island is **Road Town,** the capital of the British Virgin Islands. It's the seat of Government House and other administrative buildings, but it feels more like a small village than a town. The landfill at Wickhams Cay, a 70-acre (28-hectare) town center development and marina in the harbor, has lured a massive yacht-chartering business here and has transformed the sleepy capital into more of a bustling center.

The entire southern coast, including Road Town, is characterized by rugged mountain peaks. On the northern coast are white sandy beaches, banana trees, mangos, and clusters of palms.

Close to Tortola's eastern end, **Beef Island** is the site of the main airport for passengers arriving in the British Virgins. The tiny island is connected to Tortola by the one-lane Queen Elizabeth Bridge, which the queen dedicated in 1966. On the north shore of Beef Island is Long Bay Beach.

ESSENTIALS

VISITOR INFORMATION A **B.V.I. Tourist Board Office,** at the center of Road Town near the ferry dock (© **284/494-3134**), has information about hotels, restaurants, tours, and more. Pick up a copy of *The Welcome Tourist Guide,* which has a useful map of the island.

GETTING THERE Because Tortola is the gateway to the British Virgin Islands, the information on how to get here is covered at the beginning of this chapter.

GETTING AROUND Taxis meet every arriving flight. Government regulations prohibit anyone from renting a car at the airport, so you'll have to take a taxi to your hotel. The fare from the Beef Island airport to Road Town is $18 for 1 to 3 passengers. A **taxi tour** lasting 2½ hours costs $45 for 1 to 3 people. To call a taxi in Road Town, dial © **284/494-2322;** on Beef Island, © **284/495-2378.**

A handful of local companies and U.S.-based chains rent cars. **Itgo** (© **284/ 494-2639**) is located at 1 Wickhams Cay, Road Town; **Avis** (© **800/331-1212** in the U.S., or 284/494-3322 on Tortola; www.avis.com) maintains offices opposite police headquarters in Road Town; and **Hertz** (© **800/654-3001** in the U.S., or 284/495-4405 on Tortola; www.hertz.com) has offices outside Road Town, on the island's West End, near the ferryboat landing dock. Rental companies will usually deliver your car to your hotel. All three companies require a valid driver's license and a temporary B.V.I. driver's license, which the car-rental agency can sell you for $10; it's valid for 3 months. Because of the volume of tourism to Tortola, you should reserve a car in advance, especially in winter.

Remember to *drive on the left.* Roads are pretty well paved, but they're often narrow, windy, and poorly lit, and they have few, if any, lines, so driving at night can be tricky. It's a good idea to rent a taxi to take you to that difficult-to-find beach, restaurant, or bar.

Scato's Bus Service (© **284/494-2365**) operates from the north end of the island to the west end, picking up passengers who hail it down. Fares for a trek across the island are $1 to $3.

FAST FACTS The local **American Express** representative is Travel Plan, Waterfront Drive (© **284/494-2347**).

Local bank branches include the **Bank of Nova Scotia,** Wickhams Cay (© **284/494-2526**), or **Barclays Bank,** Wickhams Cay (© **284/494-2171**), both near Road Town. There's also a branch of **Chase Manhattan Bank** at Road Town on Wickhams Cay (© **284/494-2662**), with an ATM.

The best place for camera supplies and developing on Tortola is **Bolos Brothers,** Wickhams Cay (© **284/494-2867**).

For dental emergencies, contact **Dental Surgery** (© **284/494-3274**), in Road Town, behind the Skeleton Building and next to the *BVI Beacon,* the local newspaper.

Tortola

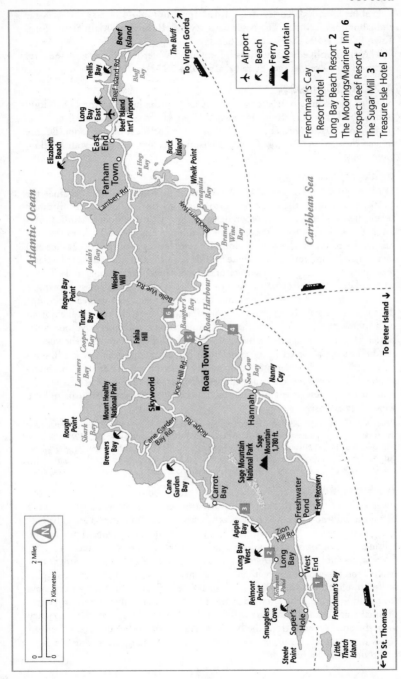

Key:
- ✈ Airport
- ⚓ Beach
- ⛴ Ferry
- ▲ Mountain

Frenchman's Cay Resort Hotel **1**
Long Bay Beach Resort **2**
The Moorings/Mariner Inn **6**
Prospect Reef Resort **4**
The Sugar Mill **3**
Treasure Isle Hotel **5**

Atlantic Ocean

Caribbean Sea

To Virgin Gorda
To Peter Island →
← To St. Thomas

Beef Island
The Bluff
Trellis Bay
Bluff Bay
Long Bay East
Beef Island Int'l Airport
Elizabeth Beach
East End
Buck Island
Fat Hogs Bay
Whelk Point
Parham Town
Lambert Rd.
Paraquita Bay
Brandy Wine Bay
Josiah's Bay
Rogue Bay Point
Wesley Will
Belle Vue Rd.
Cooper Bay
Trunk Bay
Fahia Hill
Bauguher's Bay
Blackburn Hwy.
Road Harbour
Larimers Bay
Mount Healthy National Park
Skyworld
Joe's Hill Rd.
Road Town
Rough Point
Shark Bay
Brewers Bay
Cane Garden Bay Rd.
Ridge Rd.
Sea Cow Bay
Nanny Cay
Cane Garden Bay
Carrot Bay
Sage Mountain National Park
Sage Mountain 1,780 ft.
Hannah
Apple Bay
Long Bay West
Long Bay
Zion Hill Rd.
Freshwater Pond
Fort Recovery
West End
Belmont Point
Richman Trail
Smugglers Cove
Soper's Hole
Frenchman's Cay
Steele Point
Little Thatch Island

2 Miles
2 Kilometers
0
0

191

Peebles Hospital, Porter Road, Road Town (© **284/494-3497**), has X-ray and laboratory facilities. The best pharmacy is **J. R. O'Neal,** Main Street, Road Town (© **284/494-2292**); closed Sunday.

The main **police headquarters** is located on Waterfront Drive near the ferry docks on Sir Olva Georges Plaza (© **284/494-3822**).

ACCOMMODATIONS

None of the island's hotels is as big or splashy as the hotels in the U.S. Virgin Islands, and that's just fine with most of Tortola's repeat visitors. All rates are subject to a 10% service charge and a 7% government tax on the room. Be sure to read the section "Package Deals" in chapter 2 before you book your hotel on your own.

VERY EXPENSIVE

Long Bay Beach Resort ★★   A favorite of sophisticated travelers since the 1960s, this resort is the finest on Tortola and lies on a mile-long (2km) sandy beach. It completed a recent upgrade by adding 18 new poolside studios. In a lovely setting on the north shore, about 10 minutes from West End, it's the only full-service resort on the island, a low-rise complex set in a 52-acre (21-hectare) estate. The accommodations include hillside rooms and studios, the smallest and most basic with simple furnishings, and deluxe beachfront rooms and cabanas with either balconies or patios that overlook the ocean. The resort also offers two- and three-bedroom villas complete with a kitchen, living area, and large deck with a gas grill. If you're not staying right on the beach, you'll still enjoy an ocean view from any of the other accommodations. All units have one four-poster king or two queen-size beds, plus large bathrooms with tiled showers.

The Beach Café is set in the ruins of an old sugar mill. The Garden Restaurant offers dinner by reservation only and a tantalizing variety of local and international dishes in a more elegant, alfresco setting of tropical gardens. The cuisine is among the finest of any hotel on the island, especially the fresh fish, and the wine list is extensive.

Tortola, B.V.I. © **800/729-9599** in the U.S. and Canada, or 284/495-4252. Fax 914/833-3318 in Larchmont, NY. www.longbay.com. 120 units. Winter $275–$395 double; $595–$650 2-bedroom villa; $850–$925 3-bedroom villa. Off-season $155–$210 double; $320–$350 2-bedroom villa; $450–$485 3-bedroom villa. MAP (breakfast and dinner) $48 per person extra. AE, MC, V. **Amenities:** 2 restaurants; 3 bars; 2 pools; 3 tennis courts; snorkeling; children's program (ages 3–8); car rental; babysitting; laundry. *In room:* A/C, TV, hair dryer, safe.

The Sugar Mill ★   Set in a lush tropical garden on the site of a 300-year-old sugar mill on the north side of Tortola, this secluded cottage colony sweeps down the hillside to its own little beach, with vibrant flowers and fruits brightening the grounds. Well furnished and comfortable apartments climb up the hillside. The accommodations are contemporary and well designed, ranging from suites and cottages to studio apartments, all self-contained with kitchenettes and private terraces with views. Rooms have twin or king-size beds, plus well-maintained private bathrooms with showers. Four of the units are suitable for families of four. The latest addition, the Plantation House suites, evoke traditional Caribbean architecture, with fine stone work, breezy porches, and lacy gingerbread. Just steps from the beach, a pair of two-bedroom air-conditioned suites have tropical decor and sea views. Each has a king-size bed and a large bathroom with double sinks.

Lunch or dinner is served down by the beach at Islands, which features Caribbean specialties along with burgers and salads. Dinner is also offered at the Sugar Mill Restaurant (see "Dining," below).

Apple Bay (P.O. Box 425), Road Town, Tortola, B.V.I. ℭ 800/462-8834 in the U.S., or 284/495-4355. Fax 284/495-4696. www.sugarmillhotel.com. 24 units. Winter $310 double; $325 triple; $340 quad; $635 2-bedroom villa. Off-season $190–$245 double; $240–$260 triple; $255–$275 quad; $490–$530 2-bedroom villa. AE, MC, V. Closed Aug–Sept. Children age 11 and under not accepted in winter. **Amenities:** 2 restaurants, 2 bars; pool; snorkeling; babysitting; laundry. *In room:* A/C, kitchenette, fridge, coffeemaker, hair dryer, iron and ironing board.

EXPENSIVE

Frenchman's Cay Resort Hotel ★   This intimate resort is tucked away at the windward side of Frenchman's Cay, a little island connected by bridge to Tortola. The 12-acre (5-hectare) estate enjoys delightful year-round breezes and views of Sir Francis Drake Channel and the outer Virgins. The individual one- and two-bedroom villas (actually a cluster of condos) are well furnished, each with a shady terrace, full kitchen, dining room, and sitting room. Each two-bedroom villa has two full bathrooms—a vacation in and of itself for families looking to escape the morning bathroom line. Pastel colors and tropical styling make for inviting accommodations, and each unit has good linen and shower stalls. There's a small beach with rocks offshore; it's best for snorkeling. The Clubhouse Restaurant and lounge bar are located in the main pavilion, with a good continental and Caribbean menu.

West End (P.O. Box 1054), Tortola, B.V.I. ℭ 800/235-4077 in the U.S., 800/463-0199 in Canada, or 284/495-4844. Fax 284/495-4056. www.frenchmans.com. 9 units. Winter $260 1-bedroom villa; $390 2-bedroom villa. Off-season $150–$170 1-bedroom villa; $225–$260 2-bedroom villa. MAP (breakfast and dinner) $50 per person extra. AE, DISC, MC, V. From Tortola, cross the bridge to Frenchman's Cay, turn left, and follow the road to the eastern tip of the cay. **Amenities:** Restaurant, bar; pool; tennis court; horseback riding; island tours; sailing, kayaking, windsurfing, snorkeling; car rental. *In room:* Ceiling fan, kitchen.

The Moorings/Mariner Inn ★   Near Road Town, the Caribbean's most complete yachting resort is outfitted with at least 180 sailing yachts, some worth $2 million or more. On an 8-acre (3-hectare) resort, the inn was obviously designed with the yachting crowd in mind, and it offers not only support facilities and services but also shore-side accommodations. You experience more of town life here, as opposed to the seclusion of the resorts described above; it's a lively spot that's close to restaurants, shops, and bars. The rooms are spacious; all suites have kitchenettes, and most of them open onto the water. The rooms contain refrigerators, plus shower stalls. Obviously the boaties get more attention here than do the landlubbers. The nearest beach is Cane Garden Bay, about 15 minutes away by car; you'll either have to drive there in a rental car or take a taxi.

Wickhams Cay (P.O. Box 139), Road Town, Tortola, B.V.I. ℭ 800/535-7289 in the U.S., or 284/494-2332. Fax 284/494-2226. www.moorings.com. 40 units. Winter $170 double; $230 suite. Off-season $95 double; $125 suite. Extra person $15. MC, V. **Amenities:** Restaurant, 2 bars; pool; tennis court; room service; market; dive shop that rents underwater video cameras. *In room:* A/C, fridge, hair dryer.

Treasure Isle Hotel ★   The most centrally located resort on Tortola is built at the edge of the capital on 15 acres (6 hectares) of hillside overlooking a marina (not on the beach). The core of this attractive hotel is a rather splashy and colorful open-air bar done in vibrant colors and boasting lovely views. The motel-like, midsize rooms are on two levels along the hillside terraces; a third level is occupied by more elegantly decorated suites at the crest of a hill. Tropical touches such as local art, tile floors, white stucco walls, floral upholstery, and white rattan make for an inviting atmosphere. Each has a small bathroom containing a shower stall.

Adjoining the lounge and pool area is a covered open-air dining room overlooking the harbor. The cuisine is respected here, with barbecue and full a la carte menus offered at dinner. On Wednesday, the hotel puts on a West Indian "grill out," complete with live entertainment and dancing.

Pasea Estate (P.O. Box 68), Road Town, Tortola, B.V.I. © 800/334-2435 in the U.S., or 284/494-2501. Fax 284/494-2507. www.treasureislehotel.net. 43 units. Winter $187 double; $237 suite. Off-season $104–$143 double; $137–$209 suite. Extra person $25. AE, DISC, MC, V. **Amenities:** Restaurant, bar; pool; room service; laundry. *In room:* A/C, TV.

MODERATE

Prospect Reef Resort ✦ This is the largest resort in the British Virgin Islands. It rises above a small, private harbor in a sprawling series of two-story concrete buildings scattered over 44 acres (18 hectares) of steeply sloping, landscaped terrain. The panoramic view of Sir Francis Drake Channel from the bedrooms is one of the best anywhere, but there's no beach to speak of at this hotel.

Each of the resort's buildings contains up to 10 individual accommodations and is painted in hibiscus-inspired shades. Initially designed as condominiums, there are unique studios, town houses, and villas, in addition to guestrooms. All include private balconies or patios; larger units, which are perfect for families, have kitchenettes, living and dining areas, and separate bedrooms or sleeping lofts. About a third of the rooms are air-conditioned; others are cooled by ceiling fans and the trade winds. Bathrooms are tiled and well maintained, and come with shower stalls.

The food at the hotel's Callaloo Restaurant (see "Dining," below), offering a combination of continental specialties and island favorites, was praised by *Gourmet* magazine.

Drake's Hwy. (P.O. Box 104), Road Town, Tortola, B.V.I. © **800/356-8937** in the U.S., 800/463-3608 in Canada, or 284/494-3311. Fax 284/494-5595. www.prospectreef.com. 137 units. Winter $150–$310 double; $545 2-bedroom villa for 4. Off-season $99–$250 double; $335 2-bedroom villa for 4. Ask about packages. AE, MC, V. **Amenities:** 3 restaurants, 3 bars; 3 pools; 6 tennis courts; fitness center and spa; Jacuzzi; snorkeling, sailing, scuba diving, sport-fishing, interactive dolphin programs; children's programs; dive shop; shuttle to beaches; car rental; babysitting; culinary courses. *In room:* A/C, cable TV, minibar, hair dryer, coffeemaker, iron and ironing board, safe.

DINING
EXPENSIVE

Brandywine Bay Restaurant ✦✦ ITALIAN/INTERNATIONAL This restaurant is set on a cobblestone garden terrace along the south shore, overlooking Sir Francis Drake Channel. It's the most elegant choice for romantic dining. Davide Pugliese, the chef, and his wife, Cele, the hostess, have earned a reputation for their outstanding Florentine fare. Davide changes his menu daily, based on the availability of fresh produce. The best dishes include beef carpaccio, homemade pasta, his own special calf liver dish (the recipe is a secret), and homemade mozzarella with fresh basil and tomatoes. The skillful cookery ranges from the classic to the inspired.

Brandywine Estate, Sir Francis Drake Hwy. © 284/495-2301. Reservations required. Main courses $22–$33. AE, MC, V. Mon–Sat 6–9:30pm. Closed Aug–Oct. Drive 3 miles (5km) east of Road Town (toward the airport) on South Shore Rd.

Callaloo ⚝ INTERNATIONAL   One of the best hotel restaurants on Tortola, this place is rather romantic at night, especially if it's a balmy evening and the tropical breezes are blowing. It's the kind of cliché Caribbean setting that is forever a turn-on, and the food is quite good, too. The menu is hardly imaginative, but the chefs do well with their limited repertoire. Begin with the conch fritters or shrimp cocktail, and don't pass on the house salad, which has a zesty papaya dressing. The best dishes are fresh lobster when available (not as good as the Maine variety, though), as well as coconut basil shrimp and fresh fish such as tuna, swordfish, or mahi-mahi. For dessert, make it the pumpkin crème brûlée or the key lime pie. Downstairs is the less expensive Scuttlebutt Pub.

In Prospect Reef Resort, Drake's Hwy. ⓒ **284/494-3311.** Reservations recommended. Main courses $19–$45; fixed-price lunch $13. AE, MC, V. Daily 6:30am–11pm.

Mrs. Scatliffe's Restaurant ⚝ *Finds* WEST INDIAN   This Tortola Mama offers home-cooked meals on the deck of her island home, and some of the vegetables come right from her garden, although others might be from a can. You'll be served excellent authentic West Indian dishes; perhaps spicy conch soup, followed by curried goat, "old wife" fish, or possibly chicken in a coconut shell. After dinner, your hostess and her family will entertain you with gospel singing. *Be duly warned:* This entertainment isn't for everyone, including one reader who compared the hymns to a "screeching caterwaul." Service, usually from an inexperienced teenager, is not exactly efficient.

You may also be exposed to Mrs. Scatliffe's gentle and often humorous form of Christian fundamentalism. A Bible reading and a heartfelt rendition of a gospel song might be served up with a soft custard dessert.

Carrot Bay. ⓒ **284/495-4556.** Reservations required by 5pm. Fixed-price meal $25–$30. No credit cards. 1 seating daily begins 7–8pm.

Skyworld ⚝⚝ INTERNATIONAL   Skyworld continues to be all the rage, one of the best restaurants on the island. On one of Tortola's loftiest peaks, at a breezy 1,337 feet (401m), it offers views of both the U.S. Virgin Islands and the British Virgin Islands. The restaurant is divided into two sections—a more upscale area, with a dress code for men (collared shirts and long trousers), and an enclosed garden area, where you can dine in shorts. Both sections offer the same menu.

The fresh fish chowder is an island favorite, but you can also begin with our favorite, mushrooms stuffed with conch. The fresh fish of the day is your best bet (we prefer to skip the steak with port and peaches). The best key lime pie on the island awaits you at the end of the meal, unless you succumb to the heavenly cheese cake.

Ridge Rd., Road Town. ⓒ **284/494-3567.** Reservations required. Main courses $24.75–$36. AE, MC, V. Daily 11am–3pm and 5:30–8:30pm.

Sugar Mill Restaurant ⚝ CALIFORNIA/CARIBBEAN   Transformed from a 3-century-old sugar mill (see "Accommodations," above), this is a romantic spot for dining, with many dishes that evoke recipes in *Gourmet* magazine. Colorful works by Haitian painters hang on the old stone walls, and big copper basins have been planted with tropical flowers. Before going to the dining room, once part of the old boiling house, visit the open-air bar on a deck that overlooks the sea.

Your hosts, the Morgans, know a lot about food and wine. One of their most popular creations, published in *Bon Appétit,* is a curried-banana soup. You might also begin with smoked conch pâté. Good choices for dinner are Jamaican jerk pork roast with a green-peppercorn salsa and ginger-lime scallops with pasta and toasted walnut sauce.

Lunch can be ordered by the beach at the second restaurant, **Islands,** where dinner is also served Tuesday through Saturday from 6:30 to 9pm, from January to May. Try jerk ribs or stuffed crabs here.

Apple Bay. ⓒ **284/495-4355.** Reservations required. Main courses $22–$28. AE, MC, V. Daily noon–2pm and 7–8:30pm. Closed Aug–Sept. From Road Town, drive west about 7 miles (11km), turn right over Zion Hill going north, and turn right at the T-junction opposite Sebastians; Sugar Mill is about ½ mile (.8km) down the road.

MODERATE

Gourmet picnic, anyone? **Gourmet Chandler,** Nanny Cay (ⓒ **284/494-2211**), offers fabulous fixings, including Hediard pâté terrines and fine chocolates.

Capriccio di Mare ★ ITALIAN   Created in a moment of whimsy by the more upscale Brandywine (see above), this place is small, casual, laid-back, and a local favorite. It's the most authentic-looking Italian cafe in the Virgin Islands. At breakfast time, many locals stop in for a refreshing Italian pastry along with a cup of cappuccino, or else a full breakfast. You can come back for lunch or dinner. If it's evening, you might also order the mango Bellini, a variation of the famous cocktail served at Harry's Bar in Venice (which is made with fresh peaches). Begin with such appetizers as *piedini* (flour tortillas with various toppings), then move on to fresh pastas with succulent sauces, the best pizza on the island, or even well-stuffed sandwiches. We prefer the pizza topped with grilled eggplant. If you arrive on the right night, you might even be treated to lobster ravioli in a rosé sauce. Also try one of the freshly made salads: We like the *insalata mista* with large, leafy greens and slices of fresh Parmesan.

Waterfront Dr., Road Town. ⓒ **284/494-5369.** Reservations not accepted. Main courses $8–$14. No credit cards. Mon–Sat 8am–9pm.

Pusser's Landing CARIBBEAN/ENGLISH PUB/MEXICAN   This second Pusser's (see below for the first) is more desirably located in West End, opening onto the water. In this nautical setting, you can enjoy fresh grilled fish or an English-inspired dish, like shepherd's pie. Begin with a hearty bowl of homemade soup and follow it with filet mignon, West Indian roast chicken, or a filet of mahi-mahi. Mud pie is the classic dessert here, or else try key lime pie or, even better, the mango soufflé. Some dishes occasionally miss the mark, but on the whole this is a good choice. Happy hour is daily from 5 to 7pm.

Frenchman's Cay, West End. ⓒ **284/495-4554.** Reservations recommended. Main courses $13–$24. AE, DISC, MC, V. Daily 11am–10pm.

Pusser's Road Town Pub CARIBBEAN/ENGLISH PUB/MEXICAN   Standing on the waterfront across from the ferry dock, the original Pusser's serves Caribbean fare, English pub grub, and good pizzas. This is not as fancy or as good as the Pusser's in the West End, but it's a lot more convenient and has faster service. The complete lunch and dinner menu includes English shepherd's pies and deli-style sandwiches. *Gourmet* magazine asked for the recipe for its chicken-and-asparagus pie. John Courage ale is on draft, but the drink to order here is the famous Pusser's Rum, the same blend of 5 West Indian rums that the Royal Navy has served to its men for more than 300 years. Thursday is nickel beer night.

Waterfront Dr. and Main St., Road Town. ⓒ **284/494-3897.** Reservations recommended. Main courses $7–$20. AE, DISC, MC, V. Daily 11am–10:30pm.

HITTING THE BEACH

Beaches are rarely crowded on Tortola unless a cruise ship is in port. You can rent a car or a Jeep to reach them, or take a taxi (but arrange for a time to be picked up).

Tortola's finest beach is **Cane Garden Bay** ★★★, on Cane Garden Bay Road directly west of Road Town. You'll have to navigate some roller-coaster hills to get there, but these fine white sands, with sheltering palm trees, are among the most popular in the B.V.I., and the lovely bay is beloved by yachties. There are outfitters that rent Hobie Cats, kayaks, and sailboards. Windsurfing is possible as well. Beware of crowds in high season. There are some seven places here to eat, along with a handful of bars. **Rhymer's** (© 284/495-4639) is our favorite, offering cold beer and refreshing rum drinks. If you're hungry, try the conch or lobster, black-bean gazpacho, or barbecued spareribs. The beach bar and restaurant is open daily from 8am to 9pm, with steel-drum bands entertaining on some evenings. Ice and freshwater showers are available (and you can rent towels). Ask about renting Sunfish and Windsurfers next door.

Surfers like **Apple Bay,** west of Cane Garden Bay, along North Shore Road. The beach isn't very big, but that doesn't diminish activity when the surf's up. Conditions are best in January and February. After enjoying the white sands here, you can have a drink at the Bomba Shack, a classic dive of a beach bar at the water's edge (see "Tortola After Dark," below).

Smugglers Cove, known for its tranquility and for the beauty of its sands, lies at the extreme western end of Tortola, opposite the offshore island of Great Thatch and just north of St. John. It's a lovely crescent of white sand, with calm turquoise waters. A favorite local beach, it's at the end of bumpy Belmont Road. Once you get here, a little worse for wear, you'll think the crystal clear water and the beautiful palm trees are worth the effort. Snorkelers like this beach, which is sometimes called "Lower Belmont Bay." It's especially good for beginning snorkelers, since the reef is close to shore and easily reached. You'll see sea fans, sponges, parrot fish, and elkhorn and brain corals.

East of Cane Garden Bay and site of a campground, **Brewers Bay,** reached along the long, steep Brewers Bay Road, is ideal for snorkelers and surfers. This clean, white-sand beach is a great place to enjoy walks in the early morning or at sunset. Sip a rum punch from the beach bar, and watch the world go by.

The mile-long (2km), white-sand beach at **Long Bay West,** reached along Long Bay Road, is one of the most beautiful in the B.V.I. Joggers run along the water's edge, and it's also a lovers' walk at dusk, with spectacular sunsets. The Long Bay Beach Resort stands on the northeast side of the beach; many visitors like to book a table at the resort's restaurant overlooking the water.

At the very east end of the island, **Long Bay East,** reached along Beef Island Road, is a great spot for swimming. Cross Queen Elizabeth Bridge to reach this mile-long (2km) beach with great views and white sands.

EXPLORING THE ISLAND

Travel Plan Tours, Romasco Place, Wickhams Cay 1, Road Town (© 284/494-2347), offers a 3½-hour tour that touches on the panoramic highlights of Tortola (a minimum of 4 participants is required). The cost is $28 per person, with a supplement of $5 per person if you want to extend the tour with hill climbing in the rain forest. The company also offers 2½-hour **snorkeling tours** for $35 per person, or full-day snorkeling tours for $42 per person (with lunch included). A full-day **sailing tour** aboard a catamaran that goes from Tortola to either Peter Island or Norman Island costs $80 to $85 per person; a full-day tour, which goes as far afield as The Baths at Virgin Gorda and includes lunch, costs $80 per person. And if **deep-sea fishing** appeals to you, you can go for a half-day excursion, with equipment, for 4 fishers and up to 2 "nonfishing observers" for $600 to $700.

A **taxi tour** costs $45 for 2 passengers for 2 hours, or $60 for 3 hours. To call a taxi in Road Town, dial © **284/494-2322;** on Beef Island, © **284/495-2378.**

No visit to Tortola is complete without a trip to Sage Mountain National Park ⚲, rising to an elevation of 1,780 feet (534m). Here you'll find traces of a primeval rain forest, and you can enjoy a picnic while overlooking neighboring islets and cays. Go west from Road Town to reach the mountain. Before you head out, stop by the tourist office and pick up the brochure *Sage Mountain National Park.* It has a location map, directions to the forest (where there's a parking lot), and an outline of the main trails through the park. Covering 92 acres (37 hectares), the park protects the remnants of Tortola's original forests not burned or cleared during the island's plantation era. From the parking lot, a trail leads to the main entrance to the park. The two main trails are the Rain Forest Trail and the Mahogany Forest Trail.

Shadow's Ranch, **Todman's Estate** (© **284/494-2262**), offers horseback rides through the national park or down to the shores of Cane Garden Bay. Call for details, Monday to Saturday from 9am to 4pm. The cost is from $35 per hour.

THE WRECK OF THE *RHONE* & OTHER TOP DIVE SITES

The one site in the British Virgin Islands that lures divers over from St. Thomas is **the wreck of the HMS *Rhone*** ⚲⚲, which sank in 1867 near the western point of Salt Island. *Skin Diver* magazine called this "the world's most fantastic shipwreck dive." It teems with marine life and coral formations and was featured in the 1977 movie *The Deep.*

Although it's no *Rhone*, **Chikuzen** is another intriguing dive site off Tortola. It's a 270-foot steel-hulled refrigerator ship, which sank off the island's east end in 1981. The hull, still intact under about 80 feet (24m) of water, is now home to a vast array of tropical fish, including yellowtail, barracuda, black-tip sharks, octopus, and drum fish.

Baskin in the Sun (© **800/233-7938** in the U.S., or 284/494-2858), a PADI five-star facility on Tortola, is a good outfitter, with locations at the Prospect Reef Resort, near Road Town, and at Soper's Hole, on Tortola's West End. Baskin's most popular trip is the supervised "Half-Day Scuba Diving" experience for $95, catered to beginners, but there are trips for all levels of experience. Daily excursions are scheduled to the HMS *Rhone,* as well as "Painted Walls" (an underwater canyon, the walls of which are formed of brightly colored coral and sponges) and the "Indians" (4 pinnacle rocks sticking out of the water, which divers follow 40 feet (12m) below the surface).

Underwater Safaris (© **284/494-3235**) takes you to all the best sites, including the HMS *Rhone,* "Spyglass Wall," and "Alice in Wonderland." It has two offices: "Safari Base" in Road Town and "Safari Cay" on Cooper Island. Get complete directions and information when you call. The center, connected with The Moorings (see below), offers a complete PADI and NAUI training facility. An introductory resort course and 3 dives costs $168, while an open-water certification, with 4 days of instruction and 4 open-water dives, goes for $410, plus $40 for the instruction manual.

YACHT CHARTERS

Tortola boasts the largest fleet of bareboat sailing charters in the world. The best place to get outfitted is **The Moorings,** Wickhams Cay (© **800/535-7289** in the U.S., or 284/494-2332), whose waterside resort is also recommended in "Accommodations," earlier in this chapter. This outfit, along with a handful of others, make the British Virgins the cruising capital of the world. You can choose from a fleet of sailing yachts, which can accommodate up to four couples in comfort and style. Depending on your nautical knowledge and skills, you can arrange a bareboat rental (with no crew) or a fully crewed rental with a skipper, a staff, and a cook. Boats come equipped with a portable barbecue, snorkeling gear, dinghy, linens, and galley equipment. The Moorings has an experienced staff of mechanics, electricians, riggers, and cleaners. If you're going out on your own, you'll get a thorough briefing session on Virgin Island waters and anchorages.

If you'd like sailing lessons, consider **Steve Colgate's Offshore Sailing School** (© **800/221-4326**), which offer courses in seamanship year-round.

SHOPPING

Most of Tortola's shops are on Road Town's Main Street. Unfortunately, the British Virgins have no duty-free shopping. British goods are imported without duty, and the wise shopper will be able to find some good buys among these imported items, especially in English china. In general, store hours are Monday to Friday from 9am to 4pm, Saturday from 9am to 1pm.

Sunny Caribbee Herb and Spice Company, Main Street, Road Town (© **284/494-2178**), in an old West Indian building, was the first hotel on Tortola. It's now a shop specializing in Caribbean spices, seasonings, teas, condiments, and handcrafts. You can buy two world-famous specialties here: the West Indian hangover cure and the Arawak love potion. A Caribbean cosmetics collection, Sunsations, includes herbal bath gels, island perfume, and sunscreens. With its aroma of spices permeating the air, this factory is an attraction in itself. There's a daily sampling of island products—perhaps tea, coffee, sauces, or dips. Next door is the **Sunny Caribbee Gallery,** featuring original paintings, prints, woodcarvings, and hand-painted furniture, plus crafts from throughout the Caribbean.

Caribbean Fine Arts Ltd., Main Street, Road Town (© **284/494-4240**), sells original watercolors and oils, limited-edition serigraphs and sepia photographs, and pottery and primitives. **Caribbean Handprints,** Main Street, Road Town (© **284/494-3717**), features prints hand-done by local craftspeople and sells colorful fabric by the yard.

Samarkand, Main St., Road Town (© **284/494-6415**), evokes an exotic land, but is actually a shop that's an unusual bet for jewelry and other items. Look for an intriguing selection of bracelets, pins, pendants in both silver and gold, and pierced earrings. Caribbean motifs such as palms and sea birds often appear in the designs of the jewelry. Samarkand is also known for selling authentic pieces of eight taken from sunken Spanish galleons in the B.V.I.

J. R. O'Neal, Upper Main Street, Road Town (© **284/494-2292**), is across from the Methodist church. This home-accessories store has an extensive collection of terra-cotta pottery, wicker and rattan home furnishings, Mexican glassware, baskets, ceramics, fine crystal, china, and more, all at good prices.

Bargain hunters gravitate to **Sea Urchin,** Mill Mall, Road Town (© **284/494-4108**), for print shirts and shorts, T-shirts, bathing suits, and sandals. Good prices in swimwear are also available at **Turtle Dove Boutique,** Fleming Street,

Road Town (© **284/494-3611**), which has a wide selection. Women can purchase affordable linen and silk dresses here as well.

Pusser's Company Store, Main Street and Waterfront Road, Road Town (© **284/494-2467**), has gourmet food items including meats, cheeses, fish, and a nice selection of wines. Pusser's Rum is one of the best-selling items here.

Near the very western tip of Tortola, **Caribbean Corner Spice House Co.,** Soper's Hole (© **284/495-4498**), offers the island's finest selection of spices and herbs, along with local crafts and botanical skin-care products, which you may find useful in the fierce sun. There's also a selection of Cuban cigars (though U.S. citizens will have to smoke them here because it's illegal to bring them home). **Flamboyance,** Waterfront Drive (© **284/494-4099**), is the best place to shop for perfume and upscale cosmetics.

TORTOLA AFTER DARK

Ask around to find out which hotel might have entertainment on any given evening. Steel bands and fungi or scratch bands (African Caribbean musicians who improvise on locally available instruments) appear regularly, and nonresidents are usually welcome. Pick up a copy of *Limin' Times,* an entertainment magazine listing what's happening locally; it's usually available at hotels.

Bomba's Surfside Shack, Cappoon's Bay (© **284/495-4148**), is the oldest, most memorable, and most uninhibited hangout on the island, sitting on the beach near the West End. It's covered with Day-Glo graffiti and odds and ends of plywood, driftwood, and abandoned rubber tires. Despite its makeshift appearance, the shack has the sound system to create a really great party. Every month (dates vary), Bomba's stages a full moon party, with free house tea spiked with hallucinogenic mushrooms. (The tea is free because it's illegal to sell it.) The place is also wild on Wednesday and Sunday nights, when there's live music and an $8 all-you-can-eat barbecue. It's open daily from 10am to midnight (or later, depending on business).

The bar at **The Moorings/Mariner Inn,** Wickhams Cay (© **284/494-2332**), is the preferred watering hole for some upscale yacht owners, but drink prices are low. Open to a view of its own marina, and bathed in a dim and flattering light, the place is relaxed. Another popular choice is the **Spyglass Bar,** in the Treasure Isle Hotel, Road Town (© **284/494-2501**), where a sunken bar on a terrace overlooks the pool and faraway marina facilities of this popular hotel.

The **Bat Cave,** Waterfront Drive, Road Town (© **284/494-4880**), is one of the newest hot spots, on the ground floor of Spaghetti Junction. The latest recorded hits are played nightly. On the last Friday of each month, the staff throws a big themed costume party.

Other little hot spots, worth at least a stop on a bar-hopping jaunt, include the **Jolly Roger,** West End (© **284/495-4559**), where you can hear local or sometimes American bands playing everything from reggae to blues. In the same area, visit **Stanley's Welcome Bar,** Cane Garden Bay (© **284/495-9424**), where a rowdy frat-boy crowd gathers to drink, talk, and drink some more. Finally, check out **Sebastians,** Apple Bay (© **284/495-4212**), especially on Saturday and Sunday, when you can dance to live music under the stars, at least in winter.

Rhymer's, on the popular stretch of beach at Cane Garden Bay (© **284/495-4639**), serves up cold beer or tropical rum concoctions, along with a casual menu of ribs, conch chowder, and more. The beach bar and restaurant is open daily from 8am to 9pm, with occasional steel-drum bands entertaining in the evening.

The joint is jumping at the **Tower Night Club,** West End (© 284/494-1776), on Friday to Sunday nights. The place is packed with locals and a scattering of visitors who come to listen to a DJ, but there's often live salsa and reggae as well.

3 Virgin Gorda ★★★

In 1493, on his second voyage to the New World, Columbus named this island Virgin Gorda, or "fat virgin" (from a distance, the island looks like a reclining woman with a protruding stomach). The second largest island in the cluster of British Virgin Islands, Virgin Gorda is 10 miles (16km) long and 2 miles (3km) wide, with a population of some 1,400. It's 12 miles (19km) east of Road Town and 26 miles (42km) from St. Thomas.

The island was a fairly desolate agricultural community until Laurance S. Rockefeller established the Little Dix Bay Hotel in the early 1960s, following his success with the Caneel Bay resort on St. John in the 1950s. He envisioned a "wilderness beach," where privacy and solitude would reign. In 1971, the Virgin Gorda Yacht Harbour opened. Operated by the Little Dix Bay Hotel, it accommodates 120 yachts today.

Come to Virgin Gorda for the lazy life and to escape from everything at some of the poshest and most self-contained inns in the Caribbean, if you can afford them. Life here is much slower paced than on Tortola, far less bustling, without much shopping or nightlife. The island gets far less rain, making some sections of it quite arid and filled with goats wandering among cactus and scrub brush.

Try to visit Virgin Gorda, if only for the day, to see **The Baths,** gigantic rocks and boulders shaped by volcanic pressures millions of years ago. The beach at The Baths is simply spectacular. Virgin Gorda is also quite mountainous, attracting visitors tired of flat Caribbean islands, who love the gorgeous and more dramatic scenery here.

ESSENTIALS

GETTING THERE   You can get to Virgin Gorda by air via St. Thomas in the U.S. Virgin Islands. **Air St. Thomas** (© 800/522-3084 or 340/776-2722) flies to Virgin Gorda daily from St. Thomas. A one-way trip (40 min.) costs $68; round-trip, $140.

Speedy's Fantasy (© 284/495-5240) operates a ferry service between Road Town and Virgin Gorda. Monday through Saturday, five ferries a day leave from Road Town, reduced to two on Sunday. The cost is $15 one-way or $25 round-trip. From St. Thomas to Virgin Gorda, there's service 3 times a week (on Tues, Thurs, and Sat), costing $35 one-way or $60 round-trip.

You'll also find that the more luxurious services have their own boats to take you from the airport on Beef Island to Virgin Gorda.

GETTING AROUND   Independently operated open-sided **safari buses** run along the main road. Holding up to 14 passengers, these buses charge upwards from $3 per person to transport a passenger, say, from The Valley to The Baths.

If you'd like to rent a car, try one of the local firms, including **Mahogany Rentals,** The Valley, Spanish Town (© 284/495-5469), across from the yacht harbor. This company is the least expensive on the island, beginning at around $45 daily for a Suzuki Samurai. An alternative choice is **Andy's Taxi and Jeep Rental** (© 284/495-5511), 7 minutes from the marina in Spanish Town. Rates begin at $65 daily year-round. Representatives of either agency will meet you at the airport or ferry dock and do the paperwork there.

FAST FACTS   The local **American Express** representative is **Travel Plan,** Virgin Gorda Yacht Harbour (© **284/495-5586**).

There are also **police stations** on Virgin Gorda (© **284/495-5222**) and on Jost Van Dyke (© **284/495-9345**).

Barclay Bank (© **284/495-5217**) is located in Spanish Town at the Virgin Gorda Shopping Centre. It has an ATM.

ACCOMMODATIONS
VERY EXPENSIVE

Biras Creek Estate ★★★   This private and romantic resort stands at the northern end of Virgin Gorda like a hilltop fortress, opening onto a decent beach, much of which is human-made. This sophisticated and relaxing hideaway has vastly improved after a major face-lift. This is the class joint of the island— stay here if you want a retreat from the world. (Bitter End is more family-oriented, and Little Dix Bay more of a conventional resort.) On a 150-acre (60-hectare) estate with its own marina, it occupies a narrow neck of land flanked by the sea on three sides. All the attractive, tropically decorated units have well-furnished bedrooms and private patios. Most have king-size beds, plus spacious bathrooms with inviting garden showers. There are no radios or TVs, but you do get such luxuries as ocean-view verandas and the latest editions of the *Wall Street Journal* and the *New York Times* delivered daily. Guests get their own bikes for their stay, and there are lots of hiking trails near the property.

The food has won high praise; the wine list is also excellent here. The hotel restaurant and open-air bar are quietly elegant, and there's always a table with a view. A barbecued lunch is often served on the beach.

North Sound (P.O. Box 54), Virgin Gorda, B.V.I. © **800/608-9661** in the U.S., or 284/494-3555. Fax 284/ 494-3557. www.biras.com. 33 units. Winter $750 double; $1,050 2-bedroom suite for 2; $1,650 suite for 4. Off-season $525 double; $725 suite for 2; $1,000 suite for 4. Rates include all meals and bikes. Ask about packages. AE, MC, V. Take the private motor launch from the Beef Island airport. No children under age 6. **Amenities:** 2 restaurants, 2 bars; pool; 2 tennis courts; snorkeling, Sunfish sailboats, kayaks; taxi service to launch; free trips to beaches; babysitting; laundry. *In room:* A/C, fridge, coffeemaker, hair dryer.

The Bitter End Yacht Club ★★★   This is the liveliest of B.V.I. resorts and even better equipped than the more exclusive Biras Creek. It's the best sailing and diving complex in the British chain. It opens onto one of the most unspoiled and secluded deep-water harbors in the Caribbean. Guests have unlimited use of the resort's million-dollar fleet, the Nick Trotter Sailing and Windsurfing School. The Bitter End offers an informal yet elegant experience, as guests settle into one of the hillside chalets or well-appointed beachfront and hillside villas overlooking the sound. Most units have varnished hardwood floors, sliding-glass doors, and wicker furnishings. All villas have either twin or king-size beds, plus a large dressing area and a shower with sea views.

For something novel, you can stay aboard one of the 30-foot yachts, yours to sail, with dockage and daily maid service, meals in the Yacht Club dining room, and overnight provisions. Each yacht has a shower with pressure water and can accommodate four comfortably.

You can dine on first-rate cuisine in the Clubhouse Steak and Seafood Grille, the English Carvery, or the Pub, with entertainment by a steel-drum or reggae band.

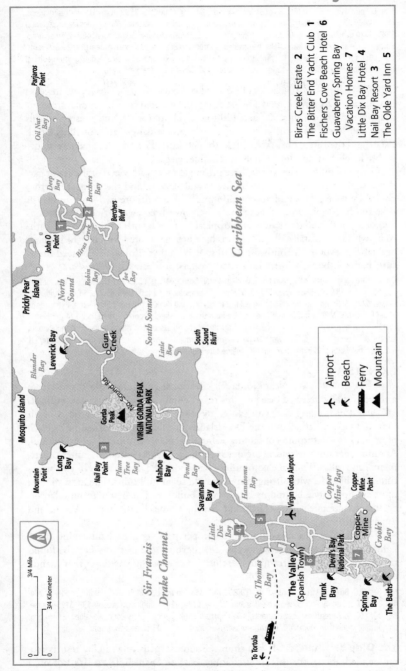

Virgin Gorda

Biras Creek Estate **2**
The Bitter End Yacht Club **1**
Fischers Cove Beach Hotel **6**
Guavaberry Spring Bay
  Vacation Homes **7**
Little Dix Bay Hotel **4**
Nail Bay Resort **3**
The Olde Yard Inn **5**

Airport
Beach
Ferry
Mountain

Caribbean Sea

Parjaros Point
Oil Nut Bay
Deep Bay
Berchers Bay
Berchers Bluff
John O Point
Biras Creek
Prickly Pear Island
Robin Bay
Joe Bay
North Sound
South Sound
Blunder Bay
Leverick Bay
Gun Creek
South Sound Bluff
Little Bay
Mosquito Island
No Sound Rd
Gorda Peak
VIRGIN GORDA PEAK NATIONAL PARK
Mountain Point
Long Bay
Nail Bay Point
Plum Tree Bay
Mahoe Bay
Pond Bay
Savannah Bay
Handsome Bay
Virgin Gorda Airport
Little Dix Bay
St Thomas Bay
The Valley (Spanish Town)
Trunk Bay
Devil's Bay National Park
Copper Mine Bay
Copper Mine Point
Copper Mine
Crook's Bay
Spring Bay
The Baths

Sir Francis Drake Channel

To Tortola

0   3/4 Mile
0   3/4 Kilometer

203

John O Point, North Sound (P.O. Box 46), Virgin Gorda, B.V.I. ✆ **800/872-2392** in the U.S. for reservations, or 284/494-2746. Fax 284/494-4756. www.beyc.com. 85 units, 3 yachts. Winter (double occupancy) $585–$770 beachfront villa, suite, yacht or hillside villa. Off-season (double occupancy) $400–$550 all units. Rates include all meals. AE, MC, V. Take the private ferry from the Beef Island airport. **Amenities:** 2 restaurants, pub; pool; fitness center; Sunfish, windsurfing, Boston whalers, reef snorkeling, scuba diving, sport-fishing; boat trips to nearby cays; babysitting; laundry. *In room:* Ceiling fan, fridge, hair dryer.

Little Dix Bay Hotel 🌟🌟   Full of low-key luxury, along a curving white-sand beach, Little Dix Bay Hotel is a resort discreetly scattered along a ½-mile, crescent-shaped, private bay on a 500-acre (200-hectare) preserve. Many guests find this resort too pricey and stuffy; we prefer the more casual elegance of Biras Creek Estate and the Bitter End Yacht Club, though Little Dix Bay does have an unde-niably lovely setting, fine service, and a quiet elegance.

All rooms, built in the woods, have private terraces with views of the sea or gar-dens. Trade winds come through louvers and screens, and the units are further cooled by ceiling fans and air-conditioning. Some units are two-story rondavels (like tiki huts) raised on stilts to form their own breezeways. Accommodations are roomy, airy, and decorated with tropical flair, each with a smart private bath-room with shower stall. All guest rooms have been renovated with new furnishings and fabrics, evoking a Southeast Asian style with beautiful wicker or reed furni-ture, bamboo beds, Balinese boxes and baskets, and ceramic *objets d'art.*

On the northwest corner of the island (P.O. Box 70), Virgin Gorda, B.V.I. ✆ **888/767-3966** in the U.S., or 284/ 495-5555. Fax 284/495-5661. www.littledixbay.com. 97 units. Winter $450–$875 double; $1,650 suite. Off-season $275–$550 double; from $800 suite. MAP (breakfast and dinner) $90 per person extra. Extra person $75. AE, DC, MC, V. Take the private ferry service from the Beef Island airport to the resort; $74 per person round-trip. **Amenities:** 3 restaurants, 2 bars; 7 tennis courts; fitness center; island tours; Sunfish sailboats, kayaks, snorkeling, scuba diving, waterskiing, deep-sea fishing; bike rental; children's programs; jeep rental; massage; babysitting; laundry. *In room:* A/C, ceiling fan, fridge, hair dryer, safe.

EXPENSIVE

Nail Bay Resort 🌟   Near Gorda Peak National Park, and a short walk from a trio of usually deserted beaches, this resort enjoys an idyllic position. From its 147-acre (59-hectare) site, you can enjoy some of the best sunset views of Sir Francis Drake Channel and the Dog Islands. All the well-furnished units, each of which has a bathroom containing a shower stall, are comfortable and tasteful. Accommodations are wide ranging, including deluxe bedrooms, suites, apart-ments, and villas. This villa community has a core of a dozen units in two struc-tures on a hillside, with sitting areas amid old sugar mill ruins. The most modest units are hotel-style bedrooms in the main building. The best accommodations are the four estate villas—Diamond Beach, Flame Trees, Sunset Watch, and Turtle Bay.

At night Nail Bay evokes a luxury property in Asia, its landscaping high-lighted by circuitous stone walkways. One devotee told us that when she found the resort, it had the "terra-ultima exclusivity of Mustique, without that island's elitism."

Nail Bay (P.O. Box 69), Virgin Gorda, B.V.I. ✆ **800/871-3551** in the U.S., 800/487-1839 in Canada, or 284/ 494-8000. Fax 284/495-5875. www.nailbay.com. Winter $125–$145 double. Off-season $99–$115 double. AE, DC, MC, V. **Amenities:** 2 restaurants, swim-up bar; pool; lighted tennis court; kayaking, snorkeling; babysitting; laundry. *In room:* A/C, TV, coffeemaker, hair dryer, iron and ironing board, safe.

The Olde Yard Inn 🌟   If you shun the super-expensive and chic resorts rec-ommended above, try this little charmer outside Spanish Town. It's not on a beach, of course, but a free shuttle hauls guests to nearby Savannah Bay, where there is an excellent white sandy beach. The inn lies a mile (2km) from the airport, surrounded by tropical gardens and a wall for privacy. Near the main house are two long bungalows with large renovated bedrooms, each with its own bathroom (shower only) and patio, done in a charming style. Half of the rooms have air-conditioning for an extra $10, and all have ceiling fans. Three of the rooms also contain fridges. You can go for a sail on a yacht or embark on a snorkeling adventure at 1 of 16 beaches nearby.

The French-accented dinners are one of the reasons for coming here. Lunch is served poolside at the Sip and Dip Grill. There's live entertainment three times a week in the dining room.

The Valley (P.O. Box 26), Virgin Gorda, B.V.I. ⓒ 800/653-9273 in the U.S., or 284/495-5544. Fax 284/495-5986. www.oldeyardinn.com. 15 units. Winter $195 double; $220 triple; $245 quad; $450 suite. Off-season $110 double; $130 triple; $150–$190 quad; $250 suite. MAP (breakfast and dinner) $55 per person extra. Honeymoon packages available. AE, MC, V. **Amenities:** 2 restaurants, bar; pool; health club; Jacuzzi; library; salon; babysitting; laundry. *In room:* Ceiling fan, no phone.

MODERATE

Fischers Cove Beach Hotel There's swimming at your doorstep in this group of units nestled near the sandy beach of St. Thomas Bay. Erected of native stone, each of the eight cottages is self-contained, with one or two bedrooms and a combination living/dining room with a kitchenette, plus a small bathroom with shower stall. You can stock up on provisions at a food store near the grounds. There are also 12 pleasant but simple rooms with views of Drake Channel. Each has its own private bathroom (with hot and cold showers) and private balcony.

The Valley (P.O. Box 60), Virgin Gorda, B.V.I. ⓒ 284/495-5252. Fax 284/495-5820. www.fischerscove.com. 20 units. Winter $160–$165 double; $190–$290 studio cottage. Off-season $100 double; $125–$205 studio cottage. MAP (breakfast and dinner) $40 per person extra. AE, MC, V. **Amenities:** Restaurant, bar; Jeeps available; bike rental; children's playground; babysitting. *In room:* A/C, TV, fridge, hair dryer.

Guavaberry Spring Bay Vacation Homes ★ Staying in one of these hexagonal, white-roofed redwood houses built on stilts is like living in a tree house, with screened and louvered walls to let in sea breezes. The Baths, with its excellent sandy beach, is nearby. Each home, available for daily or weekly rental, has one or two bedrooms; all have private bathrooms, with showers, small kitchenettes, and dining areas. Each unique vacation house also has its own elevated sundeck overlooking Sir Francis Drake Passage. Within a few minutes of the cottage colony is the beach at Spring Bay, and the Yacht Harbour Shopping Centre is a mile (2km) away.

Spring Bay (P.O. Box 20), Virgin Gorda, B.V.I. ⓒ 284/495-5227. Fax 284/495-5283. www.guavaberryspringbay. com. 18 units. Winter $185 1-bedroom house; $265 2-bedroom house. Off-season $120 1-bedroom house; $175 2-bedroom house. Extra person $17–$22. No credit cards. **Amenities:** Commissary; scuba diving, fishing, sailing; jeep rental; babysitting. *In room:* Ceiling fan, safe, no phone.

DINING
EXPENSIVE

Biras Creek Estate ★★ INTERNATIONAL With even better cuisine than that at Little Dix's The Pavillion (see below), this hilltop restaurant is our long-time island favorite, and for good reason. The resort hires the island's finest chefs, who turn out superb cuisine based on quality ingredients. The menu changes every night, but the panoramic view of North Sound doesn't: It's as super as the key lime pie with raspberry sauce served here. On our latest visit, the chef launched our meal with an appetizer of lobster medallions dressed in a bed of tomato confit enhanced with a fresh black truffle vinaigrette. Our taste buds were enthralled by the open ravioli made with octopus, scallops, vegetables, prawns, and olives.

One person at our table had an equally good (and more Caribbean) pan-roasted chicken leg served with avocado, with sweet mashed potatoes and red pepper mango salsa. Those warm berries in a champagne sauce made us not regret having passed on the pineapple mousse with an almond encrusted shell.

In Biras Creek, North Sound. ℂ 284/494-3555. Reservations required. Fixed-price dinner $59. AE, MC, V. Daily 7–11pm.

The Pavillion ✿ INTERNATIONAL   The most romantic of the dining spots on Virgin Gorda, this pavilion is our preferred choice at this deluxe resort, which also operates The Beach Grill and The Sugar Mill. At the Pavilion guests sit under a large thatched roof, with the doors open to the trade winds. A middle-aged crowd frequents the place, and there are few objections to the high prices as this resort caters to the well-heeled traveler. You don't have to be a guest to dine here. The chefs change the menu daily, so you could dine here every night and have nothing repeated. Although many of the ingredients are shipped in frozen, especially meats and some seafood, there is much that is fresh and good. The most expensive item on the menu is a perfectly prepared pan-seared red snapper with a ratatouille made not with eggplant but with christophene, "the squash of the islands." Many vegetables evoke the Pacific Rim, and the seafood keeps us returning again and again.

In the Little Dix Bay Hotel, northeast corner of the island. ℂ 284/495-5555. Reservations recommended. Main courses $29–$40. AE, MC, V. Daily noon–3pm and 7–9pm.

MODERATE

Chez Bamboo ✿ CAJUN/CREOLE   The closest approximation to a New Orleans supper club you're likely to find in Virgin Gorda is here, in a building with a big veranda and a location that's within a 5-minute walk north of the yacht club. Inside, there's a wraparound mural showing a jazz band playing within a forest of bamboo, as well as bamboo artifacts that highlight the restaurant's choice of names. Owner Rose Giacinto and chef Joyce Rodriguez concoct superb versions of dishes—such as conch gumbo, Nassau grouper *en papillotte,* and New Orleans–style strip steak that's covered with creamy Worcestershire sauce. Desserts such as apple *crostini* and crème brûlée are among the very best of their ilk on the island. Live music, usually blues or jazz, is presented every Friday night on the terrace.

In the Virgin Gorda Yacht Harbour. ℂ 284-495-5752. Reservations recommended. Main courses $19.50–$28. AE, MC, V. Tues–Sun 5–10pm.

The Flying Iguana MEDITERRANEAN/FRENCH/WEST INDIAN   The owner of this place, Puck (a.k.a. Orlington Baptiste), studied his craft in Kansas City, with the Hilton Group, before setting up this amiable restaurant overlooking the airport's landing strip and the sea. Potted hibiscus and lots of effigies of iguanas, stuffed and carved, ornament a room that's a celebration of West Indian mystique. The house drink is a "happy" concoction whose secret ingredients change according to the whim of the bartender. Whatever the recipe, it usually produces a lightheaded effect that goes well with the carefully conceived cuisine. The finest examples include fresh fish and all kinds of shellfish, including calamari, shrimp, scallops, and conch, often served in combination with one another. You'll also find the usual suspects: steak, chicken, and lamb, seasoned in a way that emulates both the Caribbean and the faraway Mediterranean. Live music is offered every Tuesday.

The Valley, at the airport. ✆ 284/495-5277. Lunch main courses $8–$18; dinner main courses $21–$32. MC, V. Daily 7am–10:30pm (last order).

Giorgio's Table ✪ ITALIAN   This is the only authentic Italian restaurant on the island. Lying a 15-minute drive north of Spanish Town, it opens onto a big covered terrace, although its varnished interior evokes a yacht. We like to sit out here at night, "star struck," gazing up at the heavens with the sounds of the surf nearby. The chef says he cooks Italian instead of "American Italian," and the food is good, despite its reliance on a lot of imported ingredients. Fresh locally caught fish is generally the best bet, although you can order an array of succulent pastas and such standard Italian staples as veal scallopine. Pizzas and sandwiches will fill you at lunch. Looking at this place, we decided its owner, Giorgio, had an appropriate last name—"Paradisio."

Mahoe Bay. ✆ 284/495-5684. Reservations recommended. Lunch main courses $13.50–$18; dinner main courses $25–$35. AE, DISC, MC, V. Daily noon–2:30pm and 6:30–9pm.

INEXPENSIVE

Bath & Turtle Pub INTERNATIONAL   At the end of the waterfront shopping plaza in Spanish Town sits the most popular pub on Virgin Gorda, packed with locals during happy hour, from 4 to 6pm. Even if you don't care about food, you might join the regulars over midmorning mango coladas or peach daiquiris. There's live music every Wednesday and Sunday night, in summer only (no cover). From its handful of indoor and courtyard tables, you can order fried fish fingers, tamarind-ginger wings, very spicy chili, pizzas, fresh pasta, barbecue chicken, steak, lobster, and daily seafood specials such as conch fritters from the simple menu here.

Virgin Gorda Yacht Harbour, Spanish Town. ✆ 284/495-5239. Reservations recommended. Breakfast $4.50–$9; main courses $7–$14 lunch, $10–$20 dinner. AE, MC, V. Daily 7:30am–11pm.

The Crab Hole WEST INDIAN   This is a clean and decent West Indian restaurant, far removed from the expense and glitter of such resorts as Little Dix Bay and Biras Creek Estate in the private home of Kenroy and Janet Millington. Order your food from the chalkboard posted above the bar. There are good days and bad days here, depending on what the market turned up. You might get stewed whelk with Creole sauce made from local spices or tomatoes, or stewed chicken, and you'll most definitely see fried fish on the menu. Stewed oxtail is sometimes on the menu, and guests, often hotel workers in the area, drop in for a noonday hamburger.

South Valley. ✆ 284/495-5307. Main courses $10–$25. No credit cards. Mon–Sat 10am–11pm. Head south along the road to The Baths, and turn left at the sign to the Crab Hole; look for a concrete house surrounded by fields and other simple private dwellings.

The Lighthouse Restaurant CONTINENTAL   A combined restaurant and beach bar, this newly renovated place is today's version of the old Pusser's, which now operates only a store here. During the day, you can enjoy all sorts of light meals, including croissant sandwiches, burgers, fried snapper, and pizza. There's also a special menu for children. At night, the menu is more ambitious, with appetizers like conch chowder and hearty main courses such as rack of barbecued ribs or penne pesto. The best food here is the fish, including mahi-mahi, wahoo, snapper, grouper, or swordfish, all prepared any way you want it (charcoal-grilled, blackened, pesto crusted, sautéed in butter, or Caribbean style with white wine and butter with pepper and onions).

Leverick Bay, North Sound. ⓒ 284/495-7154. Reservations recommended. Main courses $19–$28; lunch $8–$16; pizzas from $8. MC, V. Daily 11am–midnight. Closed Sept–Oct.

Top of The Baths CARIBBEAN This aptly named green-and-white restaurant offers a patio with a swimming pool. Locals gather here to enjoy the food they grew up on. At lunch, you can order an array of appetizers, sandwiches, and salad plates. You're invited to swim in the pool either before or after dining. At night, the kitchen turns out good home-style cookery, including fresh fish, lobster, chicken, and steaks. Look for one of the daily specials. And save room for a piece of that rum cake! Live steel bands perform on Wednesday, Thursday, and Sunday.

The Valley. ⓒ 284/495-5497. Dinner $16–$26; sandwiches and salad plates $6.50–$10. AE, MC, V. Daily 8am–10pm.

EXPLORING THE ISLAND

The northern side of Virgin Gorda is mountainous, with Gorda Peak reaching 1,370 feet (411m), the highest spot on the island. However, the southern half of the island is flat, with large boulders at every turn.

The best way to see the island if you're over for a day trip is to call **Andy Flax** at the Fischers Cove Beach Hotel. He runs the **Virgin Gorda Tours Association** (ⓒ **284/495-5151**), which will give you a tour of the island for $22.50 per person. The tour leaves twice daily, or more often if there's demand. You can be picked up at the ferry dock if you give 24-hour's notice.

HITTING THE BEACH The best beaches are at **The Baths** ★★, where giant boulders form a series of tranquil pools and grottoes flooded with seawater (nearby snorkeling is excellent, and you can rent gear on the beach). Scientists think the boulders were brought to the surface eons ago by volcanic activity.

Devil's Bay National Park can be reached by a trail from The Baths. The walk to the secluded coral-sand beach takes about 15 minutes through boulders and dry coastal vegetation.

The Baths and surrounding areas are part of a proposed system of parks and protected areas in the B.V.I. The protected area encompasses 682 acres (273 hectares) of land, including sites at Little Fort, Spring Bay, The Baths, and Devil's Bay on the east coast.

Neighboring The Baths is **Spring Bay,** one of the best of the island's beaches, with white sand, clear water, and good snorkeling. **Trunk Bay** is a wide sandy beach reachable by boat or along a rough path from Spring Bay.

Savannah Bay is a sandy beach north of the yacht harbor, and **Mahoe Bay,** at the Mango Bay Resort, has a gently curving beach with neon-blue water.

DIVING **Kilbrides Sunchaser Scuba** is located at the Bitter End Resort at North Sound (ⓒ **800/932-4286** in the U.S., or 284/495-9638). Kilbrides offers the best diving in the British Virgin Islands, at 15 to 20 dive sites, including the wreck of the ill-fated HMS *Rhone*. Prices range from $75 to $90 for a 2-tank dive on one of the coral reefs. A 1-tank dive in the afternoon costs $65. Equipment, except wet suits, is supplied at no charge, and videos of your dives are available.

HIKING Consider a trek up the stairs and hiking paths that crisscross Virgin Gorda's largest stretch of undeveloped land, **Virgin Gorda Peak National Park.**

To reach the best departure point for your uphill trek, drive north of The Valley on the only road leading to North Sound for about 15 very hilly minutes (using a four-wheel-drive vehicle is a good idea). Stop at the base of the stairway leading steeply uphill. There's a sign pointing to Virgin Gorda Peak National Park.

Depending on your climbing speed, it takes between 25 and 40 minutes to reach the summit of Gorda Peak, the highest point on the island; you'll be rewarded with sweeping views of the many scattered islets of the Virgin archipelago. There's a tower at the summit, which you can climb for enhanced views. Admire the flora and the fauna (birds, lizards, nonvenomous snakes) that you're likely to run across en route. Be sure to bring sunscreen, and consider bringing a picnic, as tables are scattered along the hiking trails.

VIRGIN GORDA AFTER DARK

There isn't a lot of action at night, unless you want to make some of your own. The **Bath & Turtle Pub,** at Yacht Harbour (© **284/495-5239**), brings in local bands for dancing on Wednesday and Sunday at 8pm. Most evenings in winter, the **Bitter End Yacht Club** (© **284/494-2746**) has live music. Reached only by boat, this is the best bar on the island. With its dark wood, it evokes an English pub and even serves British brews. Call to see what's happening at the time of your visit.

Andy's Chateau de Pirate, at the Fischers Cove Beach Hotel, The Valley (© **284/495-5252**), is a sprawling, sparsely furnished local hangout. It has a simple stage, a very long bar, and huge oceanfront windows which almost never close. The complex also houses the Lobster Pot Restaurant, the Buccaneer Bar, and the nightclub Neuso. The **Lobster Pot,** open from 11am to 2am, is a famous showcase for the island's musical groups, which perform Wednesday to Sunday from 8pm to midnight. There's a $5 cover Friday to Sunday nights. You might also check out **Pusser's at Leverick Bay,** which has live bands on Saturday night and Sunday afternoon. Call the **Olde Yard Inn** (© **284/495-5544**) to see if its Sip and Dip Grill is staging live local bands at their Sunday night barbecues.

4 Jost Van Dyke

This rugged island off the west side of Tortola was named for a Dutch settler. In the 1700s, a Quaker colony settled here to develop sugarcane plantations. One of the colonists, William Thornton, won the worldwide competition to design the U.S. Capitol in Washington, D.C. Smaller islands surround the place, including Little Jost Van Dyke, the birthplace of Dr. John Lettsome, founder of the London Medical Society.

About 150 people live on the 4 square miles (10 sq. km) of this mountainous island. On the south shore, **White Bay** and **Great Harbour** are good beaches. Although there are only a handful of places to stay, there are several dining choices, as the island is a popular stop for the yachting set and many cruise ships, including Cunard (and often some all-gay cruises). The peace and tranquility of yesteryear often disappear unless you're here when the cruise ships aren't.

ESSENTIALS

GETTING THERE   Take the ferry from either St. Thomas or Tortola. (Be warned that departure times can vary widely throughout the year, and often don't adhere very closely to the printed timetables.) Ferries from St. Thomas depart from Red Hook 2 days a week (Fri, Sat, and Sun), usually twice daily. More convenient (and more frequent) are the daily ferryboat shuttles from Tortola's isolated West End. The latter departs 3 times a day for the 25-minute trip, and costs $15 one-way. Call the **Jost Van Dyke Ferryboat Service** (© **284/494-2997**) for information about departures from any of the above-mentioned points. If all else fails, carefully negotiate a transportation fee with one of the handful of privately operated water taxis.

EMERGENCIES   In the unlikely event that you need the police, call © **284/ 495-9828.**

ACCOMMODATIONS

Sandcastle Hotel   A retreat for escapists who want few neighbors and absolutely nothing to do, these six cottages are surrounded by flowering shrubbery and bougainvillea and have panoramic views, opening onto a white sandy beach. Bedrooms are spacious, light, and airy, furnished in a tropical motif, with tile floors, local art, rattan furnishings, day beds, and king-size beds. Two units are air-conditioned. There are large, tiled bathrooms, with heated showers outside. You mix your own drinks at the beachside bar, the Soggy Dollar, and keep your own tab. Visiting boaters often drop in to enjoy the beachside informality and order a drink called The Painkiller. A line in the guest book proclaims, "I thought places like this only existed in the movies."

White Bay, Jost Van Dyke, B.V.I. © **284/495-9888.** Fax 284/495-9999. www.sandcastle-bvi.com. (For reservations and information, write or call the Sandcastle, Suite 201, Red Hook Plaza, St. Thomas, U.S.V.I. 00802-1306; © **340/495-9888**). 6 units. Winter $200–$250 double. Off-season $125–$175 double. Extra person $35–$45. 3-night minimum. MC, V. Take the private motor launch from Tortola; it's a 20-min. ride. **Amenities:** Restaurant, bar; diving, sailing, fishing trips. *In room:* Ceiling fan, no phone.

Sandy Ground   These self-sufficient apartments are along the edge of a beach on a 17-acre (7-hectare) hill site on the eastern part of Jost Van Dyke. The complex rents two- and three-bedroom villas. One of our favorites was constructed on a cliff that seems to hang about 80 feet (24m) over the beach. If you've come all this way, you might as well stay a week, which is the way the rates are quoted. The airy villas, each privately owned, are fully equipped with refrigerators and stoves. The interiors vary widely, from rather fashionable to bare bones. The living space is most generous, and extras include private balconies or terraces. Most rooms have showers only.

The managers help guests with boat rentals and watersports. Diving, day sails, and other activities can also be arranged, and there are dinghies available. Snorkeling and hiking are among the more popular pastimes.

East End (P.O. Box 594), West End, Tortola, B.V.I. © **284/494-3391.** Fax 284/495-9379. www.sandyground. com. 8 units. Weekly rates: winter $1,950 villa for 2. Off-season $1,400 villa for 2. Extra person $300 per week in winter, $200 off-season. MC, V. Take a private water taxi from Tortola or St. Thomas. **Amenities:** Diving, day sails, dinghies, snorkeling. *In room:* Ceiling fan, coffeemaker, fridge, no phone.

DINING

Abe's by the Sea WEST INDIAN   In this local bar and restaurant, sailors are satisfied with a menu of fish, lobster, conch, and chicken. Prices are low, too, and it's money well spent, especially when a fungi band plays for dancing. With each main course you also get peas and rice, coleslaw, and dessert. On Wednesday nights, Abe's will host a festive pig roast.

Little Harbour. © **284/495-9329.** Reservations recommended for groups of 5 or more. Dinner $18–$30; nightly barbecue $22. MC, V. Daily 9–11am, noon–3pm, and 7–10pm. Take the private motor launch or boat from Tortola; as you approach the east side of the harbor, you'll see Abe's on the right.

Foxy's Tamarind Bar ★★ WEST INDIAN   Arguably the most famous bar in the B.V.I., this mecca of yachties and other boat people spins entirely around a sixth-generation Jost Van Dyke native, Philicianno ("Foxy") Callwood. He opened the place some 3 decades ago, and sailors and the world have been coming back ever since. A songwriter and entertainer, Foxy is part of the draw. He creates impromptu calypso—almost in the Jamaican tradition—around his guests. If you're singled out, he'll embarrass you, but it's all in good fun. He also plays the guitar and takes a profound interest in preserving the environment of his native island.

Thursday through Saturday nights, a live band entertains. On other evenings, it's rock-and-roll, reggae, or soca. The food and drink aren't neglected, either— try Foxy's Painkiller Punch. During the day, flying-fish sandwiches, rotis, and the usual burgers are served, but evenings might bring freshly caught lobster, spicy steamed shrimp, or even grilled fish, depending on the catch of the day.

Great Harbour ✆ **284/495-9258.** Reservations recommended. Dinner $18–$25; lunch $7–$12. Daily 9am "until."

Rudy's Mariner's Rendezvous WEST INDIAN   Rudy's, at the western end of Great Harbour, serves good but basic West Indian food—and plenty of it. The place looks and feels like a private home with a waterfront terrace for visiting diners. A welcoming drink awaits sailors and landlubbers alike, and the food that follows is simply prepared and inexpensive. Conch always seems to be available, and a catch of the day is featured.

Great Harbour. ✆ **284/495-9282.** Reservations required by 6pm. Dinner $18–$30. MC, V. Daily 7pm–midnight.

Sandcastle INTERNATIONAL/CARIBBEAN   This hotel restaurant serves food that has often been frozen, but, even so, the flavors remain consistently good. Lunch is served in the open-air dining room, while lighter fare and snacks are available at the Soggy Dollar Bar. Dinner is by candlelight, featuring four courses, including such dishes as mahi-mahi Martinique (marinated in orange-lemon-lime juice and cooked with fennel, onions, and dill). Sandcastle hen is another specialty likely to appear on the menu: It's a grilled Cornish hen that's been marinated in rum, honey, lime, and garlic. But we'd skip all that for the sesame snapper, if available. Meals are served with seasonal vegetables and fresh pasta, along with a variety of salads and homemade desserts. Those desserts are luscious, and include piña-colada cheesecake and mango mousse.

At the Sandcastle Hotel, White Bay. ✆ **284/495-9888.** Reservations required for dinner by 4pm. Lunch main courses $6–$10; fixed-price dinner $32. MC, V. Daily 9:30am–3pm and 1 seating at 7pm.

5 Anegada ★

The most northerly and isolated of the British Virgins, 30 miles (48km) east of Tortola, Anegada has a population of about 250, none of whom has found the legendary treasure from the more than 500 wrecks lying off its notorious Horseshoe Reef. It's different from the other British Virgins in that it's a coral-and-limestone atoll, flat, with a 2,500-foot airstrip. Its highest point reaches 28 feet (8m), and it hardly appears on the horizon if you're sailing to it.

At the northern and western ends of the island are some good white-sand beaches, which might be your only reason for coming here. This is a remote little corner of the Caribbean: Don't expect a single frill, and be prepared to put up with some hardships, such as mosquitoes.

Most of the island has been declared off-limits to settlement and reserved for birds and other wildlife. The B.V.I. National Parks Trust has established a flamingo colony in a bird sanctuary, which is also the protected home of several different varieties of heron as well as ospreys and terns. It has also designated much of the interior of the island as a preserved habitat for Anegada's animal population of some 2,000 wild goats, donkeys, and cattle. Among the endangered species being given a new lease on life here is the rock iguana, a fierce-looking but quite harmless reptile that can grow to a length of 5 feet (2m). Although rarely seen, these creatures have called Anegada home for thousands of years.

ESSENTIALS

GETTING THERE The only carrier flying from Tortola to Anegada, **Clair Aero Service** (© **284/495-2271**), uses seven- to nine-passenger prop planes. It operates four times a week, on Monday, Wednesday, Friday, and Sunday, charging $66 per person round-trip. In addition, **Fly BVI** (© **284/495-1747**) operates a charter/sightseeing service between Anegada and Beef Island off Tortola. The one-way cost is $155 for two to three passengers.

GETTING AROUND Limited taxi service is available on the island—not that you'll have many places to go. **Tony's Taxis,** which you'll easily spot when you arrive, will take you around the island. It's also possible to rent **bicycles;** ask around.

ACCOMMODATIONS & DINING

The Anegada Reef Hotel is the only major accommodation on the island. Neptune's Treasure, below, rents tents and basic rooms.

Anegada Reef Hotel ✿ The only major hotel on the island is 3 miles (5km) west of the airport, right on the beachfront. It's one of the most remote places covered in this guide—guests who stay here are, in effect, hiding out. It's a favorite of the yachting set, who enjoy the hospitality provided by Lowell Wheatley. The hotel offers motel-like and very basic rooms with private porches, with either a garden or ocean view. Bathrooms are cramped with shower stalls. Come here for tranquility, not for pampering.

You can arrange to go inshore fishing, deep-sea fishing, or bonefishing (there's also a tackle shop); you can also set up snorkeling excursions and secure taxi service and jeep rentals.

There's a beach barbecue nightly, the house specialty is lobster, and many attendees arrive by boat. Reservations for the 7:30pm dinner must be made by 4pm. If you're visiting just for the day, you can use the hotel as a base. Call and they'll have a van meet you at the airport.

Setting Point, Anegada, B.V.I. © 284/495-8002. Fax 284/495-9362. www.anegadareef.com. 20 units. Winter $250–$275 double. Off-season $215–$250 double. Rates include all meals. MC, V. **Amenities:** Restaurant, bar. *In room:* A/C, no phone.

Neptune's Treasure *Finds* INTERNATIONAL Set near its own 24-slip marina, near the southern tip of the island in the same cluster of buildings that includes the more high-priced Anegada Reef Hotel, this funky bar and restaurant usually hosts a mix of yacht owners and local residents. Dining is in a spacious indoor area whose focal point is a bar and lots of nautical memorabilia. The drink of choice is a Pink Whoopie, composed of fruit juices and rum. The Soares family and their staff serve platters of swordfish, lobster, fish fingers, chicken, steaks, and ribs; dispense information about local snorkeling sites; and generally maintain order and something approaching a (low-key) party atmosphere.

They also offer nine simple bedrooms and about four tents for anyone looking for super-low-cost lodgings. Depending on the season, rooms with a private
bathroom rent for $90 to $105 double. Continental breakfast is included in the
rates, and discounts are offered for stays of a week or more.

Between Pomato and Saltheap points, Anegada, B.V.I. (© **284/495-9439**, or VHF Channel 16 or 68. www.
islandsonline.com. Breakfast $9; fixed-price meals $20–$40. MC, V. Daily 8–10am and 7–10pm.

6 Peter Island (★

Half of this island, boasting a good marina and docking facilities, is devoted to
the yacht club. The other part is deserted. Beach facilities are found at palm-
fringed Deadman's Bay, which faces the Atlantic but is protected by a reef. All
goods and services are at the one resort (see below).

The island is so private that except for an occasional mason at work, about
the only company you'll encounter will be an iguana or a feral cat whose ancestors
were abandoned generations ago by shippers (the cats are said to have virtually
eliminated the island's rodent population).

A hotel-operated ferry, **Peter Island Boat** (© **284/495-2000**), picks up any
overnight guest who arrives at the Beef Island airport. It departs from the pier at
Trellis Bay, near the airport. A round-trip costs $15. Other boats depart eight or
nine times a day from Baugher's Bay in Road Town. Passengers must notify the
hotel 2 weeks before their arrival so transportation can be arranged.

ACCOMMODATIONS & DINING

Peter Island Resort ★★★   This 1,800-acre (720-hectare) tropical island is
solely dedicated to Peter Island Resort guests and yacht owners who moor their
crafts here. The island's tropical gardens and hillside are bordered by five gorgeous private beaches, including Deadman's Beach (in spite of its name, it's often
voted one of the world's most romantic beaches in travel-magazine reader polls).

The resort contains 30 rooms facing Sprat Bay and Sir Francis Drake Channel (ocean-view or garden rooms) and 20 larger rooms on Deadman's Bay Beach
(beachfront). Designed with a casual elegance, each has a balcony or terrace. The
least desirable rooms are also the smallest and housed in two-story, A-frame
structures next to the harbor. Bathrooms with shower/tub combinations range
from standard motel-unit types to spectacular luxurious ones, depending on
your room assignment. The Crow's Nest, a luxurious four-bedroom villa, overlooks the harbor and Deadman Bay and features a private swimming pool. The
Hawk's Nest villas are two-bedroom villas situated on a tropical hillside.

Peter Island (P.O. Box 211), Road Town, Tortola, B.V.I. (© **800/346-4451** in the U.S., or 284/495-2000.
Fax 284/495-2500. www.peterisland.com. 54 units. Winter $800–$955 double; $1,320 2-bedroom villa;
$5,950 4-bedroom villa. Off-season $615 double; $870 2-bedroom villa; $3,150 4-bedroom villa. Rates
include all meals and transportation from the airport. AE, MC, V. **Amenities:** 2 restaurants, 2 bars; pool;
4 tennis courts; fitness center and spa; library; scuba diving, Sunfish sailboats, snorkeling gear, sea kayaks,
windsurfers, water-skiing, deep-sea fishing; room service (breakfast); massage; babysitting; laundry. *In room:*
A/C, minibar, hair dryer, safe.

7 Guana Island (★

This 850-acre (340-hectare) island, a nature preserve and wildlife sanctuary, is
one of the most private hideaways in the Caribbean. Don't come here looking
for action; rather, consider vacationing here if you want to retreat from the
world. This small island right off the coast of Tortola offers seven virgin beaches
and nature trails ideal for hiking; it abounds in unusual species of plant and

animal life. Arawak relics have been found here. Head up to the 806-foot peak of Sugarloaf Mountain for a panoramic view. It's said that the name of the island came from a jutting rock that resembled the head of an iguana.

The Guana Island Club will send a boat to meet arriving guests at the Beef Island airport (trip time is 10 min.).

ACCOMMODATIONS & DINING

Guana Island Club ★★   The sixth or seventh largest of the British Virgin Islands, Guana Island was bought in 1974 by Henry and Gloria Jarecki, dedicated conservationists who run this resort as a nature preserve and wildlife sanctuary. Upon your arrival on the island, a Land Rover will meet you and transport you up one of the most scenic hills in the region, in the northeast of Guana.

The cluster of white cottages was built as a private club in the 1930s on the foundations of a Quaker homestead. The stone cottages never hold more than 30 guests (and have only 2 phones), and because the dwellings are staggered along a flower-dotted ridge overlooking the Caribbean and the Atlantic, the sense of privacy is almost absolute. The entire island can be rented by groups of up to 30. Although water is scarce on the island, each airy accommodation has a shower. The decor is rattan and wicker, and each unit has a ceiling fan. Renting North Beach cottage, the most luxurious of the accommodations, is like renting a private home. The panoramic sweep from the terraces is spectacular, particularly at sunset. There are seven beaches, some of which require a boat to reach.

Guests will find a convivial atmosphere at the rattan-furnished clubhouse. Casually elegant dinners by candlelight are served on the veranda, with menus that include homegrown vegetables and continental and U.S. specialties.

P.O. Box 32, Road Town, Tortola, B.V.I. © 800/544-8262 in the U.S., or 284/494-2354. (For reservations, write or call the Guana Island Club Reservations Office, 10 Timber Trail, Rye, NY 10580; © 800/544-8262 in the U.S., or 914/967-6050; fax 914/967-8048.) www.guana.com. 15 units. Winter $850 double; $1,500 cottage. Off-season $640 double; $1,200 cottage. Rent the island for $11,500–$15,000. Rates include all meals and drinks served with meals. No credit cards. Closed Sept–Oct. **Amenities:** Restaurant; 2 tennis courts; massage; fishing, snorkeling, windsurfing, kayaks, sailboats, water-skiing; laundry; babysitting. *In room:* Ceiling fan, no phone.

The Cayman Islands

Despite the emergence of Grand Cayman as a major tourism destination in the 1990s, don't go to the Cayman Islands expecting fast-paced excitement. Island life focuses on the sea. Snorkelers will find a paradise, beach lovers will relish the powdery sands of Seven Mile Beach, but party-hungry travelers in search of urban thrills might be disappointed. Come to slow down and relax.

The Caymans, 480 miles (773km) due south of Miami, consist of three islands: **Grand Cayman, Cayman Brac,** and **Little Cayman.** Despite its name, Grand Cayman is only 22 miles (35km) long and 8 miles (13km) across at its widest point. The other islands are considerably smaller, of course, and contain very limited tourist facilities, in contrast to well-developed Grand Cayman. George Town on Grand Cayman is the capital and is therefore the hub of government, banking, and shopping.

English is the official language of the islands, although it's often spoken with an English slur mixed with an American southern drawl and a lilting Welsh accent.

1 Cayman Islands Essentials

VISITOR INFORMATION

The **Cayman Islands Department of Tourism** has the following offices in the United States: 6100 Blue Lagoon Dr., 6100 Waterford Bldg., Suite 150, Miami, FL 33126 (© 305/266-2300); 9525 W. Bryn Mawr, Suite 160, Rosemont, IL 60018 (© 847/678-6446); Two Memorial City Plaza, 820 Gessner, Suite 170, Houston, TX 77024 (© 713/461-1317); and 420 Lexington Ave., Suite 2733, New York, NY 10170 (© 212/682-5582).

In Canada, contact Earl B. Smith, **Travel Marketing Consultants,** 234 Eglinton Ave. E., Suite 306, Toronto, ON M4P 1K5 (© 416/485-1550).

In the United Kingdom, the contact is **Cayman Islands,** 100 Brompton Rd., London SW3 1EX (© 020/7491-7771).

The website for the Cayman Islands is **www.caymanislands.ky**.

GETTING THERE

The Cayman Islands are easily accessible. Flying time from Miami is 1 hour 20 minutes; from Houston, 2 hours 45 minutes; from Tampa, 1 hour 40 minutes; and from Atlanta, 3 hours 35 minutes. Only a handful of nonstop flights are available from the U.S. Midwest, so most visitors use Miami as their gateway.

Cayman Airways (© 800/422-9626 in the U.S. and Canada, or 345/949-2311; www.caymanairways.com) offers the most frequent service to Grand Cayman, with three daily flights from Miami, five flights a week from Tampa, two flights a week from Orlando, and three nonstop flights a week from Houston.

Many visitors also fly to Grand Cayman on **American Airlines** (© 800/433-7300; www.aa.com), which operates three daily nonstop flights from

---

Fun Fact **Ahoy, Matey!**

Cayman Islands Pirates' Week is held in late October. It's a national festival in which cutlass-bearing pirates and sassy wenches storm George Town, capture the governor, throng the streets, and stage a costume parade. The celebration, which is held throughout the Caymans, pays tribute to the nation's past and its cultural heritage. For the exact dates, contact the **Pirates Week Festival Administration** (© 345/949-5078).

Miami. **Northwest Airlines** (© 800/447-4747; www.nwa.com) flies to Grand Cayman from Detroit via Miami or Memphis, and from Memphis via Miami. **US Airways** (© 800/428-4322; www.usairways.com) offers daily nonstop flights from Charlotte, N.C. **Delta** (© 800/221-1212; www.delta.com) flies daily into Grand Cayman from its hub in Atlanta.

 FAST FACTS: The Cayman Islands

Business Hours Normally, banks are open Monday through Thursday from 9am to 2:30pm, and Friday from 9am to 1pm and 2:30 to 4:30pm. Shops are usually open Monday through Saturday from 9am to 5pm.

Currency The legal tender is the Cayman Islands dollar (**CI$**), currently valued at US$1.25 (CI80¢ equal US$1). Canadian, U.S., and British currencies are accepted throughout the Cayman Islands, but you'll save money if you exchange your U.S. dollars for Cayman Islands dollars. The Cayman dollar breaks down into 100 cents. Coins come in 1¢, 5¢, 10¢, and 25¢ denominations. Bills come in denominations of $1, $5, $10, $25, $50, and $100 (there is no CI$20 bill). Most hotels quote rates in U.S. dollars. However, many restaurants quote prices in Cayman Islands dollars, which might lead you to think that food is much cheaper than it is. *Unless otherwise noted, prices in this chapter are in U.S. dollars, rounded off.*

The cost of living in the Cayman Islands is about 20% higher than in the United States.

Documents Citizens of the United States and Canada should carry a valid passport or else a birth certificate with a raised seal along with a government-issued photo ID (we always recommend that you bring a passport). Citizens of the United Kingdom should have a valid passport. All visitors need a return or ongoing ticket.

Electricity It's 110-volt AC (60 cycles), so U.S. and Canadian appliances will not need adapters or transformers.

Emergencies For medical or police emergencies, dial © 911 or 555.

Hospital There's a hospital on Grand Cayman and another small one on Cayman Brac. Seriously ill cases on Little Cayman must be taken to Grand Cayman.

Language English is the official language of the islands.

Liquor Laws Beer, wine, and liquor are sold at most grocery and convenience stores Monday to Saturday (not on Sun). It is legal to have an open container on the beach.

Taxes A government tourist tax of 10% is added to your hotel bill. A departure tax of CI$10 (US$12.50) is collected when you leave the Caymans. There is no tax on goods and services.

Telephone To call the Cayman Islands from home, dial **1**, then the **345** area code, and the local number. **Cable and Wireless,** Anderson Square, George Town, on Grand Cayman (© 345/949-7800), is open Monday through Friday from 8:15am to 5pm, Saturday from 9am to 1pm, and Sunday from 9am to noon. Here you can purchase prepaid phone cards. Once you're on the island, to charge a long-distance call to a calling card, here are some access numbers: **AT&T** at © **800/225-5288, Sprint** at © **800/877-4646,** and **MCI** at © **800/888-8000.**

Time U.S. eastern standard time is in effect year-round; daylight saving time is not observed.

Tipping Most restaurants add a 10% to 15% charge in lieu of tipping, so check your bill carefully. Hotels also often add a 10% service charge to your bill. Taxi drivers expect a 10% to 15% tip.

Water The water in the Cayman Islands is safe to drink.

2 Grand Cayman (★(★

The largest of the three islands and a real diving mecca, Grand Cayman has become one of the hottest tourist destinations in the Caribbean in recent years. With more than 500 banks, its capital, George Town, is the offshore banking center of the Caribbean (no problems finding an ATM here!). Retirees are drawn to the peace and tranquility of this British Crown Colony, site of a major condominium development. Almost all the Cayman Islands' population of 32,000 live on Grand Cayman. The civil manners of the locals reflect their British heritage.

ESSENTIALS
GETTING THERE   See the information at the beginning of this chapter.

VISITOR INFORMATION   The **Department of Tourism** is located in the Pavilion Building, Cricket Square (P.O. Box 67), George Town, Grand Cayman, B.W.I. (© **345/ 949-0623**).

GETTING AROUND   All arriving flights are met by taxis. The fares are fixed by the director of civil aviation (© **345/949-7811**); typical one-way fares from the airport to Seven Mile Beach range from $11 to $12. Taxis (which can hold five people) will also take visitors on around-the-island tours. **Cayman Cab Team** (© **345/947-1173**) offers 24-hour service. You can also call **A.A. Transportation** at © **345/949-7222.**

Several car-rental companies operate on the island, including **Cico Avis** (© **800/331-1212** in the U.S., or 345/949-2468 on Grand Cayman; www.avis.com), **Budget** (© **800/527-0700** in the U.S., or 345/949-5605 on Grand Cayman; www.budgetrentacar.com), and **Ace Hertz** (© **800/654-3131** in the U.S., or 345/949-2280 on Grand Cayman; www.hertz.com). Each will issue the mandatory Cayman Islands driving permit for an additional US$7.50. All three require that reservations be made between 6 and 36 hours before pickup. At Avis drivers must be at least 21 and at Hertz, 25. Budget requires that drivers be between 25 and 70 years old. All three rental companies maintain kiosks within walking distance of the airport, although most visitors find it easier to take a taxi to their hotels and then arrange for the cars to be brought to them.

Remember to drive on the left and to reserve your car as far in advance as possible, especially in midwinter.

Cayman Cycle, at West Bay Road at Coconut Place (© **345/945-4021**), is open daily from 8am to 5pm, renting bikes for $15 per day or scooters and motorcycles at $25 per day.

FAST FACTS The only hospital is **George Town Hospital,** Hospital Road (© **345/949-8600**). The largest pharmacy is **Island Pharmacy,** West Shore Centre, Seven Mile Beach (© **345/949-8987**), open Monday to Saturday from 9am to 9pm, Sunday 10am to 6pm.

In George Town, the **post office** and Philatelic Bureau is located on Edward Street (© **345/949-2474**), open Monday to Friday from 8:30am to 5pm and on Saturday from 8:30am to noon. There's also a counter at the Seven Mile Beach Post Office, open the same hours.

ACCOMMODATIONS

Nearly all the hotels are lined up along Seven Mile Beach. Hotels, unlike many Caymanian restaurants, generally quote prices in U.S. dollars. When choosing a hotel, keep in mind that the quoted rates do not include the 10% government tax and the 10% hotel service tax.

Consider booking a package tour to make those expensive resorts more affordable. See the sections "Package Deals" and "Tips on Accommodations" in chapter 2 before you book.

The Ritz-Carlton chain continues its invasion of the Caribbean with the announcement that it is opening a resort and a series of condos on Grand Cayman by the winter of 2003. A nine-hole Greg Norman–designed private golf course and the island's only full-service spa facility are part of the package. A 366-room resort will be integrated with a 71-unit condo complex. The English colonial architectural and interior design will include white roofs and ivory-covered buildings, all set on 144 tropically landscaped acres (58 hectares) along Seven Mile Beach. Contact them at © **800/241-3333** for more information.

VERY EXPENSIVE

The Avalon ★★ One of Grand Cayman's best condo complexes is the Avalon, which occupies prime real estate on Seven Mile Beach. It consists of 27 oceanfront 3-bedroom/3-bathroom units, 15 of which can be rented. Only a short distance from restaurants, about a 5-minute drive from George Town, it has an architectural style and grace that's lacking in many beachfront properties. The well-appointed, spacious units have a tropical motif, plus king or twin beds. Each condo has a fully equipped open kitchen and a large, screened lanai that overlooks a stretch of the beach. Oversized tubs and separate shower stalls are in each bathroom.

West Bay Rd. (P.O. Box 31236), Grand Cayman, B.W.I. © **345/945-4171.** Fax 345/945-4189. 14 units. Winter $660 apt. for 4; $800 apt. for 6. Off-season $455 apt. for 4; $525 apt. for 6. AE, DISC, MC, V. **Amenities:** Pool; tennis court; fitness center; Jacuzzi; private garage. *In room:* A/C, TV.

Colonial Club ★★ The pastel-pink Colonial Club occupies a highly desirable stretch of the famous Seven Mile Beach. Built in 1985, it's a 3-story and rather standard condominium development about 4 miles (6km) north of George Town and some 10 minutes from the airport. First-class maintenance, service, and accommodations are provided in the apartments, all of which have

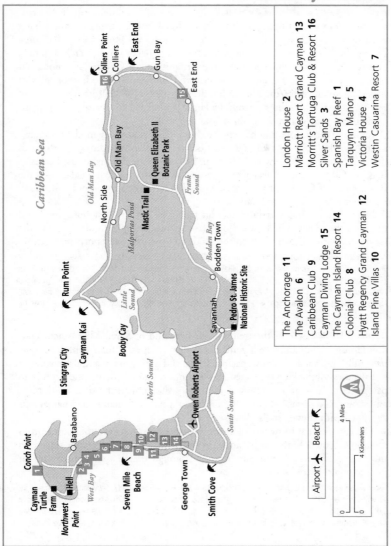

The Anchorage **11**
The Avalon **6**
Caribbean Club **9**
Cayman Diving Lodge **15**
The Cayman Island Resort **14**
Colonial Club **8**
Hyatt Regency Grand Cayman **12**
Island Pine Villas **10**

London House **2**
Marriott Resort Grand Cayman **13**
Morritt's Tortuga Club & Resort **16**
Silver Sands **3**
Spanish Bay Reef **1**
Tarquynn Manor **5**
Victoria House **4**
Westin Casuarina Resort **7**

kitchen fans, maid service, and laundry facilities. Usually only 12 of the 24 apartments are available for rent (the rest are privately owned and occupied but are sometimes rented out). You have a choice of units with two bedrooms and three bathrooms or units with three bedrooms and three bathrooms. Each unit has a well-maintained bathroom with a stall shower.

West Bay Rd. (P.O. Box 320W), Grand Cayman, B.W.I. ✆ **345/945-4660.** Fax 345/945-4839. 24 units. Winter $470–$530 apt. for 2; $520–$590 apt. for 3–4; $570–$650 apt. for 5–6. Off-season $260–$340 apt. for 2; $310–$390 apt. for 3–4; $360–$440 apt. for 5–6. Minimum stay 5 nights Dec 16–Apr 15. AE, MC, V. **Amenities:** Pool; lit tennis court; Jacuzzi. *In room:* A/C, TV, safe.

Hyatt Regency Grand Cayman ★★★   This $80 million resort is the best managed, most luxurious, and most stylish hotel in the Cayman Islands, lying on a lovely stretch of Seven Mile Beach. Two miles (3km) north of George Town, the hotel is a major component in the 90-acre (36-hectare) Britannia Resort community, which includes the Britannia Golf Course. The hotel has beautifully landscaped grounds. Dozens of Doric arcades are festooned with flowering vines that cascade beneath reflecting pools and comfortable teakwood settees. Low-rise buildings surround a large, landscaped courtyard that contains gardens, waterfalls, and the main swimming pool.

Rooms are luxurious and have private verandas but are only moderate in size. Each has a king-size or two double beds, and a spacious bathroom with a tub made of Italian marble. Two buildings and 44 rooms are devoted to the Exclusive Regency Club. The hotel also offers one- and two-bedroom luxury villas along the Britannia Golf Course or waterway. The villas have their own pool, whirlpool, laundry room, cabana, and patio area.

In the Hyatt's many restaurants and bars, you get the best hotel food and drink on the island. The Hyatt also offers the most complete watersports in the Caymans, with a Beach Club on the sands and the Red Sail Sports marina.

West Bay Rd. (P.O. Box 1588), Grand Cayman, B.W.I. ✆ **800/233-1234** in the U.S., or 345/949-1234. Fax 345/ 949-8528. www.hyatt.com. 384 units, 80 villas. Winter $415–$565 double; $585 1-bedroom villa; $755 2-bedroom villa. Off-season $220–$285 double; $295 1-bedroom villa; $385 2-bedroom villa. Ask about packages. AE, CB, DC, DISC, MC, V. **Amenities:** 6 restaurants, 4 bars; 6 pools (1 with swim-up bar); golf; tennis courts; health club and spa; 4 Jacuzzis; room service; babysitting; laundry. *In room:* A/C, minibar, TV, hair dryer, safe.

London House ★   At the tranquil northern end of Seven Mile Beach, London House is a good choice if you'd like your own upscale apartment. The units have fully equipped kitchens, spacious living and dining areas, and private patios or balconies overlooking the water. Floral prints, rattan, tile floors, and Caribbean pastels set the tone in most units. Ceiling fans supplement the air-conditioning, and daily maid service is available. Each room has well maintained bathrooms equipped with shower stalls.

The complex has its own seaside swimming pool (try to get a room away from the pool if you're bothered by noise, as house parties are sometimes staged on the patio). Many restaurants are nearby, although there's a stone barbecue for private poolside cookouts.

Seven Mile Beach, Grand Cayman, B.W.I. ✆ **345/945-4060.** Fax 345/945-4087. www.londonhouse.com.ky. 21 units. Winter $335–$375 1-bedroom apt.; $355–$475 2-bedroom apt.; $925 3-bedroom apt. Off-season $285–$305 1-bedroom apt.; $295–$360 2-bedroom apt.; $775 3-bedroom apt. Extra person $20 per day. AE, MC, V. **Amenities:** Pool; volleyball; babysitting; laundry. *In room:* A/C, TV, kitchen, fridge, coffeemaker, hair dryer.

Spanish Bay Reef ★   This is a small, intimate resort set in an isolated location amid the scrublands of the northwestern tip of Grand Cayman. It was the island's first all-inclusive resort. Rather informally run, the pale-pink, two-story stucco units are favorites with divers. (There's great snorkeling and diving right offshore from the coral beach.) The casual furnishings are in a Caribbean motif. The accommodations, which are rather simple, have balconies or patios with garden or ocean views. Don't expect grand comfort here: Rooms appeal to divers but perhaps not to those seeking resort-style accommodations and extras. Beds are comfortable, and bathrooms are a bit cramped, but contain shower/tub combinations.

Rates include all meals and beverages, island sightseeing, entertainment, use of bicycles, introductory scuba and snorkeling lessons, unlimited snorkeling or scuba diving from the shore (including tanks and weight belt), round-trip transfers, taxes, and service. If you're a diver, ask about Certified Divers Packages when making your reservations. Guests lounge around Calico Jack's Poolside Bar, and later enjoy an array of food (with lots of fish) in the Spanish Main Restaurant.

West Bay Rd. (P.O. Box 30867), Grand Cayman, B.W.I. © 800/482-3483 in the U.S., 800/424-5500 in Canada, or 345/949-3765. Fax 345/949-1842. www.caymanresorthotels.com. 63 units. Winter $250–$340 per person (nondiver); $322–$412 per person (diver). Off-season $160–$275 per person (nondiver); $230–$347 per person (diver). Children under age 12, $50 each per night in parents' room. Rates are all-inclusive. Ask about dive packages. AE, MC, V. **Amenities:** Restaurant, bar; disco; pool; Jacuzzi; snorkeling, dive shop. *In room:* A/C, TV.

Westin Casuarina Resort ★★★ The Hyatt has the edge, but this resort runs a close second. The Westin lies right on the sands on Seven Mile Beach with acres of landscaped grounds, beautiful swimming pools, and lots of sports facilities. Completed late in 1995, and designed by eminent architect Edward D. Stone, Jr., it was conceived as a direct competitor to the nearby Hyatt, which is more expensive and offers more facilities. The bedrooms are in five-story wings; most have French doors leading onto balconies. Units are a bit small for such a luxury hotel but are well equipped with quality mattresses and bed linens. Bathrooms are very spacious, with oversize marble tubs. The best rooms have ocean views; the "island view" units simply look out on the parking lot and main highway, so ask carefully when you reserve. Wheelchair-accessible rooms are available.

The most upscale of the restaurants is Casa Havana, a dinner-only gourmet restaurant that evokes the glamour of pre-Castro Cuba. One of the largest pools and poolside decks (5,000 sq. ft./450 sq. m) in the Caymans is appealingly lined with palm and date trees. Swimming pools, designed as lazy ovals or lagoons, flank the north and south sides of the hotel, each with its own cascade/waterfall. An 18-hole championship golf course, The Links at Safehaven, is across the street from the resort.

Seven Mile Beach (P.O. Box 30620), Grand Cayman, B.W.I. © 800/WESTIN-1 in the U.S., or 345/945-3800. Fax 345/949-5825. www.westin.com. 343 units. Winter $302–$426 double; from $1,000 suite. Off-season $284–$415 double; from $700 suite. AE, MC, V. **Amenities:** 3 restaurants, 3 bars; pool; 2 tennis courts; watersports, dive shop; children's programs; 24-hr. room service; laundry. *In room:* A/C, TV, minibar, coffeemaker, hair dryer, iron and ironing board.

EXPENSIVE

Caribbean Club ★★ Located right at the midpoint of gorgeous Seven Mile Beach, the low-key Bermudan-looking Caribbean Club is an exclusive compound of well-furnished villas, each with a full-size living room, dining area, patio, and kitchen. (Its only serious competition is the comparable Colonial Club.) When the owners are away, the units are rented to guests. The Caribbean Club has a long list of faithful repeat visitors who would stay nowhere else, although it is hardly deluxe. The pink villas are 3 miles (5km) north of George Town, either on or just off the beach; the 6 oceanfront units are more expensive than the others, of course. Accommodations are furnished in each owner's individual taste—which may not be yours. They contain attractive tropical furnishings, open verandas (often with barbecues), spacious closets, and combination bathrooms (tub and shower). At the core of the colony, the two-story club center, with tall, graceful arches, has picture windows that look out onto the grounds, which are planted with palm trees and flowering shrubs. The staff is one of the best and most helpful on the island.

Lantanas, the dining room, is open for lunch and dinner (see "Dining," below).

West Bay Rd. (P.O. Box 30499), Grand Cayman, B.W.I. © 345/945-4099. Fax 345/945-4443. www.caribclub. com. 18 units. Winter $260–$460 1-bedroom villa; $375–$525 2-bedroom villa. Off-season $180–$335 1-bedroom villa; $280–$375 2-bedroom villa. AE, MC, V. No children under age 12 Jan 3–Mar 15. **Amenities:** Restaurant; tennis court; laundry. *In room:* A/C, TV.

Island Pine Villas ✿

Right on Seven Mile Beach, this villa complex is comfortable and casual, far less elegant than either the Colonial Club or the Caribbean Club. At first glance (or even second glance), it looks like a motel along the Florida Turnpike. It is a family-friendly complex of one- or two-bedroom condos close to George Town. The units are well furnished with fully equipped kitchens, well-kept bathrooms with shower units, and daily maid service. There's a choice of queen- or king-size beds, and the best accommodations overlook the beach.

Seven Mile Beach (P.O. Box 30197-SMB), Grand Cayman, B.W.I. © 345/949-6586. Fax 345/949-0428. www.ipv.com.ky. 40 units. Winter $235–$270 double; Off-season $140–$180 double. AE, MC, V. **Amenities:** Dive shop; barbecue grills; laundry. *In room:* A/C, TV.

Marriott Resort Grand Cayman ✿

Way down in the pecking order from the Hyatt and Westin Casuarina, this five-story choice with an enviable location on Seven Mile Beach is still among the top ranked hotels on the island. It's a 5-minute drive north of George Town; there's good snorkeling 50 feet (15m) offshore. It's a favorite with large package-tour groups and conventions, and it has good watersports facilities. Its red-roofed, vaguely colonial design resembles a cluster of balconied town houses. Bedrooms were recently refurbished. Accommodations open onto the ocean or else the courtyard, and are decorated in cool Caribbean pastels. They have modern art, armoires, large closets, and private balconies. Bathrooms are spacious, with combination tubs and showers.

Serving a standard international cuisine, an oceanfront restaurant offers three meals a day and guests a choice of dining inside or out in the open air overlooking the water. Choose this place more for the beach out front than for the cuisine.

West Bay Rd. (P.O. Box 30371), Grand Cayman, B.W.I. © 800/333-3333 in the U.S., or 345/949-0088. Fax 345/949-0288. www.marriott.com. 309 units. Winter $375–$472 double; from $800 suite. Off-season $175–$240 double; from $500 suite. AE, DC, MC, V. **Amenities:** Restaurant, bar; pool; health club; watersports and dive shop; Jacuzzi; room service; babysitting; laundry. *In room:* A/C, TV, minibar, hair dryer, safe.

Morritt's Tortuga Club & Resort ✿

On 8 beachfront acres (3 hectares) on the east end of the island, this resort offers some of the island's best diving. This condo complex was built in the Antillean plantation style from the wreckage of a former hotel. Profiting from its position near offshore reefs teeming with marine life, it's the site of Cayman Windsurfing, which offers snorkeling and windsurfing, and rents sailboats and catamarans. Tortuga Divers, also on the premises, offers resort courses.

About a 26-mile (42km) drive from the airport, the club is composed of clusters of 3-story beachfront condos opening onto the water. Many are rented as time-share units. Each of the comfortably furnished apartments has a fully equipped kitchen, although many guests opt instead for meals in the complex's restaurant. Each unit has a small bathroom containing a shower/tub combination.

East End (P.O. Box 496GT), Grand Cayman, B.W.I. © 800/447-0309 in the U.S., or 345/947-7449. Fax 345/947-7299. www.morritt.com. 178 units. Winter $185–$195 studio; $245–$275 1-bedroom apt.; $345–$375 2-bedroom apt. Off-season $145–$155 studio; $185–$220 1-bedroom apt.; $255–$285 2-bedroom apt. AE, DISC, MC, V. **Amenities:** 2 restaurants, 3 bars; pool; watersports; room service; laundry. *In room:* A/C, TV.

Silver Sands ✪ A good choice for families, this modern 8-building complex is arranged horseshoe-fashion on the beach, 7 miles (11km) north of George Town. The well-maintained apartments are grouped around a freshwater pool. The eight apartment blocks contain either two-bedroom/two-bathroom or three-bedroom/three-bathroom units. The two-bedroom units can hold up to six people, and the three-bedroom units can house up to eight guests. Each apartment has a balcony, a fully equipped kitchen, and a small bathroom with shower. In all, this is a smoothly run operation, which, in spite of its high costs, satisfies most guests.

West Bay Rd. (P.O. Box 205GT), Grand Cayman, B.W.I. ✆ 800/327-8777 in the U.S., or 345/949-3343. Fax 345/949-1223. www.cayman.org/silversands. 15 condos. Winter $450 2-bedroom apt.; $545 3-bedroom apt. Off-season $260–$325 2-bedroom apt.; $395 3-bedroom apt. Additional person $25 extra. Children age 12 and under stay free in parents' unit. Minimum stay 7 nights in winter, 3 nights in off-season. AE, MC, V. **Amenities:** 2 tennis courts; laundry. *In room:* A/C, TV.

Victoria House ✪ Spanning 350 feet (105m) of prime oceanfront along Seven Mile Beach, this condo complex consists of one-, two-, and three-bedroom apartments, each with a bathroom containing a shower unit and tastefully furnished in a tropical motif. The resort is known for its trademark hammocks strung between the palms fronting the beach.

Seven Mile Beach, near West Bay (P.O. Box 30571-SMB), Grand Cayman, B.W.I. ✆ 800/433-DIVE in the U.S., or 345/945-4233. Fax 345/945-5328. www.victoriahouse.com. 25 units. Winter $290 1-bedroom apt.; $355 2-bedroom apt. Off-season $190 1-bedroom apt.; $215 2-bedroom apt. AE, MC, V. **Amenities:** Tennis court; snorkeling, scuba diving, deep-sea fishing. *In room:* A/C, TV.

MODERATE

The Anchorage On a tranquil part of Seven Mile Beach, this villa complex offers a series of well-furnished privately owned and individually decorated bedrooms. Each unit has two bedrooms and two baths (showers only) and each can accommodate up to four persons (great for two couples traveling together or for a family with kids). Units opening onto the garden are the least expensive; you pay more for oceanfront accommodations. Each villa has a screened porch or balcony overlooking the beach, where there's good snorkeling right offshore.

Seven Mile Beach, Grand Cayman, B.W.I. ✆ 800/433-3483 in the U.S., or 345/945-4088. Fax 345/945-5001. www.anchorage.ky. 15 units. Winter $240–$420 2-bedroom apt. Off-season $170–$310 2-bedroom apt. AE, MC, V. **Amenities:** Scuba expeditions arranged; laundry service. *In room:* A/C, TV, kitchen.

Cayman Diving Lodge This casual, laid-back place on a private coral sand beach, in the southeast corner of the island, 20 miles (32km) east of George Town, offers good value to experienced divers. The horseshoe-shaped lodge is a two-story, half-timbered building set amid tropical trees on a private coral-sand beach with a live coral barrier reef just offshore. Scuba trips include a daily two-tank morning dive of 3½ hours. The resort owns two 45-foot (14m) Garcia dive boats that are very comfortable.

In the rooms, the view of the ocean is better than the somewhat plain decor and furnishings. Linoleum floors, shower-only bathrooms, and jalousies set the tone. A few units have balconies. The bedrooms have been slightly improved recently, with new beds, furnishings, dressers, and curtains.

Chefs at the lodge's restaurant serve abundant meals and specialize in fish dishes; vegetarian food is also available.

East End (P.O. Box 11), Grand Cayman, B.W.I. ✆ 800/852-3483 in the U.S., or 345/947-7555. Fax 345/947-7560. www.divelodge.com. 12 units. Year-round with 2-tank dives, $651 double for 3 nights, $1,042 for 5 nights, $1,419 for 7 nights; with 3-tank dives, $686 double for 3 nights, $1,147 for 5 nights, $1,594 for

7 nights. Rates are per person and all-inclusive. Non-diving plans are available. AE, DISC, MC, V. **Amenities:** Restaurant; bike rental. *In room:* A/C, no phone.

Tarquynn Manor   Opening onto one of the loveliest stretches of Seven Mile Beach, this condo complex is a breezy, airy Caribbean place. The compound consists of two- or three-bedroom air-conditioned apartments, all of which are roomy and well furnished, with fully equipped kitchens. Even when you fill a unit with the six-person maximum, you'll find the large living area spacious. Each unit has a small bathroom with a shower stall.

Seven Mile Beach (P.O. Box 30435 SMB), Grand Cayman, B.W.I. ✆ **800/433-DIVE** in the U.S., or 345/945-4038. Fax 345/945-5062. www.tarquynn-manor.ky. 19 units. Winter $305 up to 4 persons; $430–$450 up to 6 persons. Off-season $265 up to 4 persons; $305 up to 6 persons. AE, MC, V. **Amenities:** Pool; sun deck. *In room:* A/C, TV.

INEXPENSIVE

The Cayman Inn and Resort *Value* *Kids*   Opened in 1992, The Cayman Inn and Resort is the closest hotel on Seven Mile Beach to the center of George Town. On rather bleak grounds, it lies 250 feet (75m) from the sands and about a 5-minute drive from the international airport. It's one of the more reasonably priced hotels on the island, offering value for your money, and it's a good choice for families. A franchise of Choice Hotels International, it offers both smoking and no-smoking rooms and units that are accessible for persons with disabilities. Furnishings are rather nondescript but perfectly comfortable. The rooms have modern tropical furnishings; the suites contain kitchenettes. Each unit has a small bathroom with a shower stall.

West Bay Rd. (P.O. Box 30111), Grand Cayman, B.W.I. ✆ **345/949-9111.** Fax 345/949-6699. www.caymaninnandresort.com. 121 units. Winter $150–$165 double; $195 suite. Off-season $109–$120 double; $179 suite. Rates include buffet breakfast. Children age 12 and under stay free in parents' room. AE, DC, DISC, MC, V. **Amenities:** 2 fast-food restaurants nearby, pool bar, pool grill; pool; dive shop; Jacuzzi; laundry/dry cleaning. *In room:* A/C, TV, safe.

DINING

Make sure you understand which currency the menu is printed in. If it's not written on the menu, ask the waiter if the prices are in U.S. dollars or Cayman Island dollars. It will make a big difference when you get your final bill; each Cayman Island dollar is currently worth US$1.25. Also note that, because virtually everything must be shipped in, Cayman Islands restaurants are among the most expensive in the Caribbean. Even so-called moderate restaurants can quickly push you into the expensive category if you order steak or lobster. For the best taste and value, opt instead for West Indian fare—items such as conch and grouper, which are invariably at the lower end of the price scale.

EXPENSIVE

Grand Old House ★★ AMERICAN/CARIBBEAN/PACIFIC RIM   This former plantation house lies amid venerable trees a mile (2km) south of George Town, past Jackson Point. Built on bedrock near the edge of the sea, it stands on 129 ironwood posts that support the main house and a bevy of gazebos. The Grand Old House is the island's premier caterer and hosts everything from lavish weddings and political functions to informal family celebrations.

The restaurant was put on the Cayman culinary map by chef Tell Erhardt, and it's often called Chef Tell's. And though the former TV celebrity chef is long gone, the Grand Old House has suffered no fallout in either food or service. The same menu has been retained, but it's been slightly updated by the new chef,

Indian-born Kandaphil Matahi. Appetizers remain the most delectable on the island, including coconut beer-battered shrimp and home-smoked marlin and salmon. Later, dig into the sautéed fresh snapper with shallots in Chardonnay white-butter sauce, or else the potato-encrusted tuna.

Petra Plantation, S. Church St. © **345/949-9333.** Reservations required. Main courses CI$18.50–CI$32.50 (US$23–US$40.60). AE, DISC, MC, V. Mon–Fri 11:45am–2pm; daily 6–10pm. Closed Sept.

Hemingway's ★★ SEAFOOD/INTERNATIONAL   The finest seafood on the island can be found 2 miles (3km) north of George Town at Hemingway's, which is named after the novelist and inspired by Key West, his one-time residence. You can dine in the open air, with a view of the sea. The menu is among the most imaginative on the island and has won acclaim from *Gourmet* magazine. Appetizers include pepperpot soup and gazpacho served with a black-bean relish. The catch of the day, perhaps snapper or wahoo, emerges from the grill to your liking. You can also order roasted rack of lamb served on fruit compote with caramelized-onion mashed potatoes. Want something more imaginative? Try grouper stuffed with crabmeat, or Cuban-spiced tenderloin served on white bean and fennel ragout.

In the Hyatt Regency Grand Cayman, West Bay Rd. © **345/949-1234.** Reservations recommended. Main courses CI$21.50–CI$28.50 (US$27–US$36); lunch CI$9.75–CI$15 (US$12–US$18.75). AE, DC, DISC, MC, V. Daily 11:30am–2:30pm and 6–10pm.

Lantanas ★★ CARIBBEAN/AMERICAN   In the middle of Seven Mile Beach is one of the best dining choices on Grand Cayman, with an imaginative menu. Begin, for example, with a jerk chicken quesadilla with jack cheese, black beans, roasted vegetables, and salsa, or roasted-garlic soup. The fish menu changes daily, offering only fresh and in-season seafood. Chances are that the seasonal menu will look like many others on the island—but look for a little more creativity here. The kitchen will even prepare an island-style jerk pork tenderloin with rice, black beans, plantains, and mango salsa. The Viennese apple strudel, called "apple pie" by the regulars, is still a specialty of the house. The upstairs has a view of Seven Mile Beach, and the downstairs has a Caribbean tropical decor.

In the Caribbean Club, West Bay Rd. © **345/949-5595.** Reservations recommended. Main courses CI$21.50–CI$27 (US$27–US$33.75). AE, DISC, MC, V. Daily 5:30–10pm.

Lighthouse at Breakers ★ CARIBBEAN/ITALIAN/SEAFOOD   On the south shore of the island, this local landmark lies about a 25-minute drive from George Town. Its creative menu features mainly fresh local seafood and an Italian cuisine. A well-trained chef, backed up by a skilled staff, offers well-prepared meals, attracting both locals and visitors. Try for a table with an ocean view. Here you can enjoy such tempting appetizers as portobello mushroom carpaccio with shaved Parmesan or else tuna sushi rolled in sesame seeds. For your main course, opt for the tender veal chop topped with gorgonzola and pancetta, or else a mixed seafood grill in a lemon butter sauce. Pastas are a strong feature on the menu, and fettuccine Mediterranean with seasonal vegetables is a particular favorite. The restaurant has one of the best wine cellars on island.

Breakers. © **345/947-2047.** Reservations recommended. Main courses CI$15–CI$40 (US$18.75–US$50). AE, DISC, MC, V. Daily 11:30am–4pm and 5:30–10pm.

Lobster Pot ★ SEAFOOD/INTERNATIONAL   Though not as good as Hemingway's, Lobster Pot is still an island favorite. It overlooks the water from its second-floor perch at the western perimeter of George Town, near what used to be Fort George. True to its name, it offers lobster prepared in many different ways: Cayman style, bisque, and salad. Conch schnitzel and seafood curry are on the menu, together with turtle steak grown commercially at Cayman Island kraals. Sometimes the seafood is a bit overcooked for our tastes, but most dishes are right on the mark. The place is also known for its prime beef steaks. For lunch, you might like the English fish-and-chips or perhaps seafood jambalaya or a pasta. The Lobster Pot's pub is a pleasant place for a drink—you may find someone up for a game of darts, too.

N. Church St. ☎ **345/949-2736.** Reservations required in winter. Main courses CI$15–CI$29 (US$18.75–US$36.25). AE, MC, V. Mon–Fri 11:30am–2:30pm; daily 5–10pm.

Ottmar's Restaurant and Lounge ★★ INTERNATIONAL/FRENCH/ CARIBBEAN   One of the island's top restaurants, Ottmar's is outfitted in a French Empire motif with lots of paneling, rich upholstery, and plenty of space between tables. There's a formal bar/lounge area decorated with deep-sea fishing trophies. This is the domain of an Austrian expatriate, Ottmar Weber, who has long abandoned the kitchen of his youth to roam the world, taking culinary inspiration wherever he finds it. The results are usually pleasing. You can order such dishes as Bavarian cucumber soup, bouillabaisse, French pepper steak, and Wiener schnitzel. Our favorite dish is chicken Trinidad, stuffed with grapes, nuts, and apples, rolled in coconut flakes, sautéed golden brown, and served in orange-butter sauce. The menu includes an array of sophisticated desserts, plus a selection of vegetarian dishes. Lunch is served at the Waterfall Restaurant. Ottmar's offers a professional welcome and attentive service. Every Friday from 5 to 8pm is happy hour, with live entertainment and free hors d'oeuvres, in addition to raffles for various prizes.

West Bay Rd. (side entrance of Grand Pavilion Commercial Centre). ☎ **345/945-5879.** Reservations recommended. Main courses $CI19–CI$32 (US$23.75–US$40). AE, MC, V. Mon–Fri 11:30am–2pm; daily 6–11pm.

The Reef Grill ★★★ SEAFOOD In the heart of Seven Mile Beach, this is one of the island's finest restaurants. The moment your first dish arrives from a seductive menu, you know you have made a good choice. Prepared from quality ingredients, the cuisine has a distinctive flavor and is imaginatively presented. You dine under the stars, listening to some of the most talented local musicians playing soca and calypso. One of the helpful, experienced staff will also guide you through one of the Cayman's best wine lists. We'd rate their appetizers the best on island, including shrimp and chicken spring rolls or hot fried calamari with a jalapeño mayonnaise. For exotic flavor, try the coconut grouper with a black bean sauce and a mango pepperpot, or the signature red snapper with a chili-laced vinaigrette. As for desserts, what on-island chef can top the almond and chocolate mousse served for a finale?

In the Royal Palms. Seven Mile Beach. ☎ **345/945-6358.** Reservations required. Main courses CI$17.60–CI$23 (US$22–US$28.95). AE, DC, MC, V. Daily 6:30–10pm.

Ristorante Pappagallo ★ NORTHERN ITALIAN/SEAFOOD   One of the island's most memorable restaurants lies on a 14-acre (6-hectare) bird sanctuary overlooking a natural lagoon, 15 minutes north of George Town. Its designers incorporated Caymanian and Aztec weaving techniques in its thatched roof. Glass doors, black marble, and polished brass mix a kind of Edwardian opulence with a Tahitian decor. You dine on black tagliolini with lobster sauce, fresh crab ravioli with asparagus sauce, lobster in brandy sauce, or perhaps Italian-style veal and chicken dishes. An occasional dish may be beyond the reach of the chef to prepare well, but the veal and seafood are generally good bets. The place strikes some diners as too pricey for what you get; we like to stop in for a nightcap.

At Villas Pappagallo, Conch Point, Barkers (near the northern terminus of West Bay Rd. and Spanish Cove, 8 miles/13km north of George Town). ✆ 345/949-1119. Reservations required. Main courses CI$14–CI$29 (US$17.50–US$36.25). AE, MC, V. Daily 6–10pm.

Smuggler's Cove ✦ INTERNATIONAL   Part of the charm of a meal at this place derives from the party-colored lights that flank the adjacent shoreline. The venue is airy, breezy, and ultra-comfortable, as witnessed by the hundreds of financial, sports-industry, and music-industry folk who have enjoyed savory meals here since the place was founded in the late 1990s. Menu items are served in generous portions and include an 8-ounce filet steak stuffed with 4 ounces of lobster tail (a glorified surf & turf), all of it drizzled with red wine sauce; a daily combination fish platter composed of at least two types of whatever fresh fish is hauled in that day; and a flavor-filled version of rack of lamb with mint sauce and rosemary. Savory beginnings include a platter of tuna and beef carpaccio with dill-flavored pesto sauce; and lobster, salmon, and blue crab cakes. You'll recognize the place by the rows of blue neon that ring its facade, its mustard-colored patio, and its location at the edge of George Town.

South Church St, South George Town. ✆ 345/949-6003. Reservations required. Main courses CI$19–CI$29 (US$23.75–US$36.25). AE, MC, V. Daily 5:30–10pm; Mon–Fri 11:30am–2:30pm.

The Wharf ✦ CARIBBEAN/CONTINENTAL   About 2 miles (3km) north of George Town, the 375-seat Wharf has been everything from a dinner theater to a nightclub. Try to catch the traditional 9pm feeding of the tarpon, which are kept in a large tank on the premises; it's quite a show. The restaurant is decorated in soft pastels and offers dining inside, out on an elevated veranda, and on a beachside terrace. The sound of the surf mingles with music from the strolling Paraguayan harpist and pan flute player and chatter from the Ports of Call Bar, located on the premises. Many diners begin with a Wharf salad of seasonal greens; others prefer the homemade black-bean soup or the home-smoked salmon. The main dishes feature everything from seafood potpourri, with lobster, shrimp, and scallops in a mild curry sauce, to veal Martinique, which is medallions of tender veal in a zesty citrus sauce. The kitchen makes a laudable effort to break away from typical, dull menu items, and for the most part they succeed.

West Bay Rd. ✆ 345/949-2231. Reservations recommended. Main courses CI$20–CI$33 (US$25–US$41.25). AE, MC, V. Daily 6–10pm.

MODERATE

Almond Tree ✦ SEAFOOD/INTERNATIONAL   Likable and unpretentious, this restaurant is supported by poles and branches, and it's lined with reeds and thatch rising into a peak. It contains a bar area accented with Trader Vic's–style artifacts and a garden lined with palmettos and flowering shrubs. Many guests prefer to dine in the garden; others like a table in the building's interior. Simple, straightforward cuisine is served, including mango chicken, conch steak, catch of the day, lobster, and filet mignon. This is not the most imaginative array of dishes ever offered, but the kitchen concentrates on what it does well. If you've never ordered it (because it's banned in the U.S.), this might be the place to request turtle steak. It's grown commercially in the Caymans and not taken from the wild.

N. Church St. (near the corner of Eastern Ave.). ✆ 345/949-2893. Reservations recommended. Main courses CI$17–CI$26 (US$21.25–US$32.50). AE, MC, V. Daily 11am–10pm.

Cracked Conch by the Sea SEAFOOD   Long a culinary landmark, this popular restaurant near the famous turtle farm in West Bay serves some of the island's freshest seafood and some of the most succulent turtle steak in the Caymans, along with burgers, chicken, steaks, and even a vegetarian pasta of the day. The menu is one of the largest on the island, and the inevitable namesake conch appears in various tasty combinations. Foods are freshly prepared—nothing frozen. The decor is a bit corny, including a cement floor made to look like "authentic" wood planking from a pirate ship. There's also a patio bar overlooking the sea, and a walkway built out so you can watch fish feeding at 8pm every evening.

West Bay Rd., near Turtle Bay Farm. © **345/945-5217.** Reservations recommended. Main courses CI$17.95–CI$33.95 (US$22–US$42). Sun brunch CI$12.95 (US$16). AE, MC, V. Daily 11:30am–10pm; Sun brunch 10am–3pm.

Crow's Nest Restaurant ★ *Value* CARIBBEAN   With a boardwalk and terrace jutting onto the sands, this informal restaurant has a view of both Sand Cay and a nearby lighthouse. It's on the island's southwesternmost tip, a 4-minute drive from George Town. The restaurant is one of those places that evoke the Caribbean "the way it used to be." There's no pretense here—you get good, honest Caribbean cooking, featuring grilled seafood. Try a daily special or perhaps sweet, tender Caribbean lobster. Other dishes include grilled tuna steak with ackee and Jamaican chicken curry with roast coconut. For dessert, try the banana toffee pie, if it's available.

South Sound. © **345/949-9366.** Reservations recommended. Main courses CI$14.95–CI$24.95 (US$19–US$31). AE, DISC, MC, V. Daily 11:30am–3pm and 5:30–10pm.

The Edge CARIBBEAN/FRENCH   At water's edge in historic Bodden Town, this French/Caymanian restaurant has received many awards since it opened in 1990. It's become well known for using the freshest seafood and the finest black angus steaks on island. You can dine inside or on a rear deck overlooking the beach and a reef in the distance. Often a diver's favorite, The Edge doesn't have great imagination in its kitchen, but exceptional products are always prepared with a finely honed technique here.

Bodden Town. © **345/947-2140.** Reservations required. CI$17.50–CI$31.95 (US$22–US$40). AE, DISC, MC, V. Daily 7:30am–10pm.

Island Taste ★ CARIBBEAN/MEDITERRANEAN   Set beside the harbor front in George Town, this restaurant sits across from the headquarters of the *Atlantis* submarine. There are indoor and outdoor bar areas and indoor tables, but the most popular seating area is on the wraparound veranda, one floor above street level. The restaurant has one of the largest starter selections on the island. Soups include both white conch chowder and turtle. Appetizers feature fresh oysters, Mexican ceviche, and calamari Vesuvio. At least seven pasta dishes are on the dinner menu, including linguine with small clams. You can also order T-bone steak and chicken parmigiana. However, most of the menu is devoted to seafood dishes. Dolphin (mahi-mahi) is served in different ways, and perennial favorites include the turtle steak and spiny lobster. This place caters more to large appetites than to picky gourmets.

S. Church St. © **345/949-4945.** Reservations recommended. Main courses CI$14–CI$29 (US$17.50–US$36.25). AE, MC, V. Mon–Sat 10:30am–4:30pm; daily 6–10pm.

INEXPENSIVE

Big Daddy's Restaurant and Sports Bar INTERNATIONAL   This bustling, big-windowed emporium of food and drink is set on the upper level of a concrete-sided building; look for the liquor store on the ground floor. One part of the restaurant is devoted to a woodsy, nautically decorated bar area, where TV screens broadcast either CNN or the day's big game. Three separate dining areas, more or less isolated from the activity at the bar, serve well-prepared food. We like the morning omelets, deli sandwiches, juicy half-pound burgers, garlic shrimp, T-bone steaks, barbecued ribs, fresh catch of the day, country-fried steak, and such pasta dishes as fettuccine alfredo.

West Bay Rd. ✆ **345/949-8511.** Main courses CI$12.95–CI$16.95 (US$16–US$21). AE, MC, V. Daily 8am–1am.

Corita's Copper Kettle ⭐ (Value) CARIBBEAN/AMERICAN   This place is generally packed in the mornings, when you can enjoy a full American breakfast or a wide selection of West Indian breakfast specialties, like green bananas served with fried dumplings, fried flying fish, and Corita's Special (ham, melted cheese, egg, and fruit jelly all presented on a fried fritter). For lunch, the menu varies from salads to chicken and beef along with conch, turtle, or lobster prepared as burgers or served up in a hearty stew.

In Dolphin Center. ✆ **345/949-7078.** Reservations required. Main courses CI$7–CI$14 (US$8.50–US$15); lunch CI$6.50–CI$8.50 (US$8–US$10.75). No credit cards. Mon–Sat 7am–5pm, Sun 7am–3pm.

HITTING THE BEACH

One of the finest beaches in the Caribbean, Grand Cayman's **Seven Mile Beach** ⭐⭐⭐, which begins north of George Town, has sparkling white sands rimmed with Australian pines and palms. (Technically, it's called West Bay Beach, but everybody just says Seven Mile Beach.) Although it's not actually 7 miles (11km) long, it is still a honey: 5½ miles (9km) of white, white sands stretching all the way to George Town. It tends to be crowded near the big resorts, but the beach is so big you can always find some room to spread out your towel. There are no peddlers to hassle you, and the beach is beautifully maintained.

Because the beach is on the more tranquil side of Grand Cayman, there is no great tide and the water is generally placid and inviting, ideal for families, even those with small children. A sandy bottom slopes gently to deep water. The water's so clear that you can generally see what's swimming in it. It's great for snorkelers and swimmers of most ages and abilities.

From one end of the beach to the other, there are hotels and condos, many with beachside bars that you can visit. All sorts of watersports concessions can be found along this beach, including places that rent snorkel gear, boats, Wind-surfers, wave runners, paddlecats, and aqua trikes. Parasailing and water-skiing are also available.

Grand Cayman also has a number of minor beaches, although they pale in comparison to Seven Mile Beach. Visit these if you want to escape the crowds. Beaches on the east and north coasts of Grand Cayman are good, filled with white sand and protected by an offshore barrier reef, so waters are generally tranquil.

One of our favorites is on the north coast, bordering the **Cayman Kai Beach Resort.** This beach is a Caribbean cliché of charm, with palm trees and beauti-ful sands, along with changing facilities. You can snorkel along the reef to Rum Point. The beach is also ideal as a Sunday-afternoon picnic spot. **Red Sail Sports** at Rum Point offers windsurfers, wave runners, sailboats, water-skiing, and even glass-bottom boat tours to see the stingrays offshore. It also offers scuba diving.

SPORTS & OTHER OUTDOOR PURSUITS

What they lack in nightlife, the Caymans make up for in watersports—the fishing, swimming, water-skiing, snorkeling, and especially diving are among the finest in the Caribbean. Coral reefs and coral formations encircle the islands and are filled with lots of marine life (which scuba divers and snorkelers are forbidden to disturb, by the way).

It's easy to dive close to shore, so boats aren't necessary, but there are plenty of boats and scuba facilities available. On certain excursions, we recommend a trip with a qualified dive master. There are many dive shops for rentals, but they won't rent you scuba gear or supply air unless you have a card from one of the national diving schools, such as NAUI or PADI. Hotels also rent diving equipment to their guests, as well as arrange snorkeling and scuba-diving trips.

Universally regarded as the most up-to-date and best-equipped watersports facility in the Cayman Islands, **Red Sail Sports** maintains its headquarters at the Hyatt Regency Grand Cayman, West Bay Road (© 877/REDSAIL in the U.S., or 345/949-8745; www.redsail.com). Other locations are at the Westin Casuarina (© **345/949-8732**) and at Rum Point (© **345/947-9203**). Red Sail has a wide range of offerings, from deep-sea fishing to sailing, diving, and more. Red Sail can also arrange water-skiing for $75 per half hour (the cost can be divided among several people) and parasailing at $60 per ride.

The following are the best options for a gamut of outdoor activities, arranged by subject.

CRUISES **Red Sail Sports** (see above) has a number of inexpensive ways you can go sailing in Cayman waters, including a glass-bottom boat ride costing $30 without snorkeling equipment or $35 with snorkeling equipment. It also offers sunset cruises costing $35. A 10am to 2pm sail to Stingray City, with snorkeling equipment and lunch included in the price of $85 per person, leaves once daily. Children under age 12 pay half price.

FISHING Grouper and snapper are most plentiful for those who bottom-fish along the reef. Deeper waters turn up barracuda and bonito. Sport-fishers from all over the world come to the Caymans for the big ones: tuna, wahoo, and marlin. Most hotels can make arrangements for charter boats; experienced guides are also available. **Red Sail Sports** (see above) offers deep-sea-fishing excursions in search of tuna, marlin, and wahoo on a variety of air-conditioned vessels with an experienced crew. Tours depart at 7am and 1pm, last half a day, and cost $600 (a full day costs $800). The fee can be split among four to six people.

GOLF The best course on the island, the **Britannia Golf Club,** next to the Hyatt Regency on West Bay Road (© **345/949-8020**), was designed by Jack Nicklaus and is unique in that it incorporates three different courses in one: a 9-hole championship layout, an 18-hole executive setup, and a Cayman course. The last was designed for play with the Cayman ball, which goes about half the distance of a regulation ball. Greens fees are a pricey $110 to play 18 holes, or $70 for 9 holes. Car rentals are included, but club rentals cost $20 for 9 holes or $40 for 18 holes.

Constantly windswept, the **Link at Safe Haven** (© **345/949-5988**) is a par-71, 6,605-yard (6,011m) course designed by Roy Case and set in what is tantamount to a botanical garden. On-site are a clubhouse, pro shop, and restaurant.

Tips   **Into the Deep: Submarine Dives**

So scuba diving's not enough for you? You want to see the real undiscovered depths of the ocean? On Grand Cayman, you can take the *Atlantis* reef dive. It's expensive, but it's a unique way to go underwater—and it might be the highlight of your trip.

One of the island's most popular attractions is the ***Atlantis XI,*** Goring Avenue (© **345/949-7700**), a submersible that's 65 feet (20m) long, weighs 80 tons, and was built at a cost of $3 million to carry 48 passengers. You can view the reefs and colorful tropical fish through the 26 large viewpoints 2 feet (.6m) in diameter, as it cruises at a depth of 100 feet (30m) through the maze of coral gardens at a speed of 1½ knots; a guide keeps you informed.

There are two types of dives. The premier dive, *Atlantis* Odyssey, features such high-tech extras as divers communicating with submarine passengers by wireless underwater phone and moving about on underwater scooters. This dive costs $89. On the *Atlantis* Expedition dive, operated both day and night, you'll experience the reef and see the famous Cayman Wall; this dive lasts 55 minutes and costs $79. Children age 4 to 12 are charged half price (no children under age 4 allowed). *Atlantis XI* dives Monday to Saturday, and reservations are recommended 2 days in advance.

Greens fees are $120 per person for 18 holes, with mandatory golf carts included. The golf course lies across Seven Mile Beach Road, opposite from the Westin Casuarina.

HIKING   The **Mastic Trail** is a restored 200-year-old footpath through a 2-million-year-old woodland area in the heart of the island. The trail lies west of Frank Sound Road, about a 45-minute drive from the heart of George Town, and showcases the reserve's natural attractions, including a native mangrove swamp, traditional agriculture, and an ancient woodland area—home to the largest variety of native plant and animal life found in the Cayman Islands. Guided tours, lasting 2½ to 3 hours and limited to 8 participants, are offered Monday to Saturday at 8:30am. Reservations are required, and the cost is $45 per person. The hike is not recommended for children under age 6, the elderly, or persons with physical disabilities. Wear comfortable, sturdy shoes and carry water and insect repellent. For reservations, call © **345/945-6588** Monday through Friday from 7 to 9am.

SCUBA DIVING & SNORKELING ✦✦   The leading dive operation in the Cayman Islands is **Bob Soto's Diving Ltd.** (© **800/262-7686** in the U.S. or 345/949-2022 to make reservations). Owned by Ron Kipp, the operation includes full-service dive shops at Treasure Island, the SCUBA Centre on North Church Street, and Soto's Coconut in the Coconut Place Shopping Centre. A full-day resort course, designed to teach the fundamentals of scuba to beginners who know how to swim, costs $120: The morning is spent in the pool and the afternoon is a one-tank dive from a boat. All necessary equipment is included. Certified divers can choose from a wide range of one-tank ($55) and two-tank

($85) boat dives daily on the west, north, and south walls, plus shore diving from the SCUBA Centre. A one-tank night dive costs $60. Nondivers can take advantage of daily snorkel trips ($30–$50), including Stingray City. The staff is helpful and highly professional.

Red Sail Sports (see above) offers beginners' scuba diving as well as excursions for the experienced. A two-tank morning dive includes exploration of two different dive sites at depths ranging from 50 to 100 feet (15–30m), and costs $85. Beginners can take a daily course that costs $120 per person. See also "Cruises," above, for information on Red Sports snorkel cruises.

The offshore waters of Grand Cayman are home to one of the most unusual (and ephemeral) underwater attractions in the world, **Stingray City** ★★. Set in the sun-flooded, 12-foot-deep (4m) waters of North Sound, about 2 miles (3km) east of the island's northwestern tip, the site originated in the mid-1980s when local fishers cleaned their catch and dumped the offal overboard. They quickly noticed scores of stingrays (which usually eat marine crabs) feeding on the debris, a phenomenon that quickly attracted local divers and marine zoologists. Today, between 30 and 50 relatively tame stingrays hover in the waters around the site for daily handouts of squid and ballyhoo from increasing hordes of snorkelers and divers. To capitalize on the phenomenon, about half a dozen entrepreneurs lead expeditions from points along Seven Mile Beach, traveling around the landmass of Conch Point to the feeding grounds. One well-known outfit is **Treasure Island Divers** (© **345/949-4456**), which charges divers $60 per one tank and snorkelers $35. Trips are made on Sunday, Wednesday, and Friday at 1pm. (Be warned that stingrays possess deeply penetrating and viciously barbed stingers capable of inflicting painful damage to anyone who mistreats them. Above all, the divers say, never try to grab one by the tail. Despite the potential dangers, divers and snorkelers seem amazingly adept at feeding, petting, and stroking the velvet surfaces of these bat-like creatures while avoiding unpleasant incidents.)

You'll find plenty of concessions offering snorkel gear for rent along Seven Mile Beach. The snorkeling is great in the clear, warm waters here. Other popular sites are Parrot's Reef and Smith's Cove, south of George Town. Lush reefs abound with parrot fish, coral, sea fans, and sponges. Also great for snorkelers is Turtle Farm Reef, a short swim from shore, offering a miniwall rising from a sandy bottom.

Another good dive outfit, **Tortuga Divers** (© **345/947-7449**), operates out of Morritt's Tortuga Club at Resort at East End. This outfitter caters to both experienced or novice divers, offering two daily dive jaunts at 9am and 2pm. Half day or full day snorkeling adventures can also be arranged at the same time, and all types of gear can be rented on the premises. The morning scuba dive costs $85, the afternoon dive going for $60. A half day's snorkeling costs $60, going up to $75 for a full day.

WINDSURFING   The best place for windsurfing on the island is the beach-front resort of **Morritt's Tortuga Club & Resort** at the East End (© **345/947-7492**). Surfing conditions here are ideal. The cost is $35 for 1 hour, $85 for 3 hours, and $130 for 5 hours. Lessons are also available for $45 for 1 hour. There's a large protected reef here opening onto a big lagoon.

EXPLORING THE ISLAND

The capital, **George Town,** can easily be explored in an afternoon; stop by for its restaurants and shops (and banks!)—not sights. The town does offer a clock monument to King George V and the oldest government building in use in the Caymans today, the post office on Edward Street. Stamps sold here are avidly sought by collectors.

The island's premier museum, the **Cayman Islands National Museum,** Harbor Drive, in George Town (© **345/949-8368**), is in a much-restored clapboard-sided antique building directly on the water. (The veranda-fronted building served until recently as the island's courthouse.) The formal exhibits include a collection of Caymanian artifacts collected by Ira Thompson beginning in the 1930s. Today the museum incorporates a gift shop, theater, cafe, and more than 2,000 items portraying the natural, social, and cultural history of the Caymans. Admission is CI$4 (US$5) for adults and CI$2 (US$2.50) for children age 7 to 12 and seniors, free for children age 6 and under. It's open Monday to Friday from 9am to 5pm and on Saturday from 10am to 2pm (last admission is half an hour prior to closing).

Elsewhere on the island, you might **go to Hell!** That's at the north end of West Bay Beach, a jagged piece of rock named Hell by a former commissioner. There the postmistress will stamp "Hell, Grand Cayman" on your postcard to send back to the U.S.

The **Cayman Turtle Farm** ✿, Northwest Point (© **345/949-3893**), is the only green sea-turtle farm of its kind in the world. Once the islands had a multitude of turtles in the surrounding waters (which is why Columbus called the islands "Las Tortugas"), but today these creatures are sadly few in number, and the green sea turtle has been designated an endangered species (you cannot bring turtle products into the United States). The turtle farm exists to provide the local market with edible turtle meat (preventing the need to hunt them in the wild) and to replenish the waters with hatchling and yearling turtles. Visitors today can observe 100 circular concrete tanks in which these sea creatures are in every stage of development; the hope is that one day their population in the sea will regain its former status. Turtles here range in size from 6 ounces to 600 pounds. At a snack bar and restaurant, you can sample turtle dishes. The turtle farm is open daily from 8:30am to 5pm. Admission is $5 for adults, free for children age 5 and under.

At **Batabano,** on the North Sound, fishers tie up with their catch, much to the delight of photographers. You can buy lobster (in season), fresh fish, and even conch. A large barrier reef protects the sound, which is surrounded on three sides by the island and is a mecca for diving and sport-fishing.

If you're driving, you might want to go along **South Sound Road,** which is lined with pines and, in places, old wooden Caymanian houses. After leaving the houses behind, you'll find good spots for a picnic.

Pedro St. James National Historic Site, Savannah (© **345/947-3329**), is a restored great house dating from 1780, when only 400 people lived on the island. It outlasted all the hurricanes until 1970 but was destroyed by fire that year. Now it's been rebuilt and is the centerpiece of a new heritage park with a visitor center and an audiovisual theater with a laser light show. Because of its size, the great house was called "the Castle" by generations of Caymanians. Its primary historic importance dates from December 5, 1831, when residents met here to elect Cayman's first legislative assembly. Therefore, Pedro St. James is the cradle of the island's democracy. The great house sits atop a limestone bluff with a panoramic view of the sea. Guests enter via a $1.5-million visitors center with a landscaped courtyard, a gift shop, and a cafe. Self-guided tours are possible. You can explore the house's wide verandas, rough-hewn timber beams, gabled framework, mahogany floors and staircases, and wide-beam wooden ceilings. Guides in 18th-century costumes are on hand to answer questions. Admission is $8 for adults, $4 for children, and free for those age 5 and under. Hours are daily from 9am to 5pm.

On the road again, you reach **Bodden Town,** once the largest settlement on the island. At Gun Square, two cannons commanded the channel through the reef. They are now stuck muzzle-first into the ground.

On the way to **East End,** just before Old Isaac Village, you'll see the onshore sprays of water shooting up like geysers. These are called blowholes, and they sound like the roar of a lion.

Later, you'll spot the fluke of an anchor sticking up from the ocean floor. As the story goes, this is a relic of the famous "Wreck of the Ten Sails" in 1788. A more recent wreck can also be seen—the *Ridgefield,* a 7,500-ton Liberty ship from New England, which struck the reef in 1943.

Old Man Bay is reached by a road that opened in 1983. From here you can travel along the north shore of the island to **Rum Point,** which has a good beach and is a fine place to end your island tour. Rum Point got its name from barrels of rum that once washed ashore here after a shipwreck. Today, it is dreamy and quaint, surrounded by towering causarina trees blowing in the trade winds. Most of these trees have hammocks hanging from their trunks, inviting you to enjoy the leisurely life. With its cays, reefs, mangroves, and shallows, Rum Point is a refuge that extends west and south for 7 miles (11km). It divides the two "arms" of Grand Cayman. The sound's many spits of land and its plentiful lagoons are ideal for snorkeling, swimming, wading, and birding. It you get hungry, drop in to the Wreck Bar for a juicy burger. After visiting Rum Point, you can head back toward **Old Man Village,** where you can go south along a cross-island road through savanna country that will eventually lead you west to George Town.

On 60 acres (24 hectares) of rugged wooded land off Frank Sound Road, North Side, the **Queen Elizabeth II Botanic Park** ⚡ (© **345/947-9462**) offers visitors a short walk through wetland, swamp, dry thicket, mahogany trees, orchids, and bromeliads. The trail is ⁸⁄₁₀ mile (1km) long. You'll likely see chick-atees, which are freshwater turtles found only on the Caymans and in Cuba. Occasionally you'll spot the rare Grand Cayman parrot, or perhaps the anole lizard, with its cobalt-blue throat pouch. Even rarer is the endangered blue iguana. The park is open daily from 9am to 5:30pm. Admission is CI$6 (US$7.50) for adults, CI$4 (US$5) for children, and free for children age 5 and under. There's a visitor center with changing exhibitions, plus a canteen for food and refreshments. It's set in a botanic park adjacent to the woodland trail and includes a heritage garden with a re-creation of a traditional Cayman home, garden, and farm; a floral garden with 1½ acres (.6 hectares) of flowering plants; and a 2-acre (.8-hectare) lake with 3 islands, home to many native birds.

GRAND CAYMAN AFTER DARK

Lone Star Bar & Grill, West Bay Road (© **345/945-5175**), is a transplanted corner of the Texas Panhandle. You can enjoy juicy burgers in the dining room or head immediately for the bar in back. Here, beneath murals of Lone Star beauties, you can sip lime and strawberry margaritas and watch several sports events simultaneously on 15 different TV screens. Monday and Thursday are fajita nights, all-you-can-eat affairs, at CI$12.99 (US$16), and Tuesday is all-you-can-eat lobster, at CI$37.97 (US$47). There's also a new volleyball court.

Legendz, West Bay Rd. (© **345/945-1950**), features traveling comedians on Wednesday, Thursday, Saturday, and Sunday nights with shows beginning at 9pm. On some of these nights live rock bands can also be heard. Another good spot is the **Royal Palms Beach Club,** West Bay Rd. (© **345/945-6358**), offering a bar open to the tradewinds where you can dance the night away in the moonlight. Local bands play here Wednesday to Saturday nights.

3 Cayman Brac ★

The "middle" island of the Caymans was given the name *Brac* (Gaelic for "bluff") by 17th-century Scottish fishers who settled here. The bluff for which the 12-mile-long (19km) island was named is a towering limestone plateau rising to 140 feet (42m) above the sea, covering the eastern half of Cayman Brac. Caymanians refer to the island simply as Brac, and its 1,400 inhabitants, a hospitable bunch of people, are called Brackers. Perhaps their laid-back lifestyle speaks to their predecessors: In the early 18th century the Caymans were occupied by pirates, and Edward Teach, the infamous Blackbeard, is supposed to have spent quite a bit of time around Cayman Brac. The island is about 89 miles (143km) east of Grand Cayman.

There are more than 170 caves honeycombing the limestone heights of the island. Some of the caves are at the bluff's foot, whereas others can be reached only by climbing over jagged limestone rock. One of the biggest is Great Cave, which has a number of chambers. Harmless fruit bats cling to the roofs of the caverns.

On the south side of the bluff you won't see many people, and the only sounds are the sea crashing against the lava-like shore. The island's herons and wild green parrots are seen here. Most of the Brackers live on the north side, many in traditional wooden seaside cottages, some built by the island's pioneers. The islanders must all have green thumbs, as attested to by the variety of flowers, shrubs, and fruit trees in many of the yards. On Cayman Brac you'll see poinciana trees, bougainvillea, Cayman orchids, croton, hibiscus, aloe, sea grapes, cactus, and coconut and cabbage palms. The gardeners grow cassava, pumpkins, breadfruit, yams, and sweet potatoes.

There are no actual towns, only settlements, such as Stake Bay (the "capital"), Spot Bay, the Creek, Tibbitts Turn, the Bight, and West End, where the airport is located.

ESSENTIALS

GETTING THERE   Flights from Grand Cayman to Cayman Brac are operated by **Cayman Airways** (© **800/422-9626** in the U.S., or 345/949-2311). The airline uses relatively large 737 jets carrying 122 passengers each. On Friday through Monday there is an evening flight here leaving at 5:40pm, plus a morning return at 6am. The round-trip cost is $107 to $141 per person and requires a 3-day advance purchase.

EMERGENCIES   There's a small hospital, the 18-bed **Faith Hospital** (© **345/948-2243**).

ACCOMMODATIONS

Brac Caribbean Beach Village ★   The largest condo project on the island offers 16 bright, spacious 2-bedroom/2-bathroom or 2-bedroom/3-bathroom condos on a white sandy beach, along with a pool and scuba-diving program. Each unit has a full-size refrigerator with an icemaker and a microwave, and

12 units open onto private balconies. A variety of items, including breakfast food, are stocked before your arrival. The master bedroom is furnished with a queen-size bed, the guest bedrooms with twin beds. Bathrooms are medium in size, each with a shower/tub combination. Maid service costs an extra $35 per day. The units are rather simply furnished in a Caribbean tropical motif.

The hotel offers some of the best dining on the island, at the Captain's Table (see below).

Stake Bay (P.O. Box 4), Cayman Brac, B.W.I. ⓒ **800/791-7911** in the U.S., or 345/948-2265. Fax 345/948-1111. www.brac-caribbean.com. 16 units. Year-round $185 apt. for 2; $245 apt. for 4. Weekly rates: $1,100 apt. for 2 adults for 7 nights; $1,600 apt. for 4 adults for 7 nights. Scuba packages from $345 for 5 dives. AE, MC, V. **Amenities:** Restaurant, bar; snorkeling; room service; laundry. *In room:* A/C, TV, coffeemaker, kitchen.

Brac Reef Beach Resort ✿

On a sandy plot of land on the south shore 2 miles (3km) east of the airport, near some of the best snorkeling in the region, this resort contains motel-style units comfortably furnished with carpeting, ceiling fans, air-conditioning, and shower/tub combination bathrooms. This is a durable resort, although frankly you'd be better housed at Walton's Mango Manor or Brac Caribbean Beach Village. Once the location was little more than a maze of sea grapes, a few of whose venerable trunks still rise amid the picnic tables, hammocks, and boardwalks. There are still lots of nature trails surrounding the resort, good for bird-watching. On the premises are the rusted remains of a Russian lighthouse tower that was retrieved several years ago from a Cuban-made trawler.

Lunches are informal affairs, and dinners are most often served buffet style under the stars. The food is not quite as good as that at the Divi Tiara (see below).

P.O. Box 56, Cayman Brac, B.W.I. ⓒ **800/327-3835** in the U.S. and Canada, or 345/948-1323. www.bracreef.com. 40 units. Winter $166 double. Off-season $134 double. Dive and meal packages available. AE, MC, V. **Amenities:** Restaurant, bar; pool; Jacuzzi; dive shop, reef fishing, snorkeling; babysitting; laundry. *In room:* A/C, TV, hair dryer.

Divi Tiara Beach Resort ✿

Part of the Divi Divi hotel chain, the Tiara, about 2 miles (3km) east of the airport, offers a white-sand beachfront. It's an excellent choice for divers, with a well-regarded dive operation. Many newcomers respond at once to the landscaping, which incorporates croton, bougainvillea, and palms. All the rather basic accommodations are housed in motel-like outbuildings; 13 of the units are time-shares, each with an ocean view, Jacuzzi, and a king-size bed. Bathrooms, with combination tubs and showers, are well maintained.

At the bar, guests gaze out to sea while sipping their drinks before heading to the Poseidon dining room to enjoy good Caribbean and American cuisine. Most meals are buffet style.

P.O. Box 238, Cayman Brac, B.W.I. ⓒ **800/367-3484** in the U.S. and Canada, or 345/948-1553. Fax 345/948-1316. www.divitiara.com. 71 units. Winter $140–$200 double. Off-season $105–$150 double. Children under age 12 stay free in parents' room. MAP (breakfast and dinner) $46 per person extra. AE, MC, V. **Amenities:** Restaurant, bar; pool; tennis court; dive shop; free bikes; laundry. *In room:* A/C, TV, hair dryer, safe.

Walton's Mango Manor ✿✿

Unique on Cayman Brac, this is a personalized, intimate B&B that's more richly decorated, more elegant, and more appealing than you might have thought was possible in such a remote place. Originally the home of a sea captain, it was moved to a less exposed location and rebuilt from salvaged materials shortly after the disastrous hurricane of 1932. Set on 3 acres (1 hectares) on the island's north shore, within a lush garden, it contains

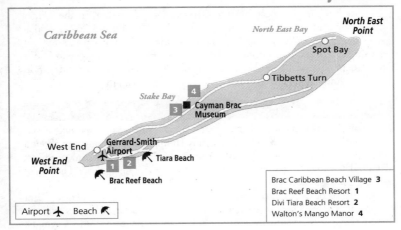

Caribbean Sea

North East Bay

North East Point

Spot Bay

Tibbetts Turn

Stake Bay

4

3 ■ Cayman Brac Museum

West End
West End Point

Gerrard-Smith Airport

Tiara Beach

1 2

Brac Reef Beach

Brac Caribbean Beach Village **3**
Brac Reef Beach Resort **1**
Divi Tiara Beach Resort **2**
Walton's Mango Manor **4**

Airport ✈ Beach ⚓

intriguing touches such as a banister salvaged from the mast of a 19th-century schooner. The most desirable accommodations are on the upper floor, partly because of their narrow balconies that offer views of the sea. Each room has a small bathroom equipped with a shower stall. Your hosts are Brooklyn-born Lynne Walton and her husband, George, a former USAF major who retired to his native Cayman Brac.

Stake Bay (P.O. Box 56), Cayman Brac. ⓒ and fax **345/948-0518**. www.waltonsmanor.com. 5 units. Winter $100–$110 double. Off-season $90–$100 double. Rates include full breakfast. AE, MC, V. *In-room:* A/C, no phone.

DINING

Captain's Table AMERICAN   The decor here is vaguely nautical, with oars over and around the bar and pieces of boats forming the restaurant's entryway. In the same building as a scuba shop and the hotel's reception desk, the restaurant offers both indoor, air-conditioned seating and outside dining by the pool. Begin with shrimp and lobster cocktail or perhaps a conch fritter, and then try one of the soups, such as black bean. Main dishes include everything from the catch of the day, often served pan-fried, to barbecue ribs. At lunch, you can order burgers and sandwiches.

In Brac Caribbean Beach Village, Stake Bay. ⓒ **345/948-1418**. Reservations recommended. Main courses CI$14.75–CI$24.50 (US$18–US$31); lunch from CI$7 (US$6). AE, MC, V. Mon–Sat 11:30am–3pm and 6–10pm; Sun noon–3pm and 6–10pm.

FUN ON & OFF THE BEACH

The biggest lure to Cayman Brac is the variety of **watersports**—swimming, fishing, snorkeling, and some of the world's best diving. There are undersea walls on both the north and south sides of the island, with stunning specimens lining their sides. The big attraction for divers is the M.V. *Tibbetts,* a 330-foot-long (99m) Russian frigate resting in 100 feet (30m) of water, a relic of the Cold War sunk in September of 1996. Hatches into the ship have been barred off to ensure diver safety. Marine life is becoming more pronounced on this relic, which now rests in a watery grave far, far from its home. The best dive center is **Dive Tiara** at the Divi Tiara Beach Resort (ⓒ **800/367-3484** in the U.S., or 345/948-1553). There's also **Brac Aquatics, Ltd.** (ⓒ **800/544-2722** in the U.S., or 345/948-1429).

History buffs might check out the **Cayman Brac Museum,** in the former Government Administration Building, Stake Bay (© **345/948-2622**), which has an interesting collection of Caymanian antiques, including pieces rescued from shipwrecks and items from the 18th century. Hours are Monday to Friday from 9am to noon and 1 to 4pm, Saturday from 9am to noon, and Sunday from 1 to 4pm. Admission is free.

4 Little Cayman ★

The smallest of the Cayman Islands, cigar-shaped Little Cayman has only about 40 permanent inhabitants. Little Cayman is 10 miles (16km) long and about a mile (2km) across at its widest point. It lies about 75 miles (121km) northeast of Grand Cayman and some 5 miles (8km) from Cayman Brac. The entire island is coral and sand.

The islands of the Caymans are mountaintops of the long-submerged Sierra Maestra Range, which runs north and into Cuba. Coral formed layers over the underwater peaks, eventually creating the islands. Beneath Little Cayman's Bloody Bay is one of the mountain's walls—a stunning sight for snorkelers and scuba divers.

The island seems to have come into its own now that fishing and diving have taken center stage; this is a near-perfect place for such pursuits. The late Jacques Cousteau hailed the waters around the little island as one of the three finest diving spots in the world. The flats on Little Cayman are said to offer the best bonefishing in the world, and a brackish inland pool can be fished for tarpon. Even if you don't dive or fish, you can row 200 yards (182m) off Little Cayman to isolated and uninhabited Owen Island, where you can swim at the sandy beach and picnic by a blue lagoon.

There may still be pirate treasure buried on the island, but it's in the dense interior of what is now the largest bird sanctuary in the Caribbean. In addition to having the largest population of rock iguanas in the entire Caribbean, which you will easily see, Little Cayman is also home to one of the oldest species of reptiles in the New World—the tree-climbing *Anulis maynardi* (which is known by no other name). This rare lizard is difficult to spot, however, because the females are green, the males brown, and, as such, they blend into local vegetation.

Blossom Village, the island's "capital," is on the southwest coast.

Most visitors fly from Grand Cayman to Little Cayman. **Island Air** (© **345/949-5252** on Grand Cayman; www.islandaircayman.com) is a charter company that charges $159 per person round-trip. Flights leave Grand Cayman four times daily at 7:45am, 9:45am, 2:35pm, and 4:35pm. The return flights are scheduled daily at 8:55am, 10:30am, 3:20pm, and 5:45pm.

ACCOMMODATIONS

Little Cayman Beach Resort ★★   Lying on the south coast, this resort is close to many of the island's diving and sporting attractions, including bonefishing in the South Hole Sound Lagoon. It's popular with anglers, divers, birdwatchers, and adventurous types. The hotel, owned by Dan Tibbetts, lies only three-quarters of a mile (2km) from the Edward Bodden Airport (really a grass airstrip), and it has a white-sand beach fringing a shallow, reef-protected bay. No-smoking units are available, and the rooms have ceiling fans. They are divided into two pastel, coral, two-story buildings with gingerbread trim. The most desirable units are the four luxurious oceanfront rooms, which go fast, since they go for the same price as the others in spite of their added comfort. Ceiling fans

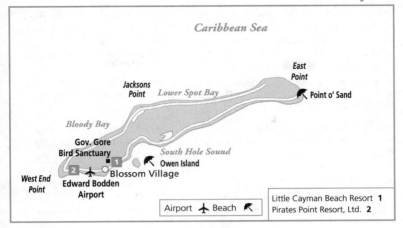

Caribbean Sea

Little Cayman Beach Resort **1**
Pirates Point Resort, Ltd. **2**

Airport ✈ Beach ✦

and tropical colors make for an inviting, airy atmosphere, and units have one king-size or two double beds, plus a combination bathroom (tub and shower).

Blossom Village, Little Cayman, Cayman Islands, B.W.I. ✆ **800/327-3835** in the U.S. and Canada, or 345/948-1033. Fax 345/948-1040. www.braclittle.com. 40 units. Winter $663–$797 per person double (diver); $483–$617 per person double (nondiver). Off-season $596–$730 per person double (diver); $416–$550 per person double (nondiver). Rates are for 3 nights and include MAP (breakfast and dinner). Longer packages are available. AE, DC, MC, V. **Amenities:** Restaurant, bar; pool; tennis court; health club, Jacuzzi; watersports; bike rental; babysitting; laundry service. *In room:* A/C, TV, coffeemaker, hair dryer, no phone.

Pirates Point Resort, Ltd. ✦   For watersports or just relaxing, this resort near West End Point offers a family environment with gourmet cuisine, although it's a notch down from Little Cayman Beach Resort. The place has remodeled rooms, and a non-air-conditioned family cottage of two large rooms, each suitable for three or four people. In addition, it has four recently built seaside cottages, with balconies overlooking Preston Bay. The bathrooms are well maintained, with shower stalls.

The resort's packages include room, three excellent meals per day with appropriate wines and all alcoholic beverages, and two-tank boat dives daily, featuring tours of the Bloody Bay Wall, the Cayman trench, and Jackson Reef. Other activities include snorkeling, bird-watching, and exploring.

The food here is excellent. The owner and manager, Gladys Howard, a graduate of Cordon Bleu in Paris, who has studied with such stars as Julia Child and the late James Beard, has written several cookbooks. She uses fresh fruits and vegetables grown locally, as well as local seafood.

Little Cayman, Cayman Islands, B.W.I. ✆ **345/948-1010.** Fax 345/948-1011. www.piratespointresort.com. 10 units. Winter $250 per person double (diver); $195 per person double (nondiver). Off-season $230 per person double (diver); $170 per person double (nondiver). Rates are all-inclusive (nondiver rates do not include bar tab); triple rates are slightly lower. DISC, MC, V. No children under age 6. **Amenities:** Restaurant; pool; Jacuzzi; diving, snorkeling, bonefishing, tarpon fishing; off-island picnics. *In room:* A/C, no phone.

DINING

Birds of Paradise AMERICAN/CONTINENTAL   This spot caters primarily to Little Cayman Beach Resort guests but welcomes anyone. The specialty is buffet-style dinners—the kind your parents might have enjoyed back in the 1950s or '60s. Saturday night features the island's most generous barbecue spread—all the ribs, fish, and Jamaican-style jerk chicken you'd want. On other nights, try the prime rib, fresh fish Caribbean style (your best bet), or chicken either Russian style (Kiev) or French style (cordon bleu). There's a freshly made salad bar, and homemade desserts are yummy, especially the key lime pie. At night, opt for an outdoor table under the stars.

At Little Cayman Beach Resort. ☎ **345/948-1033**. Reservations recommended for dinner. Dinner CI$31.25 (US$39); lunch CI$18.75 (US$23); breakfast CI$15 (US$18.75). AE, MC, V. Daily 7–8:30am, 12:30–1:30pm, and 6:30–8pm.

The Hungry Iguana AMERICAN/CARIBBEAN   At the beach, you'll spot this place immediately with its mammoth iguana mural. The island's tastiest dishes are served here, a winning combination of standard American fare along with some zesty flavors from the islands south of here. It's the rowdiest place on the island, especially the sports bar with its satellite TV in the corner, a sort of TGI Friday's atmosphere. Lunch is the usual burgers and fries along with some well-stuffed sandwiches. We always prefer the grilled chicken salad. Dinner gets a little more elaborate—there's usually a special meat dish of the day, depending on the market (supplies are shipped in once a week by barge). The chef always seems willing to prepare a steak as you like it. Try one of the seafood platters. Marinated shrimp with rémoulade is a tasty choice as well.

Paradise Resort. ☎ **345/948-0007**. Reservations recommended. Dinner CI$14–CI$27.95 (US$17.50–US$35); lunch CI$12.50–CI$16 (US$16–US$22.50). AE, MC, V. Daily noon–2:30pm and 5:30–9pm. Bar open Mon–Fri noon–1am, Sat–Sun noon–midnight.

SPORTS & OTHER OUTDOOR PURSUITS

The **Governor Gore Bird Sanctuary** ★ is home to some 5,000 pairs of red-footed boobies. As far as it is known, this is the largest colony of such birds in the western hemisphere. The sanctuary, which is near the small airport, is also home to dramatic colonies of snowy egrets and black frigates. Many bird-watchers from the U.S. fly into Little Cayman just to see these bird colonies.

The best **fishing** is at Bloody Bay, lying off the island's north coast. It is especially noted for its bonefishing and tarpon catches. For fishing, contact **Sam McCoy's Diving and Fishing Lodge** (☎ **800/626-0496**).

The **Bloody Bay Wall** ★★ is also the best dive site on island, lying just 20 minutes offshore and reached by boat. The drop here begins at only 20 feet (6m) but plunges to more than 1,200 feet (360m). This is one of the great dive spots in the Caymans. For more information about how to enjoy it, call **Paradise Divers** at ☎ **800/450-2084** in the U.S. or 345/948-0004.

10

Curaçao

Just 35 miles (56km) north of the coast of Venezuela, Curaçao, the "C" of the Dutch ABC islands of the Caribbean, is the most populous of the Netherlands Antilles. Visitors are attracted to its distinctive culture, warm people, duty-free shopping, lively casinos, and watersports. Fleets of tankers head out from its harbor to bring refined oil to all parts of the world. If you want grand high-rise resorts on spectacular beaches, head for Aruba (see chapter 5). Curaçao has a few middle-bracket resorts on the beach, mostly along the island's southern coast, but we've always found the shopping and cultural experiences here more appealing than the beaches.

A self-governing part of the Netherlands, Curaçao was spotted not by Columbus, but by two of his lieutenants, Alonso de Ojeda and Amerigo Vespucci, in 1499. The Spaniards exterminated all but 75 members of a branch of the peaceful Arawaks. However, they in turn were ousted by the Dutch in 1634, who also had to fight off French and English invasions.

The Dutch made the island a tropical Holland in miniature. Pieter Stuyvesant, stomping on his peg leg, ruled Curaçao in 1644. The island was turned into a Dutch Gibraltar, bristling with forts. Thick ramparts guarded the harbor's narrow entrance; the hilltop forts (many now converted into restaurants) protected the coastal approaches.

In the 20th century, Curaçao remained sleepy until 1915, when the Royal Dutch/Shell Company built one of the world's largest oil refineries here to process crude oil from Venezuela. Workers from some 50 countries poured onto the island, turning Curaçao into a multicultural, cosmopolitan community.

The largest of the Netherlands Antilles, Curaçao is 37 miles (60km) long and 7 miles (11km) across at its widest point. Because of all that early Dutch building, Curaçao is the most important island architecturally in the entire West Indies, with more European flavor than anywhere else. After leaving the capital, **Willemstad,** you plunge into a strange, desert-like countryside that evokes the U.S. southwest. The relatively arid landscape is studded with three-pronged cactus, spiny-leafed aloe, and divi-divi trees, with their windblown foliage. Classic Dutch-style windmills are scattered in and around Willemstad and in parts of the countryside.

Curaçao, together with Bonaire, St. Eustatius, St. Maarten, and Saba, is in the Kingdom of the Netherlands as part of the Netherlands Antilles. Curaçao has its own governmental authority, relying on the Netherlands only for defense and foreign affairs. Its population of 171,000 represents more than 50 nationalities.

1 Essentials

VISITOR INFORMATION
In the United States, contact the **Curaçao Tourist Board** at 19495 Biscayne Blvd., Suite 804, Aventuna FL 33180 (© **800/3-curacao**). You can also point your Web browser to **www.curacao-tourism.com**.

Once you're on the island, go to the **Curaçao Tourist Board,** Pietermaai 19 (© **599/9-461-6000**).

GETTING THERE
The air routes to **Curaçao International Airport,** Plaza Margareth Abraham (© **599/9-888-0101**), are still firmly linked to those leading to nearby Aruba. In recent years, however, some airlines have initiated direct or nonstop routings into Curaçao from such international hubs as Miami.

American Airlines (© **800/433-7300** in the U.S.; www.aa.com) offers a daily nonstop flight to Curaçao from its hub in Miami; it departs late enough in the day to permit easy connections from cities all over the northeastern U.S. American also offers flights to Curaçao's neighbor, Aruba, from New York, Miami, and San Juan, Puerto Rico. Once on Aruba, many travelers transfer on to Curaçao on any of ALM's many shuttle flights. American Airlines also offers discounted hotel/airfare packages. The regional affiliate of American Airlines, **American Eagle,** now flies from San Juan to Curaçao, going via Aruba.

ALM (© **800/327-7230** in the U.S.; www.airalm.com) is Curaçao's national carrier. It flies 14 times per week from Miami to Curaçao. Although 10 of these flights stop on Aruba, Bonaire, or Haiti, the others are nonstop. British travelers might take the daily British Airways flight to Amsterdam, where there are two daily **KLM** (© **800-447-4747** in the U.S.; www.klm.com) direct flights to Curaçao.

GETTING AROUND
BY RENTAL CAR   Because all points of interest on Curaçao are easily accessible via paved roads, you may want to rent a car. U.S., British, and Canadian visitors can use their own licenses, if valid. *Note: Traffic moves on the right.* International road signs are observed.

Avis (© **800/331-2112;** www.avis.com) and **Budget** (© **800/472-3325;** www.budget.com) offer some of the lowest rates. **Budget** usually offers the best deal if it has compact cars with manual transmissions in stock; **Hertz** (© **800/654-3001** in the U.S., or 599/9-8681182 on Curaçao; www.hertz.com) is also on island. Rentals are cheaper if you reserve from North America at least a week

---

Fun Fact Special Events

The big event of the year is the **Curaçao Carnival,** which starts on New Year's Day, with various festivities extending until the day before Ash Wednesday. The schedule is available at the tourism office. The most fun events, similar to hoe-downs, are called *jump-ups.* The highlight of carnival is the **Festival di Tumba,** the second week in February, in which the island's musicians vie for prizes in a hot contest. Other carnival events include the crowning of a queen and king, street parades, concerts, and even a children's carnival.

Aliva Beach Hotel **7**
Breezes Curaçao **10**
Chogogo Resort **12**
Curaçao Marriott Beach Resort
& Emerald Casino **4**
Habitat Curaçao **2**
Holiday Beach Hotel & Casino **6**
Hotel Holland **3**
Kura Hulanda Hotel and Casino **6**
Landhaus Daniel Inn **1**
Lion's Dive Hotel & Marina **11**
Plaza Hotel & Casino **8**
Sheraton Curaçao Resort **5**

before your departure, and rates vary depending on the various times of the year and seasonal promotions.

Local car-rental firms include **Rent a Yellow,** Cascoreweg 33 (© **599/9-767-3777**), whose cars are painted like a yellow cab. The lowest rates are for vehicles without air-conditioning, costing from $65 daily. Tariffs include tax and insurance.

BY TAXI Taxis are unmetered, so ask your driver to quote a price before you get in. Drivers are supposed to carry an official rate sheet, which they'll produce upon request. Charges go up by 25% after 11pm. Tipping isn't the usual custom among islanders, but from tourists, drivers will appreciate a 10% tip at your discretion, especially if they've given you help with your luggage. The fare from the airport to Willemstad is about $18, and the cost can be split among four passengers. If a piece of luggage is so big that the trunk lid won't close, you'll be assessed a surcharge of $1.

In town, the best place to get a taxi is on the Otrabanda side of the floating bridge. To summon a cab, call ℂ **599/9-869-0752.** Cabbies will usually give you a tour of the island for around $30 per hour for up to four passengers.

BY BUS Some hotels operate a free shuttle that takes you from the suburbs to the shopping district of Willemstad. A fleet of DAF yellow buses operates from Wilhelmina Plein, near the shopping center, to most parts of Curaçao. Some limousines function as C buses. If you see one listing your destination, you can hail it at any of the designated bus stops.

 FAST FACTS: Curaçao

Banking Hours Bank hours are Monday to Friday from 8:30am to noon and 1:30 to 4:30pm. However, the Banco Popular and the Bank of America remain open during the lunch hour, doing business Monday to Friday from 9am to 3pm. Banks and ATMs can be found in Willemstad.

Currency While Canadian and U.S. dollars are accepted for purchases on the island, the official currency is the Netherlands Antillean florin (NAf), also called a **guilder,** which is divided into 100 NA (Netherlands Antillean) cents. The exchange rate as of this writing is US$1 to 1.77 NAf (1 NAf = 56¢). (Just before you leave home, you can check the current exchange rates on the Web at **www.x-rates.com.**) Shops, hotels, and restaurants usually accept most major U.S. and Canadian credit and charge cards.

Documents To enter Curaçao, U.S. or Canadian citizens need proof of citizenship, such as a birth certificate or a passport, along with a return or continuing airline ticket out of the country and photo ID. (We recommend that you bring a passport.) British subjects need a valid passport.

Electricity The electricity is 110- to 130-volt AC (50 cycles), the same as in North America, although many hotels have transformers for European appliances.

Hospital The **St. Elisabeth Hospital,** Breedestraat 193 (ℂ **599/9-4624900**), near Otrabanda in Willemstad, is one of the most up-to-date facilities in the Caribbean.

Language Dutch, Spanish, and English are spoken on Curaçao, along with Papiamento, a patois that combines the three major tongues with Amerindian and African dialects. Most people in the tourism industry speak English, but you can always thank them by saying *masha danki.*

Police The police emergency number is ℂ **911.**

Safety Although Curaçao is not plagued with crime, it's wise to safeguard your valuables.

Taxes Curaçao levies a room tax of 7% on accommodations. There's a departure tax of $20 for international flights, or $5.75 for flights to other islands in the Netherlands Antilles. You can pay it in U.S. dollars.

Telephone To call Curaçao from the United States, dial **011** (the international access code), then **599** (the country code for Curaçao), and then **9** (the area code) and the local number. Once on Curaçao, to call another number on the island, only the local number is necessary; to make calls to an off-island destination, dial **021** and then the area code and number. You can reach **AT&T Direct** on the island by dialing © **800/225-5288.**

Time Curaçao is on Atlantic standard time year-round, 1 hour ahead of eastern standard time and the same as eastern daylight saving time.

Water The water comes from a modern desalination plant and is safe to drink.

Weather Curaçao has an average temperature of 81°F; trade winds keep the island quite comfortable. It's flat and arid, with an average rainfall of only 22 inches per year.

2 Accommodations

Most hotels are in the capital of Willemstad or in one of the suburbs, which lie only 10 to 15 minutes from the shopping center. The bigger hotels often have free shuttle buses running into town, and most of them have their own beaches and pools.

Curaçao is a bustling commercial center, and the downtown hotels often fill up fast with business travelers as well as visitors from neighboring countries such as Venezuela, here on a shopping holiday. So it's important to reserve well in advance.

When making reservations, ask if the 7% room tax and 12% service charge are included in the price you're quoted. There is also a $3 daily (per room) energy tax in all hotels. Be sure to take a look at the section "Package Deals" in chapter 2.

EXPENSIVE

Breezes Curaçao. ★★ *Kids* The old and fading Princess Beach Resort has reincarnated itself as the ABC islands' first major all-inclusive resort. Adjacent to both the Undersea National Park and Sea Aquarium, this big resort opens onto one of Curaçao's most beautiful beaches. This high-energy hotel has the only 1,500-foot-long (450m) beach on the island, with good snorkeling offshore. Catering to both couples and singles, the resort also welcomes families, with its Camp Breezes offering the best kiddies program on island. For those who like to gamble, it also boasts the largest casino in Curaçao.

Bedrooms and suites come in a wide configuration of rooms, including the most desirable, those overlooking the ocean; others front the hotel's gardens. Bathrooms come both with shower or else complete shower/tub combinations, and all of them open onto private patios or balconies. If the food isn't always of gourmet quality, there is at least plenty of it. It's a real all-you-can-eat type of place, from its breakfast buffets in the morning to lavish dinner feasts at night. The choice of cuisine ranges from Italian to island specialties, even Japanese, plus a beach grill. It also has an active entertainment program, complete with guest and staff talent shows.

Dr. Martin Luther King Blvd., Willemstad, Curaçao, N.A. © **599/9-736-7888.** Fax 599/9-461-7205. www. breezes.com. 41 units. Winter $600 double; from $1,040 suite. Off-season $570 double; from $990 suite. Rates are all-inclusive. AE, DC, MC, V. **Amenities:** 4 restaurants, 3 bars; 3 pools; 2 tennis courts; casino; spa; fitness center; deep-sea fishing, windsurfing, dive shop, snorkeling; kids snack bar, children's program, playground; room service; babysitting; laundry. *In room:* A/C, TV, minibar, fridge (on request), coffeemaker, hair dryer, iron (on request), safe.

Curaçao Marriott Beach Resort & Emerald Casino ★★ This is the most glamorous and most prominent hotel on the island, set beside the largest and most popular beach on Curaçao, 10 minutes from both the airport and Willemstad. The hotel is a cluster of three-story buildings whose distinctive shape and ocher color were adapted from traditional Dutch colonial architecture. The open-sided lobby was designed for optimum views of the beach and the hotel's many fountains. Scattered throughout the property are unusual, often monumental, artworks by local and international artists, and a collection of unfussy, overstuffed furniture.

Each of the colorful accommodations offers a view of the ocean and contains either one king-size or two queen-size beds, plus a spacious bathroom with a combination shower/tub.

Although never rising to any great imagination or flair, the food here is consistently good, with quality ingredients. There's also a big casino.

Piscadera Bay (P.O. Box 6003), Willemstad, Curaçao, N.A. © 800/223-6388 in the U.S., or 599/9-7368800. Fax 599/9-4627502. www.marriott.com. 57 units. Winter $259–$309 double; from $339 suite. Off-season $159–$189 double; from $219 suite. AE, DC, MC, V. **Amenities:** 3 restaurants, 2 bars; pool; 2 tennis courts; casino; 2 Jacuzzis; sauna; watersports; children's programs; car-rental desk; business center; room service (6am–1am); massage; babysitting; laundry. *In room:* A/C, TV, minibar, iron and ironing board, hair dryer, safe.

Kurá Hulanda Hotel and Casino ★★ The island's most imaginative and unusual hotel opens onto St. Anna Bay in central Willemstad near the Queen Emma Bridge. The property is the creation of Jacob Gelt Dekker, who also created the Kurá Hulanda Museum (see below). The hotel lies at the museum complex. If you'd like to escape impersonal modern hotel blocks, head here and immerse yourself in the Dutch colonial architecture of the 18th and 19th centuries. Bedrooms are beautifully furnished with Indian marble bathrooms with tub and shower, all the modern amenities, and elegant beds and furnishings. Some accommodations also have kitchenettes. You're not on a beach, but if you seek West Indian inns or hotels of character, you can do no finer in the ABC islands than you can checking in here.

Longestraat 8, Willemstad, Curaçao, N.A. © 599/9-434-7700. Fax 599/9-434-7701. www.kurahulanda.com. 100 units. Winter $275 double, $450 suite. Off-season $250 double, $425 suite. AE, DC, MC, V. **Amenities:** Restaurant, bar; small casino; 2 pools; fitness center; room service; babysitting; dry cleaning. *In room:* A/C, TV, hair dryer, safe.

Sheraton Curaçao Resort ★ Originally built in 1965, this hotel opens onto two private sandy beaches. This was one of the most famous hotels on the island—one that's sometimes credited with launching the tourism boom on Curaçao. After 30 years, it had gotten tired and a bit outdated. All that changed in 1999, when radical renovations and new management by the Sheraton group gave the place a new lease on life. Today, it rises five floors above the northern perimeter of Willemstad, amid rocky bluffs. Glass-enclosed elevators cling to the outside walls of the hotel, offering a panoramic view as you're whisked to your room. Each midsize accommodation has a view of either the ocean or the garden. Outfitted in bold tropical colors, each contains traditional furnishings, private balconies, and generously proportioned bathrooms, with tubs and showers. Rooms on the executive floor are somewhat better furnished and offer amenities like fax machines.

The food isn't great, but it's varied—everything from Italian trattoria favorites to fresh seafood. A social director organizes theme nights based on Mexican or Antillean food and dance music. There's a casino on-site.

Piscadera Bay, John F. Kennedy Blvd. (P.O. Box 2133), Willemstad, Curaçao, N.A. ℭ 800/325-3535 in the U.S. and Canada, or 599/9-462-5000. Fax 599/9-462-5846. www.curacaosheraton.com. 197 units. Winter $190–$210 double; $220–$280 suite. Off-season $140–$160 double; $180–$240 suite. AE, DC, MC, V. **Amenities:** 3 restaurants, 2 bars; pool; 2 tennis courts; casino; fitness center; dive shop, sailing, deep-sea fishing, boating; room service (7am–midnight); babysitting; laundry; free shuttle to town. *In room:* A/C, TV, hair dryer, iron, safe.

MODERATE

Avila Beach Hotel 🌟🌟   This is the only beachfront hotel in Willemstad proper, set on its own private sandy beach that offers year-round ocean swimming. To us, it has more charm, atmosphere, and personality than the resorts described so far. It consists of a beautifully restored 200-year-old mansion and a large extension, called La Belle Alliance. The mansion, built by the English governor of Curaçao during the British occupation of the island at the time of the Napoleonic wars, was converted into a hotel in 1949, and today attracts the royals of the Netherlands. In 1997 the addition of the Blues Wing further expanded the size of the hotel. Each of the new rooms has air-conditioning, TV, private bathroom with tub, minifridge, and a balcony with an ocean view; some also contain kitchenettes. The rooms in the main mansion, though rather basic and small, still have charm. Most units have a king-size bed or two twins, each fitted with a good mattress. The newer units have combination tubs and showers, whereas some of the smaller rentals are shower only. The hotel lies on the shore road leading east out of the city from the shopping center.

The romantic, open-air Belle Terrace, shaded by huge trees, features a full a la carte menu. Blues, an elevated restaurant/bar at the end of the pier, caters to small, informal parties with a taste for jazz, swing, and, of course, blues (see "Dining," below). There's also Antillean nights with local cuisine and live music, plus Saturday-night barbecues.

Penstraat 130–134 (P.O. Box 791), Willemstad, Curaçao, N.A. ℭ 800/747-8162 or 599/9-461-4377. Fax 599/9-461-1493. www.avilahotel.com. 108 units. Winter $125–$242 double; $325 suite. Off-season $115–$190 double; $260 suite. MAP (breakfast and dinner) $60 per person extra. AE, DC, MC, V. **Amenities:** 3 restaurants, 2 bars; tennis court; business service; babysitting; laundry. *In room:* A/C, TV, minibar, hair dryer, safe. From the airport, follow signs to Punda; turn left after the second traffic light in town; stay on the right side of the Plaza Smeets road and go straight. The hotel is on the right side.

Habitat Curaçao 🌟   Opening onto a private beach, this is the best choice for divers. About 20 minutes from Willemstad, on the uncrowded southwest coast, this oceanfront resort provides environmentally sensitive diving vacations. Facilities include a PADI five-star instruction center, offering diving courses from novice to instructor levels. The resort is set in manicured gardens. Accommodations include junior suites, which are tastefully furnished with two queen-size beds, a fully equipped kitchenette, a large balcony or patio, and a full bathroom. Cottages each have two bedrooms, a living room, a kitchen, a bathroom, and a large patio. All bathrooms contain shower/tub combinations.

Rif St. Marie, Curaçao, N.A. ℭ 800/327-6709 in the U.S., or 599/9-8648500. Fax 599/9-8648464. www.habitatdiveresorts.com. 71 units. $145–$165 double. 7-night packages $1,196 for divers including airport transfers, breakfast, and unlimited diving ($434 for nondivers). AE, DC, MC, V. **Amenities:** Restaurant, bar; pool; exercise room; watersports; babysitting; laundry. *In room:* A/C, TV, hair dryer, safe.

Holiday Beach Hotel & Casino   Along a sandy beach dotted with palm trees, this four-story hotel sits near a grassy peninsula jutting out to sea just west of the capital. It boasts all the facilities of a resort hotel, including a crescent-shaped beach against a backdrop of palms—all at reasonable rates. The main part of the complex houses the Casino Royale, one of the largest casinos on the island, and the property contains a handful of tennis courts.

Guest rooms are in two four-story wings, centering around a U-shaped garden with a large freshwater pool. The 30-year-old bedrooms have recently been refurbished, opening onto private balconies. A few front the water; others face the parking lot or pool. Wall-to-wall carpeting and big tile shower/tub combination bathrooms are just two of the comforts.

Pater Euwensweg 31 (P.O. Box 2178), Willemstad, Curaçao, N.A. © **599/9-4625400.** Fax 599/9-4625409. www.hol-beach.com. 200 units. Winter $160–$175 double; off-season $120 double. MAP (breakfast and dinner) $37 per person extra. AE, DC, MC, V. **Amenities:** 2 restaurants, 2 bars; casino; tennis courts; watersports; children's program; room service; babysitting; laundry. *In room:* A/C, TV, hair dryer, safe.

Lion's Dive & Beach Resort   On the island's largest white-sand beach, this hotel vies for the divers' trade with Habitat Curaçao, which has a slight edge. The hotel lies a 30-minute taxi ride southeast of the airport. This complete dive resort features programs supervised by the Underwater Curaçao staff. Each of its comfortable though standard accommodations has a sea view, a balcony or terrace, two queen-size beds, and a shower-only bath.

Bapor Kibrá, Willemstad, Curaçao, N.A. © **599/9-434-8888.** Fax 599/9-434-8889. www.lionsdive.com. 72 units. Winter $156 double; Off-season $140 double. Dive packages available. AE, DC, MC, V. **Amenities:** Restaurant, beach bar; pool; health club; seaquarium complex with marine-life encounters, dive shop, waterskiing, windsurfing, sailing; massage; babysitting; laundry. *In room:* A/C, TV, safe.

Plaza Hotel and Casino   Standing guard over the Punda side of St. Anna Bay, right in the heart of Willemstad, the Plaza is nestled in the ramparts of an 18th-century waterside fort on the eastern tip of the harbor entrance, a 15-minute drive south of the airport. In fact, it's one of the harbor's two "lighthouses." (The hotel has to carry marine collision insurance, the only accommodation in the Caribbean with that distinction.) The original part of the hotel was built in 1954, long before mass tourism swept the island, and followed the style of the arcaded fort. However, now there's a tower of rooms stacked 15 stories high. Each of the smallish bedrooms is comfortably furnished and contains a small combination bath.

The pool, with a bar and suntanning area, is inches away from the parapet of the fort. The Waterfort Grill serves standard American and continental dishes. The more formal Tournesol, which features good French cuisine for dinner only, offers a panoramic view from its location on the top floor of the hotel.

Plaza Piar (P.O. Box 813), Willemstad, Curaçao, N.A. © **599/9-4612500.** Fax 599/9-4618347. www. plazahotelcuracao.com. 243 units. Winter $125–$150 double; $200 suite. Off-season $85–$100 double; $200 suite. Rates include breakfast. AE, MC, V. **Amenities:** 6 restaurants, bar; pool; casino; sunset sails, car rental; room service (7:30–10pm); babysitting; laundry. *In room:* A/C, TV, safe.

INEXPENSIVE

Chogogo Resort   Lying on Curaçao's east end, a 2-minute walk from Jan Thiel Beach, this is for visitors seeking an apartment or a bungalow. Named after a species of local flamingo and set within an arid landscape between the oceanfront beaches and a shallow saltwater bay southeast of Willemstad, this resort caters largely to European (mostly Dutch) families who check in for at least a week and prepare their own meals. Several dozen party-colored one- and two-story buildings dot the grounds; these contain the guest bungalows, studios, and apartments, each with a kitchenette and airy, unpretentious furniture, plus a compact shower-only bath.

Jan Thiel Bay, Curaçao, N.A. © **599/9-7472844.** Fax 599/9-7472424. www.chogogo.com. Year-round $75–$90 double, $85–$100 1-bedroom apt., $115–$160 bungalow. AE, MC, V. **Amenities:** Restaurant, bar; pool; babysitting; laundry. *In room:* A/C, TV, safe.

Hotel Holland   A 2-minute drive from the airport, Hotel Holland contains the Flying Dutchman Bar, a popular gathering place, plus a casino. For a few brief minutes of every day, you can see airplanes landing from your perch at the edge of the poolside terrace, where well-prepared breakfasts, lunches, and dinners from the Cockpit Restaurant are served in good weather (see "Dining," below).

This property is the domain of former Navy frogman Hans Vrolijk and his family. Hans still retains his interest in scuba and arranges dive packages for his guests. The comfortably furnished accommodations have VCRs, fridges, shower/tub combination bathrooms, and balconies. You will probably hang around the pool, because it's a 30-minute drive to the nearest good beach. You definitely need a rental car if you stay here.

F. D. Rooseveltweg 524, Curaçao, N.A. © 599/9-8688044. 45 units. Year-round $79 double; from $117 suite. AE, DC, MC, V. **Amenities:** Restaurant, bar; pool; casino; room service; babysitting; laundry. *In room:* A/C, TV.

Landhuis Daniel Inn *Value*   South of Westpunt, near the island's westernmost point, this mustard-colored plantation house is most often visited by locals for its on-site restaurant, Landhuis Daniel Restaurant (see "Dining," below). If you don't mind a location away from the beach, it offers the best value on the island. The nearest worthwhile beaches are Porto Marie and Habitat Curaçao, which are a 7- to 10-minute drive away.

Very simple but comfortable bedrooms, located a floor above the restaurant, are tidily maintained and have small private bathrooms with shower units. Only two rooms are air-conditioned, but all units have ceiling fans—or you can rely on the trade winds to keep cool. Ask for a room in the main house: The converted slave quarters are small, but charming. This place's basic rooms and communal TV room give it something of the aura of a youth hostel; guests also play billiards and darts.

Wegnaar, Westpunt, Curaçao, N.A. © and fax 599/9-8648400. www.landhuisdaniel.com. 10 units. Year-round $60 double. AE, DC, MC, V. **Amenities:** Restaurant; bar; pool; dive shop; babysitting; laundry. *In room:* A/C, safe, no phone.

3 Dining

EXPENSIVE

Bistro Le Clochard 🎯 FRENCH/SWISS   Bistro Le Clochard fits snugly into the northwestern corner of the grim ramparts of Fort Rif, at the gateway to the harbor. De Taveerne and Fort Nassau (see below) still surpass it, but it comes in a close third in the culinary sweepstakes. Its entrance is marked with a canopy, which leads to a series of rooms, each built under the 19th-century vaulting of the old Dutch fort. Several tables have views of the Caribbean. More panoramic is the outdoor terrace, built directly at the edge of the water, with a view of the sparkling lights of the nearby town.

To begin, you might order bouillabaisse *a notre facon,* a fresh local fish soup. Among the alpine specialties are *raclette* (melted Swiss cheese served with boiled potatoes, onions, and pickles) and fondue bourguignonne; good, though a little heavy for the tropics. One section of the menu is called "Romancing the Stone." A stone is heated in the oven and brought directly to your table; then, without using oil or butter, your choice from the menu—tournedos, sirloin, T-bone steak, boneless chicken breast, or fresh fish—is cooked on the stone. Heavy or light, the food is consistently reliable and good, although we wish the prices weren't so high.

In all, this is for the diehard carnivore more than it is a dining venue for the vegetarian.

Riffort, on the Otrabanda side of the pontoon bridge. ℂ **599/9-4625666.** Reservations recommended. Main courses $25–$35. AE, DC, DISC, MC, V. Mon–Fri noon–2pm; Mon–Sat 6:30–10:45pm. Harborside Terrace, Mon–Sat 2–11pm.

Fort Nassau ★★ INTERNATIONAL   This restored restaurant and bar is built on a hilltop overlooking Willemstad in the ruins of a buttressed fort dating from 1796. It competes successfully with De Taveerne, its only equal. A great dish is the salmon steak with cane sugar glaze, a real West Indian touch, which is served with saffron rice and zesty salsa. Inside, Fort Nassau has retained an 18th-century decor; outside, from the Battery Terrace, a 360-degree panorama of the sea, the harbor, and Willemstad unfolds. You can stop by the chic bar just to enjoy a drink and watch the sunset; happy hour is Monday through Friday from 6 to 7pm.

Queen Beatrix and Crown Prince Claus of the Netherlands have dined here, and rumor has it they were more captivated by the view than by the food. One or two of the more imaginative dishes on the menu perhaps should never have been conjured up. However, we were impressed with the goat cheese in puff pastry and a cold terrine with layers of salmon and sole. The cream of mustard (yes, that's right) soup seems an acquired taste. Opt for the breast of duck with sun-dried tomatoes and basil, or even a well-prepared steak with garlic-infused mashed potatoes.

Near Point Juliana, a 5-min. drive from Willemstad. ℂ **599/9-4613086.** Reservations recommended. Main courses $20–$29. AE, DC, MC, V. Mon–Fri noon–2pm; daily 6:30–11pm.

La Pergola ★ ITALIAN   This is one of the five restaurants nestled into the weather-beaten core of the island's oldest fort, and it's thrived here for more than a decade. As the name implies, the decor is enhanced by a replica of a Renaissance-style pergola. The kitchen and one of the three dining areas are in the cellar, and two others benefit from streaming sunlight and a view over the seafront. Menu items change virtually every day, and all use truly authentic recipes. The best examples include gnocchi of chicken, fettuccine *Giulio esare* (with ham, cream, and mushrooms), a succulent version of *grigliata mista,* and a top-notch preparation of exotic mushrooms, in season, garnished with Parmesan cheese and parsley. Looking for an unusual pasta? Ask for *maltagliata* (pasta cut at random angles and lengths) served with either Gorgonzola sauce or Genoan-style pesto. In addition, a dozen pizza options await you.

In the Waterfront Arches, Waterfort Straat. ℂ **599/9-4613482.** Reservations recommended. Main courses $20–$33. AE, MC, V. Mon–Sat noon–11pm, Sun 6–11pm.

Landhuis Daniel ★ NOUVELLE CREOLE CUISINE   Surrounded by arid scrubland about a mile (2km) south of Westpunt, near the island's most northwesterly tip, this place was originally built in 1711 as an inn and tavern. Today, its mustard-colored facade, white columns, terra-cotta roof, and old-fashioned green-and-yellow dining room are carefully preserved and historically authentic. Menu items are cooked slowly, to order, in a setting of sea breezes and sunlight streaming in the big windows. Launch your repast with a spicy Caribbean bisque with fish and seafood, or else the truly delectable and regional lightly curried pumpkin soup served with garlic croutons. We generally opt for the main catch of the day, often requesting it with a basil cream sauce and pine nuts, but you might prefer the Argentina beef tenderloin with spicy pumpkin sauce or the grilled filet of mahi-mahi in sweet-and-sour tamarind ginger sauce.

In the Landhuis Daniel hotel, Wegnaar, Westpunt. © 599/9-8648400. Reservations recommended. Lunch main courses $14–$20; dinner main courses $14–$20. AE, DC, MC, V. Daily 8–2pm and 5–11pm.

Wine Cellar ⭐ INTERNATIONAL   Opposite the cathedral in the center of town is the domain of Nico and Angela Cornelisse and their son, Daniel, who offer one of the most extensive wine lists on the island. The Victorian atmosphere is reminiscent of an old-fashioned Dutch home. The kitchen turns out an excellent lobster salad and a sole meunière in a butter-and-herb sauce. You might also try fresh red snapper or U.S. tenderloin of beef with goat cheese sauce. Game dishes, imported throughout the year from Holland, are likely to include venison roasted with mushrooms, hare, and roast goose. After years of dining here, we have found the food commendable in every way—dishes are full of flavor and hearty, and there are selections for lighter appetites as well. Of course, as good as the food is, it never matches the impressive wine list.

Ooststraat/Concordiastraat, Willemstad. © 599/9-4612178. Reservations required. Main courses $23–$38. AE, MC, V. Mon–Fri noon–2:30pm and 7–10pm; Sat 7–11pm.

MODERATE

Belle Terrace ⭐ INTERNATIONAL/DANISH   This open-air restaurant, in a 200-year-old mansion on the beachfront of Willemstad, offers superb dining in a relaxed and informal atmosphere. The Schooner Bar, where you can enjoy rum punch, is shaped like a weather-beaten ship's prow looking out to sea. The restaurant, sheltered by an arbor of flamboyant branches, features Scandinavian, continental, and local cuisine, with such specialties as pickled herring, smoked salmon, and a Danish lunch platter. Local dishes, such as *keshi yena* (baked Gouda cheese with a spicy meat filling), are also on the menu. On Saturday night there's a mixed grill and a help-yourself salad bar all accompanied by live music. Fish is always fresh at Belle Terrace, and the chef prepares a seafood platter to perfection: grilled, poached, or meunière.

In the Avila Beach Hotel, Penstraat 130. © 599/9-4614377. Reservations required. Main courses $15–$27; menu *dégustation* $27 for 2 courses, $32 for 3 courses; Sat barbecue $25. AE, DC, MC, V. Daily noon–2:30pm and 7–10pm. From the airport, follow signs to Punda; turn left after the second traffic light in town; stay on the right side of the Plaza Smeets road and go straight. The hotel is on the right side.

Blues SEAFOOD/INTERNATIONAL   As you dine here on a pier jutting far out from the beachfront of the Avila Beach Hotel, water ripples beneath your seat and heaping platters of fresh seafood challenge even the heartiest of appetites. You might enjoy blue mussels cooked in wine sauce with shallots and herbs, dorado with mustard-flavored *beurre blanc,* braised lamb with blackberry sauce, or imported Maine lobster prepared with Creole herbs in a style inspired by the cuisine of New Orleans. An especially impressive dish is a "Seafood Challenge" that combines whatever fresh fish is available that day into a single huge dinner (we stuffed ourselves on flavorful portions of tuna, salmon, squid, langoustine, and scallops). If you have any room left, try the "Jam Session," a hefty sampling of every dessert on the menu, assembled onto a large platter and served for two. See also "Curaçao After Dark," later in this chapter.

In the Avila Beach Hotel, Penstraat 130. © 599/9-4614377. Reservations recommended. Main courses $16–$31; 3-course fixed price menu $35. AE, DC, MC, V. Tues–Sun 5pm–midnight. From the airport, follow signs to Punda; turn left after the second traffic light in town; stay on the right side of the Plaza Smeets road and go straight. The hotel is on the right side.

Fisherman's Wharf SEAFOOD/INTERNATIONAL   Fish lovers, look no further. This restaurant, only a few yards from the sea, offers an authentic island-style dining experience. In simple and casual surroundings, Fisherman's Wharf serves the freshest fish, just bought from the fishermen who set out daily in search of such catches as mula (similar to kingfish) and tuna. Some of the fish brought in here reach a length of 5⅓ feet (1½ m), weighing as much as 80 pounds. The kitchen also offers sashimi.

We recommend starting with the seafood soup, the most consistently reliable appetizer, or a tartar of local poached marlin, intriguingly prepared with a compote of mango. Shrimp bisque is served with old Cuban rum, or you might opt for giant mussels in cheese sauce. The catch of the day is likely to be barracuda prepared with fresh pine nuts or pan-fried tuna with a homemade tapenade of black olives and anchovy. Some meat dishes are available for those who don't want fish.

Dr. Martin Luther King Blvd. 91–93. ℂ 599/9-4657558. Reservations recommended. Main courses $16–$25. AE, MC, V. Mon–Fri noon–11pm, Sat–Sun 5–11pm.

Froet's Garden of Eaten SEAFOOD/INTERNATIONAL   Across from the Princess Beach Resort, this is a winning and inviting little eatery for an alfresco dinner. Attracting a fun-loving crowd, it serves tasty dishes that are never sublime but always satisfying. We often begin with the seafood soup or one of the fish dishes. For one price you get a starter, main course, and dessert (tiramisu or banana cake on our last visit). Succulent pastas and fresh salads are regular features, and many guests finish off with cappuccino, sometimes enjoyed with a regional plum cake flavored with cinnamon sauce.

Koraal Spechtweg 11. ℂ 599/9-461-7120. Fixed price menus $18–$27. AE, MC, V. Daily 6–10:30pm.

Pisces Seafood ✷ *Finds* CREOLE/SEAFOOD   This West Indian restaurant may be difficult to find, as it's on a flat, industrial coastline near a marina and an oil refinery, about 20 minutes from Willemstad on the island's southernmost tip. There's been a restaurant here since the 1930s, when sailors and workers from the oil refinery came for home-cooked meals. This place offers food the way the locals used to eat, long before the cruise ships started arriving and the sprawling resorts opened. The simple frame building offers seating near the rough-hewn bar or in a breeze-swept inner room. The menu depends on the catch of the day. Main courses, served with rice, vegetables, and plantains or potatoes, might include sopi, "seacat" (squid), mula (similar to kingfish), or red snapper; and the Pisces platter combines any of these in copious quantities for two or more people. Shrimp and conch are each prepared three different ways: with garlic, with curry, or Creole style. It's simple, straightforward, affordable, and often quite good.

Caracasbaaiweg 476. ℂ 599/9-7672181. Reservations recommended. Main courses $10–$22. MC, V. Tues–Sun 5–10:30pm.

Rijsttafel Restaurant Indonesia and Holland Club Bar ✷ *Value* INDONESIAN   This is the best place on the island to sample the Indonesian *rijsttafel*, the traditional rice table with all the zesty side dishes. At lunchtime, the selection of dishes is more modest, but for dinner, Japanese cooks prepare the specialty of the house—a rijsttafel consisting of 16, 20, or 25 dishes. There's even an all-vegetarian rijsttafel. Warming trays are placed on your table; the service is buffet style. You're allowed to season your plate with peppers rated hot, very hot, and palate-melting. It's best to go with a party so that all of you can share in the feast. The spicy food is a good change of pace when you tire of seafood and steak.

Mercuriusstraat 13, Salinja. (© 599/9-4612606. Reservations recommended. Main courses $16–$25; rijsttafel $22 for 16 dishes, $27 for 20 dishes, $43 for 25 dishes; all vegetarian $23 for 16 dishes. AE, DC, MC, V. Mon–Sat noon–2pm and 6–9:30pm. Take a taxi to this villa in the suburbs near Salinja, near the Princess Beach Resort & Casino southeast of Willemstad.

Small World International Cuisine ✿ *Finds* INTERNATIONAL   There is no more eclectic dining on the island than at Small World. The owner, Darryll Circkens, set out to open a restaurant that roamed the world for its culinary inspiration. He has succeeded admirably in this place, which opened in 1998. The specialties are mainly Creole, Spanish, French, and Chinese. Dinner can be outside on the terrace overlooking the sea or inside, where the ideal table is a glass top over an aquarium. Some West Indian specialties will put hair on your chest, including *lengua,* or tongue in a savory sauce. We prefer the Spanish food, especially the paella and grilled seafood. Many French dishes lean heavily on beef, such as chateaubriand and filet mignon. On our last visit we enjoyed a well-flavored Chinese chicken served with a medley of mushrooms. For us, nothing quite tops the shrimp in garlic sauce served with rice and fresh vegetables. There's a bar, so you can drop in early for a drink. Most dishes are at the lower end of the price scale.

Waterfort Boogies 18–19. (© 599/9-465-5575. Reservations recommended. Main courses $6–$26. AE, DC, MC, V. Daily 5–11pm.

INEXPENSIVE

The Cockpit *Value* DUTCH/INTERNATIONAL   The restaurant's dining room has the nose of an airplane cockpit as its focal point; there's also seating outside around the pool. Located on the scrub-bordered road leading to the airport, a few minutes from the landing strips, The Cockpit serves international cuisine with an emphasis on Dutch and Antillean specialties. Guests enjoy fresh fish in season (served Curaçao style), Dutch-style steak, Caribbean curried chicken, split-pea soup, and various pasta dishes, such as shrimp linguine in lobster sauce. All dishes are accompanied by fresh vegetables and Dutch-style potatoes. No one pretends the food is gourmet fare—it's robust, hearty, and filled with good country flavor, at a terrific value to boot.

In the Hotel Holland, F. D. Rooseveltweg 524. (© 599/9-8688044. Reservations required. Main courses $12–$25. AE, DC, MC, V. Daily 7am–11pm.

4 Beaches

Its beaches aren't the best in the Dutch Leewards, but Curaçao does have nearly 40 of them, ranging from hotel sands to secluded coves. Beaches are called *playas* or *bocas.* Playas are the larger, classic sandy beaches, and bocas are small inlets between two large rock formations. The northwest coast is generally rugged and difficult for swimming, but the more tranquil waters of the west coast are filled with sheltered bays, offering excellent swimming and snorkeling.

The man-made **Seaquarium Beach,** just to the east of the center of Willemstad, charges a fee of $2.50 for access to its complete facilities, including two bars, two restaurants, a watersports shop, beach-chair rentals, changing facilities, and showers. The calm waters make this beach ideal for swimming.

Just northwest of Willemstad, **Blauwbaai** (Blue Bay) is the largest and most popular beach on Curaçao, with enough white sand for everybody. Along with showers and changing facilities, there are plenty of shady places to retreat from the noonday sun. To get here, follow the road that goes past the Holiday Beach Hotel, heading in the direction of Juliandorp. Follow the sign that tells you to bear left for Blauwbaai and the fishing village of San Michiel.

Further up the west coast, about 30 minutes from Willemstad in the Willibrordus area on the west side of Curaçao, **Daaibooi** is a good beach, though there are no showers or changing rooms. Shade is provided by wooden umbrellas. Snorkelers are attracted to the sides of the bay, as the cliffs rise out of the surf. Small rainbow-hued fish are commonplace, and many varying corals cover the rocks. This beach gets very crowded with locals on Sunday.

A beach popular with families and a base for fishing boats, **Playa Lagun** lies well concealed in the corner of the village of Lagun as you approach from Santa Cruz. The narrow cove is excellent for swimming because of the tranquil, shallow water. Rainbow-hued fish appear everywhere, so the beach is also a favorite with snorkelers. Some concrete huts provide shelter from the scorching sun; a snack bar is open on weekends.

Knip Bay, just north of Playa Lagun, has white sands, rocky sides, and beautiful turquoise waters, making it suitable for snorkeling, swimming, and sunbathing. The beach tends to be crowded on weekends, often with locals. Manzanilla trees provide some shade, but their fruit is poisonous; never seek shelter under the trees when it rains, as drops falling off the leaves will cause major skin irritation. Changing facilities and refreshments are available.

Playa Abao, with crystal turquoise waters, is at the northern tip of the island. One of Curaçao's most popular strands, this is often called Playa Grandi ("Big Beach"). It can get very, very hot at midday, but thatched shade umbrellas provide some protection. A stairway and ramp lead down to the excellent white sands. There's a snack bar in the parking lot. Near the large cove at Playa Abao is **Playa Kenepa,** which is much smaller but gets our nod as one of the island's most beautiful strips. Partially shaded by trees, it's a good place for sunbathing, swimming, and shore diving. A 10-minute swim from the beach leads to a reef where visibility is often 100 feet (30m). Baby sea turtles are often spotted here. A snack bar is open on weekends.

Westpunt, a public beach on the northwestern tip of the island, is known for the Sunday divers who jump from its gigantic cliffs into the ocean below. You can spot rainbow-hued little boats and fishermen's nets hanging out to dry here. There are no facilities at this beach, which tends to be exceptionally hot and has no shade trees (bring lots of sunscreen). The calm waters offer excellent swimming, though they're not good for snorkeling.

South of Willemsted is **Santa Barbara Beach.** It's between the open sea and the island's primary watersports and recreational area known as Spanish Water. A mining company owns this land, which also contains Table Mountain, a

---

⌐Tips A Word of Caution to Swimmers

Beware of stepping on the spines of the sea urchins that sometimes abound in these waters. To give temporary first aid for an embedded urchin's spine, try the local remedies of vinegar or lime juice. If you're tough, you can try a burning match, as the locals advise. Although the urchin spines are not dangerous, they can give you several days of real discomfort.

remarkable landmark, and an old phosphate mine. The natural beach has pure-white sand and calm water. A buoy line protects swimmers from boats. Facilities include restrooms, changing rooms, a snack bar, and a terrace; water bicycles and small motorboats are available for rent. The beach, open daily from 8am to 6pm, has access to the Curaçao Underwater Marine Park.

5 Sports & Other Outdoor Pursuits

CRUISES   **Taber Tours,** Dokweg (© **599/9-7376637**), offers a handful of seagoing options, such as a 5-hour sunset and snorkeling cruise to a beach on Monday and Wednesday through Friday, the excursion costing $30 for adults or half price for children, including gear and one cocktail. A 2-hour sunset cruise, with wine and cheese, leaves at dusk on Friday, costing $32 for adults and $20 for children age 11 and under.

Travelers looking for an experience similar to the sailing days of yore should book a trip on the *Insulinde,* Handelskade (© **599/9-5601340** [note that this is a cellular phone and the connection may be poor]; www.insulinde.com). The 120-foot (36km) traditionally rigged sail clipper is available for day trips and chartering. On Saturday, you can enjoy a full day excursion to Klein Curaçao. The boat departs at 7am and returns at 6pm. Included in the $63 cost is break-fast, lunch, and all snorkeling gear. For a shorter trip, try the sunset cruise to Santa Barbara Beach, which departs every Thursday afternoon and makes sev-eral stops before returning by sail into the sunset. This excursion costs $43 and includes snacks and all snorkeling gear. Advance reservations are required for both trips.

Like a ghost ship from ancient times, a dual-masted, five-sailed wooden schooner cruises silently through the waters of Curaçao. It carries a name steeped in history—the *Bounty* (© **599/9-5601887**)—though it's not a replica of its famous namesake. On Friday, the 90-foot (27km), gaff-rigged schooner heads to the secluded white-sand beach of Porttomarie Bay for $25 per person. On Sun-day and Tuesday, the ship sets out for Klein Curaçao, a desert island that's a favorite of snorkelers. It costs $30 per person and includes breakfast and a bar-becued lunch.

GOLF   The **Curaçao Golf and Squash Club,** Wilhelminalaan, in Emmastad (© **599/9-737-3590**), is your best bet. Greens fees are $30, and both clubs and carts can be rented upon demand. The nine-hole course (the only nine-hole course on the island) is open to nonmembers Friday through Wednesday from 7:30am to 1:30pm, Thursday from 10:30am to sundown.

An 18-hole golf course lies at **Blue Bay Golf Course,** a par-3 course at Land-huis Blauw, on the road to Bullenbaai (© **599/9-868-1755**). This challenging course, designed by Rocky Roquemore, takes advantage of Curaçao's seaside ter-rain and views of the Caribbean. Some shots are over water. Depending on the time of year, greens fees range from $85 to $105, plus $20 to rent a cart.

HORSEBACK RIDING   At Christoffel National Park, **Rancho Alsin** (© **599/9-8640535**) specializes in private trips along unspoiled trails, riding smooth-gaited "paseo" horses suitable even for nonriders. The ride, which lasts about 2-hours, costs $30. Departures are Tuesday through Sunday at 9am. Call for reservations daily between 8am and 4pm.

TENNIS   Most of the deluxe hotels have tennis courts. Another option is the **Santa Catherine Sports Complex,** Koraal Tabac (© **599/9-7677028**), where court costs are $20 per hour.

WATERSPORTS   Most hotels offer their own watersports programs. If your hotel isn't equipped, we suggest heading for one of the most complete watersports facilities on Curaçao, **Seascape Dive and Watersports,** at the Four Points Resort Curaçao (© **599/9-462-5905**). Specializing in snorkeling and scuba diving to reefs and underwater wrecks, it operates from a hexagonal kiosk set on stilts above the water, just offshore from the hotel's beach.

Open from 8am to 5pm daily, the company offers snorkeling excursions for $25 per person in an underwater park offshore from the hotel, and jet ski rentals for $40 per half-hour. An introductory scuba lesson, conducted by a competent dive instructor with PADI certification, goes for $45; four-dive packages cost $110.

Seascape can also arrange deep-sea fishing for $336 for a half-day tour carrying a maximum of six people, $560 for a full-day tour. Drinks and equipment are included, but you'll have to get your hotel to pack your lunch.

Underwater Curaçao, in Bapor Kibrá (© **599/9-4618131**), has a complete PADI-accredited underwater sports program. A fully stocked modern dive shop offers retail and rental equipment. Individual dives and dive packages are offered, costing $35 per dive for experienced divers. An introductory dive for novices is priced at $75, and a snorkel trip costs $27.50, including equipment.

Scuba divers and snorkelers can expect spectacular scenery in waters with visibility often exceeding 100 feet (30m) at the **Curaçao Underwater Marine Park** ★★, which stretches along 12½ miles (20km) of Curaçao's southern coastline. Although the park technically begins at Princess Beach Resort and extends all the way to East Point, the island's most southeasterly tip, some scuba aficionados and island dive operators are aware of other excellent dive sites outside the official boundaries of this park. Lying beneath the surface of the water are steep walls, at least 2 shallow wrecks, gardens of soft coral, and more than 30 species of hard coral. Although access from shore is possible at Jan Thiel Bay and Santa Barbara Beach, most people visit the park by boat. For easy and safe mooring, there are 16 mooring buoys, placed at the best dive and snorkel sites. A snorkeling trail with underwater interpretive markers is laid out just east of the Princess Beach Resort & Casino and is accessible from shore. Spearfishing, anchoring in the coral, or taking anything from the reefs, except photographs, is strictly prohibited.

6 Exploring the Island

Most cruise-ship passengers see only Willemstad—or, more accurately, its shops—but you may want to get out into the *cunucu,* or countryside, and explore the towering cacti and rolling hills topped by *landhuizen* (plantation houses) built more than 3 centuries ago.

WILLEMSTAD ★★

Willemstad was originally founded as Santa Ana by the Spanish in the 1500s. Dutch traders found a vast natural harbor, a perfect hideaway along the Spanish Main, and they renamed it Willemstad in the 17th century. Not only is Willemstad the capital of Curaçao, but it's also the seat of government for the Netherlands Antilles. Today it boasts rows of pastel-colored, red-roofed town houses in the downtown area. After 10 years of restoration, the historic center of Willemstad and the island's natural harbor, Schottegat, have been inscribed on UNESCO's World Heritage List.

The easiest way to go exploring is to take a 1¼-hour **trolley tour,** visiting the highlights of the city. The open-sided cars, pulled by a silent "locomotive," make several trips each week starting at 8:30am and going throughout the day until about 4pm. The tour begins at Fort Amsterdam near the Queen Emma Pontoon Bridge. The cost is $10 for adults, $5 for children age 2 to 12. Call © **599/ 9-461-0011** for more information.

The city grew up on both sides of the canal. It's divided into **Punda** (Old World Dutch ambience and the best shopping) and **Otrabanda** ("the other side," the contemporary side). Both sections are connected by the **Queen Emma Pontoon Bridge,** a pedestrian walkway. Powered by a diesel engine, it swings open many times a day to let ships from all over the globe pass in and out of the harbor.

From the bridge, there's a view of the old **gabled houses** in harmonized pastel shades. The bright colors, according to legend, are a holdover from the time when one of the island's early governors had eye trouble, and flat white gave him headaches. The colonial-style architecture, reflecting the Dutch influence, gives the town a storybook look. The houses, built three or four stories high, are crowned by steep gables and roofed with orange Spanish tiles. Hemmed in by the sea, a tiny canal, and an inlet, the streets are narrow, and they're crosshatched by still narrower alleyways.

Except for the pastel colors, Willemstad may remind you of old Amsterdam. It has one of the most intriguing townscapes in the Caribbean. But don't let the colors deceive you: The city can be rather dirty, in spite of its fairy-tale appearance.

A **statue of Pedro Luis Brion** dominates the square known as Brionplein right at the Otrabanda end of the pontoon bridge. Born in Curaçao in 1782, Brion became the island's favorite son and best-known war hero. Under Simon Bolivar, he was an admiral of the fleet and fought for the independence of Venezuela and Colombia.

In addition to the pontoon bridge, the **Queen Juliana Bridge** opened to vehicular traffic in 1973. Spanning the harbor, it rises 195 feet (59m), which makes it the highest bridge in the Caribbean and one of the tallest in the world.

The Waterfront originally guarded the mouth of the canal on the eastern or Punda side, but now it has been incorporated into the Plaza Hotel. The task of standing guard has been taken over by **Fort Amsterdam,** site of the Governor's Palace and the 1769 Dutch Reformed church. The church still has a British cannonball embedded in it. The arches leading to the fort were tunneled under the official residence of the governor.

A corner of Fort Amsterdam stands at the intersection of Breedestraat and Handelskade, the starting point for a plunge into the island's major **shopping district.**

At some point, save time to visit the **Waterfort Arches,** stretching for a ¼ mile (.4km). They rise 30 feet (9m) high and are built of barrel-vaulted 17th-century stone set against the sea. At Waterfort, you can explore boutiques, have film developed quickly, cash a traveler's check, or purchase fruit-flavored ice cream. You can walk through to a breezy terrace on the sea for a local Amstel beer or a choice of restaurants. The grand buildings and cobbled walkways are illuminated at night.

Between the I. H. (Sha) Capriles Kade and Fort Amsterdam, at Hanechi di Snoa 29, stands the **Mikve Israel-Emanuel Synagogue** (© **599/9-4611067**), the oldest synagogue in the western hemisphere. Consecrated on the eve of Passover in 1732, it houses the oldest Jewish congregation in the New World.

Moments   The Floating Market

A few minutes' walk from the pontoon bridge, at the north end of Handelskade, is the **Floating Market** ★, where scores of schooners tie up alongside the canal, a few yards from the main shopping area. Boats arrive from Venezuela and Colombia, as well as other West Indian islands, to dock here and sell tropical fruits and vegetables—a little bit of everything, in fact, including handcrafts. The modern market under its vast concrete cap has not replaced this unique shopping expedition, which is fun to watch; arrive early or stay late.

Joaño d'Illan led the first Jewish settlers (13 families) to the island in 1651, almost half a century after their expulsion from Portugal by the Inquisition. The settlers came via Amsterdam to Curaçao. This synagogue, a fine example of Dutch colonial architecture, covers about a square block in the heart of Willemstad; it was built in a Spanish-style walled courtyard, with four large portals. Following a Portuguese Sephardic custom, sand covers the sanctuary floor, representing the desert where Israelites camped when the Jews passed from slavery to freedom. The highlight of the east wall is the Holy Ark, rising 17 feet (5m); a raised *banca,* canopied in mahogany, is on the north wall.

Adjacent to the synagogue courtyard is the **Jewish Cultural Historical Museum,** Hanechi di Snoa 29 (② 599/9-4611633), housed in two buildings dating from 1728. They were originally the rabbi's residence and the bathhouse. The 250-year-old *mikvah* (a bath for religious purification purposes) was in constant use until around 1850, when this practice was discontinued and the buildings sold. They have since been reacquired through the Foundation for the Preservation of Historic Monuments and turned into the present museum. On display are ritual, ceremonial, and cultural objects, many of which date from the 17th and 18th centuries and are still in use by the congregation for holidays and events.

The synagogue and museum are open to visitors Monday through Friday from 9 to 11:45am and 2:30 to 5pm; if there's a cruise ship in port, also on Sunday from 9am to noon. Services are Friday at 6:30pm and Saturday at 10:30am. Visitors are welcome, with appropriate dress required. There's a $3.50 entrance fee to the museum. Entrance to the synagogue is free.

Museum Kurá Hulanda, Kipstraat 9 (② 599/9-434-7765), is one of the most unusual—and one of the largest—museums in the Caribbean, housed in once-dilapidated 1800s buildings rescued from oblivion. The exhibits reflect the passion of Dr. Jacob Gelt Dekker, a Dutchman who resides next door. He has spent a great deal of his life devoted to the history and culture of Africa, and he has roamed that continent in search of cultural artifacts. At Otrabanda he has assembled his prize collection, including its most interesting exhibit, a life-size reconstruction of a slave ship that once sailed from the Ivory Coast carrying captured slaves into bondage and often death in the West. One exhibit, "Origin of Man," has a series of intriguing fossils. You can hear African music as you study the frightening wood masks, and look at everything from fertility dolls to sculptures from shona stone, along with such musical instruments as the djembe or the ballaphone. Much of the museum is devoted to objects that evoke the cultures of the former empires of West Africa. Hours are Monday to Saturday 10am to 5pm, costing adults $6 or children $3.

WEST OF WILLEMSTAD

You can walk to the tiny **Curaçao Museum,** Van Leeuwenhoekstraat (© **599/9-4623873**), from the Queen Emma Pontoon Bridge. Built in 1853 by the Royal Dutch Army Corps of Engineers as a military quarantine hospital, the building was carefully restored from 1946 to 1948 and is a fine example of 19th-century Dutch architecture, now housing paintings, objets d'art, and furniture crafted in the 19th century by local cabinetmakers. There's also a large collection from the Caiquetio tribes, the early inhabitants described by Amerigo Vespucci as 7-foot-tall (2m) giants, and a reconstruction of a traditional music pavilion in the garden, where Curaçao musicians give regular performances. It's open Monday to Friday from 8:30am to 4:30pm, Sunday from 10am to 4pm. Admission is $3 for adults, $1.75 for children age 13 and under.

The **Maritime Museum,** Van De Brandhof Straat 7 (© **599/9-4652327**), is in the historic Scharloo neighborhood of Willemstad, just off the old harbor of St. Ana Bay. More than 40 permanent displays trace the story of Curaçao, beginning with the arrival of the island's original inhabitants in 600 B.C. Video presentations cover the development of Curaçao's harbor and the role of the island as one of the largest slave depots in the Caribbean. There are also five oral histories (one from a 97-year-old Curaçaoan who served on the cargo vessel *Normandie*), antique miniatures, 17th-century ship models, and a collection of maps. Admission is $6 for adults, $4 for children age 12 to 16; free for children under 12. Hours are Tuesday to Saturday from 10am to 5pm.

On Schottegatweg West, northwest of Willemstad, past the oil refineries, lies the **Beth Haim Cemetery,** the oldest Caucasian burial site still in use in the western hemisphere. Meaning "House of Life," the cemetery was consecrated before 1659. There are some 2,500 graves on about 3 acres (1hectare) here. The carving on some of the 17th- and 18th-century tombstones is exceptional.

Country House Museum, 12 miles (19km) west of Willemstad at Doktorstuin 27 (© **599/9-8642742**), is a small-scale restoration of a 19th-century manor house that boasts thick stone walls, a thatched roof, and artifacts that represent the old-fashioned methods of agriculture and fishing. It's open Monday to Friday from 9am to 4pm, Saturday and Sunday from 9am to 6pm. Admission is $2.

En route to Westpunt, you'll come across a seaside cavern known as **Boca Tabla,** one of many such grottoes on this rugged, uninhabited northwest coast. In the Westpunt area, a 45-minute ride from Punda in Willemstad, **Playa Forti** is a stark region characterized by soaring hills and towering cacti, along with 200-year-old Dutch land houses, the former mansions that housed slave owners.

Out toward the western tip of Curaçao, a high-wire fence surrounds the entrance to the 4,500-acre (1,800-hectare) **Christoffel National Park** ★★ in Savonet (© **599/9-8640363**), about a 45-minute drive from the capital. A macadam road gives way to dirt, surrounded on all sides by abundant cactus and bromeliads. In the higher regions you can spot rare orchids. Rising from flat, arid countryside, 1,230-foot-high (369m) **St. Christoffelberg** is the highest point in the Dutch Leewards. Donkeys, wild goats, iguanas, the Curaçao deer, and many species of birds thrive in this preserve, and there are some Arawak paintings on a coral cliff near the two caves. The park has 20 miles (32km) of one-way trail-like roads, with lots of flora and fauna along the way. The shortest trail is about 5 miles (8km) long and, because of the rough terrain, takes about 40 minutes to drive through. There are also various walking trails; one takes you to the top of St. Christoffelberg in about 1½ hours. (Come early in the morning, when it isn't too hot.) The park is open Monday to Saturday from 7:30am to 4pm, Sunday from 6am to 3pm. The entrance fee is $10 per person and includes admission to the museum.

Next door, the park has opened the **National Park Shete Boka** (Seven Bays). This turtle sanctuary contains a cave with pounding waves off the choppy north coast. Admission to this park is $2.50 per person.

NORTH & EAST OF WILLEMSTAD

Just northeast of the capital, **Fort Nassau** was completed in 1797 and christened by the Dutch as Fort Republic. Built high on a hill overlooking the harbor entrance to the south and St. Anna Bay to the north, it was fortified as a second line of defense in case the waterfront gave way. When the British invaded in 1807, they renamed it Fort George in honor of their own king. Later, when the Dutch regained control, they renamed it Orange Nassau in honor of the Dutch royal family. Today, diners have replaced soldiers (see "Dining," earlier in this chapter).

Curaçao Liqueur Distillery, Landhuis Chobolobo, Saliña a Arriba (© 599/9-4613526), offers a chance to visit and taste at Chobolobo, the 17th-century *landhuis* where the famous Curaçao liqueur is made. The cordial is a distillate of dried peel of a particular strain of orange found only on Curaçao. Several herbs are added to give it an aromatic bouquet. One of the rewards of a visit here is a free snifter of the liqueur, offered Monday to Friday from 8am to noon and 1 to 5pm.

Curaçao Seaquarium, off Dr. Martin Luther King Boulevard at a site called Bapor Kibrá (© 599/9-4616666), has more than 400 species of fish, crabs, anemones, sponges, and coral on display in a natural environment. Located a few minutes' walk along the rocky coast from the Breezes Curaçao Resort, the Seaquarium is open daily from 8:30am to 4:30pm. Admission is $13 for adults, $7.25 for children age 14 and under.

A special feature of the aquarium is a "shark and animal encounter," which costs $58 for divers or $29 for snorkelers. Divers, snorkelers, and experienced swimmers can feed, film, and photograph sharks, which are separated from them by a large window with feeding holes. In the animal-encounters section, you can swim among stingrays, lobsters, tarpons, parrotfish, and other marine life, feeding and photographing these creatures in a controlled environment where safety is always a consideration. The Seaquarium is also the site of Curaçao's only full-facility, palm-shaded, white-sand beach.

Seaworld Explorer ✱ is a semisubmersible submarine that departs the Seaquarium daily at 4:30pm on hour-long journeys into the deep. You're taken on a tour of submerged wrecks off the shores of Curaçao and treated to close encounters of coral reefs with rainbow-hued tropical fish. The *Explorer* has a barge top that submerges only 5 or so feet (2m) under the water, but the submerged section has wide glass windows allowing passengers underwater views, which can extend 110 feet (33m). Reservations must be made a day in advance by calling © 599/9-4610011. It costs $33 for adults, $19 for children age 11 and under.

Curaçao Underwater Marine Park ✱✱ (© 599/9-4624242), established in 1983 with the financial aid of the World Wildlife Fund, stretches from the Breezes Curaçao Resort to the east point of the island, a strip of about 12½ miles (20km) of untouched coral reefs. For information on snorkeling, scuba diving, and trips in a glass-bottom boat to view the park, see "Sports & Other Outdoor Pursuits," earlier in this chapter.

Landhuis Brievengat ✿, Brievengat (© **599/9-7369962**), gives visitors a chance to visit a Dutch version of an 18th-century West Indian plantation house. This stately building, in a scrub-dotted landscape on the eastern side of the island, contains a few antiques, high ceilings, and a gallery facing two entrance towers, said to have been used to imprison slaves. It's open daily from 9am to noon and 3 to 6pm; admission is $1.50.

The **Hato Caves,** F. D. Rooseveltweg (© **599/9-8680379**), have been called mystical. Every hour, guides take visitors through this world of stalagmites and stalactites, found in the highest limestone terrace of the island. Actually, they were once old coral reefs, which were formed when the ocean water fell and the landmass was lifted up over the years. Over thousands of years, limestone formations were created, some mirrored in an underground lake. After crossing the lake, you enter the Cathedral, an underground cavern. The largest hall of the cave is called La Ventana ("The Window"). Also on display are samples of ancient Indian petroglyph drawings. The caves are open daily from 10am to 4pm; admission is $6.50 for adults and $5 for children age 4 to 11.

7 Shopping ✿✿

Curaçao is a shopper's paradise. Some 200 shops line the major shopping streets such as Heerenstraat and Breedestraat. Right in the heart of Willemstad is the 5-block **Punda** shopping district. Most stores are open Monday through Saturday from 8am to noon and 2 to 6pm (some from 8am–6pm). When cruise ships are in port, stores are also open for a few hours on Sunday and holidays. To avoid the cruise-ship crowds, do your shopping in the morning.

Look for good buys on French perfumes, Dutch Delft blue souvenirs, finely woven Italian silks, Japanese and German cameras, jewelry, silver, Swiss watches, linens, leather goods, liquor, and island-made rum and liqueurs, especially Curaçao liqueur, some of which has a distinctive blue color. The island is famous for its 5-pound wheels of Gouda and Edam cheeses. You'll also see wooden shoes, although we're not sure what you'd do with them. Some of the stores also stock some deals on intricate lacework imported from Portugal, China, and everywhere in between. If you're a street shopper and want something colorful, consider one of the wood carvings or flamboyant paintings from Haiti or the Dominican Republic. Both are hawked by street vendors at any of the main plazas.

Incidentally, Curaçao is not technically a free port, but its prices are often inexpensive because of its low import duty.

Kas di Arte Kursou, Breedestraat 126, Otrabanda (© **599/9-46238888**), in a 19th-century mansion in Otrobanda near the cruise-ship terminal, sells unique souvenirs such as one-of-a-kind T-shirts, all handmade by local artists. The gallery also has changing exhibits of paintings, plus a sculpture gallery.

Every garment sold in **Bamali,** Breedestraat Punda 2 (© **599/9-4612258**), is designed and, in many cases, crafted by the store owners. Influenced largely by Indonesian patterns, the airy attire includes V-neck cotton pullovers perfect for a casual, hot-weather climate, as well as linen shifts, often in batik prints, appropriate for a glamorous cocktail party. Most pieces here are for women; all are made from all-natural materials, such as cotton, silk, and linen, and there's also a limited array of sandals and leather bags. **Benetton,** Madurostraat 4 (© **599/9-4614619**), has invaded Curaçao with all its many colors. Some items are marked down by about 20% below U.S. prices (this is done to get rid of surplus stock from the previous season); in-season clothing is available as well.

Bert Knubben Black Koral Art Studio, in the Breezes Curaçao Resort, Dr. Martin Luther King Blvd. (© **599/9-4652122**), is synonymous with craftsmanship and quality. Although it's illegal to collect black coral here, an exception was made for Bert, a diver who has been harvesting corals and fashioning them into fine jewelry and objets d'art for more than 35 years. Collectors avidly seek out this type of coral, not only for the quality of its craftsmanship, but also because it's becoming increasingly rare and may one day not be offered for sale at all.

Gandelman Jewelers, Breedestraat 35, Punda (© **599/9-4611854**), is the island's best and most reliable source for jewelry, often exquisitely designed and set with diamonds, rubies, emeralds, sapphires, and other gemstones. You'll also find watches and the unique line of Prima Classe leather goods embossed with the world map.

Little Holland, Braedestraat 37, Punda (© **599/9-4611768**), specializes in silk neckties, Nautica shorts and shirts, and, most important, a sophisticated array of cigars. Crafted in Cuba, the Dominican Republic, and Brazil, they include some of the most prestigious names in smoke, including Montecristos, Cohiba, and Churchills. (Remember, it's still illegal to bring Cuban cigars into the United States; smoke them here.)

Electronics are a good buy on Curaçao, as they can be sold duty free; we recommend the very reliable **Boolchand's,** Heerenstraat 4B, Punda (© **599/9-4612262**), in business since 1930. If you can't find what you're looking for, try **Palais Hindu,** Heerenstraat 17 (© **599/9-4616897**), which sells a wide range of video and cassette recorders, photographic equipment, and watches.

Penha & Sons, Heerenstraat 1 (© **599/9-4612266**), in the oldest building in town (1708), has a history dating from 1865. It has long been known for its fine selection of perfumes, cosmetics, and designer clothing (for both men and women). It distributes such names as Calvin Klein, Yves Saint Laurent, Elizabeth Arden, Clarins, and Estée Lauder, among others.

La Casa Amarilla (The Yellow House), Breedestraat 46 (© **599/9-4613222**), operating since 1887 in a yellow-and-white 19th-century building, sells an intriguing collection of perfume and cosmetics from all over the world and is an agent of Christian Dior, Guerlain, Cartier, and Van Cleef & Arpels.

At **Landhuis Groot Santa Martha,** Santa Martha (© **599/9-8641559**), craftspeople with disabilities fashion unusual handcrafts, some evoking those found in South America.

Should you, like many visitors from Venezuela, develop a shopping craze, there are a lot more stores to check out, including **Perfume Place,** Braastraat 23 (© **599/9-461-7462**), offering all the big names in perfume and cosmetics, and **New Amsterdam,** Gomerzpein 14 (© **599/9-461-2437**), a long established store known for its Hummel figurines and hand-embroidered tablecloths among other items. For novelties and souvenirs, head for **Warenhaus Van Der Ree,** Breedestraat 5, Punda (© **599/9-461-1645**).

8 Curaçao After Dark ⟨★⟨★

Most of the action spins around the island's **casinos:** the **Marriott Beach Resort,** Piscadera Bay (© **599/9-7368800**); **Holiday Beach Hotel & Casino,** Otrabanda, Pater Euwensweg 31 (© **599/9-4625400**); **Plaza Hotel & Casino,** Plaza Piar, in Willemstad (© **599/9-4612500**); and **Breezes Curaçao Resort,** Dr. Martin Luther King Blvd. 8 (© **599/9-7367888**).

Emerald Casino at the Marriott is especially popular, designed to resemble an open-air courtyard. It features 143 slot machines, 6 blackjack tables, 2 roulette wheels, 2 Caribbean stud poker tables, a craps table, a baccarat table, and a mini-baccarat table. The casino at the Breezes Cucaçao is the liveliest on the island. These hotel gaming houses usually start their action at 2pm, and some of them remain open until 4am. The Princess Beach serves complimentary drinks.

The historic **Landhuis Brievengat** (see "Exploring the Island," above), in addition to being a museum with island artifacts, is also the site of Wednesday, Friday, and Sunday *rijsttafel* parties. They begin at 7:30pm, require an admission fee of $8 (which includes the first drink), and feature heaping portions of *rijsttafel* that start at $16.50 each. A platform is set up amid the flamboyant trees nearby, and two bands alternate with each other to provide a pleasant ambience. Call before you go, as this event is very popular, especially on Friday night.

The landlocked, flat, and somewhat dusty neighborhood of **Salinja** is now the nightlife capital of Curaçao. Among the best of them is **Blues,** in the Avila Beach Hotel, Penstraat 130 (© **599/9-4614377**), a restaurant with a hopping bar that's packed every night except Mondays. Live jazz is offered Thursday from 7pm to midnight and Saturday from 9pm to 1:30am. No cover.

Façade, Lindbergh 32 (© **599/9-4614640**), in the Salinja district, is one of the most popular discos on the island. Spread over several different levels of a modern building, it has a huge bar, three dance floors, and live music nightly. It's open Thursday and Friday from 8pm to 3am. The cover is $5 to $10.

For other nighttime diversions, begin the evening with wine and tapas served at **Rum Runners,** Otrabanda Waterfront, De Rouvilleweg 9 (© **599/9-462-3038**), which gets rowdy at times. On Friday and Saturday nights the place to be is **Ole! Ole!,** Salina (© **599/9-461-7707**), offering live music. If you like to party on the beach, head for **Hook's Hut,** Piscadera Bay (© **599/9-462-6575**). Jazz is a regular feature here, and they're also known to book the best local music on the island.

11

Dominica

The beaches aren't worth the effort to get here, but the landscape and rivers, as well as increasingly renowned scuba diving, are. Nature lovers who visit Dominica (pronounced *dom-in-EE-ka*) experience a wild Caribbean setting, as well as the rural life that has largely disappeared on the more developed islands. Dominica is, after all, one of the poorest and least developed islands in the Caribbean. There are no casinos and no mega-resorts—and hardly any road signs. In fact, it might be the only island in the Caribbean that Columbus would still recognize.

Hiking and mountain climbing are good reasons to visit Dominica; its flora is made unbelievably lush by frequent rainfall. Covered by a dense tropical rain forest that blankets its mountain slopes, including cloud-wreathed Morne Diablotin at 4,747 feet (1,424m), it has vegetation unique in the West Indies and remains the most rugged of the Caribbean islands. The mountainous island is 29 miles (47km) long and 16 miles (26km) wide, with a total land area of 290 square miles (751 sq. km), much of which has never been seen by explorers. Should you visit, you'll find clear rivers, waterfalls, hot springs, and boiling lakes.

Alec Waugh, the travel writer, wrote in 1948: "There is only one way to understand Dominica. You have to walk across it and along it. Range after range with its leaf-domed summit merges into the background of successive ranges, with each shade of green merging into another." That observation still holds true today.

With a population of 75,000, Dominica lies in the eastern Caribbean, between Guadeloupe to the north and Martinique to the south. The Caribs, the indigenous people of the Carib-bean whose numbers have dwindled to 3,000, live as a community on the northeast of the island, where the art of traditional basketry is still practiced.

Clothing is casual, including light summer wear for most of the year. However, take along walking shoes for those trips into the mountains and a sweater for cooler evenings. Locals, who are rather conservative, frown on bikinis and swimwear when worn on the streets of the capital city, **Roseau,** or in the villages.

1 Essentials

VISITOR INFORMATION

Before you go, you can contact the **Dominica Tourist Office** at 800 2nd Avenue, Suite 1802, New York, NY 10017 (© **212/949-1711**).

In England, information is available from the **Office of the Dominica High Commission London,** 1 Collingham Gardens, London SW5 0HW (© **020/ 7370-5194**).

You can also get information on the Web at **www.dominica.dm**.

Dominica

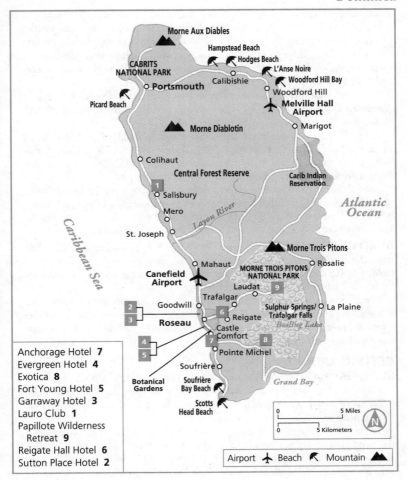

Anchorage Hotel **7**
Evergreen Hotel **4**
Exotica **8**
Fort Young Hotel **5**
Garraway Hotel **3**
Lauro Club **1**
Papillote Wilderness
    Retreat **9**
Reigate Hall Hotel **6**
Sutton Place Hotel **2**

Airport ✈ Beach ⌐ Mountain ▲▲▲

On the island, the **Dominica Tourist Information Office** is on the Old Market Plaza, Roseau, with administrative offices at the National Development Corporation offices, Valley Road (© **767/448-2045**); it's open Tuesday through Friday from 8am to 4pm, Monday from 8am to 5pm.

There are also information bureaus at **Melville Hall Airport** (© **767/ 445-7051**) and **Canefield Airport** (© **767/449-1242**).

GETTING THERE

BY PLANE   There are two airports on Dominica, neither of which is large enough to handle a jet; therefore, there are no direct flights from the U.S. or Canada. The **Melville Hall Airport** (© **767/445-7100**) is on the northeastern coast, almost diagonally across the island from the capital, Roseau, on the southwestern coast. Melville Hall is a 1½-hour taxi ride from Roseau, a drive that takes you across the island through the forest and coastal villages; the fare is $20 per person when there are four passengers. On your own, the fare could be $50.

The newer **Canefield Airport** (© 767/449-1199) is about a 15-minute taxi ride north of Roseau. The 2,000-foot (600m) airstrip accommodates smaller planes than those that can land at Melville Hall. From here, the typical taxi fare into town is $17. There's also a public bus (with an *H* that precedes the number on the license plate) that costs only $2 per person; buses come every 20 minutes and hold between 15 and 18 passengers.

For many from the U.S., the easiest way to reach Dominica is via the daily **American Eagle** (© 800/433-7300; www.aa.com) flight from American's hub in San Juan, Puerto Rico.

From Antigua, you can board one of the five daily **LIAT** (© 800/468-0482 in the U.S. and Canada, or 767/448-2421) flights to Dominica. Another possibility would be to fly via St. Maarten. From there, LIAT offers one nonstop flight daily and two other daily flights with intermediary stops.

You can also fly to Guadeloupe and make a connection on **Air Guadeloupe** (© 767/448-2181), which has two flights a day to Dominica except on Sunday, when there is no morning flight (flying time is 30 min.). If you're in Fort-de-France on Martinique, you can take a LIAT flight to Dominica.

BY BOAT   The *Caribbean Express* (© 767/448-2181 on Dominica), sailing from the French West Indies, runs between Guadeloupe in the north to Martinique in the south; Dominica is a port of call along the way. Departures are Friday to Wednesday; call for exact schedules.

In addition, car-ferries sail from Pointe-à-Pitre to Roseau five to seven times a week, depending on demand. For schedule information, contact **White Church Travel,** 5 Great Marlborough St., Roseau (© 767/448-2181). A one-way fare costs EC$152 (US$56.25).

GETTING AROUND

BY RENTAL CAR   If you rent a car, there's a fee of EC$30 (US$11) to obtain a driver's license, which is available at the airports. The island has 310 miles (499km) of newly paved roads, and only in a few areas is a four-wheel-drive vehicle necessary. *Note: Driving is on the left.*

There are also a handful of small, usually family-owned car-rental companies, the condition and price of whose vehicles vary widely. They include **Valley Rent-a-Car,** Goodwill Road, Roseau (© 767/448-3233); **Wide Range,** 79 Bath Rd., Roseau (© 767/448-2198); and **Best Deal Car Rental,** 15 Hanover St., Roseau (© 767/449-9204).

BY TAXI   You can hire a taxi at either the Melville Hall or Canefield Airport. Prices are regulated by the government (see "Getting There," above, for airport fares). If you want to see the island by taxi, rates are about $18 per car for each hour of touring, and as many as four passengers can go along at the same time.

⌒ *Fun Fact* **National Day**

National Day celebrations on November 3 commemorate both Columbus's discovery, in 1493, and independence, in 1978. Cultural celebrations of Dominica's traditional dance, music, song, and storytelling begin in mid-October and continue to Community Day, November 4, when people undertake community-based projects.

BY MINIBUS The public transportation system consists of private minibus service between Roseau and the rest of Dominica. These flamboyantly painted minibuses are filled mainly with schoolchildren, workers, and country people who need to come into Roseau. On most Caribbean islands, we don't recommend buses too zealously. But on Dominica, buses afford the best insight into local life. Taxis may be a more reliable means of transport for visitors, but there are hotels at which buses call during the course of the day. You can also just hail a bus when you see it, and tell the driver where you want to go. Fares range from $1.50 to $5. Buses are identified by the letter *H* that precedes their license numbers.

 FAST FACTS: **Dominica**

Banking Hours Banks are open Monday to Thursday from 8am to 3pm, Friday from 8am to 5pm. There are several major bank branches in Roseau, complete with ATMs that dispense EC dollars.

Currency Dominica uses the Eastern Caribbean dollar (**EC$**), worth about EC$2.70 to US$1. (Just before you leave home, you can check the current exchange rates on the Web at **www.x-rates.com**.) U.S. dollars are readily accepted, though you'll usually get change in EC dollars. *Prices in this chapter are given in U.S. dollars unless otherwise indicated.*

Customs Dominica is lenient, allowing you to bring personal and household effects, plus 200 cigarettes, 50 cigars, and 40 ounces of liquor or wine per person.

Documents To enter, U.S. and Canadian citizens must have a passport. In addition, an ongoing or return ticket must be shown. British visitors should have a valid passport.

Electricity The electricity is 220- to 240-volt AC (50 cycles), so both adapters and transformers are necessary for U.S.-made appliances. It's smart to bring a flashlight with you, in case of power outages.

Emergencies To call the police, report a fire, or summon an ambulance, dial © **999.**

Hospital There's **Princess Margaret Hospital,** Federation Drive, Goodwill (© **767/448-2231**), but those with serious medical conditions may want to forego a visit to the hospital in Dominica, as island medical facilities are often inadequate.

Language English is the official language. Locals often speak a Creole-French patois.

Pharmacies The island's best-stocked drugstore is **Jolly's Pharmacy,** in Roseau at 37 Great George St., and 12 King George V St. Both branches share the same phone number and hours (© **767/448-3388**). They're open Monday to Thursday from 8am to 4:30pm, Friday from 8am to 5pm, and Saturday from 8am to 2pm.

Safety Although crime is rare here, you should still safeguard your valuables. Never leave them unattended on the beach or in a locked car.

Taxes A 10% government room tax is added on accommodations, and a 3% tax on alcoholic drinks and food items. Anyone who remains on Dominica for more than 24 hours must pay a US$20 departure tax.

Telephone To call Dominica from the United States, dial **1**, then **767** (the country code for Dominica) and the local number. To call Dominica from another island within the Caribbean, just dial **767**, plus the seven-digit local number. International direct dialing is available on Dominica, as well as U.S. direct service through AT&T. You can contact AT&T in Dominica by dialing ✆ **800/872-2881**. MCI and Sprint are not set up on Dominica with toll-free access codes. Most hotel telephone operators throw up their hands at even placing a long-distance call for a resident. Instead, they connect their clients to the island's long-distance phone operator, who dials the call for a client, and then calls are billed directly to a client's room.

Time Dominica is on Atlantic standard time, 1 hour ahead of eastern standard time in the United States. Dominica does not observe daylight saving time, so when the United States changes to daylight saving time, clocks in Dominica and the U.S. east coast tell the same time.

Tipping Most hotels and restaurants add a 10% service charge to bills; check carefully to see if it's been added. If this charge has not been included, tipping is up to you, though an additional 5% for particularly good service is always welcome.

Water The water is drinkable from the taps and in the high mountain country. Pollution is hardly a problem here.

Weather Daytime temperatures average between 70° and 85°F. Nights are much cooler, especially in the mountains. The rainy season is June to October, when there can be warnings of hurricane activity. Regrettably, Dominica lies in the hurricane belt, and fierce storms have taken their toll on the island over the years.

2 Accommodations

The government imposes a 10% tax on hotel rooms and a 3% tax on beverages and food, which will be added to your hotel bill. Most hotels will additionally add a 10% service charge. Unless otherwise noted, the rates given below are year-round and in U.S. dollars.

If you don't want to rent a car, it's best to stay in Roseau, where you can get around better. But if you'd like to experience nature, head for one of the remote inns in exotic tropical settings.

IN ROSEAU & CASTLE COMFORT

Anchorage Hotel Recently renovated, the Anchorage is at Castle Comfort, a ½ mile south of Roseau. For the active traveler, there is no finer choice, as scuba diving, whale-watching, hiking, fishing, and bird-sighting are given great emphasis here. The Armour family provides small rooms with two double beds and a shower or bathtub, plus a balcony overlooking a pool. The best rooms open onto a view of the Caribbean Sea, and each contain two double beds. The other rooms are more standardized, each having comfortable twin beds or one double. Bathrooms are adequate, with shower/tub combinations and decent shelf space. In spite of its location at the shore, there's little or no sandy beach available, so guests spend their days around the pool. However, the hotel has its own jetty, you can swim off a pebble beach, and there's a squash court.

The hotel's French and Caribbean cuisine is simple, with an emphasis on fresh fish and vegetables. Nonresidents must ask permission to use the swimming pool, and they can also visit for meals. A West Indian band plays music twice a week for dancing. On Thursday night, there's a buffet accompanied by a live band.

Castle Comfort (P.O. Box 34), Roseau, Dominica, W.I. © 767/448-2638. Fax 767-448-5680. www. anchoragehotel.dm. 32 units. Year-round $95–$115 double. MAP (breakfast and dinner) $37 per person extra. Children age 11 and under granted 50% deductions. AE, DC, MC, V. Amenities: Restaurant, bar; pool; scuba diving; snorkeling; sailing; room service; babysitting; laundry. In room: A/C, TV.

Evergreen Hotel   This pleasant, family-run hotel looks a bit like a Swiss chalet from the outside, although inside there's an open-air restaurant with bright jungle prints, crystal teardrop chandeliers, and an Art Deco bar. The newer annex, though sterile looking, has better rooms than the main building. A few units have wraparound tile-floored verandas; all have stone accents. Accommodations are bright and airy, with two double beds and ample storage space; bathrooms have showers only. The Evergreen sits amid a cluster of other hotels about a mile (2km) south of Roseau. A stony beach is visible a few steps beyond the garden. Inside and out, the airy, comfortably modern place is trimmed with local gommier wood. Mena Winston, the Dominican-born owner, assists in preparing meals, which are well done and cost $20 to $25. Laundry service and scuba diving can be arranged. There's a pool on-site.

P.O. Box 309, Castle Comfort, Dominica, W.I. © 767/448-3288. Fax 767/448-6800. www.delphis.dm/ evergreen.htm. 17 units. Year-round $125–$150 double. Extra person $30. Rates include full breakfast. AE, DC, DISC, MC, V. Amenities: Restaurant, bar; pool; scuba diving; snorkeling; room service; babysitting; laundry. In room: A/C, TV.

Fort Young Hotel ★   Occupying a cliff-side setting, this modern hotel grew from the ruins of the 1770 Fort Young, once the island's major military installation. Traces of its former historic role remain, including cannons at the entrance. It's always attracted business travelers, but now more and more tourists are drawn to the comfortable bedrooms with ceiling fans and balconies. Here you are elevated far above the "mosquito line," so you can actually sit out and enjoy the balmy Caribbean air without being attacked. The hotel has 21 ocean-front guest rooms and 3 1-bedroom suites at the base of a cliff below the existing fort; ask for one of these newer units, which have direct ocean views facing west, a sitting area, bathrooms with shower/tub combinations and two queen-size beds. There's no beach, but there's a swimming pool with waterfalls and a shade pergola at the edge of the sea.

Fort Young Hotel Restaurant, a candlelit room with stone walls and a ceiling of wood rafters, is better than ever. The Jamaican chef not only draws on his homeland for inspiration but is also an expert at regional dishes. Much of his repertoire has a continental flair.

Victoria St. (P.O. Box 519), Roseau, Dominica, W.I. © 767/448-5000. Fax 767/448-5006. www.fortyoung hotel.com. 52 units. Year-round $125–$155 double; $230 suite. Extra person $20. AE, MC, V. Amenities: 2 restaurants, 2 bars; pool; health club; Jacuzzi; room service (7am–10pm); babysitting; laundry; island tours. In room: A/C, TV, coffeemaker, hair dryer.

⌒Tips Mosquito Warning

At night you are likely to be plagued with mosquitoes. If that's a real problem for you, check into the Fort Young Hotel (see below), which is above the "mosquito line." Most hotels offer mosquito netting. Remember, you came to Dominica for unspoiled nature, right?

Garraway Hotel   Don't faint at the news, but Dominica now offers a hotel with an elevator. Some locals like to visit just to ride up in it, even though the Garraway rises only five floors. This hotel opened in 1994, adjacent to the home of its owners, the Garraway family, who cater largely to business travelers, although it's a perfectly acceptable choice for vacationers, too. This is the best inn for those who want to be in the capital itself and who plan to rely on public transportation. Of course, it's nowhere near a beach, but no one comes to Dominica for beaches anyway. It's the closest thing to a Ramada Inn on the island. Most of the spacious guest rooms have vistas stretching all the way to Dominica's southernmost tip. Each unit is outfitted with rattan furniture and pastel floral-print fabrics, one king-size or two double beds, and a combination shower/tub bathroom. Public rooms are given an authentic island touch with artwork and locally made vetiver-grass mats. On the premises is the Balisier restaurant (see "Dining," below).

Place Heritage, The Bayfront (P.O. Box 789), Roseau, Dominica, W.I. Ⓒ **767/449-8800.** Fax 767/449-8807. www.garrawayhotel.com. 31 units. Winter $120 double; $155 suite. Off-season $101 double; $115 suite. Children under age 12 stay free in parent's room. AE, DC, MC, V. **Amenities:** Restaurant, bar; room service; babysitting; laundry. *In room:* A/C, TV, hair dryer.

Reigate Hall Hotel   On a steep hillside about a mile (2km) east of Roseau, this hotel was originally built in the 18th century as a plantation house. It was once one of the finest hotels on the island, but it now faces increased competition and has slipped a bit in terms of maintenance and service. Some people still like it for its lofty setting and panoramic views. Some parts of the original structure are left, but the building has been substantially altered. The hotel has a comfortably airy design, with hardwood floors and exposed stone. Guest rooms curve around the sides of a rectangular pool and offer ocean vistas. Two deluxe one-bedroom suites each have a fridge, wet bar, and private in-room Jacuzzi. Reigate also offers one two-bedroom apartment (without cooking facilities) that can accommodate three comfortably. Each unit has a small bathroom equipped with a shower/tub combination.

Mountain Rd. (P.O. Box 200), Reigate, Dominica, W.I. Ⓒ **767/448-4031.** Fax 767/448-4034. www.reefrainfrst. com/dominicareigate.htm. 16 units. Winter $95 double; $160 suite. Off-season $80 double; $125 suite. Rates include breakfast. AE, MC, V. **Amenities:** Restaurant, bar; pool; tennis court; sauna; room service; babysitting; laundry. *In room:* A/C, TV.

Sutton Place Hotel 🎇   This small, historic property stands in the center of town and was once a 1930s guest house run by "Mother" Harris, a matriarch who became a local legend. Destroyed by Hurricane David in 1979, the new Sutton Place was rebuilt in a traditional Caribbean style by the same Harris family, which continues the old traditions but with far greater style. Rooms are tastefully furnished with antiques, including four-poster beds, brass desk lamps, and teak furnishings in the shower-only bathrooms. Suites contain fully equipped kitchenettes. The staircase and floors of the suites are laid with a fine hardwood, tauroniro, from South America. Stylized floral arrangements, exotic prints, and luxurious fabrics contribute to the upscale style.

The restaurant, The Sutton Grill, is now one of the choice places to dine in Roseau, with a Creole/international menu that also embraces some dishes from Italy, China, and India. The nearest beach is about a mile (2km) away.

25 Old St., Roseau, Dominica, W.I. Ⓒ **767/449-8700.** Fax 767/448-3045. www.delphis.dm/sutton.htm. 8 units. Year-round $95 double; $135 suite. Rates include breakfast. AE, DISC, MC, V. **Amenities:** Restaurant, bar; room service; laundry. *In room:* A/C, TV, hair dryer.

IN THE RAIN FOREST

Papillote Wilderness Retreat ⭐ *(Finds)*   This property is run by the Jean-Baptiste family: Cuthbert, who handles the restaurant, and his wife, Anne Grey, who was a marine scientist. Their unique resort, 4 miles (6km) east of Roseau, stands right in the middle of Papillote Forest, at the foothills of Morne Macaque. In this remote setting, you're surrounded by exotic fruits, flowers, and herb gardens. The rooms have a rustic, log-cabin atmosphere, but modern comforts, such as up-to-date bathrooms with plenty of hot water, await you.

Don't expect constantly sunny weather, since this part of the jungle is known for its downpours, but that's what keeps the orchids, begonias, and brilliantly colored bromeliads lush. The 12 acres (5 hectares) of sloping and forested land have a labyrinth of stone walls and trails, beside which flow freshwater streams, a few of which come from hot mineral springs. Natural hot mineral baths are available, and you'll be directed to a secluded waterfall where you can swim in the river. The Jean-Baptistes also run a boutique that sells Dominican products, including appliquéd quilts made by local artisans. Even if you don't stay here, it's an experience to dine on the thatch-roofed terrace.

Trafalgar Falls Rd. (P.O. Box 2287), Roseau, Dominica, W.I. ✆ 767/448-2287. Fax 767/448-2285. www. papillote.dm. 7 units. Year-round $100 double; $115 suite. MAP (breakfast and dinner) $35 per person extra. AE, MC, V. Closed Sept 1–Oct 15. **Amenities:** Restaurant, bar; 2 pools; room service; laundry. *In room:* Ceiling fan, no phone.

AT MORNE ANGLAIS

Exotica ⭐ *(Finds)*   This tropical setting is home to what's called an "agro-eco" resort, with some 38 different flowers and fruit trees growing on the 4-acre (2-hectare) organic farm. When you finally reach the place after a harrowing ride, you can enjoy the cool mountain breezes at 1,600 feet (480m) above sea level, at a point some 5 miles (8km) from Roseau. In 1995, Fae and Altherton Martin built this cluster of cottages on the western slope of mount Anglais in the southern half of the island. The resort's cottages are constructed from hardwoods, cured pine, and stone to blend into their natural surroundings. Accommodations are comfortable and tastefully furnished, each with a private porch, spacious living room, kitchen, large bedroom with two double beds, and private bathrooms with shower/tub combinations. The best swimming is in a nearby river, a 5-minute walk away.

Guests can prepare their own meals or dine at the Sugar Apple Café, enjoying such delights as steamed local fish or apricot-glazed chicken with savory rice.

Morne Anglais (P.O. Box 109), Roseau, Dominica, W.I. ✆ 767/448-8839. Fax 767/448-8829. www.exotica-cottages.com. 6 units. Winter $140 double; off-season $109 double. Extra person $23. Children under age 12 stay free in parents' room. MAP (breakfast and dinner) $35 per person extra. AE, DISC, MC, V. **Amenities:** Cafe. *In room:* TV, ceiling fan, hair dryer, no phone.

AT SALISBURY

Lauro Club ⭐   Built in 1991, a short walk uphill from the island's west coast, this rustic villa complex lies about a ½ mile (2km) from the town of Salisbury (pop. 2,000), midway between Roseau and Portsmouth. It's a simple but neat compound of white-sided concrete buildings. Drawing mostly Europeans who want to get away from it all, this is a small place with no resort-type extras, there's just the beach and the lush surroundings. The studios come two to a cottage, and the one-bedroom units stand alone. None has a TV or phone, but each has a covered veranda, queen beds, and views of the water. Units range from rather small standard doubles to spacious deluxe seafront units. Tile floors and mahogany furnishings add to the stall showers and sufficient shelf space. Although the sea is nearby, it takes a 5-minute walk and a climb down a long, serpentine staircase to get to a beach that's suitable for swimming.

The Lauro Club restaurant serves Creole and international dishes.

Grande Savane, Salisbury (P.O. Box 483), Roseau, Dominica, W.I. ℂ 767/449-6602. Fax 767/449-6603. www.delphis.dm/lauroclub.htm. 10 units. Year-round $75–$85 double. AE, DC, MC, V. **Amenities:** Restaurant, bar; pool; scuba diving, snorkeling; laundry; guided island tours. *In room:* Ceiling fan, no phone.

3 Dining

If you're going out in the evening, always call to make sure your dining choice is actually open. You'll also have to arrange transportation there and back; you probably don't want to drive yourself because of the bad lighting and awful roads.

Dominica is a lush island like Grenada and grows a lot of its own foodstuff, but fish and meats are generally shipped in frozen.

IN ROSEAU

Balisier ⓐ CREOLE/INTERNATIONAL   Named after a small red flower that thrives in the jungles of Dominica, this restaurant was designed to maximize the views over Roseau's harbor. We highly recommend the food, which might include blackened tuna; chicken Garraway (breast of chicken stuffed with plantain and sweet corn); loin of pork with pineapple, mushrooms, and onions; and a choice of steak, vegetarian, or lobster entrees. Favorite local dishes include crab backs and Creole-style mountain chicken (frogs' legs). End your meal with a slice of homemade coconut-cream pie. Lunches might feature West Indian curries, fish Creole, or several kinds of salads.

In the Garraway Hotel, Place Heritage, The Bayfront. ℂ 767/449-8800. Reservations recommended. Main courses EC$45–EC$80 (US$16.65–US$29.60); lunch EC$35–EC$75 (US$12.95–US$27.75); Fri lunch buffet EC$35 (US$12.95). AE, MC, V. Daily 7am–2:30pm and 7–10pm.

Guiyave CREOLE   This airy lunch-only restaurant occupies the second floor of a wood-frame West Indian house. Rows of tables almost completely fill the narrow balcony overlooking the street outside. You can enjoy a drink at the stand-up bar on the second floor. Specialties include different preparations of conch, octopus, and lobster, spareribs, chicken, pork chops, and various Creole grills for dinner. On Saturday, rotis and "goat water" (a local goat stew) are available. The place is known for its juices, including refreshing glasses of soursop, tamarind, sorrel, cherry, and strawberry. There's also a patisserie specializing in local pastries.

15 Cork St. ℂ 767/448-2930. Reservations recommended. Lunch EC$30–EC$55 (US$11.10–US$20.35). AE, MC, V. Mon–Fri 9am–3pm, Sat 10am–2:30pm.

La Robe Creole ⓐⓐ WEST INDIAN/SEAFOOD   The best independent restaurant in the capital, La Robe Creole sits on the second floor of a colonial house, beside a sunny plaza on a slope above the sea. The staff, dressed in madras Creole costumes, serve food in a long and narrow dining room capped with heavy beams and filled with relics from the 19th century. You can enjoy pumpkin-pimento soup, callaloo with cream of coconut soup, crab backs (in season), pizzas, mountain chicken (frogs' legs) in beer batter, and shrimp in coconut with garlic sauce. The food is in the spicy Creole style. One patron found the cuisine "seductive." For dessert, try banana or coconut cake or ice cream.

A street-level section of the restaurant, **The Mouse Hole,** is a good place for food on the run. You can take out freshly made sandwiches, salads, and light meals. They make good Trinidad-inspired rotis (Caribbean burritos) here—wheat pancakes wrapped around beef, chicken, or vegetables. On Dominica, these rotis are often flavored with curry.

3 Victoria St. *(C)* **767/448-2896.** Main courses EC$25–EC$65 (US$9.25–US$24.05). DC, MC, V. Mon–Sat 11am–9:30pm. (The Mouse Hole, Mon–Sat 8am–9:30pm.)

Pearl's Cuisine ★ *Finds* CARIBBEAN   In this restored Creole house with a veranda, Chef Pearl is the hearty empress, and she enjoys a certain celebrity in town for her island delicacies. Come here for a true taste of Dominica. Begin with one of her tropical fruit juices, then go on to sample mountain chicken (frogs' legs) or perhaps freshly caught crayfish. Whenever lobster is available, it's served at dinner any way you want it. She also makes some mean pork chops, and her curried goat will make a man of you, even if you're a woman. Try the rice and spareribs or the codfish and plantains if you want to really go local.

50 King George V St., Rouseau. *(C)* **767/448-8707.** Lunch EC$6–EC$35 (US$2.20–US$12.95), dinner EC$20–EC$60 (US$7.40–US$22.20). AE, DC, MC, V. Mon–Sat 9:30am–9:30pm.

World of Food Restaurant and Bar ★ *Finds* CREOLE   This is one of the most charming Creole restaurants in town. In the 1930s the garden containing this restaurant belonged to the novelist Jean Rhys, author of *Wide Sargasso Sea*. Some say that its owner, Vena McDougal, is the best Creole cook in town, and we more or less agree, though the competition is stiff. You can have a drink at the stone-walled building at the far end of the garden if you want, but many guests select one of the tables in the shadow of a large mango tree. Specialties include steamed fish or fish steak, pork chops, chicken-filled roti, black pudding, breadfruit puffs, conch, and *tee-tee-ree* (fried fish cakes). Vena also makes the best rum punches on the island.

In Vena's Hotel, 48 Cork St. (with another entrance on Field's Lane). *(C)* **767/448-3286.** Main courses EC$25–EC$55 (US$9.25–US$20.35). MC. Daily 7:30am–10pm.

IN THE RAIN FOREST

Papillote Wilderness Retreat ★ *Finds* CREOLE/CARIBBEAN   Even if you're not staying here, come by taxi for lunch; it's only 4 miles (6km)east of Roseau. For dinner, you'll need to make arrangements. Amid exotic flowers, century-old trees, and filtered sunlight, you'll dine overlooking a gorgeous vista of rivers and mountains. The array of healthful food includes flying fish and truly delectable freshwater prawns known as *bookh*. Mountain chicken (frogs' legs) appears in season, as does kingfish. Breadfruit or dasheen puffs merit a taste if you've never tried them, and tropical salads are filled with flavor. Our favorite dishes include "the seafood symphony" and the green papaya chicken salad.

Trafalgar Falls Rd. *(C)* **767/448-2287.** Reservations recommended for lunch, required for dinner. Main courses EC$30–EC$60 (US$11.10–US$22.20). AE, DISC, MC, V. Daily 6:30am–10:30pm; dinner served at 7:30pm.

NEAR SOUFRIÈRE

Forest Bistro ★ *Finds* CARIBBEAN   On the southwestern coast, the Forest Bistro is set in a lush tropical section of the island, cozy and secluded, with cliffs as a backdrop and a panoramic vista of the Caribbean from the tables. Cows roam among the acres of lime trees, and the whole place has such a bucolic setting, you'd want to come here even if the food weren't good. But the cuisine is excellent, well prepared, and made whenever possible with the freshest of ingredients, often grown by your hosts, Andre and Joyce Charles. The restaurant on this 5-acre (2-hectare) dairy farm is actually the top floors of the Charles' home.

Joyce is a top-notch chef, having worked at some of the island's finest restaurants. Her talent is particularly obvious in her fresh fish dishes. The farm also provides an endless source of refreshing drinks, including lime squash, passion fruit, grapefruit, and fresh coconut water. At lunch, you can order delightful soups, made with either peas, pumpkin, callaloo, or papaya. Stick to the fish unless you're a total vegetarian, in which case you might opt for one of the delicious Creole-style vegetarian dishes such as a savory eggplant.

Soufrière. © **767/448-7104.** Reservations required. Main courses EC$25–EC$35 (US$9.25–US$12.95). No credit cards. Daily 1–9pm.

4 Sports & Other Outdoor Pursuits

BEACHES If you really want a great beach, you should choose another island. Dominica has some of the worst beaches in the Caribbean; most are rocky with gray-black volcanic sand. But some beaches, even though they don't have great sand or shade, are still good for diving or snorkeling in the turquoise waters surrounding the island.

The best beach on the island lies on the northwest coast. **Picard Beach** stretches for about 2 miles (3km), a strip of grayish sand with palm trees as a backdrop. It's ideal for snorkeling or windsurfing. You can drop in for food and drink at one of the hotels along the beach.

On the northeast coast, four beaches—**L'Anse Noire, Hodges Beach, Woodford Hill Bay,** and **Hampstead Beach**—are among the island's most beautiful, although none are great for swimming. Divers and snorkelers often come here, even though the water can be rough at times. Be duly warned about the strong currents here.

The southwest coast also has some beaches, but the sand here is black and studded with rocks. Nonetheless, snorkelers and scuba divers flock to **Soufrière Bay Beach** and **Scotts Head Beach** for the clear waters and the stunning underwater walls.

HIKING Wild and untamed Dominica offers hikers some of the most bizarre geological oddities in the Caribbean. Sights include scalding lava covered with a hot, thin, and not-very-stable crust; a boiling lake where mountain streams turn to vapor as they come into contact with superheated volcanic fissures; and a barren wasteland known as the "Valley of Desolation."

All these attractions are in the 17,000 heavily forested acres (6,800 hectares)of the **Morne Trois Pitons National Park,** in the island's south-central region. You should go with a guide—they're in plentiful supply, waiting for your business in the village of Laudat. Few markers appear en route, but the trek, which includes a real assortment of geological oddities, stretches 6 miles (10km) in both directions from Laudat to the Boiling Lake. Ferns, orchids, trees, and epiphytes create a tangle of underbrush; insect, bird, and reptilian life is profuse.

The hill treks of Dominica have been described as "sometimes easy, sometimes hellish," and if it should happen to rain during your climb (and it rains very frequently on Dominica), your path is likely to become very slippery. But botanists, geologists, and experienced hikers all agree that climbs through the jungles of Dominica are the most rewarding in the Caribbean. Hikers should walk cautiously, particularly in areas peppered with bubbling hot springs. Regardless of where you turn, you'll run into streams and waterfalls, the inevitable result of an island whose mountaintops receive up to 400 inches of rainfall a year. Winds on the summits are strong enough to have pushed one recreational climber to her death several years ago, so be careful.

> **Tips** **Getting a Guide**
>
> Locals warn that to proceed along the island's badly marked trails into areas that can be physically treacherous is not a good idea; climbing alone or even in pairs is not advisable. Guides should be used for all unmarked trails. You can arrange for a guide by going to the office of the **Dominica National Park,** in the Botanical Gardens in Roseau (📞 **767/448-2401**), or the Dominica Tourist Board. Forestry officials recommend **Ken's Hinterland Adventure Tours & Taxi Service,** 10A Old St., Roseau (📞 **767/448-4850**). Depending on the destination and the featured attractions, treks cost $30 to $60 per person for up to 4 participants and require 4 to 8 hours round-trip. Usually included in the price is minivan transportation from Roseau to the starting point of your hill climb.

An adventure only for the most serious and experienced hiker is to **Boiling Lake** and the Titou Gorge, a deep and very narrow ravine whose depths were created as lava flows cooled and contracted. En route, you might spot rare Sisserou and Jacquot parrots, monkeys, and vines whose growth seems to increase visibly on an hourly basis. The lake itself lies 6 miles (10km) east of Roseau, but reaching it requires about 4 hours, including some strenuous hiking. Go only with a guide, which can be arranged through the tourist office (see earlier in this chapter). Taking the Wotton Waven Road, you branch off in the direction of **Sulphur Springs,** a volcanic hot springs that are evidence of Dominica's turbulent past. Jeeps and Land Rovers can get quite close. This bubbling pool of gray mud sometimes belches smelly sulfurous fumes. The trail begins at the **Titou Gorge,** a narrow and deep gorge also formed by the island's volcanic past. At this gorge you can go for a cooling swim in a pool or enjoy the hot spring waters alongside the pool. A 5-minute swim will take you up to the gorge to a small cave with a beautiful waterfall. After the gorge the marked trail goes through the appropriately named **"Valley of Desolation"** and comes out at Boiling Lake on the far side, a trek of 2 to 3 hours one way. Sulfuric fumes in the area have destroyed much of the once flourishing vegetation in the region. **Boiling Lake** is the world's second-largest solfatara lake and the scenic attraction of the park, measuring 210 feet (63m) across. It is a bubbling cauldron with blue-gray water with vapor clouds rising. The depth of the lake is not known. The water temperature in the lake averages around 190°F. The lake is not the crater of a former volcano but a flooded fumarole. Getting to the lake is extremely difficult and even hazardous. Some visitors have even stumbled and fallen fatally into the boiling waters. The trail is most often very slippery because of rainfall. You'll encounter few visitors along this trail and, if you do, will likely be glad for the company, especially if a hiker is returning from the area where you're heading. He or she can give you advance reports of the conditions ahead of you.

See also "Exploring the Island," below, for details on gorgeous **Cabrits National Park.**

KAYAKING ⭐⭐ Dominica is probably the best place in all the Caribbean for kayaking. You can rent a kayak for $26 for a half day, then go on a unique adventure around the rivers and coastline of the lushest island in the West Indies. **Nature Island Dive,** in Roseau (📞 **767/449-8181**), offers rentals and gives the best advice. You can combine bird-watching, swimming, and snorkeling as you glide along. Consider Soufrière Bay, a marine reserve in southwest

Dominica. Off the west coast, you can discover tranquil Caribbean waters with rainbow-hued fish along the beaches in Mero, Salisbury, and in the region of the Layou and Macoucherie Rivers.

SCUBA DIVING   Diving has taken off on Dominica. The underwater terrain is spectacular. Most of the diving is on the southwestern end of the island, with its dramatic drop-offs, walls, and pinnacles. These volcanic formations are interwoven with cuts, arches, ledges, and overhangs, home to a myriad of sponges, gorgonians, and corals. An abundance of invertebrates, reef fish, and unusual sea creatures such as sea horses, frog-fish, batfish, and flying gunards attract the underwater photographer.

Dive Dominica, in the **Castle Comfort Diving Lodge** (P.O. Box 2253, Roseau), Castle Comfort, Dominica, W.I. (© **767/448-2188**), gives open-water certification (both NAUI and PADI) and instruction. Two diving catamarans and a handful of smaller boats get you to the dive sites in relative comfort. The dive outfit is part of a hotel, a 15-room lodge where at least 90% of the clientele checks in as part of a dive package. A 7-night dive package, double occupancy, begins at $995 per person, including breakfasts and dinners, 5 two-tank dives, and 1 night dive. A single tank dive goes for $45, a two-tank dive for $75, and a night dive for $50. All rooms in the lodge are air-conditioned, and have TVs and phones. On the premises is a bar (for residents and their guests only) and a Jacuzzi.

Divers from all over the world come to the **Dive Centre,** at the Anchorage Hotel in Castle Comfort (© **767/448-2638**). A fully qualified PADI and NAUI staff awaits you. A single-tank dive costs $50; a double-tank dive, $65; and a one-tank night dive, $55. A unique whale and dolphin watch from 2pm to sunset is a popular attraction. The price for a 3½-hour experience of communal straining to catch sight of the animals is $45 per person. On the way home (and not before), rum punches are served. With a pool, classrooms, a private dock, a miniflotilla of dive boats, and a well-trained and alert staff, this is the most complete dive resort on Dominica.

SNORKELING   Snorkeling sites are never very far away, regardless of where you are on Dominica. The western side of the island, where nearly all of the snorkeling takes place, is the lee side, meaning the waters are tranquil. In all, there are some 30 separate and first-rate snorkeling areas immediately off the coast. You can explore the underwater hot springs at Champagne and Toucari, the Coral Gardens off Salisbury, and the southern shoreline of Scotts Head Beach, with more than 190 species of flamboyantly colored fish. The closeness of the reefs to shore makes snorkeling here among the best in the Caribbean. Your hotel or one of the dive shops can set you up with gear.

SWIMMING   The beaches may be lousy, but Dominica has some of the best river swimming in the Caribbean. Some say the little island has 365 rivers, one for every day of the year. The best places for swimming are under a waterfall, and there are dozens of them on the island. Almost all waterfalls have a refreshing pond at the base of them, ideal for a dip. Your best bets are on the west coast at the **Picard** or the **Machoucherie Rivers.** On the east coast, the finest spot is **White River,** near the hamlet of La Plaine. Consider also the **Layou River** and its gorges. Layou is the island's largest river, ranging from tranquil beach-lined pools ideal for swimming to deep gorges and turbulent rapids. All the rivers are pristine and make nice spots for a little sunbathing or perhaps a picnic lunch to enjoy along their banks.

The staff at the tourist office (see earlier in this chapter) knows the island intimately and will help you map out a place for a picnic and a swim during your tour of the island, depending on where you're going. They'll also arm you with a good map and directions if you're heading out on your own.

Our favorite place for a dip is the **Emerald Pool Trail** (see below), which lies in the Morne Trois Pitons National Park. You reach it northeast of Pont Casse, going for 3½ miles (6km) along an unmarked road taking you north to Castle Bruce. Eventually you reach a sign pointing to the Emerald Pool Trail, the most accessible trail in this lush national park. Reached after a 30-minute hike, the trail lies off the road on the northern edge of the park. It leads to a stunning cascade of water dropping 20 feet (6m). This is Emerald Falls, where you can go for a cooling swim. Chances are, you'll have the place all to yourself.

5 Exploring the Island

Those making day trips to Dominica from other Caribbean islands will want to see the **Carib Indian Reservation** ✦, in the northeast. In 1903, Britain got the surviving Caribs to agree to live on 3,700 acres (1,480 hectares) of land. Hence, this is the last remaining turf of the once-hostile tribe for whom the Caribbean was named. Their look is Mongolian, and they are no longer "pure-blooded," as they have married outside their tribe. Today they survive by fishing, growing food, and weaving baskets and vetiver-grass mats, which they sell to the outside world. They still make dugout canoes as well. The baskets sold at roadside stands make especially good buys. Once you get here there isn't a lot to do except look at the remains of this once-famous tribe that dominated the islands of the Caribbean. Of course, they'll be staring back at you with equal interest even though they are shy people. You can get glimpses of their way of life. One of the most interesting sites is to watch the Caribs building canoes. Nothing seems to have changed in this task since the days of their forefathers.

It's like going back in time when you explore **Morne Trois Pitons National Park** ✦✦, a primordial rain forest. Mists rise gently over lush, dark-green growth, drifting up to blue-green peaks that have earned Dominica the title "Switzerland of the Caribbean." Framed by banks of giant ferns, rivers rush and tumble. Trees sprout orchids, green sunlight filters down through trees, and roaring waterfalls create a blue mist. One of the best starting points for a visit to the park is the village of **Laudat**, 7 miles (11km) from Roseau. (See also "Hiking," above.)

Deep in the park is the **Emerald Pool Trail,** a half-mile circuit loop that passes through the forest to a pool with a beautiful waterfall. Downpours are frequent in the rain forest, and at high elevations, cold winds blow. It lies 3½ miles (6km) northeast of Pont Casse. See "Swimming," above, for more details.

Five miles (8km) up from the **Roseau River Valley,** in the south-central sector of Dominica, **Trafalgar Falls** can be reached after you drive through the village of Trafalgar. Shortly beyond the hamlet of Trafalgar and up a short hill, there's a little kiosk where you can hire a guide to take you on the short walk to the actual falls. In all, allow about 1½ hours for this excursion from Trafalgar to the falls itself. This is the only road or pathway into the falls. Here, however, you have to approach on foot, as the slopes are too steep for vehicles. After a 20-minute walk past ginger plants and vanilla orchids, you arrive at the base, where a trio of falls converge into a rock-strewn pool.

For another great way to spend a half day, head for the **Papillote Wilderness Retreat** (see previous recommendation as a hotel and a restaurant). The botanical

---

Moments Searching for Moby Dick

You'll see more sperm whales, pilot whales, killer whales, and dolphins during **whale- and dolphin-watching trips** ✦ off Dominica than off any other island in the Caribbean. A pod of sperm whales can often be spotted just yards from your boat, since there are no laws here regarding the distance which you can go to "meet the whales." The best tours are offered by the **Anchorage Hotel,** at Castle Comfort (© **767/448-2638**); a 4-hour trip costs $40 (children under age 12 pay half price). The vessels leave the dock every Wednesday and Sunday at 2pm.

---

garden alone is worth the trip, as are the views of mountains and lush valleys. Near the main dining terrace is a Jacuzzi-size pool, which is constantly filled with the mineral-rich waters of a nearby hot spring. Nonguests can use the pool for EC$5 (US$1.85). Bring sturdy walking shoes in addition to a bathing suit.

On the northwestern coast, **Portsmouth** is Dominica's second-largest settlement. Once here, you can row up the Indian River in native canoes, visit the ruins of old Fort Shirley in Cabrits National Park, and bathe at Sandy Beach on Douglas Bay and Prince Rupert Bay.

Cabrits National Park ✦✦, on the northwestern coast, 2 miles (3km) south of Douglas Bay (© **767/448-2732**), is a 1,313-acre (525-hectare) protected site containing mountain scenery, tropical forests, swampland, volcanic-sand beaches, coral reefs, and the ruins of a fortified, 18th-century garrison of British, then French, construction. This is one of the great natural attractions of the area, and those with very limited time may want to head here even if they skip everything else in Dominica. The park's land area is a panoramic promontory formed by twin peaks of extinct volcanoes, overlooking beaches, with Douglas Bay on one side and Prince Rupert Bay across the headland. Part of Douglas Bay forms the marine section of the park. Fort Shirley, the large garrison last used as a military post in 1854, is being wrested from encroaching vegetation. A small museum highlights the natural and historic aspects of the park. The most interesting trail to explore is the 800-acre (320-hectare) Marine Park or reserve, lying on the north side of the park at Douglas Bay. Trails using the old tracks of the English garrisons once stationed on the island have been reopened. You'll pass an eerie ruin of the former mansion of the British military commander. Nature's gigantic roots are reclaiming the property. A dark sandy beach snakes north along Douglas Bay and is shaded by swaying palms; lots of snorkelers come here. The route beyond Douglas Bay traverses through teak plantations to Toucari Bay. The name *Cabrits* comes from the Spanish-Portuguese-French word for goat, because of the animals left here by early sailors to provide fresh meat on future visits. Entrance is EC$6 (US$2.20).

6 Shopping

Store hours are usually Monday to Friday from 8am to 5pm and Saturday from 9am to 1pm.

In Roseau, the **Old Market Plaza,** of historical significance as a former slave-trading market and more recently the site of a Wednesday-, Friday-, and Saturday-morning vegetable market, now houses three craft shops, each specializing in coconut, straw, and Carib craft products.

Tropicrafts Island Mats, 41 Queen Mary St. and Turkey Lane (© **767/448-2747**), offers the well-known grass rugs handmade and woven in several intricate patterns at Tropicrafts' factory. They also sell handmade dolls, shopping bags, and place mats, all appliquéd by hand. The Dominican vetiver-grass mats are known throughout the world, and you can watch the weaving process during store hours.

Outlets for crafts include **Dominica Pottery,** Bayfront Street at Kennedy Avenue, Roseau (no phone), run by a local priest. An array of pottery made from local clays is on sale, as well as other handcrafts. **Balisier's,** 35 Great George St., Roseau (no phone), is run by a young and talented artist, Hilroy Fingol, an expert in airbrush painting. The shop also has some of the most original T-shirts on the island, as well as an assortment of Carnival dolls and handmade jewelry. Of course, you don't come to Dominica to purchase clothing; however, **Ego Boutique**, 9 Hillsborough St. in Roseau (© **767/448-2336**), has the best selection of merchandise, much of it in the classic West Indian style, along with some crafts and home accessories, much of it made locally.

The casual shopper, seeking souvenirs and crafts, can also drop into **Island Stuff**, 25 Hanover St. in Roseau (© **767/449-9969**), a small shop that's jam-packed with intriguing items including handcrafts and fine art. Try also **The Crazy Banana**, 17 Castle St. in Roseau (© **767/449-8091**), which offers a little preview of some of the best items for which the Caribbean is known, including handcrafts, handmade jewelry, bottles of rum, and regional paintings, even cigars.

7 Dominica After Dark

It's not very lively, but there is some evening activity. A couple of the major hotels, such as the **Fort Young Hotel**, Victoria Street (© **767/448-5000**), and the **Reigate Hall Hotel,** Mountain Road (© **767/448-4031**), have entertainment on weekends, usually a combo or "jing ping" (traditional local music). In the winter season, the Castaways sponsors a weekend barbecue on the beach with live music. The **Anchorage Hotel** at Castle Comfort (© **767/448-2638**) also has live entertainment and a good buffet on Thursday. Call for details.

The clubs and bars in these hotels attract mainly foreign visitors. But if you'd like to go where the locals go, head for one of the following recommendations.

The current hot spot is **Magic Disco,** Wallhouse, Loubiere (© **767/448-7778**), housed in a long defunct old mill, now restored and reopened with a long bar and a dance floor with a DJ. It's a weekend attraction, costing a $5 cover. Both international visitors and locals ages 20 to 35 patronize this night spot.

The Warehouse, Checkhall Estate (© **767/448-5451**), a 5-minute drive north of Roseau, adjacent to Canefield Airport, is the island's major dance club, packed every Saturday. Recorded disco, reggae, and other music is played from 11pm to 5am in this 200-year-old stone building, once used to store rum. The cover is EC$10 (US$3.70).

If you're seeking more action, such as it is, head for **Wykie's Tropical Bar,** 51 Old St. (© **767/448-8015**), in Roseau. This is little more than a cramped hole-in-the-wall, yet curiously enough it draws the power brokers of the island. Happy hour on Friday is the time to show up. You might be offered some black pudding or stewed chicken to go with your local tropical drink. A homegrown calypso band is likely to entertain. You'll definitely hear some "jing ping." Try out the **Krazy Terrace,** Dame Euginia (© **767/448-8752**), if late-night disco dancing is your thing.

Other hot spots include **QClub,** corner of Bath Road and High Street, Roseau (© **767/448-2995**), the place to be on a Friday night. Records, both local and American, are played until dawn breaks. If you get bored here, head for **Symes Zee's,** 34 King George V St., Roseau (© **767/448-2494**), the domain of Symes Zee, the island's best blues man. A local band entertains with blues, jazz, and reggae. Here's your chance to smoke a reasonably priced Cuban cigar.

The Dominican Republic

Sugar-white beaches, inexpensive resorts, and rich natural beauty have long attracted visitors to the Dominican Republic. But at the same time, a not-so-fair reputation for high crime, poverty, and social unrest has scared away many travelers. So which is it: A poverty-stricken country rife with pickpockets and muggers or a burgeoning destination of beautiful beach bargains?

The answer, of course, is a little of both. The people of the Dominican Republic are among the friendliest in the Caribbean, and the hospitality here seems more genuine than in more commercialized Puerto Rico. The weather is nearly perfect year-round. And the Dominican Republic's white-sand beaches are among the finest in the Caribbean. Punta Cana/Bávaro, for example, is the longest strip of white sand in the entire region.

Safety *is* still a concern here, but it shouldn't dissuade you from planning a vacation to the Dominican Republic. Crime consists primarily of theft, robberies, and muggings, and most of it is limited to Santo Domingo (although the north coast resorts around Puerto Plata and Playa Dorada are not as safe as they should be). There is little incidence of violent crime against tourists, however. Follow simple common sense rules of safety, and you'll be fine. Lock valuables in your hotel safe, carry only a reasonable amount of cash or (better yet) one or two credit cards, and avoid dark deserted places just like you would at home. (One note: The single male will find more solicitations from prostitutes [*putas* in Spanish] here than anywhere else in the Caribbean. Putas are at their most visible and aggressive in such relatively unmonitored tourist zones as Cabarete, and within the bars and lounges of most of the deluxe hotels of Santo Domingo, especially the Jaragua.)

The combination of low prices and beautiful terrain has made the Dominican Republic one of the fastest-growing destinations in the Caribbean. Bargain-hunting Canadians, in particular, flock here in droves. Don't expect the lavish, spectacular resorts that you'll find on Puerto Rico or Jamaica, but do expect your vacation to be that much less expensive.

Often mistakenly referred to as "just a poor man's Puerto Rico," the Dominican Republic has its own distinctive cuisine and cultural heritage. Its Latin flavor is a sharp contrast to the character of many nearby islands, especially the British- and French-influenced ones.

Columbus sighted its coral-edged Caribbean coastline on his first voyage to the New World and pronounced: "There is no more beautiful island in the world." The first permanent European settlement in the New World was founded here on November 7, 1493, and its ruins still remain near Montecristi in the northeast part of the island. Natives called the island Quisqueya, "Mother Earth," before the Spaniards arrived to butcher them.

Nestled amid Cuba, Jamaica, and Puerto Rico in the heart of the Caribbean archipelago, the island of

Hispaniola (Little Spain) is divided between Haiti, on the westernmost third of the island, and the Dominican Republic, which has a lush landmass about the size of Vermont and New Hampshire combined. In the Dominican interior, the fertile Valley of Cibao (rich sugarcane country) ends its upward sweep at Pico Duarte, the highest mountain peak in the West Indies, which soars to 10,417 feet (3,125m).

Much of what Columbus first sighted still remains in a natural, unspoiled condition. One-third of the Dominican Republic's 870-mile (1,401km) coastline is devoted to beaches. The best are in Puerto Plata and La Romana, although Puerto Plata and other beaches on the Atlantic side of the island have dangerously strong currents at times.

Political turmoil kept visitors away for many years, but even that is a thing of the past. Almost from its inception, the country was steeped in misery and bloodshed, climaxing with the infamous reign of dictator Rafael Trujillo (1930–1961) and the ensuing civil wars (1960–1966). But the country has been politically stable since then, and it is building and expanding rapidly. The economic growth hasn't benefited everybody equally, though. The country is still poor, even by Caribbean standards. Every day, many Dominicans risk their lives crossing the 54-mile (87km) wide Mona Passage, hoping to land on Puerto Rico before attempting to slip into the United States.

The greatest threat to the Dominican Republic these days comes from hurricanes, which periodically flatten entire cities. The major resorts have become adept at getting back on their feet quickly after a hurricane, as evidenced by the quick rebound from the devastation of Hurricane Georges (1998). Still, if a hurricane hits the country before your trip, you might want to call ahead and make sure your room is still standing.

1 Essentials

VISITOR INFORMATION

In the United States, you can contact the **Dominican Republic Tourist Information Center** at 136 E. 57th St., Suite 803, New York, NY 10022 (© **888/374-6361** or 212/588-1012); or at 2355 Salzedo St., Suite 307, Coral Gables, FL 33134 (© **888/358-9594** or 305/444-4592; fax 305/444-4845). In Canada, try the office at 2081 Crescent St., Montréal, PQ, H39, 2B8, Canada (© **800/563-1611** or 514/499-1918; fax 514/499-1393); or at 35 Church St., Unit 53, Toronto, Ontario M5E 1TE (© **888/494-5050;** fax 416/361-2130). Don't expect too many specifics.

In England, there's an office at 20 Hand Court, High Holborn, WC1 (© **020/7242-7778**).

On the Web, check out **www.dominicanrepublic.com**.

GETTING THERE

Before you book your airline tickets, read the section "Package Deals" in chapter 2—it could save you a bundle. Even if you don't book a package, see that chapter's tips on finding the best airfare.

American Airlines (© **800/433-7300;** www.aa.com) offers the most frequent service, at least a dozen flights daily from cities throughout North America to either Santo Domingo or Puerto Plata. Flights from hubs like New York, Miami, or San Juan, Puerto Rico are usually nonstop. American also offers some good package deals.

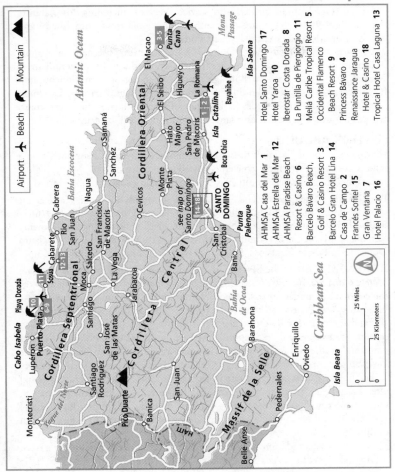

Airport ✈ Beach ✈ Mountain ◀

Hotel Santo Domingo **17**
Hotel Yaroa **10**
Iberostar Costa Dorada **8**
La Puntilla de Piergiorgio **11**
Meliá Caribe Tropical Resort **5**
Occidental Flamenco
Beach Resort **9**
Princess Bávaro **4**
Renaissance Jaragua
Hotel & Casino **18**
Tropical Hotel Casa Laguna **13**

AHMSA Casa del Mar **1**
AHMSA Estrella del Mar **12**
AHMSA Paradise Beach
Resort & Casino **6**
Barcelo Bávaro Beach,
Golf & Casino Resort **3**
Barcelo Gran Hotel Lina **14**
Casa de Campo **2**
Francés Sofitel **15**
Gran Ventana **7**
Hotel Palacio **16**

If you're heading to one of the Dominican Republic's smaller airports, your best bet is to catch a connecting flight with **American Eagle,** American's local commuter carrier. Its small planes depart every day from San Juan, Puerto Rico, for airports throughout the Dominican Republic, including Santo Domingo, Puerto Plata, La Romana, and Punta Cana.

Continental Airlines (© **800/231-0856** in the U.S.; www.continental.com) has a daily flight between Newark and Santo Domingo.

ALM (© **809/687-4569;** www.almsd.com) flies to Santo Domingo from Miami.

Iberia (© **800/772-4642** in the U.S.; www.iberia.com) offers daily flights from Madrid to Santo Domingo, making a brief stop in San Juan.

For information on flights into Casa de Campo/La Romana, see the section "La Romana & Altos de Chavón," below.

Lately, several minor airlines also service the area, including **Air Atlantic** (© **845/569-9688**; www.airatlantic.com), with flights from both Miami and San Juan on Monday, Wednesday, and Friday.

Be warned: Arriving at Santo Domingo's Las Américas International Airport is confusing and chaotic. Customs officials, who tend to be rude and over-worked, may give you a very thorough check. Stolen luggage is not uncommon here; beware of "porters" who offer to help with your bags. Arrival at La Unión International Airport, 23 miles (37km) east of Puerto Plata on the north coast, is generally much smoother and safer, but you should still be cautious.

GETTING AROUND

Getting around the Dominican Republic is not always easy if your hotel is in a remote location. The most convenient modes of transport are shuttle flights, taxis, rental cars, *públicos* (multi-passenger taxis), and *guaguas* (public buses).

BY PLANE   The quickest and easiest way to get across a difficult landscape is on one of the shuttle flights offered by **Air Santo Domingo** (© **809/683-8006**), flying from Santo Domingo to Puerto Plata, Punta Cana, La Romana, Samaná, and Santiago, among other towns. A one-way fare from Santo Domingo to Puerto Plata costs $56; to Samaná, $63, and to Punta Cana $66.50.

BY RENTAL CAR   The best way to see the Dominican Republic is to drive. *Motorists drive on the right here.* Although major highways are relatively smooth, the country's secondary roads, especially those in the east, are riddled with pot-holes and ruts. Roads also tend to be badly lit and poorly marked in both the city and the countryside. Drive carefully and give yourself plenty of time when traveling between island destinations. Watch out for policemen who may flag you down and accuse you (often wrongly) of some infraction. Many locals give these low-paid policemen a $5 *regalo*, or gift "for your children," and are then free to go.

The high accident and theft rate in recent years has helped to raise car-rental rates here. Prices vary, so call around for last-minute quotes. Make sure you understand your insurance coverage (or lack thereof) before you leave home. Your credit-card issuer may already provide you with this type of insurance; call to find out.

For reservations and more information, call the rental companies at least a week before your departure: **Avis** (© **800/331-1212** in the U.S., or 809/535-7191; www.avis.com), **Budget** (© **800/527-0700** in the U.S., or 809/549-0351; www.budget.com), and **Hertz** (© **800/654-3001** in the U.S., or 809/221-5333; www.hertz.com) all operate in the Dominican Republic. All three have offices at the Santo Domingo and Puerto Plata airports, as well as in downtown Santo Domingo. Avis and Hertz also have offices in La Romana and in Punta Cana.

Although the cars may be not as well maintained as the big three above, you can often get a cheaper deal at one of the local firms, notably **McAuto Rental Cars** (© **809/688-6518**). If you want a car with seat belts, you must ask. Your Canadian or American driver's license is suitable documentation, along with a valid credit card or a substantial cash deposit.

BY TAXI   Taxis aren't metered, and determining the fare in advance (which you should do) may be difficult if you and your driver have a language problem. You can easily hail a taxi at the airport and at most major hotels. *Don't get into an unmarked street taxi. Many visitors, particularly in Santo Domingo, have been assaulted and robbed by doing just that.* The minimum fare within Santo Domingo is RD$50 (US$3.15). In Santo Domingo, the most reliable taxi company is **Tecni-Taxi** (© 809/567-2010). In Puerto Plata, call **Tecni-Taxi** at © 809/320-7621.

BY PUBLIC TRANSPORTATION   *Públicos* are unmetered multipassenger taxis that travel along main thoroughfares, stopping often to pick up people waving from the side of the street. A *público* is marked by a white seal on the front door. You must tell the driver your destination when you're picked up to make sure the *público* is going there. A ride is usually RD$5 (30¢).

Public buses, often in the form of minivans or panel trucks, are called *guaguas* (pronounced *gwa-gwas*). For about the same price, they provide the same service as *públicos*, but they're generally more crowded. Larger buses provide service outside the towns. Beware of pickpockets on board.

 FAST FACTS: The Dominican Republic

Currency   The Dominican monetary unit is the peso (**RD$**), made up of 100 centavos. Coin denominations are 1, 5, 10, 25, and 50 centavos, and 1 peso. Bill denominations are RD$5, RD$10, RD$20, RD$50, RD$100, RD$500, and RD$1,000. Price quotations in this chapter sometimes appear in U.S. and sometimes in Dominican currency, depending on the policy of the establishment. The use of any currency other than Dominican pesos is technically illegal, but few seem to heed this mandate. At press time, we got about RD$16 to US$1 (meaning that centavos are practically worthless). *When dollar figures stand alone, they are always U.S. currency.* Bank booths at the international airports and major hotels will change your currency at the prevailing free-market rate. (Just before you leave home, you can check the current exchange rates on the Web at **www.x-rates.com**.)

Documents   To enter the Dominican Republic, citizens of the United States, Canada, and the United Kingdom need a valid passport. Upon your arrival at the airport in the Dominican Republic, you must purchase a tourist card for US$10. You can avoid waiting in line by purchasing this card when checking in for your flight to the island.

Electricity   The country generally uses 110-volt AC (60 cycles), so adapters and transformers are usually not necessary for U.S. appliances.

Emergencies   Call © **911**.

Embassies   All embassies are in Santo Domingo, the capital. The **United States** embassy is on Calle Cesar Nicholas Penson at the corner of Leopold Navarro (© **809/221-2171**). The embassy of the **United Kingdom** is located at Febrero 27, #233 (© **809/472-7111**). The embassy of **Canada** is found at Avenida Máximo Gómez 39 (© **809/685-1136**).

Language   The official language is Spanish; many people also speak some English.

Safety   The Dominican Republic has more than its fair share of crime (see "Getting There," above, for a warning about crime at airports). Avoid unmarked street taxis, especially in Santo Domingo; you could be targeted for assault and robbery. While strolling around the city, beware of hustlers selling various wares; pickpockets and muggers are common here, and visitors are easy targets. Don't walk in Santo Domingo at night.

Locals like to offer their services as guides, and it is often difficult to decline. Hiring an official guide from the tourist office is your best bet.

Taxes A departure tax of US$10 is assessed and must be paid in U.S. currency. The government imposes a 13% tax on hotel rooms, which is usually topped by an automatic 10% service charge, bringing the total tax to staggering heights.

Telephone The area code for the Dominican Republic is **809**. You place calls to or from the Dominican Republic just as you would from any other area code in North America. You can access **AT&T Direct** by dialing 🕐 **800/222-0300**. You can reach **MCI** at 🕐 **800/888-8000** and **Sprint** at 🕐 **800/877-7746**.

Time Atlantic standard time is observed year-round. Between November and March, when it's noon in New York and Miami, it's 1pm in Santo Domingo. However, during U.S. daylight saving time, it's the same time in the Dominican Republic and the U.S. east coast.

Tipping Most restaurants and hotels add a 10% service charge to your check. Most people usually add 5% to 10% more, especially if the service has been good.

Water Stick to bottled water.

Weather The average temperature is 77°F. August is the warmest month, and January the coolest month, although even then it's warm enough to swim.

2 La Romana ⭐ & Altos de Chavón ⭐⭐⭐

On the southeast coast of the Dominican Republic, La Romana was once a sleepy sugarcane town that specialized in cattle raising. Visitors didn't come near the place, but when Gulf + Western Industries opened a luxurious tropical paradise resort, the Casa de Campo, about a mile (2km) east of town, La Romana soon began drawing the jet set. It's the finest resort in the Dominican Republic, and especially popular among golfers.

Just east of Casa de Campo is Altos de Chavón, a charming and whimsical copy of what might have been a fortified medieval village in Spain, southern France, or Italy. It's the country's leading sightseeing attraction.

GETTING THERE

BY PLANE   **American Airlines** (🕐 **800/433-7300** in the U.S.; www.aa.com) offers daily service to Casa de Campo from Miami, with a travel time of about 2½ hours each way. (Yes, it's a slow plane.) **American Eagle** (same phone number) operates at least two (and in busy seasons, at least three) daily nonstop flights to Casa de Campo/La Romana airport from San Juan, Puerto Rico (see "Getting There," in chapter 17). The flight takes about 45 minutes, and it departs late enough in the day to permit transfers from other flights.

BY CAR   You can drive here in about an hour and 20 minutes from the international airport, along Las Américas Highway. (Allow another hour if you're in the center of the city.) Of course, everything depends on traffic conditions. (Watch for speed traps—low-paid police officers openly solicit bribes, whether you were speeding or not.)

LA ROMANA
ACCOMMODATIONS

AMHSA Casa del Mar 🌟 Casa de Campo (see below) dominates this coast, but this newer contender on a spectacular beach is giving the grande dame a run for its money. The golf and tennis facilities here aren't as elaborate as those at Casa de Campo, and there are no polo grounds. But the resort is beautifully landscaped, the beach palm fringed.

Casa del Mar was built in 1997 and virtually rebuilt after Hurricane Georges whacked it in 1998. Accommodations are within seven three-story buildings with yellow walls and blue-tiled roofs. Decor inside features lots of tile, varnished hardwood, wicker, and rattan, plus a neatly appointed shower-only bathroom. There's an overall cheerfulness about the place and lots of emphasis on merengue music that helps keep the good times rolling.

Everything served in all of the resort's restaurants is covered by the all-inclusive price. Michelangelo serves Italian food, Chinese is on the menu at Asia, and Saona does beachfront barbecues and grills, Dominican style. There's also a buffet restaurant and a disco.

Bayahibe Bay, La Romana, Dominican Republic. ✆ **800/472-3985** in the U.S., or 809/221-8880. Fax 809/221-8881. www.amhsamarina.com. 568 units. Year-round $130–$178 per person double; $182–$232 per person suite. Rates are all-inclusive. AE, MC, V. **Amenities:** 4 restaurants, 4 bars; 2 pools; 4 tennis courts; fitness center; Jacuzzi; sauna; horseback riding; dive shop, windsurfing, banana boat rides; bikes; children's activities; room service; babysitting. *In room:* A/C, TV, iron, minibar, hair dryer.

Casa de Campo 🌟🌟🌟 Translated as "country house," Casa de Campo, on its own beach, is the leading resort in the Dominican Republic. In the 1960s, the former Gulf + Western corporation took a vast hunk of coastal land, more than 7,000 acres (2,800 hectares) in all, and carved out this chic resort. Tiles, Dominican crafts, mahogany furniture, louvered doors, and flamboyant fabrics decorate the interior of both the public areas and the accommodations.

Rooms are divided into red-roofed, two-story *casitas,* each with four units, radiating out from the main building, and more upscale villas that dot the edges of the golf courses, the gardens near the tennis courts, and the shoreline. (Ask for one near the water if you plan to spend most of your time on the beach, or one near the links if you're an avid golfer, since the grounds are massive.) Some are clustered in a semiprivate hilltop compound with views overlooking the meadows, the sugarcane, and the fairways down to the distant sea. Accommodations have either a shower only or a shower/tub combination.

La Romana, Dominican Republic. ✆ **800/877-3643** or 809/523-3333. Fax 809/523-8548. www.casadecampo.com. 450 units. Winter $329–$427 casita for 2; $1,117 2-bedroom villa for 4. Off-season $155–$237 casita for 2; $372 2-bedroom villa for 4. Rates are all-inclusive. AE, MC, V. **Amenities:** 10 restaurants, bar; 19 pools; 2 18-hole golf courses; 13 tennis courts; health club, aerobics; sauna; theater; horseback riding, polo; bikes; fishing, snorkeling; children's programs (ages 3–12); room service (7am–midnight); massage; babysitting; laundry. *In room:* A/C, TV, minibar, coffeemaker, safe.

DINING

El Patio ⓥ**alue** CARIBBEAN/AMERICAN Originally designed as a disco, El Patio now contains a shield of lattices, banks of plants, and checkerboard tablecloths. Technically it's a glamorized bistro, offering good value, considering the quality of both the cookery and the first-class ingredients that go into meal preparations. You can feast on selections from the constantly changing menu. Try such pleasing dishes as grilled snapper in a savory lime sauce or fillet of salmon with a perfectly prepared vinaigrette. The fettuccine in seafood sauce also wins a thumbs up. If you like your dishes plainer, opt for half a roast chicken or else the classic beef tips in a mushroom-and-onion sauce.

In Casa de Campo. © 809/523-3333. Main courses RD$140–RD$345 (US$8.75–US$21.55). AE, DC, MC, V. Daily 7am–2pm and 3–10pm.

Lago Grill CARIBBEAN/AMERICAN This is ideal for breakfast; in fact, it has one of the best-stocked morning buffets in the country. Your view is of a lake, a sloping meadow, and the resort's private airport, with the sea in the distance. At the fresh-juice bar, an employee in colonial costume will extract juices in any combination you prefer from 25 different tropical fruits. Then you can select your ingredients for an omelet and an employee will whip it up while you wait. The lunchtime buffet includes sandwiches, burgers, *sancocho* (the famous Dominican stew), and fresh conch chowder. There's also a well-stocked salad bar.

In Casa de Campo. © 809/523-3333. Buffet RD$365 (US$22.80); breakfast RD$115–RD$268 (US$7.20–US$16.80). AE, DC, MC, V. Daily 7–11am and noon–4pm.

HITTING THE BEACH

La Minitas, Casa de Campo's main beach, and site of a series of bars and restaurants all its own, is a small but immaculate beach and lagoon that requires a 10-minute shuttle bus ride from the resort's central core. Transportation is provided on the bus, or you can rent an electric golf cart. A bit farther afield (a 30-min. bus ride, but only a 20-min. boat ride), **Bayahibe** is a large, palm-fringed sandy crescent on a point jutting out from the shoreline. Finally, **Catalina** is a fine beach on a deserted island, surrounded by turquoise waters; it's just 45 minutes away by motorboat. Unfortunately, many other visitors from Casa de Campo have learned of the glories of this latter retreat, so you're not likely to have the sands to yourself.

SPORTS & OTHER OUTDOOR PURSUITS

Casa de Campo is headquarters for just about any sporting activity or outdoor pursuit in the area. Call the resort's guest services staff at © **809/523-3333** for more information.

FISHING You can arrange **freshwater river-fishing trips** through Casa de Campo. Some of the biggest snook ever recorded have been caught around here. A 3-hour tour costs $31 per person, and includes tackle, bait, and whatever sodas you drink for liquid refreshment during the trip. A 4-hour deep-sea fishing trip costs $549 to $732 per boat, 8 hours going for $793 to $1,098.

GOLF *Golf* magazine declared Casa de Campo (© **809/523-3333,** ext. 3187) "the finest golf resort in the world." The **Teeth of the Dog** ✦✦✦ course has been called "a thing of almighty beauty," and it is. The ruggedly natural terrain has seven holes skirting the ocean. Opened in 1977, **The Links** ✦✦✦ is an inland course modeled after some of the seaside courses of Scotland. In the late 1990s, the resort added a third golf course to its repertoire, **La Romana Country Club,** which tends to be used almost exclusively by residents of the surrounding countryside rather than by guests of Casa de Campo.

The cost for 18 holes of golf is $100 at the Links and $150 at Teeth of the Dog or the La Romana Country Club. (Some golf privileges may be included in packages to Casa de Campo.) You can also buy a 3-day membership, which lets you play all courses for $210 per person. A 7-day membership costs $420. You can hire caddies for between $12 and $20; electric golf-cart rentals cost $20 per person per round. Each course is open 7:30am to 5:30pm daily. Call far in advance to reserve a tee time if you're not staying at the resort.

HORSEBACK RIDING   Trail rides at Casa de Campo cost RD$500 (US$31.25) per person for 1 hour, RD$800 (US$50) for 2 hours. The resort's stables shelter 250 horses, although only about 40 of them are available for trail rides. For more information, call ℂ **809/523-3333**, ext. 2249.

SNORKELING   Casa de Campo has one of the most complete watersports facilities in the Dominican Republic. You can **charter a boat** for snorkeling. The resort maintains eight charter vessels, with a minimum of eight people required per outing. Wednesday to Monday, full-day **snorkeling trips** to Isla Catalina cost $37 per snorkeler. Rental of fins and masks cost RD$100 (US$6.25) per hour, although they probably won't clock your time with a stopwatch; guests checked in on all-inclusive plans rent gear for free.

TENNIS   Casa de Campo's 13 clay courts are available from 7am to 9pm (they're lit at night). Charges are RD$400 (US$25) per court per hour during the day or RD$500 (US$31.25) at night. Lessons are RD$1,000 (US$62.50) per hour with a tennis pro, RD$900 (US$56.25) with an assistant pro, and RD$800 (US$50) with a junior pro. Call far in advance to reserve a court if you're not staying at the resort.

ALTOS DE CHAVÓN: AN ARTISTS' COLONY

In 1976 a plateau 100 miles (161km) east of Santo Domingo was selected by Charles G. Bluhdorn, then chairman of Gulf + Western Industries, as the site for a remarkable project. Dominican stonecutters, woodworkers, and ironsmiths began the task that would produce **Altos de Chavón,** a flourishing Caribbean art center set above the canyon of the Río Chavón and the Caribbean Sea.

A walk down one of the cobblestone paths of Altos de Chavón reveals architecture reminiscent of another era at every turn. Coral block and terra-cotta brick buildings house artists' studios, craft workshops, galleries, stores, and restaurants. Mosaics of black river pebbles, sun-bleached coral, and red sandstone spread out to the plazas. The **Church of St. Stanislaus** is the central attraction on the main plaza, with its fountain of the four lions, colonnade of obelisks, and panoramic views. Masses are conducted at this church every Saturday and Sunday at 5pm.

The **School of Design** at Altos de Chavón has offered a 2-year associate in applied science degree, in the areas of communication, fashion, environmental studies, product design, and fine arts/illustration, since its inauguration in 1982.

The **galleries** (ℂ **809/523-8470**) at Altos de Chavón offer an engaging mix of exhibits. In three distinct spaces—the Principal Gallery, the Rincón Gallery, and the Loggia—the work of well-known and emerging Dominican and international artists is showcased. The gallery has a consignment space where finely crafted silk-screen and other multiple works are available for sale. Exhibits change about every month.

Altos de Chavón's *talleres* are craft ateliers, where local artisans have been trained to produce ceramic, silk-screen, and woven-fiber products. From the clay apothecary jars with carnival devil lids to the colored tapestries of Dominican houses, the rich island folklore is much in evidence. The posters, note cards, and printed T-shirts that come from the silk-screen workshops are among the most sophisticated in the Caribbean. All the products of Altos de Chavón's *talleres* are sold at **La Tienda** (ℂ **809/523-3333**, ext. 5398), the foundation village store.

The Altos de Chavón **Regional Museum of Archaeology** (ℂ **809/523-8554**) houses the objects of Samuel Pion, an amateur archaeologist and collector of treasures from the vanished Taíno tribes, the island's first settlers. The timeless quality of some of the museum's objects makes them seem strangely contemporary in design—one discovers sculptural forms that recall the work of Brancusi or Arp. The museum is open Tuesday to Sunday from 9am to 8pm. Entrance is free.

At the heart of the village's performing-arts complex is the 5,000-seat open-air **amphitheater.** Since its inauguration over a decade ago by the late Frank Sinatra and Carlos Santana, the amphitheater has hosted renowned concerts, symphonies, theater, and festivals, including concerts by Julio Iglesias and Gloria Estefan. The annual Heineken Jazz Festival has brought together such diverse talents as Dizzy Gillespie, Toots Thielmans, Randy Brecker, Shakira, Carlos Ponce, Carlo Vives, and Jon Secada.

The creations at **Everett Designs** (© 809/523-8331) are so original that many visitors mistake this place for a museum. Each piece of jewelry is hand-crafted by Bill Everett in a mini-factory at the rear of the shop.

Set amid the winding cobble-covered alleyways of this pseudo-medieval village, **Coco Point** (© 809/523-8656) sells hand-painted T-shirts, swimsuits, sportswear from Dolce & Gabbana, cigars, and jewelry crafted from larimar and amber.

DINING

Because of these uncertain economic times, the following restaurants may or may not be open. Check when you arrive.

Café del Sol ITALIAN   The pizzas at this stone-floored indoor/outdoor cafe, which is positioned one flight above the medieval-looking piazza outside, are the best on the south coast. The favorite seems to be *quattro stagioni,* topped with mushrooms, artichoke hearts, cooked ham, and olives. The chef makes a soothing minestrone in the true Italian style, served with freshly made bread. To reach the café, climb a flight of stone steps to the rooftop of a building whose ground floor houses a jewelry shop.

Altos de Chavón. © 809/523-3333, ext. 5346. Pizzas RD$160–RD$255 (US$10–US$15.95). Salads RD$103–RD$250 (US$6.45–US$15.60). AE, MC, V. Daily 11am–11pm.

Casa del Río FRENCH/CARIBBEAN   The most romantic restaurant at Altos de Chavón occupies the basement of an Iberian-style 16th-century castle whose towers, turrets, tiles, and massive stairs are entwined with strands of bougainvillea. Inside, brick arches support oversized chandeliers, suspended racing sculls, and wine racks. Amid this bucolic atmosphere, you can indulge in some of the best seafood dishes on the south coast. Although the food has a slight French flair, and often a few Thai twists, everything tastes and looks firmly West Indian. Any of the seafood dishes, such as lobster lasagna, is worthy of attention. Lobster might also appear glazed with vanilla vinaigrette, which tastes a lot better than it sounds. You'll encounter innovative taste sensations here, especially in dishes involving lemongrass or coriander. Some favorites include warm goat cheese with a tossed almond and arugula salad; Provençal-style snails au gratin; and sautéed tenderloin of beef with Roquefort cheese and almonds.

Altos de Chavón. © 809/523-3333, ext. 2345. Reservations required. Main courses RD$256–RD$576 (US$16–US$36). AE, MC, V. Daily 6–11pm.

El Sombrero MEXICAN   In this thick-walled, colonial-style building, the jutting timbers and roughly textured plaster evoke a corner of Old Mexico. There's a scattering of rattan furniture and an occasional example of Mexican weaving, but the main draw is the spicy cuisine. Red snapper in garlic sauce is usually very successful. Most guests dine outside on the covered patio, within earshot of a group of wandering minstrels wearing sombreros. Chances are you've had better versions of the standard nachos, enchiladas, black-bean soup, pork chops, grilled steaks, and brochettes served here, but a margarita or two will make it a fun night out anyway.

Altos de Chavón. ✆ **809/523-3333**. Reservations recommended. Main courses RD$192–RD$400 (US$12–US$25). AE, MC, V. Daily 6–11pm.

Giacosa ITALIAN   This is the only restaurant within Altos de Chavón that's not owned and operated by Casa de Campo. As such, its owners and staff tend to try a bit harder. It's a branch of a success story based in Coral Gables, Florida, and named after one of Italy's prominent 19th-century novelists. Within a two-story stone Tuscan-style building, you can experiment with such good-tasting dishes as savory imported mussels with olive oil, garlic, white wine, parsley, and fresh tomatoes. The delectable Mediterranean cuisine is showcased here in such dishes as the seafood soup (studded with lobster and shrimp), and the risotto with shrimp and sun-dried tomatoes. A superb dish is red snapper fillet with fresh tomatoes, baked in a paper bag to seal in its aromatic flavors.

Altos de Chavón. ✆ **809/523-8466**. Reservations recommended. Main courses RD$290–RD$625 (US$18.15–US$39.05). AE, MC, V. Daily 6–11pm.

3 Punta Cana ⓕ

On the easternmost tip of the island is Punta Cana, site of several major vacation developments, including the Meliá properties, with more scheduled to arrive in the near future. Known for its 20 miles (32km) of white-sand beaches and clear waters, Punta Cana is an escapist's retreat. Its 20 miles (32km) of white sands, set against a backdrop of swaying palm trees, are unrivaled in the Caribbean, and that's the chief and perhaps only reason to come here. Within some of the most arid landscapes in the Caribbean—it rarely rains during daylight hours—Punta Cana has been recognized throughout Europe (especially Spain) and the Americas for its climate.

Capitalizing on cheap land and the virtually insatiable desire of Europeans for sunny holidays during the depths of winter, a half-dozen European hotel chains participated in something akin to a land rush, acquiring large tracts of sugarcane plantations and pastureland. Today, at least a dozen mega-hotels, most with no fewer than 500 rooms, some with even more, attract a clientele that's about 70% European or Latin American. The hotel designs here range from the not particularly inspired to low-rise mega-complexes designed by the most prominent Spanish architects.

Some of them, particularly the Meliá Tropical & Caribe and the Barcelo Bávaro complex (see below), boast some of the most lavish beach and pool facilities in the Caribbean, spectacular gardens, and relatively new concepts in architecture (focusing on postmodern interplays between indoor and outdoor spaces).

Don't expect a real town here. Although the mailing addresses for most hotels is defined as the dusty and distinctly unmemorable Higüey, very few guests at any of these hotels ever spend time there. Most remain on the premises of their hotels, as part of all-inclusive holidays where it's very tempting to never leave the confines of your resort.

If you choose to vacation in Punta Cana, you won't be alone, as increasing numbers of Latino celebrities are already making inroads there, usually renting private villas within private compounds. Julio Iglesias has been a fixture here for a while. And one of the most widely publicized feuds in the Dominican

Republic swirled a few years ago around celebrity designer Oscar de la Renta, who abandoned his familiar haunts at Casa de Campo for palm-studded new digs at Punta Cana.

Above all, don't expect a particularly North American vacation. The Europeans were here first, and many of them still have a sense of possessiveness about their secret hideaway. For the most part, the ambience is Europe in the tropics, as seen through a Dominican filter. You'll find, for example, more formal dress codes, greater interest in soccer matches than in the big football game, and red wine rather than scotch and soda at dinner. Hotels are aware of the cultural differences between their North American and European guests, and sometimes strain to soften the differences that arise between them.

ESSENTIALS

GETTING THERE   **American Eagle** (© 800/433-7300 in the U.S.; www.aa. com) offers two to six daily nonstop flights to Punta Cana from San Juan, Puerto Rico; flying time is about an hour. You can also opt for one of American Eagle's two or three (depending on the season) daily flights from San Juan to La Romana and then make the 90-minute drive to Punta Cana.

GETTING AROUND   **Star Rent-a-Car,** Catalonia, near Bávaro Resort (© 809/686-5797), rents Toyota Corollas for $70 a day, bikes go for $5 for a 2-hour ride. Most taxi fares, including those connecting the airport with most of the major hotels, range from $25 for up to four passengers. Your hotel can summon a cab for you.

ACCOMMODATIONS

Barcelo Bávaro Beach, Golf & Casino Resort ✦   This huge complex of low-rise luxury hotels occupies a spectacular 20-mile (32km) stretch of white sands along Bávaro Beach. This is the most ambitious resort colony in the Dominican Republic, a project whose scope hasn't been equaled here since the early days of Casa de Campo, a resort Barcelo Bávaro strives to outdistance but doesn't. Built between 1985 and 1996, in postmodern Spanish style, it occupies almost 4½ square miles (12 sq. km) of land, including some of the best seafront property on the island. Developed by the Barcelos Group, a group of Spanish hotel investors, it consists of five separate hotels: Bávaro Beach Hotel, Bávaro Garden Hotel, Bávaro Golf Hotel, Bávaro Casino Hotel, and the newest contender, the Bávaro Palace Hotel. Arranged within a massive park, and connected via a labyrinth of roadways and bike trails, all but one of them (the Bávaro Casino Hotel, which faces the golf course) parallel the beachfront. Neither the decor nor the gardens are as well-conceived and stylish as those within the Meliá Tropical (see below), but the effect is nonetheless comfortable and pleasant.

Accommodations in all five hotels are roughly equivalent and are outfitted in tropical furniture, with private verandas or terraces, plus an attractively tiled bathroom with tub and shower. (The Bávaro Palace's rooms are bigger and somewhat more comfortable than the others.) Bedrooms have tile floors, Dominican-made furniture, colorful upholsteries and fabrics.

Apdo. Postal 3177, Punta Cana. Higüey, Dominican Republic. © 888/228-2761 in the U.S., or 809/686-5797. Fax 809/656-5859. www.barcelo.com. 1,960 units. Winter double in Palace $241 per person. Rooms in any of the other 4 hotels $195 per person. Off-season double in Palace $111 per person. Doubles in any of the other 4 hotels $82 per person. Prices are all-inclusive. Discounts of 45% to 65% for children age 2–12 occupying parents' room. AE, DC, MC, V. **Amenities:** 14 restaurants, 16 bars; 5 pools; 18-hole golf course; 9 tennis courts; aerobics sessions; whirlpools big enough for 30 people; horseback riding; medical facilities; scuba diving, snorkeling, sailing, windsurfing, parasailing, water-skiing, deep-sea fishing; salon; massage; babysitting; laundry/dry cleaning. *In room:* A/C, TV, minibar, coffeemaker, hair dryer, iron.

Meliá Caribe Tropical Resort ⊛   This Meliá complex is less upscale than the Bávaro, but we prefer it because of its more innovative design. A series of bungalows is scattered within a spectacular garden, with palm trees, fountains, and real flamingos. When you tire of the grounds (if ever!), a little train will transport you over to the beach where topless sunbathing is commonplace. The lobby sets the fashionable tone with its lagoons, boardwalks, sculptures, and bubbling fountains. The spa is the best in the area, offering special features such as an aromatherapy massage.

Accommodations are clustered into four distinct parcels of land, two of them adjacent to the beach and the most dramatic swimming pools in the Dominican Republic. The other two lie about a ⅛ mile inland, adjacent to lobby/reception areas and a cluster of discos, cabaret stages, gift shops, and restaurants. Spacious bedrooms are among the best in Punta Cana, with intricately crafted tile and stonework, private terraces or verandas, and roomy bathrooms with tiled shower units.

Punta Cana, Dominican Republic. ℂ **800/336-3542** in the U.S., or 809/221-1290. Fax 809/221-4595. http://dominicanbreeze.com. 1,044 units. Year-round $155–$250 per person. Rates are all-inclusive. AE, DC, MC, V. **Amenities:** 5 restaurants, 4 bars; 2 pools; golf courses; 6 tennis courts; casino; health club and spa; snorkeling, windsurfing; children's programs. *In room:* A/C, TV, minibar.

Princess Bávaro ⊛   Drawing some of its architectural inspiration from Bali, this hotel opens onto a mile-long (2km) white sandy private beach. This hotel transformed all of its rooms into junior suites in 1995. The Spanish-born architect Alvaro Sanz retained most of the palms and mangrove clusters on the property and installed freshwater reservoirs, creating an oasis not only for vacationers, but also for the many species of birds that call the resort home.

All accommodations lie within 86 low-slung bungalows. The split-level suites contain refrigerators and king-size or twin beds, each fitted with comfortable furnishings. The small bathrooms have combination shower/tubs and marble counters.

Playa Arena Gorda, Punta Cana, Higüey, Dominican Republic. ℂ **809/221-2311.** Fax 809/686-5427. www.bavaroprincess.com.do. 750 units. Year-round $336–$480 double. Rates all-inclusive. AE, MC, V. **Amenities:** 7 restaurants, 5 bars, disco; 2 pools; 4 lit tennis courts; health club; land and watersports facilities; minizoo; concierge; car and scooter rentals; shopping arcade; 24-hr. room service; babysitting; laundry/dry cleaning. *In room:* A/C, TV, minibar, hair dryer, safe.

DINING

Given the wealth of restaurants in the hotels listed above, many guests never leave the premises for meals. But the following are worth a special trip.

Capitán Cook ⊛ SEAFOOD   The beauty of the cuisine derives from a battery of smoldering outdoor grills, near the entrance to a dining area whose tables are positioned beneath palm-frond gazebos overlooking a superb beach. Some guests don't bother to consult a menu, but order their meal based on whatever looks appealing, or whatever is sputtering over coals or displayed on ice, as they enter. Don't expect an elaborate cuisine or fancy sauces; the allure here is the ultrafresh nature of seafood that's simply but superbly grilled to order. Platters of grilled fish or shellfish, chicken, pork chops, or steaks are accompanied with salad, baked potatoes, or french fries. An alternative selection might be a heaping platter of paella. The shrimp and grilled calamari are superb. Beer is the perfect accompaniment for anything served here, perhaps preceded by a rum-based cocktail if you're up for it.

Playa El Cortecito, Marina El Cortecito. ℂ **809/552-0645.** Reservations recommended for dinner. Main courses RD$100–RD$720 (US$6.25–US$45). AE, DC, MC, V. Daily noon–midnight.

Restaurant Palace ✷ INTERNATIONAL   This is the showcase restaurant of one of the biggest resort complexes in the Dominican Republic. As such, you're likely to get the feeling that management poured talent, money, and taste into it. If you're not staying at one of the Barecelo hotels here, you'll have to make reservations in advance. The decor is cool and stylish, as though it were imported from a chic resort in the south of Spain. A formally dressed staff serves superb dishes that include salmon mousse in a prawn sauce, tartar of tenderloin, grilled red snapper, grouper with mustard sauce, and filet mignon with truffles and foie gras.

In the Bávaro Palace Hotel, within the Barcelo Bávaro Beach, Golf & Casino Resort. ✆ **809/686-5797.** Reservations required. Main courses RD$110–RD$450 (US$6.90–US$28.15). Buffet lunch or dinner RD$320 (US$20). AE, DC, MC, V. Daily 7–10:30pm.

HORSEBACK RIDING & GOLF

Within Punta Cana, the guest services staff at your hotel can probably arrange horseback riding for you, but if they can't, consider an equestrian jaunt at the resort's biggest stables. These are headquartered at **Rancho RN-23,** Arena Gorda (✆ **809/224-0531**). It supervises as many as 125 horses that are stabled at 3 separate "ranches," each within a reasonable distance of one another. For $25 an hour, you'll be guided on equestrian tours through groves of coconut palms near the beach and, in most cases, onto the beach itself. To reach it, you'll follow some clearly marked signs through some of the wildest terrain left in Punta Cana, down winding sandy paths to a series of palm groves, site of these stables.

　　Barcelo Bávaro Beach, Golf & Casino Resort, Bávaro Beach (✆ **809/686-5797**), isn't as great as the one at Casa de Campo, but it's the best in this part of the world. Greens fees are RD$970 (US$60) for 18 holes, with cart rentals going for US$51.25. Guests of the hotel pay only for the cart. Open daily 7am to 5pm.

PUNTA CANA AFTER DARK

Bávaro Disco, on the grounds of the Bávaro Barcelo Beach, Golf & Casino Resort (✆ **809/ 686-5797**), has emerged as the hottest, most popular, and sexiest disco in Punta Cana thanks to a superb sound system. Young-at-heart male guests, especially the single ones, have breathlessly commented on its role as a cornucopia of the best-looking women in the region, some of whom strut their stuff on elevated platforms that ring the dance floor. The venue is more European than North American, thanks to a heavy concentration of clients from Italy, Spain, and Holland. If you've been tempted to dress provocatively but never had the courage, the permissive and sexually charged ambience at this enormous club will give you the confidence to try. Painted black, with simulated stars overhead and lots of mirrors, the place is open nightly from 11pm to 5am. Entrance is free for residents of the Barcelo Hotel complex; nonresidents pay an entrance charge of US$45.

4 Puerto Plata ✷

Columbus wanted to establish a city at Puerto Plata and name it La Isabela. Unfortunately, a tempest detained him, so it wasn't until 1502 that Nicolás de Ovando founded Puerto Plata ("port of silver"), 130 miles (209km) northwest of Santo Domingo. The port became the last stop for ships going back to Europe, their holds laden with treasures taken from the New World.

　　Puerto Plata appeals to a mass-market crowd that prefers less expensive, all-inclusive resorts. More accommodations of this kind continue to pop up on this coast, and yet many are still booked solid almost year-round. An unfortunate by-product of the all-inclusive trend is that several excellent restaurants have been forced to close; in fact, the most popular dining choice along the coast now is Pizza Hut.

Most of the hotels are not actually in Puerto Plata itself but in a tourist zone called Playa Dorada, which consists of major hotels, a scattering of secluded condominiums and villas, a Robert Trent Jones, Jr.–designed golf course, and a riding stable.

Although this was the first custom-built tourist haven in the Dominican Republic, the beaches are not the greatest. They're relatively narrow, and subject—as most beaches are—to the vagaries of hurricane erosion. Don't expect Robinson Crusoe–style isolation either; you'll never be alone on a stretch of beach in Puerto Plata, since the beach is shared with the residents of at least nine hotels, each jostling for position. However, if you enjoy beige sand that's rarely too hot to walk on, and a never-ending array of watersports kiosks, chaises longues, and loudspeakers projecting merengue music, you'll be happy here. One important note: it rains a lot in Puerto Plata during the winter. If you want more guaranteed sun, go to Punta Cana or the beaches on the southern coast.

ESSENTIALS

GETTING THERE   The international airport is east of Playa Dorado on the road to Sosúa. **American Eagle** (© **800/433-7300** in the U.S.; www.aa.com) has daily flights from San Juan, Puerto Rico to Puerto Plata. The 2-hour flight costs between $215 and $360 round-trip. Most of the Puerto Plata resorts are about a 40-minute drive from the airport.

From Santo Domingo, the 3½-hour drive directly north on Autopista Duarte passes through the lush Cibao Valley, home of the tobacco industry and Bermudez rum, and through Santiago de los Caballeros, the second-largest city in the country, 90 miles (145km) north of Santo Domingo.

GETTING AROUND   **Avis** (© **800/331-1212** in the U.S., or 809/586-0214; www.avis.com), **Budget** (© **800/527-0700** in the U.S., or 809/586-0413; www.budget.com), and **Hertz** (© **800/654-3001** in the U.S., or 809/586-0200; www.hertz.com) all have offices at the airport.

You probably won't need to rent a car, however, if you're staying at one of the all-inclusive resorts. You might just like to get around Puerto Plata by **motor scooter,** although the roads are potholed. You can rent a scooter at the guest services kiosk at just about any large hotel in Puerto Plata.

Minivans are another means of transport, especially if you're traveling outside town. They leave from Puerto Plata's Central Park and will take you all the way to Sosúa. Determine the fare before getting in. Usually a shared ride between Puerto Plata and Sosúa costs RD$15 (US$1) per person. Service is daily from 6am to 9pm.

If you take a **taxi,** agree with the driver on the fare before your trip starts, as cabs are not metered. You'll find taxis on Central Park in Puerto Plata. At night, it's wise to rent your cab for a round-trip. If you go in the daytime by taxi to any of the other beach resorts or villages, check on reserving a vehicle for your return trip. A taxi from Puerto Plata to Sosúa will cost around RD$360 (US$22.50) each way (for up to four occupants).

VISITOR INFORMATION   There's an **Office of Tourism** on Playa Long Beach (© **809/586-3676**). Open Monday to Friday 8am to 4pm.

FAST FACTS   Round-the-clock **drugstore** service is offered by **Farmacia Deleyte,** Calle John F. Kennedy 89 (© **809/586-2583**). Emergency medical service is provided by **Clínica Dr. Brugal,** Calle José del Carmen Ariza 15 (© **809/586-2519**). To summon the **police** in Puerto Plata, call © **809/586-2331.**

ACCOMMODATIONS

AMHSA Paradise Beach Resort & Casino ✎ This all-inclusive resort at the beach is the best-positioned of all the Playa Dorada hotels, with superior amenities and a well-trained staff. It also boasts an eco-friendly design: a cluster of Caribbean-Victorian low-rises with white-tile roofs and lattice-laced balconies. Brick paths cut through the well-manicured, tropical grounds. Accommodations are neatly furnished with tile floors, twin or queen-size beds with excellent mattresses, refrigerators (in most cases), large closets, and tiled bathrooms with shower/tub combinations. Most rooms have French doors leading to private patios or balconies. Only the suites have views opening onto the water.

The resort has five restaurants, some of which are buffet style. The management also hosts poolside barbecues and weekly shows that include acts by singers and dancers.

Playa Dorada (Apdo. Postal 337), Puerto Plata, Dominican Republic. © **800/752-9236** in the U.S., or 809/586-3663. Fax 809/320-4858. p.beach@codetel.net.do. 440 units. Winter $92–$142 double, $102–$152 suite. Off-season $83 double, $93 suite. Rates are all-inclusive. AE, MC, V. **Amenities:** 3 restaurants (some buffet style), 4 bars, disco, poolside lounge; casino; giant pool; lit tennis courts; whirlpool; watersports; room service; babysitting; laundry/dry cleaning. *In room:* A/C, cable TV, safe.

Gran Ventana Beach Resort ✎ *Kids* Come here for the opulent style and glamour on the beach, everything set against a backdrop of 250 landscaped acres (100 hectares). If you like a hotel with some theatrical pizzazz, this is your baby. The three-story buildings are trimmed with ornate, Victorian-inspired gingerbread; each unit offers mahogany furniture, ceiling fans, a balcony or patio, and, in all but a few rooms, views of the sea. Bedrooms are compact but efficiently designed. Bathrooms are a bit small but have up-to-date plumbing with tub-and-shower combos. The gardens and lawns surrounding the site are dotted with gazebos, flowering shrubs, and tropical plants and palms.

The all-inclusive plan limits a guest to 1 hour per day of snorkeling, windsurfing, sailing, horseback riding, kayaks, and scuba diving, and it limits dining at the exclusive Octopus (the best cuisine at the resort) to once a week.

Playa Dorada (Apdo. Postal 22), Puerto Plata, Dominican Republic. © **809/320-2111.** Fax 809/320-4017. www.victoriahoteles.com.do. 506 units. Year-round $180–$300 double, $240–$420 suite. Rates all-inclusive. AE, DC, MC, V. **Amenities:** 5 restaurants, 6 bars, nightly entertainment; 3 pools; 3 tennis courts; fitness center; sauna; watersports; salon/massage facility; babysitting, nursery; kids' club. *In room:* A/C, TV, minibar in suites, coffeemaker in suites, safe.

Iberostar Costa Dorada ✎ *Kids* With easy access to the beach, this hotel represents the new architectural ideas sweeping over Puerto Plata. It opened in 1999, outside the "Zona Turistica," the gardenlike compound that until recently contained most of the resort's hotels. Owned and operated by a Madrid-based chain, it boasts one of the most exciting designs of any hotel in Puerto Plata, with some of the most intricate stone, tile, and mosaic work, and a rambling and sophisticated combination of Taíno, Andalusian, and Moorish architecture. Roofs of this hotel are often covered with woven palm fronds, amazing for a hotel of this scale, sheltering a design that opens onto views of arcades, hidden courtyards, and fountains. A day pass, which entitles you to a meal, a round of drinks, and a view of the unusual design, costs RD$610 (US$38.15) per adult, or half-price per child under age 12.

Rooms are cool and airy, with tilework floors, earth tones, brightly colored upholsteries, and wall weavings inspired by Taíno designs, and big windows. Each has a compact, shower-only bathroom.

Carretera Luperon km 2.5, Marapicá, Puerto Plata, Dominican Republic. ⓒ 888/923-2722 or 809/320-1000. Fax 809/320-2023. www.iberostar.com. 516 units. Year-round $80–$100 per person double. Rates are all-inclusive. AE, MC, V. **Amenities:** 3 restaurants, 3 bars; large pool; watersports; activities for kids. *In room:* A/C, TV, minibar, hair dryer, safe.

Occidental Flamenco Beach Resort ⭐

Opening onto a tranquil stretch of Las Papas Beach, this is one of the most upscale and consistently reliable hotels in Puerto Plata. The Occidental exudes a low-key classiness that some of its competitors lack. Operated by the Spain-based Occidental chain, it has a tasteful, discreetly elegant lobby outfitted with bouquets of flowers and reproductions of Taíno statues. Accommodations are set within clusters of three-story buildings with white walls and red terra-cotta roofs. Throughout the accommodations, there's a sense of Iberian dignity, with strong contrasts of dark paneling with white walls, blue and white tilework, and plenty of space. More expensive rooms, in the Club Miguel Ange, are somewhat larger and have upgraded amenities and round-the-clock access to a concierge. Each bathroom has a tub-and-shower combo.

Complejo Playa Dorada, Puerto Plata, Dominican Republic. ⓒ 809/320-5084. Fax 809/320-6319. www.occidental-hoteles.com. 582 units. Year-round $130–$140 per person double; $175–$205 per person suite. Rates are all-inclusive. AE, DC, MC, V. **Amenities:** 8 restaurants, 5 bars, disco; 2 pools; salon; travel agency; children's play area; laundry. *In room:* A/C, TV, minibar in suite, safe.

DINING

Acuarela ⭐ CARIBBEAN

The best and most appealing restaurant in Puerto Plata occupies the rose-colored walls of a 150-year-old former private home. The house was the birthplace and home of the nation's most famous watercolorist, Rafi Vasquez, a living artist who is widely acknowledged for his contributions to Dominican painting. Today, the site is maintained as a restaurant by the artist's son and daughter-in-law, Rafael and Linda Vasquez. You'll dine among more than 20 of the artist's oversized watercolors, some of which are for sale at prices ranging from $750 to $3,000. Menu items lean toward nouvelle cuisine, but with a definite Caribbean twist. Well-crafted starters include Camembert tropicale wrapped in prosciutto and served with guava and orange slices, and shrimp Acuarela, breaded in yucca flour and served with a tropical fruit chutney. The best main courses include a confit of crispy duck with Asian hoisin sauce; New Zealand lamb chops with chutney, tomatoes, onions, and rosemary; and a mixed seafood platter with lobster, shrimp, and calamari.

Calle Certad 3 at Calle Presidente Vasquez. ⓒ 809/586-5314. Main courses RD$145–RD$375 (US$9.10–US$23.45). AE, MC, V. Tues–Sun 6–11pm or midnight, depending on business.

Aquaceros Bar & Grill INTERNATIONAL/MEXICAN

This is one of our favorite restaurants on the Malecón, just across the busy boulevard from the sea. The menu lists such tempting food items as Creole-style conch, two different preparations of lobster, burgers, barbecued fish, burritos, quesadillas, and fajitas. Of special note is the house version of Monterrey chicken, made with chicken breast, ham, salsa, sour cream, and cheese. Rum punch and banana mamas give diners a buzz. Adobe walls, a fountain, and merengue music complete the picture.

Malecón 32. ⓒ 809/586-2796. Reservations recommended. Main courses RD$65–RD$235 (US$4.05–US$14.70). AE, MC, V. Daily 10am–2am.

Hemingway's Café INTERNATIONAL/MEXICAN   The rough-hewn character of this place stands in stark contrast to the manicured exterior of the shopping center that contains it. Inside, you'll find a dark and shadowy plank-sheathed bar and grill, dotted with accessories you might have found on a pier in Key West. We can just imagine Papa himself digging into the succulent pastas, fajitas, quesadillas, meal-sized salads, burgers, and huge New York steaks, while downing one of the "Floridita" cocktails. After around 9pm, a karaoke machine cranks out romantic or rock-and-roll favorites.

Playa Dorada Plaza. ☎ 809/320-2230. Sandwiches, salads, and pastas RD$69–RD$89 (US$4.30–US$5.55); main course platters RD$89–RD$349 (US$5.55–US$21.80). AE, MC, V. Daily noon–2am.

Le Papillon CARIBBEAN/CONTINENTAL   This is an unusual but charming restaurant set on a hillside, in a residential neighborhood about 3 miles (5km) south of Puerto Plata. It was established by Thomas Ackermann, an expatriate German whose restaurant manages to combine aspects of the Black Forest with merengue music. The best way to start a meal here is with a Brazilian *caipirinha* (brandy cocktail) at the bar beneath the cane-frond ceiling. Later, within an open-sided pavilion overlooking a forest, you'll be presented with a menu that's divided into categories that feature different preparations of pork, chicken, beef, seafood, rabbit, and even vegetarian offerings. Enduring favorites include fettuccine with lobster; "pirate" kabobs with shrimp, tenderloin of beef, and vegetables; an especially worthy chicken stuffed with shrimp and served with saffron sauce; and a four-fisted version of chateaubriand that's only prepared for two.

Villas Cofresi. ☎ 809/970-7640. Reservations recommended. Main courses RD$125–RD$295 (US$7.80–US$18.45). MC, V. Tues–Sun 6–10:30pm. From downtown Puerto Plata, drive 3 miles (5km) south, following the signs to Santiago. Turn left at the signs to Villas Cofresi.

HITTING THE BEACH

Although they face the sometimes turbulent waters of the Atlantic, and it rains a lot in winter, beaches put the north coast on the tourist map. The beaches at **Playa Dorada** are known collectively as the "Amber Coast" for all the deposits of amber that have been discovered here. Playa Dorada has one of the highest concentrations of hotels on the north coast, so the beaches here, though good, are likely to be crowded at any time of the year, both with tourists and locals. The beaches have lovely white or powdery beige sand. The Atlantic waters here are very popular for water-skiing and windsurfing. Many concession stands along the beach rent equipment.

Another good choice in the area, **Luperón Beach** lies about a 60-minute drive to the west of Puerto Plata. This is a wide beach of powdery white sand, set amid palm trees that provide wonderful shade when the noonday sun grows too fierce. It's more ideal for windsurfing, scuba diving, and snorkeling than for general swimming. Various watersports concessions can be found here, along with several snack bars.

Your watersports options in Puerto Plata are numerous. Most of the kiosks on the beach here are ultimately run by the same company, and prices don't vary among them. If there isn't one close to your hotel, try **Playa NACO Centro de Deportes Acuaticos** (☎ 809/320-2567), a rustic clapboard-sided hut on the beachfront of the Dorado NACO Hotel. Prices are as follows: banana boat rides, $7 for a 10- to 12-minute ride; water-skiing, $15.60 for a 10- to 15-minute ride; sea kayak and Sunfish sailboat rental, $10 per hour; sailboards, $18; and paragliding at $35 for a 10-minute ride.

There are watersports kiosks about every 100 yards (91m) along the beach, any of which will rent you snorkeling gear and tell you the best spots for seeing fish. Puerto Plata isn't great for snorkeling, but you can take a boat trip to some decent sites.

SPORTS & OTHER OUTDOOR PURSUITS

The north coast is a watersports scene, although the sea here tends to be rough. Snorkeling is popular, and the windsurfing is among the best in the Caribbean.

GOLF   Robert Trent Jones, Jr. designed the 18-hole **Playa Dorada** championship golf course (© **809/320-4262**), which surrounds the resorts and runs along the coast. Even nongolfers can stop at the clubhouse for a drink or a snack to enjoy the views. Greens fees are RD$950 (US$59.40) for 18 holes; a caddy costs RD$135 (US$8.45). It's best to make arrangements at the activities desk of your hotel.

The 4,888-yard (4,488m) **Playa Grande Golf Course** at Playa Grande, kilometer 9, Carretera Rio San Juan-Cabrera (© **800/858-2258** or 809/582-0860), is generating a lot of excitement. Some pros have already hailed it as one of the best courses in the Caribbean. Its design consultant was Robert Trent Jones, Jr. Ten of its holes border the Atlantic, and many of these are also set atop dramatic cliffs overlooking the turbulent waters of Playa Grande Beach. Greens fees are $90 in winter, $60 off-season.

TENNIS   Nearly all the major resort hotels have tennis courts.

SEEING THE SIGHTS

Fort San Felipe, the oldest fort in the New World, is a popular attraction. Philip II of Spain ordered its construction in 1564, a task that took 33 years to complete. Built with 8-foot-thick (2m) walls, the fort was virtually impenetrable, and the moat surrounding it was treacherous—the Spaniards sharpened swords and embedded them in coral below the surface of the water to discourage enemies from fording the moat. The doors of the fort are only 4 feet (1m) high, another deterrent to swift passage. During Trujillo's rule, Fort San Felipe was used as a prison. Standing at the end of the Malecón, the fort was restored in the early 1970s. Admission is RD$10 (65¢) (© **809/261-6043**). Open daily 8am to 5pm. Free for children under age 12.

Isabel de Torres (© **809/970-0501**), a tower with a fort built when Trujillo was in power, affords a panoramic view of the Amber Coast from a point near the top, 2,595 feet (779m) above sea level. You reach the observation point by cable car (*teleférico*), a 10-minute ascent. Once here, you're also treated to 7 acres (3 hectares) of botanical gardens. The round-trip costs RD$100 (US$6.25) for adults, RD$50 (US$3.15) for children age 12 and under. The aerial ride is operated Thursday to Tuesday from 9am to 5pm. There's often a long wait in line for the cable car, and at certain times it's closed for repairs, so check at your hotel before you head out.

You can see a collection of rare amber specimens at the **Museo de Ambar Dominicano,** Calle Duarte 61 (© **809/586-2848**), near Puerto Plata's Central Park. It's open Monday to Fri 8am to 6pm, Saturday 9am to 5pm. Guided tours in English are offered. Admission is RD$40 (US$2.50) for adults, RD$7 (45¢) for children.

SHOPPING

The neoclassical house sheltering the Museum of Dominican Amber (see above) also contains the densest collection of **boutiques** in Puerto Plata. Many of the paintings here are from neighboring Haiti, but the amber, larimar, and mahogany wood carvings are local.

Plaza Turisol Complex, the largest shopping center on the north coast, has about 80 different outlets. You may want to make this your first stop so you can get an idea of the merchandise available in Puerto Plata. This complex also has the most upscale and tasteful merchandise. You might want to stop in here if you don't have time to visit all the shopping centers. It's about 5 minutes from Puerto Plata and Playa Dorada, on the main road heading east. Nearby is a smaller shopping center, **Playa Dorada Plaza,** with about 80 shops, selling handcrafts, clothing, souvenirs, and gifts. Both it and the Plaza Turisol are open daily from 9am to 9pm. The **Amber Shop,** in the Playa Dorada Plaza (© **809/ 320-2215**), is associated with the Amber Museum. This shop sells the best collection of Dominican amber in town, artfully displayed on racks and on shelves. It features necklaces, pendants, bracelets, and rings crafted from amber ranging in color from oil-clear yellow to dark blue. **Tobacco Shop,** in the Playa Dorada Plaza (© **809/320-2216**), is the best shop selling cigars around Puerto Plata. Don't overlook the benefits of cigars rolled in the Dominican Republic from tobacco grown with Cuban seeds. They're a lot less expensive than most of the Cubans, and many of them are surprisingly good. Plus, you can take them into the U.S.

Plaza Isabela, in Playa Dorada about 500 yards (455m) from the entrance to the Playa Dorada Hotel complex, is a collection of small specialty shops constructed in Victorian gingerbread style, although much of its inventory has a Spanish inspiration or flair. Here you'll find the main branch of the Dominican Republic's premier jeweler, **Harrison's** (© **809/586-3933**), a specialist in platinum work. Madonna, Michael Jackson, and Keith Richards have all been spotted wearing Harrison's jewelry. The store has a special clearance area; tours are available. There's another branch in the Playa Dorada Plaza (© **809/320-2219**) in the Playa Dorada Hotel complex.

PUERTO PLATA AFTER DARK

AMHSA Paradise Beach Casino (© **809/586-3663**) has the most appealing design of Puerto Plata's three casinos. It is decorated in shades of hot pink, with a soaring ceiling and lots of mahogany trim and louvers. Open daily 7pm to 4am. **Allegro's Jack Tar Village,** Playa Dorada (© **809/320-3800**), has a casino as well as a disco, a European-style restaurant, and five bars. These facilities are only for guests of the hotel. It's built in Spanish-Mediterranean-colonial style with a terra-cotta roof. **Playa Dorada Casino,** in the Playa Dorada Hotel (© **809/586-3988**), has mahogany gaming tables reflected in the silver ceiling. If you have time to visit only one casino, make it this one. No shorts are permitted inside the premises after 7pm, and beach attire is usually discouraged. Access to the slot machines is at 4pm, with full casino action after 6pm.

The Playa Dorada Hotel complex contains about 20 hotels, 5 of which have **discos** that welcome anyone, guest or not, into their confines. These after-dark diversions tend to be filled mainly with foreign visitors, although it occasionally attracts locals looking to hook up with tourists. None charge a cover, and the almost-universal drink of choice, Presidente Beer, costs RD$100 (US$6.25) a bottle. **Andromeda,** in the Hotel Heaven (© **809/586-5250**), is a high-voltage club off the lobby that opens nightly at 11pm. The cover charge here ranges from RD$30 to RD$50 (US$1.90–US$3.15). **Crazy Moon,** adjacent to the lobby of the AMHSA Paradise Hotel (© **809/320-3663**), is the hottest, hippest, and most sought-after nightclub in Puerto Plata. Fronted by an artful re-creation of a clapboard-sided Creole cottage, it's open Monday to Saturday

10pm to 4am. Admission charges range from RD$20 to RD$80 (US$1.25–US$5).

La Barrica, Avenida Manolo Tavares Justo 106 (© **809/586-6660**), lies behind an ochre-colored Spanish colonial facade on the dusty highway leading from Puerto Plata to Santiago, about a mile (2km) south of the town center. It's mobbed with locals every night after 11pm. They talk, smoke, drink, flirt, and often neck with each other on any of the thousands of folding chairs, many of which you're likely to trip over. If you enjoy active, sometimes aggressive merengue bars where a man will positively never need to be alone, you might find it fascinating. Entrance is free, but know in advance that you might be frisked for weapons before you enter. Open Monday to Thursday from 6pm to 6am, Friday and Saturday 2pm to 6am.

5 Sosúa (★)

About 15 miles (24km) east of Puerto Plata is one of the finest beaches in the Dominican Republic, **Sosúa Beach.** A strip of white sand more than a ½ mile (.8km) wide, it's tucked in a cove sheltered by coral cliffs. The beach connects two strikingly disparate communities, which together make up the town known as Sosúa. As increasing numbers of visitors flock to Sosúa, mainly for its beach life, it is becoming a rival of Puerto Plata. You don't come here for history, but oh, those soft, white sands and crystal clear waters, all to be enjoyed when many northern climes are buried under snow. Sosúa also has a well-deserved reputation for resorts with much more reasonable rates than similar accommodations at Puerto Plata. You won't find the super-deluxe resorts that are commonplace in Puerto Plata, but prices in Sosúa are half what they are at the big resorts. And the beaches are just as lovely.

At one end of the beach is **El Batey,** an area with residential streets, gardens, restaurants, shops, and hotels. Real-estate transactions have been booming in El Batey and its environs, where many villas have been constructed, fronted by newly paved streets.

At the other end of Sosúa Beach lies the typical village community of **Los Charamicos,** a sharp contrast to El Batey. Here you'll find tin-roofed shacks, vegetable stands, chickens scrabbling in the rubbish, and warm, friendly people.

Sosúa was founded in 1940 by European Jews seeking refuge from Hitler. Trujillo invited 100,000 of them to settle in his country on a banana plantation, but only 600 or so Jews were actually allowed to immigrate, and of those, only about a dozen or so remained on the plantation. However, there are some 20 Jewish families living in Sosúa today, and for the most part they are engaged in the dairy and smoked-meat industries, which the refugees began during the war. Biweekly services are held in the local one-room synagogue. Many of the Jews intermarried with Dominicans, and the town has taken on an increasingly Spanish flavor; women of the town are often seen wearing both the Star of David and the Virgin de Altagracia. Nowadays many German expatriates are also found in the town.

To get here from Puerto Plata, take the autopista east for about 30 minutes. If you venture off the main highway, anticipate enormous potholes. Taxis, charter buses, and *públicos* from Puerto Plata and Playa Dorada let passengers off at the stairs leading down from the highway to Sosúa beach.

ACCOMMODATIONS

Hotel Yaroa   Clean, decent, and well managed, this hotel, a short walk from the beach, gets its name from a long-ago native village. Inside, you'll find a two-story atrium illuminated by a skylight that's shaped like a Star of David, lots of exposed wood and stone, and a well-designed garden that rings a sheltered swimming pool. Each bedroom has more space than you might expect, with a decor that's based on varnished mahogany louvers and trim, terra-cotta tile floors, white walls, and a ceiling fan. Shower-only bathrooms are cramped but serviceable, and the overall ambience is pleasant and reasonably priced.

Calle Dr. Rosen, El Batey, Sosúa, Dominican Republic. ℂ 809/571-2651. Fax 809/571-3814. www.hotel yaroa.com. 24 units. Year-round $32–$65 double. Rates include breakfast. AE, DC, MC, V. **Amenities:** Restaurant, bar; pool; scuba instruction; babysitting; laundry/dry cleaning. In room: A/C, safe.

La Puntilla de Piergiorgio 🖈 *Value* This hotel lies in a quiet residential neighborhood, within a 10-minute walk from the bustling commercial center of Sosúa. Built on a rocky promontory high above the beach, it has a neo-Victorian design that includes lots of enticing gingerbread, lattices, and whimsical grace. Accommodations are bright, large, very clean, and outfitted with white-tile floors, flowered chintz upholsteries, and a semicircular veranda with views of either the garden or the ocean. Each accommodation comes with a small, but neatly arranged tiled private bathroom with shower stalls.

Calle La Puntilla, 1 El Batey, Sosúa, Dominican Republic. ℂ **809/571-2215**. Fax 809/571-2786. 51 units. Year-round $90–$110 double. Rates include breakfast. AE, MC, V. **Amenities:** Restaurant, bar; pool; room service; babysitting; laundry/dry cleaning. In room: A/C, TV, hair dryer, safe.

DINING

La Puntilla de Piergiorgio 🖈 ITALIAN A 10-minute walk west of Sosúa's center, this place serves the best Italian food in town, attracting an animated clientele of Europeans looking for a change from Creole and Dominican cuisine. The setting, located in the hotel of the same name, is a series of outdoor terraces, some of them covered, most of them open-air, that cascade down to the edge of a seacliff. There's enough space to allow conversational privacy for virtually any intimate dinner, and a pair of gazebo-style bars that provide an ongoing supply of mimosas and rum-based drinks. It's true we've had better versions of every dish served here, but for the area it is outstanding, especially the different preparations of fresh fish caught off local waters, which you can even order barbecued. Sometimes the chef gets fancy, as when he flames the prawns with cognac, or goes continental with his filet steak in green peppercorn sauce. The cannelloni Rossini (chopped meat and spinach) isn't bad at all.

Calle La Puntilla. ℂ **809/571-2215**. Main courses RD$145–RD$275 (US$9.05–US$17.20). AE, MC, V. Daily noon–midnight.

Morua Mai INTERNATIONAL This is the most visible, and most deeply entrenched, restaurant in downtown Sosúa. Established by German entrepreneurs in the 1970s, and set at the town's busiest intersection, it incorporates the closest thing in town to a European cafe on the pavement in front. It was designed of timbers and palm thatch like an enormous Taíno teepee, under which ceiling fans slowly spin, and wicker and wooden furniture help create an ambience conducive to the consumption of leisurely tropical drinks and well-prepared food. Steaks and seafood are an ongoing staple here. Depending on the arrival of fresh supplies that day, the menu might also include four different preparations of lobster; several kinds of shrimp, including a version with spicy tomato sauce and fresh vegetables; four different preparations of sea bass, including a version flavored with Chablis; orange-flavored chicken spiced with ginger; steak Diana, flavored with bacon; and pork in mustard-flavored cream sauce. An excellent version of paella contains chunks of lobster and fresh shrimp.

Pedro Clisante 5, El Batey. © **809/571-2966**. Pizzas and pastas RD$75–RD$165 (US$4.70–US$10.30). Main courses RD$165–RD$275 (US$10.30–US$17.20). AE, MC, V. Daily 8am–midnight.

SPORTS & OTHER OUTDOOR PURSUITS

There are watersports kiosks about every 100 yards (91m) along the beach, any of which will rent you snorkeling gear and tell you the best spots for seeing fish. You can also rent sailboats, Windsurfers, and other watersports gear at any of the kiosks.

For a more active vacation than just hitting the beach, book one of the many tours offered by **Ligia Tours,** Calle Dr. Alejo Martínez (© **809/571-1038**). Their best is a rafting experience near the village of Jarabacoa on the Rio Yaque in the mountains. Eco-sensitive and trendy, the tour costs $35 and lasts all day. Many exciting river rapids alternate with more tranquil sections in valleys and canyons. The price includes the Jeep safari, lunch, and drinks.

Gipsy Ranch, Carretera Sosua-Cabarete, opposite the Coconut Palm Resort (© **809/571-1373**), is the region's largest and best-recommended riding stable, home to about 20 horses, which can be hired for equestrian treks of between 1 and 4 hours. You'll begin your experience at the stone corral about 4½ miles (7km) from Sosúa and 3 miles (5km) from Cabarete. A 1-hour jaunt goes for US$16; a 4-hour excursion through forests and along beaches costs US$34. Reservations are strongly recommended.

SHOPPING

Patrick's Silversmithy, Calle Pedro Clisante 3 (© **809/571-2121**), was established by British expatriate Patrick Fagg in 1973 as a showcase for his unusual jewelry designs. At least half of the inventory here is made within his studios, and each incorporates such local stones as larimar, amber, and black coral. About 80% of the inventory is made from silver, making these one-of-a-kind creations affordable.

The best art gallery is **Viva,** Calle Dr. Alejo Martínez (© **809/571-2581**), which sells local art and giftware. An excellent selection of Dominican masters is on sale; the giftware includes beautifully crafted wood sculptures in both mahogany and *guayacán* (ironwood). Many ceramic "faceless" dolls are also for sale.

6 Cabarete

The winds that blow constantly southward off the Atlantic swept in a hip young crowd in the 1990s, as Cabarete emerged as the premier windsurfing site in the Caribbean. But only a small portion of the visitors who come here are actually interested in the waves. Hundreds of the young, the beautiful, and the restless who throng here, mostly from Europe, never even think about jumping on a board. Instead, they come to bask in the reflected glitter, or the bare-chested sex appeal, of a hard-core cadre of young men who spend lots of time riding the waves by day, and strutting their stuff in the hyper-hip town bars by night.

To service the needs of the growing number of visitors, the town has attracted some of the most aggressive prostitutes in the Dominican Republic; all ages, all skin tones, all degrees of blatancy. If you're a heterosexual male in Cabarete, you'll absolutely never, ever, lack for female companionship, paid or unpaid.

News of Cabarete's allure has spread, some might say like a contagious virus, among the 20-something populations of Europe. Especially prevalent are visitors from northern Europe, including Germans, Dutch, Belgians, Swiss, French (some chic boutiques cater to the sense of French aesthetics), Spaniards, Italians, and Scandinavians. (There are fewer U.S. and Canadian young people here than you'd think.) The big attraction remains **Cabarete Beach,** with its white sands and ideal wind and surf conditions.

Cabarete isn't particularly distinguished architecturally, consisting of a series of relatively small-scale hotels, restaurants, and gift shops lining either side of the highway that parallels the north coast. Virtually everything in town lies along this street (Calle Principal), with the exception of small-scale shops that are found on narrow alleyways that bisect the main street. But as word of the resort has spread, there have been increasing numbers of large all-inclusive hotels built on the outskirts of town.

To reach Cabarete from Sosúa, continue east along the autopista for about 8 miles (13km). Taxis and *públicos* from Sosúa will also take you here.

ACCOMMODATIONS

AHMSA Estrella del Mar ✦   With direct access to a wide sandy beach, this is our favorite large-scale hotel in Cabarete, thanks to its central location and helpful staff. It was built by the AHMSA chain in 1997. Several four-story wings wrap around a central courtyard. Here, within high-ceilinged pavilions whose soaring steel girders seem strong enough to resist many hurricanes, you'll find the best-run hotel in town. Bedrooms are good-sized, clean, attractive, and airy, usually with white-tile floors, large bathrooms with tubs and showers, and a sense of comfort.

Calle Principal, Cabarete, Dominican Republic. ✆ 809/571-0808. Fax 809/571-0904. www.ahmsa marina.com. 164 units. Year-round $136–$172 double; $166–$202 suite for 2. Rates all-inclusive. AE, MC, V. **Amenities:** 2 restaurants, 2 bars; 3 pools; gym; room service; babysitting; laundry/dry cleaning. *In room:* A/C, TV, hair dryer, safe.

Tropical Hotel Casa Laguna *Value*   One of the better lodging values in Cabarete is this 1980s hotel, just across the street from the beach, within a pleasant walled-in garden. Each of the rooms has a refrigerator, mahogany louvers and lattices, plus functional furniture. Most have sparsely equipped kitchenettes, and each has a tiled bathroom with a combination tub and shower.

Calle Principal, Cabarete, Dominican Republic. ✆ 809/571-0956. Fax 809/571-0709. www.tropical clubs.com. 62 units. Year-round $50–$93 per double; $24 per person extra for meals. Rate includes all meals. DC, MC, V. **Amenities:** 2 restaurants, 2 bars; pool; salon; massage; babysitting; laundry. *In room:* A/C, TV, kitchenette in 12 units, fridge, safe.

DINING

Casa del Pescador SEAFOOD   Since 1988, Casa del Pescador has served sophisticated seafood in an engagingly hip environment. It's right on the beach, in the heart of town. To begin, sample the chef's flavor-filled fish consommé. He does very well with shrimp, too, either with pastis sauce or more zestily, with curry and fresh garlic. On a hot day, the seafood salads are a welcome relief and tasty, too, as are the grilled octopus in spicy Créole sauce and fresh lobster in

---

⟨*Tips*⟩ **Serious Windsurfing**

Cabarete hosts an annual weeklong windsurfing tournament every June. Only amateurs are allowed to participate. For more information, contact the **Happy Surf School,** Hotel Villa Taina, Calle Principal (✆ **809/571-0784**), or any staff member at the **AHMSA Hotel Estrella del Mar** (✆ **809/ 571-0808**).

garlic sauce (the latter spice, however, overpowers a good thing when a butter sauce might have sufficed). Although there's a full wine list, Presidente beer seems the best accompaniment to the fish, especially on hot, sultry nights.

Calle Principal. (℃ **809/571-0760**. Reservations recommended for dinner. Main courses RD$180–RD$320 (US$11.25–US$20). AE, DC, MC, V. Daily 11am–11pm.

La Casita de Don Alfredo (Chez Papy) ⭐ DOMINICAN/FRENCH   This quirky and durable bistro is one of our favorite restaurants in Cabarete. It's located on a battered pavilion directly on the sands of Cabarete's beachfront, and it's accessible from the town's Calle Principal. Don Alfredo himself, a French expatriate from Strasbourg, keeps a firm grip on things. Menu items sure to entice include spiny Caribbean lobster with garlic and saffron sauce or with pastis; filet mignon with peppercorn sauce; and an array of whatever local fishermen bring in that day. We nearly always go for the fresh fish, which can be prepared almost any way you like it. As you'd expect from an articulate Frenchman, the wines are well chosen and urbane.

Playa de Cabarete (no phone). Reservations not accepted. Main courses RD$160–RD$250 (US$10–US$15.50). No credit cards. Bar and cafe daily 8:30am–midnight. Meals 8:30–10:30am, noon–2:30pm, and 6–10:30pm.

SPORTS & OTHER OUTDOOR PURSUITS

Cabarete, the best **windsurfing** resort destination in the Caribbean, is also home to the best windsurfing school, **Carib Bic Center,** Playa Cabarete (℃ **809/571-0640**). It's devoted to teaching proper windsurfing techniques and to renting state-of-the-art equipment. Rental of equipment costs $45 a day, and instruction is given for $30 an hour.

Iguana Mama at Cabarete (℃ **809/571-0908**) offers the best **mountain biking** and hiking. Going strong since 1993, it features a trek to Mount Isabel de Torres with experienced guides, lasting a full day and costing $65 per person. If enough people book, this tour is offered daily. Another trek involves a 3,000-foot (900m) downhill cruise with time for cycling down rolling hills, costing $40 per person and held only Monday, Wednesday, and Friday.

The best **adventure tours** are offered by **Cabarete Tours** (℃ **809/571-0505**), which will take you on a day-long Jeep safari for $23 per person, exploring river banks, small caves, and a tropical rain forest. It can also take you **deep-sea fishing,** for $65 per angler. Finally, **Gipsy Ranch** (℃ **809/571-1373**) is the most complete riding stable in the Dominican Republic; they'll take you **horseback riding** at a cost of $22 per person for 2 hours.

SHOPPING

Atlantis, Calle Principal (℃ **809/571-2286**), has the largest and most intriguing repository of Haitian sculptures along the north coast of the Dominican Republic. Most of them are bas-relief cutouts fashioned from sheet metal (sometimes the tops of oil drums). Many reflect mystical and, in some cases, voodoo-related themes that are invariably intriguing and usually very dramatic. There's also elaborate jewelry from both the Dominican Republic and Haiti, and large-scale Haitian banners, many inspired by voodoo rituals, fashioned from intricate layerings of beads and sequins.

Island Clothes, Calle Principal (℃ **809/571-0921**), is run by a local family with strong ties to the United States. This shop is loaded with Dominican handcrafts, Haitian paintings, souvenirs, costume jewelry, beach accessories, and tropical-weight clothing.

CABARETE AFTER DARK

New Wave Café, Calle Principal (© 809/571-0826), attracts raucous, hip, young windsurfers from as far away as Stockholm and Los Angeles. Set between the resort's main street and the beachfront, and designed without walls beneath a simple shanty-style roof, it rocks and rolls every day of the week from 9am to 4am, but gets especially sexy and especially cool after 9pm. There's live music every Saturday, and recently released recorded music every other night of the week. There's no cover charge; drinks cost RD$35 to RD$55 (US$2.20–US$3.45).

Las Brisas, Calle Principal (© 809/571-0614), is the second-most-important and the most popular nightlife venue in Cabarete, but arrive after 10:30pm when the disco action begins. From 8am to 10:30pm, food is served daily. The dance floor is illuminated with strobe lights and lasers, and the bar is always busy. Many patrons here arrive with dates of their own, but if you're a man flying solo, never fear, as a bevy of attractive working women are invariably on hand to provide companionship.

7 Santo Domingo ⟨★★★⟩

Bartholomeo Columbus, brother of Christopher, founded the city of New Isabella (later renamed Santo Domingo) on the southeastern Caribbean coast in 1496. It's the oldest city in the New World and the capital of the Dominican Republic. Santo Domingo has had a long, sometimes glorious, more often sad, history. At the peak of its power, Diego de Velázquez sailed from here to settle Cuba, Ponce de León went forth to conquer and settle Puerto Rico and Florida, and Cortés set out for Mexico. The city today still reflects its long history— French, Haitian, and especially Spanish.

Santo Domingo is one of the Caribbean's most vibrant cities, with a 12-block Colonial Zone to rival that of Old San Juan in Puerto Rico. Come here to walk in the footsteps of Cortés, Ponce de León, and, of course, Columbus himself. Allow at least a day to capture some of the highlights of the old city such as its Alcazar and its Catedral Santa Maria la Menor.

Santo Domingo is also one of the grand shopping bazaars of the Caribbean, with such "hot" items as hand-wrapped cigars for sale virtually everywhere, along with local handcrafts. Jewelry made of larimar or amber is also much sought after. From gambling to merengue, Santo Domingo is also one of the liveliest cities in the Caribbean after dark. Be careful, however. Most of the Dominican Republic's crime is concentrated in Santo Domingo. Keep valuables in your hotel safe, carry a minimum of cash with you, don't wear flashy jewelry, and if in doubt, take a cab.

ESSENTIALS

GETTING THERE See the beginning of this chapter for details on the airlines serving Santo Domingo.

FAST FACTS There's a **24-hour drugstore** called San Judas Tadeo, Av. Independencia 57 (© 809/685-8165). An emergency room operates at the **Centro Médico Universida,** Av. Máximo Gómez 68, on the corner of Pedro Enrique Urena (© 809/221-0171). For the **police,** call © **911.**

VISITOR INFORMATION The Tourist Office is located at Avenida Mexico, Esquina Calle 30 de Marzo (© 809/221-4660), open Monday to Friday only from 8am to 6pm.

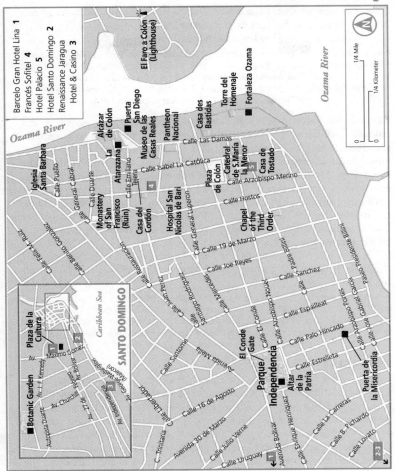

Barcelo Gran Hotel Lina **1**
Francés Sofitel **4**
Hotel Palacio **5**
Hotel Santo Domingo **2**
Renaissance Jaragua
   Hotel & Casino **3**

ACCOMMODATIONS

Remember that taxes and service charges will be added to your bill, which will make the rates about 20% higher. When making reservations, ask if they're included in the rates quoted—usually they aren't.

EXPENSIVE

Hotel Santo Domingo ★★★   Run by Premier Resorts & Hotels, the Hotel Santo Domingo has a tasteful extravagance without the glitzy overtones of the Jaragua (see below). Those seeking local character in a home-grown hotel should check in here. This waterfront hotel sits on 14 tropical acres (6 hectares), 15 minutes from the downtown area, in the La Feria district.

Oscar de la Renta helped design the interior. Most of the rooms have views of the sea, though some face the garden. Accommodations have bright floral carpets, tasteful Caribbean fabrics, and mirrored closets along with firm double beds. Bathrooms are tiled with shower/tub combinations and adequate shelf space. The superior Excel Club rooms offer sea-view balconies and other amenities. Excel guests also have access to a private lounge.

The cuisine is among the finest hotel food in the capital.

Avenida Independencia (at the corner of Abraham Lincoln), Santo Domingo, Dominican Republic. **℃ 800/877-3643** in the U.S., or 809/221-1511. Fax 809/535-4050. www.hotel.stodgo.com.do. 220 units. Year-round $195 double, $238 Excel Cub double, $366 executive suite. Rates include American breakfast. AE, MC, V. **Amenities:** Restaurant, 2 bars; Olympic-size pool; 3 lit professional tennis courts; sauna; gym; 24-hr. room service; babysitting; laundry/dry cleaning. *In room:* A/C, TV, minibar, coffeemaker, hair dryer, iron.

Renaissance Jaragua Hotel & Casino ★★ A Las Vegas–style palace, this 10-story hotel lies on the 14-acre (6-hectares) site of the old Jaragua (*ha-RA-gwa*) Hotel, which was popular in Trujillo's day. Open since 1988, it's a splashy, pink-colored waterfront palace that doesn't have the dignity and class of the Hotel Santo Domingo. For example, the casino and bars are often active with prostitutes plying their trade. Located off the Malecón and convenient to the city's major attractions and shops, the hotel consists of two separate buildings: the 10-story Jaragua Tower and the two-level Jaragua Gardens Estate. Jaragua boasts the largest casino in the Caribbean, a 1,000-seat Vegas-style showroom, a cabaret theater, and a disco.

The luxurious rooms, the largest in Santo Domingo, feature multiple phones, refrigerators, and marble bathrooms with large makeup mirrors and shower/tub combinations.

Av. George Washington 367, Santo Domingo, Dominican Republic. **℃ 800/HOTELS-1** in the U.S. and Canada, or 809/221-2222. Fax 809/686-0528. www.renaissancehotels.com. 296 units. Year-round $140–$205 double; $185–$205 junior suite, $750 suite. AE, DC, MC, V. **Amenities:** 3 restaurants, 4 bars; casino; pool; tennis center with 4 lit clay courts and a pro shop; health club and spa; salon; room service; babysitting; laundry/dry cleaning. *In room:* A/C, TV, minibar, fridge, hair dryer, safe.

EXPENSIVE

Barcelo Gran Hotel Lina ★ Rising nine floors in the heart of the capital in a sterile cinder-block design, the Lina offers a wide range of amenities. All the units contain refrigerators, and at least a third overlook the Caribbean. Bedrooms are comfortable and many of them quite spacious, but the decor is the standard motel style. The best rooms, on the 8th and 9th floors, have balconies. The tiled bathrooms have spacious marble vanities and shower/tub combinations.

The hotel boasts one of the best-known restaurants in the Caribbean, the Lina Restaurant (see "Dining," below).

Avs. Máximo Gómez and 27 de Febrero, Santo Domingo, Dominican Republic. **℃ 800/942-2461** in the U.S., or 809/563-5000. Fax 809/686-5521. www.barcelo.com. 217 units. Year-round $120 double, from $149 suite. Extra person $28. Rates include breakfast. AE, DC, MC, V. **Amenities:** 2 restaurants, bar, snack bar, piano bar; casino; pool; fitness center; Jacuzzi; sauna; 24-hr. room service; babysitting; laundry/dry cleaning. *In room:* A/C, TV, minibar, hair dryer, coffeemaker, iron, safe.

INEXPENSIVE

Francés Sofitel ★ Our favorite small hotel in the old city, this intimate inn lies within a stone-fronted town house dating from the 16th century. Sofitel has upgraded the accommodations, while retaining many of its original architectural features. Arches surround an Iberian-style fountain, and columns reach up to the second floor patios, with palms and tropical plants surrounding the rooms. You'll think you've been delivered to Seville. A gracefully winding stone staircase leads to the high-ceilinged and thick-walled bedrooms outfitted in a somber, rather dark colonial style. Accommodations are simple but tasteful, with rugs resting on tile floors; each has a somewhat cramped but tidily kept bathroom with shower and tub.

Calle las Mercedes (corner Arzobispo Merino), Santo Domingo, Dominican Republic. (C) **809/685-9331.** Fax 809/685-1289. H2137@accor-hotels.com. 19 units. Year-round $110–$130 double. AE, MC, V. **Amenities:** Restaurant, bar; room service; laundry/drycleaning. *In room:* A/C, TV, minibar, hair dryer, iron, safe.

Hotel Palacio *Value* History buffs often opt to stay here, since the hotel is within walking distance of the city's major historical sights. It's in the heart of the historic zone, only 2 blocks from the cathedral. The Palacio is also popular with business travelers. Built in the 1600s, it was the family home of a former president of the Dominican Republic, Buenaventura Báez, and still retains its original iron balconies and high ceilings. Kitchenettes were added to all rooms in the early 1990s. Not all rooms are the same size; if you want a more spacious unit, just ask. The shower-only bathrooms tend to be small.

Calle Duarte 106 (at Calle Solomé Ureña), Santo Domingo, Dominican Republic. (C) **809/682-4730.** Fax 809/687-5535. www.codetel.net.do/hotel_palacio/welcome.html. 17 units. Year-round $68–$82.50 double; $93–$150 suite. Children age 12 and under stay free in parents' room. AE, MC, V. **Amenities:** Bar; small fitness center; rooftop Jacuzzi; babysitting; laundry/dry cleaning. *In room:* A/C, TV, minibar, hair dryer, safe.

DINING

Most of Santo Domingo's restaurants stretch along the seaside, bordering Avenida George Washington, popularly known as the Malecón. Some of the best restaurants are in hotels. It's safest to take a taxi when dining out at night.

In most restaurants, casual dress is fine, although shorts are frowned upon at the fancier, more expensive spots. Many Dominicans prefer to dress up when dining out, especially in the capital.

EXPENSIVE

El Mesón de la Cava ✿ DOMINICAN/INTERNATIONAL   At first we thought this was a mere gimmicky club—you descend a perilous iron stairway into an actual cave with stalactites and stalagmites—but the cuisine is among the finest in the capital. The quality ingredients are well prepared and generously served, with accurate timing and full flavors. Recorded merengue, Latin jazz, blues, and salsa give the place a festive ambience. Launch your repast with the small shrimp sautéed in a delicate sauce of garlic or white wine, perhaps a mixed seafood or "sexy" conch gratinée. The gazpacho is also an excellent beginning, as is the bubbling *sopa de pescado* (red snapper chowder). Follow it up with the grilled Caribbean rock lobster or the double French lamb chops, which are done to tender perfection.

Mirador del Sur 1. (C) **809/533-2818.** Reservations required. Main courses at lunch cost RD$135–RD$485 (US$8.45–US$30.30), main courses at dinner cost RD$235–RD$486 (US$14.70–US$30.30). AE, DC, MC, V. Daily noon–4pm and 5:30pm–1am.

Lina Restaurant ✿✿ INTERNATIONAL/SPANISH   This is one of the most prestigious restaurants in the Caribbean. Spanish-born Lina Aguado originally came to Santo Domingo as the personal chef of the dictator Trujillo, whom she served until opening her own restaurant. Today, four master chefs, whom Dona Lina entrusted with her secret recipes, rule the kitchen of this modern hotel restaurant. The cuisine is international, with an emphasis on Spanish dishes, and the service is first rate. Try the paella Valenciana, the finest in the Dominican Republic. We're equally enticed by the sea bass flambé with brandy, and few can resist the mixed seafood medley doused with Pernod (it's cooked casserole style). Lina's cuisine even wins the approval of some hard-to-please Madrileños we know, who are a bit contemptuous of Spanish food served outside Spain.

In the Barcelo Gran Hotel Lina, Avs. Máximo Gómez and 27 de Febrero. ✆ **809/563-5000**, ext. 7250. Reservations recommended. Main courses RD$155–RD$335 (US$9.70–US$20.95). AE, DC, DISC, MC, V. Daily 11:30am–4pm and 6:30pm–midnight.

Vesuvio I ⭐ ITALIAN   Along the Malecón, the most famous Italian restaurant in the Dominican Republic draws crowds of visitors and local businesspeople in spite of its fading decor. What to order? That's always a problem here, as the Neapolitan owners, the Bonarelli family, have worked since 1954 to perfect and enlarge the menu. As they proudly claim about their food: "We like to catch it ourselves, cook it from scratch, or even grow it if that's possible." Their homemade soups are excellent. Fresh red snapper, sea bass, and oysters are prepared in enticing ways. Specialties include Dominican crayfish *a la Vesuvio* (topped with garlic and bacon). Recent menu additions feature *pappardelle al Bosque* (with porcini mushrooms, rosemary, and garlic), and black tallarini with shrimp a la crema.

The owner claims to be the pioneer of pizza in the Dominican Republic. At **Pizzeria Vesuvio** next door (✆ **809/685-7608**), he makes a unique yard-long pizza! There's also **Vesuvio II** at Ave. Tiradentes 17 (✆ **809/562-6060**).

Av. George Washington 521. ✆ **809/221-3333**. Reservations recommended Fri–Sat. Main courses RD$230–RD$475 (US$14.40–US$29.70). AE, MC, V. Daily 11am–midnight.

MODERATE

Paté Palo ⭐ INTERNATIONAL   Part of Paté Palo's charm derives from its location, overlooking Plaza Colón, the graceful arcades of the Alcazar de Colón, and the amiable clusters of Dominican families who promenade with their children every night at dusk. During the 1500s, the building was a bistro under the supervision of a mysterious Dutch buccaneer known as Peg-Leg (Paté Palo), who's credited with establishing the first tavern in the New World.

In the late 1990s, another Dutchman and his four partners transformed the place into a gregarious and engaging bistro that on weekends is one of the most crowded and popular singles bars in the country. Tables are thick-topped wooden affairs, set either on the plaza outside or within the antique walls of the dark and shadowy interior. The food is some of the best in the capital, and is usually accompanied by live guitar music every Thursday to Sunday from 6 to 10pm. Having dined here many times, we feel at home with the menu and can most recommend the sautéed shrimp in coconut curry sauce. On festive occasions, ask for the brochette of mixed meats; the meat has been marinated in fresh spices and herbs and is artfully flambéed at your table. The sea bass with white wine sauce is perfectly prepared, although the fancy continental dishes such as charbroiled steak with onion sauce and a grilled rack of lamb might be more suited for the cold Alps.

La Atarazana 25, Zona Colonial. ✆ **809/687-8089**. Burgers and salads RD$110–RD$225 (US$6.90–US$14.05). Main courses RD$195–RD$450 (US$12.20–US$28.15). AE, MC, V. Daily 11am–1:30am.

Tu Casona ARGENTINEAN/INTERNATIONAL   Set in an antique building in the colonial zone, just around the corner from the Plaza Colón, this restaurant has tiles and rough-hewn ceiling beams. Within a pair of dining rooms, you'll find simple wooden chairs, starched linens, and a cheerful Dominican staff. Menu items stress grilled beefsteak prepared in the way you might expect on the Pampas of Argentina. We don't claim the cuisine is spectacular, but it is well crafted, even heartfelt, and full of brawny flavors. You might begin with a portion of Manchego cheese or Serrano ham, followed by grilled chicken or tender grilled fillets of beef or pork (served in either 12- or 16-ounce huge portions).

Calle Emilano Tejera 101. ℂ 809/687-8970. RD$160–RD$320 (US$10–US$20). AE, DISC, MC, V. Daily noon–midnight.

INEXPENSIVE

El Conuco ✿ DOMINICAN   Come to "the countryside" (its English name) for the best-tasting and most authentic Dominican dishes in the capital. La Bahía (see below) may have better seafood, but otherwise this place is superb even if a bit corny. The waiters in costume will even dance a wicked merengue with you. Few restaurants have been as successful at commercializing the charms of rural Dominican life, and as such, it has attracted many of the country's sports and pop-music stars. You'll find it within an upscale residential neighborhood near the Malecón, close to the Jaragua Resort. Inside, you'll find everything you might need to cope with country living in the Spanish-speaking tropics: hammocks, domino tables, colorful weavings, and thatch-covered *bohios*. Familiar menu items here include six kinds of steak, and chicken "merengue," prepared with red wine, onions, and mushrooms. Only the venturesome dare try cow's foot stew. A specialty here is the "Dominican flag," a traditional platter whose various colors derive from artfully arranged portions of white rice, beans, meat, fried bananas, and salad.

Calle Casimiro de Moya 152, Gazcue. ℂ 809/686-0129. Reservations recommended. Main courses RD$95–RD$225 (US$5.95–US$14.05). Buffet RD$100 (US$6.25) at lunch, RD$180 (US$11.25) at dinner. AE, DC, MC, V. Daily noon–2am.

La Bahía ✿ *Finds* SEAFOOD   You'd never know that this unassuming place right on the Malecón serves some of the best and freshest seafood in the Dominican Republic. One predawn morning as we passed by, fishermen were waiting outside to sell the chef their latest catch. Rarely in the Caribbean will you find a restaurant with such a wide range of seafood dishes. To start, you might try *ceviche* (sea bass marinated in lime juice) or lobster cocktail. Soups usually contain big chunks of lobster as well as shrimp. Our favorite specialties include kingfish in coconut sauce, sea bass Ukrainian style, baked red snapper, and a savory kettle of seafood in the pot. The chef also works his magic with conch. Desserts are superfluous. The restaurant stays open until the last customer departs.

Av. George Washington 1. ℂ 809/682-4022. Main courses RD$90–RD$270 (US$5.65– US$16.90). AE, MC, V. Daily 11am–2am.

SPORTS & OTHER OUTDOOR PURSUITS

BEACHES   The Dominican Republic has some great beaches, but they aren't in Santo Domingo. The principal beach resort near the capital is at **Boca Chica,** less than 2 miles (3km) east of the airport and about 19 miles (31km) from the center of Santo Domingo. Here you'll find clear, shallow blue water, a white-sand beach, and a natural coral reef. The east side of the beach, known as "St. Tropez," is popular with Europeans. In recent years, the backdrop of the beach has become rather tacky, with an array of pizza and fast-food stands, beach cottages, chaise longues, watersports concessions, and plastic beach tables.

Slightly better maintained is the narrow white-sand beach of **Playa Juan Dolio** or **Playa Esmeralda,** a 20-minute drive east of Boca Chica. Several resorts have recently located here. The beach used to be fairly uncrowded, but with all the hotels now lining it, it's likely to be as crowded as Boca Chica any day of the week.

HORSE RACING   Santo Domingo's racetrack, **Hipódromo V Centenario,** on Avenida Las Américas km. 14 (ℂ 809/687-6060), schedules races Tuesday,

Moments Un, Dos, Tres Strikes You're Out

Dominicans were crazy about baseball long before their countryman Sammy Sosa set the United States on fire with his annual home run race against Mark McGwire. Almost every Major League baseball team has at least one player from the Dominican Republic on its roster these days. Pedro Martinez, Manny Ramirez, and Armando Benitez are just a few of the all-star team of players who hail from the Dominican Republic.

If you're here between October and January, you might want to catch a game in the Dominican Republic's Professional Winter League. The **Liga de Beisbol stadium** (© **809/567-6371**) is in Santo Domingo; check local newspapers for game times, or ask at your hotel. There are also games at the Tetelo Vargas Stadium in San Pedro de Macoris, known to die-hard sports fans as the "land of shortstops" for the multitude of infielders that call this tiny town home.

Thursday, and Saturday at 3:15pm. You can spend the day here and have lunch at the track's restaurant. Admission is free.

TENNIS   You can often play on the courts at the major resorts if you ask your hotel desk to call in advance for you and make arrangements.

SEEING THE SIGHTS

Prieto Tours, Av. Francia 125 (© **809/685-0102**), one of the capital's leading tour operators, offers a 3-hour tour of the **Colonial Zone,** leaving most mornings at 9am and again at 3pm if there's sufficient demand; it costs $35. A 6-hour tour visits the Colonial Zone, the **Columbus Lighthouse,** the **Aquarium,** and the city's modern neighborhoods; the $50 cost includes lunch and entrance to several well-known museums and monuments. About an hour of the tour is devoted to shopping.

THE RELICS OF COLUMBUS & A COLONIAL ERA

Santo Domingo—a treasure trove of historic, sometimes crumbling, buildings—is undergoing a major government-sponsored restoration. The old town is still partially enclosed by remnants of its original city wall. The narrow streets, old stone buildings, and forts are like nothing else in the Caribbean, except perhaps Old San Juan. The only thing missing is the clank of the conquistadors' armor.

Old and modern Santo Domingo meet at the **Parque Independencia,** a big city square whose most prominent feature is its **Altar de la Patria,** a national pantheon dedicated to the nation's heroes, Duarte, Sanchez, and Mella, who are all buried here. These men led the country's fight for freedom from Haiti in 1844. As in provincial Spanish cities, the square is a popular family gathering place on Sunday afternoon. At the entrance to the plaza is **El Conde Gate,** named for the count (El Conde) de Penalva, the governor who resisted the forces of Admiral Penn, the leader of a British invasion. It was also the site of the March for Independence in 1844, and holds a special place in the hearts of Dominicans.

In the shadow of the Alcázar, **La Atarazana** is a fully restored section of one of the New World's finest arsenals. It extends for a city block, holding within it a catacomb of shops, art galleries, boutiques, and some good regional and international restaurants.

Just behind river moorings is the oldest street in the New World, **Calle Las Damas** (Street of the Ladies), named not because it was the red light district, but for the elegant ladies of the viceregal court who used to promenade here in the evening. It's lined with colonial buildings.

Just north is the chapel of **Our Lady of Remedies,** where the first inhabitants of the city used to attend mass before the cathedral was erected.

Try to see the **Puerta de la Misericordia** (Calle Palo Hincado just north of Calle Arzobispo Portes). Part of the original city wall, this "Gate of Mercy" was once a refuge for colonists fleeing hurricanes and earthquakes.

The **Monastery of San Francisco** is but a mere ruin, lit at night. That any part of it is still standing is a miracle; it was destroyed by earthquakes, pillaged by Drake, and bombarded by French artillery. To get here, go along Calle Hostos and across Calle Emiliano Tejera; continue up the hill, and about midway along you'll see the ruins.

You'll see a microcosm of Dominican life as you head east along **Calle El Conde** from Parque Independencia to **Columbus Square (Plaza de Colón),** which has a large bronze statue honoring the discoverer, made in 1882 by a French sculptor, and the **Catedral de Santa María la Menor** (see below).

Alcázar de Colón ✿   The most outstanding structure in the old city is the Alcázar, a palace built for Columbus's son, Diego, and his wife, who was also niece to Ferdinand, king of Spain. Diego became the colony's governor in 1509, and Santo Domingo rose as the hub of Spanish commerce and culture in America. For more than 60 years, this coral limestone structure on the bluffs of the Ozama River was the center of the Spanish court, entertaining such distinguished visitors as Cortés, Ponce de León, and Balboa. The nearly two-dozen rooms and open-air loggias are decorated with paintings and period tapestries, as well as 16th-century antiques.

Calle La Atarazana (at the foot of Calle Las Damas). ✆ **809/686-8657**, ext. 232. Admission RD$20 (US$1.25). Mon–Sat 9am–5pm, Sun 9am–4pm.

Catedral Primada de America ✿   The oldest cathedral in the Americas was begun in 1514 and completed in 1540. With a gold coral limestone facade, the church combines elements of both Gothic and baroque, with some lavish plateresque styles as exemplified by the high altar chiseled out of silver. The cathedral was the center for a celebration of the 500th anniversary of the European Discovery of America in 1992.

Calle Arzobispo Meriño (on the south side of Columbus Sq.). ✆ **809/682-3848**. Free admission. Cathedral, Mon–Sat 9am–4pm, Sun masses begin at 6am; treasury, Mon–Sat 9am–4pm.

El Faro a Colón (Columbus Lighthouse)   Built in the shape of a cross, the towering 688-foot-tall (206m) El Faro a Colón monument is both a sightseeing attraction and a cultural center. In the heart of the structure is a chapel containing the Columbus tomb, and, some say, his mortal remains. The "bones" of Columbus were moved here from the Cathedral of Santa María la Menor (see above). (Other locations, including the Cathedral of Seville, also claim to possess the explorer's remains.) The most outstanding and unique feature is the lighting system composed of 149 searchlights and a 70-kilowatt beam that circles out for nearly 44 miles (71km). When illuminated, the lights project a gigantic cross in the sky that can be seen as far away as Puerto Rico.

Although the concept of the memorial is 140 years old, the first stones were not laid until 1986, following the design submitted in 1929 by J. L. Gleave, the winner of the worldwide contest held to choose the architect. The monumental lighthouse was inaugurated on October 6, 1992, the day Columbus's "remains" were transferred from the cathedral.

Av. España (on the water side of Los Tres Ojos, near the airport in the Sans Souci district). ✆ **809/591-1492.** Admission RD$20 (US$1.25) adults, RD$5 (30¢) children age 11 and under. Tues–Sun 9am–5:30pm.

Museo de las Casas Reales (Museum of the Royal Houses) Through artifacts, tapestries, maps, and re-created halls, including a courtroom, this museum traces Santo Domingo's history from 1492 to 1821. Gilded furniture, arms and armor, and other colonial artifacts make it the most interesting museum of Old Santo Domingo. It contains replicas of the *Niña,* the *Pinta,* and the *Santa Maria,* and one exhibit is said to hold part of the ashes of the famed explorer. You can see, in addition to pre-Columbian art, the main artifacts of two galleons sunk in 1724 on their way from Spain to Mexico, along with remnants of another 18th-century Spanish ship, the *Concepción.*

Calle Las Damas (at Calle Las Mercedes). ✆ **809/682-4202.** Admission RD$20 (US$1.25). Free for children under 12. Daily 9am–5pm.

SHOPPING

The best buys in Santo Domingo are handcrafted native items, especially amber jewelry. **Amber,** petrified tree resin that has fossilized over millions of years, is the national gem. Look for pieces of amber with objects like insects or spiders trapped inside. Colors range from a bright yellow to black, but most of the gems are golden in hue. Fine-quality amber jewelry, along with lots of plastic fakes, is sold throughout the country.

A semiprecious stone of light blue (sometimes a dark-blue color), **larimar** is the Dominican turquoise. It often makes striking jewelry, and is sometimes mounted with wild boar's teeth.

Ever since the Dominicans presented John F. Kennedy with what became his favorite rocker, visitors have wanted to take home a **rocking chair.** These rockers are often sold unassembled, for easy shipping. Other good buys include Dominican rum, hand-knit articles, macramé, ceramics, and crafts in native mahogany.

The best shopping streets are **El Conde,** the oldest and most traditional shop-flanked avenue, and **Avenida Mella.** In the colonial section, **La Atarazana** is filled with galleries and gift and jewelry stores, charging inflated prices. Duty-free shops are found at the airport, in the capital at the **Centro de los Héroes,** and at both the Hotel Santo Domingo and the Hotel Embajador. Shopping hours are generally Monday to Saturday from 9am to 12:30pm and 2 to 5pm.

Head first for the National Market, **El Mercado Modelo,** Avenida Mella, filled with stall after stall of crafts, spices, and produce. The merchants will be most eager to sell, and you can easily get lost in the crush. Remember to bargain. You'll see a lot of tortoiseshell work here, but exercise caution, since many species, especially the hawksbill turtle, are on the endangered-species list and could be impounded by U.S. Customs if discovered in your luggage. Also for sale here are rockers, mahogany, sandals, baskets, hats, and clay braziers for grilling fish.

Ambar Marie, Caonabo 9, Gazcue (✆ **809/682-7539**), is a trustworthy source for amber. Look for the beautiful necklaces, as well as the earrings and pins; you can even design your own setting here. **Amber World Museum,** Arzobispo Meriño 452 (✆ **809/682-3309**), lives up to its name. In the wake of the film *Jurassic Park,* more and more visitors are flocking here to see plants, insects, and even scorpions fossilized in resin millions of years ago. Although some of the displays are not for sale, in an adjoining salon you can watch craftspeople at

---

Tips   You Call That a Bargain?

Always haggle over the price of handcrafts in the Dominican Republic, particularly in the open-air markets. No stall-keeper expects you to pay the first price asked. Remember the Spanish words for too expensive: *muy caro.*

---

work, polishing and shaping raw bits of ancient amber for sale. To visit the museum costs adults RD$15 (95¢) and children RD$10 (65¢). Open Monday to Saturday 8am to 6pm and Sunday 8am to noon.

Another reliable source for stunning amber, as well as coral, is **Ambar Nacional,** Calle Restauración 110 (© **809/686-5700**). This is also the best source for purchasing larimar jewelry. In general, prices here are a bit less expensive than those at the more prestigious Amber World Museum around the corner.

In the center of the most historical section of town is the well-known **Galería de Arte Nader,** Rafael Augusto Sanchez 22 (© **809/544-0878**), which displays so many Latin paintings that they're sometimes stacked in rows against the walls. The works of the country's best-known painters and most promising newcomers are displayed here (though to be honest, the Dominican Republic is short on painters with international reputations). There is also a lot of tourist junk, shipped in by the truckload from Haiti. In the ancient courtyard in back, you can get a glimpse of how things looked in the Spanish colonies hundreds of years ago.

Nuebo, Fantino Falco 36, Naco (© **809/562-3333**), is patronized by some of the capital's most socially conscious. This shop sells a carefully chosen assortment of art objects, lamps, and furnishings, including the kind of four-poster beds that tend to be showcased in fashion layouts. With some persuasion, anything you buy here can be shipped.

Columbus Plaza (Decla, S.A.), Calle Arzobispo Meriño 204 (© **809/689-0565**), is one of the largest, supermarket-style gift and artifacts store in the country. Well-organized and imaginative, with a helpful English-speaking staff, it sprawls over three floors of a modern building divided into boutiques specializing in amber, larimar, gold and silver jewelry, cigars, paintings and sculpture, plus craft items.

Cigars are a big-selling item in Santo Domingo. The best selection of cigars is at **Cigar King,** Calle Conde 208, Baguero Building (© **809/686-4987**), in the colonial city. Its selection of Dominican and Cuban cigars in a temperature-controlled room is wide ranging. However, those Cuban stogies have to be smoked locally, as they are not allowed into the United States.

SANTO DOMINGO AFTER DARK
DANCE CLUBS

Local young people flock to the dance clubs in droves after dinner. Even the hotel discos cater to locals as well as tourists. Great dancers abound, so go and watch even if you're not as light on your feet as you wish.

La Guácara Taína, av. Mirador del Sur, in Parque Mirador del Sur (© **809/533-1051**), is the best *discoteca* in the country, drawing an equal blend of locals and visitors. Set in an underground cave within a verdant park, the specialty is merengue, salsa, and other forms of music. There are three bars, two dance floors, and banquettes and chairs nestled into the rocky walls. The cover is RD$150 (US$9.40). Open Tuesday to Sunday from 9pm; closing time varies.

Fantasy Disco, Avenida Heroes de Luperón 29, La Feria (© **809/535-5581**), is one of the capital's most popular discos, about a block inland from the Malecón. Once you get past the vigilant security staff, you'll find lots of intimate nooks and crannies, a small dance floor, and one of the country's best-chosen medleys of nonstop merengue music. Entrance is free, and beer costs RD$45 (US$2.80) a bottle. The place is open daily from 4pm till 6am.

Jet Set, Centro Comercial El Portal, Avenida Independencia (© **809/533-9707**), is one of the capital's most formal and elaborate nightclubs, admitting couples only, and nobody who is too rowdy. Most of the tables and chairs slope down toward an amphitheater-style dance floor, giving the place the feel of a bullfighting arena. The collection of live orchestras that play here are better than anywhere else in town. Entrance costs between RD$65 to RD$300 (US$4–US$18.50), depending on the artist. Opens at 9pm until the early morning.

In the colonial zone stands **Bachata Rosa,** La Atarazana 9 (© **809/688-0969**), which takes its name from a popular song on the island. In fact, Juan Luís Guerra, the Dominican merengue megastar who made the song a hit, is part owner. Currently, this is the island's best dance club, with action taking place on two floors. This club draws a heavier concentration of locals than of visitors. There's also a typical restaurant here serving local specialties. Daily 6pm to 2am.

The country's leading **gay dance club** is **Disco Free,** Avenida Ortega y Gaset (© **809/565-8100**), open Thursday to Sunday only, from 7pm until the early morning. It has some of the best music in town, and is known for its salsa and merengue.

ROLLING THE DICE

Santo Domingo has several major casinos, all of which are open nightly until 4 or 5am. We view gambling here as a very minor attraction and find the odds pretty much against you. If gambling is your raison d'être, you'd do better to plan a holiday in Puerto Rico. The most glamorous casino in the country is fittingly housed in the capital's poshest hotel: the **Renaissance Jaragua Hotel & Casino,** Av. George Washington 367 (© **809/221-2222**). You can't miss the brightly flashing sign; it's the most dazzling light along the Malecón. You can wager on blackjack, baccarat, roulette, and slot machines in either Dominican pesos or U.S. dollars. Open daily 4pm to 4am.

Another casino is at the **Hispaniola Hotel,** Avenida Independencia (© **809/221-7111**). One of the most stylish choices is the **Casino Diamante,** in the Meliá Santo Domingo Hotel & Casino, Av. George Washington 361 (© **809/221-6666**). Its bilingual staff will help you play blackjack, craps, baccarat, and keno, among other games. There's also a piano bar. These casinos are open daily 4pm to 4am.

13

Grenada

Its political troubles of the 1980s long over, this sleepy island offers fairly friendly people and the lovely and popular white sands of Grand Anse Beach. Exploring its lush interior, especially Grand Etang National Park, is also worthwhile. Crisscrossed by nature trails and filled with dozens of secluded coves and sandy beaches, Grenada has moved beyond the turbulence of the 1980s. It's not necessarily for the serious party person and definitely not for those seeking action at the casino. Instead, it attracts visitors who like snorkeling, sailing, fishing, and doing nothing more invigorating than lolling on a beach under the sun.

The "Spice Island," Grenada is an independent, three-island nation (the other two islands are Carriacou, the largest of the Grenadines, and Petite Martinique). Grenada has more spices per square mile than any other place in the world: cloves, cinnamon, mace, cocoa, tonka beans, ginger, and a third of the world's supply of nutmeg. "Drop a few seeds anywhere," the locals will tell you, "and you have an instant garden." The central area is like a jungle of palms, oleander, bougainvillea, purple and red hibiscus, crimson anthurium, bananas, breadfruit, birdsong, ferns, and palms.

Beefed up by financial aid from the United States, this island of some 100,000 people has revived a sagging tourist industry. Many improvements, including a workable phone system and better roads, have been made with the benefit of U.S. aid.

1 Essentials

VISITOR INFORMATION

In the United States, the **Grenada Tourist Office** is located at 317 Madison Ave., Suite 1522, New York, NY 10017 (© **800/927-9554** or 212/687-9554).

In London, contact the **Grenada Board of Tourism,** 1 Collingham Gardens, Earl's Court, London, SW5 0HW (© **020/771-7016**).

On the island, pick up maps, guides, and general information at the **Grenada Board of Tourism,** the Carenage, in St. George's (© **473/440-2279**), open Monday to Friday from 8am to 4pm.

You can find Grenada information on the Web at **www.grenada.org**.

GETTING THERE

Point Salines International Airport lies at the southwestern toe of Grenada. The airport is a 5- to 15-minute taxi ride from most of the major hotels.

American Airlines (© **800/433-7300** in the U.S.; www.aa.com) offers daily flights to Grenada from New York and Miami.

British Airways (© **800/247-9297** in England; www.british-airways.com) flies to Grenada every Wednesday and Friday from London's Gatwick Airport, making a single stop at Antigua en route.

Air Jamaica (© **473/444-5975**; www.airjamaica.com) offers nonstop flights from New York to Grenada two times a week.

Grenada

Allamanda Beach Resort & Spa **2**
Blue Horizons Cottage Hotel **4**
Calabash **12**
Coyaba Beach Resort **5**
Flamboyant Hotel **3**
Gem Holiday Resort **8**
Grenada Grand Beach Resort **6**
Laluna **9**
La Sagesse Nature Center **16**
LaSource **11**
No Problem Apartment Hotel **15**
Rex Grenadian **10**
Secret Harbour **14**
Spice Island Inn **7**
True Blue Bay Resort **1**
Twelve Degrees North **13**

Airport ✈ Beach 🗻 Mountain ▲▲▲

GETTING AROUND

BY TAXI   Taxi rates are set by the government. Most arriving visitors take a cab at the airport to one of the hotels near St. George's, at a cost of $15. Add 33% to the fare from 6pm to 6am. You can also use most taxi drivers as a guide for a day of sightseeing; negotiate a price beforehand.

BY RENTAL CAR   First, remember to *drive on the left.* A U.S., British, or Canadian driver's license is valid on Grenada; however, you must obtain a local permit, costing EC$30 (US$11). These permits can be obtained either from the car-rental company or from the traffic department at the Carenage in St. George's. The Carenage is both the walkway and the road that loops around the horseshoe-shaped St. George's Harbour. It is the capital's principal thoroughfare.

Avis (© 800/331-1212 in the U.S., or 473/440-3936; www.avis.com) operates out of a Shell station on Lagoon Road, on the southern outskirts of St. George's. Avis will meet you at the airport, but requires at least 24-hour notice to guarantee availability. You can also try **Dollar Rent-a-Car,** at the airport (© **800/800-4000** in the U.S., or 473/444-4786; www.dollar.com).

A word of warning about local drivers: There's such a thing as Grenadian driving machismo; the drivers take blind corners with abandon. An extraordinary number of accidents are reported in the lively local paper. Gird yourself with nerves of steel, and be extra alert for children and roadside pedestrians when driving at night. Many foreign visitors, in fact, find any night driving hazardous.

Fun Fact Carnival on Grenada

The second weekend of August brings colorful Carnival parades, music, and dancing. The festivities begin on Friday, continuing practically nonstop through Tuesday. Steel bands and calypso groups perform at Queen's Park. Jouvert, one of the highlights of the festival, begins at 5am on Monday with a parade of Djab Djab/Djab Molassi, devil-costumed figures daubed with a black substance. (*Be warned:* Don't wear nice clothes to attend this event—you may get sticky from close body contact.) The Carnival finale, a gigantic "jump-up" (like a hoedown), ends with a parade of bands from Tanteen through the Carenage into town.

BY BUS Minivans, charging EC$1 to EC$6 (US40¢–US$2), are the cheapest way to get around. The most popular run is between St. George's and Grand Anse Beach. Most minivans depart from Market Square or from the Esplanade area of St. George's.

 FAST FACTS: **Grenada**

Banks Banks in St. George's, the capital, include **Barclays,** at Church and Halifax streets (© **473/440-3232**); **Scotiabank,** on Halifax Street (© **473/440-3274**); the **National Commercial Bank (NCB),** at Halifax and Hillsborough streets (© **473/440-3566**); the **Grenada Bank of Commerce,** at Halifax and Cross streets (© **473/440-3521**); and the **Grenada Cooperative Bank,** on Church Street (© **473/440-2111**). Most have ATMs. Hours are usually Monday through Thursday from 8am to 3pm Friday from 8am to 5pm.

Currency The official currency is the Eastern Caribbean dollar (**EC$**), approximately EC$2.70 to US$1. Always determine which dollars, EC or U.S., you're talking about when someone on Grenada quotes you a price.

Documents A valid passport is required of U.S., British, and Canadian citizens entering Grenada, plus a return or ongoing ticket.

Electricity Electricity is 220- to 240-volt AC (50 cycles), so transformers and adapters will be needed for U.S.-made appliances.

Embassies & High Commissions The **U.S. Embassy** is located at L'Anse aux Epines Salines, St. George's (© **473/444-1173**). The **British High Commission** is on Church Street, St. George's (© **473/440-3536**).

Emergencies Dial © **911** for police, fire, or an ambulance.

Hospital **St. George's General Hospital** located on Grandetang Road, St. George's (© **473/440-2051**), has an X-ray department and operating room. Private doctors and nurses are available on call.

Language English is commonly spoken due to long years of British influence. Creole English, a mixture of several African dialects, English, and French, is spoken informally by the majority.

Pharmacies Try **Gittens Pharmacy,** Halifax Street, St. George's (© **473/440-2165**), open weekdays from 8am to 6pm (they close at 5pm on Thurs), and Saturday from 8am to 3pm.

Post Office The general post office, at the Pier, St. George's, is open Monday to Friday from 8am to 3:30pm.

Safety Street crime occurs here, tourists have been victims of armed robbery in isolated areas, and thieves frequently steal U.S. passports and alien registration cards in addition to money. Muggings, purse-snatchings, and other robberies occur in areas near hotels, beaches, and restaurants, particularly after dark. Don't leave valuables unattended at the beach. Be cautious when walking after dark, or take a taxi. Report a stolen or lost passport immediately to the local police and the embassy.

Taxes A 10% VAT (value-added tax) is imposed on food and beverages, and there's an 8% room tax. You'll pay a departure tax of $20 when you leave.

Telephone The area code for all of Grenada is **473**. You can call to or from Grenada like you would to any other area code in North America. Public phone and fax services are available at the Carenage offices of **Grenada Cable & Wireless** in St. George's (© **473/440-1000** for all Grentel offices). The office is open Monday to Friday from 8:00am to 4:30pm, Saturday from 8am to 1pm, and Sunday and holidays from 10am to noon.

Time Grenada is on Atlantic standard time year-round, which means it's usually 1 hour ahead of the U.S. east coast—except during daylight saving time, when the clocks are the same.

Tipping A 10% service charge is added to most restaurant and hotel bills. No additional tip is expected.

Water Stick to bottled water.

Weather Grenada has two distinct seasons: dry and rainy. The dry season is from January to May; the rest of the year is the rainy season, although the rainfall doesn't last long. The average temperature is 80°F. Because of constant trade winds, there's little humidity.

2 Accommodations

Whether you're looking for a kitchenette apartment, a small and intimate inn, or a major resort, you'll find it waiting for you in Grenada, which has some of the best and most varied accommodations in the southern Caribbean. Unless you want to stay in an atmospheric inn tucked away somewhere, opt for a hotel lined up along Grand Anse Beach. All you'll have to do is walk out the door and head for the ocean.

Your hotel or inn will probably add a service charge of 10% to your bill—ask about this in advance, so you can accurately anticipate what your final bill will look like.

VERY EXPENSIVE

Calabash ★★★ On a landscaped 8-acre (3-hectare) beach, the Calabash is today the leading hotel on Grenada. Of all the upmarket inns on the island, this is the smallest and most posh, drawing a devoted repeat clientele, especially among its English clients. Everything is refined and low key here—nothing splashy like La Source (see below). Five miles (8km) south of St. George's and only minutes from the airport, it occupies an isolated section of Prickly Bay

(L'Anse aux Epines). Foremost among the multitude of shrubs here are the scores of beautiful *calabashes* (gourds) for which the resort was named. The 8 private plunge-pool suites and 22 whirlpool-bath suites all have verandas and either one king-size bed or two double beds. Bathrooms are very spacious, with big stall showers, oversized tubs, and bidets.

The restaurant serves an excellent West Indian and continental cuisine. Entertainment, ranging from piano music to steel bands, is provided 4 or 5 nights a week.

L'Anse aux Epines (P.O. Box 382), St. George's, Grenada, W.I. (© 800/528-5835 in the U.S. and Canada, or 473/444-4334. Fax 473/444-5050. www.calabashhotel.com. 30 units. Winter $510–$870 suite for 2. Off-season $250–$525 suite for 2. Extra person $175–$215 in winter; $130 in off-season. Children under age 12 free. Breakfast and dinner $50 per person extra. AE, MC, V. Children age 12 and under not permitted in winter. **Amenities:** Restaurant, 2 bars; pool; golf privileges; tennis court; snorkeling, sailboat rentals; room service; babysitting; laundry. *In room:* A/C, minibar, hair dryer, safe.

LaLuna ★★ Grenada's newest hotel lies on an isolated, beautiful beach at Quarantine Point, near the extreme southern tip of the island. Designed along the architectural models you might have expected in Indonesia, the resort consists of 16 thatch-covered, wood-and-stone sided cottages, each with a small pool of its own, and each with artwork and furnishings including fabric-swathed four-poster beds, imported from Bali. Scattered up and down a hillside, about a mile north of the Port Salines airport, they each lie within a 2-minute walk from the beach. The resort's social and architectural centerpiece is a clubhouse larger than the cottages, the site of big verandas, a restaurant, a good-looking bar area, and check-in facilities.

La Luna opened as the brainchild of Italian-born Bernardo Bertucci, who emigrated to Grenada after a successful career marketing fashion on New York's Seventh Avenue. With clients that, since opening, have included members of the Eurythmics, English comedian Frank Skinner, and Mick Jagger's ex-wife Jerry Hall, it seems headed for a glittery, hedonistic niche with a very appealing international kind of irony and worldliness. The restaurant, which is open to non-residents who phone in advance, is artfully sited less than 40 feet (12m) from the beach, and separated from the airy bar by a communal swimming pool. For more on this, refer to "Dining," below.

Morne Rouge (P.O. Box 1500), St. George's, Grenada, W.I. © 473/439-0001. Fax 473/439-0600. www.laluna.com. 16 cottages. Winter $480–$630 cottages and suites for 1–2 people, $960 cottages for 1–4 people. Off-season $270–$370 cottages and suites for 1–2 people, $540 cottages for 1–4 people. MAP $55 extra per person per day. AE, MC, V. **Amenities:** Restaurant, bar; pool; massage facilities; windsurfing, snorkeling, boat rental; bicycle rental; shops; library; car rental. *In-room:* A/C, ceiling fan, data port, TV/VCR, CD player, minibar.

LaSOURCE ★★★ This was the first completely all-inclusive hotel on Grenada, spread across 40 acres (16 hectares) of a former cocoa and nutmeg plantation, with two white-sand beaches separated by a rocky knoll. It's not as intimate as Calabash, but if you want an all-inclusive with top spa facilities, you'll be happier here. La Source stresses revitalization of the body and mind through spa treatments and experiences with nature. Meals, drinks, watersports, entertainment, and most (but not all) spa treatments are included in the all-inclusive price. Everything's laid out for you on a platter, from diving courses to limbo dancing.

Guest rooms are located in a hillside compound of white-walled, terra-cotta-roofed buildings. Rooms are furnished with mahogany four-poster beds, Italian marble floors, and ceiling fans, evoking a dignified colonial plantation house. The marble-clad shower/tub combination bathrooms are extremely roomy with plenty of shelf space.

The plush Great House serves some of the island's best cuisine; less formal is the open-sided Terrace Restaurant.

Pink Gin Beach (P.O. Box 852), St. George's, Grenada, W.I. ✆ **800/544-2883** in the U.S. and Canada, or 473/444-2556. Fax 473/444-2561. www.lasource.com.gd. 100 units. Winter $720–$770 double; $840–$880 suite for 2. Off-season $440–$570 double; $600–$650 suite for 2. Rates are all-inclusive. AE, MC, V. **Amenities:** 2 restaurants, bar, piano bar; pool; 9-hole golf course; 2 tennis courts; health club and spa, massages; Jacuzzi, sauna; dive shop, watersports; laundry. *In room:* A/C, hair dryer.

Spice Island Inn ✿✿✿   On an estate overlooking the Caribbean, this inn is built along 1,200 feet (360m) of Grand Anse Beach. This is *the* classic beach resort, where you can run from your bungalow onto the white sands of the island's most perfect beach. It's not the most romantic or atmospheric, and it has none of the array of facilities of La Source, but for the best location on Grand Anse there is no equal. The main house, reserved for dining and dancing, has a tropical feel and lots of tasteful touches. Of the accommodations, we prefer the beach suites. Second-floor suites have terraces overlooking the ocean and the garden; 17 units have their own private plunge pools where guests can go skinny-dipping. Room furnishings are casual. The bathrooms are the largest and most luxurious on Grenada, with showers and Jacuzzis.

Grand Anse Beach (P.O. Box 6), St. George's, Grenada, W.I. ✆ **800/742-4276** in the U.S., 212/251-1800 in New York City, or 473/444-4258. Fax 473/444-4807. www.spicebeachresort.com. 66 units. Winter $570–$990 double. Off-season $470–$780 double. Rates are all-inclusive. AE, MC, V. **Amenities:** Restaurant, bar; private pools; complimentary greens fees at Grenada Golf Course; tennis court; fitness center; nonmotorized watersports; bike rentals; room service; laundry. *In room:* A/C, TV, minibar, hair dryer, safe.

EXPENSIVE

Coyaba Beach Resort ✿   On a 5½-acre (2-hectare) site on Grand Anse Beach next to the medical school, this resort, whose name means "heaven" in Arawak, is 6 miles (10km) from St. George's and 3 miles (5km) north of the airport. Opened in 1987, the hotel has views of town and of St. George's Harbor. All units have double beds with good mattresses, verandas or patios, and spacious bathrooms with tiled shower/tub combinations. For persons with disabilities, this is the best choice on the island, with its widened doorways, ramps, and three wheelchair-accessible guest rooms.

Grand Anse Beach (P.O. Box 336), St. George's, Grenada, W.I. ✆ **473/444-4129.** Fax 473/444-4808. www.coyaba.com. 70 units. Winter $210 double. Off-season $130 double. Extra person $50 in winter, $25 in off-season. Breakfast and dinner $42 per person extra. AE, DC, MC, V. **Amenities:** 2 open-air restaurants, 2 bars; tennis court; volleyball; watersports; room service; laundry. *In room:* A/C, TV, hair dryer.

Grenada Grand Beach Resort ✿   On 20 acres (8 hectares) of lush ground, this hotel stands on a desirable stretch of white sandy beachfront, across from the Grand Anse Shopping Centre. Guests are ushered between a pair of manicured formal gardens to their (often small) rooms, which are tiled and furnished with mahogany pieces. Each has a balcony or patio and a well-kept bathroom equipped with a shower/tub combination. The beach-view rooms are the most desirable, naturally. You can dine indoors or out at The Water Front, which has passable international cuisine. Entertainment is offered.

Grand Anse Beach (P.O. Box 441), Grenada, W.I. ✆ **473/444-4371.** Fax 473/444-4800. 240 units. Winter $235–$295 double; $400–$600 suite. Off-season $205–$255 double; $400–$600 suite. Rates include breakfast. AE, MC, V. **Amenities:** Restaurant, 2 bars; 2 pools; 2 tennis courts; fitness center; watersports; salon; room service; babysitting; laundry. *In room:* A/C, TV, hair dryer.

Rex Grenadian ✿   This is the largest and most bustling hotel on the island, though it's not the best. It's a convention-group favorite, set on 12 rocky, partially forested acres (5 hectares) that slope steeply down to a pair of white-sand beaches. Each of the wintergreen and pale-blue units is uniquely configured, and each is outfitted in rattan, wicker, and muted tropical fabrics. Eighty-four units offer ocean views, but not all are air-conditioned. The more expensive rooms contain shower/tub combinations. The bathrooms in other units are more compact with shower units. Adjacent to the accommodations is a 2-acre (.8-hectare) artificial lake strewn with islands that are connected to the "mainland" with footbridges.

The International serves buffets with foods from around the world. The Oriental is far better, specializing in—what else?—Asian cuisine. A bit more casual is Spicers, which offers local cuisine for lunch. The Tamarind Lounge offers cabaret singing and disco music.

Point Salines (P.O. Box 893), St. George's, Grenada, W.I. © 473/444-3333. Fax 473/444-1111. www.rex caribbean.com/index/html. 212 units. Winter $240–$360 double; $650 suite. Off-season $210–$330 double; $500 suite. AE, DC, MC, V. **Amenities:** 3 restaurants, 2 bars; 2 tennis courts; fitness center; dive shops, water-sports; room service; babysitting; laundry. *In room:* A/C, hair dryer. About a ¼ mile (.4km) from the airport.

Secret Harbour ★★ This resort evokes a Mediterranean complex on Spain's Costa del Sol—a tasteful one, that is, with white stucco arches, red-tile roofs, and wrought-iron light fixtures, with steps leading down to a good beach. Secret Harbour is a favorite of the yachting set. While many guests reside at the hotel, others stay on yachts anchored off the property. The inn is littered with antiques from all over Grenada, including some from island plantation homes. Guest rooms have generous closet space, refrigerators, and mahogany four-poster beds fitted with crisp white spreads. Each suite has wide windows with harbor views, a dressing room, living area, and patio overlooking the water. The bathrooms are luxurious and include showers and sunken tubs lined with Italian tiles.

The antique-filled Ocean View features a good international menu, often prepared with fresh produce from Grenada.

Mount Hartman Bay, L'Anse aux Epines (P.O. Box 11), St. George's, Grenada, W.I. © 473/444-4439. Fax 473/444-4819. www.secretharbour.com. 20 units. Winter $230 suite for 2. Off-season $130 suite for 2. Extra person $20. MAP (breakfast and dinner) $30 per person extra. AE, MC, V. No children under age 12 accepted. **Amenities:** 2 restaurants, bar; pool; tennis court; dive shop, water-skiing, boating, marina; room service; laundry. *In room:* A/C, fridge, hair dryer, safe.

Twelve Degrees North ★ On a very private beach, this cluster of spotlessly clean efficiency apartments is owned and operated by Joseph Gaylord, who personally greets visitors on his front lawn. Many staff members have been with Mr. Gaylord since he opened the place many years ago. They'll cook breakfast, prepare lunch (perhaps pumpkin soup and flying fish), do the cleaning and laundry, and fix regional specialties for dinner (which you can heat up for yourself later). A housekeeper/cook, assigned to each unit, arrives at 8am to perform the thousand small kindnesses that make Twelve Degrees North a favorite lair for repeat guests. All units are equipped with efficiency kitchens, large beds and shower-only bathrooms with robes. The owner prefers to rent by the week.

L'Anse aux Epines (P.O. Box 241), St. George's, Grenada, W.I. © and fax 473/444-4580 (call collect to make reservations). www.twelvedegreesnorth.com. 8 units. Winter $225 1-bedroom apt. for 2; $350 2-bedroom apt. for 4. Off-season $150 1-bedroom apt. for 2; $265 2-bedroom apt. for 4. Extra person $70. No credit cards. No children under age 16 accepted. **Amenities:** Beach bar; pool; tennis court; double-seat kayak, snorkeling, Sunfish. *In room:* Ceiling fan, hair dryer, no phone. 3 miles (5km) east of the airport.

MODERATE

Allamanda Beach Resort & Spa ★ Opening onto a wide stretch of Grand Anse Beach, this is one of the best full-service operations on the island, with everything from a watersports center to a spa. Accommodations open onto views of the water. Units come with either a little terrace or a balcony, and some are suitable for persons with disabilities. The decor is light and airy in a Caribbean tropical motif, with tile floors, well-kept bathrooms with shower/tub combinations, and, in some cases, whirlpool baths in the tiled bathrooms.

Grand Anse Beach (P.O. Box 27), St. George's, Grenada W.I. ℂ 473/444-0095. Fax 473/444-0126. www. allamandaresort.com. 50 units. Winter $155–$180 double; $340 suite. Off-season $120–$145 double, $235 suite. AE, MC, V. **Amenities:** Restaurant, bar; tennis court; health club and spa; watersports, room service; laundry. *In room:* A/C, TV, fridge, hair dryer, safe.

Blue Horizons Cottage Hotel ⋆ Co-owners Royston and Arnold Hopkin transformed this once-neglected property into one of the finest on the island. Grand Anse Beach is only a 5-minute walk away. The medium-sized units are strewn about a 6-acre (2-hectare) garden. Superior studios contain a small dining alcove and a king-size bed. The more expensive deluxe suites come with a separate living and dining area along with two king-size or double beds. Each room has an efficiency kitchen and comfortable, solid, mahogany furniture. Bathrooms, though small, are well maintained and equipped with shower/tub combinations.

Lunch is served around a pool bar, and guests who prefer to cook in their rooms can buy supplies from a Food Fair at Grand Anse, a 10-minute walk away. (Its restaurant, La Belle Creole, is described in "Dining," below.)

Grand Anse Beach (P.O. Box 41), Grenada, W.I. ℂ 800/223-9815 in the U.S., or 473/444-4316. Fax 473/444-2815. www.bluegrenada.com. 32 cottages. Winter $170–$190 double. Off-season $120–$130 double. Extra person $50 in winter, $35 in off-season. AE, DC, DISC, MC, V. **Amenities:** Restaurant, bar; room service; babysitting; laundry. *In room:* A/C, TV, hair dryer.

Flamboyant Hotel This hotel is a well-established standby. It occupies a hillside that slopes down to Grand Anse Beach, in a neighborhood peppered with other resorts. It was designed as a complex of modern, red-roofed buildings punctuated with an outdoor swimming pool. The management arranges parties, crab races, barbecues, dinner dances, and entertainment from reggae bands several nights a week. Each medium-size accommodation has a loggia-style balcony overlooking the beach, tile floors, good beds, and floral-patterned curtains and upholsteries. The apartments contain kitchenettes. Each unit has a somewhat cramped bathroom with a shower/tub combination, but maintenance is good.

Grand Anse Beach (P.O. Box 214), St. George's, Grenada, W.I. ℂ 473/444-4247. Fax 473/444-1234. www.flamboyant.com. 60 units. Winter $145 double; $300 2-bedroom apt. for 4. Off-season $105–$115 double; $185 2-bedroom apt. for 4. Extra person $25–$40. AE, DC, DISC, MC, V. **Amenities:** Restaurant, bar; pool; dive shop; free snorkeling equipment; game room; car and jeep rental; minimart; room service; babysitting; laundry. *In room:* A/C, TV, minibar, hair dryer, safe.

True Blue Bay Resort This resort takes its name from an old indigo plantation that once stood on this spot. It's still appropriately named because of the panoramic views of the blue waters of Prickly Bay. You can select one-bedroom apartments with verandas overlooking the bay, or two-bedroom cottages nestled in tropical gardens. Children are allowed in the cottages (but not in the one-bedroom apartments). The accommodations are tastefully furnished in pastels and tropical rattan pieces, with excellent beds, either king-size or twin. Each unit has a fully equipped kitchen and a tiled, shower-only bathroom.

Old Mill Ave., True Blue (P.O. Box 1414), St. George's, Grenada, W.I. ℂ 473/443-8783. Fax 473/444-5929. www.truebluebay.com. 28 units. Winter $155 1-bedroom apt.; $220 2-bedroom cottage. Off-season $105 1-bedroom apt.; $177 2-bedroom cottage. Extra person $25. MC, V. **Amenities:** Restaurant, 2 bars; pool; dive shop; room service. *In room:* A/C, TV, safe.

INEXPENSIVE

Gem Holiday Resort   Opening onto Morne Rouge Beach, this complex of self-catering apartments is family-friendly. It's owned and operated by the Beadeau family, which welcomes guests to its one- and two-bedroom apartments. The units are a bit small, but they are fully equipped, with a kitchenette, good beds, mahogany furnishings, shower-only bathrooms, and a private terrace opening onto the beach.

If you don't prepare your own meals, you can patronize Sur La Mer at the beach, which offers fresh fish and Caribbean dishes at both lunch and dinner. There is an on-site dance club, Fantazia 2001 (see "Grenada After Dark," later in this chapter).

Morne Rouge Bay (P.O. Box 58), St. George's, Grenada, W.I. ⓒ 473/444-4224. Fax 473/444-1189. www.gembeachresort.com. 20 units. Winter $126–$135 double; $180 quad. Off-season, $75–$90 double, $135 quad. Extra person $15. AE, DC, DISC, MC, V. **Amenities:** Restaurant, bar; dance club; minimart, room service (7:30am–10:30pm); babysitting; laundry/dry cleaning. *In room:* A/C, TV, kitchen, fridge, coffeemaker, hair dryer, iron and ironing board.

La Sagesse Nature Center ⭐ *Finds*   On a sandy, tree-lined beach 10 miles (16km) from the airport, La Sagesse consists of a seaside guest house, restaurant, bar, and art gallery, with watersports available. Nearby are trails for hiking and exploring, a haven for wading and shore birds, hummingbirds, hawks, and ducks. Rivers, mangroves, and a salt pond sanctuary enhance the natural beauty of the place. The original great house of what was once La Sagesse plantation contains two apartments, one with a fully equipped kitchen, and each with high ceilings and comfortable beds, plus shower-only bathrooms. Guests also have a choice of a two-bedroom beach cottage, with comfortable furnishings and a wraparound porch. The least desirable accommodations are two small, economy-priced bedrooms in back of the inn's patio restaurant.

St. David's (P.O. Box 44), St. George's, Grenada, W.I. ⓒ 473/444-6458. Fax 473/444-6458. www.caribbean connection.com 9 units. Winter $110–$125 double. Off-season $50–$80 double. MC, V. **Amenities:** Restaurant, bar; snorkeling; laundry. *In room:* Ceiling fan, no phone.

No Problem Apartment Hotel *Value*   The small one-bedroom apartments at this all-suite hotel are one of the best deals on the island. The motel-style lodging is just 5 minutes from the airport and Grand Anse Beach. The simply furnished suites open onto a pool and bar area; each has good beds and fully equipped kitchenettes, plus a small, bathroom with a shower/tub combination.

True Blue (P.O. Box 280), St. George's, Grenada, W.I. ⓒ 800/74-CHARMS in the U.S., or 473/444-4634. Fax 473/444-2803. 20 units. Winter $85 double. Off-season $65 double. Extra person $20. Breakfast and dinner $30 per person extra. AE, MC, V. **Amenities:** Coffee bar; reading room; free bikes; shuttle to the beach; laundry. *In room:* A/C, TV, hair dryer.

3 Dining

EXPENSIVE

Brown Sugar ⭐ GRENADIAN   Overlooking Grand Anse, just above the South Winds Apartments, this little eatery offers some of the most authentic island dishes in Grenada. Much of the local cookery has been updated for modern tastes, but other dishes are designed to put hair on your chest.

For great flavor, launch yourself with Ketch Ah Vaps, a hearty vegetable soup finished with coconut milk and a swirl of curried butter. "Lig-A-Rou?" you ask. (That's derived from the French word, *loupgarou,* or island werewolf.) When we ordered that, what later arrived on our plate was plaintain chips, topped with shrimp dipped in corn flour and deep-fried, accompanied by a spicy tomato sauce. It was delicious but hardly wolflike. One of our favorite dishes here is Dry-Vay, Jamaican jerk seasoned flying fish with a salad and guava vinaigrette. We couldn't resist "Too-Tool-Bay" when it was translated as "to be head over heels in love." It turned out to be pumpkin ravioli stuffed with sweet potato in a creamy pesto, topped with frizzled eggplant, chives, and steamed vegetables.

One of the two dining rooms is a replica of a plantation great house. A shuttle will be sent to your hotel to bring you here. The best nights are Tuesday, Wednesday, Friday, and Sunday, when a local band plays pan music.

Main Rd., Grand Anse. ✆ 473/444-2374. Reservations required. Main courses EC$90–EC$120 (US$33.30–US$44.40). AE, DC, MC, V. Daily 7:30–9am and 7–10:30pm.

Coconut Beach Restaurant ✦ FRENCH/CREOLE This informal restaurant occupies a pink-and-green clapboard house set directly on the sands of the beach. From the dining room, you can watch the staff at work in the exposed kitchen. They'll definitely be making callaloo soup, made with local herbs and blended to a creamy smoothness. The kitchen specializes in various kinds of lobster, including an imaginative lobster stir-fry with ginger chile. Fish predominates, including a catch of the day served with mango chutney. Chicken and meats are also savory, especially breast of chicken cooked in local herbs and lime juice.

Warning: Because of the restaurant's close proximity to several major hotels, many people opt to walk along the beach to reach it. Don't! Tourists have been attacked by machete-carrying thugs who've robbed them and threatened their lives. Even though it might be only a short ride, take a taxi instead.

Grand Anse Beach, about ½ mile (.8km) north of St. George's. ✆ 473/444-4644. Reservations recommended. Lunch platters EC$18–EC$25 (US$6.65–US$9.25); main courses EC$42–EC$75 (US$15.55–US$27.75). AE, DISC, MC, V. Wed–Mon 12:30–10pm.

La Belle Creole ✦ CREOLE/WEST INDIAN/SEAFOOD This is one of the best restaurants on Grenada for West Indian specialties, and the menu boasts a variety of continental recipes with West Indian touches. The chefs prepare one of the most creative cuisines on the island. To get you going, try chilled conch mousse if it's featured; it's delectable in every way. The lobster Creole is a classic, served in a shell, but even better is the spicy ginger pork chops with local seasonings, heightened with a touch of white wine. Another longtime favorite is the deviled fish with curry and local seasonings. Three local vegetables fresh from the lush countryside are served with each meal. Desserts, however, are nothing special.

At Blue Horizons, Grand Anse Beach. ✆ 473/444-4316. Reservations required for nonhotel guests. 5-course fixed-price dinner EC$110–EC$130 (US$40.70–US$48.10). AE, DC, MC, V. Daily 7:30–10am and 7–10pm.

Laluna ITALIAN/INTERNATIONAL This is the restaurant that feeds, nourishes, and entertains the sometimes hedonistic international clientele of one of Grenada's newest and quietly stylish cottage compounds. And it does so exceedingly well. You'll dine in a thatch-covered setting, adjacent to the sea and a swimming pool, enjoying the cookery of a Sicily-born chef with wide-ranging experience in Asia. The best examples include seafood gnocchi; spice island sushi; pasta a l'amatriciana (with salami, ham, tomatoes, capers, and olives); and seafood Benedetto, a medley of wine-and-tomato-soaked seafood served over rice.

In the La Luna Resort, Morne Rouge, P.O. Box 1500. ✆ 473/439-0001. Reservations recommended. Main courses EC$74–EC$105 (US$27.40–US$38.85). AE, MC, V. Daily noon–2:30pm and 7–9:30pm.

The Red Crab ★ WEST INDIAN/INTERNATIONAL   The Red Crab doesn't serve as fine a cuisine as the restaurants recommended above, but it's a fun place to be at night. Your companions are likely to be the liveliest on island. The Red Crab, favored by visitors and locals alike, is only a short taxi ride from the major hotels. The place is especially popular with students from the medical college. Patrons can dine inside or out under the starry night. The beefsteaks, especially the pepper steak, are among Grenada's finest. Other fine offerings include local lobster tail; *lambi* (conch); and locally caught fish such as snapper, dolphin (mahi-mahi), and grouper, though other island chefs prepare better versions of these seafood dishes.

L'Anse aux Epines. ✆ 473/444-4424. Reservations required in winter. Main courses EC$44.25–EC$95.50 (US$16.35–US$35.35). AE, MC, V. Mon–Sat 11am–2pm and 6–11pm.

Spice Island Inn ★ CREOLE/SEAFOOD   Want to dine on an uncrowded beachfront, but with a parapet over your head to protect you from sudden tropical showers? The parapet here, built of imported pine and cedar, looks like a Le Corbusier rooftop. Some of the best hotel food on the island is served in this winning setting. The view here is of one of the finest beaches in the Caribbean— miles of white sand sprouting an occasional grove of sea grape or almond trees. You can even eat your lunch in a swimsuit. Local seafood is featured on the constantly changing menu. The most generous buffet on the island, a real Grenadian spread, is served on Friday, along with live entertainment. On Saturday seafood is the specialty.

Grand Anse Beach. ✆ 473/444-4258. Reservations required for nonguests. Fixed-price breakfast EC$53 (US$19.60). Lunch EC$40–EC$53 (US$14.80–US$19.60). Fixed-price dinner EC$120 (US$44.40). AE, DC, DISC, MC, V. Daily 7:30–10am, 12:30–3:00pm, and 7–9:30pm.

MODERATE

The Boatyard ★ INTERNATIONAL   This medical student hangout overlooks the marina where the yachts are moored. It attracts a lot of visiting yachties, most of whom seem to prefer the liquid lunch. Lunch consists of a Caribbean daily special, and may include stewed pork or Creole chicken served in a tomato sauce with rice. Some of the best featured dishes are stewed and barbecued chicken, baked conch Parmesan, and grilled steak; most are served with rice, salad, and fresh vegetables. Mexican specialties and Italian pastas also appear on the menu, but they are not reason enough to come here. On Friday nights a steel-drum band plays; when they're done the sound system is cranked up for indoor-outdoor dancing until the wee hours.

L'Anse aux Epines, Prickly Bay. ✆ 473/444-4662. Main courses EC$28–EC$80 (US$10.35–US$29.60). MC, V. Daily 8:30am–midnight.

Cicely's ★★ CONTINENTAL/CARIBBEAN   On the sun-drenched Prickly Bay Beach, you can relax and be waited upon by the helpful staff here while enjoying the cuisine of Cicely Roberts, one of the island's most outstanding chefs. We can't claim it will be a life-changing experience, but what you get is worthy of any discerning palate. Although most dishes vary in origin, many have a unique West Indian flair because of the deft use of locally grown ingredients. The menus change constantly, but you are likely to be enticed by fillet of pork with fresh ginger, garlic, and guava. Begin with a lobster mousse or *christophene vichyssoise*, a squashlike vegetable regional to the Caribbean. Expect live music at least 3 nights a week.

In the Calabash Hotel, L'Anse Aux Epines. ✆ 473/444-4334. Reservations required. Main courses EC$29 (US$10.75). AE, MC, V. Daily 5:30–9:30pm.

La Dolce Vita ITALIAN   Some of the island's best Italian cuisine is served in this complex of self-contained villas built like a Mediterranean-style village. The view from here is one of the most scenic in the Caribbean. You enter tropical gardens and follow the wafting aromas coming from the kitchen of this well-run restaurant. We prefer the chef's homemade pasta dishes to all others on the island, although you may prefer to start with the constantly changing array of both hot and cold antipasti, often made with fresh vegetables. Our favorite dish is the spaghetti with chunks of lobster caught in local waters, or one of the fresh fish specials, grilled to perfection.

In the Cinnamon Hill Hotel, Grand Anse. © 473/444-3456. Reservations required. Main courses EC$21 (US$7.75). AE, MC, V. Tues–Sun 3–9pm.

The Nutmeg SEAFOOD/CREOLE   Right on the harbor, The Nutmeg is a rendezvous point for the yachting set. It's suitable for a snack or a full-fledged dinner in an informal atmosphere. The drinks are very good; try one of the Grenadian rum punches made with Angostura bitters, grated nutmeg, rum, lime juice, and syrup. There's always fresh fish, and usually callaloo or pumpkin soup, plus potato croquettes. *Lambi* (that ubiquitous conch) is done very well here. A small wine list has some California, German, and Italian selections, and you can drop in just for a glass of beer to enjoy the sea view. Sometimes, however, you'll be asked to share a table.

The Carenage, St. George's. © 473/440-2539. Main courses EC$20–EC$70 (US$7.40–US$25.90) lunch, EC$35–EC$70 (US$12.95–US$25.90) dinner. AE, MC, V. Mon–Sat 8am–11pm, Sun 4–11pm.

Rudolf's ✿ *Value* INTERNATIONAL   A longtime favorite and an excellent value for your money, Rudolf's overlooks St. George's harbor. It's a good spot for lethal rum drinks in the late afternoon. Austrian-born Rudolf is very charming, and he has a hardworking and genteel staff. The restaurant does a busy lunch business; ceiling fans cool patrons off at midday. The ceiling is sheathed in a layer of corrugated egg cartons, which adds an unconventional, appealing touch and also muffles the noise from the sometimes very crowded bar area. The menu is the most extensive on the island, the food is well prepared, and the steaks are the best in the capital. Flying fish and dolphin (mahi-mahi), prepared in several different ways, deserve the most praise. There's even a classic wiener schnitzel.

The Carenage, St. George's. © 473/440-2241. Reservations recommended. Main courses EC$26–EC$60 (US$9.60–US$22.20). MC, V. Mon–Sat 10am–midnight.

INEXPENSIVE

Aquarium Beach Club & Restaurant SEAFOOD   This beachfront club near the airport changes personalities between day and night. You can rent snorkeling equipment or ocean kayaks here in the morning and return in the afternoon for a good seafood lunch. There's always something happening around here, including a "lobster barbecue" on Sunday afternoons, instead of the typical brunch. The convivial bar fills up, often with locals, during happy hour from 5 to 6:30pm.

At dinner the place becomes slightly more formal, and a full menu is offered. Your best bet is the fresh fish of the day, which can be prepared as you like it. Lots of other good dishes emerge from the kitchen as well, including two specialties: a tender and well-flavored pepper steak, and a spinach-like callaloo cannelloni, a uniquely Caribbean concoction. Most of the main courses are inexpensive; only the barbecued lobster will tax your wallet.

Point Salines. ℂ **473/444-1410.** Reservations required for dinner. Main courses EC$24–EC$76.50 (US$8.90–US$28.30). AE, MC, V. Tues–Sun 10am–11pm.

La Boulangerie FRENCH/ITALIAN   Don't be deterred by the shopping center location. This French coffee shop and bakery is an ideal spot for a good breakfast or light lunch (served throughout the afternoon). And prices at dinner are most reasonable. In the early morning visitors throng here for the freshly brewed coffee, downed with pastries or croissants. The afternoon crowd devours well-stuffed baguettes, sandwiches, and pizzas. More substantial dishes are offered in the evening, including roast chicken and fresh fish.

Le Marquis Shopping Complex, Grand Anse Beach. ℂ **473/444-1131.** Sandwiches and pizzas EC$8–EC$17 (US$2.95–US$6.30) dinner main courses EC$16–EC$30 (US$5.90–US$11.10). No credit cards. Daily 8am–9pm.

Deyna's Tasty Food ★ *Finds* GRENADIAN   This little eatery is a closely guarded secret among locals. It's reached by heading up Melville Street to a modest three-story building overlooking the sea. You might even get invited back into the kitchen to see what's cookin'. The duenna of the stove, Deyna Hercules, looks like she lives up to her namesake and eats her own food. Where else can you get someone to fry you up a tasty batch of *titiri,* those minnow-sized fish just plucked from the Caribbean and washed down with "bush tea" steeped from black sage leaves? Her savory stuffed crabs are the island's best, and you can check out her specialties scribbled on a countertop chalkboard. Her specialty is a "fix up"—a sampling of the best food of the day, perhaps "stew fish," green plantains, and curried goat. She also serves the national dish of Grenada, an "oil down," made with salted meat and breadfruit cooked in coconut milk. Diners with hair on their chest can opt for two of her gamey specialties—*manicou* (a cross between an opossum and a large rat) and *tatou,* akin to armadillo. Stewed turtle and fried sea eggs round out this offbeat menu.

Melville St. ℂ **473/440-6795.** Reservations recommended. Main courses EC$15–EC$22 (US$5.55–US$8.15). MC, V. Mon–Sat 8am–8pm, Sun 10am–4pm.

La Sagesse ★ CARIBBEAN/CONTINENTAL   Opening onto a sandy beach, this romantic open-air spot is one of the most offbeat places to dine on island. Although it is casually run, it serves a fine cuisine based on fresh ingredients. The fresh seafood served here is some of the island's finest—and freshest. You can order freshly made salads and well-stuffed sandwiches throughout the day. The conch (a.k.a. *lambi*) is an excellent choice, but on most nights, you can choose from a full range of fish, including dolphin (mahi-mahi) and grouper. In the evening several continental dishes appear. The restaurant also caters to vegetarians.

In the La Sagesse Nature Center, St. David's. ℂ **473/444-6458.** Reservations recommended for dinner. Main courses EC$34–EC$60 (US$12.60–US$22.20). MC, V. Daily 8–10:30am, 11:30am–3:30pm, and 5:30–10:30pm.

Morne Fendue ★ *Finds* CREOLE   This plantation house is the ancestral home of the late owner, Betty Mascoll. It was built in 1912, the year Miss Mascoll was born, of carefully chiseled river rocks held together with a mixture of lime and molasses. Miss Mascoll died in 1998, but her loyal staff carries on her tradition. Of course, they need time to prepare food for your arrival, so it's imperative to give them a call to let them know you're coming by. Lunch is likely to include yam and sweet-potato casserole, curried chicken with lots of hot spices, and a hot pot of pork and oxtail. Because this is very much a private home, tipping should be done with the greatest tact. Nonetheless, the hard-working cook and maid seem genuinely appreciative of a gratuity.

St. Patrick's, 25 miles (40km) north of St. George's. (C) **473/442-9330.** Reservations required. Fixed-price lunch EC$45 (US$16.65). No credit cards. Mon–Sat 12:30–2pm. Follow the coastal road north out of St. George's. After you pass through Nonpareil, turn inland (east) and continue through Buguesng and follow the signs to Morne Fendue.

4 Beaches

The best of the 45 beaches on Grenada are in the southwestern part of the island. The granddaddy of them all is **Grand Anse Beach** ★★★, 2 miles (3km) of sugar-white sand fronting a sheltered bay. This beach is really the stuff of dreams—it's no surprise why so many of the major resort hotels are here. Many visitors never leave this part of the island. Protected from strong winds and currents, the waters here are relatively safe, making Grand Anse a family favorite. The clear, gentle waters are populated with schools of rainbow-hued fish. Palms and sea-grape trees offer shade. Watersports concessions are found here, offering water-skiing, parasailing, windsurfing, and scuba diving; vendors peddle coral jewelry, local crafts, and the inevitable T-shirts.

The beach at **Morne Rouge Bay** is less frequented but just as desirable, with its white sands bordering clear waters. Morne Rouge is noted for its calm waters and some of the best **snorkeling** in Grenada. It's about a mile (2km) south of Grand Anse Bay.

Pink Gin Beach lies near the airport at Point Salinas, bordering two large resorts, La Source and Rex Grenadian (see "Accommodations," earlier in this chapter). This is also a beach of white sand and clear waters, ideal for swimming and snorkeling. (No one seems to know why it's called Pink Gin Beach.) You'll find a restaurant and kayak rentals here.

Also on Grenada's southern coast, **La Sagesse Beach** is part of La Sagesse Nature Center. This especially powdery strip of white sand is a lovely, tranquil area; in between time spent on the beach, you can go for nature walks in most directions. A small restaurant opens onto the beach.

If you like your waters more turbulent, visit the dramatic **Pearl's Beach,** north of Grenville on the Atlantic coast. The light gray sand stretches for miles and is lined with palm trees. You'll practically have the beach to yourself.

Part of Levera National Park, **Levera Beach,** at the northeastern tip of the island, is one of the most beautiful on Grenada. Its sands front the Atlantic, which most often means rough waters. Many locals come here for Sunday picnics.

5 Sports & Other Outdoor Pursuits

DEEP-SEA FISHING   Fishers come here from November to March in pursuit of both blue and white marlin, yellowfin tuna, wahoo, sailfish, and more. Most of the bigger hotels have a sports desk that will arrange fishing trips for you. The **Annual Game Fishing Tournament,** held in January, attracts a number of regional and international participants. For more information, call Robert Miller at ((C) **473/444-2220**).

GOLF   At the **Grenada Golf Course and Country Club,** Woodlands ((C) **473/444-4128**), you'll find a nine-hole course offering views of both the Caribbean Sea and the Atlantic. Greens fees are $16 for 9 holes, or $23 if you want to play it twice (to get 18 holes). Hours are Monday to Thursday 8am to 7pm, Friday 8am to 5pm, Saturday 8am to 7pm, and Sunday from 8am to 1:30pm.

HIKING   Grenada's lushness and beauty make it one of the best Caribbean islands for hiking. If you have time for only one hiking experience on Grenada, make it the **Grand Etang National Park and Forest Preserve** ★ (© 473/440-6160). For sheer scenic beauty, our number-one choice on the island is the **Lake Circle Trail,** which makes a 30-minute circuit along Grand Etang Lake, the crater of an extinct volcano amidst a forest preserve and bird sanctuary. You're likely to see the yellow-billed cuckoo and the emerald-throated hummingbird. The park is also a playground for Mona monkeys. Of course, you can also take more elaborate hikes, perhaps to the peak of **Mount Qua Qua** at 2,373 feet (712m). Trails can be slippery after a rainfall (especially between June and November), so wear good hiking shoes and carry plenty of water with you. The park's **Grand Etang Interpretation (Nature) Centre** is open Monday to Friday from 8am to 4pm, featuring a video about the park. Admission is $1.

You can hike the shorter trails independently, but you might wish to hire a guide for the ascent to Mount Qua Qua or the even more demanding hike to Mount Catherine, at 2,757 feet (827m). The former costs $25 per person for a 4-hour hike, while the latter is $35. For information, call **Telfor Bedeau Hiking Tours** (© 473/442-6200). Good hiking trails can also be found at **Levera National Park** (see "A Spectacular Rain Forest & More," below).

SCUBA DIVING & SNORKELING   Grenada offers divers an underwater world rich in submarine gardens, exotic fish, and coral formations, sometimes with visibility stretching to 120 feet (36m). Off the coast is the wreck of the ocean liner *Bianca C,* which is nearly 600 feet (180m) long. Novice divers might want to stick to the west coast of Grenada, while more experienced divers might search out the sights along the rougher Atlantic side.

Daddy Vic's Watersports, in the Grenada Renaissance, Grand Anse Beach (© 473/444-4371, ext. 638), is the premier dive outfit on the island. It has night dives or two-tank dives for $50 and $76 respectively; PADI instructors offer an open-water certification program for $350 per person. Daddy Vic's also offers **snorkeling trips** for $21 (1½–2 hr.). You can **rent snorkel gear** from Daddy Vic's as well, even if you don't take the boat ride.

> **Tips Diving Warning**
>
> Grenada doesn't have a decompression chamber. If you get the bends, you'll have to take an excruciatingly painful flight to Trinidad.

Giving Daddy Vic's serious competition is the affable **Grand Anse Aquatics,** at the Coyaba Beach Resort on Grand Anse Beach (© 473/444-7777). There's a PADI instructor on site. The dive boat is well equipped with well-maintained gear. Both scuba diving and snorkeling jaunts to panoramic reefs and shipwrecks teeming with marine life are offered. A single dive costs $47, a resort course $75, and a night dive $55. A **snorkeling trip** can be arranged for $21. Diving instruction, including a resort course, is available.

If you'd rather strike out on your own, take a drive to Woburn and negotiate with a fisher for a ride to **Glovers Island,** an old whaling station, and snorkel away. Glovers Island is an uninhabited rock spit a few hundred yards offshore from the hamlet of Woburn.

SAILING   Two large party boats, designed for 120 and 250 passengers, operate out of St. George's harbor. The *Rhum Runner* and *Rhum Runner II,* c/o Best of Grenada, P.O. Box 188, St. George's, Grenada, W.I. (© **473/440-4FUN**), make three trips daily, with lots of emphasis on strong liquor, steel-band music, and good times. Four-hour tours, conducted every morning and afternoon, coincide with the arrival of cruise ships, but will carry independent travelers if space is available. Rides cost $25 per person and include snorkeling stops at reefs and beaches along the way. Evening tours are much more frequently attended by island locals, and are more bare-boned, louder, and usually less restrained.

TENNIS   Most big resorts have tennis courts. There are public courts, as well, both at Grand Anse and in Tanteen in St. George's.

WATERSPORTS   Daddy Vic's Watersports, in the Grenada Renaissance, Grand Anse Beach (© **473/444-4371,** ext. 638), rents sailboards or Sunfish sailboats for $21 per hour. Parasailing is $30 per 10 minutes, and water-skiing is $15 per run.

6 Exploring the Island

ST. GEORGE'S & VICINITY

The capital city of Grenada, **St. George's** ★★ is the prettiest harbor town in the West Indies. Its landlocked inner harbor is actually the deep crater of a long-dead volcano—or so one is told. In the town, you'll see some of the most charming Georgian colonial buildings in the Caribbean, still standing despite a devastating hurricane in 1955. The steep, narrow hillside streets are filled with houses of ballast bricks, wrought-iron balconies, and sloping, red-tile roofs. Many of the pastel warehouses date from the 18th century. Frangipani and flamboyant trees add to the palette of color.

The port, which some have compared to Portofino, Italy, is flanked by old forts and bold headlands. Among the town's attractions is an 18th-century pink **Anglican church,** on Church Street, and the **Market Square,** where colorfully attired farm women offer even more colorful produce for sale. **Fort George,** on Church Street, built by the French, stands at the entrance to the bay, with subterranean passageways and old guardrooms and cells.

Everyone strolls along the waterfront of the **Carenage** ★ on the inner harbor, or relaxes on its pedestrian plaza, with seats and hanging planters providing shade from the sun. The best place to sit and have a drink is **The Nutmeg** (see "Dining," above). From its large open windows you'll have great views of the harbor activity. The hamburgers and rum drinks are great, too.

On this side of town, the **Grenada National Museum,** at the corner of Young and Monckton streets (© **473/440-3725**), is set in the foundations of an old French army barracks and prison built in 1704. Small but interesting, it houses finds from archaeological digs, including petroglyphs, native fauna, the first telegraph installed on the island, a rum still, and memorabilia depicting Grenada's history. The most comprehensive exhibit traces the native culture of Grenada. Hours are Monday through Friday from 9am to 4:30pm, Saturday from 10am to 1pm. Admission is $2.

You can take a drive up to Richmond Hill and **Fort Frederick,** begun by the French in 1779 and completed by the English in 1791. From its battlements, you'll have a superb view of the harbor and of the yacht marina.

An afternoon tour of St. George's and its environs might take you into the mountains north of the capital. A 15-minute drive delivers you to **Annandale Falls** ✶, a tropical wonderland, with a cascade about 50 feet (15m) high. You can enjoy a picnic surrounded by liana vines, elephant ears, and other tropical flora and spices. The **Annandale Falls Centre** (© 473/440-2452) offers gift items, handcrafts, and samples of the indigenous spices of Grenada. Nearby, an improved trail leads to the falls where you can enjoy a refreshing swim. Swimmers can use the changing cubicles at the falls for free. The center is open daily from 8am to 4pm.

A SPECTACULAR RAINFOREST & MORE

If you head north out of St. George's along the western coast, you can take in beaches, spice plantations, and the fishing villages that are so typical of Grenada.

You'll pass through **Gouyave,** a spice town, the center of the nutmeg and mace industry. At the **Grenada Cooperative Nutmeg Association** (© 473/444-8337), near the entrance to Gouyave, huge quantities of the spice are aged, graded, and processed. This is the best place to see spices being readied for market. Workers sit on stools in the natural light from the open windows of the aging factory, and laboriously sort the raw nutmeg and its by-product, mace, into different baskets for grinding, peeling, and aging. Jams, jellies, syrups, and more are all for sale. Hours are Monday to Friday 8am to 4pm; admission is $1.

In the northeast corner of the island (just east of Sauteurs) is the palm-lined **Levera Beach,** an idyll of sand where the Atlantic meets the Caribbean. This is a great spot for a picnic lunch, but swimming can sometimes be dangerous. On the distant horizon you'll see some of the Grenadines.

Opened in 1994, the 450-acre (180-hectare) **Levera National Park** ✶ has several white-sand beaches for swimming and snorkeling, although the surf is rough here where the Atlantic meets the Caribbean. It's also a **hiker's paradise.** Go hiking here only if you've already hiked through Grand Etang National Park and Forest Preserve (see "Hiking," above), which is lusher and of far greater interest. Levera Park contains a mangrove swamp, a lake, and a bird sanctuary; perhaps you'll see a rare tropical parrot. Offshore are coral reefs and sea grass beds. The park's interpretative center (© 473/442-1018) is open Monday to Friday from 8am to 4pm, Saturday and Sunday from 8am to 4pm.

Heading down the east coast of Grenada, you reach **Grenville,** the island's second city. If you pass through on a Saturday morning, you can enjoy the hubbub of the native produce market. There's also a fish market along the waterfront. A nutmeg factory here welcomes visitors. From Grenville, you can cut inland into the heart of Grenada. Here you're in a world of luxuriant foliage, and you pass along nutmeg, banana, and cocoa plantations.

In the center of the island, reached along the major interior road between Grenville and St. George's, is **Grand Etang National Park** ✶ (© 473/440-6160), containing the island's spectacular rainforest. Beginning at the park's forest center, the short hike on the **Morne LeBaye Trail** affords a view of the 2,309-foot (693m) Mount Sinai and the east coast. Another easy hike is the **Lake Circle Trail,** which takes you through a forest preserve and bird sanctuary along Grand Etang Lake, the crater of an extinct volcano. For more information about hikes in the park, see "Hiking," above.

On your descent from the mountains, you'll pass hanging carpets of mountain ferns. Going through the tiny hamlets of Snug Corner and Beaulieu, you eventually come back to the capital.

7 Shopping

Everybody who visits Grenada goes home with a basket of **spices,** better than any you're likely to find in your local supermarket. Wherever you go, you'll be besieged by spice vendors. These hand-woven panniers of palm leaf or straw are full of items grown on the island, including the inevitable nutmeg, as well as mace, cloves, cinnamon, bay leaf, vanilla, and ginger. Grenada is no grand merchandise mart of the Caribbean like St. Thomas and St. Maarten, but you may locate some local handcrafts, gifts, and even art.

If you like to attend Caribbean markets as much as we do, head for **Market Square** at the foot of Young Street in St. George's. The market is at its liveliest on Saturday morning, but is also open Monday to Friday too. It's best to go between 8am and noon. An array of handcrafts is for sale, but fresh spices to bring home are more plentiful.

8 Grenada After Dark

Regular evening entertainment is provided by the resort hotels and includes steel bands, calypso, reggae, folk dancing, and limbo—even crab racing. Ask at your hotel desk to find out what's happening at the time of your visit.

The island's most popular nightspot is **Fantazia 2001,** Morne Rouge Beach (© 473/444-2288). It's air-conditioned, with state-of-the-art equipment, good acoustics, and fantastic disco lights, and plays the best in regional and international sounds. Live shows are presented on Friday and Saturday. The cover is EC$10 to EC$15 (US$3.75–US$5.50), depending on the entertainment.

You can also try **Boatyard,** Prickly Bay, L'Anse aux Epines (© 473/ 444-4662), down by the marina. Friday night after 11pm, a local DJ spins dance music until dawn.

Casablanca, Grand Anse (© 473/444-1631), is the island's major sports bar. It's also a piano bar. The **Beachside Terrace** at the Flamboyant Hotel, Grand Anse (© 473/444-4247), is a laid-back spot featuring **crab races** on Monday, a steel band on Wednesday and Saturday, and, our favorite, a beach barbecue with live calypso music on Friday.

One of our favorite bars is **Aquarium Beach Club & Restaurant** at Point Salines (© 473/444-1410), which also serves delectable food (see "Dining," earlier in this chapter). From the sprawl of decks open to the trade winds, you can enjoy the lights of St. George's Harbour here at night.

For those seeking culture, the 200-seat **Marryshow Folk Theatre,** Herbert Blaize Street near Bain Alley, St. George's (© 473/440-2451), offers performances of Grenadian, American, and European folk music, drama, and West Indian interpretative folk dance. Check with the theater or the tourist office to see what's on. Tickets cost EC$20 to EC$25 (US$7.40–US$9.25).

14

Guadeloupe

Guadeloupe gives travelers a taste of France in the tropics. In addition to its Gallic flair and fine Creole cuisine (among the finest in the Caribbean), it offers some excellent beaches and a mountainous, lush terrain full of gorgeous scenery. The resorts here are not as spectacular and plush as those on, say, Anguilla or Jamaica, though there are some large beachfront properties, but you can also choose small inns where locally prepared food and tranquility can give you a real island experience.

Guadeloupe is part of the Lesser Antilles, about 200 miles (322km) north of Martinique. It's actually comprised of two different islands,

separated by a narrow seawater channel known as the Rivière Salée. **Grande-Terre,** the eastern island, is full of rolling hills and sugar plantations. **Basse-Terre,** to the west, is a rugged mountainous island, dominated by the 4,800-foot (1,440m) volcano, La Soufrière, which is still alive and dotted with banana plantations. Guadeloupe's mountains are covered with tropical forests, impenetrable in many places. The island is ringed by beautiful white-sand beaches. In the unlikely event that you should grow bored on Guadeloupe, you can hop over to really remote islands offshore, including **Iles des Saintes** and **Marie-Galante.**

1 Essentials

VISITOR INFORMATION

For advance information, contact the **French Government Tourist Office** in the U.S. at 444 Madison Ave., **New York, NY** 10022 (© **212/659-7779**); 9454 Wilshire Blvd., **Beverly Hills, CA** 90212 (© **310/276-2835**); or 645 N. Michigan Ave., **Chicago, IL** 60611 (© **312/337-6339**).

In **Britain,** the address is 178 Piccadilly, London, W1V 0AL (© **020/71499-6911**). In **Canada,** contact 1981 McGill College Ave., Suite 490, Montréal, Québec H3A 2W9 (© **514/288-4264**), or 30 St. Patrick St., Suite 700, Toronto, Ontario M5T 3A3 (© **416/593-6427**).

Guadeloupe is not on the Web, but you can e-mail the tourism office at **office.tourism.guadeloupe@wanadoo.fr**.

On the island, the major tourist office is the **Office Départemental du Tourisme,** Square de la Banque 5, in Pointe-à-Pitre (© **590/82-09-30**).

GETTING THERE

To get to Guadeloupe, most U.S. travelers will have to fly to another island and transfer. You can take an **American Airlines** (© **800/433-7300** in the U.S.; www.aa.com) flight to its hub in San Juan, Puerto Rico, and then get an American Eagle flight to Guadeloupe. There are also connections available through Martinique (see chapter 16).

Air Canada (© **800/776-3000** in the U.S., or 800/268-7240 in Canada; www.aircanada.ca) flies between Montréal and Guadeloupe (but not Martinique) every Saturday year-round. When this isn't convenient, passengers from throughout Canada can route themselves through Toronto on one of the daily nonstop flights to Barbados. From there, passengers can transfer onto other carriers (usually LIAT), making the ongoing journey to points within the French West Indies.

Air France (© **590/82-61-61;** www.airfrance.com) flies into Guadeloupe every day from Paris, with efficient connecting service from Britain and the rest of Europe. Air France also—at least in theory—maintains direct service to Guadeloupe from San Juan and Miami, although in the wake of the September, 2001, bombings of New York's World Trade Center, they've been suspended. Check with Air France directly prior to your trip to see if they've been re-inaugurated.

If you're already on the islands, you can wing into Guadeloupe on **LIAT** (© **590/31-13-93;** www.liatairline.com), which flies here from Antigua, St. Maarten, St. Croix, St. Lucia, Martinique, Barbados, Grenada, Trinidad, and Dominica. **Air Caraïbes** (© **590/21-13-34;** www.aircaraibes.com) operates about a half-dozen flights a day into Guadeloupe from Martinique, as well as at least one flight a day, each, from San Juan, St. Barts, and French St-Martin.

Consider arriving in Guadeloupe like many of the locals do, on one of the daily ferryboats operated by **Express des Iles** (© **590/83-04-43**), whose vessels originate every day in Martinique at 2pm, make a 30-minute stopover in Dominica en route (departing from Dominica around 4pm), and then docking at the quays of Pointe-à-Pitre sometime between 5:45 and 6:10pm, depending on weather, tides, and the vagaries of island life.

One-way passage to Pointe-à-Pitre from Dominica costs 52.45€ (US$46.85) per person; one-way passage to Guadeloupe from Martinique is only 1.50€ (US$1.35) more per person—53.95€ (US$48.20), partly the result of government subsidies within the French-controlled *departments d'outre-mer.* For timetables and more information in Guadeloupe, call **Agence Penchard** (the local representative of Expres des Iles) at © **590/83-04-43.** For timetables and information in Martinique, contact Expres des Iles directly at © **596/63-12-11.**

GETTING AROUND

BY RENTAL CAR   You may want to rent a car on Guadeloupe so you can explore Basse-Terre; the loop around the island is one of the most scenic drives in the Caribbean. Car-rental kiosks at the airport are open to meet international flights. Rental rates at local companies might appear lower, but several readers have complained of mechanical problems, billing irregularities, and difficulties in resolving insurance disputes in the event of accidents. So we recommend reserving a car in advance through one of North America's largest car-rental companies: **Hertz** (© **800/654-3131** in the U.S., or 590/21-13-46 locally; www.hertz.com), and **Avis** (© **800/331-1212** in the U.S., or 590/21-13-54 locally; www.avis.com), each of which is headquartered at the airport. Many of the major hotels also have car-rental desks. You'll have to pay a one-time airport surcharge of 15.20€ (US$13.55) and VAT (value-added tax) of 9.5%. Prices are usually 20% to 25% lower between March and early December, but not in July and August.

As in France, *driving is on the right-hand side of the road,* and there are several gas stations along the island's main routes. Because of the distance between gas stations away from the capital, try not to let your gas gauge fall below the halfway mark.

Guadeloupe

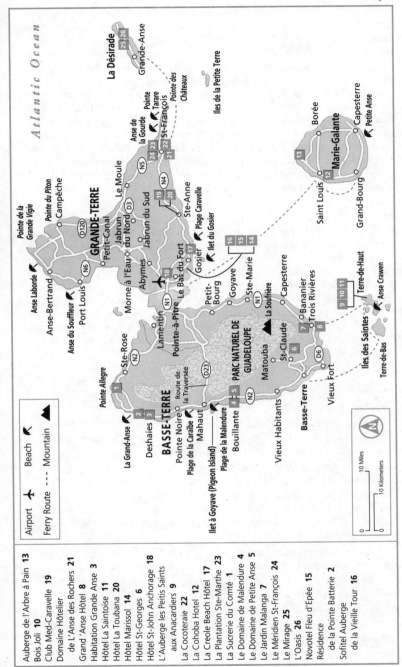

Key / Legend:

- Airport ✈
- Ferry Route - - -
- Beach ↙
- Mountain ▲

Locations on map

Atlantic Ocean

- La Désirade
- Grande-Anse — 25 26
- Pointe des Châteaux
- Iles de la Petite Terre
- Campêche
- Pointe du Piton
- Pointe de la Grande Vigie
- Anse Laborde ↙
- Anse-Bertrand
- Anse du Souffleur ↙
- Port Louis
- N6
- D120
- Petit-Canal
- **GRANDE-TERRE**
- Le Moule
- N5
- Jabrun du Nord — D3
- Jabrun du Sud
- Morne à l'Eau
- Abymes
- N4
- 19 20
- Ste-Anne
- Plage Caravelle
- Pointe Tarare
- Anse de la Gourde
- 24 23 — St-François
- 22 21
- Ilet du Gosier ↙
- Gosier
- Le Bas du Fort
- 17
- 18
- N1
- Lamentin
- Pointe-à-Pitre
- Petit-Bourg
- Goyave
- Ste-Marie
- 16 15 14
- Marie-Galante
- Borée
- Petite Anse ↙
- Capesterre
- Grand-Bourg
- Saint Louis
- 12
- 13
- Ste-Rose
- N2
- Pointe Allegre
- La Grand-Anse ↙
- 1
- Deshaies — 3
- 2
- Pointe Noire ↙
- Plage de la Caraïbe ↙
- Mahaut
- Plage de la Malendure ↙
- Bouillante
- Ilet à Goyave (Pigeon Island)
- Route de la Traversée
- D23
- **BASSE-TERRE**
- 4 5
- N2
- **PARC NATUREL DE GUADELOUPE**
- La Soufrière ▲
- Matouba
- St-Claude
- 6
- D6
- 7
- 8
- Bananier
- Trois Rivières
- Capesterre
- N1
- Vieux Habitants
- Basse-Terre
- Vieux Fort
- Iles des Saintes
- Terre-de-Haut
- Anse Crawen ↙
- 9 10 11
- Terre-de-Bas

Scale:
- 0 — 10 Miles
- 0 — 10 Kilometers
- N (compass)

BY TAXI You'll find taxis when you arrive at the airport, but no limousines or buses. From 9pm until 7am, cabbies are legally entitled to charge you 40% more. Some, but not all, taxis in Guadeloupe have meters, although the driver will either activate them or not, depending on a complicated set of parameters that depend on the time of day, your destination, and his or her whim, even though fares are technically regulated by the French government. If the taxi you're about to enter doesn't have a working meter, always agree on a price before getting in. Approximate fares are 15.20€ to 21.30€ (US$13.55–US$19) from the airport to the hotels of Gosier; or about 12.15€ (US$10.85) from the airport to anywhere within Pointe-à-Pitre. Radio taxis can be contacted throughout Guadeloupe by calling **C.D.L. Taxi** at ⓒ **590/20-74-74** or **Taxi Leader** at ⓒ **590/82-26-26.** It's possible, but very expensive, to sightsee by taxi. Usually, the concierge at your hotel will help you make arrangements. Fares are usually negotiated at the rate of around 121.60€ (US$108.60) for a 7-hour day for up to 4 passengers.

BY BUS Buses link almost every hamlet to Pointe-à-Pitre. However, you may need to know some French to use the system. From Pointe-à-Pitre, you can catch one of these jitney vans, either at the Gare Routière de Bergevin if you're going anywhere in Basse-Terre; to the Gare Routière de Mortenol if the northern half of Grande-Terre is your destination, or the *prolongement* (extension) of the Marché de la Darse if the southern end of Grande-Terre is your destination. Infrequent and somewhat erratic service is available daily from 5:30am to 7:30pm. The bus fare from the airport to the Pointe-à-Pitre terminal on rue Peynier is 1.20€ (US$1.10). Many visitors find it easier, especially when they first arrive on Guadeloupe, to take a taxi. Taxi fare from the airport to the center of Pointe-à-Pitre costs 7.60€ (US$6.80).

 FAST FACTS: **Guadeloupe**

Banking Hours Banks on Guadeloupe are usually open Monday through Friday from 9am to 3pm. There are about a dozen banks in Pointe-à-Pitre, most with ATMs (they're called *distributeurs des billets*).

Currency Because the territory of Guadeloupe falls under the same monetary system as mainland France, the island fell under the euro umbrella in January of 2002, abandoning the French franc and adopting the euro (€) as its mode of exchange. Just before you leave home, you can check the current exchange rate on the Web at **www.x-rates.com**. Banks give much better exchange rates than hotels.

Customs Items for personal use, such as tobacco, cameras, and film, are admitted without formalities or tax if not in excessive quantity.

Documents U.S., British, or Canadian residents need a passport, plus a return or ongoing plane ticket.

Electricity The local electricity is 220-volt AC (50 cycles), which means that U.S.-made appliances will need a transformer and an adapter. Some of the big resorts lend these to guests, but don't count on it.

Emergencies Call the **police** at ⓒ **17.** To report a **fire** or summon an **ambulance,** dial ⓒ **18.**

Hospitals There are 5 modern hospitals on Guadeloupe, plus 23 clinics. Hotels and the Guadeloupe tourist office can assist in locating English-speaking doctors. There's a 24-hour emergency room at the **Centre Hôpitalier Universitaire de Pointe-à-Pitre,** Abymes (© 590/89-10-10).

Language The official language is French; Creole is the unofficial second language. English is spoken only in the major tourist centers, rarely in the countryside.

Liquor Laws Liquor is sold in grocery and liquor stores on any day of the week. It's legal to have an open container, though the authorities are very strict about any littering, disorderly behavior, and drunk driving.

Pharmacies The pharmacies carry French medicines, and most over-the-counter U.S. drugs have French equivalents. Prescribed medicines can be purchased if you have the prescription with you. At least one drugstore is always open; the tourist office can tell you what pharmacies are open at what time.

Police In an emergency, call © **17.** Otherwise, call © **590/82-99-86.**

Safety Guadeloupe is relatively free of serious crime. But don't go wandering alone at night on the streets of Pointe-à-Pitre; by nightfall they are relatively deserted and might be dangerous. Purse-snatching by fast-riding motorcyclists has been reported, so exercise caution.

Taxes A departure tax, required on scheduled flights, is included in the airfares. Hotel taxes are included in all room rates.

Telephone To call Guadeloupe from the United States, dial **011** (the international access code), then **590** (the country code for Guadeloupe), then **590** again, and the rest of the local number, which will be six digits. If you want to call another island of the French Antilles, be aware that St. Barts, French St. Martin, and offshore dependencies of Guadeloupe such as Ile des Saints or La Désirade are all directly linked to the phone network of Guadeloupe. Consequently, no telephone prefix is required, and you can dial any of those islands simply by dialing the six-digit local phone number. But if you're on Guadeloupe and want to dial someone in Martinique, you'll have to punch in the prefix for Martinique (**0596**), followed by the six-digit local number. Unfortunately, you can't place collect calls to the United States from Guadeloupe, but you can use telephone calling cards, or else bill calls to your hotel room. To reach an **AT&T operator on Guadeloupe,** dial © **00011;** to use **AT&T Direct,** dial © **0800/99-00-11.** To reach **MCI,** dial © **0800/99-00-19,** and to reach **Sprint,** dial © **0800/99-00-87.** It looks like the island's phone technology will be improved soon.

Time Guadeloupe is on Atlantic standard time year-round, 1 hour ahead of eastern standard time (when it's 6am in New York, it's 7am on Guadeloupe). When daylight saving time is in effect in the U.S., clocks in New York and Guadeloupe show the same time.

Tipping Hotels usually add a 10% to 15% service charge. Restaurants always add a 15% service charge, and no additional tip is needed. Most taxi drivers who own their own cars do not expect a tip; if they've been especially helpful with your luggage, you might give them an additional 10%.

Water While on Guadeloupe, stick to bottled water only.

2 Pointe-à-Pitre

The port and chief city of Guadeloupe, Pointe-à-Pitre, lies on Grande-Terre. Unfortunately, it doesn't have the old-world charm of Fort-de-France on Martinique, and what beauty it does possess is often hidden behind closed doors.

Having been burned and rebuilt so many times, the port now lacks character. Modern apartments and condominiums form a high-rise backdrop over jerry-built shacks and industrial suburbs. The rather narrow streets are jammed during the day with a colorful crowd that creates a permanent traffic jam. However, at sunset the town becomes quiet again and almost deserted. The only charm left is around the waterfront, where you half expect to see Bogie sipping rum at a cafe table.

Most visitors just drop in to Pointe-à-Pitre for **shopping.** It's best to visit the town in the morning (you can easily cover it in half a day), taking in the waterfront and outdoor market (the latter is livelier in the early hours).

The town center is **place de la Victoire,** a park shaded by palm trees and poincianas. Here you'll see some old sandbox trees said to have been planted by Victor Hugues, the mulatto who organized a revolutionary army of both whites and blacks to establish a dictatorship. In this square he kept a guillotine busy, and the death-dealing instrument stood here (but not in use) until modern times.

With the recent completion of the **Centre St-John-Perse,** a $20 million 22.4€) project that had been on the drawing boards for many years, the waterfront of Pointe-à-Pitre has been transformed from a bastion of old warehouses and cruise-terminal buildings into an architectural complex comprising a hotel, 3 restaurants, 80 shops and boutiques, a bank, and the expanded headquarters of Guadeloupe's Port Authority. Named for Saint-John Perse, the 20th-century poet and Nobel Laureate who was born just a few blocks away, the center is designed in contemporary French Caribbean style, which blends with the traditional architecture of Pointe-à-Pitre. For brochures and maps, the **Guadeloupe tourist office** is just minutes away, at Square de la Banque 5 ((C) **590/82-09-30**).

ACCOMMODATIONS

Hôtel St-John Anchorage   This hotel rises four stories above the harbor front, near the quays. We recommend that you stay here only if you have business in town or need to be here for an early morning flight. The small rooms are clean, simple, and furnished with locally crafted mahogany pieces. Very few units have views over the sea. Shower-only bathrooms are small, with no frills. Once you check in, the laissez-faire staff will probably leave you alone until the end of your stay.

There's a simple coffee shop/cafe on street level. To reach a beach, you'll have to travel 2 miles (3km) to the east to Le Bas du Fort and the Gosier area (see below).

Centre Saint-John-Perse, quai de Croisières (at the harbor front), 97110 Pointe-à-Pitre, Guadeloupe, F.W.I. (C) **590/82-51-57.** Fax 590/82-52-61. www.saint-john-perse.com. 44 units. Year-round 76€–89.70€ (US$67.85–US$80.10) double. Rates include continental breakfast. AE, MC, V. **Amenities:** Coffee shop. *In room:* A/C, TV, safe.

DINING

Côté Jardin FRENCH/CREOLE   Because of its fine food and its sense of Gallic style, no one really cares that there isn't a water view. Surrounded by potted flowers and shrubs, with a view over palm trees and reproductions of paintings by Miró and Matisse, you'll dine in a red and green room with a hint of Provence. Menu items focus on fresh shellfish, many of them kept healthy and alive within aquariums that bubble away near the restaurant's entrance. Crayfish in spicy Creole sauce is our favorite, as are sweetbreads with morels in puff pastry. For a tasty treat, try grilled mahi-mahi served with teriyaki-flavored orange sauce.

La Marina, Pointe-à-Pitre. © 590/90-91-28. Reservations recommended. Fixed-price menus 28.80€–36€ (US$25.70–US$32.15). AE, MC, V. Mon–Fri noon–2:30pm; Mon–Sat 7:30–11pm.

Restaurant Sucré-Salé TRADITIONAL FRENCH   In the heart of Pointe-à-Pitre, adjacent to an Air France office and near several banks, this restaurant is always filled at lunchtime with dealmakers and office workers. The decorative theme revolves around jazz, with portraits of Louis Armstrong, Billie Holliday, and Miles Davis. A covered terrace overlooking the busy boulevard serves as an animated singles bar every evening after work. The charming Marius Pheron, the Guadeloupe-born owner who did an 18-year stint in Paris, offers fillets of snapper served with pommes soufflés and black pepper, meal-sized salads, entrecôte steaks, and an impressive medley of grilled fish. The restaurant hosts a jazz concert 1 evening a month; posters announcing the event appear all over town.

Bd. Légitimus. © 590/21-22-55. Reservations recommended. Main courses 9.90€–19.75€ (US$8.80–US$17.65). MC, V. Mon–Sat noon–3pm; Tues–Sat 7–9:30pm.

SHOPPING

We suggest that you skip a shopping tour of Pointe-à-Pitre if you're going to Fort-de-France on Martinique, as you'll find far more merchandise there, and perhaps friendlier service. If you're not, however, we recommend the following shops, some of which line rue Frébault.

Your best buys will be anything French—perfumes from Chanel, silk scarves from Hermès, cosmetics from Dior, crystal from Lalique and Baccarat. Though they're expensive, we've found some of these items discounted (but not often) as much as 30% below U.S. or Canadian prices. Most shops will accept U.S. dollars, and they'll give these discounts only for purchases made by traveler's check. (If you pay with a traveler's check instead of a credit card, the shop doesn't have to pay a fee to the credit card company and passes the discount on to you.) Purchases are duty free if brought directly from store to plane. In addition to the places below, there are also duty-free shops at **Raizet Airport** (© 590/21-14-66) selling liquor, rums, perfumes, crystal, and cigarettes.

Most shops open at 8:30am, close at 1pm, and then reopen between 3 and 5:30pm. They're closed on Saturday afternoon, Sunday, and holidays. When the cruise ships are in port, many eager shopkeepers stay open longer and on weekends.

One of the best places to buy French perfumes, at prices often lower than those charged in Paris, is **Phoenicia,** 8 rue Frébault (© 590/83-50-36), which has a good selection of imported cosmetics. U.S. traveler's checks will get you further discounts.

Other leading perfume shops include **Au Bonheur des Dames,** 49 rue Frébault (© 590/82-00-30), which is also known for its skin-care products.

If you're adventurous, you may want to seek out some native goods in little shops along the back streets of Pointe-à-Pitre. Collector's items are the straw hats or *salacos* made in Les Saintes islands, usually created from split bamboo. Native **doudou dolls** are also popular gift items.

Open-air stalls surround the **covered market** (Marché Couvert) at the corner of rue Frébault and rue Peynier. Here you can discover the many fruits,

Moments The Essence of Guadeloupe

At some point as you stroll through the market, order a glass of rum from one of the local vendors, and ask for *rhum agricole,* a pure form of the drink that's fermented from sugarcane juice. Savvy locals claim that the rum (whose brand name is Rhum Damoiseau) is the only kind you can drink without a hangover the next morning.

spices, and vegetables that are fun to look at as well as to taste. In madras turbans, local Creole women make deals over their strings of fire-red pimientos. The bright fabrics they wear compete with the rich colors of oranges, papayas, bananas, mangos, and pineapples. Best times to visit are Monday to Saturday 8am to noon.

3 Le Bas du Fort

Just 2 miles (3km) east of Pointe-à-Pitre is the tourist area of Le Bas du Fort, near Gosier. This is the best place to stay if you'd like to be near (but not in) the capital and if you'd like a location near the international airport. Although it has some good sandy beaches, there are far better ones further out from the center. One drawback is that the area is rather built up and you may not find the tranquility here you'll enjoy in other parts of Guadeloupe.

Aquarium de la Guadeloupe, place Créole, Marina Bas-du-Fort (© **590/ 90-92-38**), is the largest and most modern aquarium in the Caribbean. Just off the highway near Bas-du-Fort Marina, the aquarium is home to tropical fish, coral, underwater plants, huge sharks, and other sea creatures. Hours are daily from 9am to 7pm. Admission is 6.40€ (US$5.70) for adults, 3.50€ (US$3.10) for children age 6 to 12; free for kids age 5 and under.

ACCOMMODATIONS

Hôtel Marissol ✪ This secluded bungalow colony of two- and three-story structures, run by the French Novotel chain, sits near the entrance to the tourist complex of Bas du Fort on a small white-sand beach. It is operated in conjunction with the Fleur d'Epée (see below), and all the dining and amenities are shared. We prefer the more commodious accommodations at the Marissol to those at Fleur d'Epée. Set a soothing distance back from the main road, the Marissol occupies the grounds between a secondary route and the shoreline. In 2001, its summery bedrooms underwent a long-overdue renovation, bringing them up to spiffy, albeit simple, standards of comfort. The well-maintained rooms open onto views of the grounds or the water. The furnishings are simple but comfortable, the floors are tiled, and all units have either twin or double beds, each with a shower-only, tiled bathroom.

Le Bas du Fort, 97190 Gosier, Guadeloupe, F.W.I. © **800/221-4542** in the U.S., or 590/90-84-44. Fax 590/90-83-32. www.antilles-info-tourisme.com/guadeloupe/accor-gb.htm. 195 units. Winter 183€ (US$163.40) double. Off-season 134€ (US$119.65) double. Rates include continental breakfast. AE, DC, MC, V. **Amenities:** 2 restaurants, 2 bars; disco; casino; 2 pools; tennis court; fitness center; boating, snorkeling; salon; massage; babysitting; laundry. *In room:* A/C, TV, hair dryer, safe.

Novotel Fleur d'Epée ✪ This is Guadeloupe's most prominent branch of the successful French hotel chain (which also owns the Marissol, above). Even though it has a rather laid-back staff and is architecturally undistinguished, the three-story hotel is still popular with young people from France who turn up here in bikini-clad droves. It stands beside a pair of crescent-shaped bays with small white-sand beaches shaded by palms and sea-grape trees. Each small guest room is well-kept, modern, and tiled, with a simple motel-style floor plan and a terrace or balcony. The compact bathrooms have combination shower/tubs.

Bas-du-Fort Coralia, Le Bas du Fort, 97190 Gosier, Guadeloupe, F.W.I. *©* **800/221-4542** in the U.S., or 590/90-40-00. Fax 590/90-99-07. www.novotel.com. 190 units. Winter 183€ (US$163.40) double. Off-season 134€ (US$119.65) double. AE, DC, MC, V. **Amenities:** Facilities shared with Hotel Marissol (see above). *In room:* A/C, TV, hair dryer, safe.

DINING

Rosini *⚔* NORTHERN ITALIAN   This is the best Italian restaurant in the French West Indies, thanks to a sophisticated father-in-law/son-in-law team of Venice-born Luciano Rosini and Christophe Giraud, from Provence. It's contained within two air-conditioned dining rooms on the ground floor of an upscale condo complex across from the Novotel in Bas-du-Fort. Recorded opera music sets the mood for succulent versions of tournedos layered with foie gras, osso buco, and freshwater prawns served *diavolo* style in a tomato, garlic, and parsley sauce with freshly made fettuccine. Ravioli comes stuffed either with veal and herbs or with lobster. At least five types of pizza are also available for the kids. English is readily understood here.

La Porte des Caraïbes, Bas-du-Fort. *©* **590/90-87-81.** Reservations recommended. Main courses 9.10€–30.40€ (US$8.15–US$27.15). AE, DC, MC, V. Daily noon–2:30pm and 6:30–11pm.

4 Gosier

Gosier is where some of the best beachfront in Guadeloupe begins, and it's become one of the island's major resort centers, since it has nearly 5 miles (8km) of sandy but narrow beach, stretching east from Pointe-à-Pitre. All the hotels below are in easy proximity to the sands. We like the funky charm of the town, which evokes a little resort along the French Riviera. Unlike many parts of the Caribbean, this area attracts mainly French visitors, so you'll feel like you're on a Mediterranean holiday. Gosier also has some of the island's best dining and nightlife, plus a casino.

For an excursion, you can climb in 15 minutes to the semi-ruined heights of **Fort Fleur-d'Epée,** dating from the 18th century. Its dungeons and battlements are testaments to the ferocious fighting between the French and British armies in 1794. The ruins command the crown of a hill, which affords good views over the bay of Pointe-à-Pitre. If the visibility is good, you can see the neighboring offshore islands of Marie-Galante and Iles des Saintes.

ACCOMMODATIONS

La Creole Beach Hôtel *⚔* *(Kids)*   This is the largest resort on Guadeloupe, but because of the way it's divided into four distinct sections, you'll get a sense of isolation and privacy. It's located alongside two beaches within a lush setting of lawns, trees, hibiscus, and bougainvillea, and it has a strong French Creole flavor.

The most upscale of the units is Les Palmes, a section completed in 2002 with the best furnishings and the most spacious accommodations, followed by Le Creole, a three-story building with verandas influenced by French colonial architecture. Slightly less desirable is Le Mahogany, a comfortable compound with oceanfront rooms (most without kitchens). The most basic, Le Yucca, houses the family units with kitchens. Most rooms are spacious and contain two queen-size beds. All units contain a private bathroom, mainly with shower (one-fourth of them feature a shower/tub combination).

La Route des Epices serves excellent local specials and an international cuisine. Le Zawag lies just on the rocks by the sea, offering fresh fish and seafood.

Pointe de la Verdure, B.P. 61, 97190 Gosier, Guadeloupe, F.W.I. (C) 590/90-46-46. Fax 590/90-46-66. www.creole-beach.gp. 384 units. Winter 228€–282€ (US$203.60–US$251.85) double. Off-season 130€–172€ (US$116.10–US$153.60) double. Year-round 190€–343€ (US$169.65–US$306.30) duplex for 1–4. Children under age 12 stay free in parent's room. Rates include continental breakfast. AE, DC, MC, V. **Amenities:** 2 restaurants, bar; pool; tennis court; scuba diving, water-skiing, windsurfing, sailboat rentals, deep-sea fishing; room service (breakfast only); babysitting; laundry/dry cleaning. *In room:* A/C, TV, fax, kitchenette, minibar, fridge, coffeemaker.

Sofitel Auberge de la Vieille Tour ★ Though it's a Sofitel, this place grew from a family inn that was originally built around the shadow of an old sugar mill. Set on a 5-acre (20-hectare) bluff, the property encompasses a small private beach.

The older guest rooms are relatively short on charm. The better maintained units are within La Résidence, a series of town house–style accommodations set near the pool. Their desirability is rivaled only by units referred to as "luxury-class," set close to the water near the beach. Rooms have comfortable furnishings and compact bathrooms with shower stalls or shower/tub combinations.

The restaurants La Vieille Tour and Le Zagaya serve excellent French and Creole food, respectively, in relatively elegant, semiformal settings. L'Ajoupa is a grill-style indoor-outdoor affair.

Montauban, 97190 Gosier, Guadeloupe, F.W.I. (C) 800/221-4542 in the U.S., or 590/84-23-23. Fax 590/84-33-43. www.sofitel.com. 180 units. Winter 320€–400€ (US$285.75–US$357.20) double; 480€ (US$428.65) minisuite. Off-season 167€–220€ (US$149.15–US$196.45) double; 267€ (US$238.45) minisuite. Rates include continental breakfast. AE, MC, V. **Amenities:** 3 restaurants, 2 bars; pool; tennis court; watersports; laundry. *In room:* A/C, TV, minibar, hair dryer, safe.

DINING

Le Bananier CREOLE Locals flock to this restaurant where some of the most imaginative dishes in the Creole repertoire are handled with finesse and charm. Within an air-conditioned, 50-year-old clapboard-sided cottage, you'll enjoy old-fashioned staples, such as stuffed crab backs and *accras* (beignets) of codfish. Much more appealing, however, are dishes like filet mignon served with pulverized blood sausage, port wine, and a reduction of crayfish bisque; a *clafoutis* (gratinated medley) of shellfish; and a *tourtière d'oeufs aux crabes* (an omelette with breaded and baked crabmeat, fresh tomatoes, and reduction of callaloo leaves). The menu's most appealing dessert is banana flambéed in *Schrubb*, an obscure island liqueur made from fermented orange peels and prized by the owners' grandparents.

Rue Principale de Gosier, Montauban. (C) 590/84-34-85. Reservations recommended. Main courses 12.15€–27.65€ (US$10.85–US$24.70). AE, DC, MC, V. Tues–Sun noon–2:30pm and 7–10:30pm.

5 Ste-Anne

About 9 miles (14km) east of Gosier, little Ste-Anne is a sugar town and a resort offering many fine beaches and lodgings. In many ways, it's the most charming village of Guadeloupe, with its pastel-colored town hall, its church, and its principal square, **Place de la Victoire,** where a statue of Schoelcher commemorates the abolition of slavery in 1848.

All the rainbow colors of the Caribbean are for sale at **La Case à Soie** in Ste-Anne ((C) 590/88-11-31), known for its flamboyantly colored scarves and its flowing silk dresses.

ACCOMMODATIONS & DINING

Club Med La Caravelle ⭐   This chain resort, covering 45 acres (18 hectares) along a peninsula dotted with palm trees, opens onto one of the finest beaches in the French West Indies. The guest rooms tend to be small, but have good beds. (All but 10 units have twin beds; those 10 exceptions have queen-size beds.) Tiled and shower-only bathrooms are compact and short on amenities. The building known as Marie-Galante contains the resort's largest and most comfortable rooms (each with a terrace or veranda), costing about 20% more than the smaller, bland standard rooms. Children age 4 and over are welcome, but special supervision and "child-amusing" programs are in place only at specific times of the year, usually during school vacations.

The meals here are nothing if not generous. The breakfast and lunch buffet tables groan with French, continental, and Creole food. Dinner is served in the main dining room or in the candlelit, more romantic annex restaurant beside the sea. At the weekly folklore night, the Guadeloupe folklore ballet, Ballets Guadeloupeans, performs.

97180 Ste-Anne, Guadeloupe, F.W.I. ⓒ 800/CLUB-MED in the U.S., or 590/85-49-50. Fax 590/85-49-70. www.clubmed.com. 329 units. Nov–Apr 1,672€–2,432€ (US$1,493.05–US$2171.70) weekly; May–Oct 1,292€–1,824€ (US$1,153.70–US$1,628.75) weekly. Rates are per person based on double occupancy. Rates are all-inclusive. Children age 4–12 are charged 75% of the adult rate. Single supplement 25%–40% above the per person double rate. AE, MC, V. No children under age 4. **Amenities:** 2 restaurants, pub, night club; 6 tennis courts; aerobics; archery; volleyball; basketball; windsurfing; children's programs; laundry. *In room:* A/C, TV, hair dryer, safe.

Hôtel La Toubana ⭐   Built on 4 acres (2 hectares) of sloping land close to the beach (a 5-min. walk on a path carved into the cliff side), La Toubana is centered around a low-lying stone building on a rocky cliff overlooking the bay and Ste-Anne Beach. Many guests come here just for the view, which on a clear day encompasses Marie-Galante, Dominica, La Désirade, and the Iles des Saintes, but you'll quickly learn that there's far more to this charming place than just a panorama. The red-roofed bungalows lie scattered among the tropical shrubs along the adjacent hillsides (*toubana* means "small house" in Arawak); there are 20 garden units and 12 more upscale ocean-view units. Each has a kitchenette, comfortable French furnishings, a terrace, a rather compact shower/tub

---

Moments   **Begin the Beguine**

The folkloric dance troupe **Ballets Guadeloupeans** makes frequent appearances at the big hotels, whirling and moving to the rhythms of island music in colorful costumes and well-choreographed routines. Some resorts, including the Club Med La Caravelle, use their weekly visit to set the theme for the evening, serving up a banquet of traditional island dishes to accompany the dance, music, and costumes.

Ask at your hotel where the Ballets Guadeloupeans will be appearing during your stay, as their schedule tends to vary as they tour the island. You can catch them as they rotate through the hotels Arawak, Salako, L'Auberge de le Vieille Tour, and Fleur d'Epée Novotel, as well as the Club Med La Caravelle. On the night of any of these performances, you can order a drink at the bar and catch the show, or join in the hotel buffet for a flat price. Buffets usually start around 8pm, with the show beginning at 8:30pm. The troupe also performs on some cruise ships.

combination bathroom, and either two twin beds or one king-size bed. Cots for kids are available on request.

Le Baobab offers both indoor and alfresco dining of fine quality in a site overlooking the pool. It serves the best lobster on the island. The beachfront bar serves tropical drinks and occasionally hosts live entertainment.

Durivage (B.P. 63), 97180 Ste-Anne, Guadeloupe, F.W.I. ✆ **590/88-25-57**. Fax 590/88-38-90. www. toubana.gp. 32 units. Winter 176€–209.15€ (US$157.20–US$186.75) double. Off-season 111.85€–131.95€ (US$99.90–US$117.80) double. Rates include American breakfast. AE, MC, V. **Amenities:** Restaurant; bar; pool; tennis court; snorkeling; scooters; deep-sea fishing; watersports; babysitting; laundry. *In room:* A/C, hair dryer.

6 St-François 🖈

Continuing east from Ste-Anne, you'll notice many old round towers named for Father Labat, the Dominican founder of the sugarcane industry. These towers were once used as mills to grind the cane. St-François, 25 miles (40km) east of Pointe-à-Pitre, used to be a sleepy fishing village, but it's been discovered, and is known for its Creole restaurants. Then Air France discovered it and opened a Méridien hotel with a casino. That was followed by the promotional activities of J. F. Rozan, a native who invested heavily to make St-François a jet-set resort. Now the once sleepy village has first-class accommodations, as well as an airport available to private jets, a golf course, and a marina, where there's a casino (see "Guadeloupe After Dark," near the end of the chapter).

Today St-François is the golfing center of the island, and it has some good beaches. It is the site of some of the island's finest inns and hotels as well.

ACCOMMODATIONS

Domaine Hôtelier de l'Anse des Rochers   The largest hotel on Guadeloupe, opened in 1995, sprawls across 19 acres (8 hectares) of sloping land in St-François, with a nice sandy beach. (Note that it's quite a hike to the beach.) Accommodations are housed in either a half-dozen multileveled, hotel-style buildings, each of which contains 39 units, or 32 party-colored bungalows (4 units per bungalow). The decor is airy, summery, and uncluttered. Bedrooms are fairly routine, most often small, each with a tiled, shower-only bathroom. Despite the size of the resort, guests still feel a sense of isolation and intimacy, thanks to the way the place is configured into smaller blocks. Expect lots of young families with children, honeymooners, and European package-tour groups.

Domaine de l'Anse des Rochers, 97118 St-François, Guadeloupe, F.W.I. ✆ **590/93-90-00**. Fax 590/93-91-00. www.anse-des-rochers.com. 356 units. Winter 168€–208€ (US$150–US$185.75) double; 192€–238€ (US$171.45–US$212.55) villa. Off-season 114€–168€ (US$101.80–US$150) double; 130€–192€ (US$116.10–US$171.45) villa. AE, MC, V. **Amenities:** 3 restaurants; bar; live entertainment; pool; 2 tennis courts; watersports; beach volleyball; archery; car rental. *In room:* A/C, TV, kitchenette with minibar, hair dryer in some, safe.

La Cocoteraie 🖈🖈   Beside its sibling, Le Meridien St-François, this is a plush, suites-only resort, the island's finest choice for a luxury holiday. It opens onto a lagoon with two small white sandy private beaches where you can wear your most provocative swimwear. The hotel hides behind a colonial plantation style facade, flanked by a series of buildings, also in the colonial style. Twenty of the units are more desirable because they open right onto the beach. Across from the hotel lies the Robert Trent Jones golf course. Rooms are luxuriously decorated evocative of a rich Asian décor with sisal matting covering tile floors, Japanese style wood cabinets, and large Hermès octagonal bathtubs in the bow windows. Each unit comes with a spacious patio or a balcony overlooking the water or else the largest hotel pool on Guadeloupe. Some of the accommodations are equipped with a duo of shower-only baths; others have tub and shower combination.

Av. De l'Europe, St-François 97118. © 800/322-2223 or 590/88-79-81. Fax 590/88-78-33. www.le meridien.com. 50 suites. Winter 419€–960€ (US$374.15–US$857.30) double. Off-season 229€–427€ (US$204.50–US$381.30) double. AE, DC, MC, V. Closed Aug 24–Oct 23. **Amenities:** Restaurant, bar; 2 tennis courts; fitness center; car rental room service; babysitting. *In room:* A/C, TV, minibar, hair dryer, safe.

La Plantation Ste-Marthe 🏵🏵   Built in 1992 on the site of a 19th-century sugar plantation, this was one of Guadeloupe's finest major hotels. Although the manor house that once stood on the premises is now in ruins, the stables, the ruined rum distillery, and the molasses factory remain, adding character to the property. It lies 3 miles (5km) from the nearest good beach, Plage des Raisins Clairs. Monday to Friday from 9am to 5pm, the hotel runs a free shuttle van to and from this beach; on weekends, you'll have to walk, drive yourself, take a taxi, or bike.

Accommodations are in four three-story structures, whose architecture was inspired by the Creole buildings of Louisiana. Each unit has lots of exposed wood and boldly patterned tiles, plus a large terrace or balcony that many visitors end up using as an extension of their living quarters. The duplex suites feature a sleeping loft that may remind you of a big-city apartment, and the furnishings are modernized versions of antique French designs, using lots of woven cane. Most units are spacious, with king-size beds, plus small tiled bathrooms with shower/tub combinations. La Vallée d'Or serves all-you-can-eat buffets at night.

97118 St-François, Guadeloupe, F.W.I. © 590/93-11-11. Fax 590/93-11-48. 120 units. Winter 164.15€ (US$146.60) double; 182.40€ (US$162.90) duplex suite for 2. Off-season 144.40€ (US$128.95) double; 167.20€ (US$149.30) duplex suite for 2. Rates include buffet breakfast. AE, MC, V. Closed Nov–mid-Dec. **Amenities:** Restaurant, bar; pool; 2 tennis courts; horseback riding; watersports; minivan to beach; babysitting. *In room:* A/C, TV, minibar in some.

Le Méridien St-François 🏵   At five stories, this is one of the tallest buildings in the area. It stands on one of the best beaches on Guadeloupe on 150 acres (60 hectares) of land at the most easterly tip of the island, a 10-minute walk from the village of St-François. This is a competent workhorse of a hotel, albeit without the glamour and architectural flair of its sibling hotel, La Cocoteraie (see above). Rooms overlook the sea or the Robert Trent Jones, Sr.-designed golf course. Each contains many amenities and modern-style furnishings with Creole overtones. Most of the medium-size bedrooms contain twin beds, and all units are furnished comfortably. Each unit has a small but tidily maintained bathroom with a shower/tub combination. Food at the restaurants is only average.

97118 St-François, Guadeloupe, F.W.I. © 800/543-4300 in the U.S., or 590/48-05-00. Fax 590/88-40-71. www.intel-media.im-caraibes. 263 units. Winter 215€–395€ (US$192–US$352.75) double; 320€–395€ (US$285.75–US$352.75) suite. Off-season 190€–235€ (US$169.65–US$209.85) double, 265€–340€ (US$236.65–US$303.60) suite. AE, DC, MC, V. **Amenities:** 2 restaurants, 2 bars; pool; 2 tennis courts; windsurfers; golf available at course next door; nearby marina; access to additional watersports; room service (breakfast only); massage; babysitting; laundry. *In room:* A/C, TV, fridge, hair dryer.

DINING

Les Oiseaux 🏵 FRENCH/CREOLE   This place feels like a Provençal farmhouse. It offers views over the sea and the island of Marie-Galante. The walled-in front garden frames a stone-sided, low-slung building that emits an aroma of southern French and Antillean cuisine worth the detour. This is the domain of Frederick Rollé. They serve delectable dishes, each homemade, including Creole-style beef, cassoulet of seafood, and the island's finest sea urchins. Try also the marmite Robinson, inspired by Robinson Crusoe, a tasty fondue of fish and vegetables that you cook for yourself in a combination of bubbling coconut and corn oil. The Sunday bunch here is one of the best on island.

Anse des Rochers, 3½ miles (6km) west of St-François. ⑦ 590/88-56-92. Reservations recommended. Main courses 15.95€–31.90€ (US$14.25–US$28.50). MC, V. Sun noon–2:30pm, Tues–Sat 7–9:30pm. Closed Sept.

7 Pointe des Châteaux

Seven miles (11km) east of St-François is the rocky headland of Pointe des Châteaux, the easternmost tip of Grand-Terre, where the Atlantic meets the Caribbean. Here, where crashing waves sound around you, you'll see a cliff sculpted by the sea into dramatic castle-like formations, the erosion typical of France's Brittany coast. The view from here is panoramic. At the top is a cross erected in the 19th century.

You might want to walk to **Pointe des Colibris,** the extreme end of Guadeloupe. From here you'll have a view of the northeastern sector of the island, and to the east a look at La Désirade, another island that has the appearance of a huge vessel anchored far away (see the section "Side Trips from Guadeloupe," later in this chapter).

Pointe des Châteaux has miles of coved white-sand beaches. Most of these are safe for swimming, except at the point where the waves of the turbulent Atlantic encounter the tranquil Caribbean Sea, churning up the waters. There's a nudist enclave at **Pointe Tarare.**

Since there are no hotels here, you can come just for the day, to enjoy the beaches.

DINING

Iguane Café ★ (Finds) FRENCH This bistro/cafe is one of the best dining choices on the island, the equal of such stellar choices as Château de Feuilles. Owners Marie and Sylvan Serrouart offer a creative cuisine at a point on the road connecting St. François with Pointe du Châteaux. With a colorful West Indian decor and an open-air kitchen, the cafe prints menus in English. Don't come here in a rush, as food is cooked to order, and that takes time. Mellow out at the bar, with its selection of nearly two-dozen rum punches, including one flavored with cinnamon. A novelty drink comes from a large jar of rum, which contains several hibiscus flowers floating in it. On the creative and varied menu, begin with a delectable goat's cheese appetizer, battered in a crust with zesty Creole spices. You might also opt for the goose liver pâté. We always gravitate to the fresh fish of the day, perhaps snapper, aromatically cooked in a puff pastry. We avoid the rabbit or goat dishes, which are often overcooked and a bit tough. The steamed fish, flavored with five spices, is a treat, however. For dessert? The hibiscus beignets perfumed with bergamot are even better than those dear old mumsy used to make. As for the service? Order another rum punch or two and be patient.

Route de la Pointe des Châteaux, St. François. ⑦ 590/88-61-37. Reservations recommended. Main courses 18.25€–28.90€ (US$16.30–US$25.80). AE, MC. Wed–Mon 7:30–10:30pm, Sun 12:30–2:30pm. Closed Sept.

A STOP IN LE MOULE

To go back to Pointe-à-Pitre from Pointe des Châteaux, you can use an alternative route, the N5 from St-François. After a 9-mile (14km) drive, you'll reach the village of **Le Moule,** which was founded at the end of the 17th century and known long before Pointe-à-Pitre. It used to be a major shipping port for sugar. Now a tiny coastal fishing village, it never regained its importance after it was devastated in the hurricane of 1928, like so many other villages of Grand-Terre. Because it offers more than 10 miles (16km) of crescent-shaped beach, it's developing as a destination.

Specialties of this Guadeloupean village are *palourdes,* the clams that thrive in the semi-salty mouths of freshwater rivers. Known for being more tender and less rubbery than saltwater clams, they often, even when fresh, have a distinct sulfur taste not unlike that of over-poached eggs. Local gastronomes prepare them with saffron and aged rum or cognac.

Three miles (5km) from Le Moule, heading toward Campêche, the **Edgar Clerc Archaeological Museum La Rosette,** Parc de la Rosette (© **590/23-57-57**), shows a collection of both Carib and Arawak artifacts gathered from various islands of the Lesser Antilles. Hours are Tuesday to Sunday from 9am to noon and 2 to 5pm. Admission is 1.50€ (US$1.35), .75€ (US70¢); students, free for those under age 12.

To return to Pointe-à-Pitre, we suggest that you use route D3 toward Abymes. The road winds around as you plunge deeply into Grand-Terre. As a curiosity, about halfway along the way a road is signposted to **Jabrun du Nord** and **Jabrun du Sud.** These two villages are inhabited by Caucasians with blond hair, said to be survivors of aristocrats slaughtered during the Revolution. Those members of their families who escaped found safety by hiding out in Les Grands Fonds. The most important family here is named Matignon, and they gave their name to the colony known as "les Blancs Matignon." These citizens are said to be related to Prince Rainier of Monaco. Pointe-à-Pitre lies only 10 miles (16km) from Les Grand Fonds.

8 The North Coast of Grande-Terre 🖈🖈

From Pointe-à-Pitre, head northeast toward Abymes, passing next through Morne à l'Eau; you'll reach the small but not insignificant settlement of **Petit Canal** after 13 miles (21km). This is Guadeloupe's sugarcane country, and a sweet smell fills the air.

PORT LOUIS

Continuing northwest along the coast from Petit Canal, you come to Port Louis, well known for its beautiful beach, **Anse du Souffleur,** which lacks facilities. We like it best in spring, when the brilliant white sand is effectively shown off against the flaming red poinciana. During the week, the beach is an especially quiet spot. The little port town has some good restaurants.

DINING

Le Poisson d'Or 🖈 *Finds* CREOLE   You enter this white-sided Antillean house by walking down a narrow corridor and emerging into a rustic dining room lined with varnished pine. Despite the simple setting, the food is well prepared and satisfying. Don't even think of coming here at night without an advance reservation—you might find the place locked up and empty. Try the stuffed crabs or beef bouillon, topped off by coconut ice cream, which is homemade and tastes it. The place is a fine choice for an experience with Creole cuisine, complemented by a bottle of good wine.

2 rue Sadi-Carnot, Port Louis. C **590/22-88-75.** Reservations required. Main courses 9.90€–12.15€ (US$8.80–US$10.85); fixed-price menu 15.20€–18.25€ (US$13.55–US$16.30). AE, MC, V. Daily 8am–4pm and 7–9pm. Closed 3 weeks in Sept. Drive northwest from Petit-Canal along the coastal road.

ANSE-BERTRAND

About 5 miles (8km) from Port Louis is Anse-Bertrand, the northernmost village of Guadeloupe. What is now a fishing village was the last refuge of the Carib tribes, and a reserve was once created here. Everything now, however, is sleepy.

DINING

Le Château de Feuilles ★★ FRENCH/CARIBBEAN   Set inland from the sea, amid 8 rolling acres (3 hectares) of greenery and blossoming flowers, this hideaway is owned and run by a Norman-born couple, Jean-Pierre and Martine Dubost, who moved here to escape "civilization." To reach their place, which is 9 miles (14km) from Le Moule, near the eastern tip of Grande-Terre, you drive past the ruins of La Mahaudière, an 18th-century sugar mill. A gifted chef, who makes maximum use of local ingredients, Monsieur Dubost prepares pâté of warm sea urchins, sautéed conch with Creole sauce, a cassoulet of crayfish, and a traditional version of magret of duckling with fresh sugarcane. One unusual taste sensation is a *pavé of tazar* (a local fish) served with fresh garlic sauce. We've had some of our finest meals on Guadeloupe at this restaurant.

Campêche, Anse-Bertrand. C **590/22-30-30.** Reservations required, especially in summer (when meals are prepared only in anticipation of your arrival). Main courses 14.60€–20.50€ (US$13.05–US$18.30). V. Winter Tues–Sun 11am–4pm; at night, at least 10 diners must reserve before they will open. Closed Sept.

CONTINUING AROUND THE NORTHERN TIP

From Anse-Bertrand, you can drive along a gravel road heading for **Pointe de la Grande Vigie,** the northernmost tip of the island, which you'll reach after 4 miles (6km) of what we hope will be cautious driving. Park your car and walk carefully along a narrow lane that will bring you to the northernmost rock of Guadeloupe. The view of the sweeping Atlantic from the top of rocky cliffs is remarkable—you stand about 280 feet (84m) above the sea.

Afterward, a 4-mile (6km) drive south on a good road will bring you to the **Porte d'Enfer** or "gateway to hell," where the sea rushes violently against two narrow cliffs.

After this awesome experience in the remote part of the island, you can head back, going either to **Morne à l'Eau** or **Le Moule** before connecting to the road taking you back to Pointe-à-Pitre.

9 Around Basse-Terre ★★★

Leaving Pointe-à-Pitre by Route N1, you can explore the western coast and the island of Basse-Terre. Here you'll find views as panoramic as those along the corniche along the French Riviera, but without the heavy traffic and crowds. After 1½ miles (2km) you cross the Rivière Salée at Pont de la Gabarre. This narrow strait separates the two islands that form Guadeloupe. For the next 4 miles (6km) the road runs straight through sugarcane fields.

At the sign, on a main crossing, turn right on Route N2 toward **Baie Mahault.** (Don't confuse this with the town of Mahault on Basse-Terre's westernmost coast.) Head northwest to **Lamentin,** a village settled by *corsairs* (pirates) at the beginning of the 18th century. Scattered about are some colonial mansions, but neither of these villages merit a stopover.

STE-ROSE

From Lamentin, you can drive for 6½ miles (10km) to Ste-Rose, where you'll find several good **beaches.** On your left, a small road leads in a few minutes to **Sofaia,** from which you'll have a panoramic view over the coast and forest preserve. You can easily skip this, however, if you're rushed for time.

Your main reason to stop here is La Sucrerie du Comté, one of the island's most atmospheric inns, set on the ruins of a sugar factory with gardens. The nearest beach is only a 10-minute stroll away. You might also stop in Ste-Rose for lunch, as it boasts one of Basse-Terre's best restaurants, Restaurant Clara (see below).

ACCOMMODATIONS

La Sucrerie du Comté   Although you'll see the ruins of a 19th-century sugar factory (including a rusting locomotive) on this hotel's 8 acres (3 hectares) of forested land overlooking the sea, most of the resort is modern (it opened in 1991). The medium-size accommodations are in 26 pink-toned bungalows. Each cozy bungalow has chunky and rustic handmade furniture and a bay window overlooking either the sea or a garden. (Each bungalow contains two units, both with ceiling fans; none have TVs or phones.) Shower-only bathrooms are tiny but tidy. The nearest major beach is La Grand-Anse, a 10- to 15-minute drive from the hotel, but there's a small, unnamed beach within a 10-minute walk, although the swimming there isn't very good.

Comté de Loheac, 97115 Ste-Rose, Guadeloupe, F.W.I. ✆ 590/28-60-17. Fax 590/28-65-63. www.prime-invest-hotels.com. 52 units. Winter 58€–72€ (US$51.80–US$64.30) double. Off-season 38€–46€ (US$33.95–US$41.10) double. Rates include breakfast. 3-night minimum bookings. AE, MC, V. Closed Sept. **Amenities:** Restaurant, bar; pool, scuba diving, snorkeling, fishing; bike rental; car rental; babysitting; laundry/dry cleaning. *In room:* A/C, no phone.

DINING

Restaurant Clara ⚜ CREOLE   On the waterfront near the center of town is the culinary statement of Clara Lesueur. Clara lived for 12 years in Paris as a member of an experimental jazz dance troupe, but years ago she returned to Guadeloupe, her home, to set up this breezy restaurant. Try for a table on the open patio, where palm trees complement the color scheme.

Clara artfully melds the classic French style of fine dining with authentic Creole flavors. Specialties include *ouassous* (freshwater crayfish), brochette of swordfish, *palourdes* (small clams), several different preparations of conch, sea-urchin omelets, and *crabes farcis* (red-orange crabs with a spicy filling). The "sauce chien" that's served with many of the dishes is a blend of hot peppers, garlic, lime juice, and "secret things." The house drink is made with six local fruits and ample quantities of rum.

Bd. Maritime, Ste-Rose. ✆ 590/28-72-99. Reservations recommended. Main courses 9.10€–18.25€ (US$8.15–US$16.30). MC, V. Mon–Tues and Thurs–Sat noon–3pm and 7–10pm, Sun noon–3pm.

DESHAIES/LA GRAND-ANSE

A few miles farther along, you reach Pointe Allegre, the northernmost point of Basse-Terre. At **Clugny Beach,** you'll be at the site where the first settler landed on Guadeloupe. This would be a great place to break up your drive with a swim, although the waters are sometimes rough here and there are no beach facilities.

Two miles (3km) farther will bring you to **La Grand-Anse,** one of the best beaches on Guadeloupe. It is very large and still secluded, sheltered by many tropical trees, especially palms. The place is ideal either for a swim or a picnic, although, again, there are no facilities.

At **Deshaies,** immediately to the south, snorkeling and fishing are popular pastimes, but you must bring your own equipment. The narrow road alongside the beach winds up and down and has a corniche look to it, with the blue sea underneath, and the view of green mountains studded with colorful villages.

Nine miles (14km) from Deshaies, **Pointe Noire** comes into view, its name coming from black volcanic rocks. Look for the odd polychrome cenotaph in town, the only reason to stop over.

ACCOMMODATIONS

Habitation Grande Anse ⭐ Laid out like a complex of bungalows and studio apartments, with a unifying theme that evokes a Mediterranean complex of small-scale villas, each with natural-grained wood trim, this establishment lies across the coastal road from one of the island's best beaches, Grande-Anse. Studios and bungalows have kitchenettes, and all units—even the conventional bedrooms—contain rattan furniture, white walls, and a simple, summery decor that's well-suited to life close to the beach. All the accommodations have small private bathrooms with shower. Don't expect too many activities here—the focus is on restful sunbathing surrounded by tropical landscaping beside the beach, usually punctuated with entertainment you'll provide, or create, for yourself.

Localité Ziotte, 97126 Deshaies, La Guadeloupe, F.W.I. ☎ 590/28-45-36. Fax 590/28-51-17. www.Hotel Hga.com. 50 units. Winter 84€–104€ (US$75–US$92.85) double; 99€–114€ (US$88.40–US$101.80) double occupancy of a studio with kitchen; 183€–198€ (US$163.40–US$176.80) for up to 6 occupants of a 2-bedroom apartment with kitchen. Off-season, 44€–59€ (US$39.30–US$52.70) double; 53€–84€ (US$47.35–US$75) studio with kitchen; 107€–137€ (US$95.55–US$122.35) 2-bedroom apt. with kitchen for up to 6 occupants. Supplemented for half-board 27€ (US$24.10) per person per day. AE, DC, MC, V. **Amenities:** Restaurant, bar; 2 pools. *In room:* minibar, TV.

Résidence de la Pointe Batterie Built in 1996 on steeply sloping land near the edge of both the rain forest and the sea, these all-wood villas each contain a veranda, an American-built kitchen, ceiling fans, good beds, small and summery furniture made from rattan, local hardwoods, and wicker. All units have at least a shower/tub combination, the two-bedroom villas coming with that plus one additional shower unit. The nearest beach, La Grand-Anse, is a 3-minute drive, or a long uphill walk, away.

97126 Pointe Batterie, Deshaies, Guadeloupe, F.W.I. ☎ 800/322-2223 in the U.S., or 590/28-57-03. Fax 590/28-57-28. 24 units. Winter 256.90€–288.80€ (US$229.40–US$257.90) 2-bedroom villa with pool (for up to 6); 208.25€–231.05€ (US$185.95–US$206.30) 1-bedroom villa with pool (for up to 4); 156.55€–182.40€ (US$139.80–US$162.90) 1-bedroom suite without pool (for up to 4). Off-season, 144.40€ (US$128.95) 2-bedroom villa with pool (for up to 6); 118.55€ (US$105.85) 1-bedroom villa with pool (for up to 4); 89.70€ (US$80.10) 1-bedroom suite without pool (for up to 4). MC, V. **Amenities:** Restaurant, bar; communal pool (in addition to private pools associated with some of the villas); ping pong and billiard tables; tennis court within 100-yard (91m) walk from the hotel. *In room:* A/C, TV, kitchen, ceiling fans. All units have at least 1 shower/tub combination, 2-bedroom villas have 1 shower/tub combination plus 1 additional shower unit.

DINING

Chez Jackye ⭐ CREOLE/AFRICAN Named after its owner, Creole matriarch Jacqueline Cabrion, this place enjoys a loyal following. In a French-colonial house about 30 feet (9m) from the sea, it features lots of exposed wood, verdant plants, tropical furniture, and a bar that sometimes does a respectable business in its own right. Some of the dishes and spices were inspired by Africa, and others are in the classic Creole repertoire. Our favorites are the *colombo* of conch and the fricassee of conch. If it's available, go for the freshwater crayfish or several preparations of grilled fish based on the catch of the day. The ragout of lamb is a winner, as is the fresh grilled lobster. After all that, the bananas flambé are a bit much. Lighter fare includes a limited choice of sandwiches and salads, which tend to be offered only during daylight hours. The cuisine here seems to have more zest than Les Gommiers (see below). However, since it's a close tie, if there's no room at Chez Jackye, head for Les Gommiers instead. Both kitchens will feed you well on rather similar cuisine.

Anse Guyonneau, Pointe Noire. © 590/98-06-98. Reservations recommended at dinner. Main courses 7.60€–22.05€ (US$6.80–US$19.70); fixed-price menu 11.40€–18.25€ (US$10.20–US$16.30). AE, MC, V. Mon–Sat 8am–10pm, Sun 8am–5pm.

La Caféière Beausejour ★ *(Finds* CREOLE   In the green Pointe-Noire Valley, you come upon one of the dining secrets of Guadeloupe: La Caféière Beausejour. This is the domain of the hearty empress of the mountain, Bernadette Hayot-Beauzelin, who grows her own produce and herbs used in many of her nouvelle Creole dishes. On the site of a coffee plantation more than 2 centuries old, Ms. Hayot-Beauzelin welcomes you into her home. Since early morning she has been gathering up the bounty of the day—everything from tomatoes and bananas to passion fruit and avocados. The house was constructed in 1764, years after Louis XIV sent the first coffee plant to Guadeloupe in 1721. Ms. Hayot-Beauzelin is called a *bèkè*—that's a white Creole whose family came here from France some 3 centuries ago to colonize the French West Indies.

Don't expect a menu—you'll be told what the kitchen prepared that day. Chances are it'll be your most memorable meal in the French West Indies. We still remember the quiche made with fresh leeks and papaya. She also makes papaya tarts. Your main course might be a delectable smoked duck served with some pan-Asian sauce that tastes of ginger, with side dishes of fries (cut like French fries) from the breadfruit tree and pumpkin purée. Ms. Hayot-Beauzelin's coffee is the island's best. Always call for a reservation before heading up into the mountains, and get good directions.

Pointe Noire. © 590/98-10-09. Reservations required. Fixed-price menu 28.10€–38€ (US$25.10–US$33.95); set menu (Mon–Fri) 19€ (US$16.95). No credit cards. Tues–Sun 12:15–2:30pm. Dinner available for groups.

Les Gommiers CREOLE   Named after the large rubber trees (*les gommiers*) that grow nearby, this popular Creole restaurant serves up well-flavored dishes in a dining room lined with plants. You can order such Creole staples as *accras de morue* (codfish), *boudin Creole* (blood pudding), fricassee of freshwater crayfish, seafood paella, and a custard-like dessert known as *flan coucou*. Dishes inspired by France include fillet of beef with Roquefort sauce and veal scallops. We consistently return year after year, and have never detected any slip-off in the quality. One chef told us, "We are not technically perfect, but we cook from the heart."

Rue Baudot, Pointe Noire. © 590/98-01-79. Main courses 12.15€–22.80€ (US$10.85–US$20.35). Fixed-price menus 13.70€–22.80€ (US$12.20–US$20.35). MC, V. Daily 11:30am–3pm; Tues–Sat 7–10pm.

PARC NATUREL DE GUADELOUPE: A TROPICAL FOREST ★★

Four miles (6km) from Pointe Noire, you reach **Mahaut.** On your left begins the **Route de la Traversée** ★★, the Transcoastal Highway. This is the best way to explore the scenic wonders of **Parc Naturel de Guadeloupe,** passing through a tropical forest as you travel between the capital, Basse-Terre, and Pointe-à-Pitre.

To preserve Parc Naturel, Guadeloupe has set aside 74,100 acres (29,640 hectares), about one-fifth of its entire terrain. Easily accessible via modern roads, this is a huge tract of mountains, tropical forests, and gorgeous scenery, and one of the largest and most spectacular parks in the Caribbean.

The park is home to a variety of tame animals, including *titi* (a raccoon, adopted as the park's official mascot) and such birds as the wood pigeon, turtle-dove, and thrush. Small exhibition huts, devoted to the volcano, the forest, or to coffee, sugarcane, and rum, are scattered throughout the park. Parc Naturel has no gates, no opening or closing hours, and no admission fee.

You can hike for only 15 minutes or stretch out the adventure all day, as there are 180 miles (290km) of trails here, taking in rain forests and the wooded slopes of the 4,813-foot-high (1,444m) Soufrière volcano, passing by hot springs, rugged gorges, and rushing streams (see also "Hiking" under "Sports & Other Outdoor Pursuits," later in this chapter).

From Mahaut, you climb slowly in a setting of giant ferns and luxuriant vegetation. Four miles (6km) after the fork, you reach **Les Deux Mamelles (The Two Breasts),** where you can park your car and go for a hike. Some of the trails are for experts only; others, such as the **Pigeon Trail,** will bring you to a summit of about 2,600 feet (780m), where the view is impressive. Expect to spend at least 3 hours going each way. Halfway along the trail, you can stop at **Forest House;** from that point, many lanes, all signposted, branch off on trails that will take anywhere from 20 minutes to 2 hours.

The most enthralling walk in the park is to the **Chute de l'Ecrevisse,** the "Crayfish Waterfall," a little pond of very cold water at the end of a ¼-mile (.4km) path. This spot in the tropical forest is one of the beauty spots of the island. The pool found at the base of the falls is an ideal place for a cooling swim. In just 10 minutes you can reach this signposted attraction from the Corossol River Picnic Area. To the left of the Route de la Traversée, a short trail parallels the Corossol River, ending at the crayfish falls.

After the hike, the main road descends toward **Versailles,** a village about 5 miles (8km) from Pointe-à-Pitre. However, before taking this route, while still traveling between Pointe Noire and Mahaut on the west coast, you might consider the following lunch stop.

DINING

Chez Vaneau CREOLE Set in an isolated pocket of forest about 18 miles (29km) north of Pointe Noire, far from any of its neighbors, Chez Vaneau offers a wide, breezy veranda overlooking a gully. Neighbors often gather here to play cards, while steaming Creole specialties emerge from the kitchen. This is the domain of Vaneau Desbonnes, who is assisted by his wife, Marie-Gracieuse, and their children. Their best specialties include oysters with a piquant sauce, cray-fish bisque, ragout of goat, fricassee of conch, different preparations of octopus, and roast pork. All these dishes bespeak admirable talents in the kitchen, and there is an authenticity and personality that go into what is served. In 1995, they installed a saltwater tank to store lobsters, which are now featured heavily on the menu.

Mahaut/Pointe Noire. ⓒ **590/98-01-71.** Main courses 9.10€–13.70€ (US$8.15–US$12.20); fixed-price menu 15.20€–22.80€ (US$13.55–US$20.35). AE, MC, V. Daily noon–4pm and 7–10:30pm.

BOUILLANTE

If you don't take the Route de la Traversée at this time but want to continue exploring the west coast, you can head south from Mahaut until you reach the village of Bouillante, which is exciting for only one reason: You might encounter the former French film star and part-time resident, Brigitte Bardot.

ACCOMMODATIONS

Le Domaine de Malendure *Finds*   Isolated within a scrub-and-forest-covered landscape, at least 3 miles (5km) from its nearest neighbor, this hotel lies directly in front of the Reserve Jacques Cousteau, the underwater nature park beloved of scuba enthusiasts. Most of its accommodations are within a scattering of green-and-white bungalows (there are two units per bungalow), each within a few steps of a beach (Malendure Plage) that's known for its nearly black (dark gray) sands. The decor of each accommodation includes contemporary-looking furniture imported from the French mainland, white walls, tiled bathrooms (none with bathtub), and a private terrace. None of them has a kitchen. Expect a sports-oriented clientele that includes lots of scuba enthusiasts, many of whom sign up for extensive dive packages.

Morne Tarare Pigeon, 97132 Bouillante, Guadeloupe, F.W.I. (C) **590/98-92-10.** Fax 590/98-92-12. www.leaderhotels.gp. 50 units. Winter 123.75€ (US$110.50) double; off-season 101.25€ (US$90.40) double. Rates include breakfast. Supplement for half-board 26.60€ (US$23.75) per person. AE, DC, MC, V. Closed Sept. **Amenities:** Restaurant, bar; pool; an affiliated relationship with an independently operated on-site scuba facility. *In room:* A/C, TV, small fridge, private terrace.

Le Domaine de Petite-Anse   Completed in 1993, this isolated holiday compound is composed of a central, three-story core that contains the conventional bedrooms, and a scattering of cement-sided bungalows—each perched at the edge of a sandy beach—that punctuate the landscaping of the surrounding gardens. Despite the appeal of the beach, many guests prefer the large swimming pool, with its surrounding sun terrace and scantily clad visitors, most of whom come from the French mainland. Decor within the simply furnished bedrooms includes white walls, dark-stained rattan furniture, and tile-sheathed bathrooms. Bathrooms in the regular doubles contain a shower; those in the bungalows have a shower/tub combo. Expect a sports-oriented, relatively youthful clientele, lots of emphasis on quiet relaxation beside the pool or beneath the sea-fronting palms and sea grapes, and an entertainment staff that tries to include hotel guests in any of the several activities that are planned during the course of any day here. Occupants of the bungalows (each of which has its own kitchen) tend to prepare at least some of their meals in-house. Very few (only about eight) of the conventional bedrooms has a balcony or terrace.

Plage de Petite-Anse, Monchy, 97125 Bouillante, F.W.I. (C) **590/98-78-78.** Fax 590/98-80-28. 175 units. Winter 99€–155€ (US$88.40–US$138.40) double, 130€–190€ (US$116.10–US$169.65) bungalow for up to 4 occupants. Off-season 70€–90€ (US$62.50–US$80.35) double, 110€ (US$98.25) bungalow for up to 4 occupants. Rates for doubles include breakfast. Breakfast not available within bungalows. AE, DC, MC, V. Closed Sept. **Amenities:** Restaurant, bar; pool; nightclub/disco; boutique; sea kayaking; facilities for scuba instruction; windsurfing; laundry/dry cleaning. *In-room:* A/C, TV, fridge, safe.

DINING

Chez Loulouse *CREOLE*   A good choice for lunch, this place offers plenty of offhanded charm, and it stands on the well-known beach opposite Pigeon Island. Many guests prefer their rum punches on the lovely veranda, overlooking a scene of loaded boats preparing to depart and merchants hawking their wares. The equally colorful dining room inside has a ceiling of palm fronds, wraparound Creole murals, and reggae music emanating from the bar. The charming Mme Loulouse Paisley-Carbon holds court here, assisted by her children. She offers house-style Caribbean lobster, spicy versions of conch, octopus, accras (codfish), *gratin of christophine* (squash), and savory *colombos* (curries) of chicken or pork. She's perfected these dishes so well, she must have learned from her grandmother.

Malendure Plage. ☏ **590/98-70-34.** Reservations required for dinner. Main courses 7.60€–30.40€ (US$6.80–US$27.15); fixed-price menu 12.15€–34.95€ (US$10.85–US$31.20). AE, MC, V. Daily noon–3:30pm and 7–10pm.

Le Rocher de Malendure FRENCH/CREOLE   On a rocky peninsula 30 feet (9m) above the rich offshore reefs near Pigeon Island, this restaurant offers gorgeous views. Each table is sheltered from direct sunlight (and rain) by a shed-style roof, which also affords a greater sense of privacy. Much of the cuisine served here is seafood caught in offshore waters: grilled red snapper, fondues of fish, marinated marlin steaks, and different preparations of lobster and conch. Meat dishes include veal in raspberry vinaigrette and fillet of beef with any of three different sauces.

The restaurant also operates a small hotel on-site, Le Jardin Tropical, renting 11 bungalows, which cost 60.80€ (US$54.30) per night, single or double occupancy. Each small unit has a sea view, a tiny bathroom, and a simple kitchenette, where many visitors cook most of their meals. Amenities include a pool and laundry, and in each accommodation is a ceiling fan and a shower unit.

Malendure Plage, Pointe Batterie, Bouillante. ☏ **590/98-70-84.** Reservations recommended. Main courses 11.85€–22.80€ (US$10.60–US$20.35). Fixed-price menus 21.30€–33.45€ (US$19–US$29.85). AE, V. Thurs–Tues 11am–4pm; Mon–Sat 7–10pm. Closed Sept.

BASSE-TERRE ⚓

The winding coastal road brings you to **Vieux Habitants** (Old Settlers), one of the oldest villages on the island, founded in 1636. The name comes from the people who settled it: After serving in the employment of the West Indies Company, they retired here, but they preferred to call themselves inhabitants, so as not to be confused with slaves.

Another 10 miles (16km) of winding roads bring you to **Basse-Terre,** the capital of Guadeloupe. This sleepy town of some 15,000 inhabitants lies between the water and La Soufrière, the volcano. Founded in the 1640s, it's the oldest town on the island and still has a lot of charm; its market squares are shaded by tamarind and palm trees. The place, in spite of many modern buildings, still has a quaint old charm, with some grand old colonial buildings still standing.

The town suffered heavy destruction at the hands of British troops in 1691 and again in 1702. It was also the center of fierce fighting during the French Revolution, when the political changes that swept across Europe caused explosive tensions on Guadeloupe. As it did in France, the guillotine claimed many lives on the island during the infamous Reign of Terror.

In spite of the town's history, there isn't much to see in Basse-Terre except for a 17th-century **cathedral** and **Fort St-Charles,** which has guarded the city (not always well) since it was established. Much modernized and reconstructed over the years, the cathedral is only of passing interest. On the narrow streets, you can still see old clapboard buildings, upper floors of shingle-wood tiles, and wrought-iron balconies. For the most interesting views, seek out the **Place du Champ d'Arbaud** and the **Jardin Pichon.** At the harbor on the southern tier of town, you can see **Fort Delgrès,** which once protected the island from the English. There are acres of ramparts to be walked with panoramic vistas in all directions.

Originally selected as Guadeloupe's capital because of its prevailing breezes and its altitudes above the steaming lowlands of Pointe-à-Pitre, Basse-Terre is today a city that's curiously removed from the other parts of the French Antilles that it governs, and, when the business of the day is concluded, it's an almost bizarrely calm and quiet town. The neighboring municipality of **St-Claude,** in the cool heights above the capital, was always where the island's oldest families proudly maintained their ancestral homes and where they continue to live today in the same buildings. These families, direct descendants of the white, slave-owning former plantation owners who originally hailed from such major French Atlantic ports as Bordeaux and Nantes, tend to live quietly, discreetly, and separately from both the island's blacks and the French *métropolitains* whose tourist ventures have helped change the face of Guadeloupe.

ACCOMMODATIONS & DINING

Grand-Anse Hôtel ⚝   Built in the 1970s but renovated in 1996, this secluded hotel is removed from all the hordes, but near the ferryboat piers of Trois-Rivières. It doesn't have a beach, but it's one of the finest places to stay along the northern coast of Basse-Terre, where lodgings are few. It also makes one of the finest bases on island for exploring Parc Naturel de Guadeloupe. Bungalows are set in a garden with a view of the mountains and, in some cases, the sea. The small accommodations are mostly modern, with sliding-glass doors, vague hints of French colonial styling, mahogany furniture, and small, shower-only bathrooms. The closest beach, Plage Grand-Anse (with black volcanic sand), is a ½ mile (.8km) away. The hotel's location near the ferryboat departures for the Iles des Saintes makes day trips there convenient.

Grand Anse, 97114 Trois-Rivières, Guadeloupe, F.W.I. © **590/92-90-47.** Fax 590/92-93-69. 16 units. Winter 60.80€ (US$54.30) double. Off-season 45.60€–60.80€ (US$40.70–US$54.30) double. Rates include breakfast. MC, V. **Amenities:** Restaurant, bar; pool. *In room:* A/C, TV.

Le Jardin Malanga ⚝ *(Finds)*   Off-the-record lovers, honeymooners, or just lovers of nature view this as their secret hideaway in Guadeloupe. In a secluded location in the midst of a banana plantation, it overlooks the Les Saintes archipelago. The nearest beach, La plage du Vieux-Fort, lies a 15-minute drive from the hotel. Wander in a secret garden of banana trees, birds of paradise flowers, rare orchids, hibiscus (the favorite food of iguanas), and much flowering tropical foliage. Guests, for those who appreciate a place that looks like an outpost of French Guinea, will gravitate to the main house of the inn, which was constructed in 1927 and is still filled with family antiques. Day trips are spent rushing over to Iles de Saintes, or else exploring the nearby national park of Guadeloupe. You can also stay on-site, lounging at the swimming pool built into a cliff. Each of the bedrooms is comfortably and tastefully furnished, with bathrooms tiled in white. Sometimes the bathtubs open onto scenic views to be enjoyed while you scrub down. The French-Creole meals are worth a detour here (often made with produce from the hotel's own gardens).

Hermitage, Trois-Rivières 97114, Guadeloupe F.W.I. © **590/92-67-57.** Fax 590/92-67-58. www.deshotel setdesiles.com. 9 units. Year-round 170€–232€ (US$151.80–US$207.20) double. AE, DC, MC, V. Closed June 15–Oct 15. **Amenities:** Restaurant, bar/nightclub; pool; limited room service; laundry; currency exchange. *In room:* A/C, no phone.

Hotel St-Georges   Built in 1996, this tastefully modern inn is set on a hill with sweeping views over the town and the sea. A series of three-story buildings is centered around a large swimming pool. The medium-size bedrooms are outfitted, Creole style, with dark-grained and rattan furniture, tiled floors, and small bathrooms trimmed with touches of marble. Most accommodations come with a shower/tub combination, the rest with showers. Overall, this place has the feel of a business hotel. Expect lots of amiable goodwill from the 20 or 30 students registered at the hotel training school that's associated with the St-Georges.

Rue Gratien, Parize, 97120 St-Claude, Guadeloupe, F.W.I. ☎ **590/80-10-10.** Fax 590/80-30-50. perso.wanadoo.fr/hotel.st.georges. 40 units. Year-round 80.55€–100.30€ (US$71.95–US$89.60) double; 144.40€ (US$128.95) suite. MAP (breakfast and dinner) 20.50€ (US$18.30) per person extra. AE, DC, MC, V. **Amenities:** Restaurant, bar; pool; fitness center, laundry/dry cleaning. *In room:* A/C, TV, fridge.

AROUND LA SOUFRIÈRE ★★

The big attraction of Basse-Terre is the famous sulfur-puffing **La Soufrière** volcano, which is still alive, but dormant (for the moment, at least). Rising to a height of some 4,800 feet (1,440m), it's flanked by banana plantations and lush foliage.

After leaving the capital at Basse-Terre, you can drive to **St-Claude,** a suburb, **4 miles** (6km) up the mountainside at a height of 1,900 feet (570m). It has a reputation for its perfect climate and various privately owned tropical gardens in the area.

From St-Claude, you can begin the climb up the narrow, winding road the Guadeloupeans say leads to hell—that is, **La Soufrière.** The road ends at a parking area at La Savane à Mulets, at an altitude of 3,300 feet (990m). This is the ultimate point to be reached by car. Hikers are able to climb right to the mouth of the volcano. Currently, the belching beast is quiet and it's presumed safe to climb to the summit at 4,815 feet (1,445m), the tallest elevation in the Lesser Antilles. (Allow about 2 hr. for this climb.) However, in 1975, the appearance of ashes, mud, billowing smoke, and earthquake-like tremors proved that the old beast was still alive. In the resettlement process that followed the eruption, 75,000 inhabitants were relocated to safer terrain in Grande-Terre. No deaths were reported, but the inhabitants of Basse-Terre still keep a watchful eye on the smoking giant.

Even in the parking lot, you can feel the heat of the volcano merely by touching the ground. Steam emerges from fumaroles and sulfurous fumes from the volcano's "burps." Of course, fumes come from its pit and mud cauldrons as well. On the way back down, near the parking lot—but only if it's open—you can visit **La Maison du Volcan** (☎ **590/78-15-16**), a small-scale, dusty-looking museum devoted to volcanoes in general and La Soufrière in particular. Charging 2.30€ (US$2.05) per person admission, it maintains erratic hours that are, technically, every day from 9am to 5pm. More esoteric and technical information is available one day a week (Fri) between 4 and 5pm, and only with advance notification, at a government-funded laboratory, Observatoire Volcanologique le Houëlmont, 97113 Gourbeyre (☎ **590/99-11-33**). Conceived as an observation post for seismic and volcanic activities, and staffed with geologists and volcanologists from the French mainland, it can be toured without charge by anyone who's interested in the technical aspects of this science.

DINING

Chez Paul de Matouba CREOLE/INTERNATIONAL   You'll find good food in this family-run restaurant, which sits beside the banks of the small Rivière Rouge (Red River). The dining room on the second floor is enclosed by windows, allowing you to drink in the surrounding dark-green foliage of the mountains. The cooking is Creole, and the specialty is crayfish dishes, though well-prepared East Indian meals are also available. By all means, drink the mineral or spring water of Matouba. Hearty meals include perfectly executed stuffed crab, *colombo* (curried) of chicken, and an array of French, Creole, and Hindu specialties. You're likely to find the place overcrowded in winter with the tour-bus crowd.

Rivière Rouge. ⓒ **590/80-01-77**. Main courses 9.10€–22.05€ (US$8.15–US$19.70); fixed-price menu 18.25€ (US$16.30). No credit cards. Daily noon–3pm. Follow the clearly marked signs; it's beside a gully close to the center of the village.

THE WINDWARD COAST ★★

From Basse-Terre to Pointe-à-Pitre, the road N1 follows the east coast, called the Windward Coast. The country here is richer and greener than elsewhere on the island, though there's no major sight or stopover along the way. If your time is limited, you can merely drive along the coastal road savoring the views, with the sea to your right and the scenic landscapes to your left.

To reach the little town of **Trois Rivières** you have a choice of two routes: One goes along the coastline, coming eventually to Vieux Fort, from which you can see Les Saintes archipelago. The other heads across the hills, Monts Caraïbes.

Near the pier in Trois Rivières you'll see the pre-Columbian petroglyphs carved by the original inhabitants, the Arawaks. They're called merely **Roches Gravées**, or "carved rocks." In this **Parc Archéologique** at Bord de la Mer (ⓒ **590/92-91-88**), the rock engravings are of animal and human figures, dating most likely from A.D. 300 or 400. You'll also see specimens of plants, including cocoa, pimento, and banana, that the Arawaks cultivated long before the Europeans set foot on Guadeloupe. Hours are daily 9am to 5pm; admission is 1.50€ (US$1.35) for adults, free for children under age 12.

After leaving Trois Rivières, continue north on N1. Passing through the village of Bananier after a 15-minute drive, you turn on your left at Anse Saint-Sauveur to reach the famous **Les Chutes du Carbet** ★, a trio of waterfalls that are wonderful to behold year-round. If you have time for only one stopover along the route, make it this one. The road to two of them is a narrow, winding one, along many steep hills, passing through banana plantations as you move deeper into a tropical forest.

Les Chutes du Carbet are the tallest falls in the Caribbean. The waters pour down from La Soufrière at 800 feet (240m) in a trio of stages on the eastern slopes of Guadeloupe. The upper cascade falls 410 feet (123m) through a steep crevice. Drawing the most visitors and the easiest to reach is the middle falls at 360 feet (108m), dropping into a bigger canyon than the upper cascade. The second cascade in the falls is likely to be overrun with tour groups. The lower cascades drop only 65 feet (20m) and are less interesting.

You can hike to each cascade. To reach the dramatic second stage, from the little town of Saint-Sauveur, head inland via the village of Habituée, going to the end of the road. From here, follow the signs for a 30-minute walk along a marked trailway to the foot of the falls. There is a picnic area nearby.

If you have plenty of time and are in good shape, you can also reach the upper falls from here. Follow a signposted trail but note that this level of hiking takes about 1½ hours and is very steep, difficult, and often slippery to climb.

After Capesterre, a 4½-mile (7km) drive brings you to **Ste-Marie;** in the town square, you can see the statue of the first visitor who landed on Guadeloupe: Christopher Columbus, who anchored a ¼ mile (.4km) from Ste-Marie on November 4, 1493. In the journal of his second voyage, he wrote: "We arrived, seeing ahead of us a large mountain which seemed to want to rise up to the sky, in the middle of which was a peak higher than all the rest of the mountains from which flowed a living stream." However, when the Caribs started shooting arrows at him, he left quickly. If you'd like to see the same view that greeted Columbus, you can stop off here. The statue and that view are the only reasons to take a look.

After Ste-Marie, you pass through Goyave, then Petit-Bourg, seeing on your left the route de la Traversée before reaching Pointe-à-Pitre.

10 Beaches

Chances are your hotel will be right on a beach, or no more than 20 minutes from a good one. Plenty of natural beaches dot the island, from the surf-brushed dark strands of western Basse-Terre to the long stretches of white sand encircling Grande-Terre. Public beaches are generally free, but some charge for parking. Unlike hotel beaches, they have few facilities. Hotels welcome nonguests, but charge for changing facilities, beach chairs, and towels.

Sunday is family day at the beach. Topless sunbathing is common at hotels, less so on village beaches.

Most of the best beaches lie between Gosier and St-François on Grande Terre. Visitors usually head for the hotel beaches at **Gosier.** Stone jetties were constructed here to protect the beaches from erosion. Since this area has the largest concentration of tourists, it's likely to be crowded.

These beaches are not peas-in-a-pod; each one is different. There's no shade at the **Creole Beach** fronting Creole Beach Hotel, although you can retreat to the bar there for a drink. A stone retaining wall blocks access to the water. Nearby, the **Salako Beach** has more sand and is set against a backdrop of palms that offer some shade. Part of this beach also leads up to a jetty. This is a fine sandy beach, although a little too crowded at times, and it also contains a snack bar.

Also nearby, **Arawak Beach** is a gorgeous spot, with plenty of swaying palm trees providing a bit of shade on the beige sands. It, too, is protected by jetties. Close at hand, **Callinago Beach** is smaller than Arawak, but still has a pleasant crescent of beige sand and palms.

Le Bas du Fort, 2 miles (3km) east of Pointe-à-Pitre and close to Gosier, is another popular area. Its beaches, also protected by jetties, are shared by guests at the Hotels Fleu d'Epée and Marissol. This is a picture-postcard tropical beach with tranquil waters, plenty of sand, and palms for shade. There are hotel bars as well as snack bars, and vendors, too (some of whom are rather aggressive).

Some of Grande-Terre's best beaches are in the **Ste-Anne** area, site of a Club Med. **Plage Caravelle** is heaped with white sand, attracting crowds of sun-bathers; snorkelers, too, are drawn to the beach's reef-protected waters.

The French visitors here often like to go nude, and there is no finer nude beach than **Pointe Tarare,** a 45-minute drive from Gosier. This beach lies east of St-François at Pointe des Chateaux. It's one of the island's most pristine, tranquil beaches, but there's no shade to protect you from the fierce noonday sun. You can snorkel here if the water's not kicking up. There's a good restaurant by the car park. *Warning:* The tourist office doesn't recommend that women come here unaccompanied.

If you're not a nudist, you can enjoy the lovely strip of white sand at **Anse de la Gourde,** lying between St-François and Pointe des Chateaux. It has good sand, but it tends to become crowded on weekends.

The eastern coast of Grande-Terre is less desirable for swimming, as it fronts the more turbulent Atlantic. Nonetheless, the sands at **Le Moule** make for an idyllic beach because a reef protects the shoreline. There are also beach bars here—and the inevitable crowds, especially on weekends. You'll find a more secluded strip of sand north of here at **La Porte d'Enfer.**

There are two other excellent beaches on the northwestern coast: one at **Anse Laborde** just outside the village of Anse-Bertrand, the other called **Anse du Souffleur** at Port-Louis. We especially like the beach at Souffleur for its brilliant, flamboyant trees that bloom in the summer. There are no facilities here, but you can pick up provisions in the shops in the little village, then enjoy a picnic on the beach.

In Basse-Terre, a highly desirable beach is **La Grande-Anse,** just outside Deshaies, reached by heading west from Sainte Rose along the N2. You won't find any facilities here, but we think you'll enjoy the powdery sands, tranquil waters, and palm trees. Another desirable beach is **Plage de la Malendure,** on the west coast (the more tranquil side) of Basse-Terre across from Pigeon Island. This is a major center for scuba diving, but the sand tends to be dark here.

If you want to escape the crowds, seek out the spurs and shoulders produced by the mountains of Basse-Terre. In the northwest is a string of fine sandy beaches. Although small, these are highly desirable enclaves for sunbathing and swimming. Favorites include **La Plage de Cluny** (near Pointe Allegre), **Plage de la Tillette,** and **Plage de la Perle.**

South of Pointe Noire, also on the west coast, is **Plage de La Caraïbe,** with its calm waters and sandy strip. This beach has picnic facilities, a shower, and toilets.

Warning: The beaches on the north coast of Basse-Terre are exceedingly dangerous for swimming. **Plage de Clugny** is especially treacherous, and there have been several deaths by drowning.

Other good beaches are found on the offshore islands, **Iles des Saintes** and **Marie-Galante** (see the end of this chapter).

11 Sports & Other Outdoor Pursuits

DEEP-SEA FISHING   Blue marlin, wahoo (known locally as *thazar*), and yellowfin tuna can be fished throughout the year; the season for dorado is limited to December through March. Hotels can usually recommend a deep-sea outfitter or two, but one of the island's most consistently reliable is **Capitaine Valère** (© **590/95-67-26**), who moors his 38-foot (11m) Bertram in the Bas du Fort Marina in Gosier. A full-day deep-sea fishing expedition for up to four fishermen at a time, with a picnic lunch and all equipment included, costs 684€ (US$610.80).

GOLF   Guadeloupe's only public golf course is the well-known **Golf de St-François** ★★ (© **590/88-41-87**), opposite the Hôtel Méridien. The course runs alongside an 800-acre (320-hectare) lagoon where windsurfing, water-skiing, and sailing prevail. Designed by Robert Trent Jones, Sr., it's a challenging 6,755-yard (6,147m), par-71 course, with water traps on 6 of the 18 holes, not to mention massive bunkers, prevailing trade winds, and a particularly fiendish 400-yard (364m), par-4 ninth hole. The par-5 sixth is the toughest hole on the course; its 450 yards (410m) must be negotiated in the constant easterly winds. Greens fees are 38€ (US$33.95) per day per person, which allows a full day of playing time. You can rent clubs for 15.20€ (US$13.55) a day; a cart costs 33.45€ (US$29.85) for 18 holes. Hours are daily from 7:30am to 6:30pm.

HIKING   The 74,100-acre (29,640-hectare) **Parc Naturel de Guadeloupe** contains some of the best hiking trails in the Caribbean (for our favorite trail, see the touring notes on Route de la Traversée in the section "Around Basse-Terre," earlier in this chapter). The 180 miles (290km) of trails cut through the deep foliage of rain forest, passing waterfalls and cool mountain pools, hot springs, and rugged gorges along the way. The big excursion country, of course, is around the volcano, La Soufrière. Another highlight is Chutes du Carbet, one of the tallest waterfalls in the Caribbean, with a drop of 800 feet (240m).

Hiking brochures are available from the tourist office. Hotel tour desks can make arrangements. For information about this and other hikes in the national park, contact **Organisation des Guides de Montagne de la Caraïbe,** Maison Forestière, Matouba (© **590/94-29-11**).

Warning: Hikers may experience heavy downpours. The annual precipitation on the higher slopes is 250 inches per year, so be prepared with rain gear.

SCUBA DIVING   Guadeloupe is more popular for scuba diving than any of the other French-speaking islands. The allure is the relatively calm seas and **La Réserve Cousteau,** a kind of French national park with many intriguing dive sites, where the underwater environment is rigidly protected. Jacques Cousteau once described the waters off Guadeloupe's Pigeon Island as "one of the world's 10 best diving spots." Sergeant majors become visible at a depth of 30 feet (9m), spiny sea urchins and green parrot fish at 60 feet (18m), and magnificent stands of finger, black, brain, and star coral at 80 feet (24m).

The most popular dive sites include Aquarium, Piscine, Jardin de Corail, Pointe Carrangue, Pointe Barracuda, and Jardin Japonais. Although scattered around the periphery of the island, many are in the bay of Petit Cul-de-Sac Marin, south of Rivière Salée, the channel that separates the two halves of Guadeloupe. North of the Salée is another bay, Grand Cul-de-Sac Marin, where the small islets of Fajou and Caret also boast fine diving.

Reacting to the rich diversity of underwater flora and fauna, which thrive at relatively shallow, and relatively safe, depths, several entrepreneurs have set up shop. One of these is **Les Heures Saines,** Rocher de Malendure, Bouillante (© **590/98-86-63**), whose trio of dive boats departs three times a day at 10am, 12:30pm, and 3pm, for explorations of the waters within the reserve.

With all equipment included, dives—depending on the level of expertise of the participants, and the intended destination—cost from 34€–42€ (US$30.35–US$37.50) each. Novices, at least for the very first time they engage in the sport, pay 50€ (US$44.65) for what is referred to as a *baptême* (baptism). Les Heures Saines maintains its own 11-unit hotel, **Le Paradis Creole** (© **590/98-71-62**). Here, simple, motel-style accommodations rent for between 70€ and 94€ (US$62.50 and US$83.95), with breakfast included. All have air-conditioning, but no TV or phone, and very few frills. Many of them are occupied almost exclusively by avid divers on tour-group holiday from the French mainland.

This outfit's slightly larger competitor, located a short distance away, is **Centre International de la Plongée (C.I.P.),** B.P. 4, Lieu-Dit Poirier, Malendure Plage, Pigeon, Bouillante (© **590/98-81-72**). It's acknowledged as the most professional dive operation on the island. In a wood-sided house on Malendure Plage, close to a well-known restaurant, Chez Loulouse, it's well-positioned at the edge of the Cousteau Underwater Reserve. Certified divers pay 33.45€ (US$29.85) for a one-tank dive. A "resort course" for first-time divers costs 42.55€ (US$38) and is conducted one-on-one with an instructor. Packages of 6 or 12 dives are offered for 167.20€ and 304€ (US$149.30 and US$271.45), respectively.

TENNIS   If you're a guest at a large-scale hotel with courts of its own, tennis will usually be without charge, although there might be a small fee for nighttime illumination if it's available. If your hotel doesn't have a court of its own, and if you've called nearby hotels without any luck about using—even for a fee—one of their courts, try either of the two tennis courts at the **Tennis Club de St-François,** Plage des Raisins Claires, St-François (© **590/88-75-61**). Use of one of the courts costs around 6.10€ (US$5.45) per hour. If no one answers the phone, which sometimes happens here, call the local tourist office in St-François (© **590/88-75-61**).

WINDSURFING   If you're really serious about windsurfing, and if you want an intensive immersion in the sport, consider enrolling for a week-long course at the **UCPA (Union Nationale des Centres de Plein-Air),** 97118 St-François (© **590/88-64-80** or 590/88-54-84). Seven days lodging, double occupancy, with all meals, drinks, and windsurfing lessons included, costs 456€ (US$407.20) per person. Lodgings are within simple bungalows, each built in 1986, arranged around a swimming pool, dining hall, and beachfront, each with ceiling fans, but without TV, phone, air-conditioning, or any other grace note. On the premises—in addition to windsurfing equipment—are extensive facilities for the teaching and enjoyment of golf and sailing. If you're interested only in a half-day's rental of a windsurfer, the same organization can rent you one. Rentals cost 22.80€ (US$20.35) per half-day, and a 30-minute lesson, if a staff member is available, an additional 19€ (US$16.95) each.

A member of the same chain, wherein the emphasis is on scuba diving and hiking, but not on windsurfing, is the **UCPA in Bouillante** (© **590/98-89-00**), where 60 simple bedrooms, equivalent to lodgings at the UCPA branch at St-François, are available. Technically, both resorts are open only to persons aged 18 to 40, although young-at-heart and physically fit persons up to around 50 are sometimes admitted as well. This organization maintains an aggressive sales office in Paris. Consequently, its branches are likely to be filled with members of tour groups from Europe, especially France and to a lesser degree, Sweden, Switzerland, and Germany.

12 Guadeloupe After Dark

Guadeloupeans claim that the *beguine* was invented here, not on Martinique, and they dance it as if it truly were their own. Of course, there's also calypso, technically imported from points further south such as Trinidad, merengue sounds from the Dominican Republic, salsa from Puerto Rico, and fusion jazz from Cuba, too—the islanders are known for their dancing.

Ask at your hotel for details on the folkloric **Ballets Guadeloupeans** performances. This troupe makes frequent appearances at the big resorts.

An important casino, one of only two on the island, both administered by the same bureaucracy, is **Casino Gosier-les-Bains,** 43 Pointe de la Verdure, Gosier (© **590/84-79-68**). A casually elegant spot, it's open daily from 10am until 3am (until 4am on Fri and Sat), although the most interesting activities—those associated with the roulette, chemin de fer, and blackjack—don't open till 7:30pm. There's no cover, and no ID requested, for admission to the area with the slot machines, but entrance to the gaming tables and roulette wheels costs 10.50€ (US$9.35) per person, and requires the presentation of a photo ID or passport.

A smaller casino, with fewer slot machines but with the same opening hours and admission charge, is **Casino de la Marina,** avenue de l'Europe (© **590/88-41-31**), near the Hotel Méridien in St-François.

If you don't like casino action, you'll find other nighttime diversions in Guadeloupe, although these tend to be seasonal, with more offerings in the winter. **Lele Bar,** at Le Méridien in St-François (© **590/88-51-00**), is one of the most active on the island, attracting Guadeloupeans along with visitors. Newer, and more closely linked to the nighttime esprit you might have expected in Paris, are the **Zoo Rock Café** at La Marina in Gosier (© **590/90-77-77**). Sheathed in wood, and open to the outdoor breezes, it offers a revolving series of theme parties ("Midnight in Rio," and "Carnival in New Orleans" that might remind you of something in St-Tropez. Equally up-to-date and cutting-edge trendy is **Le Spy Bar,** Rte. des Hotels, Bas du Fort (© **590/59-14-25**). Associated with the hyper-stylish Hotel Le Coste in Paris, and a *de rigeur* stopover for whatever photo model happens to be in Guadeloupe at the time, it offers drinks, dancing, and dialogue about all things French and/or fashionable.

Cuban salsa and Latin dancing draw patrons to **Lollapalooza,** 122 Montauban, Gosier (© **590/84-58-58**), where pictures of dictator Fidel and the long-dead Che Guevara decorate the walls. If you get tired of this joint, try **Fanzy Bar,** Mathurin Poucette (© **590/84-41-34**), where musical styles might include 1980s-style French disco, Bob Marley reggae, and in an occasional orgy of nostalgia, Edith Piaf singing songs from the 1940s and '50s. These bars are free but the island's discos charge a uniform fee of about $20 (22€), which includes the cost of a first drink. After that, most cocktails are a pricey $10 (11.20€). Other options include **Caraïbes 2,** Carrefour de Blanchard, Bas-du-Fort (© **590/90-97-16**), whose specialty is Brazilian music, or **Zenith,** Route de la Riviera (© **590/90-72-04**), which goes in and out of fashion as a sought-after island nightclub and disco.

If you want to find some genuinely raffish local color, make it **Les Tortues,** off the N2 near Bouillante, signposted near the main road on Basse-Terre's western coast (© **590/98-82-83**). This bar is a local hangout, often filled with scuba divers downing Corsaire beer and telling tall tales of the deep. The bartender's rum specialty is *ti punch,* cut with lime and cane syrup. You can also dine here on good food, especially the catch of the day (marlin, kingfish, ray, snapper, or Caribbean lobster). Les Tortues is closed all day Sunday and on Monday night.

13 Side Trips from Guadeloupe

ILES DES SAINTES 🖈

A cluster of eight islands off the southern coast of Guadeloupe, the Iles des Saintes are certainly off the beaten track. The two main islands and six rocks are Terre-de-Haut, Terre-de-Bas, Ilet-à-Cabrit, La Coche, Les Augustins, Grand Ilet, Le Redonde, and Le Pâté. Only Terre-de-Haut ("land of high") and, to a lesser extent, Terre-de-Bas ("land below") attract visitors; **Terre-de-Haut** is the most interesting, and the only island with overnight accommodations.

Some claim that Les Saintes has one of the nicest bays in the world, a Lilliputian Rio de Janeiro with a sugarloaf. The isles, just 6 miles (10km) from the main island, were visited by Columbus on November 4, 1493, who named them "Los Santos."

The history of Iles des Saintes is very much the history of Guadeloupe itself. In years past, the islands have been heavily fortified, as they were Guadeloupe's

Gibraltar. The climate is very dry, and until the desalination plant opened, water was often rationed.

The population of Terre-de-Haut is mainly Caucasian, all fisherfolk or sailors and their families who are descended from Breton *corsairs*. The very skilled sailors maneuver large boats called *saintois* and wear hats called *salacos*, which are shallow and white, with sun shades covered in cloth built on radiating ribs of thick bamboo. Frankly, the hats look like small parasols. If you want to take a photograph of these sailors, please make a polite request (in French, no less; otherwise they won't know what you're talking about). Visitors often like to buy these hats (if they can find them) for use as beachwear.

Terre-de-Haut is a place for nature lovers, many of whom stake out their exhibitionistic space on the nude beach at **Anse Crawen.**

Some visitors travel to Ile des Saintes for the day just to go scuba diving. The island's two leading dive outfitters include **Dive-Bouteille** (© **590/99-54-25**); and **Pisquettes** (© **590/99-88-80**). Both charge competitive rates and have staffs who are well-versed in the esoterica of the region's many dive sites.

ESSENTIALS

GETTING THERE   The fastest way to get there is by plane, but at this writing, all flights into Iles des Saintes had been suspended, without notice of when they're likely to be re-inaugurated. Prior to your trip, phone the local carrier, **Air Caraïbes** (© **590/82-47-00**), for news about whether or not they've been reinstated, and know in advance that the airport is a truncated landing strip that accommodates nothing larger than small propeller planes such as a 20-seat Twin Otter.

Most islanders reach Terre-de-Haut via one of the several **ferryboats** that travel from Guadeloupe every day. Two boats depart daily from **Pointe-à-Pitre's Gare Maritime des Iles,** on quai Gatine, across the street from the well-known open-air market. The trip is 60 minutes each way, and costs 28.10€ (US$25.10) round-trip. The most popular departure time for Terre-de-Haut from Pointe-à-Pitre is daily at 8am, with returns scheduled every afternoon at 4pm. Be at the ferryboat terminal at least 15 minutes prior to the anticipated departure. Pointe-à-Pitre is not the only departure point for Terre-de-Haut: Other ferryboats (two per day) also depart daily at 9am to 4:30pm from **Trois Rivières,** and one additional boat leaves from **Basse-Terre** daily. The trip is 25 minutes each way from both of these towns, and costs 13.70€ (US$12.20) round-trip. The waters are often rough, so you may want to take Dramamine before you set out. For more information and last-minute departure schedules, contact **Frères Brudey** (© **590/90-04-48**) or **Trans Antilles Express,** Gare Maritime, quai Gatine, Pointe-à-Pitre (© **590/21-05-68**).

VISITOR INFORMATION   In the center of town and easy to spot, the **Office du Tourisme** (© **590/99-58-60**) isn't on a street plan but there's a sign out. Its information, for the most part, is in French, but a map of the island might come in handy.

GETTING AROUND   On an island that doesn't have a single car-rental agency, you get about by walking or riding a bike or motor scooter, which can be rented at hotels and in town near the pier. **Localizé,** at route Aerodrome in Terre-de-Haut (© **590/99-51-99**), rents both motorboats and scooters, costing from 22.80€ (US$20.35).

There are also minibuses called *taxis de l'Ile* (eight in all), which take six to eight passengers.

ACCOMMODATIONS ON TERRE-DE-HAUT

Bois Joli   Set on the western edge of the island, about 2 miles (3km) from the village of Bourg, this complex of pink-stucco buildings forms one of the most isolated resorts on the island. Known for housing families, some with children, from the French mainland, it offers both conventional bedrooms within the main house, plus eight outlying bungalows set into palm groves near the beach. Two of the bungalows have kitchenettes, but don't cost more than the other units. Decor includes bold-patterned fabrics, comfortable chairs, and modern but blandly international furnishings, plus small bathrooms with a shower. The food served in the dining room emphasizes simple Creole cuisine, sometimes served buffet-style, especially at midday.

97137 Terre-de-Haut, Les Saintes, Guadeloupe, F.W.I. ⓒ 590/99-50-38. Fax 590/99-55-05. www. ifrance.com/boisjoli. 31 units. Winter 174.95€ (US$156.25) double; 230.45€ (US$205.75) bungalow for 2. Off-season 88.90€ (US$79.40) double; 129.95€ (US$116.05) bungalow for 2. Rates include half board in winter, only breakfast in off-season. MC, V. **Amenities:** Restaurant, bar; pool; water-skiing, sailing, boat trips to some of the islets or rocks that form Les Saintes, snorkeling. *In room:* A/C.

Hôtel La Saintoise   Originally built in the 1960s, La Saintoise is a modern two-story building set near the almond trees and widespread poinciana of the town's main square, near the ferryboat dock, across from the town hall. As in a small French village, the inn places tables and chairs on the sidewalk, where you can sit and observe what action there is. The owner will welcome you and show you through the uncluttered lobby to one of his modest, second-floor bedrooms, each outfitted with a small shower-only bathroom. Housekeeping is good, and the comfort level is suitable. This is a friendly and unpretentious place.

Place de la Mairie, 97137 Terre-de-Haut, Les Saintes, Guadeloupe, F.W.I. ⓒ and fax 590/99-52-50. 8 units. Year-round 39.50€–54.70€ (US$35.30–US$48.85) double. Rates include continental breakfast. MC, V. *In room:* A/C.

L'Auberge les Petits Saints aux Anacardiers ⭐   The choice place to stay— and also to dine—is this antiques-filled former mayor's house set on a hillside site with a view of the turquoise bay and the adjacent beach. Surrounded by a tropical garden, a 5-minute walk north of Bourg, this is a tranquil retreat with much colonial charm. The owners, Didier Spindler and Jean-Paul Colas, have filled the house with their collection of furnishings and objects from around the world. Bedrooms have queen-size or twin beds, all except a one-bedroom bungalow and a separate guesthouse. The latter has five spacious rooms and is suitable for friends traveling together or families. All rooms have showers and toilets, but no bathtubs; corridor showers are available.

The best food on the island is here. (The restaurant is open to the public but you should call for a reservation.)

La Savane, Terre-de-haut, 97137 Guadeloupe, F.W.I. ⓒ 590/99-50-99. Fax 590/99-54-51. www.petits saints.com. 10 units. Winter 114€ (US$101.80) double. Off-season 91.20€ (US$81.45) double. MC, V. **Amenities:** Restaurant, bar; pool; sauna. *In room:* A/C, no phone.

DINING ON TERRE-DE-HAUT

Le Génois ⭐ INTERNATIONAL/FRENCH   Philippe and Chantal, refugees from the urban sprawl of mainland France, are the owners of this raffish green-and-white bistro that's set immediately adjacent to the quays where the ferryboats arrive from Guadeloupe. Views from the windows include the *génois* (mainsails) of the many sailing crafts that are moored a short distance from your table. The staff here is exceptionally cooperative, even charming. Look for meal-sized salads, an array of both sweet (i.e., dessert) and salted (i.e., starter)

> ### *Finds* An Escape to Pristine Beaches
>
> Most visitors flock to the beaches. There is none finer than **Plage de Pom-pierre,** which curves around the bay like a half moon, and is set against a backdrop of palms. The beach lies only a 15- to 20-minute walk from where the ferry docks from Guadeloupe. Unless a cruise ship is in port, the beach is generally uncrowded, filled with mainland French enjoying the powdery white sand wearing next to nothing. If you want to bare all, head for **Anse Crawen** on the western coastline. It is the legal nudist beach, although visitors often go nude on the other beaches too. The best snorkeling is on the southern coast at **Plage Figuier,** which, chances are, you'll have almost to yourself.

tartes, each freshly made on-site, that might include versions with smoked fish, tomatoes and cheese, or fruits. Grilled fish, steaks, and confits of duckling add reminders of the cuisine of the faraway French mainland. Don't hesitate to drop in here just for drinks and tapas, and expect to overhear the dialogue of (or at least see) many of the yacht-owners whose craft are moored nearby.

On the harbor front, Terre-de-Haut. *C* **590/99-53-01.** Main courses 10.65€–15.20€ (US$9.50–US$13.55). MC, V. Daily 7:30am–2pm and 7–9pm (until 10pm if there's a lot of business).

Les Amandiers CREOLE   Across from the town hall on the main square of Bourg is the most traditional Creole bistro on Terre-de-Haut. Monsieur and Madame Charlot Brudey are your hosts in this beige-painted building, with tables and chairs on the upper balconies for open-air dining. Conch (*lambi*) is prepared either in a fricassee or a *colombo,* a savory curry stew. Also offered are a court bouillon of fish, a *gâteau* (terrine) of fish, and a seemingly endless supply of grilled crayfish, a staple of the island. The catch of the day is also grilled the way you like it. You'll find an intriguing collection of stews, concocted from fish, bananas, and *christophine* (squash). A knowledge of French is helpful around here.

Place de la Mairie. *C* **590/99-51-77.** Reservations recommended. Fixed-price menu 12.15€–15.20€ (US$10.85–US$13.55). AE, MC, V. Daily noon–3pm and 7–10pm.

EXPLORING TERRE-DE-HAUT

On Terre-de-Haut, the main settlement is at **Le Bourg,** a single street that follows the curve of the harbor. A charming but sleepy village, it has little houses with red or blue doorways, balconies, and Victorian gingerbread. Donkeys are the beasts of burden, and everywhere you look, you'll see fishnets drying in the sun. After a short walk north of Le Bourg, you can also explore the ruins of **Fort Napoléon,** which is left over from those 17th-century wars, including the naval encounter known in European history books as "The Battle of the Saints." You can see the barracks and prison cells, as well as the drawbridge and art museum. Occasionally you'll spot an iguana scurrying up the ramparts. The fort is open daily from 9am to 12:30pm, costing 3.05€ (US$2.70) for admission. For more information, call *C* **590/37-99-59.** Closed in September.

  Scuba diving is not limited to mainland Guadeloupe. The underwater world off Les Saintes has attracted deep-sea divers as renowned as Jacques Cousteau, but even the less experienced may explore its challenging depths and multi-colored reefs. Intriguing underwater grottoes can be found near Fort Napoléon on Terre-de-Haut. One recommended outfitter on the island is the

Centre Nautique de la Colline, Fond-du-Curé (© **590/99-54-25**). In addition, a couple of outfitters on the "mainland" of Guadeloupe can arrange diving trips to Terre de Haut: **Blue Bubbles,** Gourbeyre, La Guadeloupe (© **590/99-06-65**), and **Club Pisquette,** près de la Maison Bâteau, in Bourg (© **590/99-88-80**).

SHOPPING ON TERRE-DE-HAUT

Few come here to shop, but there is one offbeat choice at **Kaz an Nou Gallery** on Terre-de-Haut (© **590/99-52-29**), where a local artist, Pascal Fay, makes carved miniature wooden house facades, all candy colored and trimmed in gingerbread. The most popular reproduction graces the cover of the best-selling coffee-table book *Caribbean Style.* Mr. Fay will point the way to the real house a few blocks away, which has become a sightseeing attraction all on its own due to the book's popularity. The "houses" measure about 16 by 13 inches and sell for $100 to $400 each.

If you're looking for an authentic salaco hat, head to **José Beaujour** at Terre-de-Bas (© **590/99-80-20**). At **Mahogany Artisanat,** Bourg in Terre-de-Haut (© **590/99-50-12**), you'll find Yves Cohen's batik and hand-painted T-shirts.

MARIE-GALANTE

Come to Marie-Galante to see the Caribbean the way it used to be before the advent of high-rise hotels and casinos. In just 1 hour from Pointe-à-Pitre you can be transported to a world that time seems to have forgotten. This offshore dependency of Guadeloupe is an almost-perfect circle of about 60 square miles (155 sq. km). Almost exclusively French speaking, it lies 20 miles (32km) south of Guadeloupe's Grand-Terre and is full of rustic charm.

Today, some 30,000 inhabitants live here, making their living from sugar and rum, the latter said to be the best in the Caribbean. The best distillery to visit is **Distillerie Bielle,** Section Bielle, 97112 Grand-Bourg (© **590/97-93-62**). The island's climate is rather dry, and there are many good beaches, some of the best in Guadeloupe's archipelago. One of these stretches of brilliantly white sand covers at least 5 miles (8km). However, swimming can be dangerous in some places. The best beach is at **Petite Anse,** 6½ miles (10km) from **Grand-Bourg,** the main town, with an 1845 baroque church.

ESSENTIALS

GETTING THERE **Antilles Trans Express (Exprès des Iles),** Gare Maritime, quai Gatine, Pointe-à-Pitre (© **590/83-12-45** or 590/91-13-43), operates boat service to the island with three daily round-trips between Point-à-Pitre and Grand-Bourg. The round-trip costs 27.35€ (US$24.45). Monday to Saturday, ferryboats depart from Pointe-à-Pitre for Grand-Bourg (Marie Galante), at 8am, 12:30pm, and 5pm, with Sunday departures occurring at 8am, 5pm, and 7pm. Monday to Saturday, ferryboats to Pointe-à-Pitre depart from Marie-Galante at 6am, 9am, and 3:45pm, and on Sunday, ferryboats leave from Marie-Galante at 6am, 3:45pm, and 6pm.

VISITOR INFORMATION The **Syndicate d'Initiatives** or tourist office is located at rue du Fort, BP 15, 97112 Grand-Bourg, Marie-Galante (© **590/97-56-51**).

GETTING AROUND A limited number of **taxis** are available at the airport, but the price should be negotiated before you drive off.

ACCOMMODATIONS

Auberge de l'Arbre à Pain   Set behind a clapboard facade close to the street, about a 5-minute stroll from the harbor front, this place is named after the half-dozen breadfruit trees (*les arbres à pain*) that shelter its courtyard and its simple bedrooms from the blazing sun. The place is a bit run down and in need of restoration, but choices are limited on the island, so you often have to take what you can get. Each room has uncomplicated furnishings and a private shower-only bathroom. You can walk over to nearby beaches.

34 Rue Jeanne-d'Arc, 97112 Grand-Bourg, Marie-Galante, Guadeloupe, F.W.I. ☎ **590/97-73-69.** 9 units. Year-round 45.60€ (US$40.70) double. Rates include continental breakfast. V. At the harbor, take the first street going toward the church. **Amenities:** Restaurant. *In room:* A/C, no phone.

La Cohoba Hotel   On Folle Anse, an uncrowded white-sand beach, this hotel is a bargain and a comfortable nest. The beach is edged with sea grape and mahogany trees. The hotel itself takes its name from the cohoba plant, known to the Caribs as a plant whose red pods have hallucinogenic powers. The hotel, the largest on Marie-Galante, has small suite-like rooms decorated with white tile and ghost-white walls, along with bright Caribbean colors and tiny but efficient shower-only bathrooms. Thirty of the accommodations have kitchenettes.

Folle Anse, Marie Galante, Guadeloupe, F.W.I. ☎ **800/322-2223** in the U.S., or 590/97-50-50. Fax 590/97-97-96. www.cohoba.gp. 100 units. Winter 125.25€ (US$111.85) double. Off-season 95.15€ (US$84.95) double. Rates include continental breakfast. AE, MC, V. **Amenities:** 2 restaurants; pool; 2 tennis courts. *In room:* A/C, TV, hair dryer, safe.

DINING

In addition to the following choice, the **Auberge de l'Arbre à Pain** has a popular restaurant (see above).

Le Touloulou CREOLE   Set adjacent to the beach, with a hardworking staff and a casual crowd, Le Touloulou specializes in shellfish and crayfish culled from local waters. If sea urchins or lobster are your passion, you'll find them here in abundance, prepared virtually any way you want. Other standbys include a savory, and highly ethnic, version of *bébélé* (cow tripe enhanced with breadfruit, dumplings, and plantains) and conch served either as fricassee or in puff pastry.

The inn has also added five very basic units, each with air-conditioning and a small private bathroom. In winter, a double costs 45.60€ (US$40.70); a double with kitchenette, 49.40€ (US$44.10). A two-bedroom bungalow with kitchenette, suitable for four, rents for 91.20€ (US$81.45). In the off-season, a double costs 42.55€ (US$38), with the bungalow going for 85.10€ (US$76).

Petite Anse, Marie-Galante, Guadeloupe, F.W.I. ☎ 590/97-32-63. Fax 590/97-33-59. Main courses 7.60€–22.80€ (US$6.80–US$20.35); set menu 26.60€ (US$23.75). MC, V. Tues–Sun noon–2:30pm and 7–9:30pm. Closed Sept 15–Oct 15.

LA DÉSIRADE

La Désirade is one of the few islands in the Caribbean that is not ruined or even touched by tourism of any significance. Most visitors come just for the day, to enjoy the uncrowded white sandy beach.

The ubiquitous Columbus spotted this *terre désirée* or "sought-after land" after his Atlantic crossing in 1493. The island, just 5 miles (8km) off the eastern tip of Guadeloupe proper, is less than 7 miles (11km) long and about 1½ miles (2km) wide, and it has a single potholed road running along its length.

The island has fewer than 1,700 inhabitants, including the descendants of Europeans exiled here by royal command. Most visitors come to sunbathe or perhaps tour the island's barren expanses. There are, however, a handful of exceptionally simple guest houses charging from 45.60€ (US$40.70) for overnight accommodations for two. Don't expect anything grand.

The main village is **Grande-Anse,** which has a small church with a presbytery and flower garden. **Le Souffleur** is a boat-building community, and at **Baie Mahault,** you'll see the ruins of the old leper colony (including a barely recognizable chapel) from the early 18th century.

The best **beaches** are Souffleur, a tranquil oasis near the boat-building center, and Baie Mahault, a small quintessentially Caribbean beach with white sand and palm trees.

ESSENTIALS

GETTING THERE   From Guadeloupe most passengers opt for transit to La Désirade by **ferry,** which leaves St-François every day at 8am and 5pm (and sometimes at 3pm as well, depending on the season) from the wharves at St-François, near Guadeloupe's eastern tip. Returns from La Désirade for St-François include a daily departure at 3pm, allowing convenient access for day-trippers. Trip time is around 50 minutes each way, depending on conditions at sea. Round-trip passage on the ferryboat costs 27.35€ (US$24.45). Call ✆ **590/88-48-63** for schedules, but only from 4 to 7pm daily.

GETTING AROUND   On La Désirade, three or four **minibuses** run between the airport and the towns. To get around, you might negotiate with a local driver. **Bicycles** are also available at the hotels.

ACCOMMODATIONS

Accommodations are available at **L'Oasis** (✆ **590/20-02-12**) and **Le Mirage** (✆ **590/20-01-08;** fax 590/20-07-45). Both are at Beauséjour, a ½ mile (.8km) from the airport. L'Oasis has six plain rooms and charges 44.85€ (US$40.05) for a double, including breakfast. Built in 1990 of concrete, it's simple and boxy, lying a short walk from a good beach. Le Mirage offers seven rather drab rooms and charges 41.05€ (US$36.65) for a double, including breakfast. Built of concrete around the same time as L'Oasis, it offers a simple bar and restaurant, and it lies a bit closer to the sands than its competitor. Closed in September.

15

Jamaica

Most visitors already have a mental image of Jamaica before they arrive, picturing its boisterous culture of reggae and Rastafarianism; its white, sandy beaches; and its jungles, rivers, mountains, and clear waterfalls. This island nation's art and cuisine are also remarkable.

Jamaica lies 90 miles (145km) south of Cuba and is the third largest of the Caribbean islands, with some 4,400 square miles (11,396km) of lush green land, a mountain ridge peaking at 7,400 feet (2,220m) above sea level, and, on the north coast, many white-sand beaches with clear blue waters.

It can be a tranquil and intriguing island, but there's no denying that it's plagued by crime, drugs, and muggings. There is also palpable racial tension here. But many visitors are unaffected; they're escorted from the airport to their heavily patrolled hotel grounds and venture out only on expensive organized tours. These vacationers are largely sheltered from the more unpredictable and sometimes dangerous side of Jamaica, and this kind of trip can suit you just fine if all you want is to unwind on a beautiful beach. Those who want to see "the real Jamaica," or at least see the island in greater depth, had better be prepared for some hassle. Vendors on the beaches and in the markets can be particularly aggressive.

As we went to press, Jamaica saw an eruption of violence where gun battles between police and government opponents led to at least 25 people being killed. To quell the violence, the prime minister, P. J. Patterson, ordered out the entire Jamaican army of 3,000 troops. The violence was confined to the capital of Kingston and did not spread to any of the major tourist centers, such as Ocho Rios or Montego Bay. What long-term impact, if any, this explosion of violence will have on Jamaica's $1.3 billion tourist industry is not known. We advise you to check with travel agents and consult State Department travel advisories before you go.

Should you go? Certainly. You'll want to be prudent and cautious, just as if you were visiting New York, Miami, or Los Angeles. But the island has fine hotels and a zesty cuisine. It's well geared to couples who come to tie the knot or celebrate their honeymoon. As for sports, Jamaica boasts the best golf courses in the West Indies, and its landscape offers lots of outdoor activities, like rafting and serious hiking. The island has gorgeous beaches and some of the finest diving waters in the world.

CHOOSING WHERE TO STAY ON JAMAICA

Jamaica is such a large island that you have a wide range of choices.

The grand dame of Jamaica is **Montego Bay,** which has three of the leading and poshest resorts in the Caribbean (Half Moon, Round Hill, and Tryall), plus a very good selection of moderately priced and affordable hotels. The beaches are fabulous here, though often crowded in winter due to the hotel density.

There are fine golf courses here, and the shopping is excellent for Jamaica, but the nightlife is surprisingly lackluster.

Younger and hipper than Montego Bay, **Negril** is a sleepy town (with surprisingly little in the way of dining or nightlife) that has a freewheeling, sensual personality and a spectacular stretch of beach. A row of resorts, many of them lavish all-inclusives, has sprouted up along its shores. One visitor who flies in every year claims Negril is for "sand and sex," but not necessarily in that order.

To the west, **Ocho Rios** has some of the grandest and most traditional resorts in Jamaica as well as some of the leading Sandals properties. But it doesn't have the best beaches, shops, or scenic attractions, and it's frequently overrun with cruise-ship passengers. Nonetheless, if you like the sound of a particular resort there and just plan to stay put on your resort's beach, this might be your choice.

Port Antonio is for the upscale traveler who wants to escape the mass package tours of Ocho Rios or even Montego Bay. Come here for some good beaches plus great river rafting, scuba diving, or snorkeling.

Most visitors go to **Kingston** only for business reasons. It does have interesting museums and historic sights, fine galleries, and a diverse nightlife scene. But all in all, it's a city with some serious urban problems, and probably not what you're looking for in an island vacation. You certainly wouldn't go to Kingston for beaches.

1 Essentials

VISITOR INFORMATION

Before you go, you can get information from the **Jamaica Tourist Board** at the following U.S. addresses: 500 N. Michigan Ave., Suite 1030, **Chicago, IL** 60611 (© **312/527-1296**); 1320 S. Dixie Hwy., Suite 1101, **Miami, FL** 33146 (© **305/665-0557**); 3440 Wilshire Blvd., Suite 805, **Los Angeles, CA** 90010 (© **213/384-1123**); and 801 Second Ave., **New York, NY** 10017 (© **212/856-9727**). In **Atlanta,** information can be obtained by phone only (© **770/452-7799**).

In **Canada,** contact 1 Eglinton Ave. E., Suite 616, Toronto, ON M4P 3A1 (© **416/482-7850**). Brits can contact the **London** office: 1–2 Prince Consort Rd., London SW7 2BZ (© **020/7224-0505**).

The official website of the Jamaica Tourist Board is **www.jamaicatravel.com**.

Once on the island, you'll find tourist offices at 64 Knutsford Ave., **Kingston** (© **876/929-9200**); Cornwall Beach, St. James, **Montego Bay** (© **876/952-4425**); Shop no. 29, Coral Seas Plaza, **Negril** (© **876/957-4243**); in the Ocean Village Shopping Centre, **Ocho Rios** (© **876/974-2582**); in City Centre Plaza, **Port Antonio** (© **876/993-3051**); and in Hendriks Building, 2 High St., **Black River** (© **876/965-2074**).

GETTING THERE

Before you book your own airfare, read the sections "Package Deals" and "Finding the Best Airfare" in chapter 2—you may save a bundle, because there are always lots of package deals available to Jamaica's resorts.

There are two **international airports** on Jamaica: **Donald Sangster Airport** in Montego Bay (© **876/952-3124**) and **Norman Manley Airport** in Kingston (© **876/924-8452**). The most popular flights to Jamaica are from New York and Miami. Remember to reconfirm all flights, coming and going, no later than 72 hours before departure. Flying time from Miami is 1¼ hours; from Los Angeles, 5½ hours; from Atlanta, 2½ hours; from Dallas, 3 hours; from Chicago and New York, 3½ hours; and from Toronto, 4 hours.

Some of the most convenient service to Jamaica is provided by **American Airlines** (© 800/433-7300 in the U.S.; www.aa.com) through its hubs in New York and Miami. Throughout the year, one daily nonstop flight departs from New York's JFK airport for Montego Bay, continuing on to Kingston. Return flights to New York usually depart from Montego Bay, touch down briefly in Kingston, then continue nonstop back to JFK. From Miami, at least two daily flights depart for Kingston and two daily flights for Montego Bay.

US Airways (© 800/428-4322; www.usair.com) has two daily flights from New York, stopping in Charlotte. One daily flight leaves out of Baltimore, stopping in either Charlotte or Philadelphia before continuing to Jamaica. **Northwest Airlines** (© 800/225-2525 in the U.S.; www.nwa.com) flies directly to Montego Bay from Detroit.

Air Jamaica (© 800/523-5585 in the U.S.; www.airjamaica.com) operates about 14 flights per week from New York, most of which stop at both Montego Bay and Kingston, and even more frequent flights from Miami.

Air Canada (© 888/247-2262 in the U.S. or Canada; www.aircanada.ca) flies from Toronto to Jamaica daily. **British Airways** (© 0845/773-3377 in the U.K.; www.british-airways.com) has four nonstop flights weekly to Montego Bay and Kingston from London's Gatwick Airport.

GETTING AROUND

Especially if you've booked a package at one of the big resorts, you're likely to have airport transfers from Montego Bay included. Many resorts from around the island send buses to pick up and drop off their arriving and departing guests.

BY PLANE   Most travelers enter the country via Montego Bay. If you want to fly elsewhere, you'll need to use the island's domestic air service, which is provided by **Air Jamaica Express** (© 800/523-5585), a subsidiary of Air Jamaica, whose planes usually hold between 10 and 37 passengers. Air Jamaica Express flies from the island's international airports at Montego Bay and Kingston to small airports around the island, including Port Antonio, Boscobel (near Ocho Rios), Negril, and Tinson Pen (a tiny airport near Kingston for domestic flights only). For example, there are 11 flights a day between Kingston and Montego Bay and 3 flights a day between Negril and Port Antonio. Car-rental facilities are available only at the international airports at Kingston and Montego Bay.

The most convenient air link for resort visitors to Negril is on **Air Link** (© 876/940-6660), which flies from Montego Bay (site of the international airport) to Negril.

Moments **A True Taste of Jamaica**

Wherever you go in Jamaica, you'll see ramshackle stands selling jerk pork. There is no more authentic local experience than to stop at one of these stands and order a lunch of jerk pork, preferably washed down with a Red Stripe beer. Jerk is a special way of barbecuing highly spicy meats on slats of pimento wood, over a wood fire set in the ground. You can never be quite sure what goes into the seasoning, but the taste is definitely of peppers, pimento (allspice), and ginger. You can also order jerk chicken, sausage, fish, and even lobster. The cook will haul out a machete and chop the meat into bite-size pieces for you, then throw them into a paper bag.

Jamaica

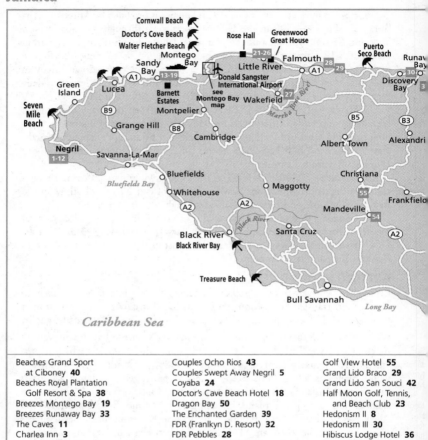

Beaches Grand Sport at Ciboney **40**	Couples Ocho Rios **43**	Golf View Hotel **55**
Beaches Royal Plantation Golf Resort & Spa **38**	Couples Swept Away Negril **5**	Grand Lido Braco **29**
	Coyaba **24**	Grand Lido San Souci **42**
Breezes Montego Bay **19**	Doctor's Cave Beach Hotel **18**	Half Moon Golf, Tennis,
Breezes Runaway Bay **33**	Dragon Bay **50**	and Beach Club **23**
The Caves **11**	The Enchanted Garden **39**	Hedonism II **8**
Charlea Inn **3**	FDR (Franlkyn D. Resort) **32**	Hedonism III **30**
Coral Cliff **22**	FDR Pebbles **28**	Hibiscus Lodge Hotel **36**
Country, Country **2**	Fern Hill Club Hotel **49**	High Hope Estate **34**
Couples Negril **7**	Goblin Hill Villas at San San **48**	Hotel Mocking Bird Hill **45**
	Goldeneye **44**	Jamaica Heights Resort **46**

BY TAXI Not all of Jamaica's taxis are metered; if yours is not, negotiate the price before you get in. In Kingston and on the rest of the island, special taxis and buses for visitors are operated by **JUTA** (Jamaica Union of Travellers Association) and have the union's emblem on the side of the vehicle. All prices are controlled, and any local JUTA office will supply a list of rates. JUTA drivers handle nearly all the ground transportation, and some offer sightseeing tours. Rates are 25% higher after midnight.

BY RENTAL CAR Jamaica is big enough, and public transportation is unreliable enough, that a car is a necessity if you plan to do much independent sightseeing. In lieu of this, you can always take an organized tour or a taxi tour to the major sights and spend the rest of the time on the beaches near your hotel.

Depending on road conditions, driving time for the 50 miles (81km) from Montego Bay to Negril is 1½ hours; from Montego Bay to Ocho Rios, 1½

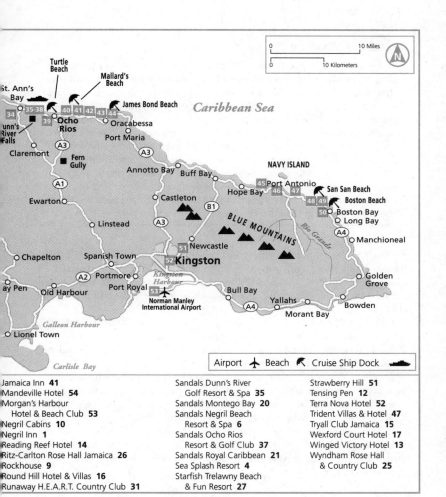

Jamaica Inn **41**	Sandals Dunn's River	Strawberry Hill **51**
Mandeville Hotel **54**	Golf Resort & Spa **35**	Tensing Pen **12**
Morgan's Harbour	Sandals Montego Bay **20**	Terra Nova Hotel **52**
Hotel & Beach Club **53**	Sandals Negril Beach	Trident Villas & Hotel **47**
Negril Cabins **10**	Resort & Spa **6**	Tryall Club Jamaica **15**
Negril Inn **1**	Sandals Ocho Rios	Wexford Court Hotel **17**
Reading Reef Hotel **14**	Resort & Golf Club **37**	Winged Victory Hotel **13**
Ritz-Carlton Rose Hall Jamaica **26**	Sandals Royal Caribbean **21**	Wyndham Rose Hall
Rockhouse **9**	Sea Splash Resort **4**	& Country Club **25**
Round Hill Hotel & Villas **16**	Starfish Trelawny Beach	
Runaway H.E.A.R.T. Country Club **31**	& Fun Resort **27**	

hours; from Ocho Rios to Port Antonio, 2½ hours; and from Ocho Rios to Kingston, 2 hours.

Unfortunately, car-rental rates on Jamaica have skyrocketed recently, making it one of the most expensive rental scenes in the Caribbean. There's also a 15% government tax on rentals. Equally unfortunate are the unfavorable insurance policies that apply to virtually every car-rental agency on Jamaica.

Try **Budget Rent-a-Car** (© **800/527-0700** in the U.S., 876/952-3838 at the Montego Bay Airport, or 876/924-8762 in Kingston; www.budgetrenta car.com); with Budget, a daily collision-damage waiver is mandatory and costs $15 per day. **Hertz** (© **800/654-3001** in the U.S.; www.hertz.com) operates branches at the airports at both Montego Bay (© **876/979-0438**) and Kingston (© **876/924-8028**).

If you'd like to shop for a better deal with one of the local companies in Montego Bay, try **Jamaica Car Rental,** 23 Gloucester Ave. (© **876/952-5586**), with

> **Tips** **A Word on Marijuana**
>
> You will almost certainly be approached by someone selling *ganja*—in fact, that's why many travelers come here. However, we should warn you that drugs (including marijuana) are illegal, and imprisonment is the penalty for possession. You don't want to experience the Jamaican penal system firsthand. Don't smoke pot openly in public. Of course, hundreds of visitors do and get away with it, but you may be the one who gets caught, and the person selling to you might even be a police informant. Above all, don't even try to bring marijuana back into the United States. There are drug-sniffing dogs stationed at the Jamaican airports, and they will check your luggage. U.S. Customs agents, well aware of the drug situation on Jamaica, have arrested many tourists who have tried to take a chance on bringing some home.

a branch at the Sangster International Airport at Montego Bay (© **876/952-9496**). Daily rates begin at $55. You can also try **United Car Rentals,** 49 Gloucester Ave. (© **876/952-3077**), which rents Mazdas, Toyotas, Hondas, and Suzuki Jeeps, costing from $48 per day for a four-door standard car with air-conditioning.

In Kingston, try **Island Car Rentals,** 17 Antigua Ave. (© **876/926-5991**), with a branch at Montego Bay's Sangster International Airport (© **876/952-7225**). It rents Hondas and Samurais with rates beginning at $66 daily in winter, $49 in the off-season.

Driving is on the left, and you should exercise more than your usual caution here because of the unfamiliar terrain. Be especially cautious at night. Speed limits in town are 30 miles per hour (48kmph), and 50 miles per hour (80kmph) outside towns. Gas is measured in the Imperial gallon (a British unit of measure that will give you 25% more than a U.S. gallon), and the charge is payable only in Jamaican dollars; most stations don't accept credit cards. Your own valid driver's license from back home is acceptable for short-term visits to Jamaica.

 FAST FACTS: Jamaica

Banks Banks island-wide are open Monday to Friday from 9am to 5pm. You'll find ATMs in all the major resort areas and towns, including Port Antonio, Ocho Rios, and Kingston. There are lots in Montego Bay, of course, and even one or two in sleepy Negril.

Currency The unit of currency on Jamaica is the **Jamaican dollar,** and it uses the same symbol as the U.S. dollar ($). There is no fixed rate of exchange for the Jamaican dollar. Subject to market fluctuations, it's traded publicly. Visitors to Jamaica can pay for any goods in U.S. dollars. When asking a price, always inquire if the quotation is in U.S. dollars or Jamaican dollars. The difference can mean whether you get robbed or not!

In this guide we've generally followed the price-quotation policy of the establishment, whether in Jamaican dollars or U.S. dollars. The symbol **J$** denotes prices in Jamaican dollars; the conversion into U.S. dollars follows in parentheses. *When dollar figures stand alone, they are always U.S. currency.*

Jamaican currency is issued in banknotes of J$50, J$100, J$500, and J$1,000. Coins are available in denominations of 10¢, 25¢, J$1, J$5, J$10, and J$20. At press time, but subject to change, the exchange rate of Jamaican currency is J$43 to US$1 (J$1 equals about 2.3¢). As this will probably fluctuate a bit during the lifetime of this edition, use this rate for general guidance only. (Just before you leave home, you can check the current exchange rates on the Web at **www.x-rates.com**.)

There are Bank of Jamaica exchange bureaus at both international airports (Montego Bay and Kingston), at cruise-ship piers, and in most hotels.

Customs Do *not* bring in or take out illegal drugs from Jamaica. Your luggage will be searched; marijuana-sniffing police dogs are stationed at the airport. Otherwise, you can bring in most items intended for personal use.

Documents U.S. and Canadian residents need a passport and a return or an ongoing ticket. In lieu of a passport, an original birth certificate plus photo ID will do, but before you rely on this, always check in case document requirements have changed. We always recommend just taking your passport. Other visitors, including British subjects, need passports, good for a maximum stay of 6 months.

Immigration cards, needed for bank transactions and currency exchange, are given to visitors at the airport arrival desks.

Electricity Most places have 110-volt AC (60 cycles), as in the United States. However, some establishments operate on 220-volt AC (50 cycles). If your hotel is on a different current from your U.S.-made appliance, ask for a transformer and an adapter.

Embassies, Consulates & High Commissions Calling embassies or consulates in Jamaica is a challenge. Phones will ring and ring before being picked up, if they are answered at all. Extreme patience is needed to reach a live voice on the other end. The embassy of the **United States** is located at the Jamaica Mutual Life Centre, 2 Oxford Rd., Kingston 5 (© **876/929-4850**). The High Commission of **Canada** is situated at 3 Wet Kings House Rd., Kingston 10 (© **876/926-1500**), and there's a consulate at 29 Gloucester Ave., Montego Bay (© **876/952-6198**). The High Commission of the **United Kingdom** is found at 28 Trafalgar Rd., Kingston 10 (© **876/926-9050**).

Emergencies For the **police**, dial © **119**; to report a **fire** or call an **ambulance**, dial © **110**.

Language Jamaicans speak English with a lovely lilt. Among themselves, they also speak patois, a fast-spoken blend of French, English, and a number of other languages.

Pharmacies Prescriptions are accepted by local pharmacies only if issued by a Jamaican doctor. Hotels have doctors on call. If you need any particular medicine or treatment, bring evidence, such as a letter from your own physician.

Safety Major resorts have security guards who protect the grounds, so most vacationers don't have any real problems. It's not wise to accept an invitation to see "the real Jamaica" from some stranger you meet on the beach. Exercise caution when traveling around Jamaica. Safeguard your valuables, and never leave them unattended on a beach. Likewise, never leave luggage or other valuables in a car, or even the trunk of a car. The U.S. State Department has issued a travel advisory about crime rates in Kingston, so don't walk around alone at night. Caution is also advisable in many north-coast tourist areas, especially remote houses and isolated villas that can't afford security.

Taxes The government imposes a 12% room tax. You'll be charged a J$1,000 (US$23) departure tax at the airport, payable in either Jamaican or U.S. dollars. There's also a 15% government tax on rental cars and a 15% tax on all overseas phone calls.

Time Jamaica is on eastern standard time year-round, so most of the year Jamaica is on the same time as the U.S. east coast. When the United States is on daylight saving time, at 6am in Miami it's 5am in Kingston.

Tipping A general 10% or 15% is expected in hotels and restaurants on occasions when you would normally tip. Some places add a service charge to the bill, so make sure you understand whether or not it's already included. Tipping is not allowed in the all-inclusive hotels. Taxi drivers expect about 10% to 15%.

Water It's usually safe to drink piped-in water, island-wide, as it's filtered and chlorinated. But, as always, it's more prudent to drink bottled water if it's available.

Weather Expect temperatures around 80° to 90°F on the coast. Winter is a little cooler. In the mountains it can get as low as 40°F. There is generally a breeze, which in winter is noticeably cool. The rainy periods generally are October and November (although it can extend into December) and May and June. Normally rain comes in short, sharp showers; then the sun shines.

2 Montego Bay ★★★

Situated on the northwestern coast of the island, Montego Bay first attracted tourists in the 1940s, when Doctor's Cave Beach became popular with wealthy vacationers who bathed in the warm water fed by mineral springs. It's now Jamaica's second-largest city.

Despite the large influx of visitors, Montego Bay still retains its own identity as a thriving business and commercial center, and it functions as the market town for most of western Jamaica. It has cruise-ship piers and a growing industrial center at the free port.

Because Montego Bay has its own airport, those who vacation here have little need to visit Kingston, the island's capital. MoBay is the most cosmopolitan of Jamaica's resort areas.

ESSENTIALS

EMERGENCIES The **Cornwall Regional Hospital** is at Mount Salem (© 876/952-5100). For medicines and prescriptions, try the **Overton Pharmacy,** 49 Union St., Overton Plaza (© 876/952-2699).

ACCOMMODATIONS

Most of the big, full-service resorts are frequently included in package tours. Booking a package will make the rates much more reasonable. See "Package Deals" and "Tips on Accommodations" in chapter 2.

VERY EXPENSIVE

Breezes Montego Bay ★★ A five-story complex, this SuperClub—defined as "a sandbox for your inner child"—is the only major hotel directly on the sands of Montego Bay's most popular public beach, Doctor's Cave. It's adult and indulgent, but without the raucous partying that's the norm at Hedonism II (a member of the same chain). Bedrooms are tastefully furnished and breezy, overlooking either the beach or the garden that separates the hotel from the traffic of Montego Bay's main commercial boulevard, Gloucester Avenue. Rooms range from intimate cabins to lavish suites. The cabin rooms, 31 in all, are similar to a ship's cabin, very intimate with a queen-size bed. Slightly larger are the deluxe rooms, with twins or a king-size bed. The best are the deluxe oceanfront rooms, with king-size beds, and the oceanfront suites.

Informal but good meals are served at Jimmy's Buffet, a terrace overlooking the pool and the beach. More formal meals, with a more refined cuisine, are dished out at the candlelit Martino's, an Italian rooftop restaurant.

Gloucester Ave., Montego Bay, Jamaica, W.I. ⓒ **800/859-SUPER** in the U.S., or 876/940-1150. Fax 876/940-1160. www.superclubs.com. 123 units. All-inclusive rates for 3 nights: Winter $1,410 double. Off-season $1,200 double. Rates include all meals, drinks, and most activities. AE, DC, DISC, MC, V. No children under age 16 accepted. **Amenities:** 2 restaurants, bar; pool; lit tennis courts; fitness center; rooftop Jacuzzi; full range of watersports, including snorkeling, windsurfing, sailing, and kayaking. *In room:* A/C, TV, coffeemaker, hair dryer, safe.

Half Moon Golf, Tennis & Beach Club ★★★ Opening onto 400 acres (16 hectares) that take in a ½-mile (.8km) of white-sand beach, this is one of the grand hotels of the Caribbean, without the snobbism of Round Hill or Tryall (see below). About 8 miles (13km) east of Montego Bay's city center and 6 miles (10km) from the international airport, this is a classic, and one of the 300 best hotels in the world, according to *Condé Nast Traveler*. It's a very grand and appealing place, a true luxury hideaway with taste and style. It has far more activities, excitement, amenities, restaurants, and a better beach than either Round Hill or Tryall.

Accommodations include conventional hotel rooms, suites, and a collection of superbly accessorized private villas (most villas have private pools and a full-time staff). Each unit is comfortably furnished with an English colonial/Caribbean motif, with a private balcony or patio, plus a state-of-the-art bathroom with a shower/tub combo. Queen Anne–inspired furniture is set off by vibrant Jamaican paintings, and many units contain mahogany four-poster beds.

The Sugar Mill restaurant, our favorite restaurant in Montego Bay, is set beside a working water wheel from a bygone sugar estate (see "Dining," later in this chapter). The Seagrape Terrace (named after the 80-year-old sea-grape trees on the property) offers delightful meals alfresco. Il Giardino, set within a convincing replica of a Renaissance palazzo, serves savory Italian cuisine. The resort also has a pan-Asian restaurant, a steakhouse, and an English pub.

Half Moon Post Office, Rose Hall, St. James, Montego Bay, Jamaica, W.I. ⓒ **800/626-0592** in the U.S., or 876/953-2211. Fax 876/953-2731. www.halfmoonclub.com. 419 units. Winter $390 double; from $590 suite; from $780 villa. Off-season $240–$290 double; from $350 suite; from $480 villa. MAP (breakfast and dinner) $70 per person extra. Ask about golf and spa packages. AE, DC, DISC, MC, V. **Amenities:** 6 restaurants, 6 bars;

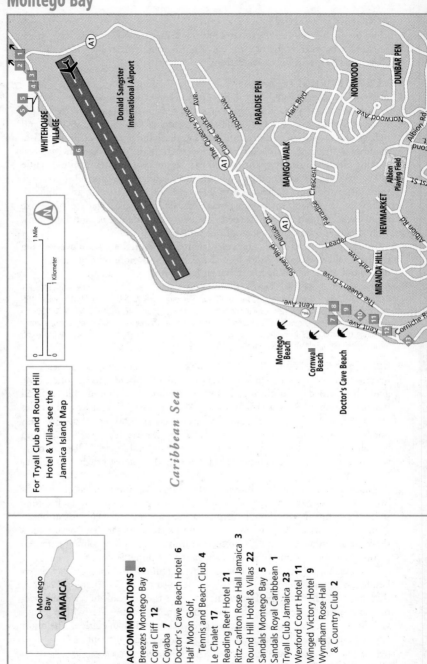

For Tryall Club and Round Hill
Hotel & Villas, see the
Jamaica Island Map

Caribbean Sea

Donald Sangster
International Airport

WHITEHOUSE
VILLAGE

A1

PARADISE PEN

NORWOOD

DUNBAR PEN

MANGO WALK

NEWMARKET

MIRANDA HILL

Albion
Playing Field

Montego
Beach

Cornwall
Beach

Doctor's Cave Beach

O Montego
Bay
JAMAICA

ACCOMMODATIONS

Breezes Montego Bay **8**
Coral Cliff **12**
Coyaba **7**
Doctor's Cave Beach Hotel **6**
Half Moon Golf,
   Tennis and Beach Club **4**
Le Chalet **17**
Reading Reef Hotel **21**
Ritz-Carlton Rose Hall Jamaica **3**
Round Hill Hotel & Villas **22**
Sandals Montego Bay **5**
Sandals Royal Caribbean **1**
Tryall Club Jamaica **23**
Wexford Court Hotel **11**
Winged Victory Hotel **9**
Wyndham Rose Hall
   & Country Club **2**

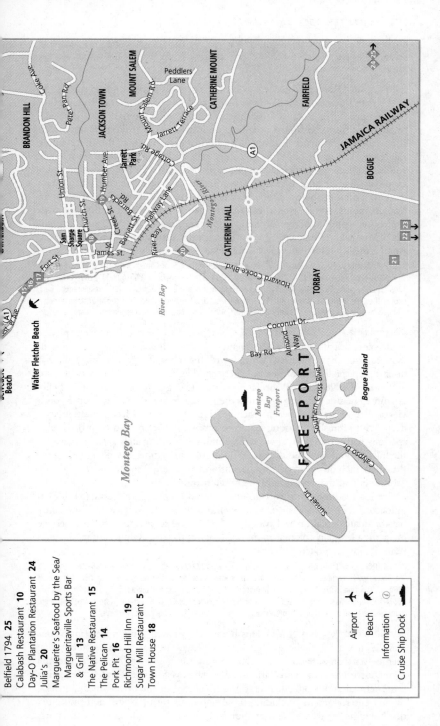

Belfield 1794 **25**
Calabash Restaurant **10**
Day-O Plantation Restaurant **24**
Julia's **20**
Marguerite's Seafood by the Sea/
Margueritaville Sports Bar
& Grill **13**
The Native Restaurant **15**
The Pelican **14**
Pork Pit **16**
Richmond Hill Inn **19**
Sugar Mill Restaurant **5**
Town House **18**

Airport ✈
Beach 🏊
Information ⓘ
Cruise Ship Dock ⚓

3 pools; 18-hole golf course; 13 tennis courts (7 lit at night); spa; Jacuzzi; horseback riding; bike rental; deep-sea fishing; car rental; room service (7am–11:30pm); babysitting; laundry. *In room:* A/C, TV, minibar, hair dryer, iron and ironing board, safe.

Ritz-Carlton Rose Hall Jamaica ★★★ The most up-to-date and spectacular of the grand dames of MoBay (and that includes Half Moon and Round Hill), this complex sprawls across a dazzling stretch of white sandy beach. Just a 10-minute ride from the airport, Ritz-Carlton lives up to its stellar reputation with this latest blitz, its major draw the White Witch golf course, a 10-minute shuttle ride away. The resort offers the ambience of a traditional Jamaican great house with all modern comforts including a full-service spa. In the old plantation country of Jamaica, the hotel is secluded, standing in carefully landscaped grounds. It's the new kid on the block for luxury options in Jamaica. First-rate guestrooms, in tropical motifs, feature stoned-columned balconies and deluxe bathrooms with shower/tub combos. Some accommodations are suitable for those with disabilities. Those who can afford it live in even greater luxury in the executive suites. Among the top resorts of Jamaica, only Half Moon equals its cuisine.

Rose Hall, Montego Bay, Jamaica, W.I. ✆ **800/241-3333** in the U.S. or Canada, or 876/953-2204. Fax 876/953-8790. www.rosehall.com. 427 units. Winter $375–$3,000 double; $845–$3,000 suite. Off-season $205–$1,250 double; $325–$1,250 suite. Children under age 12 free in room. **Amenities:** 5 restaurants, 2 bars; pool; golf course; 2 tennis courts; health club and spa; Jacuzzi; watersports; children's activities; business center; 24-hr. room service; babysitting; laundry. *In room:* A/C, TV, minibar, hair dryer, iron and ironing board, safe.

Round Hill Hotel and Villas ★★★ Opened in 1953 on its small, private white-sand beach—and now a legend—this remains the prestige address in Jamaica, even though it hasn't kept up with the times like Half Moon. Still, that doesn't stop the likes of Steven Spielberg and Harrison Ford from checking into villas on the 98-acre (39-hectare) estate. The guestrooms are in a richly appointed seaside building known as the Pineapple House, and each opens onto views of the water and beach. Each spacious, breezy unit has plantation-style decor with refinished antique furniture and a king-size or two twin beds, plus spacious bathrooms with shower/tub combinations. Privately owned villas dot the hillside, and each is individually decorated, sometimes lavishly so. Rates for the villas include the services of a uniformed maid, a cook, and a gardener. Twenty-one of these villas have their own private pools.

Breakfast is brought to your room or served on the dining terrace. Informal luncheons are held in an intimate straw hut with an open terrace in a little sandy bay. Standard Jamaican and continental dishes are served on a candlelit terrace or in the Georgian colonial room overlooking the sea. Ralph Lauren, a sometimes visitor, decorated the cocktail area.

Rte. A1 (P.O. Box 64), Montego Bay, Jamaica, W.I. ✆ **800/972-2159** in the U.S., or 876/956-7050. Fax 876/956-7505. www.roundhilljamaica.com. 74 units. Winter $420–$510 double; $600–$850 villa. Off-season $260–$310 double; $370–$550 villa. Extra person $70. MAP (breakfast and dinner) $80 per person extra. AE, DC, MC, V. **Amenities:** Restaurant, 3 bars; pool; 5 tennis courts; health club and spa; watersports; dive shop; room service (7:30am–9:30pm); babysitting; laundry. *In room:* A/C, coffeemaker, hair dryer.

Sandals Montego Bay ★ This honeymoon haven (only male-female couples) lies next to Whitehouse Village on the largest private beach in MoBay, one even better than at Sandals Royal Caribbean. On a 19-acre (8 hectare) site, the all-inclusive has a big party atmosphere, whereas Sandals Royal Caribbean is more refined and subdued. Everything is covered in the price—meals, snacks, nightly entertainment (including those notorious toga parties), and unlimited drinks, night or day, at one of four bars. Lots of entertainment and sports facilities are available on the property, so many guests never leave. There's a real drawback here, though. The resort lies literally at the edge of the main airport, with planes flying over all day, rattling the rum glasses.

The accommodations are either in villas spread along 1,700 feet (510m) of white-sand beach or in the main house, where all bedrooms face the sea and contain private balconies. Try to avoid booking into a room over the dining room; these don't have balconies and may be noisy. The best units are the grande luxe ocean or beachfront units, with private balconies or patios. Each unit is equipped with a first-rate bathroom with a shower/tub combinations. The cuisine is in the typical Sandals chain–style format—plenty of it, but nothing too imaginative. The best option is Tokyo Joe's, serving six-course Asian dinners. Oleander Deck with its "white-glove service" features Jamaican and Caribbean cuisine and is the other best bet option.

Kent Ave. (P.O. Box 100), Montego Bay, Jamaica, W.I. (C) 800/SANDALS in the U.S. and Canada, or 876/952-5510. Fax 876/952-0816. www.sandals.com. 245 units. All-inclusive rates for 4 days/3 nights: winter $1,113–$1,470 double; $2,919 suite for 2. Off-season $1,029–$1,420 double; $1,512 suite for 2. Rates include all meals, drinks, and all activities. AE, MC, V. **Amenities:** 5 restaurants, 4 bars; 2 pools; 4 tennis courts; fitness center; 4 Jacuzzis; sauna; watersports; dive shop; salon; massage; laundry. *In room:* A/C, TV, safe.

Sandals Royal Caribbean ★★   This all-inclusive, couples-only (male-female) resort, with a more tranquil atmosphere than Sandals Montego Bay, lies on its own private beach (which, frankly, isn't as good as the one at Sandals Montego Bay). Some of the British colonial atmosphere remains (the formal tea in the afternoon), but there are modern touches as well, including a private, clothing-optional island reached by boat.

The spacious rooms come in a wide range of categories, from standard to superior to deluxe. Most desirable are the grand luxe beachfront rooms, with private patios or balconies. Each unit has a small but well-equipped private bathroom with a shower/tub combination. The cuisine seems more varied here than at other MoBay Sandals, with variety such as Bali Hai, an Indonesian restaurant serving on an offshore island. The Regency Suite serves a rather good Jamaican-inspired cuisine, among other options.

Mahoe Bay (P.O. Box 167), Montego Bay, Jamaica, W.I. (C) 800/SANDALS in the U.S. and Canada, or 876/953-2232. Fax 876/953-2788. www.sandals.com. 190 units. All-inclusive rates for 4 days/3 nights: winter $1,620–$2,280 per couple; from $2,670 suite for 2. Off-season $1,440–$2,160 per couple; from $2,370

(Fun Fact Catch a Fire: Jamaica's Reggae Festivals**

Every August, Jamaica comes alive with the pulsating sounds of **Reggae Sunsplash,** the world's largest annual reggae festival. This weeklong music extravaganza has featured some of the most prominent reggae groups and artists, including Ziggy Marley, Cocoa Tea, and the Melody Makers. Sunsplash takes place at different venues; check with Jamaican tourist boards for the latest details. Some time during the second week of August, **Reggae Sunfest** takes place in Montego Bay. Usually this is a 4-day musical event. Some of the biggest names in reggae, both from Jamaica and worldwide, perform. Many local hotels are fully booked for the festival, so advance reservations are necessary.

The Jamaican Tourist Board's U.S. and Canadian offices can give you information about packages and group rates for the festivals and fill you in on other reggae concerts and events held throughout the year on Jamaica.

suite for 2. Rates include all meals, drinks, and activities. AE, MC, V. **Amenities:** 4 restaurants, 5 bars; 4 pools; 3 tennis courts; fitness center; 5 Jacuzzis; watersports; massage; laundry. *In room:* A/C, TV, safe.

Tryall Club Jamaica ★★★ With more spacious grounds than almost any other hotel on Jamaica, this stylish and upscale resort sits 12 miles (19km) west of town on the site of a 2,200-acre (880-hectare)former sugar plantation. It doesn't have the fine beach that Half Moon does, nor the elegant house-party atmosphere of Round Hill, but it's noteworthy nevertheless. Known as one of the grandest resorts of Jamaica, the property lies along a 1½-mile (2km) beachfront and is presided over by a 165-year-old Georgian-style great house. It's a top choice for vacationers who are serious about their golf game.

The accommodations in luxurious villas are decorated in cool pastels with English colonial touches. All contain ceiling fans and air-conditioning, along with picture windows framing sea and mountain views. Bedrooms are exceedingly spacious, with luxurious beds, private patios or terraces, and tile floors. Bathrooms are roomy, with plenty of counter space and a shower/tub combination. The resort's villas are set amid lush foliage and are designed for privacy, each with a private pool. The most formal of the resort's dining areas is in the great house, where a refined cuisine is presented, but it's not the equal of the options available at Half Moon and the Ritz-Carlton. There's also a beach cafe— very informal and more for convenience than for good food.

Many clients here are CEOs, so the hotel has opened an Internet room, allowing guests access to e-mail accounts and to check on stock portfolios. On other fronts, Tryall is wining recognition as one of the most eco-sensitive resorts in the Caribbean, wining acclaim as a "Green Globe Hotel."

St. James (P.O. Box 1206), Montego Bay, Jamaica, W.I. ✆ **800/238-5290** in the U.S., or 876/956-5660. Fax 876/956-5673. www.tryallclub.com. 72 villas. Winter $400–$12,000 villa. Off-season $250–$7,000 villa. MAP (breakfast and dinner) $77 per person extra. AE, DC, MC, V. **Amenities:** 2 restaurants, 4 bars, cafe; pool with swim-up bar; championship 18-hole par-71 golf course; 9 Laykold tennis courts; fitness center; windsurfing, snorkeling, deep-sea fishing; salon; room service (breakfast only); massage; babysitting; laundry. *In room:* A/C (in some), TV, kitchen, fridge, coffeemaker, hair dryer (in some), safe.

EXPENSIVE

Coyaba ★★ On a lovely strip of private beachfront, this small all-inclusive resort evokes a British colonial atmosphere. It was established in 1994 by American/Jamaican-Chinese entrepreneurs, the Robertson family, and built from scratch at a cost of $4 million. Set a 15-minute drive east of the center of Montego Bay, it's centered around an adaptation of an 18th-century great house.

Accommodations in the main building overlook the garden; those in the pair of three-story outbuildings lie closer to the beach and are somewhat more expensive. The decor is plantation style, with traditional prints, expensive chintz fabrics, French doors leading onto private patios or verandas, and mahogany furniture. Hand-carved bedsteads, often four-posters, are fitted with luxury coverings. The roomy bathrooms have combination shower/tubs. More than 30 of its bedrooms have been refurbished, and some have been upgraded to junior suites with small refrigerators and such special amenities as irons and ironing boards. The hotel's main and most formal restaurant, the Vineyard, serves first-rate Jamaican and continental dinners. Less upscale is Docks Caribbean Bar & Grill.

Mahoe Bay, Little River, Montego Bay, Jamaica, W.I. ✆ **877/COYABA-8** or 876/953-9150. Fax 876/953-2244. www.coyabaresortjamaica.com. 50 units. Winter $290–$390 double. Off-season $190–$250 double. All meals $95 per person extra. Children age 11 and under get a 50% discount. AE, MC, V. **Amenities:** 3 restaurants, 3 bars; pool; lit tennis court; health club and spa; Jacuzzi; watersports; car rental; room service (7am–10pm); massage; nanny service; laundry. *In room:* A/C, TV/VCR, coffeemaker, hair dryer, safe.

FDR Pebbles ⭐ *Kids*   No, it's not named after the U.S. president. This resort, which pioneered at Runaway Bay, has invaded Montego Bay and almost overnight became the most family-friendly place at the resort. It's even better than its parent outside Ocho Rios. FDR Pebbles lies a 35-minute drive east of the airport, opening onto the waterfront and a beach. The resort is an all-inclusive property of cedarwood accommodations designed with real Jamaican flair and style, offering spacious living and bedroom areas, shower/tub combintion bathrooms, plus generous balconies opening onto a view. It's most suited for families with two children, although a larger family can be very comfortable in adjoining units. Everything is geared towards family fun, with an array of activities including fishing and swimming in a nearby river and hiking along nature trails. Each family is assigned a "vacation nanny" (yes, that politically incorrect term is used), who assists with the housekeeping and babysitting.

Main St., Trelawny (P.O. Box 1933), Jamaica, W.I. ⓒ 888/FDR-KIDS in the U.S. or 876/617-2495. Fax 876/617-2512. www.fdrholidays.com. Winter $275–$350 double. Off-season $252–$330 double. Children under age 16 stay free. Rates all-inclusive. AE, MC, V. **Amenities:** 2 restaurants, 3 bars, dance club; tennis court; watersports; hikes; babysitting. *In room:* A/C, TV.

Starfish Trelawny Beach & Fun Resort ⭐ *Kids*   Following a $5 million and much-needed renovation, this all-inclusive is one of the best value vacations on the island. Opening onto a stretch of powder-white, soft, sandy beach, it offers activities for both children and adults. The location is 23 miles (37km) east of MoBay airport. The most spacious rooms are the cottages, housing 3 adults and 2 children, lying at the rear of the hotel. For those who must have an ocean view, the resort rents some "superior" rooms, suitable for three adults and one child, with a balcony overlooking the beach. The least expensive units have a mountain or garden view, with a balcony, each housing three adults and one child. The wide range of sports and amenities make this an alluring choice. The food is fairly standardized, but a la carte variety is achieved by its feature of both a Japanese restaurant and a Sushi Bar with Teppanyaki tables and a pasta and pizza restaurant. There's also an a la carte four-course gourmet dinner served in the Casablanca Restaurant.

North Coast Highway, Falmouth, Jamaica, W.I. ⓒ 800/659-5436 or 876/954-2450. Fax 876/954-2173. 350 units. Winter $410–$430 double, $520 cottage. Off-season $330–$370 double, $480 cottage. AE, DC, MC, V. **Amenities:** 4 restaurants, 4 bars; disco bar; pool; 4 tennis courts; fitness center; badminton court; sauna; watersports; dive shop; children's programs; babysitting; laundry. *In room:* A/C, TV, safe.

Wyndham Rose Hall & Country Club ⭐   On a thin strip of white sandy beach, this 30-acre (12-hectare) resort stands along the north-coast highway 9 miles (14km) east of the airport. On a former sugar plantation that once covered 7,000 acres (2,800 hectares), the hotel abuts the 200-year-old home of the legendary "White Witch of Rose Hall," now a historic site. If you have to be directly on a great beach, this place isn't for you. But if you want to escape the more impersonal and chain-operated all-inclusives like the Sandals clones, and want a more authentic Jamaican experience, then check in. The seven-story H-shaped structure features a large and attractive lobby on the ground floor; upstairs, guestrooms all have sea views and come with a small private balcony. The tiled bathrooms with tubs and showers are well maintained.

Facing massive competition from the newly opened Ritz-Carlton (which is far superior), Wyndham has spent millions on massive renovations, improving and upgrading its accommodations with new designer furniture. Bathrooms are receiving a makeover with granite countertops, new plumbing fixtures, and

Bath & Body Works amenities. The cuisine in all the hotel's five restaurants is generally good but not sublime.

Rose Hall (P.O. Box 999), Montego Bay, Jamaica, W.I. ✆ **800/996-3426** in the U.S., or 876/953-2650. Fax 876/953-2617. www.wyndham.com. 487 units. Winter $290–$315 double; from $445 suite. Off-season $235–$265 double; from $370 suite. MAP (breakfast and dinner) $55 per person extra. AE, DC, MC, V. **Amenities:** 6 restaurants, 6 bars; 3 pools (2 with swim-up bar); golf course; 6 lit all-weather Laykold tennis courts; fitness center; sailboats; children's programs; room service (7am–11pm); massage; babysitting; laundry. *In room:* A/C, TV, safe.

MODERATE

Doctor's Cave Beach Hotel ★ *Value*   This hotel stands across from Doctor's Cave Beach, the busiest and most crowded, but also the best sands, in the Montego Bay area. This three-story hotel offers great value and lies in the bustle of the town's commercial zone, so it's not recommended for isolationists. It has its own gardens on 4 acres (2 hectares) of tropical gardens. The well-maintained rooms are simply but comfortably furnished, and suites have kitchenettes. Rooms are rated standard or superior, the latter more spacious with balconies opening onto a view. All units have tile floors; queen-size or twin beds, and small but efficiently organized tiled bathrooms with combination shower/tubs. At its two restaurants, the food is more authentic than at the resorts recommended above.

Gloucester Ave. (P.O. Box 94), Montego Bay, Jamaica, W.I. ✆ **800/44-UTELL** in the U.S., or 876/952-4355. Fax 876/952-5204. www.doctorscave.com. 90 units. Winter $145–$155 double; $170 suite for 2. Off-season $120–$130 double; $150 suite for 2. Extra person $35. MAP (breakfast and dinner) $29 per person extra. AE, DC, MC, V. **Amenities:** Restaurant, bar. *In room:* A/C, TV, hair dryer on request.

Reading Reef Hotel ★   With style and flair, this small, informal inn is set on a 300-foot (90m) sandy beach where guests relax undisturbed by vendors. It's located on 2½ acres (1 hectare), a 15-minute drive west of Montego Bay. The complex of four buildings overlooks beautiful reefs once praised by Jacques Cousteau for their aquatic life.

The accommodations open onto views of the Caribbean. All have air-conditioning and ceiling fans and a light island motif. The luxury rooms contain minibars, and the two- and three-bedroom suites offer kitchenettes. Fine linens are found on the comfortable beds, and the medium-size bathrooms contain adequate shelf space. Each bathroom is equipped with a shower or a shower/tub combination. The cuisine at the hotel is excellent, and for variety, Jamaican dishes are featured along with an international repertoire, even including Tex-Mex.

Rte. A1, on Bogue Lagoon, at the bottom of Long Hill Rd. (P.O. Box 225), Reading, Montego Bay, Jamaica, W.I. ✆ **876/952-5909.** Fax 876/952-7217. www.montego-bay-jamaica.com/jhta/reefclub. 28 units. Winter $115–$150 double; $265 2-bedroom suite; $325 3-bedroom suite. Off-season $85–$125 double; $220 2-bedroom suite; $270 3-bedroom suite. AE, MC, V. **Amenities:** 2 restaurants, 2 bars/lounges; pool; spa; watersports; babysitting; laundry. *In room:* A/C, TV.

Winged Victory Hotel ★ *Finds*   On a hillside road in Montego Bay, in the Miranda Hill District, this tall and modern hotel doesn't reveal its true beauty until you pass through its comfortable public rooms into a Mediterranean-style courtyard in back. Here, urn-shaped balustrades enclose a terraced garden, a pool, and a veranda looking over the faraway crescent of Montego Bay. All but five have a private balcony or veranda, along with an eclectic decor that's part Chinese, part colonial, and part Iberian. The bedrooms are an average-size and are well maintained, along with average-size, shower-only bathrooms. On the hotel's veranda is the well-regarded Calabash Restaurant (see "Dining," below).

5 Queen's Dr., Montego Bay, Jamaica, W.I. ✆ **800/74-CHARMS** in the U.S., or 876/952-3891. Fax 876/952-5986. www.wingedvictory-calabash.com. 30 units. Winter $100–$110 double. Off-season $80–$90

double. MAP (breakfast and dinner) $30 per person extra. MC, V. **Amenities:** Restaurant, 2 bars; room service; laundry. *In room:* A/C, TV, no phone.

INEXPENSIVE

Coral Cliff ★ *Value*   For good value, the Coral Cliff may be your best bet in Montego Bay, lying only a 2-minute walk from Doctor's Cave Beach. The hotel grew from a colonial-style building that was once the private home of Harry M. Doubleday (of the famous publishing family). It's located about a mile (2km) west of the center of town. Many of the light, airy, and spacious bedrooms open onto sea-view balconies. The rooms, as befits a former private house, come in a wide variety of shapes and sizes, most of them containing old colonial furniture, wicker, and rattan. Most units also have twin beds. The bathrooms are small in the older bedrooms, but more spacious in the newer wing out back. Each is tidily maintained and has a combination shower/tub.

Standard—not special—Jamaican and international dishes are served at Coral Cliff's restaurant.

165 Gloucester Ave. (P.O. Box 253), Montego Bay, Jamaica, W.I. © **876/952-4130.** Fax 876/952-6532. www.coralcliffjamaica.com. 21 units. Winter $95–$150 double; $105–$150 triple; from $140 suite. Off-season $80–$90 double; $92–$105 triple; from $120 suite. MC, V. **Amenities:** Restaurant, bar. *In room:* A/C.

Wexford Court Hotel *Kids*   Especially good for families on a budget, this hotel lies within a 5-minute walk of Doctor's Cave Beach. This hotel has a small pool and a patio (where calypso is enjoyed in season). The apartments have living/dining areas and kitchenettes, so you can cook for yourself. All the rooms have patios shaded by gables and Swiss chalet-style roofs, and each has a tiled, shower-only bathroom. The restaurant serves some zesty Jamaican dishes against a restaurant decor that evokes a 1950s Howard Johnson's in America.

39 Gloucester Ave. (P.O. Box 108), Montego Bay, Jamaica, W.I. © **876/952-2854.** Fax 876/952-3637. www.montego-bay-jamaica.com/wexford. 59 units. Winter $115.50–$132 double; $170 apt. Off-season $104.50–$121 double; $115.50 apt. MAP (breakfast and dinner) $38 per person extra. AE, MC, V. **Amenities:** Restaurant, 2 bars; pool. *In room:* A/C.

DINING
EXPENSIVE

Julia's ★ ITALIAN/INTERNATIONAL   The winding jungle road you take to reach this place is part of the before-dinner entertainment. After a jolting ride to a setting high above the city and its bay, you pass through a walled-in park that was the site of a private home built in 1840 for the Duke of Sutherland. The long, low-slung modern house boasts sweeping, open-sided views over the rolling hills and faraway coastline. Neville and Gisela Roe, the Jamaican-German couple running the place, draw on the styles of both the Caribbean and central Europe to prepare fillet of fresh fish with lime juice and butter, lobster, shrimp, and about 10 different kinds of pasta. Also look for such German dishes as schnitzels of chicken and pork; goulash with noodles or dumplings; cheesecake of the day, and schwartzwald torte (Black Forest cake). The food, although competently prepared with fresh ingredients whenever possible, can hardly compete with the view.

Julia's Estate, Bogue Hill. © **876/952-1772.** Reservations required. Fixed-price dinner $50–$55. AE, MC, V. Daily 5–11pm. Private van transportation provided; ask when you reserve.

Sugar Mill Restaurant ★★ INTERNATIONAL/CARIBBEAN   This restaurant, near a stone ruin of what used to be a water wheel for a sugar plantation, is reached after a drive through rolling landscape. Despite newer, trendier restaurants in town, this remains a perpetual favorite for its lovely setting and exquisite cuisine. Guests dine by candlelight either indoors or on an open terrace with a view of a pond, the water wheel, and plenty of greenery. Lunch can be a relatively simple affair, perhaps an ackee burger with bacon, preceded by Mama's pumpkin soup and followed with homemade rum-and-raisin ice cream. For dinner, try one of the chef's zesty versions of jerk pork, fish, or chicken. He also prepares the day's catch with considerable flair. Smoked north-coast marlin is a specialty. On any given day, you can ask the waiter what's cooking in the curry pot. Chances are it will be a Jamaican specialty such as goat, full of flavor and served with island chutney.

At the Half Moon Golf, Tennis & Beach Club, Rose Hall, along Rte. A1. © 876/953-2314. Reservations required. Main courses $19.50–$44. AE, MC, V. Daily noon–3pm and 7–11pm. A minivan can be sent to most hotels to pick you up.

Town House ★ JAMAICAN/INTERNATIONAL   Housed in a redbrick building dating from 1765, the Town House is a tranquil dining choice. It offers sandwiches and salads, or more elaborate fare if your appetite demands it. At night, it's floodlit, with outdoor dining on a veranda overlooking an 18th-century parish church. You can also dine in what used to be the cellars, where old ship lanterns provide a warm atmosphere. Pepperpot or pumpkin soup is a delectable start to a meal. The chef offers a wide selection of main courses, including the local favorite, red snapper *en papillote*. We're fond of the large rack of barbecued spareribs, with the owners' special Tennessee sauce. The pasta and steak dishes are also good, especially the homemade fettuccine with whole shrimp and the perfectly aged New York strip steak.

16 Church St. © 876/952-2660. Reservations recommended. Main courses $15–$36. AE, DC, DISC, MC, V. Mon–Fri 11:30am–3:30pm; daily 6–10:30pm. Free limousine service to and from many area hotels.

MODERATE

Belfield 1794 ★ INTERNATIONAL   Here's an unusual blend of fine dining and Jamaican colonial history. Owned and operated by the prestigious Half Moon Resort, but set in the hills above Montego Bay, several miles from the hotel, it includes a tour of a late 18th-century plantation home as part of the dining experience. You'll start out with a drink at a bar that's set on what used to be the threshing floor of an antique sugarcane mill; place your order, and then you'll be ushered through a 15-minute tour of the nearby Great House. A guide will point out its construction of coral stone and mahogany and some of the mahogany furniture that was made on the premises by slaves working in the British style.

Finds Going Native on the Street

MoBay has some of the finest and most expensive dining on the island. But if you're watching your wallet and have an adventurous streak, you'll find lots of terrific street food. On **Kent Avenue** you might try authentic jerk pork or seasoned spareribs, grilled over charcoal fires and sold with extra-hot sauce; order a Red Stripe beer to go with it. Cooked shrimp are also sold on the streets of MoBay; they don't look it, but they're very spicy, so be warned. And if you have an efficiency unit with a kitchenette, you can buy fresh lobster or the catch of the day and make your own dinner.

After the tour you'll return to a different area of the sugarcane mill, to enjoy dishes that are usually served either within a "Dutchie" (a shallow cast iron pot with a tightly fitting cover) or on a carved wooden platter covered with a bread-fruit leaf. The best menu items include fillet of beef with a plantain/port wine sauce and sweet potato pudding; fillet of fish with three kinds of citrus butter (grapefruit, orange, and lime); a jerk combination platter; and curried goat. Shuttle bus service to the restaurant is offered at regular intervals from both the Half Moon and Round Hill Resorts.

Barnett Estate, Granville. ℂ 876/952-2382. Reservations recommended. Main courses $15–$20. AE, MC, V. Mon–Sat 6:30–11pm.

Day-O Plantation Restaurant ★ Finds INTERNATIONAL/JAMAICAN

Here's your chance to wander back to Jamaica's plantation heyday. This place was originally built in the 1920s as the home of the overseer of one of the region's largest sugar producers, the Barnett Plantation. Established as a restau-rant in 1994, it occupies a long, indoor/outdoor dining room that's divided into two halves by a dance floor and a small stage. Here, owner Paul Hurlock per-forms as a one-man band, singing and entertaining the crowd while his wife, Jennifer, and their three children manage the dining room and kitchen.

Every dish is permeated with Jamaican spices and a sense of tradition. Try the chicken made plantation style, with red wine sauce and herbs; fillet of red snapper in Day-O style, with olives, white wine, tomatoes, and peppers; or, even better, one of the best versions of jerked snapper in Jamaica. We also like the grilled rock lobster with garlic butter sauce.

Barnett Estate Plantation, Lot 1, Fairfield, Montego Bay. ℂ 876/952-1825. Reservations required. Main courses $14–$32. AE, DC, DISC, MC, V. Tues–Sun 7–11pm. It's an 8-min. drive west of town off the A-1 high-way toward Negril; minivan service will pick up diners at any of the Montego Bay hotels and return them after their meal.

Richmond Hill Inn INTERNATIONAL/CONTINENTAL

This planta-tion-style house dates from 1806, when it was built by owners of the Dewar's whiskey distillery, who happened to be distantly related to Annie Palmer, the "White Witch of Rose Hall." Today it's run by an Austrian family, who prepare well-flavored food for an appreciative clientele. Dinners include a shrimp-and-lobster cocktail, an excellent house salad, different preparations of mahi-mahi, breaded breast of chicken, wiener schnitzel, filet mignon, and a choice of dessert cakes. Many of the dishes are of a relatively standard international style, but oth-ers, especially the lobster, are worth the trek up the hill.

45 Union St. ℂ 876/952-3859. Reservations recommended. Main courses $17–$30. AE, MC, V. Daily 7:30am–10pm. Take a taxi (a 4-min. ride uphill, east of the town's main square) or ask the restaurant to have you picked up at your hotel.

INEXPENSIVE

Calabash Restaurant INTERNATIONAL/JAMAICAN

This is one of the most romantic places to retreat to at night. The rich and famous don't show up like they used to, but the chefs still cook as well as they ever did, and they always did a fine job. It's perched on the hillside road in Montego Bay, 500 feet (150m) above the sea. The restaurant was opened more than a quarter century ago in this Mediterranean-style courtyard and elegantly simple eagle's-nest patio. The chefs raid the cupboards for Jamaican recipes as well as international favorites. A recent dinner served up such island classics as curried goat and baked stuffed Jamaican she-crab. Our party had high praise for the lobster and seafood dishes. The chef also serves a year-round version of Jamaican Christmas cake.

In the Winged Victory Hotel, 5 Queen's Dr. ✆ **876/952-3891.** Reservations recommended. Main courses $10–$35. AE, MC, V. Daily 7am–9pm.

Le Chalet *Value* JAMAICAN/CHINESE   Forget the tacky commercial surroundings, evoking a fast-food outlet in the U.S. The cooks here dish up an array of lip-smacking good dishes, platter after platter of fresh, tasty Jamaican and Chinese food. In the densest concentration of stores and souvenir shops on Montego Bay's tourist strip, this high-ceilinged restaurant lies across Gloucester Avenue from the sea. The well-prepared food is served in copious portions: The lunch selection might include burgers, sandwiches, barbecued ribs, and salads, and the dinner choice of chicken platters, steaks, fresh fish, and lobster, which seems to taste best here if prepared with Jamaican curry.

32 Gloucester Ave. ✆ **876/952-5240.** Main courses $4–$19 at lunch, $6–$19 at dinner. AE, MC, V. Mon–Sat 10am–10pm, Sun 2–10pm.

The Native Restaurant ⋆ JAMAICAN/INTERNATIONAL   Open to the breezes, this casual restaurant with panoramic views serves some of the finest Jamaican dishes in the area. Appetizers include jerk reggae chicken and ackee and saltfish, or smoked marlin, which you can follow with steamed fish or jerk chicken. The most tropical offering is "goat in a boat" (that is, a pineapple shell). A more recent specialty is Boonoonoonoos; billed as "A Taste of Jamaica," it's a big platter with a little bit of everything—meats and several kinds of fish and vegetables.

29 Gloucester Ave. ✆ **876/979-2769.** Reservations recommended. Main courses $12–$38. AE, DISC, MC, V. Daily 7:30–10:30pm.

The Pelican JAMAICAN   A Montego Bay landmark, the family-friendly Pelican has been serving good food at reasonable prices for more than a quarter century. Most of the dishes are at the lower end of the price scale, unless you order shellfish. Many diners come here at lunch, for one of the well-stuffed sandwiches, juicy burgers, or barbecued chicken. You can also choose from a wide array of Jamaican dishes, including stewed peas and rice, curried goat, Caribbean fish, fried chicken, and curried lobster. A "meatless menu" is also featured, and includes such dishes as a vegetable plate and vegetable chili. The soda fountain serves old-fashioned sundaes with real whipped cream.

Gloucester Ave. ✆ **876/952-3171.** Reservations recommended. Main courses $12–$38. AE, DC, MC, V. Daily 7am–11pm.

Pork Pit ⋆ JAMAICAN   This joint is the best place to go for the famous Jamaican jerk pork and jerk chicken, and the location is right in the heart of Montego Bay, near Walter Fletcher Beach. Many beachgoers desert their towels at noontime and head over here for a big, reasonably priced lunch. Picnic tables encircle the building, and everything is open-air and informal. A half-pound of jerk meat, served with a baked yam or baked potato and a bottle of Red Stripe, is usually sufficient for a meal. The menu also includes steamed roast fish.

27 Gloucester Ave. ✆ **876/952-1046.** 1 lb. of jerk pork $9.20. AE, MC, V. Daily 11am–11pm.

HITTING THE BEACH

Cornwall Beach (✆ **876/952-3463**) is a long stretch of white sand with dressing rooms, a bar, and a cafeteria. The grainy sand and good swimming have made Cornwall a longtime favorite. Unlike some of Jamaica's remote, hard-to-get-to beaches, this one is near all the major hotels, especially the moderately priced ones. Unfortunately, it can be crowded in winter (mostly with tourists, not locals). This is a good beach for kids, with gentle waters and a gently sloping ocean bottom. The beach is open daily from 9am to 5pm. Admission is J$80 (US$1.85) for adults, J$40 (90¢) for children.

Doctor's Cave Beach, on Gloucester Avenue (© **876/952-2566** for the beach club), arguably the loveliest stretch of sand bordering Montego Bay, helped put Montego Bay on the map in the 1940s. Its gentle surf, golden sands, and fresh turquoise water make it one of the most inviting places to swim, and there's always a beach-party atmosphere. Placid and popular with families, it's the best all-around beach in Montego Bay. Sometimes schools of tropical fish weave in and out of the waters, but usually the crowds of frolicking people scare them away. Since it's almost always packed, especially in winter, you have to get there early to stake out a beach-blanket-sized spot. Admission is $3 for adults, $1.50 for children age 12 and under. The beach club here has well-kept changing rooms, showers, restrooms, a food court, a bar, a cyber-cafe, and a sundries shop. Beach chairs and umbrellas can be rented daily.

One of the premier beaches of Jamaica, **Walter Fletcher Beach** (© **876/979-9447**), in the heart of MoBay, is noted for its tranquil waters, which makes it a particular favorite for families with children. This is one of the most beautiful beaches along the southern coast of Jamaica. Easy to reach, it's generally crowded in winter and enjoyed by visitors and locals alike. Some people bring picnics, but be careful not to litter, as patrols might fine you. From December to March, there seems to be a long-running beach party here. Somehow, regardless of how many people show up, there always seems to be a place in the sun for them. Visitors show up in almost anything (or lack of anything), although actual nudity is prohibited. There are changing rooms, a restaurant, and lifeguards. Hours are daily from 10am to 10pm. Admission is J$100 (US$2.30) for adults, J$50 (US$1.15) for children.

Frankly, you may want to skip all these public beaches entirely and head instead for the **Rose Hall Beach Club** (© **876/680-0969** for the beach club), on the main road 11 miles (18km) east of Montego Bay. The club offers a ½ mile (.8km) of secluded white-sand beach with crystal-clear water, plus a restaurant, two bars, a covered pavilion, an open-air dance area, showers, restrooms, hammocks, changing rooms, beach volleyball courts, beach games, a full watersports program, and live entertainment. Admission is $6 for adults, $3 for children. Hours are daily from 9am to 6pm.

SPORTS & OTHER OUTDOOR PURSUITS

DEEP-SEA FISHING   **Seaworld Resorts,** whose main office is at the Cariblue Hotel, Rose Hall Main Road (© **876/953-2180**), operates flying-bridge cruisers, with deck lines and outriggers, for fishing expeditions. A half-day fishing trip costs $380 for up to four participants.

DIVING, SNORKELING & OTHER WATERSPORTS   **Seaworld Resorts** (see above) also operates scuba-diving excursions, plus sailing, windsurfing, and more. Its dives plunge to offshore coral reefs, among the most spectacular in the Caribbean. There are three certified dive guides, one dive boat, and all the necessary equipment for both inexperienced and already-certified divers. One-tank dives cost $40; night dives are $65.

Dive Jamaica (© **876/953-2021**), run by PADI-certified instructor Ben Baker, offers everything from resort courses to specialty certification, with outings to a variety of sites, including the Basket Reef, where you'll see basket sponges, sea fans, parrot fish, and perhaps even a turtle or dolphin if you're lucky.

North Coast Marine Sports (© 876/953-9266), located at the Half Moon Golf, Tennis & Beach Club, offers everything from scuba diving to Sunfish, snorkel gear, kayaks, and more. They can arrange for deep-sea fishing trips and snorkel cruises, too.

Doctor's Cave Beach is part of the **Montego Bay Marine Park,** which was established to protect the wide variety of marine life among the coral reefs right offshore from the popular beaches. You can rent snorkel gear from the beach club at Doctor's Cave, or indeed from the beach clubs at any of the local beaches.

You might also like to head across the channel to check out Cayaba Reef, Sea-world Reef, and Royal Reef, which are full of barjacks, blue and brown chromis, yellow-headed wrasses, and spotlight parrotfish. You must have a guide here, as the currents are strong and the wind picks up in the afternoon. If you're not stay-ing at a resort offering snorkeling expeditions, then Seaworld is your best bet. For a cost of usually $25 per hour, the guide swims along with you and points out the various tropical fish.

GOLF The **White Witch of Rose Hall Golf Course,** part of the Ritz-Carlton Rose Hall (© 876/953-2204), is the newest and also one of the most spectacular courses in the Caribbean, situated on 200 acres (80 hectares) of lush greenery in Jamaica's old plantation country. The course is named after Annie Palmer, the notorious "White Witch" who was the mistress of Rose Hall nearby. Five minutes from the deluxe resort by wheels, the course was created by Robert von Hagge, who designed the course to wind up and down the mountains, with panoramic vistas of the sea visible from 16 of the 18 holes. Greens fees are $175 for hotel guests, $225 for nonguests.

Wyndham Rose Hall Golf & Beach Resort ✦✦, Rose Hall (© 876/953-2650), has a noted course with an unusual and challenging seaside and mountain layout, built on the shores of the Caribbean. Its 8th hole skirts the water, then doglegs onto a promontory and a green thrusting 200 yards (182m) into the sea. The back nine are the most scenic and interesting, rising up steep slopes and falling into deep ravines on Mount Zion. The 10th fairway abuts the family burial grounds of the Barretts of Wimpole Street, and the 14th passes the vacation home of singer Johnny Cash. The 300-foot-high (90m) 13th tee offers a rare panoramic view of the sea and the roof of the hotel, and the 15th green is next to a 40-foot (12m) waterfall, once featured in a James Bond movie. Ameni-ties include a fully stocked pro shop, a clubhouse, and a professional staff. Golfers pay $100 to $125 for 18 holes, or $60 to $75 for 9 holes. Cart rental and the use of a caddy are included in the greens fees.

The excellent course at the **Tryall Club Jamaica** ✦✦✦ (© 876/956-5660), 12 miles (19km) from Montego Bay, is so regal that it's often been the site of major tournaments, including the Jamaica Classic Annual and the Johnnie Walker Tournament. For 18 holes, guests of Tryall are charged $80 in winter, $40 the rest of the year. In winter the course is usually closed to nonguests; the rest of the year, they pay a steep $150.

Half Moon, at Rose Hall (© 876/953-2560), features a championship course designed by Robert Trent Jones, Sr., with manicured and diversely shaped greens. Half Moon hotel guests pay $90 for 18 holes; nonguests pay $130. Carts cost $35 for 18 holes, and caddies (which are mandatory) are hired for $15.

The **Ironshore Golf & Country Club,** Ironshore, St. James, Montego Bay (© 876/953-3681), is another well-known 18-hole, par-72 course. Privately owned, it's open to all golfers. Greens fees for 18 holes are $80, plus $30 for a cart and $14 for a caddy.

HORSEBACK RIDING A good program for equestrians is offered at the **Rocky Point Riding Stables,** at the Half Moon Club, Rose Hall, Montego Bay (© 876/953-2286). Housed in the most beautiful barn and stables in Jamaica, it offers around 30 horses and a helpful staff. A 90-minute beach or mountain ride costs $50.

RAFTING Mountain Valley Rafting, 31 Gloucester Ave. (© 876/956-4920), offers excursions on the Great River, which depart from the Lethe Plantation, about 10 miles (16km) south of Montego Bay, but it's pretty tame and touristy.

We say skip that trip, and head over to Falmouth, 28 miles (45km) to the east, where rafting on the **Martha Brae** is an adventure. To reach the starting point from Falmouth, drive approximately 3 miles (5km) inland to **Martha Brae's Rafters Village** (© 876/952-0889). The rafts are similar to those on the Rio Grande, near Port Antonio; you sit on a raised dais on bamboo logs. The cost is $45, with two riders allowed on a raft, plus a small child if accompanied by an adult (but use caution). The trips last 1¼ hours and operate Monday to Saturday from 9am to 4pm. It's not necessary to wear swimsuits. Along the way, you can stop and order cool drinks or beer along the banks of the river. There's a bar, a restaurant, and two souvenir shops in the village.

TENNIS Half Moon Golf, Tennis & Beach Club ★★★, outside Montego Bay (© 876/953-2211), has the finest courts in the area. Its 13 state-of-the-art courts, 7 of which are lit for night games, attract tennis players from around the world. Lessons cost $25 to $35 per half hour, $50 to $65 per hour. Residents play free, day or night. The pro shop, which accepts reservations for court times, is open daily from 7am to 9pm. If you want to play after those hours, you switch on the lights yourself. If you're not a hotel guest, you must purchase a day pass ($40 per person) at the front desk; it allows access to the resort's courts, gym, sauna, Jacuzzi, pools, and beach facilities.

Tryall Club Jamaica, St. James (© 876/956-5660), offers nine hard-surface courts, three lit for night play, near its great house. Day games are free for guests; nonguests pay $30 per hour. There's a $12 per hour charge to light the courts after dark. Four on-site pros provide lessons for $15 to $30 per half hour, or $20 to $50 per hour.

Wyndham Rose Hall Golf & Beach Resort, Rose Hall (© 876/953-2650), outside Montego Bay, is an outstanding tennis resort, though it's not the equal of Half Moon or Tryall. Wyndham offers six hard-surface courts, each lit for night play. As a courtesy, nonguests are sometimes invited to play for free, but permission has to be obtained from the manager. You cannot play unless you're invited. The resident pro charges $30 per hour for lessons, or $20 for 30 minutes.

WATERSPORTS A "water world" for the family, the $20 million **Aguasol Theme Park** (© 876/940-1344), Walter Fletcher Beach, lures with its array of watersports activities, including a giant water slide, a go-kart track, along with a large sandy beach, plus planned amusements that cover everything from fashion shows to presentations of reggae. There's also an outdoor restaurant and a sports bar featuring 42 big screen televisions. An upper deck is ideal for sunbathing, and there's also a picnic area. At night a dance club dominates the action. Open daily from 10am to 10pm, the attraction charges J$100 (US$2.30) adults, J$50 (US$1.15) for children age 12 and under. Rentals of beach chairs or umbrellas go for J$100 (US$2.30) each.

Moments **Meeting Some Feathered Friends**

At the **Rocklands Wildlife Station,** about a mile (2km) outside Anchovy on the road from Montego Bay, St. James (© **876/952-2009**), it's a unique experience to have a Jamaican doctor bird perch on your finger to drink syrup, to feed small doves and finches millet from your hand, and to watch dozens of other birds flying in for their evening meal. Don't take children age 5 and under to this sanctuary, as they tend to bother the birds. Admission is J$300 (US$6.90); open daily from 2 to 5pm.

SEEING THE SIGHTS
TOURS & CRUISES

A **Hilton High Day Tour,** booked through Beach View Plaza (© **876/952-3343**), includes round-trip transportation on a scenic drive through historic plantation areas. Your day starts with continental breakfast at an old plantation house. You can roam the 100 acres (40 hectares) of the plantation and visit the German village of Seaford Town or St. Leonards village nearby. Calypso music is played throughout the day, and a Jamaican lunch is served at 1pm. The cost is $55 per person for the plantation tour, breakfast, lunch, and transportation. Tour days are Tuesday, Wednesday, Friday, and Sunday.

Day and evening cruises are offered aboard the *Calico,* a 55-foot (17m) gaff-rigged wooden ketch that sails from Margaritaville on the Montego Bay waterfront. An additional vessel, *Calico B,* also carries another 40 passengers. You can be transported to and from your hotel for either cruise. The daily voyage, which departs at 10am and returns at 1pm, offers sailing, sunning, and snorkeling (with equipment supplied). The cruise costs $35. On the *Calico's* evening voyage, which goes for $25 and is offered Wednesday to Saturday from 5 to 7pm, cocktails and wine are served as you sail through sunset. For information and reservations, call **North Coast Cruises** (© **876/952-5860**) a few days in advance.

THE GREAT HOUSES

Occupied by plantation owners, each great house of Jamaica was always built on high ground so that it overlooked the plantation itself and was in sight of the next house in the distance. It was the custom for the owners to offer hospitality to travelers crossing the island by road; travelers were spotted by the lookout, and bed and food were given freely. While these homes are intriguing and beautiful, it's important to remember that they represent the sad legacy of slavery—they were built by slaves, and the lavish lifestyle of the original owners was supported by the profits of slave labor.

The two great houses below can be toured in the same day.

Greenwood Great House ✦   Some people find the 15-room Greenwood even more interesting than Rose Hall (see below), because it's been less restored and has more literary associations. Erected on its hillside perch between 1780 and 1800, the Georgian-style building was the residence of Richard Barrett (cousin of poet Elizabeth Barrett Browning). Elizabeth Barrett Browning herself never visited Jamaica, but her family used to be one of the largest landholders here. An absentee planter who lived in England, her father once owned 84,000 acres (33,600 hectares) and some 3,000 slaves. On display is the original library of the Barrett family, with rare books dating from 1697, along with oil paintings of the family, Wedgwood china, rare musical instruments, and a fine collection of antique furniture.

On Rte. A1, 14 miles (23km) east of Montego Bay. ✆ 876/953-1077. Admission $12 adults, $6 children under age 12. Daily 9am–6pm.

Rose Hall Great House ★ The legendary Rose Hall is the most famous great house on Jamaica. The subject of at least a dozen Gothic novels, it was immortalized in the H. G. deLisser book, *White Witch of Rose Hall.* The house was built from 1778 to 1790 by John Palmer, a wealthy British planter. At its peak, this was a 6,600-acre (2,640-hectare) plantation, with more than 2,000 slaves. However, it was Annie Palmer, wife of the builder's grandnephew, who became the focal point of fiction and fact. Called "Infamous Annie," she was said to have dabbled in witchcraft. She took slaves as lovers and then killed them off when they bored her. Servants called her "the Obeah woman" (*Obeah* is Jamaican for voodoo). Annie was said to have murdered several of her husbands while they slept and eventually suffered the same fate herself. Long in ruins, the house has now been restored and can be visited by the public. Annie's Pub is on the ground floor.

Rose Hall Hwy., 9 miles (15km) east of Montego Bay. ✆ 876/953-2323. Admission $15 adults, $10 children. Daily 9am–6pm.

SHOPPING ★★

Be prepared for aggressive vendors in Montego Bay, as in all of Jamaica. There's a feverish attempt to peddle goods to potential customers, all of whom are viewed as rich. Therefore, prepare yourself for being pursued persistently.

Some so-called "duty-free" prices are actually lower than stateside prices, but then the government hits you with a 10% "general consumption tax" on all items purchased. But you can still find good duty-free items here, including Swiss watches, Irish crystal, Italian handbags, Indian silks, and liquors and liqueurs. Appleton's rums are an excellent value. Tia Maria (coffee-flavored) and Rumona (rum-flavored) are the best liqueurs. Khus Khus is the local perfume. Jamaican arts and crafts are available throughout the resorts and at the Crafts Market (see below).

The main shopping areas are at **Montego Freeport,** within easy walking distance of the pier; **City Centre,** where most of the duty-free shops are, aside from those at the large hotels; and the **Holiday Village Shopping Centre.**

Old Fort Craft Park, a shopping complex with 180 vendors (all licensed by the Jamaica Tourist Board), fronts Howard Cooke Boulevard (up from Gloucester Avenue in the heart of Montego Bay, on the site of Fort Montego). A market with a varied assortment of handcrafts, it's grazing country for both souvenirs and more serious purchases. If you have time for only one shopping complex, make it this one, as its crafts are more varied. You'll see wall hangings, hand-woven straw items, and wood sculpture. You can even get your hair braided. Vendors can be very aggressive, so be forewarned. If you want something, also be prepared to bargain.

At the **Crafts Market,** near Harbour Street in downtown Montego Bay, you can find a good selection of handmade souvenirs of Jamaica, including straw hats and bags, wooden platters, straw baskets, musical instruments, beads, carved objects, and toys. That *jipijapa* hat is important if you're going to be out in the island sun.

One of the newest and most intriguing places for shopping is an upscale minimall, **Half Moon Plaza,** on the coastal road about 8 miles (13km) east of the commercial center of Montego Bay. It caters to the guests of the Half Moon Club, and the merchandise here is upscale and expensive. On the premises are a bank and about 25 shops, each arranged around a central courtyard and selling a wide choice of carefully selected merchandise.

Klass Kraft Leather Sandals, 44 Fort St. (© **876/952-5782**), offers sandals and leather accessories made on location by a team of Jamaican craftspeople.

Golden Nugget, 8 St. James Shopping Centre, Gloucester Ave. (© **876/952-7707**), is a duty-free shop with an impressive collection of watches and a fine assortment of jewelry, plus cameras and a wide assortment of French perfumes.

Copasetic, Half Moon Shopping Village (© **876/953-3838**), is a good outlet for Jamaican crafts, including pottery and jewelry. There are also good buys here in straw products.

The best selection of native art is found at the **Gallery of West Indian Art,** 11 Fairfield Rd. (© **876/952-4547**), with a wide selection of paintings not only from Haiti and Jamaica, but Cuba as well, along with Jamaican hand-carved wooden animals—even some painted hand-turned pottery.

Another gallery, much less impressive, is **Sun Gallery** at the Half Moon Plaza (© **876/953-3455**), specializing in Jamaican art only, mainly watercolors of seascapes and landscapes. It also offers a limited selection of Jamaican pottery and handmade local clothing.

MONTEGO BAY AFTER DARK

Nightlife is not a guaranteed thing at the leading hotels of Montego Bay. It's a sometimes thing. In winter, count on the restaurants and bars of the Ritz-Carlton or Half Moon for having the most diversity of amusements. After dark it's sleepy at Round Hill and Tryall.

The following clubs attract mainly a crowd in their 20s to their 40s.

Marguerite's Seafood by the Sea and **Margueritaville Sports Bar & Grill,** Gloucester Avenue (© **876/952-4777**), the number-one night spot in MoBay, is a two-in-one restaurant across from the Coral Cliff Hotel specializing in moderately priced seafood served on a breezy terrace overlooking the sea. The sports bar and grill features a 110-foot (33m) Hydroslide, live music, satellite TV, a sundeck, a CD jukebox, and a straightforward menu of seafood, sandwiches, pasta, pizza, salads, and snacks—nothing fussy. Naturally, the bartenders specialize in margaritas.

Cricket Club, at Wyndham Rose Hall (© **876/953-2650**), is more than just a sports bar; it's where people go to meet and mingle with an international

---

Moments **Rum & Reggae—And an Escape**

When you want to escape, head for **Time 'n' Place,** just west of Falmouth (© **876/954-4371**). From Montego Bay, you'll spot the sign by the side of the road before you reach Falmouth: "If you got the time, then we got the place." On an almost deserted 2-mile (3km) beach sits this funky beach bar, built of driftwood. Sit back in this relaxed, friendly place and listen to the reggae from the local stations. You can order the island's best daiquiris, made from fresh local fruit, or stick around for peppery jerk chicken or lobster. Time 'n' Place isn't as completely undiscovered as we've made it out to be: Somehow the fashion editors of *Vogue* have swooped down on the place, using it as a backdrop for beach fashion shots.

crowd. Televised sports, karaoke sing-alongs, tournament darts, and backgammon are all part of the fun. It's open daily from 8pm to 1am; there's no cover.

We've enjoyed the atmosphere at **Walter's,** 39 Gloucester Ave. (© **876/952-9391**), which has an authentic Jamaican laid-back feel—complete with a constant flow of calypso and reggae music from as early as 10am daily (for the diehards) until 2am. There's never a cover, and they have live bands on the weekends.

The Brewery, Gloucester Avenue (© **876/940-2433**), is one of the city's most popular nightlife hangouts. It's a cross between an English pub and a Jamaican jerk pork pit. There's a woodsy looking bar where everyone is into Red Stripe and reggae, lots of neo-medieval memorabilia, and a covered veranda in back overlooking busy Gloucester Avenue.

3 Negril (★(★(★

This once-sleepy village has turned into a tourist mecca, with visitors drawn to its beaches along three well-protected bays: Long Bay, Bloody Bay (now Negril Harbour), and Orange Bay. Negril became famous in the late 1960s, when it attracted American and Canadian hippies, who liked the idea of a place with no phones and no electricity; they rented modest digs in little houses on the West End where the local people extended their hospitality. But those days are long gone, and a strip of sophisticated hotels and all-inclusive resorts has sprouted along the sands of famous **Seven Mile Beach.** You won't have to get up for anything, as somebody will be along to serve you. Perhaps it'll be the "banana lady," with a basket of fruit perched on her head. Maybe the "ice-cream man" will set up a stand right under a coconut palm. Surely the "beer lady" will find you as she strolls along the beach with a carton of Jamaican beer on her head, and hordes of young men will peddle illegal *ganja* (marijuana), whether you smoke it or not.

Situated on the western tip of the island, Negril is 50 miles (81km) and about a 2-hour drive from Montego Bay's airport, along a winding road and past ruins of sugar estates and great houses.

There are really two Negrils: The West End is the site of many little local restaurants and funky cottages that still take in visitors. This is the area to head to if you want to recapture some of the charm and freewheeling spirit first publicized here in the '60s, though you can't expect a lot of creature comforts there. The other Negril is on the east end, the first you approach on the road coming in from Montego Bay. Here are the upscale hotels, with some of the most gorgeous beachfronts. Come here if you want to experience your Negril from the confines of a luxury resort, especially an all-inclusive.

GETTING THERE

BY PLANE   If you're going to Negril, you will fly into **Donald Sangster Airport** in Montego Bay. Some hotels, particularly the all-inclusive resorts, will arrange for airport transfers from that point. Be sure to ask when you book.

If your hotel doesn't provide transfers, you can fly to Negril's small airport on the independent carrier **Air Jamaica Express,** booking your connection through Air Jamaica (© **800/523-5585** in the U.S.). The airfare is $60 one-way.

BY BUS   The 2-hour bus trip costs $21. We recommend **Tour Wise** (© **876/952-4943** or 876/952-0019 in Montego Bay, or 876/974-2323 in Ocho Rios). The bus will drop you off at your final destination once you reach Negril.

ACCOMMODATIONS
VERY EXPENSIVE

The Caves ✿ Although not on the beach, this inn still attracts international celebrities who seek out the most atmospheric and elegant small inn in Negril. A 12-minute ride into Negril will deposit you on a good beach. This place might be well suited for groups of friends traveling together or for a family reunion. This small-scale hotel was established in 1990 on 2 acres (1 hectare) of land that's perched above a honeycombed network of cliffs, 32 feet (10km) above the surf on a point near Negril's lighthouse, close to Jamaica's westernmost tip. Accommodations are in breezy units within five cement and wood-sided cottages, each with a thatched roof and sturdy furniture. Matisse could have designed them. None has air-conditioning, and the windows are without screens. A TV and VCR can be brought in if you request them. Many of the units contain alfresco showers.

In spite of its fame, there are drawbacks here. Of all the members of Chris Blackwell's Outpost hotels, generally the finest in the Caribbean, there's a sense of snobbishness, and the prices are very high when stacked up against the competition. The hotel's physical setting, though lavishly publicized, is difficult to negotiate with its stairwells and catwalks. Sumptuous meals are prepared only for guests and are included, along with domestic Jamaican drinks from the bar, as part of the all-inclusive price.

P.O. Box 15, Lighthouse Station, Negril, Jamaica, W.I. ✆ 800/OUT-POST in the U.S. and Canada, or 876/957-0270. Fax 876/957-4930. www.islandoutpost.com. 10 units. Year-round $425–$1,150 double. Rates include all meals and self-service bar. AE, MC, V. Closed Sept 8–Oct 28. **Amenities:** 2 restaurants; bar; saltwater pool; spa; Jacuzzi; sauna; bikes; airport transfers; snorkeling equipment. *In room:* Ceiling fan.

EXPENSIVE

Couples Negril ✿ If you're a man and a woman in love (others stay away!), you're welcomed at this romantic resort, lying on 1,000 feet (300m) of white sandy beach, 5 miles (8km) from the center of Negril. The formula worked in Ocho Rios (see later in this chapter), so it was repeated here. A rival of Sandals properties, this love nest site is the scene of many a wedding, or at least, a honeymoon. On 18 acres (7 hectares) facing crescent-shaped Bloody Bay, this resort caters to those who want back-to-back scheduled activities, ranging from tennis tournaments to fashion shows. Each good-sized unit has a king-size bed and a CD player (bring your own tunes), plus a balcony or patio with a view of the bay or of the lush gardens. Furnishings, though standard, are comfortable, and everything is new, including the shower/tub combination bathrooms. The best doubles are the deluxe beachfront suites, which have Jacuzzis and hammocks. No building in the complex is higher than the tallest coconut tree. On the east side of the property *au naturel* sunbathing is permitted.

The food is good, and you have a choice of three restaurants, including Otaheite, serving a Caribbean fusion cuisine. Mediterranean and continental menus are also served. A resident band plays nightly and there's special entertainment planned throughout the week, including Caribbean dinner buffets with music.

Bloody Bay, Negril, Jamaica, WI. ✆ 800/COUPLES in the U.S., or 876/957-5960. Fax 876/957-5858. www.couples.com. 234 units. All-inclusive rates for 3 nights: winter $1,780–$2,560 double; from $2,310 suite for 2. Off-season $1,550–$2,230 double; from $2,310 suite for 2. Rates include all meals, drinks, and activities. AE, DC, MC, V. **Amenities:** 3 restaurants; 5 bars; 2 pools; 2 tennis courts; fitness room with aerobics classes; basketball court; watersports, including glass-bottom boat trips and Sunfish sailing; game room, currency exchange; tour desk. *In room:* A/C, TV, CD player, coffeemaker, hair dryer, safe.

Negril

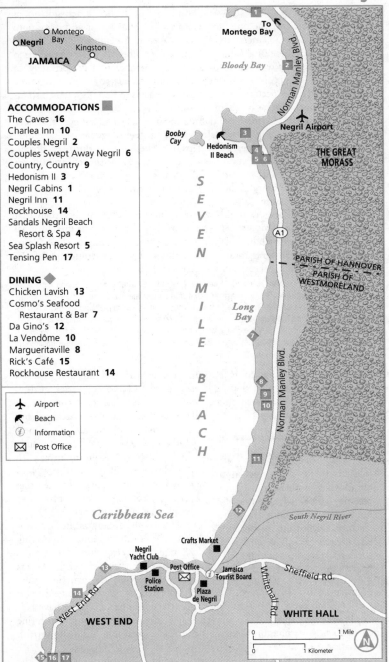

ACCOMMODATIONS ■
The Caves **16**
Charlea Inn **10**
Couples Negril **2**
Couples Swept Away Negril **6**
Country, Country **9**
Hedonism II **3**
Negril Cabins **1**
Negril Inn **11**
Rockhouse **14**
Sandals Negril Beach
  Resort & Spa **4**
Sea Splash Resort **5**
Tensing Pen **17**

DINING ◆
Chicken Lavish **13**
Cosmo's Seafood
  Restaurant & Bar **7**
Da Gino's **12**
La Vendôme **10**
Margueritaville **8**
Rick's Café **15**
Rockhouse Restaurant **14**

✈ Airport
✦ Beach
ⓘ Information
✉ Post Office

Couples Swept Away Negril ⭐⭐ This is one of the best beach-side hotels in Negril—it's certainly the one most conscious of both sports and relaxation. All-inclusive, it caters to singles and couples eager for an ambience of all possible diversions available but absolutely no organized schedule and no pressure to participate if you just want to relax. As a staff member told us (privately, of course), "We get the health-and-fitness nuts, and Sandals or Hedonism get the sex crazed." The resort occupies 20 flat and sandy acres (8 hectares), which straddle both sides of the highway leading in from Montego Bay.

The accommodations (the hotel defines them as "veranda suites" because of their large balconies) are in 26 two-story villas clustered together and accented with flowering shrubs and vines, a few steps from the 7-mile (11km) beachfront. Each lovely, airy, and spacious unit has a ceiling fan, a king-size bed, and (unless the vegetation obscures it) sea views. Wooden shutters all around let sunlight and breezes filter in. Twenty of the units contain shower/tub combinations, and the rest have showers only.

The cuisine here is more health conscious and of better quality than that served at Sandals and Hedonism II. The resort's social center is its international restaurant, Feathers, which lies inland, across the road from the sea. There's also an informal beachfront restaurant and bar, plus a veggie bar serving fresh fruit, juices, pita sandwiches, salads, and vegetarian dishes.

Norman Manley Blvd. (P.O. Box 77), Negril, Jamaica, W.I. © **800/COUPLES** in the U.S. and Canada, or 876/957-4061. Fax 876/957-4060. www.sweptaway.com. 134 units. All-inclusive rates for 3 nights: winter $1,665–$2,050 per couple. Off-season $1,470–$1,860 per couple. Ask about spa packages. AE, MC, V. No children under 18. **Amenities:** 3 restaurants, 4 bars; 2 pools; 10 tennis courts; racquetball; squash; health club and spa; 2 Jacuzzis; sauna; sailing, scuba diving, windsurfing, snorkeling, glass-bottom boat trips, water-skiing, sea kayaking; bikes; tour desk; room service (continental breakfast only); laundry; airport transfers. *In room:* A/C, coffeemaker; hair dryer, safe.

Hedonism II ⭐ Devoted to the pursuit of sophomoric pleasure, and with less class than Couples Negril, Hedonism II packs the works into a one-package deal, including all the drinks and partying anyone could want. The resort complex lies at the northern end of Negril Beach. Of all the members of the SuperClubs chain, this is the most raucous. It's a meat market, deliberately inviting its mainly single guests to go wild for a week. To provide a sense of the ambience, we'll tell you that one manager boasted that the resort holds the record for the most people in a Jacuzzi at once.

⌒ Fun Fact The Naked Truth

Nude bathing is allowed at a number of hotels, clubs, and beaches (especially in Negril), but only where there are signs stating "swimsuits optional." Elsewhere, the law will not allow even topless sunbathing.

The rooms are stacked in dull two-story clusters dotted around a sloping 22-acre (9-hectare) site about 2 miles (3km) east of the town center. This is not a couples-only resort; singles are both accepted and encouraged. The hotel will find you a roommate if you'd like to book on the double-occupancy rate. Accommodations don't have balconies but are very spacious. Each has a king-size or twin beds, fitted with fine linen, with mirrors hanging over the beds. Each bathroom has a shower/tub combination.

On one section of this resort's beach, clothing is optional. It's called the "Nude" section; the other is known as "the Prude." The resort also has a secluded beach on nearby Booby Cay, where guests are taken twice a week for picnics.

Fun Fact **How Not to Arrive in Negril**

When Jimmy Buffet flew into Negril on his private seaplane to stay at Chris Blackwell's posh Island Outpost The Caves, the singer got quite a welcome—and not one margarita. The Negril police opened fire on his plane from their "fortress" at the Negril Lighthouse. The police mistakenly thought the singer's plane was carrying illegal drugs from a neighboring island. Buffet escaped alive. The bullet-dodging incident led to a new song, *Jamaica Mistaka.*

There's nightly entertainment, along with a live band, a high-energy disco, and a piano bar. International cuisine, a bit bland, is served in daily buffets. There's also a clothing-optional bar, a prude bar, and a grill.

Negril Beach Rd. (P.O. Box 25), Negril, Jamaica, W.I. ⓒ **800/859-7873** in the U.S., or 876/957-5200. Fax 876/957-5289. www.superclubs.com. 280 units. All-inclusive rates for 4 days/3 nights: winter $2,040–$2,280 double. Off-season $1,840–$2,080 double. Rates include all meals, drinks, and activities. AE, DC, DISC, MC, V. Children not accepted. **Amenities:** 3 restaurants, 3 bars, 2 grills; 2 pools; 6 tennis courts; 2 badminton courts; basketball court; 2 indoor squash courts; volleyball court; exercise rooms, aerobics; dive shop, sailing, snorkeling, water-skiing, scuba diving, windsurfing, glass-bottom boat rides; massage; free airport transfers. *In room:* A/C, coffeemaker, safe.

Sandals Negril Beach Resort & Spa ⭐ On 13 acres (5 hectares) of prime beachfront land a short drive east of the center of Negril, Sandals Negril is an all-inclusive, couples-only (male-female) resort that attracts a basically young and unsophisticated audience. It's far more active and freewheeling than the more formal Sandals properties in Ocho Rios and Montego Bay. The crowd is usually convivial, informal, and young. The casual, well-furnished rooms have a tropical motif. Recently renovated, they come in a wide range of styles, but are generally spacious, each with a marble bathroom with a shower/tub combination. The best units open directly on the beach. Honeymooners usually end up in a Jamaican-built four-poster mahogany bed. For a balcony and sea view, you have to pay the top rates.

Rates include all meals; snacks; unlimited drinks, day and night, at one of four bars (including two swim-up pool bars); and nightly entertainment, including theme parties. Coconut Cove is the main dining room, but guests can also eat at one of the specialty rooms, including the Sundowner, offering white-glove service and Jamaican cuisine, with low-calorie health food served beside the beach. Kimono features Japanese cuisine. In the typical Sandals chain style, the food is rather standard and nearly everything is imported, but there is quite a variety and no one ever goes hungry.

Norman Manley Blvd., Negril, Jamaica, W.I. ⓒ **800/SANDALS** in the U.S. and Canada, or 876/957-5216. Fax 876/957-5338. www.sandals.com. 223 units. All-inclusive rates: $290–$375 double; from $375 suite. Off-season $260–$320 double; from $345 suite. Rates include all meals, drinks, and activities. AE, MC, V. Children not accepted. **Amenities:** 4 restaurants, 4 bars; 2 pools; 4 tennis courts; fitness center with saunas, aerobics classes; scuba diving, snorkeling, Sunfish sailing, windsurfing, canoeing; glass-bottom boat; massage; laundry; airport transfers. *In room:* A/C, TV, hair dryer, safe.

MODERATE

Charela Inn ⭐ A seafront inn reminiscent of a Spanish hacienda, this place sits on the main beach strip on 3 acres (1 hectare) of landscaped grounds. The building's inner courtyard, with a tropical garden and a round, freshwater pool, opens onto one of the widest (250 ft./75m) sandy beaches in Negril. Try for 1 of the 20 or so rooms with a view of the sea. Accommodations are generally spacious, often with a bit of Jamaican character with their wicker furnishings and ceiling fans. All the rooms have either private patios or balconies. Most of the good-sized bathrooms have shower/tub combinations, though some have shower stalls only.

Le Vendôme, facing the sea and the garden, offers both an a la carte menu and a five-course fixed-price meal that changes daily (see "Dining," below). Thursday and Saturday nights, there's live entertainment. Simplicity, a quiet elegance, and excellent value for the money are the hallmarks of the inn.

Norman Manley Blvd. (P.O. Box 33), Negril, Jamaica, W.I. © 876/957-4648. Fax 876/957-4414. www.charela.com. 49 units. Winter $158–$210 double. Off-season $108–$148 double. MAP (breakfast and dinner) $40 per person extra. 5-night minimum stay in winter. AE, MC, V. **Amenities:** Restaurant, bar; pool; sunset cruises; Sunfish sailing, windsurfing, kayaking; laundry. *In room:* A/C.

Negril Cabins Resort *(Value)* *(Kids)*   This place appeals to travelers who want to get away from it all without spending a fortune; it's an especially good choice for families with kids. These wooden cabins (which have been featured in *Architectural Digest*) are in a forest, across the road from a beach called Bloody Bay. The 9 acres (4 hectares) of gardens are planted with royal palms, bull thatch, and a rare variety of mango tree.

The simple but stylish cabins are small timber cottages, none more than two stories high, rising on stilts. Each accommodation offers two spacious and comfortable bedrooms, plus a balcony and shower-only bathroom. Many units have been recently upgraded and improved, and all are brightened with vibrant Jamaican fabrics. The best are rented as "executive suites," with a sunken living and dining area, plus a pull-out queen-size sofa bed for small families. The executive units also come with air-conditioning and an iron and ironing board.

Ruthland Point, Negril, Jamaica, W.I. © 800/382-3444 in the U.S., or 876/957-5350. Fax 876/957-5381. www.negril-cabins.com. 84 units. Winter $240 cabin for 2. Off-season $220 cabin for 2. Rates are for 3 nights, including breakfast. Children cost an additional $25 each. AE, MC, V. **Amenities:** Restaurant, bar; pool; tennis courts; fitness center; Jacuzzi; scuba and snorkeling arranged; bike rental; children's programs; car rental; room service (7am–10pm); babysitting; laundry. *In room:* A/C, TV, hair dryer, safe.

Negril Inn *★*   Located about 3 miles (5km) east of the town center in the heart of the 7-mile (11km) beach stretch, this is one of the smallest and most reasonably priced all-inclusive resorts in Negril. Because of its size, it's very low-key. The resort, not confined to couples only, offers very simple but comfortably furnished guest rooms with private balconies, in a series of two-story structures in a garden setting. Each unit has a small tiled bathroom with a shower/tub combination.

Included in the package are all meals, all alcoholic drinks (except champagne), and nightly entertainment (including a disco). The resort's only restaurant serves rather good food.

Norman Manley Blvd. (P.O. Box 59), Negril, Jamaica, W.I. © 876/957-4209. Fax 876/957-4365. 46 units. Winter $240 double; $300 triple. Off-season $180 double; $210 triple. Rates are all-inclusive, including airport transfers. AE, MC, V. Children not accepted in winter. **Amenities:** Restaurant, bar, disco; pool; 2 tennis courts; fitness center; Jacuzzi; piano room; room service (breakfast only); laundry; airport transfers. *In room:* A/C, hair dryer, no phone.

Sea Splash Resort   Partly because of its small size, this beachfront resort has a friendly, personable feeling. Much more intimate than the mega-resorts nearby, it lies on a small but carefully landscaped sliver of beachfront land planted with tropical vegetation. The suites are spacious and stylishly decorated with wicker furniture and fresh pastel colors. All are the same size and contain the same amenities—a kitchenette, a balcony or patio, large closets, and either a king-size bed or twin beds—although the suites on the upper floor have higher ceilings and feel more spacious than the others. Living areas contain sofa beds, ideal for small families. The small bathrooms come with showers.

Norman Manley Blvd. (P.O. Box 123), Negril, Jamaica, W.I. ⓒ **800/254-2786** in the U.S., or 876/957-4041. Fax 876/957-4049. www.seasplash.com. 21 units. Winter $199–$254 suite for 2. Off-season $156–$180 suite for 2. Extra person $24. Full board $65 per person extra. AE, DC, MC, V. **Amenities:** Restaurant, bar; pool; small gym; Jacuzzi; room service; babysitting; laundry. *In room:* A/C, TV, hair dryer.

Tensing Pen ★★   Our favorite nest in Negril lies on the western tip and has grown and evolved since its hippie era in the early 1970s. On a cliff, a 10-minute stroll from the landmark lighthouse, it is 3½ miles (6km) south of the center of Negril. Hidden away from the world, the place is a little gem. Those aggressive beach vendors will never find you here, hidden behind a high wall. On 2 acres (1 hectare) of grounds, you're surrounded by tropical planting. Laze in the hammocks or take a sunbath on the terraces hewn out of rock. Sleep in a rustic stone cottage covered in thatch in a four-poster draped in mosquito netting, plantation house–style. Some of the huts are elevated, evoking tree-house living. Local tiles, tropical woods, bamboo rockers, ceiling fans, and louvered windows set the tone. Bathrooms with shower/tub combinations are a bit cramped. There's a communal kitchen where guests sometimes cook for each other.

Lighthouse Rd. (P.O. Box 13), Negril, Jamaica, W.I. ⓒ **876/957-0387.** Fax 876/957-0161. www.tensing pen.com. 16 units. Winter $105–$350 double. Off-season $73.50–$245 double. MC, V. **Amenities:** Communal kitchen. *In room:* Ceiling fan.

INEXPENSIVE
Another low budget option for lodging is found at Da Gino's (see "Dining," below).

Country Country ★   The owners of this intimate hotel were determined to outclass their older competitors, so they turned to celebrity decorator Ann Hodges, the creative force behind the gorgeous decor in many of the much-more-expensive Island Outpost properties. A narrow meandering path stretches from the coastal boulevard to the white-sand beach, where watersports await. Along the way is a collection of neo-Creole, clapboard-sided buildings that drip with elaborate gingerbread and cove moldings, each inspired by an idealized vision of vernacular Jamaican colonial architecture. The buildings are a rainbow of peacock hues highlighting the separate architectural features of each building. Inside, concrete floors keep the spacious interiors cool. Each unit has a vaguely Victorian feel, with comfortable furnishings, plus a shower-only bathroom. There's a beachfront bar and grill, Arnella's by the Sea, plus the only Chinese restaurant in Negril, the Hunan Garden, offering good-tasting, moderately priced dishes in a setting that evokes Shanghai during the British colonial era.

Norman Manley Blvd., (P.O. Westmoreland), Negril Jamaica, WI. ⓒ **876/957-4273.** Fax 876/957-4342. www.countrynegril.com. 14 units. Dec 15–Apr 14 $149–$166 double. Off-season $120–$132 per night double. AE, MC, V. *In room:* A/C, fridge.

Rockhouse ★   This funky boutique inn stands in stark contrast to the hedonistic all-inclusive resorts such as Sandals, and it offers very affordable rates. It seems like a cross between a South Seas island retreat and an African village, with thatched roofs capping stone-and-pine huts. A team of enterprising young Aussies restored and expanded this place, which was one of Negril's first hotels (the Rolling Stones hung out here in the 1970s). The rooms have ceiling fans, four-poster beds draped in mosquito netting, and open-air showers. One cottage is divided into two studios; other units contain queen-size beds; and four cottages have sleeping lofts with extra queen-size beds. A ¼ mile (.4km) from the beach, Rockhouse has a ladder down to a cove where you can swim and snorkel. After a refreshing dip in the cliff-side pool, you can dine in the open-sided restaurant pavilion serving spicy and excellent local fare three times a day.

West End Rd. (P.O. Box 24), Negril, Jamaica, W.I. © and fax 876/957-4373. www.rockhousehotel.com. 28 units. Winter $130 studio; $210 villa. Off-season $95 studio; $140 villa. Children age 11 and under stay free in parents' unit. AE, MC, V. **Amenities:** Restaurant, 2 bars; pool; snorkeling. *In room:* A/C, fridge, safe.

DINING
EXPENSIVE

Le Vendôme ★ JAMAICAN/FRENCH   This place some 3½ miles (6km) from the town center enjoys a good reputation. You don't have to be a hotel guest to sample the cuisine, which owners Daniel and Sylvia Grizzle describe as a "dash of Jamaican spices" with a "pinch of French flair." Dine out on the terra-cotta terrace, where you can enjoy a view of the swaying palms on the beach. Start off with homemade pâtés, or perhaps a fresh vegetable salad, and then follow with baked snapper, duckling a l'orange, or a seafood platter. You may have had better versions of these dishes at other places, of course, but the food is quite satisfying here, and there's rarely an unhappy customer. The wines and champagnes are imported from France.

In the Charela Inn, Negril Beach. © 876/957-4648. Reservations recommended for Sat dinner. Continental breakfast $5; English breakfast $10; main courses $20–$30; fixed-price meal $24–$35. MC, V. Daily 7:30am–10pm.

Rick's Café ★ SEAFOOD/STEAKS   At sundown, everybody in Negril heads toward the lighthouse along the West End strip to Rick's Café, whether they want a meal or not. Of course, the name was inspired by the old watering hole of Bogie's *Casablanca*. There was a real Rick (Richard Hershman), who first opened this bar back in 1974, but he's long gone. This laid-back cafe was made famous in the '70s as a hippie hangout, and ever since it's attracted the bronzed and the beautiful (and some who want to be). Management claims the sunset here is the most glorious in Negril. After a few fresh fruit daiquiris, you'll agree with them. (Actually, the sunset is just as spectacular at any of the waterfront hangouts in Negril, if nothing is blocking the view.) Casual dress is the order of the day, and reggae and rock comprise the background music. If you want dinner, you can order imported steaks along with a complete menu of blackened dishes, Cajun style. The fish (red snapper, fresh lobster, or grouper) is always fresh. The food is rather standard fare, and expensive for what you get, but that hardly keeps the touristy crowds away from the sunset party. You can also buy plastic bar tokens at the door, which you can use instead of money, a la Club Med. A bit tacky, we'd say. Bogie would never have tolerated this.

West End Rd. © 876/957-0380. Reservations accepted for parties of 6 or more. Main courses $15–$28. AE, MC, V. Daily noon–10pm.

Rockhouse Restaurant ★ INTERNATIONAL   This is a gorgeous setting for enjoying some of the best food in Negril. Set on the premises of the previously recommended Rockhouse, it was developed by a team of Australian and Italian entrepreneurs who designed a bridge-like span, equivalent to a railway trestle, high above the surging tides of a rocky inlet on Negril's West End. You may even get a touch of vertigo if you lean over the railing. This place attracts a hip international crowd. Enjoy a drink or two at the Blue Maho Bar, which is built with glossy tropical hardwoods and coral stone, before your meal. Delectable menu items, which are always supplemented with daily specials, might include a seasonal platter of smoked marlin or an upscale version of Jamaican peppered pork with yams and root vegetables.

In the Rockhouse, West End Rd. ✆ 876/957-4373. Reservations required for dinner in high season; otherwise not necessary. Main courses $13.80–$23. MC, V. Daily 7am–11pm.

MODERATE

Da Gino's ITALIAN   Four octagonal, open-sided dining pavilions, separated from Negril's beachfront by a strip of trees, evolved as the escapist dream of Gino Travaini, the Brescia (Italy)-born owner. Pastas and bread are made fresh daily on the premises every day. The best chef's specialties feature linguine with lobster, fillet of beef with peppercorns, various forms of scaloppini, and heaping platters of grilled seafood.

On the premises are a dozen very simple huts, each octagonal, rustic, and camplike, that rent for between $60 and $80 each, depending on the season, double occupancy. Each has a TV and a very basic kitchenette, but no air-conditioning.

In the Hotel Mariposa Hideaway, Norman Manley Blvd. ✆ 876/957-4918. Reservations recommended. Main courses $13–$19. MC, V. Daily 7am–10pm.

Margueritaville AMERICAN/INTERNATIONAL   It's practically Disney gone Jamaican at this rowdy bar, restaurant, and entertainment complex. Thanks to the loaded buses that pull in as a field trip from some of Negril's all-inclusive hotels, it's a destination in its own right. People party here all day and night. There's an on-site art gallery where most of the works are by the very talented U.S.-born artist Geraldine Robbins, and at the gift shops you might actually be tempted to buy something. Every evening, beginning around 9pm, there's live music or perhaps karaoke. Permanently moored a few feet offshore is a pair of Jamaica's largest trampolines, whale-sized floaters that feature high-jumping contests by any participant whose party-colored cocktails haven't affected them yet. Drinks are deceptively potent. In all this party atmosphere, you don't expect the food to be that good, but it might happily surprise, even though it consists of such fare as shrimp-and-tuna kebobs. You'll find southern fried chicken, and what is known as a "Pacific paella," along with the standard club steaks and burgers.

Norman Manley Blvd. ✆ 876/957-4467. Burgers and sandwiches $6.25–$9.75. Main courses $10–$26. MC, V. Daily 9am–11pm.

INEXPENSIVE

Chicken Lavish ✵ *Finds* JAMAICAN   We've found that Chicken Lavish, whose name we love, is the best of the low-budget eateries. Just show up on the doorstep of this place along the West End beach strip, and see what's cooking. Curried goat is a specialty, as is fresh fried fish. The red snapper is caught in local waters. But the big draw is the restaurant's namesake, the chef's special Jamaican chicken. He'll tell you, and you may agree, that it's the best on the island. Ironically, this utterly unpretentious restaurant has achieved something like cult status among counterculture travelers who have eaten here since the 1970s. It's amazingly consistent, specializing in chicken, chicken, and more chicken, that's fried or served with curry or sweet-and-sour sauce. Dine on the roofed-over veranda if you want, or ask for take-out and dine elsewhere.

West End Rd. ✆ 876/957-4410. Main courses $5–$13. MC, V. Daily 10am–10pm.

Cosmo's Seafood Restaurant & Bar ⭐ SEAFOOD/JAMAICAN   One of the best places to go for local seafood is centered around a Polynesian thatched *bohío* (beach hut) open to the sea and bordering the main beachfront. In this rustic setting, Cosmo Brown entertains locals as well as visitors. You can order his famous conch soup, or conch in a number of other ways, including steamed or curried. He's also known for his savory kettle of curried goat, or you might prefer freshly caught seafood or fish, depending on what the catch turned up. Unless you order expensive shellfish, most dishes are rather inexpensive, making this place a friend of the budget traveler.

Norman Manley Blvd. ✆ **876/957-4784.** Main courses $7.40–$18.40. AE, MC, V. Daily 9am–10pm.

FUN ON & OFF THE BEACH

BEACHES   Beloved by the hippies of the 1960s, **Seven Mile Beach** ⭐⭐ is still going strong, but it's no longer the idyllic retreat it once was. Resorts now line this beach, attracting an international crowd. Nudity, however, is just as prevalent as it's always been, especially along the stretch near Cosmo's. There's a carefree, laid-back vibe in the air. On the western tip of the island, the white powdery sand stretches from Bloody Bay in Hanover to Negril Lighthouse in Westmoreland; clean, tranquil aquamarine waters, coral reefs, and a backdrop of palm trees add to the appeal. When you tire of the beach, you'll find all sorts of resorts, clubs, beach bars, open-air restaurants, and the like. Vendors will try to sell you everything from Red Stripe beer to *ganja.* Many of the big resorts have nude beaches as well. The hottest and most exotic is found at **Hedonism II,** although **Grand Lido** next door draws its fair share. Nude beaches at each of these resorts are in separate and "private" areas of the resort property. Total nudity is required for strolling the beach, and security guards keep peeping Toms at bay. Photography is not permitted. Most of the resorts also have nude bars, nude hot tubs, and nude swimming pools.

WATERSPORTS   **Watersports equipment** is easily available at any of at least seven associated kiosks that operate at strategic intervals along the sands. Each of the informal-looking outlets is operated under the umbrella of **Seatec Water Sports** (✆ **876/957-4401**). Each kiosk charges roughly the same rates, and in many cases, each of them has access to the same equipment. Jet skis cost $40 to $50 for a 30-minute ride; snorkeling is $15 per person for a 90-minute excursion by boat to an offshore reef with equipment; 20-minute banana-boat rides are $15; parasailing is $30 for a 12-minute ride; and water-skiing is $25 for a 15-minute tow-around.

The best area for **snorkeling** is off the cliffs in the West End. The coral reef here is extremely lively, with marine life visible at a depth of about 10 to 15 feet (3–5m). The waters are so clear and sparkling that just by wading in and looking down, you'll see lots of marine life. The fish are small but extremely colorful.

Negril has the best and most challenging **scuba diving** in Jamaica. Unusual dive sites within an easy boat ride of Negril include **Shallow Plane,** the site of a Cessna aircraft that crashed in 50 feet (15m) of water, and which is a diving attraction today; an underwater cave, **Throne Room,** which allows divers to enter at one end and ascend into the open air at the other; and two separate sites, each about 66 feet (20m) underwater, known as **Shark's Reef** and **Snapper Drop.** Each of these is loaded with flora and fauna whose species change as the elevations change.

Negril Scuba Centre, in the Negril Beach Club Hotel, Norman Manley Boulevard (✆ **800/818-2963** in the U.S., or 876/957-9641), is the most modern, best-equipped scuba facility in Negril. A professional staff of internationally certified scuba instructors and dive masters teach and guide divers through Negril's colorful coral reefs. Beginners' dive lessons are offered daily, as well as multiple-dive packages for certified divers. Full scuba certifications and specialty courses are also available.

A resort course, designed for first-time divers with basic swimming abilities, costs $75 and includes all instruction and equipment, a lecture on water and diving safety, and one open-water dive. It begins daily at 10am and ends at 2pm. A one-tank dive costs $30 per dive plus $20 for equipment rental (not necessary if divers bring their own gear). More economical is a 2-tank dive, which must be completed in 1 day. It costs $55, plus the (optional) $20 rental of all equipment. This organization is PADI-registered, although it accepts all recognized certification cards.

GOLF   Negril Hills Golf Course, Sheffield Rd. (© **876/957-4638**), is Negril's only golf course. Although it doesn't have the cachet of such Montego Bay courses as Tryall, it's the only golf course in western Jamaica. Greens fees for this 18 hole par-72 course are $57.50, and club rental is $18. Carts and caddies, which are not obligatory, cost $34.50 and $14, respectively. Anyone can play, but advance reservations are recommended.

HORSEBACK RIDING   Horseback riding, heretofore confined to the north shore, has come to Negril. For a close encounter with the natural beauty of this part of Jamaica, head for the local version of the OK Corral—**Rhodes Hall Plantation,** signposted at the eastern edge of the resort (© **876/957-6334**), which now offers guided excursions on horseback, a 2-hour ride across the most scenic beauty spots on the outskirts of Negril. Along the way you'll pass some of the richest vegetation in the Caribbean, including breadfruit, guava, and even wild tobacco plants. Thirsty? With his machete your guide will decapitate a young coconut for your drinking pleasure. The trail ends at the aptly named Crocodile River. Costs range from $30 to $60 per rider.

NEGRIL AFTER DARK ✦

Although smaller than MoBay, Negril is not without nightspots, though you're likely to spend most evenings enjoying the entertainment in your own resort. Fun places are easy to find, as nearly *everything* is on Norman Manley Boulevard, the only major road in Negril.

See "Dining," above, for details on **Rick's Café** and **Margueritaville.**

Alfred's Ocean Palace, Norman Manley Boulevard (© **876/957-4735**), draws mainly locals, but there's lots of intermingling and visitors are welcome. It attracts mainly a young party crowd, but if you're 80, you'll still be warmly embraced, your cold Red Stripe beer waiting. There's no cover, and in addition to grabbing a drink, you can order a bite to eat until midnight. Particularly interesting is the beach-party area, with a stage for live reggae and jazz acts. You can also boogie on the dance floor inside, shaking to hits you'll hear at clubs stateside.

Risky Business, Norman Manley Boulevard (© **876/957-3008**), sits a few feet from the waves. It can be sleepy or manic, depending on what music is playing. In season, you can order burgers and sandwiches, and the Red Stripe is cheap all year round. Basically, it's a young hangout kind of place whose traditional party nights are Monday, Thursday, and Saturday, beginning at 9pm. There's no cover, even when the place is rocking and rolling.

4 Runaway Bay

Once a mere satellite of Ocho Rios, Runaway Bay, 10 miles (16km) west of Ocho Rios, has become a destination in its own right, with white-sand beaches that are much less crowded than those in Ocho Rios, where cruise-ship crowds and aggressive vendors can intrude on your beach relaxation.

Since you're so far removed from the action, such as it is, in Ocho Rios, you stay at Runaway Bay mainly if you're interested in hanging out at a particular resort. Runaway is especially recommended to those who want to escape from the hordes, including those from cruise ships, descending on Ocho Rios.

This part of Jamaica's north coast has several distinctions: It was the first part of the island seen by Columbus, the site of the first Spanish settlement on the island, and the point of departure of the last Spaniards leaving Jamaica following their defeat by the British.

Jamaica's most complete equestrian center is the **Chukka Polo Club and Resort,** at Richmond Llandovery, St. Ann (© **876/972-2506**), less than 4 miles (6km) east of Runaway Bay. A 1-hour trail ride costs $30, while a 2-hour mountain ride goes for $40. The most popular ride is a 3-hour beach jaunt that involves riding over trails to the sea, then swimming in the surf. The $55 cost includes refreshments. A 6-hour beach ride, complete with picnic lunch, goes for $130. Polo lessons are also available, costing $50 for 30 minutes. A more recent feature is a mountain and sea adventure on a bike (90% of which is downhill). The 3-hour bike ride, costing $50, ends in a swim and some snorkeling.

Most people who stay at Runaway Bay stay at one of the all-inclusives, where meals are included. If you're not staying at such a resort, you can dine at Runaway H.E.A.R.T. Country Club, which is open to nonguests; otherwise you can drive to Ocho Rios for meals.

ACCOMMODATIONS

Breezes Runaway Bay ✧   This stylish resort is an all-inclusive. Its clubhouse is approached by passing through a park filled with tropical trees and shrubbery. The lobby is the best re-creation of the South Seas on Jamaica, with hanging wicker chairs and totemic columns. There's a mini-jungle with hammocks and a nearby nude beach, in addition to the lovely stretch of sandy beach right out front. The resort lies 2 miles (3km) east of Paradise Beach and just next door to the town's second best beach, Cardiffall.

Guest rooms are spacious, with a light, tropical motif. They're fitted with local woods, cool tile floors, and private balconies or patios. The most elegant are the suites, with Jamaican-made four-poster beds. The good-sized bathrooms have combination shower/tubs and generous marble counters.

Live music emanates from the stylish Terrace every evening at 7pm, and a nightclub offers live shows 6 nights a week at 10pm. Dine either in the beach-side restaurant or in the more formal Italian restaurant, Martino's, which is the best. Breezes now has a bar on its *au naturel* beach. Now you can order a piña colada while keeping a voyeur's eye out for your favorite nude of the day. The resort's Starlight Grill has also expanded its menu to include a vegetarian cuisine. Both these additions came about by popular demand.

P.O. Box 58 (6 miles/10km west of Ocho Rios), Runaway Bay, Jamaica, W.I. © **800/GO-SUPER** in the U.S., or 876/973-2436. Fax 876/973-2352. www.superclubs.com. 234 units. Winter $510–$890 double. Off-season $460–$850 double. Rates include all meals, drinks, and activities. AE, DISC, MC, V. No children under age 16. **Amenities:** 2 restaurants, 4 bars, 2 grills; pool; 4 tennis courts; golf and tennis schools; 3 Jacuzzis; fitness center; dive shop, scuba diving, windsurfing (with instruction), snorkeling, sailing; room service; laundry. *In room:* A/C, TV, coffeemaker, hair dryer, safe.

FDR (Franklyn D. Resort) *Kids* Located on Route A1, 17 miles (27km) west of Ocho Rios, FDR is an all-inclusive that's the number-one choice if you're traveling with children. FDR lies 2 miles (3km) east of Paradise Beach and about a ¼ mile (.4km) east of Cardiffall. Its own no-name beach stretches for about 200 yards (182m), a mixture of stone and sand. The resort, named after its Jamaican-born owner and developer, Franklyn David Rance, is on 6 acres (2 hectares) of flat, sandy land dotted with flowering shrubs and trees, on the main seaside highway. Each of the Mediterranean-inspired buildings has a terra-cotta roof, a loggia or an outdoor terrace, Spanish marble in the bathrooms, a kitchenette, and a personal attendant (called a vacation nanny), who cooks, cleans, and cares for children. Although neither the narrow beach nor the modest pools are the most desirable on the island, and most rooms lack a sea view, many visitors appreciate the spacious units and the resort's wholehearted concern for visiting kids.

Two restaurants on the property serve free wine with lunch and dinner (and offer special children's meals), and a piano bar provides music every evening. There's live music nightly.

Main St. (P.O. Box 201), Runaway Bay, St. Ann, Jamaica, W.I. ✆ **888/FDR-KIDS** in the U.S., or 876/973-4592. Fax 876/973-4600. www.fdrholidays.com. 76 units. Winter $660–$900. Off-season $500–$600. Rates are all-inclusive. Children age 15 and under stay free in parents' suite. AE, MC, V. **Amenities:** 2 restaurants, 3 bars, disco; pool; tennis court; health club; free babysitting (9:30am–4:45pm); children's center; donkey rides; free bikes. *In room:* A/C, TV, kitchen.

Grand Lido Braco ✷ Established in 1995, this is one of the most historically evocative all-inclusive resorts in Jamaica, lying on a prime stretch of sandy, 350-yard (319m) beachfront. In addition, the hotel also provides a shuttle to Paradise Beach in 45 minutes and Cardiffall in 20 minutes. Set on 85 acres (34 hectares) of land near Buena Vista, a 15-minute drive west of Runaway Bay, it's a re-creation of a 19th-century Jamaican Victorian village, with charming gingerbread architecture. A copy of a courthouse hosts entertainment, and benches line the borders of the town square, where artisans display their handiwork. The old Jamaica that's portrayed here is a rather sanitized, Disney version. Yet this is not a place for children; it is a primarily adult retreat.

Accommodations are in 12 blocks of three-story buildings, each trimmed in colonial-style gingerbread and filled with wicker furniture. All the spacious units have private patios or verandas and face the ocean, although blocks one through six are closer to the beachfront, and blocks five and six face a strip of sand designated as a "clothing-optional" area. Beds are very comfortable, with extremely good mattresses and fine linen; the bathrooms are well maintained and have showers.

Separate dining areas serve tasty Jamaican cuisine, pizza and pasta, and blander international fare; the Piacere Restaurant offers upscale dinners and has a dress code. For variety, Munahana serves Japanese sushi and Teppanyaki cuisine.

Rio Bueno (P.O. Box 226), Trelawny, Jamaica. ✆ **877/GO-SUPER** in the U.S., or 876/954-0000. Fax 876/954-0020 or 876/954-0021. www.superclubs.com. 226 units. All-inclusive rates for 3 nights: winter $2,070–$2,370 double; $2,670–$3,570 suite for 2. Off-season $825–$870 double; $960–$1,530 suite for 2. Rates include all meals, drinks, and activities. AE, MC, V. Children under age 16 not accepted. **Amenities:** 6 restaurants, 8 bars, disco; 2 pools; 9-hole golf course; 3 tennis courts; health club and spa; 4 Jacuzzis; sauna; steam room; watersports; free bikes; business center; 24-hr. room service; laundry. *In room:* A/C, TV, CD player, radio, coffeemaker, hair dryer, iron and ironing board, safe.

⌒ *Fun Fact* **Nude Nuptials**

At Hedonism III Resort (see below), couples who want to see what they're getting before they tie the knot can be married in their birthday suits. Instead of a gown and a tuxedo, suntan lotion is recommended so that any body parts, already exposed, might not become overexposed, at least to the sun. After the "I do's" are said, and the nude nuptials are out of the way, the happy couple can head for the honeymoon suite at this adults-only all-inclusive.

Hedonism III ★   Following a chain format established in Negril, this latest beachfront Hedonism bills itself as a "truly active (and slightly wicked!) vacation." Though this branch of Hedonism isn't as rowdy and raunchy as the Negril branch—it's a little more serene and isolated from the action in town—it's still for the serious party person who likes to drink all night, hang out at the beach all day, and go wild at those toga parties. Set on 15 acres (6 hectares) of landscaped gardens on the eastern end of Runaway Bay, it features ocean views from all rooms and an all-inclusive package deal. Hedonism III has its own private, slightly rocky beach stretching for some 200 yards (182m)—part of it is often nude. It lies a 15-minute drive east of Paradise Beach and a 10-minute walk west of Cardiffall.

Bedrooms are roomy and freshly decorated, with Jamaica's first-ever block of "swim-up" rooms. All swim-up rooms feature large marble tub-and-shower bathrooms with Jacuzzis and CD players. Single guests are paired up with a roommate of the same sex, or have to pay a single supplement.

The food is quite decent—everything from Italian to Japanese to Jamaican. There is even a disco with a four-story water slide!

Runaway Bay, Jamaica, W.I. ✆ **877/GO-SUPER** in the U.S., or 876/973-4100. Fax 876/973-5402. www.super clubs.com. 225 units. All-inclusive rates for 6 nights: winter $3,763–$5,283 double. Off-season $2,863–$4,263 double. Rates include all meals, drinks, and activities. AE, DC, MC, V. No children under age 18. **Amenities:** 5 restaurants, 6 bars, disco; 3 large pools; 3 tennis courts; basketball; volleyball; fitness center; Circus workshop; scuba diving, windsurfing, sailing, water-skiing, kayaking. *In room:* A/C, TV, iron and ironing board, safe.

Runaway H.E.A.R.T. Country Club ★ *Value*   This place wins hands-down as the bargain of the north coast. One of Jamaica's few training and service institutions, the club and its adjacent academy are operated by the government to provide a high level of training for young Jamaicans interested in the hotel trade. The helpful staff of both professionals and trainees offers the finest service of any hotel in the area. Runaway lies a 30-minute drive east of Paradise Beach and a 5-minute drive to Cardiffall. Free shuttles are offered only to Cardiffall.

The good-sized rooms are bright and airy. Bathrooms have generous shelf space and shower stalls. The accommodations open onto private balconies with views of well-manicured tropical gardens or vistas of the bay and golf course. Guests enjoy having a drink in the piano bar (ever had a cucumber daiquiri?) before heading for the dining room, the Cardiff Hall Restaurant, which serves superb Jamaican and continental dishes.

Ricketts Ave. (P.O. Box 98), Runaway Bay, St. Ann, Jamaica, W.I. ✆ **876/973-2671.** Fax 876/973-4704. www.discoverjamaica.com. 56 units. Winter $100–$125 double. Off-season $97–$123 double. Rates include MAP (breakfast and dinner). AE, MC, V. **Amenities:** Restaurant, bar; laundry. *In room:* A/C, TV.

BEACHES & WATERSPORTS

The two best beaches at Runaway Bay are **Paradise Beach** and **Cardiffall Lot Public Beach.** Both wide, white-sand strips are clean and well maintained—ideal spots for a picnic. There is a great natural beauty to this part of Jamaica, and many foreigners, especially Canadians, seek it out, preferring it to the crowded sands of Ocho Rios. (If you're staying in Ocho Rios and want to escape the crowds, come here.) You don't get a lot of facilities, however, so you'd better bring along whatever you need.

The waters are calm almost all year. Prevailing trade winds will keep you cool in the morning and late afternoon. Since there are no lifeguards, be especially careful if you're with children.

Runaway Bay offers some of the best areas for **snorkeling** in Jamaica. The reefs are close to shore and extremely lively with marine life, including enormous schools of tropical fish such as blue chromis, triggerfish, small skate rays, and snapper. Since boats and fishing canoes can be a problem close to shore, go on a snorkeling excursion with the best diving facility at Runaway Bay: **Resort Divers** (© 876/974-5338), along the beach. This five-star PADI facility takes you out to one of several protected reefs where the water currents aren't dangerous, and where fishing boats are required to stay at least 200 yards (182m) away from snorkelers. Resort Divers also provides sport-fishing jaunts as well as scuba-diving certification and equipment. A resort dive costs $85, with a one-tank dive going for $35 or a two-tank dive for $65. Parasailing is also available, costing $45 per 15 minutes.

SEEING THE SIGHTS

Columbus Park Museum, on Queens Highway, Discovery Bay (© 876/973-2135), is a large, open area between the main coast road and the sea at Discovery Bay. Just pull off the road and walk among the fantastic collection of exhibits; admission is free. There's everything from a canoe made from a solid piece of cottonwood (the way Arawaks did it more than 5 centuries ago) to a stone cross that was originally placed on the Barrett Estate (9 miles/14km east of Montego Bay) by Edward Barrett, brother of poet Elizabeth Barrett Browning. You'll see a tally, used to count bananas carried on men's heads from plantation to ship, as well as a planter's strongbox with a weighted lead base to prevent its theft. Other items are 18th-century cannons, a Spanish water cooler and calcifier, a fish pot made from bamboo, a corn husker, and a water wheel. Pimento trees, from which allspice is produced, dominate the park, which is open daily from 8:30am to 4:30pm.

You can also visit the **Seville Great House,** Heritage Park (© 876/972-2191). Built in 1745 by the English, it contains a collection of artifacts once used by everybody from the Amerindians to African slaves. In all, you're treated to an exhibit of 5 centuries worth of Jamaican history. Modest for a great house, it has a wattle-and-daub construction. A small theater presents a 15-minute historical film about the house. It's open daily from 9am to 5pm; admission is $4.

5 Ocho Rios ⟨★⟩

This north-coast resort is a 2-hour drive east of Montego Bay or west of Port Antonio. Ocho Rios was once a small banana and fishing port, but tourism became the leading industry long ago. Short on charm, it's now Jamaica's cruise-ship capital. The bay is dominated on one side by a bauxite-loading terminal and on the other by a range of hotels with sandy beaches fringed by palm trees.

Ocho Rios and neighboring Port Antonio have long been associated with Sir Noël Coward (who invited the world to his doorstep) and Ian Fleming, creator of James Bond (see below for details about their homes here).

Frankly, unless you're a cruise passenger, you may want to stay away from the major attractions when a ship is in port. The duty-free markets are overrun then, and the hustlers become more strident in pushing their crafts and junk souvenirs. Dunn's River Falls becomes almost impossible to visit at those times.

However, Ocho Rios has its own unique flavor and offers the usual range of sports, including a major fishing tournament every fall, in addition to a wide variety of accommodations.

In our view, you go to overrun Ocho Rios only if you want to stay put at one of the resorts here: It is home to some of the leading inns of the Caribbean as well as two stellar Sandals properties. When in the area, we prefer to stay away from the center of Ocho Rios itself, perhaps at a resort in Runaway Bay or something really special like Ian Fleming's Goldeneye.

ESSENTIALS

GETTING THERE   If you're going to Ocho Rios, you'll fly into the **Donald Sangster Airport** in Montego Bay. Some hotels, particularly the larger resorts, will arrange for airport transfers from that point. Be sure to ask when you book.

By taxi, a typical one-way fare from Montego Bay to Ocho Rios is $90. Always negotiate and agree on a fare *before* getting into the cab.

If your hotel does not provide transfers, you can go by bus for a $25 one-way fare. We recommend **Tour Wise** (© **876/979-1027** in Montego Bay, or 876/974-2323 in Ocho Rios). The bus will drop you off at your hotel; the trip takes 2 hours.

You can rent a car for the 67-mile (108km) drive east along Highway A1 (see "Getting Around" in the section "Essentials," at the beginning of this chapter).

ACCOMMODATIONS
VERY EXPENSIVE

Beaches Royal Plantation Golf Resort & Spa ★★   This hotel entrance evokes the antebellum South. At any moment, you expect Scarlett O'Hara to rush out to greet Rhett. You drive up a sweeping driveway and enter through a colonnaded portico 1½ miles (2km) east of the center. The stately inn of yesterday, a rival of the Jamaica Inn, has fallen under the Sandals umbrella and has become the chain's most upmarket property in Jamaica. A complete renovation has brought major improvements to the rooms and public areas and added a full service European spa. Accommodations are all suites, each opening onto the ocean views. Bedrooms are handsomely equipped with such extras as plush cotton robes, daily *New York Times,* fax service, Internet connections, CD players, and the like. Guests have full exchange privileges with the two other Sandals resorts in the area. The cuisine here is far superior to that at the other Sandals properties, and the atmosphere is less rowdy.

Main St., Ocho Rios, Jamaica, W.I. © **888/BEACHES** or 876/974-5601. Fax 876/974-5912. www.beaches. com. Winter $400–$1,260 double. Off-season $310–$1,010 double. 74 units. Children age 16 and over permitted. **Amenities:** 2 restaurants, bar; golf at nearby Sandals; spa; glass-bottom boat, scuba diving, and other watersports; 24-hr. room service. *In room:* A/C, cable TV, VCR, CD player, Internet connection, minibar, safe.

Goldeneye ★★   Few other hotels in the world manage to be so luxurious and yet so appealingly informal as this intimate retreat. It's centered around the villa where the most famous secret agent in the world, James Bond (007), was created in 1952 by then-owner Ian Fleming. Fleming built the imposing but simple main house in 1946, and wrote each of the 13 original James Bond books there. In the early 1990s, music publisher–turned-hotelier Chris Blackwell bought and restored the by-then dilapidated property to its original modernist dignity, retaining an airy simplicity in the main house but unleashing a series of sophisticated British decorators to enrich it with dozens of Balinese antiques and sculptures. Fleming's original desk remains, and the overall decor of oversized Indonesian furniture is enhanced, Hollywood-style, with memorabilia from what later became the most famous spy movies in the world. The main house is usually only rented as a three-bedroom whole for extended house parties, often to rock stars and other celebs.

You're more likely to rent one of the four additional villas that were built, in distinct harmony with nature, on the surrounding property. Each evokes a tropical version of a billionaire's summer camp in Maine, thanks to a juxtaposition of indoor and outdoor spaces, sofas, and well-chosen decorative pieces. Each unit has a fully equipped kitchen of its own. All drinks and food, and most activities, are included in the price.

There's a pool on the premises, but it's reserved only for occupants of the main house. Masonry paths lead to a nearby beach.

Oracabessa, St. Mary, Jamaica, W.I. ⓒ 800/688-7678 in the U.S. or 876/975-3354. Fax 876/975-3620. www.islandoutpost.com. 5 villas. Year-round $600–$700 1-bedroom villa; $850–950 2-bedroom villa; $1,300–$2,000 3-bedroom villa; $3,000 Ian Fleming's 3-bedroom house for up to 6; $6,000 for entire property of 11 bedrooms (sleeping up to 22). Rates include all meals, drinks, and activities. AE, DISC, MC, V. **Amenities:** Watersports. *In room:* Ceiling fan, TV, kitchenette, minibar, coffeemaker.

Grand Lido Sans Souci ★★★ If a cookie-cutter Sandals resort is the last thing you want, head for a classier beachfront joint: this one. Winner of four diamonds from AAA, Sans Souci (which means "without a care") is a pink, cliffside luxurious resort that recently completed a $7 million renovation. It's located 3 miles (5km) east of town on a forested plot of land whose rocky border abuts a good white-sand beach. This Grand Lido here is more elegant than the Grand Lido Negril. There's a separate clothing-optional beach, a mineral bath big enough for an elephant, and a labyrinth of catwalks and bridges stretching over rocky chasms filled with surging water.

Each unit features a veranda or patio, copies of Chippendale furniture, plush upholstery, and subdued colonial elegance. Some contain Jacuzzis. Accommodations range from rather standard bedrooms to vast suites with large living and dining areas, plus kitchens. Deluxe touches include glazed tile floors, luxurious beds, and marble bathrooms with whirlpool tubs. You'll enjoy the food at the elegant Casanova restaurant.

Rte. A3 (P.O. Box 103), Ocho Rios, Jamaica, W.I. ⓒ 876/994-1206. Fax 876/994-1544. www.superclubs.com. 146 units. All-inclusive rates for 6 nights: winter $3,551 double. Off-season $3,073 double. AE, DC, DISC, MC, V. **Amenities:** 5 restaurants, 6 bars; 4 pools; 2 tennis courts; health club and spa; 2 Jacuzzis; watersports. *In room:* A/C, TV, minibar, safe.

Jamaica Inn ★★ Built in 1950, the gracious beachfront Jamaica Inn is a series of long, low buildings set in a U-shape near the sea, 1½ miles (2km) east of town. Noël Coward, arriving with Katharine Hepburn or Claudette Colbert, was a regular, and Errol Flynn and Ian Fleming used to drop in from time to time. It's an elegant anachronism, a true retro hotel, and has remained little changed in 4 decades, avoiding the glitter of all-inclusives like Sandals.

Lovely patios open onto the lawns, and the bedrooms are reached along garden paths. Guest rooms are very spacious, with colonial two-poster beds, quality carved-wood period pieces, and balustraded balconies opening onto views. Bathrooms are elegant and roomy, gleaming with marble vanities, combination shower/tubs, robes, and deluxe toiletries. The beach is a wide, champagne-colored strip; close to the shore, the sea is almost too clear to make snorkeling an adventure, but farther out it's rewarding. The European-trained chef prepares both refined international and Jamaican dishes. The emphasis is on cuisine that uses fresh local produce. Men must wear a jacket and tie at night in winter.

Main St. (P.O. Box 1), Ocho Rios, Jamaica, W.I. © **800/837-4608** in the U.S., or 876/974-2514. Fax 876/974-2449. www.jamaicainn.com. 45 units. Winter including all meals $550–$795 double; from $1,200 suite for 2. Off-season including MAP (breakfast and dinner) $300–$445 double; from $500 suite for 2. AE, MC, V. Children age 13 and under not accepted. **Amenities:** Restaurant, 2 bars; pool; tennis court; exercise room; Sunfish, kayaks; room service; laundry. *In room:* A/C.

EXPENSIVE

Beaches Grand Sport at Ciboney ⭐   This all-inclusive lies a 1½-mile (2km) drive southeast of town, set on 45 acres (18 hectares) of tropical gardens on a private estate dotted with red-tile villas. A great house in the hills overlooks the Caribbean. Across from the imposing gate near the resort's entrance are the white sands of a private beach.

All but a handful of the accommodations are in one-, two-, or three-bedroom villas, each with a pool, a fully equipped kitchen, and a shaded terrace. Honeymoon villas have their own whirlpools. Thirty-six units are traditional single or double rooms on the third floor of the great house. Accommodations are high-ceilinged, roomy, and decorated in Caribbean colors. They're well furnished, with particularly fine beds, and bathrooms with combination shower/tubs are well maintained.

Main St. (P.O. Box 728), Ocho Rios, St. Ann, Jamaica, W.I. © **800/BEACHES** in the U.S. and Canada, or 876/974-1027. Fax 876/974-5838. 300 units. All-inclusive rates for 3 nights per couple: winter $735–$840 double; $930 junior suite; $1,005 1-bedroom villa suite; $1,185 honeymoon villa; $1,425 2-bedroom villa for 4. Off-season $615–$705 double; $765 junior suite; $840 1-bedroom villa suite; $720 honeymoon villa; $1,185 2-bedroom villa for 4. AE, MC, V. Children age 15 and under not accepted. **Amenities:** 4 restaurants, 6 bars; 9 pools; 6 tennis courts; spa; 5 Jacuzzis; 2 saunas; 2 steam rooms; watersports, scuba diving. *In room:* A/C, TV, minibar, safe.

Couples Ocho Rios ⭐   This is a couples-only resort (and management defines couples as "any man and woman in love"). Most visiting couples are married, and many are on their honeymoon. Everything is in pairs, even the chairs at night by the moon-drenched beach. Some guests slip away from the resort, which is an 18-minute drive (5 miles/8km) east of town, to Couples' private island to bask in the buff. (A shuttle boat transports visitors offshore to this beautiful little island with a fine sandy beach, a bar, a pool, and a hot tub. Security guards keep the gawkers from bothering guests here.)

In general, this is a classier operation than the more mass-market Sandals (at least the Dunn's River and the Ocho Rios versions). The bedrooms have either a king-size bed or two doubles, pleasantly traditional furnishings, and a patio fronting either the sea or the mountains. Good-sized bathrooms have showers. For a chain all-inclusive, the cuisine is above average.

Tower Isle, along Rte. A3 (P.O. Box 330), Ocho Rios, Jamaica, W.I. © **800/268-7537** in the U.S., or 876/975-4271. Fax 876/975-4439. www.couples.com. 201 units. All-inclusive rates for 3 nights: winter $1,350–$2,550 double; $2,085 suite. Off-season $1,230–$2,350 double; $1,800 suite. Rates include all meals, drinks, and activities. AE, MC, V. The hotel usually accepts bookings for a minimum of any 3 nights of the week, though most guests book by the week; a 4-day stay is sometimes required at certain peak periods, such as over the Christmas holidays. No one age 17 or under accepted. **Amenities:** 4 restaurants, 4 bars; pool; 5 tennis courts; health club and spa; 5 Jacuzzis; sauna; scuba diving, snorkeling, windsurfing, sailing, water-skiing; bike rental; room service (breakfast only); laundry. *In room:* A/C, TV, coffeemaker, hair dryer.

Sandals Dunn's River Golf Resort & Spa ★

Located on a wide, sugary beach, this is the finest of the Sandals resorts, at least in the opinion of some guests who have sampled them all. As at all Sandals resorts, only male-female couples are allowed. Set on the beachfront between Ocho Rios and St. Ann's Bay, the resort is very sports oriented. It occupies 25 well-landscaped acres (10 hectares), offering attractively furnished and often quite spacious accommodations. All the rooms have an Italianate/Mediterranean motif. The elegant guest rooms are scattered among the six-story main building, two lanai buildings, and a five-story west wing. Extras include spacious balconies, walk-in closets, king-size beds, and shower/tub combinations. Before retreating to the disco or enjoying the nightly entertainment, guests can choose among several dining options, selecting from an array of restaurants that at least attempt variety in lieu of first-rate cuisine. The International Room is elegant, with fabric-covered walls and rosewood furniture. The West Indian Terrace serves Caribbean specialties. D'Amoré offers Italian cuisine, and Restaurant Teppanyaki serves Chinese, Polynesian, and Japanese dishes.

Rte. A3 (P.O. Box 51), Ocho Rios, Jamaica, W.I. ✆ **800/SANDALS** in the U.S. and Canada, or 876/972-1610. Fax 876/972-1611. www.sandals.com. 256 units. All-inclusive rates: winter $915–$1,000 double; from $1,535 suite. Off-season $705–$765 double; from $1,215 suite. Minimum stay of 4 days/3 nights. AE, DISC, MC, V. **Amenities:** 4 restaurants, 7 bars, snack bar/grill; 2 pools; shuttle to 18-hole golf course; pitch-and-putt golf course; 12 tennis courts; health club and spa; 3 Jacuzzis; saunas; steam rooms; watersports. *In room:* A/C, TV, coffeemaker, hair dryer, safe.

Sandals Ocho Rios Resort & Golf Club ★

This resort opening onto a good sandy beach attracts a mix of unmarried and married (male-female) couples, including honeymooners. At times the place seems like a summer camp for grown-ups (or others who didn't quite grow up). This is the most low-key of the Sandals properties. Is it romantic? Most guests think so, although we've encountered other couples here whose relationship didn't survive the 3-night minimum stay.

On 13 well-landscaped acres (5 hectares) a mile (2km) west of the town center, it offers comfortably furnished but uninspired rooms with either ocean or garden views, plus some cottage units. All units are reasonably large, with king-size beds and good-size bathrooms with shower/tub combinations. You can sip drinks at an ocean-side swim-up bar. Nightly theme parties and live entertainment take place in a modern amphitheater. A unique feature of the resort is an open-air disco. The resort's main dining room is St. Anne's; Michelle's serves standard Italian food, and the Reef Terrace Grill does above-average Jamaican cuisine and fresh seafood. A more recent addition is the Arizona Steakhouse, with some sizzling good steaks.

Main St. (P.O. Box 771), Ocho Rios, Jamaica, W.I. ✆ **800/SANDALS** in the U.S. and Canada, or 876/974-5691. Fax 876/974-5700. www.sandals.com. 237 units. All-inclusive rates per couple: winter $225–$285 double; from $320 suite; summer $200–$260 double, from $285 suite. AE, MC, V. **Amenities:** 4 restaurants, 4 bars, snack bar/grill; 3 pools; tennis court; fitness center; Jacuzzis; saunas; watersports; massage; laundry. *In room:* A/C, TV, hair dryer, coffeemaker, safe, iron.

The Enchanted Garden ★★

This most verdant of Jamaican resorts sits on a secluded hilltop high above the commercial center of town. Owned and developed by Edward Seaga, former Jamaican prime minister, the land includes 20 acres (8 hectares) of rare botanical specimens, nature trails, and 14 cascading waterfalls. The hotel maintains a shuttle bus that departs at 30-minute intervals daily from 9am to 5pm, making a 12-minute run to the nearest good beach at

Mammee Bay. The lobby is housed in a pink tower accented with white ginger-bread; the interior sports marble floors, big windows, and enormous potted palms. Bisected by the Turtle River, the place is of particular interest to botanists and bird-watchers.

The bedrooms are contained in eight different low-rise buildings amid the resort's carefully landscaped grounds. All of the roomy, elegantly furnished units have sturdy rattan furniture, queen-size or king-size beds, and private patios or balconies; some contain kitchens. The spacious bathrooms have shower/tub combinations.

The resort's restaurants serve Continental, Thai, Japanese, Indonesian, and regional Chinese cuisines, and they do so rather well. Annabella's nightclub provides after-dinner entertainment in a setting like something out of *1,001 Arabian Nights*.

Eden Bower Rd. (P.O. Box 284), Ocho Rios, Jamaica, W.I. (Ⓒ *800/847-2535* in the U.S. and Canada, or 876/974-1400. Fax 876/974-5823. www.enchanted.com.jm. 113 units. All-inclusive rates per couple: Winter $310–$330 double; from $370 suite. Off-season $280 double; from $320 suite. AE, MC, V. **Amenities:** 5 restaurants, 4 bars; 2 pools; 2 tennis courts; health club and spa; Jacuzzi; walk-in aviary with hundreds of exotic birds; watersports; salon; shuttle for shopping. *In room:* A/C, TV, coffeemaker, hair dryer.

MODERATE

High Hope Estate ⚝   Because this hotel is so intimate, whether you like it will depend on whether you click with the owner and the other guests. It's conceived as a tranquil, private home that accepts paying guests, in the style of the British colonial world at its most rarefied. It was built for a socially prominent heiress, Kitty Spence, granddaughter of prairie-state populist William Jennings Bryan, and later served as the home and laboratory of a horticulturist who successfully bred 560 varieties of flowering hibiscus. The estate's 40 acres (16 hectares), set 550 feet (165m) above the coast and 7 miles (11km) west of Ocho Rios, thrive with flow-ering plants as well as memories of such luminaries as Noël Coward, who used to play the grand piano that graces one of the public areas. There are absolutely no planned activities here. Basically, it's an upscale private home, the domain of U.S. entrepreneur Dennis Rapaport, whose staff is on hand to help with supervising children, maintaining the property, and preparing meals for anyone who gives advance notice. Bedrooms are a delight—spacious, well thought out, and exceed-ingly comfortable. The excellent bathrooms have shower/tub combinations.

The nearest beach is a 10-minute ride away. You could rent the entire villa with a group of friends, and you can purchase all-inclusive packages.

Box 11, St. Ann's Bay, near Ocho Rios, Jamaica, W.I. (Ⓒ *876/972-2277.* Fax 876/972-1607. www.highhope estate.com. 5 units. Year-round $85–$155. Rates include breakfast. MC, V. **Amenities:** Dining room; pool; tennis court; TV room; room service; babysitting; laundry. *In room:* Ceiling fan, coffeemaker.

INEXPENSIVE

Hibiscus Lodge Hotel *(Value*   This inn offers more value for your money than any other resort at Ocho Rios. The intimate little inn, perched precariously on a cliff along the shore 3 blocks from the Ocho Rios Mall, has character and charm. Mallards Bay Beach, shared by residents of some of the biggest hotels in Ocho Rios, lies within a 3- to 4-minute walk of the hotel. All medium-size bed-rooms, either doubles or triples, have small, shower-only bathrooms, ceiling fans, and verandas opening to the sea.

After a day spent in a pool suspended over the cliffs, or lounging on the large sundeck, guests can enjoy a drink in the unique swinging bar. The owners pro-vide dining at the Almond Tree Restaurant (see "Dining," below).

83 Main St. (P.O. Box 52), Ocho Rios, St. Ann, Jamaica, W.I. ℂ **876/974-2676.** Fax 876/974-1874. 26 units. Winter $115–$126 double; $157 triple. Off-season $103–$115 double; $140 triple. Rates include breakfast. AE, DC, MC, V. **Amenities:** Restaurant, bar; tennis court; Jacuzzi. *In room:* A/C, TV.

DINING
MODERATE
Almond Tree Restaurant INTERNATIONAL   The Almond Tree is a two-tiered patio restaurant with a tree growing through the roof. Lobster Thermidor is the most delectable item on the menu, but we also like the bouillabaisse (made with conch and lobster). Other excellent choices are the roast suckling pig, medallions of beef Anne Palmer, and a fondue bourguignon. Jamaican plantation rice is a local specialty. The wine list offers a variety of vintages, including Spanish and Jamaican. Have a cocktail in the unique "swinging bar"—with swinging chairs, that is.

In the Hibiscus Lodge Hotel, 83 Main St. ℂ **876/974-2813.** Reservations recommended for dinner. Main courses $12–$30. AE, MC, V. Daily 7:30–10:30am, noon–2:30pm, and 6–10pm.

Evita's Italian Restaurant ⭐ ITALIAN   A 5-minute drive south of the commercial heart of Ocho Rios, in a hillside residential neighborhood that enjoys a panoramic view over the harbor and beachfronts, this is one of the most fun restaurants along the north coast of Jamaica. Its soul and artistic flair come from Eva Myers, the convivial former owner of some of the most legendary bars of Montego Bay, who established her culinary headquarters in this white gingerbread Jamaican house in 1990. An outdoor terrace adds additional seating and enhanced views. More than half the menu is devoted to pastas, including almost every variety known in northern and southern Italy. The fish dishes are excellent—especially the snapper stuffed with crabmeat and the lobster and scampi in a buttery white cream sauce. Italian (or other) wines by the bottle might accompany your main course. The restaurant lies a few steps from the Enchanted Garden resort.

Eden Bower Rd. ℂ **876/974-2333.** Reservations recommended. Main courses $10–$29. AE, MC, V. Daily 11am–11pm.

Little Pub Restaurant JAMAICAN/INTERNATIONAL   Located in a red-brick courtyard with a fishpond and a waterfall in the center of town, this indoor-outdoor pub's centerpiece is a restaurant in the dinner-theater style. Top local and international artists are featured, as are Jamaican musical plays. No one will mind if you just enjoy a drink while seated on one of the pub's barrel chairs. But if you want dinner, proceed to one of the linen-covered tables topped with cut flowers and candles. We are fond of the barbecued chicken and the grilled kingfish, but you might opt for the stewed snapper or the freshly caught lobster.

59 Main St. ℂ **876/974-2324.** Reservations recommended. Main courses $12–$28. AE, MC, V. Daily 7am–10:30pm.

Toscanini's ITALIAN   The three partners behind this place, Emanuele and Lella Guilivi and her brother, chef Pierluigi Ricci, all hail from Parma, Italy. Coming from a long line of restaurateurs, they bring style and a Continental sophistication to their food service and preparation. The restaurant is set at an art gallery along the coast. The menu offers many classic Italian dishes, supplemented by ever-changing specials, depending on what's fresh at the market. The best specialties include marinated marlin, various homemade pastas, carpaccio, gnocchi, and a strong emphasis on fresh lobster and seafood. The chef also caters to vegetarians. All this good food is backed up by a fine wine list.

In Harmony Hall, Tower Isles on Rte A3, 4 miles (6km) east of Ocho Rios. ⓒ **876/975-4785.** Main courses $10–$22; pasta dishes $9–$16. AE, MC, V. Tues–Sun noon–2:30pm and 7–10:30pm.

INEXPENSIVE

BiBiBips INTERNATIONAL/JAMAICAN   Set in the main tourist strip of Ocho Rios, this restaurant (whose name is the owner's nickname) occupies a sprawling open-air compound of porches and verandas. Lots of single folks come just to hang out at the bar. Drinks and flirtations sometimes segue into dinner at the adjacent restaurant, where well-prepared menu items include Red Stripe shrimp, which is deep-fried in a beer-based batter; coconut-curried chicken; vegetarian Rasta Pasta; and a combination Creole-style seafood platter. Lunches are a bit simpler, focusing mostly on sandwiches, salads, and an especially delicious jerk chicken burger. There's live entertainment, usually some kind of rap or reggae band, every Friday, Saturday, and Sunday beginning at 8pm.

93 Main St. ⓒ **876/974-8759.** Lunch main courses $5.30–$25.20; dinner main courses $6.05–$26.80. AE, MC, V. Daily 11am–5:30pm and 6pm–2am.

Ocho Rios Village Jerk Centre ★ *(Finds)* JAMAICAN   At this open-air restaurant, you can get the best jerk dishes along this part of the coast. When only a frosty Red Stripe beer can quench your thirst and your stomach is growling for the fiery taste of Jamaican jerk seasonings, head here—and don't dress up. Don't expect anything fancy: It's the food that counts, and you'll find fresh daily specials posted on a chalkboard menu on the wall. The dishes are hot and spicy, but not *too* hot; hot spices are presented on the side for those who want to go truly Jamaican. The barbecue ribs are especially good, and fresh fish is a delight, perfectly grilled—try the red snapper. Vegetarian dishes are also available on request, and if you don't drink beer you can wash it all down with natural fruit juices.

Da Costa Dr. ⓒ **876/974-2549.** Jerk pork $3 ¼ lb., $10 1 lb. Whole jerk chicken $13. MC, V. Daily 10am–11pm.

Parkway Restaurant JAMAICAN   Come here to eat as Jamaicans eat. This popular spot in the commercial center of town couldn't be plainer or more unpretentious, but it's always packed. Locals know they can get some of Ocho Rios's best and most affordable dishes here. It's the local watering hole, and the regulars are a bit disdainful of all those Sandals and Couples resorts, with their contrived international food. Hungry diners dig into straightforward fare such as Jamaican-style chicken, curried goat, sirloin steak, and fillet of red snapper, topping it all off with banana cream pie. The restaurant recently renovated its third floor to offer entertainment and dancing. Tuesday's Reggae Night lets local bands do their best "to let the groove ooze," as they say here.

60 DaCosta Dr. ⓒ **876/974-2667.** Lunch main courses $6–$11.25, dinner main courses $6.50–$26. AE, MC, V. Daily 8am–11:30pm.

HITTING THE BEACH

The most idyllic sands are at the often-overcrowded **Mallards Beach,** in the center of Ocho Rios and shared by hotel guests and cruise-ship passengers. Locals may steer you to the white sands of **Turtle Beach** in the south, between the Renaissance Jamaica Grande and Club Jamaica. It's smaller, more desirable, and not as overcrowded as Mallards.

The most popular spot (stay away when cruise ships are in port!) is **Dunn's River Beach,** located below the famous falls. Another great spot is **Jamaica Grande's Beach,** which is open to the public. Parasailing is a favorite sport here.

Our favorite is none of the above. We always follow the trail of 007 and head for **James Bond Beach** (© **876/975-3663**), east of Ocho Rios at Oracabessa Beach. Entrepreneur Chris Blackwell reopened writer Ian Fleming's former home, Goldeneye. For J$150 (US$5) adults, J$50 (US$2.50) children, nonguests can enjoy its sand strip any day except Monday. There's a watersports rental center here as well.

You might also escape the crowds at Ocho Rios and head to the lovely beach at nearby Runaway Bay (see the section "Runaway Bay," earlier in this chapter).

SPORTS & OTHER OUTDOOR PURSUITS

GOLF   **SuperClub's Runaway Golf Club,** at Runaway Bay near Ocho Rios on the north coast (© **876/973-7319**), charges no fee to guests who stay at any of Jamaica's affiliated SuperClubs. For nonguests, the price is $80 year-round. Any player can rent carts for $35 for 18 holes; clubs are $14 for 18 holes.

Sandals Golf & Country Club (© **876/975-0119**), a 15-minute ride from the center of the resort, is a 6,500-yard (5,915m) course, known for its panoramic scenery some 700 feet (210m) above sea level. (From the center of Ocho Rios, travel along the main bypass for 2 miles (3km) until you reach Mile End Road. A Texaco station is located at the corner of Mile End Road. Turn right and drive for another 5 miles (8km) until you come to the Sandals course on your right.) The 18-hole, par-71 course was designed by P. K. Saunders and opened in 1951 as the Upton Golf Club. Rolling terrain, lush vegetation, and flowers and fruit trees dominate the 120-acre (48-hectare) course. A putting green and driving range are available for those who wish to hone their skills first. Sandals guests play free; nonguests pay $70 for 9 holes or $100 for 18 holes.

TENNIS   **Beaches Grand Sport at Ciboney,** Main Street, Ocho Rios (© **876/974-1027**), focuses more on tennis than any other resort in the area. It offers three clay-surface and three hard-surface courts, all lit for night play. Guests play free, day or night, but nonguests must call and make arrangements with the manager. An on-site pro offers lessons for $25 an hour. Ciboney also sponsors twice-a-day clinics for both beginners and advanced players. Frequent guest tournaments are also staged, including handicapped doubles and mixed doubles.

EXPLORING THE AREA

A scenic drive south of Ocho Rios along Route A3 will take you inland through **Fern Gully** ✦, a lush gorge. This was originally a riverbed, but now the main road winds up some 700 feet (210m) among a profusion of wild ferns, a tall rain forest, hardwood trees, and lianas. There are hundreds of varieties of ferns, and roadside stands offer fruits and vegetables, carved-wood souvenirs, and basketwork. The road runs for about 4 miles (6km). At Moneague, a small town, the A1 continues south into the interior of Jamaica, but the same route number (A1) also heads back north along a different route from the A1 you just took south. This A1 northerly road lies to the west of the A1 southern route to Moneague. If you take this A1 north, you'll come to the coast on the north shore again.

Heading up A1 north, you'll pass the ruins of **Edinburgh Castle** lying 8 miles (13km) southwest of Claremont, the major town on the route back (but of no tourist interest). These ruins—not worth a detour but of passing interest only if you're driving by—are a local curiosity.

This 1763 lair was the former abode of one of Jamaica's most famous murderers, a Scot named Lewis Hutchinson, who used to shoot passersby and toss their bodies into a deep pit. At his so-called "castle," really a two-story house, Hutchinson invited his victims inside. There he would wine and dine them before murdering and then robbing them.

The authorities got wind of his activities. Although he tried to escape by canoe, Hutchinson was captured and hanged at Spanish Town on March 16, 1773. Rather proud of his achievements (evidence of at least 43 bodies was found), he left 100 British pounds and instructions for a memorial to be built in his honor. It never was.

These castle ruins can be viewed on the northern outskirts of the village of Bensonton, near the Bensonton Health Club.

Back on the A1 northern route again, you can drive to the coast, coming to it at **St. Ann's Bay,** the site of the first Spanish settlement on the island, where you can see the **statue of Christopher Columbus,** cast in his hometown of Genoa and erected near St. Ann's Hospital on the west side of town, close to the coast road. There are a number of Georgian buildings in the town—the **Court House** near the parish church, built in 1866, is the most interesting.

Brimmer Hall Estate   Some 21 miles (34km) east of Ocho Rios, in the hills 2 miles (3km) from Port Maria, this 1817 estate is an ideal place to spend a day. You can swim in the pool and sample a wide variety of brews and concoctions. The Plantation Tour Eating House offers typical Jamaican dishes for lunch, and there's a souvenir shop with a good selection of ceramics, art, straw goods, wood carvings, rums, liqueurs, and cigars. All this is on a working plantation where you're driven around in a tractor-drawn jitney to see the tropical fruit trees and coffee plants; the knowledgeable guides will explain the various processes necessary to produce the fine fruits of the island. This is a far more interesting and entertaining experience than the trip to Croydon Plantation in Montego Bay. So if you're visiting both resorts and have time for only one plantation, make it Brimmer Hall.

Port Maria, St. Mary's. ⓒ **876/994-2309.** Tours $15. Tours Mon–Fri 8am–4pm.

Coyaba River Garden and Museum   A mile (2km) from the center of Ocho Rios, at an elevation of 420 feet (126m), this park and museum were built on the grounds of the former Shaw Park plantation. The word *coyaba* comes from the Arawak name for paradise. Coyaba is a Spanish-style museum with a river and gardens filled with native flora, a cut-stone courtyard, fountains, and a crafts shop and bar. The museum boasts a collection of artifacts from the Arawak, Spanish, and English settlements in the area.

Shaw Park Rd. ⓒ **876/974-6235.** Admission $4.50, free for children age 12 and under. Daily 8am–5pm. Take the Fern Gully–Kingston road, turn left at St. John's Anglican Church, and follow the signs to Coyaba, just a ½ mile (.4km) farther.

Dunn's River Falls *Overrated*   For a fee, you can relax on the beach or climb with a guide to the top of the 600-foot (546m) falls. You can splash in the waters at the bottom of the falls or drop into the cool pools higher up between the cascades of water. The beach restaurant provides lackluster snacks and drinks, and dressing rooms are available. If you're planning to climb the falls, wear old tennis shoes or sport sandals to protect your feet from the sharp rocks and to prevent slipping.

Climbing the falls with the crowds is a chance to experience some 610 feet (183m) of cold but clear mountain water. In contrast to the heat swirling around you, the splashing water hitting your face and bare legs is cooling on a hot day. The problem here is slipping and falling, especially if you're joined to a chain of hands linking body to body. In spite of the slight danger, there seem to be few accidents. The falls aren't exactly a wilderness experience, with all the tour buses carrying cruise ship passengers here. The place is always overrun.

Rte. A3. ✆ **876/974-2857.** Admission $6 adults, $3 children age 2–11, free for children under age 2. Daily 8:30am–5pm (7am–5pm on cruise-ship arrival days). From the center of Ocho Rios, head west along Route A3.

Firefly ⭐   This vacation retreat was the home of Sir Noël Coward and his longtime companion, Graham Payn, who, as executor of Coward's estate, donated it to the Jamaica National Heritage Trust. The recently restored house is more or less as it was on the day Sir Noël died in 1973. His Hawaiian-print shirts still hang in the closet of his austere bedroom, with its mahogany four-poster. The library contains a collection of his books, and the living room is warm and comfortable, with big armchairs and two grand pianos (where he composed several famous tunes). Guests were housed at Blue Harbour, a villa closer to Port Maria; they included Evelyn Waugh, Winston Churchill, Errol Flynn, Laurence Olivier, Vivien Leigh, Claudette Colbert, Katharine Hepburn, Mary Martin, and the Queen Mother. Paintings by the noted playwright/actor/author/composer adorn the walls. An open patio looks out over the pool and the sea. Across the lawn, Sir Noël is buried under a simple white marble gravestone.

Grants Pen, in St. Mary, 20 miles (32km) east of Ocho Rios above Port Maria. ✆ **876/725-0920.** Admission $10. Mon–Thurs and Sat 9am–5pm.

Harmony Hall   This was the centerpiece of a sugar plantation in the late 19th century. Today it has been restored and is now the focal point of an art gallery and restaurant that showcases the painting and sculpture of Jamaican artists as well as a tasteful array of arts and crafts. Among the featured gift items are Sharon McConnell's Starfish Oils, which contain natural additives harvested in Jamaica. The gallery shop also carries the "Reggae to Wear" line of sportswear, designed and made on Jamaica.

Harmony Hall is also the setting for one of the best Italian restaurants along the coast, Toscanini's (see "Dining," above).

Tower Isles on Rte A3, 4 miles (6km) east of Ocho Rios. ✆ **876/975-4222.** Free admission. Gallery daily 10am–6pm; restaurant/cafe Tues–Sun 10am–2:30pm and 6–11pm.

Prospect Plantation   This working plantation adjoins the 18-hole Prospect Mini Golf Course. A visit to this property is an educational, relaxing, and enjoyable experience. On your leisurely ride by covered jitney through the scenic beauty of Prospect, you'll readily see why this section of Jamaica is called "the garden parish of the island." You can view the many trees planted by such visitors as Winston Churchill, Henry Kissinger, Charlie Chaplin, Pierre Trudeau, and Noël Coward. You'll learn about and observe pimento (allspice), bananas, cassava, sugarcane, coffee, cocoa, coconut, pineapple, and the famous leucaena ("Tree of Life"). You'll see Jamaica's first hydroelectric plant and sample some of the exotic fruit and drinks.

Horseback riding is available on three scenic trails at Prospect. The rides vary from 1 to 2¼ hours. Advance booking of 1 hour is necessary.

Rte. A3, 3 miles (5km) east of Ocho Rios, in St. Ann. ✆ **876/994-1058.** Tours $12 adults, free for children age 12 and under; 1-hr. horseback ride $20. Tours Mon–Sat at 10:30am, 2pm, and 3:30pm; Sun at 11am, 1:30pm, and 3pm.

SHOPPING

For many, Ocho Rios provides an introduction to Jamaica-style shopping. After surviving the ordeal, some visitors may vow never to go shopping again. Literally hundreds of Jamaicans pour into Ocho Rios, hoping to peddle items to cruise-ship passengers and other visitors. Be prepared for aggressive vendors. Pandemonium greets many an unwary shopper, who must also be prepared for some fierce haggling. Every vendor asks too much at first, which gives them the leeway to "negotiate" until the price reaches a more realistic level. Is shopping fun in Ocho Rios? A resounding no. Do cruise-ship passengers and land visitors indulge in it anyway? A decided yes.

In general, the shopping is better in Montego Bay. If you're not going there, wander the Ocho Rios crafts markets, although much of the merchandise is repetitive.

SHOPPING CENTERS & MALLS   There are a number of shopping plazas in Ocho Rios. We've listed them because they're here, not because we heartily recommend them. Newer ones include the **New Ocho Rios Plaza,** in the center of town, with some 60 shops; opposite is the **Taj Mahal,** with 26 duty-free stores. **Island Plaza** is another major shopping complex, as is the **Mutual Security Plaza** with some 30 shops.

Ocean Village Shopping Centre (© 876/974-2683) is one of the originals, with numerous boutiques, food stores, a bank, sundries purveyors, travel agencies, service facilities, and what have you. The **Ocho Rios Pharmacy** (© 876/974-2398) sells most proprietary brands, perfumes, and suntan lotions, among its many wares. Nearby is the major competitor of Ocean Village, the **Coconut Grove Shopping Plaza,** which is linked by walkways and shrubs. The merchandise here consists mainly of local craft items, and this center is often overrun with cruise-ship passengers. Ocean Village is slightly bigger and more upscale, and we prefer it.

Just east of Ocho Rios, the **Pineapple Place Shopping Centre** is a collection of shops in cedar-shingle-roofed cottages set amid tropical flowers.

The **Ocho Rios Craft Park** has 150 stalls for browsing. A vendor will weave a hat or a basket while you wait, or you can buy a ready-made hat, hamper, handbag, place mats, or lampshade. Other stands stock hand-embroidered goods and will make small items while you wait. Wood carvers work on bowls, ashtrays, statues, and cups.

Island Plaza, right in the heart of Ocho Rios, has some of the best Jamaican art, all paintings by local artists. You can also purchase local handmade crafts (be prepared to do some haggling), carvings, ceramics, kitchenware, and the inevitable T-shirts.

SPECIALTY SHOPS   **Swiss Stores,** in the Ocean Village Shopping Centre (© 876/974-2519), sells jewelry and all the big names in Swiss watches. The Rolex watches here are real, not those fakes touted by hustlers on the streets.

One of the best bets for shopping is **Soni's Plaza,** 50 Main St., the address of all the shops recommended below. **Casa de Oro** (© 876/974-5392) specializes in duty-free watches, fine jewelry, and classic perfumes. **Chulani's** (© 876/974-2421) sells quality watches, fine jewelry, and brand-name perfumes, although some of the leather bags might tempt you as well. **Gem Palace** (© 876/974-2850) is the place to go for diamond solitaires, tennis bracelets, and 14-karat gold chains. **Mohan's** (© 876/974-9270) offers one of the best selections of 14-karat and 18-karat gold chains, rings, bracelets, and earrings. **Soni's** (© 876/

974-2303) dazzles with gold, but also cameras, French perfumes, watches, china and crystal, linen tablecloths, and even the standard Jamaican souvenirs. **Taj Gift Centre** (© 876/974-9268) has a little bit of everything: Blue Mountain coffee, film, cigars, and hand-embroidered linen tablecloths. For something different, look for Jamaican jewelry made from hematite, a mountain stone. **Tajmahal** (© 876/974-6455) beats most competition with its name-brand watches, jewelry, and fragrances. It also has Paloma Picasso leather wear and porcelain by Lladró.

Jamaica Inn Gift Shop, in the Jamaica Inn, Main Street (© 876/974-2514), is better than most specialty shops here, selling everything from Blue Mountain coffee to Walkers Wood products, and even guava jelly and jerk seasoning. If you're lucky, you'll find marmalade from an old family recipe, plus Upton Pimento Dram, a unique liqueur flavored with Jamaican allspice. Local handcrafts include musical instruments for kids, brightly painted country cottages of tin, and intricate jigsaw puzzles of local scenes. The store also sells antiques and fine old maps of the West Indies.

OCHO RIOS AFTER DARK

A $16 million attraction, **Entertainment Village,** a massive complex of sights and amusements, is scheduled to open by the time you read this. On 4 acres (2 hectares) of land at the western end of Ocho Rios between Turtle Beach and Reynolds Pier, the site will be a re-created Jamaican village with gardens, a lagoon, and a number of entertainment options. Shops and restaurants—along with craft outlets, a theater, an amphitheater, a children's play area, and even a Cyber Center—will complete the offerings. Naturally, there will be Jamaican reggae music, both live and at a museum.

The **Sports Bar** at the Little Pub Restaurant (see earlier in this chapter) is open daily from 10am to 3am, and Sunday is disco night. Most evenings are devoted to some form of entertainment, including karaoke. Also see "Dining," earlier in this chapter, for a review of **BiBiBips,** where there's a hopping bar and live bands on Friday, Saturday, and Sunday nights.

Jamaic'N Me Crazy, at the Renaissance Jamaica Grande (© 876/974-2201), has the best lighting and sound system in Ocho Rios (and perhaps Jamaica). The crowd includes everyone from the passing yachter to the curious tourist, who may be under the mistaken impression that he or she is seeing an authentic Jamaican nightclub. It charges nonguests $30 to cover everything you can shake or drink, nightly from 10pm to 3am.

6 Port Antonio ✦

Port Antonio, sometimes called the Jamaica of 100 years ago, is a verdant and sleepy seaport on the northeast coast, 63 miles (101km) northeast of Kingston. It's the mecca of the titled and the wealthy, including European royalty and stars like Whoopi Goldberg and Peter O'Toole.

This small, bustling town is like many on the island: clean but cluttered, with sidewalks around a market filled with vendors, and tin-roofed shacks competing with old Georgian and modern brick and concrete buildings. At the market, you can browse for local craftwork, spices, and fruits.

Travelers used to arrive by banana boat and stay at the Titchfield Hotel (which burned down). Captain Bligh landed here in 1793 with the first breadfruit plants, and Port Antonio claims that the ones grown in this area are the best on the island. Visitors still arrive by water, but now it's in cruise ships that moor close to Navy Island, and the passengers come ashore just for the day.

Navy Island and the long-gone Titchfield Hotel were owned for a short time by Errol Flynn. The story is that after suffering damage to his yacht, he put into Kingston for repairs, visited Port Antonio by motorbike, fell in love with the area, and in due course acquired Navy Island (some say he won it in a bet). Later, he either lost or sold it and bought a nearby plantation, Comfort Castle, still owned by his widow, Patrice Wymore Flynn, who spends most of her time there. He was much loved and admired by the Jamaicans and was totally integrated into the community. They still talk of him in Port Antonio—his reputation for womanizing and drinking lives on.

We find Port Antonio one of the more relaxed retreats in Jamaica, certainly not as undiscovered as it was when William Randolph Hearst or J. P. Morgan visited, but a virtual Shangri-la compared to Ocho Rios or Montego Bay. It also has some of the finest beaches in Jamaica and has long been a center for some of the Caribbean's best deep-sea fishing. It's a good place to go to get away from it all.

ESSENTIALS

GETTING THERE If you're going to Port Antonio, you will fly into the **Donald Sangster Airport** in Montego Bay or the **Norman Manley International Airport** in Kingston. Some hotels, particularly the larger resorts, will arrange for airport transfers from that point. Be sure to ask when you book.

If your hotel does not provide transfers, you can fly to Port Antonio's small airport aboard **Air Jamaica Express,** booking your connection through Air Jamaica (© **800/523-5585** in the U.S.). The one-way fare is $50 from Kingston, $60 from Montego Bay.

You can also take a private bus for your transfers. The bus costs $25 one-way. We recommend a private company: **Tour Wise** (© **876/979-1027**). The bus will drop you off at your hotel. The trip takes 2 hours, but for safety's sake, we only recommend this option if you fly into Montego Bay.

You can rent a car for the 133-mile (214km) drive east along Route A1 (see "Getting Around" in the section "Essentials," at the beginning of this chapter), but we don't advise this 4-hour drive for safety's sake, regardless of which airport you fly into.

If you take a taxi, the typical one-way fare from Montego Bay is $100, but always negotiate and agree upon a fare *before* you get into the cab.

MEDICAL FACILITIES The **Port Antonio General Hospital** is at Naylor's Hill (© **876/993-2646**).

ACCOMMODATIONS

Increasingly and despite its charms, Port Antonio is suffering from a lack of business as travelers are drawn to the more famous Negril, Ocho Rios, and Montego Bay. Many of the hotels are forced to fill up empty rooms with low-cost tour groups hailing from everywhere from Italy to Canada. Because of this, we've found that some of the hotels in the area are showing signs of wear and deterioration; they don't all seem to be maintained in a state-of-the-art condition.

VERY EXPENSIVE

Trident Villas & Hotel ★★ This luxury hideaway is located on Allan Avenue, on the coast toward Frenchman's Cove. It sits regally above jagged coral cliffs with a seaside panorama. The hotel's main building is furnished with antiques and cooled by sea breezes. Your accommodations will be a studio cottage or tower, reached by a path through the gardens. In the cottages, a large bedroom with ample sitting area opens onto a private patio with a sea view. All units have ceiling fans, plenty of storage space, and tasteful Jamaican antiques and colorful chintzes. Beds are most comfortable, while bathrooms have combination shower/tubs. Trident has a horseshoe-shaped sandy beach cove at one end of its grounds, which is accessible by a path that meanders along a landscaped terrain. It's a strip of muddy bottomed seafront that's not as appealing as a dip in the hotel pool. That pool is positioned near a graceful gazebo and sits above jagged rocks where the surf crashes and churns for most of the day.

Men are required to wear jackets and ties at dinner, when silver service, crystal, and Port Royal pewter sparkle on the tables. Dinner is a multicourse, excellent fixed-price meal, so if you have dietary restrictions, make your requirements known early.

Rte. A4 (P.O. Box 119), Port Antonio, Jamaica, W.I. ℭ 800/330-8272 in the U.S., or 876/993-2602. Fax 876/993-2960. www.tridentvillas.com. 27 units. Winter $340 double; from $620 suite. Off-season $220 double; from $340 suite. Rates include MAP (breakfast and dinner). AE, MC, V. **Amenities:** Restaurant, bar; pool; tennis courts; croquet; snorkeling, deep-sea fishing, scuba diving; room service; massage; babysitting; laundry. *In room:* A/C, safe.

EXPENSIVE

Dragon Bay ⭐ Set on 55 acres (22 hectares) of forested land that slopes down to a good sandy beach, this resort has changed hands frequently during its lifetime. Today, it's a compound of bungalows and villas that caters to a mainly European crowd, most of whom check in for relatively long stays of 2 weeks or more. Accommodations are within about 30 pink-and-white, two-story bungalows, some built on flatlands beside the beach, others on the steeply sloping terrain leading uphill to the resort's "clubhouse." Furnishings are durable but comfortable; the efficiently organized bathrooms have shower stalls. All but the smallest units contain kitchens, a fact that's appreciated by guests who prepare at least some of their own meals with supplies purchased at neighborhood grocery stores. There are two restaurants, one a beach grill and one a bit more substantial. There are three bars—our favorite is the "Cruise Bar," which was used as a set for Tom Cruise in that silly film, *Cocktail.*

P.O. Box 176, Port Antonio, Jamaica, W.I. ℭ 876/993-8751. Fax 876/993-8971. www.dragonbay.com. 90 units. Winter $175–$205 double; $240–$270 1-bedroom suite; $360 2-bedroom suite; $440 3-bedroom suite. Off-season $120–$150 double; $200 1-bedroom suite; $250 2-bedroom suite; $320 3-bedroom suite. AE, MC, V. **Amenities:** 2 restaurants, 3 bars; pool; 2 tennis courts; aerobics classes; dive shop. *In room:* A/C.

Goblin Hill Villas at San San ⭐ This green and sunny hillside—once said to shelter goblins—is now filled with Georgian-style vacation homes on San San Estate. The pool is surrounded by a vine-laced arbor, which lies just a stone's throw from an almost impenetrable forest. A long flight of steps leads down to the crescent-shaped sands of San San beach. This beach is now private, but guests of the hotel receive a pass. Everything has the aura of having last been fixed up in the 1970s, but the resort is still comfortable. The accommodations are town-house style; some have ceiling fans and king-size beds, but none have phones or TVs. The generally roomy units are filled with handmade pine pieces, along with a split-level living and dining area with a fully equipped kitchen. Housekeepers prepare and serve meals and attend to chores in the villas.

San San (P.O. Box 26), Port Antonio, Jamaica, W.I. ℭ 876/925-8108. Fax 876/925-6248. www.goblinhill.com. 42 units. Winter $110–$195 1-bedroom villa; $185–$245 2-bedroom villa. Off-season $90–$165 1-bedroom villa; $145–$195 2-bedroom villa. AE, MC, V. **Amenities:** Restaurant, bar; pool; 2 tennis courts; car rental; room service (8am–8pm); babysitting; laundry/dry cleaning. *In room:* A/C, kitchenette, fridge, no phone.

INEXPENSIVE

Fern Hill Club Hotel   Airy and panoramic but showing signs of wear, Fern Hill occupies 20 forested acres (8 hectares) high above the coastline, attracting primarily a British and Canadian tour group clientele. The nearest beach is San San, a 5-minute drive east of the hotel. There's no shuttle but the reception desk can arrange for a taxi to take you there. This is a far less elegant choice than its main competitor, Goblin Hill (see earlier in this chapter), though you can almost always get better rates here. Technically classified as a private club, it's comprised of a colonial-style clubhouse and three outlying villas, plus a comfortable annex at the bottom of the hill. The accommodations come in a wide range of configurations, including standard rooms, junior suites, spa suites, and villas with cooking facilities. All units are highly private and attract many honeymooners. Bathrooms, mainly with shower, are adequate with plenty of shelf space.

See "Dining," below, for a review of the hotel restaurant, Fern Hill Club, which offers a standard international menu.

Mile Gully Rd., San San (P.O. Box 100), Port Antonio, Jamaica, W.I. © **876/993-7374.** Fax 876/993-7373. fernhill@cwj.com. 31 units. Year-round $99–$121 double. AE, MC, V. Drive east along Allan Ave. and watch for the signs. **Amenities:** Restaurant; bar; 3 pools; tennis court; shuttle to beach. *In room:* A/C, TV.

Jamaica Heights Resort *(Finds)*   This affordable but sophisticated retreat might be full of rock stars from Düsseldorf or up-and-coming filmmakers cranking out tomorrow's cult film. It's set at the top of a rutted and very steep series of roads, the best of which were privately built by the very worldly owner, Helmut Steiner, former professor of literature and philosophy in Berlin, who built the place between 1984 and 1996 after skippering his own sailboat around the world. The resort is not on a beach but provides transportation to two of the finest beach strips of sand at Port Antonio, including Frenchman's Cove and San San.

Today, with his wife, Charmaine, he maintains the funkiest, most amusing, and hippest guesthouse in town. Scattered amid the wedge-shaped 8-acre (3-hectare) property are a half-dozen buildings, each white-walled with shutters, gazebos, climbing vines, and a pavilion for meditating over views of the forested terrain that cascades down to Port Antonio's harbor. The garden sports exotic palms, a stream with its own waterfalls, the most elegant Ping-Pong pavilion in the world, and dozens of botanical oddities from around the world. The minimalist accommodations are spotlessly clean. Each has a four-poster bed and funky lighting fixtures, plus shower/tub combination bathrooms. Doors can be opened or closed to create suites with between two and four bedrooms.

Spring Bank Rd, Port Antonio, Jamaica, WI. © **876/993-3305.** Fax 876/993-3563. aaaja@ jamaicaheights.com. 8 units. $60–$75 double. No credit cards. **Amenities:** Restaurant; pool; watersports can be arranged. *In room:* Ceiling fan, no phone.

Hotel Mocking Bird Hill *(⋆)*   A 6-mile (10km) drive east of Port Antonio, this hotel occupies the much-renovated premises of what was originally built in 1971 as the holiday home of an American family. The inn lies a 5-minute drive from Frenchman's Cove Beach. In 1993, two imaginative women transformed the place into a blue-and-white enclave of good taste, reasonable prices, and ecological consciousness. Set about 600 feet (180m) above the coastline on a hillside laden with tropical plants, the place attracts a clientele of mostly German and Dutch visitors, who seem to revel in the artsy and ecologically conscious setting. The accommodations are simple but tasteful, and other than their ceiling fans, they're utterly devoid of the electronic gadgets that prevail in the urban world. Much of the establishment's interior, including its restaurant (Mille Fleurs), is decorated with Ms. Walker's artworks, and as this hotel grows, the gallery aspect will probably be expanded. You can participate in rafting tours, day hikes, or classes in painting and papermaking, or you can just relax and enjoy a herbal massage or the sweeping views out over the Blue Mountains and the Jamaican coastline.

Mocking Bird Hill, North Coast Hwy. (east of Port Antonio), Port Antonio, Jamaica, W.I. ℂ 876/993-7267. Fax 876/993-7133. www.hotelmockingbirdhill.com. 10 units. Winter $180–$230 double. Off-season $125–$160. AE, MC, V. **Amenities:** Restaurant. *In room:* A/C in some, ceiling fans, no phone.

DINING

All hotel restaurants welcome outside guests for dinner, but reservations are required.

Fern Hill Club INTERNATIONAL/JAMAICAN   One of the finest dining spots in Port Antonio offers a sweeping view of the rugged coastline, with great sunsets. Well-prepared specialties are served: jerk chicken, jerk pork, grilled lobster, and Creole fish. Depending on who's in the kitchen, the food here can be quite satisfactory, though once in a while, especially off-season, the cuisine might be a bit of a letdown. The club also offers entertainment, with a calypso band and piano music during the week and disco music on weekends.

In the Fern Hill Club Hotel, Mile Gully Rd. ℂ 876/993-7374. Reservations recommended. Main courses $5–$10 lunch, $12–$27.50 dinner. AE, MC, V. Daily 7:30am–10:30pm. Head east on Allan Ave.

Trident Hotel Restaurant ⋆ INTERNATIONAL   The elegant Trident Hotel Restaurant still serves a fine cuisine evoking the Jamaica of the '50s. The high-pitched wooden roof set on white stonewalls holds several ceiling fans that gently stir the air. The antique tables are set with old china, English silver, and Port Royal pewter. The formally dressed waiters will help you choose your wine and whisper the name of each course as they serve it: Jamaican salad, mahi-mahi with mayonnaise-and-mustard sauce, steak with broccoli and sautéed potatoes, and peach Melba and Blue Mountain coffee with Tia Maria, a Jamaican liqueur. The six-course dinner menu changes daily. The cuisine is always fresh and prepared with first-class ingredients, though the setting and the white-gloved service are generally more memorable than the food.

In Trident Villas & Hotel, Rte. A4. ℂ 876/993-2602. Reservations required. Jackets and ties required for men. Fixed-price dinner $44. AE, MC, V. Daily 7:30am–4pm and 8–9:30pm. Head east on Allan Ave.

Yachtsman's Wharf INTERNATIONAL   This restaurant beneath a thatch-covered roof is at the end of an industrial pier, near the departure point for ferries to Navy Island. The rustic bar and restaurant is a favorite of the expatriate yachting set. Crews from many of the ultra-expensive boats have dined here and have pinned their ensigns on the roughly textured planks and posts. The kitchen opens for breakfast and stays open all day, serving menu items such as burgers,

---

Moments   **A Dip in the Blue Lagoon**

Remember the young Brooke Shields? She made the film *The Blue Lagoon* in a calm, protected cove 10 miles (16km) east of Port Antonio. The water is so deep, nearly 20 feet (6m) or so, that it turns a cobalt blue; there's almost no more scenic spot in all of Jamaica. The Blue Lagoon, with its small, intimate beach, is a great place for a picnic (you can pick up plenty of jerk pork, smoked at various shacks along the Boston Bay Beach area).

ceviche, curried chicken, and ackee with saltfish. Main dishes include vegetables. Come here for the setting, the camaraderie, and the usual array of tropical drinks; the food is only secondary.

16 West St. ✆ **876/993-3053**. Main courses $9–$36. No credit cards. Daily 7:30am–10pm.

HITTING THE BEACH

Port Antonio has several white-sand beaches, including the famous **San San Beach,** which has recently gone private. Guests of certain hotels are admitted with a pass, or else you pay a fee of $3.

Boston Beach is free, and it often has light surfing; there are picnic tables as well as a restaurant and snack bar. On your way here, stop and get the makings for a picnic lunch at the most famous center for peppery jerk pork and chicken on Jamaica. These rustic shacks also sell the much rarer jerk sausage. It's 11 miles (18km) east of Port Antonio and the Blue Lagoon.

Also free is **Fairy Hill Beach** (Winnifred), with no changing rooms or showers. **Frenchman's Cove Beach** attracts a chic crowd to its white-sand beach combined with a freshwater stream. Nonguests are charged $3.

Navy Island, once Errol Flynn's personal hideaway, is a fine choice for swimming (one beach is clothing optional) and snorkeling (at **Crusoe's Beach**). Take the boat from the Navy Island dock on West Street across from the Exxon station. It's a 7-minute ride to the island; a one-way fare is 30¢. The ferry runs 24 hours a day.

SPORTS & OTHER OUTDOOR PURSUITS

DEEP-SEA FISHING   Northern Jamaican waters are world renowned for their game fish, including mahi-mahi, wahoo, blue and white marlin, sailfish, tarpon, barracuda, and bonito. The **Jamaica International Fishing Tournament** and **Jamaica International Blue Marlin Team Tournaments** run concurrently at Port Antonio every September or October. Most major hotels from Port Antonio to Montego Bay have deep-sea-fishing facilities, and there are many charter boats.

A 40-foot-long (12m) **sport-fishing boat** (✆ **876/993-3209**) with a tournament rig is available for charter rental. Taking out up to six passengers at a time, it charges $900 per half day or $1,600 per day, with crew, bait, tackle, and soft drinks included. It docks at Port Antonio's Marina, off West Palm Avenue, in the center of town. Call for bookings.

RAFTING   Although it's not exactly adventurous (it's a tame and safe outing), this is the best rafting experience on the island and the most fun. Rafting started on the Rio Grande as a means of transporting bananas from the plantations to the waiting freighters. In 1871, a Yankee skipper, Lorenzo Dow Baker, decided that a seat on one of the rafts was better than walking, but it was not until Errol Flynn arrived that the rafts became popular as a tourist attraction. Flynn used to hire the craft for his friends, and he encouraged the rafters to race down the Rio Grande, betting on the winners. Now that bananas are transported by road, the raft skipper makes one or maybe two trips a day down the waterway. If you want to take a trip, contact **Rio Grande Tours,** Berrydale (✆ **876/913-5434**).

The rafts, some 33 feet (10m) long and only 4 feet (1m) wide, are propelled by stout bamboo poles. There's a raised double seat about two-thirds of the way back. The skipper stands in the front, trousers rolled up to his knees, the water washing his feet, and guides the craft down the lively river, about 8 miles (13km) between steep hills covered with coconut palms, banana plantations, and flowers, through limestone cliffs pitted with caves, through the "Tunnel of Love," a narrow cleft in the rocks, then on to wider, gentler water.

Trips last 2 to 2½ hours and are offered from 9am to 5pm daily at a cost of $45 per raft, which holds two passengers. A fully insured driver will take you in your rented car to the starting point at Berrydale, where you board your raft. If you feel like it, take a picnic lunch, but bring enough for the skipper, too, who will regale you with lively stories of life on the river.

SNORKELING & SCUBA DIVING   The best outfitter is **Lady Godiva's Dive Shop** in Dragon Bay (© 876/993-8988), 7 miles (11km) from Port Antonio. Full dive equipment is available. Technically, you can snorkel off most of the beaches in Port Antonio, but you're likely to see much more further offshore. The very best spot is San San Bay by Monkey Island. The reef here is extremely active and full of a lot of exciting marine life. Lady Godiva offers two excursions daily to this spot for $12 per person. Snorkeling equipment costs $9 for a full day's rental.

EXPLORING THE AREA

Athenry Gardens and Cave of Nonsuch   Twenty minutes from Port Antonio, it's an easy drive and an easy walk to see the stalagmites, stalactites, fossilized marine life, and evidence of Arawak civilization in Nonsuch. The cave is 1.5 million years old, and you can explore its underground beauty by following railed stairways and concrete walkways on a 30-minute walk. The place is dramatically lit. Although the United States and Europe have far greater cave experiences, this is as good as it gets in Jamaica. From the Athenry Gardens, there are panoramic views over the island and the sea. The gardens are filled with coconut palms, flowers, and trees, and complete guided tours are given.

Portland. © 876/993-3740. Admission (including guide for gardens and cave) $8 adults, $3 children age 11 and under. Daily 10am–4pm. From Harbour St. in Port Antonio, turn south in front of the Anglican church onto Red Hassel Rd. and proceed approximately a mile (2km) to Breastworks community (fork in road); take the left fork, cross a narrow bridge, go immediately left after the bridge, and proceed approximately 3½ miles (6km) to Anthenry Estates.

PORT ANTONIO AFTER DARK

It was bound to happen. Down by the sea east of Port Antonio, at **Dragon Bay** (© 876/993-8751), the cocktail bar has been renamed "Cruise Bar" in honor of the movie *Cocktail,* which starred Tom Cruise. Cruise and a Hollywood cast came to the resort's 55 acres (22 hectares) to shoot the movie. Two other films were shot here, the remake of *Lord of the Flies* and *Club Paradise.* Regrettably, Cruise himself is no longer here serving those rum punches. Come here for a "sundowner," and you may fall in love with the place—or the bartender—and stick around for dinner. Another recently opened bar, drawing a fashionable crowd, is the **Tree Bar,** on the grounds of Goblin Hill Villas at San San (© 876/925-8108), high on a hill commanding a panoramic view of 12 acres (5 hectares). The aptly named bar is wrapped around huge ficus trees, whose mammoth aerial roots dangle over the drinking area. Giant-leafed pothos climb down the trunks. It's a sort of "Me Tarzan, You Jane" kind of place and should prove increasingly popular.

7 Kingston & Vicinity

Kingston, the largest English-speaking city in the Caribbean, is the capital and cultural, industrial, and financial center of Jamaica. It's home to more than 750,000 people, including those living on the plains between Blue Mountain and the sea.

The buildings here are a mixture of the modern, graceful, old, and just plain ramshackle. It's a busy city, as you might expect, with a natural harbor that's the seventh largest in the world. The University of the West Indies has its campus on the edge of the city.

Few other cities in the Caribbean carry as many negative connotations for North American travelers as Kingston, thanks to widely publicized, and sometimes exaggerated, reports of violent crime. Marry that with urban congestion, potholed roads, and difficult-to-decipher directional signs that make it hard to navigate, and you've got a bad reputation.

But if you're an urban dweller who copes with everyday life in, say, New York, Atlanta, or Los Angeles, you already know how to deal with city life, and Kingston doesn't have to be that scary. It offers resources and charms that can't be found anywhere else. It is here that Jamaica is at its most urban and confident, its most witty, its most exciting, and its most challenging. No other place in Jamaica offers as many singles bars, dance clubs, and cultural outlets—it's the nation's creative cauldron, wherein ideas and opinions are sharply focused. If you're truly interested in Jamaican culture, Kingston can be very stimulating, as it's very far removed from the tourist-oriented economies of Negril, Ocho Rios, and Montego Bay.

We've carefully screened the recommendations contained within this guidebook, eliminating any that lie within the most dangerous neighborhoods. So keep an open mind about Kingston—it can be a lot of fun and very exciting.

ESSENTIALS

GETTING THERE   See "Getting There" in section 1 of this chapter for details on the airlines that serve Kingston's international airport.

GETTING AROUND   Because Kingston is a rather confusing place to negotiate, many visitors rely on taxis.

MEDICAL NEEDS   The **University Hospital** is at Mona (© 876/927-1620). **Moodie's Pharmacy** is in the New Kingston Shopping Centre (© 876/926-4174).

ACCOMMODATIONS

All leading hotels in security-conscious Kingston have guards.

Terra Nova Hotel   This house is on the western edge of New Kingston, near West Kings House Road. Built in 1924 as a wedding present for a young bride, it was converted into a hotel in 1959. Set in 2½ acres (1 hectare) of gardens with a backdrop of greenery and mountains, it's now one of the best small Jamaican hotels, although the rooms are rather basic and not at all suited for those who want a resort ambience. Most of the bedrooms are in a new wing. The Spanish-style El Dorado Room, with a marble floor, wide windows, and spotless linen, offers local and international food.

17 Waterloo Rd., Kingston 10, Jamaica, W.I. © 876/926-2211. Fax 876/929-4933. www.cariboutpost.com/terra_nova. 35 units. Year-round $150 double. AE, MC, V. **Amenities:** Restaurant, bar; pool. *In room:* A/C, TV, VCR.

IN NEARBY PORT ROYAL

Morgan's Harbour Hotel & Beach Club   The yachtie favorite, this hotel is in Port Royal, once believed to be the wickedest city on earth. On the premises is a 200-year-old redbrick building once used to melt pitch for His Majesty's navy, a swimming area defined by docks and buoys, and a series of wings whose eaves are accented with hints of gingerbread. Set on 22 acres (9 hectares) of flat and rocky seashore, the resort contains the largest marina facility in Kingston, plus a breezy waterfront restaurant and a popular bar (where ghost stories about the old Port Royal seem especially lurid as the liquor flows on Friday night). Longtime residents quietly claim that the ghosts of soldiers killed by a long-ago earthquake are especially visible on hot and very calm days, when British formations seem to march out of the sea.

The well-furnished bedrooms are laid out in an 18th-century Chippendale-Jamaican style. Medium-size bathrooms are tidily maintained, each with a shower bath. The Buccaneer Scuba Club organizes dives to some of the 170-odd wrecks lying close to shore.

Port Royal, Kingston 1, Jamaica, W.I. © 800/44-UTELL in the U.S., or 876/967-8030. Fax 876/967-8073. 51 units. Year-round $180 double; $210 suite. AE, DISC, MC, V. Take the public ferryboat that departs every 2 hr. from near Victoria Pier on Ocean Blvd.; many visitors arrive by car or taxi. **Amenities:** Restaurant, bar; deep-sea fishing charters. *In room:* A/C, TV, minibar.

DINING

Norma's on the Terrace ★★ JAMAICAN   This is the creation of Jamaica's most famous businesswoman, Norma Shirley, purveyor of food to stylish audiences as far away as Miami. It's housed beneath the wide porticos of the gallery surrounding Kingston's most famous monument, Devon House. Ms. Shirley has taken the old, woefully dusty gardens and transformed them, so now they're manicured like something you'd expect on an English estate. Menus change with the season, but usually reflect Ms. Shirley's penchant for creative adaptations of her native Jamaican cuisine. Stellar examples include Jamaican chowder with crabmeat, shrimp, conch, and lobster; grilled whole red snapper encrusted with herbs and served with a thyme and caper sauce; or grilled smoked pork loin in a teriyaki/ginger sauce, served with caramelized apples.

In Devon House, 26 Hope Rd. © 876/968-5488. Reservations recommended. Main courses $14.95–$41.40. AE, MC, V. Daily 11am–11pm.

HITTING THE BEACH

You don't really come to Kingston for beaches, but there are some here. To the southwest of the sprawling city are black sandy **Hellshire Beach** and **Fort Clarence.** Both of these beaches are very popular with the locals on weekends. Both have changing rooms, heavy security, and numerous food stands. The reggae concerts at Fort Clarence are legendary on the island.

Just past Fort Clarence, the fisherman's beach at **Naggo Head** is an even hipper destination, or so Kingston beach buffs claim. After a swim in the refreshing waters, opt for one of the food stands selling "fry fish" and *bammy* (cassava bread). The closest beach to the city (although it's not very good) is **Lime Cay,** a little island on the outskirts of Kingston Harbour, approached after a short boat ride from Morgan's Harbour at Port Royal.

SEEING THE SIGHTS

Even if you're staying at Ocho Rios or Port Antonio, you may want to visit Kingston for brief sightseeing and for trips to nearby Port Royal and Spanish Town.

From Kingston, you can make excursions into the Blue Mountains. See the section "The Blue Mountains," below.

IN TOWN

One of the major attractions, **Devon House,** 26 Hope Rd. (© **876/929-6602**), was built in 1881 by George Stiebel, a Jamaican who made his fortune mining in Latin America, becoming one of the first black millionaires in the Caribbean. A striking classical building, the house has been restored to its original beauty by the Jamaican National Trust. The grounds contain crafts shops, boutiques, two restaurants, shops that sell the best ice cream in Jamaica (in exotic fruit flavors), and a bakery and pastry shop with Jamaican puddings and desserts. The main house also displays furniture of various periods and styles. Admission to the main house is $6; hours are Tuesday to Saturday from 9:30am to 5pm. Admission to the grounds (the shops and restaurants) is free.

Almost next door to Devon House are the sentried gates of **Jamaica House,** residence of the prime minister, a fine, white-columned building set well back from the road.

Continuing along Hope Road, at the crossroads of Lady Musgrave and King's House roads, turn left and you'll see a gate on the left with its own personal traffic light. This leads to **King's House,** the official residence of the governor-general of Jamaica, the queen's representative on the island. The outside and front lawn of the gracious residence, set in 200 acres (80 hectares) of well-tended parkland, is sometimes open for viewing, Monday to Friday from 10am to 5pm. The secretarial offices are housed next door in an old wooden building set on brick arches. In front of the house is a gigantic banyan tree in whose roots, legend says, *duppies* (ghosts) take refuge when they're not living in the cotton trees.

Between Old Hope and Mona roads, a short distance from the Botanical Gardens, is the **University of the West Indies** (© 876/927-1660), built in 1948 on the Mona Sugar Estate. Ruins of old mills, storehouses, and aqueducts are juxtaposed with modern buildings on what must be the most beautifully situated campus in the world. The chapel, an old sugar-factory building, was transported stone by stone from Trelawny and rebuilt. The remains of the original sugar factory here are well preserved and give a good idea of how sugar was made in slave days.

National Library of Jamaica (formerly the West India Reference Library), Institute of Jamaica, 12 East St. (© 876/967-2494), a storehouse of the history, culture, and traditions of Jamaica and the Caribbean, is the finest working library for West Indian studies in the world. It has the most comprehensive, up-to-date, and balanced collection of materials on the region, including books, newspapers, photographs, maps, and prints. It's open Monday to Thursday from 9am to 5pm, Friday from 9am to 4pm.

Bob Marley Museum, 56 Hope Rd. (© 876/927-9152), is the most-visited sight in Kingston, but if you're not a Marley fan, it may not mean much to you. The clapboard house with its garden and high surrounding wall was the famous reggae singer's home and recording studio until his death on May 11, 1981, in a Miami hospital. You can tour the house and view assorted Marley memorabilia, and you may even catch a glimpse of his children, who often frequent the grounds. Hours are Monday to Saturday from 9:30am to 4pm. Admission is J$400 (US$9.20) for adults, J$300 (US$6.90) ages 13 to 18, J$200 (US$4.60) ages 4 to 12. It's reached by bus no. 70 or 75 from Halfway Tree, but take a cab to save yourself the hassle of dealing with Kingston public transport.

IN PORT ROYAL

From West Beach Dock in Kingston, a ferry ride of 20 to 30 minutes will take you to Port Royal, whose name in pirate lore conjures up visions of swashbuckling pirates led by Henry Morgan, swilling grog in harbor taverns. This was once one of the largest trading centers of the New World, with a reputation for being the wickedest city on earth. Blackbeard stopped here regularly on his Caribbean trips. But it all came to an end on June 7, 1692, when a third of the town disappeared underwater as the result of a devastating earthquake. Nowadays, Port

Royal, with its memories of the past, has been designated by the government for redevelopment as a tourist destination.

Today Port Royal is a small fishing village at the end of the Palisades strip. Some 2,000 residents live here with what many locals claim are a "lot of ghosts." Port Royal's seafaring traditions continue, and it's known for its seafood and ramshackle and much-battered architecture of yesterday. Once there were six forts here with a total of 145 guns, some of which can be seen today. Only fort Charles (see below) still stands, however.

As you drive along the Palisades, you arrive first at **St. Peter's Church.** It's usually closed, but you may persuade the caretaker, who lives opposite, to open it if you want to see the silver plate, said to be spoils captured by Henry Morgan from the cathedral in Panama. In the ill-kept graveyard is the tomb of Lewis Galdy, a Frenchman swallowed up and subsequently regurgitated by the 1692 earthquake.

Fort Charles (© 876/967-8438), the only remaining fort of Port Royal's six original ones, has withstood attack, earthquake, fire, and hurricane. Built in 1656 and later strengthened by Morgan for his own purposes, the fort was expanded and further armed in the 1700s, until its firepower boasted more than 100 cannons, covering both the land and the sea approaches. In 1779, Britain's naval hero, Horatio Lord Nelson, was commander of the fort and trod the wooden walkway inside the western parapet as he kept watch for the French invasion fleet. Scale models of the fort and ships of past eras are on display. The fort is open daily from 9am to 5pm; admission is J$100 (US$2).

Part of the complex, **Giddy House,** once the Royal Artillery storehouse, is another example of what the earth's movements can do. Walking across the tilted floor is an eerie and strangely disorienting experience.

IN SPANISH TOWN

From 1662 to 1872, Spanish Town was the capital of the island. Originally founded by the Spaniards as Villa de la Vega, it was sacked by Cromwell's men in 1655, and all traces of Roman Catholicism were obliterated. The English cathedral, surprisingly retaining a Spanish name, **St. Jago de la Vega,** was built in 1666 and rebuilt after being destroyed by a hurricane in 1712. As you drive into the town from Kingston, the ancient cathedral catches your eye with its brick tower and two-tiered wooden steeple, which was not added until 1831. Since the cathedral was built on the foundation and remains of the old Spanish church, it is half English and half Spanish, and displays two distinct styles: Romanesque and Gothic. Of cruciform design and built mostly of brick, it's one of the most interesting buildings on the island. The black-and-white marble stones of the aisles are interspersed with ancient tombstones, and the walls are heavy with marble memorials that are almost a chronicle of Jamaica's history, dating back as far as 1662.

After visiting the cathedral, walk 3 blocks north along White Church Street to Constitution Street and the **Town Square.** This little square is surrounded by towering royal palms. On the west side is old **King's House,** gutted by fire in 1925, although the facade has been restored. This was the residence of Jamaica's British governors until 1872, when the capital was transferred to Kingston.

Beyond the house is the **Jamaica People's Museum of Craft & Technology,** Old King's House, Constitution Square (© 876/922-0620), open Monday to Friday from 9am to 4pm. Admission is J$100 (US$2.30) for adults, J$40 (90¢) for children. The garden contains examples of old farm machinery, an old watermill wheel, a hand-turned sugar mill, a fire engine, and more. An outbuilding houses a museum of crafts and technology, together with a number of smaller agricultural implements. In the small archaeological museum are old prints, models, and maps of the town's grid layout from the 1700s.

The streets around the old Town Square contain many fine Georgian town houses intermixed with tin-roofed shacks. Nearby is the **market,** so busy in the morning that you'll find it difficult, almost dangerous, to pass through. It provides, however, a bustling scene of Jamaican life.

SHOPPING

Downtown Kingston, the old part of the town, is centered around Sir William Grant Park, formerly Victoria Park, a showpiece of lawns, lights, and fountains. Covered arcades lead off from King Street, but everywhere is a teeming mass of people going about their business. There are some beggars and the inevitable hucksters who sidle up and offer "hot stuff, mon," frequently highly polished brass lightly dipped in gold and offered at high prices as real gold.

For many years, the richly evocative paintings of Haiti were viewed as the most valuable contribution to the arts in the Caribbean. There is on Jamaica, however, a rapidly growing perception of itself as one of the artistic leaders of the Third World. An articulate core of Caribbean critics is focusing the attention of the art world on the unusual, eclectic, and sometimes politically motivated paintings being produced here.

Frame Centre Gallery, 10 Tangerine Place (© **876/926-4644**), is one of the most important art galleries on Jamaica. Its founder and guiding force, Guy McIntosh, is widely respected today as a patron of the Jamaican arts. There are three viewing areas and a varied collection of more than 300 works.

Kingston Crafts Market, at the west end of Harbour Street (reached via Straw Avenue, Drummer's Lane, or Cheapside), is a large, covered area of small stalls, selling all kinds of island crafts: wooden plates and bowls; pepper pots made from mahoe (the national wood of the island); straw hats, mats, and baskets; batik shirts; banners for wall decoration, inscribed with the Jamaican coat-of-arms; and wood masks with elaborately carved faces. You should bargain a bit, and vendors will take something off the price, but not very much.

The **Shops at Devon House,** 26 Hope Rd. (© **876/929-6602**), ring the borders of a 200-year-old courtyard once used by slaves and servants. Associated with one of the most beautiful and historic mansions on Jamaica, a building operated by the Jamaican National Trust, 4 of these 10 or so shops are operated by Things Jamaican, a nationwide emporium dedicated to the enhancement of the country's handcrafts. Shops include the Cookery, offering island-made sauces and spices, and the Pottery, selling crockery and stoneware. Look for pewter knives and forks, based on designs of pewter items discovered in archaeological digs in the Port Royal area in 1965. Other outlets include a children's shop, a leather shop, a stained-glass shop, and a gallery.

8 The Blue Mountains ⟨★⟨★⟨★

Just a short drive north of Kingston is some of the most varied and unusual topography in the Caribbean; it is a beautiful mountain range laced with rough rivers, streams, and waterfalls. The 192,000-acre (76,800-hectare) Blue Mountain–John Crow Mountain National Park is maintained by the Jamaican government. The mountainsides are covered with coffee fields, producing a blended version that's among the leading exports of Jamaica. But for the nature enthusiast, the mountains reveal an astonishingly complex series of ecosystems that change radically as you climb from sea level into the fog-shrouded peaks.

The most popular, the most scenic, and our favorite climb begins at **Whitfield Hall** (© 876/927-0986), a high-altitude hostel and coffee estate about 6 miles (10km) north of the hamlet of **Mavis Bank.** Reaching the summit of Blue Mountain Peak (3,000 ft./900m above sea level) requires between 4 and 5 hours, each way. Of course, you can also take much shorter versions of this tour if you don't want to see "everything" (see below). En route, hikers pass through acres of coffee plantations and forest, where temperatures are cooler than you might expect, and where high humidity encourages thick vegetation. Along the way, watch for an amazing array of bird life, including hummingbirds, many species of warblers, rufous-throated solitaires, yellow-bellied sapsuckers, and Greater Antillean pewees.

Dress in layers and bring bottled water. If you opt for a 2am departure in anticipation of watching the sunrise from atop the peak, carry a flashlight as well. Sneakers are usually adequate, although many climbers bring their hiking boots. Be aware that even during the "dry" season (from Dec–Mar), rainfall is common. During the "rainy" season (the rest of the year), these peaks can get up to 150 inches of rainfall a year, and fogs and mists are frequent.

You can opt to head out alone into the Jamaican wilderness, but considering the dangers of such an undertaking, and the crime you might encounter en route, it isn't advisable. A better bet involves engaging one of Kingston's best-known specialists in eco-sensitive tours, **Sunventure Tours,** 30 Balmoral Ave., Kingston 10 (© **876/960-6685**). The staff here can always arrange an individualized tour for you or your party, but offers a mainstream roster of choices as well. The **Blue Mountain Sunrise Tour** involves a camp-style overnight in one of the most remote and inaccessible areas of Jamaica. For a fee of $150 per person, participants are retrieved at their Kingston hotels, driven to an isolated ranger station, Wildflower Lodge, that's accessible only via four-wheel-drive vehicle, in anticipation of a two-stage hike that begins at 2pm. A simple mountaineer's supper is served at 6pm around a campfire at a ranger station near Portland Gap. At 3am, climbers hike by moonlight and flashlight to a mountaintop aerie that was selected for its view of the sunrise over the Blue Mountains. Climbers stay aloft until around noon that day, then head back down the mountain for an eventual return to their hotels in Kingston by 4pm. A 4-hour trek, costing from $25 to $30 per person, can also be arranged.

At no point do we recommend that you hike alone in the Blue Mountains, even if you're an experienced hiker having conquered the alpine peaks of Central Europe. Weather conditions can change rapidly, and hiking maps are in general very poor. Since there are so few discernible landmarks, it is easy to lose your direction.

Security is a major concern for an unaccompanied hiker, especially for those hiking on the Kingston side of the mountain. A guide will not only clear an overgrown path for you, but may keep you out of harm's way. You could be robbed by bandits. These robbers can then disappear into the vast wilderness of the Blue Mountains and are hard, if not impossible, to track down. If you appeal to local authorities, you will probably face indifference and a belated suggestion that "You should have used a guide."

A second popular offering from the same company involves an excursion from Kingston **"Y's Waterfall"** on the Black River, in southern Jamaica's Elizabeth Parish. Participants congregate in Kingston at 6:30am for a transfer to a raft and boating party near the hamlet of Lacovia, and an all-day waterborne excursion to a region of unusual ecological interest. Depending on the number of participants, fees range from $80 to $100 per person, including lunch.

Blue Mountain Bike Tours (© 876/974-7075) offers all-downhill bike tours through the Blue Mountains—you peddle only about a half dozen times on this several-mile trip. Visitors are driven to the highest navigable point in the Blue Mountains, where they are provided bikes and protective gear. Lunch, snacks, and lots of information about coffee, local foliage, and history are provided. The cost is about $85 per person.

ACCOMMODATIONS

Strawberry Hill ★★ Music-industry mogul turned hotelier extraordinaire Chris Blackwell worked here to re-create an idealized version of Jamaica that he remembered from his childhood. The setting is a former coffee plantation in the Blue Mountains, on precariously sloping rain forest terrain 3,100 feet (930m) above the sea. Views from its terraces overlook the capital's twinkling lights. Eco-sensitive and fully self-contained, it has its own power and water-purification system, a small-scale spa, and elaborate botanical gardens. One former guest described this exclusive resort as a "home away from home for five-star Robinson Crusoes." Maps and/or guides are provided for tours of nearby coffee plantations, hiking and mountain biking through the Blue Mountains, and tours by night or by day of the urban attractions of nearby Kingston.

Accommodations are lavishly nostalgic, draped in bougainvillea and Victorian-inspired gingerbread, and outfitted with gracious mahogany furniture like what you'd have expected in a 19th-century Jamaican Great House. Local craftspeople fashioned the cottages and furnished them in classic plantation style, with canopied four-poster beds and louvered mahogany windows. The elegant bathrooms, each designed in an artfully old-fashioned motif, come with shower/tub combinations. The food served in the hotel's glamorous restaurant is good enough to draw foodies from throughout eastern Jamaica.

Irish Town, Blue Mountains, Jamaica, W.I. © 800/OUTPOST in the U.S., or 876/944-8400. Fax 876/944-8408. www.strawberryhillresort.com. 16 units. Year-round $295–$775. AE, MC, V. Guests are personally escorted to the hotel in a customized van or via a 7-min. helicopter ride. It's a 50-min. drive from the Kingston airport or 30 min. via mountain roads from the center of the city. **Amenities:** Restaurant, bar; pool; spa with hydrotherapy facilities and massage; bike rental; room service; laundry. *In room:* TV (on request), kitchenette, minibar, hair dryer, safe.

DINING

Blue Mountain Inn ★ CARIBBEAN/INTERNATIONAL About a 20-minute drive north from downtown Kingston is an 18th-century coffee-plantation house set high on the slopes of Blue Mountain. Surrounded by trees and flowers, it rests on the bank of the Mammee River. On cold nights, log fires blaze, and the dining room gleams with silver and sparkling glass. The inn is one of Jamaica's most famous restaurants, not only for its food but also for its atmosphere and service. The effort of dressing up is worth it, and the cool night air justifies it; women are advised to take a wrap. The cuisine features the fresh seafood and vegetables from the gardens of Jamaica, and menus change monthly. Top off your meal with one of the fresh-fruit desserts or homemade ice creams.

Gordon Town Rd. © 876/927-1700. Reservations required. Main courses $20–$40. AE, MC, V. Mon–Sat 7–9:30pm. Head north on Old Hope Rd. into the mountains.

Martinique

With beautiful white-sand beaches and a culture full of French flair, Martinique is part of the Lesser Antilles and lies in the semitropical zone; its western shore faces the Caribbean, and its eastern shore fronts the more turbulent Atlantic. The surface of the island is only 420 square miles (1,088 sq. km)—50 miles (81km) at its longest point and 21 miles (34km) at its widest point.

The terrain is mountainous, especially in the rain-forested northern part, where the volcano Mount Pelée rises to a height of 4,656 feet (3,297m). In the center of the island, the mountains are smaller, with Carbet Peak reaching a 3,960-foot (1,188m) summit. The high hills rising among the peaks or mountains are called *mornes.* The southern part of Martinique has big hills that reach peaks of 1,500 feet (350m) at Vauclin and 1,400 feet (420m) at Diamant. The irregular coastline of the island has five bays, dozens of coves, and miles of sandy beaches. Almost a third of the island's year-round population of 360,000 lives in the capital and largest city, Fort-de-France.

The climate is relatively mild, with the average temperature in the 75° to 85°F range. At higher elevations, it's considerably cooler. The island is cooled by a wind the French called *alizé,* and rain is frequent but doesn't last very long. Late August to November might be called the rainy season. April through September are the hottest months.

The early Carib peoples, who gave Columbus such a hostile reception, called Martinique "the island of flowers," and indeed it has remained so. The lush vegetation includes hibiscus, poinsettias, bougainvillea, coconut palms, and mango trees. Almost any fruit can sprout from Martinique's soil, including pineapples, avocados, bananas, papayas, and custard apples.

Bird-watchers are often pleased at the number of hummingbirds, and visitors can also see the mountain whistler, the blackbird, and the mongoose. Multicolored butterflies flit about, and after sunset, there's a permanent concert of grasshoppers, frogs, and crickets.

1 Essentials

For advance information, contact the **French Government Tourist Office** in the U.S. at 444 Madison Ave., New York, NY 10022 (© **212/659-7779**); 9454 Wilshire Blvd., Suite 715, Beverly Hills, CA 90212 (© **310/276-2835**); or 645 N. Michigan Ave., Chicago, IL 60611 (© **312/337-6339**). In Britain, contact 178 Piccadilly, London, W1V OAL (© **020/71499-6911**). In Canada, write to 1981 McGill College Ave., Suite 490, Montréal, Québec H3A 2W9 (© **514/288-4264**), or 30 St. Patrick St., Suite 700, Toronto, Ontario M5T 3A3 (© **416/593-6427**).

In **Canada,** contact the **Martinique Tourist Office,** 2159 rue Mackay, Montréal, Québec H3G 2J2 (© **800/361-9099** or 514/844-8566); or 1 Dundas St. W., Suite 2405, Toronto, ON M5G 1ZE (© **800/361-9099** or 416/593-4723).

On the Web, go to **www.martinique.org**.

On the island, the **Office Départemental du Tourisme** (tourist office) is on Boulevard Alfassa in Fort-de-France, across the waterfront boulevard from the harbor (© **596/63-79-60**); it's open Monday to Friday from 8am to 5pm, Saturday from 8am to noon. The information desk at Lamentin Airport is open daily until the last flight comes in.

GETTING THERE

BY PLANE Before you book your own airfare, read the sections "Package Deals" and "Finding the Best Airfare" in chapter 2.

Lamentin International Airport is outside the village of Lamentin, a 15-minute taxi ride east of Fort-de-France and a 40-minute taxi ride northeast of the island's densest concentration of resort hotels (the Les Trois-Ilets peninsula). Most flights to Martinique and Guadeloupe require a transfer on a neighboring island—usually Puerto Rico, but occasionally Antigua. Direct or nonstop flights to the French islands from the U.S. mainland are rare.

American Airlines (© 800/433-7300 in the U.S.; www.aa.com) flies into its busy hub in San Juan from many points throughout North America. From here, passengers bound for Martinique transfer onto one or two daily **American Eagle** (same phone number) flights to Guadeloupe. From Guadeloupe, they transfer again onto 1 of up to 10 daily flights from Guadeloupe to Martinique on **Air Caraïbes** (formerly known as Air Guadeloupe). American can book all the legs of this complicated series of transfers (call the 800 number listed above).

Air France (© 800/237-2747 in the U.S.; www.airfrance.com) operates separate nonstop flights from Paris to both Martinique and Guadeloupe. These depart at least once a day, and in some cases, depending on the season and the day of the week, twice a day. The airline also maintains three weekly flights from Port-au-Prince, Haiti, to Martinique, and three flights a week, depending on the season, between Cayenne, in French Guyana, and Martinique.

Antigua-based **LIAT** (© 800/468-0482 in the U.S. and Canada, 268/462-0700, or through the reservations department of **American Airlines** © 800/433-7300 in the U.S.) flies from Antigua and Barbados to both Martinique and Guadeloupe several times a day. Depending on the season, flights to the two islands are either separate or combined into a single flight, with touchdowns en route. Both Antigua and Barbados are important air-terminus links for such larger carriers as American Airlines (see above).

Another option for reaching either Martinique or Guadeloupe involves flying **BWIA** (© 800/538-2942 in the U.S.; www.bwee.com), the national airline of Trinidad and Tobago, from either New York or Miami nonstop to both Barbados and Antigua, and from there, transferring onto a LIAT flight to either of the French-speaking islands.

British Airways (© 800/247-9297 in the U.S., or 0845/773-3377 in England; www.british-airways.com) flies separately to both Antigua and Barbados three times a week from London. From either of those islands, LIAT connects to either Guadeloupe or Martinique.

BY FERRY One particularly evocative means of travel between Martinique and Guadeloupe involves taking one of the motorized catamarans that are maintained by a local operator, **Exprés des Iles.** Carrying between 395 and 495 passengers, depending on the boat, they require 3¾ hours of waterborne transit, which includes an intermediate stopover on either Dominica or Terre de Haut, in the Iles

Martinique

Airport ✈ Beach ⚲ Mountain ▲▲

Martinique Passage

Macouba
Grand-Rivière
Basse-Pointe
Le Lorrain
Leyritz
17
Montagne Pelée ▲▲
Ajoupa-Bouillon
Le Marigot
16
N1
Le Prêcheur
Morne Rouge
Ste-Marie
Tartane
Caravelle Nature Preserve

Atlantic Ocean

Morne des Esses
Caravelle Peninsula
St-Pierre
Musée Gaugin
Trinité
15
Le Carbet
N2
N3
Balata
N4
Gros-Morne
Bellefontaine
Carbet Peak
St-Joseph
N1
Case-Pilote
Schoelcher
N1
Lamentin
Le François
13 14
Fort-de-France
1 2
Lamentin International Airport
Pointe du Bout ⚲
Anse Mitan ⚲
3-6
N5
Mt. Vauclin ▲
N6
Anse-à-l'Ane ⚲
7
Vauclin
Les Trois-Ilets
D7
Grande Anse
Anses-d'Arlets
8 9
D7
Rivière-Pilote
D37
Le Diamant
Le Marin
Diamond Beach ⚲
Ste-Luce
Cap Chevalier ⚲
Diamond Rock ■
10
11
Les Salines ⚲
Ste-Anne
12
Petrified Forest
Pointe des Salines

Caribbean Sea

St. Lucia Channel

0 — 5 Miles
0 — 5 Kilometers

Auberge de L'Anse Mitan **7**
Club Med Les Boucaniers **10**
Frégate Bleue **13**
Habitation La Grange **16**
Hôtel Diamant Les Bains **8**
Hôtel L'Impératrice **1**
Hôtel Plantation de Leyritz **17**
La Dunette **11**
La Pagerie **7**

Le Lafayette **2**
Le Méridien Trois-Ilets **4**
L'Habitation de L'Ilet Thierry **14**
Manoir de Beauregard **12**
Novotel Coralia Carayou **5**
Novetel Coralia Diamant **9**
Saint-Aubin Hôtel **15**
Sofitel Bakoua Coralia **3**

des Saintes. The company operates one (and sometimes two) itineraries a day between the two largest islands of the French West Indies.

Morning departures from Pointe-à-Pitre for Fort-de-France are usually at 8am, and departures from Fort-de-France for Pointe-à-Pitre are usually at 2pm, although the schedule can vary unexpectedly according to the season and the day of the week. Fares are 82.10€ ($73.30) round-trip or 53.95€ ($48.20) one way. For details and reservations, contact **Exprés des Iles,** Gare Maritime, quai Gatine, 97110 Pointe-à-Pitre, Guadeloupe (© **590590/83-12-45**), or **Terminal Inter-Iles,** Bassin de Radoub, 97200 Fort-de-France, Martinique (© **596/63-12-11**).

GETTING AROUND

BY RENTAL CAR   Unless you never plan to leave your hotel's beach, you probably want to rent a car to explore the island. Martinique has several local car-rental agencies, but clients have complained of mechanical difficulties and billing irregularities. We recommend renting from one of the U.S.-based firms. An international driver's license is required. *Driving in Martinique is on the right side of the road.*

Budget has an office at 12 rue Félix-Eboué, Fort-de-France, in addition to an airport location (© **800/527-0700** in the U.S., or 596/63-69-00 locally; www.budgetrentacar.com). **Avis** is located at Lamentin Airport (© **800/331-1212** in the U.S., or 596/42-16-92 locally; www.avis.com), as is **Hertz** (© **800/654-3001** in the U.S., or 596/51-01-01 locally; www.hertz.com). Of the three outfitters, Hertz has more branches (about five) than either of its other competitors.

Regardless of which company you choose, you'll be hit with a value-added tax (VAT) of 8.5% on top of the final bill, plus either a charge of around 22.80€ ($20.35) if you ask the car to be delivered to your hotel, or an airport pickup charge of about 15.20€ ($13.55) if you retrieve your car at the airport. Collision damage waivers (CDWs), which eliminate some or all of your financial responsibility in the event of an accident, cost a minimum of between 9.10€ and 10.65€ ($8.15 and $9.50) per day at Budget and Hertz, and a whopping 33.60€ ($30) per day at Avis.

BY TAXI   Local laws demand that any bona-fide *Martiniquais* cab must contain a working meter. For specific itineraries—wherein a passenger tells the driver where he or she wants to go—the meter must be "on" and functioning properly. **Radio Taxi** (© **596/63-63-62**), the island's largest dispatcher of taxis, advises us that if a taxi driver quotes a flat rate to a passenger instead of activating the meter, that you're being robbed, and you should immediately get out and find another cab. But for an idea of prices, a taxi ride for up to four passengers between Lamentin Airport and any of the hotels in Pointe du Bout will cost about 30.40€ ($27.15) during the day, and about 41.05€ ($36.65) between 7pm and 6am, when 40% surcharges are added to the day fare.

The rule about using a taxi's meter does not apply to passengers who want to hire a taxi for a general tour of the island. If that is your goal, expect to pay between 27.35€ and 31.90€ ($24.45 and $28.50) per hour for up to four passengers, depending on the itinerary and routing you negotiate with the driver.

BY BUS & TAXI COLLECTIF   There are two types of buses operating on Martinique. Regular buses, called *grands busses,* hold about 40 passengers and cost .75€ to 1.20€ (70¢–$1.10) anywhere within the city limits of Fort-de-France. To travel beyond the city limits, *taxis collectifs* are used. These are privately owned minivans that traverse the island and bear the sign *TC.* Their routes are flexible and depend on passenger need. A one-way fare from Fort-de-France to

---

Fun Fact Carnival

If you like masquerades and dancing in the streets, you should be here to attend **Carnival**, or *Vaval,* as it's known here. Carnival begins in early January and runs through the first day of Lent. Each village prepares costumes and floats. Weekend after weekend, frenzied celebrations take place, reaching fever pitch just before Lent. Fort-de-France is the focal point for Carnival, but the spirit permeates the whole island. On Ash Wednesday, the streets of Fort-de-France are filled with *diablesses,* or she-devils (portrayed by members of both sexes). Costumed in black and white, they crowd the streets to form King Carnival's funeral procession. As devils cavort about and the rum flows, a funeral pyre is built at La Savane. When it's set on fire, the dancing of those she-devils becomes frantic (many are thoroughly drunk at this point). Long past dusk, the cortége takes the coffin to its burial, ending Carnival until next year.

Ste-Anne is 5.30€ to 6.10€ ($4.75–$5.45). *Taxis collectifs* depart from the heart of Fort-de-France from the parking lot of Pointe Simon. There's no phone number to call for information about this unpredictable means of transport, and there are no set schedules. Traveling in a *taxi collectif* is for the adventurous visitor—these vehicles are crowded and not very comfortable.

BY FERRY The least expensive—and most colorful—way to transfer between Fort-de-France and the hotel and tourist district of Pointe du Bout is via one of the ferryboats (*vedettes*) that depart from quai d'Esnambuc in Fort de France. Transit costs 3.65€ ($3.25) one way or 5.80€ ($5.15) round-trip. Schedules for the ferryboats, at least 20 of which are scheduled at regular intervals every day between 6:30am and midnight, are printed in the free visitor's guide *Choubouloute,* which is distributed by the tourist office. Because they're so frequent, most visitors dispense with attempting to understand the schedule at all, and meander down to the waterfront to wait for the next boat.

There's also a smaller ferryboat that runs between Fort-de-France and the unpretentious resorts of Anse Mitan and Anse-à-l'Ane, both across the bay and home to many two- and three-star hotels and modest Creole restaurants. A boat departs from quai d'Esnambuc in Fort-de-France at intervals of between 20 and 30 minutes every day from 7:30am to 6pm. The trip takes about 20 minutes. One way and round-trip passage costs 3.65€ ($3.25) and 5.80€ ($5.15), respectively. If seas are extremely rough, or if there's a hurricane warning, all ferryboat services may be suspended.

For more information, call **Somatour,** 14 rue Blenac, 97200 Fort-de-France (© **596/73-05-53**).

BY BICYCLE & MOTORBIKE You can rent motor scooters from **Funny** at branches that include 80 rue Ernest-Deproge, Fort-de-France (© **596/63-33-05**) and 14 rue Félix Éboué, also in Fort-de-France (© **596/73-68-30**). Scooters are available with either 125cc or 150cc engines. Depending on their size and horsepower, they're priced at between 25.85€ ($23.05) and 33.45€ ($29.85) per day. Renters must leave a deposit, either in cash or in the form of a credit card, of between 228€ ($203.60) and 380€ ($339.35). From time to time, these branches rent bicycles as well, although in hilly Martinique, where roads are narrow and traffic whizzes by at a sometimes terrifying speed, bike rentals are not particularly popular.

FAST FACTS: **Martinique**

Banks Most of the banks of Martinique maintain the following hours: Monday to Friday from 7:30am to noon, and from 2:30 to 4pm, but in recent years, a few of them have opted to close on Wednesday afternoon. Others maintain a policy of remaining closed all day Monday, but to open their doors every Saturday morning between 7:30am and noon. There are about 10 ATM machines, maintained by several different banks, in Fort-de-France, at least 3 at Lamentin airport, and a scattering of others throughout the island, usually in such touristed areas as Pointe du Bout, Le Diamant, and Ste-Anne. **Change Caraïbes** maintains full-service foreign currency divisions, as well as ATMs, at both Lamentin Airport (© 596/42-17-11) and at 4 rue Ernest Deproge, in the center of Fort-de-France (© 596/60-28-40), across the street from the tourist office.

Currency In February of 2002, the Euro (€) went into usage as the currency of France, replacing the traditional monetary unit of the French franc. All the French islands of the Caribbean, including Martinique and Guadeloupe, also came under the Euro umbrella. Currently US$1 is converted at 1.12€.

Just before you leave home, you can check the current exchange rate on the Web at **www.x-rates.com**. Banks give much better exchange rates than hotels, and there's a money-exchange service, **Change Caraïbes** (© 596/42-17-11), available at Lamentin Airport. Its downtown branch is at 4 rue Ernest Deproge (© 596/60-28-40).

Customs Items for personal use, such as tobacco, cameras, and film, are admitted without formalities or tax if not in excessive quantity.

Documents U.S. and Canadian citizens need a valid passport. A return or ongoing ticket is also necessary. British citizens need only an identity card.

Electricity Electricity is 220-volt AC (50 cycles), the same as that used on the French mainland. However, check with your hotel to see if it has converted the electrical voltage and outlets in the bathrooms (some have). If it hasn't, bring your own transformer and adapter for U.S. appliances.

Emergencies Call the **police** at © **17**, report a **fire** by dialing © **18**, and summon an **ambulance** at © **17** or **18**.

Hospitals There are 18 hospitals and clinics on the island, and there's a 24-hour emergency room at **Hôpital Pierre Zobda Quikman,** Châteauboeuf, 3 miles (5km) from Fort-de-France (© **596/55-20-00**), on the road to Lamentin Airport.

Language French, the official language, is spoken by almost everyone. The local Creole patois uses words borrowed from France, England, Spain, and Africa. In the wake of increased tourism, English is occasionally spoken in the major hotels, restaurants, and tourist organizations—but don't count on driving around the countryside and asking for directions in English.

Liquor Laws Liquor is sold in grocery and liquor stores on any day of the week. It's legal to have an open container in public, though the authorities will be very strict with any littering, disorderly behavior, or drunk driving.

Pharmacies Try the **Pharmacie de la Paix,** at the corner of rue Perrinon and rue Victor-Schoelcher in Fort-de-France (© **596/71-94-83**), open Monday to Friday from 7:15am to 6:15pm and on Saturday from 7:45am to 1pm.

Safety Crime is hardly rampant on Martinique, yet there are still those who prey on unsuspecting tourists. Follow the usual precautions here, especially in Fort-de-France and in the tourist-hotel belt of Pointe du Bout. It's wise to protect your valuables and never leave them unguarded on the beach.

Taxes & Service Charges Most hotels include a 10% service charge in the bill; all restaurants include a 15% service charge. There's also a resort tax; this varies from place to place, but it never exceeds $1.50 per person per day.

Telephone To call Martinique from the United States, dial **011** (the international access code), then **596** (the country code for Martinique), and finally the six-digit local number. When making a call from one place on Martinique to another on the island, just dial the six-digit local number. To call the United States from Martinique, dial **19-1**, then the area code, then the seven-digit local number. You can reach **AT&T Direct** at ☏ **0800/99-00-11**. To reach **MCI**, dial ☏ **0800/99-00-19**, and to reach **Sprint**, dial ☏ **0800/99-00-87**.

Time Martinique is on Atlantic standard time year-round, 1 hour earlier than eastern standard time except when daylight saving time is in effect in the U.S. Then, Martinique time is the same as on the east coast of the United States.

Tipping Restaurants generally add a 15% service charge to all bills, which you can supplement if you think the service is outstanding. Some hotels also add a 10% service charge to your bill. Tip taxi drivers at least 15% of the fare.

Water The water is safe to drink throughout the island.

Weather The climate is relatively mild—the average temperature is in the 75° to 85°F range.

2 Fort-de-France

With its iron-grille-work balconies overflowing with flowers, Fort-de-France, the largest town on Martinique, seems like a cross between New Orleans and a town on the French Riviera. It lies at the end of a large bay surrounded by evergreen hills.

The proud people of Martinique are even more fascinating than the town of Fort-de-France, although today the Creole women are likely to be seen in jeans instead of their traditional turbans and Empress Joséphine–style gowns, and they rarely wear those massive earrings that used to jounce and sway as they sauntered along.

Narrow streets climb up the steep hills, where houses have been built to catch the overflow of the capital's more than 100,000 inhabitants.

ACCOMMODATIONS

Rates are sometimes advertised in U.S. dollars, sometimes in Euros, and sometimes in a combination of both. Be sure to check out the "Package Deals" and "Tips on Accommodations" sections in chapter 2.

Don't stay in town if you want a hotel near a beach (see the hotels listed below for beach resorts). If you do opt to stay in Fort-de-France, you'll have to take a ferryboat to reach the beaches at **Pointe du Bout** (see the section "Pointe du Bout & Les Trois-Ilets," later in this chapter). The one exception to this is the Hôtel La Bateliére, which opens onto a small beach, but it's in the suburb of Schoelcher.

Hôtel L'Impératrice   Favored by businesspeople without unlimited expense accounts, this stucco-sided, five-story hotel faces a landscaped mall in the heart of town, near the water's edge. L'Impératrice was originally built in the 1950s and named in honor of one of Martinique's most famous exports, Joséphine. Its balconies overlook the traffic at the western edge of the sprawling promenade known as La Savane. The small- to medium-size guestrooms are modern and functional. The front rooms tend to be noisy, but they do offer a look into life along La Savane. Bathrooms are compact, with a combination shower/tub. Don't expect outstanding service here. Almost no one on staff speaks English, and they all seem a bit jaded. But despite the confusion in the very noisy lobby, and the unremarkable decor of the simple bedrooms, you might end up enjoying the unpretentiousness of this place.

The hotel's restaurant, Le Joséphine, does a brisk business with local shoppers in town for the day.

15 place de la Savane, rue de la Liberté, 97200 Fort-de-France, Martinique, F.W.I. (C) **596/63-06-82.** Fax 596/72-66-30. 24 units. Winter 65.35€–79.05€ ($58.35–$70.60) double. Off-season 54.70€–68.40€ ($48.85–$61.10) double. Rates include breakfast. AE, DC, MC, V. **Amenities:** Restaurant, bar. *In room:* A/C, TV.

Le Lafayette   You'll enter this modest downtown hotel, located right on La Savane, through rue Victor-Hugo; the reception hall is up a few terra-cotta steps. The hotel was renovated in 2000 and 2001, and its bedrooms are tidy and clean. Most units contain comfortable twin beds, with small, pure-white, shower-only bathrooms. The overall impression is neat but simple and unpretentious. The inn is the oldest continuously operating hotel on Martinique, originally built in the 1940s with quasi–Art Deco hints that are now slightly dowdy. There's no on-site restaurant, but several eateries are within a short walk.

5 rue de la Liberte, 97200 Fort-de-France, Martinique, F.W.I. (C) **596/73-80-50.** Fax 596/60-97-75. 24 units. Winter 55€ ($49.10) double. Off-season 46€ ($41.10) double. AE, MC, V. *In room:* A/C, TV, fridge.

DINING
FORT-DE-FRANCE

La Belle Epoque ★★ FRENCH   In a turn-of-the-century house, this elegant choice features a haute cuisine menu. In the affluent suburb of Didier, this colonial style restaurant stands high above the capital of Fort-de-France. The dining room is filled with crystal, silver, and beautiful tiles, along with white linens, the room opening onto a terrace with a view of the garden. Guests savor the expert, superbly prepared cuisine with many inventive creations. A delectable and delicate salmon ravioli appears in a Breton crab spider's shell, or else you can enjoy puff pastry stuffed with curried shrimp or red snapper flambéed in an antique rum. The fish dishes are the finest in the area, particularly filet of John Dory steamed with fresh basil and thyme and served with a lime butter. Some classic beef dishes are also offered, cooked to order and appearing with sauces that often contain foie gras and truffles. The best of these is filet of beef Périgourdine with foie gras and truffles. Roasted stuffed pigeon is as good as anything this side of Morocco, and a rack of lamb is perfectly glazed in honey and lemon.

97 Route de Didier. (C) **596/64-41-19.** Reservations required. Main courses 14.45€–25.10€ ($12.90–$22.40). AE, MC, V. Mon–Fri noon–2:15pm; Mon–Sat 7:45–9:30pm.

La Mouina FRENCH/CREOLE   *La Mouina* (Creole for "meeting house") is a venerable restaurant established some 20 years ago by members of the French-Swiss-Hungarian Karschesz family. Next to the police station in the suburb of Redoute, about 1½ miles (2km) south of Fort-de-France, this 70-year-old colonial house is the domain of one of the island's most experienced groups of chefs. You might begin with *crabes farcis* (stuffed crabs) or *escargots de Bourguignon,* then follow with a classic tournedos Rossini, *rognon de veau entier grillé* (whole grilled veal kidneys), or duckling in orange sauce. The owners are particularly proud of their version of red snapper baked in parchment, and served with coconut sauce and yellow bananas. Ask at your hotel for good directions before setting out (or even better, take a taxi), as it's hard to find.

127 rte. de Redoute. ⓒ **596/79-34-57.** Reservations recommended for Sat–Sun dinner. Main courses 14.45€–31.15€ ($12.90–$27.80). MC, V. Mon–Fri noon–2:30pm, 7:30–9:15pm. Closed Aug.

Le Planteur ⭐ FRENCH/CREOLE   A growing number of local fans and members of the island's business community appreciate this restaurant's location on the southern edge of La Savane, in the commercial core of Fort-de-France. Established in 1997, it contains several somewhat idealized painted depictions of colonial Martinique. The hardworking, somewhat distracted staff run around hysterically trying to be all things to all diners. Menu items are fresh, filled with flavor, and usually received with approval. They feature a hot *velouté* (soup) concocted from shrimp and *giraumons,* a green-skinned tropical fruit with a succulent yellow core; a cassoulet of minced conch; fillet of *daurade* with coconut; and a *blanquette* (white, slow-simmered stew) of shellfish that's available only when the local catch makes such a dish possible.

1 rue de la Liberté. ⓒ **596/63-17-45.** Reservations recommended. Main courses 11.40€–19.75€ ($10.20–$17.65); set menus 13.70€ ($12.20) lunch only, 19.75€ ($17.65), and 28.10€ ($25.10). AE, MC, V. Mon–Fri noon–2:30pm; daily 7–10:30pm. Mar–Nov. Closed Sat–Sun.

Marie-Sainte ⭐ *Finds* CREOLE   You'd expect to find this place out in the countryside, not right in the capital. Your hostess is Agnés Marie-Sainte, a venerable Creole cook whose recipes for *boudin Créole, daube de poisson,* and colombo of mutton were derived from her ancestors. In a simple dining room that's likely to be crowded with locals, she offers fixed-price lunches with a strong emphasis on fresh fish (grilled or fried), and perhaps a fricassee of conch, always accompanied by a medley of fresh beans, dasheen, breadfruit, and *christophine.* This is about as authentic as it gets and also as inexpensive as you're likely to find for meals of such quality.

Although we highly recommend this place for its Creole-style lunches, consider "going local" and dropping in for an "Antillean" breakfast instead. Served every Monday to Saturday from 8am till noon, it welcomes many of the construction and office workers of the neighborhood, tempting them with dishes that include *un macadam morue,* made with sticky rice and codfish served with a thick tomato sauce; or slabs of either fried fish or fried beef served with raw vegetables.

160 rue Victor-Hugo. ⓒ **596/70-00-30.** Breakfast platters 6.85€–9.10€ ($6.10–$8.15); fixed-price lunch 10.65€ ($9.50); lunch main courses 6.85€–30.40€ ($6.10–$27.15). AE, MC, V. Mon–Sat 8am–noon (breakfast) and noon–3pm (lunch).

OUTSIDE FORT-DE-FRANCE (LAMENTIN)

La Canne à Sucre ⭐⭐ FRENCH/CREOLE   Chef-owner Gerard Virginius brings sophisticated française style to this stellar choice, having moved here from Guadeloupe, where his spicy Creole and French cuisine is surely missed.

Much of this cuisine has a definite nouvelle twist, but not alarmingly so. His specialty is such exotica as ostrich with shrubb (a zesty local orange liqueur), or red snapper flavored with vanilla. Well-informed foodies on Martinique flock here for the latest offerings, and they're delivered with style, flair, and flavor, especially sea urchin mousse and a filet of tazar (a local fish whose name doesn't translate) served with a passionfruit sabayon. For dessert we are yet to see a better concoction on Martinique than the crème brûlée with passion fruit.

Patio de Cluny, route Schoelcher. © 596/63-33-95. Reservations required. Main courses 21.30€–25.10€ ($19–$22.40). AE, DC, MC, V. Mon–Fri noon–3pm; Mon–Sat 8–10pm.

SPORTS & OTHER OUTDOOR PURSUITS

If it's a beach you're looking for, take the ferry to **Pointe du Bout** (see the section "Pointe du Bout & Les Trois-Ilets," below). The island's only **golf course** is located in Les Trois-Ilets, also discussed in the next section.

DEEP-SEA FISHING Most hotels maintain a list of the yachts and skippers who will take groups out for a day on the wide blue sea. If yours doesn't offer such arrangements, call the staff at **Caribtours,** B.P. 292, Lamentin (© **596/50-93-52**). The cost of renting such a boat, in which all equipment is usually included, is 114€ ($101.80) for a full-day charter for up to six anglers, with a brief stopover in St. Lucia included. Most game fish tend to be most active very early in the morning, and many experienced fishermen claim that it's not worth going after 10am, so departures tend to leave before breakfast, around 6am. Note, however, that this sport is in decline in waters around Martinique because of overfishing.

HIKING Inexpensive guided hikes are organized year-round by the personnel of the **Parc Naturel Régional de la Martinique,** 9 Bd. Du General de Gaulle, Fort-de-France (© **596/70-54-88**); special excursions can be arranged for small groups.

EXPLORING FORT-DE-FRANCE

At the heart of town is **La Savane,** a broad garden with many palms and mangos, playing fields, walks, and benches, plus shops and cafes lining its sides. In the middle of this grand square stands a statue of Josèphine, "Napoleon's little Creole," made of white marble by Vital Debray. With the grace of a Greek goddess, the statue poses in a Regency gown and looks toward Les Trois-Ilets, where she was born. The statue was beheaded, though, in 1991, probably because islanders felt she championed slavery. Near the harbor, at the edge of the park, you'll find vendors' stalls with handmade crafts, including baskets, beads, bangles, woodcarvings, and straw hats.

Your next stop could be the 1875 **Cathédrale St-Louis,** on rue Victor-Schoelcher. The religious centerpiece of the island, it's an extraordinary iron building, which someone once likened to "a sort of Catholic railway station." A number of the island's former governors are buried beneath the choir loft.

A statue in front of the Palais de Justice is of the island's second main historical figure, **Victor Schoelcher** (you'll see his name a lot on Martinique), who worked to free the slaves more than a century ago. **Bibliothèque Schoelcher,** 1 rue de la Liberté (© **596/70-26-67**), also honors this popular hero. Functioning today as the island's central government-funded library, the elaborate structure was first displayed at the Paris Exposition of 1889. The Romanesque portal, the Egyptian lotus-petal columns, even the turquoise tiles were imported piece by piece from Paris and reassembled here. It's open Monday from 1 to 5:30pm,

Tuesday through Thursday from 8:30am to 5:30pm, Friday from 8:30am to 5pm, and Saturday from 8:30am to noon.

Guarding the port is **Fort St-Louis,** built in the Vauban style on a rocky promontory. In addition, **Fort Tartenson** and **Fort Desaix** stand on hills overlooking the port.

Musee Departemental de la Martinique, 9 rue de la Liberte (© **596/71-57-05**), the one bastion on Martinique that preserves its pre-Columbian past, has relics left from the early settlers, the Arawaks, and the Caribs. The era the museum celebrates is from 3000 B.C. to A.D. 1635. Everything here stops shortly after the arrival of the first French colonials on the southern tip of Martinique in the early 1600s. In other words, it's mostly an ethnological museum, which was enlarged and reorganized into a more dynamic and up-to-date place in 1997. The museum faces La Savane and is open Monday to Friday from 8am to 5pm and on Saturday from 9am to noon; admission is 3.05€ ($2.70) for adults, 2.30€ ($2.05) for students, and 1.50€ ($1.35) for children ages 3 to 12.

Sacre-Coeur de Balata Cathedral, at Balata, overlooking Fort-de-France, is a copy of the one looking down from Montmartre upon Paris—and this one is just as incongruous, maybe more so. It's reached by going along route de la Trace (route N3). Balata is 6 miles (10km) northwest of Fort-de-France.

A few minutes away on route RN3, **Jardin de Balata** (© **596/64-48-73**) is a tropical botanical park, created by Jean-Philippe Thoze on land that the jungle was rapidly reclaiming around a Creole house that belonged to his grandmother. He has also restored the house, furnishing it with antiques and historic engravings. The garden contains a profusion of flowers, shrubs, and trees, offering a vision of tropical splendor. It's open daily from 9am to 5pm. Admission is 6.45€ ($5.75) for adults, 2.50€ ($2.25) for children age 7 to 12, and free for children 6 and under.

SHOPPING

Your best buys on Martinique are French luxury imports, such as perfumes, fashions, Vuitton luggage, Lalique crystal, and Limogès dinnerware. Sometimes (but don't count on it) prices are as much as 30% to 40% below those in the United States.

If you pay in U.S. dollars, store owners supposedly will give you a 20% discount; however, the exchange rates vary considerably from store to store, and almost invariably they are far less favorable than the rate offered at the local banks. You're usually better off shopping in the smaller stores, where prices are 8% to 12% lower on comparable items, and paying in francs that you have exchanged at a local bank.

FORT-DE-FRANCE AFTER DARK

The most exciting after-dark activity is seeing a performance of the folkloric troupe **Grand Ballets de Martinique** (see "Begin the Beguine," above).

The popularity of individual bars and dance clubs in Martinique rises and falls almost monthly. Many of them charge a cover of 15.20€ ($13.55), although that's often ignored if business is slow, and if you're a particularly appealing physical specimen. **Le Yucca Bar** (also known as Le Piano Bar), 24 bd. Allegre, in the Fort de France suburb of Rivière Roche (© **596/60-48-36**), is also a restaurant that draws both locals and visitors from mainland France. Very nearby, also in the suburb of Rivière Roches, is **Le Palacio,** Zone Industrielle, Rivière Roche (© **596/50-90-95**), a disco where absolutely, positively no one

Begin the Beguine

The sexy and rhythmic *beguine* was *not* an invention of Cole Porter. It's a dance of the islands—though exactly which island depends on whom you ask. Popular wisdom and the encyclopedia give the nod to Martinique, though Guadeloupeans claim it as their own, too.

Everybody who goes to Martinique wants to see the show performed by **Les Grands Ballets Martiniquais,** a troupe of about 2 dozen dancers, along with musicians, singers, and choreographers, who tour the island regularly. Their performances of the traditional dances of Martinique have been acclaimed in both Europe and the United States. With a swoosh of gaily striped skirts and clever acting, the dancers capture all the exuberance of the island's soul. The group has toured abroad with great success, but they perform best on their home ground, presenting tableaux that tell of jealous brides and faithless husbands, demanding overseers and toiling cane cutters. Dressed in traditional costumes, the island women and men dance the spirited mazurka, which was brought from the ballrooms of Europe, and, of course, the exotic beguine.

Les Grands Ballets Martiniquais usually perform Monday at the Novotel Coralia Diamant, Wednesday at the Novotel Coralia Carayou, Thursday at the Meridien Trois-Ilets, and Friday at the Bakoua Beach, but these schedules can vary, so check locally. In addition, the troupe gives mini-performances aboard visiting cruise ships. The cost of dinner and the show is usually 39.50€ ($41.50). Most performances are at 9pm, with dinners at the hotels beginning at 7:30pm.

appears before around 11pm. A nightclub where anyone can be a star, at least for a few minutes, is **Le Karaoke Café California,** Immeuble Les Coteaux, Lamentin (© 596/50-07-71).

And in downtown Fort-de-France, check out a pair of bars and dance clubs where live bands alternate with recorded music for an evening of getting down with the locals. They include **Le Latin Club,** 11 rue Lamartine (© 596/63-18-60), where the music of choice is salsa and merengue. A final choice is **La Cheyenne,** 8 rue Joseph Compère (© 596/70-31-19), a cavernous disco where several bars and dance floors provide lots of visual distractions.

If you want to gamble, or at least move around an environment where other people will gamble, head for Martinique's newest casino, **Casino Bâtelière Plaza,** at Schoelcher (© 596/61-73-23), a 10-minute drive from the center of Fort-de-France. You'll need a passport and 10.65€ ($9.50) to enter the gaming rooms, where a jacket and necktie are encouraged for men. A special area reserved just for slot machines and their fans is open daily, without charge, from noon to 3am. A more formal gambling area, with French baccarat, roulette, and blackjack, is open daily from 8:30pm to 3am. Access to the slot machines is free.

If you opt for an evening at the casino, you won't go hungry. On-site are two restaurants, the relatively expensive and upscale restaurant **Club Seven,** and the less formal, more ethnic **Case Navier.**

3 Pointe du Bout ⟨★⟩ & Les Trois-Ilets

Pointe du Bout is a narrow peninsula across the bay from the busy capital of Fort-de-France. It's the most developed resort area of Martinique, with at least four of the island's largest hotels, an impressive marina, about a dozen tennis courts, pools, facilities for horseback riding, and all kinds of watersports. There's also a handful of independent restaurants, a casino, boutiques, and in nearby Les Trois-Ilets, a Robert Trent Jones, Sr.–designed golf course. Except for the hillside that contains the Sofitel Bakoua Caralia, most of the district is flat and verdant, with gardens and rigidly monitored parking zones. All the hotels listed below are near the clean white-sand beaches of Pointe du Bout. Some of the smaller properties are convenient to the white sandy beaches of Anse Mitan. Nearby is also Les Trois-Ilets, the birthplace of Joséphine, the empress of France and wife of Napoleon Bonaparte.

GETTING THERE

If you're driving from Fort-de-France, take Route 1, which crosses the plain of Lamentin—the industrial area of Fort-de-France and the site of the international airport. Often the air is filled with the fragrance of caramel, from the large sugarcane factories in the surrounding area. After 20 miles (32km), you reach Les Trois-Ilets, Joséphine's hometown. Three miles (5km) farther on your right, take Route D38 to Pointe du Bout.

The **ferry service** runs all day long until midnight from the harbor front (quai d'Esnambuc) in downtown Fort-de-France. Round-trip fare is 5.80€ ($5.15). See "Getting Around" in section 1, earlier in this chapter, for details.

ACCOMMODATIONS
EXPENSIVE

Sofitel Bakoua Coralia ⟨★⟩   Its reputation for French chic now seems a thing of the past, but this is still the area's finest hotel, even if airline crews fill up many of its rooms today. It's known for the beauty of its landscaping and its somewhat isolated hillside location, and it's the only really upscale hotel in the area. Run by the Sofitel chain, it consists of three low-rise buildings in the center of a garden, plus another pair of bungalow-type buildings set directly on the beach. Accommodations come in a wide range of sizes, from small to spacious. Rooms have balconies or patios, extra comfortable beds, and small tiled bathrooms with showers. We'd choose this place over Le Méridien (see below).

Pointe du Bout, 97229 Trois-Ilets, Martinique, F.W.I. ⟨©⟩ **800/221-4542** in the U.S., 0181/283-4500 in London, or 596/66-02-02. Fax 596/66-00-41. www.sofitel.com. 142 units. Nov 1–Dec 23 182.40€–273.60€ ($162.90–$244.30) double; 562.40€–684€ ($502.20–$610.80) suite. Dec 24–May 3 319.20€–478.80€ ($285.05–$427.55) double; 729.60€–760€ ($651.50–$678.65) suite. May 4–Oct 31 189.40€–279.20€ ($169.10–$249.35) double; 562.40€–684€ ($502.20–$610.80) suite. Rates include continental breakfast. MAP (breakfast and dinner) 37.85€ ($33.80) per person extra. AE, DC, MC, V. **Amenities:** 2 restaurants, bar; pool; shuttle to golf course; 2 tennis courts; snorkeling, dive shop, water-skiing; salon; babysitting; laundry/ dry cleaning. *In room:* A/C, TV, minibar, safe.

Le Méridien Trois-Ilets ⟨★⟩   This is the largest and tallest (at seven stories) building in the resort community of Pointe du Bout, and it offers extensive facilities. But despite its prominence, we definitely don't find it the most desirable place to stay. The Sofitel Bakoua Coralia (see above) remains a more desirable choice. However, between 2000 and 2001 the fifth, sixth, and seventh floors of Le Meridian were renovated. So try, if possible, for these accommodations as they are infinitely more desirable. Because some rooms aren't renovated yet, the hotel maintains a two-tier pricing system, including standard or not yet renovated units and superior or renovated rooms. All rooms are midsize regardless of their price.

The hotel has a slightly shabby reception area that opens onto the palm-fringed pool, the waters of the bay, and the faraway lights of Fort-de-France. The hotel is slightly angled to follow the contours of the shoreline, so each bedroom overlooks either the Caribbean or the bay. Each unit contains a private balcony and conservatively modern furnishings with tropical accents. Rooms have comfortable beds, most often doubles, plus roomy tiled bathrooms containing bidets, shower/tub combinations, and toiletries.

Pointe du Bout, Trois-Ilets (B.P. 894, 97229 Fort-de-France), Martinique, F.W.I. © **800/543-4300** in the U.S. and Canada, or 596/66-06-00. Fax 596/66-00-74. www.lemeridien-hotels.com. 279 units. Winter 268€–299€ ($239.30–$267)double; from 389€ ($347.40) suite. Off-season 192€–223€ ($171.45–$199.15) double; from 229€ ($204.50) suite. Rates include buffet breakfast. AE, DC, MC, V. **Amenities:** 2 restaurants, bar; casino; pool; 2 tennis courts; sauna; dive shop, 100-foot (30m) marina, sailing, snorkeling, water-skiing, wind-surfing; massage; laundry. *In room:* A/C, TV, hair dryer, safe.

Novotel Coralia Carayou ⓐ A member of France's biggest hotel chain, the Accor Group, this hotel, popular with families and groups, has always prided itself on its lush gardens and glamorous garden setting. The accommodations aren't the most attractive in the area, but they are housed in a series of three-story outbuildings, each encircled by large lawns dotted with coconut or palm trees and flowering shrubs. The seaside rooms are the best, and some of the units are air-conditioned. Against a setting of wood trim and whitewashed walls, the rooms are generally small but well maintained. Each bathroom is equipped with a shower/tub combination, a bidet, toiletries, and large mirrors. The property has a small beach.

Creole dishes, especially the seafood items, are prepared here with flair.

Pointe du Bout, 97229 Trois-Ilets, Martinique, F.W.I. © **800/221-4542** in the U.S., or 596/66-04-04. Fax 596/66-00-57. www.novotel.com. 201 units. Winter 115€–148€ ($102.70–$132.15) double. Off-season 115€ ($102.70) double. Rates include American buffet. AE, DC, MC, V. **Amenities:** 2 restaurants, bar; pool; tennis court; watersports; children's programs; laundry/dry cleaning. *In room:* A/C, TV, safe.

MODERATE

La Pagerie The facilities here are relatively modest compared to those in some of the larger and more expensive hotels of Pointe du Bout, but guests can compensate by visiting the many restaurants, bars, and sports facilities in the area. Set close to the gardens of the Sofitel Bakoua Caralia (see above) and a 16-mile (26km) drive from the airport, this hotel offers comfortably modern bedrooms. Although the walls are thin, the units are neat and uncomplicated, with tile floors, small fridges, and balconies with views opening onto the bay. About two-thirds of the units contain tiny kitchenettes, at no extra charge. The accommodations are outfitted with floral prints, low-slung furnishings, and louvered closets. The tiled bathrooms have combination shower/tubs, marble vanities, bidets, and wall-mounted showerheads. Guests usually walk 5 minutes to Novotel Coralia Carayou (see above) for watersports and access to the beach.

Pointe du Bout, 97229 Trois-Ilets, Martinique, F.W.I. © **800/221-4542** in the U.S., or 596/66-05-30. Fax 596/66-00-99. 94 units. Winter 122.65€–147.60€ ($109.55–$131.80) double. Off-season 78.75€–86.65€ ($70.30–$77.35) double. Rates include buffet breakfast. AE, DC, MC, V. **Amenities:** 2 restaurants, bar; pool; laundry/dry cleaning. *In room:* A/C, TV, fridge, kitchenette (in some).

INEXPENSIVE

Auberge de L'Anse Mitan Many guests like this hotel's location at the isolated end of a road whose more commercial side is laden with restaurants and a bustling nighttime parade. The hotel was built in 1930, but it has been renovated several times since by the hospitable Athanase family. What you see today is a three-story concrete box–type structure. Six of the units are studios with kitchens and TVs; all have private showers. Rooms are boxy, but the beds are comfortable. Bathrooms are very small and cramped, but tidy. You don't get anything special here, but the price is right.

Anse Mitan, 97229 Trois-Ilets, Martinique, F.W.I. ℂ **596/66-01-12.** Fax 596/66-01-05. www.aubergean semitan.com. 25 units. Winter 68.40€ ($61.10) double; 63.85€ ($57) studio. Off-season 50.15€ ($44.80) double; 45.60€ ($40.70) studio. Room (but not studio) rates include breakfast. AE, DC, MC, V. **Amenities:** Restaurant, bar; laundry. *In room:* A/C.

DINING

There isn't a great choice of restaurants in Pointe du Bout, but here's the pick of the litter.

Au Poisson d'Or CREOLE   Its position near the entrance of the resort community of Pointe du Bout makes it easy to find. There's no view of the sea and the traffic runs close to the edge of the veranda and terrace, but the reasonable prices and the complete change of pace make up for that. The rustic dining room offers such classics as grilled fish, grilled conch scallops sautéed in white wine, poached local fish, and flan. These ordinary dishes are prepared with flair and served with style.

L'Anse Mitan. ℂ **596/66-01-80.** Reservations recommended. Main courses 12.90€–22.80€ ($11.55–$20.35); fixed-price menu 11.40€–28.90€ ($10.20–$25.80). AE, MC, V. Tues–Sun noon–2pm and 7–9:30pm. Closed July.

La Villa Creole ⭐ CREOLE/FRENCH   This restaurant, which lies a 3- or 4-minute drive from the hotels of Pointe du Bout, has thrived since the late 1970s, offering a colorful, small-scale respite from the island's high-rise resorts. Set within a simple but well-maintained Creole house, with no particular views other than the small garden that surrounds it, the restaurant serves fairly priced set-price menus of such staples as *accras de morue* (beignets of codfish), *boudin creole* (blood sausage), and *feroce* (a local form of pate concocted from fresh avocados, pulverized codfish, and manioc flour). A special delight is the red snapper prepared either with tomato sauce or grilled. Owner Guy Bruère-Dawson, a singer and guitarist, entertains as you dine.

L'Anse Mitan. ℂ **596/66-05-53.** Reservations recommended. Main courses 12.90€–28.90€ ($11.55–$25.80); set menus 12.90€–33.45€ ($11.55–$29.85). AE, MC, V. Tues–Sat noon–2pm; Tues–Sun 7–10:30pm.

Pignon sur Mer CREOLE   Simple and unpretentious, this is an intimate Creole restaurant containing about 15 tables, set within a rustically dilapidated building beside the sea (it's a 12-min. drive from Pointe du Bout). Menu items are island-inspired, and might include *delices du Pignon,* a platter of shellfish, or whatever grilled fish or shellfish was hauled in that day. *Lambi* (conch), shrimp, and crayfish are almost always available, and brochettes of chicken are filling and full of flavor.

Anse-a-l'Ane. ℂ **596/68-38-37.** Main courses 10.65€–27.35€ ($9.50–$24.45). MC, V. Tues–Sun 12:15–4pm; Tues–Sat 7–9:30pm.

Sapori d'Italia ⭐ ITALIAN   In Creole Village in Les Trois-Ilets, this restaurant is worth the expense, as its savory viands are well crafted and a refreshing change of pace from the typical French and Creole food. Dig into any of the delights, many of which seem inspired by the kitchens of Milan. We like to open with "Valentina," the best antipasti on the menu, with an assortment of bruschette, various types of salami and cheese, and very ripe olives. The house lasagna is the best on the island, and you can also take delight in the gnocchi or the tortellini alle noce (with nuts). There are, in fact, 20 types of pasta. If the night is right, opt for a table on the outdoor terrace.

Village Creole, Pointe du Bout. ©️ **596/66-15-85.** Reservations required. Main courses 15.20€–27.35€ ($13.55–$24.45). Thurs–Mon noon–2:30pm; daily 7–10:30pm. AE, MC, V. Closed June and 2 weeks in Oct.

HITTING THE BEACH

The clean white-sand beaches of **Pointe du Bout,** site of the major hotels of Martinique, were created by developers and tend to be rather small. Most of the tourists head here, so the narrow beaches are among the island's most crowded. It doesn't help that Pointe du Bout also has several marinas lining the shore, as well as the docking point for the ferry from Fort de France. Even if you don't find a lot of space on the beach, with its semi-clear waters, you will find toilets, phones, restaurants, and cafes galore. The waters suffer from industrial usage, although apparently the pollution is not severe enough to prevent people from going in. You'll often see the French standing deep in the water, smoking cigarettes—perhaps not your idea of an idyllic beach vacation.

To the south, however, the golden-sand beaches at **Anse Mitan** have always been welcoming to visitors, including many snorkelers. The beaches here are far less crowded and more inviting, with cleaner waters. However, the steepness of Martinique's shoreline leaves much to be desired by its swimmers and snorkelers. The water declines steeply into depths, no reefs ring the shores, and fish are rarely visible. Nonetheless, beaches here are ideal for sunbathing.

The neighboring beach to Anse-Mitan is **Anse-à-l'Ane,** an ideal place for a picnic on the white sands.

SPORTS & OTHER OUTDOOR PURSUITS

GOLF Robert Trent Jones, Sr., designed the 18-hole **Golf de l'Impératrice-Josèphine,** at Trois-Ilets (©️ **596/68-32-81**), a 5-minute drive from Pointe du Bout and about 18 miles (29km) from Fort-de-France. The only golf course on Martinique, the greens slope from the birthplace of Empress Joséphine (for whom it's named) across rolling hills with scenic vistas down to the sea. Amenities include a pro shop, a bar, and a restaurant. Greens fees are 41.05€ ($36.65) for 18 holes. There are also three rather battered tennis courts, which cost 12.15€ ($10.85) per hour if you wish to play on them.

HORSEBACK RIDING The premier riding facility on Martinique is **Ranch Jack,** Esperanza, Trois-Ilets (©️ **596/68-37-69**). It offers morning horseback rides for both experienced and novice riders, at a cost of 53.20€ ($47.50) for a 3-hour ride. Jacques and Marlene Guinchard make daily promenades across the beaches and fields of Martinique, with a running explination of the history, fauna, and botany of the island. Cold drinks are included in the price, and transportation is usually free to and from the hotels of nearby Pointe du Bout. Four to 15 participants are needed to book a tour. This is an ideal way to discover both the botany and geography of Martinique.

SCUBA DIVING & SNORKELING The beachfront of the Hotel Meridien (at Pointe du Bout) is the headquarters for the island's best-recommended dive outfit, **Espace Plongée Martinique** (©️ **596/60-00-00**), which welcomes anyone who shows up, regardless of where they happen to be staying. Daily dive trips, depending on demand, leave from Hotel Meridien's pier every day at 9am, returning at noon, and at 3pm, returning at 5pm. Popular dive sites within a reasonable boat ride, with enough diversity and variation in depth to appeal to divers of all degrees of proficiency, include *La Baleine* (The Whale) and *Cap Solomon.* A dive shop stocks everything you'll need to take the plunge, from weight belts and tanks to wet suits and underwater cameras. Divers pay between 30.40€ and 38€ ($27.15 and $33.95) per session. Instruction for novice divers, which is conducted in Le Méridien's pool every day from noon to 12:30pm, is free.

Snorkeling equipment is usually available free to hotel guests, who quickly learn that coral, fish, and ferns abound in the waters around the Pointe du Bout hotels.

TENNIS   Tennis pros at Bathy's Club at the **Hotel Meridien,** Pointe du Bout (© **596/66-00-00**), usually allow nonguests to play for free if the courts are otherwise unoccupied.

You can also play on one of the three courts at **Golf de l'Impératrice-Joséphine,** at Trois-Ilets (© **596/68-32-81**). It costs 12.15€ ($10.85) per hour to play, and no racquet rentals are available.

WINDSURFING   An enduringly popular sport in the French West Indies, windsurfing (*"la planche à voile"*) is available at most of the large-scale hotels. One of the best equipped is **Fanatic Board Center** (also known as "Just in Fun, S.A.R.L."), which occupies a site directly on the beachfront of the Hotel Méridien, Pointe du Bout (© **596/66-00-00**). Lessons cost 15.20€ ($13.55) per hour, and boards, depending on their make and model, rent for 15.20€ to 19.75€ ($13.55–$17.65) per hour. You can also experiment with a sport that's relatively new in Martinique, kite-surfing, wherein impossibly light sailboards are attached to very large sails. Don't even think of attempting this without some advance instruction. The team at the Fanatic Board Center proposes that you take 15 hours of lessons, divided into three 5-hour blocks, for a net fee of 304€ ($271.45), including all equipment.

A VISIT TO LES TROIS-ILETS

Marie-Josephe-Rose Tascher de la Pagerie was born here in 1763. As Joséphine, she was to become the wife of Napoleon I and empress of France from 1804 to 1809. Six years older than Napoleon, she pretended that she'd lost her birth certificate so he wouldn't find out her true age. Although many historians call her ruthless and selfish, she is still revered by some on Martinique as an uncommonly gracious lady. Others have less kind words for her—because Napoleon is said by some historians to have "reinvented" slavery, they blame Joséphine's influence.

Twenty miles (32km) south of Fort-de-France, you reach Les Trois-Ilets, a charming little village. A mile (2km) outside the village, turn left to La Pagerie, where the small **Musee de la Pagerie** (© **596/68-34-55**) has been installed in the former estate kitchen, where Josephine gossiped with her slaves and played the guitar. Along with her childhood bed, you'll see a passionate letter from Napoleon and other mementos. The collection was compiled by Dr. Robert Rose-Rosette.

Still remaining are the partially restored ruins of the Pagerie sugar mill and the church (in the village itself) where she was christened in 1763. The plantation was destroyed in a hurricane. The museum is open Tuesday through Friday from 9am to 5:30pm, Saturday and Sunday from 9am to 1pm and 2:30 to 5:30pm. Admission is 3.05€ ($2.70).

A botanical garden, the **Parc des Floralies,** is adjacent to the golf course (see above), as is the museum devoted to Joséphine (see above).

Maison de la Canne, Pointe Vatable (© **596/68-32-04**), is on the road to Trois-Ilets. Located on the premises of an 18th-century distillery, its permanent exhibitions tell the story of sugarcane and the sweeping role it played in the economic and cultural development of Martinique. It's open Tuesday to Sunday from 9am to 5:30pm, charging an admission of 3.05€ ($2.70) for adults, .75€ (70¢) for children age 5 to 12, free for children age 5 and under.

The Marina complex has a number of interesting boutiques; several sell handcrafts and curios from Martinique. They're sometimes of good quality, but are quite expensive, particularly the enameled jewel boxes and some of the batiks of natural silk.

At Christmastime, many of the island's traditional foie gras and pastries are presented in crocks made by Martinique's largest earthenware factories, the **Poterie de Trois-Ilets,** Habitation, Trois-Ilets (© **596/68-25-41**). At least 90% of its production is devoted to brick making. However, one small-scale offshoot of the company devotes itself to producing earth-toned stoneware and pottery whose colors and shapes have contributed to the folklore of Martinique. In theory, the studios are open Monday through Saturday from 9am to 5:30pm, but call before you set out to make sure they'll accept visitors.

POINTE DU BOUT AFTER DARK

Martinique has one of the dullest casinos in the French West Indies, **Casino Trois-Ilets,** Hotel Meridien Trois-Ilets, Pointe du Bout (© **596/66-00-30**). Slot machines, for which entrance is free, are open daily from 10am to 3am. Roulette and blackjack ("*les grands jeux*"), for which there's an entrance charge of 10.65€ ($9.50), and for which a visitor must present ID or a passport, are open daily from 9pm to 3am.

A mellow piano bar atmosphere is found at **L'Amphore,** in the rear of Sofitel Bakoua Caralia, Pointe du Bout (© **596/66-03-09**).

4 The South Loop

South of Pointe du Bout you can find sun and beaches. Resort centers here include Le Diamant and Ste-Anne.

From Trois-Ilets, you can follow a small curved road that brings you to **Anse-à-l'Ane, Grande Anse,** and **Anses-d'Arlets.** At any of these places, you'll find small beaches, which are quite safe and usually not crowded.

ANSES-D'ARLETS

The scenery is beautiful here. Brightly painted fishing boats (*gommiers*) draw up on the white-sand beach, and the nets are spread out to dry in the sun. Children swim and adults fish from the good-size pier. The waters off Anses-d'Arlets are a playground for divers, with a wide variety of small tropical fish and colorful corals.

The area itself has been a choice spot for weekend "second homes" for many years, and is now beginning to develop touristically. The little village features a pretty steepled church, a bandstand for holiday concerts, and a smattering of modest little dining spots. Aficionados of Martinique come here to see "the way it used to be" on the island. Unspoiled and folkloric, the hamlet still retains its *charm typique martiniquaise.*

From Anses-d'Arlets, Route D37 takes you to Le Diamant, along a panoramic road.

DINING

Fatzo ★★ *Finds* INTERNATIONAL   The best restaurant in the fishing port of Anse d'Arlets occupies a 1890s blue-and-white house that was originally built by island merchants and planters, the Clement family, directly across the street from La Mairie (City Hall), and immediately adjacent to the town's only pharmacy. Inside, you'll find at least 20 framed sepia-toned photographs depicting local catastrophes (hurricanes, volcanic eruptions) of decades past, entire walls covered with a collection of straw hats, and memorabilia of the island's colonial past. Named after a German-born former owner (who everyone called "Fatzo" despite the fact that he wasn't particularly hefty), the place specializes in the kind of savory Creole and international food that tastes wonderful in hot, humid weather. Examples include grilled fish with spicy Creole sauce; flambéed shrimp with pastis and thyme sauce; rack of lamb; *involtini* of chicken with leeks; grilled filet of peppercorn-studded beef; and magret of duckling with honey sauce. The *cous-cous royal,* served every Friday night, draws loyal fans from throughout the region who appreciate its North African–style combination of semolina grain garnished with *merguez* (spicy sausages), lamb, chicken, raisins, seven vegetables, and spices.

11 rue Félix Éboué, Anses-d'Arlets. © **596/68-62-79.** Reservations recommended. Main courses 11.40€–16.70€ ($10.20–$14.95). AE, DC, MC, V. Tues–Sun 7–11pm (last order).

LE DIAMANT

Set on the island's southwestern coast, this village offers a good beach, open to the prevailing southern winds. The village is named after one of Martinique's best-known geological oddities, **Le Rocher du Diamant** (Diamond Rock), a barren offshore island that juts upward from the sea to a height of 573 feet (172m). Sometimes referred to as the Gibraltar of the Caribbean, it figured prominently in a daring British-led invasion in 1804, when British mariners carried a formidable amount of ammunition and 110 sailors to the top. Despite frequent artillery bombardments from the French-held coastline, the garrison held out for 18 months, completely dominating the passageway between the rock and the coast of Martinique. Intrepid foreigners sometimes visit Diamond Rock, but the access across the strong currents of the channel is risky.

Diamond Beach ★★★, on the Martinique mainland, offers a sandy bottom, verdant groves of swaying palms, and many different surf and sunbathing possibilities. The entire district has developed in recent years into a resort, scattered with generally small hotels.

ACCOMMODATIONS

Hotel Diamant Les Bains   This is an unpretentious, family-style hotel with direct access to a sandy beach. From the edge of the resort's pool, you can enjoy a view of the offshore island of Diamond Rock. Twenty units are in outlying motel-style bungalows set either in a garden or beside the beach; the others are in the resort's main building, which also houses the restaurant and bar. Two rooms are outfitted for travelers with disabilities. Accommodations have furnished terraces or patios, white-tile floors, small fridges, and built-in furniture made from polished fruitwood. Most rooms are medium in size except for the small units on the second floor of the main building, which are often rented to business travelers from the French mainland. The most ideal are the 10 rustic bungalows directly above the beach. Bathrooms, which are aging but still work just fine, are accented with blue tiles and equipped with such extras as bidets; each has a shower stall.

The cuisine at the hotel restaurant is for the most part Creole, with some French dishes thrown in.

97223 Le Diamant, Martinique. F.W.I. ✆ **596/76-40-14.** Fax 596/76-27-00. www.wwte.com/select/ diamant1.htm. 27 units. Winter 120.10€ ($107.25) double; 136.80€ ($122.15) bungalow. Off-season 91.20€ ($81.45) double; 101.85€ ($90.95) bungalow. Rates include continental breakfast. MAP (breakfast and dinner) 18.25€–24.30€ ($16.30–$21.70) per person extra. MC, V. Closed 10 days in June and Sept 1–early Oct. **Amenities:** Restaurant, bar; pool. *In room:* A/C, TV, fridge.

Novotel Coralia Diamant   On 6 acres (2 hectares) of forested land, 2 miles (3km) outside the village and 18 miles (29km) south of Fort-de-France, this low-rise building is in one of the most beautiful districts on Martinique. It's the ultimate in laissez-faire management—guests, often tour groups from France, are basically left to fend for themselves. Guestrooms, housed in four three-story wings, face either the pool or the coast, with its view of Diamond Rock. From many of the rooms, the views are more evocative of the South Pacific than of the Caribbean. The inviting units have tropical decor, white-tile floors, whitewashed walls, roomy closets, and rattan furnishings, plus adequate desk space. Bathrooms have shower/tub combinations and full-length mirrors.

Outside the hotel, the neighboring beaches aren't too crowded. They consist of white sand but are rather narrow. The taxi ride from the airport should take about 40 minutes.

97223 Le Diamant, Martinique, F.W.I. ✆ **800/221-4542** in the U.S., or 596/76-42-42. Fax 596/76-22-87. www.novotel.com. 181 units. Winter 195€–230€ ($174.15–$205.40) double; with a supplement of 30€–70€ ($26.80–$62.50) for a suite. Off-season 110€ ($98.25) double; with a supplement of 30€–50€ ($26.80–$44.65) for a suite. Rates include breakfast. AE, DC, MC, V. **Amenities:** 2 restaurants, 2 bars; large swimming pool; 2 tennis courts; watersports; laundry. *In room:* A/C, TV, hair dryer, safe.

STE-ANNE

From Le Marin, a 5-mile (8km) drive brings you to Ste-Anne, at the extreme southern tip of Martinique. This sleepy little area is known for the white-sand beaches of Les Salines (those to the north are more grayish in color). In many ways, these are Martinique's finest. The climate is arid like parts of Arizona, and the beaches are almost always sunny, perhaps too much so at midday. The name comes from Étang des Salines, a large salt pond forming a backdrop to the strip of sand. Manchineel trees are found at the southeastern end of the beach. Under no circumstances should you go under these trees for protection in a rainfall. When it's sunny you can seek shade here, but when it rains, drops falling from the poisonous tree will be like acid on your tender skin.

Holidays and weekends tend to be crowded, as many islanders and their families flock to this beach. Unfortunately, it's not big enough to handle the hordes.

Les Salines is also the site of Martinique's only real **gay beach.** Drive to the far end of the parking lot, near the sign labeled Petite Anse des Salines. Here you'll find a trail leading through thick woods to a sun-flooded beach often populated by naked gay men, with an occasional lesbian couple or two. Technically, there are no legal nudist beaches on Martinique, so it's possible you could be arrested for going nude, although authorities don't seem to enforce this law. (Throughout the island, however, the European custom of topless bathing is not uncommon on any of the beaches or even around hotel pools.)

Ste-Anne opens onto views of the Sainte Lucia Canal, and nearby is the Petrified Savanna Forest, which the French call **Savane des Petrifications.** It's a field of petrified volcanic boulders in the shape of logs. The eerie, desert-like site is studded with cacti.

ACCOMMODATIONS

Club Med Les Boucaniers ✷   Set on a peaceful cove at the southernmost tip of Martinique, about a 50-minute drive from the airport, this resort is designed as a series of scattered outbuildings reminiscent of a Creole village. The club is on the 48-acre (19-hectare) site of a former pirate's hideaway at Buccaneer's Creek, amid a forest of coconut palms. Bedrooms are a bit spartan but comfortable; bathrooms are compact with shower stalls. Although many Club Meds welcome children, this particular one does not accept kids age 11 and under, and it is geared more toward single guests or couples, some of whom like the *au naturel* beach nearby. The emphasis is often on group activities. In a domed two-level building in the heart of the resort, you'll find an amusement center, theater, dance floor, and bar. A walk along rue du Port (the main street of Club Med) leads to Tour du Port, a bar that overlooks the sailboat fleet anchored in the marina.

Pointe Marin, 97227 Ste-Anne, Martinique, F.W.I. ✆ 800/CLUB-MED in the U.S., or 596/76-72-72. Fax 596/76-83-36. www.clubmed.com. 299 units. All-inclusive weekly rates: Winter $775–$945. Off-season $740–$810. Rates are per person and based on double occupancy. AE, MC, V. **Amenities:** 2 restaurants, 3 bars; nightclub with disco and karaoke; 7 tennis courts; dive shop, water polo; water-skiing; boating; snorkeling; volleyball; basketball; softball; massage; laundry; guided tours and cruises (at additional cost) to other parts of Martinique and nearby islands. *In room:* A/C, safe.

La Dunette *Value*   A motel-like stucco structure directly beside the sea, this hotel appeals to guests who appreciate its simplicity and its isolation from the more built-up resort areas of other parts of Martinique. A three-story building originally constructed in the late 1960s, it's near the Club Med and the white-sand beaches of Les Salines. An unpretentious seaside inn with a simple, summery decor, the hotel is accented with a garden filled with flowers and tropical plants. The furnishings are casual and modern, although some rooms are quite small. The private shower-only bathrooms, although cramped, are well maintained. The in-house restaurant is better than you might expect, thanks to the culinary finesse of the Tanzania-born owner, Gerard Kambona.

97227 Ste-Anne, Martinique, F.W.I. ✆ 596/76-73-90. Fax 596/76-76-05. 18 units. Winter 76€ ($67.85) double. Off-season 45.60€ ($40.70) double. Rates include continental breakfast. MC, V. **Amenities:** Restaurant, bar. *In room:* A/C, TV, hair dryer.

Manoir de Beauregard ✷✷   One of the most venerable and historic hotels on Martinique lies within the massive walls of a manor house that once administered many acres of surrounding sugarcane fields. It was originally built between 1720 and 1800 by a prominent French family, and almost resembles a medieval church. A fire in 1990 completely gutted the building's interior and led to 4 years of restoration. Today, there are three bedrooms on the upper floors of the original house, and another eight within a modern, less inspired one-story annex. Rooms within the annex, although not as dignified, have antique West Indian beds and direct views over the garden. Most units are roomy with double or twin beds, plus a compact tiled bathroom with a combination tub/shower. A truly superb beach, Plage des Salines, is a 5-minute drive to the south, and a slightly less appealing beach, Plage de Sainte-Anne, is within a 15-minute walk.

Meals here are conservative, traditional, tried-and-true Creole cuisine, with dishes like codfish fritters, boudin Creole (blood sausage), grilled fish in Creole sauce, curries, and fresh lobster.

Chemin des Salines (a 10-min. walk south of Ste-Anne), 97227 Ste-Anne, Martinique, F.W.I. ✆ 596/76-73-40. Fax 596/76-93-24. www.martinique-hotels.com. 11 units. Winter 98.80€–136.80€ ($88.20–$122.15) double. Off-season 83.60€–106.40€ ($74.65–$95) double. Rates include breakfast. AE, MC, V. **Amenities:** Restaurant, bar; pool. *In room:* A/C.

5 The North Loop

As we swing north from Fort-de-France, our main targets are **Le Carbet, St-Pierre, Montagne Pelée,** and **Leyritz.** However, we'll sandwich in many stopovers along the way.

From Fort-de-France, there are three ways to head north to Montagne Pelée. The first is to follow route N4 up to St-Joseph. There you take the left fork for 3 miles (5km) after St-Joseph and turn onto Route D15 toward Le Marigot.

Another way to Montagne Pelée is to take Route N3 through the vegetation-rich *mornes* (hills) until you reach Le Morne Rouge. This road is known as "Route de la Trace" and is now the center of the Parc Naturel de la Martinique.

Yet a third route to Montagne Pelée is via route N2 along the coast. This is the route we'll follow, and the order in which we'll list the towns along the way. Near Fort-de-France, the first town you reach is **Schoelcher.** Farther along route N2 is **Case-Pilote,** and then Bellefontaine. This portion, along the most popular drive in Martinique—that is, Fort-de-France to St-Pierre—is very reminiscent of the way the French Riviera used to look. **Bellefontaine** is a small fishing village, with boats stretched along the beach. Note the many houses also built in the shape of boats.

LE CARBET

Leaving Bellefontaine, a 5-mile (8km) drive north will deliver you to Le Carbet. Columbus landed here in 1502, and the first French settlers arrived in 1635. In 1887, Gauguin lived here for 4 months before going on to Tahiti. You can stop for a swim at an Olympic-size pool set into the hills, or watch the locals scrubbing clothes in a stream. The town lies on the bus route from Fort-de-France to St-Pierre.

Centre d'Art Musee Paul-Gauguin, Anse Turin, Le Carbet (© **596/78-22-66**), is near the beach represented in the artist's *Bord de Mer.* The landscape hasn't changed in 100 years. The museum, housed in a five-room building, commemorates the French artist's stay on Martinique in 1887, with books, prints, letters, and other memorabilia. There are also paintings by René Corail, sculpture by Hector Charpentier, and examples of the work of Zaffanella. Of special interest are faience mosaics made of once-white pieces that turned pink, maroon, blue, and black in 1902 when the fires of Montagne Pelee devastated St-Pierre. There are also changing exhibits of works by local artists. Hours are daily from 9:30am to 5:30pm; admission is 3.05€ ($2.70) for adults, 1.50€ ($1.35) for students, .75€ (70¢) children under age 8.

ST-PIERRE ✦

At the beginning of this century, St-Pierre was known as the "Little Paris of the West Indies." Home to 30,000 inhabitants, it was the cultural and economic capital of Martinique. On May 7, 1902, the citizens read in their daily newspaper that "Montagne Pelée does not present any more risk to the population than Vesuvius does to the Neapolitans."

However, on May 8, at 8am, the southwest side of Montagne Pelée exploded into fire and lava. At 8:02am, all 30,000 inhabitants were dead—that is, all except one. A convict in his underground cell was saved by the thickness of the walls. When islanders reached the site, the convict was paroled and left Martinique to tour in Barnum and Bailey's circus.

St-Pierre never recovered its past splendor. It could now be called the Pompeii of the West Indies. Ruins of the church, the theater, and some other buildings can be seen along the coast.

One of the best ways to get an overview of St-Pierre involves riding a rubber-wheeled "train," the **Cyparis** *Exprès* (© **596/55-50-92**), which departs on tours from the base of the Musee Volcanologique. Tours cost 7.60€ ($6.80) for adults, 3.80€ ($3.40) for children 11 and under, and run Monday through Friday from 11am to 1pm and 2:30 to 7pm. Tours last about an hour, and depart every Monday to Friday at 11am and 2:30pm, from a point immediately adjacent to the Musée Volcanologique. In winter or during periods of high demand, additional tours might be added.

Musée Volcanologique, rue Victor-Hugo, St-Pierre (© **596/78-15-16**), was created by the American volcanologist Franck Alvard Perret, who turned the museum over to the city in 1933. Here, in pictures and relics dug from the debris, you can trace the story of what happened to St-Pierre. Dug from the lava is a clock that stopped at the exact moment the volcano erupted. The museum is open daily from 9am to 5pm; admission is 1.50€ ($1.35) for adults, free for children age 7 and under.

LE PRÊCHEUR

From St-Pierre, you can continue along the coast north to Le Prêcheur. Once the home of Madame de Maintenon, the mistress of Louis XIV, it's the last village along the northern coast of Martinique. Here you can see hot springs of volcanic origin and the **Tombeau des Caraïbes (Tomb of the Caribs),** where, according to legend, the collective suicide of many West Indian natives took place after they returned from a fishing expedition and found their homes pillaged by the French.

MONTAGNE PELÉE ✦

A panoramic and winding road (route N2) takes you through a tropical rain forest. The curves are of the hairpin variety, and the road is not always kept in good shape. However, you're rewarded with tropical flowers, baby ferns, plumed bamboo, and valleys so deeply green you'll think you're wearing cheap sunglasses.

The village of **Morne Rouge,** right at the foot of Montagne Pelée, is a popular vacation spot for Martiniquais. From here on, a narrow and unreliable road brings you to a level of 2,500 feet (750m) above sea level, 1,600 feet (480m) under the round summit of the volcano that destroyed St Pierre. Montagne Pelée itself rises 4,575 feet (1,373m) above sea level.

If you're a serious mountain climber and you don't mind 4 or 5 hours of hiking, you can scale the peak, though you should hire an experienced guide to accompany you. Realize that this is a real mountain, that rain is frequent, and that temperatures drop very low. Tropical growth often hides deep crevices in the earth, and there are other dangers. The park service maintains more than 100

Fun Fact **Photo Ops**

Martinique is a photographer's dream—certainly the French fashion magazines know it, because crews are always around on shoots. The most picturesque sites are **La Savane,** in Fort-de-France; **St-Pierre,** the best place to photograph towering Mount Pelée; **La Pagerie,** with its decaying ruins of a sugar factory; and from the panoramic overlooks along **La Trace,** the serpentine road winding through the entire rain forest.

miles (161km) of trails. Although the hikes up from Grand-Rivière or Le Prêcheur are generally the less arduous of the three options leading to the top, most visitors opt for departures from Morne Rouge, a landlocked village set to the south of the summit, because it doesn't take as long to finish the trip. It's steeper, rockier, and more exhausting, but you can make it in just 2½ hours versus the 5 hours it takes from the other two towns. There are no facilities other than these villages, so it's vital to bring water and food with you. Your arduous journey will be rewarded at the summit with sweeping views over the sea and panoramas that sometimes stretch as far as mountainous Dominica to the south. As for the volcano, its deathly eruption in 1902 apparently satisfied it—at least for the time being!

Upon your descent from Montagne Pelée, drive down to **Ajoupa-Bouillon,** one of the most beautiful towns on Martinique. Abounding in flowers and shrubbery with bright yellow and red leaves, this little village is the site of the remarkable **Gorges de la Falaise.** These are mini-canyons on the Falaise River, up which you can travel to reach a waterfall. Ajoupa-Boullion also makes a good lunch stop.

DINING

Le Fromager ★ *Finds* CREOLE/FRENCH   Set about a half mile uphill (east) of the center of St Pierre, this indoor–outdoor villa, owned by the Rene family, welcomes luncheon guests with a humor and charm that's half French, half Martiniquais. The restaurant, which resembles a covered open-air pavilion, has a sweeping view of the town. Good-tasting menu items include marinated octopus, grilled conch or lobster, curried goat or chicken, and whatever grilled fish is available that day. This is a good lunch stopover during your tour of the island.

Route de Fonds-St-Denis, St-Pierre. ℂ 596/78-19-07. Reservations recommended. Fixed-price menu 15.20€–28.90€ ($13.55–$25.80); main courses 12.15€–19.75€ ($10.85–$17.65). AE, DC, MC, V. Daily noon–3pm.

LEYRITZ

If you continue east toward the coast, near the town of Basse-Pointe in northeastern Martinique turn left a mile before Basse-Pointe and follow a road that goes deep into sugarcane country to Leyritz, where you'll find one of the best-restored plantations on Martinique.

ACCOMMODATIONS

Hôtel Plantation de Leyritz   Dating from the 18th century, this plantation, converted to a hotel, remains one of the most famous in the Caribbean, but is in a bit of a decline, a condition we hope is temporary. Its dilapidated main house is closed with progress on restoration moving at the pace of an *escargot.* It's still a working plantation that often attracts tour groups. There are 16 acres (6 hectares) of tropical gardens with views that sweep across the Atlantic and take in the fearsome Montagne Pelée. At the core of the grounds is the shuttered great house. About half the accommodations are in a series of small outbuildings which presumably were slave quarters; others, a bit sterile, are in a series of modern bungalows. All the units come with sun terraces. Bathrooms are small and equipped with showers instead of tubs. A pool is on-site, but the nearest beach, Plage de la Tartane, is a 25-minute drive from the hotel.

97218 Basse-Pointe, Martinique, F.W.I. ℂ 596/78-53-92. Fax 596/78-92-44. www.fwinet.com/leyritz.htm. 55 units. Winter 79.05€ ($70.60) double. Off-season 71.15€ ($63.50) double. Rates include continental breakfast. AE, MC, V. **Amenities:** Restaurant; bar; laundry. *In room:* A/C, TV, minibar (in some).

GRAND-RIVIÈRE

After Basse-Pointe, the town you reach on your northward trek is Grand-Rivière. From here you must turn back, but before doing so, you may want to stop at a good restaurant right at the entrance to the town.

DINING

Yva Chez Vava ⭐ *Finds* FRENCH/CREOLE   Directly west of Basse-Pointe, in a low-slung building painted the peachy-orange of a paw-paw fruit, Yva Chez Vava is a combination private home and restaurant. It represents the hard labor of three generations of Creole women. Infused with a simple country-inn style, it was established in 1979 by a well-remembered, long-departed matron, Vava, whose daughter, Yva, is now assisted by her own daughter, Rosy. Family recipes are the mainstay of this modest bistro. A la carte items include Creole soup, blaff of sea urchins, lobster, and various colombos or curries. Local delicacies used in the kitchen include *z'habitants* (crayfish), *vivaneau* (red snapper), *tazard* (kingfish), and *accras de morue* (cod fritters).

In 2000, the establishment added four simple studio apartments onto their restaurant, each equipped with A/C but without TV, phone, or any other accessory. Each rents for 45.60€ ($40.70) double occupancy, with breakfast, per night, or 258.40€ ($230.75) per week. There's no pool, and few amenities, but clients can bathe in the nearby river, or walk to an unnamed strip of sand, the nearest beach, which lies about a ¼ mile (.4km) from the restaurant.

Blvd. Charles-de-Gaulle. ✆ 596/55-72-72. Reservations recommended. Main courses 9.90€–27.35€ ($8.80–$24.45); fixed-price menu 12.15€–27.35€ ($10.85–$24.45). AE, DC, MC, V. Daily noon–6pm.

LE MARIGOT

After passing back through Basse-Pointe and Le Lorrain, you come to a small village that was relatively ignored by tourists until hotelier Jean-Louis de Lucy used France's tax-shelter laws to restore a landmark plantation and turn it into one of the finest hotels on the island. True, the nearest good beach is at Trinité, a 30-minute drive from the hotel, but guests of the Habitation LaGrange don't seem to mind.

ACCOMMODATIONS & DINING

Habitation LaGrange ⭐⭐⭐   One of the most unusual and historic properties of Martinique, this hotel lies in isolation about a mile (2km) north of the village of Le Marigot. It's set on 6 acres (2 hectares) of land whose edges are engulfed by acres of banana fields. About 1½ miles (2km) inland from the coast, it was originally built in 1928 as part of the last sugar plantation and rum distillery on Martinique. Today, the ruins of that distillery rise a short distance from the Louisiana-style main house. This hotel is the *ne plus ultra* of Martinique, superior in style and class to Leyritz, to which it bears some resemblance.

Rooms are either in the main house or in a comfortable annex, which was erected in 1990. In addition to that, another two very large rooms are in what used to be the stables. We actually prefer these rooms, as they have been beautifully restored and on occasion photographs of them have appeared in architectural magazines. Each unit is different, and contains antique or reproduction furniture crafted from mahogany, baldachin-style (canopy) beds, and accessories steeped in the French colonial style. All units have verandas or patios, with ample vistas over a tropical landscape of gardens and faraway banana groves. As a conscious effort to preserve the calm and quiet, no units contain TVs or radios. Bathrooms are among the island's finest, with wood paneling, four-footed tubs equipped with showers, and pedestal sinks. Meals are prepared in the Creole style by local chefs, then served in the Ajoupa, an open-sided pavilion.

97225 Le Marigot, Martinique, F.W.I. 𝐶 **596/53-60-60.** Fax 596/53-50-58. (For reservations, contact Caribbean Inns, P.O. Box 7411, Hilton Head Island, SC 29983; 𝐶 **800/633-7411** in the U.S.) www.habitation-lagrange.com. 12 units. Winter 243.20€–266€ ($217.15–$237.55) double; 319.20€ ($285.05) suite. Off-season 190€–212.80€ ($169.65–$190) double; 266€ ($237.55) suite. Rates include breakfast. MAP (breakfast and dinner) 30.40€ ($27.15) per person extra. AE, MC, V. **Amenities:** Dining room, daytime restaurant at poolside, bar; pool; tennis court; library. *In room:* A/C, minibar, safe.

STE-MARIE

Heading south along the coastal road, you'll pass Le Marigot en route to the little town of Ste-Marie. **Musee du Rhum Saint-James,** route de l'Union at the Saint James Distillery (𝐶 **596/69-30-02**), displays engravings, antique tools and machines, and other exhibits tracing the history of sugarcane and rum from 1765 to the present. When inventories of rum are low and the distillery is functioning (only 4 months of the year, from early March to late June), guided tours of the distillery are offered every day, whenever clients show up, between 9am and 5pm. Tours cost 3.05€ ($2.70) per person. Admission to the museum (open daily, year-round, from 9am–5pm, regardless of whether the distillery is functioning) is free. Rum is available for purchase on-site.

From here you can head out the north end of town and loop inland a bit for a stop at Morne des Esses, or continue heading south straight to Trinité.

DINING

Restaurant La Decouverte/Chez Tatie Simone ★ *Finds* CREOLE   Set near Martinique's northeastern tip, 2½ miles (4km) north of Ste-Marie, this restaurant prepares superb versions of traditional Creole cuisine. The cement-sided house, built in the early 1980s, is the showcase for the cuisine created by "Auntie" (*Tatie*) Simone Adelise. Since she is now semi-retired, her daughter, Mady Adelise, is usually on hand to supervise the food preparation. In a dining room accented with white wainscoting and folkloric paintings, you'll enjoy her *boudin rouge* (blood sausages, in this case accented with habañero chiles and cinnamon), *boudin blanc* (sausages made from pulverized conch and spices), couscous with *fruits de mer* (garnished with shrimp, crayfish, sea urchins, clams, and octopus), and a succulent array of grilled fish.

A member of the staff may propose a short stroll after your meal, along a well-marked trail dotted with signs that give the names of specific trees and plants. At its end, you'll be rewarded with sweeping panoramas over sea and coastline. Estimated round-trip time for the hike, not counting stops to admire the view, is 40 minutes.

Foret la Philippe, Route du Marigot, Ste-Marie. 𝐶 **596/69-44-04**. Reservations recommended. Main courses 12.15€–25.10€ ($10.85–$22.40). Fixed-price menu 18.25€–30.40€ ($16.30–$27.15). Daily noon–3:30pm. Dinner only by arrangement.

TRINITÉ

Passing through Morne des Esses, continue south, then turn east, or from Ste-Marie head south along the coastal route (N1), to reach Trinité. The town is the gateway to the Caravelle peninsula, where the **Caravelle Nature Preserve,** a well-protected peninsula jutting into the Atlantic Ocean from the town of Trinité, has safe beaches and well-marked trails through tropical wetlands and to the ruins of historic Chateau Debuc. It offers excellent hiking and one of the only safe beaches for swimming on the Atlantic coast. It would hardly merit an actual stop were it not for the Saint-Aubin Hotel.

ACCOMMODATIONS

Saint Aubin Hôtel ⭐ A former restaurant owner, Normandy-born Guy Forêt, sunk his fortune into restoring this three-story Victorian house which is now one of the loveliest inns in the Caribbean. Painted a vivid pink with fancy gingerbread, the hotel was originally built in 1920 of brick and poured concrete as a replacement for a much older wood-sided house, which served as the seat of a large plantation. It sits on a hillside above sugarcane fields and the bay, 2 miles (3km) from the village of Trinité itself. The nearest beach is plage Cosmy, lying three-fourths of a mile (2km) from the hotel. All the good-size bedrooms sport wall-to-wall carpeting and modern (not antique) furniture; views are of either the garden or the sea. There are some family rooms as well. All but two of the bedrooms have shower/tub combinations, the remaining two with shower.

97220 Trinité, Martinique, F.W.I. ✆ 596/69-34-77. Fax 596/69-41-14. 15 units. Winter 72.95€–88.15€ ($65.15–$78.70) double. Off-season 57.75€–72.95€ ($51.60–$65.15) double. Rates include continental breakfast. AE, DC, MC, V. **Amenities:** Pool; laundry. *In room:* A/C.

DINING

La Caravelle INTERNATIONAL/FRENCH   Set about a ½ mile (.8km) east of the fishing village of Tartane, this is the most easterly hotel and restaurant on the La Caravelle peninsula, a rocky spur that juts out from Martinique's eastern edge. The setting, as created by Paris-born Jean-Luc Combaluzier and his wife, Nicole, is a blue-and-white hotel and restaurant complex, built in the 1980s, which is well known for the quality and sophistication of its cuisine. You can drop in here for the lunchtime salad and crepe bar, experimenting with any of several well-conceived salads and crepes, although the main culinary zest is visible during the dinner hour. Then, the menu might include a Colombo (spicy Creole stew) of shark; callaloo soup with crabmeat; several preparations of shrimp or fish, or red snapper cooked in parchment and stuffed with sea urchins. Desserts include, among others, a soufflé flavored with aged, orange-flavored rum. You'll dine within a garden, or on a veranda that's ringed with artful landscaping. From there, you'll have sweeping views over the sea, thanks to the establishment's location on a steep hillside, atop a low cliff at the edge of the sea. On-site are 15 studio apartments, each with telephone and a small kitchenette. Accommodations rent for between 40€ and 74€ ($35.70 and $66.10) per day, for up to four occupants.

Route du Château Dubuc, L'Anse l'Étang, Tartane (Trinité). ✆ 596/58-07-32. http://perso.wanadoo.fr/hotel caravelle. Reservations recommended. Lunch salads and crepes 5.80€–9.90€ ($5.15–$8.80); dinner main courses 11.85€–30.10€ ($10.60–$26.85); set dinners 18.25€ ($16.30). AE, MC, V. Salad and crepe bar daily noon–4pm; restaurant daily 7–9:30pm (last order).

LE FRANÇOIS

Continuing your exploration of the east coast of Martinique, you can stop over in Le François to visit the **Musée Rhum Clement** at the Domaine de l'Acajou (✆ 596/54-62-07), about 1½ miles (2km) south of the village center. The distillery is in the cellar of an 18th-century mansion with period furnishings. The setting for this museum is an outmoded distillery that the Clement Rum Company closed in the early 1990s, when it shifted its production to a newer plant (which cannot be visited) about a mile (2km) away. A Christopher Columbus exhibit is set up in caves, and other exhibits trace the institution of slavery in the islands. The museum is located in a botanic park; you could easily spend 2 or 3 hours exploring the exhibits and grounds. It's open daily from 9am to 6pm. Admission is 6.10€ ($5.45) adults, 3.05€ ($2.70) children 12 to 16 (free, ages 11 and under).

ACCOMMODATIONS

Frégate Bleue ★ *(Finds)* This is the closest thing to a European B&B on the island. It's a calm and quiet choice with touches of personal, old-fashioned charm. It's not the place for vacationers looking for nightlife and lots of activities—it's for escapists who don't mind the 10-minute drive to the beaches of St-François or the prevailing sense of isolation. Much of this ambience is the work of owner Yveline de Lucy de Fossarieu, an experienced veteran of the hotel industry. Her house is a 5-minute drive inland from the sea, and it overlooks several chains of deserted off-shore islands (including Les Ilets de St-François and Les Ilets de l'Impératrice). Bedrooms are small but cozy, each with a compact bathroom with a shower stall. The site is perched in a quiet residential neighborhood high on a hill. Each room has either a terrace or a balcony with sweeping views over the coast. Three nights a week, between December and April, Mme de Fossarieu (who speaks perfect English) prepares an evening meal, served to whomever requests it in advance. She quotes her rates in U.S. dollars.

Route de Vauclin, Le François 97240, Martinique, F.W.I. ⓒ **800/633-7411** in the U.S., or 596/54-54-66. Fax 596/54-78-48. www.caribbeaninns.com. 7 units. Winter $200–$225 double. Off-season 134€–157€ ($120–$140) double. Extra person 18.25€ ($16.30). Rates include continental breakfast. MC, V. **Amenities:** Pool; laundry. *In room:* A/C, TV, kitchenette

L'Habitation de L'Ilet Thierry ★ *(Finds)* The setting of this hotel on a remote, offshore island is the most offbeat location in Martinique. The island's only beach is a sandy cove about a ½ mile (.8km) from this inn. Around 1900, a Martinique-based merchant and planter from *la France metropolitaine* decided to build a clapboard- and stucco-covered, veranda-ringed second home on an isolated island off the southeastern coast of Martinique. In 1989, a trio of investors from the French mainland, taking advantage of the tax benefits that accompany an investment in the offshore *departements* of France, bought and transformed it into one of the most isolated hotels in the French-speaking Caribbean. In 1999, it was renovated and upgraded into a mostly white, somewhat spartan-looking temple for rest, contemplation, relaxation, and (if you bring your own companion) romance. Accommodations are large, high-ceilinged, and filled with rustic furniture that's sometimes covered with rattan. Each has direct access to either of the building's two levels of wraparound verandas, and none has any electronic amenities. Each has a sink and a toilet, but showers are shared facilities off each hallway. You can swim and snorkel off the nearby pier or at any of several gravel-covered bays closer to home. If you want to kayak, sail, or windsurf, you can inform your hosts in advance, and they'll arrange to have a suitable craft (for a fee) delivered in advance of your arrival. The island itself, covering a scrub-covered expanse of about 37 acres (15 hectares), is the most distant of the 7 islands of the Le François archipelago, and lies within a 12-minute boat ride from the Le François marina. It's there that—upon prior reservation—an employee of the hotel will fetch you and up to five other passengers in a motorboat.

Non-guests can come to this isolated site only for lunch, but if you do, you'll have to reserve at least 48 hours in advance, and pay 38€ ($33.95) for round-trip transportation, a price that's valid for up to six passengers.

L'Ilet Thierry, B.P. 26, 97240 Le François, La Martinique, FWI. ⓒ **596/65-88-54** or 596/27-66-07. www.ilet-thierry.com. 5 units. Year-round 197.60€ ($176.45) double. Rates include round-trip transport from the "mainland" of Martinique and breakfast. Supplements of 38€ ($33.95) per person per day for breakfast and dinner and 68.40€ ($61.10) per person per day for full board. No credit cards. Closed 4 weeks Oct–Nov.

DINING

La Maison de L'Ilet Oscar ★ *Finds* INTERNATIONAL/FRENCH   There are many similarities between this establishment and the one we also recommend on l'Ilet Thierry. Both lie on nearly adjacent islands off the southeast coast of Martinique; both are accessed by motorboat from the Marina at Le François; both are centered around antique Creole houses, and both offer overnight accommodations in charming but somewhat spartan settings that appeal to off-beat adventurers. They're even owned by the same absentee investors from mainland France. Less imposing than its sibling hotel on the Ilet Thierry, this one is more amenable to day-trippers who want a meal, but not necessarily an overnight, on the island.

If you make advance reservations, you'll be hauled on a 12-minute boat ride to the island, stopping at an emerald-colored tidal pool where legend says that Joséphine, eventual wife of Napoleon I, once went swimming. You'll then head to the island's only dwelling, a one-story wood-sided house that was originally built in 1898 on nearby Ilet Thierry, and disassembled and floated, beam by beam, across to Ilet Oscar and reassembled there in 1935. Menu items focus on Creole specialties like an all-fish menu, an all-shrimp menu, or an all-lobster menu, but if you desire food inspired by the traditions of mainland France, Brittany-born Bruno de Lussy and his staff will whip you up fried foie gras with peaches, potatoes *dauphinoise,* magret of duckling, or whatever else happens to be in the larder. If you want to overnight, the five bedrooms (all with shower, toilet, and double sinks) rent for 152€ ($135.75) per person, per day, with full board included. None has TV, phone, or air-conditioning.

L'Ilet Oscar, B.P. 12, 97240 Le François, La Martinique. ℂ 596/65-82-30. www.ilet-oscar.com. Reservations essential 1 day in advance. Set-price menu 30.40€–45.60€ ($27.15–$40.70) per person; round-trip transport from Le Marina du François 45.60€ ($40.70) for up to 6 passengers. AE, MC, V. Daily 11am–3pm and 6–9:30pm.

Le Plein Soleil ★ *Finds* INTERNATIONAL   The meal you'll consume here will be entirely sited on a wide veranda of a 1980s French-colonial-style house that sits on a hillside about 300 feet (90m) from the seafront. Your hosts are a trio of France- and Martinique-born entrepreneurs (Eric, José, and Jean-Christophe) who will welcome you, organize your meal (only if you phone in your intentions a day in advance), and cook sublime food. Menu items combine the aesthetics of France and the Antilles. The best examples include pork with a lemon-flavored honey sauce and a confit of onions; and filets of red snapper or grouper with white vermouth and fish broth. There are also 12 bedrooms, each with private bathroom (shower only, no tubs) and telephone, but without TV or any other amenities. (A few of them are air-conditioned.) Depending on the season and their layouts, rooms rent for 95€ to 144.40€ ($84.85–$128.95) each, double occupancy. There's a beach within a walk of about 300 yards (274m) , and a formal-looking, rectangular swimming pool, but in most cases, whatever distractions and diversions appeal to you, you'll have to organize on your own.

Villa Lagon S.A.R.L., Pointe Thalemont, 97240 Le François. ℂ 596/38-07-77. Reservations required at least 1 day in advance. Set-price lunches 23.55€ ($21.05); set-price dinners 28.10€ ($25.10). MC, V. Daily 12:30–3pm, Mon–Sat 7:30–9pm. Closed Sept. Lies 3 miles (5km) north from Le François, following signs first to *Le Robert,* then veering eastward when you see the signs to *Thalemont, Manssard,* and *Plein Soleil.*

17

Puerto Rico

No one has ever suffered from boredom on Puerto Rico. It has hundreds of beaches, a mind-boggling array of watersports, miles of golf courses, acres of tennis courts, a huge variety of resorts, and casinos galore. It has more discos than any other place in the Caribbean, and it has shopping bargains to equal St. Thomas. And all this fun and variety comes with a much more reasonable price tag than it does on many of the other islands.

Lush, verdant Puerto Rico is half the size of New Jersey and is located some 1,000 miles (161km) southeast of the tip of Florida. With 272 miles (438km) of Atlantic and Caribbean coastline and a culture some 2,000 years old, Puerto Rico is packed with attractions. Old San Juan is its greatest historic center, with 500 years of history, as reflected in its restored Spanish colonial architecture.

It's also a land of contrasts. There are 79 cities and towns on Puerto Rico, each with a unique charm and flavor. The countryside is dotted with centuries-old coffee plantations, sugar estates still in use, a fascinating tropical rain forest, and foreboding caves and enormous boulders with mysterious petroglyphs carved by the Taíno peoples, the original settlers.

Dorado Beach, Cerromar Beach, and Palmas del Mar are the chief centers for those who've come for golf, tennis, and beaches. San Juan's hotels on the Condado/Isla Verde coast also have, for the most part, a complete array of watersports. The continental shelf, which surrounds Puerto Rico on three sides, contributes to an abundance of coral reefs, caves, sea walls, and trenches for scuba diving and snorkeling.

San Juan is the world's second-largest home port for cruise ships, and the old port of San Juan recently underwent a $90 million restoration.

In this chapter, we start out in San Juan, and then move west, counter-clockwise around the island, until we reach Ponce. Then we turn our attention to attractions east of San Juan, and head clockwise around the island. You can base yourself at one resort and still do a lot of exploring elsewhere, if you don't mind driving for a couple hours. It's possible to branch out and see a lot of the island even if you're staying in San Juan.

For even more comprehensive coverage, consider getting yourself a copy of *Frommer's Puerto Rico.*

1 Essentials

VISITOR INFORMATION

For information before you leave home, contact one of the following **Puerto Rico Tourism Company** offices: 666 Fifth Ave., **New York, NY** 10103 (© **800/223-6530** in the U.S. or 212/586-6262); 3575 W. Cahuenga Blvd., Suite 405, **Los Angeles, CA** 90068 (© **800/874-1230**); or 901 Ponce de León Blvd., Suite 604, **Coral Gables, FL** 33134 (© **800/815-7391** or 305/445-9112). In **Canada** you can stop by 230 Richmond St. W, Suite 902, Toronto,

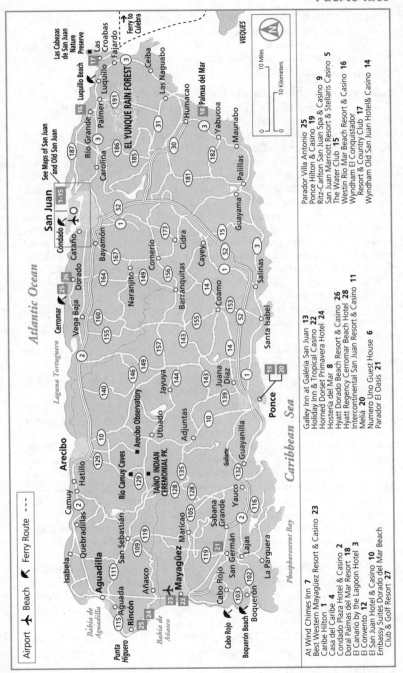

Puerto Rico

Atlantic Ocean

Caribbean Sea

San Juan — See Maps of San Juan and Old San Juan **1-15**

Airport ✈ Beach ⚓ Ferry Route ---

467

At Wind Chimes Inn **7**
Best Western Mayagüez Resort & Casino **23**
Caribe Hilton **1**
Casa del Caribe **4**
Condado Plaza Hotel & Casino **2**
Doral Palmas del Mar Resort **18**
El Canario by the Lagoon Hotel **3**
El Convento **12**
El San Juan Hotel & Casino **10**
Embassy Suites Dorado del Mar Beach Club & Golf Resort **27**

Galley Inn at Galería San Juan **13**
Holiday Inn & Tropical Casino **22**
Horned Dorset Primavera Hotel **24**
Hostería del Mar **8**
Hyatt Dorado Beach Resort & Casino **26**
Hyatt Regency Cerromar Beach Hotel **28**
Intercontinental San Juan Resort & Casino **11**
Meliá **20**
Numero Uno Guest House **6**
Parador El Oasis **21**

Parador Villa Antonio **25**
Ponce Hilton & Casino **19**
Ritz-Carlton San Juan Spa & Casino **9**
San Juan Marriott Resort & Stellaris Casino **5**
The Water Club **15**
Westin Rio Mar Beach Resort & Casino **16**
Wyndham El Conquistador Resort & Country Club **17**
Wyndham Old San Juan Hotel & Casino **14**

ON M5V 1V6 (© **800/667-0394** in the U.S. or 416/368-2680), for information. The official website is **www.prtourism.com**.

On the island, it's best to go to the local city hall for tourist information. Ask for a copy of *Qué Pasa,* the official visitors' guide.

GETTING THERE

Before you book your own airfare, read the section "Package Deals" in chapter 2—it can save you a bundle! There are more package deals to Puerto Rico than almost any other island except for Jamaica.

Puerto Rico is by far the most accessible of the Caribbean islands, with frequent airline service. **American Airlines** (© **800/433-7300** in the U.S.; www.aa.com) has designated San Juan as its hub for the entire Caribbean. American offers nonstop daily flights to San Juan from Baltimore, Boston, Chicago, Dallas–Fort Worth, Hartford, Miami, Newark, New York (JFK), Orlando, Philadelphia, Tampa, Fort Lauderdale, and Washington (Dulles), plus flights from both Montréal and Toronto with changes in Chicago or Miami. There are also at least two daily flights from Los Angeles to San Juan that touch down in Dallas or Miami.

American also offers many money-saving packages that include your hotel or resort; contact **American Airlines FlyAway Vacations** (© **800/321-2121** in the U.S.; www.aavacations.com) to find out about their current offerings.

American Eagle (© **800/433-7300** in the U.S.) is the undisputed leader among the short-haul local commuter flights of the Caribbean. Collectively, American Eagle, along with its larger associate, American Airlines, offers service to dozens of destinations on more than 30 islands of the Caribbean and the Bahamas.

Delta (© **800/221-1212** in the U.S.; www.delta.com) has four daily nonstop flights from its international hub in Atlanta. Delta has six nonstops on Saturday, and four on Sunday. Ask about their packages by calling **Delta Vacations** at © **800/872-7786** in the U.S. (www.deltavacations.com).

United Airlines (© **800/241-6522** in the U.S.; www.ual.com) offers daily nonstop flights from Chicago to San Juan. **Northwest** (© **800/225-2525** in the U.S.; www.nwa.com) has one daily nonstop to San Juan from Detroit, as well as at least one (and sometimes more) connecting flights to San Juan from Detroit. Northwest also offers flights to San Juan, some of them nonstop, from both Memphis and Minneapolis, with a schedule that varies according to the season and the day of the week. **US Airways** (© **800/428-4322** in the U.S.; www.usairways.com) also competes, with daily flights between Charlotte, North Carolina and San Juan (but doesn't require a change of planes). The airline also offers three daily nonstop flights from Philadelphia, and one from Pittsburgh. You can also ask about packages offered by **US Airways Vacations** (© **800/455-0123** in the U.S.).

Lufthansa (© **800/645-3880** in the U.S. or 01-803-803-803 in Germany) passengers can fly on Saturday (one weekly flight) from Frankfurt to San Juan via Condor (a subsidiary operating the flight). British travelers can take a **British Airways** (© **0845/773-3377** in the U.K., 800/247-9297 in the U.S.) weekly flight direct from London to San Juan on Sunday.

Finally, **Iberia** (© **800/772-4642** in the U.S.; www.iberia.com) has two weekly flights from Madrid to San Juan, leaving on Thursday and Saturday.

GETTING AROUND

BY PLANE   American Eagle (© **787/749-1747**) flies from Luís Muñoz International Airport to Mayagüez in 40 minutes, the gateway to western Puerto

Value **Great Discounts Through the LeLoLai VIP Program**

For the $10 it will cost you to join Puerto Rico's **LeLoLai VIP** (Value in Puerto Rico) program, you can enjoy the equivalent of up to $250 in travel benefits. Of course, most of the experiences linked to LeLoLai are of the rather touristy type, but it can still be a good investment. You'll get discounts on admission to folklore shows, guided tours of historic sites and natural attractions, lodgings, meals, shopping, activities, and more.

Paradores Puertorriqueños, the island's modestly priced network of country inns, give cardholders 10% to 20% discounts on room rates Monday to Thursday. Discounts of 10% to 20% are offered at many restaurants, from San Juan's toniest hotels to several *mesones gastronómicos:* government-sanctioned restaurants serving Puerto Rican fare. Shopping discounts are offered at many stores and boutiques, and cardholders get 10% to 20% discounts at many island attractions. The card also entitles you to free admission to some of the island's folklore shows.

For more information about this card, call ☎ **787/722-1709** or go to the El Centro Convention Center at Ashford Avenue on the Condado. Although you can call for details before you leave home, you can only sign up for this program when you reach Puerto Rico. Many hotel packages include participation in this program as part of their offerings.

Rico. Fares vary widely, but expect to pay between $155 and $196 round-trip, per person, and try to book your passage as early as possible.

BY RENTAL CAR Some local car-rental agencies may tempt you with slashed prices, but if you're planning to tour the island, you won't find any local branches to help you should you run into car trouble. Plus, some of the agencies advertising low-cost deals don't take credit cards and want cash in advance. You also have to watch out for hidden extras and the insurance problems that sometimes proliferate among the smaller and not very well known firms.

The old reliables include **Avis** (☎ **800/331-1212** in the U.S., or 787/791-2500; www.avis.com), **Budget** (☎ **800/527-0700** in the U.S., or 787/253-5926; www.budgetrentacar.com), or **Hertz** (☎ **800/654-3131** in the U.S., or 787/791-0840; www.hertz.com). Each offers minivan transport to its office from the San Juan airport. Another alternative is **Kemwel Holiday Auto** (☎ **800/678-0678;** www.kemwel.com in the U.S.). None of these companies rents Jeeps, four-wheel-drive vehicles, or convertibles. Note that car theft is high on Puerto Rico, so extra precaution is always a good idea.

Distances in Puerto Rico are often posted in kilometers rather than miles (a kilometer is 0.62 miles), but speed limits are in miles per hour.

BY PUBLIC TRANSPORTATION *Públicos* are cars or minibuses that provide low-cost transportation and are designated with the letters *P* or *PD* following the numbers on their license plates. They usually operate only during daylight hours, carry up to six passengers at a time, and charge rates that are loosely governed by the Public Service Commission. Although prices are low, this option is slow, with frequent stops, often erratic routing, and lots of inconvenience.

Locals are adept at figuring out their routes along rural highways, and in some cases, they simply wave at a moving *público* that they suspect might be headed in their direction. Unless you're fluent in Spanish and feeling adventurous, we suggest that you phone either of the numbers below, describe where and when you want to go, and agree to the prearranged price between specific points. Then, be prepared to wait. Although, at least in theory, a *público* might be arranged between most of the towns and villages of Puerto Rico, by far the most popular routes are between San Juan and Ponce and San Juan and Mayagüez. Fares vary according to whether a *público* will make a detour to pick up or drop off a passenger at a specific locale. If you want to deviate from the predetermined routes, you'll pay more than if you wait for a *público* at vaguely designated points beside the main highway, or at predefined points that include airports and, in some cases, the main plaza (central square) of a town.

Information about *público* routes between San Juan and Mayagüez is available from **Lineas Sultana,** Calle Esteban González 898, Urbanización Santa Rita, Rio Piedras (© 787/765-9377). Information about *público* routes between San Juan and Ponce is available from **Choferes Unidos de Ponce,** terminal de carros públicos, Calle Vive in Ponce (© 787/721-2400 or 787/764-0540). Fares from San Juan to Ponce cost $15 to $25.

SIGHTSEEING TOURS   If you want to see more of the island but don't want to rent a car or deal with public transportation, perhaps an organized tour is for you. **Castillo Sightseeing Tours & Travel Services,** Calle Laurel 2413, Punta La Marias, Santurce (© 787/726-5752), maintains offices at some of San Juan's major hotels. They can also arrange pickup at other accommodations in one of their six air-conditioned buses. One of the most popular half-day tours runs from San Juan to El Yunque Rain Forest; it departs in the morning, lasts 4 to 5 hours, and costs $35 per person. The company also offers a 4-hour city tour of San Juan that costs $35 and includes a stopover at the Bacardi rum factory. Full-day snorkeling tours to the reefs near the coast of a deserted island off Puerto Rico's eastern edge aboard one of two sail- and motor-driven catamarans go for $69, with lunch, snorkeling gear, and piña coladas included.

Fun Fact **Special Events**

The annual **Casals Festival** in June is the Caribbean's most celebrated cultural event. The bill at San Juan's Performing Arts Center includes a glittering array of international guest conductors, orchestras, and soloists who come to honor the memory of Pablo Casals, the renowned cellist who was born in Spain to a Puerto Rican mother, and who died in Puerto Rico in 1973. Tickets range from $20 to $40; a 50% discount is offered to students, seniors, and persons with disabilities. Call © 787/721-7727 for tickets.

The island's **Carnival** celebrations feature float parades, dancing, and street parties in the week leading up to Ash Wednesday. The festivities in **Ponce** are marked by masqueraders wearing brightly painted horned masks, the crowning of a Carnival queen, and the closing "burial of the sardine." Hotel rates go up at this time of year, sometimes considerably. For more information, call © 787/284-4141. Ash Wednesday falls on February 12 in 2003.

FAST FACTS: **Puerto Rico**

Banks Most major U.S. banks have branches with ATMs in San Juan, and are open Monday to Friday from 8:30am to 2:30pm.

Currency The **U.S. dollar** is the coin of the realm. Canadian currency is accepted by some big hotels in San Juan, although reluctantly.

Documents Since Puerto Rico is part of the United States, American citizens do not need a passport or visa. Canadians, however, should carry some form of identification, such as a birth certificate and photo ID, though we always recommend carrying your passport. Citizens of the United Kingdom should have a passport.

Electricity The electricity is 110-volt AC (60 cycles), the same as in the United States and Canada.

Emergencies Call ⓒ **911.**

Language English is understood at the big resorts and in most of San Juan, though it's polite to at least greet people in Spanish and ask if they speak English before you make assumptions. Out in the island, Spanish is still *número uno.*

Safety Use common sense and take precautions. Muggings are commonly reported on the Condado and Isla Verde beaches in San Juan, so you might want to confine your moonlit-beach nights to the fenced-in and guarded areas around some of the major hotels. The countryside of Puerto Rico is safer than San Juan, but caution is always the rule. Avoid small and narrow little country roads and isolated beaches day or night.

Taxes There's a government tax of 9% in regular hotels or 11% in hotels with casinos. The airport departure tax is included in the price of your ticket.

Telephone Puerto Rico is on the North American telephone system; the area code is **787.** Place a call to or from Puerto Rico just as you would from within the United States or Canada.

Time Puerto Rico is on Atlantic standard time year-round, putting it 1 hour ahead of U.S. eastern standard time. In winter, when it's noon in Miami, it's 1pm in San Juan. But from April until late October (during daylight saving time on the U.S. east coast), Puerto Rico and the east coast keep the same time.

Tipping Some hotels add a 10% service charge to your bill. If they don't, you're expected to tip for services rendered. Tip as you would in the United States (15%–20%).

Water The water in Puerto Rico is generally safe to drink, although you may prefer bottled water.

Weather Puerto Rico is cooler than most of the other Caribbean islands because of its northeast trade winds. Sea, land, and mountain breezes also help keep the temperatures at a comfortable level. The climate is fairly stable all year, with an average temperature of 76°F. The only variants are found in the mountain regions, where the temperature fluctuates between 66° and 76°F, and on the north coast, where the temperature ranges from 70° to 80°F. There is no real rainy season, but August is the wettest month.

2 San Juan ✰✰✰

Puerto Rico's capital is a major city—actually an urban sprawl of several munic-ipalities that lies along the island's north coast. Its architecture ranges from clas-sic colonial buildings that recall the Spanish empire to modern beachfront hotels reminiscent of Miami Beach.

SAN JUAN ESSENTIALS

ARRIVING   Dozens of taxis line up outside the airport to meet arriving flights, so you rarely have to wait. The island's **Public Service Commission** (© 787/756-1401) sets flat rates between the Luís Muñoz Marin Airport and major tourist zones as follows: From the airport to any hotel in Isla Verde, $8; to any hotel in the Condado district, $12; and to any hotel in Old San Juan, $16. Tips of between 10% and 15% of that fare are expected.

   Airport Limousine Service (© 787/791-4745) offers minivan transport from the airport to various neighborhoods of San Juan for prices that are lower than taxis. You'll have to wait until they get a minimum of 8 to 10 passengers to fill the van, however. The fare is $35 to $55 per van to any hotel in Isla Verde, $55 to $75 per van to the Condado or Old San Juan. The sign-up desk is near the American Airlines arrival facilities.

   For conventional limousine service, **Bracero Limousine** (© 787/253-1133) offers upholstered cars with drivers to meet you at the arrivals terminal for lux-urious and strictly private transport to your hotel or anywhere you specify in Puerto Rico. This luxury and convenience will cost you, though. The price for going anywhere in San Juan ranges from $85 to $105; rates to other points on the island vary from $150 to $275, depending on the time and distance.

VISITOR INFORMATION   Tourist information is available at the **Luís Muñoz Marín Airport** (© 787/791-1014). Another office is at **La Casita,** Pier 1, Old San Juan (© 787/722-1709). Open Sunday to Wednesday 9am to 8pm, Thursday and Friday 9am to 5:30pm.

ORIENTATION   The city center is on **San Juan Island,** connected to the rest of the metropolitan area by causeways. The western half of San Juan Island con-tains the walled city of **Old San Juan.** The eastern half is known as **Puerto de Tierra,** and contains many government buildings. Across the causeways is the neighborhood of **Miramar,** which fronts the Laguna del Condado. **Condado** is the narrow peninsula that loops around the top of Miramar almost all the way back to San Juan Island. It's where you'll find many of the best beaches. Just east of Condado is the residential neighborhood of **Ocean Park.** South of Condado and Ocean Park is **Santurce.** To the east is the International Airport, and even further east is **Isla Verde,** home of some of the Caribbean's most upscale resort hotels, connected to the rest of San Juan by an isthmus.

GETTING AROUND   Walking is the best way to get around Old San Juan. The historic core of the old city is very compact. If your feet tire of the cobble-stoned old streets, board one of the free open-air trolleys that slowly make their way through the old city. You can board a trolley at any point along its route (either side of the Calle Fortaleza or Calle San José are good bets), or you can go to either the Marina or La Puntilla for departures.

   The rest of the city is not so pedestrian-friendly. You'll want to take buses, taxis, or your own car to get around the rest of San Juan, including Condado and Isla Verde. The **Metropolitan Bus Authority** (© 787/767-7979) operates buses in the greater San Juan area. Bus stops are marked by upright metal signs

Tren Urbano in 2003: The Way to Go

San Juan will be linked to its major suburbs such as Santurce, Bayamón, and Guaynabo in the summer of 2003 by a $1.25 billion urban train called "Tren Urbano." This will be the first mass transit project in the history of Puerto Rico. The new train system is designed to bring a fast and easy mode of transportation to the most congested areas of metropolitan San Juan. Trains will run every 4 minutes during peak hours in morning and afternoon. The line is expected to carry some 115,000 passengers daily. For more information, call © **787/765-0927.**

or yellow posts that say *parada*. Bus terminals in San Juan are in the dock area and at Plaza de Colón. A typical fare is 25¢ to 50¢. The higher fee is for the faster buses that make fewer stops; call for more information about routes and schedules.

Taxis are metered; tips between 10% and 15% of the fare are customary. The initial charge for destinations in the city is $1, plus 10¢ for each ¹⁄₁₀ mile (.16km) and 50¢ for every suitcase, with a minimum fare of $3. Taxis are invariably lined up outside the entrance to most of the island's hotels, and if not, a staff member can almost always call one for you. If you want to arrange a taxi on your own, call the **Mejor Cab Company** (© **787/723-2460**). If you want to take a cab to a destination outside the city, you must negotiate a flat fee with the driver. For complaints or questions, contact the **Public Service Commission** (© **787/751-5050**), which regulates cabs.

FAST FACTS   One of the most centrally located **pharmacies** is the **Puerto Rico Drug Co.,** Calle San Francisco 157 (© **787/725-2202**), in Old San Juan; open Monday to Friday from 7am to 9:30pm, Saturday from 8am to 9:30pm, and Sunday from 8:30am to 7:30pm. **Walgreen's,** 1130 Ashford Ave., Condado (© **787/725-1510**), is a 24-hour pharmacy.

In a **medical emergency,** call © **787/721-2116.** Ashford Memorial Community Hospital, 1451 Ashford Ave. (© **787/721-2160**), maintains a 24-hour emergency room.

American Express services are handled by the **Travel Network,** 1035 Ashford Ave., Condado (© **787/725-0960**). The office is open Monday to Friday from 9am to 5pm and on Saturday from 9 to 11am.

ACCOMMODATIONS

All hotel rooms on Puerto Rico are subject to a 7% to 9% tax, which is not included in the rates listed in this chapter. Most hotels also impose a 10% service charge. Before you book a hotel, refer back to the section "Package Deals" in chapter 2. Packages can save you a lot of money, especially if you want to stay at one of the big resorts.

IN OLD SAN JUAN

El Convento ⋆   This landmark is back. Puerto Rico's most famous hotel had deteriorated into a shabby version of its former self, but it came majestically back to life when it was restored and reopened in 1997. Built in 1651, this hotel in the heart of the old city was once the New World's first Carmelite convent. Over the years El Convento played many roles when it ceased being a convent—everything from dance hall to flophouse to parking lot for garbage trucks. Rescued from ruin, it opened as a hotel, thanks to backing by the Woolworth

San Juan

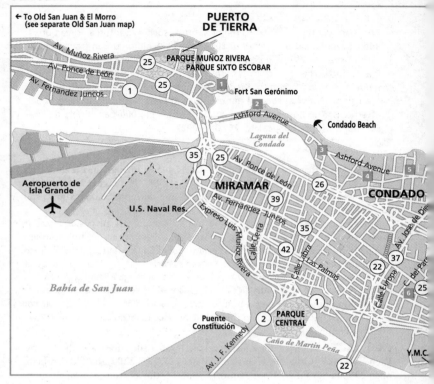

← To Old San Juan & El Morro
(see separate Old San Juan map)

PUERTO
DE TIERRA

Av. Muñoz Rivera

PARQUE MUÑOZ RIVERA
PARQUE SIXTO ESCOBAR

Av. Ponce de León

Av. Fernandez Juncos

Fort San Gerónimo

Ashford Avenue

Condado Beach

Laguna del
Condado

Ashford Avenue

Aeropuerto de
Isla Grande

Av. Ponce de León

MIRAMAR

CONDADO

U.S. Naval Res.

Av. Fernandez Juncos

Expreso Luis Muñoz Rivera

Calle Cerra

Calle Labra

Las Palmas

Av. José de Diego

Calle Europa

C. del Parque

Bahía de San Juan

Puente
Constitución

PARQUE
CENTRAL

Av. J. F. Kennedy

Caño de Martín Peña

Y.M.C.

family, in 1962, but didn't make money and was seized by the government for back taxes.

Now restored at the cost of around $275,000 per room, El Convento offers some of the most charming and historic hotel experiences anywhere in the Caribbean. Handcrafted in Spain, room furnishings are in traditional Spanish style, with mahogany beams, elaborate dark-stained paneling, and handmade terra-cotta tile floors. Each unit contains doubles or twins, each fitted with a comfortable mattress and fine linen, and such extras as VCRs and stereos. The small bathrooms contain scales, second phones, and shower/tub combinations. The interior courtyard is again open to the sky, as it was in the 1600s. Of course, you won't have the same resort facilities here that you'd find in a blockbuster hotel on the Condado or in Isla Verde. The lower two floors feature a collection of shops, bars, and restaurants.

100 Cristo St., San Juan, PR 00901. ✆ 800/468-2779 or 787/723-9020. Fax 787/721-2877. www.el convento.com. 58 units. Winter $315–$375 double, from $500 suite. Off-season $220–$285 double, from $400 suite. AE, DC, DISC, MC, V. Parking $10. Bus: Old Town trolley. **Amenities:** 3 restaurants, 2 bars; pool; Jacuzzi; fitness center; massage. *In room:* A/C, TV, VCR, stereo, coffeemaker, hair dryer, iron and ironing board, safe.

Gallery Inn at Galería San Juan ★ *Finds*   This hotel's location and ambience are unbeatable. We suggest booking one of the least expensive doubles here— even the least expensive units are fairly roomy and attractively furnished, with good beds and small but adequate bathrooms, some with shower, some with tub.

To Isla Verde →

Set on a hilltop in the Old Town, with a sweeping sea view, this unusual hotel contains a maze of verdant courtyards. In the 1700s, it was the home of an aristocratic Spanish family. Today, it's one of the most whimsically bohemian hotels in the Caribbean. All courtyards and rooms are adorned with hundreds of sculptures, silk-screens, or original paintings, usually for sale. The nearest beach is a 15-minute ride away, however.

Calle Norzagaray 204–206, San Juan, PR 00901. © 787/722-1808. Fax 787/722-1808. www.thegallery inn.com. 22 units. Year-round $145–$270 double; $350 suite. Rates include continental breakfast. AE, DC, MC, V. There are 6 free parking spaces, plus parking on the street. Bus: Old Town trolley. **Amenities:** Breakfast dining room. *In room:* A/C, hair dryer, safe.

Wyndham Old San Juan Hotel & Casino ★ Opened in 1997, this dignified nine-story waterfront hotel is part of a $100 million renovation of San Juan's cruise-port facilities. Most (but not all) of the major cruise ships dock nearby, making this a worthwhile choice if you want to spend time in San Juan before boarding a ship.

Upper floors of this hotel are closely attuned to hotel guests. But on days when cruise ships pull into port, the lobby and its bars are likely to be jammed with passengers. The hotel's triangular floor plan surrounds an inner courtyard that floods light into the tasteful and comfortable beige-and-white bedrooms, each of which has two phone lines and a modem connection for laptop computers. Other than that, the rooms lack character and are a bit bandboxy and small, although each comes with a comfortable bed, plus a compact bathroom with shower and tub. Think of a typical Holiday Inn geared for business travelers instead of a luxury resort. If you want Old Town character and atmosphere head for the El Convento instead. Most of the lobby level is devoted to a 10,000-square-foot (900 sq. m) casino. The upscale dining room serves a perfectly fine if unremarkable international cuisine with some regional specialties.

100 Brumbaugh St., San Juan, PR 00902. ⓒ **800/996-3426** or 787/721-5100. Fax 787/721-1111. www.wyndham.com. 240 units. Winter $230–$340 double; $290–$390 suite. Off-season $135–$200 double; $185–$290 suite. AE, DC, DISC, MC, V. Free parking; valet parking $15. Bus: A7. **Amenities:** 8 restaurants, 14 bars, nightclub; casino; 2 pools; 3 tennis courts; fitness center; 5 Jacuzzis; room service (6:30am–11:30pm). *In room:* A/C, TV, minibar, coffeemaker, hair dryer, iron.

IN PUERTO DE TIERRA

Caribe Hilton ★★   After rivers of money were poured into its radical renovation, this deluxe hotel is one of the most up-to-date spa and convention hotels in San Juan.

Thanks to an unusual configuration of natural barriers and legal maneuverings, the hotel has the only private beach on the island (and the only garden incorporating an antique naval installation, the semi-ruined colonial Fort San Gerónimo). The Caribe's size (17 acres/7 hectares of parks and gardens) and sprawling facilities often attract conventions and tour groups. Only the Condado Plaza and the Hotel El San Juan rival it for nonstop activity.

Rooms were radically upgraded in the late 1990s; variations in price are a function of the views outside and the amenities within. Each room has a larger-than-expected bathroom with a shower/tub combination, and comfortable tropical-inspired furniture. In the Caribe Terrace Bar, you can order the bartender's celebrated piña colada, which was once enjoyed by the likes of movie legends Joan Crawford and Errol Flynn. A newly restored oceanfront spa and fitness center is the only beachside spa in Puerto Rico, featuring such tantalizing delights as couples massages, body wraps, hydrotherapy tub treatments, and soothing cucumber sun therapies. A 12,400-square-foot (1,116 sq. m) casino is adjacent to the lobby atrium area.

Calle Los Rosales, San Juan, PR 00902. ⓒ **800/HILTONS** in the U.S. and Canada, or 787/721-0303. Fax 787/725-8849. www.caribehilton.com. 644 units. Winter $265–$405 double, $325–$1,000 suite. Off-season $154–$303 double, $270–$900 suite Children 16 and under stay free in parents' room (maximum 4 people per room). AE, DC, DISC, MC, V. Self-parking $10; valet parking $20. Bus: A5. **Amenities:** 6 restaurants, 4 bars; casino; pool; 6 tennis courts; health club and spa; playground; business center (6am–1am); babysitting; laundry/dry cleaning. *In room:* A/C, TV, minibar, hair dryer, safe.

IN CONDADO

Once this was a wealthy residential area, but with the construction of El Centro, the Puerto Rico Convention Center, all that changed. Private villas were torn down to make way for high-rise hotels, restaurants, and nightclubs. The Condado shopping area, along Ashford and Magdalena avenues, became the center of an extraordinary number of boutiques. There are bus connections into Old San Juan, or you can take a taxi.

Very Expensive

Condado Plaza Hotel & Casino ★★   This is one of the busiest hotels on Puerto Rico, with enough facilities, restaurants, and distractions to keep a visitor occupied for weeks. It's a favorite of business travelers, tour groups, and conventions, but it also attracts independent travelers. The Hilton is its major rival, but we prefer this hotel's style and flair, especially after its recent $40-million overhaul. All units have private terraces and are spacious, bright, and airy, fitted with deluxe beds and mattresses, either king-size or doubles, but most often twins. The good-sized bathrooms contain shower/tub combinations. The complex's most deluxe section, the Plaza Club, has 80 units (including 5 duplex suites), a VIP lounge for guests, and private check-in/check-out.

Only Hotel El San Juan has a more dazzling array of dining options. This place is known for creating charming restaurants with culinary diversity that many local residents flock to sample. The hotel's premier restaurant, a hot ticket on San Juan's dining scene, is Cobia, winner of several culinary awards.

999 Ashford Ave., San Juan, PR 00907. ⓒ 800/468-8588 in the U.S., or 787/721-1000. Fax 787/721-4613. www.condadoplaza.com. 570 units. Winter $325–$475 double; $460–$1,350 suite. Off-season $225–$390 double; $350–$945 suite. AE, DC, DISC, MC, V. Valet parking $10. Bus: A7. **Amenities:** 6 restaurants, 3 bars; casino; 3 pools; 2 tennis courts; health club and spa; 3 Jacuzzis; watersports; car rental; children's programs; salon; 24-hr. room service; laundry/dry cleaning. *In room:* A/C, TV, minibar, coffeemaker, hair dryer, iron and ironing board, safe.

San Juan Marriott Resort & Stellaris Casino ✪   It's the tallest building on the Condado, a 21-story landmark that Marriott spent staggering sums to renovate in a radically different format after a tragic fire gutted the premises in 1989. The current building packs in lots of postmodern style, and one of the best beaches on the Condado is right outside. Furnishings in the soaring lobby were inspired by Chippendale. If there's a flaw, it's the decor of the comfortable but bland bedrooms, with pastel colors that look washed out when compared to the rich mahoganies and jewel tones of the rooms in the rival Condado Plaza Hotel. Nonetheless, the units here boast one of the most advanced telephone networks on the island, and good security and fire-prevention systems. They're generally spacious, with good views of the water, and each comes with a tiled bathroom with a shower/tub combination. We suggest having only one dinner in-house—at Ristorante Tuscany; see "Dining," below.

1309 Ashford Ave., San Juan, PR 00907. ⓒ 800/464-5005 or 787/722-7000. Fax 787/722-6800. www. marriottpr.com. 538 units. Winter $205–$340 double. Off-season $180–$225 double. Year-round $610 suite. Suite rate includes breakfast. AE, DC, DISC, MC, V. Parking $10. Bus: B21. **Amenities:** 3 restaurants, 2 bars; casino; 2 pools; 2 tennis courts; health club; Jacuzzi; sauna; concierge; tour desk; car rental; salon; 24-hr. room service; babysitting; laundry/dry cleaning. *In room:* A/C, TV, minibar, hair dryer, coffeemaker, iron and ironing board, safe.

Moderate

El Canario by the Lagoon Hotel   A relaxing, informal European-style hotel, El Canario is in a quiet residential neighborhood just a short block from Condado Beach. This is one of the better B&Bs in the area, although it still charges affordable rates. The hotel is very much in the Condado styling, which evokes Miami Beach in the 1960s. The bedrooms are generous in size and have balconies. Most of them have twin beds and bathrooms are sleek and contemporary, with shower stalls and enough space to spread out your stuff. If the hotel doesn't have room for you, it can book you into its sibling properties, either El Canario Inn or El Canario by the Sea.

Calle Clemenceau 4, Condado, San Juan, PR 00907. ⓒ 800/533-2649 in the U.S., or 787/722-5058. Fax 787/723-8590. www.canariohotels.com. 40 units. Winter $145 double. Off-season $90.50–$105 double. Rates include continental breakfast and morning newspaper. AE, DISC, MC, V. Bus: B-21 or C-10. **Amenities:** Access to health club; tour desk; laundry. *In room:* A/C, TV, safe.

Inexpensive

At Wind Chimes Inn ✪   This restored and renovated Spanish manor, 1 short block from the beach and 3½ miles (5km) from the airport, is one of the best guesthouses on the Condado. Upon entering a tropical patio, you'll find tile tables surrounded by palm trees and bougainvillea. There's plenty of space on the deck and a covered lounge for relaxing, socializing, and eating breakfast. Dozens of decorative wind chimes add melody to the daily breezes. The good-sized rooms offer a choice of size, beds, and kitchens; all contain ceiling fans and air-conditioning. Beds are comfortable and come in four sizes ranging from twin to king-size. The shower-only bathrooms, though small, are efficiently laid out.

1750 Ashford Ave., Condado, San Juan, PR 00911. ✆ **800/946-3244** or 787/727-4153. Fax 787/728-0671. www.atwindchimesinn.com. 13 units. Winter $80–$129 double, $125–$140 suite. Off-season $65–$110 double, $120 suite. Rates include continental breakfast. AE, DISC, MC, V. Parking $5. Bus: B21 or A5. **Amenities:** Pool. *In room:* A/C, TV.

Casa del Caribe *Value*   Don't expect the Ritz, but if you're looking for a bargain on the Condado, this is it. This renovated guesthouse was built in the 1940s, later expanded, then totally refurbished with a tropical decor late in 1995. A very Puerto Rican ambience has been created, with emphasis on Latin hospitality and comfort. On a shady side street just off Ashford Avenue, behind a wall and garden, you'll discover Casa del Caribe's wraparound veranda. The small but cozy guest rooms have ceiling fans and air-conditioners, and most feature original Puerto Rican art. The bedrooms are most inviting, with comfortable furnishings and efficiently organized shower-only bathrooms. The front porch is a social center for guests, and you can also cook out at a barbecue area. The beach is a 2-minute walk away, and the hotel is also within walking distance of some mega-resorts with their glittering casinos.

Calle Caribe 57, San Juan, PR 00907. ✆ **787/722-7139.** Fax 787/723-2575. 13 units. Winter $72–$130 double. Off-season $55–$99 double. Rates include continental breakfast. AE, DISC, MC, V. Parking $5. Bus: B21. **Amenities:** Babysitting; laundry/dry cleaning. *In room:* A/C, TV.

IN OCEAN PARK

Hostería del Mar ✿   Lying a few blocks from the Condado casinos are the white walls of this distinctive landmark. It's in a residential seaside community that's popular with locals looking for beach action on weekends. The hotel boasts medium-size ocean-view rooms. Those on the second floor have balconies; those on the first floor open onto patios. The guest-room decor is invitingly tropical, with wicker furniture, good beds, pastel prints, and ceiling fans, plus small but efficient bathrooms, some with shower, some with tub. The most popular unit is no. 208, with a king-size bed, private balcony, kitchenette, and a view of the beach, idyllic for a honeymoon. There's no pool, but a full-service restaurant here is known for its vegetarian, macrobiotic, and Puerto Rican plates, all freshly made. The place is simple, yet with its own elegance, and the hospitality is warm.

1 Tapia St., Ocean Park, Santurce, San Juan, PR 00911. ✆ **877/727-3302.** or 787/727-3302. Fax 787/268-0772. www.travelguides.com/inns/full/PR/1704.html. 8 units. Winter $75–$125 double without ocean view; $165–$185 double with ocean view; $195–$240 apt. Off-season, $75–$90 double without ocean view; $120–$130 double with ocean view; $185–195 apt. Children age 11 and under stay free in parents' room. AE, DC, DISC, MC, V. Bus: A5. **Amenities:** Restaurant, room service, babysitting; laundry/dry cleaning. *In room:* A/C, TV, coffeemaker (in some), safe.

Número Uno Guest House ✿   As a translation of its name implies, this is the best of the small-scale, low-rise guesthouses in Ocean Park. It was originally built in the 1950s in a prestigious residential neighborhood adjacent to the wide sands of Ocean Park Beach, on a knoll that avoids the occasional flooding that's the curse of other homes nearby. Much of this is thanks to the owner, Ester Feliciano, who cultivates a garden within her walled compound, replete with fountains, a small swimming pool, and manicured shrubbery and palms.

Stylish-looking bedrooms contain white tile floors, wicker furniture, and comfortable beds, plus tiled, shower-only bathrooms. Two of the units are apartments, suitable for families. Some repeat guests, many of whom are gay, refer to it as their fantasy version of a private villa beside a superb and usually convivial beach.

Calle Santa Ana 1, Ocean Park, San Juan PR 00911. ℂ **787/726-5010.** Fax 787/727-5482. 13 units. Winter $115–$135 double, $265 apt. Off-season $60–$80 double, $165 apt. $20 each additional occupant of a double room. Rates include continental breakfast. AE, MC, V. Bus: A5. **Amenities:** Restaurant, bar; pool; babysitting. *In room:* A/C, TV, minibar, hair dryer, iron, safe.

IN ISLA VERDE

Isla Verde, right on the beach, is closer to the airport than the other sections of San Juan, but it's farther from Old Town. Some of the Caribbean's most upscale hotels are here. If you plan to spend most of your time on the beach rather than exploring the city, consider one of the following hotels.

Very Expensive

Intercontinental San Juan Resort & Casino ⭐   Today, thanks to an extensive $15.2 million restoration, this resort competes with El San Juan Hotel next door, but doesn't overtake it. You'll get the sense of living in a sophisticated beach resort rather than a hotel where the sun rises and sets around the whims of high-rolling gamblers.

Most of the comfortable, medium-size rooms have balconies and terraces and tastefully conservative furnishings with a lot of pizzazz. Top floor rooms are the most expensive, even though they lack balconies. Bathrooms have power showerheads, deep tubs, and scales. The most desirable units are in the Plaza Club, a mini-hotel within the hotel that sports a private entrance, concierge service, complimentary food and beverage buffets, and suite/spa and beach facilities. Dining within any of this hotel's six restaurants merits attention, although the choice is vaster at the neighboring El San Juan Hotel.

5961 Isla Verde Ave., Isla Verde, PR 00937. ℂ **800/443-2009** in the U.S., or 787/791-6100. Fax 787/253-2510. www.intercontinentalsj.com. 400 units. Winter $269–$489 double; $409–$1,699 suite. Off-season $199–$339 double; $279–$450 suite. AE, DC, DISC, MC, V. Self-parking $10; valet parking $15. Bus: A7, M7, or T1. **Amenities:** 6 restaurants, 3 bars; the Caribbean's largest free-form pool; gym; scuba diving; limousine service; business center; room service (6am–2pm and 5pm–2am); massage; baby sitting; laundry/dry cleaning. *In room:* A/C, TV, coffeemaker, hair dryer, iron and ironing board, safe.

Ritz-Carlton San Juan Spa & Casino ⭐⭐⭐   The Ritz-Carlton is one of the most spectacular deluxe hotels in the Caribbean. Set on 8 acres (3 hectares) of prime beachfront, within a 5-minute drive from the airport, it was designed to appeal to both business travelers and vacationers. The hotel decor reflects Caribbean flavor and the Hispanic culture of the island, with artwork from prominent local artists. More visible, however, is an emphasis on continental elegance. Some of the most opulent public areas anywhere include wrought-iron balustrades and crystal chandeliers.

Beautifully furnished guest rooms open onto ocean views or the gardens of nearby condos. Rooms are very large, with excellent furnishings, fine linen, and data ports. The bathrooms are exceptionally plush, with shower/tub combinations, scales, bathrobes, and deluxe toiletries. Some rooms are accessible for guests with disabilities. Preferred accommodations are in the 9th-floor Ritz-Carlton Club, which has a private lounge and personal concierge staff.

The scope and diversity of dining here is second only to the El San Juan, and as for top-shelf dining venues, the Ritz-Carlton has no equal. The Vineyard

Room is one of the finest restaurants in San Juan. The hotel has the Caribbean's largest casino (see later in this chapter).

6961 avenida de los Gobernadores, no. 187, Isla Verde, Carolina, PR 00979. © 800/241-3333 or 787/253-1700. Fax 787/253-0700. www.ritzcarlton.com. 414 units. Winter $199–$299 double. Off-season $279–$399 double. Year-round from $975 suite. AE, DC, DISC, MC, V. Valet parking $15. Bus: A7, M7, or T1. **Amenities:** 3 restaurants, 3 bars, nightclub; large casino; 7,200-square-foot (648m) pool; 2 tennis courts; gym; children's programs; salon; 24-hr. room service; babysitting; laundry/dry cleaning. *In room:* A/C, TV, minibar, hair dryer, iron, safe.

The Water Club ★★★ A refreshing change from the mega-chain resorts of San Juan, this ultra-chic hotel is hip and contemporary. It's the city's only "boutique hotel" on a beach. We find much to praise at this small and exclusive hotel because of its highly personalized and well-trained staff. Although avant-garde, the design is not daringly provocative. Behind glass are "waterfalls," even on the elevators, and inventive theatrical-style lighting is used to bring the outdoors inside. The one-of-a-kind glass art doors are from Murano, the fabled center of glassmaking outside Venice. Overlooking Isla Verde's best beach area, all the bedrooms are spacious, opening onto views of the water and containing custom-designed beds positioned to face the ocean. Bathrooms are tiled and elegant, with shower/tub combinations. Unique features are the open-air 11th-floor exotic bar with the Caribbean's only rooftop fireplace. The pool is a level above; it's like swimming in an ocean in the sky.

Jose M. Tartak St. 2, Isla Verde, Puerto Rico 00979. © 888/265-6699 or 787/253-0100. Fax 787/253-0220. www.waterclubsanjuan. Winter $395–$485 double, $995 suite. Off-season $205–$310 double, $825 suite. AE, DC, MC, V. Bus: T1 or A5. **Amenities:** Restaurant, 2 bars; pool; Jacuzzi; fitness center; room service; babysitting; laundry/dry cleaning . *In room:* A/C, TV, minibar, hair dryer, safe.

Wyndham El San Juan Hotel & Casino ★★★ *Kids*   One of the best hotels in Puerto Rico, this place evokes Havana in its heyday. Built in the 1950s, it was restored with an infusion of millions—some $80 million in 1997 and 1998 alone. It's also a great choice for (well-to-do) families, with lots of activities for children. The beachfront hotel is surrounded by 350 palms, century-old banyans, and gardens. Its 700-yard-long (637m) sandy beach is the finest in the San Juan area. The hotel's river pool, with its currents, cascades, and lagoons, evokes a jungle stream, and the lobby is the most opulent and memorable in the Caribbean. Entirely sheathed in red marble and hand-carved mahogany paneling, the public rooms stretch on almost endlessly.

The large, well-decorated rooms have intriguing touches of high-tech; each contains three phones and a VCR. Bedrooms are the ultimate in luxury in San Juan with honey-hued woods and rattans and king-size or double beds. Bathrooms have all the amenities, shower/tub combinations; a few feature Jacuzzis. About 150 of the units, designed as comfortable bungalows, are in the outer reaches of the garden. Known as *casitas,* they include Roman tubs, atrium showers, and access to the fern-lined paths of a tropical jungle a few steps away. A 17-story, $60 million wing with 120 suites, all oceanfront, was completed late in 1998. The ultra-luxury tower features 103 one- or two-bedroom units, 8 garden suites, 5 governor's suites, and 4 presidential suites.

No other hotel in the Caribbean offers such a rich diversity of dining options and such high-quality food. Japanese, Italian, Mexican, and 24-hour American/Caribbean restaurants are just a few of the choices.

6063 Isla Verde Ave., San Juan, PR 00979. © 800/468-2818 or 787/791-1000. Fax 787/791-0390. www. wyndham.com. 389 units. Winter $415–$565 double; from $625 suite. Off-season $145–$495 double; from $515 suite. AE, DC, DISC, MC, V. Self-parking $10; valet parking $15. Bus: A7, M7, or T1. **Amenities:** 8 restaurants,

3 bars; 2 pools; tennis courts; health club and spa; steam room; sauna; watersports; children's club; 24-hr. room service; massage; babysitting; dry cleaning. *In room:* A/C, TV, minibar, coffeemaker, hair dryer, safe.

DINING

IN OLD SAN JUAN

Very Expensive

Chef Marisol ✿✿ INTERNATIONAL   Marisol Hernández is one of the top chefs of Puerto Rico. Trained in Hilton properties, including one in London, she broke away to become an independent restaurateur in Old San Juan. In a Spanish colonial building, with a courtyard patio for dining, her eight-table restaurant is warm and intimate. Service is low key and slightly formal. Her list of appetizers is Old Town's finest selection, including peppers stuffed with codfish and a creamy Italian polenta with a wild mushroom fricassee. One of our favorite dishes here is the Cajun spiced blackened shrimp and andouille sausages with linguini or the loin of veal medallions with shiitake mushrooms and oven-dried tomatoes. Another delight is the curried chicken breast with basmati rice and a homemade mango chutney.

Calle del Cristo 202. ✆ 787/725-7454. Reservations required. Main courses $25–$40. AE, MC, V. Thurs–Sat noon–2:30pm; Tues–Sun 7–10pm. Bus: A7, T1, or 2.

Expensive

Parrot Club ✿✿ PUERTO RICAN   The hottest restaurant in Old San Juan is this bistro and bar serving a Nuevo Latino cuisine that blends traditional Puerto Rican cookery with Spanish, Taíno, and African influences. It's set in a stately-looking 1902 building that was originally a hair-tonic factory. Today, you'll find a cheerful-looking dining room where San Juan's mayor and the governor of Puerto Rico can sometimes be spotted, and a verdantly landscaped courtyard where tables for at least 200 diners are scattered amid potted ferns, palms, and orchids. Live music, either Brazilian, salsa, or Latino jazz, is offered nightly, as well as during the popular Sunday brunches.

Menu items are updated interpretations of old-fashioned Puerto Rican specialties. They include ceviche of halibut, salmon, tuna, and mahi-mahi; delicious crab cakes; *criolla*-style flank steak; and pan-seared tuna served with a sauce made from dark rum and essence of oranges. Everybody's favorite drink is a "parrot passion," made from lemon-flavored rum, triple sec, oranges, and passion fruit.

Calle Fortaleza 363. ✆ 787/725-7370. Reservations not accepted. Main courses $17–$29 at dinner, $12–$20 at lunch. AE, DC, MC, V. Daily 11:30am–3pm and 6–11pm. Closed 2 weeks in July. Bus: Old Town Trolley.

Trois Cent Onze ✿ FRENCH/INTERNATIONAL   This former film studio lures some of the most demanding foodies to its Art Deco surroundings. A European-style eatery is the realization of a life-long dream of Sylma Pérez and Christophe Gourdain. The bill of fare offers a variety of dishes half influenced by the light, provincial cuisine of southern France. Other dishes evoke the provinces of Normandy and Burgundy. The repertoire reflects a commitment to creative flavors. We like such appetizers as a delightful tuna tartare marinated in olive oil and lemon juice, or avocado stuffed with tomato, basil, and balsamic vinaigrette. From the extensive list of main courses, you can select such delicacies as roasted baby chicken with herbs and olive oil, perhaps the roast rack of lamb with potato crust, and most definitely the Maine lobster stew with a mushroom gratin.

Calle Fortaleza 311. ✆ 787/725-7959. Reservations required. Main courses $14.50–$29.50. AE, DISC, MC, V. July–Dec 15 Tues–Thurs 6–10:30pm, Fri–Sat 6–11:30pm, Sun noon–4pm (brunch) and 4–10pm (dinner). Dec 16–June Mon–Thurs 6–10:30pm, Fri–Sat 6–11:30pm, Sun noon–4pm (brunch) and 4–10pm (dinner). Bus: T1 or 2.

Moderate

Amadeus ✦ CARIBBEAN   Housed in a brick-and-stone building that was constructed in the 18th century by a wealthy merchant, Amadeus offers Caribbean ingredients with a nouvelle twist. The appetizers alone are worth the trip here, especially the Amadeus dumplings with guava sauce and arrowroot fritters. The chef will even prepare a smoked-salmon-and-caviar pizza. One zesty specialty is pork scaloppini with sweet-and-sour sauce.

Calle San Sebastián 106 (across from the Iglesia de San José). ✆ **787/722-8635**. Reservations recommended. Main courses $12–$26. AE, MC, V. Mon 6pm–2am, Tues–Sun noon–2am (kitchen closes at midnight). Bus: M2, M3, or A5.

Carli Café Concierto ✦ INTERNATIONAL   This stylish restaurant at the base of the Banco Popular building in Old San Juan is a new arena for the music of owner Carli Muñoz. The gold disc hanging on the walls attests to Carli's success in his previous role as a pianist for The Beach Boys. Nowadays, he entertains his dinner guests with a combination of standards, romantic jazz, and original material on his grand piano. Diners can choose to sit outside on the Plazoleta, where they can enjoy a panoramic view of the bay, or they can eat inside against a backdrop of a tasteful decor of terra-cotta walls, black marble tables, and a black-and-white tiled floor. The chef tempts visitors with an imaginative international menu, including such delights as a quail rockettes stuffed with dried fruits and sage or else a classic filet mignon with wild mushrooms. The filet of salmon and a mouth-watering rack of lamb are among the finest main dishes. Carli plays every night. The bar, with its mahogany and brass fittings, is an ideal spot to kick back and chill out.

Edificio Banco Popular, Plazoleta Rafael Carrion, calle Recinto Sur. ✆ **787/725-4927**. Reservations recommended. Main courses $17–$29. AE, MC, V. Mon–Thurs 4–11:30pm, Fri–Sat 4pm–1:30am. Bus: M2 or M3.

La Mallorquina PUERTO RICAN   This is San Juan's oldest restaurant, founded in 1848, and it has been run by the Rojos family since 1900. If you look carefully at the floor adjacent to the old-fashioned mahogany bar, you'll see the building's original gray-and-white marble flooring that the owners are laboriously restoring, square foot by square foot, to its original condition. Lunches here tend to attract a following of local office workers; dinners are more cosmopolitan and more leisurely, with many residents of the Condado and other modern neighborhoods selecting this place specifically because of its old-fashioned, old-world charm.

The food has changed little here over the decades, with special emphasis on *asopao* made with rice and either chicken, shrimp, or lobster and shrimp. *Arroz con pollo* (rice with chicken) is almost as popular. Begin with either garlic soup or gazpacho, end with a flan, and you'll have composed a meal that's authentically Puerto Rican.

Calle San Justo 207. ✆ **787/722-3261**. Reservations not accepted at lunch, recommended at dinner. Dinner main courses $14.95–$36 (highest price is for lobster). AE, MC, V. Mon–Sat noon–10pm. Closed Sept. Bus: Old Town Trolley.

Inexpensive

Hard Rock Cafe AMERICAN   If you must, here it is. On days when cruise ships pull into port (usually Tues and Sun), the place is likely to be mobbed.

Calle Recinto Sur 253. ✆ **787/724-7625**. Burgers, sandwiches, and platters $7–$21.99. AE, DISC, DC, MC, V. Daily 11am–11pm. Bus: Old Town Trolley.

La Bombonera ✦ *Value* PUERTO RICAN   This place offers exceptional value in its homemade pastries, well-stuffed sandwiches, and endless cups of coffee and has done so since 1902. Its atmosphere evokes turn-of-the-century Castile transplanted to the New World. The food is authentically Puerto Rican, homemade, and inexpensive, with regional dishes like rice with squid, roast leg of pork, and seafood *asopao*. For dessert, you might select an apple, pineapple, or prune pie, or one of many types of flan. Service is polite, if a bit rushed, and the place fills up quickly at lunchtime.

Calle San Francisco 259. ✆ 787/722-0658. Reservations recommended. American breakfast $4–$8; main courses $6.95–$14.95. AE, DISC, MC, V. Daily 7:30am–8pm. Bus: M2 or M3.

IN CONDADO
Very Expensive

La Belle Epoque ★★★ FUSION/FRENCH   Twice in recent years, master chef Jeremie Cruz has been voted "Caribbean Chef of the Year," and he currently reigns supreme as Puerto Rico's greatest talent in the kitchen. Expect spectacular dining at this elegant enclave of exquisitely prepared cuisine. The Condado setting is one of Murano chandeliers, hand-painted custom-made plates, and Italian damask tablecloths. In addition to two exquisite dining rooms, there is also a Smoker Terrace with a wide collection of fine cigars, plus a cozy wine cellar with a selection of more than 1,000 vintage bottles. Even a basic onion soup for an appetizer is prepared with flair, although you can order more luxurious concoctions such as lobster bisque. Another starter might be in seafood mousse resting under a brown potato crust or perhaps a watercress and arugula salad studded with walnuts and savory bits of blue cheese. For a main course, opt for the poached salmon with "lobster potatoes," one of the best dishes we've ever sampled here. Other options might include a classic coq au vin (chicken with wine) given added dimension by the use of wild mushrooms, or else seared bay scallops with spinach and a saffron-laced mussel sauce. Between courses a palate cleanser is served, a refreshing fermented cider with frozen white grapes. Desserts are among the most unusual, delicious, and imaginative on island— take the lemongrass soup with sorbet, pieces of fresh fruit, and candied carrots.

Casabella Building, 1400 Magdalena Ave., Condado. ✆ 787/977-1765. Reservations required. Main courses $17–$25. AE, MC, V. Mon–Sat noon–3pm and 5–11pm. Bus: B21.

Pikayo ★★★ PUERTO RICAN/CAJUN   This is an ideal place to go for the new generation of Puerto Rican cookery, with a touch of Cajun thrown in for spice and zest. This place not only keeps up with the latest culinary trends, but often sets them, thanks to the inspired guidance of owner and celebrity chef Wilo Benet. Formal but not stuffy, and winner of more culinary awards than virtually any other restaurant in Puerto Rico, Pikayo is a specialist in the *criolla* cuisine of the colonial age, emphasizing the Spanish, Indian, and African elements in its unusual recipes. Appetizers include a dazzling array of taste explosions: witness shrimp spring rolls with a peanut sofrito sauce; crab cake with aïoli; or perhaps a ripe plantain, goat cheese, and onion tart. Main course delights feature charred rare yellowfin tuna with an onion escabeche or red snapper fillet with sweet potato purée served with foie gras butter. Our favorite remains the grilled shrimp with polenta and a barbecue sauce made with guava.

Museum of Art of Puerto Rico, 299 De Diego Ave. ✆ 787/721-6194. Reservations recommended. Main courses $29–$34; set-price menus $65. AE, DC, MC, V. Tues–Sun noon–3pm, Tues–Sat 6–11pm. Closed 2 weeks in Dec–Jan. Bus: M2, A7, or T1.

Ramiro's ★ SPANISH/INTERNATIONAL   This restaurant boasts the most imaginative menu on the Condado. Its refined "New Creole" cooking is a style pioneered by owner and chef Jesús Ramiro. You might begin with breadfruit *mille-feuille* with local crabmeat and avocado. For your main course, any fresh fish or meat can be charcoal-grilled for you on request. Some of the latest menu specialties include paillard of lamb with spiced root vegetables and guava sauce, charcoal-grilled black Angus steak with shiitake mushrooms, or grilled striped sea bass with a citrus sauce. Among the many homemade desserts are caramelized mango on puff pastry with strawberry-and-guava sauce, and "four seasons" chocolate.

Ave. Magdalena 1106. ✆ **787/721-9049**. Reservations recommended off-season, required in winter. Main courses $23–$40. AE, DC, MC, V. Sun–Fri noon–3pm and 6–10pm; Mon–Fri noon–3pm and 6:30–11pm; Sat 6:30–11pm. Bus: A7, T1, or M2.

Expensive

Ajili Mojili ✦ PUERTO RICAN/CREOLE   This restaurant is devoted exclusively to *la cucina criolla,* the starchy, down-home cuisine that developed on the island a century ago. It's set in the heart of the Condado tourist strip, across from the convention center. Though the building housing it is quite modern, look for artful replicas of the kind of crumbling brick walls you'd expect in Old San Juan, and a bar that evokes Old Spain. The staff will willingly describe menu items in colloquial English. Locals come here for a taste of the food they enjoyed at their mother's knee, like *mofongos* (green plantains stuffed with veal, chicken, shrimp, or pork), *arroz con pollo* (stewed chicken with saffron rice), *medallones de cerdo encebollado* (pork loin sautéed with onions), *carne mechada* (beef rib eye stuffed with ham), and *lechon asado con maposteado* (roast pork with rice and beans). Wash it all down with an ice-cold bottle of local beer.

1052 Ashford Ave. (at the corner of Calle Joffre). ✆ **787/725-9195**. Reservations recommended. Main courses $16–$35. Children's menu $5.95. AE, MC, V. Mon–Fri 11:30am–3pm; Mon–Sat 6–10pm; Sun 12:30–4pm and 6–10pm. Bus: B21.

Chayote's ✦ PUERTO RICAN/INTERNATIONAL   The cuisine of this restaurant is among the most innovative in San Juan. It draws local business leaders, government officials, and celebs like Sylvester Stallone and Melanie Griffith. It's an artsy, modern, basement-level bistro in a surprisingly obscure hotel (the Olimpo). The restaurant changes its menu every 3 months, but you might find appetizers like a yucca turnover stuffed with crabmeat and served with a mango and papaya chutney, or a ripe plantain stuffed with chicken and served with a fresh tomato sauce. For a main dish, you might try a red snapper fillet with a citrus vinaigrette made of passion fruit, orange, and lemon. An exotic touch appears in the pork fillet seasoned with dried fruits and spices in a tamarind sauce and served with a green banana and taro root timbale. To finish off your meal, there's nothing better than the mango flan served with macerated strawberries.

In the Olimpo Hotel, Ave. Miramar 603. ✆ **787/722-9385**. Reservations recommended. Main courses $21–$28. AE, MC, V. Tues–Fri noon–2:30pm; Tues–Sat 7–10:30pm. Bus: 5.

La Compostela ✦ INTERNATIONAL   This restaurant offers formal service from a battalion of well-dressed waiters. Established by a Galician-born family, the pine-trimmed restaurant has gained a reputation as one of the best in the capital. The chef made his name on the roast peppers stuffed with salmon mousse. Equally delectable is duck with orange and ginger sauce or baby rack of lamb with fresh herbs. Of course, any shellfish grilled in a brandy sauce is a sure winner. The chef also makes two different versions of paella, both savory. The wine cellar, comprised of some 10,000 bottles, is one of the most impressive in San Juan.

Avenida Condado 106. **787/724-6088.** Reservations required. Main courses $23.95–$38.95. AE, MC, V. Mon–Fri noon–2:30pm; Mon–Sat 6:30–10:30pm. Bus: M2.

Ristorante Tuscany ✿ NORTHERN ITALIAN   This is the showcase restaurant of one of the most elaborate hotel reconstructions in the history of Puerto Rico, and the kitchen continues to rack up culinary awards. Try grilled veal chops with shallots and a glaze of Madeira, or grilled chicken breast in a cream sauce with chestnuts, asparagus, and brandy, surrounded with fried artichokes. The seafood selections are excellent, especially the fresh red snapper sautéed in olive oil, garlic, parsley, and lemon juice. The risottos are the finest on the island, especially the one made with seafood and herbs. The cold and hot appetizers are virtual meals unto themselves, with such favorites as grilled polenta with sausages or fresh neck clams and mussels simmered in herb-flavored tomato broth.

In the San Juan Marriott Resort, 1309 Ashford Ave. **787/722-7000.** Reservations recommended. Main courses $19.50–$34. AE, DC, DISC, MC, V. Daily 6–11pm. Bus: B21.

Zabó ✿ INTERNATIONAL   This restaurant enjoys citywide fame thanks to its blend of bucolic charm and superb innovative food. It's set in a dignified villa that provides some low-rise dignity in a sea of skyscraping condos. The creative force here is owner and chef/culinary director Paul Carroll, who built the place from its origins as a simple deli into one of the most sought-after restaurants on the Condado. Menu items fuse the cuisines of the Mediterranean, the Pacific Rim, and the Caribbean into a collection that includes dishes like blinis stuffed with medallions of lobster with ginger, thyme, and beurre blanc; carpaccio of salmon with mesclun salad and balsamic vinegar; and baked chorizo stuffed with mushrooms, sherry, paprika, and cheddar. The black bean soup is among the very best in Puerto Rico, served with parboiled cloves of garlic marinated in olive oil, that melt in your mouth almost like candy.

Calle Candina 14 (entrance is via an alleyway leading from Ashford Ave. between Calles Washington and Cervantes). **787/725-9494.** Reservations recommended. Main courses $19.95–$29 at dinner, $8.75–$29 at lunch. AE, MC, V. Tues–Wed 6–10pm, Thurs–Sat 6–11pm. Also Fri noon–3pm. Bus: A7.

IN SANTURCE

La Casona ✿ SPANISH/INTERNATIONAL   In a turn-of-the-century mansion surrounded by gardens, La Casona offers the kind of dining usually found in Madrid, complete with a strolling guitarist. The much-renovated but still charming place draws some of the most fashionable diners on Puerto Rico. Paella marinara, prepared for two or more, is a specialty, as is *zarzuela de mariscos* (seafood medley). Or you might select fillet of grouper in Basque sauce, octopus vinaigrette, *osso buco* (veal shanks), or rack of lamb. Grilled red snapper is a specialty, and you can order it with almost any sauce you want, although the chef recommends one made from olive oil, herbs, lemon, and toasted garlic. The cuisine here has both flair and flavor.

Calle San Jorge 609. **787/727-2717.** Reservations required. Main courses $17–$48. AE, DC, MC, V. Mon–Fri noon–3pm; Mon–Sat 6–11pm. Bus: 1.

IN OCEAN PARK

Pamela's ✿ CARIBBEAN FUSION   A sense of cachet and style is very pronounced at this restaurant, a fact that's somewhat surprising considering its out-of-the-way location. Part of its allure derives from a sophisticated blend of Caribbean cuisines that combines local ingredients with Puerto Rican flair and a sense of New York style. Menu items include a salad that marries vine-ripened and oven-roasted tomatoes, each drizzled with a roasted garlic and cilantro vinaigrette; club sandwiches stuffed with barbecued shrimp and cilantro-flavored mayonnaise; plantain-encrusted crab cakes with a spicy tomato-herb emulsion; and grilled island-spiced pork loin served with guava glaze and fresh local fruits. Beer or any of a wide array of party-colored drinks go well with this food.

In the Número Uno Guest House, Calle Santa Ana 1, Ocean Park. ✆ **787/726-5010.** Reservations recommended. Sandwiches and salads at lunch $10–$14. Main course platters $20–$29. AE, MC, V. Daily noon–3pm and 7–10:30pm. Bus: A5.

IN ISLA VERDE
Very Expensive

The Vineyard ★★ CALIFORNIA/MEDITERRANEAN Within the realm of *haute cuisine* served with impeccable European credentials, this is the finest restaurant in San Juan. The Vineyard Room duplicates the gourmet citadels of Italy and France more accurately than any other restaurant in Puerto Rico, thanks to a staff of culinary luminaries spearheaded by Philippe Trosch, a prize catch that Ritz-Carlton worked hard to get. The wait staff is the best trained in Puerto Rico. The wine-tasting menus, either four or five courses, are the best on the island. Select innovative appetizers like potato cannelloni filled with Caribbean lobster risotto, or a summer salad of cavallion melon, serrano ham, mozzarella, and olive pesto with ciabatta toast. The main courses are equally appealing to your taste buds: Nantucket sea bass with a barley tapenade and a black olive sabayon, or apple-smoked rabbit with a cannellini bean mash. You might precede (or end) an experience here at the bar, where the dark paneling and deep leather seats emulate an Edwardian-era men's club in London.

In the Ritz-Carlton San Juan Spa & Casino, 6961 State Rd. #187, Isla Verde, Carolina. ✆ **787/253-1700.** Reservations required. Main courses $34–$37. Fixed-price menus $45, $55, $65, $75. AE, DC, MC, V. Mon–Thurs 6–10pm, Fri–Sun 6–11pm. Bus: A7, M7, or T1.

Expensive

Back Street Hong Kong ★ MANDARIN/SZECHUAN/HUNAN To reach this restaurant, you head down a re-creation of a backwater street in Hong Kong—disassembled from its original home at the 1964 New York World's Fair, and rebuilt here with its original design intact. A few steps later, you enter one of the best Chinese restaurants in the Caribbean, serving consistently good food, filled with fragrance and flavor. Beneath a soaring redwood ceiling, you can enjoy pineapple fried rice served in a pineapple, scallops with orange sauce, Szechuan beef with chicken, or Dragon and Phoenix (lobster with shrimp).

In El San Juan Hotel & Casino, Isla Verde Ave. ✆ **787/791-1000,** ext. 1758. Reservations recommended. Main courses $18–$29. AE, MC, V. Mon–Sat 5pm–midnight, Sun 1pm–midnight. Bus: M7 or T1.

La Piccola Fontana ★ NORTHERN ITALIAN Right off the luxurious Palm Court in the El San Juan Hotel, this restaurant takes classic northern Italian cuisine seriously and delivers plate after plate of delectable food nightly. From its white linen to its classically formal service, it enjoys a fine reputation. The food is straightforward, generous, and extremely well prepared. You'll dine in one of two neo-Palladian rooms whose wall frescoes depict Italy's ruins and landscapes. Menu items range from the appealingly simple (grilled fillets of fish or grilled veal chops) to more elaborate dishes such as *tortellini San Daniele,* made with veal, prosciutto, cream, and sage; or *linguine scogliere,* with shrimp, clams, and seafood. Grilled medallions of filet mignon are served with braised arugula, Parmesan cheese, and balsamic vinegar.

In El San Juan Hotel & Casino, Isla Verde Ave. ☎ 787/791-0966. Reservations required. Main courses $28.95–$39.95. AE, DC, MC, V. Daily 6–11pm. Bus: T1.

Moderate

Ciao Mediterranean Café ★ MEDITERRANEAN   In its own informal and breezy way, this is the most charming restaurant in Isla Verde. It's draped with bougainvillea and set directly on the sands, attracting both hotel guests and locals wandering in barefoot from the beach. Overall, the place is chic, charming, and popular—one of our enduring favorites. The visual centerpiece is an open-air kitchen set within the confines of an oval-shaped bar. Here, a crew of cheerfully animated chefs mingle good culinary technique with Latino theatricality. (Xandra Lopez is one of the few female head chefs in Puerto Rico.)

Pizzas and pastas are enduringly popular here, but more appealing are such dishes as seafood salad, wherein shrimp, scallops, calamari, peppers, onions, and lime juice create something you might have expected in the south of Italy. Greek-style squid (*kalamarakia tiganita*) consists of battered and deep-fried squid served with ratatouille and spicy marinara sauce. Provençal-style rack of lamb, with ratatouille, polenta, and Provençal herbs; and a mixed grill of seafood are evocative of what you'd expect in Marseilles, thanks to its roe-enhanced aïoli and couscous.

Intercontinental San Juan Grand Resort and Casino, 187 Isla Grande Ave. ☎ 787/791-5000. Reservations recommended for dinner. Breakfast $5–$8; pizzas and salads $8–$17; main courses $16–$25. AE, MC, V. Daily 6:30am–10pm. Bus: A7, M7, or T1.

Inexpensive

Metropol CUBAN/PUERTO RICAN/INTERNATIONAL   This is part of a restaurant chain known for serving the island's best Cuban food, although the chefs prepare a much wider range of dishes. Metropol is the happiest blend of Cuban and Puerto Rican cuisine we've ever had. The black-bean soup is among the island's finest, served in the classic Havana style with a side dish of rice and chopped onions. Endless garlic bread accompanies most dinners, likely to include Cornish game hen stuffed with Cuban rice and beans or perhaps marinated steak topped with a fried egg (reportedly Castro's favorite). Smoked chicken or chicken fried steak are also heartily recommended; portions are huge. Plantains, yucca, and all that good stuff accompany most dishes. Finish with a choice of thin or firm custard. Most dishes are at the low end of the price scale.

Ave. Isla Verde. ☎ 787/791-4046. Main courses $6.95–$28.90. AE, MC, V. Daily 11:30am–10:30pm. Bus: C41, B42 or A5.

MIRAMAR

Augusto's Cuisine ★ FRENCH/INTERNATIONAL   This is one of Puerto Rico's most elegant and glamorous restaurants, with a European flair. Austrian-born owner/chef Augusto Schreiner operates from a gray-and-green dining room set on the lobby level of a 15-story hotel in Miramar, a suburb near the island's main airport. Menu items are concocted from strictly fresh ingredients, and include such dishes as lobster risotto, rack of lamb with aromatic herbs and fresh garlic, an oft-changing cream-based soup of the day (one of the best is corn and fresh oyster soup), and a succulent version of medallions of veal Rossini style, prepared with foie gras and Madeira sauce. The wine list is one of the most extensive on the island.

In the Hotel Excelsior, 801 Ave. Ponce de León, Miramar. ☎ 787/725-7700. Reservations recommended. Main courses $24–$36. AE, MC, V. Tues–Fri noon–2pm; Tues–Sat 7–9:30pm. Bus: A5 or T1.

HITTING THE BEACH

Some public stretches of shoreline around San Juan are overcrowded, especially on Saturday and Sunday; others are practically deserted. If you find that secluded, hidden beach of your dreams, proceed with caution. Muggings have been known to occur on sparsely populated sands. For more information about the island's many beaches, call the **Department of Sports and Recreation** (© 787/728-5668).

All beaches on Puerto Rico, even those fronting the top hotels, are open to the public, although you will be charged for parking and for use of *balneario* facilities, such as lockers and showers. Public beaches shut down on Monday; if Monday is a holiday, the beaches are open for the holiday but close the next day, Tuesday. Beach hours are from 9am to 5pm in winter, to 6pm off-season. Major public beaches in the San Juan area have changing rooms and showers; Luquillo Public Beach (see below) also has picnic tables.

Famous among beach buffs since the 1920s, **Condado Beach** put San Juan on the map as a tourist resort. Backed up by high-rise hotels, it seems more like Miami Beach than any other in the Caribbean. You can book all sorts of watersports at kiosks along the beach or at the activities desk of the various hotels. There are also plenty of outdoor bars and restaurants when you tire of the sands. Condado is especially busy wherever a high-rise resort is located. People-watching seems a favorite sport along these golden strands.

At the end of Puente Dos Hermanos, the westernmost corner of the Condado is the most popular strip. This section of the beach is small and shaded by palms, and a natural rock barrier calms the turbulence of the waters rushing in, making for protected, safe swimming in gin-clear waters. The lagoon on the other side of the beach is ideal for windsurfing and kayaking.

A favorite of San Juaneros themselves, golden-sand **Isla Verde Beach** is also ideal for swimming, and it, too, is lined with high-rise resorts and luxury condos. Isla Verde has picnic tables, so you can pick up the makings of a lunch and make it a day at the beach. This strip is also good for snorkeling because of its calm, clear waters; many kiosks will rent you equipment. Isla Verde Beach extends from the end of Ocean Park to the beginning of a section called Boca Cangrejos. The best beach at Isla Verde is in front of the Hotel El San Juan. Most sections of this long strip have separate names, such as El Alambique, which is often the site of beach parties, and Punta El Medio, bordering the new Ritz-Carlton, also a great beach and very popular even with the locals. If you go past the luxury hotels and expensive condos behind the Luís Muñoz Marín International Airport, you arrive at the major public beach at Isla Verde. Here you'll find a balneario with parking, showers, fast-food joints, and watersports equipment. The sands here are whiter than the golden sands of the Condado, and are lined with coconut palms, sea-grape trees, and even almond trees, all of which provide shade from the fierce noonday sun.

Tips Let the Swimmer Beware

You have to pick your spots carefully if you want to swim along Condado Beach. The waters along the Condado Plaza Hotel are calmer than in other areas because of a coral breakwater. However, the beach near the Marriott is not good for swimming because of rocks and an undertow. Proceed with caution.

One of the most attractive beaches in the Greater San Juan area is **Ocean Park,** a mile (2km) of fine gold sand in a neighborhood east of Condado. This beach attracts both young people and a big gay crowd. Access to the beach at Ocean Park has been limited recently, but the best place to enter is from a section called El Ultimo Trolley. This area is also ideal for volleyball, paddleball, and other games. The easternmost portion, known as Punta Las Marias, is best for windsurfing. The waters at Ocean Park are fine for swimming, although they can get rough at times.

Rivaling Condado and Isla Verde beaches, **Luquillo Public Beach** ★★ is the grandest in Puerto Rico and one of the most popular. It's 30 miles (48km) east of San Juan near the town of Luquillo. Here you'll find a mile-long (2km) half-moon bay set against a backdrop of coconut palms. Saturday and Sunday are the worst times to go, as hordes of San Juaneros head here for fun in the sun. Water-sports kiosks are available, offering everything from windsurfing to sailing. Facilities include lifeguards, an emergency first-aid station, ample parking, showers, and toilets. You can easily have a local lunch here at one of the beach shacks offering cod fritters and tacos.

SPORTS & OTHER OUTDOOR PURSUITS

CRUISES   For the best cruises of San Juan Bay, go to **Caribe Aquatic Adventures** (see "Scuba Diving," below). Bay cruises start at $25 per person.

DEEP-SEA FISHING   Deep-sea fishing here is top-notch! Allison tuna, white and blue marlin, sailfish, wahoo, mahi-mahi, mackerel, and tarpon are some of the fish that can be caught in Puerto Rican waters, where 30 world records have been broken. Charter arrangements can be made through most major hotels and resorts.

Capt. Mike Beñitez, who has chartered out of San Juan for more than 40 years, is one of the most qualified sport-fishing captains in the world. Past clients have included Jimmy Carter. Contact **Beñitez Fishing Charters** directly at P.O. Box 9066541, Puerto de Tierra, San Juan, PR 00906 (© **787/723-2292** until 6pm). The captain offers a 45-foot (14m) air-conditioned deluxe Hatteras, the *Sea Born.* Fishing tours for parties of up to six cost $490 for a half-day excursion and $850 for a full day, with beverages and all equipment included.

HORSE RACING   Great thoroughbreds and outstanding jockeys compete all year at **El Comandante,** Avenida 65 de Infantería, Route 3, kilometer 15.3, at Canovanas (© **787/724-6060**), Puerto Rico's only racetrack, a 20-minute drive east of the center of San Juan. Post time varies from 2:15 to 5:30pm on Monday, Wednesday, Friday, Saturday, and Sunday.

SCUBA DIVING   In San Juan, the best outfitter is **Caribe Aquatic Adventures** (© **787/281-8858**), which operates a dive shop in the rear lobby of the Radisson Normandie Hotel. The company offers diving certification from both PADI and NAUI as part of 40-hour courses priced at $465 each. A resort course for first-time divers costs $100. They have a variety of full-day diving expeditions to various reefs off the east coast of Puerto Rico. If your time is severely limited, you can take a half-day dive of sites near San Juan. But since the best dive sites are further away, the serious scuba diver will want to take a full-day tour. They also offer windsurfing excursions (see below).

SNORKELING   Snorkeling is better in the outlying portions of the island than in overcrowded San Juan. But if you don't have time to explore greater Puerto Rico, you'll find that most of the popular beaches, such as Luquillo and Isla Verde, have pretty good visibility. One of the best places is the San Juan Bay marina near the Caribe Hilton. Snorkeling equipment generally costs $15 per

---

Finds A Side Trip to Mona Island

Known locally as "the Galápagos of the Caribbean," **Mona Island** enjoys many legends of pirate treasure and is known for its white-sand beaches and marine life. The island is virtually uninhabited, except for two policemen and a director of the institute of natural resources. Although the island is closer to Mayagüez than to San Juan, most boat tours of the island leave from the capital.

The island attracts hunters seeking pigs and wild goats, along with big-game fishers. But mostly it's intriguing to anyone who wants to escape civilization. **Playa Sardinera** on Mona Island was a base for pirates. On one side of the island, at **Playa de Pajaros,** are caves where the Taíno people left their mysterious hieroglyphs. Everything needed, including water, must be brought in, and everything, including garbage, must be taken out. For further information, call the **Puerto Rico Department of Natural Resources** at © 787/721-5495.

Encantos Ecotours (© 787/272-0005 or 787/808-0005) offers bare-bones but ecologically sensitive tours to Mona Island at sporadic intervals that vary according to the demand of clients who are interested. The experience includes ground transport to and from San Juan, sea transport departing from Cabo Rojo (a few miles south of Mayagüez), plus a half-day tour of the island. The approximately 4-hour tour costs $50 per person.

---

day and is available from the kiosks on the public beaches. Watersports desks at the big San Juan hotels at Isla Verde and Condado can make arrangements for equipment rental and can also point you to the best places for snorkeling. If your hotel doesn't offer such services, you can contact **Caribe Aquatic Adventures** (see "Scuba Diving," above), which caters to both snorkelers and scuba divers. Other possibilities for equipment rentals are at **Caribbean School of Aquatics,** Taft No. 1, Suite 10F, in San Juan (© **787/728-6606**).

TENNIS Nonguests can use the courts at the **Caribe Hilton & Casino,** Puerta de Tierra (© **787/721-0303**), and at the **Condado Plaza Hotel & Casino,** 999 Ashford Ave. (© **787/721-1000**), if they make reservations. There are also 17 public courts, lighted at night, at **San Juan Central Municipal Park,** at Calle Cerra (exit on Route 2; © 787/722-1646). Fees are $4 an hour from 8am to 6pm, $5 per hour from 6 to 10pm.

WINDSURFING A favorite spot is the sheltered waters of the Condado Lagoon in San Juan. Throughout the island, many of the companies featuring snorkeling and scuba diving also offer windsurfing equipment and instruction, and dozens of hotels offer facilities on their own premises. Another good spot is at the Radisson Normandie Hotel, where **Caribe Aquatic Adventures** has its main branch (see "Scuba Diving," above). Board rentals cost $25 to $30 per hour; lessons cost $45.

STEPPING BACK IN TIME: EXPLORING THE HISTORIC SITES OF SAN JUAN

The Spanish moved to Old San Juan in 1521, and the city played an important role as Spain's bastion of defense in the Caribbean. Today, the streets are narrow and teeming with traffic, but a walk through Old San Juan (El Viejo San Juan) is like a stroll through 5 centuries of history. You can do it in less than a day. In

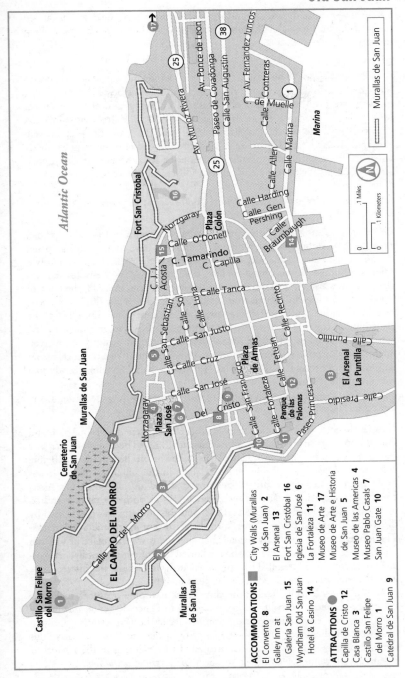

Atlantic Ocean

Castillo San Felipe del Morro **1**

Cemeterio de San Juan

EL CAMPO DEL MORRO

Murallas de San Juan

Calle del Morro

Murallas de San Juan

Fort San Cristóbal

Norzagaray

Calle O'Donell

Plaza Colón

C. Tamarindo

C. Capilla

C.J.J. Acosta

Calle Tanca

Calle San Sebastián

Calle Sol

Calle Luna

Calle San Justo

Calle Cruz

Calle San José

Plaza San José

Norzagaray

Del Cristo

Calle San Francisco

Plaza de Armas

Calle Tetuan

Calle Recinto

Calle Puntillo

Calle San Francisco

Parque de las Palomas

Calle Fortaleza

Calle Cristo

Paseo Princesa

El Arsenal

La Puntilla

Calle Presidio

Av. Muñoz Rivera

Av. Ponce de Leon

Paseo de Covadonga

Calle San Augustin

Av. Fernandez Juncos

C. de Contreras

C. de Muelle

Calle Marina

Calle Allen

Marina

Calle Harding

Calle Gen. Pershing

Calle Braumbaugh

25

38

17

25

16

15

5

4

6 7

8

9

10

11

12

13

14

1

2

2

3

Murallas de San Juan

.1 Miles

.1 Kilometers

a 7-square-block landmark area in the westernmost part of the city, you can see many of Puerto Rico's chief historical attractions, and do some shopping along the way.

CHURCHES

Capilla de Cristo   The chapel was built to commemorate what legend says was a miracle. In 1753, a young rider lost control of his horse in a race down this very street during the fiesta of St. John's Day, plunging over the precipice. Moved by the accident, the secretary of the city, Don Mateo Pratts, invoked Christ to save the youth, and had the chapel built when his prayers were answered. Today it's a landmark in the old city and one of its best-known monuments. The chapel's gold-and-silver altar can be seen through its glass doors. Since the chapel is open only on Tuesdays, most visitors have to settle for a view of its exterior.

Calle del Cristo (directly west of Paseo de la Princesa). *℘* **787/722-0861**. Free admission. Tues 10am–2pm. Bus: Old Town trolley.

Catedral de San Juan   San Juan Cathedral was begun in 1540 and has had a rough life. Looting, a lack of funds, and hurricanes have continually hampered its construction and reconstruction. Over the years, a circular staircase and two adjoining vaulted Gothic chambers have been added. Many beautiful stained-glass windows also escaped pillagers and natural disasters. In 1908, the body of Ponce de León was disinterred from the nearby Iglesia de San José and placed here in a marble tomb near the transept, where it remains. Since 1862, the cathedral has contained the wax-covered mummy of St. Pio, a Roman martyr persecuted and killed for his Christian faith. To the right of the mummy, you might notice a bizarre wooden statue of Mary with four swords stuck in her bosom. The cathedral faces Plaza de las Monjas (the Nuns' Square), a shady spot where you can rest and cool off.

Calle del Cristo 153 (at Caleta San Juan). *℘* **787/722-0861**. Free admission. Daily 8:30am–4pm. Bus: Old Town trolley.

Iglesia de San José   Initial plans for this church were drawn in 1523, and Dominican friars supervised its construction in 1532. (The church is currently closed for extensive renovations; check its status before heading here.) Before entering, look for the statue of Ponce de León in the adjoining plaza—it was made from melted-down British cannons captured during Sir Ralph Abercromby's unsuccessful attack on San Juan in 1797. Both the church and its monastery were closed by decree in 1838, and the property was confiscated by the royal treasury. Later, the Crown turned the convent into a military barracks. The Jesuits restored the badly damaged church. This was the place of worship for Ponce de León's descendants, who are buried here under the family's coat-of-arms. The conquistador, killed by a poisoned arrow in Florida, was interred here until his removal to the Catedral de San Juan in 1908.

Although it was badly looted, the church still has some treasures, including *Christ of the Ponces,* a carved crucifix presented to Ponce de León; four oils by José Campéche, the leading Puerto Rican painter of the 18th century; and two large works by Francisco Oller, the stellar artist of the late 19th and early 20th centuries. Many miracles have been attributed to a painting in the Chapel of Belém, a 15th-century Flemish work called *The Virgin of Bethlehem.*

Plaza de San José, Calle del Cristo. *℘* **787/725-7501**. Free admission. Church and Chapel of Belém, Mon–Wed and Fri 7am–3pm, Sat 8am–1pm. Bus: Old Town trolley.

(Moments **Jogger's Trail or Romantic Walk**

El Morro Trail, a jogger's paradise, provides Old Town's most scenic views across the harbor. The first part of the trail extends to the San Juan Gate. The walk then goes by El Morro, a 16th-century fort, and eventually reaches a scenic area known as Bastion de Santa Barbara. The walk passes El Morro's well-preserved walls, and the trail ends at the entrance to the fortress. The walkway is designed to follow the undulating movement of the ocean, and sea grapes and tropical vegetation surround benches. The trail is romantic at night, when the walls of the fortress are illuminated. Stop in at the tourist office for a map and set off on the adventure.

FORTS

Castillo San Felipe del Morro ⭐   Called "El Morro," this fort stands on a rocky promontory dominating the entrance to San Juan Bay. Constructed in 1540, the original fort was a round tower, which can still be seen deep inside the lower levels of the castle. More walls and turrets were added, and by 1787, the fortification attained the complex design you see today. This fortress was attacked repeatedly by both the English and the Dutch.

The National Park Service protects the fortifications of Old San Juan, which have been declared a World Heritage Site by the United Nations. You'll find El Morro an intriguing labyrinth of dungeons, barracks, ramps, and vaults, with lookouts that provide some of the most dramatic views in the Caribbean. Historical information is provided in a video in English and Spanish. The nearest parking is the underground facility beneath the Quincentennial Plaza at the Ballajá barracks (Cuartel de Ballajá) on Calle Norzagaray. Sometimes park rangers lead hour-long tours for free, although you can also visit on your own. Your ticket here also entitles you to free admission to Fort San Cristóbal (see below) on the same day.

At the end of Calle Norzagaray. ⓒ **787/729-6960.** Admission $2 adults, $1 seniors and ages 13–17, free for children age 12 and under. Daily 9am–5pm. Bus: A5, B21, or B40.

Fort San Cristóbal ⭐   This huge fortress, begun in 1634 and reengineered in the 1770s, is one of the largest the Spanish ever built in the Americas. Its walls rise more than 150 feet (45m) above the sea. San Cristóbal protected San Juan against attackers coming by land as a partner to El Morro, to which it is linked by a ½ mile (.8km) of monumental walls and bastions filled with cannon-firing positions. A complex system of tunnels and dry moats connects the center of San Cristóbal to its "outworks," defensive elements arranged layer after layer over a 27-acre (11-hectare) site. You'll get the idea if you look at the scale model on display. Like El Morro, the fort is administered and maintained by the National Park Service.

Be sure to see the Garita del Diablo, or the Devil's Sentry Box, one of the oldest parts of San Cristóbal's defenses, and famous in Puerto Rican legend. The devil himself, it is said, would snatch away sentinels at this lonely post at the edge of the sea. In 1898, the first shots of the Spanish–American War in Puerto Rico were fired by cannons on top of San Cristóbal during an artillery duel with a U.S. Navy fleet. Sometimes park rangers lead hour-long tours for free, although you can visit on your own.

In the northeast corner of Old San Juan (uphill from Plaza de Colón on Calle Norzagaray). ✆ **787/729-6960.** Admission $2 adults, $1 ages 13–17, free for children age 12 and under. Daily 9am–5pm. Bus: A5, B21, or B40; then the free trolley from Covadonga station to the top of the hill.

OTHER HISTORIC SITES

The **city walls** around San Juan (*murallas de San Juan*) were built in 1630 to protect the town against both European invaders and Caribbean pirates, and indeed were part of one of the most impregnable fortresses in the New World. Even today, they're an engineering marvel. At their top, notice the balconied buildings that served for centuries as hospitals and also residences of the island's various governors. The thickness of the walls averages 20 feet (6m) at the base and 12 feet (4m) at the top, with an average height of 40 feet (12m) . Between Fort San Cristóbal and El Morro, bastions were erected at frequent intervals. The walls come into view as you approach from San Cristóbal on your way to El Morro. To get here, take the T1 bus.

San Juan Gate, Calle San Francisco and Calle Recinto Oeste, built around 1635, just north of La Fortaleza, several blocks downhill from the cathedral, was the main gate and entry point into San Juan—that is, if you arrived by ship in the 18th century. The gate is the only one remaining of the several that once pierced the fortifications of the old walled city. To get here, take the B21 bus.

Casa Blanca Ponce de León never lived here, although construction of the house (built in 1521) is sometimes attributed to him. The house was erected 2 years after the explorer's death; work was ordered by his son-in-law, Juan García Troche. The parcel of land was given to Ponce de León as a reward for services rendered to the Crown. His descendants lived in the house for about 2½ centuries, until the Spanish government took it over in 1779 for use as a residence for military commanders. The U.S. government also used it as a home for army commanders. On the first floor, the Juan Ponce de León Museum is furnished with antiques, paintings, and artifacts from the 16th through the 18th centuries. In back is a garden with spraying fountains, offering an intimate and verdant respite from the monumental buildings of old San Juan.

Calle San Sebastián 1. ✆ **787/724-5477.** Admission $2. Tues–Sat 9am–noon and 1–4:30pm. Bus: B21.

El Arsenal The Spaniards used shallow craft to patrol the lagoons and mangroves in and around San Juan. Needing a base for these vessels, they constructed El Arsenal in the 19th century. It was at this base that they staged their last stand, flying the Spanish colors until the final Spaniard was removed in 1898, at the end of the Spanish–American War. Changing art exhibitions are held in the building's three galleries.

La Puntilla. ✆ **787/723-3068.** Free admission. Wed–Sun 8:30am–4:30pm. Bus: B21.

La Fortaleza The office and residence of the governor of Puerto Rico is the oldest executive mansion in continuous use in the western hemisphere, and has served as the island's seat of government for more than 3 centuries. Yet its history goes back even farther, to 1533, when construction began on a fortress to protect San Juan's Spanish settlers during raids by Carib tribesmen and pirates. The original medieval towers remain, but as the edifice was subsequently enlarged into a palace, other modes of architecture and ornamentation were also incorporated, including baroque, Gothic, neoclassical, and Arabian. La Fortaleza has been designated a national historic site by the U.S. government. Informal but proper attire is required.

Calle Fortaleza, overlooking San Juan Harbor. ✆ **787/721-7000**, ext. 2211. Free admission. 30-min. tours of the gardens and building (conducted in English and Spanish) given Mon–Fri, every hour 9am–3:30pm. Bus: B21.

MUSEUMS

Museo de Arte ★★   Puerto Rico's most important gallery, which opened in 2000 and was constructed at a cost of $55 million, is a state-of-the-art showcase for the island nation's rich cultural heritage as reflected mainly through its painters. Housed in a former city hospital in Santurce, the museum features both a permanent collection and temporary exhibitions. Prominent local artists are the star—for example, Francisco Oller (1833–1917), who brought a touch of Cézanne or Camille Pissarro to Puerto Rico (Oller actually studied in France with both of these Impressionists). Another leading star of the permanent collection is Jose Campeche, a late 18th-century classical painter. The museum is like a living textbook of Puerto Rico, beginning with its early development and going on to showcase camp aspects such as the poster art created here in the mid-20th century. All the important modern island artists are also presented, including the best known, the late Angel Botello, but also such contemporaries as Rafael Tufiño and Arnaldo Roche Rabell.

299 Av. Jose de Diego, Santurce. ✆ **787/977-6277**. Admission $5 adults, $3 children under age 12. Tues and Thurs–Sat 10am–5pm, Wed 10am–8pm, Sun 11am–6pm. Bus: A5.

Museo de las Americas   One of the major new museums of San Juan, Museo de las Americas showcases the artisans of North, South, and Central America, featuring everything from carved figureheads from New England whaling ships to dugout canoes carved by Carib Indians in Dominica. It is unique in Puerto Rico and well worth a visit. Also on display is a changing collection of paintings by artists from throughout the Spanish-speaking world, some of which are for sale, and a permanent collection called "Puerto Rican *Santos*," which includes a collection of carved wooden depictions of saints.

Cuartel de Ballajá. ✆ **787/724-5052**. Free admission, but donations accepted. Tues–Sun 10am–4pm. Bus: Old Town trolley.

Museo Pablo Casals   Adjacent to Iglesia de San José, this museum is devoted to the memorabilia left to the people of Puerto Rico by the musician Pablo Casals. The maestro's cello is here, along with a library of videos (played upon request) of some of his festival concerts. This small 18th-century house also contains manuscripts and photographs of Casals. The annual Casals Festival draws worldwide interest and attracts some of the greatest performing artists; it's still held during the first 2 weeks of June.

Plaza San José, Calle San Sebastián 101. ✆ **787/723-9185**. Admission $1 adults, 50¢ children. Tues–Sat 9:30am–5pm. Bus: Old Town trolley.

Museo de Arte e Historia de San Juan   Located in a Spanish colonial building at the corner of Calle MacArthur, this cultural center was the city's main marketplace in the mid-19th century. Local art is displayed in several galleries, and audiovisual materials (in English and Spanish) reveal the history of the city (hourly from 9am–4pm Mon–Fri). Sometimes major cultural events are staged in the museum's large courtyard.

Calle Norzagaray 150. ✆ **787/724-1875**. Free admission, but donations accepted. Tues–Sun 9am–4pm. Bus: Old Town Trolley, then a short walk.

Finds **El Yunque Tropical Rain Forest**

Some 25 miles (40km) east of San Juan lies the **Caribbean National Forest** ⭐⭐⭐, known as El Yunque, the only tropical forest in the U.S. National Forest Service system. It was given its status by former president Theodore Roosevelt. Within its 28,000 acres (11,200 hectares) are some 240 tree species (only half a dozen of which are found on the mainland United States). In this world of cedars and satinwood, draped in tangles of vines, you'll hear chirping birds, see wild orchids, and perhaps hear the song of the tree frog, the *coquí*. The entire forest is a bird sanctuary and may be the last retreat of the rare Puerto Rican parrot.

El Yunque offers a number of walking and hiking trails, high above sea level. The most scenic is the rugged El Toro Trail, which passes through four different forest systems en route to the 3,523-foot (1,057m) Pico El Toro, the highest peak in the forest. The signposted El Yunque Trail leads to three of the recreation area's most spectacular lookouts, and the Big Tree Trail is an easy walk to panoramic La Mina Falls. Just off the main road is La Coca Falls, a sheet of water cascading down mossy cliffs. You can be fairly sure you'll encounter rain—more than 100 billion gallons of rain falls here annually—but showers are usually brief, and there are plenty of shelters in the park.

Nearby, the Sierra Palm Interpretive Service Center offers maps and information and arranges for guided tours of the forest. A 45-minute drive southeast from San Juan (near the intersection of Route 3 and Route 191), El Yunque is a popular half-day or full-day outing. Major hotels provide guided tours.

El Portal Tropical Forest Center, Route 191, Rio Grande (© **787/888-1880**), an $18 million exhibition and information center, opened its doors in the tropical rain forest, with 10,000-square-feet (900 sq. m) of exhibition space. Three pavilions offer exhibits and bilingual displays. The actor Jimmy Smits narrates a documentary called *Understanding the Forest*. The center is open daily from 9am to 5pm, and it charges an admission of $3 for adults and $1.50 for children.

SHOPPING ⭐⭐

U.S. citizens don't pay duty on items they purchase in Puerto Rico and bring back to the United States. And you can still find great bargains on Puerto Rico, where the competition among shopkeepers is fierce.

The streets of **Old Town,** such as Calle San Francisco and Calle del Cristo, are the major venues for shopping. Note, however, that most stores in Old San Juan are closed on Sunday.

Local handcrafts can be good buys, including needlework, straw work, ceramics, hammocks, papier-mâché fruits and vegetables, and paintings and sculptures by Puerto Rican artists. Puerto Rican *santos* (saints) are sought by collectors. These carved wooden religious idols vary greatly in shape and size, and devout locals believe they have healing powers—often the ability to perform *milagros* or miracles.

The biggest and most up-to-date shopping plaza in the Caribbean Basin is **Plaza Las Americas,** in the financial district of Hato Rey, right off the Las Americas Expressway. The complex, with its fountains and advanced architecture, has more than 200 mostly upscale shops. The stores here (and their wares) are about what you'd find in a big mall back home. Prices are comparable to those stateside.

Art

If you're interested in acquiring Puerto Rican art, there are many possibilities. **Galería Botello,** 314 av. Franklin D. Roosevelt at Hato Rey (© 787/723-2879), is a contemporary Latin American gallery, a living tribute to the late Angel Botello, one of Puerto Rico's most outstanding artists. His paintings and bronze sculptures, evocative of his colorful background, are done in a style uniquely his own. On display are his and other local artists' paintings and sculptures, as well as a large collection of Puerto Rican antique *santos.*

Galería Fosil Art, Calle Cristo 200B (© 787/725-4252), is a specialty gallery, displaying unique art pieces from limestone and coral that may have existed at the time of the dinosaurs. The work is the creation of Radamés Rivera. One of the gallery's most noted artists is Yolanda Velasquez, who paints in an abstract style. The gallery also showcases the work of some 40 other artists, ranging from Mexico to Cuba.

Galería Palomas, Calle del Cristo 207 (© 787/724-8904), is another leading choice. Works range from $300 and include some of the leading painters of the Latin American world, and are rotated every 2 to 3 weeks. The setting is a 17th-century colonial house. Of special note are works by such local artists as Homer, Moya, and Alicea. **Galería San Juan,** at the Gallery Inn, Calle Norzagaray 206 (© 787/722-1808), specializes in the sculpture and paintings of Jan D'Esopo, a Connecticut-born artist who has spent much of her time in Puerto Rico. Many of her fine pieces are in bronze.

Books

For travel guides, maps, and just something to read on the beach, there are two good bookstores. Try **Bell, Book & Candle,** 102 de Diego Ave., Santurce (© 787/728-5000), a large general-interest bookstore that carries fiction and classics in both Spanish and English, plus a huge selection of postcards. **Libreria Cronopios,** Calle San José 255 (© 787/724-1815), is the leading choice in the old town, with the largest selection of titles. It sells a number of books on Puerto Rican culture as well as good maps of the island.

Coffee & Spices

Spicy Caribbee, Calle Cristo 154 (© 787/725-4690), offers the best selection of Puerto Rican coffee, which is gaining an increasingly good reputation among aficionados. It also has the Old Town's best array of hot spicy sauces of the Caribbean.

Fashion

Nono Maldonado, 1051 Ashford Ave. (midway between the Condado Plaza and the Ramada Hotel, © 787/721-0456), is named after its owner, a Puerto Rican designer who worked for many years as the fashion editor of *Esquire* magazine. This is one of the most fashionable and upscale haberdashers in the Caribbean. Selling both men's and women's clothing, it has everything from socks to dinner jackets, as well as ready-to-wear versions of Maldonado's twice-a-year collections. There is also a Maldonado boutique in the El San Juan Hotel

in Isla Verde. **Polo Ralph Lauren Factory Store,** Calle del Cristo 201 (© 787/
722-2136), has prices that are often 35% to 40% less what you'd find on the
U.S. mainland. You can find even greater discounts on irregular or slightly damaged garments. One upstairs room is devoted to home furnishings. **Speedo
Authentic Fitness,** Calle Fortaleza 65 at the corner of Calle Cristo (© 787/
724-3089), sells sportswear for women and men, specializing in shorts, jackets,
and swimwear. There's also one of the town's best collections of sandals here.

Gifts, Arts & Crafts

Butterfly People, Calle Fortaleza 152 (© 787/723-2432), is a gallery/cafe in a
handsomely restored building in Old San Juan. Butterflies, preserved forever in
artfully arranged boxes, range from $20 for a single mounting to thousands of
dollars for whole-wall murals. Most of these butterflies come from farms around
the world, some of the most beautiful from Indonesia, Malaysia, and New
Guinea. Tucked away, on the same premises, is **Malula Antiques.** Specializing
in tribal art from the Moroccan sub-Sahara and Syria, it contains a sometimes
startling collection of primitive and timeless crafts and accessories.

    Barrachina's, Calle Fortaleza 104, between Calle del Cristo and Calle San José
(© 787/725-7912), is more than a jewelry store. This is also the birthplace, in
1963, of the piña colada. It's a favorite of cruise-ship passengers, offering one of
the largest selections of jewelry, perfume, cigars, and gifts in San Juan. There's a
patio for drinks, plus a Bacardi rum outlet selling bottles cheaper than stateside,
but at the same prices as the Bacardi distillery. You'll also find a costume-jewelry
department, a gift shop, a restaurant, and a section for authentic silver jewelry.

    Xian Imports, Calle de la Cruz 153 (© 787/723-2214), is set within a jum-
bled, slightly claustrophobic setting where you'll find compactly arranged porcelain, sculptures, paintings, and Chinese furniture, much of it antique. It's
favored by the island's decorators as a source for unusual art objects.

    El Artesano, Calle Fortaleza 314 (© 787/721-6483), is a curiosity. You'll
find Mexican and Peruvian icons of the Virgin Mary; charming depictions of
fish and Latin American birds in terra-cotta and brass; all kinds of woven goods;
painted cupboards, chests, and boxes; and mirrors and Latin dolls.

    Bóveda, Calle del Cristo 209 (© 787/725-0263), is a long narrow space
crammed with exotic jewelry, clothing, greeting cards of images of life in Puerto
Rico, some 100 handmade lamps, antiques, Mexican punched tin and glass, and
art-nouveau reproductions, among other items.

    Olé, Calle Fortaleza 105 (© 787/724-2445), deserves an olé. Browsing this
store is a learning experience. Practically everything comes from Puerto Rico or
Latin America. If you want a straw hat from Ecuador, hand-beaten Chilean silver, Christmas ornaments, or Puerto Rican *santos* (saints), this is the place.

    Puerto Rican Arts & Crafts, Calle Fortaleza 204 (© 787/725-5596), set in
a 200-year-old colonial building, is one of the premier outlets on the island for
authentic artifacts. Of particular interest are papier-mâché carnival masks from
Ponce. Taíno designs inspired by ancient petroglyphs are incorporated into most
of the sterling silver jewelry sold here. There's an art gallery in back, with silk-
screened serigraphs by local artists, and a gourmet Puerto Rican food section
with such items as coffee, rum, and hot sauces. The store also exhibits and sells
small carved *santos,* representations of the Catholic saints and the infant Jesus,
laboriously carved by artisans in private studios around the island.

    Libreria y Tienda de Artesania del Instituto de Cultura Puertorriqueña,
Calle Norzagaray 98 (© 787/721-6866), next to the Convento de los Domini-
cos, has not only a collection of books on Puerto Rico, but a good display of

crafts in the Old Town, including *santos* (saints), Indian artifacts, carnival masks (many from Ponce), and baskets. All pieces are said to be made in Puerto Rico, and not in places such as Taiwan, as is so often the case.

Jewelry

Bared & Sons, Calle Fortaleza 65 (at the corner of Calle San Justo; © 787/ 724-4811), now in its fourth decade, is the main outlet of a chain of at least 20 upscale jewelry stores on Puerto Rico. On the ground floor are gemstones, gold, diamonds, and watches. One floor up, there's a monumental collection of porcelain and crystal. It's a great source for hard-to-get and discontinued patterns discounted from Christofle, Royal Doulton, Wedgwood, Limoges, Royal Copenhagen, Lalique, Lladró, Herend, Baccarat, and Daum.

R. Kury, Calle Fortaleza 201 (© 787/977-4873), is a direct factory outlet for the oldest jewelry factory on Puerto Rico, the Kury Company. Don't expect a top-notch jeweler here: Many of the pieces are replicated in endless repetition. But don't overlook the place for 14-karat-gold ornaments. Some of the designs are charming, and prices are about 20% less than at retail stores in the U.S.

Joyería Riviera, Calle La Cruz 205 (© 787/725-4000), is an emporium of 18-karat gold and diamonds, and the island's leading jeweler. Adjacent to Plaza de Armas, the shop has an impeccable reputation. This is the major distributor of Rolex watches on Puerto Rico.

Eduardo Barquet, Calle Fortaleza 200 (at the corner of Calle La Cruz) (© 787/723-1989), is known as a leading value-priced place to buy fine jewelry in Old San Juan. **Mounts and Gems,** Calle Fortaleza 205 (© 787/724-1377), sells convincing, glittering fake diamonds for those who don't want to wear or can't afford the real thing. It also stocks real diamond chips, emeralds, sapphires, and rubies, too.

Joseph Manchini, Calle Fortaleza 101 (© 787/722-7698), displays the works of its namesake and the shop's owner. He conceives almost anything you'd want in gold, silver, and bronze. Some of old town's most imaginative rings, bracelets, and chains are displayed here. If you don't like what's on sale, you can design your own jewelry, including pieces made from sapphire, emerald, and rubies.

Lace & Linens

Linen House, Calle Fortaleza 250 (© 787/721-4219), specializes in napery, bed linens, and lace, and has the island's best selection. Some of the more delicate pieces are expensive, but most are moderate in price. Inventories include embroidered shower curtains and lace doilies, bun warmers, placemats, and tablecloths that workers took weeks to complete. Some astonishingly lovely items are available for as little as $30. The aluminum/pewter serving dishes have beautiful Spanish-colonial designs. Prices here are sometimes 40% lower than those on the North American mainland.

SAN JUAN AFTER DARK
THE PERFORMING ARTS

Qué Pasa, the official visitor's guide to Puerto Rico, lists cultural events, including music, dance, theater, film, and art exhibits. It's distributed free by the tourist office.

A major cultural venue in San Juan is **Teatro Tapía,** Avenida Ponce de León (© 787/721-0169), across from Plaza de Colón, one of the oldest theaters in the western hemisphere (built about 1832). Much of Puerto Rican theater history is connected with the Tapía, named after the island's first prominent playwright,

Alejandro Tapía y Rivera. Various productions, some musical, are staged here throughout the year and include drama, dance, and cultural events. You'll have to call the box office (open Mon–Fri 10am–6pm) for specific information. Tickets generally range in price from $30.

San Juan Chateau, 9 Chardon Avenue in Hato Rey (© **787/751-2000**), is the best venue in the city for merengue and salsa. The cover charge, ranging from $8 to $20, depends on what group is appearing. You no longer get Ricky Martin, incidentally. On Friday and Saturday, live Latin groups perform, but Sunday night the club goes gay with drag shows and the like. The club attracts a wide age range from late teenagers to the middle aged. The club has no set closing hours but opens on Friday at 5pm and on Saturday and Sunday after 9pm.

Another glitzy scene unfolds at the **Hacienda Country Club,** a 25-minute drive out of San Juan on the signposted road to Caguas (© **787/747-9692**). You can't miss the club along the highway. Live musicians entertain here in an alfresco setting surrounded by mountains. A mainly 20- to 30-year old crowd is attracted to a club evocative of the one where Ricky Ricardo might have appeared in the '50s. The cover, ranging from $5 to $30, depends on the entertainment being offered. Sometimes they have some of the hottest Latin groups in the Caribbean appearing here. The club opens Saturday at 7:30pm and Sunday at 3pm, with no set closing hours.

THE CLUB & MUSIC SCENE

Modeled after an artist's rendition of the once-notorious city of Mesopotamia, **Babylon,** in El San Juan Hotel & Casino, 6063 Isla Verde, Isla Verde (© **787/791-1000**), is circular, with a central dance floor and a wraparound balcony where onlookers can scope out the action below. The crowd is usually in the 25-to-45 age group. This place has one of the best sound systems in the Caribbean. You might want to make a night of it, stopping into the El San Juan's bars and casino en route. The club is open from Thursday to Saturday from 10pm to 3am. Guests of the hotel enter free; otherwise, there's a $10 cover.

Houlihan's, 1309 Ashford Ave., Condado, (© **787/723-8600**), is a two-story casual hangout along the Condado, which is one of the best places to hear merengue, Spanish rock music, or salsa. The second floor is used like a pub but only Thursday to Saturday, attracting a relatively young, fun-loving group of both visitors and locals. If you're having dinner or drinks downstairs, you can enter the pub for free; otherwise you pay a $5 cover. In addition to the bar, Houlihan's also serves reasonably good food, such as grilled salmon with vegetables, pasta with chicken, or sirloin steak with a Cabernet sauce and fresh mushrooms. Main courses cost from $10 to $20. It's open Monday to Thursday from 5 to 10pm, Friday and Saturday from 5pm to 12:30am, and Sunday from 2 until 10pm (Bus: B21 or C10).

Laser, Calle del Cruz 251 (© **787/725-7581**), is set in the heart of the old town near the corner of Calle Fortaleza. This disco is especially crowded when cruise ships pull into town. Once inside, you can wander over the three floors, listening to whatever music happens to be hot, with lots of additional merengue and salsa thrown in as well. Depending on the night, the age of the crowd varies. It's open Thursday to Saturday from 9pm to 4am. Women enter free after midnight on Saturday. The cover ranges from $8 to $10.

St. Mick's, 2473 Loíza St., Punta Las Marias (© **787/727-6620**), is a local dive featuring food, fun, and rock 'n roll. It's like an Irish pub near Ocean Park drawing an under-25 crowd to its simple precincts decorated in wood. It's mainly a bar, but the kitchen on site serves food including churrasco (braised meat) with potatoes, chicken breast with mozzarella, and a selection of nachos, tapas, and burgers. When live music is featured on Wednesday and Saturday, there's a $2 to $3 cover. Open Tuesday to Sunday 5pm (no set closing). Bus: B21.

Star Gate, Avenida Robert Todd, Santurce (© **787/725-4664**), is where the young man of San Juan takes his date. Both often dress up to patronize this disco-bar, where they dance and drink until the late hours. Wednesday night is the most casual, Friday and Saturday the most formal nights. Cover charge is $12. Open Friday to Sunday 9:30pm to 4am. Some of the best live music along the Condado is played here.

THE BAR SCENE

Two of the most dramatic bars in San Juan are at **El San Juan Hotel & Casino,** 6063 Isla Verde Ave., Isla Verde (© **787/791-1000**). There is no more beautiful bar in the Caribbean than the **Palm Court** here, open daily 5pm to 4am. Set in an oval wrapped around a sunken bar area, amid marble and burnished mahogany, it offers a view of one of the world's largest chandeliers. After 9pm Tuesday to Saturday, live music, often salsa and merengue, emanates from an adjoining room (the El Chico Bar). There's also a fine **Cigar Bar,** with a magnificent repository of the finest cigars in the world. Some of the most fashionable women in San Juan—and men, too—can be seen puffing away in this chic rendezvous, while sipping a cognac.

Ireland and its ales meet the tropics at **Shannon's Irish Pub,** Calle Bori 46, Río Piedras (© **787/281-8466**). This is definitely a Gallic pub with a Latin beat. A sports bar, it's the regular watering hole of many university students, a constant supplier of high-energy rock-n-roll and 10 TV monitors. There's live music Wednesday through Sunday—everything from rock to jazz to Latin. There are pool tables, and a simple cafe serves inexpensive food daily from 11:30am to 1am. A $3 cover is imposed after 7pm.

We're not so keen on the food served here any more (and neither are our readers), but we still like to visit old town's **El Patio de Sam,** Calle San Sebastian 102 (© **787/723-1149**), one of the most popular late-night joints with a good selection of beers. Live entertainment is presented here Monday to Saturday. This is one of the most enduring of the old town eateries and it remains a fun joint—that is, if you dine somewhere else before coming here.

HOT NIGHTS IN GAY SAN JUAN

The Beach Bar, on the ground floor of the Atlantic Beach Hotel, 1 Calle Vendig (© **787/721-6900**), is the site of a hugely popular Sunday afternoon gathering that gets really crowded beginning around 4pm, and which stretches into the wee hours. There's an occasional drag show on a dais at one end of the outdoor terrace. There's also an open-air rectangular bar. The Beach Bar is open daily from 11am to at least 1am.

Cups, Calle San Mateo 1708, Santurce (© **787/268-3570**), is a Latin tavern, the only place in San Juan that caters almost exclusively to lesbians. Men (gay or straight) aren't particularly welcome. Although the club is open Wednesday through Saturday from 7pm to 4am, entertainment such as live music or cabaret is presented only on Wednesday at 9pm or Friday at 10pm.

Eros, 1257 Ponce de León, Santurce (© **787/722-1131**), is the town's most popular gay disco, with strippers and shows. Most of the crowd is in its late 20s. Rum-based drinks, merengue, and the latest dance tunes are on tap; the place really gets going after around 10:30pm. It's open Wednesday to Sunday from 10pm to 5am. The cover is $5.

CASINOS ★★

Gambling is big in Puerto Rico. Many people come here to do little more than that. As a result, there are plenty of options.

The casino generating all the excitement today is the 18,500-square-foot (1,665 sq. m) **casino at Ritz-Carlton San Juan Spa & Casino,** 6961 State Rd., Isla Verde (© **787/253-1700**), the largest in the whole Caribbean. It combines the elegant decor of the 1940s with tropical fabrics and patterns. This is one of the plushest and most exclusive entertainment complexes in the Caribbean. You almost expect to see Joan Crawford arrive, on the arm of Clark Gable. It features traditional games such as blackjack, roulette, baccarat, craps, and slot machines.

One of the splashiest of San Juan's casinos is at the **Wyndham Old San Juan Hotel & Casino,** Calle Brumbaugh 100 (© **787/721-5100**). Five-card stud competes with some 240 slot machines and roulette tables.

You can also try your luck at **El San Juan Hotel & Casino,** Isla Verde Avenue (© **787/791-1000**), in Isla Verde (one of the most grand), and the **Condado Plaza Hotel & Casino,** 999 Ashford Ave. (© **787/721-1000**). There are no passports to flash or admissions to pay, as in European casinos.

The Stellaris Casino at the **San Juan Marriott Resort,** 1309 Ashford Ave. (© **787/722-7000**), is a newer casino than those above., as is **El Tropical Casino** at Crown Plaza Hotel & Casino, Route 187, km 1.5, Isla Verde (© **787/253-2929**). El Tropical is open 24 hours a day and is the only theme casino in San Juan, re-creating El Yunque Tropical Rain Forest.

Most casinos are open daily from noon to 4pm and again from 8pm to 4am. Jackets for men are requested after 6pm.

3 Dorado ⟨★

Along the north shore of Puerto Rico, about a 40-minute (22-mile/35km) drive west of San Juan, a world of luxury resorts and villa complexes unfolds. The big properties of the Hyatt Dorado Beach Hotel and Hyatt Regency Cerromar Beach Hotel sit on the choice white sandy beaches here. Many guests of these hotels only pass through San Juan on arrival and departure, though if you're a first-time visitor to Puerto Rico, you may want to spend a day or so sightseeing and shopping in San Juan before heading for one of these complete resort properties, since, chances are, once you're at the resort you'll never leave the grounds. These are the only lodging options in Dorado; the only choice you have to make is which Hyatt you'd like to stay at.

GETTING THERE

If you don't have a car, call **Dorado Transport Corp.,** which is on the site shared by the Hyatt Hotels (© **787/796-1234**). It offers frequent shuttle service between the Hyatt Hotels and the San Juan airport every day between 11am and 10pm. The charge is $20 per person, but a minimum of three passengers must make the trip for the bus to operate.

ACCOMMODATIONS

Lodgings in Dorado are pretty much limited to the two Hyatts. Either is a good choice for families. They both offer family getaway packages at Camp Coquí, the Puerto Rican version of Camp Hyatt, featuring professionally supervised day and evening programs for children age 3 to 12. Children also receive a 50% discount on meals. A shuttle bus runs back and forth between the two resorts every half hour, and guests can use the facilities at either hotel.

Families interested in massive facilities and the best sports-oriented program in Puerto Rico gravitate to the Cerromar Beach, which is more like a conventional resort hotel. It also attracts more conventions. Those interested in a more peaceful, relaxing ambience cast their vote for the Dorado Beach, whose low-rise buildings sprawl across a former plantation, amidst palms, pine trees, purple bougainvillea, all within a short walk of a 2-mile (3km) sandy beach. If forced to choose, we prefer the Dorado, especially since you can take the shuttle to the Cerromar's fabulous pool area even if you don't stay there.

Hyatt Dorado Beach Resort & Casino ★★ *Kids*   Hyatt has spent millions on improvements here. This is the more elegant and subdued of the two Hyatt properties, the Cerromar attracting more families and rowdy conventions bent on having a good time. The renovated guest rooms have marble bathrooms and terra-cotta floors throughout. Accommodations are available on the beach or in villas tucked in and around the lushly planted grounds. They're fairly spacious and bathrooms have everything from tubs to bathrobes, deluxe toiletries to power showers. The *casitas* are a series of private beach or poolside houses.

Dinner is served in a three-tiered main dining room where you can watch the surf. Hyatt Dorado chefs have won many awards, and the food at the hotel restaurants is among the most appealing in Puerto Rico.

Dorado, PR 00646. ⓒ **800/233-1234** in the U.S., or 787/796-1234. Fax 787/796-6560. www.hyatt.com. 298 units, 17 *casitas*. Winter $395–$595 double; from $705 *casita* for 2. Off-season $175–$365 double; from $375 *casita* for 2. MAP (mandatory in winter) $70 extra per day for adults, $35 extra per day for children. AE, DC, DISC, MC, V. **Amenities:** 3 restaurants, 2 bars; 2 pools; 2 18-hole championship golf courses; 7 all-weather tennis courts; spa; windsurfing school; children's camp; 24-hr. room service; babysitting; laundry/dry cleaning. *In room:* A/C, minibar, hair dryer, iron and ironing board, safe.

Hyatt Regency Cerromar Beach Hotel ★★ *Kids*   The name Cerromar is a combination of two Spanish words—*cerro* (mountain) and *mar* (sea)—and true to its name, it's surrounded by mountains and ocean. Approximately 22 miles (35km) west of San Juan, the high-rise hotel shares the 1,000-acre (400-hectare) former Livingston estate with the more elegant Dorado, so guests can enjoy the Robert Trent Jones, Sr., golf courses and other facilities at the hotel next-door.

All rooms have first-class appointments and are well maintained; most have private balconies. The floors throughout are tile, the furnishings casual tropical, in soft colors and pastels. Many units are wheelchair accessible, and some are reserved for nonsmokers. Bathrooms are equipped with tubs and power showers; the Regency Club units also have robes and hair dryers.

Even if you're trapped at your resort every night because of the isolation of Dorado itself, you'll find a wide variety of cuisine here ranging from Asian to Italian. The fare is relatively standard but adequate. The water playground contains the world's longest freshwater swimming pool: a 1,776-foot-long (533m) fantasy pool with a riverlike current in five connected free-form pools. It takes 15 minutes to float from one end of the pool to the other. There are also 14 waterfalls, tropical landscaping, a subterranean Jacuzzi, water slides, walks, bridges, and a children's pool. A full-service spa and health club provides services for all manner of body and skin care, including massages.

Dorado, PR 00646. ⓒ **800/233-1234** in the U.S., or 787/796-1234. Fax 787/796-4647. www.hyatt.com. 506 units. Winter $375–$535 double; from $805 suite. Spring and fall $255–$350 double; from $600 suite. Summer $200–$250 double; from $455 suite. MAP (breakfast and dinner) $70 extra for adults, $35 extra for children. AE, DC, DISC, MC, V. **Amenities:** 4 restaurants, 3 bars, dance club; casino; 2 golf courses; 14 tennis courts; health club and spa; snorkeling; children's programs; 24-hr. room service; babysitting; laundry/dry cleaning. *In room:* A/C, TV, minibar, safe.

DINING

El Malecón PUERTO RICAN   If you'd like to discover an unpretentious local place serving good Puerto Rican cuisine, then head for El Malecón, a simple concrete structure minutes away from a small shopping center. It has a cozy family ambience and is especially popular on weekends. Some members of the staff speak English, and the chef is best with fresh seafood. The chef might also prepare a variety of items not listed on the menu. Most of the dishes are at the lower end of the price scale; only the lobster is expensive. On Wednesday and Friday a live band plays for dancing.

Rte. 693, km 8.2 Marginal Costa de Oro. © 787/796-1645. Main courses $10–$37. AE, MC, V. Daily 11am–11pm.

Steak Co. ⭐ STEAKS   This restaurant offers the best beef of the Hyatts' fine restaurants. Frequented by an upscale, usually well-dressed clientele, it occupies a soaring, two-story room with marble and Italian-tile floors. Diners enjoy views of venerable trees draped in Spanish moss, a landscaped pond, and a waterfall, while dining on well-conceived cuisine. The best steaks and prime ribs in this part of Puerto Rico are served here. Most dishes are at the lower end of the price scale. The most expensive main course—called "Sea and Earth"—consists of a tender filet mignon and a lobster tail. Most dishes are accompanied by large, perfectly baked (not soggy) potatoes and great sourdough bread. In the highly unlikely possibility you have room for dessert, you'll be glad you do.

In the Hyatt Regency Cerromar. © 787/796-1234, ext. 3240. Reservations required. Main courses $20–$48. AE, DC, DISC, MC, V. Daily 6–10pm.

Su Casa Restaurant ⭐⭐⭐ SPANISH/PUERTO RICAN   This is a restored version of the 19th-century Livingston family plantation home. Today it offers the finest dining at all the Hyatt's Dorado properties. It's an attractive setting, an old oceanfront hacienda with a red-tile roof, graceful staircases and a courtyard, and verandas in the Spanish style. Strolling musicians add to the romantic ambience, as does the candlelight. The Rockefellers used to entertain their formally dressed guests at this posh Dorado beach hideaway, but today the dress is casual (no shorts). The chef produces an innovative cuisine, using Puerto Rican fruits and vegetables whenever possible. Dining here is such an event patrons make an evening of it. For a refreshing starter, try the white gazpacho with grapes or else a tropical green salad with papaya, avocado, and Caribbean spices. The kitchen whips up a delectable seafood and chicken paella, or else you can order mahimahi (dorado) with a spicy corn sauce served with couscous and a spinach timbale. Meats are also savory, especially the roasted pork chops flavored with a tamarind sauce.

In the Hyatt Dorado Beach Hotel. © 787/796-1234. Reservations required. Main courses $27–$48. AE, DC, MC, V. Daily 6:30–10pm.

SPORTS & OTHER OUTDOOR PURSUITS

GOLF   The Robert Trent Jones, Sr.–designed courses at the **Hyatt Regency Cerromar** and the **Hyatt Dorado Beach** ⭐⭐ match the finest anywhere. The two original courses, known as east and west (© 787/796-8961 for tee times), were carved out of a jungle and offer tight fairways bordered by trees and forests, with lots of ocean holes. The somewhat newer and less noted north and south courses (© 787/796-8915 for tee times) feature wide fairways with well-bunkered greens and an assortment of water traps and tricky wind factors. Each course has a 72 par. The longest is the south course, at 7,047 yards (6,213m). Guests of the Hyatt hotels get preferred tee times and lower fees than nonguests. On the north and south courses, guests pay $70 to $90, with non-guests charged $85 to $115. On the east and west courses guests pay $126 to $145, with non-guests paying from $151 to $181. Golf carts at any of the courses rent for $25, whether you play 9 or 18 holes. The north and south, and the east and west courses each maintain separate pro shops, each with a bar and snack-style restaurant. Both are open daily from 7am until dusk.

WINDSURFING & OTHER WATERSPORTS The best place on the island's north shore is along the well-maintained beachfront of the Hyatt Dorado Beach Hotel near the 10th hole of the east golf course. Here, **Penfield Island Adventures** (© 787/382-4631, ext. 3262, or 787/796-2188) offers 90-minute **windsurfing lessons** for $80 each; board rentals cost $50 per half day. Well-supplied with a wide array of Windsurfers, including some designed specifically for beginners and children, the school benefits from the almost uninterrupted flow of the north shore's strong, steady winds and an experienced crew of instructors. A **kayaking/snorkeling** trip (© 787/796-4645), departing daily at 9:15am and 11:45am and lasting 2 hours, costs $69. Two-tank **boat dives** go for $95 per person. **Waverunners** can be rented for $60 per half hour for a single rider, and $75 for two riders. A **Sunfish** rents for $50 for 1 hour, $68 for 2 hours.

4 Rincón ⭐

At the westernmost point of the island, Rincón, 6 miles (10km) north of Mayagüez and 100 miles (161km) west of San Juan, has one of the most exotic beaches on the island, which draws surfers from around the world. In and around this small fishing village are some unique accommodations.

GETTING THERE

If you rent a car at the San Juan airport, it will take approximately 2½ hours to drive here via the busy northern Route 2, or 3 hours via the scenic mountain route (no. 52) through Ponce to the south. We recommend the southern route.

In addition, there are 4 flights daily from San Juan to Mayagüez on **American Eagle** (© 800/352-0714). These flights take 40 minutes, and round-trip airfares range from $155 to $196. From the Mayagüez airport, Rincón is a 30-minute drive to the north on Route 2 (go left or west at the intersection with Route 115).

ACCOMMODATIONS

Horned Dorset Primavera ⭐⭐⭐ This is the most sophisticated hotel on Puerto Rico and one of the most exclusive and elegant small properties anywhere in the Caribbean. It opens onto a secluded semiprivate beach, and it was built on the massive breakwaters and seawalls erected by a local railroad many years ago. The hacienda evokes an aristocratic Spanish villa, with wicker armchairs, hand-painted tiles, ceiling fans, seaside terraces, and cascades of flowers. Accommodations are in a series of suites that ramble amid lush gardens. The decor is tasteful, with four-poster beds and brass-footed tubs in marble-sheathed bathrooms, with showers and tubs. Rooms are spacious and luxurious, with Persian rugs over tile floors, queen-size sofa beds in the sitting areas, and fine linen and tasteful fabrics on the elegant beds.

The eight-suite Casa Escondida villa, set at the edge of the property, adjacent to the sea, is decorated with an accent on teakwood and marble. Some of the units have private plunge pools; others offer private verandas or sundecks. Each contains high-quality reproductions of colonial furniture by Baker.

The hotel's restaurant, also called Horned Dorset Primavera, is one of the finest on Puerto Rico (see "Dining," below).

Hotel Rte. 429 (P.O. Box 1132), Rincón, PR 00677. ℂ **800/633-1857** or 787/823-4030. Fax 787/823-5580. www.horneddorset.com. 31 units. Winter $380–$440 double; $540–$800 suite for 2. Off-season $280–$340 double; $420–$650 suite for 2. MAP (breakfast and dinner) $82 per person extra. AE, MC, V. Children under age 12 not accepted. **Amenities:** 2 restaurants, bar; 2 pools; tennis court; fitness center; library; deep-sea fishing; room service (breakfast and lunch); massage; laundry. *In room:* A/C, minibar, hair dryer, iron, safe.

Parador Villa Antonio Ilia and Hector Ruíz offer apartments by the sea in this privately owned and run *parador.* The beach outside is nice, but the local authorities don't keep it as clean as they ought to. Surfing and fishing can be enjoyed just outside your front door, and you can bring your catch right into your cottage and prepare a fresh seafood dinner in your own kitchenette (there's no restaurant). This is a popular destination with families from Puerto Rico who crowd in on the weekends, occupying the motel-like rooms with balconies or terraces. Furnishings are well used but offer reasonable comfort, and bathrooms are small with shower stalls.

Rte. 115, km 12.3 (P.O. Box 68), Rincón, PR 00677. ℂ **787/823-2645.** Fax 787/823-3380. www.villa-antonio.com. 61 units. Year-round $85–$117.50 double, $120 suite. AE, DISC, MC, V. **Amenities:** Pool; 2 tennis courts; playground; babysitting; laundry. *In room:* A/C, TV, coffeemaker, iron, safe.

DINING

Horned Dorset Primavera ★★ FRENCH/CARIBBEAN This is the finest restaurant in western Puerto Rico, so romantic that people sometimes come from San Juan just for an intimate dinner. A masonry staircase sweeps from the garden to the second floor, where soaring ceilings and an atmosphere similar to that within a private villa awaits you.

The menu, which changes virtually every night based on the inspiration of the chef, might include chilled parsnip soup, a fricassee of wahoo with wild mushrooms, grilled loin of beef with peppercorns, and medallions of lobster in an orange-flavored beurre-blanc sauce. The grilled breast of duckling with bay leaves and raspberry sauce is also delectable. Dorado (mahi-mahi) is grilled and served with a ginger-cream sauce on a bed of braised Chinese cabbage. It's delicious, as is the grilled squab with tarragon sauce.

In the Horned Dorset Primavera hotel, Rte. 429. ℂ **787/823-4030.** Reservations recommended. Main courses $22–$35; fixed-price dinner $136 for 2. AE, MC, V. Daily noon–2pm and 7–9pm.

HITTING THE BEACH & THE LINKS

One of Puerto Rico's most outstanding surfing beaches is at **Punta Higuero,** on Route 413 near Rincón. In the winter months especially, uninterrupted Atlantic swells with perfectly formed waves averaging 5 to 6 feet (2m) in height roll shoreward, and rideable swells sometimes reach 15 to 25 feet (5–8m).

Punta Borinquén Golf Club, Route 107 (ℂ **787/890-2987**), 2 miles (3km) north of Aguadilla's center, across the highway from the city's airport, was originally built by the U.S. government as part of the Ramey Air Force Base. Today, its 18 holes function as a public golf course, open daily from 7am to 6:30pm. Greens fees are $20 for an all-day pass. Rental of a golf cart that can carry two passengers is $26 for 18 holes, or $14 for 9 holes. Clubs can be rented for $10. The clubhouse contains a bar and a simple restaurant.

5 Mayagüez

The port city Mayagüez, not architecturally remarkable, is the third largest city on Puerto Rico; it lies 98 miles (158km) southwest of San Juan. It was once the needlework capital of the island, and there are still craftspeople who sew fine embroidery. Mayagüez is also the honeymoon capital of Puerto Rico for certain tradition-minded Puerto Rican couples. If we were honeymooning, we'd rather stay in the Greater San Juan area or at one of the posh north coast resorts, but this island tradition dates from the 16th century. It's said that when local fathers needed husbands for their daughters, they kidnapped young Spanish sailors who were en route to Latin America.

GETTING THERE

American Eagle (© **800/352-0714**) flies four times daily throughout the year between San Juan and Mayagüez. Flight time is 40 minutes, although there are often delays on the ground at either end of the itinerary. Depending on restrictions and the season you book your flight, round-trip fares range from $159 to $196 per person.

If you rent a car at the San Juan airport and want to **drive** to Mayagüez, it's fastest and most efficient to take the northern route that combines sections of the newly widened Route 22 with the older Route 2. Estimated driving time for a local resident is about 90 minutes, although newcomers usually take about 30 minutes longer. The southern route, which combines the modern Route 52 with a transit across the outskirts of historic Ponce, and a final access into Mayagüez via the southern section of Route 2, requires a total of about 3 hours and affords some worthwhile scenery across the island's mountainous interior.

ACCOMMODATIONS

Mayagüez Resort & Casino ★ Except for the ritzy Horned Dorset Primavera (see above), this is the largest and best general hotel resort in western Puerto Rico, appealing equally to business travelers and vacationers. In 1995 local investors took over what was then a sagging Hilton and radically renovated it to the tune of $5 million. The hotel benefits from its redesigned casino, country-club format, and 20 acres (8 hectares) of tropical gardens. The landscaped grounds have been designated an adjunct to the nearby Mayagüez Institute of Tropical Agriculture. There are five species of palm trees, eight kinds of bougainvillea, and numerous species of rare flora, set adjacent to the Institute's collection of tropical plants, which range from a pink torch ginger to a Sri Lankan cinnamon tree.

The hotel's well-designed bedrooms open onto views of the swimming pool, and many units have private balconies. Guest rooms tend to be small, but they have good beds. Some units are suitable for nonsmokers, while others are accessible for people with disabilities. The restored bathrooms are well equipped with makeup mirrors, scales, and shower/tub combinations.

For details about El Castillo, the hotel's restaurant, see "Dining," below. The hotel is the major entertainment center of Mayagüez. Its casino has free admission and is open daily from noon to 4am. You can also drink and dance at the Victoria Lounge.

Rte. 104 (P.O. Box 3781), Mayagüez, PR 00709. © **888/689-3030** or 787/832-3030. Fax 787/834-3475. www.mayaguezresort.com. 140 units. Year-round $169–$189 double; $260 suite. AE, DC, DISC, MC, V. Parking $5. **Amenities:** Restaurant, 3 bars, nightclub; Olympic-size pool, children's pool; 3 tennis courts; small fitness room; Jacuzzi; deep-sea fishing, skin-diving, surfing, scuba diving; playground; room service (6:30am–10:30pm); babysitting; laundry. *In room:* A/C, TV, minibar, coffeemaker.

Holiday Inn & Tropical Casino   This six-story hotel competes with the Mayagüez Resort & Casino, though we like the previous recommendation better. The Holiday Inn is well-maintained, contemporary, and comfortable. It has a marble-floored, high-ceilinged lobby, an outdoor pool with a waterside bar, and a big casino, but its lawn simply isn't as dramatically landscaped as the Mayagüez resort's surrounding acreage. Bedrooms here are comfortably but functionally outfitted in motel style; they've recently been refurbished. Each unit is equipped with a tiled bathroom with a shower/tub combinations.

2701 Rte. 2, km 149.9, Mayagüez, PR 00680-6328. ✆ 800/HOLIDAY in the U.S. and Canada, or 787/833-1100. Fax 787/833-1300. www.holiday-inn.com. 142 units. Year-round $99.50–$130.50 double; $210–$260 suite. AE, DC, MC, V. **Amenities:** Restaurant, 2 bars; casino; pool; gym; room service; laundry. *In room:* A/C, TV, coffeemaker, hair dryer, safe.

DINING

El Castillo   INTERNATIONAL/PUERTO RICAN   This is the best-managed large-scale dining room in western Puerto Rico, as well as the main restaurant for the largest hotel and casino in the area. Known for its generous lunch buffets, El Castillo serves only a la carte items at dinner, including seafood stew served on a bed of linguine with marinara sauce, grilled salmon with a mango-flavored Grand Marnier sauce, and fillets of sea bass with a cilantro, white wine, and butter sauce. Steak and lobster are served on the same platter, if you want it. The food has real flavor and flair, and isn't the typical bland hotel fare so often dished up.

In the Mayagüez Resort & Casino, Rte. 104. ✆ 787/832-3030. Breakfast buffet $11.25. Mon–Fri buffet lunch $14; Sat–Sun brunch buffet $25; main courses $13.50–$32. AE, MC, V. Daily 6:30am–11pm.

EXPLORING THE AREA: BEACHES & TROPICAL GARDENS

Along the western coastal bends of Route 2, north of Mayagüez, lie the best surfing **beaches** in the Caribbean. Surfers from as far away as New Zealand come to ride the waves. You can also check out panoramic **Punta Higuero** beach, nearby on Route 413, near Rincón (see above).

The chief sight in Mayagüez is the **Tropical Agriculture Research Station** (✆ **787/831-3435**), located on Route 65, between Post Street and Route 108, adjacent to the University of Puerto Rico at Mayagüez campus and across the street from the **Parque de los Próceres** (Patriots' Park). At the administration office, ask for a free map of the tropical gardens, which contain a huge collection of tropical species useful to people, including cacao, fruit trees, spices, timbers, and ornamentals. The grounds are open Monday to Friday from 7am to 5pm, and there is no admission charge.

6 San Germán

Only an hour's drive from Ponce or Mayagüez and the beaches of the southern coast, and just over 2 hours from San Juan, San Germán, Puerto Rico's second-oldest town, has been compared to a small-scale outdoor museum. It was founded in 1512 and destroyed by the French in 1528. Rebuilt in 1570, it was named after Germain de Foix, the second wife of King Ferdinand of Spain. Once the rival of San Juan, but without the benefit of Old San Juan's lavish restoration budgets, San Germán harbored many pirates, who pillaged the ships that sailed off the nearby coastline. Indeed, many of today's residents are descended from the smugglers, poets, priests, and politicians who lived here.

Although the pirates and sugar plantations are long gone, the city retains some colorful reminders of those former days. Today it has settled into a slumber, albeit one that has preserved the feel of the Spanish colonial era. Flowers brighten some of the patios here as they do in Seville. Also as in a small Spanish town, many of the inhabitants stroll through the small but choice historic zone in early evening. Nicknamed "Ciudad de las Lomas," or City of the Hills, San Germán boasts verdant scenery that provides a pleasant backdrop to a variety of architectural styles—Spanish colonial (1850s), criollo (1880s), neoclassical (1910s), art deco (1930s), and international (1960s)—depicted in the gracious old world–style buildings that line some of its streets. So significant are these buildings that San Germán is only the second Puerto Rican city (the other is San Juan) to be included in the National Register of Historic Places.

ACCOMMODATIONS

Parador El Oasis   Although it's not state-of-the-art, this hotel evokes some appealing doses of Spanish colonial charm. If you'd like to anchor into this quaint old town, far removed from the beaches, it's a decent place to stay. A three-story building constructed around a pool and patio area, the hotel originated in the late 1700s as a privately owned mansion. The older rooms, positioned close to the lobby, show the wear and tear of the years. The more modern rooms, located in the back, are without character, but are cleaner and more spacious than the older units. Three of the units have private balconies, and each of the accommodations come with a tiled, shower-only bathroom. The hotel sits on the town's overcrowded main street, about 2 blocks from the historic churches of San Germán. The in-house restaurant is not the most imaginative choice in town, but it emerges year after year as the most reliable and consistent of those within the town center.

Calle Luna 72, San Germán, PR 00683. (C) 787/892-1175. 52 units. Year-round $73.03–$74.95 double. Extra person $10. Children age 11 and under stay free in parents' room. Rates include continental breakfast. AE, DC, DISC, MC, V. **Amenities:** Restaurant, bar; pool; babysitting. *In room:* A/C, TV, hair dryer.

SEEING THE SIGHTS

The city's 249 noteworthy historical treasures are within easy walking distance of one another, though you'll only see most of them from the outside. If some of them are actually open, count yourself fortunate, as they have no phones, keep no regular hours, and are staffed by volunteers who rarely show up. Also, be aware that most of the city's architectural treasures lie uphill from the impossibly congested main thoroughfare (Calle Luna), that streets in the old town tend to run only one way (usually the way you don't want to go), and that you're likely to be confused by the bad signs and dilapidated condition of many of the historic buildings. We usually try to park on the town's main street (Carretera 102, which changes its name within the border of San Germán to Calle Luna), and then proceed on foot through the city's grimy-looking commercial core before reaching the architectural highlights described below.

One of the most noteworthy churches in Puerto Rico is **Iglesia Porta Coeli (Gate to Heaven)** ✿ ((C) 787/892-0160), which sits atop a knoll at the eastern end of a cobble-covered square, the Parque de Santo Domingo. Dating from 1606, in a form inspired by the Romanesque architecture of northern Spain, this is the oldest church in the New World. Restored by the Institute of Puerto Rican Culture, and sheathed in a layer of salmon-colored stucco, it contains a museum of religious art with a collection of ancient *santos,* the carved figures of saints that have long been a major branch of Puerto Rican folk art. Look for the 17th-century portrait of St. Nicholas de Bari, the French Santa Claus. Inside, the original palm-wood ceiling and tough, brown ausobo-wood beams draw the eyes upward. Other treasures include early choral books from Santo Domingo, a primitive carving of Jesus, and 19th-century Señora de Monserrate (Black Madonna and Child) statues. Admission costs $1; free for children age 12 and under. It's open Wednesday through Sunday from 8:30am to noon and 1 to 4:30pm.

Less than 100 feet (30m) downhill from the church, at the bottom of the steps that lead from its front door down to the plaza below, is the **Casa Morales** (it's also known as the **Tomás Vivoni House,** after its architect), San Germán's most popular and widely recognized house. It was built in 1913 (during a period of agrarian prosperity), and named for the local architect who designed it. Edwardian style, with wraparound porches, elaborate gables, and elements that might remind you of a Swiss chalet, it was built in 1913, reflecting the region's turn-of-the-century agrarian prosperity.

The long and narrow, gently sloping plaza that prefaces the Iglesia Porta Coeli is the **Parque de Santo Domingo,** one of San Germán's two main plazas. Street signs also identify the plaza as the Calle Ruiz Belvis. Originally a marketplace, the plaza is paved with red and black cobblestones, and bordered with cast-iron benches and portrait busts of some of the prominent figures in the town's history. This plaza merges gracefully with an equivalently shaped, identically sized twin, which street signs and maps identify simultaneously as the **Plaza Francisco Mariano Quiñones,** the Calle José Julian Acosta, or the Plaza Principal. Separating the two plazas is the unused, gray-and-white bulk of San Germán's **Viejo Alcaldia (Old Town Hall).** Built late in the 19th century, and awaiting a new vision, perhaps as a museum or public building, it's closed to the public.

San Germán's most impressive church—and the most monumental building in the region—is **San Germán de Auxerre** (© **787/892-1027**), which rises majestically above the western end of the Plaza Francisco Mariano Quiñones. Designed in the Spanish baroque style, it was founded in 1573 in the form of a simple chapel with a low-slung thatch roof. Much of what you'll see today is the result of a rebuilding in 1688 and a restoration in 1737 that followed a disastrous earthquake. Inside, you'll find 3 naves, 10 altars, 3 chapels, and a belfry that was rebuilt in 1939 following the collapse of the original during another earthquake in 1918. The central chandelier, made from rock crystal and imported from Barcelona in 1866, is the largest in the Caribbean. The pride of the church is the *trompe l'oeil* ceiling, which was elaborately restored in 1993. The building's restoration was completed in 1999 with the insertion of a series of stained glass windows with contemporary designs. The church can be visited daily 7am or 7:30pm at either mass.

A handful of lesser sights within or near the town's two main squares will distract you as well. They include the **Farmacia Martin,** a modern pharmacy that's incongruously set within the shell of a graceful but battered art deco building at the edge of the Parque Santo Domingo (22 Calle Ruiz Belvis; © **787/892-1122;** Mon–Fri 9am–10pm; Sat 9am–9pm). A cluster of dilapidated clapboard-sided houses line the southern side of the Calle Dr Ueve. The most important of these is at no. 66, the **Casa Acosta y Fores** house. Also noteworthy is a substantial-looking house at the corner of the Calle Dr Ueve and Parque Santo Domingo, the **Casa Juan Perichi.** Both were built around 1917, of traditional wood construction, and are fine examples of Puerto Rican adaptations of Victorian architecture. Both, regrettably, are in seriously dilapidated condition, although that might change as San Germán continues the slow course of its historic renovations.

7 Ponce (★)

Puerto Rico's second-largest city, Ponce ("The Pearl of the South"), was named after Loíza Ponce de León, grandson of Ponce de León. Today it's Puerto Rico's principal shipping port on the Caribbean Sea, located 75 miles (121km) south-west of San Juan. The city is well kept and attractive, with many plazas, parks, and public buildings. It has the air of a provincial Mediterranean town. Look for the *rejas* (framed balconies) of the handsome colonial mansions. Ponce is a city, not a beach resort, and should be visited mainly for its sights.

ESSENTIALS

GETTING THERE   Ponce is 75 miles (121km) southwest of San Juan and is reached by Route 52. Allow at least 1½ hours if you **drive. Cape Air** ((℃ **800/ 352-0714**) offers four daily flights between San Juan and Ponce (flight time is approximately 35 minutes) for $124 round-trip.

VISITOR INFORMATION   Maps and information can be found at the **tourist office,** Paseo del Sur Plaza, Suite 3 ((℃ **787/843-0465**). Open Monday to Friday 8am to 5pm.

ACCOMMODATIONS

Meliá   A city hotel with southern hospitality, the Meliá, which has no con-nection with the international hotel chain, attracts businesspeople. The location is a few steps away from the Cathedral of Our Lady of Guadalupe and from the Parque de Bombas (the red-and-black firehouse). Although this old and some-what tattered hotel was long ago outclassed by the more expensive Hilton, many people who can afford more upscale accommodations still prefer to stay here for its old-time atmosphere. The lobby floor and all stairs are covered with Spanish tiles of Moorish design. The desk clerks speak English. The small rooms are comfortably furnished and pleasant enough, and most have a balcony facing either busy Calle Cristina or the old plaza. Bathrooms are tiny, each with a shower stall. Breakfast is served on a rooftop terrace with a good view of Ponce, and Mark's at the Meliá thrives under separate management (see "Dining," below). You can park your car in the lot nearby. There's no pool here.

Calle Cristina 2, Ponce, PR 00731. (℃ 800/742-4276 in the U.S., or 787/842-0260. Fax 787/841-3602. www.home.coqui.net/melia. 75 units. Year-round $82–$131 double. Rates include continental breakfast. AE, DC, MC, V. Parking $3. **Amenities:** Restaurant. bar; room service; babysitting; laundry/dry cleaning. *In room:* A/C, TV, hair dryer, iron, safe.

Ponce Hilton & Casino (★★)   On an 80-acre (32-hectare) tract of land right on the beach at the western end of Avenida Santiago de los Caballeros, about a 10-minute drive from the center of Ponce, this is the most glamorous hotel in southern Puerto Rico. Designed like a miniature village, with turquoise-blue roofs, white walls, and lots of tropical plants, ornamental waterfalls, and gar-dens, it welcomes conventioneers and individual travelers alike. Accommoda-tions contain tropically inspired furnishings, ceiling fans, and terraces or balconies. All the rooms are medium to spacious, with adequate desk and stor-age place, tasteful fabrics, good upholstery, and fine linen. The ground-floor rooms are the most expensive. Each is equipped with a generous bathroom in tile with shower/tub combinations.

The food is the most sophisticated and refined on the south coast of Puerto Rico. All the waiters seem to have an extensive knowledge of the menu and will guide you through some exotic dishes—of course, you'll find familiar fare, too.

1150 Avenida Caribe (P.O. Box 7419), Ponce, PR 00732. © **800/HILTONS** in the U.S. and Canada, or 787/259-7676. Fax 787/259-7674. www.hilton.com. 153 units. Year-round $185–$280 double; $475 suite. AE, DC, DISC, MC, V. Self-parking $5; valet parking $10. **Amenities:** 2 restaurants, 3 bars; casino; lagoon-shaped pool ringed with gardens; 4 tennis courts; fitness center; watersports; bike rentals; playground; summer camp for children; business center; room service (7am–midnight); babysitting; laundry/dry cleaning. *In room:* A/C, TV, minibar, hair dryer, coffeemaker, safe.

DINING

El Ancla ★ PUERTO RICAN/SEAFOOD   This is one of Ponce's best restaurants, with a lovely location 2 miles (3km) south of the city center, on soaring piers that extend from the rocky coastline out over the surf. As you dine, the sound of the sea rises literally from beneath your feet.

Menu items are prepared with real Puerto Rican zest and flavor. A favorite here is red snapper stuffed with lobster and shrimp, served either with fried plantain or mashed potatoes. Other specialties are fillet of salmon in caper sauce, and a seafood medley of lobster, shrimp, octopus, and conch. Most of the dishes are reasonably priced, especially the chicken and conch. Lobster tops the price scale. The side orders, including crabmeat rice and yucca in garlic, are delectable.

805 Hostos Ave., Playa Ponce. © **787/840-2450**. Main courses $13–$36. AE, DC, MC, V. Sun–Thurs 11am–9:30pm, Fri–Sat 11am–11pm.

La Cava ★★ INTERNATIONAL   Designed like a hive of venerable rooms within a 19th-century coffee plantation, this is the most appealing and elaborate restaurant in Ponce. There's a well-trained staff, a sense of antique charm, well-prepared cuisine, and a champagne-and-cigar bar where the bubbly sells for around $6 a glass. Menu items change every 6 weeks, but might include duck foie gras with toasted brioche, Parma ham with mango, cold poached scallops with mustard sauce, a fricassee of lobster and mushrooms in a pastry shell, and grilled lamb sausage with mustard sauce on a bed of couscous. Dessert could be a black-and-white soufflé or a trio of tropical sorbets.

In the Ponce Hilton, 1150 Avenida Caribe. © **787/259-7676**. Reservations recommended. Main courses $24–$39. AE, DISC, DC, MC, V. Mon–Sat 6:30–10:30pm.

La Montserrate PUERTO RICAN/SEAFOOD   Beside the seafront, in a residential area about 4 miles (6km) west of the town center, this restaurant draws a loyal following from the surrounding neighborhood. A culinary institution in Ponce since it was established 20 years ago, it occupies a large, airy, modern building divided into two different dining areas. The first of these is slightly more formal than the next. Most visitors, however, head for the large room in back, where windows on three sides encompass a view of some offshore islands. Specialties, concocted from the catch of the day, might include octopus salad, four different kinds of *asopao*, a whole red snapper in Creole sauce, or a selection of steaks and grills. Nothing is innovative, but the cuisine is typical of the south of Puerto Rico, and it's a family favorite. The fish dishes are better than the meat selections.

Sector Las Cucharas, Rte. 2. © **787/841-2740**. Main courses $15–$25. AE, DC, DISC, MC, V. Daily 11am–10pm.

Mark's at the Meliá ★★★ INTERNATIONAL   Mark French (isn't that a great name for a chef?) elevates Puerto Rican dishes into haute cuisine at this eatery, which is certainly off the beaten path. You'd think he'd been entertaining the celebs in San Juan instead of cooking at what is somewhat of a Caribbean backwater. French was hailed as "Chef of the Caribbean 2000" in

Fort Lauderdale. With his constantly changing menus, and his insistence that everything be fresh, he's still a winner. You'll fall in love with this guy when you taste his tamarind barbecued lamb with yucca mojo. Go on to sample his lobster pionono with tomato and chive salad or his freshly made sausage with pumpkin, cilantro, and chicken. All over Puerto Rico you get fried green plantains, but here they come topped with sour cream and a dollop of caviar. The corn-crusted red snapper with yucca purée and tempura jumbo shrimp with Asian salad are virtual signature dishes. The desserts are spectacular, notably the vanilla flan layered with rum sponge cake and topped with a caramelized banana, and the award-winning bread pudding soufflé with coconut vanilla sauce.

In the Meliá Hotel, calle Cristina. © 787/284-6275. Reservations recommended. Main courses $14–$30. AE, MC, V. Wed–Sat noon–3pm and 6–10:30pm, Sun noon–5pm.

BEACHES & OTHER OUTDOOR PURSUITS

A 10-minute drive west of Ponce will take you to **Playa de Ponce,** a long strip of white sand opening onto the tranquil waters of the Caribbean. This beach is usually better for swimming than the Condado in San Juan. There's little in the way of organized sports here, however.

The city owns two **tennis complexes,** one at Poly Deportivos, with nine hard courts, and another at Rambla, with six courts. Both are open from 9am to 10pm and are lit for night play. You can play for free. For more information and for road directions from wherever you are, call the Secretary of Sports at © 787/840-4400.

Golfers have their choice of two nine-hole courses, one 30 miles (48km) east of Ponce, the other 30 miles (48km) west. The one to the east is **Aguirre Golf Club,** Route 705, Aguirre (© 787/853-4052), 30 miles (48km) east of Ponce (take Highway 52). It's open from 7am to 5pm daily, charges greens fees of $15 Monday through Friday, going up to $18 on weekends and holidays. The one to the west is **Club Deportivo,** Carretera 102, kilometer 15.4, Barrio Jogudas, Cabo Rojo (© 787/254-3748), open daily from 7am to 6pm. Greens fees are $30 daily.

SEEING THE SIGHTS

A $40 million project has restored more than 1,000 buildings in town to their original turn-of-the-century charm. Architectural styles that combine neoclassical with "Ponce Creole" and art deco give the town a distinctive ambience.

Any Ponceño will direct you to their **Museo de Arte de Ponce** ✪, Avenida de las Americas 25 (© 787/848-0505), which has a fine collection of European and Latin American art, the best on the island. Among the nearly 400 paintings, sculptures, and artworks on display are exceptional pre-Raphaelite and Italian baroque paintings. The building was designed by Edward Durell Stone, and has been called the "Parthenon of the Caribbean." It's open daily from 10am to 5pm. Adults pay $4; children age 11 and under are charged $2.

Most visitors head for the **Parque de Bombas,** Plaza de las Delicias (© 787/284-4141), the main plaza of Ponce. This fantastic old black-and-red firehouse was built for a fair in 1883. It's open Wednesday through Monday from 9:30am to 5:30pm.

Around the corner from the firehouse, a trail will lead you to the **Cathedral of Our Lady of Guadalupe,** Calle Concordia/Calle Union (© 787/842-0134). Designed by architects Francisco Porrata Doría and Francisco Trublard in 1931, and featuring a pipe organ installed in 1934, it remains an important place for prayer. It's open Monday to Friday from 6am to 3:30pm and on Saturday and Sunday from 6am to 1pm and 3 to 8pm.

El Museo Castillo Serrallés, El Vigía 17 (© 787/259-1774), the largest and most imposing building in Ponce, was constructed high on a hilltop above town by the Serrallés family (owners of a local rum distillery) in the 1930s. This is one of the architectural gems of Puerto Rico and the best evidence of the wealth produced by the turn-of-the-century sugar boom. Guides will escort you through the Spanish Revival house, where Moorish and Andalusian details include panoramic courtyards, a baronial dining room, and a small cafe and souvenir shop. Hours are Tuesday to Thursday 9:30am to 5pm, Friday and Sunday 9:30am to 5:30pm. Admission is $3 for adults, $2 for seniors over age 62, and $1.50 for students and children age 15 and under. From the Plaza las Delicias de Ponce, a free trolley bus runs frequently throughout the day, taking visitors to the museum.

The oldest cemetery in the Antilles, excavated in 1975, is near Ponce on Route 503 at kilometer 2.7. The **Tibes Indian Ceremonial Center** (© 787/840-2255) contains some 186 skeletons, dating from A.D. 300, as well as pre-Taíno plazas from A.D. 700. Guided tours in English and Spanish are conducted through the grounds. Shaded by trees are seven rectangular ball courts and two dance areas. The arrangements of stone points on the dance grounds, in line with the solstices and equinoxes, suggest a pre-Columbian Stonehenge. A re-created Taíno village includes not only the museum but also an exhibition hall where you can see a documentary about Tibes; you can also visit the cafeteria and souvenir shop. The museum is open Tuesday to Sunday from 9am to 4pm. Admission is $2 for adults and $1 for children.

Hacienda Buena Vista, Route 10, kilometer 16.8 (© 787/284-7020 or 787/722-5882), is a 30-minute drive north of Ponce. Built in 1833, it preserves an old way of life, with its whirring waterwheels and artifacts of 19th-century farm production. Once it was one of the most successful plantations on Puerto Rico, producing coffee, corn, and citrus. It was a working coffee plantation until the 1950s, and 86 of the original 500 acres (200 hectares) are still part of the estate. The rooms of the hacienda have been furnished with authentic pieces from the 1850s. Tours, lasting 2 hours, are conducted Saturday and Sunday at 8:30am, 10:30am, 1:30pm, and 3:30pm (in English only at 1:30pm). Reservations are required. Tours cost $5 for adults, $2.50 for seniors, $2 for children. The hacienda lies in the small town of Barrio Magüeyes, on Route 10 between Ponce and Adjuntas.

If you feel a yen for **shopping,** head for the **Fox Delicias Mall,** at the intersection of calle Reina Isabel and Plaza de Las Delicias de Ponce, the city's most innovative shopping center.

8 Las Croabas & Luquillo Beach ★★

From San Juan, Route 3 leads east toward the fishing town of Fajardo, where you'll turn north to Las Croabas, about 31 miles (50km) from the capital.

You'll be near **Luquillo Beach,** one of the island's best and most popular public stretches of sand. From here, you can also easily explore El Yunque Rain Forest. See the section "San Juan," earlier in this chapter, for details on both.

GETTING THERE

The two big resort hotels in this area run buses to and from the San Juan airport, based on the arrival times of incoming flights. It's $25 per person each way to the Westin Rio Mar Beach, and $28 per person to the Wyndham El Conquistador. A taxi from the airport will cost approximately $70 to either hotel. Private limousine service costs $225 per carload.

If you are driving from San Juan, go past the San Juan airport, following the signs to "Carolina," which will lead to Route 3 going east. To reach the El Conquistador hotel, follow the signs to Fajardo, then to "Las Croabas." To reach the Westin, follow signs to El Yunque, then signs to the Westin.

ACCOMMODATIONS

Embassy Suites Dorado del Mar Beach & Golf Resort ★★ This is the only all-suite beachfront resort in Puerto Rico, a success since it opened in 2001. Clustered within the 500-acre (200-hectare) Westin Rio Mar Beach Resort, the oceanfront villas are located between the signature 16th hole of the resort's oceanfront course and the larger Westin Rio Mar resort itself. The one-, two-, and three-bedroom villas range in size from 860 to 2,250 square feet (77–203 sq. m), and are tastefully and comfortably decorated, each opening onto an oceanfront balcony. Bathrooms are tiled and fitted with shower/tub combinations. Guests here have full charging privileges at the adjoining Westin Resort, making it easy to enjoy its vast entertainment and recreation venues.

201 Dorado del Mar Blvd., Dorado, PR 00646. ⓒ 787/796-6125. Fax 787/796-6145. www.Hilton.com. 174 units. Winter $240–$295 double, $345–$420 suite, $605 apt. Off-season $160–$200 double, $169–$265 suite, $420 apt. Rates include breakfast. AE, DC, MC, V. **Amenities:** See "amenities" of Westin Rio Mar Beach Resort & Casino (below). *In room:* A/C, TV, fridge, wet bar, coffeemaker, hair dryer, iron and ironing board, safe.

Westin Rio Mar Beach Resort & Casino ★★★ Marking Westin's debut in the Caribbean, this $180 million, 481-acre (192-hectare) resort lies on a relatively uncrowded neighbor (Rio Mar Beach) of the massively popular Luquillo Beach, a 5-minute drive away. It was designed to compete with the Hyatt hotels at Dorado and El Conquistador, with which it's frequently compared. It's the newest, freshest, and best property in the area.

Landscaping includes several artificial lakes situated amid tropical gardens. More than 60% of the guest rooms look out over palm trees to the Atlantic. Other units open onto the mountains and forests of nearby El Yunque National Park (just a 15-minute drive away). Throughout, the style is Spanish hacienda with nods to the surrounding jungle, incorporating unusual art and sculpture that alternates with dark woods, deep colors, rounded archways, big windows, and tile floors. In the bedrooms, muted earth tones, wicker, rattan, and painted wood furniture add to the ambience. Bedrooms are spacious, with balconies or terraces, and good mattresses, plus shower/tub combinations in the spacious bathrooms.

For diversity of cuisine, the only hotel in Puerto Rico that outpaces it is Wyndham's El Conquistador (see below). The resort encompasses the Rio Mar Country Club, site of two important golf courses. The older of the two, the Ocean Course, was designed by George and Tom Fazio as part of the original resort, and has been a staple on Puerto Rico's professional golf circuit since the 1960s. In 1997, Westin opened the property's second 18-holer, the slightly more challenging River Course, the first Greg Norman–designed course in the Caribbean. The resort also has a 6,500-square-foot (585 sq. m) casino.

6000 Rio Mar Blvd. (19 miles/31km east of Luis Muñoz Marin International Airport, with entrance off Puerto Rico Hwy. 3), Rio Grande, PR 00745. ⓒ 800/WESTIN-1 or 787/888-6000. Fax 787/888-6600. www.westin riomar.com. 694 units. Year-round $395–$675 double; from $900 suite. AE, DC, DISC, MC, V. **Amenities:** 8 restaurants, 6 bars; casino; 13 tennis courts; health club and spa; deep-sea game fishing; sailing; nearby horseback riding; children's programs; 24-hr. room service; laundry/dry cleaning. *In room:* A/C, TV, hair dryer, coffeemaker, minibar, iron and ironing board, safe.

Wyndham El Conquistador Resort & Country Club ★★★ *(Kids)*   One of the most impressive resorts anywhere in the Caribbean, with a flash and glitter that always remains supremely tasteful, El Conquistador is a destination unto itself, with an incredible array of facilities. Rebuilt in 1993 at a cost of $250 million by Kumagai/Mitsubishi, it encompasses 500 acres (20 hectares) of forested hills sloping down to the sea. Accommodations are divided into five separate sections that share a common theme of Mediterranean architecture and lush landscaping. Most of them lie several hundred feet above the sea. At the same altitude, a bit off to the side, is a replica of an Andalusian hamlet, Las Casitas Village, which seems straight out of the south of Spain; these plush, pricey units, each with a full kitchen, are a self-contained enclave unto themselves.

A short walk downhill takes you to a circular cluster of tastefully modern accommodations, Las Olas Village. And at sea level, adjacent to an armada of pleasure craft bobbing at anchor, is La Marina Village, whose balconies seem to hang directly over the water. The accommodations are outfitted with comfortable and stylish furniture, soft tropical colors, and robes. All the far-flung elements of the resort are connected by serpentine, landscaped walkways, and by a railroad-style funicular that makes frequent trips up and down the hillside.

The resort contains an array of restaurants and lounges. You could live here for a month and always sample something new and different by dining around. One of the most comprehensive spas in the world, The Golden Door, maintains a branch in this resort. The hotel is sole owner of a "fantasy island" (Palomino Island), with caverns, nature trails, horseback riding, and watersports such as scuba diving, windsurfing, and snorkeling. About a ½ mile (.8km) offshore, the island is connected by free private ferries to the main hotel at frequent intervals. There's also a 25-slip marina.

1000 Conquistador Avenue, Las Croabas, Fajardo, PR 00738. **©** **800/468-5228** in the U.S., or 787/863-1000. Fax 787/863-6500. www.wyndham.com. 915 units. Winter $455–$765 double; from $1,375 suite for 1–4; from $1,195 *casita*, with kitchen, for 1–6. Off-season $295–$525 double; from $1,125 suite for 1–4; $325–$1,025 *casita*, with kitchen, for 1–6. MAP (breakfast and dinner) $92 extra per adult per day, $46 extra per child age 12 and under. Children age 15 and under stay free in parents' room. AE, DC, DISC, MC, V. Parking $10 per day. **Amenities:** 6 restaurants, 7 bars, night club; casino; 6 pools; golf course; 6 tennis courts; health club and spa; watersports, fishing, sailing, dive shop; children's programs; room service; massage; laundry/dry cleaning. *In room:* A/C, TV, minibar, coffeemaker, hair dryer, iron and ironing board, safe.

DINING

Isabela's Grill ★ AMERICAN STEAKHOUSE   Of all the restaurants in El Conquistador Resort, this is the most "American." If Ike were to miraculously return, he'd feel comfortable with this 1950s menu. The severely dignified baroque room was inspired by an aristocratic monastery in Spain. The massive gates are among the most spectacular pieces of wrought iron on Puerto Rico. The service is impeccable, the steaks tender, and the seafood fresh.

Special care is taken with the beef dishes, even though the meat has to be imported frozen. You can begin with the lobster bisque or French soup, then move on to the thick cut of veal chop or the perfectly prepared rack of lamb. Prime rib of beef is a feature, as are the succulent steaks, especially the New York strip or the porterhouse.

In the El Conquistador Resort, Las Croabas. **©** **787/863-1000.** Reservations recommended. Main courses $24–$35. Parking $2.50–$15. AE, DISC, MC, V. Mon–Sat 6–10pm, Sun 6pm–midnight.

Otello's ⋆ NORTHERN ITALIAN   Here you can dine by candlelight in the old-world tradition, with a choice of both indoor and outdoor seating. The decor is neo-Palladian. You might begin with one of the soups, perhaps pasta fagioli, or select one of the zesty Italian appetizers, such as an excellently prepared clams Posillipo. Pastas can be ordered as a half-portion appetizer or as a main dish, and they include the likes of homemade gnocchi or fettuccine with shrimp. The chef is known for his superb veal dishes. A selection of poultry and vegetarian food is offered nightly, along with several shrimp and fish dishes. The salmon filet in champagne sauce has beautiful accents, as does the veal chop in an aromatic herb sauce.

In the Wyndham El Conquistador Resort. ℂ **787/863-1000**. Reservations required in winter, recommended off-season. Main courses $19.95–$36.95. AE, DISC, MC, V. Daily 6–11pm.

TO THE LIGHTHOUSE: EXPLORING LAS CABEZAS DE SAN JUAN NATURE RESERVE ⋆

Better known as El Faro or "The Lighthouse," this preserve in the northeastern corner of the island, north of Fajardo off Route 987, is one of the most beautiful and important areas on Puerto Rico. A number of different ecosystems flourish in the vicinity. Surrounded on three sides by the Atlantic Ocean, the 316-acre (126-hectare) site encompasses forestland, mangroves, lagoons, beaches, cliffs, offshore cays, and coral reefs. El Faro serves as a research center for the scientific community. It's home to a vast array of flora and fauna, including sea turtles and other endangered species.

The nature reserve is open Wednesday to Sunday; reservations are required, so call before going. For reservations throughout the week, call ℂ **787/722-5882;** for reservations on Saturday and Sunday, ℂ **787/860-2560** (reservations on weekends can be made only on the day of your intended visit). Admission is $5 for adults, $2 for children age 12 and under, and $2.50 for seniors. Guided tours are conducted at 9:30am, 10am, 10:30am, and 2pm (in English at 2pm).

9 Palmas del Mar ⋆

The residential resort community of Palmas del Mar lies on the island's eastern (Caribbean) shore, outside the town of Humacao. It's about an hour's drive from the San Juan airport, 45 miles (72km) east of San Juan.

You'll find plenty to do: golf, tennis, scuba diving, sailing, deep-sea fishing, horseback riding—the list goes on and on. The beach, an excellent strip of white sand, is ideal for sunbathing and swimming, though there isn't much snorkeling to speak of. Hiking on the resort's grounds is another favorite activity, and there's a forest preserve with giant ferns, orchids, and hanging vines. There's even a casino.

The Doral Palmas del Mar Resort is not what it was in its heyday in the early 1990s. Today it is virtually a real estate conglomerate, promoting vacation properties to investors. Many of the occupants are residents of San Juan who come here on weekends. Tourists are welcome, but most first-time visitors will find better accommodations up the coast at the Westin Rio Mar or the Wyndham El Conquistador (see "Las Croabas & Luquillo Beach," above).

GETTING THERE

Humacao Regional Airport is 3 miles (5km) from the northern boundary of Palmas del Mar. Its 2,300-foot (690m) strip will accommodate private planes; no regularly scheduled airline currently serves the Humacao airport. Palmas del

Mar will arrange minivan or bus transport from Humacao to the San Juan airport for $36 per person for two passengers or $24 per person for four passengers. For reservations call ✆ **787/285-4323.** Call the resort if you want to be met at the airport.

ACCOMMODATIONS

Doral Palmas del Mar Resort ✪ Although the acreage within the Palmas del Mar development contains thousands of privately owned villas, many of which can be rented or purchased outright by investors, this is the only conventional, full-service hotel in Palmas del Mar. At least some of its business derives from newcomers who want to experience firsthand what Palmas del Mar is like before buying a villa. It was radically renovated in 1997, and again in 1999 by the Wyndham group. None of the well-furnished bedrooms overlook the sea, but many have private patios or verandas, and most are roomier than you might expect. Rooms have tile floors, tropical furnishings, large closets, fine linens, and either king- or queen-size beds, plus tiled bathrooms with shower/tub combinations.

The beach, tennis center, and golf courses are close at hand. There is also the highly visible presence of a cadre of salespeople showing off the charms of a development that's moving more and more into the role of a full-time residential community, with less and less emphasis on temporary hotel guests. There's a restaurant within the hotel, Palma's Café (see "Dining," below), although it's only one of the panoply of dining options.

170 Candalero Dr., Palmas del Mar, Humacao, PR 00791. ✆ **800/725-6273** in the U.S., or 787/852-6000. Fax 787/852-6320. www.palmasdelmar.com. 102 units. Winter $225–$260 double. Off-season $160–$195 double. MAP (breakfast and dinner) $45 per person extra. AE, DC, MC, V. **Amenities:** Restaurant, 2 bars; casino; pool; 2 18-hole golf courses; 20 tennis courts; health club; horseback riding; dive shop; fishing; bikes; kids' program; car rental; room service (6am–10pm); babysitting; laundry/dry cleaning. *In room:* A/C, TV, hair dryer.

DINING

All the restaurants are open during the winter season; however, in summer only three or four may be fully functional. For a complete rundown, ask when you make your booking.

Barracuda Bistro PUERTO RICAN/INTERNATIONAL The most active bar scene in the early evening takes place here, as yachters gather to talk about the adventures of the day. After downing more margaritas than Jimmy Buffett, you can also eat well here. The sautéed mahi-mahi in tequila butter and lime sauce is worth the trip alone. Fresh red snapper is sautéed in butter and lemon zest, and you can also count on the chef throwing a T-bone steak on the grill. You can also order both Mexican and Creole specialties including roast pork and fajitas with either chicken or beef. If you're visiting at lunch or during the afternoon, you can also order fast food too, including hot dogs, sandwiches, and burgers.

La Marina. ✆ **787/850-4441.** Main courses $5–$30. DC, MC, V. Daily noon–10pm.

Chez Daniel/Le Grill ✪ FRENCH It's French, it's fun, and it's the favorite of the folks who tie up their yachts at the adjacent pier. Normandy-born Daniel Vasse, the owner, along with his French Catalonian wife, Lucette, maintain twin dining rooms that in their way are the most appealing at Palmas del Mar. Le Grill is a steakhouse with a Gallic twist and lots of savory flavor in the form of béarnaise, garlic, or peppercorn sauces, or whatever else you specify. It keeps the same hours as Chez Daniel (see below) but is open only December to April.

Chez Daniel shows a more faithful allegiance to the tenets of classical French cuisine, placing an emphasis on such dishes as the bouillabaisse (both the Catalonian and Marseillaise versions), onion soup, and snails, as well as lobster and chicken dishes. For dessert, consider a soufflé au Cointreau.

Marina de Palmas del Mar. *C* 787/852-6000. Reservations required. Main courses $22–$35 at dinner, $8–$11 at lunch. AE, MC, V. Wed–Sun noon–3pm and Wed–Mon 6:30–10pm. Closed June.

Palma's Café INTERNATIONAL   Cooled by trade winds, this restaurant overlooking a courtyard and pool is an ideal choice for any casual meal. Lunch always includes sandwiches and burgers; if you want heartier fare, ask for the Puerto Rican specialty of the day, perhaps red snapper in garlic butter, preceded by black-bean soup. Dinner is more elaborate. Begin with stuffed jalapeños or chicken tacos, followed by Caribbean lobster, New York sirloin, paella, or the catch of the day. The cooking, although of a high standard, is never quite gourmet—it's just good, hearty food.

In Doral Palmas del Mar Resort, Palmas del Mar. *C* 787/852-6000, ext. 50. Reservations required only for groups of 6 or more. Main courses $12–$17. AE, DC, DISC, MC, V. Daily 6:30–11am, noon–5pm, and 6–10:30pm.

SPORTS, ON & OFF THE WATER

Nonguests of the **Palmas del Mar** resorts can still use these hotel facilities, but should call ahead first. The main office can help you arrange deep-sea diving and other activities.

Few other real estate developments in the Caribbean devote as much attention and publicity to their golf facilities as the **Palmas del Mar Golf Club** ⭐ (*C* **787/285-2256**). Today, both the older course, the Gary Player–designed Palm Course, and the newer course, the Reese Jones–designed Flamboyant, have pars of 72 and layouts of around 6,800 feet (612m) each. Crack golfers consider holes 11 to 15 of the older course among the toughest 5 successive holes in the Caribbean. The pro shop that services players on both courses is open daily from 7am to 5:30pm. The Flamboyant course costs $175 for 18 holes; the Palm Course, $160 for 18 holes.

The **Tennis Center** at Palmas del Mar (*C* **787/852-6000**, ext. 51), the largest on Puerto Rico, features 15 hard courts and 5 clay courts. Fees for hotel guests are $20 per hour during the day or $25 per hour at night. Equivalent fees for non-guests are $24 for daytime play or $29 at night. Special tennis packages, which include accommodations, are available. Call for more information.

PALMAS DEL MAR AFTER DARK

The **casino** in the Palmas del Mar complex, (*C* **787/852-6000**, ext. 10142), has 12 blackjack tables, 2 roulette wheels, a craps table, and dozens of slot machines. The casino is open daily year-round, Sunday through Thursday from 4pm to 2am and Friday and Saturday from 6pm to 3am. Under Puerto Rican law, alcoholic beverages cannot be served in a casino.

18

Saba

An extinct volcano, with no beaches or flat land, cone-shaped Saba is 5 square miles (13 sq. km) of rock carpeted with lush foliage like orchids, giant elephant ears, and Eucharist lilies. At its zenith, Mount Scenery, it measures 2,900 feet (870m). Under the sea, the volcanic walls that form Saba continue a sheer drop to great depths, making for some of the most panoramic diving in the Caribbean.

Unless you're a serious hiker or diver, you might confine your look at Saba to a day trip from St. Maarten (and flee as the sun sets). If you're a self-sufficient type who demands almost no artificial amusement, then sleepy Saba might be your hideaway.

One of the smallest islands of the Netherlands Antilles, Saba is 150 miles (242km) east of Puerto Rico and 90 miles (145km) east of St. Croix. Most visitors fly from St. Maarten, 28 miles (45km) to the north.

The official language of Saba is Dutch, but because so many English missionaries and Scottish seamen from the Shetland Islands settled here, Saba has always been English-speaking. All those European settlers have resulted in a population that is 60% Caucasian, many with red hair and freckled fair skin.

1 Essentials

VISITOR INFORMATION

The **Saba Tourist Board** is located at Lambees Place in the heart of Windwardside (© **599/416-2231**). It's open Monday through Thursday from 8am to noon and 1 to 5pm, Friday from 8am to noon and 1 to 4:30pm.

Saba is on the Web at **www.turq.com/saba**.

GETTING THERE

BY PLANE You'll have to get to St. Maarten before you can get to Saba. **American Airlines** (© **800/433-7300** in the U.S.; www.aa.com) offers direct flights from New York's JFK; **Continental Airlines** (© **800/231-0856** in the U.S; www.flycontinental.com) flies out of Newark. From Queen Juliana Airport on St. Maarten, you can take the 12-minute hop to Saba on **Winair** (Windward Islands Airways International; © **599/416-2255**). There are at least five flights per day, depending on volume; fares are $96 round-trip.

Saba's **Juancho Yrausquin Airport** (© **599/416-2255**) is one of the shortest landing strips in the world, stretching only 1,312 feet (394m) along the aptly named Flat Point, one of the few level areas on the island.

Many guests at hotels on St. Maarten fly over to Saba on the morning flight, spend the day sightseeing, then return to St. Maarten on the afternoon flight. Winair connections can also be made on Saba to both St. Kitts and St. Eustatia.

BY BOAT You can also take a high-speed ferry from St. Maarten's Pelican Marina at Simpson Bay to Fort Bay on Saba; you'll arrive in about an hour.

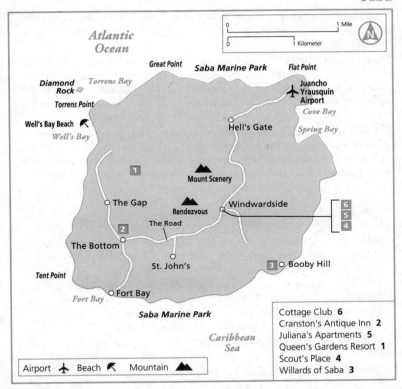

Atlantic Ocean

Saba Marine Park

Great Point   Flat Point

Diamond Rock

Torrens Bay

Juancho Yrausquin Airport

Torrens Point

Cove Bay

Well's Bay Beach

Well's Bay

Hell's Gate

Spring Bay

1

Mount Scenery

The Gap

Rendezvous

Windwardside

6
5
4

The Road

2

The Bottom

St. John's

3 Booby Hill

Tent Point

Fort Bay

Fort Bay

Saba Marine Park

Caribbean Sea

Airport ✈   Beach 🏖   Mountain ▲▲

Cottage Club **6**
Cranston's Antique Inn **2**
Juliana's Apartments **5**
Queen's Gardens Resort **1**
Scout's Place **4**
Willards of Saba **3**

The Edge (© 599/416-2640) departs Wednesday, Friday, and Sunday at 9am, returning at 4pm, making a day trip to Saba possible. Sometimes the waters are turbulent, making passengers seasick. The round-trip fare is $60 per person. Bigger than the ferry and giving you a bit of a smoother ride are **Voyager I,** a 150-passenger catamaran, and **Voyager II,** a 100-passenger powerboat. *Voyager I* sails from Marigot in French St. Martin for Fort Bay on Tuesday at 8:30am, returning at 4:30pm, and *Voyager II* leaves Phillipsburg in Saint Maarten for Saba Thursday at 8:30am, returning at 4:30pm. The cost is $60 round-trip. For information and bookings, call © 599/542-3436.

GETTING AROUND

BY TAXI   Taxis meet every flight. Up to four people are allowed to share a cab. The fare from the airport to Windwardside is $8, or $12.50 to The Bottom. A taxi from Windwardside to The Bottom costs $6.50. There is no central number to call for service

BY RENTAL CAR   None of the major U.S. firms operate on Saba, partly because most visitors opt to get around by taxi. In the unlikely event that you should dare to drive a car on Saba, locally operated companies include **Johnson's Rental,** Windwardside (© 599/416-2269), renting about six Mazdas, starting at $50 per day and including a full tank of gas and unlimited mileage. Some insurance is included in the rates, but you might be held partly responsible in the event of an accident. Because of the very narrow roads and dozens of cliffs, it's crucial to exercise caution when driving on Saba. Note that traffic moves on the right, the same as in the United States.

BY HITCHHIKING Hitchhiking has long been an acceptable means of transport on Saba, where everybody seemingly knows everybody else. And if you hitchhike, you'll probably get to know everybody else, too. On our most recent sightseeing tour, our taxi rushed a sick child to the plane and picked up an old man to take him up the hill because he'd fallen and hurt himself.

ON FOOT The traditional means of getting around on Saba—walking—is still much in evidence. But we suggest that only the sturdy in heart and limb walk from The Bottom up to Windwardside. Many do, but you'd better have some shoes with good traction, particularly after a recent rain.

 FAST FACTS: Saba

Banks The main bank on the island is **Barclays,** Windwardside (© 599/416-2216), open Monday to Friday from 8:30am to 3:30pm. *Note:* There are no ATMs on Saba. The closest ATM is on St. Martin.

Currency Saba, like the other islands of the Netherlands Antilles, uses the **Netherlands Antilles guilder (NAf),** valued at NAf 1.77 to US$1. However, unless otherwise specified, *rates in this chapter are quoted in U.S. dollars,* since U.S. money is accepted by almost everybody here.

Customs You don't have to go through Customs in Saba, as this is a free port.

Documents The government requires that all U.S. and Canadian citizens show proof of citizenship, such as a passport or a birth certificate with a raised seal, along with a government-issued photo ID. A return or ongoing ticket must also be provided. United Kingdom citizens must have a valid passport.

Electricity Saba uses 110-volt AC (60 cycles), so most U.S.-made appliances don't need transformers or adapters.

Hospital Saba's hospital complex is the **A. M. Edwards Medical Centre,** The Bottom (© 599/416-3289).

Language The official language on Saba is Dutch, but you'll find English widely spoken.

Pharmacies Try **The Pharmacy,** The Bottom (© 599/416-3289), open Monday through Friday from 7:30am to 5:30pm.

Police Call © 599/416-3237 for the police.

Safety Crime on this island, where everyone knows everyone else, is practically nonexistent. But who knows? A tourist might rob you. It is always wise to safeguard your valuables.

Taxes The government imposes an 8% tourist tax on hotel rooms. If you're returning to St. Maarten or flying over to Statia, you must pay a $5 departure tax. If you're going anywhere else, however, a $10 tax is imposed.

Telephone You can make international phone calls at **Antelecon,** The Bottom (© 599/416-3211). To call Saba from the United States, dial **011** (the international access code), then **599** (the country code for the Netherlands Antilles), and finally **416** (the area code for all of Saba) and the 4-digit local number. To make a call within Saba, only the 4-digit local number is necessary.

Time Saba is on Atlantic standard time year-round, 1 hour earlier than eastern standard time. When the United States is on daylight saving time, clocks on Saba and the U.S. east coast read the same.

Water The water on Saba is generally safe to drink.

2 Accommodations

If you're looking for a hotel on the beach, you've come to the wrong island. Saba's only beach, Well's Bay Beach, is tiny and can be reached from most hotels only via a $10 taxi ride.

Cottage Club ✷   Small, intimate, and immersed in the architectural and aesthetic traditions of Saba, this hotel complex occupies about a ½ acre (.2 hectares) of steeply sloping and carefully landscaped terrain, a 2-minute walk from the center of the island's capital. Only its lobby evokes a historic setting: Designed of local stone, and set at an altitude above the other buildings of the complex, it's filled with a collection of island antiques and lace curtains.

Each medium-sized studio apartment has a semiprivate patio, a living-room area, and a queen-size bed. Bathrooms have showers and are well maintained. These units are housed in clapboard replicas of antique cottages—two studios per cottage—with red roofs, green shutters, white walls, and yellow trim. The interiors are breezy, airy, and comfortable. If you'd like a room with an ocean view, request numbers 1 or 2. There's no bar or restaurant on the premises, but a nearby supermarket will deliver supplies on request. The owners of the establishment are three Saban brothers (Gary, Mark, and Dean) whose extended families all seem to assist in the maintenance of the place.

Windwardside, Saba, N.A. ✆ **599/416-2486.** Fax 599/416-2476. www.cottage-club.com. 10 units. Winter $118 studio apt. for 2. Off-season $105 studio apt. for 2. Third and fourth person $25 each. Children 12 and under stay free in parents' room. MC, V. **Amenities:** Pool; laundry. *In room:* Ceiling fan, TV, kitchenette.

Cranston's Antique Inn ✷ *(Finds*   Everyone congregates for rum drinks and gossip on the front terrace of this inn near the village roadway, on the west coast north of Fort Bay. It's an old-fashioned house, more than 100 years old, with antique four-poster beds in all the rooms. Mr. Cranston, the owner, will gladly rent you the same bedroom where Queen Juliana once spent a holiday in 1955. Aside from the impressive wooden beds, the furnishings are mostly hit or miss, and not much has changed since the queen checked in oh-so-long ago. The bedrooms are quite tiny, although the floral spreads jazz them up a bit. Come here for the old-time atmosphere and the cheap prices, not for any grand style. The biggest improvement is that all the rooms now have private—but extremely cramped—shower-only bathrooms.

Mr. Cranston has a good island cook, who makes use of locally grown spices. Island dishes include goat meat, roast pork from Saba pigs, red snapper, and broiled grouper.

The Bottom, Saba, N.A. ✆ **599/416-3203.** Fax 599/416-3469. 6 units. Winter $130 double. Off-season $99 double. DISC, MC, V. **Amenities:** Restaurant, bar; pool. *In room:* A/C, TV.

Juliana's Apartments Built in 1985, this hostelry is set on a hillside. Each guest room is modern, immaculate, and simply but comfortably furnished. All have access to a sundeck and balconies opening onto beautiful views of the Caribbean, except numbers 1, 2, and 3, which are in the rear. Opt for one of the upper-level rooms (7, 8, or 9), as they offer the best views. The shower-only bathrooms are small but adequate, and housekeeping wins high marks here. Also available are a 2½-room apartment, complete with kitchenette; and a renovated original Saban cottage, with 2 bedrooms, a spacious living room, a dining room, a TV, and a fully equipped kitchen.

Windwardside, Saba, N.A. ✆ **599/416-2269.** Fax 599/416-2389. www.julianas-hotel.com. 12 units. Winter $125 double; $150 apt.; $165 cottage. Off-season $100 double; $125 apt.; $145 cottage. Extra person $20. Dive packages available. DISC, MC, V. **Amenities:** Restaurant, bar; pool; recreation room; car rental. *In room:* Ceiling fan, TV, fridge, no phone.

Queen's Gardens Resort ⚐ It's still outclassed by Willard's of Saba, but this is a classy joint as well. One of the most massive engineering projects in Saba's recent memory included the placement of a rock-sided terrace on this plot of forested, steeply sloping land 1,200 feet (360m) above the sea. The result, early in 1997, was a well-conceived cluster of white-walled, red-roofed bungalows angled for sweeping views, and clustered around the semicircular edges of the largest pool on Saba, with north-facing views over the island's capital and the sea. From a distance, the compound evokes a fortified village in Iberia; close-up, it's charming and much, much more comfortable. Accommodations are simple, modern, airy, and clean, each decorated in pastel colors. Most units are split-level, with large living rooms; all have kitchenettes and fine double or twin beds. Bathrooms are large but have showers only. On the premises is a restaurant, the Mango Royale (see "Dining," below).

P.O. Box 4, Troy Hill, The Bottom, Saba, N.A. ✆ **599/416-3494.** Fax 599/416-3495. www.queensaba.com. 12 units. Winter $200 double; $250 1-bedroom suite for 2; $350 2-bedroom suite for up to 4. Off-season $210 double; $270 1-bedroom suite for 2; $370 2-bedroom suite for up to 4. AE, MC, V. **Amenities:** Restaurant, bar; pool; Jacuzzi; dive shop; room service (7:30am–9pm); babysitting; laundry. *In room:* TV, kitchen, minibar, coffeemaker, hair dryer.

Scout's Place Right in the center of Windwardside, funky Scout's Place is hidden from the street and set on the ledge of a hill. With only 13 rooms, it's still the second-largest inn on the island. The old house has a large, covered, open-air dining room, where every table has a view of the sea. It's informal with a decor ranging from Surinam hand-carvings to red-and-black wicker peacock chairs to silver samovars. Guest rooms open onto an interior courtyard filled with flowers, and each has a view of the sea. The rooms are small and rather plain, except for the four-poster beds; many have linoleum floors and tiny TVs. The best units are on the lower floor, as they have French doors opening onto balconies fronting the ocean. Furniture is haphazard. Bathrooms are small, with showers only. The apartment with kitchenette is suitable for up to five.

Windwardside, Saba, N.A. ✆ **599/416-2740.** Fax 599/416-2388. www.sabadivers.com. 13 units. Winter $114 double; $129 cottage. Off-season $102 double; $117 cottage. Extra person $30. Rates include continental breakfast. MC, V. **Amenities:** Restaurant, bar; pool; dive shop. *In room:* Ceiling fan, TV, fridge, no phone.

Willard's of Saba ⚐⚐ This is Saba's only pocket of posh. Until Brad Willard arrived, Saba never had anything remotely up to the standards here. Willard is the great-grandson of Henry Augustus Willard, who built his namesake hotel in Washington, D.C. The Saba hotel opened in 1994 and became an immediate sellout, attracting visitors, often celebrities, who might not have set foot on the island before. Guest rooms have *Casablanca*-like ceiling fans; furnishings are not of the highest standard, but are still comfortable. Because of the hotel's location (in a garden high on a hill overlooking the island's southwestern coastline), each room has sweeping views and access to almost constant ocean breezes. Much care went into the design of this place, making use of everything from cedar from the U.S. Northwest to original island paintings.

The least expensive units are the two rooms in the main building, which are quite spacious. The other five units are in a concrete building designed in the island's distinctive style, with red roofs, white walls, and green shutters. For the most luxurious living, ask for the VIP Room overlooking the pool, with its own large balcony. Lower Cliffside units are the smallest, but have good views from their private balconies. The Room in the Sky is the choice of honeymooners. Bathrooms are small, with shower only.

The Corazon restaurant and its bar are recommended in "Dining," below.

Booby Hill, Saba, N.A. ⓒ **599/416-2498**. Fax 599/416-2482. www.willardsofsaba.com. 7 units. Winter $400 double; $350–$450 bungalow; $600 honeymoon suite. Off-season discounts of around 20%. Extra person $50. AE, DISC, MC, V. Children age 12 and under not accepted. **Amenities:** Restaurant, bar; pool; tennis court; Jacuzzi. *In room:* Ceiling fan, no phone.

3 Dining

Brigadoon Pub & Eatery ⚝ CARIBBEAN/AMERICAN   This is the island's best dining choice. An array of Caribbean, American, and other international flavors combine to form a savory cuisine in this century-old colonial building with an open front. Whenever possible, fresh local ingredients are used, including herbs, spices, fruits, and farm-fresh vegetables. Fresh local fish is generally the preferred course, or you can order live local lobster from the island's only live lobster tank (prices vary). Steaks are flown in weekly. You might also prefer the Saba fish pot, a variety of fresh catch from Saba's waters in a basil-and-tomato sauce. Other main courses include mahi-mahi (dolphin) with citrus butter sauce (justifiably very popular) and Thai shrimp in a coconut-curry sauce.

Windwardside. ⓒ **599/416-2380**. Main courses $12–$33. AE, MC, V. Wed–Mon 6:30–9:30pm.

Corazon ⚝ ANTILLEAN/ASIAN/INTERNATIONAL   This restaurant features a breezy island decor, a sweeping high-altitude view of Saba's southeastern coastline, and some of the freshest fish and lobster on the island. Most of the catch featured on the "island-inspired" menu comes from the boats of local fisherfolk. Entrees change with the availability of the ingredients, although grouper, snapper Florentine, and lobster Thermidor are usually featured, as are two recently sampled and truly savory dishes: pork loin with a champagne-and-caper sauce, and Chinese-style beef with oyster sauce. You can cool down with a crepe stuffed with banana and jackfruit, then fried and served with home-made ice cream. The restaurant takes its name from Corazon de Johnson, manager and chef. Although born in the Philippines, she doesn't limit her inspiration to her homeland, but roams the world for ideas for her fusion cuisine. There's a pleasant bar on the premises where you might enjoy a round of before-dinner drinks.

In the Willard's of Saba hotel, Booby Hill. ⓒ **599/416-2498**. Reservations required. Main courses $23–$35. AE, DISC, MC, V. Daily 11:30am–3pm and 6:30–9:30pm.

Mango Royale INTERNATIONAL   Part of this restaurant's allure has to do with its placement beside the largest pool on Saba, its high-altitude views that sweep northward over the sea, and its flaming torches that add a flickering glamour to the site during the dinner hour. You can dine on an indoor/outdoor terrace, or—for more privacy—within a lattice-covered structure inspired by a gazebo. Menu items at lunch include salads, sandwiches, and relatively simple versions of grilled fish. Evening meals are more elaborate, with offerings such as goat meat with mint sauce, lobster bisque, Saba spiced shrimp with Peking dumplings, grilled chicken with tropical herbs, barbecued beef kebabs, and fettuccine with cream sauce.

In the Queen's Gardens Resort, Troy Hill, The Bottom. ✆ 599/416-3494. Reservations recommended. Lunch platters $10–$13; dinner main courses $16–$27. AE, DC, MC, V. Daily 7am–2pm and 7–9:30pm.

Saba Chinese Bar & Restaurant (Moo Goo Gai Pan) CHINESE   Amid a cluster of residential buildings on a hillside above Windwardside, this place is operated by a family from Hong Kong. It offers some 120 dishes, an unpretentious decor of plastic tablecloths and folding chairs, and food so popular that many residents claim this is their most frequented restaurant. Meals include an array of Cantonese and Indonesian specialties—lobster Cantonese, Chinese chicken with mushrooms, sweet-and-sour fish, conch chop suey, several curry dishes, roast duck, and *nasi goreng*. It doesn't rank with the great Chinese restaurants of New York, San Francisco, and Hong Kong, but it's good, change-of-pace fare.

Windwardside. ✆ 599/416-2353. Main courses $8–$20. V. Tues–Sun 11am–10pm.

Scout's Place INTERNATIONAL   This is a popular dining spot among day-trippers to the island, so you should have your driver stop by early to make a reservation for you. Lunch at Scout's is simple, good, and filling, and the prices are low, too. Dinner is more elaborate, with tables placed on an open-sided terrace, the ideal spot for a drink at sundown. Fresh seafood is a specialty, as is curried goat. The sandwiches are the island's best, made with fresh-baked bread. Locals come from all over the island to sample them. Each day, a selection of homemade soups is also offered, perhaps pumpkin or pigeon pea. Scout's chef is proud of his ribs as well. Fresh local fruits and vegetables are used whenever possible. Even if you don't like the food, it's the best place on the island to catch up on the latest gossip.

In the Scout's Place hotel, Windwardside. ✆ 599/416-2740. Reservations recommended. Lunch $6–$15; fixed-price dinner $10–$25. MC, V. Daily 7am–11pm.

4 Sports & Other Outdoor Pursuits

If it's beaches you're seeking, forget it: It's better to remain on the sands of St. Maarten. Saba's only beach, Well's Bay Beach, disappears entirely during the winter. Sports here are limited primarily to diving and hiking.

DIVING & SNORKELING ★★

Circling the entire island and including four offshore underwater mountains (seamounts), the **Saba Marine Park,** Fort Bay (✆ **599/416-3295**), preserves the island's coral reefs and marine life. The park is zoned for various pursuits. The all-purpose recreational zone includes **Well's Bay Beach,** Saba's only beach, but it's seasonal—it disappears with the winter seas, only to reappear in late spring. There are two anchorage zones for visiting yachts and Saba's only harbor. The five dive zones include a coastal area and four seamounts, a mile (2km) offshore. In these zones are more than two-dozen marked and buoyed dive sites and a snorkeling trail. You plunge into a world of coral and sponges, swimming with parrot fish, doctorfish, and damselfish.

The **snorkel trail,** however, is not for the neophyte. It can be approached from Well's Bay Beach but only from May to October. Depths of more than 1,500 feet (450m) are found between the island and the seamounts, which reach a minimum depth of 90 feet (27m). There's a $3 per dive visitor fee. Funds are also raised through souvenir sales and donations. The park office at Fort Bay is open Monday to Friday from 8am to 4pm, Saturday from 8am to noon, and Sunday from 10am to 2pm. There's also a fully operational decompression chamber/hyperbaric facility located in the Fort Bay harbor.

Sea Saba Dive Center, Windwardside (© **599/416-2246**), has nine experienced instructors eager to share their knowledge of Saba Marine Park: famous deep and medium-depth pinnacles, walls, spur-and-groove formations, and giant boulder gardens. Their two 40-foot (12m), uncrowded boats are best suited for a comfortable day on Saba's waters. Daily boat dives are made between 9:30am and 1:30pm, allowing a relaxing interval for snorkeling. Courses range from resort through dive master. Extra day and night dives can be arranged. A 1-tank dive costs $50, a 2-tank dive $90.

Saba Deep Dive Center, P.O. Box 22, Fort Bay, Saba, N.A. (© **599/416-3347**), is a full-service dive center that offers scuba diving, snorkeling, equipment rental/repair, and tank fills. Mike Myers and his staff of NAUI and PADI instructors and dive masters make an effort to provide personalized service and great diving, whether you're an old pro or with an entire family of first-timers. A certification course goes for $400. A single-tank dive costs $50; a 2-tank dive, $90. Night dives are $70. The center is open daily from 8am to 6pm. On the same property, the **In Two Deep Restaurant** and the **Deep Boutique** offer air-conditioned comfort, a view of the harbor area and the Caribbean Sea, good food and drink, and a wide selection of clothes, swimwear, lotions, and sunglasses. The restaurant is open for breakfast and lunch.

HIKING

Saba is as beautiful above the water as it is below. It offers many trails, both for the neophyte and the more experienced hiker, all reached by paths leading off from "The Road." There's nothing more dramatic than the hike to the top of **Mount Scenery,** a volcano that erupted 5,000 years ago. Allow at least 3 hours and take your time climbing the 1,064 sometimes-slippery concrete steps up to the cloud-reefed, 2,855-foot (857m) mountain. You'll pass through a lush rain forest of palms, bromeliads, elephant ears, heliconia, mountain raspberries, lianas, and tree ferns. Queen Beatrix of the Netherlands climbed these steps in her pumps and, upon reaching the summit, declared: "This is the smallest and highest place in my kingdom." On a clear day, you can see the neighboring islands of St. Kitts, St. Eustatius, St. Maarten, and even St. Bart's. Ask your inn to pack you a picnic lunch, and bring water. The higher you climb, the cooler it grows, about a drop of 1°F every 328 feet (98m); on a hot day this can be an incentive.

One of our favorite hikes—with some of Saba's most panoramic views—is the **Crispeen Track,** reached from Windwardside as the main road descends to the hamlet of St. John's. Once at St. John's, the track heads northeast going through a narrow but dramatic gorge covered in thick tropical foliage. The vegetation grows lusher and lusher, taking in banana and citrus fields. As you reach the higher points of a section of the island called Rendezvous, the fields are no longer cultivated and resemble a rain forest, covered with such flora as philo-dendron, anthurium, and the wild mammee. Hiking time to Rendezvous is about an hour.

If you don't want to explore the natural attractions of the island on your own, the **Saba Tourist Office,** P.O. Box 527, Windwardside (© **599/416-2231**), can arrange tours of the tropical rain forests. Jim Johnson (© **599/416-3307**), a fit, 40-ish Saban guide, conducts most of these tours, and knows the terrain better than anyone else on the island (he's sometimes difficult to reach, however). Johnson will point out orchids, golden heliconia, and other flora and fauna, as well as the rock formations and bromeliads you're likely to see. Tours can accom-modate one to eight hikers and usually last about half a day; depending on your particular route and number of participants, the cost can be anywhere from $50 to $90. Actual prices, of course, are negotiated.

5 Exploring the Island

Tidy white houses cling to the mountainside, and small family cemeteries adjoin each dwelling. Lace-curtained, gingerbread-trimmed cottages give a Disneyland aura.

The first Jeep arrived on Saba in 1947. Before that, Sabans went about on foot, climbing from village to village. Hundreds of steps had been chiseled out of the rock by the early Dutch settlers in the 1640s.

Past storybook villages, this road goes over the crest to **The Bottom.** Derived from the Dutch word *botte,* which means "bowl-shaped," this village is nestled on a plateau and surrounded by rocky volcanic domes. It occupies about the only bit of ground, 800 feet (240m) above the sea. It's also the official capital of Saba, a charming Dutch village of chimneys, gabled roofs, and gardens.

From The Bottom, you can take a taxi up the hill to the mountain village of **Windwardside,** perched on the crest of two ravines about 1,500 feet (450m) above sea level. This village of red-roofed houses, the second most important on Saba, is the site of the two biggest inns and most of the shops.

From Windwardside, you can climb steep steps cut in the rock to yet another village, **Hell's Gate,** teetering on the edge of a mountain. There's also a ser-pentine road from the airport to Hell's Gate, where you'll find the island's largest church. Only the most athletic climb from here to the lip of the volcanic crater.

Moments **A Road That's a Roller Coaster**

Regardless of what road you travel in the Caribbean, there's nothing to compare with 19-mile-long (31km) "The Road." Its hairpin curves climb from the little airport up the steep, steep hillside to the lush interior of Saba. In days of yore, engineer after engineer came to the island and told Sabans they'd have to forget ever having a road on their volcanic moun-tain. Josephus Lambert Hassell, a local, had high hopes. In the 1930s he began to take a correspondence course in engineering while he plotted and planned The Road. Under his guidance, his fellow islanders built The Road over the next 2 decades or so. In recent years, it's been necessary to reconstruct The Road, but it's there waiting to thrill you. At the top of The Road stands Windwardside at 1,804 feet (541m), Saba's second largest settlement and the island's midpoint.

6 Saba After Dark

If you want to do a lot of partying on your vacation, you might want to consider another island. Saba is known for its tucked-away, relaxed, and calm atmosphere. However, don't be too dismayed; there's still something to do at night.

Scout's Place, Windwardside (© 599/416-2740), is the place to hang out if you want to relax, enjoy a drink, and have a laugh, especially on weeknights. A hotel and restaurant, Scout's Place moonlights as a local watering hole, entertaining tourists and locals alike with a distinct Saban/Caribbean atmosphere. You won't do much dancing (well, that actually depends on how much you've had to drink), but it's much better than the weeknight alternative: nothing. It's open daily from 8am to around midnight (but actual closing hours depend on business or the lack thereof). There's no cover.

Normally a pizzeria, **Guido's,** near Scout's Place, Windwardside (© 599/416-2230), serves simple food and drinks weeknights, but becomes the most happening place on island on Friday and Saturday nights, as it's really your only option to get a drink *and* boogie down. As a disco, it's known as Mountain High Club. There's a dance floor, a sound system, and even a disco ball. Weeknights are similar to Scout's Place: a simple dining crowd. Hours are Monday through Thursday from 6pm to midnight, and Friday and Saturday from 6pm to 2am. There's no cover.

If you'd like to combine the ambience of a British pub with a saloon that might have been found in the Arizona Badlands, head for **Swinging Doors,** Windwardside (© 599/416-2506). Saba's good ol' boy watering hole, where locals start consuming the brew at 9am and keep drinking until late at night (no set closing hour). If you get hungry along the way, you can go for those jalapeño poppers.

19

St. Barthélemy

For luxury with minimum hassle, albeit at a high price tag, St. Barts is rivaled only by Anguilla. It's the ultimate in sophistication in the tropics: chic, rich, and very Parisian. Forget such things as historic sites or ambitious watersports programs here. You go to St. Barts for the relaxation, the French cuisine, the white-sand beaches, and the ultimate in comfort.

New friends call it "St. Barts," while old-time visitors prefer "St. Barths." Either way, it's short for St. Barthélemy, named by its discoverer Columbus in 1493 and pronounced *San Bar-te-le-MEE*. For the most part, St. Bartians are descendants of Breton and Norman fisherfolk. Many are of French and Swedish ancestry, the latter evident in their fair skin, blond hair, and blue eyes. The mostly Caucasian population is small, about 3,500 living in some 8 square miles (21 sq. km), 15 miles (24km) southeast of St. Martin and 140 miles (225km) north of Guadeloupe.

Occasionally you'll see St. Bartians dressed in the provincial costumes of Normandy and speaking Norman French. In little **Corossol,** more than anywhere else, people sometimes follow customs brought from 17th-century France. You might see elderly women wearing the traditional starched white bonnets, at least on special occasions. The bonnets, known as *quichenottes* (a corruption of "kiss-me-not"), served as protection from the close attentions of English or Swedish men on the island. The bonneted women can also be spotted at local celebrations, particularly on August 25, **St. Louis's Day.** Many of these women are camera-shy, but they offer their homemade baskets and hats for sale to visitors.

For a long time, the island was a paradise for a few millionaires, such as David Rockefeller, who has a hideaway on the northwest shore, and Edmond de Rothschild, who occupies some fabulous acres at the "other end" of the island. Nowadays, however, St. Barts is developing a broader base of tourism as it opens more hotels. Nevertheless, the island continues to be a favorite of celebrities, attracting the likes of Tom Cruise, Harrison Ford, and Mikhail Baryshnikov.

St. Barts also attracts a lot of star-seeking paparazzi, who stalk celebrities not only at their private villas, but also at the beach, including Grand Saline beach, where the late John F. Kennedy, Jr., was photographed bathing in the nude (which is common and legal at this beach). On another occasion, the paparazzi caught Brad Pitt sunning in the nude at his private villa, with then-girlfriend Gwyneth Paltrow. In February, the island guest list reads like a roster from *Lifestyles of the Rich and Famous.*

The island's capital is **Gustavia,** named after a Swedish king. It's St. Barts' only town and seaport. A sheltered harbor, it has the appearance of a little dollhouse-scale port.

Airport ✈ Beach ↖ Mountain ▲▲ Ferry Route ----

Carl Gustaf **5**	Hôtel Manapany Cottages **4**	Le Toiny **15**
Eden Rock **6**	Hôtel Normandie **10**	Le Village St-Jean **8**
El Sereno Beach Hotel **14**	Hôtel St. Barth Isle de France **3**	Manoir de St. Barthélémy **12**
Filao Beach Hotel **7**	La Banane **9**	Sofitel Coralia Christopher **11**
François Plantation **1**	Le P'tit Morne **2**	Tropical Hôtel **5**
Hôtel Guanahani **13**		

1 Essentials

VISITOR INFORMATION

For information before you go, contact the **French Government Tourist Office** (© **202/659-7779;** www.francetourism.com). There are offices at 444 Madison Ave., **New York, NY** 10022 (© **212/838-7800**); 9454 Wilshire Blvd., Suite 715, **Beverly Hills, CA** 90212 (© **310/271-6665**); or 676 N. Michigan Ave., Suite 3360, **Chicago, IL** 60611 (© **312/751-7800**).

On the island, go to the **Office du Tourisme,** in the commercial heart of Gustavia, adjacent to La Capitanerie (the Port Authority Headquarters), quai du Général-de-Gaulle (© **590/27-87-27**).

GETTING THERE

BY PLANE   Before you book your own airfare, read the section on package tours in chapter 2—it can save you a bundle!

The makeshift landing strip on St. Barts has been the butt of many jokes. It's short and accommodates only small aircraft; the biggest plane it can land is a 19-seater. And even on these small planes, landing on St. Barts has often been compared (and not favorably) to touching down on an aircraft carrier. No landings or departures are permitted after dark.

Therefore, it goes without saying that there are no nonstop flights from North America. From the United States, the principal gateways are

St. Maarten, St. Thomas, and Guadeloupe (see the individual chapters on these islands). At any of these islands, you can connect to St. Barts via inter-island carriers.

From St. Maarten, your best bet is **Windward Islands Airways International** (known by everybody as **Winair** © 590/27-61-01), which usually offers 18 daily flights to St. Barts. Round-trip passage costs $107; flight duration is a mere 10 minutes.

Air Caraïbes (© 590/27-61-90; www.aircaraibes.com) flights depart four or five times a day from Pointe-à-Pitre's Le Raizet Airport. One-way passage from Guadeloupe to St. Barts costs $125; trip time is 55 minutes. Air Caraïbes also offers about three flights a day to St. Barts from the small Esperance Airport on the French side of St. Martin. A one-way fare costs $103.

Air St. Thomas (© 800/522-3084 in the U.S. or 590/27-71-76) offers two flights a day to St. Barts from both San Juan and St. Thomas. However, customers have complained that the airline's schedule is unpredictable. The fare from St. Thomas to St. Barts is $255 round-trip; from San Juan to St. Barts, $340 round-trip.

BY BOAT The *Voyager* vessels (© 590/27-77-24), which operate from a base in Gustavia harbor, make frequent (usually daily) runs between St. Barts and either side of St. Maarten/St. Martin. The schedule varies according to the season and the whim of the proprietors, but the *Voyager II* (a catamaran with room for 150 passengers) usually departs Marigot Harbor for St. Barts every morning at 9am, arriving in Gustavia at 10:30am. *Voyager I,* a single-hulled sailboat with room for 110 passengers, travels from Philipsburg Harbour to Gustavia every day at approximately the same hours. Both vessels charge around $57 round-trip. Advance reservations are a good idea, particularly since the schedule is so iffy.

GETTING AROUND

BY TAXI Taxis meet all flights and are not super-expensive, mostly because destinations aren't far from one another. Dial © 590/27-66-31 for taxi service. A typical rate, St-Jean to Cul-de-Sac, is 11.40€ ($10.20). Night fares between 7pm and midnight are 50% higher. Except under rare circumstances, taxi service isn't available between midnight and 7am.

Virtually every cab driver is aware of the official prices that the island government imposes on **tours by taxi.** Many travelers simply approach a likely looking taxi driver and ask him to show them around. The official rates for 1 to 3 passengers are 38€ ($33.95) for 45 minutes, 45.60€ ($40.70) for 60 minutes, and 60.80€ ($54.30) for 90 minutes. For 4 or more passengers, add 7.60€ ($6.80) to each of the above-mentioned prices.

BY RENTAL CAR Nowhere will you see so many open-sided Mitsubishi Mini-Mokes and Suzuki Samurais as on St. Barts. You'll enjoy driving one, too, as long as you're handy with a stick shift and don't care about your coiffure.

Budget (© 800/472-3325 in the U.S., or 590/27-66-30; www.budget rentacar.com) offers the least stringent terms for its midwinter rentals, and some of the most favorable rates. It rents Suzuki Samurais and Mitsubishis for $60 a day or $420 a week, with unlimited mileage. A collision-damage waiver (CDW; in French, *une assurance tous-risques*), absolving renters of all but $400 of responsibility in the event of an accident, costs 10.65€ ($9.50) a day. For the lowest rate, you should reserve at least 3 business days before your arrival.

Hertz (© **800/654-3001** in the U.S.; www.hertz.com) operates on St. Barts through a local dealership, **Henry's Car Rental,** with branches at the airport and in St-Jean (© **590/27-71-14**). It offers open-sided Suzuki Samurais for 62€ ($55.35) a day, and more substantial Suzuki Sidekicks for 71€ ($63.40) per day. The CDW is about $10 per day (with a $500 deductible). To guarantee the availability of a car in winter, Hertz insists that a deposit of $100 (payable in the form of a cashier's check or a debit held against a valid credit or charge card) be phoned or mailed directly to the local rental agent 3 weeks before your arrival on the island.

At **Avis** (© **800/331-1212** in the U.S., or 590/27-71-43; www.avis.com), you'll need a reservation a full month in advance during high season, plus a $100 deposit in advance. In the winter, cars range from $78 to $110 a day, with weekly rentals going from $400 to $500. In the off-season, rentals are $50 to $70 a day, with weekly rentals from $330 to $600. The CDW costs $10 extra per day (with a $500 deductible).

Never drive with less than half a tank of gas on St. Barts. There are only two gas stations on the island, and they're closed on Sunday and open only from 7:30am to noon and 2 to 5:30pm on other days of the week. (Remarkably, though, you can pay at the pump during business hours if you have a Visa card.) One gas station is near the airport; the other is near L'Orient. All valid foreign driver's licenses are honored. Honk your horn furiously while going around the island's blind corners to avoid having your fenders sideswiped.

BY MOTORBIKE & SCOOTER   **Denis Dufau** operates two affiliates (© **590/27-70-59** and © **590/27-54-83**). Call either number to make arrangements for rentals. A helmet is provided, and renters must either leave an imprint of a valid credit card or pay a 456€ ($407.20) deposit. Rental fees vary from 22.05€ to 27.35€ ($19.70–$24.45) per day, depending on the size of the bike. For all but the smallest models, presentation of a valid driver's license is required.

 FAST FACTS: **St. Barthélemy**

Banks   The two main banks are both in Gustavia. The **Banque Francaise Commerciale,** rue du General-de-Gaulle (© **590/27-62-62**), is open Monday through Friday from 8am to 12:30pm and 2 to 4:30pm; it's closed Wednesday afternoon. The **Banque Nationale de Paris,** rue du Bord-de-Mer (© **590/27-63-70**), is open Monday through Friday from 8am to noon and 2 to 3:30pm; closes at noon on Wednesday.

Currency   In 2002, St. Barts, as a political part of mainland France, abandoned its historic French franc and joined the Euro umbrella. The current rate of exchange is 1.12€ to US$1.

Documents   U.S., British, and Canadian citizens need only a passport to enter St. Barts. If you're flying in, you'll need to present your return or ongoing ticket.

Electricity   The electricity is 220-volt AC (50 cycles); U.S.-made appliances will require adapter plugs and transformers.

Emergencies   Dial © **16** for police or medical emergencies, © **18** for fire emergencies.

Hospital St. Barts is not the greatest place to find yourself in a medical emergency. Except for vacationing doctors escaping their own practices in other parts of the world, it has only seven resident doctors and about a dozen on-call specialists. The island's only hospital, with the only emergency facilities, is the **Hopital de Bruyn,** rue Jean-Bart (© **590/27-60-35**), about a ¼ mile (.4km) north of Gustavia. Serious medical cases are often flown out to St. Maarten, Martinique, Miami, or wherever the accident victim or his/her family specifies.

Language The official language is French, but English is widely spoken.

Pharmacies The **Pharmacie de Saint-Barth** is on quai de la Republique, Gustavia (© **590/27-61-82**). Its only competitor is the **Pharmacie de l'Aeroport,** adjacent to the airport (© **590/27-66-61**). Both are open Monday through Saturday from 8am to 8pm; on Sunday, one or the other remains open for at least part of the day.

Safety Although crime is rare here, it would be wise to protect your valuables. Don't leave them unguarded on the beach or in parked cars, even if locked in the trunk.

Taxes There's an airport departure tax of 4.55€ ($4.05), but no hotel tax.

Telephone St. Barts is linked to the Guadeloupe telephone system. To call St. Barts from the United States, dial **011** (the international access code), then **590** (the country code for Guadeloupe), then **590** again (the area code for St. Barths), and finally the 6-digit local number. To make a call to anywhere in St. Barts from within St. Barts, dial only the 6-digit local number, and ignore the prefix 590. To reach an AT&T operator from anywhere on the island, dial © **0800-99-00-11.** To reach **MCI,** dial © **0800-99-00-19,** and to reach **Sprint,** dial © **0800-99-0087.**

Time When standard time is in effect in the United States and Canada, St. Barts is 1 hour ahead of the U.S. east coast. Thus, when it's 7pm on St. Barts, it's 6pm in New York. When daylight saving time is in effect in the United States (Apr–Dec), clocks in New York and St. Barts show the same time.

Tipping Hotels usually add a service charge of 10% to 15%; always ask if this is included in the price you're quoted. Restaurants typically add a service charge, too. Taxi drivers expect a tip of 10% of the fare.

Water The water on St. Barts is generally safe to drink.

Weather The climate of St. Barts is ideal: dry with an average temperature of 72° to 86°F.

2 Accommodations

With the exception of a few of the really expensive hotels, most places here are homey, comfortable, and casual. Everything is small, as tiny St. Barts is hardly in the mainstream of tourism. In March, it's often hard to stay on St. Barts unless you've made reservations far in advance. Accommodations throughout the island, with some exceptions, tend to be exceptionally expensive, and a service charge of between 10% and 15% is usually added to your bill.

St. Barts has a sizable number of villas, beach houses, and apartments for rent by the week or month. Villas are dotted around the island's hills—very few are on the beach. Instead of an oceanfront bedroom, you get a panoramic view. One of the best agencies to contact for villa, apartment, or condo rentals is **St. Barth Properties,** 2 Master Dr., Franklin, MA 02038 (© **800/421-3396** in the U.S. and Canada, or 508/528-7727). Peg Walsh, a longtime aficionado of St. Barts, assisted by her capable son, Tom Smyth, will let you know what's available. She can also make arrangements for car rentals and air travel to St. Barts. When you arrive, she can book babysitters and restaurant reservations. Rentals can range from a one-room "studio" villa away from the beach, for $980 per week off-season, up to $40,000 per week for a mini-palace at Christmas. Yes, that $40,000 is right, but it's for a very unusual, antique-furnished luxury home. Most rentals are far cheaper, averaging between $2,500 and $4,000 a week between mid-December and mid-April, with discounts of 30% to 50% the rest of the year. In addition to villas, Ms. Walsh can also arrange accommodations in all categories of St. Barts's hotels.

VERY EXPENSIVE

Carl Gustaf ✦✦✦   The most glamorous hotel in Gustavia rises above the town's harbor from its position on a steep hillside. Each state-of-the-art unit is in one of a dozen pink or green, red-roofed villas whose facilities include a private kitchenette, two phones, a fax machine, two stereo systems, a private terrace, a private pool, two TVs, and comfortably plush rattan furniture. Access to each building is via a central staircase, which tests the stamina of even the most active of guests. The wood-frame units are angled for maximum views of the boats bobbing far below in the bay and panoramic sunsets. Bedrooms aren't as large as might be expected at such prices, but they are exceedingly well furnished, especially suites no. 30 through 33. You'll walk across Italian marble floors under a pitched ceiling to reach your luxurious bed with elegant fabrics. Bathrooms are also well equipped, with mosaic-clad showers (no tubs), and makeup mirrors. Beach facilities are within a 10-minute walk. The mood is French, not unlike what you'd find on the coast of Provence.

The cuisine is French and Creole. Often a well-known chef from Paris appears in winter.

Rue des Normands, 97099 Gustavia, St. Barthélemy, F.W.I. © 800/322-2223 in the U.S., or 590/27-82-83. Fax 590/29-79-00. www.carlgustaf.com. 14 units. Winter $950–$1,000 1-bedroom suite; $1,300–$1,400 2-bedroom suite. Off-season $660 1-bedroom suite; $900 2-bedroom suite. Rates include continental breakfast. AE, MC, V. **Amenities:** Restaurant; bar; pool; health club; sauna; plunge pools; helicopter rides; scuba diving, deep-sea fishing, water-skiing, sailing, windsurfing; 24-hr. room service; massage; laundry/dry cleaning. *In room:* A/C, TV, VCR, stereo, fax machine, kitchenette, minibar, fridge, hair dryer, safe.

Eden Rock ✦   Greta Garbo long ago checked out, but this legendary hotel still occupies the most spectacular site on St. Barts, flanked by two perfect beaches. Many years ago, when the island's former mayor, Remy de Haenen, bought the quartzite promontory this hotel sits on from an old woman, she laughed at him for paying too much. Today, the story is part of island lore. Offering the best panoramas on the island, it's surrounded on three sides by the waters of St. Jean Bay.

The building atop the pinnacle looks like an idealized version of a Provençal farmhouse. The stone house contains a collection of French antiques and paintings left over from the de Haenen family, plus English antiques and paintings imported by new owners. The decor in each guest room includes a stylish mixture of tasteful antiques and reproductions, and fabrics and accessories pulled together with flair. Some are right on the beach, with their own access to the sand. The best and most expensive are the ocean suites with private balconies.

The least expensive are the small and cozy cabins. Bathrooms are compact and have showers.

97133 St-Jean, St. Barthélemy, F.W.I. ℂ 590/29-79-89. Fax 590/27-88-37. www.edenrockhotel.com. 16 units. Winter $340–$1,500 double. Off-season $275–$1,200 double. Rates include buffet breakfast. AE, MC, V. **Amenities:** 4 restaurants, 2 bars; pool; windsurfing, snorkeling; room service; laundry/dry cleaning. *In room:* A/C, TV, hair dryer, minibar, safe.

François Plantation ⋆⋆   This complex re-creates the plantation era, standing on a steep hill with panoramic views of the beach below. It's inland from the beach, but the management throws in a free rental car (in summer only) for the price of the room. Just pick up your car at the airport. Twelve bungalows, each decorated in an elegant West Indian style, surround a tropical garden. Eight of the units have sea views, and the others look out over a garden. Spacious bedrooms contain mahogany four-posters, ceiling fans, and Moroccan rugs on marble or tile floors make the places extra cozy. Marble bathrooms come with bidets, open showers, and dual basins. The owners are Françoise and François (you read it right) Beret, longtime residents of St. Barts.

The hotel has an exceptional restaurant, La Route des Epices (see "Dining," later in this chapter).

Colombier, 97133 St. Barthélemy, F.W.I. ℂ 590/29-80-22. Fax 800/207-8071 in the U.S. or 590/27-61-26. www.francois-plantation.com. 12 units. Winter $350–$450 bungalow for 2. Off-season $280–$320 bungalow for 2. Rates include American breakfast and free use of a rental car in summer only. AE, MC, V. Closed Jul 31–Oct 31. **Amenities:** Restaurant, bar; pool; health club; room service (breakfast only); laundry. *In room:* A/C, TV, minibar, coffeemaker, hair dryer, safe.

Hôtel Guanahani ⋆⋆   Better equipped than its nearest rival, Hôtel Manapany Cottages (see below), this is the largest hotel on St. Barts, opening onto two scenic beaches. It, along with the Sofitel Coralia Christopher (see below) are the most commercial properties on island. Isolated in the northeast part of the island, the hotel is spread over 7 steeply sloping acres (3 hectares) on its own peninsula, dotted with a network of 50 Lilliputian cottages trimmed in gingerbread and painted in bold, tropical colors. Don't consider this place if you have mobility problems or just don't relish the idea of puffing up and down steep slopes. But if that's not a problem, the views over the sea from each unit are broad and sweeping. Most units, at least those on the resort's upper slopes, are self-contained in their own individual cottages. The bungalows closest to the beach, a private white-sand strip on a reef-protected bay, sometimes contain two units each. Every accommodation has a fridge, ceiling fans, and a private patio or balcony. Queen Anne–style desks and tables, tasteful upholstery, and four-poster beds spell deluxe living, as do the fine linen and comfortable beds. Bathrooms are brightly tiled with shower/tub combinations.

Grand Cul-de-Sac, 97133 St. Barthélemy, F.W.I. ℂ 800/223-6800 in the U.S., or 590/27-66-60. Fax 590/27-70-70. www.leguanahani.com. 75 units. Winter $446.50–$714.40 double; from $803.70 suite. Off-season 300€–500€ $267.90–$446.50 double; $535.80 suite. Rates include American breakfast and round-trip airport transfers. AE, MC, V. **Amenities:** 2 restaurants, 3 bars; 2 pools; 2 tennis courts; fitness center; Jacuzzi; watersports, windsurfing; bike rental; boat rental; car rental; salon; 24-hr. room service; massage; babysitting; laundry/dry cleaning. *In room:* A/C, TV, minibar, hair dryer, safe.

Hôtel Manapany Cottages ⋆   This resort climbs a steep, well-landscaped hillside on the northwestern side of the island, a 10-minute taxi ride north of the airport. This is one of the most stylish hotels on St. Barts, although not in the league of Carl Gustaf or Hotel Christopher. It's small, intimate, and accommodating; the name, translated from Malagese, means "small paradise." The place was designed as a minivillage of gingerbread-trimmed Antillean cottages, set either on a steeply sloping hillside or beside the water. The rambling verandas and open-sided living rooms allow you to enjoy the trade winds off the sea, while the bedrooms have air-conditioning in case it gets too hot. The furnishings include both white rattan and Caribbean colonial pieces carved from mahogany and imported from the Dominican Republic. Mosquito netting covers most of the four-poster beds for a romantic touch. Rooms come with large-screen TVs with in-house video movies, and kitchenettes. Bathrooms are quite luxurious, most with shower/tub combinations.

Anse des Cayes, 97098 St. Barthélemy, F.W.I. (© 800/847-4249 in the U.S., or 590/27-66-55. Fax 590/27-75-28. www.lemanapany.com. 47 units. Winter $465–$515 double; $730–$950 junior suite; $920–$1,050 cottage. Off-season $270–$300 double; $425–$540 junior suite; $530–$600 cottage. Rates include continental breakfast. AE, DC, MC, V. **Amenities:** Restaurant, bar; tennis court; small spa; 24-hr. room service; babysitting; laundry. *In room:* A/C, TV, fridge, hair dryer, safe.

Hôtel St. Barth Isle de France ⚘

Like François Plantation (see above), this resort evokes colonial era charm, but François does it more elegantly. This small, family-run hotel is completely isolated from a chain-hotel mentality, with unusually spacious guest rooms for St. Barts. Each top-notch unit contains a private patio or terrace, and an individual decor with antique mahogany and rattan furniture and engravings collected from neighboring islands. Beds are luxurious, fitted with fine linen. Clad in marble, bathrooms are spacious and well equipped with dual basins, large tubs (in some cases with whirlpool jets) and showers.

Meals are charming and sophisticated (with strong French overtones), despite their informality.

97098 Anse des Flamands, St. Barthélemy, F.W.I. (© 800/810-4691 in the U.S., or 590/27-61-81. Fax 590/27-86-83. www.isle-de-france.com. 30 units. Winter $545–$825 double; $990 suite; $545–$775 bungalow. Off-season $440–$620 double; $805 suite; $390–$565 bungalow. Rates include continental breakfast. AE, MC, V. **Amenities:** Restaurant, bar; 2 pools; tennis court; exercise room; car rental; 24-hr. room service; babysitting; laundry. *In room:* A/C, TV/DVD, stereo, minibar, fridge, coffeemaker, hair dryer, safe.

Le Toiny ★★★

This posh retreat is in a dead heat for supremacy with Carl Gustaf. One of the most glamorous and chillingly expensive resorts on St. Barts, it contains only a dozen suites, which are scattered among a half-dozen buildings clinging to a gently sloping hillside near Plage des Gouverneurs. The nearest beach for swimming is a 5-minute drive away at Grande Saline, the only sanctioned nude beach on the island.

All the suites here have floors of either wide planks or terra-cotta tiles, kitchenettes, bathrooms with shower/tub combinations, and mahogany four-posters draped with mosquito netting. Each provides plenty of privacy, with lots of space and shrubbery between units.

Anse de Toiny, 97133 St. Barthélemy, F.W.I. (© 800/278-6469 or 590/27-88-88. Fax 590/27-89-30. www.letoiny.com. 13 suites. Winter $1,321.65 1-bedroom suite for 2; $2,232.50 3-bedroom suite for up to 6. Off-season $642.95 1-bedroom suite; $1,160.90 3-bedroom suite. AE, DC, MC, V. Closed Sept 1–Oct 22. **Amenities:** Restaurant, bar; pool; bike rental; car rental; 24-hr. room service; babysitting; laundry/dry cleaning. *In room:* A/C, TV/VCR/DVD, kitchenette, minibar, coffeemaker, hair dryer, safe.

Sofitel Coralia Christopher ★★★

Set on a dramatic promontory above the ocean, this full-service hotel offers views of St. Martin and nearby islets. Built and managed by Sofitel, it offers a French-colonial decor and a low-rise design that incorporates four slate-roofed, white-sided buildings arranged in a semicircle above a rocky coastline. The hotel is not adjacent to the water; guests must drive about 10 minutes to reach a good beach, Plage de l'Orient. Most of the resort's activities revolve around the swimming pool. The roomy accommodations, with king-size beds, fall into two categories: deluxe oceanfront with

---

Fun Fact **Oh, Those Paparazzi**

We wouldn't call Le Toiny snobbish, although they did turn away the late Princess Di when she showed up on the doorstep seeking shelter. Brad Pitt, on the other hand, might have wished he'd been turned away. Cliff-climbing paparazzi photographed him in the nude with Gwyneth Paltrow, and he ended up as a nude centerfold (against his wishes, of course) in *Playgirl*.

---

patio or deluxe ocean view with terrace. All are furnished in a Creole style and have ceiling fans. The differences between the two categories of rooms are most pronounced in the bathrooms. The oceanfront rooms have separate shower/tub combinations, while the ocean views have small garden areas opening directly off the bathrooms.

The resort's pool, a 4,500-square-foot (405 sq. m) pair of interconnected ovals with a bridge, is the largest on the island.

Pointe Milou (B.P. 571), 97133 St. Barthélemy, F.W.I. ⓒ **800/221-4542** in the U.S., or 590/27-63-63. Fax 590/27-92-92. www.accorhotels.com. 42 units. Winter $460–$550 double; from $930 suite. Off-season $295–$355 double; $610 suite. Rates include American breakfast. 1 child under age 12 can stay free in parents' room. AE, DC, MC, V. Closed Sept–Oct 15. **Amenities:** 2 restaurants, bar; pool; room service (7am–9:30pm); massage; laundry. *In room:* A/C, TV, minibar, hair dryer, safe.

EXPENSIVE

El Sereno Beach Hotel ⓐ   Sereno's low-slung pastel facade and its isolated location create the aura of St-Tropez in the Antilles. The Riviera crowd is attracted to its location on a good beach with calm waters. More of the units overlook the gardens than the sea, but they're so comfortable that no one seems to mind. Each unit contains two beds with firm mattresses, and a fridge. The compact, shower-only bathrooms are tidily maintained. The feeling is a bit like a private compound, whose social center is an open-air bar and poolside restaurant.

Grand Cul-de-Sac (B.P. 19), 97133 St. Barthélemy, F.W.I. ⓒ **800/322-2223** in the U.S., or 590/27-64-80. www.serenobeach.com. Fax 590/27-75-47. 32 units. Winter $250–$480 double. Off-season $180–$330 double. Rates include continental breakfast. Extra person $75. AE, MC, V. Closed Sept–Oct 31. **Amenities:** 2 restaurants, 2 bars; pool; exercise room; room service; babysitting; laundry/dry cleaning. *In room:* A/C, TV, minibar, hair dryer, safe.

Filao Beach Hotel ⓐ   This bungalow hotel is set on 4 flat acres (2 hectares) next to one of the island's most important beaches, the oh-so-chic St. Jean Beach. Established in 1982, this is one of the few Relais & Châteaux hotels in the Caribbean. But although the staff is charming and the setting is supremely comfortable, the hotel simply can't maintain the standards of a Relais & Châteaux property in France. Critics complain that despite the management's efforts, the place has a subtle dowdiness that prevents it from being one of St. Barts's avidly sought-out hotels.

The accommodations, many of which suggest a nice motel room, were refitted with new floor tiles and upholsteries in the late 1990s. All units are modern, with large closets, ceiling fans, and sun-flooded terraces where you can order breakfast. Some units are subject to traffic noise; only a few open right onto the beach. The staff is most welcoming, providing a bottle of rum, slippers, and a robe in each bedroom. Bathrooms are small but well appointed, with oversized tubs with showers.

Baie de St-Jean (B.P. 1005), 97012 St. Barthélemy, F.W.I. © **590/27-64-84.** Fax 590/27-62-24. www.filaobeach.com. 30 units. Winter $330.40–$384 double. Off-season $232.20–$267.90 double. Rates include continental breakfast and airport transfers. AE, DC, MC, V. Closed Aug 30–Oct 15. **Amenities:** Restaurant, bar; pool; scuba diving, snorkeling, windsurfing, water-skiing; car rental; room service; babysitting; laundry/dry cleaning. *In room:* A/C, TV/VCR, fridge, hair dryer, safe.

La Banane ⭐ On the outskirts of the village of Lorient lies this intimate and well-furnished hotel. Because of its small size and carefully restricted access, many aspects of this place might remind you of a private, and very Parisian, house party. The in-house restaurant is reserved only for residents or their guests.

Set on a flat, low-lying, and somewhat steamy landscape, the hotel grounds are richly planted with bananas, flowering shrubs, and palms. It's about a 3-minute walk from the beach. The accommodations here are delightful and quite roomy, and are filled with some of the most stylish antiques on the island. Our favorite unit contains a large mahogany four-poster bed whose trim was made from a little-known Central and South American wood called angelique. The other units are less spacious, but each has some Haitian art, a mixture of antique and modern designs, a fridge, a private terrace, and louvered windows overlooking the garden; some are air-conditioned. Decorated in Mexican tiles, shower-only bathrooms are open to private gardens with alfresco tubs and showers.

97133 Lorient, St. Barthélemy, F.W.I. © **590/27-68-25.** Fax 590/27-68-44. www.labanane.com. 9 units. Winter $420 double. Off-season $330 double. Rates include breakfast. AE, MC, V. **Amenities:** Bar; pool; room service; babysitting; laundry. *In room:* A/C, ceiling fan, TV, minibar, hair dryer.

MODERATE (FOR ST. BARTS)

Le Village St-Jean ⭐ *Value* This family-owned cottage colony hideaway, a mile (2km) from the airport toward St.-Jean, continues to attract a distinguished clientele. Lying in the most central part of St. Barts, a 5-minute drive uphill from Saint-Jean Beach, it offers one of the best values on this high-priced resort island. The cottages contain kitchens, sundecks or gardens, terraced living rooms, balconies, and ceiling fans. Furnishings are modest but comfortable, and the living space is generous. The tiled shower-only bathrooms are compact, and some have bidets. Although the rates here are modest compared to other places on the island, don't be surprised to see a media headliner here; after all, some of them like to save money, too. The complex has a well-managed restaurant and bar, Terrazza, with a sprawling terrace on a platform above the sloping terrain (see "Dining," below).

Baie de Saint-Jean (B.P. 623), 97098 St. Barthélemy, F.W.I. © **590/27-61-39.** Fax 590/27-77-96. www.village stjeanhotel.com. 31 units. Winter $160 double; $190–$360 1-bedroom cottage; $490 2-bedroom cottage; $390 suite. Off-season $95 double; $130–$250 1-bedroom cottage; $300 2-bedroom cottage; $280 suite. Extra person $40. AE, MC, V. **Amenities:** Restaurant, bar; pool; Jacuzzi; car rental; room service (7:30–10:30am); babysitting; laundry. *In room:* A/C, fridge, hair dryer.

Tropical Hôtel The facade of this small, unpretentious hotel looks like a picture-postcard Caribbean colonial inn. Originally built in 1981, and restored in 1997, it's perched on a hillside about 50 yards (46m) above St-Jean Beach. Each room contains a private shower-only bathroom, a king-size bed with a good mattress, tile floors, and a fridge. Nine units have sea views and balconies; no. 11 has a porch that opens onto a garden that's so lush it looks like a miniature jungle.

The hotel has a hospitality center where guests read, listen to music, or order drinks at a paneled bar surrounded by antiques. The pool is small, but watersports are available on the beach.

St-Jean (B.P. 147), 97095 St. Barthélemy, F.W.I. ℂ **800/223-9815** in the U.S., or 590/27-64-87. Fax 590/27-81-74. www.st-barths.com/tropicalhotel. 21 units. Winter $175–$200 double. Off-season $135–$185 double. Rates include continental breakfast. AE, MC, V. **Amenities:** Snack bar; pool; car rental; babysitting; laundry. *In room:* A/C, TV, fridge, hair dryer.

INEXPENSIVE (RELATIVELY, ANYWAY)

Hôtel Normandie   This modest, unassuming, family-owned hotel offers no facilities other than the clean but somewhat dreary accommodations. But what do you want for this kind of money on St. Barts? This is what the French call an *auberge antillaise.* Set near the intersection of two major roads, about 100 yards (91m) from Lorient Beach, it offers motel-inspired bedrooms of casual comfort. The more expensive units are larger, lie adjacent to the hotel's modest pool, and contain TVs. The less expensive, smaller rooms are next to the highway. The shower-only bathrooms are really too small, but they're well kept.

97133 Lorient, St. Barthélemy, F.W.I. ℂ **590/27-61-66.** Fax 590/27-98-83. 8 units. Winter $61.10 double; $69.90 triple. Off-season $54.30 double; $65.15 triple. MC, V. **Amenities:** Pool. *In room:* A/C.

Le P'tit Morne *Finds*   This is hardly the most luxurious or stylish lodging on an island that's legendary for its glamour and its five-star hotels. But the hotel's three-star format, its relatively low rates, and the warm welcome extended by its island-born owner, Marie-Joëlle, make it a worthy vacation site, lying a 10-minute drive to the beach. And you won't have to mortgage your home to pay for it. The guest rooms are filled with completely unpretentious furniture and generally comfortable beds, but don't expect deluxe living. There's plenty of elbow room, however, and units were built to catch the trade winds. Bathrooms are compact and have shower stalls.

Colombier (P.O. Box 14), 97098 St. Barthélemy, F.W.I. ℂ **590/27-62-64.** Fax 590/27-84-63. www. st-barths.com/ptit-morne. 15 units. Winter $145.55 double. Off-season $66.10 double. Off-season rates include daily breakfast and unlimited use of a car. AE, MC, V. Closed June. *In-room:* A/C, TV, kitchen.

Manoir de St. Barthélemy *Value*   If this place looks like it was built in Normandy, it was. Originally constructed as the centerpiece of a large farm in 1610, it was disassembled and rebuilt a minute's walk from the sands of Lorient Plage in the 1970s by a then-individual homeowner. Shortly thereafter, eight half-timbered bungalows, each in an ersatz Norman style, were erected in the garden, each facing a reflecting pool accented with water lilies, a fountain, and nearby palms and bougainvillea. Guests of the property won't have a lot to do with the main house, other than to check in and chitchat from time to time with the on-site managers. But each will probably construct a beach-going life that's private, isolated, and cost-efficient, thanks to the presence of kitchens within most of the units. In 2000, new owners (the de la Mazure family) renovated much of the decor, giving it a valued "refreshing." Accommodations are Antillean rustic, with brown and white color schemes, hints of antique Normandy, white linen hassocks, beds draped in tulle, and a sense of romance. Each unit has a small, shower-only bathroom. Six of the accommodations have their own kitchens, and two are equipped with refrigerators. Usually, meals are not served on the premises, although with advance notification, something can be arranged.

Route de Saline, Lorient, 97133 St. Barthélemy, F.W.I. ℂ **590/27-79-27.** www.lemanoir-st-barth.com. 8 units. Winter $122.15–$169.65 double. Off-season 67.85–$142.50 double. $27.15 per person for third and fourth occupants. AE, V. **Amenities:** Babysitting; laundry. *In-room:* A/C, ceiling fan, kitchen, no phone.

3 Dining

IN GUSTAVIA

Au Port FRENCH/CREOLE   This restaurant is one of the culinary staples of the island, having survived for many years, thanks to a straightforward and unpretentious ambience that focuses on good cooking, generous portions, and an utter lack of snobbery. Set one floor above street level, in the center of town, it features a neocolonial decor with models of sailboats, antique accessories, and flavorful cuisine. The best menu items may include foie gras of duckling, *boudin* of conch and lobster, crayfish in green curry sauce, lobster tail with morels, and magret of duckling with a honey-flavored butter sauce. The fish soup makes a worthwhile beginning.

Rue Sadi-Carnot. © **590/27-62-36.** Reservations recommended, especially for veranda tables. Main courses 15.20€–25.85€ ($13.55–$23.05); menu Creole 29.65€ ($26.45). AE, MC, V. Mon–Sat 6:30–10pm. Closed June 15–July 31.

La Mandala ★★ THAI/EUROPEAN   This is one of the most exciting restaurants on St. Barts. It occupies a house on the steepest street in Gustavia, high above the harbor. If you drive your own car up to the entrance, a valet will park it for you. Its name derives from the Mandala, symbol of Buddhist harmony, whose design of a square within a circle is duplicated by the position of the dining deck above a swimming pool visible from above. The owners and chefs are partners Kiki and Boubou (Christophe Barjetta and Olivier Megnin), whose nicknames belie their formidable training at some of the grandest restaurants of France. Gastronomes on St. Barts have watched the menu here make many sophisticated detours from the Mediterranean theme that was the norm during its earliest years. Today, the cuisine is Thai and European. Examples include tempura of crayfish with mango salad and coriander sauce; a traditional Thai dish, *tataki,* composed of deliberately undercooked fish with a ginger-flavored vinaigrette, shallots, and sesame oil; dorado with mushroom risotto; and rack of lamb with exotic spices and a cold purée of cucumbers and mint. Everybody's favorite dessert is the warm chocolate tart.

Rue Courbet. © **590/27-96-96.** Reservations recommended. Main courses 21.30€–28.90€ ($19–$25.80). AE, DC, MC, V. Daily 5pm–midnight; tapas and cocktails daily 5–7pm.

La Route des Boucaniers ★ *Finds* FRENCH/CREOLE   What a discovery! Near the harbor, this bistro is the domain of Francis Delage, who is the definitive authority on Creole cuisine, having written a five-volume primer. Wonderful ingredients turn up here, and they are concocted into a medley of local dishes whose flavors are not found elsewhere in this island where some chefs feel that "being French" is passport enough to their places. The decor evokes some rum shack—there's even a boat wreck—but these "pirate" artifacts don't suggest the sophistication of the cuisine. Our avocado salad was reason to return the following night. It was given added zest by chewy flakes of dried cod in a hot Creole sauce. "We're a little bit French, a whole lot Creole, and a hell of a lot good," one of the staff accurately praised the joint. For the main course, the chef's pride and joy is a large bowl of fresh fish and shellfish huddled together with red bean purée, everything blended into a smooth texture that is properly seasoned and delicious. Other surprises await, especially the Cajun mahi-mahi with coin-shaped sautéed yucca. What makes everything taste so good? Maybe you don't want to know. It's *beurre rouge, lardons* that have been heavily salted and spiced. Not what your doctor ordered, but they are irresistible to the palate.

Rue de Bord de Mer, Gustavia. ☎ **590/27-73-00.** Reservations required. Main courses 15.70 €–26.90€ ($14–$24). MC, V. Daily 9am–11pm.

Le Rivage ⭐ FRENCH/CARIBBEAN This restaurant offers the kind of offhanded charm and oversized Gallic egos that you'd expect in a chic but somewhat disorganized beach resort in the south of France. It's set on a covered veranda built on piers above the waters of the lagoon. About half the tables are open to views of the stars. During the day, no one objects to bathing suits at the table; at night, fashionably casual is the preferred dress. With a rapidly changing menu, items that might merit raves include carpaccio of beef and a tempting roster of "supersalads," the most justifiably popular of which combines shrimp with smoked salmon and melted goat cheese. There's also a seafood platter of raw shellfish (scallops, clams, and crayfish), artfully arranged on a bed of seaweed; grilled crayfish, *daurade,* snapper, and tuna; and a full complement of such Creole specialties as *boudin noir* (blood sausage), *accras de morue* (beignets of codfish), and *court bouillon* of fish.

In the St. Barth Beach Hotel, Grand Cul de Sac. ☎ **590/27-82-42.** Reservations recommended. Main courses 15.20€–45.60€ ($13.55–$40.70). AE, V. Daily noon–6pm and 7–10pm.

Le Sapotillier ⭐⭐ FRENCH/SEAFOOD This West Indian house beside the less frequented part of the harbor is the domain of Austrian-born Adam Rajner, who runs one of the best-known restaurants in Gustavia. Le Sapotillier is near the top of the list for every visiting gourmet. Dine outside on the candlelit patio or inside the clapboard-covered Antillean bungalow that was transported from the outlying village of Corossol.

Chef Rajner, in the best tradition of European innkeeping, pays strict attention to the quality and presentation of his food. Your meal might begin with a homemade duck-liver pâté, or perhaps the fish soup. Among the more interesting meat dishes are a whole young pigeon imported from Bresse, France, and a filet of young lamb with ratatouille.

Rue Sadi-Carnot. ☎ **590/27-60-28.** Reservations required. Main courses 27.05€–36.50€ ($24.15–$32.60). DISC, MC, V. Tues–Sun 6:30–10:30pm; daily 6:30–10:30pm Christmas–Easter. Closed mid-May–Oct.

L'Escale ITALIAN/FRENCH Some villa owners cite L'Escale, a sometimes raucous, and always irreverent hangout for the wealthy, as their favorite restaurant on the island. It's set in a simple, industrial-looking building on the relatively unglamorous south side of Gustavia's harbor, adjacent to dozens of moored yachts. You can dine lightly and inexpensively here, but you can also spend a lot of money. Typical fare might include one of about a half-dozen pizzas or meal-size salads, as well as such well-received pastas as lasagna, *penne a l'arrabiata,* or any of several gnocchis. Also available are carpaccio of raw marinated fish and beef, Milanese-style veal, and a wide roster of grilled meats and fish (such as a whole snapper, grilled and served with Creole sauce and rondelles of lemon). Thursday nights feature Canadian lobster, flown in specially from Newfoundland. The dessert specialty is the island's most theatrical version of flambéed bananas: Lights are dimmed and the shooting flames of the ritual's burning rum illuminate the entire restaurant.

Rue Jeanne-d'Arc, La Pointe. ☎ **590/27-81-06.** Reservations required in high season. Main courses 25.85€–45.60€ ($23.05–$40.70). AE, MC, V. Thurs–Tues 7pm–midnight.

Le Toiny ⭐ FRENCH   This restaurant opens its doors to folks who want to dine among the rich and jaded, but aren't willing to mortgage their future for a room at St. Barts's most upscale and expensive hotel. Guests dine in an open-air pavilion adjacent to the resort's pool, with a view that sweeps out over the wide blue sea. The emphasis is French, casually stylish, and offhanded in a way that might remind you of a particularly rich version of bohemian Paris. At lunchtime, menu items might include eggplant ravioli with tomato coulis and Parmesan, a *tarte fine* with tomatoes and feta, or prawns in "an Oriental nest" with sage and onion sauce. After dark, choices are even more exquisite. Examples include crab-meat salad with fennel, ravioli stuffed with conch and served with a garlicky cream sauce, sea bass with cauliflower and caramelized balsamic vinegar, and roasted rack of lamb with truffle sauce and Parmesan. The cuisine, the setting, the first-rate ingredients: Everything works to make a memorable meal here.

In Le Toiny hotel, Anse de Toiny. ⓒ 590/27-88-88. Reservations required. Main courses 16.70€–22.80€ ($14.95–$20.35) lunch; 25.85€–38€ ($23.05–$33.95) dinner. AE, MC, V. Daily noon–2:30pm and 7–11pm. Closed Sept 1–Oct 23.

L'Iguane JAPANESE/INTERNATIONAL   Set adjacent to three upscale shops, this restaurant and cafe offers an international menu that includes sushi, American breakfasts, and California-style sandwiches and salads. The walls are ocher and blue, and the lighting fixtures are filtered to flatter even the most weather-beaten skin. The sometimes-glamorous clients all seem to be watching their waistlines. The ambience grows more Asian as the evening progresses. Sushi, imported twice a week from suppliers in Miami and served according to time-honored Japanese techniques, is the main allure here, with special emphasis on tuna, snapper, salmon, and eel.

Carre d'Or, quai de la Republique. ⓒ 590/27-88-46. Reservations recommended for dinner. Continental breakfast 5.30€ ($4.75); sushi 2.30€–3.05€ ($2.05–$2.70) per piece; main courses 22.80€–30.40€ ($20.35–$27.15). AE, MC, V. Mid-Nov–Aug, cafe daily 8–11am; restaurant daily 11am–11pm. Off-season, cafe Mon–Sat 8–11am; restaurant Mon–Sat 11am–3pm, daily 7–11pm. Closed Sept–Oct.

IN THE ST-JEAN BEACH AREA

Terrazza *Value* ITALIAN/PIZZA   Proudly positioned as the centerpiece of a charming and not particularly expensive hotel (see "Accommodations," earlier in this chapter), Terrazza has a deserved reputation for well-conceived food. Examples include spaghetti with squid ink and eggplant, ravioli stuffed with spiny crayfish meat, *saltimbocca* (veal and ham) alla Romana, an unusual version of

---

⌐Finds **Picnic Fare on St. Barts**

St. Barts is so expensive that many visitors opt to buy at least one of their meals (perhaps a "gourmet lunch to go" package) from a take-out deli. The most centrally located of the island's epicurean delis is **La Rôtisserie,** rue Oskar-II (ⓒ **590/27-63-13**), which is proud of its endorsement by Fauchon, the world-famous food store in Paris. On display are bottles of wine, crocks of mustard, pâté, herbs, and exotic oils and vinegars, as well as take-out (and very French) platters sold by the gram. *Plats du jour* cost around 9.10€ to 18.25€ ($8.15–$16.30) for a portion suitable for one. Set on a narrow street behind the eastern edge of Gustavia's harbor, the place is open Monday through Saturday from 6:30am to 7pm, Sunday from 7am to 1pm. American Express, MasterCard, and Visa are accepted.

spaghetti *en papillote* with fresh vegetable sauce, and one of our personal favorites, chicken breast with rosemary potatoes. There's a rotating choice of unusual pizzas as well, including versions that feature asparagus or freshwater crayfish with parsley. Desserts usually include a homemade tiramasu.

In Le Village St-Jean hotel, St-Jean Hill. ✆ **590/27-70-67.** Reservations required. Main courses 12€–23€ ($10.70–$20.55). AE, MC, V. Thurs–Tues 6:30–10pm. Closed Sept.

AT MORNE LURIN

La Route des Epices ✿ FRENCH   Since 1995, Françoise and François Beret have been promoting a cuisine that many diners consider an enjoyable departure from the ubiquitous French/Creole. Their dining room, adapted from part of the old plantation that stood here, makes a point of flavoring many dishes with spices not usually seen in the French repertoire. Exact components change frequently but might include an aromatic, highly spicy version of fish soup; a stir-fry of jumbo shrimp with lime-and-ginger sauce; or local red snapper roasted in its own skin. The food is as cerebral as it is satisfying. The wine, the service, and the quality of ingredients used in the dishes presented are top-notch.

In the François Plantation, Colombier. ✆ **590/29-80-22.** Reservations required. Main courses 33.45€–44.10€ ($29.85–$39.35). AE, MC, V. Daily 6:30–11pm. Closed May 31–Oct 30.

Santa Fe AMERICAN   Set inland from the sea, atop one of the highest elevations on the island, this burger house and sports bar enjoys a formidable niche for itself with the island's English-speaking clientele. It features wide-screen TVs that show events like the Super Bowl to as many as 450 viewers. After the hurricanes of 1995, Santa Fe's roof, wraparound decks, and bar tops were completely rebuilt of teakwood, and a more nautical flair was introduced. You can take in the view of the surrounding landscapes for free, but most clients stop for one of the well-recommended hamburgers or steak, shrimp, or barbecued-chicken dishes. This place earned its reputation on its burgers and fresh-made fries, which some diners compare to the best available in the United States.

Morne Lurin. ✆ **590/27-61-04.** Burgers 4.55€–8.35€ ($4.05–$7.45); meal platters 11.40€–19€ ($10.20–$16.95) No credit cards. Thurs–Tues noon–2pm and 5–10pm. Closed for lunch Apr–Oct.

IN THE GRANDE SALINE BEACH AREA

Le Tamarin ✿ FRENCH/CREOLE   One of the island's genuinely offbeat restaurants is Le Tamarin, a deliberately informal bistro that caters to a clientele from the nearby Plage de Saline. It's isolated amid rocky hills and forests east of Gustavia, in a low-slung cottage whose eaves are accented with gingerbread. Inside, a teak-and-bamboo motif prevails. Lunch is the more popular and animated meal here, with most customers dining in T-shirts and bathing suits. If you have to wait, you can order an aperitif in one of the hammocks stretched under a tamarind tree (hence the name of the restaurant). The menu focuses on light, summery meals that go well with the streaming sunlight and tropical heat. Examples include gazpacho, Cajun-style tuna with Creole sauce and baby vegetables, a carpaccio of fish that includes very fresh portions of marinated salmon and tuna, and chicken roasted with lemon and ginger. There's a broad-based wine list, plus a chocolate cake dessert specialty that appeals to dyed-in-the-wool chocoholics. Service can be hectic, but if you're in a rush, you shouldn't be here. It's the perfect place for a lazy afternoon on the beach.

Plage de Saline. ✆ **590/27-72-12.** Reservations required for dinner. Main courses 21.30€–28.90€ ($19–$25.80). MC, V. Nov 1–May 30, daily noon–4pm and Fri–Sun 7–9:30pm. Closed May 30–Oct 30.

IN THE GRAND CUL-DE-SAC BEACH AREA

Bartolomeo ⚔ PROVENCAL/NORTHERN ITALIAN   Although this is the deluxe dining choice for one of the most exclusive and expensive hotels on the island, Bartolomeo works hard to be unthreatening, informally sophisticated, and gracefully upscale. A live pianist plays soothing music while diners choose from a menu that changes frequently. Examples include lobster cannelloni on a bed of spinach with lobster sauce, sea scallops with Szechuan peppers and crepe-studded risotto, filet mignon with green peppercorns and a gratin of *pommes dauphinoise,* and roasted rack of lamb with goat-cheese ravioli. Wednesday features a sweeping array of cold antipasti, and the chef will prepare any pasta you want from an artfully arranged display of seafoods, meats, herbs, wines, and cream.

In the Hôtel Guanahani, Grand Cul-de-Sac. ⓒ 590/27-66-60. Reservations required, especially for nonguests. Main courses 31.90€–36.50€ ($28.50–$32.60). AE, DC, MC, V. Daily 7:30–10pm. Closed Sept.

Boubou's ⚔ *Finds* INTERNATIONAL   This place is high camp (remember that expression?). A former Parisian, Boubou himself has established his Aladdin's tent of fantasy here, with Persian carpets and animal-print fabrics. On the beach of the Sereno Beach Hotel, this exotic Berber-like decor is a backdrop for a little theater and surprisingly good cuisine. Drop in for lunch, and get your fill of grilled fish in Creole sauce or plenty of sushi; or perhaps try light Thai salad if the day is hot. Boubou races about in all-white flowing Moroccan garb. In the evening the chefs really strut their stuff, turning out some of the most succulent pastas on the island, as well as an excellent risotto primavera. Try the gnocchi au pistou. After dinner many patrons linger long into the evening at the bar.

Grand Cul de Sac. ⓒ 590/29-83-01. Reservations required. Main courses 18.25€–28.90€ ($16.30–$25.80). AE, MC, V. Daily 7am–3pm and 7pm–midnight.

Club Lafayette FRENCH/CREOLE   This is no fast-food beach joint. Lunching in the sun here, at a cove on the eastern end of the island, east of Marigot, is like taking a meal at your own private beach club—and a very expensive beach club at that. After a dip in the ocean or pool, you can order a *planteur* in the shade of a sea grape, and later proceed to lunch itself. You might begin with a *tarte fine aux tomates, mozzarelle, et herbes de Provence* that's lighter and more flavorful than most pizzas. (The congenial owners and chefs, Toulouse-born Nadine and Georges Labau, would be horrified to hear it compared to a pizza.) There's also warm foie gras served with apples, grilled chicken breast with mushroom sauce, lobster served with basil-flavored pasta, and one of the best meal-size lobster salads on the island. Desserts include everything from simple, refreshing citrus-flavored sherbet to rich, crisp (and definitely fattening) *croustillant au chocolate.*

Grand Cul-de-Sac. ⓒ 590/27-62-51. Reservations recommended. Main courses 31.90€–57€ ($28.50–$50.90). AE, MC, V. Daily noon–4pm and 7–10pm. Closed May–Oct.

IN VITET

Hostellerie des Trois Forces ⭐ *Finds* FRENCH/CREOLE/VEGETARIAN Isolated from the bulk of St. Barts's tourism, this restaurant lies midway up the island's highest mountain (Morne Vitet). The place has a resident astrologer, a French provincial decor, terraces accented with gingerbread, and food that won its owner/chef an award from France's prestigious *Confrérie de la Marmite d'Or* in 1995. The heart and soul of the place is Hubert de la Motte, who arrived from Brittany with his wife to create a hotel where happiness, good food, comfort, and conversation are a way of life. Even if you don't stay here, you might want to drive over for a meal. The setting is a compound that contains seven pastel-colored, gingerbread-trimmed cottages, each named after a different sign of the zodiac, in a high-altitude setting of bucolic charm. Although the same menu is available throughout the day and evening, dinners are more formal than lunches, and might include fish pâté, beef shish kebab with curry sauce, grilled fresh lobster, veal kidneys flambé with cognac, a cassoulet of snails, and desserts such as crepes Suzette flambé. "Each dish takes time," in the words of the owner, as it's prepared fresh. Count on a leisurely meal and a well-informed host who has spent years studying astrology.

Vitet. © 590/27-61-25. Reservations required. Main courses 15.20€–36.50€ ($13.55–$32.60); fixed-price menu 34.95€ ($31.20). AE, MC, V. Mon–Sat noon–3pm and 6–10:30pm.

IN THE PUBLIC BEACH AREA

Maya's ★★ *Finds* CREOLE   This is the most surprising restaurant on St. Barts, thanks to its artful simplicity and glamorous clients. This much-rebuilt green-and-white Antillean house with almost no architectural charm attracts crowds of luminaries from the worlds of media, fashion, and entertainment. This is the kind of place you might find on Martinique, because that's where its French Creole chef, Maya Beuzelin-Gurley, grew up. Maya's stresses "clean, simple" food with few adornments other than its freshness and a flavor-filled sprinkling of island herbs and lime juice. You might begin with the salad of tomatoes, arugula, and endive, then follow with grilled fish in sauce *chien* (hot), or a grilled filet of beef. Maya also prepares what she calls "sailor's chicken," a marinated version made with fresh chives, lime juice, and hot peppers. Almost no cream is used in any dish, a fact that makes the place beloved by the fashion models and actors who hang out here. You'll find the place directly west of Gustavia, close to the island's densest collection of factories and warehouses. Views face west and south, ensuring glorious sunset-watching.

Public Beach. © 590/27-75-73. Reservations required. Main courses 25.10€–31.90€ ($22.40–$28.50). AE, MC, V. Mon–Sat 6–10pm. Closed Sept–Oct.

4 Beaches

St. Barts has 14 white-sand beaches. Few are ever crowded, even in winter; all are public and free. Topless sunbathing is quite common. The most famous beach is **St-Jean Beach** ★★, which is actually two beaches divided by the Eden Rock promontory. It offers watersports, restaurants, and a few hotels, as well as some shady areas. **Flamands Beach,** to the west, is a very wide, long beach with a few small hotels and some areas shaded by lantana palms. In winter, the surf here can be a bit rough, although it is rarely hazardous. **Lorient Beach,** on the north shore, is quiet and calm, with shady areas. It's popular with surfers and swimmers who like rolling waves. **Marigot Beach,** also on the north shore, is narrow but offers good swimming and snorkeling.

For a beach with hotels, restaurants, and watersports, **Grand Cul-de-Sac Beach,** on the northeast shore, fits the bill. This is a narrow beach protected by a reef.

North of the commercial port at Gustavia, the rather unromantic sounding **Public Beach** is a combination of sand and pebbles. This beach is more popular with boaters than swimmers—it's the location of the St. Barts Sailing School. There is no more beautiful place on the island, however, to watch the boats at sunset. Located near a small fishing village, **Corossol Beach** offers a typical glimpse of French life, St. Barts style. This is a calm, protected beach, with a charming little **seashell museum.**

South of Gustavia, **Shell Beach** or **Grand Galet** is awash with seashells. Rocky outcroppings protect this beach from strong waves. It's also the scene of many a weekend party.

Gouverneur Beach, on the southern coast, can be reached by driving south from Gustavia to Lurin. Turn at the Santa Fe restaurant (see "Dining," above) and head down a narrow road. The beach is gorgeous and completely uncrowded, but there's no shade. **Grande Saline Beach,** to the east of Gouverneur Beach, is reached by driving up the road from the commercial center in St-Jean; a short walk over the sand dune and you're here. Like Gouverneur Beach, Saline Beach offers some waves but no shade. This beach is full of beautiful sunbathers, all in the nude.

Colombier Beach is difficult to get to but well worth the effort. It can only be reached by boat or by taking a rugged goat path from Petite Anse past Flamands Beach, a 30-minute walk. Shade and snorkeling are found here, and you can pack a lunch and spend the day. Locals call it Rockefeller's Beach because for many years David Rockefeller owned the property surrounding it.

5 Sports & Other Outdoor Pursuits

FISHING   Anglers are fond of the waters around St. Barts. From March to July, they catch mahi-mahi; in September, wahoo. Atlantic bonito, barracuda, and marlin also turn up with frequency. **Marine Service,** quai du Yacht-Club, Gustavia (© **590/27-70-34**), rents a 29-foot (9m) Phoenix that is specifically outfitted for big-game fishing. A full day for four costs 665€ ($593.85), which includes a captain and first mate. The outfitter also offers shore fishing on a 21-foot (6m) day cruiser, which tends to remain close to the island's shoreline, searching for tuna, barracuda, and other fish. A full-day excursion, with fishing and scuba gear for up to four participants, costs 500.10€ ($446.55).

SCUBA DIVING   **Marine Service,** quai du Yacht-Club, in Gustavia (© **590/ 27-70-34**), is the most complete watersports facility on the island. It operates from a one-story building set directly on the water at the edge of a marina, on the opposite side of the harbor from the more congested part of Gustavia. Tailoring its dives for both beginners and advanced divers, the outfit is familiar with at least 20 unusual sites scattered at various points offshore. The most interesting of these include the Grouper, a remote reef west of St. Barts, close to the rich reef life surrounding the uninhabited cay known as Ile Forchue. The island has only one relatively safe wreck dive, the rusting hulk of *Kayali*, a trawler that sank offshore in 1994. Set in deep waters, it's recommended only for experienced divers. A resort course, including two open-water dives, costs 115€ ($102.70). A "scuba review," for certified divers who are out of practice, goes for 60€ ($53.60), while a one-tank dive for certified divers begins at 50€ ($44.65). Multidive packages are available.

SNORKELING   You can test your luck at hundreds of points offshore, simply by donning a mask, fins, and a snorkel. **Marine Services,** quai du Yacht-Club, Gustavia (© **590/27-70-34**), runs daily snorkeling expeditions. A 7-hour excursion (9am–4pm), including a full French-style picnic, all equipment, and exploration of two separate snorkeling sites, costs 77€ ($68.75). They can also rent you snorkeling gear and tell you where to go by yourself.

WINDSURFING   Windsurfing is one of the most popular sports here. Try **Wind Wave Power,** Grand Cul de Sac (© **590/27-82-57**), open daily from 9am to 5pm. Windsurfing costs 22.80€ ($20.35) per hour, and professional instructors are on hand.

6 Shopping

You don't pay any duty on St. Barts, so it's a good place to buy liquor and French perfumes, at some of the lowest prices in the Caribbean—often cheaper than in France itself. You'll find good buys in sportswear, crystal, porcelain, watches, and other luxuries. The only trouble is that selections are limited. If you're in the market for **island crafts,** try to find the fine straw hats St. Bartians like to wear. You may also see some interesting block-printed resort clothing in cotton.

Diamond Genesis/Kornerupine, 12 rue du General-de-Gaulle/Les Suites du Roi-Oskar-II (© **590/27-66-94**), a well-respected gold, gemstone, and diamond shop, maintains an inventory of designs strongly influenced by European tastes. Although the prices can go as high as $60,000, a particularly appealing best-seller is an 18-karat-gold depiction of St. Barts, which sells for around $20. It's one of the few shops on the island where jewelry is handcrafted on the premises. You can also peruse the selection of watches by Corum and Jaeger Lecoultre (both of which are available only through this store), as well as Breitling and Tag Heuer.

For handcrafts, **Made in St-Barth,** Villa Creole (© **590/27-56-57**), is the best place to shop. The women of the hamlet of Corossol have this outlet here for their intricate straw work, including those ever-so-fashionable wide-brim beach hats. Other crafts include local paintings and decorative ornaments.

Gold Fingers, rue de la France (© **590/27-64-66**), is the largest purveyor of luxury goods on St. Barts. The entire second floor is devoted to perfumes and crystal, the street level to jewelry and all kinds of watches. Prices are usually 15% to 20% less than equivalent retail goods sold stateside. Smart shoppers immediately ask what sales promotions are in effect at the time of their visit.

The elegant, upscale **Le Comptoir du Cigare,** 6 rue du Général-de-Gaulle (© **590/27-50-62**), caters to the December-to-April crowd of villa and yacht owners who flock to St. Barts. It's sheathed in exotic hardwood, and enhanced with a glass-sided, walk-in humidor for the storage of thousands of cigars. Cigars hail from Cuba and the Dominican Republic; the connoisseur-quality rums come from Martinique, Cuba, and Haiti. Smoke the Cubans on the island—it's illegal to bring them back to the United States. There's also a worthy collection of silver ornaments suitable for adorning the desk of a CEO, artisan-quality Panama hats from Ecuador, and the most beautiful collection of cigar boxes and humidors in the Caribbean.

La Boutique Couleur des Îles, 8 rue du Général-de-Gaulle (© **590/27-51-66**), tucked off a courtyard adjacent to one of the main streets of Gustavia, sells shirts and blouses with hand-embroidered references to the flora and fauna of St. Barts. Suitable for both men and women to wear to a "casually elegant" onboard cocktail party, they sell for between $35 and $55. Also available are what might be the most elegant beach towels in the world, each a thirsty mass of terry cloth embroidered in gold letters.

Laurent Eiffel, rue du Général-de-Gaulle (© **590/27-54-02**), is faux fashion. Despite the elegance of this store and the tact of its employees, nothing sold here is original—everything is either "inspired by" or crafted "in imitation of" designer models that usually cost 10 times as much. Look for belts, bags, and accessories that are copies of Versace, Prada, Hermès, Gucci, and Chanel, sold at prices much lower than what you'd pay in Paris.

St. Barts Style, rue Lafayette, near rue du Port (© **590/27-76-17**), offers racks of beachwear by such makers as Jams World and Vicidomine in citrus colors of lemon, lime, grapefruit, and orange, and psychedelic-looking T-shirts from about a dozen different manufacturers.

Sud, Etc., Galerie du Commerce (adjacent to the airport), St-Jean (© **590/ 27-98-75**), is known for its stylish clothing, both day and evening wear. Most of the inventory is for women, although a selection of swim trunks and Bermuda shorts are stocked for men. If you're a high-fashion model, or an heiress who's trying to look like one, chances are this boutique will have something that might appeal.

7 St. Barts After Dark

Most guests consider a French Creole dinner under the stars enough of a nocturnal adventure. Beyond that, there isn't a lot of excitement here.

In Gustavia, the most popular gathering place is **Le Select,** rue de la France (© **590/27-86-87**), apparently named after its more famous granddaddy in the Montparnasse section of Paris. It's utterly simple: Tables are set on the gravel in the open-air garden, near the port, and a game of dominoes might be under way as you walk in. You never know who might show up here—perhaps Mick Jagger. Beer begins at 1.50€ ($1.35), and the place is open Monday to Saturday from 10am to 11pm. The locals like it a lot; they allow outsiders, but don't necessarily embrace you until they get to know you a bit. If you want to spread a rumor and have it travel fast across the island, start it here.

La Cantina, rue du Bord-de-Mer (© **590/27-55-66**), is one of the more charming watering holes in Gustavia. It's set along the waterfront, with a decor that includes artifacts from Mexico. The mood is "Cote d'Azur in the 1970s" (before it was ruined by tour operators). The menu is set up like something aboard a cruise ship, and is very, very simple, featuring only sandwiches, salads, and drinks. Don't expect gourmet fare, but come to check out the people and the scenery from this portside perch in the heart of Gustavia. Salads and platters range from 10.65€ to 22.80E ($9.50–$20.35); the place opens daily from 7am to 10pm.

Bar de l'Oubli, 5 rue de la Republique (© **590/27-70-06**), occupies the most prominent corner in Gustavia, at the intersection of streets that are so well known that most local residents don't even know their names—they refer to it simply as "Centre-Ville." The setting is hip and Gallic, the color scheme is marine blue and white, and the background music might be the Rolling Stones. Sandwiches and salads are served. It's open daily from 8am (when breakfast is served to clients recovering from various stages of their hangovers) to 10 or 11pm, depending on business.

20

St. Eustatius

Called "Statia," this Dutch-held island is a mere 8-square-mile (21 sq. km) pinpoint in the Netherlands Antilles, still basking in its 18th-century heritage as the "Golden Rock." One of the true backwaters of the West Indies, it's just awakening to tourism.

You might want to visit first on a day trip from St. Maarten to see if you'd like it for an extended stay. The volcanic, black-sand beaches aren't especially alluring, and as Caribbean islands go, it's rather dull here, with no nightlife. Some pleasant strips of beach exist on the Atlantic side, but the surf here is dangerous for swimming.

If you're a hiker or a diver, the outlook on Statia improves considerably. You can hike around the base of the Quill, an extinct volcano on the southern end of the island. Wandering through a tropical forest, you'll encounter wild orchids, philodendron, heliconia, anthurium, fruit trees, ferns, wildlife, and birds, along with the inevitable oleander, hibiscus, and bougainvillea.

The island's reefs are covered with corals and enveloped by marine life. At one dive site, known as Crack in the Wall, or sometimes "the Grand Canyon," pinnacle coral shoots up from the floor of the ocean. Darting among the reefs are barracudas, eagle rays, black-tip sharks, and other large ocean fish.

Statia is located 150 miles (242 km) east of Puerto Rico, 38 miles (61km)

south of St. Maarten, and 17 miles (27km) southeast of Saba. The two extinct volcanoes, the Quill and "Little Mountain," are linked by a sloping agricultural plain known as De Cultuurvlakte, where yams and sweet potatoes grow.

Overlooking the Caribbean on the western edge of the plain, **Oranjestad** (Orange City) is the capital and the only village, consisting of both an Upper and Lower Town, connected by stone-paved, dogleg Fort Road.

Columbus sited Statia in 1493, on his second voyage, and Jan Snouck claimed the island for the Netherlands in 1640. The island's history was turbulent before it settled down to peaceful slumber under Dutch protection; from 1650 to 1816, Statia changed flags 22 times! Once the trading hub of the Caribbean, Statia was a thriving market, both for goods and for slaves.

Before the American Revolution, the population of Statia did not exceed 1,200, most of whom were slaves engaged in raising sugarcane. When war came and Britain blockaded the North American coast, Europe's trade was diverted to the Caribbean. Dutch neutrality lured many traders, leading to the construction of 1½ miles (2km) of warehouses in Lower Town. The American revolutionaries obtained gunpowder and ammunition through Statia—perhaps one of the first places anywhere to recognize the United States of America as a new nation.

1 Essentials

VISITOR INFORMATION

On the island, the **Tourist Bureau** is located at 3 Fort Oranjestrat (© **599/ 318-2433**), open Monday through Friday from 8am to noon and 1 to 5pm (4:30 on Fri). The Internet address for Statia is **www.turq.com/statia**.

GETTING THERE

St. Eustatius can be reached from Dutch St. Maarten's Queen Juliana Airport via the 20-seat planes of **Windward Islands Airways International (Winair)** (© **599/318-2362**). The little airline, launched in 1961, has an excellent safety record. Always reconfirm your return passage once you're on Statia. The 5 flights a day take only 20 minutes to hop the waters to Statia's Franklin Delano Roosevelt Airport (© **599/318-2362**). There are usually two flights a day between Statia and Saba, and two per week between Statia and St. Kitts, but schedules are very irregular. To be sure of getting to another island from Statia, you'll want to go to St. Martin first.

GETTING AROUND

BY TAXI   Taxis meet all incoming flights. Taxi rates are low, probably no more than $3.50 to $5 from the airport to your hotel. On the way to the hotel your driver may offer himself as a guide. If you book a 2- to 3-hour tour (long enough to cover all the sights on Statia), the cost is about $40 per vehicle. To summon a taxi, call **Rainbow Taxis** (© **599/318-2811**) or **Josser Daniel** (© **599/ 31802358**).

BY RENTAL CAR   Rainbow Car Rental (© **599/318-2811**) or **Walters** (© **599/318-2719**) are your best bets if you want to reserve a car in advance. Drivers must be 21 years old and present a valid license and credit or charge card. Walter's rents both cars and Jeeps.

 FAST FACTS: St. Eustatius

Banks **Barclay's Bank,** Wilhelminastraat, Oranjestad (© **599/318-2392**), the only bank on the island, is open Monday to Friday from 8:30am to 3:30pm. On weekends, most hotels will exchange money.

Currency The official unit of currency is the **Netherlands Antilles guilder (NAf),** at NAf 1.77 to each US$1, but nearly all places will quote you prices in U.S. dollars.

Customs There are no Customs duties since the island is a free port.

Documents U.S. and Canadian citizens need proof of citizenship, such as a passport or a birth certificate with a raised seal and a government-authorized photo ID, along with an ongoing ticket. British subjects need valid passports.

Electricity It's 100-volt AC (60 cycles), the same as in the United States.

Hospital A licensed physician is on duty at the **Queen Beatrix Medical Center,** 25 Princessweg, in Oranjestad (© **599/318-2211**).

Language Dutch is the official language, but English is commonly spoken as well.

Safety Although crime is rare here, it's wise to secure your valuables and take the kind of discreet precautions you would anywhere. Don't leave valuables unguarded on the beach.

Taxes & Service Charges There's a $5 tax if you're returning to the Dutch-held islands of St. Maarten or Saba; if you're going elsewhere, the tax is $10. Hotels on Statia collect a 7% government tax. Most hotels, guest-houses, and restaurants add a 10% service charge.

Telephone St. Eustatius maintains a 24-hours-per-day telephone service—and sometimes it takes about that much time to get a call through! To access **AT&T Direct** for calls to the United States from Statia, call ☎ **001-800-872-2881.**

To call Statia from the U.S., dial **011** (the international access code), then **599** (the country code for the Netherlands Antilles), and finally **318** (the area code for Statia) and the 5-digit local number. To make a call within Statia, only the 5-digit local number is necessary.

Time St. Eustatius operates on Atlantic standard time year-round. Between November and March, when it's 6pm in Oranjestad it's 5pm in New York. During daylight saving time (Apr–Oct) the island keeps the same time as the U.S. east coast.

Water The water here is safe to drink.

Weather The average daytime temperature ranges from 78° to 82°F. The annual rainfall is 45 inches.

2 Accommodations

Don't expect deluxe hotels or high-rises—Statia is strictly for escapists. Guests are sometimes placed in private homes. A 15% service charge and 7% government tax are added to hotel bills.

Golden Era Hotel   Set directly on the water, this modern hotel is clean, serviceable, and comfortable. Twelve units offer full or partial sea views (the most stunning panorama is from no. 205). All accommodations are tasteful and spacious, with king-size or queen-size beds. Regrettably, the shower-only bathrooms are so tiny that it's hard to maneuver. You can, if you wish, sit on the toilet and wash your face at the same time. Lunch and dinner are served daily in the simply decorated bar and dining room.

Lower Town, Oranjestad, St. Eustatius, N.A. ☎ **599/318-2345.** Fax 599/318-2445. goldera@goldenrock.net. 20 units. Winter $88–$100 double; $104 triple. Off-season $75 double; $90 triple. MAP (breakfast and dinner) $30 per person extra. AE, DISC, MC, V. **Amenities:** Restaurant, bar; pool; laundry. *In room:* A/C, TV, fridge.

Kings Well Resort ⭐   This is the choice address on Statia, surpassing The Old Gin House. Set on the Caribbean side of the island, about a ½ mile (.8km) north of Oranjestad, this secluded choice occupies about ⅔ acre (.3 hectare) perched on an oceanfront cliff, 60 feet (18m) above the surf. Construction on the hotel started in 1994 and has progressed slowly ever since. If you're looking for a laid-back, escapist vacation, this is your place. (Your nearest neighbors will be in the local cemetery.) Most views look out to the southwest, ensuring colorful sunsets that tend to be enhanced by drinks served from the bar at the Kings Well Restaurant (see "Dining," below).

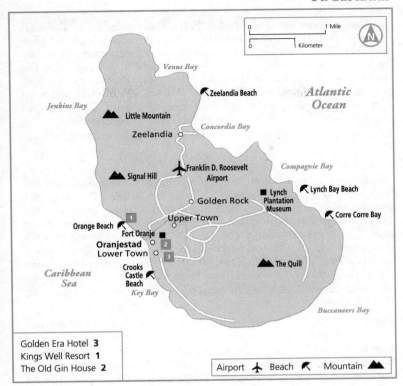

Golden Era Hotel **3**
Kings Well Resort **1**
The Old Gin House **2**

Airport ✈ · Beach ⚓ · Mountain ▲▲

There are no room keys, so don't expect much security. The accommodations are small and rather sparsely furnished; each is unique. Beds are draped with mosquito netting; rooms 1 and 4 contain waterbeds. The rooms in the rear are larger and face the sea, and those in front open onto a shared sea-view balcony. Bathrooms are small, with showers only.

Oranje Bay Rd-1, Oranjestad, St. Eustatius, N.A. ℂ and fax **599/318-2538**. 14 units. Winter $84–$102 double; $115–$140 efficiency. Off-season $65–$100 double; $115 efficiency. Rates include breakfast. DISC, MC, V. **Amenities:** Restaurant, bar; pool; fishing; boating; laundry. *In room:* TV, fridge.

The Old Gin House ★ For years the premier resort of Statia, The Old Gin House, a historic landmark, is now open after a long slumber. The inn is a faithful reconstruction of an 18th-century building that once housed a cotton gin. The bricks that went into the construction were once used by sailing ships as ballast. Surrounded by tropical gardens, including palms and bougainvillea, the hotel enjoys a central but tranquil location. All the good-size bedrooms are comfortably furnished, with queen-size beds, direct-dial phones, and restored shower-only bathrooms.

Oranjebaai 1, St. Eustatius, N.A. ℂ **599/318-2319**. Fax 599/318-2135. www.oldginhouse.com. 17 units. Year-round $135–$165 double; $275 suite. Rates include breakfast. AE, MC, V. **Amenities:** Restaurant, bar; pool; dive shop across the street. *In room:* A/C, TV.

3 Dining

Chinese Bar & Restaurant CHINESE   This place caters to locals and offers standard Chinese-restaurant fare with a bit of local influence thrown in, including such dishes as curried shrimp. The atmosphere is very laid back. For instance, even though the terrace isn't set up for dining, you can request to have your table moved there for an alfresco meal. The portions are hearty and range from the typical sweet-and-sour pork and a variety of shrimp dishes to chop suey and chow mein. This is the best place on the island for vegetarian food.

Princess Weg, Oranjestad. ✆ 599/318-2389. Main courses $8–$12. No credit cards. Mon–Sat 11am–3pm and 7:30–11pm.

Kings Well Restaurant INTERNATIONAL   The restaurant here is more successful and more complete than the simple hotel in which it's housed (see "Accommodations," above). Set about a ½ mile (.8km) north of Oranjestad, and perched on a cliff about 60 feet (18m) above the surf, it features an open kitchen and great sunset panoramas. Enjoy a fruity drink from the rustic bar before your meal. Lunches feature deli-style sandwiches and a selection of platters from the dinner menu, which is more elaborate. Dishes might include grilled Colorado beefsteaks, fresh lobster, pan-fried grouper or snapper with parsley-butter sauce, plus a few German meat dishes like *sauerbraten.*

Oranje Bay Rd., Oranjestad. ✆ 599/318-2538. Lunch platters $6–$12; dinner main courses $10–$19. DISC, MC, V. Daily 6–8:30pm.

L'Etoile CREOLE   Caren Henriquez's simple second-floor restaurant is well known on Statia for its local cuisine, but you don't run into too many tourists here. Favored main dishes include the ubiquitous "goatwater" (a stew), mountain crab, stewed whelks, tasty spareribs, and Caribbean-style lobster. Caren is also known for her *pastechis*—deep-fried turnovers stuffed with meat. Expect a complete and very filling meal.

6 Van Rheeweg, northeast of Upper Town. ✆ 599/318-2299. Reservations required. Main courses $7–$20. No credit cards. Thurs–Tues 7am–3am.

The Old Gin House Restaurant ✿ INTERNATIONAL/FRENCH/ASIAN For something exotic, escape here for some of the more imaginative dishes on an island that tends to be devoted to a basic Antillean cuisine. It' a popular spot for divers, who can usually be found at the bar watching Winston preparing their favorite drinks. This beautiful old bar, Mooshay Pub, is in the main building, a former warehouse that has been restored. It used to house sugar, cotton, and indigo. The dining room and kitchen are also found here. You can enjoy a candlelit dinner at poolside if the night is right. Fresh lobster appears almost daily on the menu in winter, and the catch of the day, which can be grilled, typically includes the likes of red snapper, mahi-mahi, and kingfish. You can see the fishermen bringing in the catch to sell to the chef in the kitchen.

Oranjebaai 1. ✆ 599/318-2319. Reservations required. Main courses $7–$25. AE, MC, V. Daily 7am–1:30am.

Yellow Bell Bar & Restaurant ✿ INTERNATIONAL   Set beside the beach, in a wood-sided Antillean house brightly painted in neon shades of blue and yellow, this restaurant combines West Indian funkiness with a polite staff and well-prepared cuisine. Menu items are whimsical and charming, and rely on culinary inspiration from around the world. The best examples include grilled chicken Caesar salads, spicy Thai-style fish, beef skewers in a peanut-based satay sauce, and grilled steaks and fish.

Bay Rd., Lower Town, Oranjestad. ℂ **599/318-2873**. Main courses $4.50–$12.50 lunch, $12–$20 dinner. MC, V. Tues–Sun 10am–11pm. Bar daily 10am–11pm.

4 Beaches

Most of the beaches of Statia are small, narrow strips of sand, either volcanic black or a dull mud-like gray. Regrettably, the preferred beaches are not on the tranquil Caribbean side, but on the turbulent Atlantic side, where the waters are often too rough for swimming.

Beachcombers delight, however, in their search for the fabled **blue-glass beads,** which were manufactured in the 1600s by a Dutch West Indies Company. These beads were used as money for the trading of such products as tobacco, cotton, and rum. They were even used to purchase slaves. These beads—real collector's items—often are unearthed after a heavy rainfall or tropical storm.

Orange Beach is also called Smoke Alley Beach. On the Caribbean side of the island, it lies directly off Lower Town. This is one of the small volcanic beaches on the southwest shore, with beige or black sands and waters suitable for a leisurely swim. You virtually have the beach to yourself until late afternoon, when locals start to arrive for a dip.

Also on the leeward, or Caribbean, side is **Crooks Castle Beach,** south of Oranjestad. The waters, filled with giant yellow sea fans, sea whips, and pillar coral, attract snorkelers, while beachcombers are drawn to the many blue beads that have been unearthed here.

On the southeast Atlantic side of the island, **Corre Corre Bay** has a strip of dark golden sand. It's about half an hour down Mountain Road and is worth the trip to get here, although the waters are often too churned up for comfortable swimming. Two bends north of this beach, the light-brown-sand **Lynch Bay Beach** is more sheltered from the wild swells of the Atlantic. Nonetheless, the surf here is still almost always rough, plus there's a dangerous undertow; this beach is better used for sunbathing than swimming.

Also on the Atlantic side, **Zeelandia Beach** is 2 miles (3km) long and filled with dark, dark beige and volcanic-black sand. One tourist promotion speaks of its "exciting Atlantic surf and invigorating trade winds," but fails to warn of the dangerous undertow. Only one small, designated section is safe for swimming. The beach is suitable, however, for wading, hiking, and sunbathing. The place is nearly always deserted.

5 Sports & Other Outdoor Pursuits

HIKING   Hiking is the most popular outdoor activity on the island. Those with the stamina can climb the slopes of the **Quill,** the highest point on Statia. Its extinct volcanic cone harbors a crater filled with a dense tropical rain forest, containing towering kapok trees and a dozen or more species of wild orchids, some quite rare. It's also home to at least 50 species of bird life, including the rare blue pigeon, known to frequent the breadfruit and cottonwood trees here. Islanders once grew cocoa, coffee, and cinnamon in the crater's soil, but today bananas are the only crop. The **tourist office** (ℂ **599/318-2433**) will supply you with a list of a dozen trails of varying degrees of difficulty and can also arrange for a guide. You'll have to negotiate the fee; it's usually $20 and up.

We're perfectly serious: If you're interested, you can join Statians in a crab hunt. The Quill's crater is the breeding ground for these large crustaceans. At night they emerge from their holes to forage, and that's when they're caught. Either with flashlights or relying on moonlight, crab hunters climb The Quill, catch a crab, and take the local delicacy home to prepare stuffed crab-back. Your hotel can usually hook you up with this activity.

WATERSPORTS   **Dive Statia** is a full PADI diving center on Fishermen's Beach in Lower Town (© **599/318-2435**), offering everything from beginning instruction to dive master certification. Its professional staff guides divers of all experience levels to spectacular walls, untouched coral reefs, and historic shipwrecks. Dive Statia offers 1- and 2-tank boat dives, costing $45 to $75, including equipment. Night dives and snorkel trips are also available.

Statia is mostly a divers' island, but there is some decent **snorkeling** on the Caribbean side. You can explore the remnants of an 18th-century man-of-war and the walls of warehouses, taverns, and ships that sank below the surface of Oranje Bay more than 200 years ago. The best place to go is **Crooks Castle Beach,** southwest of Lower Town. Any dive shop can rent you snorkeling gear.

Water-skiing is expensive on Statia. **Dive Statia,** operating out of the Golden Era Hotel, Bay Road, Lower Town (© **599/318-2435**), will hook you up for around $90 per hour.

TENNIS   Statia maintains tennis courts at the **Community Center,** Rosemary Laan in Upper Town (© **599/318-2249**), costing only $2 per hour. You'll have to bring your own rackets and balls, but there is a changing room.

6 Exploring the Island

Oranjestad stands on a cliff looking out on a beach and the island's calm anchorage, where in the 18th century you might have seen 200 vessels offshore. **Fort Oranje** was built in 1636 and restored in honor of the U.S. bicentennial celebration of 1976. Perched atop the cliffs, its terraced rampart is lined with the old cannons.

St. Eustatius Historical Foundation Museum, Upper Town (© **599/ 318-2288**), is also called the Donker House in honor of its former tenant, Simon Donker. After British Admiral Rodney sacked Statia for cooperating with the United States, he installed his own headquarters here. Today, the 18th-century house and museum stands in a garden, with a 20th-century wing crafted from 17th-century bricks. There are exhibits on the process of sugar refining and shipping and commerce, a section devoted to the pre-Columbian period, archaeological artifacts from the colonial period, and a pair of beautiful rooms furnished with 18th-century antiques. In the annex is a massive piece of needlework by American Catherine Mary Williams, showing the flowers of Statia. The museum is open Monday to Friday from 9am to 5pm, Saturday and Sunday from 9am to noon; admission is $2 for adults, $1 for children.

A few steps away, a cluster of 18th-century buildings surrounding a quiet courtyard is called **Three Widows' Corner.**

Nearby are the ruins of the first **Dutch Reformed church,** on Kerkweg ("Church Way"). To reach it, turn west from Three Widows' Corner onto Kerkweg. Tilting headstones record the names of the characters in the island's past. The St. Eustatius Historical Foundation recently completed restoration of the church. Visitors may climb to the top level of the tower and see the bay as lookouts did many years before.

Statia once had a large colony of Jewish traders, and you can explore the ruins of **Honen Dalim,** the second oldest Jewish synagogue in the western hemisphere. Built around 1740 and damaged by a hurricane in 1772, the synagogue stands beside Synagogpad, a narrow lane whose entrance faces Madam Theatre on the square.

The walls of a *mikvah* (ritual bath) rise beside the **Jewish burial ground** on the edge of town. Most poignant is the memorial of David Haim Hezeciah de Lion, who died in 1760 at the age of 2 years, 8 months, 26 days; carved into the baroque surface is an angel releasing a tiny songbird from its cage.

You can also visit **Lynch Plantation Museum** at Lynch Bay (© **599/ 318-2338**), but you'll have to call to arrange a tour. Donations are accepted; otherwise, admission is free. Locals still call this place the Berkel Family Plantation, although today it's a museum depicting life on Statia a century ago, through antiques, fishing and farming equipment, pictures, and old Bibles. Usually Ismael Berkel is on hand to show you around. This is still very much a residence, rather than some dead, dull museum.

7 Shopping

At **Mazinga Giftshop,** Fort Oranje Straat, Upper Town (© **599/318-2245**), you'll find an array of souvenirs—T-shirts, liquor, costume jewelry, 14-karat-gold jewelry, cards, drugstore items, beachwear, children's books, handbags, and paperback romances. You may have seen more exciting stores in your life, but this is without parallel for Statia. You can buy books and magazines at the **Paper Corner,** Van Tonningenweg, Upper Town (© **599/318-2208**).

8 St. Eustatius After Dark

As for after-dark fun on Statia, Las Vegas it ain't. Nightlife pickings here are among the slimmest in the Caribbean. Weekends are the best—maybe the only—time to go out on Statia. The local hot spot is known as **Elegant Club,** Paramiraweg, Upper Town (© **599/318-2195**), which rocks and rolls on weekends. There's dancing to a DJ, plus a little restaurant. The pool table is forever engaged. **The Stone Oven,** 16A Feaschweg, Upper Town, Oranjestad (© **599/ 318-2543**), often has dancing and local bands on weekends; you can also enjoy simple West Indian fare here. For local flavor, try **Cool Corner** (© **599/ 318-2523**), across from the St. Eustatius Historical Foundation Museum, in the center of town. Another option is **Largo Heights**, Chapel Piece, (© **599/ 318-2811**).

21

St. Kitts & Nevis

The two islands of St. Kitts and Nevis were British possessions until 1983, when they became a tiny, independent two-island nation (a ministate, really), complete with UN membership. But British traditions remain in evidence. Cricket is still fiercely popular, and motorists drive on the left.

For decades St. Kitts and Nevis slumbered as backwaters of the Caribbean. The country's economy was dependent entirely on sugarcane, making it especially vulnerable to the ravages of hurricanes (Hurricane Hugo, in 1990, caused particularly serious damage). But in recent years, tourists, especially celebrities, have discovered the islands' average year-round temperature of 79°F, low humidity, white-sand beaches, and unspoiled natural beauty.

This doesn't mean that St. Kitts and Nevis are playgrounds for the rich and famous—not yet. But people who can go anywhere have been spotted here in the near past:

the late Princess Di, Oprah Winfrey, Sylvester Stallone, Danny Glover, Robert DeNiro, Michael J. Fox, and Gerald and Betty Ford, to name a few.

Of the two islands, Nevis is the sleepier. It has less direct access from North America, fewer luxury hotel choices, and almost no nightlife to speak of. It also has a reputation as being a money-laundering haven for drug traffickers and other suspicious businesses (despite righteous denials by Nevis officials). The tiny island has some 9,000 offshore businesses—about one business per inhabitant—registered and operating under strict secrecy laws.

In fact, disagreements about controls over offshore banking activities triggered a rift between the two islands that almost led to Nevis's secession. In the most recent referendum on the issue, in 1998, a majority of Nevisians (but not the two-thirds required) voted for independence from St. Kitts.

1 St. Kitts & Nevis Essentials

VISITOR INFORMATION

Information is available from the tourist board's stateside offices at 414 E. 75th St., **New York, NY** 10021 (© **800/582-6208** or 212/535-1234).

In **Canada,** an office is located at 133 Richmond St., Suite 311, Toronto, ON, M5H 2L3 (© **416/368-6707**), and in the **United Kingdom** at 10 Kensington Court, London, W8 5DL (© **020/7376-0881**).

The website for both St. Kitts and Nevis is **www.stkitts-nevis.com**.

FAST FACTS: St. Kitts & Nevis

Currency   The local currency is the **Eastern Caribbean dollar (EC$)**, pegged at $2.70 to the U.S. dollar. Many prices, however, including those of hotels, are quoted in U.S. dollars. Always determine which "dollar" locals are talking about.

Customs   You are allowed in duty-free with your personal belongings. Sometimes luggage is subjected to a drug check. If you clear customs in one of the islands, you don't have to do it again if you visit the other.

Documents   U.S. and Canadian citizens can enter with proof of citizenship, such as a passport or birth certificate with a raised seal accompanied by a government-issued photo ID. British subjects need a passport, but not a visa.

Electricity   Electricity on St. Kitts is 220-volt AC (60 cycles), so you'll need an adapter and a transformer for U.S.-made appliances. However, most hotels on the islands have outlets that will accept North American appliances. Check with your hotel to see if it has converted its voltage and outlets.

Emergencies   Dial *(*) **911** for emergencies.

Language   English is the language of both islands, and it is spoken with a decided West Indian lilt; patois is commonly spoken as well.

Safety   This is still a fairly safe place to travel. Most crimes against tourists—and there aren't a lot—are robberies on Conaree Beach on St. Kitts, so exercise the usual precautions. It's wise to safeguard your valuables, and women should not go jogging alone along deserted roads. Crime is rare on Nevis.

Taxes   The government imposes a 7% tax on rooms and meals, plus another $16.50 airport departure tax. (You don't pay the departure tax when you travel between the islands.)

Telephone   The area code for St. Kitts and Nevis is **869.** You can make calls to or from the United States as you would for any other area code in North America. To access **AT&T Direct,** call *(*) **800/872-2881** and to reach MCI dial *(*) **800/888-8000.**

Time   St. Kitts and Nevis are on Atlantic standard time year-round. This means that in winter, when it's 6am in Basseterre, it's 5am in New York. When the United States goes on daylight saving time, St. Kitts and Nevis are on the same time as the east coast of the United States.

Tipping   Most hotels and restaurants add a service charge of 10% to cover tipping. If not, tip 10% to 15%.

Water   The water on St. Kitts and Nevis is so good that Baron de Rothschild's chemists selected St. Kitts as their only site in the Caribbean to distill and produce CSR (Cane Sugar Rothschild), a pure sugarcane liqueur. In the 1700s, Lord Nelson regularly brought his fleet to Nevis just to collect water, and Nevis still boasts of having Nelson spring water.

Weather   St. Kitts and Nevis are tropical, and the warm climate is tempered by the trade winds. The average air temperature is 79°F; the average water temperature, 80°F. Dry, mild weather is usually experienced from November to April; May to October it's hotter and rainier.

2 St. Kitts

St. Kitts has become a resort mecca in recent years. Its major crop is sugar, a tradition dating from the 17th century. But tourism may overwhelm it in the years to come, as its southeastern peninsula, site of the best sugar-white-sand beaches, has been set aside for massive resort development. Most of the island's other beaches are of gray or black volcanic sand.

At some point during your visit you should eat sugar directly from the cane—any farmer will sell you a huge stalk. There are sugarcane plantations all over the island—just ask your taxi driver to take you to one. Strip off the hard exterior of the stalk, bite into it, chew on the tasty reeds, and swallow the juice. It's best with a glass of rum.

The Caribs, the early settlers, called the island Liamuiga, or "fertile isle." Its mountain ranges reach up to nearly 4,000 feet (1200m), and its interior contains virgin rain forests, alive with hummingbirds and wild green vervet monkeys. The monkeys were brought in as pets by the early French settlers but were set free when the British took control of the island in 1783. These native African animals have proliferated and can be seen at the Estridge Estate Behavioral Research Institute. The British brought in mongooses to control rats in the sugarcane fields, only to discover that the predators slept during the rats' most active forays. Wild deer are found in the mountains.

The capital of St. Kitts, **Basseterre,** lies on the Caribbean shore near the southern end of the island, about a mile (2km) from the airport. With its white colonial houses with toothpick balconies, it looks like a Hollywood version of a West Indian port.

ST. KITTS ESSENTIALS

GETTING THERE   There are no nonstop flights to St. Kitts from North America. To get here, you'll have to stop or change planes in Antigua, St. Maarten, or Puerto Rico. **American Airlines** (© 800/433-7300 in the U.S.; www.aa.com) has dozens of daily flights to San Juan. From here, **American Eagle** (© 800/433-7300 in the U.S.; www.aa.com) makes four daily nonstop flights into St. Kitts.

Windward Islands Airways International (known to everybody as **Winair;** © 869/465-8010) flies to St. Kitts from St. Maarten. The Antigua-based carrier, **LIAT** (© 869/465-8200; www.liatairline.com), flies to St. Kitts from Antigua, Guadeloupe, San Juan, and St. Maarten. **Nevis Express** (© 869/469-9755; www.nevisexpress.com) flies from Guadeloupe, San Juan, and St. Maarten. Nevis Express also operates seven **shuttle flights** each way daily between St. Kitts and Nevis. A round-trip ticket costs $50. LIAT also flies twice a day between St. Kitts and Nevis islands.

Air Canada (© 514/422-5000 in Canada; www.aircanada.ca) flies from Toronto to Antigua, and **British Airways** (© 800/247-9297 in the U.S.; www.british-airways.com) flies from London to Antigua. From Antigua, you can make connections on LIAT or WinAir (see above).

You can also use the **interisland ferry service** between St. Kitts and Nevis. Ferry schedules are subject to change without notice, and follow no obvious patterns. The **M.V. *Sea Hustler*** makes at least three trips per day, and sometimes four. There is usually one morning crossing and one afternoon crossing from each island. Travel time is 1 hour. The **M.V. *Caribe Queen*** makes the crossing in 45 minutes, but it doesn't run on Thursdays or Sundays. Its schedule is also different every day—it generally makes one round-trip in the morning (usually

Airport ✈ Beach 🏄 Ferry Route --- Mountain ▲▲

0   5 Miles
0   5 Kilometers

Dieppe Bay

Sandy Bay

St. Paul's

Sadlers

Newton Ground

Hermitage Bay

Mount Liamuiga

Ottley's

Sandy Point Town

Brimstone Hill Fortress

Cayon

Keys

Atlantic Ocean

Half-Way Tree

Carib Rock Drawings

Middle Island

Old Road Town

St. Peter's

Conaree Bay

Challengers

North Frigate Bay

Basseterre

North Friar's Bay

Frigate Bay

Turtle Beach

Caribbean Sea

South Friar's Bay

Sand Bank Bay

Great Salt Pond

Booby Shoals

White House Bay

St. Anthony's Peak

Cockleshell Bay

Nag's Head

Banana Bay

To Nevis ↘

Bird Rock Beach Hotel **8**
Coconut Beach Club **6**
Frigate Bay Resort **7**
Golden Lemon Inn & Villas **2**
Jack Tar Royal St. Kitts
   Hotel & Casino **5**
Morgan Heights Condo Resort **4**
Ocean Terrace Inn **9**
Ottley's Plantation Inn **3**
Rawlins Plantation **1**

7 or 7:30am) and at least one trip each way in the afternoon (at 4, 5, or 6pm, depending on the island). The fare is $8 round-trip for either ferry. Contact the tourist office on either island for exact schedules.

GETTING AROUND Since most **taxi** drivers are also guides, this is the best means of getting around. You don't even have to find a driver at the airport— one will find you. Drivers also wait outside the major hotels. Before heading out, however, you must agree on the price, since taxis aren't metered. Also, ask if the rates quoted to you are in U.S. or Eastern Caribbean dollars. The fare from the airport to Basseterre is about EC$16 (US$5.90); to Sandy Point, EC$37 (US$13.70) and up. For more information, call the **St. Kitts Taxi Association** (📞 **869/465-8487**).

   Avis, South Independence Square (📞 **800/331-1212** in the U.S., or 869/465-6507), charges from $50 per day, $300 per week, plus $15 per day for collision damage, with a $950 deductible. Tax is 5% extra. The company offers free delivery service to either the airport or to any of the island's hotels; drivers must be between ages 25 and 75. Avis will also arrange for a rental exchange if you go to Nevis too.

   Delisle Walwyn & Co., Liverpool Row, Basseterre (📞 **869/465-8449**), is a local company offering cars and Jeeps starting at $45 per day. Tax and insurance are extra. This might be your best deal on the island. You can also check two other local companies: **Sunshine,** Cayon Street in Basseterre and a kiosk at the

---

Fun Fact **Party Times in St. Kitts**

Carnival in St. Kitts is celebrated not in the days leading up to Ash Wednesday, but from Christmas Eve until January 2nd. The festivities include parties, dancing, talent shows, and the crowning of the Carnival Queen. The final day of the celebration is known as "Last Lap," and features a repeat of many of the activities, including a multitude of bands jamming in the streets of Basseterre.

Another popular party time is the **St. Kitt's Music Festival,** held the last weekend in June (Thurs–Sun). The Soca/Calypso night is usually the festival's opening event, and its most popular. You can also hear reggae, jazz, rhythm and blues, and gospel performances over the 4 days. For more information about the 2003 festival, call the Department of Tourism at ✆ **869/465-4040.**

---

airport (✆ **869/465-2193**), and **TDC Rentals,** West Independence Square in Basseterre (✆ **869/465-2991**).

Remember that *driving is on the left!* You'll need a local driver's license, which can be obtained at the **Traffic Department,** on Cayon Street in Basseterre, for EC$30 (US$11.10). Usually a member of the staff at your car-rental agency will drive you to the Traffic Department to get one.

FAST FACTS **Banks** on St. Kitts are open Monday to Thursday from 8am to noon and on Friday from 8am to noon and 3 to 5pm. You can place **international telephone calls, including collect calls,** at **Skantel,** Cayon Street, Basseterre (✆ **869/465-1000**), Monday to Friday from 8am to 5pm, Saturday from 8am to noon.

Parris Pharmacy, Central Street at Basseterre (✆ **869/465-8569**), is open Monday to Wednesday from 8am to 9pm, Thursday from 8am to 1pm, Friday from 8am to 5:30pm, and Saturday from 9am to 6pm. You can also try **City Drug,** Fort Street in Basseterre (✆ **869/465-2156**), open Monday to Wednesday and Friday to Saturday from 8am to 7pm, Thursday from 8am to 5pm, and Sunday from 8 to 11am.

There's a 24-hour **emergency room** in Basseterre at **Joseph N. France General Hospital,** Cayon Street (✆ **869/465-2551**).

The **St. Kitts tourist board** operates at Pelican Mall, Bay Road in Basseterre (✆ **869/465-4040**). It's open Monday and Tuesday from 8am to 4:30pm and Wednesday through Friday from 8am to 4pm.

ACCOMMODATIONS
VERY EXPENSIVE

Golden Lemon Inn & Villas ★★★ *Sophisticated* and *elegant* describe both the Golden Lemon and its clientele. Arthur Leaman, one-time decorating editor of *House & Garden* magazine, has used his taste and background to create a hotel of great charm in this once-busy shipping port. The 1610 French manor house with an 18th-century Georgian upper story is set back from a coconut grove and a black volcanic-sand beach, on the northwest coast of St. Kitts. Flanking the great house are the Lemon Court and Lemon Grove Condominiums, where you can rent luxuriously furnished suites surrounded by manicured gardens; most have private pools.

The spacious rooms are furnished with antiques and always contain fresh flowers, but are not air-conditioned. Bedrooms have recently been redecorated with new fabrics, rugs, and accessories. The names of rooms—such as Victorian, Paisley, and Lemon—evoke their themes. Many beds are raised four-posters draped in mosquito netting in the old plantation style; each is equipped with fine linen. Most of the tiled bathrooms are huge; they contain deluxe toiletries, shower/tub combinations, and dressing areas. The larger villas even have sunken tubs, kitchens, and dishwashers. The Golden Lemon Restaurant serves fine continental and Caribbean cuisine (see "Dining," below).

Dieppe Bay, St. Kitts, W.I. © **800/633-7411** in the US or 869/465-7260. Fax 869/465-4019. www.golden lemon.com. 26 units. Winter $300–$395 double; $465–$765 suite. Off-season $245 double; $395 suite. Rates include American breakfast. Extra person $125. 4-night minimum stay required in winter. Honeymoon packages available. AE, MC, V. Children age 15 and under not usually accepted. **Amenities:** Pool; horseback riding; rain-forest trips; day trips to other islands; snorkeling, catamarans, scuba diving; car rental; room service (7am–midnight); massage; laundry. *In room:* Ceiling fan, fridge, hair dryer.

Jack Tar Royal St. Kitts Hotel & Casino ⭐   The largest hotel on St. Kitts, and the showcase of the much-touted Frigate Bay development, this all-inclusive chain resort lies 1½ miles (2km) east of the airport. It's set on a flat, sandy isthmus between the sea and a saltwater lagoon. It's almost completely self-contained, giving the feeling of a frenetic private country club. Each unit has a patio or balcony and simple tropical furniture. Most visitors prefer the second-floor rooms, which have higher ceilings than the first-floor rooms. The bandbox rooms are hardly the island's most glamorous, but they are comfortable with double or king-size beds and combination shower/tub bathrooms.

The resort has two restaurants, serving cuisine that's more bountiful than gourmet, and it has the island's only casino.

Frigate Bay (P.O. Box 406), St. Kitts, W.I. © **800/858-2258** in the U.S., or 869/465-8651. Fax 869/466-9016. www.jacktar.com/jtv_s/st_kitts. 270 units. Winter $266–$346 double. Off season $226–$254 double. Rates include meals, golf fees, drinks, and most watersports. AE, MC, V. **Amenities:** 2 restaurants, 2 grills, 3 bars; casino; 2 pools; golf course nearby; 4 tennis courts; babysitting; laundry/dry cleaning. *In room:* A/C, TV, hair dryer, safe.

Ottley's Plantation Inn ⭐⭐⭐   This is clearly the island's finest place to stay, even outdistancing the more mellow and time-seasoned Golden Lemon. Six miles (10km) north of the airport, and near a rain forest, it occupies a 35-acre (14-hectare) site on a former 18th-century West Indian plantation. Those seeking charm and tranquility will like the nine rooms in an 1832 great house. Other units are divided among three cottages, with air-conditioning and overhead fans. In winter 1997, two cottages with four new suites were constructed, each with modern amenities, including private pools and panoramic views. Two of the suites are truly deluxe, with their own Jacuzzis. Rooms are elegantly appointed and very spacious with queen- or king-size beds; the bathrooms have shower/tub combinations and deluxe toiletries.

The plantation operates one of the best restaurants on the island, The Royal Palm (see "Dining," below), that offers a Sunday champagne brunch.

Ottley's (P.O. Box 345), Basseterre, St. Kitts, W.I. © **800/772-3039** in the U.S., or 869/465-7234. Fax 869/465-4760. www.ottleys.com. 24 units. Winter $295–$485 double; $740 suite. Off-season $230–$375 double; $535 suite. Rates include breakfast; $50 per person daily for dinner plan. Wedding, honeymoon, and other packages available. AE, DISC, MC, V. Children under age 9 discouraged. **Amenities:** Restaurant, 2 bars; pool; tennis court; croquet lawn; free dirt bikes; room service (8:30am–9pm); massage; babysitting; laundry; shuttle to beach. *In room:* A/C, TV (by advance request), coffeemaker, hair dryer, iron and ironing board, safe.

Rawlins Plantation ★★   This hotel near Dieppe Bay is situated among the remains of a muscovado sugar factory on the northeast coast, with a good sandy beach just a short drive away. The rather isolated former plantation is 350 feet (105m) above sea level and enjoys cool breezes from both ocean and mountains. Behind the grounds, the land rises to a rain forest and Mount Liamuiga.

A 17th-century windmill has been converted into a charming accommodation, complete with private bathroom and sitting room; the boiling houses, formerly used to distill cauldrons of molasses, have been turned into a cool courtyard, where guests dine amid flowers and tropical birds. Other accommodations are in pleasantly decorated cottages equipped with modern facilities. There's no air-conditioning, but ceiling fans and cross-ventilation keep the place comfortable. Each unit, generous in size, is decorated in a Caribbean country-house style with antiques, stone or white walls, floral prints, local art, and rattan furnishings. Many bedrooms have mahogany four-posters; all have fine linen. Bathrooms are superb, with plenty of shelf space, toiletries, and shower/tub combinations.

P.O. Box 340, Mount Pleasant, St. Kitts, W.I. ✆ **800/346-5358** in the U.S., 0207/730-7144 in London, or 869/465-6221. Fax 869/465-4954. www.rawlinsplantation.com. 10 units. Winter $450 double. Off-season $330 double. Rates include breakfast, dinner, and afternoon tea. AE, MC, V. Closed Sept–Oct. No children under age 12. **Amenities:** Restaurant; pool; tennis court; croquet; laundry. *In room:* Ceiling fan, hair dryer, no phone.

MODERATE

Bird Rock Beach Hotel   Set on a secluded, half-moon-shaped beach 2 miles (3km) southeast of Basseterre, this small resort is uncomplicated and easygoing. Views from the balconies of most of the bedrooms are either of the Bay of Basseterre and the capital, or of the water stretching toward Nevis. All units have private patios or balconies and rather bland furniture inspired by the tropics. Bedrooms carry out the Caribbean motif with flowery fabrics and paintings of birds, and shower/tub combination bathrooms are small but adequate. Each superior room has one king-size or two double beds, and each studio suite offers a queen-size bed plus a sofa bed and a full kitchen. Each efficiency apartment has two double beds, a microwave, a toaster, a coffeemaker, and a small fridge.

P.O. Box 227, Basseterre, St. Kitts, W.I. ✆ **800/621-1270** in the U.S., or 869/465-8914. Fax 869/465-1675. www.birdrockbeach.com. 46 units. Winter $160 double; $175 efficiency apt.; $185 studio suite for 2; $305 1-bedroom apt.; $325 3-bedroom apt. Off-season $85 double; $90 efficiency apt.; $100 studio suite for 2; $135 1-bedroom apt.; $200 3-bedroom apt. AE, MC, V. **Amenities:** Restaurant, 2 bars, grill; pool; tennis court. *In room:* A/C, TV, hair dryer.

Frigate Bay Resort   On a verdant hillside east of Basseterre, Frigate Bay has standard rooms and condo suites administered as hotel units for their absentee owners. The older units are more spacious than the newer accommodations. Rooms are nicely furnished to the taste of the owners and painted in cool colors. Nautical prints, tile floors, flowery prints, and private terraces or balconies make the place alluring. The small shower-only bathrooms are well maintained. Many units contain fully equipped kitchens with breakfast bars. The central core of the resort has a large pool and a swim-up bar.

Frigate Bay (P.O. Box 137), Basseterre, St. Kitts, W.I. ✆ **869/465-8935.** Fax 869/465-7050. www.frigate bay.com. 64 units. Winter double $160–$210; from $295–$400 suite. Off-season $105–$145 double; from $230 suite. Breakfast and dinner for $52 per person extra. Packages available. AE, MC, V. **Amenities:** Restaurant, bar; pool; car rental; babysitting; laundry. *In room:* A/C, TV, hair dryer, fridge.

Ocean Terrace Inn ★   This inn is affectionately known as the "OTI" by its mainly business clients. If you want to be near Basseterre, it's the best hotel around the port, with oceanfront verandas and a view of the harbor and the capital. It's so compact that a stay here is like a house party on a great liner. Terraced into a landscaped hillside above the edge of Basseterre, the hotel also has gardens and well-kept grounds. All the handsomely decorated rooms have a light, tropical feel and overlook a well-planted terrace. Beds are a wide variety of sizes, and bathrooms, with shower/tub combinations, are compact and tidily maintained. The hotel also offers apartments at the Fisherman's Wharf and Village, a few steps from the nearby harbor. These units are filled with most of the comforts of home.

P.O. Box 65, Fortlands, St. Kitts, W.I. © 869/465-2754. Fax 869/465-1057. www.oceanterrace.com. 78 units. Winter $170–$300 double. Off-season $135–$240 double. Dive, honeymoon, and eco-safari packages available. AE, DC, DISC, MC, V. Go west along Basseterre Bay Rd. past the Cenotaph. **Amenities:** 3 restaurants, 2 bars; 3 pools; fitness center; Jacuzzi; windsurfing, water-skiing. *In room:* A/C, TV, hair dryer.

INEXPENSIVE

Coconut Beach Club   Located at the foot of a green mountain, 3 miles (5km) east of Basseterre, this condo resort is a family favorite. Though short on island atmosphere, it opens onto one of the finest beaches on St. Kitts. Naturally, the most sought-after units in this complex are those opening directly onto the beach, with swimming, sailing, and watersports at your doorstep. There's also a pool, and an 18-hole golf course is just a short drive away. The rooms are furnished in a Caribbean motif, and the larger accommodations have kitchens. Units here are time-shares, so there are no routine extras. All rooms have medium-size bathrooms with shower/tub combinations.

Frigate Bay (P.O. Box 1198), Basseterre, St. Kitts, W.I. © 869/465-8597. Fax 869/466-7085. www.timothy beachresort.com. 62 units. Winter $110–$135 double; $170 studio suite; $190 1-bedroom apt. for up to 4; $290 2-bedroom apt. for up to 6. Off-season $90–$105 double; $125 studio suite; $140 1-bedroom apt. for up to 4; $205 2-bedroom apt. for up to 6. AE, MC, V. **Amenities:** Restaurant; pool; golf nearby; babysitting; laundry. *In room:* Ceiling fan, no phone.

Morgan Heights Condo Resort   Despite the name, Morgan Heights is more of a condo complex than a resort. There's a minimum of assistance from the staff. But each of the small- to medium-sized units is well maintained and fairly inviting. Most units have good beds and small, shower/tub combination bathrooms. The two-bedroom apartments each have wicker furniture, covered patios overlooking the Atlantic Ocean, and a kitchen. The suites are a more recent addition. Although there's a view of the water, the beach is a 10-minute drive away.

Canada Estate (P.O. Box 735), Basseterre, St. Kitts, W.I. © 869/465-8633. Fax 869/465-9272. www.morgan heights.com. 14 units. Winter $100 1-bedroom condo; $175 suite. Off-season $85 1-bedroom condo; $135 suite. Extra person $20 in winter, $15 off-season. AE, DC, MC, V. **Amenities:** Restaurant; pool; laundry. *In room:* A/C, TV, minibar.

DINING
VERY EXPENSIVE

The Royal Palm ★★ CARIBBEAN FUSION   On the grounds of Ottley's Plantation Inn, the Royal Palm is an island favorite, serving the most creative and best cuisine on St. Kitts. It also has a colorful setting: Gaze through the ancient stone arches to the ocean on one side and Mount Liamuiga and the inn's great house on the other. The menu changes daily, so you won't know what the inspiration of the moment will be. You might start with Brazilian gingered-chicken soup or chile-flavored shrimp corn cakes, each equally tempting. If featured, the lobster quesadillas, made with local lobster, are worth crossing the island to sample. Main courses tend to be impeccably prepared, especially the French roast of lamb or the breast of chicken Molyneux with almonds, country ham, mozzarella, and mushroom stuffing.

In Ottley's Plantation Inn, north of Basseterre, on the east coast. ✆ 869/465-7234. Reservations required. Lunch main courses $10–$25; Sun champagne brunch $29; fixed-price dinner from $60. AE, DISC, MC, V. Mon–Sat 8am–3pm, Sun brunch 11am–3pm; daily dinner seating 7:30–8:30pm.

EXPENSIVE

Ballahoo Restaurant ✦ CARIBBEAN   Overlooking the town center's Circus Clock, the Ballahoo is about a block from the sea, on the second story of a traditional stone building. Its open-air dining area is one of the coolest places in town on a hot afternoon, thanks to the sea breezes. One of the best and most reliable dishes is blue parrot fish fillet. The chef also makes some of the best chili and baby back ribs in town. Seafood platters, such as chile shrimp or fresh lobster, are served with a coconut salad and rice. For more elegant fare, there's Italian-style chicken breast topped with pesto tomatoes and cheese and served with a pasta and salad. The service is casual. Because of its central location, this restaurant draws the cruise-ship crowd.

The Circus, Fort St., Basseterre. ✆ 869/465-4197. Reservations recommended. Main courses EC$22–EC$70 (US$8.15–US$25.90). MC, V. Mon–Sat 8am–10pm.

Fisherman's Wharf Seafood Restaurant and Bar ✦ SEAFOOD/ CARIBBEAN   At the west end of Basseterre Bay Road, the Fisherman's Wharf is between the sea and the white picket fence of the Ocean Terrace Inn. Near the busy buffet grill, hardworking chefs prepare fresh seafood. An employee will take your drink order, but you personally place your food order at the grill. It's a bit like eating at picnic tables, but the fresh fish selection is excellent, caught locally and grilled to order over St. Kitts chosha coals. Spicy conch chowder is a good starter; grilled lobster is an elegant main course choice, but you may prefer the grilled catch of the day, often snapper. Grilled swordfish steak is always a pleaser, as is the combination platter, which includes lobster, barbecued shrimp kebab, and calypso chicken breast.

Fortlands, Basseterre. ✆ 869/465-2754. Reservations recommended. Main courses EC$42–EC$80 (US$5.55–US$29.60). AE, DISC, MC, V. Daily 7–11pm.

The Georgian House ✦ INTERNATIONAL   This is the best place in town for lunch. Begin with conch ceviche (marinated in lime juice and flavored with cilantro) or opt for the freshly made soup of the day. House salads are always a winner here, especially the Caesar or the grilled chicken salad. From the grill emerges a classic burger or the catch of the day, prepared as you like it. At dinner, the cuisine is more elaborate and always filled with flavor. Pastas are succulent, and the chef specializes in lobster and steaks from the grill. The menu uses quality ingredients in familiar dishes, including the likes of New York strip, grilled pork chop, and lobster Thermidor.

S. Independence Sq., Basseterre. ✆ 869/465-4049. Reservations recommended. Lunch main courses EC$18–EC$35 (US$6.65–US$12.95); dinner main courses EC$30–EC$60 (US$11.10–US$22.20). AE, MC, V. Mon–Sat 10:30am–9:30pm, Sun 5–9pm.

The Golden Lemon ✦ CONTINENTAL/CREOLE   This 17th-century house has been converted into a fine hotel on the northern coast (see "Accommodations," above). The food is very good, and the service polite. It's a great lunch stop on a tour of the island. Dinner is served in an elegant, candlelit dining room, in the garden, or on the gallery. The cuisine features Creole, continental, and American dishes, with locally grown produce. Many of the recipes were created by the hotel's sophisticated owner. The menu changes daily, but is likely to include baked Cornish hen with ginger, fresh fish of the day, and Creole sirloin steak with a spicy rum sauce. Vegetarian dishes are also available. Dress is casually chic.

In the Golden Lemon hotel, Dieppe Bay. © 869/465-7260. Reservations usually required; walk-ins accepted if space available. Lunch main courses $7–$25; fixed-price dinner $40–$60; Sun brunch $24. AE, MC, V. Mon–Sat 7:30–10am, noon–3pm and 7–10pm, Sun noon–3pm and 7–10pm.

Manhattan Gardens ⚸ CARIBBEAN/INTERNATIONAL This 18th-century island home is painted in flamboyant colors and extends a hearty welcome to its generally satisfied patrons. The ideal time to go is for the Caribbean food fest, and the place to eat it is the rear garden opening onto a view of the water. Chef/owner Rosalind Warner has some real local dishes such as curried mutton, although you might opt for the fresh catch of the day instead. We're fond of her shrimp with white wine or else garlic butter. Her boneless chicken stuffed with spinach is another winner, as are her homemade soups, especially the pumpkin.

Main Street, Old Road. © 869/465-9121. Reservations required. Main courses EC$35–EC$60 (US$12.95–US$22.20). No credit cards. Mon–Sat 10:30am–3pm and 7–11pm.

Ocean Terrace Inn ⚸ CARIBBEAN/INTERNATIONAL Some of the finest cuisine in Basseterre is found here, along with one of the best views from its open-air veranda, especially at night when the harbor is lit up. The kitchen is best when preparing the real down-home dishes of the island instead of the blander international specialties. Dinner might include tasty fish cakes, accompanied by breaded carrot slices, creamed spinach, a stuffed potato, a cornmeal dumpling known as johnnycake, and a green banana in a lime-butter sauce, topped off by a tropical fruit pie and coffee. The less venturesome can stick with Arawak chicken, chateaubriand, and steak Diane. The special night to attend is Friday, which features a Caribbean night with an all-you-can-eat buffet and a steel band at a cost of $21. Some form of entertainment is often presented.

Fortlands. © 869/465-2754. Reservations recommended. Main courses EC$52–EC$78.50 (US$19.25–US$29.05); fixed-price lunch EC$40.50 (US$15); fixed-price dinner EC$67.50 (US$25). AE, DISC, MC, V. Daily 7–10am, noon–2pm, and 7–10:30pm. Drive west on Basseterre Bay Rd. to Fortlands.

Rawlins Plantation Restaurant ⚸ This previously recommended plantation inn serves some of the finest regional cuisine in the area, dishes full of a real West Indian flavor. It is especially known for its buffet lunch, and is also ideally located, as it lies only a 10-minute drive from Brimstone Hill. For those diners tired of so-called international menus, this is an ideal choice. In an elegant setting, you can order a rum punch and immerse yourself in the old Caribbean lifestyle, later enjoying a meal with ingredients often from the kitchen gardens, or else bounty gathered from nearby farmers or local fishermen. The lunchtime buffet is a special delight, beginning with such appetizers as shrimp fritters in a mango salsa, or else plantains baked with pecans. For a main dish, try perhaps pork with pineapple and hot chili peppers, or else lobster and spinach crepes. The dinner menu is limited but choice, likely to feature such dishes as rack of lamb with a spicy herb crust, followed by local stewed guavas with a Grand Marnier cream sauce.

Mount Pleasant. © 869/465-6221. Reservations recommended. Lunch buffet $25. Set dinner $50. AE, MC, V. Lunch daily 12:30–2pm; dinner nightly at 8pm. Guests are requested not to wear shorts at dinner.

Stonewalls ⚸ *Finds* CARIBBEAN/INTERNATIONAL Surrounded by ancient stonewalls, this casual, open-air bar in a tropical garden in Basseterre's historical zone is cozy and casual. It's the type of Caribbean bar that you think exists but can rarely find. In a garden setting of banana, plantain, lime, and bamboo trees, Wendy and Garry Speckles present an innovative and constantly changing menu. The fare might be Caribbean, with fresh kingfish or tuna and a zesty gumbo, or an authentic, spicy Dhansak-style curry. Hot-off-the-wok stir-fries are served along with sizzling Jamaican-style jerk chicken. Appetizers might include piquant conch fritters. A small but carefully chosen wine list is available. The bar here is one of the most convivial places on the island for a drink.

Princes St. © **869/465-5248.** Reservations recommended. Main courses EC$42–EC$65 (US$15.55–US$24.05). AE, MC, V. Mon–Fri 5–11pm.

Turtle Beach Bar & Grill ✷ SEAFOOD   Set directly on the sands above Turtle Beach, this airy, sun-flooded restaurant is one of the most popular lunch stops for those doing the whirlwind tour of St. Kitts. Many guests spend the hour before their meal swimming or snorkeling beside the offshore reef; others simply relax on the verandas or in hammocks under the shade trees, perhaps with a drink in hand. Scuba diving, ocean kayaking, windsurfing, and volleyball are available, and a flotilla of rental sailboats moor nearby. Menu specialties are familiar stuff, but prepared with an often scrumptious flavor. Typical dishes might be stuffed broiled lobster, conch fritters, barbecued swordfish steak, pasta salads, and barbecued honey-mustard spareribs.

Southeastern Peninsula. © **869/469-9086.** Reservations recommended. Main courses EC$27–EC$63 (US$10–US$23.30). AE, MC, V. Daily 10am–6pm. Follow the Kennedy Simmonds Hwy. over Basseterre's Southeastern Peninsula; then follow the signs.

INEXPENSIVE

The Atlantic Club SEAFOOD/WEST INDIAN   Nevisian Genford Gumbs worked at the deluxe Golden Lemon for 15 years before striking out on his own and opening this enterprise in the early 1990s. On St. Kitts's east coast, a 5-minute drive from the Basseterre or the airport, this restaurant overlooks—what else?—the Atlantic Ocean. The cuisine is West Indian, with some seafood such as fresh fish, conch, and lobster usually available. The atmosphere is relaxed and casual, and the portions are large. A lot of locals show up on Saturday for the special: goat water (goat stew) and *souse* (pickled pigs' feet, ear, and head, sometimes compressed into a loaf similar to a terrine). Less-adventurous visitors may want to skip this treat and instead order the burgers, soups, salads, and sandwiches, or even a Black Angus steak.

At the Morgan Heights Condominiums, Canada Estate. © **869/465-8633.** Reservations required for dinner. Main courses EC$22–EC$75 (US$8.15–US$27.75). AE, MC, V. Mon–Sat 11am–10pm.

Glimbara Diner CARIBBEAN   Don't expect grand cuisine from this workaday but honest eatery. Established in 1998 in a simple family-run guesthouse in the heart of Basseterre, it has become a local favorite, thanks to the hardworking staff and down-to-earth food. Small and cozy, and painted in shades of pink and white, it serves Creole cuisine that varies with the mood and inspiration of the cook, plus conventional American-style platters, including hamburgers and hot dogs, usually served with fries and soda. Examples might include large or small portions of the stew-like goatwater, pumpkin or bean soup, and several kinds of fried or grilled fish, which might be accompanied by coleslaw or green salad. Ask for a local fruit punch known as *fairling* or the bottled sugary grapefruit-drink called Ting.

In the Glimbara Guest House, Cayon St., Basseterre. © **869/465-1786.** Main courses EC$14–EC$20 (US$5.20–US$7.40). AE, MC, V. Daily 7am–11pm.

BEACHES

Beaches are the primary concern of most St. Kitts visitors. The narrow peninsula in the southeast that contains the island's salt ponds also boasts the best white-sand beaches. All beaches, even those that border hotels, are open to the public. However, if you use the beach facilities of a hotel, you must obtain permission first and will probably have to pay a small fee.

For years, it was necessary to take a boat to enjoy the beautiful, unspoiled beaches of the southeast peninsula. But in 1989, the Dr. Kennedy Simmonds Highway (named for the nation's first prime minister), a 6-mile (10km) road beginning in the Frigate Bay area, opened to the public. To traverse this road is one of the pleasures of a visit to St. Kitts. Not only will you take in some of the island's most beautiful scenery, but you'll also pass lagoon-like coves and fields of tall guinea grass. If the day is clear (and it usually is), you'll have a panoramic vista of Nevis. The best beaches along the peninsula are **Frigate Bay, Friar's Bay, Sand Bank Bay, White House Bay, Cockleshell Bay,** and **Banana Bay.** Of all these, **Sand Bank Bay** ✦ gets our nod as the finest strip of sand.

Both **Cockleshell Bay** and **Banana Bay** also have their devotees. These two beaches run a distance of 2 miles (3km), all with powder-white sands. So far, in spite of several attempts, this area hasn't filled with high-rise resorts.

A live steel band plays on Sundays from 12:30 to 3pm at the **Turtle Beach Bar and Grill,** Turtle Bay, making this the place for afternoon cocktails on the beach.

For excellent **snorkeling,** head to the somewhat rocky **White House Bay,** which opens onto reefs. Schools of rainbow-hued fish swim around a sunken tugboat from long ago—a stunning sight.

South Friar's Bay is lovely, although its pristine qualities may be forever disturbed by the construction of a new Hyatt. Friar's has powder-fine sand as well, and many locals consider it their favorite. **Frigate Bay,** with its powder-white sand, is ideal for swimming as well as windsurfing and water-skiing.

As a curiosity, you may want to visit **Great Salt Pond** at the southeastern end of St. Kitts. This is an inland beach of soft white sand, opening onto the Atlantic Ocean in the north and the more tranquil Caribbean Sea in the south.

The beaches in the north of St. Kitts are numerous but are of gray volcanic sand and much less frequented than those of the southeast peninsula. Many beachcombers like to frequent them, and they can be ideal for sunbathing, but swimming is much better in the southeast, as waters in the north, sweeping in from the Atlantic, can often be turbulent.

The best beach on the Atlantic side is **Conaree Bay,** with a narrow strip of gray-black sand. Bodysurfing is popular here. **Dieppe Bay,** another black-sand beach on the north coast, is good for snorkeling and windsurfing but not for swimming. This is the site of the island's most famous inn, the Golden Lemon, which you might want to visit for lunch. If you should be on this beach during a tropical shower, do not seek shelter under the dreaded machineel trees, which are poisonous. Rain falling off the leaves will feel like acid on your skin.

SPORTS & OTHER OUTDOOR PURSUITS

BOATING   Most outfitters are found at Frigate Bay on the southeast peninsula. The best of these is the provocatively named **Mr. X Watersports** (© 869/465-0673 or 869/662-3306), where you can rent kayaks for $15 an hour, arrange windsurfing for the same price, rent a Sunfish for $20 per hour, or hook up with a snorkeling tour lasting 2 hours and costing $25 per person.

GOLF   The **Royal St. Kitts Golf Course,** Frigate Bay (© **869/465-8339**), is an 18-hole championship course that opened in 1976, covering 160 acres (64 hectares). It features 10 water hazards, not including the Caribbean Sea and the Atlantic Ocean, which border it. It's open daily from 7am to 7pm. Greens fees are $40 for 18 holes. Cart rentals cost $50 for 18 holes, plus another $25 for clubs. A bar and an on-site restaurant open daily at 7am.

HIKING   Kris Tours (© **869/465-4042**) takes small groups into the crater of Mount Liamuiga, through a rain forest to enjoy the lushness of the island, or to Verchild's Mountain, which isn't a difficult trek. A full-day tour costs $50 per person.

HORSEBACK RIDING   Trinity Stables (© **869/465-3226**) charges $50 for a half-day tour through a rain forest. You might also get to see the wild lushness of the North Frigate Bay area and the rather desolate Conaree Beach. You must call for a reservation; you'll then be told where to meet and offered any advice, including what to wear.

SCUBA DIVING, SNORKELING & OTHER WATERSPORTS   Some of the best dive spots include **Nag's Head,** at the south tip of St. Kitts. This is an excellent shallow-water dive starting at 10 feet (3m) and extending to 70 feet (21m). A variety of tropical fish, eagle rays, and lobster are found here. The site is ideal for certified divers. Another good spot for diving is **Booby Shoals,** off the Southeast Atlantic coast near Cockleshell Bay. Booby Shoals has abundant sea life, including nurse sharks, lobster, and stingrays. Dives are up to 30 feet (9m) in depth, ideal for both certified and resort divers.

A variety of activities are offered by **Pro-Divers,** at Turtle Beach (© **869/ 466-3483**). You can swim, float, paddle, or go on scuba-diving and snorkeling expeditions from here. A two-tank dive costs $80; night dives are $50. A PADI certification is available for $350, and a resort course costs $90. Three-hour snorkeling trips are $35.

Pro-Divers will also rent you snorkeling gear and tell you the best places to go **snorkeling.** One particular spot we like is **Dieppe Bay,** at the northern tip of St. Kitts.

EXPLORING THE ISLAND

The British colonial town of **Basseterre** is built around a so-called **Circus,** the town's round square. A tall green Victorian clock stands in the center of the Circus. After Brimstone Hill Fortress, **Berkeley Memorial Clock** is the most photographed landmark of St. Kitts. In the old days, wealthy plantation owners and their families used to promenade here.

At some point, try to visit the **marketplace,** especially on a Saturday morning. Here, country people bring baskets brimming with mangos, guavas, soursop, mammy apples, and wild strawberries and cherries just picked in the fields, and tropical flowers abound.

Another major landmark is **Independence Square.** Once an active slave market, it's surrounded by private homes of Georgian architecture.

You can negotiate with a taxi driver to take you on a tour of the island for about $60 for a 3-hour trip; most drivers are well versed in the lore of the island. You might want to make lunch reservations at either the Rawlins Plantation Inn or the Golden Lemon. For more information, call the **St. Kitts Taxi Association,** the Circus, Basseterre (© **869/465-8487** until 10pm).

Brimstone Hill Fortress ⭐ (© **869/465-6211**), 9 miles (14km) west of Basseterre, is the major stop on any tour of St. Kitts. This historic monument, among the largest and best preserved in the Caribbean, is a complex of bastions, barracks, and other structures ingeniously adapted to the top and upper slopes of a steep-sided 800-foot (240m) hill. The fortress dates from 1690, when the British attempted to recapture Fort Charles from the French.

Today, the fortress is the centerpiece of a national park of nature trails and a diverse range of plant and animal life, including the **green vervet monkey.** It's also a photographer's paradise, with views of mountains, fields, and the Caribbean Sea. On a clear day, you can see six neighboring islands.

Visitors will enjoy self-guided tours among the many ruined or restored structures, including the barrack rooms at Fort George, which comprise an interesting museum. The gift shop stocks prints of rare maps and paintings of the Caribbean. Admission is $5, half price for children. The Brimstone Hill Fortress National Park is open daily from 9:30am to 5:30pm.

In the old days, a large tamarind tree in the hamlet of **Half-Way Tree** marked the boundary between the British-held sector and the French half, and you can visit the site.

It was near the hamlet of **Old Road Town** that Sir Thomas Warner landed with the first band of settlers and established the first permanent colony to the northwest at Sandy Point. Sir Thomas's grave is in the cemetery of St. Thomas Church.

A sign in the middle of Old Road Town points the way to **Carib Rock Drawings,** all the evidence that remains of the former inhabitants. The markings are on black boulders, and the pictographs date from prehistoric days.

INTO THE VOLCANO

Mount Liamuiga was dubbed "Mount Misery" long ago, but it sputtered its last gasp around 1692. This dormant volcano on the northeast coast is today one of the major highlights for hikers on St. Kitts. The peak of the mountain often lies under cloud cover.

The ascent to the volcano is usually made from the north end of St. Kitts at Belmont Estate. The trail winds through a rain forest and travels along deep ravines up to the rim of the crater at 2,625 feet (788m). The actual peak is at 3,792 feet (1,138m). Figure on 5 hours of rigorous hiking to complete the round-trip walk.

The caldera itself is some 400 feet (120m) from its rim to the crater floor. Many hikers climb or crawl down into the dormant volcano. However, the trail is steep and slippery, so be careful. At the crater floor is a tiny lake along with volcanic rocks and various vegetation.

Greg's Safaris, P.O. Box Basseterre (© **869/465-4121**), offers guided hikes to the crater for $80 per person (a minimum of 6 people needed), including breakfast and a lavish picnic at the crater's rim. The same outfit also offers half-day

---

Tips Island Hopping

Most visitors to St. Kitts or Nevis like to spend at least 1 day on the neighboring island. **LIAT** (© **800/468-0482** in the U.S.), provides twice-daily flights to and from Nevis, and **Nevis Express** (© **869/469-9755**) runs shuttle service seven times a day from each island. You can also take a ferry between islands if you'd rather not fly on puddle jumper–style planes. See "Getting There," earlier in this chapter, for details. It's possible, though it makes for a whirlwind day, to do Nevis as a day trip from St. Kitts. If you do this, you'll probably want to fly. The plane trip isn't that much faster than the ferry, but there are more flights than ferries each day.

rain-forest explorations for $40 per person. **Kris Tours** (© 869/465-4042) offers similar tours for $50, but without the breakfast or the luxurious picnic spread.

SHOPPING

The good buys here are in local handcrafts, including leather (goatskin) items, baskets, and coconut shells. Some good values can also be found in clothing and fabrics, especially Sea Island cottons. Store hours vary, but are likely to be Monday to Saturday from 8am to noon and 1 to 4pm.

If your time is limited, head first for the **Pelican Shopping Mall,** Bay Road, which contains some two dozen shops. Opened in 1991, it also offers banking services, a restaurant, and a philatelic bureau. Some major retail outlets in the Caribbean, including Little Switzerland, have branches here. Also check out the offerings along the quaintly named **Liverpool Row,** which has some unusual merchandise, and **Fort Street.**

Linen and Gold Shop, in the Pelican Mall (© 869/465-9766), offers a limited selection of gold and silver jewelry, usually in bold modern designs. But the real appeal of this shop is the tablecloths, doilies, and napkins, laboriously handcrafted in China from cotton and linen. The workmanship is as intricate as anything you'll find in the Caribbean.

Ashburry's, the Circus/Liverpool Row, Basseterre (© 869/465-8175), is a local branch of a chain of luxury-goods stores based on St. Maarten. This well-respected emporium sells fragrances, fine porcelain, Baccarat crystal, Fendi handbags, watches, and jewelry, at prices 25% to 30% below what you might pay in retail stores in North America; the selection is similar to dozens of equivalent stores throughout the Caribbean.

Cameron Gallery, 10 N. Independence Sq., Basseterre (© 869/465-1617), is a leading art gallery. On display are scenes of St. Kitts and Nevis by Brit Rosey Cameron-Smith, along with works by 10 to 15 other artists. Rosey is well known on the island for her paintings of Kittitian Carnival clowns, and she also produces greeting cards, postcards, and calendars.

The finest gallery on St. Kitts is **Kate Design,** Mount Pleasant (© 869/465-7740), set in an impeccably restored West Indian house, on a hillside below the Rawlins Plantation. Virtually all the works on display are by English-born Kate Spencer, who is well known throughout North America and Europe. Her paintings of island scenes range in price from $200 to $3,000 and have received critical acclaim. Also for sale are a series of Ms. Spencer's silk-screened scarves, each crafted from extra-heavy stonewashed silk.

Beachworks, in the Palms Arcade, Basseterre (© 869/465-2599), specializes in island things, including handcrafts, amber jewelry, West Indies spices, teas, and perfumes. Also available is some tropical clothing, and a wealth of souvenirs.

Island Hopper, the Circus, below the popular Ballahoo Restaurant, Basseterre (© 869/465-1640), is one of St. Kitts's most patronized shops, with the biggest inventory of any store on the island. Notice the all-silk, shift-style dresses from China and the array of batiks made on St. Kitts. About half of the merchandise is from the islands.

Romney Manor, Old Road, 10 miles (16km) west of Basseterre (© 869/465-6253), is the most unusual factory in St. Kitts. It was built around 1625 as a manor house for sugar baron Lord Romney. For years, it has been used as the headquarters and manufacturing center for a local clothier, Caribelle Batik, whose tropical cottons sell widely to cruise-ship passengers and tourists from at least three outlets in the eastern Caribbean. The merchandise ranges from scarves to dresses, along with an extensive collection of wall hangings. In 1995, a tragic fire and hurricane completely gutted the historic building. The manor has now been rebuilt and extended. Consider a stopover here if only to admire the 5 acres (2 hectares) of lavish gardens, where 30 varieties of hibiscus, rare orchids, huge ferns, and a 250-year-old saman tree still draw horticultural enthusiasts. Entrance to the gardens is free.

ST. KITTS AFTER DARK

The **Ocean Terrace Inn's Fisherman's Wharf,** Fortlands (© **869/465-2754**), has a live band every Friday from 8 to 10pm and a DJ from 10pm. The **Turtle Beach Bar and Grill,** Turtle Bay (© **869/465-9086**), on the southeast peninsula, has a popular seafood buffet on Sunday afternoon with a live steel band from 12:30 to 3pm; on Saturday, it's beach disco time. There's no cover at either place.

If you're in the mood to gamble, head for St. Kitts's only casino, at the **Jack Tar Village,** Frigate Bay (© **869/465-8651**). It's open to all visitors, who can try their luck at roulette, blackjack, poker, craps, and slot machines. The casino is open daily from 10:30am to 2am. There's no cover.

A few other nightspots come and go (mostly go). Currently, **Henry's Night Spot,** Dunn's Cottage, Lower Cayon Street, in Basseterre (© **869/465-3508**), is one of the island's most frequented dance clubs. **Bayembi Cultural Entertainment Bar & Café,** just off the Circus in Basseterre (© **869/466-5280**), couldn't look junkier, but it's a hot and happening place. Every Thursday is oldies night and every Friday is reggae night. Its daily happy hours pack 'em in at sunset.

On Friday and Saturday nights, locals often head for **J's Place,** Romney Grounds across from Brimstone Hill (© **869/465-6264**). The place is often jumping until the early hours. Another fun joint is **Doo-Wop Days,** Memory Lane, Frigate Bay (© **869/465-1960**), painted in sherbet colors. The place looks like a junkyard, with its old 1940s photos of Frank Sinatra and Chuck Berry. Note the velvet Elvis paintings and guitar-shaped pillows. Many nights there's live music, especially from doo-wop groups of yesterday. Saturday is karaoke night.

3 Nevis

A local once said that the best reason to go to Nevis was to practice the fine art of *limin'.* To him, that meant doing nothing in particular. Limin' might still be the best reason to venture over to Nevis. Once here, you can stay at the lovely Four Seasons or find lodging in one of the old plantation houses, now converted to inns, and experience the calm still found on this small volcanic island. If you want to lie out in the sun, head for reef-protected Pinney's Beach, a 3-mile (5km) strip of dark-gold sand set against a backdrop of palm trees, with panoramic views of St. Kitts.

Columbus sighted Nevis (*NEE-vis*) in 1493. He called it Las Nieves, Spanish for *snows,* because its mountains reminded him of the snow-capped range in the Pyrenees. From St. Kitts, the island appears to be a perfect cone, rising gradually to a height of 3,232 feet (970m). A saddle joins the tallest mountain to two smaller peaks, Saddle Hill (1,250 ft./375m) in the south and Hurricane Hill (only 250 ft./75m) in the north.

Nevis is an island of beauty and has remained relatively unspoiled. Coral reefs rim the shoreline, and there's mile after mile of palm-shaded white-sand beaches. Natives of Nevis, for the most part, are descendants of African slaves.

Settled by the British in 1628, the volcanic island is famous as the birthplace of Alexander Hamilton, the American statesman who wrote many of the articles contained in *The Federalist Papers* and was George Washington's treasury secretary. Nevis is also the island on which Admiral Horatio Lord Nelson married Frances Nisbet, a local woman, in 1787, an episode described in James Michener's *Caribbean* (the historical facts are romanticized, of course).

In the 18th century, Nevis, the "Queen of the Caribees," was the leading spa of the West Indies, made so by its hot mineral springs. The island was also once peppered with prosperous sugarcane estates, but they're gone now—many have been converted into some of the most intriguing hotels in the Caribbean. Sea Island cotton is the chief crop today.

On the Caribbean side, **Charlestown,** the capital of Nevis, was fashionable in the 18th century, when sugar planters were carried around in carriages and sedan chairs. A town of wide, quiet streets, this port only gets busy when its major link to the world, the ferry from St. Kitts, docks at the harbor.

NEVIS ESSENTIALS

GETTING THERE   There are no nonstop flights to Nevis from North America. To get here, you'll have to stop or change planes in Antigua, St. Maarten, or Puerto Rico. **American Airlines** (© 800/433-7300 in the U.S.; www.aa.com) has dozens of daily flights to San Juan. From here, you can catch a propeller plane to Nevis. The Antigua-based carrier, **LIAT** (© 869/465-1330 or 869/465-5978), flies to Nevis from Antigua, Guadeloupe, San Juan, and St. Maarten. **Nevis Express** (© 869/469-9755; www.nevisexpress.com) flies from Guadeloupe, St. Maarten, and San Juan (usually with a stop in St. Kitts). Any major North American airline can arrange your flight on either of these two carriers. Nevis Express also operates seven **shuttle flights** each way daily between St. Kitts and Nevis. A round-trip ticket costs $50. LIAT also flies twice a day between St. Kitts and Nevis. The flight lasts only 7 minutes.

You can also use the **interisland ferry service** between St. Kitts and Nevis. Ferry schedules are subject to change without notice, and follow no obvious patterns. The **M.V.** *Sea Hustler* makes at least three trips per day, and sometimes four. There is usually one morning crossing and one afternoon crossing from each island. The duration of the crossing is 1 hour. The **M.V.** *Caribe Queen* makes the crossing in 45 minutes, but it doesn't run on Thursdays or Sundays. Its schedule is also different every day—it generally makes one round-trip in the morning (usually 7 or 7:30am) and at least one trip each way in the afternoon (at 4, 5, or 6pm, depending on the island). Fare is $8 round-trip for either ferry. Contact the tourist office on either island for exact schedules.

GETTING AROUND   **Taxi** drivers double as guides, and you'll find them waiting at the airport for the arrival of every plane. The fare between Newcastle Airport and Charlestown is EC$38 (US$14.05); between Charlestown and Old Manor Estate, EC$32 (US$11.85); and from Charlestown to Pinney's Beach, EC$19 (US$7.05). Between 10pm and 6am, 50% is added to the prices. Call © 869/469-5521 for more information.

If you're prepared to face the winding, rocky, potholed roads of Nevis, you can arrange for a **rental car** from a local firm through your hotel. Or you can check with **Skeete's Car Rental,** Newcastle Village, near the airport (© 869/469-9458). To drive on Nevis, you must **obtain a permit** from the traffic department, which costs EC$50 (US$18.50) and is valid for a year. Car-rental companies will handle this for you. *Remember to drive on the left side of the road.*

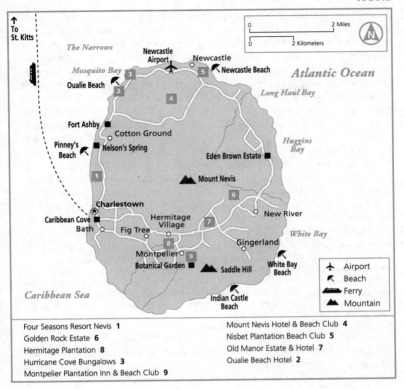

Accommodations	
Four Seasons Resort Nevis **1**	Mount Nevis Hotel & Beach Club **4**
Golden Rock Estate **6**	Nisbet Plantation Beach Club **5**
Hermitage Plantation **8**	Old Manor Estate & Hotel **7**
Hurricane Cove Bungalows **3**	Oualie Beach Hotel **2**
Montpelier Plantation Inn & Beach Club **9**	

FAST FACTS   **Banks** are usually open Monday to Saturday from 8am to 3pm; most are also open on Friday from 3:30 to 5:30pm. Normal store hours are Monday to Friday from 8am to noon and 1 to 4pm. On Thursday some places close in the afternoon, and on Saturday some stay open to 8pm. Most are closed Sunday.

The **post office** is on Main Street in Charlestown. It's open Monday to Friday from 8am to 3pm (it closes at 11 am on Thurs), and Saturday from 8am to noon. You can make **international phone calls,** including collect calls, from the **Cable & Wireless office,** Main Street, Charlestown (© **869/469-5000**). It's open Monday to Friday from 8am to 5pm, Saturday from 8am to noon.

If you need a pharmacy, try **Evelyn's Drugstore,** Charlestown (© **869/ 469-5278**), open Monday to Thursday from 8am to 6pm, Saturday from 8am to 7pm, and Sunday for only 1 hour, from 7 to 8pm, to serve emergency needs.

There's a 24-hour **emergency room** at **Alexandra Hospital,** Government Road, in Charlestown (© **869/469-5473**).

The **Nevis Tourist Bureau** is on Main Street in Charlestown (© **869/ 469-1042** or 869/469-7550).

ACCOMMODATIONS
VERY EXPENSIVE

Four Seasons Resort Nevis ★★★ *Kids*   This hotel is one of the Caribbean's world-class properties and hands-down the best choice on the island. Located on

Nevis's west coast, it's set in a palm grove beside Pinney's Beach, the finest sandy beach on Nevis. On an island known for its small and intimate inns, this 1991 low-rise resort stands out as the largest and best-managed hotel, with the most complete sports facilities (including a fabulous golf course). Designed in harmony with the surrounding landscape, the accommodations offer rich but conservative mahogany furniture, touches of marble, carpeting, and wide patios or verandas overlooking the beach, the golf course, or Mount Nevis. The spacious guest rooms have generous closet space, full-length mirrors, luxurious upholstery and fabrics, and queen-size, king-size, or double beds. The roomy bathrooms have shower/tub combinations, double sinks, makeup mirrors, and Bulgari toiletries. The public areas include rooms inspired by paneled libraries in London, complete with one of the few working fireplaces on Nevis.

Guests have the largest choice of bars and dining venues on Nevis. The resort's centerpiece is the plantation-inspired great house, which contains the most formal restaurant, The Dining Room (see "Dining," below). The resort's Kids for All Seasons is one of the most carefully planned youth programs in the Caribbean, and there's a supervised children's hour at 6pm daily in the Grill Room.

Pinney's Beach, Charlestown, Nevis, W.I. © **800/332-3442** in the U.S., 800/268-6282 in Canada, or 869/469-1111. Fax 869/469-1112. www.fourseasons.com. 196 units. Winter $715–$775 double; from $1,375 suite. Off-season $325–$425 double; from $525 suite. MAP (breakfast and dinner) $85 per person extra. Up to 2 children under 18 stay free in parents' room. AE, DC, MC, V. **Amenities:** 3 restaurants, 2 pools; 18-hole golf course; 10 tennis courts; health club; sauna; Jacuzzi; scuba; fishing; horseback riding; children's programs; salon; 24-hr. room service; massage; babysitting; laundry/dry cleaning. *In room:* A/C, TV, minibar, coffeemaker, hair dryer, safe.

Hermitage Plantation ★★ This much-photographed, frequently copied historians' delight is said to be the oldest all-wood house in the Antilles, and was built amid the high-altitude plantations of Gingerland in 1740. Some believe it once welcomed Alexander Hamilton and Horatio Nelson. Today, former Philadelphian Richard Lupinacci and his wife, Maureen, have assembled one of the best collections of antiques on Nevis here. Wide-plank floors, intricate latticework, and high ceilings add to the hotel's beauty. The accommodations are in nine glamorous buildings designed like small plantation houses. Many contain huge four-poster beds, antique accessories, and colonial louvered windows. The spotlessly maintained private bathrooms contain shower/tub combinations. The most luxurious and expensive unit is a yellow manor house on a ½ acre (.2 hectares) of private gardens with its own ceramic-tile pool, two large bedrooms furnished with antique canopy beds, oversize bathrooms with dressing rooms, a comfortable living room, dining room, full kitchen, and laundry.

Complimentary beach transportation is provided because the best nearby beach is a 15-minute drive away. The on-site restaurant is one of the finest hotel dining rooms on island (see "Dining," below).

Hermitage Village, St. John's Parish, Nevis, W.I. © **800/682-4025** in the U.S., or 869/469-3477. Fax 869/469-2481. www.hermitagenevis.com. 15 units, manor house. Winter $325–$450 double; $790 manor house. Off-season $170–$260 double; $650 manor house. AE, MC, V. Take the main island road 4 miles (6km) from Charlestown. **Amenities:** Restaurant, bar; pool; tennis court; stables; laundry. *In room:* TV, fridge, coffeemaker, hair dryer, safe.

Montpelier Plantation Inn & Beach Club ★★ One of the Plantation Inns of Nevis, the Montpelier stands in the hills, 700 feet (210m) high, with grandstand views of the ocean. It's owner-managed, and a house-party atmosphere prevails. The 18th-century plantation is in the center of its own 100-acre (40-hectare) estate, which contains 10 acres (4 hectares) of ornamental gardens that surround the cottage units. Accommodations are generally spacious and brightened with fresh flowers, along with luxuries including expansive desks, coffeemakers, comfortable chairs, and dressing tables. Bathrooms, with glass-enclosed shower/tub combinations, are kept sparkling clean.

Montpelier prides itself on its food, wine, and service. At the restaurant that shares the name of the resort, much use is made of fresh local produce (see "Dining," below).

St. John Figtree (P.O. Box 474), Montpelier, Nevis, W.I. © **869/469-3462.** Fax 869/469-2932. www.montpeliernevis.com. 17 units. Winter $350 double. Off-season $240 double. Year-round $300–$410 suite. Rates include breakfast. MC, V. Closed Aug–Sept. Children under age 8 not accepted in winter. **Amenities:** Restaurant, 2 bars; pool; tennis court; horseback riding; windsurfing; room service (breakfast only); laundry; transport to private beach. *In room:* Ceiling fan, coffeemaker, hair dryer, safe.

Nisbet Plantation Beach Club ⭐⭐ A respect for fine living prevails in this gracious estate house on a coconut plantation, which is the only plantation-style house that lives up to the grace notes of Montpellier Plantation Inn. This is the former home of Frances Nisbet, who, at the age of 22, married Lord Nelson. Although enamored of Miss Nisbet when he married her, Lord Nelson later fell in love with Lady Hamilton (as detailed in the classic film *That Hamilton Woman*).

The present main building was rebuilt on the foundations of the original 18th-century great house. The ruins of a circular sugar mill stand at the entrance, covered with bougainvillea, hibiscus, and poinciana. Guest cottages are set in the palm grove. All rooms are brightly decorated and beautifully appointed, with king-size beds and firm mattresses. The bathrooms, with shower/tub combinations, are tidily maintained.

Newcastle, St. James's Parish, Nevis, W.I. © **800/742-6008** in the U.S. and Canada, or 869/469-9325. Fax 869/469-9864. www.nisbetplantation.com. 38 units. Winter $475–$625 double; from $645 suite. Off-season $290–$355 double; from $390 suite. Rates include MAP (breakfast and dinner). AE, MC, V. Turn left out of the airport and go 1 mile (2km). **Amenities:** 3 restaurants, 2 bars; pool; golf at Four Seasons; tennis court; horseback riding; snorkeling, scuba diving, sport-fishing, sailing; babysitting; laundry. *In room:* A/C, minibar, coffeemaker, hair dryer, safe.

EXPENSIVE

Golden Rock Estate ⭐ This place doesn't have the polish and glaze of such choices as the Hermitage (see above), but it has down-home qualities and quiet charm. This former sugar estate, built in 1815, has little razzle-dazzle, but it's lushly set in the hills of Nevis, only a 15-minute drive east of Charlestown. Set on 100 tropical acres (40 hectares), it fronts a 25-acre (10-hectare) garden. The original stone tower windmill has been turned into a duplex honeymoon suite (or accommodations for a family of four), with a four-poster bed. Cottages are scattered about the garden, and each has a four-poster king-size bed made of bamboo. Rooms have large porches with views of the sea as well. Fabrics are island-made, with tropical flower designs. Guests live in fairly spacious surroundings here, in a setting of pineapple friezes, island crafts, family heirlooms, and tile flowers. Bathrooms are a bit small, with shower stalls.

The hotel lies at the beginning of a rain-forest walk; it takes about 3 to 4 hours to follow the trail round-trip (the hotel provides a map). If you want to go to the beach, the complimentary hotel shuttle will take you to either Pinney's Beach (on the leeward side) or White Bay Beach (a.k.a. Windward Beach), which has good surfing. The shuttle also stops in Charlestown if requested.

West Indian meals are served at the 175-year-old "long house." Saturday night from December to June, there's a West Indian buffet, served plantation style, while a string band plays outside under the stars.

P.O. Box 493, Gingerland, Nevis, W.I. © **869/469-3346.** Fax 869/469-2113. www.golden-rock.com. 15 units. Winter $300 double; $365 suite. Off-season $230 double; $265 suite. Rates include MAP (breakfast and dinner). Children under age 2 stay free in parents' room. AE, MC, V. **Amenities:** Restaurant, bar; pool; tennis court; horseback riding; scuba, snorkeling, windsurfing, sailing; babysitting; laundry. *In room:* No phone.

Mount Nevis Hotel & Beach Club ★ This family-owned and -run resort dating from 1989 is on the slopes of Mount Nevis, a 5-minute drive southwest of Newcastle Airport. It's known for the quality of its accommodations, for its panoramic views, and for serving some of the best food on Nevis. Near the historic fishing village of Newcastle, it offers standard rooms and junior suites, the latter with fully equipped kitchens and space enough to accommodate at least four guests comfortably, making it an ideal family choice. The rooms have such amenities as VCRs and ceiling fans, and are furnished in a tropical motif, with wicker and colorful island prints. The tidily maintained private bathrooms are well equipped and contain shower stalls.

See "Dining," below, for a review of the hotel's main restaurant, Mount Nevis Hotel Restaurant. Just a 5-minute drive from the hotel, the Mount Nevis Beach Club offers a site on Newcastle Bay and features a beach pavilion, bar, and restaurant. It pretty much introduced pizza to the island.

Newcastle (P.O. Box 494), Charlestown, Nevis, W.I. © **800/75-NEVIS** in the U.S. and Canada, 212/874-4276 in New York City, or 869/469-9373. Fax 869/469-9375. www.mountnevishotel.com. 32 units. Winter $235–$300 double; $300 suite. Off-season $165–$210 double; $210 suite. Extra person $35. AE, MC, V. **Amenities:** Restaurant, bar; pool; exercise room; beach shuttle. *In room:* A/C, TV, VCR, hair dryer.

Old Manor Estate & Hotel ★ The least elaborate of the plantation-style inns of Nevis, this hotel is the most evocative of a *Gone with the Wind* Nevisian life. East of Charlestown and north of Gingerland, at a cool and comfortable elevation of 800 feet (240m), the Old Manor Estate & Hotel has an old-world grace. When Nevis was originally colonized, the forested plot of land on which the hotel sits was granted to the Croney family in 1690 by the king of England. The estate thrived as a working sugar plantation until 1936. Today, the stately ruins of its great house, once described by British historians as "the best example of Georgian domestic architecture in the Caribbean," complement the hotel's outbuildings.

Since its acquisition by new owners in 1995, the hotel has been renovated and now has a far more cheerful, tropical appearance. Ongoing improvements are being made, since the property had fallen into decline. Accommodations contain wide-plank floors of tropical hardwoods, reproduction furniture, and high ceilings. Bathrooms come neat and tidy; some are shower-only.

The Old Manor runs a complimentary shuttle to town and to its beach bar and grill on Pinney's Beach, 15 to 20 minutes away.

P.O. Box 70, Gingerland, Nevis, W.I. © **800/892-7093** in the U.S., or 869/469-3445. Fax 869/469-3388. 12 units. Winter $204–$283 double. Off season $155–$195 double. Rates include full breakfast. AE, MC, V. **Amenities:** 2 dining rooms; pool; Jacuzzi; room service; babysitting; laundry. *In room:* Ceiling fan, hair dryer.

MODERATE

Hurricane Cove Bungalows This cluster of self-contained bungalows is set on a hillside with a world-class ocean view, a far better sight than the complex's rather ramshackle facade. It's located on the northernmost point of Nevis, a 5-minute drive west of the airport. Each bungalow is wood-sided and vaguely Scandinavian in design, with a tile roof and a massive foundation that anchors it into the rocky hillside. No meals are served, but each unit has a full kitchen; guests can dine out every night or prepare meals themselves, either in their own kitchens or at a poolside barbecue grill. Each bungalow has a queen-size bed, a covered porch, and a ceiling fan. The small, compact bathrooms are efficiently organized, with adequate shelf space and a shower stall. A freshwater pool is built into the foundation of a 250-year-old fortification, and the beach lies at the bottom of a steep hillside. The three-bedroom villa has its own small, but private, pool.

Oualie Beach, Nevis, W.I. © and fax **869/469-9462.** www.hurricanecove.com. 12 units. Winter $175–$285 1-bedroom bungalow; $275–$325 2-bedroom bungalow; $485 3-bedroom villa. Off-season $95–$155 1-bedroom bungalow; $155–$205 2-bedroom bungalow; $225 3-bedroom villa. MC, V. **Amenities:** Pool. *In room:* Ceiling fan, kitchen, fridge, coffeemaker, no phone.

Oualie Beach Hotel   This place is often fully booked several months in advance by European sun-worshipers. The Oualie Beach Hotel is set on flatlands adjacent to the white sands of its namesake, the island's second-most-famous beach. Each medium-size unit is clean and simple, with tiled floors and small fridges; a few have kitchenettes. Extras include full-length mirrors, mahogany furnishings, and double or four-poster queen-size beds. Bathrooms are small and have showers only. The resort's centerpiece is its well-recommended restaurant and bar, where doors open directly onto a view of the beach (see "Dining," below).

Oualie Bay, Nevis, W.I. © **800/682-5431** in the U.S., or 869/469-9735. Fax 869/469-9176. www.oualie.com. 33 units. Winter $195–$245 double; $205–$305 studio. Off-season $145–$195 double; $165–$205 studio. AE, MC, V. **Amenities:** Restaurant, bar; babysitting; laundry. *In room:* A/C, TV, fridge, hair dryer, iron and ironing board, safe.

DINING
VERY EXPENSIVE
The Dining Room ★★ INTERNATIONAL/CARIBBEAN/ASIAN   Set beneath a soaring, elaborately trussed ceiling, this is the largest and most formal dining room on Nevis, and the island's best and most expensive restaurant. Decorated in a Caribbean interpretation of French Empire design, it offers rows of beveled-glass windows on three sides, massive bouquets of flowers, hurricane lamps with candles, a fireplace, a collection of unusual paintings, and impeccable service.

The fusion cuisine, with lots of nouvelle touches, roams the world for inspiration. Only quality ingredients are used, and some dishes are low in fat and calories. The menu changes nightly, but appearing with frequency are savory seafood gumbo, or Cuban black-bean soup with applewood-smoked bacon. The pan-seared salmon with a curried fruit relish is incomparably fragrant, although the grilled mahi-mahi (dolphin) with wasabi-mango sauce is equally tempting. Vegetarians also have options here, perhaps vegetable cannelloni gratinée with a purple basil–tomato sauce. Dessert might be a flaming meringue "Mount Nevis." The service and the wine selection are the island's best.

In the Four Seasons Resort Nevis, Pinney's Beach. © **869/469-1111.** Reservations recommended. Main courses EC$75–EC$128 (US$27.75–US$47.35). AE, DC, DISC, MC, V. Daily 6–10pm.

Hermitage Plantation ★ INTERNATIONAL   At this restaurant, you can combine an excellent dinner with a visit to the oldest house on Nevis, now one of the island's most unusual hotels (see "Accommodations," above). Meals are served on the latticed porch of the main house, amid candles and good cheer. Maureen Lupinacci, who runs the place with her husband, Richard, combines continental recipes with local ingredients. Enjoy a before-dinner drink in the colonial-style living room, then move on to the likes of snapper steamed in banana leaves, carrot-and-tarragon soup, brown-bread ice cream, and a delectable version of rum soufflé. Many people turn up on Wednesday for the roast-pig dinner.

In the Hermitage Plantation hotel, Hermitage Village, St. John's Parish. © **869/469-3477.** Reservations required. Lunch EC$40–EC$65 (US$14.80–$US24.05), dinner EC$148 (US$54.75). AE, MC, V. Daily 8–10am, noon–3pm, and dinner at 8pm. Go south on the main island road from Charlestown.

Miss June's ★★ CARIBBEAN/INTERNATIONAL This charming venue, midway between the Four Seasons Resort and the airport, is the private home of June Mestier, a Trinidad-born grande dame, and probably wouldn't exist if it had not been for an enthusiastic visit from Oprah Winfrey. On a recent trip, Oprah heard that Ms. Mestier was the finest cook on the island and arranged a private dinner; after being served an excellent meal, Oprah urged her to open a restaurant.

A dinner in Mestier's home, which is adorned with latticework and Victorian gingerbread, requires advance reservations; some visitors call before they even arrive on Nevis. Guests at these dinner parties assemble for canapés and drinks in an airy living room, then sit down for soup and sherry. The tables hold from 2 to 10 diners, and the silver and porcelain are quaintly elegant and charmingly mismatched. Fish and wine follow. All this is followed with samples of about 20 to 30 buffet dishes that hail from Trinidad, New Orleans, India, and the French isles. Mestier's comments on the food are one of the evening's most delightful aspects. After dinner, guests retire to a lounge for dessert and port. Many visitors find the meal to be one of the highlights of their visit to Nevis.

Jones Bay. © **869/469-5330.** Reservations required. Fixed-price meal EC$175 (US$64.75). MC, V. 3 to 5 evenings a week, depending on business, beginning around 7:30pm.

Montpelier Plantation Inn & Beach Club ★ INTERNATIONAL This hotel, a mile (2km) off the main island road to Gingerland, provides some of the finest dining on the island. You sit by candlelight on the verandas of a grand old West Indian mansion, overlooking floodlit gardens, the lights of Charlestown, and the ocean. Lobster and fish are served the day the catch comes in, and the foreign and Nevisian chefs conspire to produce delectable tropical dishes. The best menu items include Cajun prawns, fresh tuna salad, curried ackee, suckling pig, and soursop-and-orange mousse for dessert. There's one seating for dinner, so try to show up on time. An excellent and well-balanced wine list is available.

In the Montpelier Plantation Inn & Beach Club hotel, Montpelier. © **869/469-3462.** Reservations recommended for lunch, required for dinner. Fixed-price dinner EC$130–EC$159 (US$48.10–US$58.85). MC, V. Daily 8:30–9:30am and 12:30–2pm, and dinner at 8:15pm. Closed Aug–Sept.

EXPENSIVE

The Cooperage ★ INTERNATIONAL/CARIBBEAN Directly east of Charlestown and north of Gingerland, The Cooperage is set in a reconstructed 17th-century building where coopers once made barrels for the sugar mill. The dining room has a high, raftered ceiling and stonewalls. The food doesn't even try to compete with that at the Four Seasons, but it's good and reliable. Some of the appetizers are those 1950s favorites: French onion soup or shrimp cocktail. For a main course, you can order a 12-ounce New York strip steak or charcoal-grilled filet mignon with a béarnaise sauce. The grilled Caribbean lobster is also appealing, as is the Nevisian pork. The menu harks back to the days when appetites were more robust. Main dishes are served with fresh vegetables of the day and your choice of twice-baked potato, rice, or pasta. Few leave hungry, especially after finishing with Old Manor's cheesecake, which has been sampled by all the movers and shakers on the island.

In the Old Manor Estate, Gingerland. (© **869/469-3445.** Reservations recommended, especially for nonguests. Main courses EC$32–EC$81 (US$11.85–US$29.95). AE, MC, V. Daily 8am–10pm.

Mount Nevis Hotel Restaurant ✪ CARIBBEAN/CONTINENTAL   This hotel restaurant is a discovery, serving some of the finest cuisine on Nevis, with menus that change every night. The chef has done a wonderful job of embracing the local tastes with a big-city gourmet twist. Just steps above the pool, the restaurant offers vistas of palm groves and the Caribbean Sea from its bar and dining terrace. You never know what's likely to be featured: A very smooth and spicy conch chowder might get you going, or an equally delectable coconut-fried lobster with grilled pineapple and green-chile salsa, providing a sweet island flavor. The standard fillet of grouper, snapper, or mahi-mahi that occupies every menu in the Caribbean is also here, as the chef tends to prepare only what he can obtain locally. A lamb shank, another fairly standard menu item, is also delectable here, with an array of local vegetables. The duck confit salad is also worth a try. The lunch menu is more limited but still filled with some surprises—tannia fritters (instead of conch), for example.

In the Mount Nevis Hotel & Beach Club, Newcastle. (© **869/469-9373.** Reservations recommended for dinner. Main courses EC$19–EC$40 (US$7.05–US$14.80) lunch, EC$48–EC$100 (US$17.75–US$37) dinner. AE, MC, V. Daily 8–10am and 11:30am–2:30pm; Mon–Sat 6:30–9pm.

Oualie Beach Hotel INTERNATIONAL/NEVISIAN   This restaurant is the centerpiece of the Oualie Beach Hotel (see "Accommodations," earlier in this chapter), the only lodging adjacent to Oualie Beach. The airy building contains a bar area and a screened-in veranda just a few steps from the ocean. The pleasant staff can offer recommendations, or point you to the chalkboard menu with the day's specials. Depending on the catch that day, it might be broiled wahoo. The chef also prepares several lobster dishes, and the Creole conch stew is the island's best. Pastas appear frequently on the menu, along with some fairly bland international dishes such as spinach-stuffed chicken breast. Every day, however, the chef prepares a creative menu with real Caribbean flair, so you may want to study it closely before ordering. An array of brightly colored rum drinks are available, and you can get a reasonably priced breakfast or lunch here, too.

In the Oualie Beach Hotel, Oualie Bay. (© **869/469-9735.** Reservations recommended for dinner. Breakfast EC$16–EC$30 (US$5.90–US$11.10); lunch EC$24–EC$43 (US$8.90–US$15.90); dinner main courses EC$38–EC$65 (US$14.05–US$24.05). AE, MC, V. Daily 7–10am, noon–4pm, and 7–11pm.

INEXPENSIVE

Newcastle Bay Marina Restaurant INTERNATIONAL   This open-air restaurant on the water, housed in a concrete-block building with cathedral ceilings, is part of the Mount Nevis Beach Club. From the deck, you can take in a panoramic sea view. The informal cuisine is usually prepared with flair by the hardworking chef. Examples are a roster of meal-sized pizzas big enough for two (try the version with seafood) as well as chicken parmigiana with pasta, shrimp with salsa verde, and Mexican platters piled high with quesadillas, tacos, flautas, and spicy beef. The best way to begin a meal is with one of the colorful margaritas.

Newcastle Marina, Charlestown. (© **869/469-9395.** Reservations recommended. Main courses EC$20–EC$38 (US$7.40–US$14.05); pizzas for 2 EC$25–EC$55 (US$9.25–US$20.35). AE, MC, V. Thurs–Tues 6–10pm.

Sunshine's Bar & Grill ✪ *Finds* WEST INDIAN   Sunshine is really Llewellyn Caines, and he runs this hot-spot bar and grill on Nevis, where you can always find an eclectic mix of people and music. It's really a shack on Pinney's Beach, but it lures even the richest guests from the Four Seasons, who want to "git down low." It all started when this Rasta man began cooking fresh lobster for beach-goers. He rounded up a few chairs from the junkyard, fashioned some tables out of tree stumps, and put a palm roof over it. Hurricanes love to blow away this joint, but Sunshine keeps rebuilding. As for the decor? Everything's painted, even the palm trees, and someone nailed up some old Jimi Hendrix and Mal-colm X posters. Who started the buzz about this place? Believe it or not, the late Princess Di did, when she strolled in one day and loved it. Yes, there's food—still that fresh lobster (the best on island), along with chicken spiced to its zesty best before facing the open fire. Count yourself lucky if you're there on any night Sunshine roasts corn or sweet potatoes. As for his conch fritters or red snapper Creole, those dishes don't get much better than the versions served here.

Pinney's Beach. ⓒ 869/662-8383. Reservations needed for dinner. Main courses EC$27–EC$54 (US$10–US$20). No credit cards. Daily noon–midnight.

Tequila Sheila's WEST INDIAN/INTERNATIONAL This restaurant is on the premises of the Inn at Cades Bay, set on a wooden platform less than 60 feet (18m) from the seafront, with a covered parapet but without walls. It offers panoramic views as far away as St. Kitts, and a menu that incorporates West Indian, Mexican, and international cuisine. Lunchtime brings dishes such as rôti, enchiladas, grilled or jerk chicken, and lobster quesadillas. Dinner platters include vegetable-stuffed chicken, lobster, filet mignon with horseradish sauce or béarnaise sauce, and fish. Flying fish, wahoo, and mahi-mahi are very fresh here, and prepared as simply as possible—usually grilled with nothing more than lemon juice and herbs. The bar, fashioned from an overturned fishing boat, offers margaritas, various brands of tequila, and all the usual party-colored drinks you'd expect.

Cades Bay. ⓒ 869/469-8139. Reservations recommended. Main courses EC$27–EC$40 (US$10–US$14.80) lunch, EC$40–EC$80 (US$14.80–US$29.60) dinner. AE, MC, V. Mon–Sat noon–3pm and 6:30–9:30pm, Sun 11:30am–4pm.

BEACHES

Most hotels in Nevis have their own private beaches that you may be able to use for a fee if you're not a hotel guest. But there are several fabulous public beaches on the island as well. The best one—in fact, one of the best in the Caribbean—is the reef-protected **Pinney's Beach,** which has crystal-clear water, golden sands, and a gradual slope. It's no accident that the Four Seasons chose this loca-tion for its chic and super-expensive Nevis Resort.

Pinney's is just a short walk north of Charlestown on the west coast. You'll have 3 miles (5km) of sand (often virtually to yourself) that culminates in a sleepy lagoon, set against a backdrop of coconut palms. It's almost never crowded, and its calm, shallow waters are perfect for swimming and wading, which makes it a family favorite. It's best to bring your own sports equipment; the hotels along this beach are stocked with limited gear that may be in use by its guests. You can go snorkeling or scuba diving here among damselfish, tangs, grunts, blue-headed wrasses, and parrot fish, among other species. The beach is especially beautiful in the late afternoon, when flocks of cattle egrets fly into its north end to roost at the freshwater pond at **Nelson's Spring.**

If your time on Nevis is limited, go to Pinney's Beach. But if you're going to be around for a few more days, you might want to search out the other beaches, notably beige-sand Oualie Beach, known especially for its diving and snorkeling.

The location is north of Pinney's and just south of Mosquito Bay. The beach is well maintained and rarely crowded; you can purchase food and drink, as well as rent watersports equipment, at the Oualie Beach Hotel.

Indian Castle Beach, at the southern end of Nevis, is rarely sought out. It has an active surf and a swath of fine-gray sand. Indian Castle is definitely for escapists—chances are you'll have the beach all to yourself except for an indigenous goat or two, who may be very social and interested in sharing your picnic lunch.

Newcastle Beach is by the Nisbet Plantation, at the northernmost tip of the island on the channel that separates St. Kitts and Nevis. Snorkelers flock to this strip of soft, beige sand set against a backdrop of coconut palms.

The beaches along the east coast aren't desirable. They front Long Haul Bay in the north and White Bay in the south. These bays spill into the Atlantic Ocean and are rocky and too rough for swimming, although they're rather dramatic to visit if you're sightseeing. Of them all, White Bay Beach (sometimes called Windward Beach), in the southeastern section, east of Gingerland, is the best (especially for surfers). But be careful, as the waters can suddenly turn turbulent.

SPORTS & OTHER OUTDOOR PURSUITS

BOATING **Scuba Safaris,** an outfit that operates independently on the premises of the Oualie Beach Hotel (© **869/469-9518**), offers boat charters to Banana Bay and Cockleshell Bay, which can make for a great day's outing; it costs $50 round-trip.

FISHING **Nevis Water Sports** (© **869/469-9060**) offers the best deep-sea fishing aboard its custom 31-foot (9m) fishing boat. The boat holds up to six; a 4-hour trip costs $350, while an 8-hour trip is $700.

GOLF The **Four Seasons Golf Course** ⭐⭐⭐, Pinney's Beach (© **869/469-1111**), has one of the most challenging and visually dramatic golf courses in the world. Designed by Robert Trent Jones, Jr. (who called it "the most scenic golf course I've ever designed"), this 18-hole championship course wraps around the resort and offers panoramic ocean and mountain views at every turn. From the first tee (which begins just steps from the sports pavilion), through the 660-yard (601m), par-5, to the 18th green at the ocean's edge, the course is, in the words of one avid golfer, "reason enough to go to Nevis." Guests of the hotel pay $125 for 18 holes; nonguests are charged $150. Rental clubs are available, costing $40 for 18 holes.

HIKING & MOUNTAIN CLIMBING Hikers can climb **Mount Nevis,** 3,232 feet (970m) up to the extinct volcanic crater, and enjoy a trek to the rain forest to watch for wild monkeys. This hike is strenuous and is recommended only to the stout of heart. Ask your hotel to pack a picnic lunch and arrange a guide (who will charge about $35 per person). The hike takes about 5 hours; at the summit you'll be rewarded with views of Antigua, Saba, Statia, St. Kitts, Guadeloupe, and Montserrat. Of course, you've got to reach that summit, which means scrambling up near-vertical sections of the trail requiring handholds on not-always-reliable vines and roots. It's definitely not for acrophobes! Guides can also be arranged at the **Nevis Historical and Conservation Society,** based at the Museum of Nevis History, Main Street, Charlestown (© **869/469-5786**).

Eco-Tours Nevis (© **869/469-2091**) offers three uniquely different walking tours of the 36-mile (58km) island. The expeditions explore the shore, tropical forests, and historic ruins. They're taken at a leisurely pace, requiring only an average level of fitness. The 2½-hour "Eco-Ramble," on the windswept, uninhabited east coast, covers the 18th-century New River and Coconut Walk Estates. Participants will see the diverse ecology of Nevis, discover archaeological evidence of pre-Colombian Amerindian settlers, and visit the remains of the last working sugar factory on Nevis. The cost is $30.

The easy, 2½-hour "Montravers Hike" takes a close look at Montravers House, one of the hidden secrets of Nevis. These great-house ruins are spectacular. The cost for this walk is $25.

"Historic Charlestown," 1½ hours, takes you through the charming, Victorian-era capital to explore its rich and turbulent past: 300 years of fire, earthquake, hurricanes, and warfare. The cost is $15.

Shorts, socks, and closed shoes are suitable for all three walking tours. A hat is a welcome addition; suitable casual attire is appreciated in Charlestown (no swim suits). The "Eco-Ramble" is recommended for children over age 12; the other tours are not suitable for kids. All walking tours are offered on a reservation-only basis.

HORSEBACK RIDING   You can ride English saddle at the **Nisbet Plantation Beach Club,** Newcastle (© **869/469-9325**). A guide takes you along mountain trails to visit sites of long-forgotten plantations. The cost is $60 per person for 45 minutes.

SCUBA DIVING & SNORKELING   Some of the best dive sites on Nevis include **Monkey Shoals,** 2 miles (3km) west of the Four Seasons. This is a beautiful reef, starting at 40 feet (12m), with dives up to 100 feet (30m) in depth. Angelfish, turtles, nurse sharks, and extensive soft coral can be found here. **The Caves** are on the south tip of Nevis, a 20-minute boat ride from the Four Seasons. A series of coral grottoes with numerous squirrelfish, turtles, and needlefish make this ideal for both certified and resort divers. **Champagne Garden,** a 5-minute boat ride from the Four Seasons, gets its name from bubbles created from an underwater sulfur vent. Because of the warm water temperature, large numbers of tropical fish are found here. Finally, **Coral Garden,** 2 miles (3km) west of the Four Seasons, is another beautiful coral reef with schools of Atlantic spadefish and large sea fans. The reef is at a maximum depth of 70 feet (21m) and is suitable for both certified and resort divers.

Snorkelers should head for Pinney's Beach. You might also try the waters of Fort Ashby, where the settlement of Jamestown is said to have slid into the sea; legend has it that the church bells can still be heard, and the undersea town can still be seen when conditions are just right. So far, no diver, to our knowledge, has ever found the conditions just right.

Scuba Safaris, Oualie Beach (© **869/469-9518**), on the island's north end, offers PADI scuba diving and snorkeling in an area rich in dive sites. It also offers resort and certification courses, dive packages, and equipment rental. A one-tank scuba dive costs $45; a two-tank dive, $80. Full certification courses cost $450 per person. Snorkeling trips cost $35 per person. Boat charters to Banana Bay and Cockleshell Bay are offered.

TENNIS   There are no public courts on Nevis. Guests at the big hotels play on their courts for free. Nonguests can play on the courts at the **Hermitage Plantation** (© **869/469-3477**) for free.

WINDSURFING   The waters here are often ideal for this sport, especially for beginners and intermediates. **Windsurfing Nevis** at the Oualie Beach Hotel (© **869/469-9682**) offers the best equipment, costing $20 for 1 hour.

EXPLORING THE ISLAND

It's a good idea to negotiate with a taxi driver to take you around Nevis. The distance is only 36 miles (58km), but you may find yourself taking a long time if you stop to see specific sights and talk to all the people who will want to chat with you. A 3-hour sightseeing tour around the island will cost $60; the average taxi holds up to four people. No sightseeing bus companies operate on Nevis, but a number of individuals own buses that they use for taxi service. Call **John's Taxis** (© **869/469-7357** or 869/662-8396) for information.

The major attraction is the **Museum of Nevis History,** in the house where Alexander Hamilton was born, on Main Street in Charlestown (© **869/ 469-5786**), overlooking the bay. Hamilton was the illegitimate son of a Scotsman and Rachel Fawcett, a Nevisian of Huguenot ancestry. The family immigrated to St. Croix, and from there Alexander made his way to the North American colonies, where he became the first Secretary of the U.S. Treasury. His picture, of course, appears on the $10 bill. The lava-stone house by the shore has been restored. The museum, dedicated to the history and culture of Nevis, houses the island's archives. Hours are Monday to Friday from 9am to 4pm, Saturday from 9am to noon. Admission is $2 for adults, $1 for children.

Eden Brown Estate, about 1½ miles (2km) from New River, is said to be haunted. It was once the home of a wealthy planter, whose daughter was to be married, but her husband-to-be was killed in a duel at the prenuptial feast. The mansion was then closed forever and left to the ravages of nature. Only the most adventurous come here on a moonlit night.

At one time, Sephardic Jews who came from Brazil made up a quarter of the island's population, and it's believed that Jews introduced sugar production to the Leeward Islands. Outside the center of Charlestown, at the lower end of Government Road, the **Jewish Cemetery** has been restored and is the resting place of many of the early shopkeepers of Nevis. Most of the tombstones date from 1690 to 1710.

An archaeological team from the United States believes that an old stone building in partial ruin on Nevis is probably the oldest **Jewish synagogue** in the Caribbean. Preliminary findings in 1993 traced the building's history to one of the two oldest Jewish settlements in the West Indies, and current work at the site plus historic documents in England establish its existence before 1650. The site is located adjacent to the government administration building in Charlestown.

One of the island's newest attractions is the 8-acre (4-hectare) **Botanical Garden of Nevis** (© **869/469-3509**), 3 miles (5km) south of Charlestown on the Montpelier Estate. Rain-forest plants grow in re-created Mayan ruins on a hillside site overlooking the Caribbean. The on-site restaurant serves an English tea with scones and double Devon cream. You can also order a ploughman's lunch (French bread, pickled onions, and cheese). If you patronize the restaurant and gift shop, you don't have to pay the admission of $9 to the gardens. The garden is open Monday to Saturday from 9am to 4pm.

Nevis Jockey Club organizes and sponsors thoroughbred races every month. Local horses as well as some brought over from other islands fill out a typical five-race card. If you want to have a glimpse at what horse racing must have been like a century or more ago, you'll find the Nevis races a memorable experience. For information, contact Richard Lupinacci, a Jockey Club officer and owner and operator of the Hermitage Plantation (© **869/469-3477**).

SHOPPING

For original art, visit **Eva Wilkins's Studio,** Clay Ghaut, Gingerland (© 869/ 469-2673). Wilkins was the island's most famous artist; even Prince Charles showed up to look at her work. Until her death in 1989, she painted island people, local flowers, and scenes of Nevis life. Prints are available in some of the local shops, but originals sell for $100 and up. You can visit her former atelier, on the grounds of an old sugar-mill plantation near Montpelier.

In a stone building about 200 feet (60m) from the wharf, near the marketplace, **Nevis Handicraft Cooperative Society,** Cotton House, Charlestown (© 869/469-1746), contains locally made gift items, including unusual objects of goatskin, local wines made from a variety of fruits grown on the island, hot-pepper sauce, guava cheese, jams, and jellies.

Hand-painted, tie-dyed, and batik clothing are featured at **Island Hopper,** in the T.D.C. Shopping Mall, Main Street, Charlestown (© 869/469-0893), which also has locations on St. Kitts and Antigua. From beach wraps to souvenirs, a wide selection of products is available.

Those interested in stamp collecting can go to the **Nevis Philatelic Bureau,** Head Post Office, Market Street (next to the public market), Charlestown (© 869/469-5535), to see the wide range of colorful stamps. They feature butterflies, shells, birds, and fish.

NEVIS AFTER DARK

Nightlife is not the major reason to visit Nevis. Summer nights are quiet, but there's organized entertainment in winter, often with steel bands performing at the major hotels.

Most action takes place at the **Four Seasons Resort,** Pinney's Beach (© 869/ 469-1111), on Friday and Saturday nights. The **Old Manor Estate,** Gingerland (© 869/469-3445), often brings in a steel band on Friday nights. On Saturday, the action swings over to the **Golden Rock,** Gingerland (© 869/469-3346), where a string band enlivens the scene.

Oualie Beach Hotel, Oualie Beach (© 869/469-9735), offers a Saturday buffet with a live string band entertaining guests. Disco reigns supreme at **Tequila Sheila's** at Cades Bay (see "Dining," above) on Saturday night.

One of the best beach bars on island is the **Beachcomber,** Pinney's Beach (© 869/469-1192), known for its happy hour and barbecues. Sometimes live bands appear.

We've saved the best for last. Head for **Sunshine's Bar & Grill** (see earlier in this chapter) and order "The Killer Bee." Sunshine, the owner, won't tell you what goes into it. "First there's a little rum, maybe a lot of rum, and then some passion fruit juice. And that's all I'm tellin'." When you arrive in Nevis, check to see if Sunshine is throwing one of his "Full Moon" parties, a raucous island event, with a roaring bonfire and a limbo contest. But, even without the party, Sunshine's bar is the most fun place to be on Nevis on any night, even a Monday. "Monday, Sunday, it's all the same at Sunshine's," one of the staff told us.

22

St. Lucia

In recent years, St. Lucia (pronounced *LOO-sha*) has become one of the most popular destinations in the Caribbean, with some of its finest resorts. The heaviest tourist development is concentrated in the northwest, between the capital, **Castries,** and the northern end of the island, where there's a string of white-sand beaches.

The rest of St. Lucia remains relatively unspoiled, a checkerboard of green-mantled mountains, valleys, banana plantations, a bubbling volcano, wild orchids, and fishing villages. There's a hint of the South Pacific about the island, as well as a mixed French and British heritage.

A mountainous island of some 240 square miles (623 sq. km), St. Lucia has about 120,000 inhabitants. The capital, Castries, is built on the southern shore of a large harbor surrounded by hills.

Native son Derek Walcott was born in Castries. His father was an unpublished poet who died when Walcott was just a year old, and his mother was a former headmistress at the Methodist school on St. Lucia. In 1992, Walcott won the Nobel Prize for literature. He prefers, however, not to tout the charms of St. Lucia, telling the press, "I don't want everyone to go there and overrun the place." Alas, his warning has come too late.

1 Essentials

VISITOR INFORMATION

In the **United States,** the St. Lucia Tourist Board office is located at 800 Second Ave., New York, NY 10017 (© **800/456-3984** or 212/867-2950). In the **United Kingdom,** contact the tourist office at 421A Finchley Rd., London NW3 6HJ (© **0870/900-7697**). In **Canada,** information is provided at the tourist board at 8 King St. East, Suite 700, Toronto, Ontario M5V 1B5 (© **416/362-4242**).

On the island, the main tourist office is at Sureline Building, Vive Boutielle, Castries Harbour (© **758/452-4094**). In **Soufrière,** there's a branch on Bay Street (© **758/459-7419**). St. Lucia information is on the Web at **www.stlucia.org**.

GETTING THERE

Before you book your own airfare, read the section "Package Deals" in chapter 2—it can save you a bundle.

The island maintains two separate airports, whose different locations cause endless confusion to many newcomers. Most international long-distance flights land at **Hewanorra International Airport** (© **758/454-6355**) in the south, 45 miles (72km) from Castries. If you arrive here and you're booked into a hotel in the north, you'll have to spend about an hour and a half traveling along the potholed East Coast Highway. The average taxi fare is $60 for up to four passengers.

Flights from other parts of the Caribbean usually land at the somewhat antiquated **Vigie Airport** (© 758/452-2596), in the northeast. Its location just outside Castries affords much more convenient access to the capital and most of the island's hotels.

You'll probably have to change planes somewhere else in the Caribbean to get to St. Lucia. **American Eagle** (© 800/433-7300 in the U.S., or 758/452-1820; www.aa.com) serves both of the island's airports with nonstop flights from San Juan. Connections from all parts of the North American mainland to the airline's enormous hub in San Juan are frequent and convenient. American also offers some good package deals.

Air Canada (© 800/776-3000 in the U.S., 800/268-7240 in Canada, or 758/454-6038; www.aircanada.ca) has one nonstop weekly flight to St. Lucia that departs from Toronto.

British Airways (© 0845/773-3377 in England, or 758/452-7444; www.british-airways.com) offers three flights a week from London's Gatwick Airport to St. Lucia's Hewanorra Airport. All these touch down briefly on Antigua before continuing to St. Lucia.

LIAT (© 800/468-0482 in the U.S. and Canada; www.liatairline.com) has small planes flying from many points throughout the Caribbean into Vigie Airport. Points of origin include such islands as Barbados, Antigua, St. Thomas, St. Maarten, and Martinique. On some LIAT flights, you may visit all these islands before arriving in St. Lucia.

Air Jamaica (© 800/523-5585 in the U.S., or 758/454-8869; www.air jamaica.com) serves the Hewanorra Airport with nonstop service from either New York's JFK or Newark daily, except Wednesday and Friday.

Another option is **BWIA** (© 800/538-2942 in the U.S.; www.bwia.com), which has one weekly flight from New York's JFK to Hewanorra, two weekly flights from Miami, and two weekly flights from London's Heathrow Airport. All flights make a quick stopover in Barbados. At least, we hope it's quick.

GETTING AROUND

BY TAXI   Taxis are ubiquitous on the island, and most drivers are eager to please. The drivers have to be quite experienced to cope with the narrow, hilly, switchback roads outside the capital. They also have special training that allows them to serve as guides. Their cabs are unmetered, but tariffs for all standard trips are fixed by the government. From Castries, the fare to Marigot Bay should be approximately $25 to $30; to Rodney Bay, the fare is $18 to $20. Always determine if the driver is quoting a rate in U.S. dollars or Eastern Caribbean dollars (EC$).

Most day tours of the island cost $129.50 per carload; you can also negotiate a half-day rate. One company that specializes in these tours is **Toucan Travel,** The Marina in Castries (© 758/452-9962).

BY RENTAL CAR   *Remember to drive on the left,* and try to avoid some of the island's more obvious potholes. Drive carefully and honk your horn while going around the blind hairpin turns. You'll need a St. Lucia driver's license ($20), which you can purchase at either airport when you pick up your rental car.

Avis (© 800/331-1212 in the U.S., or 758/452-2700; www.avis.com), **Budget** (© 800/527-0700 in the U.S., or 758/452-0233; www.budgetrentacar. com), and **Hertz** (© 800/654-3001 in the U.S., or 758/452-0679; www.

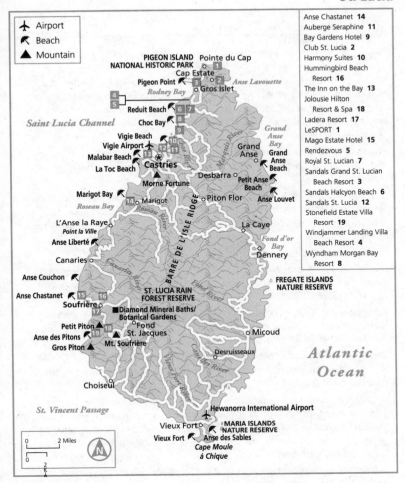

Airport
Beach
Mountain

Anse Chastanet **14**
Auberge Seraphine **11**
Bay Gardens Hotel **9**
Club St. Lucia **2**
Harmony Suites **10**
Hummingbird Beach
　Resort **16**
The Inn on the Bay **13**
Jolousie Hilton
　Resort & Spa **18**
Ladera Resort **17**
LeSPORT **1**
Mago Estate Hotel **15**
Rendezvous **5**
Royal St. Lucian **7**
Sandals Grand St. Lucian
　Beach Resort **3**
Sandals Halcyon Beach **6**
Sandals St. Lucia **12**
Stonefield Estate Villa
　Resort **19**
Windjammer Landing Villa
　Beach Resort **4**
Wyndham Morgan Bay
　Resort **8**

hertz.com) have offices at (or will deliver cars to) both of the island's airports. Each also has an office in Castries and, in some cases, at some of the island's major hotels.

You can sometimes get lower rates by booking through one of the local car-rental agencies, where rates begin at $60 per day. Try **C.T.L. Rent-a-Car,** Grosislet Highway, Rodney Bay Marina (© **758/452-0732**). **Cool Breeze Car Rental,** New Development, Soufrière (© **758/459-7729**), is also a good bet if you're staying in the south.

BY BUS　Minibuses (with names like "Lucian Love") and jitneys connect Castries with such main towns as Soufrière and Vieux Fort. They're cheap, but they're generally overcrowded and often filled with produce on its way to market. Buses for Cap Estate, in the northern part of the island, leave from Jeremy Street in Castries, near the market. Buses going to Vieux Fort and Soufrière depart from Bridge Street in front of the department store.

FAST FACTS: St. Lucia

Banks Banks are open Monday to Thursday from 8am to 1pm and on Friday from 8am to noon and 3 to 5pm.

Currency The official monetary unit is the **Eastern Caribbean dollar (EC$)**, which is pegged at EC$2.70 per U.S. dollar. Most of the prices quoted in this section are in U.S. dollars, as they are accepted by nearly all hotels, restaurants, and shops. Always be clear on which dollar is being used when discussing prices.

Customs At either airport, Customs may be a hassle if there's the slightest suspicion, regardless of how ill-founded, that you're carrying illegal drugs.

Documents U.S., British, and Canadian citizens need valid passports, plus an ongoing or return ticket.

Electricity St. Lucia runs on 220- to 230-volt AC (50 cycles), so bring an adapter if you plan to use U.S. appliances.

Emergencies Call the police at ℂ **999**.

Hospitals There are 24-hour emergency rooms at **St. Jude's Hospital**, Vieux Fort (ℂ **758/454-6041**), and **Victoria Hospital**, Hospital Road, Castries (ℂ **758/452-2421**).

Language Although English is the official tongue, St. Lucians probably don't speak it the way you do. Islanders also speak a French-Creole patois, similar to that heard on Martinique.

Pharmacies The best is **M&C Drugstore**, Bridge Street, in Castries (ℂ **758/458-8147**), open Monday through Friday from 8am to 5pm, and Saturday from 8am to 12:30pm.

Safety St. Lucia has its share of crime, like every other place these days. Use common sense and protect yourself and your valuables. If you've got it, don't flaunt it! Don't pick up hitchhikers if you're driving around the island. The use of narcotic drugs is illegal, and their possession or sale could lead to stiff fines or jail.

Taxes The government imposes an 8% occupancy tax on hotel rooms, and there's a $20 departure tax for both airports.

Telephone The area code for St. Lucia is **758**. Make calls to or from St. Lucia just like you would with any other area code in North America. On the island, dial all seven digits of the local number. If your hotel won't send a fax for you, try **Cable & Wireless,** in the SMC Building on the waterfront in Castries (ℂ **758/452-3301**). To access **AT&T Direct**, call ℂ **800/225-5288**; to reach **MCI**, dial ℂ **800/888-8000**.

Time St. Lucia is on Atlantic standard time year-round, placing it 1 hour ahead of New York. However, when the United States is on daylight saving time (April–Oct), St. Lucia matches the clocks of the U.S. east coast.

Tipping Most hotels and restaurants add a 10% service charge (ask if it's been included in the initial hotel rate you're quoted). If you're pleased with the service in a restaurant, by all means, supplement with an extra 5%. Taxi drivers expect 10% of the fare.

Water Water here is generally considered safe to drink; if you're unsure or have a delicate constitution, stick to bottled water.

Weather This little island, lying in the path of the trade winds, has year-round temperatures of 70° to 90°F.

2 Accommodations

Most of the leading hotels on this island are pretty pricey; you have to really search for the bargains. However, many of the big resorts here are frequently featured in packages (see the section "Package Deals," in chapter 2). Once you reach your hotel, chances are you'll feel pretty isolated, which is exactly what most guests want. Many St. Lucian hostelries have kitchenettes where you can prepare simple meals. Prices are usually quoted in U.S. dollars. As mentioned above, an 8% hotel tax and a 10% service charge are added to your bill.

VERY EXPENSIVE

Anse Chastanet ★★   One of the few places that merits the cliché "tropical paradise," this is not only St. Lucia's premier dive resort, but also an exceptional Caribbean inn. It offers warm service, excellent food, a beach location, and first-class facilities. It lies 18 miles (29km) north of Hewanorra International Airport (a 50-minute taxi ride), 2 miles (3km) north of Soufrière on a forested hill, and a 103-step climb above palm-fringed Anse Chastanet Beach. You're surrounded by coffee trees, mangos, papayas, banana plants, breadfruit, grapefruit, coconut palms, and hibiscus. The core of the house is a main building decorated in a typical island style, with a relaxing bar and dining room.

Guests can stay on the beach in spacious accommodations styled like West Indian plantation villas. Other units, constructed like octagonal gazebos and cooled by ceiling fans, have views of the Pitons. The spacious rooms are comfortably appointed with locally made furniture crafted from island woods. They have tropical hardwood floors, wooden jalousie louvers, king-size beds, and roomy private bathrooms with shower stalls and dual sinks.

You can dine or drink on a wind-cooled terrace, built like a tree house over the tropical landscape, in the Pitons Bar and Restaurant. Even if you're not a guest of the hotel, consider stopping at the beachside restaurant, Trou au Diable, which offers West Indian cuisine and a barbecue grill, plus a twice-weekly Creole dinner buffet.

Anse Chastanet Beach (P.O. Box 7000), Soufrière, St. Lucia, W.I. © 800/223-1108 in the U.S., or 758/459-7000. Fax 758/459-7700. www.ansechastanet.com. 49 units. Winter $440–$670 double; from $790 suite. Off-season $245–$420 double; from $540 suite. Winter rates include breakfast and dinner. AE, MC, V. **Amenities:** 2 restaurants; 2 bars; tennis court; spa; dive shop; sailboat rentals; babysitting; laundry; airport transfers. *In room:* Ceiling fan, hair dryer, safe; no phone.

Jalousie Hilton Resort & Spa ★★★   For visitors to St. Lucia's southwest coast who require a bit more luxury than can be found at Ladera or Anse Chastenet, Hilton offers this recently refurbished (for $6 million) sprawling resort. Among other improvements, Hilton has added an inviting, gently sloping white-sand beach. The location, between the Pitons, is one of the most scenic in the Caribbean. The property is so large (325 acres/130 hectares) that vans constantly circulate to shuttle guests around. Most of the resort's accommodations are in individual villas or villa suites (slightly larger, with separate sitting rooms) that dot the hillside. All the tile-floored villa rooms have four-star luxuries, including remote-controlled air-conditioning, fold-out sofas, and shower/tub combinations. All villas and suites also have private plunge pools. Our only complaint is that the degree of privacy is not always enough to allow, say, nude sunbathing. In addition to the villas, 12 Sugar Mill double rooms are in 2 buildings; they're slightly smaller than the other rooms, but they still have private terraces. The staff here is especially friendly and helpful.

The chef's inventive cuisine is ambitious but best when it concentrates on flavor-filled, locally available ingredients.

P.O. Box 251, Soufrière, St. Lucia, W.I. (C) **888/744-5256** in the U.S. for reservations only, or 758/456-8000. Fax 758/459-7667. www.hilton.com. 112 units. Winter $460 double; $515 villa; $675 villa suite. Off-season $275 double; $380 villa; $470 villa suite. Breakfast and dinner for $80 per person extra. Honeymoon, dive, and spa packages available. AE, DC, DISC, MC, V. Small pets allowed. **Amenities:** 4 restaurants, 4 bars; pool; par-3 executive golf course; 4 Laykold tennis courts; squash court; health club and spa; Jacuzzi; sauna; watersports; children's activities; tour desk; car rental; business center; salon; 24-hr. room service; babysitting; laundry/ dry cleaning. *In room:* A/C, satellite TV, VCR, dataport, minibar, coffeemaker, bathrobes, hair dryer, safe.

Ladera Resort ✿✿✿   The Ladera is an exercise in luxurious simplicity on St. Lucia's southwest end, a frequent retreat for the rich and famous who seek total privacy from the outside world: There are no phones or TVs in the rooms. Outside the town of Soufrière, this hideaway is perched on a hillside 1,100 feet (330m) above sea level. Sandwiched between the Pitons, the resort has views of Jalousie Bay—perhaps the most stunning vistas you are likely to find on St. Lucia. The villas and suites are completely open to the views of the Pitons and cooling breezes (units are not air-conditioned). You don't come here for the beach—it's a 15- to 20-minute complimentary shuttle ride away—but for the lovely setting, gracious service, and privacy.

Accommodations are constructed of tropical hardwoods, stone, and tile, and are furnished with 19th-century French furniture, wicker, and accessories built by local craftspeople. You'll find interesting touches in all the rooms: sinks made of shells, or open, rock-walled showers. All units afford total privacy and have indoor gardens and plunge pools, plus shower/tub combinations. Many rooms have four-poster queen-size beds draped in mosquito netting, and most have fridges. To get in here in winter, reserve 4 months in advance. We're not kidding.

The Dasheene Restaurant & Bar offers fine dining, specializing in a local Creole and continental cuisine. The seafood is caught fresh daily. Guests enjoy high tea in Ladera's botanical garden.

P.O. Box 225, Soufrière, St. Lucia, W.I. (C) **800/738-4752** in the U.S. and Canada, or 758/459-7323. Fax 758/459-5156. www.ladera-stlucia.com. 25 units. Winter $395–$560 1- or 2-bedroom suite; $600–$820 villa. Off-season $240–$330 1- or 2-bedroom suite; $375–$565 villa. Extra person $35. Breakfast and dinner plan for $65 per person extra (3-night minimum). 7-night minimum stay Dec 18–Jan 4. AE, DISC, MC, V. **Amenities:** Restaurant, 2 bars; pool; horseback riding; scuba diving; snorkeling; sailing; fishing charters; shuttle service to the beach at Anse de Pitons. *In room:* Plunge pool, no phone.

LeSPORT ✿✿✿   Following a multimillion-dollar renovation and expansion, this luxury all-inclusive spa resort, now called The Body Holiday at LeSPORT, is better than ever. It's all the way at the northernmost tip of the island, an 8-mile (13km) drive from Castries. Guests seem to prefer this isolation.

The resort makes a promise faithfully kept: Everything you "do, see, enjoy, drink, eat, and feel" is included in the price—that means not only accommodations, three meals a day, all refreshments, and bar drinks, but also use of sports equipment, facilities, and instruction, and most (though not all) of the spa treatments. Units are in a four-story building on a hill site fronting a long palm-fringed beach. Bedrooms are roomy and beautifully appointed, with fridges, wicker furnishings, and king-size or paired twin beds. Bathrooms are spacious, with tubs and showers and dual basins. To cater to the rapidly growing singles market, the resort has created rooms especially for these solo travelers.

Meals are served in an open-air restaurant overlooking the Caribbean. Breakfast and lunch are buffet style; dinner offers a choice between lighter-style dishes and "not-so-light" options. A more recent addition is Tao, an East/West fusion restaurant, open only at dinner, where advance reservations are needed. Nonguests who reserve can dine here. The food is arguably the best of that offered by the all-inclusive resorts. There's live entertainment, including a piano bar that's popular until late at night.

Cariblue Beach (P.O. Box 437), St. Lucia, W.I. ⓒ 800/544-2883 in the U.S. and Canada, or 758/450-8551. Fax 758/450-0368. www.thebodyholiday.com. 154 units. Winter $700–$770 double; $990–$1,020 suite. Off-season $500–$570 double; $610–$640 suite. Children age 6–11 get a 50% discount, age 5 and under $35 per day. Rates are all-inclusive. AE, DISC, MC, V. **Amenities:** 2 restaurants, 2 bars; 3 pools; fencing; archery; health club and spa; scuba diving, windsurfing, water-skiing, snorkeling, sailing; room service (breakfast only); babysitting; laundry; airport transfers. *In room:* A/C, hair dryer, safe.

Royal St. Lucian ★★   A fine resort with a new spa, the Royal St. Lucian lies north of Castries. Standing in its own gardens of royal palms and tropical foliage, it opens onto a dramatic lobby. All the accommodations are luxury suites, the best of which have sea views and balconies. There are eight even more spacious and deluxe suites right at beachfront, each with a private terrace. Some of the units are split-level, with spacious bathrooms containing tubs and jet showers, cream-colored tile floors, rattan furniture, and woven rugs, all of which make the accommodations look inviting. Everywhere you look, the setting is lush. The food is among the best hotel cuisine on the island, and candlelit beach dinners are a feature. The chefs are also known for their West Indian and Italian buffets. Jazz can be heard in the chic cocktail lounge, and the spa offers everything from hydrotherapy to herbal body wraps.

Rodney Bay (P.O. Box 977), Castries, St. Lucia, W.I. ⓒ 800/255-5859 in the U.S., or 758/452-9999. Fax 758/452-9639. www.travelhop.com. 96 units. Winter $475–$715 double. Off-season $390–$630 double. AE,

---

Moments **Soft Adventures in the Wild**

LeSPORT at Cariblue Beach (ⓒ **800/544-2883**) has introduced several "soft adventures" that include scenic walks, mountain climbing, and turtle-watching. Two river walks, with wading, go deep into the rainforest. One is along the River Doree in the southern part of St. Lucia and the other is along Anse la Raye River, which is mid-island. Mountain climbing takes you to Gros Piton, one of the island's two dramatic sugarloaf peaks, where overnights are often arranged so you can wake up to a spectacular sunrise from a lofty vantage point.

These excursions often pass by waterfalls, providing hikers with an opportunity to swim in their pools. Many tropical birds can be observed, including the St. Lucia parrot, which once was nearly extinct. During turtle-watching season, from April to September, LeSPORT guests can camp overnight at Grand Anse beach, with the prospect of watching the huge Leatherback turtles lay eggs. Escorts from the hotel set up Arabian-like tents and a barbecue dinner is served.

Adventures cost from $45 to $90 per person.

DC, MC, V. **Amenities:** 2 restaurants, 2 bars; pool; health club and spa; room service; laundry. *In room:* A/C, TV, minibar, hair dryer, safe.

Sandals Grand St. Lucian Beach Resort ★★★

The popular chain, Sandals, is leaving its footprints all over the sands of the island. In the summer of 2002, Jamaican hotelier Butch Stewart invaded St. Lucia for the third time, opening yet another couples-only (male/female) all-inclusive. Compared to the other two, this new one is the best of the lot. This luxury resort lies at the causeway on the northern tip of St. Lucia, linking the "mainland" with Pigeon Island, with the tranquil Caribbean Sea on one side and the often more turbulent Atlantic Ocean on the other side. Set on a landscaped 3-acre (1-hectare) lagoon, the megaresort took over a new and already existing property, Hyatt Regency, at a point 6 miles (10km) northwest of Castries at Rodney Bay. When Hyatt decided to pull out of St. Lucia, Stewart moved in, thinking he could make a go of it.

Everything is here, so the aim seems to be to keep you "grounded" during your entire vacation with a private golden sandy beach, the most lavish lagoon-style swimming pool on the island, a state-of-the-art spa, a spacious, elegant casino, and a choice of four restaurants featuring cuisines that span the world for inspiration.

Even the standard bedrooms are spacious, with antique reproductions in a plantation style. Local art brightens the walls, and there is plenty of comfort, including luxurious full bathrooms. For the best of the lot, select one of the fourth-floor rooms for better views, service, space, and comfort. Or for the ultimate, ask for one of the two dozen "swim-up" units with their own free-form pools and terraces. Inquire about the stay at one play at two program where you stay at one Sandals property but are able to use the other properties as well.

Pigeon Island Causeway, Gros Islet, St. Lucia. W.I. © **800/SANDALS.** www.sandals.com. 284 units. Winter $425–$650 double; from $1,500 suite. Off-season $290–$375 double; from $420 suite. Rates are per person and all-inclusive. AE, MC, V. Children not accepted. **Amenities:** 4 restaurants, 3 bars; casino; pool; golf privileges; 4 tennis courts; health club and spa; dive shop, snorkeling, windsurfing, deep-sea fishing; laundry; airport shuttle. *In room:* A/C, TV, minibar, hair dryer, iron and ironing board, safe.

Sandals Halcyon ★

Within walking distance of Palm Beach and a 15-minute drive northeast of Castries, this is the smaller of the three Sandals properties on St. Lucia, and it has fewer facilities. But you can always take the free, 15-minute minibus ride to Sandals St. Lucia if you want to use the nine-hole golf course and extensive facilities there. Guest rooms come in a wide range of categories, usually with a king-size mahogany four-poster bed. Each room has a full bathroom with a tub and shower. The food is copious but not of the highest quality. The best place to dine here is the Pier Restaurant, a West Indian–style restaurant atop a 150-foot (45m) pier. Children, singles, and gay and lesbian couples are not permitted.

Choc Bay (P.O. Box GM 910), Castries, St. Lucia, W.I. © **800/SANDALS** or 758/453-0222. Fax 758/451-8435. www.sandals.com. 170 units. All-inclusive rates for 3 nights: winter $1,860–$2,670 double. Off-season $1,680–$2,490 double. AE, MC, V. **Amenities:** 3 restaurants, 4 bars; dance club; 2 pools; golf privileges; 2 tennis courts; fitness center; 3 Jacuzzis; watersports; laundry; transfers to airport. *In room:* A/C, TV, coffeemaker, hair dryer, safe.

Sandals St. Lucia ★★

The Jamaica-based Sandals chain opened this clone on a forested 155-acre (62-hectares) site that slopes steeply down to the sea. This is larger and more upscale than the Sandals Halcyon, but not as spiffy as the newest Sandals Grand St. Lucian Beach Resort. However, the male-female couples thing is just as strongly emphasized here. The hotel is near Castries, on the island's northwestern coast. The center of the resort is a gazebo-capped pool that incorporates an artificial waterfall, a swim-up bar, and a dining pavilion. Larger-than-expected guest rooms contain king-size four-poster beds with mahogany headboards, balconies or patios, and a pastel tropical decor. Bathrooms are spacious, with shower/tub combinations.

The resort's six restaurants are infinitely superior to the cuisine served at Sandals Halcyon (see above). The most upscale, La Toc, features French cuisine. Kimonos offers Japanese food cooked on a heated table top, teppanyaki style. The Arizona Restaurant, as befits its name, features the cuisine of the U.S. Southwest. After dark, guests gravitate to Jaime's, the nightclub/disco, or to Herbie's Piano Bar. Inquire about the stay at one play at two program where you stay at one Sandals property but are able to use the other properties as well.

La Toc Rd. (P.O. Box 399), Castries, St. Lucia, W.I. ✆ 800/SANDALS in the U.S. and Canada, or 758/452-3081. Fax 758/452-1012. www.sandals.com. 328 units. All-inclusive rates for 3 nights: winter $1,980–$2,820 double; $3,000–$4,680 suite. Off-season $300–$410 per person per night double; $430–$775 per person per night suite. AE, MC, V. Children not accepted. **Amenities:** 6 restaurants, 10 bars, night club; 3 pools; 9-hole golf course; 5 tennis courts; health club and spa; 4 Jacuzzis; watersports; salon; massage; laundry. *In room:* A/C, TV, hair dryer, safe.

Stonefield Estate Villa Resort ★ *(Finds*

Nestled at the base of Petit Piton, this place is for escapists. In the southwestern part of the island, it stands on its own 26 acres (10 hectares), complete with a nature trail and some of the most striking panoramas on the island. Secluded away from the overrun resort areas, it lies only a 5-minute drive from the little fishing village of Soufrière yet close enough to the Jalousie Hilton that Stonefield guests can use the beach there, which lies a free 5-minute shuttle ride away. The estate's plantation houses are surrounded by tropical greenery, and each of the cottages available for rent has its own character and privacy. One of the island's oldest sites, the estate here still has a well-preserved Petroglyph dating from pre-Columbian times. All the accommodations come with antiques, high ceilings, verandas, bedrooms, and full bathrooms, with intimate outdoor garden showers and fully furnished kitchens. Villas are identical in layout, except they range in size from one to three bedrooms.

Stonefield Villas, P.O. Box 228, Soufrière, St. Lucia, W.I. ✆ 758/459-5648. Fax 758/459-5550. www.stonefieldvillas.com. Winter $240–$340 1-bedroom villa; $250–$490 2-bedroom villa; $475–$800 3-bedroom villa. Off-season $159–$210 1-bedroom villa; $170–$320 2-bedroom villa; $310–$530 3-bedroom villa. AE, MC, V. **Amenities:** Restaurant, bar; pool; library; babysitting; laundry. *In room:* Ceiling fan, no phone.

Wyndham Morgan Bay Resort ★

Set a 10-minute drive north of Castries, on 45 landscaped acres (18 hectares) partially shaded with trees and flowering shrubs, this all-inclusive resort draws more Europeans than Americans. Opened in 1992 and operated by the Wyndham chain, it offers guest rooms in six different annexes. Standard features include patios or verandas, rattan and wicker furnishings, fridges, and queen-size or paired twin beds. The spacious marble-trimmed bathrooms contain shower/tub combinations. Unlike some other all-inclusive hostelries on the island, this one welcomes children. The beach here is small, with murky water.

You can dine elegantly by candlelight at the resort's premier restaurant, the Trade Winds, overlooking the garden. The cuisine is resort standard, nothing more. Local musicians, steel bands, and calypso singers often perform live in the Sundowner Bar.

Choc Bay (P.O. Box 2167), Gros Islet, St. Lucia, W.I. ✆ 800/822-4200 in the U.S., or 758/450-2511. Fax 758/450-1050. www.wyndham.com. 238 units. Winter $490–$560 double. Off-season $390–$450 double. Year-round $650–$660 suite for 2. Rates are all-inclusive. Winter children age 13–18 staying in parents' room $80, children age 3–12 $55, children under age 3 stay free in parents' room. Off-season children age 17 and under stay free in parents' room. AE, DC, DISC, MC, V. **Amenities:** 2 restaurants, 3 bars; pool; 4 tennis courts; fitness center; Jacuzzi; spa; watersports; kids' club; laundry; airport shuttle. *In room:* A/C, TV, coffeemaker, hair dryer, safe.

EXPENSIVE

Club St. Lucia ⚱   Beefed up by a $6 million renovation, this all-inclusive resort sits in Cap Estate on a 65-acre (26-hectare) site, with 2 beaches in an area near LeSPORT. It's 8 miles (13km) north of Vigie Airport at the northern tip of the island. Very sports- and entertainment-oriented, the hotel opens onto a curved bay where smugglers used to bring in brandies, cognacs, and cigars from Martinique. The club's core is a wooden building with decks overlooking a free-form pool. The accommodations are in simple bungalows scattered over land-scaped grounds. Each features one king-size or two twin beds, air-conditioning and/or ceiling fans, and patios or terraces. Bathrooms have recently been upgraded, with makeup mirrors, marble vanities, and excellent shower/tub combinations.

The inclusive package is impressive, offering all meals, even snacks, along with unlimited beer, wine, and mixed drinks, both day and night. The food is standard resort fare, but you'll never go hungry here. To break the monotony, guests are often transported to the Great House, a restaurant at Cap Estate, where they receive a discount on meals.

Smugglers Village (P.O. Box 915), St. Lucia, W.I. ✆ **800/777-1250** in the U.S., or 758/450-0551. Fax 758/450-0281. www.splashresorts.com. 369 units. Winter $410–$440 double. Off-season $360–$390 double. Rates are all-inclusive. AE, DC, MC, V. **Amenities:** 5 restaurants, 8 bars, dance club; 4 pools; 9 tennis courts; fitness center; watersports; children's club; babysitting; laundry; airport shuttle. *In room:* A/C, TV, coffeemaker, hair dryer, iron and ironing board, safe.

Rendezvous ⚱⚱   On Malabar Beach, Rendezvous is an all-inclusive hotel for heterosexual couples only (no children, singles, or gay couples allowed). This is the down-market version of LeSPORT (see above) and suffers from its location at the end of the airport runway. Most guests are between the ages of 25 and 40, but you'll occasionally see some older folks who still enjoy spending every minute of every day with each other. There are several price categories, depend-ing on the season and the accommodation; top rates are charged for oceanfront luxury suites for two. A recent major refurbishment has involved the installation of marble floors, replacement of furnishings, and a general upgrading. Many beds are four-poster king-sizes draped in mosquito netting. The bathrooms are small but have combination shower/tubs, lighted makeup mirrors, and dual basins. Balconies and terraces are common to all units. The resort is north of Vigie Airport, near Castries, set within a 7-acre (3-hectare) tropical garden on the edge of a large, sandy beach.

The Trysting Place, a classical colonial-style dining room, is highlighted by polished brass chandeliers. The informal, open-air Terrace Restaurant features pastas as well as traditional favorites. For live entertainment 6 nights a week, guests frequent the piano bar.

Malabar Beach (P.O. Box 190), St. Lucia, W.I. ✆ **800/544-2883** in the U.S. and Canada, or 758/452-4211. Fax 758/452-7419. www.rendezvous.com.lc. 100 units. Winter $388–$478 double; $500 suite for 2. Off-season $240–$420 double; $446 suite for 2. Rates are all-inclusive. AE, DISC, MC, V. **Amenities:** 2 restau-rants, 3 bars; 2 pools; 2 tennis courts; fitness center; sauna; scuba-diving facilities, water-skiing, windsurfing; bicycle tours; laundry. *In room:* A/C, TV, hair dryer, safe.

Windjammer Landing Villa Beach Resort ⚱⚱⚱   Windjammer, set on 55 tropical acres (22 hectares) north of Reduit Beach, about a 15-minute drive from Castries, is a quiet, luxurious retreat, one of the most glamorous in the West

Indies. The resort was designed with a vaguely Moorish motif, heavily influenced by Caribbean themes; pastel colors predominate. It's composed of a cluster of white villas climbing a forested hillside above a desirable beach. This is an all-suite/villa resort (the larger villas have private plunge pools), making it a good choice for families or anyone who likes a lot of space. Standard features include ceiling fans, fridges, and queen-size or paired twin beds. The roomy villas offer separate living and dining rooms, full kitchens, cassette players, and VCRs upon request. All bedrooms adjoin private bathrooms and open onto sun terraces. Some bathrooms have showers only.

The resort contains more restaurants per capita than most of its competitors. The most elegant of the lot is Mango Tree. Papa Don's is an Italian trattoria specializing in pizza and pasta. Jammer's restaurant and bar is a nautically styled, informal bar/steakhouse/grill.

Labrelotte Bay (P.O. Box 1504), Castries, St. Lucia, W.I. ℭ **800/743-9609** in the U.S., 800/267-7600 in Canada, 0207/771-7000 in the United Kingdom, or 758/452-0913. Fax 758/452-9454. www.windjammer-landing.com. 234 units. Winter $220 double; $395 1-bedroom villa for 2; $640 2-bedroom villa for 4. Winter rates are 15%–20% higher Dec 20–Jan 3. Off-season $160 double; $275 1-bedroom villa for 2; $420 2-bedroom villa for 4. Up to 2 extra occupants are allowed in the villas (but not in the double rooms) at $50 each per night. Breakfast and dinner for $55 extra. AE, MC, V. **Amenities:** 4 restaurants, 3 bars; 4 pools; 2 tennis courts; fitness center; Jacuzzi; watersports; children's programs; room service; massage; babysitting; laundry. *In room:* A/C, TV, coffeemaker, hair dryer, safe.

MODERATE

Bay Gardens Hotel ⭐ *(Value)* This hotel offers one of the best values, as well as some of the best service, on the island. It's not right on the sands, but Reduit Beach, one of St. Lucia's finest beaches, is a 5-minute walk or a complimentary 2-minute shuttle ride away. One of the newest and most up-to-date hotels on the island, Bay Gardens opens onto a large atrium lobby with a designer fountain pool and bamboo furnishings. Joyce and Desmond Destang are among the most hospitable hosts on the island. Their medium-size bedrooms in vivid florals contain a terrace or balcony, and tropical art and accessories. Bathrooms are tiled with a combination tub and shower. Families might want to consider one of the eight apartments, each a self-contained unit with a kitchenette. One child is accommodated without charge. Its international restaurant, Spices, serves some of the island's best hotel food. Look for weekly rum punches, barbecues, Caribbean buffets, and live music on occasion.

Rodney Bay (P.O. Box 1892), Castries, St. Lucia. W.I. ℭ **800/223-9815** in the U.S., or 758/452-8060. Fax 758/452-8059. www.baygardenshotel.com. 71 units, 8 apartments. Winter $110–$150 double. Off-season $95–$140 double. AE, MC, V. **Amenities:** Restaurant, bar, ice cream shop; 2 pools; Jacuzzi; library; car rental; room service (7am–9:30pm); babysitting; laundry. *In room:* A/C, TV, dataport, fridge, coffeemaker, hair dryer, safe.

Harmony Suites ⭐ This complex of two-story buildings offers well-maintained accommodations at reasonable rates, a short walk from one of the island's finest beaches at Reduit. The suites, decorated in rattan, wicker, and florals, sit adjacent to a saltwater lagoon, where boats find refuge from the rough waters of the open sea. Each unit offers a patio or balcony with views of moored yachts, the lagoon, and surrounding hills. Those on the top floor have more privacy. All suites, except the VIP/honeymoon units, have sofa beds. Each VIP suite features a double Jacuzzi, a four-poster queen-size bed on a pedestal, a sundeck, white rattan furnishings, and a bidet. Eight of the suites contain kitchenettes, complete with coffeemakers, fridges, and wet bars—ideal for families on a budget. Shower/tub combination bathrooms are small, of the routine motel variety, but are tidily maintained.

Rodney Bay Lagoon (P.O. Box 155), Castries, St. Lucia, W.I. ℂ **758/452-0336.** Fax 758/452-8677. www. harmonysuites.com. 30 units. Winter $124–$165 double. Off-season $95–$135 double. Extra person $25. AE, MC, V. **Amenities:** Restaurant, bar; pool; laundry. *In room:* A/C, TV, hair dryer, safe.

Hummingbird Beach Resort ⭐ *Finds*   Set on ¾ acre (.3 hectare) of verdantly landscaped grounds, this is a small, charming, and carefully maintained inn that enjoys direct access to a sandy strip of beachfront, on the northern edge of Soufrière on St. Lucia's southwest coast. Originally conceived as the private vacation home of a Canadian investor, it was transformed in the mid-1970s into this hotel. There's a restaurant, The Hummingbird, on the premises (see "Dining," below). Bedrooms are sheathed in white stucco and accented with varnished hardwoods like mahogany. Views are of the water or the soaring nearby heights of Petit Titon and the rugged landscape of southern St. Lucia. Each has a ceiling fan and mosquito netting that's artfully draped over the sometimes elaborately carved bedsteads. Regrettably, the low wattage in the bedside lamps makes nighttime reading difficult. Bathrooms are very compact but have shower/tub combinations and adequate shelf space.

P.O. Box 280, Soufrière, St. Lucia, W.I. ℂ **758/459-7232.** Fax 758/459-7033. www.nvo.com/pitonresort. 11 units. Winter $90 double; $160 suite; $285 cottage for 2–4. Off-season $60 double; $110 suite; $175 cottage for 2–4. AE, DISC, MC, V. **Amenities:** Restaurant, 2 bars; pool; access to nearby health club; car rental; room service (7am–10pm); babysitting; laundry. *In room:* Ceiling fan, TV.

The Inn on the Bay   This small-scale inn is perched 300 feet (90m) above the waters of Marigot Bay on a site that required massive retaining walls to buttress. It's the creative statement of Montréal-born Normand Viau and his wife, Louise Boucher. Abandoning careers as a lawyer and social worker, respectively, they designed the hotel themselves, modeling its blue roof and veranda-ringed style on the island's plantation-house tradition. Today, the centerpiece of their establishment is an open-air terrace, site of a small pool and semiprivate dinners available only to hotel guests. Bedrooms, with 10-foot (3m) ceilings, are spacious, comfortably furnished, and airy. Each has a ceiling fan and ample windows for cross-ventilation. Some bathrooms are shower only. This makes for a great romantic escape.

Seaview Ave., Marigot Bay (P.O. Box RB2377), Castries, St. Lucia, BWI. ℂ **758/451-4260.** Fax 758/438-3828. www.saint-lucia.com. 5 units. Winter $145 double. Off-season $120 double. MC, V. Children under age 18 not accepted. **Amenities:** Breakfast room; pool; room service. *In room:* Ceiling fan, fridge, hair dryer, no phone.

Mago Estate Hotel *Finds*   Just above the fishing village of Soufrière, German-born Peter Gloger runs this glamorous little inn, which had been his vacation paradise. Named Mago, which is patois for mango, it is unique to St. Lucia. It is a true Caribbean Shangri-La, overlooking one of the Pitons. The property is surrounded by tropical trees, not only mango, but mahogany, papaya, maracuya, and banana. It would be ideal for a honeymoon. You sleep in a four-poster underneath a ceiling of painted clouds. Each accommodation has only three walls; the other side of the room is open to a view of the mountains and sea. Mosquito netting protects you at night from insects, and each unit comes with a small shower-only bathroom. Attached to each unit is a spacious private terrace. The food is excellent, and it's served at communal tables surrounded by carved African chairs.

Palm Mist, Soufrière. ℂ **758/459-5880.** Fax 758/459-7352. www.mago-hotel.com. 6 units. Winter $150–$350 double. Off-season $100–$250 double. Rates include breakfast and beach shuttle service. MAP (Caribbean breakfast and dinner) $20 per person extra. MC, V. **Amenities:** Dining room, bar; pool; laundry. *In room:* Ceiling fan, fridge, no phone.

Auberge Seraphine This two-story concrete-sided building painted cerulean blue and white is a 15-minute walk from Vigie Beach, overlooking the marina and the harbor of Castries. Owned and operated by the St. Lucia–born Joseph family, whose hotel skills derived from a long sojourn in England, the hotel offers well-maintained but very simple accommodations. They're generally spacious and decorated with bright colors, often tropical prints. The bathrooms, though small, are clean and have tiled showers. Most activities surround an open terrace whose surface is sheathed with terra-cotta tiles ringing a small round-sided pool. Don't expect too many extras, as the place's charm derives from its simplicity.

Vigie Cove (Box 390), Castries, St. Lucia, W.I. © 758/453-2073. Fax 758/451-7001. www.sluonestop. com/auberg. 28 units. Year-round $100 double, $120 suite for 2. AE, MC, V. **Amenities:** Restaurant, bar; pool; room service; babysitting; laundry. *In room:* A/C, TV, hair dryer.

3 Dining

IN CASTRIES

Green Parrot ✪ CONTINENTAL/CARIBBEAN About 1½ miles (2km) east of the center of town, Green Parrot overlooks Castries Harbour and remains the local hot spot for visitors, expatriates, and locals. It takes about 12 minutes to walk here from downtown, but the effort is worth it. This elegant place is run by chef Harry, who had many years of training in prestigious restaurants and hotels in London, including Claridge's. Guests take their time and make an evening of it; many enjoy a before-dinner drink in the Victorian-style salon. You might like to try a Grass Parrot (made from coconut cream, crème de menthe, bananas, white rum, and sugar). An evening in the English-colonial dining room usually includes free entertainment, which might be a limbo contest or a fire-eating show. All this may sound gimmicky, but the food doesn't suffer for all the activity. There's an emphasis on St. Lucian specialties and homegrown produce. Try the *christophine au gratin* (a Caribbean squash with cheese) or the Creole soup made with callaloo and pumpkin. There are five kinds of curry with chutney, as well as a selection of omelets and sandwiches at lunch.

Green Parrot also offers some of the island's least expensive lodging; rooms have air-conditioning and phones. In winter, doubles are $100; in off-season, $80.

Red Tape Lane, Morne Fortune. © 758/452-3399. Reservations recommended. Lunch main courses EC$35–EC$80 (US$12.95–US$29.60); fixed-price dinner EC$90–EC$110 (US$33.30–US$40.70). AE, MC, V. Daily 7am–midnight.

IN THE SOUFRIÈRE AREA

Camilla's Restaurant & Bar WEST INDIAN Set a block inland from the waterfront, one floor above street level, this is a decent Caribbean-style restaurant with simple, unpretentious food. It's operated by a local matriarch, Camilla Alcindor, who will welcome you for coffee, a soda, or Perrier. The food is straightforward but flavorful. Opt for the fish and shellfish (Caribbean fish Creole or lobster Thermidor) rather than the beef, although the chicken curry is a savory choice. Lunches are considerably less elaborate and include an array of sandwiches, salads, omelets, and burgers. Our favorite tables are the pair that sit on a balcony overlooking the energetic activities in the street below. Otherwise, the inside tables can get a bit steamy on a hot night, as there's no air-conditioning.

7 Bridge St., Soufrière. © 758/459-5379. Main courses EC$30–EC$85 (US$11.10–US$31.45). AE, DISC, MC, V. Daily 8am–10:30pm.

Dasheene Restaurant & Bar ✦ CARIBBEAN/CALIFORNIAN   One of the most widely heralded restaurants on St. Lucia, and definitely the one with the most dramatic setting, this mountaintop hideaway offers some of the most refined and certainly the most creative cuisine on St. Lucia, taking as inspiration the best of the Caribbean/Creole kitchen plus the innovations of California. Start with a garden salad of locally grown greens or the *christophene* and coconut soup. We're especially fond of the chilled Creole seafood soup, which is reminiscent of gazpacho. Moving on to main dishes, the chef has a special flair for seafood pasta or marinated sirloin steak, and chicken appears stuffed with bread crumbs, sweet peppers, and onions. But the best bet is the catch of the day, likely to be kingfish or red snapper, and grilled to perfection. The chocolate soufflé flambé for dessert makes the night out all the more festive.

In the Ladera Resort, between Gros and Petit Piton. ✆ 758/459-7323. Reservations recommended. Main courses EC$60–EC$80 (US$22.20–US$29.60). AE, MC, V. Daily 7:30–10am, noon–2:30pm, and 6:30–9pm.

The Hummingbird CARIBBEAN/INTERNATIONAL   The restaurant is the best part of the Hummingbird Beach Resort complex. Tables are set on a stylish veranda adjacent to the sands of Hummingbird Beach. The cuisine focuses on such West Indian dishes as Creole-style conch, lobster, burgers, steaks, and fillets of both snapper and grouper, punctuated with such American staples as burgers and BLTs. A tiny gift shop on the premises sells batik items crafted by members of the staff.

At the Hummingbird Beach Resort, on the waterfront just north of the main wharf at Soufrière. ✆ 758/459-7232. Platters EC$41–EC$93 (US$15.15–US$34.40). AE, DISC, MC, V. Daily 8–11pm.

The Still ✦ *Finds* CREOLE   This is the most authentic and atmospheric place for lunch while touring the Soufrière area in the south. The first thing you'll see as you drive up the hill from the harbor is a very old rum distillery set on a platform of thick timbers. The site is a working cocoa and citrus plantation that has been in the same St. Lucian family for four generations. The front blossoms with avocado and breadfruit trees, and a mahogany forest is a few steps away. The bar near the front veranda is furnished with tables cut from cross-sections of mahogany tree trunks. In the more formal and spacious dining room, you can feast on excellently prepared St. Lucian specialties, depending on what's fresh at the market that day. Try to avoid the place when it's overrun with cruise-ship passengers or tour groups. There are far better restaurants on St. Lucia, but if it's lunchtime and you're near Diamond Falls, you don't have a lot of choices.

Soufrière. ✆ 758/459-7224. Main courses EC$20–EC$65 (US$7.40–US$24.05). AE, DC, DISC, MC, V. Mon–Fri 8am–5pm, Sat–Sun 8am–11pm.

IN RODNEY BAY

The Bistro (On the Waterfront) SEAFOOD/INTERNATIONAL   This popular restaurant is designed as a long, thin veranda, and as such offers more waterfront tables than any other place on the island. The owners are English, but the bistro has a decidedly French cafe atmosphere, with a comfortable bar area. Many of the owners of the luxury yachts moored alongside the restaurant dine here, knowing that the Bistro has the freshest ingredients available. Our favorite appetizer is scallops, lobster, shrimp, and crab au gratin, chopped finely and baked in a creamy sauce with cheese. The seafood bisque is excellent, as are all the homemade pastas, including fettuccine with shrimp, mussels, and calamari. In honor of the owners' origins, pub grub such as steak-and-kidney pie is featured as well. And here's your chance to sample a traditional hot and spicy West

Indian pepper pot, with beef, lamb, and chicken. Finally, the potato-crusted snapper in a tomato-basil sauce is sublime.

Rodney Bay. ✆ **758/452-9494.** Reservations recommended. Main courses EC$47–EC$110 (US$17.40–US$40.70). AE, MC, V. Fri–Wed 5:30–10:30pm.

Capone's ✪ ITALIAN/CARIBBEAN   This trattoria looks like a 1930s-era Miami Beach speakeasy. It could have been inspired by *Some Like It Hot*. North of Reduit Beach, near the lagoon, it's brightly lit at night. At the entrance is a self-service pizza parlor that also serves burgers and well-stuffed pita-bread sandwiches daily from 11am to 1pm. However, we recommend that you head to the back for a really superb Italian or Caribbean meal, beginning with a drink, perhaps Prohibition Punch or a St. Valentine's Day Massacre, served by "gangster" barmen, who will later present the check in a violin case. A player piano enlivens the mood. If you feel that all this atmosphere is a little too cute and gimmicky, rest assured that the dishes here are well prepared, with fresh, quality ingredients. The Little Caesar salad leads off many a meal, and the creamy lasagna is a special favorite. The best bet is the fresh local charcoal-grilled fish or some of the best steaks on the island.

Reduit Beach, Rodney Bay. ✆ **758/452-0284.** Reservations recommended. Main courses EC$48–EC$78 (US$17.75–US$28.85). AE, MC, V. Tues–Sun 3pm–midnight.

The Charthouse AMERICAN/CREOLE   In a large building with a sky-lit ceiling and a mahogany bar, the Charthouse is one of the oldest restaurants in the area and one of the island's most popular dining venues. This outpost of the international chain was built several feet above the bobbing yachts of the lagoon, without walls, to allow an optimal view of the water. The helpful staff serves simple, honest, good food in large portions. The specialties might include callaloo soup, St. Lucian crab backs, "meat-falling-off-the-bone" baby back spareribs, and fresh local lobster (from Sept–Apr, you can often witness the live lobster being delivered from the boat at around 5pm). If you fancy a well-cooked charcoal-broiled steak, you'll see why this dish made the restaurant famous. Of course, traditionalists visit The Charthouse for one reason only—its roast prime rib of beef, which is good, but never better on St. Lucia than in the U.S.

Reduit Beach, Rodney Bay. ✆ **758/452-8115.** Reservations recommended. Main courses EC$60–EC$110 (US$22.20–US$40.70). AE, MC, V. Mon–Sat 5–10:30pm.

The Lime ✪ AMERICAN/CREOLE   This bistro stands north of Reduit Beach in an area that's known as restaurant row. Some of these places are rather expensive, but the Lime continues to keep its prices low, its food good and plentiful, and its service among the finest on the island. Both locals and visitors come here for "limin'," or hanging out. West Indian in feeling and open-air in setting, the restaurant features a "lime special" drink in honor of its namesake. Specialties include stuffed crab backs and fish steak Creole, as well as shrimp, steaks, lamb and pork chops, and *róti* (Caribbean burritos). The steaks are done over a charcoal grill. Nothing is fancy, nothing is innovative, and nothing is nouvelle—just like the savvy local foodies like it. It's less expensive than the more touristy Capone's.

Rodney Bay. ✆ **758/452-0761.** Reservations recommended for dinner. Main courses EC$35–EC$85 (US$12.95–US$31.45). MC, V. Wed–Mon 8am–1am.

The Mortar & Pestle CARIBBEAN/INTERNATIONAL   Set on the waterfront of Rodney Bay Lagoon, this restaurant offers indoor–outdoor dining with a view of the boats moored at the nearby marina. The menu includes select recipes from the various islands of the southern Caribbean, with their rich medley of African, British, French, Spanish, Portuguese, Dutch, Indian, Chinese, and even Amerindian influences. To get you going, try the rich and creamy conch chowder, followed by crab *farci* (a delicious stuffed crab in the shell). To sample something truly regional, try the Barbados *souse*, with marinated pieces of lean cooked pork. A steel band or some other local band sometimes accompanies the meals.

In the Harmony Suites, Rodney Bay Lagoon. ✆ 758/452-8711. Reservations recommended. Main courses EC$35–EC$85 (US$12.95–US$31.45). MC, V. Daily 7am–11pm.

Razmataz! INDIAN   Across from the Royal St. Lucian Hotel, this welcome entry into the island cuisine features delectable tandoori dishes, among other offerings. It's in an original Caribbean colonial timbered building with lots of gingerbread, decorated in a medley of colors and set in a garden, a 2-minute walk from the beach. A tempting array of starters greets you, everything from fresh local fish marinated in spicy yogurt and cooked in the tandoor to mulligatawny soup (made with lentils, herbs, and spices). Tandoori delights include shrimp, fresh fish such as snapper or mahi-mahi, chicken, and mixed grill, not to mention the best assortment of vegetarian dishes on the island. There's live music on weekends, and the owner is often the entertainer.

Rodney Bay Marina. ✆ 758/452-9800. Reservations recommended. Main courses EC$24–EC$55 (US$8.90–US$20.35). MC, V. Fri–Wed 4–11pm.

IN GROS ISLET

Great House ✿ FRENCH/CREOLE/INTERNATIONAL   Built on the foundation stones of the original plantation house of Cap Estate, this restaurant lies under a canopy of ampeche and cedar trees. The inviting ambience extends to the formal dining room, which opens onto a tranquil patio overlooking the sea. French cuisine is served here with Caribbean flair. The service, food, and wine are first rate. The menu is adjusted frequently to take advantage of the freshest ingredients. Begin with a callaloo cream soup or local crab back, with chives and a vinaigrette sauce. Creatively prepared main courses include a seafood casserole with coconut milk. To go local, try the St. Lucian beef, savory chicken, or pork pepper pot. For dessert, the coconut cheesecake with a tropical fruit topping is without equal.

Cap Estate. ✆ 758/450-0450. Reservations recommended. Main courses EC$39–EC$108 (US$14.45–US$39.95). AE, DC, DISC, MC, V. Tues–Sun 7–10pm.

4 Beaches

Since most of the island hotels are built right on the beach, you won't have to go far to swim. All beaches are open to the public, even those along hotel properties. However, if you use any of the hotel's beach equipment, you must pay for it. We prefer the beaches along the western coast, as a rough surf on the windward (east) side makes swimming there potentially dangerous. The best hotels are all on the western coast for a reason.

Leading beaches include **Pigeon Point Beach** off the north shore, part of the **Pigeon Island National Historic Park** (see below). The small beach here has white sand and is an ideal place for a picnic. Pigeon Island is joined to the mainland of St. Lucia by a causeway, so it's easy to reach.

The most frequented beach is **Reduit Beach** at Rodney Bay, a mile (2km) of soft beige sand fronting very clear waters. Many watersports kiosks can be found along the strip bordering Royal St. Lucian Hotel. With all its restaurants and bars, you'll find plenty of refueling stops.

Choc Bay is a long stretch of sand and palm trees on the northwestern coast, convenient to Castries and the big resorts. Its tranquil waters lure swimmers and especially families (including locals) with small children.

The 2-mile (3km) white-sand **Malabar Beach** runs parallel to the Vigie Airport runway, in Castries, to the Rendezvous resort. **Vigie Beach,** north of Castries Harbour, is also popular. It has fine beige sands, sloping gently into crystalline water. **La Toc Beach,** just south of Castries, opens onto a crescent-shaped bay containing golden sand.

Marigot Bay is the quintessential Caribbean cove, framed on three sides by steep emerald hills and skirted by palm trees. There are some small but secluded beaches here. The bay itself is an anchorage for some of the most expensive yachts in the Caribbean.

One of the most charming and hidden beaches of St. Lucia is the idyllic cove of **Anse Chastanet,** north of Soufrière. This is a beach connoisseur's delight. Towering palms provide shade from the fierce noonday sun, and lush hills are a refreshing contrast to the dark sandy strip.

The dramatic crescent-shaped bay of **Anse des Pitons** is at the foot of and between the twin peaks of the Pitons, south of Soufrière. The Jalousie Hilton transformed the natural black-sand beach by covering it with white sand; walk through the resort to get to it. It's popular with divers and snorkelers. While here, you can ask about a very special beach reached only by boat, the black volcanic sands and tranquil waters of **Anse Couchon.** With its shallow reefs, excellent snorkeling, and picture-postcard charm, this beach has become a hideaway for lovers. It's south of Anse-le-Raye.

You'll discover miles of white sand at the beach at **Vieux Fort,** at the southern end of the island. Reefs protect the crystal-clear waters here, making them tranquil and ideal for swimming. At the southern end of the windward side of the island is **Anse des Sables,** which opens onto a shallow bay swept by trade winds that make it great for windsurfing.

5 Sports & Other Outdoor Pursuits

BOATING   The most dramatic trip offered is aboard the 140-foot (42m) **Brig** *Unicorn* (© **758/452-5566**), used in the filming of the famous *Roots* TV miniseries. Passengers sail from Vigie Cove in Castries to Soufrière and the twin peaks of the Pitons, among other natural attractions of the island. A full-day sail costs $90.

CAMPING   Camping is now possible on St. Lucia courtesy of the **Environmental Educational Centre,** a division of the St. Lucia National Trust (© **758/452-5005**). This reserve, opened in 1998, features 12 campsites (with many more to be added) along a beautiful stretch of beach on historic Anse Liberté, in the fishing town of Canaries, 25 miles (40km) southwest of Castries and 8 miles (13km) north of Soufrière. Beachfront campsites, available for around $25 per night, offer a view of the harbor and of Martinique on a clear day. There are nearby community bathrooms and community cooking areas. The reserve has 5 miles (8km) of hiking trails; staff members give tours of the area and explain the rich history of the Anse Liberté, which literally translated means "freedom harbor." Camping equipment is available for rent.

DEEP-SEA FISHING   The waters around St. Lucia are known for their game fish, including blue marlin, sailfish, mako sharks, and barracuda, with tuna and kingfish among the edible catches. Most hotels can arrange fishing expeditions. Call **Mako Watersports** (© 758/452-0412), which offers half-day fishing trips for $360 and full-day trips for $720. **Captain Mike's** (© 758/452-7044) also conducts fishing trips, renting boats by the half day for $400 to $560, or a whole day in the $750 to $1,000 price range.

GOLF   St. Lucia has an 18-hole golf course (6,815 yards/6,202m, par 71) at the **Cap Estate Golf Club,** at the northern end of the island (© 758/450-9905). Greens fees are $95 for 18 holes, $70 for 9 holes; there are no caddies. Carts are included, and clubs can be rented for $20. Hours are from 7am to 6pm daily. Reservations are needed.

HIKING   A tropical rain forest covers a large area in the southern half of St. Lucia, and the St. Lucia Forest & Lands Department has proven to be a wise guardian of this resource. This forest reserve divides the western and eastern halves of the island. There are several trails, the most popular of which is the **Barre De L'Isle Trail,** located almost in the center of St. Lucia, southeast of Marigot Bay; it's a fairly easy trail that even children can handle. There are four panoramic lookout points, where you'll have a dramatic view of the sea where the Atlantic Ocean meets the Caribbean. It takes about an hour to walk this mile-long (2km) trail, which lies about a 30-minute ride from Castries. Guided hikes can usually be arranged through the major hotels or through the **Forest and Lands Department** (© 758/450-2231 or 758/450-2078).

HORSEBACK RIDING   North of Castries, you can ride at **Cas-En-Bas.** To make arrangements, call René Trim (© 758/450-8273). The cost is $40 for 1 hour, $50 for 2 hours. Ask about a picnic trip to the Atlantic, with a barbecue lunch and drinks included, for $70. Departures on horseback are at 8:30am, 10am, 2pm, and 4pm.

PARASAILING   Some say the most panoramic view of the northwest coast is from a point high over Rodney Bay. Parasailing is the key to this, and it's available at the watersports kiosk at the **Royal St. Lucian Hotel** at Rodney Bay (© 758/452-8351). The cost is $40.

SCUBA DIVING   In Soufrière, **Scuba St. Lucia,** in the Anse Chastanet Hotel (© 758/459-7000), offers one of the world's top dive locations at a five-star PADI dive center. At the southern end of Anse Chastanet's ¼-mile-long (.4km), secluded beach, it features premier diving and comprehensive facilities for divers of all levels. Some of the most spectacular coral reefs of St. Lucia, many only 10 to 20 feet (3–6m) below the surface, lie a short distance from the beach.

Many professional PADI instructors offer four dive programs a day. Photographic equipment is available for rent (film can be processed on the premises), and instruction is offered in picture taking. Experienced divers can rent any equipment they need. PADI certification courses are available. A 2- to 3-hour introductory lesson costs $85 and includes a short theory session, equipment familiarization, development of skills in shallow water, a tour of the reef, and all equipment. Single dives cost $35. Hours are from 8am to 5:45pm daily.

Another full-service scuba center is now available on St. Lucia's southwest coast at the new **Jalousie Hilton,** at Soufrière (© 758/459-7666). The PADI center offers dives in St. Lucia's National Marine Park; there are numerous shallow reefs near the shore. The diver certification program is available to hotel guests and other visitors ages 12 and up. Prices range from a single dive for $60 to a certification course for $535. Monday through Saturday, there's a daily resort course for noncertified divers that includes a supervised dive from the beach; it costs $83. All prices include equipment, tax, and service charges.

TENNIS   The best place for tennis on the island is the **St. Lucia Racquet Club,** adjacent to Club St. Lucia (© **758/450-0551**). It opened in 1991 and quickly became one of the finest tennis facilities in the Lesser Antilles. Its seven courts are maintained in state-of-the-art condition, and there's also a good pro shop on site. You must reserve 24 hours in advance. Guests of the hotel play for free; nonguests are charged $55 for a full day pass. Tennis racquets rent for $8 per hour.

If you're in the southern part of the island, a good, new program is offered by the **Jalousie Hilton,** at Soufrière (© **758/459-7666**). Vernon Lewis, the top-ranked player in St. Lucia, is the pro. You'll find four brand-new Laykold tennis courts (three lit for night play). Hotel guests play for free (though they pay for lessons). Nonguests can play for $35 per hour.

OTHER WATERSPORTS   The best all-around watersports center is **St. Lucian Watersports,** at the Rex St. Lucian Hotel (© **758/452-8351**). Water-skiing costs $15 for a 10- to 15-minute ride. Windsurfers can be rented for $18 for half an hour or $27 an hour. Snorkeling is free for guests of the hotel; nonguests pay $10 per hour for equipment.

6 Exploring the Island

Lovely little towns, beautiful beaches and bays, mineral baths, banana plantations—St. Lucia has all this and more. You can even visit a volcano.

Most hotel front desks will make arrangements for tours that take in all the major sights of St. Lucia. For example, **Sunlink Tours,** Reduit Beach Avenue (© **758/452-8232**), offers many island tours, including full-day boat trips along the west coast of Soufrière, the Pitons, and the volcano; the cost is $85 per person. Jeep safaris can be arranged for $100 apiece. One of the most popular jaunts is a rain-forest ramble for $55 by bus or $85 by Jeep. There's also a daily shopping tour for $25. The company has tour desks and/or representatives at most of the major hotels.

CASTRIES

The capital city has grown up around its **harbor,** which occupies the crater of an extinct volcano. Charter captains and the yachting set drift in here, and large cruise-ship wharves welcome vessels from around the world. Because it has been hit by several devastating fires (most recently in 1948) that destroyed almost all the old buildings, the town today has a look of newness, with glass-and-concrete (or steel) buildings replacing the French colonial or Victorian look typical of many West Indian capitals.

Castries may be architecturally dull, but its **public market** is one of the most fascinating in the West Indies, and our favorite people-watching site on the island. It goes full blast every day of the week except Sunday, and is most active on Friday and Saturday mornings. The market stalls are a block from Columbus Square along Peynier Street, running down toward the water. The country women dress up in traditional garb and cotton headdresses; the number of knotted points on top reveals their marital status (ask one of the locals to explain it to you). The luscious fruits and vegetables of St. Lucia may be new to you; the array of color alone is astonishing. Sample one of the numerous varieties of bananas: on St. Lucia, they're allowed to ripen on the tree, and taste completely different from those picked green and sold at supermarkets in the United States. You can also pick up St. Lucian handcrafts such as baskets and unglazed pottery here.

To the south of Castries looms **Morne Fortune,** the inappropriately named "Hill of Good Luck." In the 18th century, some of the most savage battles between the French and the British took place here. You can visit the military cemetery, a small museum, the old powder magazine, and the "Four Apostles Battery" (a quartet of grim muzzle-loading cannons). Government House, now the official residence of the governor-general of St. Lucia, is one of the few examples of Victorian architecture that escaped destruction by fire. The private gardens are beautifully planted, aflame with scarlet and purple bougainvillea. Morne Fortune also offers what many consider the most scenic lookout perch in the Caribbean. The view of the harbor of Castries is panoramic: You can see north to Pigeon Island or south to the Pitons; on a clear day, you may even spot Martinique. To reach Morne Fortune, head east on Bridge Street.

PIGEON ISLAND NATIONAL HISTORIC PARK ✪

St. Lucia's first **national park** is joined to the mainland by a causeway. On its west coast are two white-sand beaches (see "Beaches," above). There's also a restaurant, Jambe de Bois, named after a wooden-legged pirate who once used the island as a hideout.

Pigeon Island offers an **Interpretation Centre,** equipped with artifacts and a multimedia display on local history, ranging from the Amerindian occupation of A.D. 1000 to the Battle of the Saints, when Admiral Rodney's fleet set out from Pigeon Island and defeated Admiral De Grasse in 1782. The Captain's Cellar Olde English Pub lies under the center and is evocative of an 18th-century English bar.

Pigeon Island, only 44 acres (18 hectares) in size, got its name from the redneck pigeon, or ramier, that once made this island home. It's ideal for picnics, weddings, and nature walks. The park is open daily from 9am to 5pm, charging an entrance fee of EC$13.50 (US$5). For more information, call the **St. Lucia National Trust (© 758/452-5005).**

RODNEY BAY ✪

This scenic bay is a 15-minute drive north of Castries. Set on a man-made lagoon, it has become a chic center for nightlife, hotels, and restaurants—in fact, it's the most active place on the island at night. Its marina is one of the top watersports centers in the Caribbean, and a destination every December for the Atlantic Rally for Cruisers, when yachties cross the Atlantic to meet and compare stories.

MARIGOT BAY ✪

Movie crews, including those for Rex Harrison's *Dr. Doolittle* and Sophia Loren's *Fire Power,* have used this bay, one of the most beautiful in the Caribbean, for background shots. Eight miles (13km) south of Castries, it's narrow yet navigable by yachts of any size. Here Admiral Rodney camouflaged his ships with palm leaves while lying in wait for French frigates. The shore, lined with palm trees, remains relatively unspoiled, although some building sites have been sold. It's a delightful spot for a picnic. A 24-hour ferry connects the bay's two sides.

SOUFRIÈRE

This little fishing port, St. Lucia's second-largest settlement, is dominated by two pointed hills called **Petit Piton** and **Gros Piton** ✪✪✪. The Pitons, two

Finds Discovering "Forgotten" Grande Anse

The northeast coast is the least visited and least accessible part of St. Lucia, but it contains dramatic rockbound shores interspersed with secret sandy coves. The government has set Grand Anse aside as a nature reserve so that it will never be developed. The terrain is arid and can be unwelcoming, but it is fascinating nonetheless. Grande Anse is home to some rare bird species, notably the white-breasted thrasher, as well as the fer-de-lance, the only poisonous snake on the island (but visitors report rarely seeing them). Its beaches—Grande Anse, Petite Anse, and Anse Louvet—are nesting grounds for endangered sea turtles, including the hawksbill, the green turtle, the leatherback, and the loggerhead. Nesting season lasts from February to October. Many locals tackle the poor road in a four-wheel-drive vehicle, especially the bumpiest part from Desbarra to Grande Anse.

volcanic cones rising to 2,460 and 2,619 feet (738m and 696m), have become the very symbol of St. Lucia. Formed of lava and rock, and once actively volcanic, they are now covered in green vegetation. Their sheer rise from the sea makes them a landmark visible for miles around, and waves crash at their bases. It's recommended that you attempt to climb only Gros Piton, but doing so requires the permission of the **Forest and Lands Department** (© 758/450-2078) and the company of a knowledgeable guide.

Near Soufrière lies the famous "drive-in" volcano, **Mount Soufrière** ★★, a rocky lunar landscape of bubbling mud and craters seething with sulfur. You literally drive your car into a millions-of-years-old crater and walk between the sulfur springs and pools of hissing steam. Entrance costs EC$7 (US$2.60) per person and includes the services of your guide, who will point out the blackened waters, among the few of their kind in the Caribbean. Hours are daily from 9am to 5pm; for more information, call © 758/459-7200.

Nearby are the **Diamond Mineral Baths** (© 758/452-4759) in the **Diamond Botanical Gardens** ★. Deep in the lush tropical gardens is the Diamond Waterfall, one of the geological attractions of the island. Created from water bubbling up from sulfur springs, the waterfall changes colors (from yellow to black to green to gray) several times a day. The baths were constructed in 1784 on the orders of Louis XVI, whose doctors told him these waters were similar in mineral content to the waters at Aix-les-Bains; they were intended to provide recuperative effects for French soldiers fighting in the West Indies. The baths have an average temperature of 106°F. For EC$10 (US$3.70), you can bathe and try out the recuperative effects for yourself.

From Soufrière in the southwest, the road winds toward Fond St-Jacques, where you'll have a good view of mountains and villages as you cut through St. Lucia's Cape Moule-Chique tropical rain forest. You'll also see the Barre de l'Isle divide.

NATURE RESERVES

The fertile volcanic soil of St. Lucia sustains a rich diversity of bird and animal life. Some of the richest troves for ornithologists are in protected precincts off the St. Lucian coast, in either of two national parks, Fregate Islands Nature Reserve and the Maria Islands Nature Reserve.

The **Fregate Islands** are a cluster of rocks a short distance offshore from Praslin Bay, midway up St. Lucia's eastern coastline. Barren except for tall grasses that seem to thrive in the salt spray, the islands were named after the scissor-tailed frigate birds (*Fregata magnificens*) that breed here. Between May and July, large colonies of the graceful birds fly in well-choreographed formations over islands that you can only visit under the closely supervised permission of government authorities. Many visitors believe that the best way to admire the Fregate Islands (and to respect their fragile ecosystems) is to walk along the nature trail that the St. Lucian government has hacked along the cliff top of the St. Lucian mainland, about 150 feet (45m) inland from the shoreline. Even without binoculars, you'll be able to see the frigates wheeling overhead. You'll also enjoy eagle's-eye views of the unusual geology of the St. Lucian coast, which includes sea caves, dry ravines, a waterfall (which flows only during rainy season), and a strip of mangrove swamp.

The **Maria Islands** are larger and more arid and are almost constantly exposed to salt-laden winds blowing up from the equator. Set to the east of St. Lucia's southernmost tip, off the town of Vieux Fort, they contain a strictly protected biodiversity. The approximately 30 acres (12 hectares) of cactus-dotted land comprising the two largest islands (Maria Major and Maria Minor) are home to more than 120 species of plants, lizards, butterflies, and snakes that are believed to be extinct in other parts of the world. These include the large ground lizard (*Zandolite*) and the nocturnal, nonvenomous kouwes snake (*Dromicus ornatus*).

The Marias are also a bird refuge, populated by such species as the sooty tern, the bridled tern, the Caribbean martin, the red-billed tropicbird, and the brown noddy, which usually builds its nest under the protective thorns of prickly pear cactus.

Tours to either island must be arranged through the staff of the **St. Lucia National Trust** (© 758/454-5014). Full-day excursions, including the boat ride to the refuge and the guided tour, cost $70 for the Fregates and $85 for the Marias (the Marias jaunt includes lunch).

7 Shopping

Most of the shopping is in **Castries,** where the principal streets are William Peter Boulevard and Bridge Street. Many stores will sell you goods at duty-free prices (providing you don't take the merchandise with you but have it delivered to the airport or cruise dock). There are some good (but not remarkable) buys in bone china, jewelry, perfume, watches, liquor, and crystal.

Built for the cruise-ship passenger, **Pointe Seraphine, in Castries,** has the best collection of shops on the island, along with offices for car rentals, organized taxi service (for sightseeing), a bureau de change, a philatelic bureau, an information center, and international phones. Cruise ships berth right at the shopping center. Under red roofs in a Spanish-style setting, the complex requires that you present a cruise pass or an airline ticket to the shopkeeper when purchasing goods. Visitors can take away their purchases, except liquor and tobacco, which will be delivered to the airport. The center is open in winter, Monday to Friday from 8am to 5pm and Saturday from 8am to 2pm; off-season, Monday to Saturday from 9am to 4pm. It's also open when cruise ships are in port.

On Gros Islet Highway, 2 miles (3km) north of Castries, **Gablewoods Mall** contains three restaurants and one of the densest concentrations of shops on the island.

8 St. Lucia After Dark

There isn't much nightlife in St. Lucia besides the entertainment offered by hotels. In the winter, at least one hotel has a steel band or calypso music every night of the week. Otherwise, check to see what's happening at **Capone's** (© 758/452-0284) or the **Green Parrot** (© 758/452-3167), both in Castries.

Indies, at Rodney Bay (© 758/452-0727), is a split-floor, soundproof dance club with a large wooden dancing area and stage. There's also a trio of bars, with smoking and no-smoking sections. The DJs keep the joint jumping, with both West Indian and international sounds, often American. The action gets going Wednesday, Friday, and Saturday from 11pm to 4am. There's a cover costing men EC$25 (US$9.25), women EC$15 (US$5.55). Indies has opened a bar around the side of the building called the **Back Door,** featuring alternative music and reggae. A sort of rock and sports bar, it serves snacks until 3am.

One of the island's most action-packed dance clubs is **Folley,** Rodney Bay (© 758/450-0022), adjoining La Creole Restaurant. Patrons age 21 and up can enter to enjoy a wide array of music from reggae to rock. Entrance is EC$20 (US$7.40).

If you'd like to go barhopping, begin at **Banana Split,** on St. George's Street in Castries (© 758/450-8125). This is a popular hangout that often offers live entertainment, as does **Shamrocks Pub,** Rodney Bay (© 758/452-8725). This Irish-style pub is especially popular among boaters and gets really lively on weekends.

Up on Pigeon Island is **Captain's Cellar** (© 758/458-0078), not very St. Lucian, but it draws a lot of expats to its informal English pub site, especially on weekends when live jazz is featured.

Among the dance clubs, **Late Lime,** Reduit Beach (© 758/452-0761), is heavily patronized by the islanders themselves, although visitors go here as well. A DJ plays dance music nightly. **The Chalet,** Rodney Bay (© 758/450-0022), near La Creole Restaurant, lies at Rodney Bay marina, luring dancing feet to its wild disco nights. Some of the best zouk and salsa are played here.

St. Maarten/St. Martin

For an island with a big reputation for its restaurants, hotels, and energetic nightlife, St. Maarten is small—only 37 square miles (96 sq. km), about half the area of Washington, D.C. An island divided between the Netherlands and France, St. Maarten (Sint Maarten) is the Dutch half, and St. Martin is French. Legend has it that a gin-drinking Dutchman and a wine-guzzling Frenchman walked around the island to see how much territory each could earmark for his country in a day; the Frenchman out-walked the Dutchman, but the canny Dutchman got the more valuable piece of property.

The divided island is the smallest territory in the world shared by two sovereign states. The only way you'll know you're crossing an international border is when you see the sign BIENVENUE PARTIE FRANÇAISE, attesting to the peaceful coexistence between the two nations. The island was officially split in 1648, and many visitors still ascend Mount Concordia, near the border, where the agreement was reached. Even so, St. Maarten changed hands 16 times before it became permanently Dutch.

Returning visitors who haven't been to the island for a while are often shocked when they see today's St. Maarten. No longer a sleepy Caribbean backwater, it's become a boomtown in recent years. Many hotels and restaurants sustained serious structural damage from Hurricane Luis in September 1995 but have since reopened, with freshly renovated facilities, new and often better menus, and energized staffs. A sense of freshness and rejuvenation now permeates the island.

Duty-free shopping has turned the island into a virtual mall, and the Dutch capital, Philipsburg, is often bustling with cruise-ship hordes. The nightlife is among the best in the Caribbean, with lively happy hours and casinos galore. Sunshine is pretty much guaranteed year-round on St. Maarten, so you can swim, snorkel, and sail almost any day. The island's 36 white-sand beaches remain unspoiled, and the clear turquoise waters are even more enticing.

Despite its natural beauty, much has been lost to the bulldozer on St. Maarten, too. This is obviously not an island for people who don't like crowds, so if you want to get away from it all, we suggest heading over to the nearby Dutch islands of St. Eustatius (Statia) and Saba (or choosing another getaway, such as the British Virgin Islands). Even the French side of the island would suit you much better. Nevertheless, in spite of its problems, including crime, occasional storms, traffic congestion, and corruption, St. Maarten continues to attract massive numbers of visitors who want a Caribbean island vacation with a splash of Las Vegas.

The Dutch capital, **Philipsburg,** curves like a toy village along Great Bay. The town lies on a narrow sand isthmus separating Great Bay and the Great Salt Pond. The capital was founded in 1763 by Commander John Philips, a Scot in Dutch employ. To protect Great Bay, Fort Amsterdam was built in 1737.

The main thoroughfare is busy **Front Street,** which stretches for about a mile (2km) and is lined with stores selling international merchandise, such as French fashions and Swedish crystal. More shops are along the little lanes, known as *steegijes,* that connect Front Street with Back Street, another shoppers' haven.

The French side of the island has a slightly different character. It's been undergoing a building boom of late, with lots of new hotels opening, but for now at least, it's still much sleepier than the Dutch side. Most hotels here tend to be quieter and more secluded than their Dutch counterparts, and you won't be overwhelmed with cruise-ship crowds. There are no dazzling sights, there's no spectacular nightlife. Even the sports scene on St. Martin isn't as well organized as on many Caribbean islands (though the Dutch side has golf and other diversions). Most people come to St. Martin just to relax on its many white-sand beaches. Mostly they come to sample "France in the tropics."

French St. Martin does, however, boast some of the best cuisine in the Caribbean, with an extraordinary number of good bistros and restaurants. It has a distinctly French air. Police officers, for example, wear *képis.* The towns have names like Colombier and Orléans, the streets are *rues,* and the French flag flies over the *gendarmerie* in **Marigot,** the capital. Its advocates cite it as distinctly more sophisticated, prosperous, stylish, and cosmopolitan than its neighboring *départements d'outre-mer,* Guadeloupe and Martinique.

French St. Martin is governed from Guadeloupe and has direct representation in the government in Paris. The principal town on the French side is Marigot, the seat of the subprefect and municipal council. Visitors come here not only for shopping, as the island is a free port, but also to enjoy the excellent cookery in the Creole bistros.

Marigot is not quite the same size as its counterpart, Philipsburg, in the Dutch sector. It has none of the frenzied pace of Philipsburg, which is often overrun with cruise-ship passengers. In fact, Marigot looks like a French village transplanted to the Caribbean. If you climb the hill over this tiny port, you'll be rewarded with a view from the old fort.

About 20 minutes by car beyond Marigot is **Grand-Case,** a small fishing village that's an outpost of French civilization, with many good restaurants and a few places to stay.

1 Essentials

VISITOR INFORMATION

If you're going to either **Dutch St. Maarten** or **French St Martin,** contact the St. Maarten/St Martin Tourist Office, 675 Third Ave., Suite 1807, New York, NY 10017 (© 800/786-2278 or 212/953-2084 for the department servicing the Dutch side, and © 877/956-1234 or 212/475-8970 for the department servicing the French side). In Canada, the office for information about both sides of the island is located at 703 Evans Ave., Suite 106, Toronto, Ontario M9C 5E9 (© 416/622-4300 for information about life on either side of the island.) Once on the island, go to the **Tourist Information Bureau,** Vineyard Park, 33 W. G. Buncamper Road, Philipsburg, St. Maarten, N.A. (© 599/54-22337), open Monday to Friday from 8am to noon and 1 to 5pm.

The tourist board on French St. Martin, called the **Office du Tourisme,** is at Route de San dy Ground, Marigot, 97150 St. Martin (© 590/ 87-57-21), open Monday to Friday from 8:30am to 1pm and 2:30 to 5:30pm, Saturday from 8am to noon.

St. Maarten/St. Martin

ST. MAARTEN

ACCOMMODATIONS
Belair Beach Hotel **8**
Caravanserai Beach Resort **17**
Divi Little Bay Beach Resort **9**
Holland House **3**
Horny Toad Guesthouse **13**
Maho Beach Hotel & Casino **20**
Mary's Boon Beach Plantation **15**
Oyster Bay Beach Resort **1**
Pasanggrahan **2**
The Pelican **11**

DINING
Antoine's **5**
The Boathouse **16**
Cheri's Café **18**
Da Livio Ristorante **7**
Kangaroo Court **4**
La Vista **10**
Le Perroquet **19**
Saratoga **14**
Wajang Doll **6**

ST. MARTIN

ACCOMMODATIONS
Captain Oliver's Resort Hotel **54**
Club Orient Naturist Resort **51**
Esmeralda Resort **47**
Grand Case Beach Club **36**
Hotel Beach Plaza **25**
Hotel L'Esplanade Caraïbes **34**
Hotel St-Tropez des Caraïbes **50**
La Plantation Orient Bay Resort **52**
La Résidence **26**
La Samanna **21**
Le Méridien L'Habitation/
    Le Domaine **46**
Le Mississippi **53**
Le Petit Hotel **37**
Le Royale Louisiana **27**
Mercure Simson Beach Coralia **23**
Nettlé Bay Beach Club **22**

DINING
Calmos Café **33**
Friar's Bay Beach Café **32**
Hélvéa **38**
Il Nettuno **39**
Kakao **49**
Kon Tiki **48**
La Brasserie de Marigot **28**
La Marine **40**
La Vie en Rose **30**
Le Cottage **41**
Le Pressoir **42**
Le Tropicana **31**
L'Oizeau Rare **29**
Mahogany **53**
Mario's Bistro **24**
Michael's Café **43**
Rainbow Café **44**
The Rib Shack **35**
Sunset Café **45**
Turtle Bar Pier
    & Restaurant **12**

Pointe
Arago

Pointe
du Bluff

Pointe du Plum

Baie aux
Prunes

Baie Rouge

22 *Baie Nettlé*

*Baie de
Marigot*

Mari

26-31

25

Nettlé Beach

23

Marigot
Fort ■

24

Baie Longue

21

Cupecoy Bay Beach

Simpson Bay Lagoon

Mullet Bay Beach

Queen Juliana
International
Airport

20 19

■ Border
Monume

Caribbean Sea

Maho Bay Beach

18 ✈

17

12-16

Simpson
Bay Beach

Koolba

11

10

*Cole
Bay*

C. A. Cannegieter St.

Schrijnwerkersteeg

Back St.

Walter Nisbet Rd.

Front St.

7 6 5

Back St.

Front St.

St. Jansteeg

Great Bay Beach

4

Kerksteeg

3

Philipsburg

2

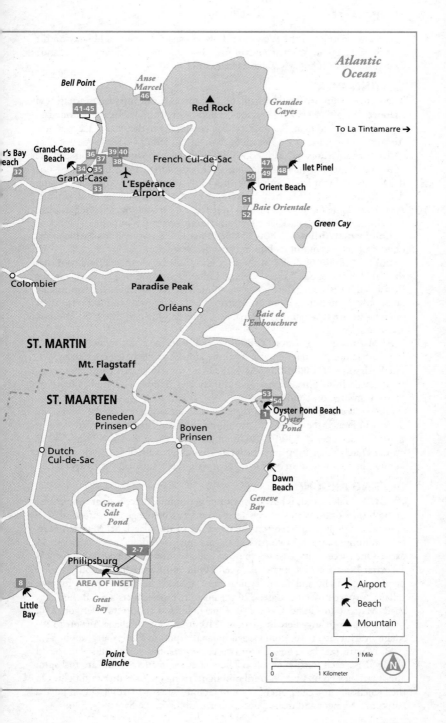

Atlantic
Ocean

Bell Point

*Anse
Marcel*
46

Red Rock

*Grandes
Cayes*

To La Tintamarre →

r's Bay
each

**Grand-Case
Beach**

32

36 37

39 40
38

34 35

Grand-Case

33

French Cul-de-Sac

47
49 48

Ilet Pinel

50

Orient Beach

**L'Espérance
Airport**

51

Baie Orientale

52

Green Cay

Colombier

Paradise Peak

Orléans

*Baie de
l'Embouchure*

ST. MARTIN

Mt. Flagstaff

ST. MAARTEN

**Beneden
Prinsen**

**Boven
Prinsen**

53
54

Oyster Pond Beach

1

*Oyster
Pond*

Dutch
Cul-de-Sac

**Dawn
Beach**

*Geneve
Bay*

*Great
Salt
Pond*

2-7

Philipsburg

AREA OF INSET

8

**Little
Bay**

*Great
Bay*

**Point
Blanche**

✈ Airport

☂ Beach

▲ Mountain

| 0 | | 1 Mile |
| 0 | | 1 Kilometer |

N

For information on the Web about how to creatively spend a holiday on the French side, go to **www.st-martin.org**. For information about the island's Dutch side, search out **www.st-maarten.com**.

GETTING THERE

There are two airports on the island. St. Maarten's **Queen Juliana International Airport** (© 599/54-54211) is the second-busiest airport in the Caribbean, topped only by San Juan, Puerto Rico. You can also fly to the smaller **L'Espérance Airport,** in Grand-Case on French St. Martin (© 590/87-53-03).

American Airlines (© 800/433-7300 in the U.S.; www.aa.com) offers more options and more frequent service into St. Maarten than any other airline—one daily nonstop flight from both New York's JFK and Miami. Additional nonstop daily flights into St. Maarten are offered by American and its local affiliate, **American Eagle** (© 800/433-7300 in the U.S.; www.aa.com), from San Juan. Ask about American's package tours, which can save you a bundle.

Continental Airlines (© 800/231-0856 in the U.S.; www.flycontinental.com) offers daily flights out of its hub in Newark, New Jersey.

LIAT (© 800/468-0482 in the U.S. and Canada; www.liatairline.com) has three flights out of San Juan, non-stop. Other flights stop first at Tortola in the British Virgin Islands before going on to St. Maarten. Even so, the trip usually takes only 90 minutes. From St. Martin, LIAT, often with connections, offers ongoing service to Anguilla, Antigua, St. Croix, San Juan, St. Kitts, St. Thomas, and Dominica.

ALM Antillean Airlines (© 800/327-7230 in the U.S.; www.alm-airlines. com) offers nonstop daily service from the airline's home base on Curaçao.

US Airways (© 800/428-4322 in the U.S.; www.usairways.com) offers non-stop service from Philadelphia on Saturday and Sunday and from Charlotte, North Carolina, on Sunday.

If you're coming from St. Barts, there's at least one airline serving the short route directly to French-speaking St. Martin. It includes **Air Caraïbes** (formerly known as Air Guadeloupe; © 590/87-10-36 on the French side, and © 599/54-54212 on the Dutch side). It operates between 15 and 20 daily flights, each about 10 minutes in duration, from St. Barts, about a third of which land at L'Espérance.

GETTING AROUND

BY TAXI   Taking taxis is how most visitors get around. Since taxis are unmetered on both sides of the island, always agree on the rate before getting into a cab.

Rates are slightly different on the two sides of the island. **St. Maarten taxis** have minimum fares for two passengers, and each additional passenger pays $4 extra. One piece of luggage per person is allowed free; each additional piece is $1 extra. Fares are 25% higher between 10pm and midnight, and 50% higher between midnight and 6am. Typical fares around the island are as follows: Juliana Airport to Grand Case: $20 for up to two passengers and all their luggage; Marigot to Grand Case, $10; Queen Juliana airport to Marigot, $10; Juliana airport to anywhere in Marigot, $10; from Queen Juliana Airport to the Maho Beach Hotel is $6; from Queen Juliana Airport to Philipsburg, about $12.

St. Martin taxi fares are also for two passengers, but you should plan to add about $1 for each suitcase or valise. These fares are in effect from 7am to 10pm; after that, they go up by 25% until midnight, rising by 50% after midnight. On the French side, the fare from Marigot to Grand-Case is $10, from Queen Juliana Airport to Marigot and from Queen Juliana Airport to La Samanna, $20.

For late-night cab service on St. Maarten, call © **599/ 54-54317. Taxi Service & Information Center** operates at the port of Marigot (© **590/87-56-54**) on the French side of the island.

BY RENTAL CAR   Especially if you want to experience both the Dutch and the French sides of the island, you might want to rent a car. The taxi drivers' union strictly enforces a law that forbids anyone from picking up a car at the airport. As a result, every rental agency delivers cars directly to your hotel, where an employee will complete the paperwork. If you prefer to rent a car on arrival, head for one of the tiny rental kiosks across the road from the airport, but beware of long lines.

Budget (© **800/472-3325** in the U.S., 599/54-54030 on the Dutch side, or 590/87-38-22 on the French side; www.budgetrentacar.com), **Hertz** (© **800/ 654-3131** in the U.S., 599/54-54314 on the Dutch side, or 590/87-83-71 on the French side; www.hertz.com), and **Avis** (© **800/331-1084** in the U.S., 599/54-52847 on the Dutch side, or 590/87-50-60 on the French side; www.avis.com) all maintain offices on both sides of the island. **National** (© **800/328-4567** in the U.S., 599/54-42168 in Cole Bay, or 599/54-96856 at Queen Juliana Airport; www.nationalcar.com) has offices only on the Dutch side. All these companies charge roughly equivalent rates.

All three major car-rental agencies require that renters be at least 25 years old. Your credit-card issuer may provide insurance coverage, so check before your trip; otherwise, it may be wise to buy the fairly cheap collision-damage waiver (CDW) when you rent.

Drive on the right-hand side on both the French and Dutch sides of the island, and expect traffic jams near the major towns. International road signs are observed, and there are no Customs formalities at the border between the two sides of the island.

BY MINIBUS   Minibus is a reasonable means of transport on St. Maarten/St. Martin if you don't mind inconveniences and overcrowding at times. Buses run daily from 7am to midnight and serve most of the major locations on both sides of the island. The most popular run is from Philipsburg on the Dutch side to Marigot on the French side. Privately owned and operated, minibuses tend to follow specific routes, with fares ranging from $1.50 to $2.50, depending on how far you travel.

BY SCOOTER   Some of the best bike deals are at Eugene Motos, at Baie Nettlé (© **590/29-65-89**), and at Location des Roues, Centre Commerciale Baie Nettlé (© **590/87-20-59**), both just across the border on the French side. Both of rent scooters for $24 per day, with motorbikes (here, defined as something bigger than a scooter) beginning around $40 a day.

 FAST FACTS: **St. Maarten/St. Martin**

Banks On the Dutch side, most banks are open Monday to Thursday from 8:30am to 1pm, Friday from 8:30am to 1pm and 4 to 5pm. On the French side, they are also usually open every weekday afternoon from 2 to 4 or 5pm. It's easy to find ATMs. On the Dutch side, several banks are clustered along Front Street in Philipsburg. On the French side, most banks are along rue de la République in Marigot.

Currency Despite the dominance of the Euro since January 2002 within the mother country, Holland, the legal tender on the Dutch side is still the **Netherlands Antilles guilder (NAf)**; the official exchange rate is NAf 1.77 for each U.S.$1. Despite its status as the Dutch side's official currency, U.S. dollars are widely accepted, and prices in hotels and most restaurants and shops are widely designated in dollars as well. On the French side, the official monetary unit is the Euro, with most establishments widely quoting and accepting either dollars or Naf guilders as well. At press time, the U.S. dollar converted into Euros at a rate of $1 US = 1.12 Euros (or 1€ = 89.3¢). (Just before you leave home, you can check the current exchange rates on the Web at **www.x-rates.com**.) *Prices throughout this chapter are given in U.S. currency for establishments on the Dutch side, and in either Euros or dollars for establishments on the French side.*

Documents U.S., British, and Canadian citizens should have a passport, plus an ongoing or return ticket and a confirmed hotel reservation. In lieu of a passport, U.S. citizens can get away with presenting two pieces of photo I.D., but frankly, we get the strong feeling that local authorities prefer presentation of a passport instead. We always recommend that you travel with your passport.

Electricity Dutch St. Maarten uses the same voltage (110-volt AC, 60 cycles) with the same electrical configurations as the United States, so adapters and transformers are not necessary. However, on French St. Martin, you'll usually need transformers and adapters. To simplify things, many hotels on both sides of the island have installed built-in sockets suitable for both European and North American appliances.

Emergencies On the Dutch side, call the **police** at ☎ **599/54-22222** or an **ambulance** at ☎ **599/54-22111**. On the French side, you can reach the **police** by dialing ☎ **17** or 590/87-50-06. In case of **fire**, dial ☎ **18**.

Hospitals On the Dutch side, go to the **Medical Center**, Welegen Road, Cay Hill (☎ **599/54-31111**). On the French side, the local hospital is **Hôpital de Marigot**, Rue de l'Hôpital in Marigot (☎ **590/87-50-07**).

Language The language on the St. Maarten side is officially Dutch, and it's officially French on St. Martin. But most people speak English. A French-based patois is spoken by a small segment of the local populace.

Liquor Laws On both sides of the island, liquor is sold in grocery and liquor stores on any day of the week. It's legal to have an open container in public, though the authorities are very strict with any littering, disorderly behavior, or drunk driving.

Safety If possible, avoid night driving—it's particularly unwise to drive on remote, unlit, back roads at night. Also, let that deserted, isolated beach remain so. You're safer in a crowd, although under no circumstances should you ever leave anything unguarded on the beach.

Taxes & Service Charges There is no departure tax imposed for departures from Espérance Airport on the French side. However, for departures from Queen Juliana Airport on the Dutch side, there's a departure tax of $20 ($6 if you're leaving the island for St. Eustatius or Saba).

On the Dutch side, a government tax of between 5% and 8%, depending on the category of hotel you stay in, is added to hotel bills. On the

French side, hotels must levy a *taxe de séjour;* this differs from hotel to hotel, depending on its classification, but is often $4 a day. In addition to these taxes, most hotels add a (mandatory) service charge of around 15% to your hotel bill as well.

Telephone To call Dutch St. Maarten from the United States, dial **011** (the international access code), then **599** (the country code for the Netherlands Antilles), followed by **54** and then the five-digit local number. To make a local call on Dutch St. Maarten, dial **54,** then the five-digit local number. But if you're calling "long distance" from the Dutch side of the island to the French side of the island, dial **00,** followed by **590590** (the most prevalent international access code for French St. Martin) or in rare instances **590690,** followed by the six-digit local number.

If you're on the French side of the island and want to call anyone on the Dutch side, dial **00,** followed by **599,** then **54** and the five-digit local number. Know in advance that calls between the French and Dutch sides are considered long-distance calls and are much, much more expensive than you might have imagined, considering the relatively short distances involved.

French St. Martin is linked to the Guadeloupe telephone system. To call French St. Martin from the United States, dial **011** (the international access code), then **590590** (the country code for Guadeloupe) and the six-digit local number. To make a call from French St. Martin to any point within French St. Martin, no codes are necessary; just dial the local six-digit French number.

To call the United States from the island, dial **AT&T Direct** at ✆ **0800/ 99-00-11.** To reach **MCI,** dial ✆ **0800/99-00-19,** and to reach **Sprint,** dial ✆ **0800/99-0087.**

Tipping Most hotels on both sides on the island add a 10% or 15% service charge to your bill; make sure you understand whether or not it's already included in the original price quoted to you. Most restaurants automatically add a service charge to your bill. If service has not been added (unlikely), it's customary to tip around 15% in restaurants. Taxi drivers also expect a 15% tip.

Time St. Maarten and St. Martin operate on Atlantic standard time year-round. Thus in winter, if it's 6pm in Philipsburg, it's 5pm in New York. During daylight saving time in the United States, the island and the U.S. east coast are on the same time.

Water The water on the island is safe to drink. In fact, most hotels serve desalinated water.

Weather The island has a year-round temperature of about 80°F.

2 Accommodations

IN DUTCH ST. MAARTEN

Remember, a government tax of between 5% and 8%, plus a service charge of 10% to 15% will be added to your hotel bill. Ask whether it's included in the original rates you're quoted to save yourself a shock when you check out.

VERY EXPENSIVE/EXPENSIVE

Belair Beach Hotel ⭐ *Kids*   Many visitors find this place a good value, especially families, who appreciate the kitchens and the fact that children stay free. Originally built in 1980, a 10-minute drive from the airport, this hotel has lasted because of excellent management, good maintenance, and a reputation for quality and good value. With some unusual Middle Eastern architectural touches, it rises above a smallish swimming pool and beach. The units are all two-bedroom suites, each with a rather large master bedroom, two full bathrooms with shower/tub combinations, a fully equipped kitchen (there's an on-site grocery store), and a 21-foot (6m) terrace with a sweeping view of the sea. The suites are either time-shares or privately owned condos that are rented to visitors when their owners are not on the island.

Belair (P.O. Box 940), Philipsburg, St. Maarten, N.A. ✆ **800/933-3264** in the U.S., or 599/54-23362. Fax 599/54-25295. www.sxmhotels.com. 72 units. Winter $375 1-bedroom suite; $409–$499 2-bedroom suite. Off-season $209 1-bedroom suite; $249–$389 2-bedroom suite. Children age 17 and under stay free in parents' suite (subject to availability). AE, DC, DISC, MC, V. **Amenities:** Restaurant, bar; pool; 2 tennis courts; watersports; car rental; babysitting; laundry. *In room:* A/C, TV, radio, hair dryer.

Caravanserai Beach Resort ⭐   This long-time favorite at the airport keeps getting blown away by hurricanes, but it has bounced back once again to claim its place as one of the island's leading hostelries. It fronts a small beach where the hotel has erected a sea wall to prevent any more incursions from the sea. The place has a fresh new look, with a spa, freshly planted palms, waterfalls, and rock pools. Accommodations are spacious and tastefully furnished, with shower/tub combinations, a mixture of pastel colors and dark-stained wood trim, and much comfort. You can choose between sea-view rooms and units opening onto the gardens.

2 Beacon Hill Rd., St. Maarten, N.A. ✆ **800/616-1154** in the U.S., or 599/54-54000. Fax 599/54-54001. www.caravan-sxm.com. 66 units. Winter $210–$270 double; $395 1-bedroom apt. Off-season $160–$190 double; $350 1-bedroom apt. AE, MC, V. **Amenities:** 2 restaurants, 3 bars; casino; 3 pools; 2 tennis courts; spa with massage facilities; 3 Jacuzzis. *In room:* A/C, TV, hair dryer, unstocked fridge, ironing board, safe.

Divi Little Bay Beach Resort ⭐   Built on a desirable peninsula about a 10-minute drive east of the airport, this hotel sits on a sandy beach that's rocky in part. It originated as a simple guesthouse in 1955, and it soon became famous as the vacation home of the Netherlands' Queen Juliana, Prince Bernhard, and Queen Beatrix. After several massive enlargements and modifications, it was severely damaged during the hurricanes of the early 1990s, and then it was rebuilt in 1997 as the flagship of the Divi chain (though it feels as if the hotel continues to try to find itself—it keeps changing its image and marketing strategies). Its new design evokes a European seaside village, with pastel stucco walls and terra-cotta roofs, with some Dutch colonial touches. In the upper reaches of the property are the ruins of Fort Amsterdam, once Dutch St. Maarten's most prized military stronghold and today a decorative historical site. Gardens are carefully landscaped, and Divi has improved the nearby beach after it suffered massive erosion.

This hotel development is larger than its 235 units imply, since part of it is devoted to the maintenance and marketing of time-share units. Sometimes it evokes a large residential apartment complex that's enhanced with hotel-style amenities and services. Accommodations are airy, accented with ceramic tiles and pastel colors; most units have kitchens. Bathrooms tend to be small and compact, but have adequate shelf space and a shower/tub combination.

Little Bay (P.O. Box 961), Philipsburg, St. Maarten, N.A. ✆ **800/367-3484** in the U.S., or 599/54-22333. Fax 599/54-25410. www.diviresorts.com. 235 units. Winter $210 double; $215–$302 1-bedroom apt.; $425

2-bedroom apt.; Off-season $155 double, $180–$235 1-bedroom apt.; $375 2-bedroom apt.; AE, DC, MC, V.
Amenities: Restaurant, bar; 3 pools; 2 tennis courts; watersports; laundry. *In room:* A/C, TV.

Horny Toad Guesthouse ★ *Value*   This place is homey and welcoming. It's
run by an expatriate from Maine, Betty Vaughan. Seven well-maintained units
are in an amply proportioned beachside house originally built in the 1950s as a
private home by the island's former governor. The eighth room is in half of an
octagonal "round house," with large windows and views of the sea. Guestrooms
range from medium-size to spacious, and each has a kitchenette, a good-quality
mattress, and a small but well-kept shower-only bathroom. There's no pool, no
restaurant, and no organized activities of any kind, although the beach is a few
steps away, and there are often impromptu get-togethers around the pair of gas-
fired barbecues. The only drawback is that the hotel is near the airport, but the
roar of jumbo jets is heard only a few times a day for a few moments. Children
age 7 and under are not encouraged, but families with children over age 7 often
retreat here to avoid the mega-resorts, and second-timers quickly become "part
of the family."

2 Vlaun Dr., Simpson Bay, St. Maarten, N.A. ✆ **800/417-9361** in the U.S., or 599/54-54323. Fax 599/54-53316.
www.thehornytoadguesthouse.com. 8 units. Winter $198 double. Off-season $107 double. Extra person $40
in winter; $25 in off-season. DC, MC, V. No children under age 7. *In room:* Ceiling fan; kitchenette, no phone.

La Vista ★   A recent discovery, this is a small West Indian–style complex that
lies at the foot of Pelican Cay. Guests often stay at this inn, but use the more
elaborate facilities of the nearby Pelican Resort (for a charge), with its health spa,
casino, tennis courts, restaurants, and watersports facilities. A good, sandy
beach lies only a 2-minute walk from La Vista. Rooms with a view come in
seven different categories, including a junior suite, deluxe suite, penthouse, or
cottage. Accommodations feature fully equipped kitchenettes and medium-
sized bathrooms with shower. Our preference is the one-bedroom Antillean
cottage with its front porch (suitable for occupancy by four).

53 Billy Folly Rd., Pelican Cay (P.O. Box 2086), Simpson Bay, St. Maarten, NA ✆ 599/54-43005. Fax 599/
54-43010 www.lavistaresort.com. 32 suites. Winter $180 double; $210–$330 for 4. Off-season $140 double;
$160–$225 for 4. Children under 12 free when sharing with 2 adults. AE, MC, V. **Amenities:** Restaurant; large
pool; laundry. *In room:* A/C TV, kitchenette.

Maho Beach Hotel & Casino ★   Separated into three distinct sections, each
built over an 8-year period beginning in the mid-1980s, this mega-resort, with its
sprawling convention facilities, is the largest hotel on the island. Even with its fail-
ings, it's the closest thing on either side of the island to a Las Vegas–style block-
buster resort. It has a rather anonymous feeling (it's always full of conventioneers
and giant tour groups), but it is completely modern and up-to-date, with lots of
facilities that were enhanced after a $30 million upgrade that was completed in
2001. Set on a 10-acre (4-hectare) tract that straddles the busy, and often congested, coastal road adjacent to the crescent-shaped Maho Beach, the hotel's
scattered structures are all painted a trademark yellow and white.

   The rooms are fairly spacious and conservatively but comfortably furnished.
Each has wicker furniture, Italian tiles, a large (i.e., 25 in.) TV, comfortable
upholstered pieces, a walk-in closet, and good soundproofing (which is important, since you hear the thundering noise of planes landing at the nearby airport
several times a day when you're on the hotel's beach). Bathrooms are spacious,
with bidets and shower/tub combinations.

   Because of its size, the hotel contains three separate restaurants that are managed directly by the hotel, with another half-dozen on-site that are independently

managed. The Casino Royale, across the street from the hotel's accommodations, is the largest casino on the island, with a recently enlarged cabaret theater for glittery shows loaded with girls, razzmatazz, and glitter. The Q-Club, attached to the Casino Royale, is the island's splashiest, most electronically sophisticated late-night spot for drinking and dancing, complete with light shows and cat-walks looking down on the action below.

Maho Bay, Philipsburg, St. Maarten, N.A. ⓒ 800/223-0757 in the U.S., or 599/54-52115. Fax 599/54-53180. www.mahobeach.com. 600 units. Winter $235–$330 double; $390–$515 suite; from $845 2-bedroom unit. Off-season $190–$260 double; $330–$400 suite; from $625 2-bedroom unit. AE, DC, MC, V. **Amenities:** 9 restaurants, 3 bars, dance club; casino; 2 pools; 4 tennis courts; fitness center; business services; watersports; babysitting; laundry. *In room:* A/C, TV, safe.

Oyster Bay Beach Resort ⓐ   At the end of a twisting, scenic road, a 1-minute walk from Dawn Beach, this elegant retreat was originally designed for vacationers who don't like overly commercialized mega-resorts, like Maho Beach Hotel. Once an intimate inn, it's been growing by leaps and bounds, having witnessed a five-fold increase in size since it was established as an isolated inn in the 1960s. It can't be considered intimate anymore, but it's still not overwhelming. On a circular harbor on the eastern shore, near the French border, the fortress-like structure stands guard over a 35-acre (14-hectare) protected marina. There's a central courtyard and an alfresco lobby, with white wicker and fine paintings. There's an intense focus here on marketing some of the units as time-shares.

More than half the units have kitchens, and most have West Indian decor with lots of rattan and wicker. The bedrooms offer balconies overlooking the pond or sea; the deluxe and superior rooms are preferable to the tower suites. Rooms are airy and fairly spacious, and each has a bathroom with a tub and a shower.

Oyster Pond (P.O. Box 239), Philipsburg, St. Maarten, N.A. ⓒ 877/478-6669 in the U.S., or 599/54-36040. Fax 599/54-36695. www.oysterbaybeachresort.com. 33 inn units (plus 84 time-shares). Winter $200–$300 double; $310–$600 suite. Off-season $120–$175 double; $190–$400 suite. Children under age 12 stay free in parents' room. AE, DISC, MC, V. **Amenities:** Restaurant, bar; pool; fitness center; laundry. *In room:* A/C, TV, coffeemaker, hair dryer.

MODERATE/INEXPENSIVE

Holland House   Located in the congested heart of Philipsburg, this well-managed hotel rents cozy medium-size apartments decorated with mostly rattan furniture. Units either face the street or the beach, and most contain tiny kitchenettes, ideal for light cooking (and best of all, the kitchenette units don't cost any more than the regular rooms). The suites are very spacious. Shower-only bathrooms are small but efficiently arranged. Each room has a veranda, many of them overlooking the sea. It also has the most beautiful hardwood floors in St. Maarten, made from a well-finished Guyanan hardwood. Rooms are really very attractive, sometimes filled to capacity with U.S. naval officers and staff from some of the ships that periodically moor offshore. Good beaches are a 10- to 15-minute drive away. (You may want to arrange for a taxi to drop you off and pick you up at a prearranged time, since the lack of parking in Philipsburg makes it tough to have a car here.)

An open-air dining terrace fronts Great Bay, and the hotel is near all the major restaurants and shops of Philipsburg. Even if you're not staying here, you might want to call and reserve a table for dinner; this is one of the few hotels that serves authentic Dutch specialties at its Three Ladies Restaurant. International and Indonesian specialties are also featured.

Front St. (P.O. Box 393), Philipsburg, St. Maarten, N.A. ⓒ 800/223-9815 in the U.S., or 599/54-22572. Fax 599/54-24673. www.hhbh.com. 60 units. Winter $155–$170 for up to 3; $200 suite. Off-season $80–$109 for up to 3; $139 suite. AE, DISC, MC, V. **Amenities:** Restaurant, lounge; babysitting; laundry. *In room:* A/C, TV, kitchen, fridge.

Mary's Boon Beach Plantation ✿

This is the most charming and well-managed small inn on Dutch St. Maarten. It's very near the airport (so you do get the sounds of jets taking off and landing a few times a day), and it's also only minutes from casinos, shops, and restaurants. Mary's Boon draws a loyal repeat clientele that appreciates its sense of intimacy and understated elegance. Everything's relaxed and informal, though the service is alert and attentive.

Accommodations have verandas or terraces, but each varies in architectural style. Those facing the sea directly are breezy, high-ceilinged, and comfortably unpretentious, with furnishings like what you'd expect in a 1970s-era Florida motel. Try to get one of the newer units, set within the garden; they're very stylish indeed, showing the deft touch of a professional decorator. Done in jewel tones, they usually contain four-poster cherrywood beds and Balinese woodcarvings. Regardless of their age, most units have king-size beds. The inn enjoys direct access to one of the best beaches on St. Maarten, with white sands. The family-style restaurant offers good-value fixed-price dinners (with seconds included).

117 Simpson Bay Rd., St. Maarten, N.A. (or P.O. Box 523882, Miami, FL 33152). Ⓒ **599/54-54235.** Fax 599/54-53403. www.marysboon.com. 20 units. Winter $150–$250 double. Off-season $75–$175 double. AE, MC, V. Take the first right-hand turn as you head from the airport toward Philipsburg, then follow the signs to Mary's Boon. **Amenities:** Restaurant, bar. *In room:* A/C, TV.

Pasanggrahan ✿ (Value)

Pasanggrahan is the Indonesian word for guesthouse, and this West Indian–style guesthouse lies 50 feet (15m) from a private beach. A small, informal place, it's right on the busy, narrow main street of Philipsburg, toward the end of the mountainside of Front Street. It's set back under tall trees, with a white wooden veranda. The interior has peacock bamboo chairs, Indian spool tables, and a gilt-framed oil portrait of Queen Wilhelmina. So many guests asked to see the bedroom where the queen and her daughter, Juliana, stayed during World War II, that the management turned it into a cozy, Dutch colonial–style bar. The small- to medium-size renovated bedrooms have queen-size, double, or king-size beds with good mattresses and four-poster designs; some are in the main building and others are in an adjoining annex. All accommodations have ceiling fans, and all but six are air-conditioned. Bathrooms are small but tidy, and 10 have shower/tub combinations; the remainder have only showers. Set among the wild jungle of palms and shrubbery is the Pasanggrahan Restaurant.

15 Front St. (P.O. Box 151), Philipsburg, St. Maarten, N.A. Ⓒ **599/54-23588.** Fax 599/54-22885. 31 units. Winter $128–$168 double. Off-season $88–$110 double. MC, V. Closed Sept. **Amenities:** Restaurant, bar. *In room:* A/C, TV, ceiling fan.

The Pelican

This resort, built in 1979 on 12 acres (5 hectares) of land near the airport, is the largest time-share facility on St. Maarten, and the staff appears at times more interested in hawking these properties than in running a hotel. Nevertheless, it's a good value, with lots of amenities, and it's a good backup choice if the other resorts are full. Although many of the suites are leased for predesignated periods throughout the year, others are rented by the on-site managers as they become available. Accommodations, which contain ceiling fans, shower-only bathrooms, and full kitchens, are arranged into village-style clusters separated from other units by lattices, hibiscus hedges, and bougainvillea. Each unit is fairly spacious, equipped with straightforward furnishings and comfortable king-size or double beds; most units have patios or verandas, and some have hair dryers. Scattered around the property are a lily pond, many small waterways, and an orchid garden, not to mention the beachfront.

Simpson Bay (P.O. Box 431), Philipsburg, St. Maarten, N.A. © **800/550-7088** in the U.S., or 599/54-42503. Fax 599/54-42133. www.pelicanresort.com. 342 units. Winter $125–$160 studio for 2; $200–$220 1-bedroom suite for up to 4; $300–$330 2-bedroom suite for up to 6; $400 3-bedroom suite for up to 8. Off-season $85–$110 studio for 2; $100–$170 1-bedroom suite for 4; $215–$235 2-bedroom suite for 6; $260–$290 3-bedroom suite for 8. Holiday rates higher. AE, DISC, MC, V. **Amenities:** 2 restaurants, 5 bars; casino; 5 pools; 4 tennis courts; spa; dive shop, windsurfing; playground; car rentals; babysitting; laundry. *In room:* A/C, TV.

IN FRENCH ST. MARTIN

Hotels on French St. Martin add a 10% service charge and a *taxe de séjour*. This visitors' tax on rooms differs from hotel to hotel, depending on its classification, but is often $4 a day.

VERY EXPENSIVE

Esmeralda Resort ✦ Originally conceived as a site for a single private villa, and then for a semiprivate club, this hillside housing development gives the appearance of a well-maintained compound of Creole-inspired villas on sloping terrain that's interspersed with lush gardens. It lies within a 25-minute taxi ride northeast of Queen Juliana Airport. Opening onto Orient Beach, the Esmeralda blossomed into a full-scale resort in the early 1990s, offering views over Orient Bay and a decidedly French focus. Each of the 18 Spanish mission–style, tile-roofed villas can be configured into four separate units by locking or unlocking the doors between rooms. Each individual unit contains a king-size or two double beds, a kitchenette, a shower-only bathroom, a terrace, and a private entrance. Each villa has a communal pool, which creates the feeling of a private club.

Parc de la Baie Orientale (B.P. 5141), 97150 St. Martin, F.W.I. © 590/87-36-36. Fax 590/87-35-18. www.sxm hotels.com. 65 units. Winter $300–$450 double; from $550 suite. Off-season $200–$270 double; from $320 suite. AE, MC, V. **Amenities:** 2 restaurants; 17 pools; 2 tennis courts; horseback riding; scuba diving, water-skiing, snorkeling; concierge; room service; massage; babysitting; laundry. *In room:* A/C, TV, safe.

La Samanna ✦✦✦ Luxurious, sybaritic, and spectacularly expensive, this world-class resort features Mediterranean-style architecture on a 1½-mile (2km) stretch of one of St. Martin's finest beaches. The resort was acquired by Orient Express Hotels and made especially competitive with regular and massive infusions of cash. Since then, the resort has earned a reputation as a sleek, sexy, and stylish complex where celebrities sometimes come to hide out and unwind. Although the place is pricey, it's not particularly stuffy. Many aspects of the place feel like they've been transplanted directly from the French Riviera.

Rows of mature royal palms enhance the 55-acre (22-hectare) property's front entrance. As you enter, you're greeted by lavish art objects from Morocco and Thailand. Regardless of their size, most units have private terraces. Suites and villas have spacious bedrooms with luxurious beds, fully equipped kitchens, living and dining rooms, VCRs, and large patios. The bathrooms are simpler than might be expected, but they're well designed nonetheless, with bidets, hand-painted Mexican tiles, and shower/tub combinations. The fourth floor of the main building is the site of one of the grandest suites in the Caribbean.

Guests enjoy superb French cuisine alfresco, on a candlelit terrace overlooking Baie Longue. After dinner, the bar becomes a disco. At the poolside grill, waiters serve food, St-Tropez style, on the beach.

Baie Longue (B.P. 4077), 97064 St. Martin CEDEX, F.W.I. © **800/854-2252** or 590/87-64-00. Fax 590/87-87-86. www.orient-expresshotels.com. 81 units. Winter $745–$835 double; from $1,115 suite or villa. Off-season $395–$640 double; from $725 suite or villa. Rates include breakfast. AE, MC, V. Closed Sept 2–Oct. 31.

Amenities: Restaurant, bar; pool; 3 tennis courts; fitness center; water-skiing, windsurfing, sailing, snorkeling; library; 24-hr. room service; massage; babysitting; laundry. *In room:* A/C, TV, minibar, safe.

Le Méridien L'Habitation/Le Domaine ★★★ *Kids*   This is the largest resort on the French side of the island; it's often packed with French-speaking tour groups. It's tucked under Pigeon Pea Hill, opening onto a beautiful white-sand beach. The older section (L'Habitation), with less panoramic bedroom views, was erected in the mid-1980s on a 150-acre (60-hectare) tract of rugged scrubland nestled between the sea and a mountain ridge. In the early 1990s, after the project had been purchased by Air France, work began on Le Domaine, a few steps to the west of the original complex. Today, both resorts are fully integrated, sharing all entertainment, dining, drinking, and recreational facilities.

Accommodations at both resorts are in a string of neo-Victorian two- and three-story buildings ringed with lattices, gingerbread, and verandas. Most of the rooms in Le Domaine overlook the ocean, and are thus more expensive. The rooms in L'Habitation mostly open onto a 120-slip marina and a garden. All rooms and suites are comfortably and stylishly furnished, each with quality beds, soundproofing, a balcony or terrace, a two-sink bathroom with a shower/tub combo, an airy, tropical decor, and in many cases, kitchens. Thanks to some special children's programs that combine activities for children with limited child-minding services, this is an ideal place for families.

Anse Marcel (B.P. 581, 97056 Marigot), St. Martin, F.W.I. © **800/543-4300** in the U.S., or 590/87-67-67. Fax 590/87-67-88. www.lemeridien-lhabitation.com. 396 units. Winter $296–$384 double; $494–$741 suite. Off-season $138–$192 double; $213–$378 suite. AE, DC, DISC, MC, V. Closed Sept. **Amenities:** 4 restaurants, 3 bars, dance club; 2 pools; 6 tennis courts; health club and spa; Jacuzzi; 120-slip marina; watersports; room service (7am–11pm); babysitting; laundry. *In room:* A/C, TV, kitchen, minibar, fridge, hair dryer.

Le Mississippi ★   Here you get a wooden cottage on a hill, looking down from its perch over Oyster Pond. The complex consists of a series of wooden cottages, some of them octagonal, and each inspired by the vernacular Creole architecture of long ago. Floors, walls, and ceilings are for the most part crafted from mahogany. Mosquito netting drapes romantically over four-poster beds, and throughout, there's a sense of discreet privacy that's perfect for romance. It's an intimate, luxurious, and completely relaxing place, great for those who just want to rest and unwind (there isn't a lot to do, other than dining and going to the beach). The nearest beach (Dawn Beach) is a 12- to 15-minute walk from the hotel, down a steep and winding pathway, on the Dutch side of the island.

Six of the units are independent cottages, each with its own Jacuzzi. Suites are spacious, with posh features that include marble and tile floors, luxury beds, VCRs, and stereos. Bathrooms are adorned with pink Portuguese marble and come with whirlpool tubs. Cottages are equally luxurious, with king-size beds and antique-style tubs. Some accommodations have sweeping water views that extend as far as St. Barts and Saba, as does the terrace of the appealing restaurant, Mahogany (see "Dining," below).

Oyster Pond, 97150 St. Martin, F.W.I. © **590/87-33-81.** Fax 590/87-31-52. www.lemississippi.com. 19 units. Winter $286–$343 double; $680–$720 suite for 2. Off-season $200–$279 double; $280–$480 suite for 2. An $86–$114 supplement is charged for each additional person, up to a total of 4, in any suite. AE, MC, V. Closed Sept. **Amenities:** Restaurant, bar. *In room:* A/C, TV, minibar.

EXPENSIVE

Captain Oliver's Resort Hotel ★ *Kids*   A quiet, intimate place, this is one of the most appealing, upper-middle-bracket hotels of French St. Martin, in some ways likened to the Esmeralda Resort, to which it's sometimes compared. At the

French–Dutch border 10 miles (16km) east of Queen Juliana Airport, this hotel is near the Dutch side's Oyster Bay Beach Hotel. The pink bungalows, with a bit of gingerbread, are set in a labyrinth and connected by boardwalks. High on a hill, they command panoramic views, and from the large terraces you can gaze over to St. Barts. The accommodations, which are clustered three to a bungalow, are furnished in white rattan and decorated with local prints, and come with kitchenettes, marble-trimmed full bathrooms with double sinks, large double closets, and many amenities. Each junior suite has two beds and a sofa bed, which makes them perfect for families.

Oyster Pond, 97150 St. Martin, F.W.I. ✆ 590/87-40-26. Fax 590/87-40-84. www.captainolivers.com. 50 units. Winter $175–$205 junior suite for 2. Off-season $120–$150 junior suite for 2. Rates include buffet breakfast. AE, DC, MC, V. **Amenities:** Restaurant, snack bar; pool; scuba diving; hairdresser; room service (7am–10:30pm); babysitting; laundry; private taxi boat to beach. *In room:* A/C, TV, minibar, coffeemaker, hair dryer.

Club Orient Naturist Resort ★ (Finds)

Occupying an isolated spot, this is the only true nudist resort in the French West Indies. Established in the late 1970s by a Dutch-born family, and completely rebuilt after its devastation by hurricanes in 1995, it welcomes a European and North American clientele. There's an excellent beach here and a restaurant, the Papagayo, where you can dine alfresco (literally). However, most guests opt to cook their own meals, as each unit has its own kitchenette (there's a mini-market on-site). Accommodations, set in red-pine chalets imported from Finland, are utterly plain and simple; all have outside showers and most have both front and back porches. This is definitely *not* a wild, swinging, or actively partying kind of place. It's very clean, decent, middle-class, and even family friendly. Very few single guests check in here, so if you're looking for partners to play with, don't be fooled into thinking that this is a good place to meet someone. Despite their lack of clothing, many of the guests here are very conservative—definitely looking for a quiet, reclusive getaway with like-minded nudists. There's no pool on the premises, but the chalets are right on the beach.

Baie Orientale, 97150 St. Martin, F.W.I. ✆ 800/452-9016 in the U.S., or 590/87-33-85. Fax 590/87-33-76. www.cluborient.com. 136 units. Winter $205 studio; $240–$260 minisuite; $305–$340 chalet. Off-season $110–$150 studio; $120–$180 minisuite; $145–$215 chalet. AE, DC, DISC, MC, V. **Amenities:** Restaurant. *In room:* A/C, ceiling fan, kitchen.

Grand Case Beach Club ★

This restored condo complex, five motel-like buildings with white trim, sits directly on the sands of Grand-Case Beach. The entire place was rebuilt after the hurricanes of 1995, with ongoing renovations every year since. The medium-size accommodations contain private patios or balconies, kitchenettes, mostly white and rather simple decor, and views of either the garden or the sea. Guestrooms have king-size or double beds, foldout couches, and white-tiled bathrooms with tubs and showers. Everything here is extremely informal, if a little staid: This is the kind of place where you don't need much more than a bathing suit.

Rue du Petit-Plage Grand-Case, 97150 St. Martin, F.W.I. ✆ 800/447-7462 in the U.S., or 590/87-51-87. Fax 590/87-59-93. www.gcbc.com. 75 units. Winter $250–$325 double; $305–$355 1-bedroom suite; $460–$475 2-bedroom suite. Off-season $115–$130 double; $130–$160 1-bedroom suite; $240–$255 2-bedroom suite. Rates include continental breakfast. AE, DISC, MC, V. **Amenities:** Restaurant, bar; pool; tennis court; watersports; babysitting; laundry. *In room:* A/C, TV, kitchen, safe.

Hotel Beach Plaza ★

This is our favorite hotel within a reasonable distance of Marigot's commercial center. A three-story hotel that's centered around a soaring atrium festooned with live banana trees and climbing vines, it's within a cluster of buildings mostly composed of condominiums. Built in 1996, and painted in shades of blue and white, it's set midway between the open sea and the lagoon, giving all rooms water views. Inside, the decor is pure white, accented with varnished, dark-tinted woods and an inviting tropical motif. Each room contains a balcony, tile floors, native art, a private safe, and simple hardwood furniture, including a writing desk and comfortable beds. Bathrooms have showers and generous shelf space.

Baie de Marigot, 97150 St. Martin, F.W.I. ✆ 590/87-87-00. Fax 590/87-18-87. www.hotelbeachplazasxm. com. 144 units. Winter $215–$295 double; from $453 suite. Rates higher between Christmas and New Years. Off-season $160–$224 double; from $357 suite. Rates include buffet breakfast. MAP (dinner) $33 per person per day. AE, MC, V. **Amenities:** Restaurant, 2 bars; pool; watersports; bike rentals; car rentals; room service; babysitting; laundry. *In room:* A/C, TV, minibar, hair dryer.

Hôtel L'Esplanade Caraïbe 🏵

This elegant collection of suites lies on a steeply sloping hillside above the road leading into the village of Grand-Case from Marigot. Covered with cascades of bougainvillea, and accented with a vaguely Hispanic overlay of white walls, hand-painted tiles, and cream-colored roofs, the resort's various elements are connected by a network of concrete steps that add to the layout's drama. There's a pool, a series of gorgeous terraced gardens, and access to a beach that you reach after a 6-minute walk on a winding, stair-dotted pathway. There's no restaurant (only a bar that's open in midwinter), but the village of Grand-Case is known for its restaurants.

All views from the guestrooms and their terraces are angled out toward the sea and the sunset. Each unit contains a kitchen with a large fridge, up-to-date cookware, plus exposed mahogany and wicker furniture; and especially comfortable queen-size beds. Bathrooms are beautifully equipped right down to elegant toiletries baskets, bidets, and showers. The loft suites on the upper floors are worth the cost, as they include a sofa bed that can sleep extra guests, an upstairs master bedroom with a king-size bed, and a partial bathroom downstairs.

Grand-Case, (B.P. 5007), 97150 St. Martin, F.W.I. ✆ 866/596-8365 or 590/87-06-55. Fax 590/87-29-15. www.lesplanade.com. 24 units. Winter $270–$320 double studio; $370 suite. Off-season $170–$220 double studio; $270 suite. AE, MC, V. **Amenities:** Bar; pool; car rentals; room service (8am–10am); babysitting; laundry/dry cleaning. *In room:* A/C, TV, fridge, coffeemaker, hair dryer.

Le Petit Hotel 🏵

Set on a small parcel of property that's squeezed between other buildings, with direct access to the sands of Grand-Case Beach, this is a stylish, well-managed, thoughtfully designed hotel that opened late in 1996. Much of its appeal derives from its hard-working and articulate manager, Kristin Petrelluzi, who offers advice on any of two-dozen restaurants in nearby Grand-Case (since there's no restaurant on site). Nine of the spacious units are studios, while the tenth is a one-bedroom apartment. Each has a kitchenette with everything from a can opener to champagne glasses, as well as a microwave, fridge, and a two-burner stove. (There's no oven, but guests never seem inspired to actually cook during their stay here.) All units have balconies or outdoor terraces, plus furnishings that are both durable and comfortable. The small bathrooms come with shower stalls.

248 bd. de Grand-Case, Grand-Case, 97150 St. Martin, F.W.I. ✆ 590/29-09-65. Fax 590/87-09-19. www.le petithotel.com. 10 units. Winter $260–$280 studio for 2; $360 1-bedroom apt. for up to 4. Off-season $170–$220 studio for 2; $270 1-bedroom apt. for up to 4. Children under 7 stay free. AE, MC, V. *In-room:* A/C, TV, kitchenette, coffeemaker, hair dryer.

MODERATE/INEXPENSIVE

Hôtel St.-Tropez des Caraïbes

In the early 1990s, a much larger hotel here split up into three parts after its managers dissolved their partnership. This hotel is one of the three separate entities, and the background explains why it's flanked on either side with two very similar-looking properties. The St.-Tropez des

Caraïbes is the best maintained of the three. Don't expect too many hotel-style amenities here, as there's no bar, very little to do, and in terms of dining, only a very simple poolside pizzeria—but with the sweeping sands of Orient Beach at your disposal, you may not care. None of the units has a kitchen, but many bars and restaurants are within a short walk. Seven units lie within each of eight neo-Romanesque buff- and pink-colored buildings. Rooms are genuinely appealing, each with bright but soft tones of pink and green, floral upholsteries, a balcony, and a bathroom with a shower/tub combination. The best accommodations, with the highest ceilings and the greatest sense of space, lie on the top (third) floor of each of the eight buildings.

Baie Orientale (B.P. 5137), 97070 St. Martin, F.W.I. ⓒ **590/87-42-01.** Fax 590/87-41-69. www.st-tropez-caraibes.com. 56 units. Winter $166–$216 double. Off-season $134–$166 double. AE, DISC, MC, V. **Amenities:** Pizzeris (dinner only); pool. *In room:* A/C, TV, fridge, hair dryer.

La Plantation Orient Bay Resort ⭐

Although it requires a few minutes' walk to reach the gorgeous white-sand beach here, this is one of the most attractive and appealing hotels at Orient Bay. It's set on a steep, carefully landscaped slope, and designed like an upscale and rather charming condo complex. Seventeen colonial-style villas are scattered around the tropically landscaped grounds and pool; each villa contains a suite and two studios, which can be rented separately or combined. The spacious units are stylishly furnished in a South Seas/Polynesian theme, complete with hand-painted or hand-stenciled murals, and each sports its own ocean-view terrace. Studios have kitchenettes and queen-size or twin beds; the suites have separate bedrooms with king-size beds, spacious living rooms, full kitchens, and beautifully tiled full bathrooms.

C 5 Parc de la Baie Orientale, Orient Bay, 97150 St. Martin, F.W.I. ⓒ **590/29-58-00.** Fax 590/29-58-08. www.la-plantation.com. 54 units. Winter $165–$250 studio for 2; $230–$305 suite. Off-season $145 studio, $190 suite. Rates include breakfast. DISC, MC, V. Closed: Sept 1–mid-Oct. **Amenities:** 2 restaurants, beach bar and grill; pool; golf privileges; horseback riding; health club; windsurfing; diving; bike rental; massage. *In room:* A/C, TV, kitchen, fridge, coffeemaker, hair dryer.

La Résidence

In the commercial center of Marigot (and favored by business travelers for its location), La Résidence's concrete facade is enlivened with neo-Victorian gingerbread fretwork. A bar with a soaring tent serves drinks to guests relaxing on wicker and bentwood furniture. The small bedrooms are arranged around a landscaped central courtyard with a fish-shaped fountain. Each room contains minimalist decor, and all but a few have sleeping lofts and a duplex design of mahogany-trimmed stairs and balustrades. About half were renovated early in 2002. Bathrooms are also small, with shower stalls.

Rue du Général-de-Gaulle (B.P. 679, 97150 Marigot), 97150 St. Martin, F.W.I. ⓒ **590/87-70-37.** Fax 590/87-90-44. laresidence@wanadoo.fr. 22 units. Year-round $88 double. Rates include continental breakfast. AE, MC, V. **Amenities:** Restaurant. *In room:* A/C, TV, minibar.

Le Royale Louisiana

Occupying a prominent position in the center of Marigot, 10 miles (16km) north of Queen Juliana Airport, this hotel is designed in a hip-roofed French-colonial Louisiana style; its rambling balconies are graced with ornate balustrades. It's about a 10-minute drive to the nearest good beach; you'll want a car if you stay here. Each small- to medium-size guestroom contains big sunny windows and modern furniture. Standard rooms have either king- or queen-size beds, and in many cases, small verandas. Duplexes, ideal for families, have a sitting room with a sofa bed on the lower floor, with a bedroom and bathroom on the upper level. Note that duplex rates are not based on the number of occupants. Bathrooms are well maintained but a bit cramped, with shower stalls.

Rue du Général-de-Gaulle, Marigot, 97150 St. Martin, F.W.I. ⓒ **590/87-86-51.** Fax 590/87-96-49. louisiana@top-saint-martin.com. 58 units. Winter $73 double; $105 duplex. Off-season $62 double; $89 duplex. Rates include continental breakfast. AE, MC, V. **Amenities:** Restaurant, bar. *In room:* A/C, TV.

Mercure Simson Beach Coralia   One of the most stylish hotels in its price bracket on the French side of the island is operated by the French hotel conglomerate Accor. It's good value for the money, especially since each unit contains a kitchenette. The complex occupies a flat, sandy stretch of land between a saltwater lagoon and the beach, 5 miles (8km) west of Queen Juliana Airport. Decorated throughout in ocean-inspired pastels, its five three-story buildings are each evocative of a large, many-balconied Antillean house. In its center, a pool serves as the focal point for a bar built out over the lagoon, an indoor/outdoor restaurant, and a flagstone terrace that hosts steel bands and evening cocktail parties. Each unit, in addition to the kitchenette, offers ceiling fans and simple, durable wicker furniture, plus a tiled, shower-only bathroom. The most desirable accommodations, on the third (top) floor, contain sloping ceilings sheltering sleeping lofts and two bathrooms.

Baie Nettlé (B.P. 172), 97150 Marigot, St. Martin, F.W.I. ⓒ **800/221-4542** in the U.S., or 590/87-54-54. Fax 590/87-92-11. www.mercure-simson-beach.com. 178 units. Winter $162 studio for 2; from $204 duplex. Off-season $118 studio for 2; $157 duplex. Rates include buffet breakfast. AE, DC, MC, V. **Amenities:** Restaurant, bar; tennis court; dive shop, snorkeling, windsurfing; bikes; car rental; babysitting; laundry. *In room:* A/C, TV, kitchen.

Nettlé Bay Beach Club   This is a stylish and appealing colony of villas scattered across a landscaped garden that opens onto four bays, each fronted with its own swimming pool. Each villa is a two-story Creole-style cottage set with some degree of privacy into its own garden. Each villa can be rented as a complete two-story, two-bedroom house that's very comfortable for four occupants. Either the upper floor or the lower floor can be rented as a self-contained studio or one-bedroom apartment, respectively. If your plan is to rent just one floor of any of these cottages, try to book the lower floors, which are larger and more comfortable. Regardless of their size, each unit has terra-cotta floors, wicker furniture, shower-only bathrooms, and a veranda or terrace. All the apartments have kitchens, as do some of the studios.

Baie Nettlé, (B.P. 4081), 97064 St. Martin, F.W.I. ⓒ **590/87-68-68.** Fax 590/87-21-51. www.karibea.com. 140 units. Year-round $79–$160 studio; $90–$183 1-bedroom apt. for 2; $179–$353 2-bedroom villa for up to 6. AE, MC, V. **Amenities:** Restaurant, snack bar, bar; 4 lit Laykold tennis courts. *In room:* A/C, TV.

3 Dining

IN DUTCH ST. MAARTEN
EXPENSIVE

Antoine's ⓐ FRENCH/CREOLE/ITALIAN   This restaurant offers fine cuisine in a lovely setting by the sea. Antoine's has a certain sophistication and style, backed up by first-class service and an impressive wine list. Start off with a cocktail in the bar while you peruse the menu of old continental favorites. The Gallic specialties with Creole overtones are among the best on the island, even holding their own with the better restaurants in the French zone. The Italian dishes, however, are better at Da Livio (see below). We always start with the chef's savory kettle of fish soup, or his homemade pâté would also make a suitable opening. If it's featured, try the baked red snapper fillet, which is delicately flavored with white wine, lemon, shallots, and a butter sauce. Although the veal and beef dishes are shipped in frozen, they're fashioned into rather delectable choices, especially the veal scaloppini with a mustard-and-cream sauce that's smooth and perfectly balanced.

119 Front St., Philipsburg. © **599/54-22964.** Reservations recommended, especially in winter. Lunch main courses $7–$13; dinner main courses $22–$37. AE, DISC, MC, V. Daily 11am–4pm and 6–10pm.

Da Livio Ristorante ✦ ITALIAN   This is the finest Italian dining on the Dutch side of St. Maarten, even though we prefer Il Nettuno, an Italian competitor on the French side. The food is consistently excellent, and the staff is graciousness itself. The place is as Italian as they come, even if all the staff isn't. Bergamasco Livio himself hails from near Venice, and he purchases most of his ingredients from the finest suppliers in his home country. At the western edge of Front Street, with a panoramic view of the Great Bay, the restaurant sets a romantic mood in the evening with background music. Since 1979, and in spite of hurricanes, Da Livio has been turning out the classics and offering daily specials with an emphasis on fresh pastas and fresh local fish. We love the homemade manicotti della casa, filled with ricotta, spinach, and a zesty tomato sauce. For a main course, we suggest you tear into fra diavolo with linguine or the tender and juicy veal chop with sage-flavored butter. Tony Bennett and even Eddie Murphy have sung the praises of these dishes. This is obviously a kitchen staff who cares, even going so far as to grow tomatoes in their own garden.

189 Front St., Philipsburg. © **599/54-22690.** Reservations recommended for dinner. Main courses $18–$27. AE, MC, V. Mon–Fri noon–2pm; Mon–Sat 6–10pm.

Le Perroquet ✦ FRENCH   One of St. Maarten's finest restaurants is in a typical West Indian house with shutters open to the trade winds blowing around Simpson Bay Lagoon. Dutch-born Thea Castagne, a restaurateur of exceptional ability, offers dishes that include a savory fish soup, a delectable onion tart, scallops in a shallot and white wine sauce, or a fresh mâche salad. You can move on to lobster ravioli, savory duck with Grand Marnier orange sauce, or perfectly cooked red snapper in garlic sauce. Some of the specialties are wheeled in on a table so you can make a visual selection—a nice touch.

106 Airport Rd., a short walk from the airport. © **599/54-54339.** Reservations recommended. Main courses $19–$25. AE, DISC, MC, V. Tues–Sun 6–10pm. Closed May–Oct.

Saratoga ✦ AMERICAN   This is the most creative and cutting-edge restaurant in St. Maarten; it's laid-back and intensely choreographed at the same time. It's a beautiful setting, resembling a Spanish colonial structure from the outside, and lined with rich mahogany inside. You might like a predinner drink ("ultra-premium margaritas" and vodka martinis are the house specialties) in the bar. Seating is either indoors or on a marina-side veranda. The menu changes daily, but there's always an artfully contrived low-fat selection like onion-crusted salmon served on a compote of lentils and sweet corn. Yellowfin tuna might be grilled with basmati rice or wasabi-flavored butter and daikon leaves. Long Island duckling is served with a sauce that varies from night to night, depending on the inspiration of the chef. Another dish is crispy-fried black sea bass with an Asian-style sauce of fermented black beans and scallions. Rack of venison is often featured with port sauce or some other sauce concocted by owner/chef John Jackson, who hails from Saratoga Springs, New York.

Simpson Bay Yacht Club, Airport Rd. © **599/54-42421.** Reservations recommended. Main courses $20–$26. AE, MC, V. Mon–Sat 6:30–10:30pm. Closed Aug–mid-Oct.

MODERATE/INEXPENSIVE

The Boathouse AMERICAN/INTERNATIONAL   Funky, irreverent, and friendly, this is one of the Dutch side's most enduringly popular bars and restaurants The seafaring theme of the interior includes a soaring network of heavy timbers accented with soft pinks, blues, greens, and lots of nautical accessories. Come here for the bar, a wraparound affair that attracts good-natured expatriates and locals alike, and for the generous portions dished up by the hardworking kitchen staff. Lunches consist of sandwiches, pastas, and salads. (Especially worthwhile are the shrimp salad and the grilled chicken Caesar salad.) Main courses at dinner are more substantial, including filet mignon, pepper steak, surf and turf, and red snapper that's either charcoal-grilled or stuffed with shrimp and crabmeat and served with a white-wine cream sauce. Live bands usually play most Fridays after 11pm, when the already-active bar gets even busier.

74 Airport Rd., Simpson Bay. © 599/54-45409. Reservations recommended for dinner, not necessary at lunch. Lunch main courses $7–$15; dinner main courses $14–$29. MC, V. Mon–Sat 11:30am–2:30pm; daily 5:30–10:30pm.

Cheri's Café ⭐ AMERICAN   American expatriate Cheri Batson's island hot spot is the best bar on the island. Touristy but fun and sassy, a great place to meet people, it's outfitted in an irrepressible color scheme of hot pink and white. This open-air cafe, serving some 400 meals a night, is really only a roof without walls, and it's not even on a beach. But people flock to it anyway, devouring 18-ounce steaks, burgers (one of the most popular things on the menu), and grilled fresh-fish platters. The clientele covers everybody from rock bands to movie stars, high rollers at the casino to beach bums. Some come for the cheap eats, others for the potent drinks, many to dance and flirt. The bartender's special is a frozen "Straw Hat" made with vodka, coconut, tequila, pineapple and orange juices, and strawberry liqueur. Maybe even one more ingredient, we suspect—although nobody's talking. There's live music every night beginning at 8pm, and ending around 10:15pm.

45 Cinnamon Grove Shopping Centre, Maho Beach. © 599/54-53361. Reservations not accepted. Main courses $9.75–$22. MC, V. Wed–Mon 11am–10pm (until midnight Fri–Sat). Closed Sept.

Kangaroo Court SANDWICHES/SALADS   Simple and unpretentious, this cafe and sandwich shop is set on a side street between Front and Back Streets, adjacent to the courthouse. The thick 200-year-old walls that shelter it are among the oldest in town, crafted of black stone that has withstood many a hurricane. Within an interior that's brightly painted in vibrant Creole colors, you'll find display racks loaded with fresh-baked pastries and espresso machines that chug out endless cups of caffeine. Salads (including versions with sesame chicken, or shrimp, avocado, and papaya) and sandwiches (beef, turkey, tuna, and grilled chicken) are sold at a roaring pace, mostly to passengers from the nearby cruise ship docks, throughout the day.

Hendrick's Straat 6, Philipsburg. © 599/54-27557. Sandwiches and salads $4.95–$12.95. AE, DISC, MC, V. Mon–Fri 7:30am–5:30pm, Sat 8am–4pm.

Turtle Bar Pier & Restaurant AMERICAN/SEAFOOD ⭐ *(Finds*   No, they don't serve the endangered turtle, although turtles swim in a large protected pool in the nearby lagoon. They're not destined for the stew pot, but are released when they become adults. They do offer one of the island's best menus of fresh seafood, much of which is caught in waters off neighboring islands. The location is not its greatest asset, across from the Juliana airport, but once inside, you forget all about jets. Located on a pier beside the water, the place evokes a small zoo, with chattering parrots, macaws, cockatoos, even rabbits, monkey, and guinea pigs. Wednesday is lobster night and this succulent creature is prepared in many different ways. Because they're shipped in containers of seawater by air or sea, they're the freshest-tasting on the island. At night, you can go for the Creole-style conch soup, a savory kettle, or else launch yourself with some tuna sashimi. Fish such as mahi-mahi, tuna, or grouper can be grilled, poached, served meunière, or blackened. Duck is also a specialty. Our favorite is pan-seared duck breast in a sauce made from local guavaberry liqueur. Chops, lamb or pork, and some succulent steaks round out the menu.

Turtle Pier, Simpson Bay. 114 Airport Rd. ℂ **599/54-52562.** Main courses $11.50–$17.25 at lunch, $11.95–$22 at dinner. No credit cards. Daily 7am–10pm.

Wajang Doll ⭐ *Value* INDONESIAN   Housed in a cement-sided West Indian building on the main street of town, Wajang Doll is the best Indonesian restaurant in the Caribbean. A low-slung front porch lets you watch the pedestrian traffic outside, and the big windows in back overlook the sea. The restaurant is known for its 19-dish dinner, known as a *rijsttafel* (rice table), in which rice is served with a medley of small dishes containing everything from beef curry to mango chutney. The chef crushes his spices every day for maximum pungency, according to an ancient craft. The specialties include fried red snapper with ginger, chile, onions, garlic, and lemongrass; a variety of omelets stuffed with curry; Sumatran-style beef with white rice, a spicy seafood tofu, tempura made from soy bean, plus zestily flavored Javanese chicken dishes.

167 Front St., Philipsburg. ℂ **599/54-22687.** Reservations required. Lunch main courses $10.50–$17; set-price 14-dish *rijsttafel* dinner $20, 19-dish *rijsttafel* dinner $26. AE, MC, V. Mon–Sat noon–2pm and 6:45–10pm. Closed Sept.

IN FRENCH ST. MARTIN

No other town in the Caribbean features as many restaurants, per capita, as the ramshackle-looking village of Grand-Case, set near French St. Martin's northernmost tip. Don't be put off by the town's first impression: Behind the slowly decaying clapboards of its Creole architecture are French-, Italian-, and American-style restaurants managed by some extremely canny entrepreneurs, many of whom are extremely sophisticated cooks. If you're a real foodie and you want a decadent vacation, check into one of Grand-Case's hotels, go to a topless beach every day, and dine at a different restaurant every night.

EXPENSIVE

La Vie en Rose ⭐⭐ FRENCH   The dining room in this balconied second-floor restaurant evokes a tropical version of Paris in the 1920s, thanks to ceiling fans, candlelight, and a well-developed sense of culinary showmanship. The menu is classic French, although Caribbean flavors and overtones often creep in. Lunches are relatively simple affairs, with an emphasis on fresh, meal-sized salads, simple grills like beefsteak with mustard sauce, brochettes of fresh fish, pastas, sandwiches, and salads. Dinners are more elaborate, and might begin with fried foie gras with pears marinated in red wine. Main courses include grilled fillet of red snapper in puff pastry with fresh basil sauce; breast of duck with an orange/walnut sauce; fresh medallions of smoked lobster with fresh-made pasta and herbs; boneless breast of duck with raspberry sauce and fried bananas; and an unusual version of roasted rack of lamb with a gratin of goat cheese and sliced potatoes. A particularly worthwhile beginner at either lunch or dinner is the house version of lobster bisque.

Blvd. de France at rue de la République, Marigot. © **590/87-54-42.** Reservations recommended, especially in winter and as far in advance as possible. Main courses 10€–20€ ($8.95–$17.85) lunch, 21€–38€ ($18.75–$33.95) dinner. AE, MC, V. Mon–Sat 11:30am–2:30pm; daily 6:30–10pm.

Mahogany ✿ FRENCH/CREOLE   This is an elegant, stylish, and extremely French restaurant, with an aesthetic that you might have expected in faraway Paris. It lies on an isolated hillside, in a rambling, woodsy set of connected verandas with views extending out over neighboring St. Barts and Saba. Tables are arranged into a labyrinth of cubbyholes that allow privacy. The menu has been influenced by the grand culinary traditions of Paris. Examples include a platter lined with different types of homemade foie gras; a broth of scallops with coconut milk and curry; "crème brûlée" of crayfish in an herbal infusion of verveine flavored with bacon; a crispy version of free-range chicken and crayfish with fresh morels; suprême of red snapper with a crystalline of fresh vegetables; and rosettes of Peking duck with lavender-flavored honey and a sherry-flavored vinaigrette. Two particularly successful desserts include warm chocolate and raspberry cake, and an apple *chaud-froid* with pistachio cream and chocolate. The cuisine remains always inventive, always consistently good.

In Le Mississippi hotel, Oyster Pond. © **590/87-33-81.** Reservations recommended. Main courses 23€–36€ ($20.55–$32.15);. MC, V. Wed–Mon noon–2pm and 6:30–10pm. Closed Sept.

MODERATE

Hévéa ✿ FRENCH   Normandy-born restaurateurs own this formal place, the most obviously French restaurant in Grand-Case. There's a touch of class here, with Louis XV chairs, Norman artifacts, and candlelight. There are fewer than a dozen tables, so advance reservations are usually crucial. Start with the Caesar salad, which remains the best on the island. In honor of their Norman roots, the owners prepare such classic dishes as cassoulet of scallops with fumet of crab and Noilly Prat; *darne* of kingfish; scallops *Dieppoise* (with cream-flavored mussel sauce); filet steak served with a sauce made from three kinds of pepper; and one of the great dishes of the conservative French repertoire, escalopes of veal *Pays d'Auge,* made with apple brandy (Calvados) and cream. You might also try more experimental dishes such as mahi-mahi with a sauce made from acacia-flavored honey; or lasagna with two kinds of salmon. To remind you that you're in the West Indies, there's a set-price all-Creole menu, as well as set menus focusing on traditional French food from *La France Métropolitaine,* and a set-price lobster menu.

163 Blvd. de Grand-Case, Grande-Case. © **590/87-56-85.** Reservations required. Main courses 13€–22€ ($11.60–$19.65); Set-price menus 22€–45€ ($19.65–$40.20). AE, MC, V. Oct–June Mon–Sat 6:30–9:30pm. Closed July–Sept.

Il Nettuno ✿ ITALIAN   This is the most elaborate, best-managed, and most appealing Italian restaurant on either side of the island, coping gracefully with a cosmopolitan, international crowd. It was established by a seasoned Italian restaurateur, Raymond Losito, whose career included a 25-year stint at a French restaurant in Washington, D.C., where he developed a deep attachment to the Washington Redskins football team, whose banners and memorabilia decorate the walls of the restaurant's bar. It's a great watering hole, outfitted in the colors of the Italian flag, and drawing a fervent crowd of sports fans for U.S. football games.

Meals are served on a large, rambling wooden veranda that the owners bravely refurbish after each hurricane that hits the island. It serves the best blackened tuna we've ever had, as well as grilled portobello mushrooms, mussels in white wine sauce, fresh Chilean sea bass or fillet of sea wolf cooked in parchment, fillet of grouper with prosciutto, and a worthy version of veal pizzaiola. The pastas are superb. There's an especially worthwhile version of sea bass baked in rock salt, prepared for a minimum of two diners.

70 Blvd. de Grand-Case, Grande-Case. ✆ 590/87-77-38. Reservations recommended. Main courses 18€–28€ ($16.05–$25). AE, DISC, MC, V. Daily noon–2:30pm and 6–10:30pm. Closed for lunch Apr–Oct; completely closed in Sept.

La Marine FRENCH   Set on the seaward side of the main road running through Grand-Case, this is an attractive restaurant occupying an antique, much-enlarged Creole house with a blue-and-white color scheme. Much of the cuisine focuses on the succulent grills that emerge, with finesse, from the kitchens. The best menu items include anise-marinated salmon filets; a crisp-skinned version of codfish served, with onions and herbs, as a *brandade;* magret of duckling with tropical fruits; grilled beefsteak with red wine sauce, grilled sea bream or sea bass served with sweet spices; and a *pierrade* of assorted fish that's prepared and cooked tableside on a hot stone.

158 Blvd. de Grand-Case, Grande-Case. ✆ 590/87-02-31. Reservations recommended. Main courses 16€–22€ ($14.30–$19.65); set-price menu 23€ ($20.55). AE, MC, V. Daily 6–10:30pm. Closed May 15–Oct 15.

Le Cottage ⭐ FRENCH/CREOLE   One of our favorite restaurants in a town that's loaded with worthy contenders is set in what looks like a private house, on the inland side of the main road running through Grand-Case. Its atmosphere is at least partly influenced by the Burgundy-born wine steward, Stephane Émorine, who shows a canny intuition at recommending the perfect wine by the glass to complement each course of the French and Caribbean cuisine. Menu items include both rustic *cuisine du terroir* (such as roasted rack of lamb with either a rosemary or a cream-based *pistou* sauce) and Creole dishes, including a fillet of local dorado served with a reduction of crayfish, or a *blaff* (stew) of red snapper flavored with Creole herbs. Other dishes seem to go beyond Creole classics, onto a creative level all their own: Witness the scallops in puff pastry, with a unique form of tea that's brewed from flap mushrooms and mint leaves. Meals tend to begin dramatically with such dishes as a *charlotte* of crayfish and avocados with a citrus sauce or a tartar of tuna and salmon with mustard-flavored vinaigrette.

97 Blvd. de Grand-Case, Grande-Case. ✆ 590/29-03-30. Reservations recommended. Main courses 20€–24€ ($17.85–$21.45). AE, DC, MC, V. Daily 6:30–11pm. Closed Sun May–Sept.

Le Pressoir FRENCH   This bistro occupies a charming, old-fashioned Creole house painted yellow and blue. Favored by locals, it presents a combination of old and new French cuisine that includes sliced foie gras with wine sauce; marinated salmon carpaccio with pink peppercorns; rolled sea scallops in a mango-flavored butter sauce; and roasted rack of lamb in a mustard-enhanced vinaigrette. Fresh products are deftly handled, and their natural flavors enhanced by the use of imaginative flavorings. The restaurant's signature dish assembles very fresh versions of grilled shellfish and fish in a stew pot with beurre blanc.

Blvd. de Grand-Case, Grande-Case. ✆ 590/87-76-62. Reservations recommended. Main courses 19€–35€ ($16.95–$31.25) AE, MC, V. Daily 6–10:30pm.

Le Tropicana FRENCH   Despite formidable competition from about 20 other restaurants that flank the edge of the marina, this one draws a lot of repeat business, thanks to relatively reasonable prices and flavorful food. Gilles Artu is the French entrepreneur who runs this little hideaway, whose location at the most distant edge of the marina gives it a quiet atmosphere. A simple nautical decor sets the tone for a *croustillant* of Brie with cassis sauce; fish soup with garlicky rouille; a seafood *pot au feu;* and a rack of lamb with goat cheese and rosemary garnish.

Marina Port La Royale, Marigot. ☎ 590/87-79-07. Reservations recommended. Lunch main courses 8€–21€ ($7.15–$18.75); dinner main courses 11€–23€ ($9.80–$20.55). AE, MC, V. Mon–Sat noon–3pm and 6–10pm.

Mario's Bistro FRENCH/INTERNATIONAL   Airy and chic, this restaurant is full of breezy and sometimes arch references to mainland French glamour. It occupies a cement-sided building that's directly adjacent to an inland canal (the Sandy Ground Canal) that funnels boats between a saltwater estuary and the open sea. Menu items are flavorful and well prepared: grilled filet of tuna with melted blue cheese on a bed of gnocchi in a tomato sauce with *fines herbes;* braised lamb shank with red wine and garlic sauce; and a half-duckling cooked on the bone with a honey-garlic glaze, garlic-flavored mashed potatoes, and a sweet-and-sour sauce.

Sandy Ground Bridge, Sandy Ground. ☎ 590/87-06-36. Reservations recommended. Main courses 23€–28€ ($20.55–$25) MC, V. Mon–Sat 6:30–10pm. Closed mid-June to mid-Aug, and also closed Sun–Mon mid-Aug to late Oct.

Rainbow Café FRENCH/INTERNATIONAL   Set on the northeastern end of the row of restaurants that line either side of the main road of Grand-Case, this little bistro thrives under the direction of Dutch-born Fleur Radd, and Buffalo, New York–born David Hendricks. The house containing the cafe opens onto views over the sea. Meals are served in an artfully simple dining room outfitted in shades of dark blue and white. Menu items evolve almost every evening—perhaps chopped lamb with mashed potatoes and an onion-garlic marmalade; snapper in Parmesan-onion crust with tomato-flavored vinaigrette or chicken breast marinated in lemongrass and ginger, with grilled balsamic-glazed vegetables. There's also salmon in puff pastry with spinach and citrus-dill butter sauce, and fricassee of scallops and shrimp served with Caribbean chutney.

176 blvd. de Grand-Case, Grand-Case. ☎ 590/87-55-80. Reservations recommended. Main courses 26€–30€ ($23.20–$26.80). MC, V. Daily 6–11pm. Closed Sun Apr–Nov.

INEXPENSIVE

Kakao *Finds* INTERNATIONAL   This French Polynesian–style open-air pavilion beside the sands of Orient Beach is always hopping, always hip. Amid dark-stained timbers, thatch-covered roofs, and nautical pieces that include the artifacts from several demolished or sunken yachts, you can drink, eat, sun, lie on lounge chairs, or simply gossip with the Euro-Caribbean crowd that hangs out here. Frozen piña coladas go for $6 each, beer for $2.50, and no one will mind if you just have a liquid lunch. But if you're hungry, a menu lists pizzas, grilled steaks and fish, burgers, ice cream, and banana splits. This place is a bit more family friendly, and a bit less irreverent and raunchy, than the Kon Tiki, next door.

Orient Beach. ☎ 590/87-43-26. Pizzas 10€–14.50€ ($8.95–$12.95); main courses 14.30€–22€ ($12.75–$19.65). AE, DISC, MC, V. Daily 8am–6pm.

Kon Tiki FRENCH/INTERNATIONAL   From the parking lots where you'll leave your car, this is the most distant of the several bars that flank the sands of Orient Bay. Inside, you'll find everything you'll need to amuse yourself for a day at the beach. Facilities include three bars, a watersports facility, volleyball courts, and a bandstand where there's often live music. Chaises longues with mattresses rent for $6 for a full day's use, and there's a staff member who'll bring you such party-colored drinks as a Sex on the Beach ($5). If you opt to spend part of a day here, you won't be alone: Previous clients have included the late John F. Kennedy, Jr., Diana Ross, Miss France, and French singer and heart-throb Johnny Halliday. Sundays here are particularly animated, thanks to a live band that plays between 8pm and around midnight, and a mousse machine that spits out dozens of gallons of foam onto the party animals gathered on the outdoor deck.

Orient Plage. ✆ 590/87-43-27. Burgers, sandwiches, pizzas, platters 6€–18€ ($5.35–$16.05). AE, MC, V. Daily 8am–7pm (until 9pm Nov–May; until 1am every Sun year-round)

La Brasserie de Marigot FRENCH   Gruff but friendly, this is a well-managed, fast-paced brasserie right in the heart of Marigot, with sidewalk tables. It's an excellent choice for good food at reasonable prices, and it draws local French-speaking residents, many from the French mainland. This building was originally a bank, and it still has a marble-and-brass decor, and a retro 1950s-style with green leather banquettes. Menu items include a succulent version of garlicky fish soup, frogs' legs in garlic sauce, snails in garlic butter sauce, breast of duckling in orange sauce, Provençal-style shrimp, pot-au-feu, and fillet of beef with mushroom sauce, all those good dishes that the French enjoy at blue-collar bistros. Naturally, you can order interesting terrines here, and wine is sold by the glass, carafe, or bottle. The kitchen also prepares a handful of Caribbean dishes, such as swordfish in garlic sauce. If it's on the menu, check out the tartar of shark, seasoned with onions, chives, and an ample dose of lime juice. There's also a U.S. inspired version of a "surf & turf."

11 rue du Général-de-Gaulle, Marigot. ✆ 590/87-94-43. Main courses 9.15€–28€ ($8.15–$25). AE, MC, V. Mon–Sat 7:30am–9pm.

L'Oizeau Rare ★ *(Value)* FRENCH   Overall, this is a rather grand, upscale restaurant that seems like a breezy, stylish restaurant along the Côte d'Azur. French cuisine is served in a blue-and-ivory-colored antique house with a view of three artfully landscaped waterfalls in the garden. The tables are dressed with snowy cloths and Limoges china. At lunch, served on the covered terrace, you can choose from a number of salads as well as fish and meat courses. Dinner choices include fresh fish, such as snapper, salmon, or fresh-caught mahi-mahi with lemon-flavored coconut sauce; thin-sliced carpaccio of salmon; fillet of pork with pineapple sauce; and fillets of lamb with Provençal herbs. Duck with mango or raspberries has always been a specialty, as has bouillabaisse or giant shrimp in garlic butter. The cooking is grounded firmly in France, but there are Caribbean twists and flavors, which come as delightful surprises. The wine list has an extensive selection of imported French options at moderate prices. Many guests come here at sundown to enjoy the harbor view.

Blvd. de France, Marigot. ✆ 590/87-56-38. Reservations recommended. Main courses 10€–24€ ($8.95–$21.45) lunch, 13€–32€ ($11.60–$28.60) dinner. AE, DISC, MC, V. Mon–Sat 11:30am–2:30pm and 6–10:30pm. Closed Sept.

Michael's Café *(Kids)* AMERICAN   This is the most Americanized hangout in Grand-Case. Breakfast is a daily highlight here, attracting beach boys, surfers, Americans and American wannabes, lots of repeat visitors, and even a handful of cruise ship passengers taxiing in from Marigot. You'll dine within a blue-and-white seafront enclave that's the personal domain of Boston-bred Mike Petone and his wife, Marilyn. (He cooks, she waits tables and tends bar.) Breakfast showcases an all-American medley of bacon, eggs, ham, and toast. Lunch might feature chili, Caesar salad, pepper steak sandwiches, and fish soup. Happy hour, Monday to Saturday from 4 to 6pm, provides one of the genuinely sociable venues in Grand-Case. Dinners are relatively free form, consisting of whatever the owners feel like cooking that night, as filtered through their perceptions of how busy the evening might be. If it's available, try the linguine in clam sauce—it's usually excellent.

48 blvd. de Grand-Case, Grand-Case. ℂ 590/87-23-68. Breakfast platters 7€–9€ ($6.25–$8.05); lunch and dinner main courses 9€–17€ ($8.05–$15.20). No credit cards. Tues–Sat 9am–7pm, Sun 9am–11pm

Sunset Café INTERNATIONAL   Set on the sands at the Grand-Case Beach Club, this open-air restaurant and bar wraps around the rocky peninsula that divides Grand-Case Beach from Petite Plage. Tables are strewn along a narrow veranda-style terrace that affords sweeping views of the setting sun. A planter's punch will make the fish soup, locally smoked fish, snails with Roquefort sauce, or red snapper fillet with vanilla sauce taste even better. Lunch items are simpler, with emphasis on sandwiches, burgers, melon with slices of Parma ham, pastas, and salads. The hotel here tends to be a little staid, so this place is better suited to a quiet and romantic dinner than it is to a wild party.

In the Grand-Case Beach Club, rue de Petit-Plage, Grande-Case. ℂ 590/87-51-87. Reservations recommended only for weekend dinners in winter. Lunch main courses 7€–11€ ($6.25–$9.80); dinner main courses 16€–24€ ($14.30–$21.45). AE, MC, V. Daily 7:30am–10pm.

4 Beaches 🌟🌟

The island has 36 beautiful white-sand beaches, and it's fairly easy to find a place to park your beach towel. Most beaches have recovered from the erosion caused by the 1995 hurricane. *Warning:* If it's too secluded, be careful. It's unwise to carry valuables to the beach; there have been reports of robberies on some remote strips.

Regardless of where you stay, you're never far from the water. If you're a beach sampler, you can often use the changing facilities at some of the bigger resorts for a small fee. Nudists should head for the French side of the island, although the Dutch side is getting more liberal about such things. Here's a rundown of the best, starting on the Dutch side of the island.

The popular **Cupecoy Bay Beach** is very close to the Dutch–French border, on the western side of the island. It's a string of three white-sand beaches set against a backdrop of caves, beautiful rock formations, and cliffs that provide morning shade. There are no restaurants, bars, or other facilities here, but locals come around with coolers of cold beer and soda for sale. The beach has two parking lots, one near Cupecoy and Sapphire beach clubs, the other a short distance to the west. Parking costs $2. You must descend stone-carved steps to reach the sands. Cupecoy is also the island's major gay beach.

Also on the west side of the island, west of the airport, **Mullet Bay Beach** is filled with white sand and shaded by palm trees. Once it was the most crowded beach on the island, but St. Maarten's largest resort, Mullet Bay, remained closed at press time, so the crowds aren't so bad anymore. Weekdays are best, as many locals flock here on weekends. Watersports equipment can be rented at a kiosk here.

Another lovely spot near the airport, **Maho Bay Beach,** at the Maho Beach Hotel and Casino, is shaded by palms and is ideal in many ways, if you don't mind the planes taking off and landing nearby. This is one of the island's busiest beaches, buzzing with windsurfers. Food and drink can be purchased at the hotel.

Stretching the length of Simpson Bay Village are the mile-long (2km) white sands of crescent-shaped **Simpson Bay Beach,** west of Philipsburg before you reach the airport. This beach is popular with windsurfers, and it's an ideal place for a stroll or a swim. Watersports equipment rentals are available here, but there are no changing rooms or other facilities.

Great Bay Beach is preferred if you're staying along Front Street in Philipsburg. This mile-long (2km) beach is sandy, but since it borders the busy capital, it may not be as clean as some of the more remote choices. On a clear day, you'll have a view of Saba. Immediately to the west, at the foot of Fort Amsterdam, is picturesque **Little Bay Beach,** but it, too, can be overrun with tourists. When you tire of the sands here, you can climb up to the site of Fort Amsterdam itself. Built in 1631, it was the first Dutch military outpost in the Caribbean. The Spanish captured it 2 years later, making it their most important bastion east of Puerto Rico. Only a few of the fort's walls remain, but the view is panoramic.

On the east side of the island, **Dawn Beach** is noted for its underwater life, with some of the island's most beautiful reefs immediately offshore. Visitors talk ecstatically of its incredible sunrises. Dawn is suitable for swimming and offers year-round activities such as sand-castle-building contests and crab races. There's plenty of wave action for both surfers and windsurfers. The road to this beach is bumpy, but worth the effort. Nearby are the pearly white sands of **Oyster Pond Beach,** near the Oyster Bay Beach Resort. Bodysurfers like the rolling waves here.

Top rating on St. Martin goes to **Baie Longue** on the west side of the island, a beautiful beach that's rarely overcrowded. Chic and very expensive La Samanna opens onto this beachfront. Its reef-protected waters are ideal for snorkeling, but there is a strong undertow. Baie Longue is to the north of Cupecoy Bay Beach, reached via the Lowlands Road. Don't leave any valuables in your car, as many break-ins have been reported along this occasionally dangerous stretch of highway.

If you continue north along the highway, you'll reach another long and popular stretch of sand and jagged coral, **Baie Rouge.** Swimming is excellent here, and snorkelers are drawn to the rock formations at both ends of the beach. This intimate little spot is especially lovely in the morning. There are no changing facilities, but a local kiosk sells cold drinks.

Isolated, but well-known among St. Martin's beach-going crowd, **Friar's Bay Beach** lies at the end of a winding country road; its clearly signposted entrance intersects with the main highway between Grand-Case and Marigot. Although you certainly won't be alone here, this is a less-visited beach with ample parking. There's some topless sunbathing, depending on who happens to show up.

White-sand **Grand-Case Beach** is right in the middle of the town of Grand-Case and is likely to be crowded, especially on weekends. The waters are very calm here, making swimming excellent, and making it a good choice for families with kids. A small but select beach, it has its own charm, with none of the carnival-like atmosphere found on other beaches.

On the eastern side of the island, **Orient Beach** is the island's only official nudist beach, so anything (or nothing, as it were) goes in terms of attire. There's steady action here: bouncy Caribbean bands, refreshments of all kinds, watersports, and clothing, crafts, and jewelry vendors. Everyone comes to enjoy this stretch of velvety white sands. The coral reef off the beach here is teeming with marine life, making for great snorkeling. Club Orient, the nude resort, is at the end of the beach; voyeurs from cruise ships can always be spotted here. This is also a haven for windsurfers.

Finally, for the most isolated and secluded beach of all, you have to leave St. Martin. **Ilet Pinel,** off the coast at Cul-de-Sac, is reached by a boat ride off the northeast coast (you can hire a local boatman to take you from Cul-de-Sac for about $5 one way). The island has no residents (except wild goats), phones, or electricity. You will find fine white-sand beaches, idyllic reefs with great snorkeling, and waters great for bodysurfing. There are even two beach bars that rent lounge chairs and serve dishes such as lobster, ribs, and grilled chicken.

5 Sports & Other Outdoor Pursuits

DEEP-SEA FISHING   **Pelican Watersports,** on the Dutch side, at the Pelican Resort and Casino, Simpson Bay (© 599/54-42640), is part of one of the island's most comprehensive resorts. Their 40-foot (12m) *Kratuna* is available for deep-sea-fishing expeditions priced at $600 for a half-day (7–11am) or $1,200 for a full day (7am–3pm) excursion.

GOLF   The **Mullet Bay Resort** (© 599/54-53069), on the Dutch side, has the island's only golf course. It's a slightly battered, slightly dusty 18-hole Joseph Lee–designed course, whose fate has hung in the balance, based on some ongoing court battles, for years. Although the resort itself is closed, the golf course is still operational. Mullet Pond and Simpson Bay Lagoon provide both beauty and hazards. Greens fees are $40 for 9 holes or $70 for 18 holes, for players who opt to walk instead of ride. Renting an electric cart, serviceable for up to two players at a time, will cost an additional $30 to $36, depending on how many holes you play. Club rentals cost $21 for 9 holes or $26 for 18 holes.

HORSEBACK RIDING   Increasingly popular, horseback riding is possible at **Bayside Riding Club,** Route Galion Beach, Orientale (© 590/87-36-64). Rides along the beach are a highlight, and prices start at $50 for a 2-hour ride.

SCUBA DIVING   Scuba diving is excellent around **St. Martin,** with reef, wreck, night, cave, and drift diving; the depth of dives is 20 to 70 feet (6–21m). Off the northeastern coast on the French side, dive sites include Ilet Pinel, for shallow diving; Green Key, a barrier reef; and Tintamarre, for sheltered coves and geologic faults. To the north, Anse Marcel and neighboring Anguilla are good choices. Most hotels will arrange scuba excursions on request.

The island's premier dive operation is **Marine Time,** whose offices are immediately adjacent to the West Indies Mall, Chemin du Port, Marigot (© 590/87-20-28). Operated by Englishman Philip Baumann, it offers morning and afternoon dives in deep and shallow water, wreck dives, and reef dives, at a cost of $45 per dive. A resort course for first-time divers with reasonable swimming skills costs $80 and includes 60 to 90 minutes of instruction in a swimming pool, then a one-tank dive above a coral reef. Full PADI certification costs $400, an experience that requires 5 days and includes classroom training, sessions with a scuba tank within the safety of a swimming pool, and three open-water dives. Snorkeling trips cost $25 for a half day or $75 for a full day, plus $10 for equipment rental. This organization will also arrange rentals, with a skipper and crew if necessary, of yachts and catamarans for sea-borne jaunts to neighboring islands.

You can also try **Blue Ocean Watersport & Dive Center,** BP 4079, Baie Nettlé, St. Martin (© 590/87-89-73). A certified one-tank dive costs $45, including equipment. A PADI certification course is available for $336, and takes 4 to 5 days. Three one-tank dives are offered for $120, five dives for $180. Snorkeling trips, more modestly priced at $35, are conducted daily from 9am to noon, and from 2:30 to 5:30pm.

St. Maarten's crystal-clear bays and countless coves make for good scuba diving as well as snorkeling. Underwater visibility runs from 75 to 125 feet (23–38m). The biggest attraction for divers is the 1801 British man-of-war,

HMS *Proselyte,* which came to a watery grave on a reef a mile (2km) off the coast. Most of the big resorts have facilities for scuba diving and can provide information about underwater tours, photography, as well as night diving.

SNORKELING ★★ The calm waters ringing the shallow reefs and tiny coves found throughout the island make it a snorkeler's heaven. The waters off the northeastern shores of French St. Martin have been classified as a regional underwater nature reserve, **Réserve Sous-Marine Régionale,** which protects the area around Flat Island (also known as Tintamarre), Ilet Pinel, Green Key, Proselyte, and Petite Clef. Equipment can be rented at almost any hotel, and most beaches have watersports kiosks.

One of St. Martin's best sources for snorkeling and other beach diversions is **Carib Watersports** (© 590/87-51-87), a clothing store, art gallery, and watersports kiosk on the beachfront of the Grand-Case Beach Club. Its French and U.S. staff, which includes Michigan-born Marla Welch, provides information on island activities and rents kayaks for $15 an hour, paddleboats for $20 an hour, and snorkeling equipment for $10 a day. The main allure, however, are the guided snorkeling trips to St. Martin's teeming offshore reefs, including Creole Rock, an offshore clump of reef-ringed boulders rich in underwater fauna. The 2-hour trips depart daily at 11am and cost $20, with all equipment included. Reservations are recommended.

TENNIS You can try the courts at most of the large resorts, but you must call first for a reservation. Preference, of course, is given to hotel guests.

On the Dutch side, there are three lit courts at **The Pelican,** Simpson Bay (© 599/54-42503); another three lit courts at the **Divi Little Bay Beach Resort,** Little Bay Road (© 599/54-22333); and yet another three at the **Maho Beach Hotel,** Maho Bay (© 599/54-52115).

On the French side, the **Privilège Resort & Spa,** Anse Marcel (© 590/87-38-38), offers four lit tennis courts and two squash courts; the **Hotel Mont Vernon,** Baie Orientale (© 590/87-62-00), has two courts; and the **Nettlé Bay Beach Club,** Baie Nettlé (© 590/87-68-68), has three lit Laykold courts.

WATER-SKIING & PARASAILING Most of French St. Martin's large beachfront hotels maintain facilities for water-skiing and parasailing, often from kiosks that operate on the beach.

Two independent operators on Orient Bay, close to the cluster of hotels near the Esmeralda Hotel, include **Kon Tiki Watersports** (© 590/87-46-89) and **Bikini Beach Watersports** (© 590/87-43-25). They both rent jet skis for around $45 per half-hour; parasailing costs $50 for 10 minutes or $80 if two go together.

Jet-skiing and water-skiing are also especially popular in Dutch St. Maarten. The unruffled waters of Simpson Bay Lagoon, the largest lagoon in the West Indies, are ideal for these sports, and outfitters have facilities right on the sands.

WINDSURFING Most windsurfers gravitate to the eastern part of the island, most notably Coconut Grove Beach, Orient Beach, and to a lesser extent, Dawn Beach, all in French St. Martin. The best of the several outfitters here is **Tropical Wave,** Coconut Grove, Le Galion Beach, Baie de l'Embouchure (© 590/87-37-25). Set midway between Orient Beach and Oyster Pond, it has an ideal combination of wind and calm waters. Tropical Wave is the island's leading sales agent for Mistral Windsurfers. They rent for $20 an hour, with instruction offered at $30 an hour.

In St. Maarten, visitors usually head to Simpson Bay Lagoon for windsurfing.

7 Shopping ★★★

IN DUTCH ST. MAARTEN

Not only is St. Maarten a free port, but it also has no local sales taxes. Prices are sometimes lower here than anywhere else in the Caribbean, except possibly St. Thomas. On some items (fine liqueurs, cigarettes, Irish linen, German cameras, French perfumes), we've found prices 30% to 50% lower than in the United States or Canada. Many well-known shops on Curaçao have branches here.

Except for the boutiques at resort hotels, the main shopping area is in the center of **Philipsburg.** Most of the shops are on **Front Street** (called Voorstraat in Dutch), which is closer to the bay, and **Back Street** (Achterstraat), which runs parallel.

In general, the prices marked on the merchandise are firm, though at some small, very personally run shops, where the owner is on site, some bargaining might be in order.

Antillean Liquors, Queen Juliana Airport (© **599/54-54267**), has a complete assortment of liquor and liqueurs, cigarettes and cigars. Prices are generally lower here than in other stores on the island, and the selection is larger. The only local product sold is the Guavaberry island liqueur.

Del Sol St-Maarten, 23 Front St. (© **599/54-28784**), sells men's and women's sportswear. Embedded into the mostly black-and-white designs are organic crystals that react to sunlight (specifically, ultraviolet light), which transforms the fabric into a rainbow of colors. Step back into the shadows, and your T-shirt will revert to its original black-and-white design. The same technology is applied to yo-yos, which shimmer psychedelically when you bob them up and down.

Colombian Emeralds International, Old Street Shopping Center (© **599/ 54-23933**), sells unmounted emeralds from Colombia, as well as emerald, gold, diamond, ruby, and sapphire jewelry. Prices are approximately the same as in other outlets of this famous Caribbean chain, and if you're seriously shopping for emeralds, this is the place. There are some huckster vendors around the island pawning fakes off on unsuspecting tourists; Colombian Emeralds offers the genuine item.

Belgian Chocolate Shop, 109 Old St. (© **599/54-28863**), is the best of its kind on island. Contrary to popular rumor, only *some* of the velvety chocolates sold in this upscale shop are pornographic, portraying parts of the human anatomy. Chocolates seem to fly out of this shop, especially on days when cruise ships are berthed at the nearby piers.

Guavaberry Company, 8–10 Front St. (© **599/54-22965**), sells the rare "island folk liqueur" of St. Maarten, which for centuries was made only in private homes. Sold in square bottles, the product is made from rum that's given a unique flavor with rare berries usually grown in the hills in the center of the island. (Don't confuse guavaberries with guavas—they're very different.) The liqueur has a fruity, woody, almost bittersweet flavor. You can blend it with coconut for a unique guavaberry colada or pour a splash into a glass of icy champagne.

Greenwich Galleries, 20 Front St. (© **599/54-23842**), is the most interesting and sophisticated art gallery on either side of the island, with Bajan pottery in tones of sea greens and blues, replicas of Taínoartifacts, enamelled metal cutouts that are both quirky and perplexing, and a range of paintings and lithographs from artists as far away as Holland and Britain.

Little Switzerland, 52 Front St. (© **599/54-22523**), is part of a chain of stores spread throughout the Caribbean. These fine-quality European imports are made even more attractive by the prices, often 25% or more lower than stateside. Elegant famous-name watches, china, crystal, and jewelry are for sale, plus perfume and accessories. Little Switzerland has the best overall selection of these items of any shop on the Dutch side.

The **Caribbean Camera Centre,** 79 Front St. (© **599/54-25259**), has a wide range of merchandise, but it's always wise to know the prices charged back home before making a major purchase. Cameras here may be among the cheapest on St. Maarten; however, if you're going to St. Thomas, we've discovered better deals there.

Little Europe, 80 Front St. (© **599/54-24371**), is an upscale purveyor of all the "finer things" in life. It's favored by cruise-ship passengers because its prices are inexpensive compared to North American boutiques. Inventory includes porcelain figurines by Hummel, jewelry, and watches by Concorde, Piaget, Corum, and Movado.

At the **Shipwreck Shop,** Front Street (© **599/54-22962**), you'll find West Indian hammocks, beach towels, salad bowls, baskets, jewelry, T-shirts, postcards, books, wood carvings, native art, sea salt, cane sugar, and spices—in all, a treasure trove of Caribbean handcrafts. If you're looking for affordable gifts or handcrafts in general, this might be your best bet.

IN FRENCH ST. MARTIN

Many day-trippers come over to Marigot from the Dutch side of the island just to visit the French-inspired boutiques and shopping arcades. Because St. Martin is also a duty-free port, you'll find some of the best shopping in the Caribbean here as well. There's a wide selection of European merchandise, much of it luxury items such as crystal, fashions, fine liqueurs, and cigars, sometimes at 25% to 50% less than in the United States and Canada. Whether you're seeking jewelry, perfume, or St. Tropez bikinis, you'll find it in one of the boutiques along **rue de la République** and **rue de la Liberté** in Marigot. Look especially for French luxury items, such as Lalique crystal, Vuitton bags, and Chanel perfume.

Prices are often quoted in U.S. dollars, and salespeople frequently speak English. Credit cards and traveler's checks are generally accepted. When cruise ships are in port on Sundays and holidays, some of the larger shops stay open.

At harborside in Marigot, there's a lively **morning market** with vendors selling spices, fruit, shells, and handcrafts. Shops here tend to be rather upscale, catering to passengers of the small but choice cruise ships that dock offshore.

At **Port La Royale,** the bustling center of everything, mornings are even more active: Schooners unload produce from the neighboring islands, boats board guests for picnics on deserted beaches, a brigantine sets out on a sightseeing sail, and a dozen different little restaurants are readying for the lunch crowd. The largest shopping arcade on St. Martin, it has lots of boutiques.

Havane Boutique, 50 Marina Port La Royale (© **590/87-70-39**), is a hyper-stylish menswear store, more couture than ready-to-wear. **Serge Blanco "15" Boutique,** Marina Port La Royale (© **590/29-65-49**), is a relatively unknown name in North America, but in France, Blanco is revered as one of the most successful rugby players of all time. His menswear is sporty, fun, and elegant. Everything is manufactured in or near Blanco's hometown of Biarritz in southwestern France. Clothes include polo shirts, shorts, and truly wonderful latex jackets. **Gingerbread & Mahogany Gallery,** 4–14 Marina Royale (© **590/**

87-73-21), is among the finest galleries on the island. Owner Simone Seitre is one of the most knowledgeable purveyors of Haitian art in the Caribbean. Even if you're not in the market for an expensive piece, you'll find dozens of charming and inexpensive handcrafts. The little gallery is a bit hard to find (on a narrow alleyway at the marina), but it's worth the search.

Another complex, the **Galerie Périgourdine,** facing the post office, also has a cluster of boutiques. Here you might pick up designer wear for both men and women, including items from the collection of Ted Lapidus.

Act III, 3 rue du Général-de-Gaulle (© **590/29-28-43**), is perhaps the most glamorous women's boutique in St. Martin. It prides itself on its evening gowns and chic cocktail dresses. If you've been invited to a reception aboard a private yacht, this is the place to find the right outfit. Designers include Alaïa, Thierry Mugler, Gianni Versace, Christian Lacroix, Cerruti, and Gaultier. The bilingual staff is accommodating, tactful, and charming.

J'Aime Ça by Bettina, Passage Louisiane (© **590/87-29-76**), sells lace garments, the kind that are demure when worn with undergarments and more than a bit naughty when worn without them. Lace, lace, and more lace—in colors that include white, ecru, and black—is fashioned into skirts, tops, jumpsuits, shirts and blouses, and even "summer coats" that have lots of style but virtually no warmth, thanks to the peek-a-boo holes artfully crafted into each square yard.

La Romana, 12 rue de la République (© **590/87-88-16**), specializes in chic women's clothing that's a bit less pretentious and more fun and lighthearted than the selection at Act III. Italian rather than French designers are emphasized, including lines such as Anna Club and Ritmo de la Perloa, plus La Perla swimwear, Moschino handbags, and perfumes. A small collection of menswear is also available. The popular chain **Little Switzerland** has a branch here on rue de la République (© **590/87-50-03**). This outlet is different from the one on the Dutch side, with a concentration on French products. The widest array of duty-free luxury items in French St. Martin is available here, including French perfume and leather goods. **Maneks,** 24 rue de la République (© **590/ 87-54-91**), has a little bit of everything: video cameras, electronics, household appliances, liquors, gifts, souvenirs, beach accessories, film, watches, T-shirts, sunglasses, and Majorca pearls. The staff even sells Cuban cigars, but these can't be brought back into the United States. **Roland Richardson Paintings and Prints,** 6 rue de la République (© **590/87-84-08**), has a beautiful gallery. A native of St. Martin, Mr. Richardson is one of the Caribbean's premier artists, working in oil, watercolors, pastels, and charcoal. Called a "modern-day Gauguin," he is known for his landscapes, portraits, and colorful still-lifes. His work has been exhibited in more than 70 one-man and group exhibitions in museums and galleries around the world.

A charming roadside Creole cottage is home to **Gloria Lynn Studio,** 83 bd. de Grand-Case (© **590/87-77-24**), which offers some of the most interesting paintings in Grand-Case. Inside, you'll find artworks produced by four members of the Lynn family (Gloria, Marty, Peter, and Robert). Their shared theme is island life and island sociology.

8 St. Maarten/St. Martin After Dark ⓐⓐ

After-dark activities begin early here, as guests start off with a sundowner, perhaps on the garden patio of **Pasanggrahan** (see "Accommodations," earlier in this chapter). The most popular bar on the island is **Cheri's Café** (see "Dining," earlier in this chapter).

Many hotels sponsor **beachside barbecues** (particularly in season) with steel bands, native music, and folk dancing. Outsiders are welcomed at most of these events, but call ahead to see if it's a private affair.

The **Casino Royale,** at the Maho Beach Hotel on Maho Bay (© **599/54-52115**), has 16 blackjack tables, 6 roulette wheels, and 3 craps and 3 Caribbean stud-poker tables. The casino offers baccarat, mini-baccarat, and more than 250 slot machines. It's open daily from 1pm to 4am. The **Casino Royale Cabaret Theater,** newly inaugurated in 2001, is the largest and most technologically sophisticated theater on either side of St Maarten/St. Martin, with glittery shows whose schedule changes according to whatever act has been booked at the time. Within the same building is the island's most block-busting disco, the **Q-Club.** Containing wraparound catwalks that look down on the dance floor, multiple bars, colored lights, and very danceable music, it's open nightly from around 10pm, attracting dance-a-holics from both sides of the island. A cover charge of between $5 and $10 is sometimes imposed, depending on the season and the night of the week.

One of the island's most visited casinos, the **Dolphin,** is at The Caravanserai on Beacon Hill Rd. (© **599/54-54000**). Gamblers start pouring in here at 1pm daily, some staying until 3 the next morning.

The **Sunset Beach Bar,** 2 Beacon Hill Rd., Airport Beach (© **599/54-53998**), is set directly on the sands of airport beach, and resembles an oversized gazebo. This place is mobbed most afternoons and evenings with office workers, off-duty airline pilots, beach people, and occasional celebs like Sandra Bullock. No one seems to mind the whine of airplane engines overhead, or the fumes that filter down from aircraft that seem to fly at precarious altitudes just a few dozen feet overhead. Drinks are cheap, and you can order burgers, sandwiches, steaks, fish, chicken, and hot dogs from an outdoor charcoal grill. Many local residents time their arrival here for sundown (usually beginning around 6:30pm), when "shooters of the day," cost only $1 each.

The **Pelican Resort Club,** Simpson Bay (© **599/54-42503**), has a popular Vegas-style casino with a panoramic view of the bay. It offers 2 craps tables, 3 roulette tables, 9 blackjack tables, 2 stud-poker tables, and 120 slot machines. The Pelican also features horse racing, bingo, and sports nights with events broadcast via satellite, plus nightly dancing on the Pelican Reef Terrace and island shows featuring Caribbean bands. It's open daily from 1pm to 3am.

Indiana Beach Restaurant & Bar and Indy's Bar, Kimshore, Simpson Bay (© **599/54-42797**), are immediately adjacent to one another and set beside the sands of Simpson's Bay. They jointly reign as queen (or king) of the night every Thursday after 8:30pm, when they're mobbed with singles, who enjoy the two-for-one frozen margaritas after 10pm. The decor combines aspects of Harrison Ford's *Indiana Jones and the Temple of Doom* (theme-ish looking flaming torches, statues of Polynesian demigods, caged alligators, and so on) with thatch-covered

Moments **Waiting with Ernest at the Bar**

Each evening, visitors watch for the legendary **green flash,** an atmospheric phenomenon described by Hemingway that sometimes occurs in these latitudes just as the sun drops below the horizon. Guests have been known to break into a round of applause at a particularly spectacular sunset.

bohios set directly on the sands of the beach. If you want a full-fledged meal, Indiana Beach serves lunch and dinner daily.

The Roman-themed **Coliseum Casino,** on Front Street in Philipsburg (© **599/54-32102**), tries to attract high rollers, and has the highest table limits ($1,000 maximum) on St. Maarten. The Coliseum features more than 200 slot machines, 4 blackjack tables, 3 poker tables, and 2 roulette wheels. The Coliseum is open daily from 11am to 3am.

Right in the heart of Philipsburg's shopping-crazed Front Street, **Rouge et Noir** (© **599/54-22952**) has a futuristic design. It offers slot machines, a Sigma Derby horse machine, video Keno, and video poker. It opens Monday to Saturday at 9am and Sunday at 11am to snag cruise-ship passengers.

On the French side, in the heart of Grand-Case, **Portofino,** bd. de Grand-Case (© **590/29-08-28**), is a lot of fun. A few nights a week, live rock and roll and country-western music is presented, with a French accent, between 10pm and 1am. There's no cover charge, and the cross-cultural pollination is charming. A menu lists all kinds of pizzas and pastas to stave off starvation.

Also in Grand-Case, **Calmos Café,** blvd. du Grand-Case no. 4 (© **590/29-01-85**), is funky and low-key. This beachfront shack draws a young, hip crowd, with an occasional pop icon like Linda Evangelista dropping in. (In this case, she arrived with her then-fiancé, soccer star Fabien Barthez.) Management posts a sign that says "no snobs" near the entrance. In winter, there's sometimes live music after 9:30pm. Most people come just to flirt, gossip, and drink, but there's also good, affordable food, such as a Greek salad, a tuna salad, and "New Wave burgers" that are slathered with goat cheese. Also popular is an Ocean Salad, combining salad greens with three kinds of grilled fish plus shrimp. The house special drink is a Ti Punch that's a local variation on an old-fashioned rum punch. It's open daily from 10am to 11pm.

St. Vincent & The Grenadines

One of the major British Windward Islands, sleepy St. Vincent is just beginning to awaken to tourism. Sailors and the yachting set have long known of St. Vincent and the Grenadines, and until recently it was a well-kept vacation secret.

You visit St. Vincent for its lush beauty, and the Grenadines for the best sailing waters in the Caribbean. Don't come for nightlife, grand cuisine, or fabled beaches. There are some white-sand beaches near Kingstown on St. Vincent, but most of the other beaches ringing the island are of black sand. The yachting crowd seems to view St. Vincent merely as a launching pad for the 40-plus-mile (64km) string of the Grenadines, but the island still has a few attractions that make it worth exploring on its own.

Unspoiled by the fallout that mass tourism sometimes brings, the people actually treat visitors like human beings: Met with courtesy, they respond with courtesy. British customs predominate, along with traces of Gallic cultural influences, but all with a distinct West Indian flair.

South of St. Vincent, the small chain of islands called the Grenadines extends for more than 40 miles (64km). The islands are strung like a necklace of precious stones and have such romantic-sounding names as Bequia, Mustique, Canouan, and Petit St. Vincent. We'll explore Union and Palm Islands, and Mayreau as well. A few of the islands have accommodations, but many are so small and so completely undeveloped that they attract only beachcombers and stray boaters.

Populated by the descendants of African slaves and administered by St. Vincent, the Grenadines collectively add up to a landmass of 30 square miles (78 sq. km). These specks of land, often dots on nautical charts, may lack natural resources, but they're blessed with white-sand beaches, coral reefs, and their own kind of sleepy beauty. If you don't stay overnight in the Grenadines, at least try to visit one of them on a day trip, and enjoy a picnic lunch (which your hotel will pack for you) on your own quiet stretch of sand.

1 St. Vincent & The Grenadines Essentials

VISITOR INFORMATION

In the United States, you can get information at the **St. Vincent and Grenadines Tourist Office,** 801 Second Ave., 21st Floor, New York, NY 10017 (© **800/729-1726** or 212/687-4981).

The website for St. Vincent and the Grenadines is **www.svgtourism.com.**

On St. Vincent, the local **Department of Tourism** is on Upper Bay Street, Government Administrative Centre, Kingstown (© **784/457-1502**). Open Monday to Friday from 8am to 4:30pm.

GETTING THERE

In the eastern Caribbean, St. Vincent—the "gateway to the Grenadines" (the individual islands are discussed later in this chapter)—lies 100 miles (161km) west of Barbados. **American Eagle** (© **800/433-7300** in the U.S., or 784/456-5000; www.aa.com) has one flight daily from San Juan, making it more convenient than ever to get here. If that flight doesn't work for you, you may fly to Barbados first where you can make connections to St. Vincent's **E. T. Joshua Airport** and on to the Grenadines. For details on getting to Barbados from North America, see chapter 6.

Air Martinique (© **784/458-4528**) runs chartered service between Martinique, St. Lucia, St. Vincent, and Union Island.

Dependable **Mustique Airways** (© **784/458-4380;** www.mustique.com) makes frequent runs from St. Vincent to the major airports of the Grenadines. With advance warning, Mustique Airways will arrange reasonably priced special charters to and from many of the surrounding islands (including Grenada, Aruba, St. Lucia, Antigua, Barbados, Trinidad, and any others in the southern Caribbean). The price of these chartered flights is less than you might expect and often matches the fares on conventional Caribbean airlines. The airline currently owns seven small aircraft, none of which carries more than nine passengers.

GETTING AROUND ST. VINCENT

BY TAXI   The government sets the rates for fares, but taxis are unmetered, so be sure to agree on the fare before getting in. Figure on spending $10 or more to go from the E. T. Joshua Airport to your hotel. You should tip about 12% of the fare.

You can also hire taxis to take you to the island's major attractions. Most drivers seem to be well-informed guides (it won't take you long to learn everything you need to know about St. Vincent). You'll spend from $15 per hour for a car holding two to four passengers.

BY RENTAL CAR   Driving on St. Vincent is a bit of an adventure because of the narrow, twisting roads (don't be shy about sounding your horn as you make the sharp hairpin turns). *Drive on the left.* If you present your valid driver's license from home at the police department, on Bay Street in Kingstown, and pay an EC$50 (US$18.50) fee, you'll get a temporary permit to drive.

Avis (© **800/331-1084** in the U.S., or 784/456-2929 locally; www.avis.com) has a branch at the airport. One local rental firm is **Star Garage,** on Grenville Street in Kingstown (© **784/456-1743**). Make sure your car has a spare tire because the roads are full of potholes.

BY BUS   Flamboyantly painted "alfresco" buses travel the principal roads of St. Vincent, linking the major towns and villages. The price is low, depending on where you're going, and the experience will connect you with the locals. The central departure point is the bus terminal at the New Kingstown Fish Market. Fares range from EC$1 to EC$6 (US35¢–US$2.20).

Fun Fact   **Special Events**

Late June brings St. Vincent's weeklong **Carnival,** one of the largest such celebrations in the eastern Caribbean. The festivities include steel-band and calypso competitions, parades, costumes, and the crowning of the king and queen of the carnival. The fun extends through the first 2 weeks in July, culminating in a huge street party.

FAST FACTS: **St. Vincent & The Grenadines**

Banks Most banks are open Monday to Thursday from 8am to either 1 or 3pm, and Friday from either 8am to 5pm or 8am to 1pm and 3 to 5pm. There are a few banks with ATMs on Halifax Street in Kingstown on St. Vincent (plus one at the airport), and there are also a few on Bequia and Union Island.

Currency The official currency of St. Vincent is the **Eastern Caribbean dollar (EC$)**, pegged at about $2.70 per U.S. dollar. *Most of the quotations in this chapter appear in U.S. dollars, unless marked EC$.* Most restaurants, shops, and hotels will accept payment in U.S. dollars or traveler's checks.

Documents British, Canadian, and U.S. citizens should have a passport and a return or ongoing airplane ticket. A birth certificate with a raised seal is often accepted with a photo ID, but we always recommend traveling with your passport overseas.

Electricity Electricity is 220-volt AC (50 cycles), so if you're traveling with U.S. appliances, you'll need an adapter and a transformer. Some hotels have transformers, but it's best to bring your own.

Emergencies In an emergency, dial ☎ **999.**

Hospitals There is one hospital on St. Vincent in Kingstown: **Kingstown General Hospital** (☎ **784/456-1185**).

Language English is the official language.

Liquor Laws Liquor can be sold on any day of the week. It's legal to have an open container on the beach as long as you don't get rowdy or litter.

Pharmacies On St. Vincent, try **Deane's Pharmacy,** Halifax Street, Kingstown (☎ **784/457-2056**), open Monday to Friday from 8:30am to 4:30pm and Saturday from 8:30am to 12:30pm. There are a few other drugstores to choose from in Kingstown as well.

Post Office The **General Post Office,** on Halifax Street in Kingstown (☎ **784/456-1111**), is open Monday to Friday from 8:30am to 3pm and Saturday from 8:30 to 11:30am. There are smaller post offices in 56 districts throughout the country, including offices on the Grenadine islands of Bequia, Mustique, Canouan, Mayreau, and Union Island.

Safety St. Vincent and its neighboring islands of the Grenadines are quite safe. Even in Kingstown, the capital of St. Vincent, chances are you'll encounter little serious crime. However, take the usual precautions and never leave valuables unguarded.

Taxes & Service Charges The government imposes an airport departure tax of EC$30 (US$11.25) per person. A 7% government occupancy tax is charged for all hotel accommodations. Hotels and restaurants almost always add a 10% to 15% service charge. Ask whether or not it's included in the initial hotel rates you're quoted. If it's not already added at a restaurant, tip at that rate.

Telephone To call St. Vincent from the United States, dial **1**, then **784** (the area code for St. Vincent) and the local seven-digit number. Once on St. Vincent, you can access **AT&T Direct** at ☎ **800/872-2881.** To reach **MCI,** dial ☎ **800/888-8000.**

Time Both St. Vincent and the Grenadines operate on Atlantic standard time year-round: When it's 6am on St. Vincent, it's 5am in New York. During daylight saving time in the United States, St. Vincent keeps the same time as the U.S. east coast.

Water In St. Vincent and the Grenadines, stick to bottled water.

Weather The climate of St. Vincent and the Grenadines is pleasantly cooled by the trade winds year-round. The tropical temperature is in the 78° to 82°F range. The rainy season is May to November.

2 St. Vincent Accommodations

Don't expect high-rise resorts here; everything is small. The places are comfortable, not fancy, and you usually get a lot of personal attention from the staff. Most hotels and restaurants add a 7% government tax and a 10% to 15% service charge to your bill; ask whether these taxes are included in the prices quoted.

If you want a luxurious resort, head for the Grenadines. Except for Young Island, most resorts here are fairly simple affairs, and since most people are only in St. Vincent for a night or two, you may prefer to be located directly in the center in the capital of Kingstown.

VERY EXPENSIVE

Petit Byahaut ★ *Finds* This ecologically sensitive place attracts snorkelers, scuba divers, and anyone who wants to truly get away from it all and get back to nature. (All that simplicity is awfully expensive, though.) Lying 4½ miles (7km) north of Kingstown on the leeward coast and accessible only by boat, Petit Byahaut accepts no more than 14 guests at a time. Guests are housed in roomy tents with queen-size beds, screened windows and doors, and large covered decks with hammocks. In various nooks and crannies built into the hills are your outdoor freshwater shower, sink, and toilet. Lush foliage between the tents provides privacy; hummingbirds and other winged creatures often visit the tropical flowers blooming on the grounds. Opening onto a horseshoe-shaped bay, where more hammocks await on the sands, the complex stands in a 50-acre (20-hectare) private valley. A seaside bar and restaurant offers wholesome, healthy meals, picnics are prepared during the day, and dinner is served by candlelight. The reef right off the beach provides excellent snorkeling and scuba diving, and watersports equipment is provided. Rain forest trips, boating, and guided snorkeling and scuba trips can be arranged.

Petit Byahaut Bay, St. Vincent, W.I. Ⓒ and fax **784/457-7008.** www.petitbyahaut.com. 4 units: 3 tents, 1 patio dwelling. Year-round $380 double per day, or $1,500 for 5 days/4 nights. Rates are all-inclusive. Scuba packages available. 3-night minimum stay. MC, V. **Amenities:** Restaurant, bar; dive shop; boating, snorkeling; airport shuttle. *In room:* No phone.

Young Island Resort ★★ On its own private island off Villa Beach, this resort is as good as it gets in St. Vincent. It far surpasses in both style and comfort its nearest competitor, Grand View Beach Hotel. This 32-acre (13-hectare) resort, its grounds full of lush fruit trees, white ginger, hibiscus, and ferns, is supposedly where a Carib tribal chieftain kept his harem. It lies just 200 yards (182m) off the south shore of St. Vincent; a ferry makes the 5-minute run from the pier right on Villa Beach. Hammocks are hung under thatched roofs, and the beach is of brilliant white sand. Set in a tropical garden are wood-and-stone Tahitian cottages (all for couples), with bamboo decor and outdoor showers in little rock grottoes—very romantic. Floors are of tile and terrazzo, covered with rush rugs. The spacious accommodations come with queen- or king-size beds (rarely a twin) and generous storage space. Some units open onto the beach; others are on a hillside. Some guests have complained of hearing noises from the rooms adjoining them. For your shower, you slip into a romantic little rock grotto. Exhibitionists will be disappointed to learn they are open but hidden from public view.

Food and service are not always of a high standard, despite the longtime fame of this hotel. Dining is by candlelight, and dress is informal. Sometimes a steel band plays for after-dinner dancing, and strolling singers serenade diners.

P.O. Box 211, Young Island, St. Vincent, W.I. ℂ **800/223-1108** in the U.S. and Canada, or 784/458-4826. Fax 784/457-4567. www.youngisland.com. 29 units. Winter $475 cottage for 2. Off-season $345–$390 cottage for 2. Extra person $100. Rates include breakfast and dinner. Ask about packages. AE, MC, V. **Amenities:** Restaurant, 2 bars; pool; tennis court; access to nearby health club; snorkeling, boating, windsurfing; car rental; room service; babysitting; laundry; airport shuttle. *In room:* Ceiling fan, fridge, hair dryer, safe, no phone.

EXPENSIVE

Camelot Inn ⭐ The island's oldest inn is now its most charming guesthouse, having the intimacy that Young Island doesn't and the atmosphere and character that Grand View Beach Hotel lacks. Set in an upscale residential neighborhood on the sloping heights above Kingstown, with a view sweeping out over the capital and the blue Caribbean, this guesthouse opened in 1996. It's not on a beach, and the nearest sands are a 15-minute drive away. Originally built in 1781 as a private villa by the island's first French governor, and radically renovated in the mid-1990s, it retains most of its original stonework. It has a gleaming white clapboard exterior, plus modern bathrooms whose terra-cotta basins were hand-painted by friends of the owners. Each pastel bedroom has a private patio that opens directly onto a garden, where afternoon tea is served amid flowering shrubbery. St. Vincent's most elegant accommodations are handsomely decorated with ceiling fans, Spanish rattan, frames of Mexican silver, and in some cases antique phones and love seats. Each unit has a shower/tub combination.

Kingstown Park St. (P.O. Box 787), Kingstown, St. Vincent, W.I. ℂ **784/456-2100.** Fax 784/456-2233. www.vincy.com/camelot. 20 units. Year-round $175–$275 double; $325–$410 suite. Rates include MAP (breakfast and dinner) and afternoon tea. AE, MC, V. **Amenities:** 2 restaurants, bar; pool; fitness center; sauna; library; salon; shuttle to Young Island beach. *In room:* A/C, TV, hair dryer, safe.

Grand View Beach Hotel ⭐ Owner/manager F. A. (Tony) Sardine named this place well: The "grand view" promised is of islets, bays, yachts, Young Island, headlands, lagoons, and sailing craft. On well-manicured grounds, this resort is set on 8 acres (3 hectares) of gardens, just steps from the beach. The converted plantation house is a large, white, two-story mansion. The most luxurious guest rooms are in a Mediterranean-style modern wing. The other units are on the upper level of a former great house; these have a B&B feel. The beds are dressed with crisp white sheets and most of the bathrooms have showers only. The West Indian fare served here is average.

P.O. Box 173, Villa Point, St. Vincent, W.I. ℂ **800/223-6510** in the U.S., or 784/458-4811. Fax 784/457-4174. www.grandviewhotel.com. 19 units. Winter $175–$240 double. Off-season $150–$185 double. MAP (breakfast and dinner) $45 per person extra. AE, MC, V. Villa Point is 5 min. from the airport and 10 min. from

Kingstown. **Amenities:** Restaurant, bar; pool; tennis and squash courts; fitness center; sauna; bike rental; car rental; room service (7:30am–8:30pm); massage; babysitting; laundry/dry cleaning. *In room:* A/C, TV, dataport, hair dryer, safe.

MODERATE

Lagoon Marina & Hotel   A two-story group of rambling modern buildings crafted from local wood and stone, this hotel lies 4 miles (6km) from the airport on the main island road, opening onto a narrow, curved, black-sand beach. There's a pleasantly breezy bar that's often filled with sailors and yachties. As you relax, you'll overlook a moored armada of boats tied up at a nearby marina. A lagoon-shaped, two-tiered pool is terraced into a nearby hillside. Snorkeling, windsurfing, and daily departures on sailboats to Mustique and Bequia can be arranged through the hotel. Each of the recently refurbished medium-size, high-ceilinged guest rooms has a balcony. The bedrooms have ceramic-tile floors and good furnishings. Bathrooms are in the standard motel style, with shower/tub combinations.

P.O. Box 133, Blue Lagoon, St. Vincent, W.I. © and fax **784/458-4308**. www.lagoonmarina.com. 19 units. Winter $120 double. Off-season $95 double. MC, V. **Amenities:** Restaurant, 2 bars; 2 pools; snorkeling, boating; bike rental; car rental; room service; laundry. *In room:* A/C, cable TV, dataport, coffeemaker, hair dryer.

Villa Lodge Hotel   Set on a residential hillside a few minutes southeast of the center of Kingstown and the E. T. Joshua Airport, this place is a favorite of visiting businesspeople. Because of its access to a beach and its well-mannered staff, it evokes the feeling of a modern villa. It's ringed with tropical, flowering trees and shrubs growing in the gardens. The air-conditioned rooms have ceiling fans, king-size beds, comfortable rattan and local mahogany furniture, and small bathrooms equipped with a shower/tub combination. The hotel also rents eight apartments in its Breezeville Apartments complex, charging year-round prices of $145 for a double, $160 for a triple, and $195 for a quad.

P.O. Box 1191, Villa Point, St. Vincent, W.I. © **784/458-4641**. Fax 784/457-4468. www.villalodge.com. 10 units. Year-round $110 double; $140 triple; $160 apt. for 4. AE, MC, V. **Amenities:** Restaurant, bar; room service; babysitting; laundry. *In room:* A/C, TV, fridge, hair dryer, safe.

INEXPENSIVE

Beachcombers Hotel ★ (Value   Richard and Flora Gunn operate this place in a tropical garden right on the beach. A pair of chalet-like buildings house the small- to medium-size accommodations, all with private bathrooms and tasteful decor. They're cooled by ceiling fans, and a few rooms have air-conditioning as well. The rooms are spotless and well maintained. Try for rooms no. 1, 2, or 3, as they open onto the water. Two units have small kitchenettes. Bathrooms are a bit cramped, with showers only. The hotel has a health spa (Mrs. Gunn is a massage and beauty therapist). And, astonishingly for a B&B, the Beachcombers offers a steam room, sauna, and even facials and aromatherapy. The Beachbar & Restaurant, a favorite gathering place for locals, fronts an open terrace, and serves an excellent cuisine. Curtis Chas, who mastered his cooking skills in the Caribbean, is the chef.

Villa Beach (P.O. Box 126), Kingstown, St. Vincent, W.I. © **784/458-4283**. Fax 784/458-4385. www.beach combershotels.com. 14 units. Year-round $90 double. AE, MC, V. **Amenities:** Restaurant, bar; pool; spa; steam room; sauna; library; room service; babysitting; laundry. *In room:* A/C, ceiling fan, TV, kitchenette, fridge.

Cobblestone Inn   Originally built as a warehouse for sugar and arrowroot in 1814, the core of this historic hotel is made of stone and brick. Today, it's one of the most famous hotels on St. Vincent, known for its labyrinth of passages, arches, and upper hallways. To reach the high-ceilinged reception area, you pass from the waterfront through a stone tunnel into a chiseled courtyard. At the top of a massive sloping stone staircase, you're shown to one of the simple, old-fashioned bedrooms. Most of the small units contain TVs, and some have windows opening over the rooftops of town. The most spacious is no. 5, but it opens onto a noisy street. Furnishings are comfortable, and the bathrooms are tiny, with shower/tub combinations. Meals are served on a third-floor aerie, high above the hotel's central courtyard. The bar here is one of the most popular in town. The hotel is convenient to town, but it's a 3-mile (5km) drive to the nearest beach.

Bax St. (P.O. Box 867), Kingstown, St. Vincent, W.I. © **784/456-1937.** Fax 784/456-1938. www.thecobble stoneinn.com. 20 units. Year-round $65 double; $75 triple. AE, DISC, MC, V. **Amenities:** Restaurant, bar; babysitting; laundry. *In room:* A/C, TV.

Coconut Beach Hotel This owner-occupied inn, restaurant, and bar is 5 minutes south of the airport and 5 minutes from Kingstown. It grew out of a villa constructed in the 1930s by one of the region's noted eccentrics, and it lies across the channel from the much more expensive Young Island. Its seaside setting makes it a choice for swimming and sunbathing. Island tours, such as sailing the Grenadines, can be arranged, as can diving, snorkeling, and mountain climbing. There's minimum comfort here: Each small guest room is furnished in a straightforward modern style, with a tiny bathroom with a shower only.

Indian Bay (P.O. Box 355), Kingstown, St. Vincent, W.I. © and fax **784/457-4900.** 11 units. Year-round $70 double. Rates include breakfast. AE, MC, V. **Amenities:** Restaurant, bar; laundry. *In room:* A/C, ceiling fan, no phone.

Heron Hotel This respectable but slightly run-down hotel is among the most historic buildings on St. Vincent. Built of local stone and tropical hardwoods, it served as a warehouse in the late 18th century, then later provided lodgings for colonial planters doing business along the wharves of Kingstown. Some of the simple and rather small rooms overlook an inner courtyard; others face the street. Room no. 15 is the largest of the lot. Accommodations have timeworn furnishings, rather garish floral draperies, single beds, and cramped bathrooms with shower stalls. Although you don't get grand comfort here, the price is hard to beat, and the staff most hospitable. The hotel attracts a clientele of moderately eccentric guests, some of whom conduct business in the heart of the island's capital, and others who want to be near the docks in time for early morning departures. The on-site restaurant is busiest at lunch (it may close after dusk, so dinner reservations are important). Overall, this place exudes a sense of old-fashioned timelessness you'll almost never find in modern resorts.

Upper Bay St. (P.O. Box 226), Kingstown, St. Vincent, W.I. © **784/457-1631.** Fax 784/457-1189. 8 units. Year-round $70 double. Rates include full breakfast. AE, MC, V. **Amenities:** Restaurant, bar; laundry. *In room:* A/C, TV.

3 St. Vincent Dining

Most guests eat at their hotels on the Modified American Plan (breakfast and dinner), and many Vincentian hostelries serve authentic West Indian cuisine. There are also a few independent restaurants, but not many.

Basil's Bar & Restaurant ⭐ SEAFOOD/INTERNATIONAL This enclave is a less famous annex of the legendary Basil's Beach Bar on Mustique. It's set within the early 19th-century walls of an old sugar warehouse, beneath the previously recommended Cobblestone Inn. The air-conditioned interior is accented with exposed stone and brick, soaring arches, and a rambling mahogany bar, which remains open throughout the day. The food is quite acceptable, but nowhere near as good as that enjoyed by Princess Margaret or Mick Jagger at Basil's other bar on Mustique. The menu might include lobster salad, shrimp in garlic butter, sandwiches, hamburgers, and barbecued chicken. Dinners feature grilled lobster, escargots, shrimp cocktail, grilled red snapper, and grilled filet mignon, all fairly standard dishes of the international repertoire. You can order meals here throughout the day and late into the evening—until the last satisfied customer leaves.

Bay St., Kingstown. ⓒ 784/457-2713. Reservations recommended. Main courses EC$37–EC$65 (US$13.70–US$24.05). AE, MC, V. Mon–Sat 8am–10:30pm.

Bounty AMERICAN/WEST INDIAN   In the redbrick Troutman Building in the center of Kingstown, you'll find the extremely affordable Bounty serving the local workers (the true power-lunch venue is Basil's, recommended above). A friendly local staff greets you, and people who work nearby frequent the place, making it their second home. Fill up on pastries of all kinds, rôtis, hot dogs, hamburgers, and sandwiches, along with homemade soups, pastas, quiche, and pizza. The cooking is just as simple as the surroundings. The interesting collection of drinks includes passion fruit. An on-site gallery sells works by local artists.

Egmont St., Kingstown. ⓒ 784/456-1776. Snacks and sandwiches EC$3.50–EC$16 (US$1.30–US$5.90); main courses EC$20.25–EC$43.20 (US$7.50–US$16). No credit cards. Mon–Fri 8am–5pm, Sat 8am–1:30pm.

French Restaurant ✦ FRENCH/SEAFOOD   In a clapboard waterfront house 2 miles (3km) from the airport, near the pier where the ferry from Young Island docks, this is one of the most consistently good restaurants on the island. It offers a long, semi-shadowed bar, which you pass on your way to the rear veranda. Here, overlooking the moored yachts off the coast of Young Island and surrounded by vine-laced lattices, you can order well-seasoned dishes like seafood casserole or curried conch, shrimp in garlic sauce, fresh fish in a ginger and peppercorn sauce, or lobster fresh from the tank. Lunch is simpler and cheaper, with fresh fish, seafood kebabs, grilled cheese steak, and spicy pineapple conch. The staff is inexperienced, but the food makes up for it.

Villa Beach. ⓒ 784/458-4972. Reservations recommended. Lunch EC$18–EC$75 (US$6.65–US$27.75); dinner main courses EC$38–EC$85 (US$14.05–US$31.45). AE, MC, V. Mon–Sat noon–2pm and 6–9:30pm. Closed Sept–Oct.

Juliette's Restaurant WEST INDIAN   Set amid the capital's cluster of administrative buildings, across from the National Commercial Bank, this restaurant caters to office workers on their lunch breaks. Meals are served in a clean and respectable dining area headed by a veteran of the restaurant trade, Juliette Campbell. (Campbell's husband is the island's well-known attorney general.) Menu items include soups, curried mutton, an array of fish, stewed chicken, stewed beef, and sandwiches. Many of the platters are garnished with fried plantains and rice. Although Juliette's opens early, it doesn't serve breakfast, offering only snacks and lunch-type items in the morning.

Egmont St., Kingstown. ⓒ 784/457-1645. Rôtis and sandwiches EC$6–EC$9 (US$2.20–US$3.35); fixed-price menu EC$10–EC$15 (US$3.70–US$5.55). No credit cards. Mon–Fri 8am–5pm, Sat 8:30am–noon.

King Arthur's Restaurant ✦ INTERNATIONAL   This is your best bet for a taste of contemporary cookery when you've had too many plates of beans and rice. Set on a terrace whose views sweep over a garden, the faraway sea, and the commercial core of downtown Kingstown, this restaurant is in a prosperous-looking house that was built in the 1790s by St. Vincent's first governor under the French regime. More stylish and a bit more formal than many of its competitors, it focuses on international cuisine and set-price menus that change according to the seasons and the inspiration of the chef. Choices may include pumpkin soup, Chinese spring rolls, several kinds of salads, filet of fresh salmon with chef's potatoes, and baked Vienna-style chicken served with glazed vegetables.

In the Camelot Inn, Kingstown Park St. (a 10-min. drive from the center of town), Kingstown. © **784/ 456-2100.** Reservations recommended. Set-price lunch EC$54 (US$20); set-price dinner EC$94.50 (US$34.95). AE MC, V. Daily 7am–2:30pm and 6:30–10pm.

Lime N' Pub Restaurant ⭐ (*Value* WEST CARIBBEAN/INDIAN   This is one of the island's most popular restaurants, and it sits opposite the super-expensive Young Island Hotel, right on Young Island Channel. It's the most congenial pub on St. Vincent, with a wide selection of pub grub, including pizza. There's even a live lobster pond. A local band livens things up a few times a week in winter. In the more formal section of this indoor and alfresco restaurant, you can partake of some good West Indian food, along with dishes from India or the international kitchen. The rôtis win high praise, but we always order the fresh fish and lobster dishes instead. Coconut shrimp is generally excellent. Service is among the most hospitable on the island.

Opposite Young Island at Villa Beach. © **784/458-4227.** Main courses EC$55–EC$95 (US$20.35–US$35.15). AE, DISC, MC, V. Daily 10am–midnight.

Rooftop Restaurant & Bar WEST INDIAN/INTERNATIONAL   This restaurant does a thriving business, thanks to its well-prepared food and its location three stories above the center of Kingstown. After you climb some flights of stairs, you'll see a bar near the entrance, an indoor area decorated in earth tones, and a patio open to the prevailing breezes. Lunches stress traditional Creole recipes using fresh fish, chicken, mutton, beef, and goat. Dinners are more international, and may include lobster, excellent snapper with lemon-butter and garlic sauce, steaks with onions and mushrooms, and several savory preparations of pork. Every Wednesday and Friday, there's a karaoke sing-along; Saturday is family night, with a barbecue and a steel band after 6pm. In addition, 60 different drinks are featured at the bar.

Bay St., Kingstown. © **784/457-2845.** Reservations recommended for dinner. Lunch platters EC$25 (US$9.25); dinner main courses EC$20–EC$60 (US$7.40–US$22.20). AE, DISC, MC, V. Mon–Wed 9am–10pm, Thurs–Fri 9am–1am, Sat 10am–4pm,.

4 Exploring St. Vincent

BEACHES

All beaches on St. Vincent are public, and many of the best ones border hotel properties, where you can order drinks or lunch. Most of the resorts are in the south, where the beaches have golden-yellow sand. The only real white-sand beach on St. Vincent is Young Island, which is private (see "St. Vincent Accommodations," earlier in this chapter, for a review of this expensive resort property). Many of the beaches in the north have sands of a lava-ash color. The safest swimming is on the leeward beaches; the surf on the windward or eastern beaches is often rough and can be quite dangerous.

The island's most popular strip is narrow **Villa Beach,** only a 10-minute drive from Kingstown. Its tranquil Caribbean waters make swimming safe here, and

Beachcombers Hotel **9**
Camelot Inn **3**
Cobblestone Inn **2**
Coconut Beach Hotel **6**
Grand View Beach Hotel **8**
Heron Hotel **4**
Lagoon Marina & Hotel **10**
Petit Byahaut **1**
Villa Lodge Hotel **7**
Young Island **5**

numerous simple cafes and watersports stands are ready to serve you. The drawback to this beach: Its sands can barely accommodate the crowds who flock here; weekends can be particularly bad.

Nearby **Indian Bay Beach** is similar to Villa Beach and also attracts lots of Vincentians on weekends. Monday through Thursday, however, you'll probably have plenty of room on this narrow strip. The sand here is slightly golden in color, but tends to be rocky. The reef-protected tranquil waters are ideal for both swimming and snorkeling. You'll find both bars and restaurants here.

Heading north from Kingstown, you'll reach **Buccament Bay Beach,** where the waters are clean, clear, and tranquil enough for swimming. This beach is very tiny, however, and its sand is of the black volcanic variety. In the same area, **Questelle's Bay Beach** (pronounced *keet-ELLS*) is also on the leeward, tranquil Caribbean side of the island. The black-sand beach, next to Camden Park, is very similar to Buccament Bay.

Only diehards head for the beaches on the east coast, or windward side, where the big breakers roll in from the Atlantic. Don't plan to go swimming in these rough waters; you might just enjoy a beach picnic instead. The best beaches, all with black volcanic sand, are found at **Kearton's Bay, Peter's Hope,** and **Richmond Beach,** all reached along the leeward highway running up the west coast of St. Vincent.

SPORTS & OTHER OUTDOOR PURSUITS

FISHING   It's best to go to a local fisherman for advice if you're interested in this sport, which your hotel can also arrange for you. The government of St. Vincent doesn't require visitors to have a fishing license. It's sometimes possible to accompany a fisherman on a trip, perhaps 4 or 5 miles (6 or 8km) from shore. A modest fee should suffice. The fishing fleet leaves from the leeward coast at Barrouallie. People have been known to return to shore with everything from a 6-inch redfish to a 20-foot (6m) pilot whale.

HIKING   Exploring St. Vincent's hot volcano, **La Soufrière,** is an intriguing adventure. As you travel the island, you can't miss its cloud-capped splendor. This volcano has occasionally captured the attention of the world. The most recent eruption was in 1979, when it spewed ashes, lava, and hot mud that covered the vegetation on its slopes. Belching rocks and black curling smoke filled the blue Caribbean sky. About 17,000 people were evacuated from a 10-mile (16km) ring around the volcano.

Fortunately, the volcano is in the sparsely settled northern part of the island. It lies away from most of the tourism and commercial centers of St. Vincent, and even if it should erupt again, vulcanologists don't consider it a danger to visitors lodged at beachside hotels along the leeward coast.

At the rim of the crater, you'll be rewarded with one of the most panoramic views in the Caribbean—that is, if the wind doesn't blow too hard and make you topple over into the crater itself! *Take extreme caution.* Looking inside, you can see the steam rising from the crater.

Even if you're an experienced hiker, don't attempt to explore the volcano without a guide. Also, wear suitable hiking clothes and be sure that you're in the best of health before making the arduous journey. The easiest route is the 3-mile-long (5km) eastern approach from Rabacca. The more arduous trail, longer by half a mile (2km), is the western trail from Chateaubelair, which definitely requires a guide. The round-trip to the crater takes about 5 hours.

St. Vincent Forestry Headquarters, in the village of Campden Park, about 3 miles (5km) from Kingstown along the west coast (© **784/457-8594**), offers a pamphlet on hiking to La Soufrière. It's open Monday to Friday from 8am to noon and 1 to 4pm. **HazEco Tours** (© **784/457-8634**) offers guided hikes up to La Soufrière, costing $120 per couple, including lunch.

If you don't want to face Soufrière, the best hikes are the **Vermont Nature Trails.** These marked trails (get a map at the tourist office) take you through a rain forest and pass long-ago plantations reclaimed by nature. If it's your lucky day, you might even see the rare St. Vincent parrot with its flamboyant plumage. Wear good hiking shoes and lots of mosquito repellent.

SAILING & YACHTING ✦✦   St. Vincent and the Grenadines are one of the great sailing centers of the Caribbean. If you want to go bare-boating, you can obtain a fully provisioned yacht. If you're a well-heeled novice, you can hire a captain and a crew. Rentals are available for a half-day, a full day, overnight, or even longer.

The longest established yacht-chartering company in St. Vincent, **Barefoot Yacht Charters,** Blue Lagoon (© **784/456-9526**), is better than ever, and is now granting substantial discounts for last-minute or walk-in bookings, notably $165 per day for a 32-foot (10m) yacht in off-season. The outfitter has a fleet of 20 yachts run by the American Sailing Association and offers charters with or without a crew. Its operation is at its own custom-built marina with docks and moorings, along with a restaurant opening onto a panoramic vista of Bequia. There's even an Internet cafe. The charter company also offers its own airline, **SVG Air,** one of the longest established airlines in the region, and will fly you in modern craft of five- to nine-seaters to any island within the Eastern Caribbean. It is especially popular for services through the Grenadines.

We'd also suggest **Nicholson Yacht Charters** ✰✰ (© **800/662-6066** in the U.S.) and the **Lagoon Marina and Hotel,** in the Blue Lagoon area (© **800/ 327-2276** in the U.S., or 784/458-4308). The latter offers 44-foot (13m) crewed sloops, costing $100 per person per day (minimum of five people).

SNORKELING & SCUBA DIVING ✰✰   St. Vincent's 30 or so dive sites are sprinkled along its leeward shore, where you might spot seahorses and frogfish. The best area for snorkeling and scuba diving is the Villa/Young Island section on the southern end of the island.

Dive St. Vincent, on the Young Island Cut (© **784/457-4928**), has been owned and operated by a transplanted Texan, Bill Tewes, for more than a decade. The oldest and best dive company, it now has two additional dive shops: **Dive Canouan,** at the Tamarind Beach Hotel on Canouan Island (© **784/ 458-8044**), and **Grenadines Dive,** at the Sunny Grenadines Hotel on Union Island (© **784/458-8138**). The shops have a total of six instructors and three dive masters, as well as seven dive boats. All shops offer dive/snorkel trips as well as sightseeing day-trips and dive instruction. Single-tank dives cost $50 and two-tank dives go for $90, including all equipment and instructors and/or dive master guides. Dive packages are also available.

EXPLORING KINGSTOWN

Lush and tropical, the capital isn't as architecturally fascinating as St. George's on Grenada. Some English-style houses do exist, many of them looking as if they belonged in Penzance or Cornwall, instead of in the Caribbean. You can still meet old-timers if you stroll on Upper Bay Street. White-haired and bearded, they can be seen loading their boats with produce grown on the mountain, before heading to some secluded beach in the Grenadines. This is a chief port and gateway to the Grenadines, and you can see the small boats and yachts that have dropped anchor here. On Saturday morning, the **market** at the south end of town is at its most active.

At the top of a winding road on the north side of Kingstown, **Fort Charlotte** (© **784/456-1165**) was built on Johnson Point around the time of the American Revolution. The ruins aren't much to inspect; the reason to come here is the view. The fort sits atop a steep promontory some 640 feet (192m) above the sea. From its citadel, you'll have a sweeping view of the leeward shores to the north, Kingstown to the south, and the Grenadines beyond. On a clear day, you can even see Grenada. Three cannons used to fight off French troops are still in place. You'll see a series of oil murals depicting the history of black Caribs. Admission is free, and the fort is open daily 6am to 6pm.

The second major sight is the **Botanic Gardens** ✰, on the north side of Kingstown at Montrose (© **784/457-1003**). Founded in 1765 by Gov. George Melville, these are the oldest botanic gardens in the West Indies. You'll see 20 acres (8 hectares) of such tropical exotics as teak, almond, cinnamon, nutmeg, cannon-ball, and mahogany; some of the trees are more than 200 years old. One of the breadfruit trees was reputedly among those original seedlings brought to this island by Captain Bligh in 1793. There's also a large *Spachea perforata* (the

Soufrière tree), a species believed to be unique to St. Vincent and not found in the wild since 1812. The gardens are open daily from 6am to 6pm; admission is free.

THE LEEWARD HIGHWAY ★★

The leeward, or sheltered, west side of the island has the most dramatic scenery. North of Kingstown, you rise into lofty terrain before descending to the water again. There are views in all directions. Here you can see one of the finest petro-glyphs in the Caribbean: the massive **Carib Rock,** with a human face carving dating from A.D. 600.

Continuing north, you reach **Barrouallie,** where there's a Carib stone altar. Even if you're not into fishing, you might want to spend some time in this village, where some whalers still occasionally set out in brightly painted boats armed with harpoons, Moby Dick–style, to seek the elusive whale. While Bar-rouallie may be one of the few outposts in the world where whaling is still car-ried on, Vincentians point out that it doesn't endanger an already endangered species, since so few are caught each year. If one is caught, it's an occasion for festivities.

The highway continues to **Chateaubelair,** the end of the line. Here you can swim at the attractive **Richmond Beach** before heading back to Kingstown. In the distance, the volcano, La Soufrière, looms menacingly in the mountains.

The adventurous set out from here to see the **Falls of Baleine,** 7½ miles (12km) north of Richmond Beach on the northern tip of the island, accessible only by boat. Baleine is a freshwater falls that comes from a stream in the vol-canic hills. If you're interested in making the trip, check with the tourist office in Kingstown for tour information.

THE WINDWARD HIGHWAY

The Windward Highway runs along the eastern Atlantic coast from Kingstown. Waves pound the surf, and panoramic seascapes are all along the rocky shores. If you want to go swimming on this often-dangerous coast, stick to the sandy spots, as they offer safer shores. This road will take you past coconut and banana plantations and fields of arrowroot.

North of Georgetown is the **Rabacca Dry River,** which shows the flow of lava from the volcano when it erupted at the beginning of the 20th century. The journey from Kingstown to here is only 24 miles (39km), but it will seem like much longer. If you want to go the final 11 miles (18km) along a rugged road to **Fancy,** the northern tip of the island, you'll need a really rugged four-wheel-drive vehicle.

MARRIQUA VALLEY ★

Sometimes known as the Mesopotamia Valley, the Marriqua Valley is one of the lushest cultivated valleys in the eastern Caribbean. Surrounded by mountain ridges, the drive takes you through a landscape planted with nutmeg, cocoa, coconut, breadfruit, and bananas. The road begins at the Vigie Highway, east of the airport; surrounded by mountain ridges, it opens onto a panoramic view of Grand Bonhomme Mountain, rising 3,180 feet (954m). At Montréal, you'll come upon natural mineral springs where you can have lunch and take a dip. Only rugged vehicles should make this trip.

Around Kingstown, you can also enjoy the **Queen's Drive,** a scenic loop into the high hills to the east of the capital. From here, the view is panoramic over Kingstown and its yacht-clogged harbor to the Grenadines in the distance.

SHOPPING

You don't come to St. Vincent to shop, but once here, you might pick up some of the Sea Island cotton fabrics and clothing that are local specialties. In addition, Vincentian artisans make pottery, jewelry, and baskets.

Since Kingstown consists of about 12 small blocks, you can walk, browse, and see about everything in a single morning's shopping jaunt. Try to be in town for the colorful, noisy **Friday-morning market.** You might not purchase anything, but you'll surely enjoy the riot of color.

Noah's Arkade, Bay Street, Kingstown (© **784/457-1513**), sells gifts from the West Indies, including wood carvings, T-shirts, and a wide range of books and souvenirs.

At **Sprott Brothers,** Homeworks, Bay Street (© **784/457-1121**), you can buy clothing designed by Vincentians, along with an array of fabrics, linens, and silk-screened T-shirts, and even Caribbean-made furniture. In fact, there's a little bit of everything here.

St. Vincent Philatelic Services, Bonadie's Building, Bay Street (© **784/ 457-1911**), is the largest operating bureau in the Caribbean, and its issues are highly acclaimed by stamp collectors around the world.

Y. de Lima, Bay and Egmont streets (© **784/457-1681**), is well stocked with cameras, stereo equipment, toys, clocks, binoculars, and the best selection of jewelry on the island.

Typical Caribbean duty-free goods are found at **Voyager,** Halifax Street (© **784/456-1686**), including quality jewelry, French perfumes, leather goods, and Swiss watches.

ST. VINCENT AFTER DARK

Most nightlife centers around the hotels, where activities are likely to include barbecues and dancing to steel bands. In season, at least one hotel seems to have something planned every night during the week. Beer is extremely cheap at all the places noted below.

Aquatic Club, adjacent to the departure point of the ferryboat from St. Vincent to Young Island (© **784/458-4205**), is the loudest and most raucous nightspot on St. Vincent, with frequent live bands playing reggae, soca, and calypso. It's a source of giddy fun to its fans and a sore bone of contention to nearby hotel guests, who claim they can't sleep because of the noise. On Friday, Saturday, and Sunday nights, things heat up by 11pm and continue until as late as 3am. During the other nights of the week, the place functions as a bar. Centered around an open-sided veranda and an outdoor deck, it's open every night from 10pm to 2 or 3am. No cover.

The **Attic,** in the Kentucky Building, Melville and Back streets, Kingstown (© **784/457-2558**), features jazz and easy-listening music. Music is live only on Friday and Saturday; Tuesday and Thursday it's recorded, and Wednesday is karaoke night. Fish and burgers are available. There's usually a cover of EC$10 to EC$15 (US$3.70–US$5.55).

Emerald Valley Casino, Penniston Valley (© **784/456-7824**), is not one of the Caribbean's glamorous casinos. This "down-home" spot offers a trio of roulette tables, three blackjack tables, and one Caribbean stud poker table. You can also play craps here. There's also a bar, and you can order food. If you've got nothing else to do, you might consider a visit any time Wednesday through Monday from 8pm to 4am.

5 The Grenadines

GETTING THERE

BY PLANE   Four of the Grenadines—Bequia, Mustique, Union Island, and Canouan—have small airports. Service from St. Vincent is by small inter-island carriers including **Mustique Airways** (© 784/458-4380), which serves Canouan and Mustique. **Air Martinique** (© 784/458-4528) flies to Union Island.

BY BOAT   The ideal way to go, of course, is to hire your own yacht, as many wealthy visitors do. A far less expensive option is to take a mail, cargo, or passenger boat, as the locals do, but you'll need time and patience. However, boats do run on schedules. The **government mail boat,** MV *Baracuda* (© 784/456-5180), leaves St. Vincent on Monday, Wednesday, and Friday at 10:30am, stops at Bequia, Canouan, and Mayreau, and arrives at Union Island at about 3:45pm. On Tuesday, Thursday, and Saturday, the boat leaves Union Island at about 6:30am, stops at Mayreau and Canouan, reaches Bequia at about 10:45am, and makes port at St. Vincent at noon. One-way fares from St. Vincent to Bequia are EC$15 (US$5.55). To Canouan, it's EC$30 (US$11.10); Mayreau; EC$20 (US$7.40); and Union Island, EC$25 (US$9.25).

Monday through Saturday, you can also reach Bequia on the *Admiral I* and *II.* For information on these sea trips, inquire at the **Tourist Board,** Upper Bay Street, in Kingstown (© 784/457-1502).

BEQUIA 🖈🖈

Only 7 square miles (18 sq. km) of land, Bequia (pronounced *BECK-wee*) is the largest of the Grenadines. It's the northernmost island in the chain (only 9 miles/14km south of St. Vincent), offering quiet lagoons, reefs, and long stretches of nearly deserted beaches. Its population of some 6,000, descended from seafarers and other early adventurers, will give you a friendly greeting. Of the inhabitants, 10% are of Scottish ancestry, who live mostly in the Mount Pleasant region. A feeling of relaxation and informality prevails on Bequia.

ESSENTIALS

VISITOR INFORMATION   Before going to your hotel, drop in at the circular **Tourist Information Centre,** Port Elizabeth (© 784/458-3964). Here you can ask for a driver who's familiar with the attractions of the island (all of them are). You should negotiate the fare in advance.

GETTING AROUND   **Rental cars,** owned by locals, are available at the port, or you can hire a **taxi** at the dock to take you around the island or to your hotel. Taxis are reasonably priced, but an even better bet are the so-called **dollar cabs,** which take you anywhere on the island for a small fee. They don't seem to have a regular schedule—you just flag one down.

BANKS   There are a few bank branches on Bequia, mostly in Port Elizabeth.

SPECIAL EVENTS   The **Easter Regatta** is held over Easter weekend, with boat races, food, and music. Bequia's **Carnival** celebrations are a 4-day affair, held just before St. Vincent's party in late June.

ACCOMMODATIONS

Frangipani Hotel 🖈🖈   This local favorite of yachties is a great hangout spot, its ambience created by James Mitchell, longtime prime minister of the island chain. The core of this pleasant guest house originated as the home of a 19th-century sea captain. Since it was transformed into a hotel, it has added

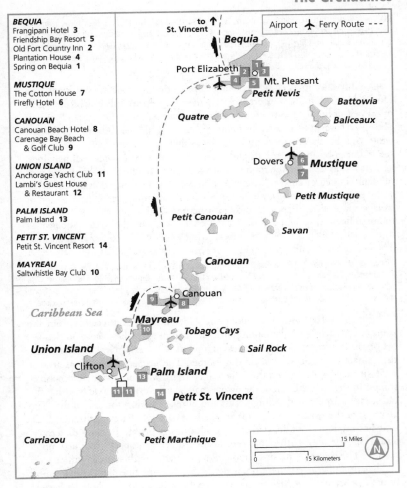

BEQUIA
Frangipani Hotel **3**
Friendship Bay Resort **5**
Old Fort Country Inn **2**
Plantation House **4**
Spring on Bequia **1**

MUSTIQUE
The Cotton House **7**
Firefly Hotel **6**

CANOUAN
Canouan Beach Hotel **8**
Carenage Bay Beach
  & Golf Club **9**

UNION ISLAND
Anchorage Yacht Club **11**
Lambi's Guest House
  & Restaurant **12**

PALM ISLAND
Palm Island **13**

PETIT ST. VINCENT
Petit St. Vincent Resort **14**

MAYREAU
Saltwhistle Bay Club **10**

Airport ✈ Ferry Route - - -

to ↑
St. Vincent

Bequia
Port Elizabeth
Mt. Pleasant
Petit Nevis
Quatre
Battowia
Baliceaux
Dovers **Mustique**
Petit Mustique
Petit Canouan
Savan
Canouan
Canouan
Caribbean Sea
Mayreau
Tobago Cays
Sail Rock
Union Island
Clifton
Palm Island
Petit St. Vincent
Carriacou
Petit Martinique

0   15 Miles
0   15 Kilometers

accommodations that border a sloping tropical garden in back. The complex overlooks the island's most historic harbor, Admiralty Bay, and draws many clients who return to it every year. The five rooms in the original house are smaller and much less glamorous (and less expensive) than the better-outfitted accommodations in the garden. The garden units are handcrafted from local stone and hardwoods, and have tile floors, carpets of woven hemp, wooden furniture (some made on St. Vincent), and balconies. Most of the rooms have a small private bathroom with a shower; otherwise, corridor bathrooms are adequate and tidily maintained.

The open-sided restaurant, Frangipani, overlooks the yacht harbor (see "Dining," below). Guests can play tennis or arrange scuba dives, sailboat rides, or other watersports nearby. (The nearest scuba outfitter, Sunsports, is fully accredited by PADI.) There's live music every Monday night in winter and an outdoor barbecue, with a steel band, every Thursday night.

P.O. Box 1, Bequia, The Grenadines, St. Vincent, W.I. ✆ **784/458-3255.** Fax 784/458-3824. www.frangipani. com. 15 units. Winter $55 double without bathroom, $150–$175 double with bathroom. Off-season $45 double without bathroom, $90–$130 double with bathroom. Extra person $25. Children age 12 and under $15. AE, DISC, MC, V. **Amenities:** Restaurant, bar; tennis court; boating, dive shop; babysitting; laundry. *In room:* Ceiling fan, safe, no phone.

Friendship Bay Resort ⭐ Lacking some of the sophistication of Plantation House, but with more comfort and style than Frangipani, this beachfront resort offers well-decorated rooms with private verandas, nestled in 12 acres (5 hectares) of tropical gardens. The complex stands on a sloping hillside above one of the best white-sand beaches on the island, at Friendship Cove. Guests have a view of the sea and neighboring islands. Brightly colored curtains, handmade wall hangings, and grass rugs decorate the rooms, which are cooled by the trade winds and ceiling fans (in lieu of air-conditioning). Driftwood and various flotsam art, along with sponge-painted walls, evoke the sea. The accommodations have generous storage space, beds draped in mosquito netting, and small, shower-only bathrooms. The most requested units are those set directly on the ocean. The owners have added a beach bar and offer a local string band on Wednesday and Saturday. The food is good, and the menu features many island specialties.

Friendship Cove (P.O. Box 9), Bequia, The Grenadines, St. Vincent, W.I. ✆ **784/458-3222.** Fax 784/458-3840. www.friendshipbay.com. 28 units. Winter $200–$250 double; $325 suite. Off-season $140–$185 double; $250 suite. Rates include continental breakfast. AE, MC, V. **Amenities:** 2 restaurants, 2 bars; pool; tennis court; dive shop, windsurfing, water-skiing, boating; room service; babysitting; laundry. *In room:* Ceiling fan, no phone.

Old Fort Country Inn ⭐ This special hideaway has been created from the ruins of a French-built plantation house commanding the best views on Bequia. Set on 30 tropical acres (12 hectares) at a point 450 feet (135m) above the sea, the climate is excellent, with no mosquitoes. The property dates from at least 1756 (it may be older), and the 3-foot-thick (.9m) walls are made from cobblestones. In the reconstruction, the owner matched the original style by using the old stones with exposed ceiling beams and rafters, creating a medieval feel. The views from the spacious bedrooms are the best of any hotel on the island. Each unit has modern Scandinavian-style furnishings, a private balcony or terrace, and a shower-only bathroom. An unstocked fridge can be supplied upon request. The rooms aren't air-conditioned, but trade winds seem to suffice.

The atmospheric restaurant holds eight tables, serving fine four- or five-course dinners of Creole and Mediterranean specialties, including a whole barbecued fish. On the property are nature trails, a beach that's a 10-minute hike from the hotel, and a 15-by-30-foot (5 by 9m) pool, with views of the ocean on three sides.

Mount Pleasant, Bequia, The Grenadines, St. Vincent, W.I. ✆ **784/458-3440.** Fax 784/457-3340. www.old fortbequia.com. 6 units. Winter $190–$250 double. Off-season $160–$200 double. Rates include breakfast and dinner. MC, V. **Amenities:** Restaurant; pool; 24-hr. room service; babysitting; laundry. *In room:* Ceiling fan, hair dryer upon request, safe, no phone.

Plantation House ⭐⭐ This is the island's most sophisticated address. The exquisite house is on Admiralty Bay, just a 5-minute walk from the center of town. It offers an informal elegance, and caters to a well-heeled international clientele (they say their "exquisite seclusion is only for the fortunate few"). Although everything's completely modernized, there's a nice dash of nostalgic, gracious charm here. The gingerbread trim and the traditional verandas overlooking the manicured tropical gardens add a romantic touch; hammocks beckon for you to relax. The accommodations consist of 17 peach-and-blue West Indian cottages (each with its own private porch), 5 luxury beachfront units with fans, and 5 deluxe air-conditioned rooms in the main house. Spacious guest rooms have a kind of colonial elegance and fresh-looking Caribbean style, with vibrant colors, bamboo, and floral prints, plus VCRs and satellite TV. Two of the rooms share a private terrace overlooking Admiralty Bay. The tiled, shower-only bathrooms are stocked with deluxe toiletries.

The dining room, also called Plantation House, serves excellent cuisine and has a fine wine list (see "Dining," below); it's one of the finest restaurants in the Grenadines.

Admiralty Bay (P.O. Box 16), Bequia, The Grenadines, St. Vincent, W.I. ☎ **784/458-3425.** Fax 784/458-3612. www.hotel-plantation.com. 27 units. Winter $407 double. Off-season $306 double. Rates include breakfast. AE, MC, V. **Amenities:** 2 restaurants, 2 bars; pool; tennis court; windsurfing, boating, water-skiing, snorkeling; bicycles; babysitting; laundry; airport shuttle. *In room:* A/C, satellite TV, VCR, minibar, hair dryer, safe.

Spring on Bequia ★ *Finds* The name alone attracts us to this place. In the late 1960s, the Frank Lloyd Wright design of this hotel won an award from the American Institute of Architects. Fashioned from beautifully textured honey-colored stone, it has a flattened hip roof inspired by the old plantation houses of Martinique. Constructed on the 18th-century foundations of a West Indian homestead, it sits in the middle of 28 acres (11 hectares) of hillside orchards, producing oranges, grapefruit, bananas, breadfruit, plums, and mangos. Thanks to the almost constant blossoming of one crop or another, it always feels like spring here (hence the name). From the main building's stone bar and open-air dining room, you might hear the bellowing of a herd of cows.

All guest rooms have terraces; the three units in the main building are less spacious and darker than the others. Each room is ringed with stone and contains Japanese-style screens to filter the sun. The high pyramidal ceilings and the constant trade winds keep things cool in the rooms (which lack fans and air-conditioning). The twin or double platform beds are draped in mosquito netting, and the bathrooms have stone-grotto-like showers that use solar-heated water. All remains very quiet and tranquil here, as the place has long since been bypassed by other more glitzy resorts in the Grenadines. The sandy beach is a 3-minute walk away through a coconut grove, but it's too shallow for good swimming.

Spring Bay, Bequia, The Grenadines, St. Vincent, W.I. ☎ **784/458-3414,** or 612/823-1202 in Minneapolis. Fax 784/457-3305. 9 units. Winter $130–$230 double. Off-season $70–$140 double. MAP (breakfast and dinner) $45 per person extra. AE, DISC, MC, V. Closed end of June–Oct. **Amenities:** Restaurant, bar; pool; tennis court; snorkeling; laundry. *In room:* Ceiling fan, no phone.

DINING

The food is good and healthy here—lobster, chicken, and steaks from such fish as mahi-mahi, kingfish, and grouper, plus tropical fruits, fried plantains, and coconut and guava puddings made fresh daily. Even the beach bars are kept spotless.

Frangipani ★ CARIBBEAN This waterside dining room, always full of yachties who've come ashore, is one of the best restaurants on the island. With the exception of the juicy steaks imported for barbecues, only local food is used in the succulent specialties. Lunches, served throughout the day, include sandwiches, salads, and seafood platters. Dinner specialties include conch chowder, baked chicken with rice-and-coconut stuffing, lobster, and an array of fresh fish. A Thursday-night barbecue with live entertainment is an island event.

In the Frangipani Hotel, Port Elizabeth. ☎ **784/458-3255.** Reservations required for dinner. Breakfast EC$18–EC$21.60 (US$6.65–US$8); lunch EC$32.40–EC$81 (US$12–US$30); dinner main courses EC$32.40–EC$81 (US$12–US$29.95); fixed-price dinner EC$45–EC$94.50 (US$16.65–US$34.95). AE, MC, V. Daily 7:30am–5pm and 7–9pm. Closed Sept.

Friendship Bay Resort INTERNATIONAL/WEST INDIAN   Guests here dine in a candlelit room high above a sweeping expanse of seafront on a hillside rich with the scent of frangipani and hibiscus. Lunch is served at the Spicy 'n Herby beach bar, but dinner is more elaborate. Meals, based on fresh ingredients, might include grilled lobster in season, curried beef, grilled or broiled fish (served Creole style with a spicy sauce), shrimp curry, and charcoal-grilled steak flambé. Dishes are flavorsome and well prepared. An island highlight is the Friday- and Saturday-night "jump-up" (a Caribbean version of a hoedown) and barbecue.

Port Elizabeth. ✆ **784/458-3222.** Reservations required for dinner. Main courses EC$30–EC$48 (US$11.10–US$17.75) lunch, EC$40–EC$90 (US$14.80–US$33.30) dinner. AE, MC, V. Daily 8am–10pm. Closed Sept–Oct 29.

Le Petit Jardin ✿ INTERNATIONAL   Set in a varnished wooden house behind the post office, this restaurant is the slow-moving but likable creation of the Belmar family, who focus on as many fresh ingredients as the vagaries of the local fishing fleet will allow. You'll dine within view of a garden, in a likable ambience inspired by both the British and French West Indies. Menu items include grilled swordfish with lemon sauce; grilled lobster; shrimp and vegetable kabobs; chipped steak in cream sauce; and conventional grilled sirloin.

Backstreet, Port Elizabeth. ✆ **784/458-3318.** Reservations recommended. Main courses EC$70–EC$85 (US$25.90–US$31.45). AE, DC, MC, V. Daily 11:30am–2pm and 6:30–9:30pm.

Plantation House ✿✿ CREOLE/INTERNATIONAL/CARIBBEAN   This is the premier dining spot on the island. Although informal, evenings here are the most elegant on Bequia. The chef emphasizes fresh ingredients, a blend of some of the finest of European cookery along with West Indian spice and flair. Try the chicken cordon bleu with mousseline potatoes, *christophene* (a squash-like vegetable) in cheese sauce, and buttered pumpkin, or the roast breast of duck with orange sauce. Curried conch is a local specialty.

In the Plantation House hotel, Admiralty Bay. ✆ **784/458-3425.** Reservations required. Main courses EC$35–EC$75 (US$12.95–US$27.75). AE, MC, V. Daily 7–10:30am, noon–2:30pm and 7–9:30pm.

Whaleboner Inn WEST INDIAN/SEAFOOD   An enduring favorite, the Whaleboner is still going strong, serving dishes with the most authentic island flavor on Bequia. Inside, the bar is carved from the jawbone of a giant whale, and the barstools are made from the vertebrae. The owners offer the best pizza on the island, along with a selection of fish-and-chips and well-made sandwiches for lunch. At night, you may want one of the wholesome dinners, including a choice of lobster, fish, chicken, or steak. We prefer the curried-conch dinner beginning with the callaloo soup. The bar often stays open later than 10:30pm, depending on the crowd.

Next to the Frangipani Hotel, Admiralty Bay, Port Elizabeth. ✆ **784/458-3233.** Reservations required for dinner. Main courses EC$52–EC$89 (US$19.25–US$32.95). MC, V. Daily 7am–10pm.

EXPLORING BEQUIA

Obviously, the secluded beaches are at the top of everyone's list of Bequia's attractions. As you walk along the beaches, especially near Port Elizabeth, you'll see craftspeople building boats by hand, a method passed on by their ancestors. Whalers sometimes still set out from here in wooden boats with hand harpoons, just as they do from a port village on St. Vincent. Other beaches require a taxi ride. You might check out the uncrowded, pristine white sands at **Friendship Bay,** where you can rent watersports equipment or order a drink from the bar at the hotel there. **Industry Bay** and **Lower Bay** are both gorgeous beaches shaded by palm trees, offering good swimming and snorkeling.

Dive Bequia, Gingerbread House, Admiralty Bay (P.O. Box 16), Bequia (© **784/458-3504**), specializes in diving and snorkeling on the lush reefs of Bequia, where you might spot manta rays. Scuba dives cost $55 for one, $90 for two in the same day, and $400 for a 10-dive package. Introductory lessons go for $20 per person; a four-dive open-water certification course is $400. Snorkeling trips are $20 per person. These prices include all the necessary equipment.

The main harbor village, **Port Elizabeth,** is known for its safe anchorage, Admiralty Bay. The bay was a haven in the 17th century for the British, French, and Spanish navies, as well as for pirates. Descendants of Captain Kydd (a.k.a. Kidd) still live on the island. Today, the yachting set anchors here.

There aren't many sights after you leave Port Elizabeth, so you'll probably have your driver, booked for the day, drop you off for a long, leisurely lunch and some time on a beach. You will pass a fort with a harbor view as well as Industry Estates, which has a Beach House restaurant serving a fair lunch. At **Paget Farm,** you can wander into an old whaling village and maybe inspect a few jawbones left over from the catches of yesterday.

At **Moonhole,** there's a vacation and retirement community built into the cliffs like a free-form sculpture. These are private homes, of course, and you're not to enter without permission. For a final look at Bequia, head up an 800-foot (240m) hill that the local people call **"The Mountain."** From that perch, you'll have a 360-degree view of St. Vincent and the Grenadines to the south.

SHOPPING

The **Crab Hole,** next door to the Plantation House, Admiralty Bay (© **784/ 458-3290**), is the best of the shops scattered along the water. Guests can visit the silk-screen factory in back, then make purchases at the shop in front, including sterling-silver and 14-karat-gold jewelry.

At **Noah's Arkade,** in the Frangipani Hotel, Port Elizabeth (© **784/458-3424**), island entrepreneur Lavinia Gunn sells Vincentian and Bequian batiks, scarves, hats, T-shirts, pottery, dolls, baskets, and homemade jellies concocted from grapefruit, mango, and guava, plus West Indian cookbooks and books on tropical flowers and reef fish.

Anyone on the island can show you the way to the workshops of **Sargeant's Model Boatshop Bequia,** Front Street, Port Elizabeth (© **784/458-3344**), west of the pier past the oil-storage facility. Sought out by yacht owners looking for a scale-model reproduction of their favorite vessel, Lawson Sargeant is the self-taught wood carver who established this business. The models are carved from a soft local wood called gumwood, then painted in brilliant colors. When a scale model of the royal family's yacht, *Britannia,* was commissioned in 1985, it required 5 weeks of work and cost $10,000. You can pick up a model of a Bequia whaling boat for much less. The Sargeant family usually keeps 100 model boats in many shapes and sizes in inventory.

MUSTIQUE ★★★

This island of luxury villas, which someone once called "Georgian West Indian," is so remote and small that it would be unknown—if it didn't attract the likes of Princess Margaret, Paul Newman, Mick Jagger, Raquel Welch, Richard Avedon, Tommy Hilfiger, and Prince Andrew, many of whom have cottages here.

The island, privately owned by a consortium of businesspeople, is only 3 miles (5km) long and a mile (2km) wide, and it has only one major hotel. It's located 15 miles (24km) south of St. Vincent. After settling in, you'll find many good white-sand beaches against a backdrop of luxuriant foliage. Our favorite is **Macaroni Beach,** where the water is turquoise, the sands are pure white, and a few trees shade the picnic tables. If you've come over on a day trip, you might choose **Britannia Bay,** which is next to the jetty and close to Basil's Bar.

On the northern reef of Mustique lies the wreck of the French liner *Antilles,* which ran aground on the Pillories in 1971. Its massive hulk, now gutted, can be seen cracked and rusting a few yards offshore—an eerie sight.

If you want to tour the small island, you can rent a **Mini-Moke** to see some of the most elegant homes in the Caribbean, including the late Princess Margaret's place, **Les Jolies Eaux** (Pretty Waters).

GETTING THERE & GETTING AROUND

Mustique Airways (© **784/458-4380** in St. Vincent) runs two daily commuter flights between St. Vincent and Mustique. Flights depart St. Vincent daily at 7:30am and 4:30pm, landing on Mustique about 10 minutes later, then heading immediately back to St. Vincent. The airport closes at dusk.

Once here, you can call **Pecky's** (© **784/458-4621,** ext. 448), but chances are someone at the Cotton House will already have seen you land.

ACCOMMODATIONS

The Cotton House ✷✷✷   The Caribbean's most exclusive hotel is as casually elegant and sophisticated as its clientele. The 18th-century main house is built of coral and stone, and it was painstakingly restored, reconstructed, and redecorated by Oliver Messel, uncle by marriage to Princess Margaret. The entire property was again renovated in 1996. The style of the hotel is set by the antique loggia, arched louvered doors, and cedar shutters. The decor includes everything from Lady Bateman's steamer trunks to a scallop-shell fountain on a quartz base, where guests sit and enjoy their sundowners, perhaps after an afternoon on the tennis court or in the pool. Guests go between two beaches, each only a couple of minutes away on foot—Endeavour Bay, on the leeward side, with calmer waters, and L'Ansecoy, on the other side.

Guest rooms are in two fully restored Georgian houses, a trio of cottages, a newer block of four rooms, and a five-room beach house, all of which open onto windswept balconies or patios. Extras include king-size beds dressed in Egyptian cotton and swathed in netted canopies, robes, slippers, and toiletries from Floris in London. Some of the more romantic units have wrought-iron four-posters, and some of the bathrooms offer private outdoor showers. The Tower Suite is the most luxurious accommodation, filling the entire second floor.

The hotel enjoys an outstanding reputation for its Caribbean/continental food and service. Nonguests are welcome to dine here but must make reservations. The hotel also has three bars—you might find Mick Jagger at one of them.

Mustique, The Grenadines, St. Vincent, W.I. © **800/826-2809** in the U.S., or 784/456-4777. Fax 784/456-5887. www.cottonhouse.net. 20 units. Winter $900–$1,150 double. Off-season $590–$900 double. Rates include MAP (breakfast and dinner). AE, MC, V. **Amenities:** 2 restaurants, 3 bars; spa; horseback riding; library; dive shop, boating, snorkeling, deep-sea fishing, windsurfing; massage; babysitting. *In room:* A/C, ceiling fan, minibar, hair dryer, safe.

Firefly Hotel ✷ *Finds*   This stone house, constructed in 1972, is one of the first homes ever built by an expatriate English or North American on

Mustique. It functioned as a simple, not particularly glamorous B&B until the late 1990s, when Sussex-born Elizabeth Clayton spent huge sums of money to upgrade and enlarge the hotel and its restaurant. Although it contains only four bedrooms, it thrives as one of the most consistently popular bars and restaurants on an island where lots of the expatriate residents enjoy partying 'til the wee hours. (The restaurant is recommended in "Dining," below.) Each of the guest rooms has Caribbean decor, ceiling fans, mahogany furniture, an antique four-poster bed, and a bathroom with a sunken Jacuzzi, plus floors and countertops crafted from smooth-worn pebbles set into beds of mortar. The ambience of the place is more that of a private home than a hotel, and an added advantage is the easy accessibility to one of the island's most animated bars and restaurants.

Brittania Bay (P.O. Box 349), Mustique, The Grenadines, W.I. © 784/456-3414. Fax 784/456-3514. www.mustiquefirefly.com. 4 units. Oct–Apr $600–$700 double, $850 suite; May–Sept $500 double, $750 suite. Rates include breakfast and dinner. AE, MC, V. **Amenities:** Restaurant, bar; 2 pools; room service; laundry. *In room:* Ceiling fan, hair dryer, minibar, safe.

DINING

Basil's Beach Bar SEAFOOD/CARIBBEAN Nobody ever visits this island of indigenous farmers and fisherfolk without spending a night drinking at Basil's, which looks straight out of the South Seas with its wooden deck, open-air dance floor, and thatched roof. Princess Margaret and Mick Jagger are long gone, but the memories linger on in this gathering place for boaters, built on piers above the sea. Some people come here to drink and take in the panoramic view, but Basil's also has a reputation as one of the finest seafood restaurants in the Caribbean. Everything is simple, but well prepared. You can dine under the open-air sunscreens or with the sun blazing down on you. On Wednesday night in winter you can "jump-up" at a barbecue, and there's live music on Mondays. A boutique is also on the premises.

13 Britannia Bay. © 784/458-4621. Reservations recommended. Main courses EC$75–EC$95 (US$27.75–US$35.15). AE, MC, V. Daily 8am–10:30pm. Bar daily 8am "until very late."

The Restaurant at Firefly *Finds* FRENCH/INTERNATIONAL This is one of the island's most consistently popular restaurants, characterized by its bright tropical colors and open-air terraces, a busy bar area where you're likely to see Mustique's glitterati at play, and a menu that's the by-product of a European-trained chef whose earlier venues were very grand and very prestigious. Some of the establishment's tried-and-true dishes include spicy Caribbean crab cakes and pineapple-shrimp curry with rice. Other entrées change with the season and the inspiration of the chef. The drink that's forever associated with this place is the Firefly Special, made with coconut cream, two kinds of rum, fresh papaya, and nutmeg.

In the Firefly hotel, Britannia Bay. © 784/456-3414. Reservations recommended for dinner. Main courses EC$70–EC$90 (US$25.90–US$33.30). AE, MC, V. Daily 8am–1:30pm. Bar daily 8am–midnight.

CANOUAN

In the shape of a half circle, Canouan rises from its sandy beaches to the 800-foot-(240m) high peak of Mount Royal in the north, where you'll find unspoiled forests of white cedar. Fourteen miles (23km) south of St. Vincent and 20 miles (32km) north of Grenada, Canouan has a population of fewer than 2,000 people, many of whom fish for a living and reside in **Retreat Village,** the island's only village.

Only 3½ by 1½ miles (6 by 2km), Canouan is surrounded by long ribbons of absolutely gorgeous powdery white-sand beaches and blue lagoons. The surrounding coral reefs teem with life, making for great snorkeling and diving. **Canovan Dive Center,** in the Grand Bay (© **784/458-8044**), offers resort courses, equipment rentals, and all kinds of dive and snorkel trips.

GETTING THERE

Reaching Canouan by air is slightly different from traveling to the other islands of the Grenadines. **Mustique Airways** no longer makes passenger flights from St. Vincent to Canouan; these flights are now flown by **S.V.G.A. Airways** in St. Vincent (© **784/456-4942**). S.V.G.A. makes two daily flights to Canouan at a cost of EC$160 (US$59.20) round-trip. However, **Mustique Airways** (© **784/458-4380**) does charter flights from St. Vincent to Canouan at a cost of $295 one-way, for up to five passengers.

ACCOMMODATIONS

Canouan Beach Hotel ⭐ At the southwesterly end of Canouan, this all-inclusive resort fills up mainly with French visitors but is open to all. As the first hotel to open on the island, it doesn't have the glitter of Carenage Bay Beach or even Tamarind Beach, but it opens onto one of the best sandy beaches in the Grenadines. Opened in 1984 on 7 acres (3 hectares) of glaringly white beachfront on a peninsula jutting out into the Caribbean, it does a thriving business with escapists. There's blessedly little to do besides sleep, swim, sunbathe, snorkel, sail, and reminisce about the life you've left behind. The resort's social center is beneath the sunscreen of a mahogany-trussed parapet whose sides are open to views of the water. A pair of lush, uninhabited islands lie offshore.

Accommodations are in stone-sided buildings with sliding-glass doors and simple furnishings. The spacious bedrooms have tile floors, high ceilings, king-size or twin beds, and basic, shower-only bathrooms. The sunsets here are beautiful, but you'll have to enjoy them with the mosquitoes. All meals and soft drinks are included in the rates (there's an extra charge for alcohol). Expect buffet lunches and barbecue-style suppers.

South Glossy Bay, Canouan, St. Vincent, W.I. (c/o Mr. Joe Nadal, Manager, Canouan Beach Hotel, Canouan Post Office, St. Vincent, W.I.). © **784/458-8888.** Fax 784/458-8875. www.grenadines.net/canouan/canouan beachhotelhomepage.htm. 40 units. Winter $400 double; off-season $370 double. Rates are all-inclusive, except for alcohol. AE, MC, V. Guests fly to Barbados, where a chartered plane takes them on to Canouan (the hotel will arrange this in advance of your arrival); the price is $160 per person one way from Barbados to Canouan; from the airport, take a 5-min. taxi ride. **Amenities:** Restaurant, bar; tennis court; dive shop, marina, snorkeling, windsurfing, boating. *In room:* A/C, minibar, no phone.

Carenage Bay Beach & Golf Club ⭐⭐⭐ On 800 private acres (320 hectares) is the new choice in luxury lodgings on the island, a 155-villa resort at the beach. The American Academy of Hospitality Sciences has already granted a five-star "Diamond Award" to the property, although we think Petit St. Vincent (see below) is still the class act of the Grenadines. The resort's one- or two-story villas are arranged around the Carenage Bay shoreline, each unit with its own terrace and a panoramic ocean vista. Terra-cotta tile floors, wood furnishings, well kept bathrooms with shower/tub combinations, along with a bright explosion of Caribbean fabrics, give a resort look to this remote retreat. Since its opening it has dwarfed the local competition and brought hundreds of visitors to this island that was once one of the most remote in the Grenadines. The food, often standard resort fare, doesn't quite match the opulence of the surroundings, but it's not bad either. Surprise of surprises, you'll find the first and only European-style casino in the Americas here, and an 18-hole, par-72 golf course, half of which flanks the coastline.

Carenage Bay, Canouan, St. Vincent, W.I. (C) 800/336-4571, or 784/458-8000. Fax 784/458-8885. www.canouan.com. 155 units. Winter $475–$650 double, $875–$1,225 suite. Off-season $275–$375 double, $675–$875 suite. AE, MC, V. **Amenities:** 4 restaurants, 4 bars, night club; casino; pool; 18-hole golf course; 3 tennis courts; health club and spa; marina; boating, windsurfing; scuba diving; airport shuttle. *In room:* A/C, TV, minibar, hair dryer, safe.

MAYREAU 🖈

A tiny cay, 1½ square miles (4 sq. km) of land, Mayreau is a privately owned island shared by a hotel and a little hilltop village of about 170 inhabitants. It's on the route of the mail boat that plies the seas to and from St. Vincent, visiting Canouan and Union Island as well. It's completely sleepy unless a cruise ship anchors offshore and hustles its passengers over for a lobster barbecue on the beach.

ACCOMMODATIONS & DINING

Saltwhistle Bay Club 🖈 *(Finds*   This is a last frontier for well-heeled people seeking a tropical island paradise. Set back from the beach, the accommodations were built by local craftspeople, using local stone and such tropical woods as purpleheart and greenheart. All units are cooled by ceiling fans. Inside, the spacious cottages have an almost medieval feel, with thick stone walls and dark wood furnishings. Bathrooms are large, with cylindrical stone showers. Slightly less formal and less expensive than the Petit St. Vincent Resort on Petit St. Vincent (see below), to which it's frequently compared, the place caters to escapists with money. You can spend your days just lolling in one of the hammocks strung among the trees in the 20-acre (8-hectare) tropical garden, perhaps taking a swim off the expanse of white-sand beaches that curve along both the leeward and windward sides of the island, or the staff will take you to a little uninhabited island nearby for a Robinson Crusoe–style picnic.

The dining room at the hotel is made up of circular stone booths topped by thatch canopies, where you can enjoy seafood fresh from the waters around Mayreau: lobster, curried conch, and grouper.

Mayreau, The Grenadines, St. Vincent, W.I. (C) 784/458-8444. Fax 784/458-8944. www.saltwhistlebay.com. 8 units. Winter $480 double. Off-season $360 double. Children under age 18 pay half. Rates include MAP (breakfast and dinner). AE, MC, V. Closed Sept–Oct. Take the private hotel launch from the airport on Union Island ($50 per person round-trip). **Amenities:** Restaurant, bar; boating, snorkeling, scuba diving; babysitting; laundry. *In room:* Ceiling fan, hair dryer, no phone.

UNION ISLAND

Midway between Grenada and St. Vincent, Union Island is one of the southernmost of the Grenadines. It's known for its dramatic 900-foot (270m) peak, Mount Parnassus, which yachters can often see from miles away. For those cruising in the area, Union is the port of entry for St. Vincent. Yachters are required to check in with Customs upon entry.

ESSENTIALS

GETTING THERE   The island is reached by chartered or scheduled aircraft, cargo boat, private yacht, or mail boat (see "Getting There" at the beginning of this section). **Air Martinique** ((C) 784/458-4528) flies to Union Island from Martinique. **Mustique Airways** ((C) 784/458-4380 on St. Vincent) makes one flight per day Monday through Thursday; the fare is $60 round-trip (children under age 12 pay half).

SPECIAL EVENTS Over Easter weekend, **Easterval** features boat races, a calypso competition, and the Big Drum Dance, a festive cultural show that highlights the islanders' African heritage.

ACCOMMODATIONS & DINING

Anchorage Yacht Club This club occupies a prominent position a few steps from the bumpy landing strip that services at least two nearby resorts (Petit St. Vincent and Palm Island) and about a half dozen small islands nearby. Something of an airline-hub aura permeates the place, as passengers shuttle between their planes, boats, and the yacht club's bar and restaurant. Although at least two other hotels are nearby, this is the best. It has a threefold function as a hotel, a restaurant, and a bar, with a busy marine-service facility in the same compound under different management.

Each of the small guest rooms, set between a pair of airy verandas, has white-tile floors and simple, somewhat sun-bleached modern furniture. Shower-only bathrooms are very small and towels a bit thin, but in this remote part of the world, you're grateful for hot water. The better units are the bungalows and cabanas beside the beach.

The yachting set meets in the wood-and-stone bar, which serves breakfast, lunch, and dinner daily.

Clifton, Union Island, The Grenadines, St. Vincent, W.I. ℭ **784/458-8221.** Fax 784/458-8365. www.ayc-hotels-grenadines.com. 15 units. Winter $110 double; $165 bungalow or apt. Off-season $90 double; $120 bungalow or apt. Extra person $40. Rates include continental breakfast. MC, V. **Amenities:** Restaurant, bar; marina, fishing, snorkeling; laundry. *In room:* A/C.

Lambi's Guest House & Restaurant *Value* CREOLE/SEAFOOD Built partially on stilts on the waterfront in Clifton, this is the best place to sample the local cuisine. *Lambi* means conch in Creole patois, and naturally it's the specialty here—if you've never tried this shellfish before, this is a good place to sample it. You can order various other fresh fish platters as well, depending on the catch of the day, and lobster and crab are frequently available. You can also order the usual chicken, steak, lamb, or pork chops, but all this is shipped in frozen. Fresh vegetables are used whenever possible. In winter a steel band entertains nightly in the bar, and limbo dancers or even fire dancing will enthrall you.

Upstairs are 41 dormitory-style rooms for rent, each with 2 double beds, ceiling fans, and a tiny, tiny bathroom. Year-round, they go for EC$50 (US$18.50) single, EC$75 (US$27.75) double, and EC$90 (US$33.30) triple.

Clifton Harbour, Union Island, The Grenadines, St. Vincent, W.I. ℭ **784/458-8549.** Fax 784/458-8395. Main courses EC$30–EC$60 (US$11.10–US$22.20); 50-dish buffet EC$45 (US$16.65). MC, V. Daily 7am–11pm.

PALM ISLAND ⋆

Is this island a resort or is the resort the island? Casual elegance prevails on these 130 acres (52 hectares) in the southern Grenadines. Surrounded by five white-sand beaches, the island is sometimes called "Prune," so we can easily understand the more appealing name change. This little islet offers complete peace and quiet with plenty of sea, sand, sun, and sailing.

To get to Palm Island, you must first fly to Union Island. From Union Island, a hotel launch will take you to Palm Island.

ACCOMMODATIONS

Palm Island ⋆⋆⋆ Tranquility reigns at this all-inclusive resort with its five white-sand beaches. The old Palm Island Beach Club was completely razed to the ground and rebuilt in 1999, reopening in January 2000. This exclusive and remote retreat on a private island has come a long way since its founder, John Caldwell (called "Coconut Johnny"), began planting palms here to give the island a lush, tropical look. Now under new developers, the posh retreat consists of a cluster of 40 units contained in 22 Caribbean cottages. Bedrooms capture the spirit of the Grenadines, with units in both standard guest rooms and "tree houses," each with ceiling fans, custom-designed bamboo and rattan furnishings, colorful balconies or patios opening onto the view, shower-only bathrooms, and bathrobes. The resort also offers a series of romantic tree houses with high-peaked ceilings and breezy balconies with hammocks, along with an interior containing a four-poster bamboo bed. In addition to the regular accommodations, the Plantation House boasts four bedrooms, each with queen-size beds.

Good-quality cuisine is served in the Grenadines Restaurant, with specialties from the Caribbean, the U.S., and Europe. As one guest wrote, "if you don't dig the vittles here, you can rent a boat for the night to take you over to Union Island or else crack open a coconut." Chances are you won't have to do either, as the cuisine is great (a vast improvement over what it was in the past). From the pink grapefruit with honey rum sauce that begins your breakfast to that concluding coconut mousse after dinner, you dine "high on the hog," as the chef says.

Palm Island, The Grenadines, St. Vincent, W.I. © **800/345-0356,** or 784/458-8824. Fax 784/458-8804. www.palmislandresort.com. 40 units. Winter $700–$900 double. Off-season $560–$780 double. Rates are all-inclusive. AE, DC, MC, V. **Amenities:** 2 restaurants, 2 bars; pool; tennis court; snorkeling, marina, fishing, windsurfing; bikes; laundry. *In room:* A/C, minibar, hair dryer, safe, no phone.

PETIT ST. VINCENT ⚐

A private island 4 miles (6km) from Union Island in the southern Grenadines, this speck of land is rimmed with white-sand beaches. On 113 acres (45 hectares), it's an out-of-this-world corner of the Caribbean that's only for self-sufficient types who want to escape from just about everything.

The easiest way to get to Petit St. Vincent is to fly to Union Island via St. Vincent. Make arrangements with the hotel to have its "PSV boat" pick you up on Union Island. This is the southernmost of St. Vincent's Grenadines.

ACCOMMODATIONS

Petit St. Vincent Resort ★★★   This resort enjoys a nautical chic. It was conceived by Hazen K. Richardson, who had to do everything from planting trees to laying cables on the 113-acre (45-hectare) property. Open to the trade winds, this self-contained cottage colony was designed by a Swedish architect, Arne Hasselquist, who used purpleheart wood and the local stone, called blue bitch (yes, that's right), for the walls. This is the only place to stay on the island, and if you don't like it and want to check out, you'd better have a yacht waiting. But we think you'll be pleased.

Some cottages are built on a hillside, with great views, and some are set conveniently close to the beach. Cottages open onto big outdoor patios and are cooled by trade winds and ceiling fans. Each spacious accommodation has an ample living area, two daybeds, a good-size bedroom with two queen-size beds, a shower-only bathroom, a dressing room, Caribbean-style wicker and rattan furnishings, and a large patio with a hammock for lying back and taking it easy. For payment, personal checks are accepted and preferred. When you need something (perhaps a picnic lunch made up for your day on the beach), you simply write out your request, place it in a slot in a bamboo flagpole, and run up the yellow flag. A staff member will arrive on a motorized cart to take your order.

This resort always has a top-notch chef, and menus are changed every day. Although the food has to be shipped in, the fine U.S. and Continental dishes taste fresh and are very well prepared. The chefs are always sensitive to special requests and special diets.

Petit St. Vincent, The Grenadines, St. Vincent, W.I. (For reservations, P.O. Box 12506, Cincinnati, OH 45212.) © 800/654-9326 or 784/458-8801. Fax 784/458-8428. www.psvresort.com. 22 units. Winter $890 cottage for 2. Off-season $580 cottage for 2. Rates are all-inclusive. AE, MC, V. Closed Sept–Oct. **Amenities:** Dining room, bar; tennis court; fitness trail; watersports center. *In room:* Ceiling fan, minibar, hair dryer, no phone.

25

Trinidad & Tobago

Trinidad, birthplace of calypso, steel-drum music, and the limbo, used to be visited only by business travelers in Port-of-Spain. The island was more interested in its oil, natural gas, and steel industries than in tourism. But that has all changed now. Trinidad has become a serious vacation destination, with a spruced-up capital and a renovated airport. The island's sophistication and cultural mélange, which is far greater than that of any other island in the southern Caribbean, is also a factor in increased visitor volume.

Conversely, Tobago, its sibling island, is just as drowsy as ever, and that's its charm. Through the years, the country has been peopled by immigrants from almost every corner of the world: Africa, the Middle East, Europe, India, China, and the Americas. It's against such a background that the island has become the fascinating mixture of cultures, races, and creeds that it is today.

Trinidad, which is about the size of Delaware, and its neighbor island, even tinier Tobago, 20 miles (23km) to the northeast, together form a nation popularly known as "T&T." South African Bishop Desmond Tutu once dubbed it "The Rainbow Country," for its abundance of floral growth and the diversity of its population. The islands are the southernmost outposts of the West Indies. Trinidad lies only 7 miles (11km) from the Paria Peninsula of Venezuela, to which it was physically connected in prehistoric times.

The Spanish founded Trinidad in 1592 and held it longer than they did any of their other real estate in the Caribbean. The English settled Tobago in 1642, and they captured Trinidad in 1797. Both islands remained in British hands until the two-island nation declared its independence in 1962. The British influence is still clearly visible today, from the strong presence of the British dialect to the islanders' fondness for cricket.

1 Trinidad & Tobago Essentials

VISITOR INFORMATION

There is no Trinidadian tourism office that can be visited directly in the U.S., but you can call the **Trinidad & Tobago Tourism Office** (© **800/748-4224** or 888/595-4TNT) for information. The islands are also on the Web at **www.visit.tnt.com**.

Canadians can get information from **Taurus House,** 512 Duplex Ave., Toronto, Ontario M4R 2E3 (© **800/267-7600** or 416/485-7827).

There's also an office in **England** at **Morris Kevan International,** 66 Abbey Road, Bush Hill Park, Enfield, Middlesex EN1 2RQ (© **020/8350-1000**).

Once you're on Trinidad, you can stop by **TIDCO,** 10–14 Phillips St., Port-of-Spain (© **868/623-1932**). There's also an information desk at Piarco Airport (© **868/669-5196**).

On Tobago, go to the **Tobago Division of Tourism,** N.I.B. Mall, Level 3, Scarborough (© **868/639-2125**), or the information desk at Crown Point Airport (© **868/639-0509**).

 FAST FACTS: **Trinidad & Tobago**

Currency The **Trinidad and Tobago dollar (TT$)** has an exchange rate of about US$1 = TT$6.28 (TT$1 = 16¢). Ask what currency is being referred to when rates are quoted. We've used both in this chapter, depending on the establishment. U.S. and Canadian dollars are often accepted, particularly in Port-of-Spain. However, you'll usually do better by converting your Canadian or U.S. dollars into local currency. British pounds should be converted into the local currency. *Unless otherwise specified, dollar quotations appearing in this chapter are in U.S. currency.*

Customs Readers have reported long delays in clearing Customs on Trinidad. Visitors may bring in 200 cigarettes or 50 cigars plus 1 quart of spirits.

Documents Citizens of the United States, Britain, and Canada need passports and an ongoing or return ticket to enter Trinidad and Tobago. A visa is not required for tourist/business stays shorter than 6 weeks. Save the carbon copy of the immigration card you fill out when you arrive: you'll have to return it to immigration officials when you depart.

Electricity The electricity is either 110- or 230-volt AC (60 cycles), so ask when making your hotel reservations if you'll need transformers and/or adapters.

Embassies & High Commissions In Port-of-Spain on Trinidad, the **U.S. Embassy** is located at 7–9 Marli St., 15 Queen's Park West (© **868/622-6371**); the **Canadian High Commission** is situated at Maple House, 3 Sweet Briar Rd., St. Clair (© **868/622-6232**); and the **British High Commission** is found at 19 St. Clair Ave., St. Clair (© **868/622-2748**).

Emergencies On either Trinidad or Tobago, call the **police** at © **999;** to report a **fire** or summon an **ambulance**, dial © **990.**

Language English is the official language, although you'll hear it spoken with many different accents, especially British. Chinese, French, Spanish, Hindi, and a local dialect, Trinibagianese, are also spoken.

Safety As a general rule, Tobago is safer than its larger neighbor, Trinidad. Crime does exist on Tobago, but it's not of raging dimensions. If you can, avoid the downtown streets of Port-of-Spain at night, especially those around Independence Square, where muggings have been reported. Evening jaunts down Wilson Street and the Market of Scarborough are also discouraged. Visitors are open prey for pickpockets during Carnival time, so be alert during large street parties. It would also be wise to safeguard your valuables and never leave them unattended at the beach or even in a locked car.

Taxes & Service Charges The government imposes a 15% value-added tax (VAT) on room rates. It also imposes a departure tax of TT$100 (US$16) on every passenger more than 5 years old. The big hotels and restaurants add a 10% to 15% service charge to your final tab.

Telephone   The area code for Trinidad and Tobago is **868**. Make calls to or from the islands like you would to any other area code in North America. On either island, just dial the local seven-digit number.

Time   Trinidad and Tobago are in the Eastern time zone; from November through March, time here is the same as the U.S. east coast. From April through October (daylight saving time in the United States), when it's 6am in Miami or New York, it's 5am in T&T.

Tipping   Tip taxi drivers 10% to 15% of the fare, and tip waiters 10% to 15% of the cost of a meal. Tip skycaps and bellboys $1 per bag.

Water   On Trinidad and Tobago, stick to bottled water.

Weather   Trinidad has a tropical climate all year, with constant trade winds maintaining mean temperatures of 84°F during the day and 74°F at night. It rarely gets above 90° or below 70°F. The rainy season runs from May to November, but it shouldn't deter you from visiting; the rain usually lasts no more than 2 hours before the sun comes out again. However, carry along plenty of insect repellent if you visit then.

2 Trinidad

Trinidad is completely different from the other islands of the Caribbean, and that forms part of its charm and appeal. It's not for everyone, though. Because **Port-of-Spain,** the capital, is one of the most bustling commercial centers in the Caribbean, more business travelers than tourists are drawn here. The island, 50 miles long and 40 miles wide (81 and 64km), does have beaches, but the best of them are far away from the capital. The city itself, with a population of about 120,000, is hot, humid, and slightly on the dirty side. With the opening of its $2 million cruise-ship complex, Port-of-Spain has become a major port of call for Caribbean cruise lines.

Although Port-of-Spain, with its shopping centers, fast-food joints, modern hotels, and active nightlife, draws mixed reviews from readers, the countryside is calmer. Far removed from the traffic jams of the capital, you can explore the fauna and flora of the island. It's estimated that there are some 700 varieties of orchids alone, plus 400 species of birds.

Prices on Trinidad are often lower than on many other islands in the West Indies. Port-of-Spain abounds in inexpensive inns and guesthouses. Since most of the restaurants cater to locals, dining prices reflect the low wages.

The people are part of the attraction on Trinidad, the most cosmopolitan island in the Caribbean. The island's polyglot population includes Syrians, Chinese, Americans, Europeans, East Indians, Parsees, Madrasis, Venezuelans, and the last of the original Amerindians, the early settlers of the island. You'll also find Hindustanis, Javanese, Lebanese, African descendants, and Creole mixes. The main religions are Christianity, Hinduism, and Islam. In all, there are about 1.2 million inhabitants, whose language is English, although you may hear speech in a strange argot, Trinibagianese.

One of the most industrialized nations in the Caribbean, and one of the biggest exporters of oil in the western hemisphere, Trinidad is also blessed with the huge 114-acre (46-hectare) Pitch Lake, the source of most of the world's asphalt. It's also the home of Angostura Bitters, the recipe for which is a closely guarded secret.

TRINIDAD ESSENTIALS

GETTING THERE   From North America, Trinidad is one of the most distant islands in the Caribbean. Because of the legendary toughness of Trinidadian Customs, it's preferable to arrive during the day (presumably when your stamina is at its peak) if you can schedule it. Most passengers from eastern North America fly **American Airlines** (© **800/433-7300** in the U.S., or 868/627-7013; www.aa.com), which has one daily nonstop flight from San Juan and another from Miami.

Air Canada (© **888/247-2266** in the U.S., 800/268-7240 in Canada, or 868/664-4065; www.aircanada.ca) offers one nonstop flight per week from Toronto to Port-of-Spain.

BWIA (© **868/625-1010**; www.bwee.com) offers service from New York to Port-of-Spain. Some of these flights are nonstop; most of them touch down en route, usually on Barbados or Antigua, before continuing on to Trinidad, the airline's home base. From Miami, BWIA usually offers a daily nonstop flight to Port-of-Spain.

Trinidad is the transfer point for many passengers to Tobago. For information about getting to Tobago, see the section "Tobago," later in this chapter.

GETTING AROUND   Trinidad **taxis** are unmetered, and they're identified by their license plates, which begin with the letter *H*. There are also "pirate taxis" as well: private cars that cruise around like regular taxis and pick up passengers. Whether you take an official taxi or a pirate taxi, make sure you agree on the fare beforehand, otherwise you're likely to get ripped off. Maxi Taxis, or vans, can also be hailed on the street. A fare from Piarco Airport into Port-of-Spain generally costs $20 ($30 after 10pm).

To avoid the anxiety of driving, you can **hire a local driver** for your sightseeing jaunts. Although it costs more than doing it yourself, it alleviates the hassles of badly marked (or unmarked) roads and the sometimes-bizarre local driving patterns. Most drivers will serve as guides. Their rates, however, are based on route distances, so get an overall quotation and agree on the actual fare before setting off.

If you're brave enough to set out via **rental car,** arm yourself with a good map and *be prepared to drive on the left*. Visitors with a valid international driver's license or a license from the United States, Canada, France, or the United Kingdom may drive without extra documentation for up to 3 months.

Since the island is one of the world's largest exporters of asphalt, Trinidad's some 4,500 miles (7,245km) of roads are well paved. However, outback roads should be avoided during the rainy season, as they're often narrow, twisting, and prone to washouts. Inquire about conditions, particularly if you're headed for the north coast. The fierce traffic jams of Port-of-Spain are legendary, and night driving anywhere on the island is rather hazardous.

The major U.S.-based car-rental firms currently have no franchises on the island, so you'll have to make arrangements with a local firm (go over the terms and insurance agreements carefully). Count on spending about $40 to $60 per day or more, with unlimited mileage included. Your best bet is one of the firms maintaining offices at Piarco Airport. These include **Econo-Car Rentals** (© **868/669-2342**), **Thrifty** (© **868/669-0602**), and the simply named **Auto Rentals** (© **868/669-2277**). *A word of warning:* Although these local car-rental firms technically accept reservations, a car may not be waiting for you even if you reserve ahead of time.

Trinidad

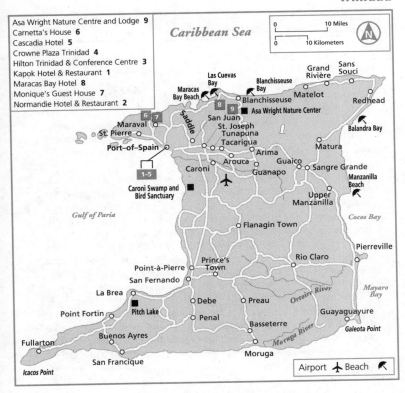

Asa Wright Nature Centre and Lodge **9**
Carnetta's House **6**
Cascadia Hotel **5**
Crowne Plaza Trinidad **4**
Hilton Trinidad & Conference Centre **3**
Kapok Hotel & Restaurant **1**
Maracas Bay Hotel **8**
Monique's Guest House **7**
Normandie Hotel & Restaurant **2**

Caribbean Sea

0   10 Miles
0   10 Kilometers

Grand Rivière   Sans Souci
Las Cuevas Bay   Blanchisseuse Bay
Maracas Bay Beach   Matelot
Blanchisseuse   Redhead
Asa Wright Nature Center
San Juan   Balandra Bay
St. Joseph
Maraval   Tunapuna
St. Pierre   Tacarigua
Port-of-Spain   Arima   Matura
Arouca   Guaico
Caroni   Guanapo   Sangre Grande
Manzanilla Beach
Caroni Swamp and Bird Sanctuary   Upper Manzanilla

Gulf of Paria
Flanagin Town   *Cocos Bay*
Pierreville
Prince's Town   Rio Claro
Point-à-Pierre   *Mayaro Bay*
San Fernando   *Ortoire River*
La Brea   Debe   Preau
Point Fortin   Pitch Lake   Guayaguayure
Penal   Galeota Point
Basseterre   *Moruga River*
Fullarton   Buenos Ayres
San Francique   Moruga
Icacos Point

Airport ✈ Beach ☂

All the cities of Trinidad are linked by regular **bus service** from Port-of-Spain. Fares are low (about 50¢ for runs within the capital). However, the old buses are likely to be very overcrowded. Try to avoid them at rush hours, and beware of pickpockets.

FAST FACTS   Most **banks** are open Monday to Thursday from 8am to 2pm and Friday from 9am to noon and 3 to 5pm. **Citibank** has offices at 12 Queen's Park East, Port-of-Spain (© 868/625-1046 or 868/625-1049), and 18–30 High St., San Fernando (© 868/652-3691). **Republic Bank Ltd.** (9–17 Park St.; © 868/625-4411) and **Royal Bank of Trinidad & Tobago Ltd.** (Royal Court, 19–21 Park St.; © 868/623-1322) are two of the many banks in Port-of-Spain with ATMs. You'll also find ATMs at some big supermarkets.

There is no 24-hour **pharmacy** on either island. In Port-of-Spain, **Star Lite Drugs** at Four Roads (© 868/632-0516) is open Monday to Saturday from 8am to 10pm, Sunday 8am to 1pm.

The **Port-of-Spain General Hospital** is located at 169 Charlotte St. (© 868/623-2951). Medical care is sometimes limited, and physicians and health-care facilities expect immediate cash payment for services. Medical insurance from the United States is not always valid outside the country, but supplemental medical insurance with specific overseas coverage is available. Contact the U.S. Embassy for updates.

Fun Fact **The Carnival of Trinidad**

Called "the world's most colorful festival," the **Carnival of Trinidad** is a spectacle of dazzling costumes and gaiety. Hundreds of bands of masqueraders parade through the cities on the Monday and Tuesday preceding Ash Wednesday, bringing traffic to a standstill. The island seems to explode with music, fun, and dancing.

Some of the Carnival costumes cost hundreds of dollars. "Bands" might depict the birds of Trinidad, such as the scarlet ibis and the keskidee, or a bevy of women might come out in the streets dressed as cats. Costumes are also satirical and comical.

Trinidad, of course, is the land of calypso, which grew out of the folk songs of the African–West Indian immigrants. The lyrics command great attention, as they're rich in satire and innuendo. The calypsonian is a poet-musician, and lyrics have often been capable of toppling politicians from office. In banter and bravado, the calypsonian gives voice to the sufferings and aspirations of his people. At Carnival time, the artist sings his compositions to spectators in tents. There's one show a night at each of the calypso tents around town, from 8pm to midnight. Tickets for these are sold in the afternoon at most record shops.

Carnival parties, or fêtes, with three or four orchestras at each one, are public and are advertised in the newspaper. For a really wild time, attend a party on Sunday night before Carnival Monday. To reserve tickets, contact the **National Carnival Committee,** Queen's Park Savannah, Port-of-Spain, Trinidad (© **868/627-1358**). Hotels are booked months in advance, and most inns raise their prices—often considerably—at the time.

You can attend rehearsals of steel bands at their headquarters, called panyards, beginning about 7pm. Preliminary band competitions are held at the grandstand of Queen's Park Savannah in Port-of-Spain and at Skinner Park in San Fernando, beginning 2 weeks before Carnival.

The main **post office** (© **868/625-2121**) is on Wrightson Road, Port-of-Spain, and is open Monday to Friday from 7am to 5pm.

If your hotel can't send or receive faxes for you, try **TSTT Communications,** 1 Edward St., Port-of-Spain (© **868/639-1195**).

ACCOMMODATIONS

The number of hotels on Trinidad is limited, and you shouldn't expect your Port-of-Spain room to open directly onto a white-sand beach. The nearest beach is a long, costly taxi ride away. Don't forget that a 15% government tax and a 10% service charge will be added to your hotel and restaurant bills. All hotels raise their rates, often considerably, during Carnival (the week before Ash Wednesday).

EXPENSIVE

Asa Wright Nature Centre and Lodge ★ *Finds* There really isn't anything else like this in the Caribbean. Known to bird-watchers throughout the world, this center sits on 196 remote acres (74 hectares) of protected land at an elevation of

1,200 feet (360m) in the rain-forested northern mountain range of Trinidad, 10 miles (16km) north of Arima, beside Blanchisseuse Road. Hummingbirds, toucans, bellbirds, manakins, several varieties of tanagers, and the rare oilbird are all on the property. Back-to-basics accommodations are available in the lodge, in the 1908 Edwardian main house, and in the cottages built on elevated ground above the main house. Even though they offer less privacy than other rooms, we prefer the two rooms in the main house, which offer more atmosphere and are outfitted with dark wood antiques and two king-size beds each. Furnishings in the cottages are rather plain but comfortable. Shower-only bathrooms are a bit cramped, but you generally get hot water—count yourself lucky.

Guided tours are available on the nature center's grounds, which contain several well-maintained trails and a natural waterfall with a pool in which guests can swim (getting to the beach involves a 90-min. drive to the coast). The minimum age accepted is 12 if accompanied by an adult, or 17 if unaccompanied.

Spring Hill Estate, Arima, Trinidad, W.I. (For information or reservations, call the toll-free number or write Caligo Ventures, 156 Bedford Rd., Armonk, NY 10504.) ℂ 800/426-7781 in the U.S., or 868/667-4655. Fax 868/667-4540. www.asawright.org. 24 units. Winter $240 double. Off-season $180 double. Rates include all meals, afternoon tea, and a welcoming rum punch. MC, V. **Amenities:** Dining room; swimming pond; laundry. *In room:* Ceiling fan, no phone.

Crowne Plaza Trinidad ✷   This bland but modern inn is a favorite with business travelers, who tolerate the noise and congestion for the convenient location, a 5-minute walk from the city center. The recently renovated bedrooms, tastefully decorated in pastels, contain private balconies, along with two double beds. The hotel has added two executive floors and such luxuries as trouser presses, magnifying mirrors, mahogany furniture, and brass lamps. The bathrooms have shower/tub combinations and dual basins in faux marble or granite.

The Olympia Restaurant is adorned with Roman-style pillars, with plants cascading over the top. La Ronde, with a French decor, is the only revolving restaurant in the Caribbean and serves standard international cuisine.

Wrightson Rd. at London Rd. (P.O. Box 1017), Port-of-Spain, Trinidad, W.I. ℂ 800/2-CROWNE in the U.S. and Canada, or 868/625-3366. Fax 868/625-4166. www.crowneplaza.com. 245 units. Year-round $189.50 double; $285 suite. AE, MC, V. **Amenities:** 2 restaurants, 2 bars; pool; fitness center; business center; room service; babysitting; laundry. *In room:* A/C, TV, hair dryer.

Hilton Trinidad & Conference Centre ✷✷   This is the most dramatic and architecturally sophisticated hotel on Trinidad. The lobby is on the uppermost floor, while the guestrooms are staggered in rocky but verdant terraces that sweep down the steep hillside. The location just above Queen's Park Savannah affords most of its rooms a view of the sea and mountains. The higher rooms are cheaper than lower ones. This is not the greatest Hilton in the world, or even in the Caribbean, but all rooms still meet international first-class standards, with queen-size or twin beds, balconies, generous closet space, and modern tiled bathrooms with combination shower/tubs. Accommodations in the main wing are the most sought after, as they have good views over Queen's Park Savannah. Executive Floor rooms have upgraded services and amenities.

The main dining room, La Boucan (see "Dining," below), contains museum-quality murals by Geoffrey Holder, one of the island's best-known artists.

Lady Young Rd. (P.O. Box 442), Port-of-Spain, Trinidad, W.I. ℂ 800/HILTONS in the U.S. and Canada, or 868/624-3211. Fax 868/624-4485. www.hilton.com. 394 units. Year-round $185–$205 double; from $350 suite. AE, DC, MC, V. **Amenities:** 2 restaurants, 3 bars; pool; 2 tennis courts; fitness center; sauna; car rentals; massage; babysitting; laundry. *In room:* A/C, TV, minibar, hair dryer, safe.

MODERATE

Cascadia Hotel   This modern hotel is another businessperson's favorite, but it houses those who obviously aren't generating the same sales as guests of the Trinidad Hilton. The hotel is past its prime, but still reasonably comfortable. Each of the pleasant bedrooms contains two phones, a balcony, and unpretentious wicker furniture. The decor is vaguely English. Bathrooms are rather standard fare, although they do contain second phones along with shower/tub combinations. On the premises is an oval pool with a "swim-through" bar and a water slide.

Ariapita Rd., St. Ann's, Trinidad, W.I. ⓒ **868/624-0940.** Fax 868/627-8046. www.cascadiahotel.com. 68 units. Year-round $114–$138 double; $186–$462 suite for 2. AE, MC, V. Located about 5 miles (8km) northwest of the center of Port-of-Spain. **Amenities:** Restaurant, bar; pool; 2 squash courts; fitness center; sauna; car rental; room service (7am–11pm); babysitting; laundry/dry cleaning. *In room:* A/C, TV, dataport, fridge on request, minibar on request, hair dryer.

Kapok Hotel & Restaurant 𝒢   This modern but unpretentious nine-floor hotel, in the residential suburb of St. Clair, is an efficient, well-maintained operation run by the Chan family. It's located away from the worst traffic of the city, near the zoo, the Presidential Palace, and just north of Queen's Park Savannah. From its lounge, you'll have panoramic views of the Savannah and the Gulf of Paria. The comfortably appointed, spacious rooms have wicker furnishings and private bathrooms with combination shower/tubs. For a hotel of this price range, it comes as a surprise to find phones with voice mail and data ports, and even room service until 10pm. The rooftop restaurant, Tiki Village, serves Chinese and Polynesian food. In the back is an expanded pool area with a waterfall, garden, menagerie, and sundeck.

16–18 Cotton Hill, St. Clair, Trinidad, W.I. ⓒ **868/622-6441.** Fax 868/622-9677. www.kapok.co.tt. 94 units. Year-round $127–$160 double, $180 suite. Additional person $15 per night. AE, MC, V. **Amenities:** Restaurant; pool; fitness center; business services; room service (7am–10pm); babysitting; laundry/dry cleaning. *In room:* A/C, TV, dataport, hair dryer.

Maracas Bay Hotel   This is the only beachfront hotel in all of Trinidad, and even here, you'll have to walk across the coastal road to reach the sands. If you want a real beach resort vacation, you should go to Tobago. But if you'd like to sightsee in Trinidad and also be on the beach, Maracas Bay Hotel is a decent choice. Owned and operated by a local family, it's nestled in a valley on sloping terrain across the road from Maracas Bay. As the crow flies, it's only 7 miles (11km) north of Port-of-Spain. But dense traffic and a winding road makes this at least a 45-minute drive from the commercial center of the capital. There's a bar/lounge accented with Hindu art, and an unpretentious dining room. Bedrooms contain simple furnishings, spartan white walls, and terra-cotta tile floors. Each unit has two queen-size beds and a tiled bathroom with a shower/tub combination. The beach, a wide strip of white sand bordered by palm trees, is a lovely oasis from the bustle of Port-of-Spain. The inn provides chaises and beach umbrellas for its guests, though nobody will be taking your drink order on the sands.

Maracas Bay, Trinidad, W.I. ⓒ **868/669-1914.** Fax 868/669-1643. 40 units. Year-round $70–$130 double. Extra person (up to a total of 4) $16. AE, MC, V. **Amenities:** Restaurant, bar. *In room:* A/C, no phone.

INEXPENSIVE

Carnetta's 𝒢 *(Finds)*   This home is in the suburb of Andalusia in cool and scenic Maraval, about a 15-minute ride from the central business district and a 45-minute ride to Maracas Beach. It's owned by Winston and Carnetta Borrell— both are keen naturalists (he was a former director of tourism) and both have a wealth of information about touring the island. Winston is a grand gardener, filling his property with orchids, ginger lilies, and anthuriums, among other plant life. Carnetta grows her own herbs to produce some of the finest meals around. The rooms have floral themes and are furnished in a tropical style. For the most privacy, request a guest room on the upper floor. The others are on the ground level. Our preferred nest is "Le Flamboyant," opening onto the little inn's patio. Most of the rooms are medium in size, and each has a small and immaculately maintained bath. Mountain bikes can be rented for $7 per day as can cars for $50 per day.

28 Scotland Terrace, Andalusia, Maraval, Trinidad, W.I. ℂ 868/628-2732. Fax 868/628-7717. www.carnetta. com. 14 units. Year-round $50–$60 double. Dinner $12 extra. AE, DC, MC, V. **Amenities:** Restaurant, bar; laundry. *In room:* A/C, TV.

Monique's Guest House   In the lush Maraval Valley just an 8-minute (3-mile/5km) drive north of the center of Port-of-Spain, Monique's offers 20 newly rebuilt bungalow-style rooms. Some are large enough to accommodate up to 4 people, and 10 rooms offer kitchenettes with their own porches. The biggest are units 25 and 26, which could possibly sleep up to 6, though that would be a bit crowded. One room is designed for elderly travelers or those with disabilities. Accommodations have open balconies so you can enjoy the tropical breezes and scenic hills. The bathrooms are well organized and spotless, each with a shower. The air-conditioned dining room and bar offers a medley of local and international dishes, and Maracas Beach is only a 25-minute drive away. Mike and Monica Charbonné will be here to welcome you.

114–116 Saddle Rd., Maraval, Trinidad, W.I. ℂ 868/628-3334. Fax 868/622-3232. www.best-caribbean.com. 20 units. Year-round $66–$73 double. AE, DC, MC, V. **Amenities:** Restaurant, bar; laundry. *In room:* A/C, TV.

Normandie Hotel & Restaurant   This inn rises around a banyan- and banana-filled courtyard that surrounds an oval-shaped pool. Each guest room has a balcony or patio, plus standard furnishings (mostly twin beds). The more spacious superior units have tiny lofts with queen-size beds. Bathrooms are a bit lackluster with shower/tub combinations and low water pressure. The cheaper rooms have drawn fire from some readers, especially for the noisy air-conditioning.

Calm and cosmopolitan, the hotel sits 3½ miles (6km) northwest of the city center, next to one of the best art galleries on Trinidad; a skylight-covered shopping center; an attractive restaurant, La Fantasie (see "Dining," below); the botanical gardens of Port-of-Spain; and the official residence of the prime minister of Trinidad and Tobago. In addition, brunch, lunch, or tea can be ordered in the hotel's cafe, and the Cascade Club offers entertainment on Friday and Saturday nights.

10 Nook Ave., St. Ann's (P.O. Box 851), Port-of-Spain, Trinidad, W.I. ℂ 868/624-1181. Fax 868/624-0108. www.normandiett.com. 53 units. Year-round $76–$90 double; $120 loft studio for 3. Children age 11 and under stay free in parents' room. AE, DC, MC, V. **Amenities:** Restaurant, cafe. *In room:* A/C, TV, hair dryer.

DINING

The food in Trinidad should probably be better than it is, considering all the different culinary backgrounds that shaped the island, including West Indian, Chinese, French, and Indian.

Stick to local specials such as stuffed crabs and *chip-chip* (tiny clamlike shellfish), but skip the armadillo and opossum stews. Spicy Indian rôtis filled with vegetables or ground meat seem to be everyone's favorite lunch, and the drink of choice is a fresh rum punch flavored with the natively produced Angostura Bitters. Except for a few fancy places, dress tends to be very casual.

EXPENSIVE

La Boucan ✿ INTERNATIONAL The finest hotel restaurant on Trinidad, with some of the most lavish buffets, this establishment satisfies the eye as well as the palate. Taking its name from the smoking process by which pirates and buccaneers used to preserve meat for long voyages, La Boucan incorporates this smoky flavor into many of its West Indian dishes. Against one of its longest walls stretches a graceful mural by Geoffrey Holder, one of the most famous artists and dancers of the Caribbean. Not all dishes reflect the nurturing and refinement they should, but most diners are satisfied with the results. Typical choices include lobster (grilled or Thermidor); a daily selection of fish (usually grouper or snapper), which is grilled, poached, or pan-fried according to your wishes and served with herb-butter sauce; and prime rib of beef. The desserts are sumptuous, especially the chocolate crème brûlée and a rich and creamy cheesecake. Live music from a pianist (and on weekends from a dance band) provides entertainment.

In the Hilton Trinidad, Lady Young Rd. © 868/624-3211. Reservations required. Lunch buffet TT$94.20 (US$15); main courses at dinner TT$37.70–TT$163.30 (US$16–US$26). AE, MC, V. Tues–Sat 7–11pm.

Plantation House Restaurant ✿ CARIBBEAN This 1920s gingerbread colonial building forms an elegant setting for the excellent cuisine served here. The chefs search for quality ingredients, which they manage to cook without destroying natural flavors. One of our favorite dishes is red snapper stuffed with crabmeat in ginger sauce. For real island taste, however, we suggest grilled chicken in a Cajun sauce or a kebab of fresh shrimp and scallops. In addition to seafood, game specialties, when available, also appear on the menu. But only the most adventurous palates will try some of them. Creole-style rabbit is common on some American menus and doesn't come as much of a shock. But stewed agouti is only for the experimental palate, as agouti is a Trinidad-based rodent—and a big one at that. A real spicy and refreshing appetizer is strips of raw conch marinated in a mixture of lime juice and red peppers.

38 Ariapita Avenue, Woodbrok. © 868/628-5551. Reservations recommended. Main courses TT$65.80–TT$188.40 (US$10.55–US$30.15). AE, MC, V. Mon–Sat 11:30am–2:30pm and 6:30–10:30pm.

Solimar ✿ INTERNATIONAL By some estimates, this restaurant offers the most creative cuisine in Trinidad and Tobago. Established by Joe Brown, an English-born chef who worked for many years in the kitchens of Hilton hotels around the world, it occupies a garden-style building cooled by open walls and ceiling fans. As you dine, you'll hear the sound of an artificial waterfall that cascades into a series of fish ponds.

The menu, which changes every 3 months, presents local ingredients inspired by the cuisines of the world. The results are usually very convincing. Dishes might include an English-inspired combination of grilled breast of chicken and jumbo shrimp dressed with a lobster sauce, and a Sri Lankan dish of herb-flavored chicken vindaloo. The restaurant's double-chocolate mousse is the highlight of any meal here.

6 Nook Ave. (next to the Normandie Hotel and Restaurant, 3½ miles (6km) northwest of the city center), St. Ann's. © 868/624-6267. Reservations recommended. Main courses TT$90–TT$300 (US$14.40–US$48). AE, MC, V. Mon–Sat 6:30–10:30pm, Fri opening at noon. Closed the last week in May and 2 weeks in mid-Aug (exact dates vary).

Tamnak Thai ★★ ASIAN   In the landmark center at Queen's Park Savannah, this upmarket restaurant lies in a restored colonial home and is the island nation's finest Asian restaurant, specializing in the regional fare of Thailand. In an elegant tasteful setting evocative of old Saigon, a refined cuisine is beautifully served in luxuriant surroundings, especially if you select a table on the patio. The kitchen makes the most of excellent ingredients, fashioning them into subtle dishes like red curry chicken in coconut milk or stir-fried lobster with spring onions. Our favorite dish is the steamed mussels in a clay pot with fresh herbs such as lemon grass. If you're in a party, you can order a large selection of hors d'oeuvres—tasty Thai tidbits—that are full of zest and flavor. Many dishes are real spicy, filled with fiery chilies, but palates preferring milder fare are also satisfied here.

13 Queen's Park East. ✆ **868/625-9715**. Reservations required. Main courses TT$70–TT$175 (US$11.20–US$28). Set dinner TT$165 (US$26.40), set lunch TT$95 (US$15.20). AE, MC, V. Tues–Fri and Sun 11am–11pm; Mon–Sat 6–11pm.

Vidalia ★ INTERNATIONAL   Off Queen's Park Savannah, Vidalia is loaded with style and features a tempting modern Creole cuisine. Many of Trinidad's usually heavy, deep-fried dishes are given a light touch here, creating a sort of *cuisine nouvelle Creole*. The changing menu might include filet mignon with a tamarind-flavored sauce, lamb loin with a tomato relish, chicken Creole, locally caught salmon in a wine-based sauce with sultana raisins and bananas, and shrimp with bread crumbs and shredded coconut served with lemon juice. "Fish walk up the hill" is grilled fish with chopped herbs, while "drunken fish" fillet is in a crepe with a white Creole sauce. End with a Trinidadian fruitcake with a rum-flavored custard, a dish especially popular at Christmas. Our only complaint: You're not exactly pampered here, and service has drawn complaints from readers.

In Normandie Hotel & Restaurant, 10 Nook Ave., St. Ann's Village. ✆ **868/624-1181**, ext. 3306. Reservations recommended. Main courses TT$80–TT$225 (US$12.80–US$36). AE, DISC, MC, V. Daily 3–11pm.

MODERATE
Restaurant Singho CHINESE   This restaurant, with an almost mystically illuminated bar and aquarium, is on the second floor of one of the capital's largest shopping malls, midway between the commercial center of Port-of-Spain and the Queen's Park Savannah. For Trinidad, this cuisine isn't bad: It's better than your typical chop suey and chow mein joint, and many of its dishes are quite tasty and spicy. A la carte choices include shrimp with oyster sauce, shark-fin soup, stewed or curried beef, almond pork, and spareribs with black-bean sauce. The to-go service is one of the best in town. The Wednesday-night buffet offers an enormous selection of main dishes, along with heaps of rice and fresh vegetables. Even dessert is included in the set price.

Long Circular Mall, Level 3, Port-of-Spain. ✆ **868/628-2077**. Main courses TT$75–TT$100 (US$12–US$16); Wed night buffet TT$98 (US$15.70). AE, MC, V. Daily 11am–10pm.

Veni Mangé ★★ CREOLE/INTERNATIONAL   Originally built in the 1930s and set about a mile (2km) west of Port-of-Spain's center, Veni Mangé (whose name means "come and eat") is painted in coral tones and has louvered windows on hinges that ventilate the masses of potted plants. It was established by two of the best-known women in Trinidad, Allyson Hennessy and her sister, Rosemary Hezekiah. Allyson, the Julia Child of Trinidad, hosts a daily TV talk show that's broadcast throughout the island.

Start with the bartender's special, a coral-colored fruit punch that's a rich, luscious mixture of papaya, guava, orange, and passion-fruit juices. The authentic callaloo soup, according to Trinidadian legend, can make a man propose marriage. With a menu that changes daily the main courses might be curried crab or West Indian hot pot (a variety of meats cooked Creole style), or perhaps a vegetable lentil loaf. The helpings are large, but if you still have room, order the pineapple upside-down cake. Dinner is served only on Wednesday nights and is something of a social event among regulars. On Friday, the bar buzzes, but the only foods served are snacks and finger foods, nicknamed "cutters" because they cut the appetite so you can drink more punch.

67A Ariapata Ave. ⓒ 868/624-4597. Reservations recommended. Main courses TT$55–TT$85 (US$8.80–US$13.60). AE, MC, V. Mon–Fri 11:30am–3pm; Wed 7:30–10pm; Fri open for bar service only 6–11:30pm.

HITTING THE BEACH

Trinidad isn't thought of as beach country, yet it has more beach frontage than any other island in the West Indies. The only problem is that most of its beaches are undeveloped and located in distant, remote places, far removed from Port-of-Spain. The closest of the better beaches, **Maracas Bay,** is a full 18 miles (29km) from Port-of-Spain on the North Coast Road. It's a delight to visitors, with its protected cove and quaint fishing village. The only drawbacks are the crowds and the strong current. Facilities include restrooms and snack bars.

Farther up the North Coast Road is **Las Cuevas Bay,** which is far less crowded. The narrow beach is set against a backdrop of palm trees. There are changing rooms and vendors selling luscious tropical fruit juices.

To reach the other beaches, you'll have to range farther afield, perhaps to **Blanchisseuse Bay** on the North Coast Road. This narrow strip of sand set against palms is excellent for a picnic, although there are no facilities here for visitors.

Balandra Bay, on the northeast coast, is frequented by bodysurfers, but the waters generally aren't good for more pedestrian swimming.

Manzanilla Beach, along the east coast of Trinidad, north of Cocos Bay and south of Matura Bay, is not ideal for swimming. Nonetheless, it has some picnic facilities, and the view of the water is dramatic.

SPORTS & OTHER OUTDOOR PURSUITS

For serious golf and tennis, we recommend that you try another island.

DEEP-SEA FISHING   Some of the best fishing in the Caribbean is possible in the waters off the northwest coast of Trinidad—or at least Franklin D. Roosevelt used to think so. Try **TNT Charters,** Bayshore, Trinidad & Tobago Yacht Club (ⓒ 868/637-3644), where Robert Nuñez takes fishers out in his 31-foot (9m) boat. Full gear is included in the rates: $225 for 4 hours, $325 for 6 hours, and $425 for 8 hours. The boat is well maintained with air-conditioning and a microwave, and no more than eight people are taken out at a time.

GOLF   The oldest golf club on the island, **St. Andrew's Golf Course,** Moka Estate (ⓒ 868/629-2314), is in Maraval, about 2 miles (3km) from Port-of-Spain. This 18-hole course has been internationally acclaimed ever since it hosted the 1976 Hoerman Cup Golf Tournament. There's a full-service clubhouse on the premises. Greens fees are TT$300 (US$48) for 18 holes. Club rental costs TT$100 (US$16). Hours are daily 7am to 6pm.

TENNIS   At the **Trinidad Country Club,** Champs-Elysées, Maraval (ⓒ 868/622-3470), six courts are lit at night. You must purchase a day pass for TT$30 (US$4.80) and pay an additional TT$5 (80¢) per hour of play during the day or TT$12 (US$1.90) per hour at night. Visitors can also obtain a temporary pass for 1 month at the cost of TT$175 (US$28). There are public courts in Port-of-Spain on the grounds of the Prince's Building (ask at your hotel for directions).

EXPLORING TRINIDAD
ORGANIZED TOURS

Sightseeing tours are offered by **Trinidad & Tobago Sightseeing Tours,** 12 Western Main Road, St. James (© **868/628-1051**), in late-model sedans with a trained driver/guide. Several different tours are offered, including a daily city tour that takes you past (but not inside) the main points of interest of Port-of-Spain. The 2-hour tour costs $25 per person for two, or $20 per person for three or more.

You'll see tropical splendor at its best on a Port-of-Spain/Maracas Bay/Saddle Road jaunt leaving at 9am or 1pm daily, lasting 3½ hours. The tour begins with a drive around Port-of-Spain, passing the main points of interest in town and then going on through the mountain scenery over the "Saddle" of the northern range to Maracas Bay, a popular beach. The cost is $35 per person for two, or $30 per person for three or more.

An **Island Circle Tour** is a 7- to 8-hour journey that includes a lunch stop (though the tour price doesn't include lunch) and a welcome drink. Leaving at 9am daily, your car goes south along the west coast with a view of the Gulf of Paria, across the central plains, through Pointe-à-Pierre and San Fernando, and on eastward into rolling country overlooking sugarcane fields. You then go down into the coconut plantations along the 14-mile-long (23km) Mayaro Beach, enjoy a swim and lunch, and return along Manzanilla Beach and back to the city. The cost is $65 per person for two, or $60 per person for three or more.

An especially interesting trip is the 4-hour trek by car and flat-bottomed boat to the Caroni Swamp and Bird Sanctuary, where you'll see rich Trinidad bird life. The guides recommend long pants and long-sleeved, casual attire, along with lots of insect repellent. The cost is $35 per person for two.

PORT-OF-SPAIN 🐦

One of the busiest harbors in the Caribbean, Trinidad's capital, Port-of-Spain, can be explored on foot. Start out at **Queen's Park Savannah** 🐦, on the northern edge of the city. "The Savannah" consists of 199 acres (80 hectares), complete with soccer, cricket, and rugby fields, and vendors hawking coconut water and rôtis. This was once a sugar plantation, until it was swept by a fire in 1808 that destroyed hundreds of homes.

Among the Savannah's outstanding buildings is the pink-and-blue **Queen's Royal College** 🐦, containing a clock tower with Westminster chimes. Today a school for boys, it stands on Maraval Road at the corner of St. Clair Avenue. On the same road, the family home of the Roodal clan is affectionately called **"the gingerbread house"** by Trinidadians. It was built in the baroque style of the French Second Empire.

Nearby stands **Whitehall,** which was once a private mansion but today has been turned into the office of the prime minister of Trinidad and Tobago. In the Moorish style, it was erected in 1905 and served as the U.S. Army headquarters here during World War II. These houses, including Hayes Court, the residence of the Anglican bishop of Trinidad, and others, form what is known as the **"Magnificent Seven"** 🐦 big mansions standing in a row.

On the south side of Memorial Park, a short distance from the Savannah and within walking distance of the major hotels, stands the **National Museum and**

Art Gallery, 117 Frederick St. (© **868/623-5941**), open Tuesday to Saturday from 10am to 6pm, Sunday from 2 to 6pm. The free museum contains a representative exhibition of Trinidad artists, including an entire gallery devoted to Jean Michel Cazabon (1813–88), permanent collections of artifacts giving a general overview of the island's history and culture, Amerindian archaeology, British historical documents, and a small natural-history exhibition including geology, corals, and insect collections. There's also a large display filled with costumes dedicated to the colorful culture of Carnival.

At the southern end of Frederick Street, the main artery of Port-of-Spain's shopping district, stands **Woodford Square.** The gaudy **Red House,** a large neo-Renaissance structure built in 1906, is the seat of the government of Trinidad and Tobago. Nearby stands **Holy Trinity Cathedral,** whose Gothic look may remind you of the churches of England.

Another of the town's important landmarks is **Independence Square,** dating from Spanish days. Now mainly a parking lot, it stretches across the southern part of the capital from the **Cathedral of the Immaculate Conception** to Wrightson Road. The Roman Catholic church was built in 1815 in the neo-Gothic style and consecrated in 1832.

The cathedral has an outlet that leads to the **Central Market,** on Beetham Highway on the outskirts of Port-of-Spain. Here you can see all the spices and fruits for which Trinidad is known. It's one of the island's most colorful sights, made all the more so by the wide diversity of people who sell their wares here.

North of the Savannah, the **Royal Botanical Gardens** (© **868/622-4221**) cover 70 acres (28 hectares) and are open daily from 6am to 6pm; admission is free. The park is filled with flowering plants, shrubs, and rare and beautiful trees, including an orchid house. Seek out also the raw beef tree: An incision made in its bark is said to resemble rare, bleeding roast beef. Guides will take you through and explain the luxuriant foliage. In the gardens is the **President's House,** official residence of the president of Trinidad and Tobago. Victorian in style, it was built in 1875.

Part of the gardens is the **Emperor Valley Zoo** (© **868/622-3530**), in St. Clair, which shows a good selection of the fauna of Trinidad as well as some of the usual exotic animals from around the world. The star attractions are a family of mandrills, a reptile house, and open bird parks. You can take shady jungle walks through tropical vegetation. Admission is TT$4 (65¢) for adults, TT$2 (30¢) for children age 3 to 12, and free for children under age 3. It's open daily from 9:30am to 5:30pm.

AROUND THE ISLAND

One of the most popular attractions in the area is the **Asa Wright Nature Centre** ✦ (© **800/426-7781** in the U.S.; www.asawright.org); see "Accommodations," earlier in this chapter. If you're not a guest of the hotel, you can call and reserve a space for its noonday lunch, for TT$50 (US$8), or its Sunday buffet, for TT$75 (US$12). It's also possible to reserve one of the daily guided tours of the sanctuary at 10:30am or 1:30pm, which costs TT$58 (US$9.30).

On a peak 1,100 feet (330m) above Port-of-Spain, **Fort George** was built by Governor Sir Thomas Hislop in 1804 as a signal station in the days of the sailing ships. Once it could be reached only by hikers, but today it's accessible by an asphalt road. From its citadel, you can see the mountains of Venezuela. Locals refer to the climb up the winding road as "traveling up to heaven." The drive is only 10 miles (16km), but to play it safe, allow about 2 hours.

Pointe-à-Pierre Wild Fowl Trust, 42 Sandown Rd., Point Cumana (© **868/ 658-4230,** ext. 2512), is a 26-acre (10-hectare) bird sanctuary, 2 hours by car south of Port-of-Spain. The setting is unlikely, near an industrial area of the state-owned Petrotrin oil refinery, with flames spouting from flare stacks in the sky. However, in this seemingly inhospitable clime, wildfowl flourish amid such luxuriant vegetation as crape myrtle, flamboyant soursop and mango trees, even black sage bushes said to be good for high blood pressure. You can spot the yellow-billed jacana, plenty of Muscovies, and, if you're lucky, such endangered species as the toucan or the purple gallinule. Admission is $5, or $2 for kids under age 12. Hours are Monday to Friday from 8am to 5pm, Saturday and Sunday by appointment only from 11am to 4pm.

Enhanced by the blue and purple hues of the sky at sunset, clouds of scarlet ibis, the national bird of Trinidad and Tobago, fly in from their feeding grounds to roost at the 40-square-mile (104 sq. km) **Caroni Bird Sanctuary** ⚐ (© **868/ 645-1305**), a big mangrove swamp interlaced with waterways. The setting couldn't be more idyllic, with blue, mauve, and white lilies; oysters growing on mangrove roots; and caimans resting on mudbanks. Visitors are taken on a launch through these swamps to see the birds (bring along insect repellent). The most reliable tour operator is **James Meddoo,** Bamboo Grove Settlement, 1 Butler Hwy. (© **868/ 662-7356**), who has toured the swamps for some 25 years. His 2½-hour tour leaves daily at 4pm and costs $10 per person, or $5 for kids. The sanctuary is about a half-hour drive (7 miles/11km) south of Port-of-Spain.

Pitch Lake ⚐ is on the west coast of Trinidad, with the village of Le Brea on its north shore. To reach it from Port-of-Spain, take the Solomon Hocoy Highway. It's about a 2-hour drive, depending on traffic. One of the wonders of the world, with a surface like elephant skin, the lake is 300 feet (90m) deep at its center. It's possible to walk on its rough side, but we don't recommend that you proceed far. Legend has it that the lake devoured a tribe of Chayma Amerindians, punishing them for eating hummingbirds in which the souls of their ancestors reposed. The lake was formed millions of years ago, and it's believed that at one time it was a huge mud volcano into which muddy asphaltic oil seeped. Churned up and down by underground gases, the oil and mud eventually formed asphalt. According to legend, Sir Walter Raleigh discovered the lake in 1595 and used the asphalt to caulk his ships. Today, the bitumen mined here is used to pave highways throughout the world. A 120-mile (193km) tour around the lake takes 5 hours. You can tour Pitch Lake on your own, or you can request a guided tour by calling © **868/ 648-7426.** Cost is approximately $5 per person. **Trinidad & Tobago Tours** (© **868/628-1051**) also runs tours of Pitch Lake. You'll find some bars and restaurants at Le Brea.

The **Saddle** ⚐ is a humped pass on a ridge dividing the Maraval and the Santa Cruz valleys. Along this circular run, you'll see luxuriant grapefruit, papaya, cassava, and cocoa trees. Leaving Port-of-Spain by Saddle Road, going past the Trinidad Country Club, you pass through Maraval Village and its St. Andrew's Golf Course. The road rises to cross the ridge at the spot from which the Saddle gets its name. After going over the hump, you descend through Santa Cruz Valley (rich with giant bamboo), into San Juan, and back to the capital along Eastern Main Road or Beetham Highway. You'll see panoramic views in every direction; the 18-mile (29km) tour takes about 2 hours.

Nearly all cruise-ship passengers are hauled along Trinidad's "Skyline Highway," the **North Coast Road.** Starting at the Saddle, it winds for 7 miles (11km) across the Northern Range and down to Maracas Bay. At one point, 100 feet (30m) above the Caribbean, you'll see on a clear day as far as Venezuela to the west or Tobago in the east, a sweep of some 100 miles (161km).

Most visitors take this route to the beach at **Maracas Bay,** the most splendid beach on Trinidad. Enclosed by mountains, it has the expected charm of a Caribbean fantasy: white sands, swaying coconut palms, and crystal-clear water (see "Hitting the Beach," above).

SHOPPING

One of the largest bazaars of the Caribbean, Port-of-Spain has luxury items from all over the globe, including Irish linens, English china, Scandinavian crystal, French perfumes, Swiss watches, and Japanese cameras. Even more interesting are the Asian bazaars, where you can pick up items in brass. Reflecting the island's culture are calypso shirts, sisal goods, woodwork, cascadura bracelets, silver jewelry in local motifs, and saris. For souvenirs, visitors often like to bring back figurines of limbo dancers, carnival masqueraders, or calypso singers.

Stecher's, Gulf City (© **868/657-6993**), is the best bet for luxury items—crystal, watches, jewelry, perfumes, Georg Jensen silver, Lladró, Wedgwood, Royal Doulton, Royal Albert—all of which can be delivered to the airport upon your departure. You can find other branches at Long Circular Mall and West Mall. You can also pay a last-minute call at their tax-free airport branches or at the cruise-ship complex at the Port-of-Spain docks.

Y. De Lima, 23 Queen St. (© **868/623-1364**), is a good store for duty-free cameras and watches, but the main focus is local jewelry. Its third-floor workroom will make whatever you want in jewelry or bronze. You might emerge with anything from steel-drum earrings to a hibiscus-blossom brooch.

Art Creators and Suppliers, Apt. 402, Aldegonda Park, 7 St. Ann's Rd., St. Ann's (© **868/624-4369**), is in a banal apartment complex, but the paintings and sculptures here are among the finest in the Caribbean. Among the artistic giants displayed are Glasgow, Robert Mackie, Boscoe Holder, Sundiata, Keith Ward, Jackie Hinkson, and many others.

Lovers of Caribbean art also flock to the **101 Art Gallery,** 101 Tragarete Rd. (© **868/628-4081**), in Port-of-Spain. This is the best showcase for the hottest local talent, both men and women. Some of the art of Sarah Beckett, local artist, is viewed so highly by the government that her abstract oils appear on regional stamps. Often you can meet some of the artists here, especially on Tuesday evening during openings. The gallery is closed on Sunday and Monday.

Gallery 1-2-3-4, in the Normandie Hotel, 10 Nook Ave., St. Ann's Village (© **868/625-5502**), is more iconoclastic and less conservative than any other gallery on the island. Since it opened in 1985, it has attracted the attention of the art world for its wide selection of Caribbean artists.

The Market, 10 Nook Ave., St. Ann's (© **868/624-1181**), is one of the most fashionable shopping complexes on Trinidad. Some 20 boutiques represent the best jewelers, designers, and art dealers on the island. You'll find a wide assortment of clothing, cosmetics, bags, shoes, china, tableware, handcrafts, and accessories. The complex forms an interconnected bridge among the Normandie Hotel and Restaurant, the restaurant La Fantasie, and Gallery 1-2-3-4.

The Boutique, 43 Syndeham Ave., St. Ann's (© **868/624-3274**), is a notable handcrafts outlet and a showcase for batik silks created by Althea Bastien, one of Trinidad's finest artisans. Her fabric art is highly prized but reasonable in price.

If you'd like to go home with some music of Trinidad, head for **Rhyner's Record Shop,** 54 Prince St. (© **868/623-5673**), which has the best selection of soca and calypso. There's another branch at the airport (© **868/669-3064**).

TRINIDAD AFTER DARK

Hilton Trinidad, Lady Young Road, Port-of-Spain (© **868/624-3211**), stages a poolside fiesta show every Monday night, with a folkloric performance beginning at 9pm and continuing live until midnight. It features lots of live music, calypso, a steel band, and limbo. It's the most spectacular on Trinidad. The cover (including a buffet dinner with grills) is TT$140 (US$22.50).

You can catch us having a beer at **Mas Camp Pub,** corner of French St. and Avenue Ariapata in Woodbrook (© **868/623-3745**). This place has a big stage where some of the best live bands in Trinidad frequently appear (or else a DJ rules the night). If you haven't eaten, you'll find a reliable kitchen here as well, dishing up local specialties for nighttime revelers.

Local joints come and go with alarming frequency, but currently locals flock to **The Base,** Main St. (no phone), lying at Chaguaramas, a 20-minute drive or taxi ride west of Port-of-Spain. The joint takes its name from its former role as a WWII air base. Open 10pm until "late" Wednesday to Sunday. Also on the base is its competitor, **Anchorage,** Point Gourde Rd. (© **868/634-4334**), which is a popular gathering spot for "sundowners." Later on groups head from here to **Pier 1,** Williams Bay (© **868/634-4426**), for dancing. Pier 1 is also on this old air base.

Back in town, **Pelican,** 2–4 Coblentz Ave., St. Ann's (© **868/624-7486**), is a British pub-type place that is the hot drinking spot in town, especially on the weekend. It draws a very mixed crowd including both singles and businessmen (who wish they were at least for the night), plus a colony of Trinidadian gays.

3 Tobago

Dubbed "the land of the hummingbird," Tobago lies 20 miles (16km) northeast of Trinidad, to which it's connected by frequent flights. It has long been known as a honeymooner's paradise. The physical beauty of Tobago is stunning, with its forests of breadfruit, mango, cocoa, and citrus, through which a chartreuse-colored iguana will suddenly dart. Tobago's idyllic natural beauty makes it one of the greatest escapes in the Caribbean. It's for those who like a generous dose of sand, sun, and solitude, in a mellow atmosphere. Snorkelers especially will find plenty here to entertain them.

Unlike bustling Trinidad, Tobago is sleepy, and Trinidadians come here, especially on weekends, to enjoy the wide, sandy beaches. The legendary home of Daniel Defoe's Robinson Crusoe, Tobago is only 27 miles (43km) long and 7½ miles (12km) wide. The people are hospitable, and their villages are so tiny that they seem to blend in with the landscape.

The island's village-like capital and main port, **Scarborough,** lies on the southern coast. Surrounded by mountains, its bay provides a scenic setting, but the town itself is rather plain. Most of the shops are clustered in streets around the local market.

TOBAGO ESSENTIALS

GETTING THERE   LIAT (© **800/468-0482** in the U.S. and Canada, or 868/639-0276) has two daily flights from Trinidad to Tobago. If you'd like to skip Trinidad completely, you can book a LIAT flight with direct service to Tobago from either Barbados or Grenada.

American Eagle (© 800/433-7300 in the U.S.; www.aa.com), the regional affiliate of American Airlines, operates daily round-trip flights between San Juan, Puerto Rico and Tobago. **American Airlines** also operates one daily non-stop flight between Miami and Trinidad and another between New York and Trinidad (see "Trinidad & Tobago Essentials," earlier in this chapter). From Trinidad, you can make a connecting flight into Tobago.

Tobago's small **airport** lies at Crown Point (© 868/639-0509), near the island's southwestern tip.

It's possible to travel between Trinidad and Tobago by **ferry service,** although the trip takes 5½ to 6 hours. Call the **Port Authority of Trinidad and Tobago** (© 868/639-2416 in Scarborough, Tobago, or 868/623-2901 in Port-of-Spain) for departure times. The round-trip fare is TT$60 (US$9.60) in economy or TT$160 (US$25.60) in tourist class.

GETTING AROUND   From the airport to your accommodations, you can take a **taxi,** which will cost $8 to $36, depending on the location of your hotel (like in Trinidad, taxis here are unmetered). You can also arrange (or have your hotel do it for you) a **sightseeing tour by taxi.** Rates must be negotiated on an individual basis.

To **rent a car** you have to rely on local companies—no international car rental agencies are here as of yet. Options include **Rattan's Car Rentals** at Crown Point Airport (© 868/639-8271), and **Singh's Auto Rentals,** Grafton Beach Resort (© 868/639-0191). One final possibility is **Thrifty,** Rex Turtle Beach Hotel, Courtland Bay, Black Rock (© 868/639-8507).

Inexpensive **public buses** travel from one end of the island to the other several times a day. Expect an unscheduled stop at any passenger's doorstep, and never, never be in a hurry.

FAST FACTS   Most **banks** are open Monday to Thursday from 8am to 2pm and Friday from 9am to noon and 3 to 5pm. **Royal Bank of Trinidad & Tobago** (Main Road in Scarborough; © 868/639-2404) and **Republic Bank Ltd.** (Carrington Street, Scarborough; © 868/639-2811) both have **ATMs.**

You can send mail from the **Tobago Post Office** (© 868/660-7377) at Scarborough Wilser Road in the capital. If your hotel is unable to send faxes for you, try **TSTT Phone Company** (© 868/639-1759) at the end of Wilson St. in Scarborough.

Tobago County Hospital is on Fort George Street, Scarborough (© 868/639-2551). Medical care is sometimes limited, and physicians and health-care facilities expect immediate cash payment for services. Medical insurance from the United States is not always valid outside the country, but supplemental medical insurance with specific overseas coverage is available. Contact the U.S. Embassy for updates.

ACCOMMODATIONS

To save money, it may be best to take the breakfast and dinner (MAP) plan when reserving a room. There's a 15% value-added tax (VAT) on all hotel bills, and often a service charge of about 10%. Don't forget to ask if the VAT and service charge are included in the prices quoted to you.

VERY EXPENSIVE

Hilton Tobago ★★★   On a 20-acre (8-hectare) site 2½ miles (4km) east of the airport is the once-sleepy island's first international hotel. A luxury resort, built at the cost of $35 million, the five-star hotel lies on a 5,000-foot (1,500m)

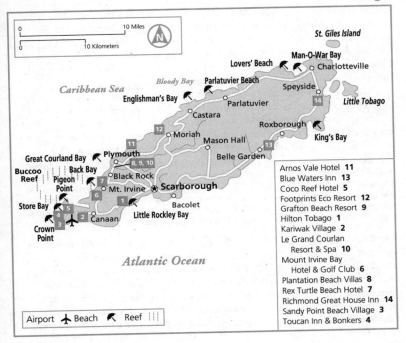

Arnos Vale Hotel **11**
Blue Waters Inn **13**
Coco Reef Hotel **5**
Footprints Eco Resort **12**
Grafton Beach Resort **9**
Hilton Tobago **1**
Kariwak Village **2**
Le Grand Courlan
   Resort & Spa **10**
Mount Irvine Bay
   Hotel & Golf Club **6**
Plantation Beach Villas **8**
Rex Turtle Beach Hotel **7**
Richmond Great House Inn **14**
Sandy Point Beach Village **3**
Toucan Inn & Bonkers **4**

Airport ✈ Beach ✿ Reef ¦¦¦

beach, set against the backdrop of a 60-acre (24-hectare) mangrove forest. The hotel is on the island's southwest coast and is part of a 750-acre (300-hectare) development that embraces a 90-acre (36-hectare) natural lagoon.

With an 18-hole, par-72 championship PGA golf course, the hotel attracts golfers away from the traditional favorite, Mount Irvine Bay. Hilton also lies in the heart of some of the best scuba-diving waters in the southern Caribbean. Rooms are tastefully and luxuriously furnished, and every suite has a Jacuzzi. Each unit opens onto ocean views and has a shower/tub combination.

The food is the finest on the island in terms of quality products, although we still prefer our favorite local eateries, some mere dives. The best local bands are brought in, and Hilton has more activities than all its rivals.

Lowlands, Scarborough, Tobago, W.I. ✆ **800/HILTONS** in the U.S., or 868/660-8500. Fax 868/660-8503. www.hilton.com. 200 units. Winter $205–$245 double, $550 suite. Off-season $185–$225 double; $350 suite. Ask about discount rates and promotional rates. AE, DC, MC, V. **Amenities:** 2 restaurants, 4 bars; 3 pools; 18-hole golf course; 2 tennis clubs; sauna; glass-bottom boat tours, scuba diving, deep-sea fishing, snorkeling; children's activities; massage; room service; babysitting; laundry/dry cleaning. *In room:* A/C, TV, minibar, hair dryer, coffeemaker, safe.

Le Grand Courlan Resort & Spa ★★ Operated by the same owners as the Grafton Beach Resort (see below), this pricey hotel is definitely five-star and definitely deluxe. For those who want to live in style but don't want a mega-resort like the new Hilton, Courlan remains the top gun. It's named for the bay on which it sits, on the western edge of the island. A soft, sandy beach is at its door, and everything is set against a backdrop of bougainvillea, white frangipani, and hibiscus. Constructed to fit in with its natural surroundings, the hotel was built of stone and teak harvested from farms on Trinidad, then furnished with handcrafted mahogany pieces and decorated with original artwork. The floors are covered in Italian porcelain tile, and the ceilings are made from Guyanan hardwood. The bedrooms are handsomely tropical in decor, with two phones, king-size beds, and large balconies. Bathrooms are small, but equipped with robes, scales, phones, and shower/tub combinations.

The hotel offers a Caribbean-style bistro and an international a la carte restaurant. The food is among the best on the island. There's also nightly entertainment.

The spa specializes in cell therapy. It has a koi pond and aerobics and offers consultations in nutrition, fitness coaching, and ozone-and-steam detoxing, and even fresh-fruit facials and full-body compression "release" massages.

Black Rock (P.O. Box 25), Scarborough, Tobago, W.I. © 800/223-6510 in the U.S., 800/424-5500 in Canada, or 868/639-9667. Fax 868/639-9292. www.legrandeourlan-resorts.com. 70 units. Winter $636–$804 double; $888 suite. Off-season $348–$384 double; $660 suite. Extra person $50. Children age 4 and under stay and dine free. Includes all meals, beverages, 1 spa treatment, and 1 scuba dive daily. AE, MC, V. **Amenities:** 3 restaurants, 2 bars; pool; golf privileges; 2 tennis courts; spa; steam room and sauna; watersports, dive shop, fishing; bikes; car rental; salon; massage; laundry. *In room:* A/C, TV, minibar, hair dryer, safe.

Plantation Beach Villas ⭐   At the edge of a tropical rainforest, between a bird sanctuary and the Caribbean, this shell pink–and-white cottage complex stands above a palm-fringed beach. The resort is reminiscent of the plantation era, with its British colonial architecture, rocking chairs on the front porch, four-poster beds, and louvered doors. Two sailing buddies and native Tobagonians, Jennier Avey and Brenda Farfan, created this little gem, furnishing it with handmade pieces and original art work. Each spacious villa has three bedrooms, a trio of baths with showers, and a teak-covered front porch with a sea view. It's like living in your own private vacation retreat. A member of the staff will even prepare breakfast and lunch or come back to make dinner, but that costs extra. The site is a 15-minute drive from the airport.

P.O. Box 434, Scarborough, Tobago, W.I. © 800/633-7411 in the U.S. or 868/639-9377. Fax 868/639-0455. www.plantationbeachvillas.com. 6 villas. $495–$600 up to 4 persons, $500–$650 up to 6 persons. Off-season $240–$275 up to 4 persons; $360–$420 up to 6 persons. AE, MC, V. **Amenities:** Bar; pool; babysitting; laundry. *In room:* A/C, TV, kitchenette, no phone.

Rex Turtle Beach Hotel ⭐   This hotel lies in an isolated location on the north shore of the southwestern corner of the island, adjacent to the tawny-colored sands of Courland Beach. The medium-size rooms have balconies or patios, cream-colored floor tiles, pastel walls, teakwood ceilings, louvered doors, spacious closets, tropical-patterned upholstery, and simple, summery furnishings. The small bathrooms have individual heaters for hot water, and most contain shower/tub combinations. The hotel's pool is so small as to be almost ornamental.

Great Courland Bay (P.O. Box 201), Scarborough, Tobago, W.I. © 868/639-2851, or 305/471-6170 for reservations. Fax 868/639-1495. www.rexcaribbean.com. 125 units. Winter $320 double. Off-season $200 double. Rates include meals. AE, MC, V. **Amenities:** 2 restaurants, 2 bars; small pool; watersports; volleyball court; bikes. *In room:* A/C, hair dryer.

EXPENSIVE

Arnos Vale Hotel ⭐   This inn—one of the first hotels of Tobago's modern tourist age—sprawls over 450 acres (180 hectares) of very private land. It's named after a township in England, although tour groups from Italy often fill up its chambers. This place was once an exclusive and closely guarded secret of the Caribbean. But it was a long time ago that Princess Margaret took her honeymoon here. The other celebs who used to flock here are off in Anguilla these days. Rooms, each with a private patio or veranda, are furnished with a wide spectrum of furniture, including some pieces dating back to the early 1960s, retained because many clients appreciate their slightly battered charm. Only a few of the units are actually on the beach. Suites are in a handful of individual bungalows. Not all bathrooms have tubs, so ask beforehand if you must have one. Most of the socializing occurs at the likable bar, where you'll find a TV, strong drinks, and a loyal clientele that returns year after year.

Arnos Vale Rd., Plymouth, Tobago, W.I. © 868/639-2881. Fax 868/639-4629. www.arnosvalehotel.com. 29 units. Winter $260 double; $320–$380 suite. Off-season $200 double; $250–$300 suite. Rates include breakfast. AE, MC, V. **Amenities:** Restaurant, 2 bars; pool; tennis court; room service; babysitting; laundry. *In room:* A/C.

Coco Reef Resort ★★
This is one of the largest beachfront hotels on the island, with a certain South Florida pizzazz about it. It's on Tobago's northern shore, near the airport. Most accommodations are in the two- and three-story main building, although about a half dozen villas are scattered over the surrounding acreage. The designer incorporated a number of environmentally friendly features, including the use of recycled materials. The bedrooms are spacious and airy, filled with wicker furniture, the big bathrooms are tiled in white and have shower/tub combinations, and each room has an intricately trimmed balcony. In 1998, the hotel added 25 new suites with large balconies and patios overlooking the Caribbean and lush tropical gardens. The new suites contain marble bathrooms equipped with shower/tub combinations, modern extras, and are embellished with hand-painted murals and custom-designed wicker furniture. The complex is near a trio of the island's best beaches—Store Bay, Pigeon Point, and Coconut Beach itself, which is just steps from your room.

Tamara's, the resort's most formal restaurant, offers some of the most sophisticated food in Trinidad and Tobago (see "Dining," below).

Coconut Beach (P.O. Box 434), Tobago, W.I. © 800/221-1294 in the U.S., or 868/639-8571. Fax 868/639-8574. www.cocoreef.com. 137 units. Winter $263–$297 double; from $420–$487 suite or villa. Off-season $203–$259 double; $393–$417 suite or villa. Breakfast and dinner for $57 per person, $35 for children age 5–12. Extra person $55 per day. AE, MC, V. **Amenities:** 2 restaurants, 2 bars; 2 tennis courts; health club and spa; dive shop, snorkeling; car rental; salon; room service; babysitting; laundry/dry cleaning. *In room:* A/C, TV, minibar, hair dryer.

Footprints Eco Resort ★ (Finds)
The island's first "eco-resort" sprawls across some 60 acres (24 hectares) on Culloden Bay. A local doctor and his daughter carved this "environmentally responsible" resort out of a dense forest of cocoa and fruit trees in 1997. The result is a rustic and charming compound of wood-sided, thatch-roofed cottages. Each unit is artfully built of recycled lumber, some of it obtained from the local telephone company, with a distinct emphasis on termite-resistant hardwoods such as wallaba and teak. Accommodations are rough-hewn but comfortable, with wooden floors and a lot of idiosyncratic charm.

Rooms range from standard doubles to king superior units with fridges. Some rooms have garden showers, and others have two full bathrooms with shower/tub combinations. On-site luxuries include the excellent Cocoa House restaurant (see "Dining," below), a network of nature trails that fan out across the nearby hills, and a mini-museum that contains Amerindian artifacts uncovered during the excavations on the property. Most guests opt to swim in the resort's pool, although worthwhile beaches, including both Courland Bay and Castara Bay, are a 15-minute drive away.

Golden Lane, Colloden Bay Rd., Tobago, W.I. © 800/814-1396 in the U.S., or 868/660-0118. Fax 868/660-0027. www.footprintseco-resort.com. 7 units. Winter $140–$300 double, $332 villa. Off-season $114–$223 double,

$332 villa. MAP (breakfast and dinner) $35 extra per day. AE, MC, V. **Amenities:** Restaurant, bar; 2 pools; yoga lessons; Jacuzzi; library; rain-forest tours; massage; babysitting; laundry. *In room:* A/C, ceiling fan.

Grafton Beach Resort ⭐   Still going strong although it's outclassed now by so many others, this complex sprawls across a beach shoreline set against a backdrop of palms. Next to the Hilton, it draws the most Europeanized clientele on island, and is under the same ownership as the neighboring and superior Le Grand Courlan Resort (Grafton guests can use Courlan's spa). Rooms are in three- and four-story buildings scattered over 5 acres (2 hectares) descending to a nice white-sand beach. The well-furnished units contain ceiling fans, sliding-glass doors opening onto balconies, and handcrafted teak furniture. Most bathrooms are small but well appointed, with combination shower/tubs, mirrored closets, and retractable laundry lines.

The resort's pool is ringed with cafe/restaurant tables, and there is a swim-up bar. Both a fine regional and international cuisine are served in the Ocean View and Neptunes restaurants. Limbo dancing and calypso, or some other form of entertainment, is featured nightly.

Black Rock (P.O. Box 25), Scarborough, Tobago, W.I. ☎ **868/639-0191.** Fax 868/639-0030. www.grafton-resort.com. 108 units. Winter $168 per person. Off-season $140 per person. Suite supplement $70 per person. Rates are all-inclusive. AE, MC, V. Located 4 miles (6km) from the airport. **Amenities:** 2 restaurants, 3 bars, pool; golf privileges; dive shop, boating, windsurfing, snorkeling; babysitting; laundry. *In room:* A/C, TV, mini-bar, hair dryer, safe.

Mount Irvine Bay Hotel & Golf Club ⭐⭐   This 16-acre (6-hectare) resort, established in 1972, stands on the site of an 18th-century sugar plantation. The surrounding Mount Irvine Golf Course is one of the finest courses in the Caribbean. But the hotel lost its front-ranking position to Le Grand Courlan Resort and now the upstart mega-resort, the Hilton, long ago. Mount Irvine still maintains its loyal clientele, however, with many guests returning every year. The center of the resort is a luxurious oval pool and the ruins of a stone sugar mill. The grounds slope down to a good sandy beach. On the hill leading to the beach are the newer and better-maintained cottage suites, covered with heliconia. Most accommodations are in the main building, a two-story, hacienda-inspired wing of rather large but standard guest rooms, each with a view of green lawns and flowering shrubbery. Some of the better units have Queen Anne–style furniture with two-posters. Bathrooms have shower/tub combinations.

The hotel maintains a high standard of international cuisine. There's dancing almost every evening, and calypso singers are often brought in to entertain guests.

Mount Irvine (P.O. Box 222), Scarborough, Tobago, W.I. ☎ **868/639-8871.** Fax 868/639-8800. www.mount irvine.com. 105 units. Winter $250 double; $385 cottage; $570 1-bedroom suite; $1,050 2-bedroom suite. Off-season $206 double; $335 cottage; $470 1-bedroom suite; $750 2-bedroom suite. AE, MC, V. About a 5-mile (8km) drive northwest of the airport. **Amenities:** 3 restaurants, 5 bars; pool; 18-hole golf course; 2 tennis courts; sauna; windsurfing, fishing, snorkeling, water-skiing; salon; room service (7am–10pm); massage; babysitting; laundry. *In room:* A/C, TV, hair dryer, safe.

MODERATE

Blue Waters Inn ⭐ *(Finds)*   Attracting nature lovers, this family-run property on the northeastern coast of Tobago is nestled along the shore of Batteaux Bay, where a private 1,000-foot-long (300m) beach beckons guests. This charming and rustic retreat extends onto acres of tropical rain forest with myriad exotic birds, butterflies, and other wildlife. The building's entrance almost appears to drop over a cliff, and birds may actually fly through the open windows of the driftwood-adorned dining room. It's a very informal place, so leave your fancy resort wear at home. The inn now offers several newly renovated units with kitchenettes, suitable for families. Two rooms are wheelchair accessible, and all of the basic, no-frills accommodations have ceiling fans and small private showers; several are air-conditioned as well. The second-floor rooms open onto lovely views of the water. The inn is about 24 miles (39km) from the airport, a 75-minute drive along narrow, winding country roads.

Batteaux Bay, Speyside, Tobago, W.I. ✆ 800/742-4276 in the U.S., or 868/660-4341. Fax 868/660-5195. www.bluewatersinn.com. 42 units. Winter $160 double; $230 efficiency; $330 1-bedroom suite; $490 2-bedroom suite. Off-season $100 double; $130 efficiency; $205 1-bedroom suite; $305 2-bedroom suite. Additional person $20 per day. Children age 5–12, $15. Breakfast and dinner for $36 per person. AE, MC, V. **Amenities:** Restaurant, bar; tennis court; dive shop, boating, snorkeling, kayaks, windsurfing; car rental; TV room; library; tanning beds. *In room:* A/C on request, ceiling fan, no phone.

Kariwak Village ★ *Finds*

This cluster of cottages evoking the South Pacific is about a 6-minute walk from the beach on the island's west end, a 2-minute drive from the airport. The name is a combination of the two native tribes that originally inhabited Tobago, the Caribs and the Arawaks. In this "village" Cynthia and Allan Clovis run a "holistic" haven as well as an inn. Come here, among other reasons, for Hatha Yoga, Qi Gong, and various stretching and relaxing exercises. Two on-site massage therapists give you all your favorite massages. If you're a vegetarian headed for Tobago, this is the place for you. You can even walk through Cynthia's garden, where she grows fresh herbs and vegetables for the meals served here (see "Dining," below). Nine of the accommodations are hexagonal cabanas with two rooms each, opening onto the pool. The units are quite spacious, with king-size beds, and the shower-only bathrooms are bright and well maintained.

Live entertainment is provided on Friday and Saturday year-round. The food served in the **Village Restaurant** is among the best on the island, and you may want to come by for a bite even if you aren't staying here.

Local Rd., Store Bay (P.O. Box 27), Scarborough, Tobago, W.I. ✆ 868/639-8545. Fax 868/639-8441. www. kariwak.co.tt. 24 units. Winter $125 double. Off-season $90 double. Children age 12 and under stay free in parents' room. AE, MC, V. **Amenities:** Restaurant, bar; pool; Jacuzzi; wellness classes; massage; laundry. *In room:* A/C, safe.

Richmond Great House Inn ★ *Value*

One of the most charming accommodations on the island is this 18th-century home set on 6 acres (2 hectares), part of a cocoa- and coconut-growing estate. Near Richmond Beach, on the southern (windward) coast, it's owned by Dr. Hollis R. Lynch, a Tobago-born professor of African history at Columbia University. As befits his profession, Dr. Lynch has decorated the mansion with African art, along with island antiques. Guests are free to explore the garden and grounds and to enjoy the pool and the barbecue. Most rooms have hardwood floors, country estate–style furnishings, and tasteful, colorful fabrics. Shower-only bathrooms are small and strictly functional, with somewhat dated plumbing. Families might want to consider one of the three small, basic family units in the extension to the main house. On the premises are two 19th-century tombs containing the remains of the original English founders of the plantation.

Both regional and international cuisine are served. Because it's such a small place, the cook asks guests about their culinary preferences.

Belle Garden, Tobago, W.I. ✆ and fax 868/660-4467. 10 units. Winter $165 double; $195 suite for 2; $225 family unit. Off-season $130 double; $175 suite for 2; $205 family unit. Room and suite rates include breakfast and dinner. MC, V. Located a 45-min. drive from the airport. **Amenities:** Dining room; pool; room service; laundry. *In room:* Ceiling fan, no phone.

INEXPENSIVE

In Scarborough, the **Old Donkey Cart House** restaurant (see "Dining," below) rents out apartment suites for $90 to $140 double, including breakfast and taxes. Call ✆ **868/639-3551** for more information.

Sandy Point Beach Village   This miniature vacation village somewhat resembles a Riviera condominium complex. It's just a 3-minute ride from the airport, but its shoreside position on the island's southwestern coast makes it seem remote. Airport noise, however, can be a problem. The little village of peaked and gabled roofs is landscaped all the way down to the sandy beach, where the rustic Steak Hut serves meals throughout the day and evening. The fully equipped accommodations have patios that open toward the sea, living and dining areas with Jamaican wicker furniture, and satellite TV. All but six of the units (those at poolside) contain kitchenettes, and each has a shower-only bathroom. Some of the studios have a rustic open stairway leading to a loft with bunk beds, with a twin-bedded room on the lower level as well.

Crown Point, Tobago, W.I. ✆ **868/639-8533.** Fax 868/639-8496. www.sandypt.net. 44 units. Winter $66 double studio; $77 double suite; $88 2-bedroom apt. Off-season $44 double studio; $55 double suite; $66 2-bedroom apt. Extra adult $15. Children age 11 and under stay in parents' room for $5. MAP (breakfast and dinner) $25 per person extra. AE, MC, V. **Amenities:** Restaurant, bar, dance club; 2 pools; fitness center; room service; laundry. *In room:* A/C, TV.

Toucan Inn & Bonkers ★ *Value*   This combination restaurant and hotel is one of Tobago's best values. An inn of charm and grace, it lies close to the airport surrounded by attractively landscaped gardens. If you stay here, you'll be just a short drive from some of the island's best sandy beaches. The staff will be helpful in directing you where to go. Bedrooms are done in a modern style with comfortable though streamlined furniture; rooms come in various shapes and sizes, each with a queen-size or double bed and a small but efficiently organized private bathroom with shower. The hotel offers you a choice of well-furnished bedrooms, with tiled shower bathrooms, one cluster facing the garden. These are more secluded, but even so many guests prefer the cabanas around the pool. Teak furnishings predominate in the bedrooms. The on-site Bonkers is one of the most frequented restaurants and bars in Tobago. Live entertainment is presented about 3 nights a week, and savory regional fare includes the likes of sweet curried lamb or sizzling blackened shrimp.

Store Bay Local Rd., Crown Point, Tobago, W.I. ✆ **868/639-7173.** Fax 868/639-8933. www.toucan-inn-com/rooms.htm. 20 units. Winter $80 double. Off-season $60 double. AE, MC, V. **Amenities:** Restaurant, bar; pool; room service; laundry. *In room:* A/C, TV.

DINING
EXPENSIVE

The Cocoa House ★ WEST INDIAN/TOBAGONIAN   Proud of its eco-sensitivity (waste water and paper trash are recycled here), this restaurant is a worthy choice for its allegiance to tried-and-true Tobagan food that's prepared in a style endorsed by many of the island's matriarchs and grandmothers. Its name comes from its unusual roof, made from the fronds of the Timit palm. On balmy evenings, the roof here retracts (just like it might at an old-fashioned cocoa pod drying room), allowing views of the setting sun and, a bit later, of the moon and stars. Well-flavored menu items include jerk versions of shrimp, chicken, and pork; duck with either orange or pineapple sauce; and *pelau,* a French-inspired dish that combines rice, chicken, and beef, all of it bound together with rice. For a dish that many Tobagans remember from their child-hood, try pork and dumplings.

In Footprints Eco Resort, Golden Lane, Colloden Bay Rd. ⓒ 868/660-0118. Reservations recommended for lunch, required for dinner before 1pm on the day of your intended arrival. Main courses TT$17–TT$40 (US$2.70–US$6.40) lunch, TT$50–TT$150 (US$8–US$24) dinner. AE, MC, V. Daily 8am–8pm.

Dillon's ⓖ INTERNATIONAL   Set in a simple house near the Coco Reef Resort and the airport, this restaurant is run by one of Tobago's leading opera-tors of a deep-sea-fishing boat. Consequently, the fish is sure to be fresh. There's both an indoor, air-conditioned room with framed memorabilia of the island's tradition of steel-pan music, and an outdoor terrace with views over the garden. Menu items include fresh snapper with lemon-butter sauce; tenderloin steak with a spinach-bacon ragout; pan-fried or grilled shrimp served with grilled parmesan polenta, basmati rice, and a tomato/basil sauce; and a dessert specialty of ice cream garnished with slices of local fruit.

Milford Rd., near Crown Point. ⓒ 868/639-8765. Reservations recommended. Main courses TT$65–TT$160 (US$10.40–US$25.60). AE, MC, V. Daily 6–10pm. Closed 6 weeks May–June.

Le Beau Rivage ⓖ FRENCH/CARIBBEAN   This restaurant is in a former golf clubhouse with sweeping views of one of Tobago's most historic inlets, Mount Irvine Bay. The food is more competent than exciting, but still quite good. Menu choices vary daily, but might include local ingredients combined with continental inspirations, such as grilled Caribbean lobster, pork tenderloin, and veal cutlet. Dessert may be fresh fruit salad, coconut pie, coconut tart, or fresh mango flan floating on a coulis of tropical fruits.

In the Mount Irvine Bay Hotel, Tobago Golf Course, Buccoo Bay. ⓒ 868/639-8871. Reservations required. Main courses TT$120–TT$240 (US$19.20–US$38.40). AE, MC, V. Daily 6–11pm. Located 5 min. northwest of the airport.

Tamara's ⓖ INTERNATIONAL   One of the most appealing restaurants on Tobago occupies a two-tiered, stone-and-timber gazebo whose curved edges are open on all sides for maximum exposure to cool breezes and views of the nearby sea. It serves some of the most sophisticated food in Trinidad and Tobago. The cuisine is based on West Indian traditions, with lots of international touches. Start, perhaps, with homemade veal and bacon terrine or pan-fried shrimp with wilted greens and wasabi sauce. Try the lamb loin set on couscous, the charcoal-grilled ocean snapper with a cream mushroom and lemongrass sauce, or most definitely the pork tenderloin garnished with a lima-bean ragout.

In the Coco Reef Resort, Coconut Beach. ⓒ 868/639-8571. Reservations recommended. Fixed-price dinner TT$136–TT$300 (US$21.75–US$48). AE, MC, V. Daily 7–10pm.

MODERATE

The Blue Crab ⓖ CARIBBEAN/INTERNATIONAL   One of our favorite restaurants in the capital, this family-run spot occupies an Edwardian-era house with an oversize veranda. The menu makes the most of local ingredients and regional spices, and is dictated by whatever is available that day in the market-place. The good, homemade food includes fresh conch, stuffed crab backs, an array of Creole meat dishes grilled over coconut husks, flying fish in a mild curry-flavored batter, shrimp with garlic butter or cream, and a vegetable rice dish of the day. Lobster sometimes appears on the menu.

Robinson St., Scarborough. ⓒ 868/639-2737. Reservations required for dinner. Lunch TT$30–TT$45 (US$4.80–US$7.20); dinner main courses TT$100–TT$150 (US$16–US$24). AE, MC, V. Mon–Fri 11am–3:30pm; daily 7–10pm (but call first to be sure).

Kariwak Village Restaurant ★ CARIBBEAN Even if you're not a guest here, consider visiting at dinnertime. The chefs here prepare one of the choicest menus on the island, a four-course repast that changes nightly, based on what's best and freshest at the market. On our latest rounds, we began with creamy breadfruit soup, followed by freshly grilled fish, rice, stuffed butternut pumpkin, and *christophene* (a squash-like vegetable). The price even included dessert and coffee, a very good value. In an open-air setting, you can enjoy recorded music from Trinidadian steel bands. The owner, Cynthia Clovis, grows herbs and vegetables in an on-site organic garden. The Friday or Saturday evening buffet is one of the best spreads on the island, with live music to boot. Shrimp and steak are favorites, but save room for the specialty green banana salad, seasoned with fresh herbs.

In the Kariwak Village hotel, Local Rd., Store Bay. ⓒ 868/639-8442. Reservations recommended. Breakfast TT$62.80 (US$10.05), lunch TT$30–TT$55 (US$4.80–US$8.80), 4-course dinner TT$116–TT$130 (US$18.55–US$20.80). AE, MC, V. Daily 7am–11pm.

Old Donkey Cart House INTERNATIONAL This unusual and noteworthy restaurant occupies a green-and-white Edwardian house about a ½ mile (.8km) south of Scarborough. Its owner, Gloria Jones-Knapp, was once a fashion model in Europe. "Born, bred, and dragged up" on Tobago, she is today the island's leading authority on selected European wines. Her restaurant also serves freshly made fruit drinks laced with the local rum. You get the standards here: grilled steaks, stir-fried shrimp, stuffed crab back, homemade pasta, fresh fish, lamb Creole in mushroom sauce, salads, and callaloo soup with crab. Guests dine either in the palm garden or on the verandas of the Hibiscus Bar.

Bacolet St., Scarborough. ⓒ 868/639-3551. Fax 868/639-6124. Reservations required. Main courses TT$80–TT$190 (US$12.80–US$30.40). AE, MC, V. Daily 8am–11pm.

Roussell's ★ WEST INDIAN/INTERNATIONAL Set in a white-sided building that was originally conceived as a private home, a 2-minute drive south of Scarborough's center, this restaurant is the creative statement of Trinidad-born partners Bobbie Evans and Charlene Goodman. Inside, four dining and drinking rooms open onto an outdoor terrace, where the view sweeps down over the coast and the sea. Look for sculptures by island artists, lots of local business, and extremely good food. Specific dishes change with the availability of ingredients and the whim of the chefs, but are likely to include broiled grouper with fresh Creole sauce, baked chicken with gingered carrots and garlic-coated green beans, and several different preparations of lobster. Dessert might be pineapple mousse or a guava cheesecake. Just looking for drinks and a friendly chat with a local? The bar stocks wines by the glass, as well as a frothy-looking and deceptively potent pink libation known as Roussell's punch. It's almost guaranteed to change your mind if you thought you never had any particular taste for rum.

Old Windward Rd., Bacolet. ⓒ 868/639-4738. Reservations recommended. Main courses TT$85–TT$240 (US$13.60–US$38.40). MC, V. Restaurant and bar Tues–Sat 7–11pm.

INEXPENSIVE

Arnos Vale Water Wheel Restaurant INTERNATIONAL This restaurant occupies the weathered premises of a former 19th-century water mill used to crush sugarcane. You'll dine in the wheelhouse, with an antique oven and the wheel's original machinery still in place, while overlooking the verdant banks of the Franklin River. Menu items include Cornish hen, shaved pear and Parmesan salad, deviled chicken, honey-roasted duck breast, caramelized breast of chicken with polenta and callaloo sauce, grilled fish served with a medley of sauces, and at least three different shrimp and lobster dishes. Three times a week, there's a performance of live Trinidadian/Tobagan music and dance; the animated sounds perk up the otherwise calm and quiet landscape of chirping tree frogs and splashing water.

Arnos Vale Rd., Plymouth. © 868/660-0815. Reservations recommended. Main courses TT$120–TT$250 (US$19.20–US$40). AE, MC, V. Daily 8–10am, 11:45am–2:45pm, and 6:30–10pm. The restaurant is a 5-min. drive from the Arnos Vale Hotel.

Jemma's Seaview Kitchen ⭐ *Finds* TOBAGONIAN   A short walk north of the hamlet of Speyside, on Tobago's northeastern coast, this is one of the very few restaurants in the Caribbean designed as a tree house. Although the simple kitchen is firmly anchored to the shoreline, the dining area is set on a platform nailed to the massive branches of a 200-year-old almond tree that leans out over the water. Some 50 tables are available on a wooden deck that provides a roof-like structure for shelter from the rain. The charming staff serves up main courses that come with soup or salad. Lunch platters include shrimp, fish, and chicken, while dinners feature more elaborate portions of each, as well as steaks, curried lamb, grilled or curried kingfish, lamb chops, and lobster served grilled or Thermidor style. Most dishes are at the lower end of the price scale. No liquor is served.

Speyside. © 868/660-4066. Reservations recommended. Main courses TT$50–TT$200 (US$8–US$32). MC, V. Sun–Fri 8am–9pm.

Papillon SEAFOOD/INTERNATIONAL   Located near the Tobago Golf Club on the corner of Buccoo Bay Road and Mount Irvine, this restaurant offers international specialties with an emphasis on seafood, including kingfish steak, stuffed flying fish, and lobster Buccoo Bay (marinated in sherry wine and broiled with garlic, herbs, and butter sauce). The interior is adorned with pictures that refer to the novel and film *Papillon,* a story about a convict who settles in the Caribbean. For a change of pace, try curried shrimp, beef Stroganoff, or grilled lamb and beef. There's a patio for alfresco dining.

Buccoo Bay Rd., Buccoo Bay. © 868/639-0275. Reservations recommended. Main courses TT$35–TT$60 (US$5.60–US$9.60) lunch, TT$65–TT$130 (US$10.40–US$20.80) dinner. MC, V. Daily 7:30am–2:30pm and 7–10pm.

HITTING THE BEACH ⭐⭐

On Tobago, you can still feel like Robinson Crusoe in a solitary sandy cove—at least until Saturday, when the Trinidadians fly over for a weekend on the beach.

Pigeon Point, on the northwestern shore, is the best-known bathing area, with a long coral beach. It's public, but to reach it you must enter a former coconut estate, which charges a fee of TT$10 (US$1.60). Set against a backdrop of royal palms, this beach is becoming increasingly commercial. Facilities include food kiosks, crafts shops, a diving concession, paddleboat rentals, changing rooms in thatched shelters, and picnic tables. Pigeon Point is also the jumping off point for snorkeling cruises to **Buccoo Reef.**

Another good beach, **Back Bay,** is an 8-minute walk from the Mount Irvine Bay Hotel on Mount Irvine Bay. Along the way, you'll pass a coconut plantation and an old cannon emplacement. Snorkeling is generally excellent here, even in winter. There are sometimes dangerous currents here, but you can always explore Rocky Point and its brilliantly colored parrot fish. In July and August, the surfing here is the finest in Tobago; it's also likely to be good in January and April. Stop in Scarborough for picnic fixings, which you can enjoy at the picnic tables here; a snack bar sells cold beer and drinks.

Great Courland Bay is known for its calm, gin-clear waters, and is flanked by **Turtle Beach,** named for the sea creatures who nest here. Near Fort Bennett and south of Plymouth, Great Courland Bay is one of the longest sandy beaches on the island and the site of several hotels and a marina.

The locals and the fishing boats make the setting at half-moon-shaped **Parlatuvier Beach** (on the north side of the island) more bucolic than the swimming. If you can't stand crowds, head for **Englishman's Bay,** on the north coast just west of Parlatuvier. We don't know why this beach is virtually deserted: It's charming, secluded, and good for swimming.

Man-O-War Bay is one of the finest natural harbors in the West Indies, at the opposite end of the island, near the little fishing village of Charlotteville. It has a long sandy beach and a government-run rest house. Sometimes local fishermen will hawk the day's catch (and clean it for you as well). Nearby **Lovers' Beach** is accessible only by boat and is famous for its pink sand, formed long ago from crushed sea shells. Negotiate a fee with one of the local boatmen; expect to pay around $25.

The true beach buff will head for **King's Bay** in the northeast, south of the town of Speyside near Delaford. Against a backdrop of towering green hills, the crescent-shaped grayish-sand beach is one of the best places for swimming.

SPORTS & OTHER OUTDOOR PURSUITS

GOLF   Tobago is the proud possessor of an 18-hole, 6,800-yard (6,188m) course at Mount Irvine. Called the **Tobago Golf Club** (© **868/639-8871**), it covers 150 breeze-swept acres (60 hectares) and was featured in the *Wonderful World of Golf* TV series. Even beginners agree the course is friendly to duffers. Well-heeled golfers should stay at the Mount Irvine Bay Hotel, where guests are granted temporary membership, use of the clubhouse and facilities, and a 30% discount on greens fees. The course is also open to nonguests, who pay $55 for 18 holes or $34 for 9 holes. Cart rentals are $41 for 18 holes or $23 for 9 holes; clubs cost $17 for 18 holes or $11 for 9 holes. By the time you read this, a competitive course should have opened at the Tobago Hilton (see earlier in this chapter). Call the hotel for details.

SCUBA DIVING, SNORKELING ✦✦ **& OTHER WATERSPORTS**   The unspoiled reefs off Tobago teem with a great variety of marine life. Divers can swim through rocky canyons 60 to 130 feet (18–39m) deep, underwater photographers can shoot pictures they won't find anywhere else, and snorkelers can explore the celebrated **Buccoo Reef** (off Pigeon Point), which teems with gardens of coral and hundreds of fish in the waist-deep water. Nearly all the major hotels arrange boat trips here.

Wreck divers have a new adventure to enjoy with the sinking of the former ferryboat *Maverick,* in 100 feet (30m) of water near Mount Irvine Bay Hotel on Tobago's southwest coast.

Dive Tobago, Pigeon Point (© **868/639-0202**), is the oldest and most established operation on Tobago, operated by Jay Young, a certified PADI instructor. It offers easy resort courses, single dives, and dive packages, along with equipment rentals. A basic resort course costs $55, although for certification you must pay $350. A one-tank dive goes for $40.

Tobago Dive Experience, at the Turtle Beach Hotel, Black Rock (© **868/639-7034**), offers scuba dives, snorkeling, and boat trips. All dives are guided, with a boat following. Exciting drift dives are available for experienced divers. A one-tank dive costs $39 without equipment or $46 with equipment; a two-tank dive starts at $70; and a resort course costs $65.

Man Friday Diving, Charlotteville (© **868/660-4676**), is a Danish-owned dive center with certified PADI instructors and dive masters. It's located right on the beach of Man-O-War Bay at the northernmost tip of Tobago. With more than 40 different dive sites, it's always able to find suitable locations, no matter what the water conditions are. Guided boat trips for certified divers go out Monday to Saturday at 9:30am and 1pm. A resort course costs $75; a PADI open-water certification, $375; a one-tank dive, $35; and a night dive, $50.

TENNIS   The best courts on the island are at the **Mount Irvine Bay Hotel** (© **868/639-8871**). Nonguests may use the two courts here for TT$11.50 (US$1.85) per half hour or TT$23 (US$3.70) per hour.

EXPLORING TOBAGO

If you'd like a close-up view of Tobago's exotic and often rare tropical birds, as well as a range of other island wildlife and lush tropical flora, naturalist-led field trips are the answer. Each 2- to 3-hour trip leads you to forest trails and coconut plantations, along rivers and past waterfalls; one excursion goes to two nearby islands. Trips cost $30 to $40. For details, contact **Newton George,** Man-O-War Bay Cottages, Charlotteville (© **868/660-4327** or 868/660-5463).

Tobago's capital, **Scarborough,** need claim your attention only briefly before you climb up the hill to **Fort King George,** about 430 feet (129m) above the town. Built by the English in 1779, it was later captured by the French, then was tossed back and forth among various conquerors until nature decided to end it all in 1847, blowing off the roofs of its buildings. You can see artifacts displayed in a gallery, plus the ruins of a military hospital.

From Scarborough, you can drive northwest to **Plymouth,** Tobago's other town. Perched on a point at Plymouth is **Fort James,** which dates from 1768. Now it's mainly in ruins.

From Speyside in the north, you can make arrangements with a local fisher to go to **Little Tobago** ⭐, a 450-acre (180-hectare) offshore island whose bird sanctuary attracts ornithologists. The 20-minute crossing is likely to be rough, but the effort is worth it. Threatened with extinction in New Guinea, many birds, perhaps 50 species in all, were brought over to this little island in the early part of last century. The islet is arid and hilly, with a network of marked trails.

Off Pigeon Point in the south lies **Buccoo Reef** ⭐⭐, where sea gardens of coral and hundreds of fish can be seen in waist-deep water. This is the natural aquarium of Tobago, offering the island's best **snorkeling** and **scuba diving.** Nearly all the major hotels arrange boat trips here. Even nonswimmers can wade knee-deep in the waters. Remember to protect your head and body from the sun and to guard your feet against the sharp coral.

After about half an hour at the reef, passengers reboard their boats and go over to **Nylon Pool,** with its crystal-clear waters. Here in this white-sand-bottom spot, about a mile (2km) offshore, you can enjoy a dip in water only 3 or 4 feet (1m) deep.

Eco-consciousness on the island was enhanced by the opening of the **Franklyn Water Wheel and Nature Park,** at Arnos Vale Estate, Franklyn Road, Plymouth (© **868/660-0815**). This is the site of Tobago's best-preserved water wheel, which once provided power to a sugar estate. The 12-acre (5-hectare) estate has walking trails, a restaurant, an outdoor theater, and the old machinery, for the most part still in place. On the trails, you may see butterflies and iguanas, plus mango and citrus orchards where you can pick your own fresh fruit. Admission is TT$10 (US$1.60) for adults, free for children. You can visit any time during the day and gain entrance to the site as long as the restaurant is open (before 10pm).

SHOPPING

In Tobago's capital, Scarborough, you can visit the local **market** Monday to Saturday mornings and listen to the sounds of the Creole patois. Scarborough's stores have a limited range of merchandise, more to tempt the browser than the serious shopper.

Farro's, Wilson Road (no phone), across from the marketplace, offers the tastiest condiments on the island, packed into little straw baskets for you to carry back home. Sample the delectable lime marmalade, any of the hot sauces, the guava jelly, and most definitely the home-canned and homemade chutney from the tamarind fruit.

If you're seeking handcrafts, especially straw baskets, head for the **Souvenir & Gift Shop,** Port Mall (© 868/639-5632), also in Scarborough.

Cotton House Fashion Studio, Old Windward Road, in Bacolet (© 868/639-2727), is the island's best choice for "hands-on" appreciation of the fine art of batik. In the Indonesian tradition, melted wax is brushed onto fabric, resisting dyes and creating unusual colors and designs. This outlet contains the largest collection of batik clothing and wall hangings on Tobago. Dying techniques are demonstrated to visitors, who can then try their skills at the art form.

TOBAGO AFTER DARK

Your best bet for entertainment is at the **Mount Irvine Bay Hotel** at Mount Irvine Bay (© 868/639-8871), where you might find some disco action or a steel band performing by the beach or pool.

The Grafton Beach Resort at Black Road owns one of the island's most charming bars, **Buccaneer's Beach Bar** (© 868/639-0191), across from the resort. Here you'll find a wide wood terrace sheltered by a grove of almond trees. Daily specials written up on a surfboard include burgers, fried fish, and the like (don't expect the elegant beachside Creole cooking of Martinique). The resort itself offers cabaret-like entertainment nightly. Catch if you can a local troupe, Les Couteaux Cultural Group, which performs a version of Tobagonian history set to dance.

The best place on a weekend is **The Deep,** at Sandy Point Hotel in Crown Point (© 868/639-8533). Sit here, sip your rum punch, and listen to the sounds of soca, pop, or rock. In between gigs, you can hear the breakers unfurling on a distant reef.

Want some local action? Try **Bonkers,** Store Bay Road at Crown Point (© 868/639-7173), an active bar where you'll hear the best soca, reggae, or jazz. If you've been "bad," the DJ might order you to walk the gangplank into the pool. Disco nights are occasionally held at **The Lush,** Shirvan Road in Mount Irvine (© 868/639-9087), one of the island's friendliest alfresco pubs. Drop in to see what's happening.

26

The U.S. Virgin Islands

The U.S. Virgin Islands are known for their sugar-white beaches, among the finest in the world, and also for duty-free shopping. The most developed island in the chain is **St. Thomas,** whose capital, Charlotte Amalie, is the shopping mecca of the Caribbean. With a population of some 50,000 and thousands more cruise-ship passengers arriving on any given day, tiny St. Thomas isn't exactly a secluded tropical retreat; you'll hardly have its beautiful beaches to yourself. It abounds in bars and restaurants, including fast-food joints, and has a vast selection of hotels in all price ranges.

St. Croix is bigger, but more tranquil, than St. Thomas. A favorite with cruise-ship passengers (as is St. Thomas), St. Croix touts its shopping and has more stores than most islands in the Caribbean, especially in and around Christiansted, although it's not as dense with stores as Charlotte

Amalie. Its major attraction is Buck Island, a U.S. National Park that lies offshore. St. Croix is peppered with inns and hotels and is condo heaven.

St. John, the smallest of the three islands, is also the most beautiful and the least developed. It has only two big hotels. Some two-thirds of this island is set aside as a U.S. National Park. Even if you visit only for the day while based on St. Thomas, you'll want to sample the island's dreamy beach, Trunk Bay.

The U.S. Virgin Islands lie in two bodies of water: St. John is entirely in the Atlantic Ocean, St. Croix is entirely in the Caribbean Sea, and St. Thomas separates the Atlantic and the Caribbean. Directly in the belt of the subtropical, easterly trade winds, these islands enjoy one of the most perfect year-round climates in the world. The U.S. Virgins are some 60 miles (97km) east of Puerto Rico and 1,100 miles (1,771km) southeast of Miami.

1 U.S. Virgin Islands Essentials

VISITOR INFORMATION

Before you go, contact the **U.S. Virgin Islands Division of Tourism,** at 1270 Ave. of the Americas (suite 2108), **New York, NY** 10020 (© 212/332-2222). Branch offices are located at: 225 Peachtree St. NE, Suite 260, **Atlanta, GA** 30303 (© 404/688-0906); 500 N. Michigan Ave., Suite 2030, **Chicago, IL** 60611 (© 312/670-8784); 2655 Le Jeune Rd., Suite 907, **Coral Gables, FL** 33134 (© 305/442-7200); 3460 Wilshire Blvd., Suite 412, **Los Angeles, CA** 90010 (© 213/739-0138); and 900 17th St. NW, Suite 500, **Washington, D.C.** 20006 (© 202/624-3590).

In **Canada,** there's an office at 3300 Bloor St. West, Suite 3120, Centre Tower, Toronto, ON M8X 2X3, Canada (© 416/622-7600). In **Britain,** contact the office at 2 Cinnamon Row, Plantation Wharf, York Place, London SW11 3TW (© 020/7978-5262).

On the Web, you can get information at **www.usvi.net.**

GETTING THERE

Before you book your airline ticket on your own, refer to the section "Package Deals," in chapter 2. You might save a bundle.

It's possible to fly from the mainland of the U.S. directly to St. Thomas and St. Croix, but the only way to get to St. John is by a ferry from St. Thomas or from Jost Van Dyke or Tortola in the British Virgin Islands.

TO ST. THOMAS OR ST. CROIX FROM THE U.S. **American Airlines** (© 800/433-7300 in the U.S.; www.aa.com) offers frequent service to St. Thomas and St. Croix from the U.S. mainland, with five daily flights from New York to St. Thomas in high season. Passengers originating in other parts of the world are usually routed to St. Thomas through American's hubs in Miami or San Juan, both of which offer nonstop service (often several times a day) to St. Thomas. (American Eagle has 13 nonstop flights daily from San Juan to St. Thomas.) A convenient nonstop flight from Miami, available only June through August, departs Miami at 5pm and continues to St. Croix, where the plane stays overnight. This late-afternoon departure from Miami allows for connections to the U.S. Virgin Islands from many other destinations within the United States. American can also arrange great discount packages that include both airfare and hotel.

Delta (© 800/221-1212 in the U.S.; www.delta.com) offers two daily nonstop flights between Atlanta and St. Thomas in winter. **US Airways** (© 800/428-4322 in the U.S.; www.usairways.com) has one nonstop flight from Philadelphia to St. Thomas.

Cape Air (© 800/352-0714 in the U.S.; www.flycapeair.com) has service between St. Thomas and Puerto Rico. This Massachusetts-based airline offers seven flights daily. Cape Air has expanded its service to include flights from San Juan to St. Croix and flights between St. Croix and St. Thomas.

In 1999, **United Airlines** (© 800/241-6522 in the U.S.; www.united.com) launched nonstop service on Saturday and Sunday to St. Thomas from Chicago and Washington, D.C.

Continental Airlines (© 800/525-0280 in the U.S.; www.continental.com) also launched flights to St. Thomas in 1999, flying daily from Newark International Airport to St. Thomas.

TO ST. CROIX FROM ST. THOMAS It's now easier than ever before to travel between St. Thomas and St. Croix. **American Eagle** (© 800/433-7300 in the U.S.) has three flights a day, costing $90 to $120 one way. In addition, **Seaborne Seaplane** (© 340/773-6442) offers 10 or 11 round-trip flights daily, going for $75 to $150 one way. Flight time is 30 minutes.

A **ferry** service between Charlotte Amalie in St. Thomas and Puerto Rico, with a stop in St. John, is available about once every 2 weeks (sometimes more often in high season). The trip takes about 2 hours, costing $60 one way or $100 round-trip, including ground transportation to the San Juan airport or Condado. Children pay $60 round-trip. For more information, call © 340/776-6282.

TO ST. JOHN The easiest and most common way to get to St. John is by **ferry** (© 340/776-6282), which leaves from the Red Hook landing pier on St. Thomas's eastern tip; the trip takes about 20 minutes each way. Beginning at 6:30am, boats depart more or less every hour. The last ferry back to Red Hook departs from St. John's Cruz Bay at 11pm. The service is frequent and efficient enough that even cruise-ship passengers temporarily anchored in Charlotte Amalie can visit St. John for a quickie island tour. The one-way fare is $3 for adults, $1 for children age 12 and under. Schedules can change without notice, so call in advance.

To reach the ferry, take the **Vitran** bus from a point near Market Square (in Charlotte Amalie) directly to Red Hook. The cost is $1 per person each way. In addition, privately owned taxis will negotiate a price to carry you from virtually anywhere to the docks at Red Hook.

If you've just landed on St. Thomas and want to go straight to the ferry dock, your best bet is to take a cab from the airport (Vitran buses run from Charlotte Amalie but don't serve the airport area). After disembarking from the ferry on St. John, you'll have to get another cab to your hotel. Depending on the traffic, the cab ride on St. Thomas would take 30 to 45 minutes, and would cost about $14.

It's also possible to board a **boat** for St. John directly at the Charlotte Amalie waterfront for a cost of $7 each way. The ride takes 45 minutes. The boats depart from Charlotte Amalie at 9am and continue at intervals of between 1 and 2 hours, until the last boat departs around 5:30pm. (The last boat to leave St. John's Cruz Bay for Charlotte Amalie departs at 3:45pm.) Call ✆ **340/776-6282** for more information.

FAST FACTS: The U.S. Virgin Islands

Banks Banks are generally open Monday to Thursday from 9am to 2:30pm, Friday from 9am to 2pm and 3:30 to 5pm. It's not hard to find a bank with an ATM on St. Thomas or St. Croix. Chase Manhattan Bank has branches, with ATMs, on all three islands.

Currency The **U.S. dollar** is the unit of currency in the Virgin Islands.

Customs Every U.S. resident can bring home $1,200 worth of duty-free purchases, including 5 liters of liquor per adult. If you go over the $1,200 limit, you pay a flat 5% duty, up to $1,000. You can also mail home gifts valued at up to $100 per day, which you don't have to declare. (At other spots in the Caribbean, U.S. citizens are limited to $400 or $600 worth of merchandise and a single bottle of liquor.)

Documents U.S. and Canadian citizens are required to present some proof of citizenship to enter the Virgin Islands, such as a birth certificate with a raised seal along with a government-issued photo ID. A passport is not strictly required, but carrying one is a good idea. The requirements for other citizens are the same as for foreigners entering the U.S. mainland; travelers from the United Kingdom, Australia, and New Zealand need valid passports, but not visas.

Electricity It's the same as on the U.S. mainland: 120-volt AC (60 cycles). No transformer, adapter, or converter is needed for U.S. appliances.

Emergencies In an emergency, dial ✆ **911.**

Liquor Laws Liquor is sold 7 days a week, and it is not permitted on beaches.

Safety The U.S. Virgin Islands have more than their share of crime. Travelers should exercise extreme caution both day and night, especially in the backstreets of Charlotte Amalie on St. Thomas, and in Christiansted and Frederiksted on St. Croix. Muggings are commonplace. Avoid strolling at night, especially on the beaches.

Taxes There is no departure tax for the U.S. Virgin Islands. Hotels add on an 8% tax (always ask if it's included in the original price you're quoted).

Telephone The phone system for the U.S. Virgin Islands is the same as on the U.S. mainland. The area code is **340.** To reach AT&T dial ✆ **800/872-2881,** to reach Sprint dial ✆ **800/999-9000,** and to reach MCI dial ✆ **800/877-8000.**

Time The U.S. Virgins are on Atlantic standard time, which is 1 hour ahead of eastern standard time. However, the islands do not observe daylight saving time, so in the summer, the Virgin Islands and the U.S. east coast are on the same time. In winter, when it's 6am in Charlotte Amalie, it's 5am in Miami; during daylight saving time, it's 6am in both places.

Tipping Tip as you would on the U.S. mainland (15% in restaurants, 10% to 15% to taxi drivers, $1 or $2 per round to bartenders, at least $1 or $2 per day for chambermaids). Some hotels add a 10% to 15% surcharge to cover service, so check before you wind up paying twice.

Water Most visitors drink the local tap water with no harmful aftereffects. Those with more delicate stomachs might want to stick to bottled water.

Weather From November to February, temperatures average about 77°F. Sometimes in August the temperature peaks in the high 80s, but the subtropical breezes keep it comfortably cool in the shade. The temperature in winter may drop into the low 60s, but this rarely happens.

2 St. Thomas ★★★

St. Thomas, the busiest cruise-ship destination in the West Indies, is not the largest of the U.S. Virgins (St. Croix, 40 miles/64km south, holds that distinction). But bustling Charlotte Amalie is the capital of the U.S. Virgin Islands, and the shopping hub of the Caribbean. The beaches on this island are renowned for their white sand and calm, turquoise waters, including the very best of them all, **Magens Bay.** Despite all the overdevelopment, *National Geographic* rated St. Thomas as one of the top destinations in the world for sailing, scuba diving, and fishing.

Charlotte Amalie, with its white houses and bright red roofs glistening in the sun, is one of the most beautiful towns in the Caribbean. It's most famous for its shopping, but the town is also filled with historic sights, like Fort Christian, an intriguing 17th-century building constructed by the Danes. The town's architecture reflects the island's culturally diverse past. You'll pass Dutch doors, Danish red-tile roofs, French iron grillwork, and Spanish-style patios.

Because of St. Thomas's thriving commercial activity, as well as its lingering drug and crime problems, the island is often referred to as the most "unvirgin" of the Virgin Islands. Charlotte Amalie's Main Street is virtually a 3- to 4-block-long shopping center. But while this area tends to be overcrowded, for the most part, the island's beaches, major hotels, restaurants, and entertainment facilities are removed from the cruise-ship chaos. And you can always find seclusion at a resort in more remote sections of the island. Hotels on the north side of St. Thomas look out at the Atlantic; those on the south side front the calmer Caribbean Sea.

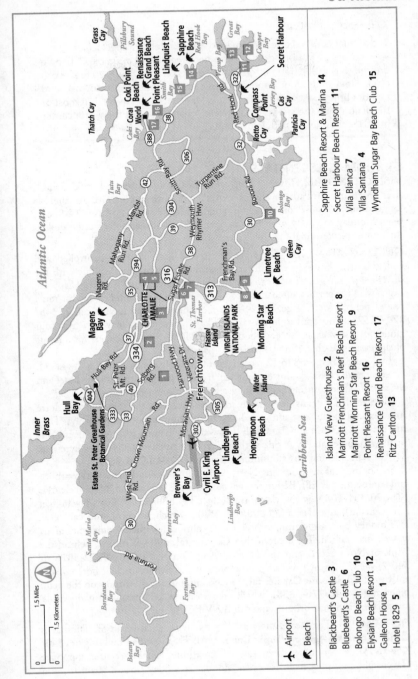

St. Thomas

Sapphire Beach Resort & Marina **14**
Secret Harbour Beach Resort **11**
Villa Blanca **7**
Villa Santana **4**
Wyndham Sugar Bay Beach Club **15**

Island View Guesthouse **2**
Marriott Frenchman's Reef Beach Resort **8**
Marriott Morning Star Beach Resort **9**
Point Pleasant Resort **16**
Renaissance Grand Beach Resort **17**
Ritz Carlton **13**

Blackbeard's Castle **3**
Bluebeard's Castle **6**
Bolongo Beach Club **10**
Elysian Beach Resort **12**
Galleon House **1**
Hotel 1829 **5**

> ⟨*Fun Fact* Carnival
>
> The annual **Carnival** celebration, held after Easter, is a spectacular event, with echoes of the islanders' African heritage. "Mocko Jumbies," people dressed as spirits, parade through the streets on stilts nearly 20 feet (6km) high. Steel and fungi bands, "jump-ups" (Caribbean hoedowns), and parades bring the event to life. Events take place islandwide, but most of the action is on the streets of Charlotte Amalie. Contact the visitor center in St. Thomas for a schedule of events.

ST. THOMAS ESSENTIALS

VISITOR INFORMATION   Stop off at the **Grand Hotel,** at Tolbod Gade 1, near Emancipation Park, on the waterfront in downtown Charlotte Amalie. No longer a hotel, it now contains shops and a **visitor center** (① **340/774-8784**), open Monday to Friday from 8am to 5pm. There's also an information desk at the cruise-ship terminal.

GETTING AROUND   **Taxis** are unmetered, but fares are controlled and widely posted; however, we still recommend that you negotiate a fare with the driver before you get into the car. A typical fare from Charlotte Amalie to Sapphire Beach is $8 per person. Surcharges, from $2 to $3, are added after midnight. You'll pay $1 per bag for luggage. For 24-hour radio dispatch taxi service, call ① **340/ 774-7457.** If you want to hire a taxi and a driver (who just may be a great tour guide) for a day, expect to pay about $30 to $40 for two passengers for 2 hours of sightseeing; each additional passenger pays $20.

　Taxi vans transport 8 to 12 passengers to multiple destinations on the island. It's cheaper to take a van instead of a taxi if you're going between your hotel and the airport. The cost for luggage ranges from 50¢ to $1 per bag.

　Buses, called **Vitrans,** leave from street-side stops in the center of Charlotte Amalie, fanning out east and west along all the most important highways. They run between 5:30am and 7pm daily, but waits can be very long and this is a difficult way to get about. A ride within Charlotte Amalie is 75¢, anywhere else, $1. For schedule and bus-stop information, call ① **340/774-5678.**

　St. Thomas has many leading North American **car-rental firms** at the airport, and competition is stiff. Before you go, compare the rates of the "big three": **Avis** (① **800/331-1084;** www.avis.com), **Budget** (① **800/527-0700;** www.budget rentacar.com), and **Hertz** (① **800/654-3001;** www.hertz.com). You can often save money by renting from a local agency, although vehicles sometimes aren't as well maintained. Try **Dependable Car Rental,** 3901 B Altona, behind the Bank of Nova Scotia and the Medical Arts Complex (① **800/522-3076** or 340/774-2253), which will pick up renters at the airport or their hotel; or the aptly named **Discount Car Rental,** 14 Content, outside the airport on the main highway (① **340/776-4858**), which grants drivers a 12% discount on rivals' rates. There is no tax on car rentals in the Virgin Islands.

FAST FACTS   The local **American Express** representative on St. Thomas is **Caribbean Travel Agency/Tropic Tours,** 14AB The Guardian Building (① **340/ 774-1855**), a 5-minute drive east of Charlotte Amalie's center, opposite Havensight shopping mall; it's open Monday to Friday from 8:30am to 5pm and Saturday from 8:30am to noon.

Royal Roy Lester Schneider Hospital, 48 Sugar Estate, Charlotte Amalie (© **340/776-8311**), a 5-minute drive east of the town's commercial center, is the largest hospital with the best-equipped emergency room.

ACCOMMODATIONS

Nearly every beach on St. Thomas has its own hotel, and the island also has more quaint inns than anyplace else in the Caribbean. If you want to stay here on the cheap, consider one of the guesthouses in the Charlotte Amalie area. All the glittering, expensive properties lie in the east end.

Remember that hotels in the Virgin Islands slash their prices in summer by 20% to 60%. Unless otherwise noted, the rates listed below do *not* include the 8% government tax.

VERY EXPENSIVE

Marriott Frenchman's Reef Beach Resort ★★★   Lying 3 miles (5km) east of Charlotte Amalie on the south shore, this is the largest hotel in the U.S. Virgin Islands. The resort has an excellent location, on a bluff overlooking both the harbor and the Caribbean. This is a full-service, American-style mega-resort; it's not suited to those seeking cozy island ambience. Go to Hotel 1829 for that. Everywhere you look are facilities devoted to the good life. To reach the private beach, for example, you take a glass-enclosed elevator. The bedrooms vary greatly, but in general are traditionally furnished and quite comfortable, though we find the rooms at the hotel's neighbor, the Marriott Morning Star (see below), more luxurious. Nonetheless, the accommodations here have all you'll need for comfort, and the bathrooms with combination shower/tubs are generally spacious. All units have private balconies with sea views.

There is enough variety in dining to make a stay here intriguing even if you don't leave the premises. The cuisine has been much improved. In general, we prefer the seafood to the frozen meat imported from the U.S. mainland.

Estate Bakkeroe, Flamboyant Point (P.O. Box 7100), St. Thomas, U.S.V.I. 00801. © **800/524-2000** in the U.S., or 340/776-8500. Fax 340/715-6191. www.marriott.com. 408 units. Winter $339–$529 double; $495–$1,500 suite. Off-season $155–$245 double; from $300 suite. MAP (breakfast and dinner) $61 per person extra. Ask about packages. AE, DC, DISC, MC, V. **Amenities:** 5 restaurants, 9 bars; 3 pools; 2 tennis courts; health club and spa; sauna; steam room; watersports; children's program, car rental; 24-hr. room service; babysitting; laundry/dry cleaning. *In room:* A/C, TV, dataport, minibar, coffeemaker, hair dryer, safe.

Tips Drivers Beware

Remember to *drive on the left*. This comes as a surprise to many U.S. visitors, who expect that U.S. driving practices will hold here. Speed limits are 20 miles per hour (.02kmph) in towns, 35 miles per hour (.03kmph) outside towns. St. Thomas has a high accident rate, as tourists are not used to driving on the left, the hilly terrain hides blind curves and entrance ramps, roads are narrow and poorly lit, and drivers often get behind the wheel after too many drinks. Double-check whether your own car insurance will cover you on the island, or whether your credit card will provide coverage. If not, to be on the safe side, consider getting **collision-damage insurance,** which usually costs an extra $15 to $20 per day. Be aware that even with this insurance, you could still get hit with a whopping deductible: The Hertz deductible is the full value of the car; at Avis and Budget, it's $500.

Marriott Morning Star Beach Resort ★★★ Built right on white sands, this is the even better neighbor of the Marriott Frenchman's Reef Beach Resort. If you're a guest you can wander between the two, which gives you a broader range of restaurant choices and facilities than any other hotel on island can offer. Recently upgraded to the tune of $6 million, this beachside enclave has been enhanced with a striking new Caribbean decor. Both its public areas and its plushly outfitted accommodations are among the best on the island. Its five cottage-style buildings each contain between 16 and 24 units. Guests have the amenities and attractions of the large hotel nearby, yet maintain the privacy of this more intimate property. Each unit has rattan furniture and views of the garden, beach, or the lights of Charlotte Amalie from your own veranda. Bedrooms are roomy and spacious, with fine furnishings and tasteful fabrics, plus extras such as phones with voice mail and data ports; tiled bathrooms have shower/tub combinations.

#5 Estate Bakkeroe, Flamboyant Point (P.O. Box 7100), St. Thomas, U.S.V.I. 00801. © **800/524-2000** or 340/776-8500. Fax 340/715-6101. www.marriott.com. 96 units. Winter $369–$529 double. Off-season $175–$245 double. MAP (breakfast and dinner) $61 per person extra. AE, DC, DISC, MC, V. **Amenities:** Shared with Frenchman's Reef (see above). *In room:* A/C, TV, minibar, coffeemaker, hair dryer, safe.

Renaissance Grand Beach Resort ★★★ This resort, which occupies 34 acres (14 hectares) on the northeast shore of St. Thomas, is perched on a steep hillside above a beautiful though small white-sand beach. In luxury it is outpaced by the Ritz-Carlton. Grand Beach has a friendlier layout and design than does one of its major competitors, Wyndham Sugar Bay Beach Club. The accommodations, all stylishly outfitted, are in seven two-story buildings designed like beach houses and staggered so that each unit has its own view. The Bougainvillea section is adjacent to the beach, while the units in the Hibiscus section are literally carved into the hillside. All rooms have quality mattresses, marble foyers, wall-to-wall carpeting, marble bathrooms with tubs and showers, private safes, mini-fridges, robes, and private patios or balconies with views of the Caribbean. The two-story town-house suites and one- or two-bedroom suites have whirlpool spas. This is a good family resort; trained counselors operate a free year-round children's program for ages 3 to 14.

Rte. 38, Smith Bay Rd. (P.O. Box 8267), St. Thomas, U.S.V.I. 00801. © **800/421-8181** in the U.S., or 340/775-1510. Fax 340/775-2185. www.renaissancehotels.com. 290 units. Winter $329–$369 double; $430 1-bedroom suite; $495 2-bedroom suite. Off-season $299–$339 double; $380 1-bedroom suite; $455 2-bedroom suite. MAP (breakfast and dinner) $75 per person extra. Ask about packages. AE, DC, DISC, MC, V. **Amenities:** 2 restaurants, 2 bars; pool; 6 tennis courts; health club and spa; sauna; steam room; watersports; children's program; 24-hr. room service, babysitting; laundry. *In room:* A/C, TV, minibar, hair dryer, iron and ironing board, safe.

Ritz-Carlton ★★★ Fronted by white-sand beaches, this is the toniest resort in all the U.S. Virgin Islands. To all other luxury hotels on the island, it can say, "Eat my dust." The chic Ritz-Carlton took over the Grand Palazzo, a 15-acre (6-hectare) oceanfront estate at the island's eastern tip, 4½ miles (7km) southeast of Charlotte Amalie. The Ritz is set amid landscaped gardens, blending European elegance with Caribbean style. Bubbling fountains and hidden courtyards create the feel of a Mediterranean villa.

Accommodations are in half a dozen three-story villas designed with Italian Renaissance motifs and Mediterranean colors. Guests register in a reception palazzo, whose arches and accents were inspired by a Venetian palace. From the monogrammed bathrobes to the digital in-room safes, the accommodations here have more extras than those at any other hotel on the island. They all have full marble bathrooms with fine toiletries, excellent-quality linens, and balconies with resort or sea views. Service is up to usual high Ritz-Carlton standards.

The elegant dining room captures the best scenic views of Great Bay and St. John, and serves a refined and deluxe cuisine that's complemented by an excellent wine list.

Great Bay, St. Thomas, U.S.V.I. 00802. ⓒ 800/241-3333 or 340/775-3333. Fax 340/775-4444. www.ritz carlton.com. 152 units. Winter $545–$695 double; $2,000 suite. Off-season $220–$400 double; $950 suite. Ask about packages. AE, DC, DISC, MC, V. **Amenities:** 4 restaurants, 3 bars; pool; 3 tennis courts; fitness center; Jacuzzi; deep-sea fishing; watersports; children's programs; 24-hr. room service; massage; babysitting; laundry/dry cleaning. In room: A/C, TV, minibar, hair dryer, safe.

Wyndham Sugar Bay Beach Club ⭐⭐   At the east end of the island, a 5-minute ride from Red Hook, this hotel is much improved but still lags behind the Marriotts. It has panoramic views, although its secluded beach is really too small for a resort of this size. Many of the attractive rooms are decorated with rattan pieces and pastels, and they have roomy marble bathrooms with shower stalls. After a recent $5 million renovation, guestrooms have new carpeting, furnishings, electronics, wall treatments, and plumbing.

6500 Estate Smith Bay, St. Thomas, U.S.V.I. 00802. ⓒ 800/WYNDHAM in the U.S., or 340/777-7100. Fax 340/ 777-7200. www.wyndham.com. 300 units. All-inclusive rates: winter $560–$650 double; from $725 suite. Off-season $496–$536 double; from $755 suite. Rates include all meals, snacks, drinks, activities, tax, and service. AE, DC, DISC, MC, V. **Amenities:** 2 restaurants, 2 bars; 3 pools; tennis stadium, 6 lit Laykold tennis courts; fitness center; spa; watersports; dive shop; children's club; babysitting; laundry/dry cleaning. In room: A/C, TV, dataport, fridge, coffeemaker, hair dryer, safe.

EXPENSIVE

Blackbeard's Castle ⭐   Once a private residence, this is now one of the most charming and atmospheric inns in the Virgin Islands. Perched high on a hillside above the town, it lies at the site of a 1679 tower that the Danish governor ordered erected of chiseled stone. The tower served as a lookout for unfriendly ships, and legend says that Blackbeard himself lived in the tower half a century later. It's not located on the sands, and the nearest beach is a 10-minute taxi ride away (you can rely on cabs if you don't want to rent a car). Most of the well-furnished bedrooms and all the suites are spacious. The garden rooms are much smaller than other rooms and have no balconies, though they're located near a private pool area; travelers on a budget might choose these. Accommodations are decorated with tile floors or dark wood, with much use made of Caribbean mahogany furnishings. Each unit is equipped with a well-maintained, shower-only bathroom. Blackbeard's is also the site of one of the most romantic restaurants in St. Thomas (see "Dining," below).

Blackbeard's Hill (P.O. Box 6227), Charlotte Amalie, St. Thomas, U.S.V.I. 00801. ⓒ 800/344-5771 in the U.S., or 340/776-1234. Fax 340/776-1234. www.blackbeardscastle.com. 11 units. Winter $115 garden room; $160–$200 balcony or junior suite. Off-season $95 garden room; $135–$160 balcony or junior suite. AE, MC, V. **Amenities:** Restaurant, bar; pool; room service. In room: A/C, TV, minibar.

Bluebeard's Castle ⭐   This is a popular resort set on the side of the bay overlooking Charlotte Amalie (it's not on a beach, but it offers free shuttle service to Magens Bay). It was once the island's number-one hotel, but it's long been surpassed by newer, more deluxe east end resorts, such as the Ritz-Carlton. The hill surrounding the hotel is now heavily built up with everything from offices to time-shares. The guestrooms come in a wide variety of shapes and sizes, all pleasantly but blandly decorated. All bathrooms are neatly kept with shower/tub combinations. Many units have a sitting room.

Serving international cuisine, the Banana Tree Grille is our favorite restaurant here (see "Dining," below).

Bluebeard's Hill (P.O. Box 7480), Charlotte Amalie, St. Thomas, U.S.V.I. 00801. © **800/524-6599** in the U.S., or 340/774-1600. Fax 340/774-5134. www.equivest.com. 170 units. Winter $169–$275 double. Off-season $129–$200 double. Extra person $25. AE, DISC, MC, V. **Amenities:** 3 restaurants, bar; pool; 2 tennis courts; fitness center. *In room:* A/C, TV, hair dryer.

Bolongo Beach Club ⋆ *Value*   This is an unpretentious, barefoot kind of place. You'll find a half-moon-shaped white-sand beach and a cluster of pink two- and three-story buildings, plus some motel-like units closer to the sands. There's also a social center consisting of a smallish pool and a beachfront bar, replete with palm fronds. It's a relatively small property, but it offers all the facilities of a big resort. Many guests check in on the continental plan, which includes breakfast; others opt for all-inclusive plans that include all meals, drinks, a sailboat excursion to St. John, and use of scuba equipment. Rooms are simple, summery, and filled with unremarkable but comfortable furniture. Each unit has its own balcony or patio, a refrigerator, and one king-size or two double beds, plus tiled, shower-only bathrooms. Some of the units on the beach come with kitchenettes. Villas, in a three-story building are apartment-style condos with full kitchens.

7150 Bolongo, St. Thomas, U.S.V.I. 00802. © **800/524-4746** or 340/775-1800. Fax 340/775-3208. www. bolongo.com. 75 units, 20 villas. Winter $245 double with no meals; $450 all-inclusive double; $245 studio villa; $295 1-bedroom villa; $345 2-bedroom villa. Off-season $145 double with no meals; $350 all-inclusive double; $175–$190 studio villa; $195–$225 1-bedroom villa; $245–$265 2-bedroom villa. Ask about packages and various meal plans. AE, MC, V. **Amenities:** 2 restaurants, 2 bars; 3 pools; 2 tennis courts; fitness center; dive shop; scuba diving; snorkeling; boating, windsurfing, deep-sea fishing; babysitting. *In room:* A/C, TV, fridge, coffeemaker, hair dryer, safe.

Elysian Beach Resort ⋆   This time-share resort on Cowpet Bay in the east end, a 20-minute drive from Charlotte Amalie, is imbued with a certain European Resort chic. The beautiful white-sand beach is the most compelling reason

---

Tips Renting a Condo, an Apartment, or a Villa

Sometimes you can make a deal on a moderately priced condo, apartment, or villa. We've found that **Calypso Realty** (© **800/747-4858** or 340/774-1620; www.calypsorealty.com) has the best offers, especially on rentals from April to mid-December. A condo overlooking St. John often goes for $800 and up per week.

Another source to check is **McLaughlin Anderson Vacations Ltd.** (© **800/666-6246** or 340/776-0635; www.mclaughlinanderson.com), which has rentals not only on St. Thomas, but on St. John and St. Croix as well. A two-bedroom villa begins at $1,600 per week in winter, with off-season rates at $1,200.

You can also contact **Paradise Properties of St. Thomas** (© **800/ 524-2038** or 340/779-1540; fax 340/779-6109; www.st-thomas.com/ paradiseproperties), which currently represents six condo complexes. Rental units range from studio apartments to four-bedroom villas suitable for up to eight people; each has a fully equipped kitchen. A minimum stay of 3 days is required in any season, and 7 nights around Christmas. The prices range from $175 to $535 per day in winter and from $125 to $445 per day in the off-season.

to stay here. Also stay here if you seek tranquility and seclusion without all the razzle-dazzle of other east end competitors. The thoughtfully planned bedrooms contain balconies, and 14 offer sleeping lofts that are reached by a spiral staircase. The decor is tropical, with rattan and bamboo furnishings, ceiling fans, and natural-wood ceilings. The rooms are in a bevy of four-story buildings connected to landscaped gardens. Of the various units, 43 can be converted into one-bedroom suites, 43 into two-bedroom suites, and 11 into three-bedroom suites. Designer fabrics and white ceramic-tile floors make the tropical living quite grand. Try to avoid rooms in buildings V, W, X, Y, and Z, as they are some distance from the beach. Each unit has a full, tiled bathroom.

6800 Estate Nazareth, Cowpet Bay, St. Thomas, U.S.V.I. 00802. © **800/524-6599** or 340/775-1000. Fax 340/776-0910. www.equivest.com. 180 units. Winter $169–$199 double; $269 suite. Off-season $139–$159 double; $209 suite. AE, DC, DISC, MC, V. **Amenities:** 2 restaurants, 2 bars; pool; tennis court; fitness center; snorkeling gear, canoes, Sunfish sailboats; massage; laundry/dry cleaning; open-air shuttle to town. *In room:* A/C, TV, safe.

Point Pleasant Resort ★   This is a very private, unique resort on Water Bay, on the northeastern tip of St. Thomas, just a 5-minute walk from lovely Stouffer's Beach. These condo units, which are rented when their owners are not in residence, are set on a 15-acre (6-hectare) bluff with flowering shrubbery, century plants, frangipani trees, secluded nature trails, old rock formations, and lookout points. The villa-style accommodations have light and airy furnishings, mostly rattan and floral fabrics. They all have full kitchens with microwaves and full bathrooms. Beds are very comfortable with fine linen. From your living room, you'll have a gorgeous view over Tortola, St. John, and Jost Van Dyke.

The restaurant, Agavé Terrace, is one of the finest on the island. The cuisine, featuring seafood, is a blend of nouvelle American dishes and Caribbean specialties. Local entertainment is provided Tuesday and Thursday night.

6600 Estate Smith Bay, St. Thomas, U.S.V.I. 00802. © **800/777-1700** or 340/775-7200. Fax 340/776-5694. www.pointpleasantresort.com. 64 units. Winter $255–$275 junior or superior suite; $355 deluxe suite; $529 2-bedroom suite. Off-season $180–$195 junior or superior suite; $255 deluxe suite; $355 2-bedroom suite. Ask about package deals. Children under age 12 stay free in parents' room. AE, DC, DISC, MC, V. **Amenities:** 2 restaurants, 2 bars; 3 pools; tennis courts; fitness center; laundry. *In room:* A/C, TV, coffeemaker, hair dryer, iron and ironing board, safe.

Secret Harbour Beach Resort ★ *Kids*   This all-suites combo resort is on the stunning white-sand beach at Nazareth Bay, just outside Red Hook Marina. All four contemporary buildings have southwestern exposure (great for sunsets), and each unit has a private deck or patio. You'll be just steps from the sand, and great snorkeling is right offshore. There are three types of accommodations: studio apartments, one-bedroom suites, and two-bedroom suites. Each studio apartment has a bedroom/sitting-room area, patio, and dressing-room area; each one-bedroom suite has a living/dining area, a separate bedroom, and a sundeck; and each luxurious two-bedroom suite has two bathrooms with shower/tub combinations and a private living room. Honeymooners are likely to show up in the winter months. In summer this is a family-friendly place, as children under 12 stay free.

6280 Estate Nazareth, Nazareth Bay, St. Thomas, U.S.V.I. 00802. © **800/524-2250** or 340/775-6550. Fax 340/775-1501. www.secretharbourvi.com. 60 units. Winter $255–$295 studio double; $275–$345 1-bedroom suite; $455–$555 2-bedroom suite. Off-season $135–$195 studio double; $179–$219 1-bedroom suite; $279–$329 2-bedroom suite. AE, MC, V. **Amenities:** Restaurant, bar; pool; 4 tennis courts; fitness center; Jacuzzi; dive shop, snorkeling, windsurfing; massage; babysitting. *In room:* A/C, TV, kitchen, fridge, coffeemaker, hair dryer, safe.

MODERATE/INEXPENSIVE

Galleon House   The rates at Galleon House are among the most competitive around, so if you don't mind a place operated without state-of-the-art maintenance and a staff attitude many readers have complained about, this is a good place to stay. You walk up a long flight of stairs to reach a concrete terrace that doubles as the reception area. The small rooms are in scattered hillside buildings, each with a ceiling fan, a firm mattress, and so-so air-conditioning, plus a cramped shower-only bath. Breakfast is served on a veranda overlooking the harbor, and Magens Beach is 15 minutes by car or taxi from the hotel.

Government Hill Pl. (P.O. Box 6577), Charlotte Amalie, St. Thomas, U.S.V.I. ℂ **800/524-2052** in the U.S., or 340/774-6952. Fax 340/774-6952. www.galleonhouse.com. 14 units, 12 with bathroom. Winter $79 double without bathroom; $99–$129 double with bathroom. Off-season $59 double without bathroom; $89 double with bathroom. Rates include continental breakfast. AE, DISC, MC, V. **Amenities:** Bar; pool; laundry. *In room:* A/C, TV.

Hotel 1829 ⋆   This national historic site is one of the leading small hotels in the Caribbean. It was designed by an Italian architect in a Spanish motif, with French grillwork, Danish bricks, and sturdy Dutch doors. Danish and African labor completed the structure in 1829 (hence the name), and since then it has entertained the likes of Edna St. Vincent Millay and Mikhail Baryshnikov. The place stands right in the heart of town, on a hillside 3 minutes from Government House. Magens Bay Beach is about a 15-minute drive or taxi ride away. It's a bit of a climb to the top of this multitiered structure—note that there are many steps, but no elevator. Amid a cascade of flowering bougainvillea are the upper rooms, which overlook a central courtyard that has a miniature pool. The rooms in the main house are well designed and attractive, and most face the water. All have old island decor, such as wood beams and stone walls. The smallest units, in the former slave quarters, are the least comfortable. Each unit has a small, tiled bathroom with a shower stall. One of the most historic restaurants on St. Thomas is located here (see "Dining," below).

Kongens Gade (P.O. Box 1567), Charlotte Amalie, St. Thomas, U.S.V.I. 00804. ℂ **800/524-2002** in the U.S., or 340/776-1829. Fax 340/776-4313. www.hotel1829.com. 15 units. Winter $100–$180 double; from $225 suite. Off-season $75–$135 double; from $670 suite. Rates include continental breakfast. AE, DISC, MC, V. **Amenities:** Restaurant, bar; pool; laundry. *In room:* A/C, TV, fridge.

Island View Guesthouse ⋆ *Value*   The casual Island View is located in a hilly neighborhood of private homes and villas about a 7-minute drive west of Charlotte Amalie and a 20-minute drive from the nearest beach, at Magens Bay. Set 545 feet (164m) up Crown Mountain, it has sweeping views over Charlotte Amalie and the harbor. It contains main-floor rooms (two without private bathrooms) and some poolside rooms, plus six units in a recent addition (three with kitchens and all with balconies). The bedrooms are cooled by breezes and fans, and the newer ones have air-conditioning; each has a shower-only bathroom. Furnishings are very basic, but the price is right. A self-service, open-air bar on the gallery operates on the honor system. A terrace, with gorgeous views, is the site for breakfast each morning and cocktails in the evening. The staff will help you arrange all kinds of outings and excursions.

11-C Contant (P.O. Box 1903), Charlotte Amalie, St. Thomas, U.S.V.I. 00803. ℂ **800/524-2023** for reservations only, or 340/774-4270. Fax 340/774-6167. www.st-thomas.com/islandviewguesthouse. 15 units (13 with private bathroom). Winter $77 double without bathroom; $110 double with bathroom; $115 suite. Off-season $55 double without bathroom; $80 double with bathroom; $90 suite. Rates include continental breakfast. AE, MC, V. From the airport, turn right onto Rte. 30; then cut left and continue to the unmarked Scott Free Rd., where you turn left; look for the sign. No children under age 14. **Amenities:** Pool; laundry. *In room:* Ceiling fan, TV.

Villa Blanca ★ *(Value)*   Small, intimate, and charming, this hotel lies east of Charlotte Amalie on 3 secluded acres (1 hectare) of hilltop land, among the most panoramic areas on the island, with views over the harbor and the green rolling hills. The hotel's main building served as the private home of its present owner, Blanca Terrasa Smith, between 1973 and 1985. After the death of her husband, Mrs. Smith added a 12-room annex in the garden and opened her grounds to paying guests. Today, a homey and caring ambience prevails. Each room contains tile floors, a ceiling fan and/or air-conditioning, a shower-only tiled bathroom, a well-equipped kitchenette, and a private balcony or terrace with sweeping views either eastward to St. John or westward to Puerto Rico and the harbor of Charlotte Amalie. No meals are served. On the premises are a freshwater pool and a large covered patio where you can enjoy the sunset. The closest beach is Morning Star Bay, about a 4-mile (6km) drive away.

4 Raphune Hill, Rte. 38, Charlotte Amalie, St. Thomas, U.S.V.I. 00801. © 800/231-0034 in the U.S., or 340/776-0749. Fax 340/779-2661. www.st-thomas.com/villablanca. 14 units. Winter $115–$145 double. Off-season $75–$115 double. Rates include continental breakfast. AE, DC, MC, V. **Amenities:** Pool; sport-fishing; laundry. *In room:* A/C, ceiling fan, TV, kitchenette.

Villa Santana ★   This unique country villa is an all-suites property. It was originally built by Gen. Antonio Lopez de Santa Anna of Mexico in the 1850s. It offers a panoramic view of Charlotte Amalie and the St. Thomas harbor. The shopping district in Charlotte Amalie is just a 5-minute walk away, and Magens Beach is a 15-minute drive. Guest rooms are located at La Mansion, the former library of the general; La Terraza, originally the wine cellar; La Cocina de Santa Anna, once the central kitchen for the entire estate; La Casa de Piedra, once the bedroom of the general's most trusted attaché; and La Torre, the old pump house that has been converted into a modern lookout tower. All rooms have fully equipped kitchens and tiled shower-only bathrooms. The Mexican decor features clay tiles, rattan furniture, and stonework. The property has a pool, sundeck, and small garden with hibiscus and bougainvillea.

Denmark Hill, Charlotte Amalie, St. Thomas, U.S.V.I. 00802. © and fax **340/776-1311**. www.st-thomas.com/villasantana. 8 units. Winter $125–$195 suite for 2. Off-season $85–$135 suite for 2. AE, MC, V. **Amenities:** Pool. *In room:* Ceiling fan, TV, kitchen, no phone.

DINING

The St. Thomas dining scene these days is among the best in the West Indies, but it has its drawbacks. Fine dining, and even not-so-fine dining, tends to be expensive, and the best spots (with a few exceptions) are not right in Charlotte Amalie, and thus can only be reached by taxi or car.

IN CHARLOTTE AMALIE

If you must go, the local branch of the **Hard Rock Café** chain is at the International Plaza, the Waterfront (© **340/777-5555**). It features live music on Friday and Saturday nights.

Banana Tree Grille INTERNATIONAL   This place offers candlelit dinners, sweeping views over the busy harbor, and a decor that includes genuine banana plants artfully scattered through the two dining rooms. The cuisine is creative, the patrons are often hip and laid-back. Start with one of the aptly named "fabulous firsts," such as bacon-wrapped horseradish shrimp grilled and dancing over mango glaze. Main dishes are filled with flavor, especially the house specialties: lobster tail tempura with orange sambal sauce or mango-mustard–glazed salmon. Try the aïoli shank, a house specialty, if it's offered: The shank of lamb is slowly braised in Chianti and served with aïoli sauce over white beans and garlic mashed potatoes. The desserts are truly decadent.

In Bluebeard's Castle, Bluebeard's Hill. © **340/776-4050**. Reservations recommended. Main courses $16–$31. AE, MC, V. Tues–Sun 6–9:30pm.

Beni Iguana's Sushi Bar JAPANESE   It's the only Japanese restaurant on St. Thomas, a change of pace from the Caribbean, steak, and seafood choices nearby. Along with a handful of shops, it occupies the sheltered courtyard and an old cistern across from Emancipation Square Park. You can eat outside or pass through wide Danish colonial doors into a red-and-black-lacquered interior devoted to a sushi bar and a handful of simple tables. A perennial favorite is the "13" roll, stuffed with spicy crabmeat, salmon, lettuce, cucumbers, and scallions.

In the Grand Hotel Court, Veteran's Dr. © **340/777-8744**. Reservations recommended. Sushi $4–$15 per portion (2 pieces); main courses $8–$17; combo plates for 4 to 5 diners $25.50–$35.50 each. AE, MC, V. Mon–Sat 11:30am–9:30pm.

Blackbeard Castle's Restaurant ★★   CONTINENTAL/ASIAN   Here you can enjoy "tower dining," eating while taking in the most stunning view of the port of Charlotte Amalie. The castle's open-air tower has been turned into the setting for a romantic gourmet dinner. It is said that the pirate Blackbeard once kept watch for invaders from this tower. Chefs roam the world for inspiration, and try to pack a lot of flavor into every dish without destroying an item's natural goodness. Try the orange and sugar cane–marinated duck with mashed sweet potatoes, or dig into the grilled tuna ancho with chile and tomatillo sauces. Those old American favorites such as filet mignon or stuffed Caribbean lobster appear on the menu, but we gravitate more to the red snapper baked with nut crust.

In Blackbeard's Castle, Blackbeard's Hill. © **340/776-1234**. Reservations needed 1 week in advance. Main courses $19–$28. AE, MC, V. Daily 11am–2pm; Mon–Sat 6–10pm.

Hervé Restaurant & Wine Bar ★   AMERICAN/CARIBBEAN/FRENCH This is the hottest restaurant on St. Thomas, surpassing all the competition in town, including its next-door neighbor, the Hotel 1829. A panoramic view of Charlotte Amalie and a historic setting are minor benefits—it's the cuisine that matters here. Hervé P. Chassin, whose experience has embraced such stellar properties as the Hotel du Cap d'Antibes, is a restaurateur with a vast classical background. Here in his own unpretentious setting, he offers high-quality food at reasonable prices.

There are two dining areas: a large open-air terrace and a more intimate wine room. Contemporary American dishes are served with the best of classic France, along with Caribbean touches. Start with the pistachio-encrusted brie, shrimp in a stuffed crab shell, or conch fritters with mango chutney. From here, you can let your taste buds march boldly forward with red snapper poached with white wine, or a delectable black-sesame-crusted tuna with a ginger/raspberry sauce. Well-prepared nightly specials of game, fish, and pasta are features. Desserts here are equally divine—you'll rarely taste a creamier crème caramel or a lighter, fluffier mango or raspberry cheesecake.

Next to Hotel 1829, Government Hill. © **340/777-9703**. Reservations requested. Main courses $5.50–$16.50 at lunch, $19–$26 at dinner. AE, MC, V. Daily 11am–3pm and 6–10pm.

Hotel 1829 ★   CONTINENTAL/CARIBBEAN   This restaurant is graceful and historic, and it serves some of the finest food on St. Thomas. Guests head for the attractive bar for cocktails before being seated on a 19th-century terrace or in the main room, with walls made from ships' ballast and a floor crafted from

200-year-old Moroccan tiles. The constantly changing menu has a distinctively European twist, with many dishes prepared and served from trolleys beside your table. This is one of the few places in town that serves the finest caviar; other appetizers include goat-cheese bruschetta with roasted-red-pepper hummus. A ragout of swordfish is made more inviting with pine-nut/basil pesto, and the sautéed snapper in brown butter is always a reliable choice. Mint-flavored roast rack of lamb and chateaubriand for two are other possibilities.

In Hotel 1829, Kongens Gade (at the east end of Main St.). *(C)* **340/776-1829.** Reservations recommended, but not accepted more than 1 day in advance. Fixed-price dinner $50–$75. AE, DISC, MC, V. Daily 6–10pm. Closed Jun 1–Dec 1.

Virgilio's ✰ NORTHERN ITALIAN   Virgilio's is the best northern Italian restaurant in the Virgin Islands. Its neobaroque interior is sheltered under heavy ceiling beams and brick vaulting. A well-trained staff attends to the tables. Owner Virgilio del Mare serves meals against a backdrop of stained-glass windows, crystal chandeliers, and soft Italian music. The *cinco peche* (clams, mussels, scallops, oysters, and crayfish simmered in a saffron broth) is a delectable house special, while the alfredo fettuccine here is the best there is. Classic dishes are served with a distinctive flair—the rack of lamb, for example, is filled with a porcini mushroom stuffing and glazed with a roasted garlic aïoli. The marinated grilled duck is served chilled. You can even order an individual margarita pizza.

18 Dronningens Gade (entrance on a narrow alley running between Main St. and Back St.). *(C)* **340/776-4920.** Reservations recommended. Main courses $11–$23 at lunch, $16–$35 at dinner. AE, MC, V. Mon–Sat 11am–10:30pm.

IN FRENCHTOWN

Alexander's ✰ AUSTRIAN/ITALIAN/SEAFOOD   West of Charlotte Amalie, this restaurant offers 12 tables in air-conditioned comfort, with picture windows overlooking the harbor. There's a heavy emphasis on seafood, plus an increasing Italian slant to the menu. If available the bacon-wrapped chicken breast stuffed with spinach and Swiss cheese is prepared to perfection, as is the pan-seared herb-crusted lamb tenderloin with a mint port sauce. At lunch, you can enjoy marinated tuna steak or penne in a basil pesto cream sauce, or go for one of the sandwiches, such as a veggie burger. The top dish, however, is the seafood pasta with an array of mussels, shrimp, clams, crab, and fresh fish. The vegetarian spring rolls are mouthwateringly good.

Rue de St. Barthélemy. *(C)* **340/776-4211.** Reservations recommended. Main courses $12–$20 at lunch, $16–$27 at dinner. AE, MC, V. Mon–Sat 11:30am–3pm and 5:30–10pm.

Craig & Sally's ✰ INTERNATIONAL   This Caribbean cafe is set in an airy, open-sided pavilion in Frenchtown. Its eclectic cuisine is, according to the owner, "passionate" and "not for the faint of heart, but for the adventurous soul." Views of the sky and sea are complemented by a cuisine that ranges from pasta to seafood, with influences from Europe and Asia. Roast pork with clams, filet mignon with macadamia-nut sauce, and grilled swordfish with a sauce of fresh herbs and tomatoes are examples from a menu that changes every day. The lobster-stuffed, twice-baked potatoes are inspired. The wine list is the most extensive and sophisticated on St. Thomas.

22 Honduras. *(C)* **340/777-9949.** Reservations recommended. Main courses $15–$28. AE, MC, V. Wed–Fri 11:30am–3pm; Wed–Sun 5:30–10pm.

The Pointe at Villa Olga STEAKS/SEAFOOD   This upscale restaurant is known for serving the finest cut of prime rib on island. But it also features grilled seafood, which on occasion is even better. The stripped-down 19th-century villa that contains the Chart House was the Russian consulate during the island's Danish administration. It lies a short distance beyond the most densely populated area of Frenchtown village. The dining gallery is a spacious open terrace fronting the sea. Cocktails start daily at 5pm, when the bartender breaks out the ingredients for his special Bailey's banana colada. Calamari, pasta dishes, coconut shrimp, and Hawaiian chicken are part of the expanded menu. For dessert, order the famous mud pie.

Villa Olga. ✆ **340/774-4262.** Reservations recommended. Main courses $17–$29; fixed-price menu $19.95. AE, DC, MC, V. Daily 6–10pm.

ON THE NORTH COAST

The Old Stone Farmhouse AMERICAN/INTERNATIONAL   Set in a wooded valley, close to the 11th hole of the Mahogany Run Golf Course, this restaurant dates from the 1750s. Once it was a stable for a nearby Danish sugar plantation, with walls more than 2 feet (.6km) thick. Ceiling fans and breezes blowing through the valley keep the place cool. For more than a quarter of a century, it has been feeding golfers and those who love them from an eclectic menu that is rotated to take advantage of the best of a season's produce. Various fresh fish dishes are always the best option. Innovative items such as sushi have been added to the menu. Begin, perhaps, with snails in garlic butter or something trendier, such as grilled Portobello mushrooms with Asian duck. Of course, many of the regulars come here for a well-prepared steak.

Mahogany Run. ✆ **340/777-6277.** Reservations recommended. Main courses $17–$29. AE, MC, V. Tues–Sun 5:30–10pm.

Romanos Restaurant ITALIAN   Located near Coral World, this hideaway is owned by New Jersey chef Tony Romano, who specializes in a flavorful and herb-laden cuisine that some diners yearn for after too much Caribbean cooking. House favorites include linguine con pesto, four-cheese lasagna, a tender and well-flavored osso buco, scaloppini Marsala, and broiled salmon. All desserts are made on the premises. This restaurant, marked by exposed brick and well-stocked wine racks, always seems full of happy, lively diners.

97 Smith Bay Rd. ✆ **340/775-0045.** Reservations recommended. Main courses $19–$30; pastas $14.95–$21. AE, MC, V. Mon–Sat. 6–10:30pm. Closed Aug and 1 week in Apr for Carnival. Take the Vitran bus.

IN & AROUND RED HOOK BAY (THE EAST END)

Agavé Terrace ✪ CARIBBEAN   Perched high above a steep and heavily forested hillside on the eastern tip of St. Thomas, this restaurant, one of the island's best, offers a sweeping panorama and unparalleled romance. The house drink is Desmond Delight, a combination of Midori, rum, pineapple juice, and a secret ingredient. After a few Delights, you may opt for the house appetizer: An Agavé sampler prepared for two, which includes portions of crabmeat, conch fritters, and shrimp cocktail. Six different types of fish turn up as catches of the day; they can be prepared in any of seven different ways, including grilled with a choice of nine different sauces. Some of the island's best steaks are served here, ranging from tenderloin to Kansas City strip. One dish after another delights, including red snapper with lobster medallions and jumbo prawns sautéed in garlic cream sauce with linguine. All diners are served with freshly baked breads and the house pasta or rice. There are also vegetarian selections. The wine list is extensive. A live steel drum band draws listeners Tuesday and Thursday nights.

In the Point Pleasant Resort, 6600 Estate Smith Bay, St. Thomas, U.S.V.I. 00802. ✆ **800/777-1700** or 340/775-4142. Reservations recommended. Main courses $18–$32. AE, MC, V. Daily 6–10pm.

Duffy's Love Shack ★ *Finds* AMERICAN/CARIBBEAN This is a fun and happening place where you can mingle with the locals. As the evening wears on, the customers become the entertainment, often dancing on tables or forming conga lines. Yes, Duffy's also serves food, standard American cuisine with Caribbean flair and flavor. The restaurant is open-air, with lots of bamboo and a thatched roof over the bar. Even the menu appears on a bamboo stick, like an old-fashioned fan. Start with a Caribbean egg roll or honey-barbecued ribs, then move on to cowboy steak or junkanoo chicken (in a coconut-and-pineapple sauce). Surf-and-turf here means jerk tenderloin and mahi-mahi. After 10pm, a late-night menu of mostly sandwiches appears. The bar business is huge, and the bartender is known for his lethal rum drinks.

650 Red Hook Plaza, Rte. 38. ✆ 340/779-2080. Main courses $8–$16. No credit cards. Daily 11:30am–2am.

The Frigate ★ AMERICAN/CARIBBEAN In the center of Red Hook, within the Game Fishing Building, this seaside restaurant manages to secure some of the best beef in the U.S. islands, as well as some of the freshest fish. As you dine overlooking the harbor at Red Hook and the island of St. John, your choice might be the fattest lobster caught that day or a steak on the level of The Palm in New York. Want something lighter? Make it chicken teriyaki. Hemingway clones opt for the grilled wahoo. The chefs amuse with a seafood kebab nightly. This is a spacious dining area with a nautical decor. Art on the walls—mainly seascapes—is for sale.

6501 Red Hook Plaza. ✆ 340/775-6124. Main courses $15–$30. AE, DC, MC, V. Daily 5:30–10:30pm.

Fungi's on the Beach CARIBBEAN Opening onto Pineapple Beach, this is a funky native bar. It's a lot of fun and the food is good too. Come here for some of the juiciest burgers on the island and the most delectable pizza. You can also order Caribbean specialties such as conch in butter sauce and roast suckling pig, along with such island favorites as johnnycakes, plantains, rice and beans, and callaloo soup. Stewed chicken is a local favorite. The place has an outdoorsy atmosphere with a reggae theme. Nightly entertainment—reggae and more reggae—is also a feature.

Point Pleasant. ✆ 340/775-7200. Main courses $8–$20. AE, MC, V. Daily 11:30am–10pm.

Molly Malone's IRISH/CARIBBEAN At the Red Hook American Yacht Harbour, you can join the good ol' boys and dig into the best baby back ribs on the island. If you're nostalgic for the Emerald Isle, go for the shepherd's pie. The conch fritters are also the best in the east end, and no one can drink more brew than the boisterous crowd that assembles here every night to let the good times roll. Begin with a bowl of savory conch chowder, and the night is yours. In one of the wildest culinary offerings we've seen lately, an "Irish/Caribbean stew" is a nightly feature. If the catch netted a big wahoo, those game fish steaks will be on the menu that night at Molly's. You can dine outdoors under a canopy on the dock at the eastern end of Red Hook where the ferry from St. John pulls in. The only time the place closes is when a hurricane comes along and blows it away.

6100 Red Hook Quarter. ✆ 340/775-1270. Main courses $15–$25. AE, MC, V. Daily 7am–1am.

Off the Hook ★ ASIAN/CARIBBEAN Diners enjoy an eclectic medley of specialties inspired by Asia, although the chefs concoct dishes using some of the freshest and finest ingredients of the West Indies. In an open-air dining room near the American Yacht Harbor, close to the departure point for the ferry to St. John, the fresh catch of the day—hauled off the little fishing boats just pulling in—is delivered to the kitchen where it's grilled to perfection. The yellow fin tuna keeps us coming back. The chef is also adept at preparing a tuna and salmon sushi platter. The black angus steak is always a pure delight. The decor is rustic, with outdoor dining and wooden tables.

6300 Estate Smith Bay. (© 340/775-6350. Reservations required. Main courses $16–$25. AE, MC, V. Daily 5:30–10pm. Closed Sept 15–Oct 15.

AT COMPASS POINT

Raffles ⭐ CONTINENTAL/SEAFOOD   Named after the legendary hotel in Singapore, this place is filled with South Seas accents. Peacock chairs and ceiling fans set the mood. We always look for the nightly specials, such as fresh West Indian–style fish (with tomato, garlic, and herbs). Starters might include sautéed conch and the lobster bisque. Everything is accompanied by homemade bread. The chef's marinated Portobello mushrooms with fresh baby vegetables in a balsamic reduction sauce is exquisite. The Thai curry chicken is a delight. One specialty rarely encountered in the Caribbean is beef Wellington in a delectable mushroom duxelle in puff pastry. The pièce de resistance is marinated duck, which is steamed, baked, and served with orange-ginger sauce.

6300 Frydenhoj, Compass Point, off Rte. 32 (a mile/2km west of Red Hook). (© 340/775-6004. Reservations recommended. Main courses $20–$29. AE, MC, V. Tues–Sun 5:30–10:30pm.

HITTING THE BEACH

Chances are your hotel will be right on the beach, or very close to one. All the beaches in the Virgin Islands are public, and most lie anywhere from 2 to 5 miles (3 –8km) from Charlotte Amalie.

THE NORTH SIDE   The gorgeous white sands of **Magens Bay** ⭐⭐ lie between two mountains 3 miles (5km) north of the capital. *Condé Nast Traveler* named this beach one of the world's 10 most beautiful. The turquoise waters here are calm and ideal for swimming, though the snorkeling isn't as good. The beach is no secret, and it's usually terribly overcrowded, though it gets better in the mid-afternoon. Changing facilities, snorkeling gear, lounge chairs, paddleboats, and kayaks are available. There is no public transportation to get here (though some hotels provide shuttle buses); from Charlotte Amalie, take Route 35 north all the way. The gates to the beach are open daily from 6am to 6pm (after 4pm, you'll need insect repellent). Admission is $1 per person and $1 per car. Don't bring valuables, and certainly don't leave anything of value in your parked car.

A marked trail leads to **Little Magens Bay,** a separate, clothing-optional, beach that is especially popular with gay and lesbian visitors. This is also former president Clinton's preferred beach on St. Thomas (no, he doesn't go nude).

Coki Point Beach, in the northeast near Coral World, is good but often very crowded. It's noted for its warm, crystal-clear water, ideal for swimming and snorkeling (you'll see thousands of rainbow-hued fish swimming among the beautiful corals). Locals even sell small bags of fish food, so you can feed the sea creatures while you're snorkeling. From the beach, there's a panoramic view of offshore Thatch Cay. Concessions can arrange everything from water-skiing to parasailing. An East end bus runs to Smith Bay and lets you off at the gate to Coral World and Coki. Watch out for pickpockets.

Also on the north side is luscious **Renaissance Grand Beach,** one of the island's most beautiful. It opens onto Smith Bay and is near Coral World. Many watersports are available here. The beach is right off Route 38.

THE EAST END   Small and special, **Secret Harbour** is near a collection of condos. With its white sand and coconut palms, it's the epitome of Caribbean charm. The snorkeling near the rocks is some of the best on the island. No public

⌢ Moments   Two Great Escapes

Water Island, ¾ mile (.2km) off the coast from the harbor of Charlotte Amalie, is the fourth largest island of the U.S. Virgins, with 500 acres (200 hectares) of land. At palm-shaded **Honeymoon Beach,** you can swim, snorkel, sail, water ski, or sunbathe, then order lunch or a drink from the beach bar. A ferry runs between Crown Bay Marina and Water Island several times a day. (Crown Bay Marina, ℂ **340/774-2255,** is part of the St. Thomas submarine base.)

In the same bay, and even closer to shore, is **Hassel Island.** It's almost completely deserted, and it is protected as part of a U.S. National Park. There are no hotels or services of any kind here, and swimming is limited to narrow, rocky beaches. Even so, many visitors hire a boat to drop them off for an hour or two. A hike along part of the shoreline is a welcome relief from the cruise-ship congestion of Charlotte Amalie. Bring water and food if you plan to spend more than 3 hours here. A ferry service at Crown Bay Marina (see above) makes the trip here as well.

---

transportation stops here, but it's an easy taxi ride east of Charlotte Amalie heading toward Red Hook.

Sapphire Beach is set against the backdrop of the Doubletree Sapphire Beach Resort and Marina, where you can have lunch or order drinks. There are good views of offshore cays and St. John, a large reef is close to the shore, and windsurfers like this beach a lot. Snorkeling gear and lounge chairs can be rented. Take the East end bus from Charlotte Amalie, going via Red Hook. Ask to be let off at the entrance to Sapphire Bay; it's not too far to walk from here to the water.

White-sand **Lindquist Beach** isn't a long strip, but it's one of the island's prettiest. It's between Wyndham Sugar Bay Beach Club and the Sapphire Beach Resort. Many films and TV commercials have used this photogenic beach as a backdrop. It's not likely to be crowded, as it's not very well known.

THE SOUTH SIDE   Morning Star Beach (also known as Frenchman's Bay Beach) is near the Marriott Frenchman's Reef Beach Resort, about 2 miles (3km) east of Charlotte Amalie. Here, among the often-young crowds (many of whom are gay), you can don your skimpiest bikini. Sailboats, snorkeling equipment, and lounge chairs are available for rent. The beach is easily reached by a cliff-front elevator at Frenchman's Reef.

Limetree Beach, set against a backdrop of sea-grape trees and shady palms, lures those who want a serene spread of sand where they can bask in the sun and even feed hibiscus blossoms to iguanas. Snorkeling gear, lounge and beach chairs, towels, and drinks are available. There's no public transportation, but the beach can easily be reached by taxi from Charlotte Amalie.

WEST OF CHARLOTTE AMALIE   Near the University of the Virgin Islands in the southwest, **Brewer's Bay** is one of the island's most popular beaches. The strip of white coral sand is almost as long as the beach at Magens Bay. Unfortunately, this isn't the place for snorkeling. Vendors sell light meals and drinks. From Charlotte Amalie, take the Fortuna bus heading west; get off at the edge of Brewers Bay, across from the Reichhold Center.

Lindbergh Beach, which has a lifeguard, restrooms, and a bathhouse, lies at the Island Beachcomber Hotel and is used almost exclusively by locals, who sometimes stage political rallies here, as well as Carnival parties. It's not good for snorkeling. Drinks are served on the beach. Take the Fortuna bus route west from Charlotte Amalie.

SPORTS & OTHER OUTDOOR PURSUITS

DEEP-SEA FISHING The U.S. Virgins have excellent deep-sea fishing—some 19 world records (8 for blue marlin) have been set in these waters in recent years. Outfitters abound at the major marinas like Red Hook. We recommend angling off the *Fish Hawk* (© 340/775-9058), which Captain Al Petrosky sails out of Fish Hawk Marina Lagoon on the East end. His 43-foot (13m) diesel-powered craft is fully equipped with rods and reels. All equipment (but not meals) is included in the price: $550 per half day for up to six passengers. Full-day excursions start at $1,000.

GOLF **Mahogany Run,** on the north shore at Mahogany Run Road (© 800/253-7103), is an 18-hole, par-70 course. This beautiful course rises and drops like a roller coaster on its journey to the sea; cliffs and crashing sea waves are the ultimate hazards at the 13th and 14th holes. Former president Clinton pronounced this course very challenging. Greens fees are $115 for 18 holes, reduced to $90 in the late afternoon. Carts are included. Club rental costs $35.

SAILING ★★ **American Yacht Harbor** ★★, Red Hook (© 800/736-7294 or 340/775-6454), offers both bareboat and fully crewed charters. It leaves from a colorful yacht-filled harbor set against a backdrop of Heritage Gade, a reproduction of a Caribbean village. The harbor is home to numerous boat companies, including day-trippers, fishing boats, and sailing charters. There are also five restaurants on the property, serving everything from continental to Caribbean cuisine. Another reliable outfitter is **Charteryacht League** ★★, at Crown Bay Marina (© 800/524-2061 in the U.S., or 340/774-3944).

Sailors may want to check out the *Yachtsman's Guide to the Virgin Islands*, available at major marine outlets, at bookstores, through catalog merchandisers, or directly from **Tropic Isle Publishers,** P.O. Box 610938, North Miami, FL 33261-0938 (© 305/893-4277). This annual guide, which costs $15.95, is supplemented by sketch charts, photographs, and landfall sketches and charts showing harbors and harbor entrances, anchorages, channels, and landmarks, plus information on preparations necessary for cruising the islands.

⟅Finds Hidden Beach Discoveries

At this point you'd think all the beaches of overrun St. Thomas had been destroyed. But there are two less trampled strands of sand we recently came upon. A sparkling beach of white sand, **Vessup Bay,** is found at the end of Bluebeard's Road (Route 322) as it branches off Route 30 near the hamlet of Red Hook. Against a rocky backdrop, the beach curves around a pristine bay studded with vegetation including cacti, agave plants, and seagrape. One end of the beach is less populated than the other. A watersports concessionaire operates here. Another find is **Hull Bay,** on the north shore, just west of Magens Bay, which is overpopulated these days with cruise-ship passengers. Surfers are attracted to the waves along the western tip of Hull Bay, and local St. Thomas fishermen anchor in the more tranquil strands. Part of the beach is in shade. Don't expect much in watersports, but there is a combined restaurant and open-air bar.

> ### *Moments* Bringing Out the Sir Francis Drake in You
>
> Tired of escorted tours? **Nauti Nymph Powerboat Rentals,** American Yacht Harbor, Red Hook (© **800/734-7345** in the U.S., or 340/775-5066), reaches out to the independent traveler and adventurer. The knowing staff here will assist in designing your personal itinerary for a bare-boat rental, or can hook you up with a captained day trip if you've been doing well in the stock market. A choice of Coast Guard–approved and fully equipped vessels ranging in size from 25 to 29 feet (9m) await you as you become your own mariner. Boats are kept in top-of-the-line condition. On your own you can explore the British Virgin Islands, including such little-known islands as Jost van Dyke and Norman Island, in the tradition of Sir Francis Drake. Norman Island, incidentally, was the inspiration for Robert Louis Stevenson's *Treasure Island.*

SCUBA DIVING   The best scuba diving site off St. Thomas, especially for novices, has to be **Cow and Calf Rocks,** off the southeast end (45 minutes from Charlotte Amalie by boat); here you'll discover a network of coral tunnels riddled with caves, reefs, and ancient boulders encrusted with coral. The *Cartanser Sr.,* a sunken World War II cargo ship that lies in about 35 feet (11m) of water, is beautifully encrusted with coral and now home to a myriad of colorful resident fish. Another popular wreck dive is the *Maj. General Rogers,* the stripped-down hull of a former Coast Guard cutter.

Experienced divers may want to dive at exposed sheer rock pinnacles like **Sail Rock** and **French Cap Pinnacle,** which are encrusted with hard and soft corals and frequented by lobsters and green and hawksbill turtles. They are also exposed to open-ocean currents that can make these very challenging dives.

St. Thomas Diving Club, 7147 Bolongo Bay (© **877/LETTSDIVE** in the U.S., or 340/776-2381), is a full-service, PADI five-star IDC center, the best on the island. An open-water certification course, including four scuba dives, costs $385. An advanced open-water certification course, including five dives that can be accomplished in 2 days, goes for $275. On request, participants are taken on an all-day scuba excursion that includes a two-tank dive to the wreck of the **HMS *Rhone*** in the British Virgin Islands; the trip costs $130. A scuba tour of the 350-foot (105m) wreck of the *Witshoal* is offered every Saturday for experienced divers only; the cost is $80. You can also enjoy local snorkeling for $30.

DIVE IN!, in the Sapphire Beach Resort & Marina, Smith Bay Road, Route 36 (© **800/524-2090** in the U.S., or 340/775-6100), is a well-recommended, complete diving center that offers some of the finest services in the U.S. Virgin Islands, including professional instruction (beginner to advanced), daily beach and boat dives, custom dive packages, underwater photography and videotapes, snorkeling trips, and a full-service PADI dive center. An introductory course costs $65, with a one-tank dive going for $55, two-tank dives for $75. A six-dive pass costs $203.

SEA KAYAKING   Virgin Island Ecotours (© **340/779-2155**) offers 2½-hour kayak trips through a mangrove lagoon on the southern coastline. The cost is $50 per person. The tour is led by professional naturalists who allow enough time for 30 minutes of snorkeling.

SNORKELING ★★ With 30 spectacular reefs just off St. Thomas, this is a spectacular destination for snorkeling. We like the waters off **Coki Point** ★★, on the northeast shore of St. Thomas; especially enticing are the coral ledges near Coral World's underwater tower. **Magens Bay** also has great snorkeling year-round. If your hotel doesn't provide snorkel gear, it's easy to rent on most of the island's popular beaches.

You may also want to take a snorkeling cruise. Many leave from the Red Hook and Yacht Haven marinas. The 50-foot (15m) *Yacht Nightwind,* Sapphire Marina (© **340/775-4110,** 24 hours a day), offers full-day sails to St. John and the outer islands. The $100 price includes a continental breakfast, a champagne buffet lunch, and an open bar aboard. You're also given free snorkeling equipment and instruction.

New Horizons, 6501 Red Hook Plaza, Suite 16, Red Hook (© **340/ 775-1171**), offers wind-borne excursions amid the cays and reefs of the Virgin Islands. The two-masted, 63-foot (19m) ketch has circumnavigated the globe and has been used as a design prototype for other boats. Owned and operated by Canadian Tim Krygsveld, it contains a hot-water shower, serves a specialty drink called a New Horizons Nooner (with a melon-liqueur base), and carries a complete line of snorkeling equipment for adults and children. A full-day excursion, with an Italian buffet lunch and an open bar, costs $100 per person. Children age 2 to 12, when accompanied by an adult, pay $55. Excursions depart daily, weather permitting, from the Sapphire Beach Resort & Marina. Call ahead for reservations and information. New Horizons has another vessel, *New Horizons II,* a 44-foot (13m) custom-made speedboat that takes you on a full-day trip to some of the most scenic highlights of the British Virgin Islands, costing $120 for adults or $95 for children age 2 to 12.

You can avoid the crowds by sailing aboard the *Fantasy,* 6700 Sapphire Village, no. 253 (© **340/775-5652;** fax 340/775-6256), which departs from the American Yacht Harbor at Red Hook at 9:30am daily. It takes a maximum of six passengers to St. John and nearby islands for swimming, snorkeling, beachcombing, and trolling. Snorkel gear with expert instruction is provided, as is a champagne lunch; an underwater camera is available. The full-day trip costs $100 per person. A half-day sail, morning or afternoon, lasts 3 hours and costs $65. Sunset tours are also popular, with an open bar and hors d'oeuvres, costing $60 per person.

TENNIS The best tennis on the island is at the **Wyndham Sugar Bay Beach Club** ★★, 6500 Estate Smith Bay (© **340/777-7100**), which has the Virgin Islands' first stadium tennis court, seating 220, plus six additional Laykold courts lit at night. The cost is $10 an hour for nonguests of the hotel. There's also a pro shop.

Another good resort for tennis is the **Bolongo Bay Beach Resort,** Bolongo Bay (© **340/775-1800**), which has two courts that are lit until 10pm. They're free to members and hotel guests but cost $10 for nonguests.

Marriott Frenchman's Reef Tennis Courts, Flamboyant Point (© **340/ 776-8500**), has four courts. Again, nonguests are charged $10 per hour per court. Lights stay on until 10pm.

WINDSURFING Windsurfing is available through the major resorts and at some public beaches, including Brewer's Bay, Morning Star Beach, and Limetree Beach. The **Renaissance Grand Beach Resort,** Smith Bay Road, Route 38 (© **340/775-1510**), is the major hotel offering windsurfing. It's available to guests with no charge and to non-guests at $20 per hour. You might want to stay here if you plan to do a lot of windsurfing.

EXPLORING ST. THOMAS
CHARLOTTE AMALIE ✪

The capital, Charlotte Amalie, where most visitors begin their sightseeing, has all the color and charm of an authentic Caribbean waterfront town. In days of yore, seafarers from all over the globe flocked here, as did pirates and members of the Confederacy, who used the port during the American Civil War. (Sadly, St. Thomas was the biggest slave market in the world.)

The old warehouses once used for storing pirate goods still stand, and today, many of them house shops. In fact, the main streets are now a virtual shopping mall and are usually packed. (See "Shopping," below, for our specific recommendations.) Sandwiched among these shops are a few historic buildings, most of which can be covered on foot in about 2 hours.

American Caribbean Museum   The cultures of the U.S. and the Caribbean are united in this museum, whose exhibits trace the history of the Virgin Islands from their volcanic beginnings through the Indian settlements and the discovery of the archipelago by Christopher Columbus. The museum also traces Danish colonization of the islands. Memorabilia concerns Alexander Hamilton, who was reared on St. Croix. Displays also show the transfer of the Virgin Islands from Denmark to the United States under President Wilson in 1917. You learn that this transfer of the landmass was the result of a tortured 50-year negotiation starting with President Lincoln. Lincoln was assassinated by John Wilkes Booth just 3 months before he was to begin negotiations for the purchase of the islands. The museum also traces the impact of the American Revolution on the Virgin Islands, including Benedict Arnold's link to the islands, and the impact of the Civil War. Finally, the museum shows what happened when the United States bought the islands, with visits by presidents ranging from Hoover to Clinton. Photographs show the landing of Charles Lindbergh in his plane *The Spirit of St. Louis* in 1928. The great aviator touched down at Mosquito Bay, whose name was later changed to Lindbergh Bay. Life-like historical figures explain the history.

32 Raadets Gade (between Waterfront and Main sts.). ✆ **340/714-5150.** Admission $8 for adults, $4 for children. Daily 9am–3pm.

Fort Christian   This imposing structure, which dates from 1672, dominates the center of town. It was named after the Danish king Christian V and has been everything from a fort to a governor's residence to a jail. It became a national historic landmark in 1977, but still functioned as a police station, court, and jail until 1983. Now a museum, the fort houses displays on the island's history and culture. Cultural workshops and turn-of-the-century furnishings are just some of the exhibits. A museum shop features local crafts, maps, and prints.

In the town center. ✆ **340/776-4566.** Free admission. Mon–Fri 8:30am–4:30pm.

Paradise Point Tramway   This contraption affords visitors a dramatic view of Charlotte Amalie harbor, with a ride to a 697-foot (209m) peak. The tramway, similar to those used at ski resorts, operates four cars, each with a 10-person capacity, for the 15-minute round-trip ride. It transports customers from the Havensight area to Paradise Point, where they can disembark to visit shops and the popular restaurant and bar.

✆ **340/774-9809.** Round-trip $15 adults, $7.50 children age 6–12 years. Daily 9am–5pm.

Seven Arches Museum   Browsers love checking out the private home of longtime residents Philibert Fluck and Barbara Demaras. This is an 18th-century Danish house, restored to its original condition and furnished with West Indian

---

Moments **Into the Deep for Nondivers**

For the first time nondivers can get some of the thrill long known to scuba aficionados by participating in **Sea Trek at the Coral World Marine Park & Underwater Observatory** (② 340/775-1555). For $68 you can get a full immersion undersea with no experience needed. Participants are given a helmet and a tube to breathe through. The tube is attached to an air source at the observatory tower. You then enjoy a 200-yard (182m), 20-minute stroll in water 18 feet (5m) deep. You're on the sea floor taking in the rainbow-hued tropical fish and the coral reefs as you go along. It's a marvelous way to experience the world as seen from the eyes of a fish.

---

antiques. You can walk through the yellow ballast arches and visit the great room, with its wonderful view of the busiest harbor in the Caribbean. Night-blooming cacti and iguanas are on the roof of the slave quarters. The admission includes a cold tropical drink served in a walled garden filled with flowers.

Government Hill. ② 340/774-9295. Admission $5. Daily 10am–4pm or by appointment.

Synagogue of Beracha Veshalom Vegmiluth Hasidim ✮   This is the oldest synagogue in continuous use under the American flag and the second oldest in the western hemisphere. It was erected in 1833 by Sephardic Jews, and it still maintains the tradition of having sand on the floor, commemorating the exodus from Egypt. The structure was built of local stone, along with ballast brick from Denmark and mortar made of molasses and sand. Next door, the **Weibel Museum** showcases 300 years of Jewish history. It keeps the same hours as the synagogue.

16 Crystal Gade. ② 340/774-4312. Free admission. Mon–Fri 9am–4pm.

ELSEWHERE ON THE ISLAND

Route 30 (Veterans Drive) will take you west of Charlotte Amalie to **Frenchtown.** (Turn left at the sign to the Admiral's Inn.) Early French-speaking settlers arrived on St. Thomas from St. Bart's after they were uprooted by the Swedes. Many island residents today are the direct descendants of those long-ago immigrants, who were known for speaking a distinctive French patois. This colorful village contains a number of restaurants and taverns. Because Charlotte Amalie has become somewhat dangerous at night, Frenchtown has picked up its after-dark business and is the best spot for dancing and other local entertainment.

Coral World Marine Park & Underwater Observatory ✮   This marine complex features a three-story underwater observation tower 100 feet (30m) offshore. Inside, you'll see sponges, fish, coral, and other aquatic creatures in their natural state. An 80,000-gallon reef tank features exotic marine life of the Caribbean; another tank is devoted to sea predators, with circling sharks and giant moray eels. Activities include daily fish and shark feedings and exotic bird shows. The latest addition to the park is a semi-submarine that lets you enjoy the panoramic view and the "down under" feeling of a submarine without truly submerging.

Coral World's guests can take advantage of adjacent **Coki Beach** for snorkel rentals, scuba lessons, or simply swimming and relaxing. Lockers and showers are available. Also included in the marine park are the Shark Bar, duty-free shops, and a nature trail.

6450 Coki Point, a 20-min. drive from Charlotte Amalie off Route 38. ✆ **340/775-1555**. Admission $18 adults, $9 children age 3–12. Daily 9am–5pm.

Estate St. Peter Greathouse Botanical Gardens ★

This estate consists of 11 acres (4 hectares) set at the foot of volcanic peaks on the northern rim of the island. The grounds are laced with self-guided nature walks that will acquaint you with some 200 varieties of West Indian plants and trees, including an umbrella plant from Madagascar. From a panoramic deck in the gardens, you can see some 20 of the Virgin Islands, including Hans Lollick, an uninhabited island between Thatched Cay and Madahl Point. The house itself, filled with local art, is worth a visit.

At the corner of Rte. 40 (6A St. Peter Mountain Rd.) and Barrett Hill Rd. ✆ **340/774-4999**. Admission $10 adults, $6 children age 4–12 years. Daily 9am–4pm.

SHOPPING ★★★

The discounted, duty-free shopping in the Virgin Islands makes St. Thomas a shopping mecca. It's possible to find well-known brand names here at savings of up to 60% off mainland U.S. prices. But be warned—savings are not always so good. Before you leave home, check prices in your local stores if you think you might want to make a major purchase, so you can be sure that you are in fact getting a good deal. Having sounded that warning, we'll mention some St. Thomas shops where we have found really good buys.

The best buys include china, crystal, perfume, jewelry (especially emeralds), Haitian art, fashion, watches, and items made of wood. Cameras and electronic items, based on our experience, are not the good buys they're reputed to be. St. Thomas is also the best place in the Caribbean for discounts on porcelain, but remember that U.S. brands may often be purchased for 25% off the retail price on the U.S. mainland. Look for the imported patterns for the biggest savings.

Most shops, some of which occupy former pirate warehouses, are open Monday to Saturday from 9am to 5pm. Some stores open Sunday and holidays if a cruise ship is in port. *Note:* Friday is the biggest cruise-ship day at Charlotte Amalie (we once counted eight ships in port at once), so try to avoid shopping then. It's a zoo.

⌐Tips Getting to the Bottom of It

The air-conditioned *Atlantis* submarine will take you on a 1-hour voyage (the whole experience is really 2 hours, when you include transportation to and from the sub) to depths of 90 feet (27m), where an amazing world of exotic marine life unfolds. You'll have up-close views of coral reefs and sponge gardens through the sub's 2-foot (.6m) windows. *Atlantis* divers swim with the fish and bring them close to the windows for photos.

Passengers take a surface boat from the West Indies Dock, right outside Charlotte Amalie, to the submarine, which is near Buck Island (the St. Thomas version, not the more famous Buck Island near St. Croix). The fare is $72 for adults, $36 for children age 4 to 17; children age 3 and under are not allowed. The *Atlantis* operates daily November through April, Tuesday through Saturday May through October. Reservations are a must (the sub carries only 30 passengers). For tickets, go to the Havensight shopping mall, building 6, or call ✆ **340/776-5650**.

Nearly all the major shopping is along the harbor of Charlotte Amalie. Cruise-ship passengers mainly shop at the **Havensight Mall** at the eastern edge of town. The principal shopping street is **Main Street,** or Dronningens Gade (its old Danish name). To the north is another merchandise-loaded street called **Back Street,** or Vimmelskaft. Many shops are also spread along the **Waterfront Highway** (Kyst Vejen). Between these major streets is a series of side streets, walkways, and alleys, all filled with shops. You might also browse along Tolbod Gade, Raadets Gade, Royal Dane Mall, Palm Passage, Storetvaer Gade, and Strand Gade.

It's illegal for most street vendors (food vendors are about the only exception) to ply their trades outside the designated area called **Vendors Plaza,** at the corner of Veterans Drive and Tolbod Gade. Hundreds of vendors converge here at 7:30am; they usually pack up around 5:30pm, Monday to Saturday.

When you completely tire of French perfumes and Swiss watches, head for **Market Square,** also called Rothschild Francis Square. Under a Victorian tin roof, locals with machetes slice open fresh coconuts, while women wearing bandanas sell akee, cassava, and breadfruit.

All the major stores in St. Thomas are located by number on an excellent map in the publication *St. Thomas This Week,* distributed free to all arriving plane and boat passengers and at the visitor center. A lot of the stores on the island don't have street numbers, or don't display them, so look for their signs instead.

Bernard K. Passman, 38A Main St. (② **340/777-4580**), is the world's leading sculptor of black-coral art and jewelry. He's famous for his *Can Can Girl* and his four statues of Charlie Chaplin. After being polished and embellished with gold and diamonds, some of Passman's work has been treasured by royalty. There are also simpler and more affordable pieces for sale.

Gallery Camille Pissarro, Caribbean Cultural Centre, 14 Dronningens Gade (② **340/774-4621**), is located in the house where Pissarro was born in 1830. In three high-ceilinged and airy rooms, you can view many prints of local artists, and the gallery also sells original batiks, alive in vibrant colors.

Mango Tango Art Gallery, Al Cohen's Plaza, Raphune Hill, Route 38 (② **340/777-3060**), is one of the largest galleries on island, closely connected with a half-dozen internationally recognized artists who spend at least part of the year in the Virgin Islands. Original works begin at $100; prints and posters are cheaper.

Blue Turtle Gallery, Government Hill (② **340/774-9440**), is a showcase of the works of Virgin Island painters, notably Lucina Schutt, best known for her Caribbean land and seascapes. At this gallery, to the west of Marisol Restaurant, Schutt not only sells artwork beginning at $15, but teaches water coloring to students.

Native Arts and Crafts Cooperative, Tarbor 1 (② **340/777-1153**), is the largest arts-and-crafts emporium in the U.S. Virgin Islands, offering the output of 90 different artisans. It specializes in items small enough to be packed into a suitcase or trunk, such as spice racks, lamps crafted from conch shells, salad bowls, crocheted goods, and straw goods.

Caribbean Marketplace, Havensight Mall, building 3 (② **340/776-5400**), carries the best selections of handcrafts, including the Sunny Caribbee line, a vast array of condiments and botanical products. Other items range from wooden Jamaican jigsaw puzzles to Indonesian batiks, and bikinis from the Cayman Islands. (Don't expect very attentive service.)

The aromas will lead you to **Down Island Traders,** Veterans Drive (② **340/ 776-4641**), which has Charlotte Amalie's most attractive array of spices, teas, candies, jellies, jams, and condiments, most of which are packaged in natural Caribbean products. There are also local cookbooks, silk-screened T-shirts and bags, Haitian metal sculpture, handmade jewelry, Caribbean folk art, and children's gifts.

The clutter and eclecticism of **Carson Company Antiques,** Royal Dane Mall, off Main Street (© **340/774-6175**), may appeal to you. The shop is loaded with merchandise, tasteless and otherwise, from virtually everywhere. Bakelite jewelry is cheap and cheerful, and the African artifacts are often interesting.

A. H. Riise Gift & Liquor Stores, 37 Main St. (© **800/524-2037** or 340/776-2303), is St. Thomas's oldest outlet for luxury items, and offers the best liquor selection on the island. The store carries fine jewelry and watches from Europe's leading craftspeople, including Vacheron Constantin, Bulgari, Omega, and Gucci, as well as a wide selection of gold, platinum, and precious gemstone jewelry. Imported cigars are stored in a climate-controlled walk-in humidor. Waterford, Lalique, Baccarat, and Rosenthal are featured in the china and crystal department. Specialty shops in the complex sell Caribbean gifts, books, clothing, food, prints, note cards, and designer sunglasses. Delivery to cruise ships and the airport is free.

One of the island's most famous outlets, **Al Cohen's Discount Liquors,** Long Bay Road (© **340/774-3690**), occupies a big warehouse at Havensight with a huge selection of liquor and wine. The wine department is especially impressive. You can also purchase fragrances, T-shirts, and souvenirs.

Tropicana Perfume Shoppe, 2 Main St. (© **800/233-7948** or 340/774-0010), offers all the famous names in perfumes, skin care, and cosmetics, including Lancôme and La Prairie. Men will also find Europe's best colognes and aftershave lotions here.

Royal Caribbean, 33 Main St. (© **340/776-4110**), is the largest camera and electronics store in the Caribbean. It carries Nikon, Minolta, Pentax, Canon, and Panasonic products, plus watches by Seiko, Movado, Corum, Fendi, Philippe Charriol, and Zodiac. There are also leather bags, Mikimoto pearls, 14- and 18-karat jewelry, and Lladró figurines. Another branch is located at the Havensight Mall (© **340/776-8890**).

Often called the Tiffany's of the Caribbean, **Cardow Jewelers,** 39 Main St. (© **340/776-1140**), boasts the largest selection of fine jewelry in the world. This fabulous shop, where more than 20,000 rings are displayed, offers savings because of its worldwide direct buying, large turnover, and duty-free prices. Unusual and traditional designs are offered in diamonds, emeralds, rubies, sapphires, and pearls. The Treasure Cove has cases of fine gold jewelry priced under $200.

Cardow's leading competitor is **H. Stern Jewellers,** Havensight Mall (© **800/ 524-2024** or 340/776-1223), the international chain with some 175 outlets. Besides this branch, there are two more on Main Street and one at Marriott's Frenchman's Reef. Stern gives worldwide guaranteed service, including a 1-year exchange privilege.

For a decade, the owners of **Blue Carib Gems and Rocks,** 2 Back St., behind Little Switzerland (© **340/774-8525**), have scoured the Caribbean for gemstones. The raw stones are cut, polished, and fashioned into jewelry by the lost-wax process. You can see craftspeople at work and view their finished products. A lifetime guarantee is given on all handcrafted jewelry. Since the items are locally made, they are duty free and not included in the $1,200 Customs exemption.

Colombian Emeralds International, Havensight Mall (© **340/774-2442**), is renowned throughout the Caribbean for its collection of Colombian emeralds, both set and unset. Here you buy direct from the source, which can mean significant savings. The shop also stocks fine watches. There's another outlet on Main Street. Another good place to browse for gemstones is **Pierre's,** 24 Palm Passage (© **800/300-0634** or 340/776-5130), one of the most impressive repositories of collector's items in the Caribbean. Look for Alexandrites (garnets in three shades of green); spinels (pink and red); sphenes, yellow-green sparklers from Madagascar that are as reflective as high-quality diamonds; and tsavorites, green stones from Tanzania.

Cosmopolitan, Drakes Passage and the waterfront (© **340/776-2040**), carries Bally shoes and handbags; women's and men's swimwear by Gottex, Hom, Lahco, and Fila; ties by Versace and Pancaldi (at least 30% less than the U.S. mainland price); and Timberland sportswear for men (discounted 10%).

The Linen House, A. H. Riise Mall (© **340/774-1668**), is considered the best store for linens in the West Indies. You'll find a wide selection of place mats, decorative tablecloths, and many hand-embroidered goods, many of them crafted in China.

If you need a beach read, head for the well-stocked **Dockside Bookshop,** Havensight Mall (© **340/774-4937**), near the cruise-ship dock. You'll find everything from mysteries to a wide selection of children's books here.

Modern Music, across from Havensight Mall and the cruise-ship docks (© **340/774-3100**), features nearly every genre, from rock to jazz to classical, and especially Caribbean. You'll find new releases from island stars such as Jamaica's Byron Lee and the Virgin Islands' The Violators, as well as U.S. groups. There is another branch at the Nisky Center (© **340/777-8787**).

Among stores that have vastly upgraded their stock is **Amsterdam Sauer,** Main Street (© **340/774-2222**), where the Sauer family still remains a leader in jewelry and gems. They've reached out to stock their store with some of the most world-renowned designers of jewelry. The Sauers also offer the largest selection of unset gems in the Caribbean. Hot on their trail is the vastly improved stock at **Artistic Jewelers,** 32 Main St. (© **800/653-3113**), which carries exclusive designer jewelry lines, including the "classics" from David Yurman.

Mr. Tablecloth, 6 Main St. (© **340/774-4343**), has received new shipments of top-quality linen from the Republic of China (also Hong Kong). Now it has the best selection of tablecloths and accessories, plus doilies, place mats, aprons, and runners in Charlotte Amalie. **Mussfeldt Design,** International Plaza Mall, near the Hard Rock Café (© **340/774-9034**), has stocked its shelves with the latest resort wear from around the world—mainly Mexico, Australia, and, of course, the Caribbean itself. Especially delectable are the unique embroideries and prints designed by Peter Mussfeldt himself.

It had to happen. **The Virgin Islands Brewing Company,** across from Fat Tuesdays at Royal Dane Mall (© **340/714-1683**), was originally founded on St. Croix but has invaded St. Thomas with two local beers, Blackbeard Ale and Foxy's Lager. At the Company store, you're given free samples and can purchase six-packs of the home-brewed suds along with T-shirts, caps, and polo shirts.

Outside of Charlotte Amalie, another noteworthy destination is **Tillett Gardens,** a virtual oasis of arts and crafts—pottery, silk-screened fabrics, candles, watercolors, jewelry, and more. It's located on the highway across from Four Winds Shopping Center (take Route 38 east from Charlotte Amalie). A major island attraction in itself is the **Jim Tillett Art Gallery and Silk Screen Print Studio** (© **340/775-1929**), which displays the best work of local artists, including originals in oils, watercolors, and acrylics. The prints are all one of a kind, and prices start as low as $15. The famous Tillett maps on fine canvas are priced from $30.

ST. THOMAS AFTER DARK ★★

St. Thomas has more nightlife than any other island in the Virgins, U.S. and British, but not as much as you might think. Charlotte Amalie is no longer the swinging town it used to be. Many of the streets are dangerous after dark, so visitors have mostly abandoned the town except for a few places. Much of the action has shifted to **Frenchtown,** which has some great restaurants and bars. However, just as in Charlotte Amalie, some of these little hot spots are along dark, badly lit roads.

Note: Sexual harassment can be a problem in certain bars in Charlotte Amalie, where few single women would want to be alone at night anyway. Any of the major resort hotels are generally safe.

The big hotels, such as Marriott's Frenchman's Reef Beach Resort and Bluebeard's, have the most lively after-dark scene. After a day of sightseeing and shopping in the hot West Indies sun, sometimes your best bet is just to stay at your hotel in the evening, perhaps listening to a local calypso band. You might also call the **Reichhold Center for the Arts,** University of the Virgin Islands, 2 John Brewer's Bay (© 340/693-1559), or check with the tourist office to see what's on during your visit. Their Japanese-inspired amphitheater is set into a natural valley, with seating space for 1,196. Several different repertory companies of music, dance, and drama perform here. Performances usually begin at 8pm. Tickets range from $5 to $65.

In Charlotte Amalie, head to the **Bar at Paradise Point** (© 340/777-4540) at sunset. It's located 740 feet (222m) above sea level (a tram takes you up the hill), across from the cruise-ship dock, and provides excellent photo ops and panoramic views. Get the bartender to serve you his specialty, a Bushwacker. Sometimes a one-man steel band is on hand to serenade the sunset watchers. You can also order inexpensive food, such as barbecued ribs, hot dogs, and hamburgers. Happy hour, with discounted drinks, begins at 5pm.

We recommend only a few other places in Charlotte Amalie. They include **Fat Tuesday,** 26A Royal Dane Mall (© 340/777-8676), on the waterfront, with fun, silly specialty drinks and different special events every night. The **Greenhouse,** Veterans Drive (© 340/774-7998), a bar/restaurant that's also directly on the waterfront, features different entertainment every night, ranging from reggae to disco. There's no cover except on Wednesday and Friday nights, when you pay $5 to $10 for the live reggae. The intimate, dimly lit, two-level bar at **Creations** night club, 3 Trompeter Gade (© 340/774-5025), attracts locals, often gay men, in summer, drawing more off-island visitors in winter. It's about 100 yards (91m) from the island's famous synagogue, in a clapboard town house built around 1935. The music here ranges from the 1950s to the 1970s. Upstairs you can enjoy drinks and a convivial atmosphere at Walter's Livingroom.

The scenic **Dungeon Bar,** Bluebeard's Hill (© 340/774-1600), overlooking the yacht harbor, offers piano-bar entertainment nightly. It's a popular gathering spot for both locals and visitors. You can dance from 8pm to midnight on Thursday and from 8pm to 1am on Saturday. Entertainment varies from month to month, but a steel band usually comes in on some nights, while other nights are devoted to karaoke or jazz. It's open Tuesday to Friday from 4pm to midnight and Saturday to Monday from 4pm to 1am. There's no cover.

During the day **Iggie's Bolongo,** in the Bolongo Beach Resort, 7150 Bolongo (© 340/775-1800), is an informal, open-air restaurant, serving hamburgers, sandwiches, and salads. After dark, it presents karaoke and offers pool tables and night volleyball. It's also one of the most active sports bars on island.

West of Charlotte Amalie, in Frenchtown, **Epernay,** rue de St. Barthélemy, next to Alexander's Restaurant (© **340/774-5348**), is a stylish watering hole with a view of the ocean. You can order vintage wines and at least six different brands of champagne by the glass. Also available are appetizers, including sushi and caviar, main courses, and tempting desserts, such as chocolate-dipped strawberries.

Latitude 18, Red Hook Marina (© **340/779-2495**), is the hot spot on the east coast, where the ferryboats depart for St. John. The ceiling is adorned with boat sails. This casual place is both a restaurant and bar, with live entertainment almost nightly and a crowd that includes some locals.

The popular **Turtle Rock Bar,** in the Mangrove Restaurant at the Wyndham Sugar Bay Beach Club, 6500 Estate Smith Bay (© **340/777-7100**), presents live music, steel bands, and karaoke. There's space to dance, but most folks just sway and listen to the steel-pan bands that play from 2pm to closing, or the more elaborate bands that play on Tuesday, Sunday, and some other nights. Thursday night is karaoke. Burgers, salads, steaks, and grilled fish are available at the Mangrove Restaurant a few steps away. There's no cover. Happy hour is 4 to 6pm every night.

Near Coki Beach on the northeast shore, the posh **Baywinds,** at the Renaissance Grand Beach Resort, Smith Bay Road (© **340/775-1510**), is a romantic place to be in the evening. Couples dance at the side of the luxurious pool as moonlight glitters off the ocean in the background. Music ranges from jazz to pop. It's open nightly, with live music and dinner from 6pm to midnight.

On the northwest shore, **Larry's Hideaway,** 10 Hull Bay (© **340/ 777-1898**), has a laid-back, casual atmosphere. Many locals like to spend lazy Sunday afternoons here at this bar. It's also a cheap place to eat; hot dogs and hamburgers are served until 9pm.

The major venue for nightlife in St. Thomas is **The Old Mill,** 193 Contant (© **340/776-3004**), the largest and newest entertainment complex to open on island, with three separate venues. The courtyard sports bar offers a variety of games, including four pool tables. The more elegant wine and champagne bar is in a restored 18th-century historic sugar mill, where guests can relax to the sound of jazz and blues. More than 100 different types of wines and champagnes from all over the world are served here. There's also a dance club, the largest of its kind in the U.S. Virgins, featuring a sunken dance floor combined with a state-of-the-art lighting and sound system. Open Thursday to Sunday, with no set closing times. Go after 9pm.

3 St. Croix ★★★

At 84 square miles (218 sq. km), St. Croix is the largest of the U.S. Virgin Islands. At the east end (which actually is the easternmost point of the United States), the terrain is rocky and arid. The west end is lusher, and even includes a small "rain forest" of mango, mahogany, tree ferns, and dangling lianas. Between the two extremes are beautiful beaches, rolling hills, pastures, and, increasingly, miles of condos.

Columbus named the island *Santa Cruz* (Holy Cross) when he landed here on November 14, 1493. He anchored his ship off the north shore but was quickly driven away by the spears, arrows, and axes of the Carib Indians. The French laid claim to the island in 1650, and the Danes purchased it from them in 1773. Under Danish rule, slave labor and sugarcane fields proliferated during

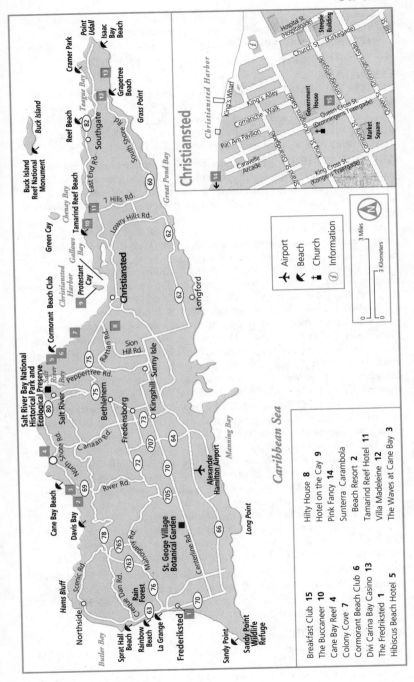

St. Croix

Christiansted

Airport
Beach
Church
Information

Hospital St. (Hospitalgade)
Steeple Building
Church St. (Kirkegade)
King's Wharf
King's Alley
Comanche Walk
Pan Am Pavilion
Caravelle Arcade
Government House
Queen Cross St. (Dronningens Gade)
Market Square
King Cross St. (Kongens Tvaergade)

Christiansted Harbor
Christiansted

Point Udall
Isaac Bay Beach
Cramer Park
Reef Beach
Grapetree Beach
Grass Point
Southgate
Reef Beach
Teague Bay
Buck Island
Buck Island Reef National Monument
Cheney Bay
Tamarind Reef Beach
Green Cay
Gallows Bay
Protestant Cay
Christiansted Harbor
Longford

South Shore Rd.
East End Rd.
1 Hills Rd.
Lowry Hills Rd.
Great Pond Bay

Cormorant Beach Club
Salt River Bay National Historical Park and Ecological Preserve
Salt River
Salt River Bay
Peppertree Rd.
Bethlehem
Fredensborg
Canaan Rd.
North Shore Rd.
Cane Bay Beach
Davis Bay
Rattan Rd.
Sion Hill Rd.
Sunny Isle
Kingshill
River Rd.
Alexander Hamilton Airport
Manning Bay

Hams Bluff
Northside
Butler Bay
Sprat Hall Beach
Rainbow Beach
La Grange
Frederiksted
Sandy Point
Sandy Point Wildlife Refuge
Scenic Rd.
Rain Forest
Creque Dan Rd.
Mahogany Rd.
St. Geoge Village Botanical Garden
Centerline Rd.
Long Point

Caribbean Sea

Breakfast Club **15**
The Buccaneer **10**
Cane Bay Reef **4**
Colony Cove **7**
Cormorant Beach Club **6**
Divi Carina Bay Casino **13**
The Fredriksted **1**
Hibiscus Beach Hotel **5**
Hilty House **8**
Hotel on the Cay **9**
Pink Fancy **14**
Sunterra Carambola Beach Resort **2**
Tamarind Reef Hotel **11**
Villa Madeleine **12**
The Waves at Cane Bay **3**

731

a golden era for both planters and pirates, which came to an end in the latter half of the 19th century. Danish influence still permeates the island today.

See "Getting There" at the beginning of the chapter for details on flights to St. Croix.

ESSENTIALS

VISITOR INFORMATION   You can begin your explorations at the **visitors bureau,** Queen Cross Street, in Christiansted (© 340/773-0495), a yellow-sided building with a cedar-capped roof near the harbor. It was originally built as the Old Scalehouse in 1856. In its heyday, all taxable goods leaving and entering the harbor were weighed here. Open Monday to Friday 8am to 5pm.

GETTING AROUND   At Alexander Hamilton Airport, you'll find official taxi rates posted. From the airport, expect to pay about $15 for a ride to Christiansted and about $10 to Frederiksted. As the cabs are unmetered, agree on the rate before you get in. The **St. Croix Taxicab Association** (© 340/778-1088) offers door-to-door service.

Air-conditioned **buses** run between Christiansted and Frederiksted about every 30 minutes daily between 6am and 9pm. They start at Tide Village, to the east of Christiansted, and go along Route 75 to the Golden Rock Shopping Center. They then make their way to Route 70, with stopovers at the Sunny Isle Shopping Center, La Reine Shopping Center, St. George Village Botanical Garden, and Whim Plantation Museum, before reaching Frederiksted. The fare is $1, or 55¢ for seniors. For more information, call © **340/778-0898.**

St. Croix offers moderately priced car rentals, even on cars with automatic transmission and air-conditioning. However, because of the island's higher-than-normal accident rate, insurance costs are a bit higher than usual. If you're not covered under your existing insurance policies or by your credit card, you should consider paying for the collision damage waiver. **Avis** (© **800/331-2112;** www.avis.com), **Budget** (© **888/227-3359** or 340/778-9636; www.budget. com), and **Hertz** (© **800/654-3001** or 340/778-1402; www.hertz.com) all maintain headquarters at the airport; look for their kiosks near the baggage-claim areas. Not to beat a dead horse, but do remember: *Driving is on the left.* In most rural areas, the speed limit is 35 miles per hour (.03kmph); certain parts of the major artery, Route 66, are 55 miles per hour (.05kmph). In towns and urban areas, the speed limit is 20 miles per hour (.02kmph). Keep in mind that if you're going into the "bush country," you'll find the roads very difficult. Sometimes the government smoothes the roads out before the rainy season begins (often in Oct or Nov), but they deteriorate rapidly.

St. Croix Bike and Tours, 5035 Cotton Valley, Christiansted (© **340/ 772-2343**), offers bike rentals. Its 21-speed mountain bikes are best suited for the rugged terrain of St. Croix. The company also features guided bike tours.

FAST FACTS   The local **American Express** representative is Southerland, Chandler's Wharf, Gallows Bay (© **800/260-2603** or 340/773-9500).

If you need medical assistance, go to the **Governor Juan F. Luis Hospital & Health Center,** 6 Diamond Ruby (© **340/778-6311**).

ACCOMMODATIONS

All rooms are subject to an 8% hotel room tax, which is not included in the rates given below.

If you're interested in a villa or condo rental, contact the places reviewed below or **Island Villas,** Property Management Rentals, 6 Company St., Christiansted,

St. Croix, U.S.V.I. 00820 (© **800/626-4512** or 340/773-8821; fax 340/773-8823), which offers some of the best accommodations on the island. Some are very private residences with pools; many are on the beach. They range from one-bedroom units to seven-bedroom villas, with prices from $1,000 to $15,000 per week year-round.

VERY EXPENSIVE

The Buccaneer ★★★ *Kids*   This large, luxurious, family-owned resort boasts three of the island's best beaches, and the best sports program on St. Croix. The property was once a cattle ranch and a sugar plantation; its first estate house, which dates from the mid–17th century, stands near a freshwater pool. Accommodations are either in the main building or in one of the beachside properties. The baronially arched main building has a lobby opening onto drinking or viewing terraces, with a sea vista on two sides and Christiansted to the west. The rooms are fresh and comfortable, though some of the standard units are a bit small. All have wicker furnishings and full bathrooms. The best bathrooms are in the Beachside Doubloons, and come complete with whirlpool tubs. A free Kid's Camp is available year-round.

2 miles (3km) east of Christiansted on Rte. 82 (P.O. Box 25200), Gallows Bay, Christiansted, St. Croix, U.S.V.I. 00824. © **800/255-3881** in the U.S., or 340/773-2100. Fax 340/778-8215. www.thebuccaneer.com. 138 units. Winter $280–$660 double; $550–$660 suite. Off-season $205–$215 double; $320–$475 suite. Rates include American breakfast. **Amenities:** 4 restaurants; bar; 2 pools; 18-hole golf course; 8 tennis courts; fitness center; watersports; children's program. *In room:* A/C, TV, fridge, coffeemaker, hair dryer, safe.

Sunterra Carambola Beach Resort ★   This hotel is set on 28 acres (11 hectares) above Davis Bay, about a 30-minute drive from Christiansted. It's one of the largest hotels on St. Croix, and it lies adjacent to an outstanding golf course, in a lovely, lush setting on a white-sand beach whose turquoise waters boast fine snorkeling. Try as it may, this resort never achieves the class and style of the Buccaneer in spite of a spectacular physical location. Originally built as a Rock Resort, it has suffered hurricane attacks and management changes, and today it is hot on the trail of the time-share market. Guests are housed in red-roofed, two-story buildings, each of which contains six units. The accommodations are furnished in rattan and wicker, with pastel colors; each has a balcony partially concealed from outside view, overlooking either the garden or the sea. Rooms have an upscale flair, with louvered doors, tile floors, mahogany trim, and sometimes such extras as screened-in porches with rocking chairs. Bathrooms are luxurious and roomy, with oversized showers (with seats) and tiled vanities. If you want the very finest room here, ask for the Davis Bay Suite, which was a former Rockefeller private beach home. Its veranda alone is capable of entertaining 100 people, should that many drop in on you.

P.O. Box 3031, Kingshill, St. Croix, U.S.V.I. 00851. © **888/503-8760** in the U.S., or 340/778-3800. Fax 340/778-1682. www.sunterra.com. 151 units. Winter $230–$370 double; $600 suite. Off-season $176–$206 double; $420 suite. AE, DC, DISC, MC, V. **Amenities:** 2 restaurants; pool; golf course; 4 tennis courts; fitness center; library; dive shop, snorkeling, fishing; car rentals; 24-hr. room service; massage; babysitting; laundry/dry cleaning. *In room:* A/C, TV, fridge, coffeemaker, hair dryer, safe.

Villa Madeleine ✿✿   This deluxe 6½-acre (3-hectares) property has some of the island's poshest rooms. When it first opened, The Villa showed great promise of overtaking the Buccaneer. That never happened. The place remains distinguished, but service here has fallen off greatly and the Buccaneer still sails mightily above it. The Villa is very independent of everything else on St. Croix—guests check in here and never leave the grounds. Many of the well-heeled occupants are retirees who live here full-time. The focal point is the great house, whose Chippendale balconies and proportions emulate the Danish colonial era. Inside, a splendidly conceived decor incorporates masses of English chintz and mahogany paneling.

Each stylish one- or two-bedroom villa has its own kitchen, privacy wall, and plunge pool. The marble bathrooms have double dressing areas and oversized shower/tub combinations. The villas comprising the resort are handled by different management companies; therefore, standards can vary greatly, depending on which one you're assigned. Beach-lovers willingly travel a ⅓ mile (.5km) to the nearest beaches, Reef and Grapetree.

8 miles (13km) east of Christiansted at Teague Bay (P.O. Box 26160), St. Croix, U.S.V.I. 00824. ✆ 800/496-7379 or 340/778-8782. Fax 340/773-2150. www.villamadeleinehotel.com. 43 units. Winter $275 1-bedroom villa; $375 2-bedroom villa. Off-season $200 1-bedroom villa; $275 2-bedroom villa. MC, V. Children age 11 and under discouraged. **Amenities:** Restaurant, bar; golf course nearby; tennis court; library; babysitting; laundry. *In room:* A/C, TV, kitchen, fridge, coffeemaker.

EXPENSIVE

Colony Cove ✿   Of all the condo complexes on St. Croix, Colony Cove is the most like a full-fledged hotel, with a relatively large staff on hand. Its four three-story buildings ring a pool next to a palm-shaded beach. Each apartment has a washer and dryer (rare for St. Croix), a modern kitchen with microwave, an enclosed veranda or gallery, two air-conditioned bedrooms, and a pair of full bathrooms. All have a light, airy, tropical feel.

3221 Estate Golden Rock (about a mile/2km west of Christiansted), St. Croix, U.S.V.I. 00820. ✆ 800/828-0746 in the U.S., or 340/773-1965. Fax 340/773-5397. www.usvi.net/hotel/colony. 60 units. Winter $195 apt. for 2; $255 apt. for 4. Off-season $135 apt. for 2; $165 apt. for 4. Extra person $20 in winter, $10 in summer. Children under age 6 stay free. AE, MC, V. Go east on Rte. 75 heading toward Christiansted as far as Five Corners; turn left and pass Mill Harbor; Colony Cove is the next driveway to the left. **Amenities:** Snack bar; pool; 2 tennis courts nearby; snorkeling. *In room:* A/C, TV, kitchen, microwave, washer and dryer.

Cormorant Beach Club ✿   This is the poshest gay resort in the Caribbean Basin, dwarfing all competition. About 70% of its clients are gay males, mostly from the eastern United States and California. The 12-acre (5-hectares) property is designed in a boxy, modern-looking series of rectangles, with strong horizontal lines and outcroppings of exposed natural stone. It strikes a well-coordinated balance between seclusion and accessibility. Long Reef lies a few hundred feet offshore from the resort's sandy beachfront. Bedrooms contain a restrained decor of cane and wicker furniture, spacious bathrooms with tubs and showers, and sliding-glass doors that flood the interior with sunlight.

The social life here revolves around an open-air clubhouse, with views of the sea. Off the central core is a bar (see "St. Croix After Dark," later in this chapter) and an airy dining room. The restaurant is St. Croix's leading gay eatery (see "Dining," below).

4126 La Grande Princesse (about 3 miles (5km) northwest of Christiansted, beside route 75), St. Croix, U.S.V.I. 00820. ✆ **800/548-4460** in the U.S., or 340/778-8920. Fax 340/778-9218. www.cormorantbeachclub.com. 38 units. Winter $180–$210 double; $265 suite. Off-season $130–$160 double; $225 suite. Extra bed $20. AE, DC, DISC, MC, V. Dive, golf, scuba, and "commitment ceremony" packages available. **Amenities:** Restaurant, bar; 2 tennis courts; snorkeling. *In room:* A/C, TV, safe.

Divi Carina Bay Casino ✪   Set along 1,000 feet (300m) of sugar-white beach, this resort brings gambling to the U.S. Virgin Islands. That fact seems to obscure its success as a place of barefoot elegance and a top new resort property. The new resort was built on the ruins of the former Grapetree Shores, which was wiped away by Hurricane Hugo. The new Divi has both smoking and non-smoking rooms available, and opens onto a good beach. Accommodations feature oceanfront guest rooms and villa suites with views of the Caribbean. Rooms are good sized and well equipped with computer/fax lines, VCRs, a small kitchen, full bathrooms, and balconies. We prefer the accommodations on the ground floor as they are closer to the water's edge. The 20 villas across the street are about a 3-minute walk from the sands. There's not only that casino, but a spa, where experts work you over to create a new you.

25 Estate Turner Hole, St. Croix, U.S.V.I. 00820. ✆ **800/823-9352** in the U.S., or 340/773-9700. Fax 340/773-6802. www.diviresorts.com. 146 units. Winter $225–$250 double, from $400 suite. Off-season, $175–$200 double, from $275 suite. AE, DC, MC, V. **Amenities:** 3 restaurants, 2 bars; casino; 2 pools; 2 tennis courts, health club and spa; watersports; game room; room service; massage; laundry. *In room:* A/C, TV, fridge, safe.

Hibiscus Beach Hotel ✪   This hotel, located on one of the island's best beaches, attracts a lively clientele. The accommodations are in five two-story pink buildings. Each guest room is a retreat unto itself, with a private patio or balcony and a view of the Caribbean, plus tasteful Caribbean furnishings and floral prints. Shower-only bathrooms are small but well maintained.

4131 La Grande Princesse (next to the Cormorant, 10 minutes from Christiansted), St. Croix, U.S.V.I. 08820. ✆ **809/442-0121** or 340-/773-4042. Fax 340/773-7668. www.1hibiscus.com. 36 units. Winter $180–$190 double; $290–$340 efficiency. Off-season $130–$140 double; $220–$270 efficiency. Honeymoon, dive, and golf packages available. AE, DISC, MC, V. **Amenities:** Restaurant, bar; pool; snorkeling; laundry. *In room:* A/C, TV, minibar, hair dryer, safe.

MODERATE

Cane Bay Reef ✪ *(Finds)*   This is one of the little gems of the island, offering large suites, each with a living room, a full kitchen, and a balcony overlooking the water. It's located on the north shore of St. Croix, about a 20-minute taxi ride from Christiansted, fronting the rocky Cane Bay Beach near the Waves at Cane Bay. Sunsets are beautiful here, and the snorkeling's great. The decor is breezily tropical, with cathedral ceilings, overhead fans, and Chilean tiles. Bedrooms are spacious, cool, and airy, with comfortable beds; living rooms also contain futons. The shower-only bathrooms are medium in size and excellently maintained. There's a golf course nearby, and there's a dive shop within walking distance. You can cook in your own kitchen, barbecue, or dine at the in-house restaurant, "Bogey's."

P.O. Box 1407, Kingshill, St. Croix, U.S.V.I. 00851. ✆ **800/253-8534** in the U.S., or 340/778-2966. Fax 340/778-2966. www.canebay.com. 9 units. Winter $165–$250 daily; $970–$1,600 weekly. Off-season $110–$160 daily; $700–$990 weekly. Extra person $20. AE, DISC, MC, V. **Amenities:** Restaurant, bar; pool; laundry. *In room:* A/C, ceiling fan, TV, kitchenette, fridge, coffeemaker, no phone.

Hilty House ✪✪   This tranquil B&B perches on a hilltop surrounded by mountains, west of Christiansted, a 15-minute ride from the airport. The place is housed in a 200-year-old building that was once a rum distillery. Upon arriving, guests pass through a shaded courtyard to a set of iron gates that lead to the inn's gardens. The beautifully appointed plantation-style house has a high-ceilinged living room and an enormous fireplace. The master bedroom is the most lavish room, with a four-poster bed and sunken shower over which hangs a chandelier. There are also two self-catering cottages that can be rented. Accommodations are generous in size, containing fine beds and small but beautifully kept shower-only bathrooms. The Danish Kitchen, one of the cottages, has a covered porch, TV, and phone. A three-course dinner is usually served on Monday night. The overall atmosphere here is very homey and warm.

Questa Verde Rd. (P.O. Box 26077), Gallows Bay, St. Croix, U.S.V.I. 00824. ✆ and fax **340/773-2594**. 6 units. Winter $120 double; $145 cottage. Off-season $95 double; $110 cottage. 3-night minimum stay in cottages. Extra person $25. No children under age 12. Room rates include continental breakfast. No credit cards. **Amenities:** Dining room; pool. *In room:* Ceiling fan, no phone.

Hotel on the Cay With its buff-colored stucco, terra-cotta tiles, and archways, this rather sterile-looking hotel evokes Puerto Rico or the Dominican Republic, but it's the most prominent building on a 3-acre (1-hectare) island set in the middle of Christiansted Harbor. Reaching it requires a 4-minute boat ride from a well-marked quay in the town center (hotel guests ride free; nonguests pay $3 round-trip). Its position in the clear waters of the harbor is both its main plus and its main drawback: Its wide sandy beaches provide the only pollution-free swimming in the town center, but it's the first hotel to be wiped off the map when a hurricane strikes.

In theory, this battered old place should be a lavishly landscaped, upscale retreat; unfortunately, it's not. Nonetheless, it does provide adequate, simple, and clean accommodations near the beach. Units are fairly roomy; most have two double beds, glass tables, wicker armchairs, desks and bureaus, adequate closet space, and laminated shower/tub combination bathrooms. Rooms open onto small metal-railed balconies with a view of the garden or the Christiansted harbor.

Protestant Cay, Christiansted, St. Croix, U.S.V.I. 00820. ✆ **800/524-2035** or 340/773-2035. Fax 340/773-7046. www.st-croix.com/hotelonthecay. 55 units. Winter $189 double; $225 suite. Off-season $130 double; $165 suite. Extra person $25. AE, DISC, MC, V. **Amenities:** Restaurant, bar; pool; 2 tennis courts. *In room:* A/C, TV.

Tamarind Reef Hotel There's a sandy beach at the Tamarind Reef's doorstep and good snorkeling along the reef. Each motel-style room features a garden patio or private balcony, affording guests a view of the blue Caribbean. In addition, 19 of the suites provide fully equipped kitchenettes for up to 4 people. All units have well maintained bathrooms with shower stalls. Guests can relax by the pool and enjoy cocktails, light lunches, and snacks from the poolside bar and grill. For those who want to explore St. Croix underwater, the hotel offers complimentary watersports equipment. Adjoining the hotel is the Green Cay Marina, where guests can charter boats for deep-sea fishing or sailing expeditions.

5001 Tamarind Reef, St. Croix, U.S.V.I. 00820. ✆ **800/619-0014** in the U.S., or 340/773-4455. Fax 340/773-3989. www.usvi.net/hotel/tamarind. 46 units. Winter $188–$220 double. Off-season $155–$171 double. Includes daily continental breakfast. Extra person $30. Children under age 7 stay free in parents' room. Ask about dive, golf, and honeymoon packages. AE, MC, V. **Amenities:** 2 restaurants; bar; pool; tennis court; snorkeling; windsurfing. *In room:* A/C, TV, fridge, coffeemaker, hair dryer, iron and ironing boards, safe.

Waves at Cane Bay This intimate and tasteful condo property is about 8 miles (13km) from the airport, midway between the island's two biggest towns. It's set on a well-landscaped plot of oceanfront property on Cane Bay, the heart of the best scuba and snorkeling at Cane Bay Beach, though the beach here is rocky and tends to disappear at high tide. There's a PADI dive shop on the property. Accommodations are in two-story units with screened-in verandas, all directly on the ocean. The high-ceilinged and very large rooms have well-stocked kitchens, private libraries, tile floors, and shower-only bathrooms, and fresh flowers are added for new guests. A two-room villa next to the main building has a large ocean-side deck. The beachside bar serves as the social center, and a restaurant on the premises is open Monday to Saturday in the evenings.

Cane Bay (P.O. Box 1749), Kingshill, St. Croix, U.S.V.I. 00851. © 800/545-0603 in the U.S., or 340/778-1805. Fax 340/778-4945. www.canebaystcroix.com. 12 units. Winter $140–$195 double. Off-season $75–$140 double. Extra person $20. AE, MC, V. From the airport, go left on Rte. 64; after a mile (2km), turn right on Rte. 70; after another mile (2km), go left at the junction with Rte. 75; after 2 miles (3km), turn left at the junction with Rte. 80; follow for 5 miles (8km). **Amenities:** Restaurant, bar; pool; dive shop; room service; babysitting. In room: A/C, TV, kitchenette, safe.

INEXPENSIVE

Breakfast Club ⚡ (Value)   Here you'll get the best value of any bed-and-breakfast on St. Croix. This comfortable place combines a 1950s compound of efficiency apartments with a traditional-looking stone house that was rebuilt from a ruin in the 1930s. Each of the units has a kitchenette, a cypress-sheathed ceiling, white walls, a beige tile floor, and simple, summery furniture. Shower-only bathrooms are small and adequately maintained. The centerpiece of the place is the hot tub on a raised deck, where impromptu parties are likely to develop at random hours of the day or night, and where views stretch as far off as St. John. Toby Chapin, the Ohio-born owner, cooks one of the most generous and appealing breakfasts on the island; try the banana pancakes or the chile rellenos.

18 Queen Cross St., Christiansted, St. Croix, U.S.V.I. 00820. © 340/773-7383. Fax 340/773-8642. www.nav.to/thebreakfastclub. 9 units. Year-round $75 double. Rates include breakfast. AE, MC, V. Free parking. **Amenities:** Hammocks. In room: Fridge, kitchen, no phone.

The Frederiksted   This contemporary four-story inn is a good choice for the heart of historic Frederiksted. It's located in the center of town, about a 10-minute ride from the airport. Much of the activity takes place in the outdoor tiled courtyard, where guests enjoy drinks and listen to live music on Friday and Saturday nights. The cheery rooms are like those of a motel on the U.S. mainland, perhaps showing a bit of wear, and with good ventilation but bad lighting. They're done in a tropical motif of pastels and are equipped with small fridges. The best (and most expensive) rooms are those with ocean views; they're subject to street noise but have the best light. Each accommodation comes with a small, tiled shower-only bathroom. The nearest beach is Dorch Beach, a mile (2km) walk or a 5-minute drive from the hotel, along the water.

20 Strand St., Frederiksted, St. Croix, U.S.V.I. 00840. © 800/595-9519 in the U.S., or 340/772-0500. Fax 340/772-0500. www.frederikstedhotel.com. 40 units. Winter $100–$110 double. Off-season $90–$100 double. Extra person $10. AE, DISC, MC, V. **Amenities:** Restaurant; bar; pool; laundry. In room: A/C, TV, fridge, microwave.

Pink Fancy ⚡   This small, unique hotel is a block from the Annapolis Sailing School. You get more atmosphere here than anywhere else in town. The oldest part of the four-building complex is a historic 1780 Danish town house. In the 1950s, the hotel became a mecca for writers and artists, including, among others, Noël Coward. The owners have made major renovations, installing more antiques and fine furnishings. Guest rooms have a bright, tropical feel, with ceiling fans, floral prints, and rattan furnishings. The deluxe rooms are furnished with canopy or iron beds, as well as antiques and art work. The medium-size bathrooms have combination shower/tubs. A 3-minute launch ride takes guests to the beach on the Cay, a sandy islet in Christiansted's harbor.

27 Prince St., Christiansted, St. Croix, U.S.V.I. 00820. © **800/524-2045** in the U.S., or 340/773-8460. Fax 340/773-6448. www.pinkfancy.com. 12 units. Winter $95–$150 double. Off-season $85–$120 double. Extra person $20. Rates include continental breakfast. Ask about packages and weekly rates. AE, DC, DISC, MC, V. **Amenities:** Pool; laundry. *In room:* A/C, ceiling fan, TV, kitchenette, fridge, hair dryer.

DINING
IN CHRISTIANSTED

Comanche Club CARIBBEAN/CONTINENTAL Relaxed yet elegant, Comanche is one of the island's most popular restaurants. It's not the best, but the specialties are eclectic—everything from fish and conch chowder to shark cakes. Each night, a different special and a different local dish is featured. Other choices include salads, curries, fish sautéed with lemon butter and capers, and typical West Indian dishes such as conch Creole with fungi. There are also standard international dishes such as filet mignon in béarnaise sauce.

1 Strand St. © **340/773-2665.** Reservations recommended. Main courses $10–$27; lunch from $12. AE, DC, MC, V. Mon–Sat 11:30am–2:30pm and 5:30–9:30pm.

Indies ★★ CARIBBEAN Dan Finnegan is one of the best chefs on the island, and through his kitchen you're likely to get your finest meal on St. Croix. Indies is a welcoming retreat, set in a 19th-century courtyard lined with antique cobblestones. You dine adjacent to a carriage and cookhouse from the 1850s in a sheltered courtyard protected from the noise of the street outside. The menu changes depending on what's fresh. The fresh fish and lobster are caught in Caribbean waters, and local seasonal fruits and vegetables are featured. Try the swordfish with fresh artichokes, shiitake mushrooms, and thyme, or perhaps the baked wahoo with lobster curry and fresh chutney and coconut. Soup choices may include an excellent island lobster and shrimp bisque or a spicy black-bean soup. A different pasta dish is offered nightly. All the desserts are freshly made.

55–56 Company St. © **340/692-9440.** Reservations recommended. Main courses $18–$28. AE, DISC, MC, V. Mon–Fri 11:30am–2:30pm; Wed–Mon 6–10pm.

Kendricks FRENCH/CONTINENTAL This restaurant, the island's toniest, lies in the historic Quin House complex at King Cross and Company streets. It has both upstairs and downstairs dining rooms, the downstairs being more informal. Some of its recipes have been featured in *Bon Appétit,* and deservedly so. You'll immediately warm to such specialties as pan-seared Thai shrimp with cucumber relish and coconut-infused rice, and grilled filet mignon with black truffle in bordelaise sauce. The signature appetizer is seared scallops and artichoke hearts in lemon–cream sauce. Another great choice is the pecan-crusted roast pork loin with ginger mayonnaise.

2132 Company St. © **340/773-9199.** Reservations required for dinner upstairs. Main courses $22–$29. AE, MC, V. Mon–Sat 6–10pm.

Luncheria Mexican Food *Value* MEXICAN/CUBAN/PUERTO RICAN This Mexican restaurant offers great value. You get the usual tacos, tostadas, burritos, nachos, and enchiladas, as well as chicken fajitas, enchiladas verde, and *arroz con pollo* (spiced chicken with brown rice). Daily specials feature both low-calorie and vegetarian choices (the chef's refried beans are lard-free), and whole-wheat tortillas are offered. The complimentary salsa bar has mild to hot sauces, plus jalapeños. More recently, some Cuban and Puerto Rican dishes have appeared on the menu, including a zesty chicken curry, black-bean soup, and roast pork. The bartender makes the island's best margaritas.

In the historic Apothecary Hall Courtyard, 2111 Company St. ℂ **340/773-4247**. Main courses $5–$12. No credit cards. Mon–Sat 11am–9pm.

Nolan's Tavern INTERNATIONAL/WEST INDIAN   This is the best place to go for a warm, cozy tavern with no pretensions. It's across from the capital's most prominent elementary school, the Pearl B. Larsen School. Your host is Nolan Joseph, a Trinidad-born chef who makes a special point of welcoming guests and offering "tasty food and good service." No one will mind if you stop in just for a drink. Mr. Joseph, referred to by some diners as "King Conch," prepares that mollusk in at least half a dozen ways, including versions with curry, Creole sauce, and garlic-pineapple sauce. He reportedly experimented for 3 months to perfect a means of tenderizing the conch without artificial chemicals. His ribs are also excellent.

5A Estate St. Peter (2 miles/3km east of Christiansted's harbor), Christiansted East. ℂ **340/773-6660**. Reservations recommended only for groups of 6 or more. Burgers $7–$10; main courses $12.75–$20. AE, DISC, MC, V. Kitchen daily 5–9pm. Bar from 3pm.

Paradise Café DELI/AMERICAN   This neighborhood favorite draws locals seeking good food and great value. Its brick walls and beamed ceiling were originally part of an 18th-century great house. New York–style deli fare is served during the day. Enjoy the savory homemade soups or freshly made salads, to which you can add grilled chicken or fish. At breakfast, you can select from an assortment of omelets, or try the steak and eggs. Dinners are more elaborate. The 12-ounce New York strip steak and the freshly made pasta specialties are good choices. Appetizers include mango chicken quesadillas and crab cakes.

53B Company St. (at Queen Cross St., across from Government House). ℂ **340/773-2985**. Breakfast $4–$9.50; lunch $5–$10; dinner $14–$20. No credit cards. Mon–Sat 7:30am–10pm.

Tutto Bene ITALIAN   In the heart of town, this place seems more like a bistro-cantina than a full-fledged restaurant. The owners, Smokey Odom and Kelly Williams, believe in simple, hearty, and uncomplicated *paisano* dishes, the kind mammas fed their sons in the old country. You'll dine on wooden tables covered with painted tablecloths, amid warm colors and often lots of hubbub. Menu items are written on a pair of oversize mirrors against one wall. A full range of delectable pastas and well-prepared seafood is offered nightly. Fish might be served parmigiana, or you can order tutto di mare with mussels, clams, and shrimp in a white wine/pesto sauce over linguine. The large mahogany bar in back does a brisk business of its own.

2 Company St. ℂ **340/773-5229**. Reservations accepted only for parties of 5 or more. Main courses $14.95–$26.95. AE, MC, V. Daily 6–10pm.

IN FREDERIKSTED

Blue Moon INTERNATIONAL/CAJUN   The best little bistro in Frederiksted becomes a hot, hip spot during Sunday brunch and on Friday nights, when it offers entertainment. The 200-year-old stone house on the waterfront is a favorite of visiting jazz musicians, and tourists have now discovered (but not ruined) it. It's decorated with funky, homemade art from the U.S., including a trash-can–lid restaurant sign. The atmosphere is casual and cafe-like. Begin with the "lunar pie," with feta, cream cheese, onions, mushrooms, and celery in phyllo pastry, or the artichoke-and-spinach dip. Main courses include the catch of the day and, on occasion, Maine lobster. The clams served in garlic sauce are also from Maine. Vegetarians opt for the spinach fettuccine. There's also the usual array of steak and chicken dishes. Save room for the yummy apple spice pie.

17 Strand St. ✆ **340/772-2222.** Reservations recommended. Main courses $17.50–$31.50. AE, DISC, MC, V. Tues–Fri 11:30am–2pm, Sun 11am–2pm; Tues–Sat 5–9:30pm, Sun 6–9pm; Fri 9:30pm–2am. Closed Aug.

Le St. Tropez FRENCH/MEDITERRANEAN This is the most popular bistro in Frederiksted. It's small, so call ahead for a table. If you're visiting for the day, make this bright little cafe your lunch stop, and enjoy crepes, quiches, soups, or salads in the sunlit courtyard. At night, the atmosphere glows with candlelight and becomes more festive. Try the paté de champagne and escargots Provençale, or one of the freshly made soups. Main dishes are likely to include rack of lamb with mushrooms, the fish of the day, or a magret of duck. Ingredients are always fresh and well prepared.

Limetree Court, 227 King St. ✆ **340/772-3000.** Reservations recommended. Main courses $15–$27. AE, MC, V. Mon–Fri 11:30am–2:30pm and 6–10pm, Sat 6–10pm.

Villa Morales PUERTO RICAN This inland spot is one of the premier Puerto Rican restaurants on St. Croix. You can choose between indoor and outdoor seating areas. No one will mind if you come here just to drink; a cozy bar is lined with the memorabilia collected by several generations of the family who maintain the place. Look for a broad cross-section of Hispanic tastes here, including many that Puerto Ricans remember from their childhood. Savory examples include fried snapper with white rice and beans, stewed conch, roasted or stewed goat, and stewed beef. Meal platters are garnished with beans and rice. Most of the dishes are at the lower end of the price scale. About once a month, the owners transform the place into a dance hall, bringing in live salsa and merengue bands (the cover ranges from $5 to $15).

Plot 82C, off Route 70 (about 2 miles/3km from Frederiksted), Estate Whim. ✆ **340/772-0556.** Reservations recommended. Breakfast $4–$8; lunch main courses $7–$14; dinner main courses $8–$25. MC, V. Thurs–Sat 8am–10pm.

AROUND THE ISLAND

Cormorant Beach Club Restaurant ⨂INTERNATIONAL This is the premier gay restaurant on St. Croix. Both the restaurant and its bar are a mecca for gay and gay-friendly people who appreciate its relaxed atmosphere, well-prepared food, and gracefully arched premises overlooking the sea. The menu changes nightly with new flavorful and generous food items. Lunch specialties may include meal-size salads, club sandwiches, burgers, and fresh fish. Dinner might begin with carrot-ginger soup or Caribbean spring rolls with chutney; main courses could include steak au poivre, chicken breast stuffed with spinach and feta, grilled New Zealand lamb chops, and grilled fillets of salmon with roasted poblano orange sauce. Desserts feature tropical fruits baked into tempting pastries.

In the Cormorant Beach Club, 4126 La Grande Princesse. ✆ **340/778-8920.** Reservations recommended. Main courses $7–$12 lunch, $14–$24 dinner. AE, DC, DISC, MC, V. Daily 7:30am–9pm.

Duggan's Reef CONTINENTAL/CARIBBEAN This is one of the most popular restaurants on St. Croix. It's set only 10 feet (3m) from the still waters of Reef Beach and makes an ideal perch for watching windsurfers and Hobie Cats. At lunch, an array of salads, crepes, and sandwiches is offered. The more elaborate night menu features the popular house specialties: Duggan's Caribbean lobster pasta and Irish whiskey lobster. Begin with fried calamari or conch chowder. Main dishes include New York strip steak, veal piccata, and pastas. The local catch of the day can be baked, grilled, blackened Cajun style, or served island style (with tomato, pepper, and onion sauce).

East End Rd., Teague Bay. ✆ 340/773-9800. Reservations required for dinner in winter. Main courses $16–$33; pastas $15–$18. AE, MC, V. Daily 11am–3pm and 6–9:30pm. Bar daily 11am–11:30pm. Closed for lunch in summer.

The Galleon FRENCH/NORTHERN ITALIAN This restaurant, which overlooks the ocean, is a local favorite, and deservedly so. It offers the cuisine of northern Italy and France, including osso buco, just as good as that served in Milan. Freshly baked bread, two fresh vegetables, and rice or potatoes accompany main dishes. The menu always includes at least one local fish, such as wahoo, tuna, swordfish, mahi-mahi, or even fresh Caribbean lobster. Or you might order a perfectly done rack of lamb, which will be carved right at your table. There's an extensive wine list, including many sold by the glass. Music from a baby grand accompanies your dinner.

East End Rd., Green Cay Marina, 5000 Estate Southgate. ✆ 340/773-9949. Reservations recommended. Main courses $17–$40. AE, MC, V. Daily 6–10pm. Go east on Rte. 82 from Christiansted for 5 min.; after going a mile (2km) past the Buccaneer, turn left into Green Cay Marina.

Sprat Hall Beach Restaurant ✰ *(Finds* CARIBBEAN This informal spot is on the west coast, near Sprat Hall Plantation. It's the best place on the island to combine lunch and a swim. The restaurant has been in business since 1948, feeding both locals and visitors. Try such local dishes as conch chowder, pumpkin fritters, tannia soup, and the fried fish of the day. These dishes have authentic island flavor, perhaps more so than any other place on St. Croix. You can also get salads and burgers. The bread is baked fresh daily. The owners allow free use of the showers and changing rooms.

A mile (2km) north of Frederiksted on Rte. 63. ✆ 340/772-5855. Lunch $7–$14; main courses $14–$24. Daily 11:30am–2:30pm and 5:30–10pm.

HITTING THE BEACH

The most celebrated beach is offshore **Buck Island,** part of the U.S. National Park Service network. Buck Island is actually a volcanic islet surrounded by some of the most stunning underwater coral gardens in the Caribbean. The white-sand beaches on the southwest and west coasts are beautiful, but the snorkeling is even better. The islet's interior is filled with such plants as cactus, wild frangipani, and pigeonwood. There are picnic areas for those who want to make a day of it. Boat departures are from Kings Wharf in Christiansted; the ride takes half an hour. For more information, see the section "Buck Island," later this chapter.

Your best choice for a beach in Christiansted is the one at the **Hotel on the Cay.** This white-sand strip is on a palm-shaded island. To get here, take the ferry from the fort at Christiansted; it runs daily from 7am to midnight. The 4-minute trip costs $3, free for guests of the Hotel on the Cay. Five miles (8km) west of Christiansted is the **Cormorant Beach Club,** where some 1,200 feet (360m) of white sand shaded by palm trees attracts a gay crowd. Since a reef lies just off the shore, snorkeling conditions are ideal.

We highly recommend both **Davis Bay** and **Cane Bay,** with swaying palms, white sand, and good swimming and snorkeling. Because they're on the north shore, these beaches are often windy, and their waters are not always tranquil. The snorkeling at Cane Bay is truly spectacular; you'll see elkhorn and brain corals, all lying some 250 yards (228m) off the "Cane Bay Wall." Cane Bay adjoins Route 80 on the north shore. Davis Beach doesn't have a reef; it's more popular among bodysurfers than snorkelers. There are no changing facilities. It's near Carambola Beach Resort.

On Route 63, a short ride north of Frederiksted, lies **Rainbow Beach,** which offers white sand and ideal snorkeling conditions. Nearby, also on Route 63, about 5 minutes north of Frederiksted, is another good beach, called **La Grange.** Lounge chairs can be rented here, and there's a bar nearby.

Sandy Point, directly south of Frederiksted, is the largest beach in all the U.S. Virgin Islands. Its waters are shallow and calm, perfect for swimming. Try to concentrate on the sands and not the unattractive zigzagging fences that line the beach. Take the Melvin Evans Highway (Route 66) west from the Alexander Hamilton Airport.

There's an array of beaches at the east end of the island; they're somewhat difficult to get to, but much less crowded. The best choice here is **Isaac Bay Beach,** ideal for snorkeling, swimming, or sunbathing. Windsurfers like **Reef Beach,** which opens onto Teague Bay along Route 82, East End Road, a half-hour ride from Christiansted. You can get food at Duggan's Reef. **Cramer Park** is a special public park operated by the Department of Agriculture. It's lined with sea-grape trees and has a picnic area, a restaurant, and a bar. **Grapetree Beach** is off Route 60 (the South Shore Road). Watersports are popular here.

SPORTS & OTHER OUTDOOR PURSUITS

Some of the best snorkeling, diving, and hiking are found on Buck Island. See the section "Buck Island," later this chapter.

FISHING   The fishing grounds at **Lang Bank** are about 10 miles (16km) from St. Croix. Here you'll find kingfish, dolphin fish, and wahoo. Using light-tackle boats to glide along the reef, you'll probably turn up jack or bonefish. At **Clover Crest,** in Frederiksted, local anglers fish right from the rocks.

Serious sportfishers can board the *Fantasy,* a 38-foot (11m) Bertram special available for 4-, 6-, or 8-hour charters, with bait and tackle included. It's anchored at St. Croix Marina, Gallows Bay. Reservations can be made by calling © **340/773-2628** during the day, or 340/773-0917 at night. The cost for up to six passengers is $400 for 4 hours, $550 to $600 for 6 hours, and $800 for 8 hours.

GOLF   St. Croix has the best golf in the U.S. Virgins. Guests staying on St. John and St. Thomas often fly over for a day's round on one of the island's three courses.

The **Carambola Golf Course,** on the northeast side of St. Croix (© **340/778-5638**), was created by Robert Trent Jones, Sr., who called it "the loveliest course I ever designed." It's been likened to a botanical garden. The par-3 holes here are known to golfing authorities as the best in the tropics. The greens fee of $100 in winter, or $58 in summer, allows you to play as many holes as you like. Carts are included.

Buccaneer, Gallows Bay (© **340/773-2100,** ext. 738), 2 miles (3km) east of Christiansted, has a challenging 5,810-yard (5,287m), 18-hole course with panoramic vistas. Nonguests of this deluxe resort pay $65 in winter or $45 off-season, plus $15 for use of a cart.

The **Reef,** on the east end of the island at Teague Bay (© **340/773-8844**), is a 3,100-yard (2,821m), 9-hole course, charging greens fees of $20 including carts. The longest hole here is a 579-yard (527m) par 5.

HIKING   Scrub-covered hills make up much of St. Croix's landscape. The island's western district, however, includes a dense, 15-acre (6-hectare) forest known as the **"Rain Forest"** (though it's not a real one). The network of footpaths here offer some of the best nature walks in the Caribbean. For more details on hiking in this area, see "The Rain Forest," below. **Buck Island** (see the section "Buck Island," below), just off St. Croix, also offers some wonderful nature trails.

The **St. Croix Environmental Association,** Arawak Building, Suite 3, Gallows Bay (© 340/773-1989), has regularly scheduled hikes from December to March. A minimum of four people are required, costing $12 per person.

HORSEBACK RIDING   **Paul and Jill's Equestrian Stables,** 2 Sprat Hall Estate, Route 58 (© 340/772-2880), the largest equestrian stable in the Virgin Islands, is known throughout the Caribbean for the quality of its horses. It's set on the sprawling grounds of the island's oldest plantation great house. The operators lead scenic trail rides through the forests, past ruins of abandoned 18th-century plantations and sugar mills, to the tops of the hills of St. Croix's western end. Beginners and experienced riders alike are welcome. A 2-hour trail ride costs $50. Tours usually depart daily in winter at 10am and 3pm, and in the off-season at 4pm, with slight variations according to demand. Reserve at least a day in advance.

KAYAKING   The beauty of St. Croix is best seen on a kayak tour offered by **Caribbean Adventure Tours** (© 340/773-4599). You use stable, sit-on-top ocean kayaks, which are a blast to use. These enable you to traverse the tranquil waters of Salt River of Columbus landfall fame and enjoy the park's ecology and wildlife, including going into secluded estuaries and mangrove groves. Some of the landscape was used as ancient Indian burial grounds. The highlights of the trip are snorkeling on a pristine beach and paddling to where Christopher Columbus and his crew came ashore some 500 years ago. The tour, lasting 3 hours, costs $50 per person.

SAFARI TOURS   The best are offered by **St. Croix Safari Tours** (© 340/773-6700) in a 25-passenger open-air bus tour run by a hip tour guide who knows all about the botany, cuisine, and history of the island. Tours crisscross the island with stops at plantation houses, historic Frederiksted, the Salt River landfall of Columbus, and a drive through the rain forest, with a stop for lunch. There are lots of photo ops. The cost of the tour is $40 per person.

SNORKELING & SCUBA DIVING ★★   Sponge life, black coral (the finest in the West Indies), and steep drop-offs into water near the shoreline make St. Croix a snorkeling and diving paradise. The island is home to the largest living reef in the Caribbean, including the fabled north-shore wall that begins in 25 to 30 feet (7.5–9m) of water and drops to 13,200 feet (3,960m), sometimes straight down. See "Hitting the Beach," above, for information on good snorkeling beaches. The **St. Croix Water Sports Center** (see "Windsurfing," below) rents snorkeling equipment for $20 per day if your hotel doesn't supply it.

Buck Island ★★ is a major scuba-diving site, with a visibility of some 100 feet (30m). It also has an underwater snorkeling trail. All the outfitters offer scuba and snorkeling tours to Buck Island. See the section "Buck Island," below.

Other favorite dive sites include the historic **Salt River Canyon** (northwest of Christiansted at Salt River Bay), which is for advanced divers. Submerged canyon walls are covered with purple tube sponges, deep-water gorgonians, and black coral saplings. You'll see schools of yellowtail snapper, turtles, and spotted eagle rays. We also like the gorgeous coral gardens of **Scotch Banks** (north of Christiansted), and **Eagle Ray** (also north of Christiansted), the latter so named because of the rays that cruise along the wall there. **Cane Bay** ★★ is known for its coral canyons.

Davis Bay is the site of the 12,000-foot-deep (3,600m) Puerto Rico Trench. **Northstar Reef,** at the east end of Davis Bay, is a spectacular wall dive, recommended for intermediate or experienced divers only. The wall here is covered with stunning brain corals and staghorn thickets. At some 50 feet (15m) down, a sandy shelf leads to a cave where giant green moray eels hang out.

The ultimate night dive is at the **Frederiksted Pier.** The old pier was damaged by Hurricane Hugo and torn down to make way for a new one. The heavily encrusted rubble from the old pier remains beneath the new one, carpeted with rainbow-hued sponges and both hard and soft coral, preserving a fantastic night dive where you're virtually guaranteed to see seahorses and moray eels.

At **Butler Bay,** to the north of the pier on the west shore, three ships were wrecked: the *Suffolk Maid,* the *Northwind,* and the *Rosaomaira,* the latter sitting in 100 feet (30m) of water. These wrecks form the major part of an artificial reef system made up mostly of abandoned trucks and cars. This site is recommended for intermediate or experienced divers.

Anchor Dive, Salt River National Park (© **800/523-DIVE** in the U.S., or 340/778-1522), is located within the most popular dive destination in St. Croix., They operate four boats including the 27-foot (11m) dive boat *Queen Bee.* The staff offers complete instruction, from resort courses through full certification, as well as night dives. A resort course is $85, with a two-tank dive going for $125. Scuba trips to Buck Island cost $65, and dive packages begin at $320 for five dives.

Other recommended outfitters include the **Cane Bay Dive Shop** (© **340/ 773-9913**) and **St. Croix Ultimate Bluewater Adventure** (© **877/789-7282**).

TENNIS Some authorities rate the tennis at the **Buccaneer** ★★, Gallows Bay (© **340/773-2100,** ext. 736), as the best in the Caribbean. This resort offers a choice of eight courts, two lit for night play, all open to the public. Nonguests pay $18 per person per hour; you must call to reserve a court. A tennis pro is available for lessons, and there's also a pro shop.

WINDSURFING Head for the **St. Croix Water Sports Center** (© **340/ 773-7060**), located on a small offshore island in Christiansted Harbor and part of the Hotel on the Cay. It's open daily from 10am to 5pm. Windsurfing rentals are $30 per hour. Lessons are available. Sea Doos that seat two can be rented for $45 to $55 per half hour. The center also offers parasailing for $65 per person, and rents snorkeling equipment for $25 per day.

EXPLORING ST. CROIX

Taxi tours are the ideal way to explore the island. The cost is around $60 for 2 hours or $100 for 3 hours for one or two passengers. All prices should be negotiated in advance. For more information, call the **St. Croix Taxi Association** at © **340/778-1088.**

CHRISTIANSTED ★★

One of the most picturesque towns in the Caribbean, **Christiansted** is an old, handsomely restored (or at least in the process of being restored) Danish port. On the northeastern shore of the island, on a coral-bound bay, the town is filled with Danish buildings erected by prosperous merchants in the booming 18th century. These red-roofed structures are often washed in pink, ocher, or yellow. Arcades over the sidewalks provide shade for shoppers. The whole area around the harbor front has been designated a historic site, including **Government House** (© **340/ 773-1404**), which is looked after by the U.S. National Park Service.

Steeple Building   This building's full name is the Church of Lord God of Sabaoth. It was built in 1753 as St. Croix's first Lutheran church, and it was deconsecrated in 1831; the building subsequently served at various times as a bakery, a hospital, and a school. Today, it houses exhibits relating to island history and culture.

On the waterfront off Hospital St. ℭ **340/773-1460**. Admission $2 (also includes admission to Fort Christiansvaern). Mon–Fri 8:30am–4:30pm.

Fort Christiansvaern   This fortress overlooking the harbor is the best-preserved colonial fortification in the Virgin Islands. It's maintained as a historic monument by the U.S. National Park Service. Its original four-pronged, star-shaped design was in accordance with the most advanced military planning of its era. The fort is now the site of the St. Croix Police Museum, which has exhibits on police work on the island from the late 1800s to the present.

ℭ **340/773-1460**. Admission $2 Daily 8am–4:45pm.

St. Croix Aquarium   This aquarium has expanded with many new exhibits, including one devoted to "night creatures." In all, it houses some 40 species of marine animals and more than 100 species of invertebrates. A touch pond contains starfish, sea cucumbers, brittle stars, and pencil urchins. The aquarium allows you to become familiar with the marine life you'll see while scuba diving or snorkeling.

Caravelle Arcade. ℭ **340/773-8995**. Admission $5 adults, $2 children. Tues–Sat 11am–4pm.

FREDERIKSTED ⊛

This former Danish settlement at the western end of the island, about 17 miles (27km) from Christiansted, is a sleepy port town that comes to life only when a cruise ship docks at its shoreline. Frederiksted was destroyed by a fire in 1879. Its citizens subsequently rebuilt it with wood frames and clapboards on top of the old Danish stone and yellow-brick foundations.

Most visitors begin their tour at russet-colored **Fort Frederik,** at the northern end of Frederiksted next to the cruise-ship pier (ℭ **340/772-2021**). This fort, completed in 1760, is said to have been the first to salute the flag of the new United States. When a U.S. brigantine anchored at port in Frederiksted hoisted a homemade Old Glory, the fort returned the salute with cannon fire, violating the rules of neutrality. Also, it was here on July 3, 1848, that Governor-General Peter von Scholten emancipated the slaves in the Danish West Indies, in response to a slave uprising led by a young man named Moses "Buddhoe" Gottlieb. In 1998, a bust of Buddhoe was unveiled here. The fort has

---

Moments **Exploring Under Water Without Getting Wet**

St. Croix Water Sports Center (& 340/773-7060), located at the Hotel on the Cay, features the Oceanique, a semi-submersible vessel that acts as part submarine and part cruiser. It takes visitors on 1-hour excursions through Christiansted harbor and along Protestant Cay. The inch-thick windows lining the vessel's underwater observation room provide views of St. Croix's colorful marine life, in a cool and dry environment. This trip is especially popular with children and nonswimmers. Day and night excursions are available for $45 for adults and $35 for children. Call for reservations.

The Heritage Trail

A trail that leads into the past, St. Croix Heritage Trail, launched at the millennium, helps visitors relive the Danish colonial past of the island. All you need are a brochure and map, available at the tourist office in Christiansted (see p. 732), and you can set out on this 72-mile (116km) road which teems with historical and cultural sights. The St. Croix Heritage Trail is 1 of the 50 nationwide Millennium Legacy Trails launched in 2000.

The route, among other of the trail's historic sites, connects the two major towns of Christiansted and Frederiksted, going past the sites of former sugar plantations.

The trail traverses the entire 28-mile (45km) length of St. Croix, passing cattle farms, suburban communities, even industrial complexes and resorts. So it's not all manicured and pretty. But much of it is scenic and worth the drive. Allow at least a day for this trail, with stops along the way.

Nearly everyone gets out of the car at Point Udall, the easternmost point under the U.S. flag. You'll pass an eclectic mix of churches and even a prison. The route consists mainly of existing roadways, and that pamphlet you picked up will identify everything you're seeing.

The highlight of the trail is the Estate Mount Washington (see p. 748), a strikingly well-preserved sugar plantation. Another highlight is Estate Whim Plantation (see p. 749), one of the best of the restored great houses with a museum and gift shop. Another stop along the way is along Salt River Bay, which cuts into the northern shoreline. This is the site of Columbus's landfall in 1493.

Of course, you'll want to stop and get to know the locals. We recommend a refreshing stop at Smithens Market along the trail. Lying off Queen Mary Highway, vendors here offer freshly squeezed sugarcane juice and sell locally grown fruits and homemade chutneys.

been restored to its 1840 appearance and is today a national historic landmark. You can explore the courtyard and stables. A local history museum has been installed in what was once the Garrison Room. Admission is free. It's open Monday to Friday from 8:30am to 4:30pm.

The **Customs House,** just east of the fort, is an 18th-century building with a 19th-century two-story gallery. To the south of the fort is the **visitors' bureau,** at Strand Street ((C) **340/772-0357**), where you can pick up a free map of the town.

BUCK ISLAND ★★★

The crystal-clear water and white coral sand of **Buck Island,** a satellite of St. Croix, are legendary. Some call this island the single most important attraction of the Caribbean. Only ⅓ mile (.5km) wide and a mile (2km) long, Buck Island lies 1½ miles (2km) off the northeastern coast of St. Croix. A barrier reef here shelters many reef fish, including queen angelfish and smooth trunkfish. In years past, the island was frequented by the swashbuckling likes of Morgan, Blackbeard, and even Captain Kidd.

Buck Island's greatest attraction is its **underwater snorkeling trails,** which ring part of the island and provide some of the most beautiful underwater views in the Caribbean. Plan on spending at least two-thirds of a day at this extremely famous ecological site, which is maintained by the U.S. National Park Service. There are also many labyrinths and grottoes for **scuba divers.** The sandy beach has picnic tables and barbecue pits, as well as restrooms and a small changing room.

You can follow **hiking trails** through the tropical vegetation that covers the island. Circumnavigating the island on foot takes about 2 hours. Buck Island's trails meander from several points along its coastline to its sunny summit, affording views over nearby St. Croix. *A couple of warnings:* Wear lots of sunscreen. Even more important, don't rush to touch every plant you see. The island's western edge has groves of poisonous machineel trees, whose leaves, bark, and fruit cause extreme irritation to human skin that comes into contact with them.

Small boats run between St. Croix and Buck Island. Nearly all charters provide snorkeling equipment and allow for 1½ hours of snorkeling and swimming. **Mile Mark Watersports,** in the King Christian Hotel, 59 King's Wharf, Christiansted (© **800/523-DIVE** or 340/773-2628), conducts two different types of tours. The first option is a half-day tour aboard a glass-bottom boat departing from the King Christian Hotel, daily from 9:30am to 1pm and 1:30 to 5pm; it costs $35 per person. The second is a full-day tour, offered daily from 10am to 4pm on a 40-foot (12m) catamaran, for $65. Included in this excursion is a small picnic on Buck Island's beach.

Captain Heinz (© **340/773-3161** or 340/773-4041) is an Austrian-born skipper with more than 25 years of sailing experience. His trimaran, *Teroro II,* leaves the Green Cay Marina "H" Dock at 9am and 2pm, never filled with more than 23 passengers. This snorkeling trip costs $50 for adults, $30 for children age 10 and under. The captain is not only a skilled sailor but also a considerate host. He will even take you around the outer reef, which the other guides do not, for an unforgettable underwater experience.

THE "RAIN FOREST" ⌾

The island's western district contains a dense, 15-acre (6-hectare) forest, called the "Rain Forest" (though it's not a real one). The area is thick with mahogany trees, *kapok* (silk-cotton) trees, turpentine (red-birch) trees, *samaan* (rain) trees, and all kinds of ferns and vines. Sweet limes, mangoes, hog plums, and breadfruit trees, all of which have grown in the wild since the days of the plantations, are also interspersed among the larger trees. Crested hummingbirds, pearly eyed thrashers, green-throated caribs, yellow warblers, and perky but drably camouflaged banana quits nest here. The 150-foot-high (45m) Creque Dam is the major man-made sight in the area.

The "Rain Forest" is private property, but the owner lets visitors go inside to explore. To experience its charm, some people opt to drive along Route 76 (also known as Mahogany Road), stopping beside the footpaths that meander off on either side of the highway into dry riverbeds and glens. It's advisable to stick to the best-worn of the footpaths. You can also hike along some of the little-traveled four-wheel-drive roads in the area. Three of the best for hiking are the **Creque Dam Road** (routes 58/78), the **Scenic Road** (route 78), and the **Western Scenic Road** (routes 63/78).

Our favorite trail in this area takes about 2½ hours one way. From Frederiksted, drive north on route 63 until you reach Creque Dam Road, where you turn right, park the car, and start walking. About a mile (2km) past the 150-foot

(45m) Creque Dam, you'll be deep within the forest's magnificent flora and fauna. Continue along the trail until you come to the Western Scenic Road. Eventually, you reach Mahogany Road (Route 76), near St. Croix Leap Project. Hikers rate this trail moderate in difficulty.

You could also begin near the junction of Creque Dam Road and Scenic Road. From here, your trek will cover a broad triangular swath, heading north and then west along Scenic Road. First, the road will rise, and then descend toward the coastal lighthouse of the island's extreme northwestern tip, **Hams Bluff.** Most trekkers decide to retrace their steps after about 45 minutes of northwesterly hiking. Real diehards, however, will continue all the way to the coastline, then head south along the coastal road (Butler Bay Road), and finally head east along Creque Dam Road to their starting point at the junction of Creque Dam Road and Scenic Road. Embark on this longer expedition only if you're really prepared for a hike lasting about 5 hours.

SANDY POINT WILDLIFE REFUGE ✿
St. Croix's rarely visited southwestern tip is composed of salt marshes, tidal pools, and low vegetation inhabited by birds, turtles, and other forms of wildlife. More than 3 miles (5km) of ecologically protected coastline lie between Sandy Point (the island's most westerly tip) and the shallow waters of the Westend Salt-pond. The area is home to colonies of green, leatherback, and hawksbill turtles. It's one of only two such places in U.S. waters. It's also home to thousands of birds, including herons, brown pelicans, Caribbean martins, black-necked stilts, and white-crowned pigeons. As for flora, Sandy Point gave its name to a rare form of orchids, a brown/purple variety.

This wildlife refuge is only open on Saturday and Sunday from 8am to 6pm. To get here, drive to the end of Route 66 (Melvin Evans highway) and continue down a gravel road. For guided weekend visits, call the **St. Croix Environmental Association** (© **340/773-1989** or 340/773-4554).

AROUND THE ISLAND
North of Frederiksted, you can drop in at **Sprat Hall,** the island's oldest planta-tion, or else continue along to the "Rain Forest" (see above). Most visitors come to the area to see the jagged estuary of the northern coastline's **Salt River.** The Salt River was where Columbus landed on November 14, 1493. Marking the 500th anniversary of Columbus's arrival, former president George Bush signed a bill creating the 912-acre (365-hectare) **Salt River Bay National Historical Park and Ecological Preserve.** The park contains the site of the original Carib village explored by Columbus and his men, including the only ceremonial ball court ever discovered in the Lesser Antilles. Also within the park is the largest mangrove forest in the Virgin Islands, sheltering many endangered animals and plants, plus an underwater canyon attracting divers from around the world. Call the **St. Croix Environmental Association,** 3 Arawak Building, Gallows Bay (© **340/773-1989**), for information on tours of the area. Tours cost $25 for adults, $12 for children under age 10.

Estate Mount Washington Plantation is the island's best-preserved sugar plantation and a highlight along the St. Croix Heritage Trail. It flourished from 1780 to 1820 when St. Croix was the second largest producer of sugar in the West Indies. The on-site private residence is closed to the public, but you can go on a self-guided tour of the 13 acres (5 hectares) at any time of the day you wish (there is no admission charge, although donations are appreciated). You'll see what is the best antique store on St. Croix, but you can visit only if you call

Moments   **The Easternmost Point of the United States**

The rocky promontory of **Point Udall,** jutting into the Caribbean Sea, is the easternmost point of the United States. Diehards go out to see the sun rise, but considering the climb via a rutted dirt road, you may want to wait until there's more light before heading here. Once at the top, you'll be rewarded with one of the best views in the U.S. Virgin Islands. On the way to the lookout point, you'll see "The Castle," a local architectural oddity, owned by the island's most prominent socialite, the Contessa Nadia Farbo Navarro. Point Udall is signposted along Route 82.

C **340/772-1026** and ask for an appointment. The plantation site lies at the very southwestern tip of the island, off Route 63, a mile (2km) inland from the highway that runs along the Frederiksted coast.

St. George Village Botanical Garden   This is a 16-acre (6-hectare) Eden of tropical trees, shrubs, vines, and flowers. The garden is a feast for the eye and the camera, from the entrance drive bordered by royal palms and bougainvillea to the towering kapok and tamarind trees. It was built around the ruins of a 19th-century sugarcane workers' village. Self-guided walking-tour maps are available at the entrance to the garden's great hall. Facilities include restrooms and a gift shop.

127 Estate St. (just north of Centerline Road, 4 miles (6km) east of Frederiksted), Kingshill. *C* **340/692-2874.** Admission $6 adults, $1 children age 12 and under; donations welcome. Dec–May daily 9am–5pm; Jun–Nov Tues–Sat 9am–3pm.

Cruzan Rum Factory   This factory distills the famous Virgin Islands rum, which some consider the finest in the world. Guided tours depart from the visitors' pavilion; call for reservations and information. There's also a gift shop.

W. Airport Rd., Rte. 64. *C* **340/692-2280.** Admission $4. Tours given Mon–Fri 9–10:30am and 1–4:15pm.

Estate Whim Plantation Museum   This restored great house is unique among those of the many sugar plantations whose ruins dot the island. It's composed of only three rooms. With 3-foot-thick (.9m) walls made of stone, coral, and molasses, the house resembles a luxurious European château. A division of Baker Furniture Company used the Whim Plantation's collection of models for one of its most successful reproductions, the "Whim Museum–West Indies Collection." A showroom here sells the reproductions, plus others from the Caribbean, including pineapple-motif four-poster beds, cane-bottomed planters' chairs with built-in leg rests, and Caribbean adaptations of Empire-era chairs with cane-bottomed seats.

Also on the premises is a woodworking shop that features tools and exhibits on techniques from the 18th century, the estate's original kitchen, a museum store, and a servant's quarters. The ruins of the plantation's sugar-processing plant, complete with a restored windmill, also remain.

Centerline Rd. (2 miles/3km east of Frederiksted). *C* **340/772-0598.** Admission $6 adults, $2 children. Jun–Oct Tues–Fri 10am–3pm; Nov–May Tues–Sat 10am–3pm.

SHOPPING ✰✰✰

In Christiansted, the emphasis is on hole-in-the-wall boutiques selling one-of-a-kind merchandise; the selection of handmade items is especially strong. Knowing that it can't compete with the volume of Charlotte Amalie on St. Thomas, Christiansted has forged its own identity as the chic spot for merchandise in the

Caribbean. All its shops are within about a ½ mile (.8km) of each other. The relatively new **King's Alley Complex** (© 340/778-8135) is a pink-sided compound filled with the densest concentration of shops on St. Croix.

In recent years, **Frederiksted** has also become a popular shopping destination. Its urban mall appeals to cruise-ship passengers arriving at Frederiksted Pier. The mall is on a 50-foot (15m) strip of land between Strand and King streets, the town's bustling main thoroughfare.

Below are our favorite shops in Christiansted.

The operators of **Folk Art Traders,** Strand Street (© 340/773-1900), travel throughout the Caribbean ("in the bush") to add to their unique collection of local art and folk-art treasures: Carnival masks, pottery, ceramics, original paintings, hand-wrought jewelry, batiks from Barbados, and high-quality iron sculpture from Haiti. There's nothing else like it in the Virgin Islands.

At the hip and eclectic **From the Gecko,** 1233 Queen Cross St. (© 340/778-9433), you can find anything from hand-painted local cottons and silks to that old West Indian staple, batiks. We found the Indonesian collection here among the most imaginative in the U.S. Virgin Islands—everything from ornate candle holders to hemp linens.

Many Hands, in the Pan Am Pavilion, Strand Street (© 340/773-1990), sells West Indian spices and teas, locally made shellwork, stained glass, hand-painted china, pottery, and handmade jewelry. The collection of local paintings is intriguing, as is the year-round "Christmas tree."

Purple Papaya, 39 Strand St., Pan Am Pavilion (© 340/713-9412), is the best place to go for inexpensive island gifts. It has the biggest array of embroidered T-shirts and sweatshirts on island. Although you're in the Caribbean and not Hawaii, there is a large selection of Hawaiian shirts and dresses, along with beachwear for the whole family, plus island souvenirs.

Royal Poinciana, 1111 Strand St. (© 340/773-9892), looks like an antique apothecary. You'll find hot sauces, seasoning blends for gumbos, island herbal teas, Antillean coffees, and a scented array of soaps, toiletries, lotions, and shampoos. There's also a selection of museum-reproduction greeting cards and calendars, plus educational but fun gifts for children.

About 60% of the merchandise at **Gone Tropical,** 55 Company St. (© 340/773-4696), is made in Indonesia (usually Bali). Prices of new, semi-antique, or antique sofas, beds, chests, tables, mirrors, and decorative carvings are the same as (and sometimes less than) those of new furniture in conventional stores. Gone Tropical also sells art objects, jewelry, batiks, candles, and baskets.

The small West Indian cottage of **Crucian Gold,** 59 Kings Wharf (© 340/773-5241), holds the gold and silver creations of island-born Brian Bishop. His most popular item is the Crucian bracelet, which contains a "True Lovers' Knot" in its design. The shop also sells hand-tied knots (bound in gold wire), rings, pendants, and earrings.

Elegant Illusions Copy Jewelry, 55 King St. (© 340/773-2727), a branch of a hugely successful chain based in California, sells convincing fake jewelry. The look-alikes range in price from $9 to $1,000, and include credible copies of the baroque and antique jewelry your great-grandmother might have worn. If you want the real thing, you can go next door to **King Alley Jewelry** (© 340/773-4746), which is owned by the same company and specializes in fine designer jewelry, including Tiffany and Cartier.

Sonya Hough of **Sonya Ltd.,** 1 Company St. (© 340/778-8605), has a group of loyal local fans who wouldn't leave home without wearing one of her bracelets. She's most famous for the sterling-silver and gold versions of her C-clasp bracelet. Locals say that if the cup of the "C" is turned toward your heart, it means you're emotionally committed; if the cup is turned outward, it means you're available. Prices range from $20 to $2,500.

Everything sold at **Waterfront Larimar Mines,** the Boardwalk/King's Walk (© **340/692-9000**), is produced by the largest manufacturer of gold settings for larimar in the world. Discovered in the 1970s, larimar is a pale-blue pectolyte prized for its color. It comes from mines located in only one mountain in the world, on the southwestern edge of the Dominican Republic. Prices range from $25 to $1,000. Although other shops sell the stone as well, this place has the widest selection.

Coconut Vine, Pan Am Pavilion (© **340/773-1991**), is one of the most colorful and popular little boutiques on the island. Hand-painted batiks for both men and women are the specialty.

Urban Threadz/Tribal Threadz, 52C Company St. (© **340/773-2883**), is the most comprehensive clothing store in Christiansted's historic core, with a two-story, big-city scale and appeal. It's where island residents prefer to shop for hip, urban styles. Men's items are on the street level, women's upstairs. The inventory includes everything from Bermuda shorts to lightweight summer blazers and men's suits. The store carries Calvin Klein, Nautica, and Oakley, among other brands.

White House, King's Alley Walk (© **340/773-9222**), is about fashion, not politics. Everything is white or off-white—nothing darker than beige is allowed on the premises. The women's clothing here ranges from casual and breezy to dressy.

ST. CROIX AFTER DARK

St. Croix doesn't have the nightlife of St. Thomas. To find the action, you might have to consult the publication *St. Croix This Week,* which is distributed free to cruise-ship and air passengers and is also available at the tourist office.

Try to catch a performance of the **Quadrille Dancers,** a real cultural treat. Their dances have changed little since plantation days. The women wear long dresses, white gloves, and turbans, while the men wear flamboyant shirts, sashes, and tight black trousers. After you've learned their steps, you're invited to join the dancers on the floor. Ask at your hotel if and where they're performing.

The 1,100-seat **Island Center** amphitheater, a ½ mile (.6km) north of Sunny Isle (© **340/773-5272**), continues to attract big-name entertainers. Its program is widely varied, ranging from jazz and musical revues to Broadway plays. Consult *St. Croix This Week* or call the center to see what's being presented. The Caribbean Community Theatre and Courtyard Players perform here regularly. Tickets range from $10 to $30.

The big nightlife news of St. Croix is the opening of the **Divi Casino,** the first on St. Croix, at the new Divi Carina Bay Resort, 25 Estate Turner Hole (© **340/773-9700**). After much protest and controversy, gambling was introduced in spring 2000. The 10,000-square-foot (3,000 sq. km) casino boasts 12 gaming tables and 275 slot machines. St. Croix has traditionally taken a back seat to St. Thomas when it comes to tourism, and it is hoped that the casino will generate more visitors to the island.

If you're looking to hear some live music, try **Blue Moon,** 17 Strand St. (© **340/772-2222**), a hip little dive and also a good bistro. It's currently the hottest spot in Frederiksted on Fridays, when a five-piece ensemble entertains. There's no cover.

The **Terrace Lounge,** in the Buccaneer, Route 82, Estate Shoys (© **340/773-2100**), off the main dining room of one of St. Croix's most upscale hotels, welcomes some of the Caribbean's finest entertainers every night, often including a full band.

2 Plus 2 Disco, at the La Grande Princess (© 340/773-3710), is a real Caribbean disco. It features the regional sounds of the islands, not only calypso and reggae but also salsa and *soca* (a hybrid of calypso and reggae). Usually there's a DJ, except on weekends when local bands are brought in. The place isn't fancy or large. Come here for *Saturday Night Fever.* Hours are Thursday and Sunday from 8:30pm to 2am and Friday and Saturday from 8pm to either 5 or 6am. The cover is $5 to $10 when there's a live band.

For a sunset cocktail, head to the **Marina Bar,** in the King's Alley Hotel, King's Alley/The Waterfront (© 340/773-0103). It has a great position on the waterfront, on a shaded terrace overlooking the deep-blue sea and Protestant Cay. It's open throughout the day, but the most appealing activities begin right after the last seaplane departs for St. Thomas, around 5:30pm, and continue until 8:30pm. Cocktails made with rum, mango, banana, papaya, and grenadine are the drinks of choice. You can also stave off hunger pangs with burgers, sandwiches, and West Indian–style platters. There's live entertainment most nights, usually street bands. On Monday, you can bet on crab races.

Cormorant Beach Club Bar, 4126 La Grande Princesse (© 340/778-8920), is set in a predominantly gay resort about 3 miles (5km) northwest of Christiansted. It caters both to resort guests and to gay men and women from other parts of the island. You can sit at tables overlooking the ocean or around an open-centered mahogany bar, adjacent to a gazebo. Excellent tropical drinks are mixed here, including the house specialty, a Cormorant Cooler, made with champagne, pineapple juice, and Triple Sec.

4 St. John (★)(★)(★)

A few miles east of St. Thomas, across a glistening, turquoise channel known as Pillsbury Sound, lies St. John, the smallest and least densely populated of the three main U.S. Virgin Islands.

St. John is a wonder of unspoiled beauty. Along its rocky coastline are beautiful crescent-shaped bays and white-sand beaches, and the interior is no less impressive. The variety of wildlife here is the envy of naturalists around the world. And there are miles of serpentine hiking trails, leading past the ruins of 18th-century Danish plantations to magnificent panoramic views. At scattered intervals along the trails, you can even find mysteriously geometric petroglyphs, of unknown age and origin, incised into boulders and cliffs.

Today, St. John (unlike the other U.S. islands) remains truly pristine, its preservation rigidly enforced by the U.S. Park Service. Thanks to the efforts of Laurance Rockefeller, who purchased acres of land here and donated them to the United States, the island's shoreline waters, as well as more than half its surface area, comprise the **Virgin Islands National Park.** The hundreds of coral gardens that surround St. John are protected rigorously—any attempt to damage or remove coral from the water is punishable with large and strictly enforced fines.

Despite the unspoiled beauty of much of St. John, the island manages to provide visitors with modern amenities and travel services, including a sampling of restaurants, car-rental kiosks, yacht-supply facilities, hotels, and campgrounds. **Cinnamon Bay,** founded by the U.S. National Park Service in 1964, is the most famous campsite in the Caribbean. In addition, the roads are well maintained, and there's even a small commercial center, **Cruz Bay,** on the island's western

St. John

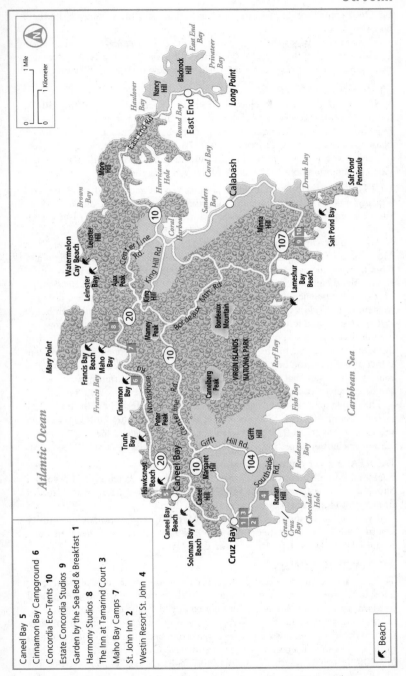

- Caneel Bay **5**
- Cinnamon Bay Campground **6**
- Concordia Eco-Tents **10**
- Estate Concordia Studios **9**
- Garden by the Sea Bed & Breakfast **1**
- Harmony Studios **8**
- The Inn at Tamarind Court **3**
- Maho Bay Camps **7**
- St. John Inn **2**
- Westin Resort St. John **4**

↖ Beach

Atlantic Ocean

Caribbean Sea

Long Point

East End

Blackrock Hill

Nancy Hill

East End Bay

Privateer Bay

Round Bay

Hanlover Bay

Brown Bay

More Hill

Hurricane Hole

Leinster Hill

Watermelon Cay Beach

Leinster Bay

Ajax Peak

Coral Bay

Sanders Bay

Calabash

Salt Pond Peninsula

Drunk Bay

Minna Hill

Salt Pond Bay

Mary Point

Francis Bay Beach

Maho Bay

Cinnamon Bay

Leinster Bay

Mamey Peak

King Hill

Bordeaux Mountain

Lameshur Bay Beach

Coral Harbour

VIRGIN ISLANDS NATIONAL PARK

Reef Bay

Camelberg Peak

Trunk Bay

Peter Peak

Francis Bay

Fish Bay

Hawksnest Beach

Gifft Hill

Gifft Hill Rd.

Margaret Hill

Rendezvous Bay

Southside Rd.

Roman Hill

Chocolate Hole

Caneel Bay

Caneel Bay Beach

Soloman Bay Beach

Great Cruz Bay

Cruz Bay

North Shore Rd.

Center Line Rd.

East End Rd.

King Hill Rd.

Bordeaux Mtn. Rd.

Center Line Rd.

Caneel Bay

10

20

7

8

10

10

20

104

107

9

10

6

5

1 Mile

1 Kilometer

753

tip. Don't come here for nightlife, though: St. John is definitely sleepy, and that's why people love it.

To get to St. John, you first pass through St. Thomas, then take the ferry. (There are also ferries from the British Virgin Islands.) See the "Getting There" section at the beginning of this chapter for information on how to get to St. Thomas.

ST. JOHN ESSENTIALS

VISITOR INFORMATION The **tourist office** (© **340/776-6450**) is located near the Battery, a 1735 fort that's a short walk from the St. Thomas ferry dock. It's open Monday to Friday from 8am to 1pm and 2 to 5pm. A **National Park Visitors Center** (© **340/776-6201**) is also found at Cruz Bay, offering two floors of information and wall-mounted wildlife displays, plus a video presentation about the culture of the Virgin Islands.

GETTING AROUND The most popular way to get around is by the local **Vitran** service, the same company that runs bus service on St. Thomas. Buses run between Cruz Bay and Coral Bay, costing $1 for adults and 75¢ for children.

An open-air **surrey-style taxi** is more fun, however. Typical fares are $9 to Trunk Bay, $12 to Cinnamon Bay, or $18 to Maho Bay. Between midnight and 6am, fares are increased by 40%. Call © **340/693-7530** for more information.

The island's undeveloped roads offer some of the best views anywhere. Because of this, many people opt to rent a vehicle (sometimes with four-wheel drive) to tour the island. Most visitors need a car for only a day or two. Just remember to *drive on the left* and follow posted speed limits, which are generally very low.

Unless you need to port around luggage, which should probably be locked away in a trunk, you might consider one of the sturdy, open-sided, Jeep-like vehicles that offer the best view of the surroundings and the most fun way to tour St. John. Note that most of these vehicles have manual transmission, which can be especially tricky in a car built to drive on the left side of the road.

The two largest car-rental agencies on St. John are **Hertz** (© **800/654-3131** in the U.S., or 340/693-7580; www.hertz.com) and **Avis** (© **800/331-1212** in the U.S., or 340/778-9355; www.avis.com). If you want a local firm, try **St. John Car Rental,** across from the post office in Cruz Bay (© **340/776-6103**).

FAST FACTS If you need a **pharmacy,** or want to purchase film, magazines, books, and other daily necessities, head to **St. John Drugcenter,** in the Boulon Shopping Center, Cruz Bay (© **340/776-6353**). It's open Monday to Saturday from 9am to 6pm and Sunday from 10am to 2pm.

If you need a **hospital,** go to **St. John Myrah Keating Smith Community Health Clinic,** 28 Sussanaberg (© **340/693-8900**), which can be reached along Route 10, 7 miles (11km) east of Cruz Bay.

ACCOMMODATIONS

There are actually more villa and condo beds available on St. John than there are hotel beds. These units offer spaciousness and comfort, as well as privacy and freedom, and they often come with fully equipped kitchens, dining areas, bedrooms, and such amenities as VCRs and patio grills. Rentals range from large multiroom resort homes to simply decorated one-bedroom condos. In addition to the condo and villa complexes reviewed below, **Caribbean Villas & Resorts** (© **800/338-0987** in the U.S., or 340/776-6152; fax 340/779-4044), the island's biggest real-estate agency, is an excellent choice. Most condos go for around $200 per night, though private homes are more expensive.

VERY EXPENSIVE

Caneel Bay ★★★   Conceived by megamillionaire Laurance S. Rockefeller in 1956, this is the Caribbean's first eco-resort. Though it's long been one of the premier resorts of the Caribbean, Caneel Bay is definitely not one of the most luxurious. A devoted fan once told us, "It's like living at summer camp." That means no phones or TVs in the rooms. Nevertheless, the movers and shakers of the world continue to descend on this place, though younger people tend to head elsewhere. To attract more families, young children are now allowed here. Go to Westin Resort St. John (see below) for the glitz and glitter; head here for a touch of class.

The resort lies on a 170-acre (68-hectare) portion of the National Park, offering a choice of seven beaches. Surrounded by lush greenery, the main buildings are strung along the bays, with a Caribbean lounge and dining room at the core. Other buildings housing guest rooms stand along the beaches. Try to get one of the six rooms in cottage no. 7, overlooking two of the most idyllic beaches, Scott and Paradise. Most rooms, however, are set back on low cliffs or headlands. The decor within is understated, with Indonesian wicker furniture, hand-woven fabrics, sisal mats, and plantation fans. All have neatly kept bathrooms with showers.

The resort has consistently maintained a high level of cuisine, often quite formal for the laid-back Caribbean. In recent years the food has been considerably improved and modernized, and the menus now include more variety and more healthy choices (see "Dining," below).

Virgin Islands National Park, St. John, U.S.V.I. 00831. © **340/776-6111.** Fax 340/693-8280. www.caneel bay.com. 166 units. Winter $450–$1,100 double. Off-season $300–$700 double. MAP (breakfast and dinner) $90 per person extra. 1 child under age 16 can stay free in parents' room. AE, DC, MC, V. **Amenities:** 3 restaurants, 2 bars; 11 tennis courts; fitness center; boating, dive shop, snorkeling, windsurfing, kayaking, deep-sea fishing; children's play area; babysitting; laundry. *In room:* A/C, minibar, coffeemaker, hair dryer, no phone.

Westin Resort St. John ★★★   Come here if you like megaresort flash and glitter as opposed to the "old-school ties" of Caneel Bay. Madonna would check in here; Walter Kronkite would prefer Caneel Bay. This is the most architecturally dramatic and visually appealing hotel on St. John. The complex is set on 34 gently sloping, intricately landscaped acres (14 hectares) on the southwest side of the island. It consists of 13 cedar-roofed postmodern buildings, each with ziggurat-shaped angles, soaring ceilings, and large windows. Herringbone-patterned brick walkways connect the gardens (with 400 palms imported from Puerto Rico) with the 1,200-foot (360m) white-sand beach and the largest pool in the Virgin Islands. Some of the stylish accommodations contain fan-shaped windows and curved ceilings. Most units open onto private balconies, and some have their own whirlpools. All bedrooms have full, deluxe bathrooms.

Cuisine is more versatile here than at Caneel Bay, but it's not always as good. Expect nouvelle cuisine, buffets, and even New York deli sandwiches.

Great Cruz Bay, St. John, U.S.V.I. 00831. © **800/808-5020** in the U.S., or 340/693-8000. Fax 340/693-8888. www.westinresortstjohn.com. 349 units. Winter $379–$559 double; $939–$1,139 suite. Off-season $249–$500 double; $525–$929 suite. AE, DISC, DC, MC, V. Round-trip shuttle bus and private ferryboat transfers from St. Thomas airport $65 per person. **Amenities:** 4 restaurants, 3 bars; pool; 6 tennis courts; fitness center; dive shop, sailboats, windsurfing, snorkeling, fishing; children's programs, 24-hr. room service; babysitting; laundry. *In room:* A/C, TV, minibar, coffeemaker, hair dryer, iron and ironing board, safe.

MODERATE/EXPENSIVE

Estate Concordia Studios   This environmentally sensitive 51-acre (20-hectare) development has been widely praised for its integration with the local ecosystem. Its elevated structures were designed to coexist with the stunning southern edge of St. John. The secluded property is nestled on a low cliff above a salt pond, surrounded by hundreds of acres of pristine National Park. It's best for those with rental vehicles. Each building was designed to protect mature trees and is connected to its neighbors with boardwalks. The nine studios are contained in six postmodern cottages. Each unit has a kitchen, a shower-only bathroom, a balcony, and a ceiling fan; some have an extra bedroom. On-site management assists with activity suggestions. For information on the on-site **Eco-Tents,** refer to "Campgrounds," below.

20–27 Estate Concordia, Coral Bay, St. John, U.S.V.I. 00830. ⓒ **800/392-9004** in the U.S. and Canada, or 212/472-9453 in New York City. Fax 212/861-6210 in New York City. www.maho.org. 9 units. Winter $135–$190 studio for 2. Off-season $95–$150 studio for 2. Extra person $25 in winter, $15 in off-season. MC, V. **Amenities:** Pool; laundry. *In room:* Ceiling fan, kitchenette, no phone.

Garden by the Sea Bed & Breakfast ★ *Finds*

Overlooking the ocean, this little B&B lies a 10-minute walk south from the little port Cruz Bay. It has easy access to the north shore beaches and lies between Frank and Turner Bays. From the gardens of the house, a 1-minute path along Audubon Pond leads to Frank Bay Beach. Be sure to reserve a room ahead, as it offers only three bedrooms. Each bedroom features elephant bamboo canopy beds, Japanese fountains, hardwood floors, and well-kept bathrooms with shower stalls. Artifacts from around the world have been used to furnish the units. Don't expect phones or TVs, as this is a getaway, not a communications center. The 1970s house is designed in a Caribbean gingerbread style with cathedral beamed ceilings. Breakfast is served on the veranda (try the homemade muffins and quiche).

P.O. Box 1469 Cruz Bay, St. John, U.S.V.I. ⓒ 340/779-4731. www.gardenbythesea.com. 3 units. Winter $180–$200 double. Off-season $130–$150 double. No credit cards. *In room:* Ceiling fan, no phone.

Harmony Studios ★

Built on a hillside above the Maho Bay Camps, this is a small-scale cluster of 12 luxury studios in 6 two-story houses with views sweeping down to the sea. The complex is designed to combine both ecological technology and comfort; it's one of the few resorts in the Caribbean to operate exclusively on sun and wind power. Most of the building materials are derived from recycled materials, including reconstituted plastic and glass containers, newsprint, old tires, and scrap lumber. The managers and staff are committed to offering educational experiences, as well as the services of a small-scale resort. The studios contain tiled shower-only bathrooms, kitchenettes, dining areas, and outdoor terraces. Guests can walk a short distance downhill to use the restaurant, grocery store, and watersports facilities at the Maho Bay Camps.

P.O. Box 310, Cruz Bay, St. John, U.S.V.I. 00831. ⓒ **800/392-9004** in the U.S. and Canada, 212/472-9453 in New York City, or 340/776-6226. Fax 340/776-6504, or 212/861-6210 in New York City. www.maho.org. 12 units. Winter $185–$210 studio for 2. Off-season $110–$140 studio for 2. Extra person $25. 7-night minimum stay in winter. AE, DISC, MC, V. **Amenities:** Restaurant; windsurfing, sailing; snorkeling. *In room:* Ceiling fan, no phone.

INEXPENSIVE

The following places offer just the basics, but they're fine if you're not too finicky.

The Inn at Tamarind Court

Right outside Cruz Bay but still within walking distance of the ferryboat dock, this modest place consists of a small hotel and an even simpler West Indian inn. Bedrooms are small, evoking those in a little country motel. Most have twin beds. Shower-only bathrooms in the inn are shared; units in the hotel have small private bathrooms. The social life here revolves around its courtyard bar and the in-house restaurant under the same name. From the hotel, you can walk to shuttles that take you to the beaches.

South Shore Rd. (P.O. Box 350), Cruz Bay, St. John, U.S.V.I. 00831. ☏ 800/221-1637 or 340/776-6378. Fax 340/776-6722. www.tamarindcourt.com. 20 units, 14 with bathroom. Winter $108 double; $138 apt.; $158 suite. Off-season $78 double; $98 apt.; $128 suite. Rates include continental breakfast. AE, DISC, MC, V. **Amenities:** Restaurant, bar. *In room:* Ceiling fan, no phone.

St. John Inn *Value*   The old Cruz Inn, once the budget staple of the island, enjoys a new lease on life. Although its rates have gone up, it has also been much improved. The inn overlooks Enighed Pond, only a few blocks from the Cruz Bay dock area. Accommodations have a light, airy, California feel. The small- to medium-size bedrooms have wrought-iron beds, handcrafted pine armoires, and a touch of Ralph Lauren flair to make for an inviting nest. The junior suites have full sofa beds, kitchenettes, and sitting areas. Shower-only bathrooms are small.

P.O. Box 37, Cruz Bay, St. John, U.S.V.I. 00831. ☏ 800/666-7688 in the U.S., or 340/693-8688. Fax 340/693-9900. www.stjohninn.com. 13 units. Winter $120–$195 double. Off-season $70–$120 double. Extra person $15. AE, DISC, MC, V. **Amenities:** Bar; pool. *In room:* A/C, TV, fridge, coffeemaker, hair dryer on request.

CAMPGROUNDS

Cinnamon Bay Campground ✦   This National Park Service campground is the most complete in the Caribbean. The site is directly on the beach, surrounded by thousands of acres of tropical vegetation. Life is simple here: You have a choice of a tent, a cottage, or a bare site. At the bare campsites, you basically get just the site, with no fancy extras. Each canvas tent is 10 by 14 feet (3 by 4m) and has a floor as well as a number of extras, including all cooking equipment; your linen is even changed weekly. Each cottage is 15 by 15 feet (5 by 5m), consisting of a room with two concrete walls and two screen walls. Each cottage contains cooking facilities and four twin beds with thin mattresses; two cots can be added. Lavatories and cool-water showers are in separate buildings nearby. Camping is limited to a 2-week period in any given year.

P.O. Box 720, Cruz Bay, St. John, U.S.V.I. 00831. ☏ 340/776-6330. Fax 340/776-6458. www.cinnamon-bay.com. 126 units, none with bathroom. Winter $110 cottage for 2; $80 tent site; $25 bare site. Off-season $70 cottage for 2; $58 tent site; $25 bare site. Extra person $17. AE, MC, V. **Amenities:** Restaurant; grocery store; snorkeling; hiking; sailing; windsurfing; no phone.

Concordia Eco-Tents   This is the newest addition to Stanley Selengut's celebrated Concordia development project on the southern tip of St. John, overlooking Salt Pond Bay and Ram Head Point. These solar- and wind-powered tent-cottages combine sustainable technology with some of the most spectacular views on the island. The light framing, fabric walls, and large screened-in windows lend a tree-house atmosphere to guests' experience. Set on the windward side of the island, the tent-cottages enjoy natural ventilation from the cooling trade winds. Inside, each has two twin beds with rather thin mattresses in each bedroom, one or two twin mattresses on a loft platform, and a queen-size futon in the living-room area (each unit can sleep up to six people comfortably). Each kitchen is equipped with a running-water sink, propane stove, and cooler. In addition, each Eco-Tent has a small private shower, rather meager towels, and a composting toilet. The secluded hillside location, surrounded by hundreds of acres of pristine National Park land, requires guests to arrange for a rental vehicle. Beaches, hikes, and the shops and restaurants of Coral Bay are only a 10-minute drive from the property. (If you're interested in regular on-site studios, see Estate Concordia Studios, above.)

20–27 Estate Concordia, Coral Bay, St. John, U.S.V.I. 00830. ☏ 800/392-9004 or 212/472-9453 for reservations. Fax 212/861-6210. www.maho.org. 11 tent-cottages. Winter $120 tent for 2. Off-season $75–$85 tent for 2. Extra person $25 in winter, $15 in off-season. AE, DISC, MC, V. **Amenities:** Pool, no phone.

Maho Bay Camps ⭐ Right on Maho Bay, this is an interesting concept in ecology vacationing, where you camp close to nature, but with considerable comfort. It's set on a hillside above the beach surrounded by the Virgin Islands National Park. To preserve the existing ground cover, all 114 tent-cottages are on platforms, above a thickly wooded slope. Utility lines and pipes are hidden under wooden boardwalks and stairs. Each tent-cottage, covered with canvas and screens, has two twin beds with thin mattresses, a couch, electric lamps and outlets, a dining table, chairs, a propane stove, an ice chest (cooler), linen, thin towels, and cooking and eating utensils. Guests share communal bathhouses. Maho Bay Camps is more intimate and slightly more luxurious than its nearest competitor, Cinnamon Bay.

P.O. Box 310, Cruz Bay, St. John, U.S.V.I. 00831. © 800/392-9004, 212/472-9453 in New York City, or 340/776-6226. Fax 340/776-6504, or 212/861-6210 in New York City. www.maho.org. 114 tent-cottages, none with bathroom. Winter $108–$123 tent-cottage for 2 (minimum stay of 7 nights). Off-season $75 tent-cottage for 2. Extra person $15. AE, DISC, MC, V. **Amenities:** Restaurant; snorkeling; walking tours; sailing; windsurfing; no phone.

DINING

St. John has some posh dining, particularly at the luxury resorts like Caneel Bay, but it also has West Indian establishments with plenty of local color and flavor. Many of the restaurants here command high prices, but you can lunch almost anywhere at reasonable rates. Dinner is often an event on St. John, since it's about the only form of nightlife the island has.

EXPENSIVE

Asolare ⭐ FRENCH/ASIAN This is the most beautiful and elegant restaurant on St. John, with the hippest and best-looking staff. It sits on a hill overlooking Cruz Bay and some of the British Virgin Islands. *Asolare* translates as "the leisurely passing of time without purpose," and that's what many diners prefer to do here. The chef roams the world for inspiration, and cooks with flavor and flair, using some of the best and freshest ingredients available on island. To begin, try the grilled Asian barbecued shrimp and scallion wonton or the marinated vegetable spring rolls. For a main course, you might be tempted by crispy Peking duckling with sesame glaze or the peppercorn dusted filet of beef. Two truly excellent dishes are the lime-sautéed chicken with yellow curry sauce and sashimi tuna on a sizzling plate with plum-passion fruit-sake vinaigrette. For dessert, try the frozen mango guava soufflé or chocolate pyramid cake.

Cruz Bay. © 340/779-4747. Reservations required. Main courses $27–$35. AE, MC, V. Daily 5:30–9pm.

Ellington's ⭐ CONTINENTAL This restaurant is set near the neocolonial villas of Gallows Point, to the right after you disembark from the ferry. Its exterior has the kind of double staircase, fan windows, louvers, and low-slung roof found in an 18th-century Danish manor house. Drop in at sunset for a drink on the panoramic upper deck, where an unsurpassed view of St. Thomas and its neighboring cays unfolds. The dinner menu changes often, to accommodate the freshest offerings of the sea. Brie in a puff pastry or toasted ravioli might get you started, or else you could opt for one of the soups—none finer than a Caribbean seafood chowder. For a main course, we always go for the Caribbean mixed grill, with lobster, shrimp, and fresh fish grilled to perfection. Blackened swordfish and wahoo or mahi-mahi with Cajun spices are also excellent choices, as are the pastas. Live music is featured nightly.

Gallows Point, Cruz Bay. © 340/693-8490. Reservations required only for seating upstairs. Main courses $13–$45. AE, MC, V. Daily 4:30–10pm.

Equator ✿ CARIBBEAN This restaurant lies behind the tower of an 18th-century sugar mill, where ponds with water lilies fill former crystallization pits for hot molasses. A flight of stairs leads to a monumental circular dining room, with a wraparound veranda and sweeping views of a park. In the center rises the stone column that horses and mules once circled to crush sugarcane stalks. In its center the restaurant grows a giant poinciana-like Asian tree of the *Albizia lebbeck* species. Islanders call it "woman's tongue tree."

The cuisine is the most daring on the island, and for the most part, the chefs pull off their transcultural dishes. A spicy and tantalizing opener is lemon grass and ginger cured salmon salad (get *Gourmet* magazine on the phone). A classic Caribbean callaloo soup is offered, and the salads use fresh ingredients such as roma tomatoes and endive. Daily Caribbean selections are offered, or you can opt for such fine dishes as seared Caribbean mahi-mahi with a lentil or pumpkin mélange, or penne pasta with shiitake mushrooms and roasted tomatoes in an herb garlic cream sauce. There's always a dry, aged Angus steak or a grilled veal chop for the more traditional palate.

In the Caneel Bay hotel, Caneel Bay. ✆ 340/776-6111. Reservations required. Main courses $22–$32. Dec 15–Jan 10 daily 6:30–9pm. The rest of the year Wed–Thurs and Sun 6:30–9pm.

Le Château de Bordeaux ✿ CONTINENTAL/CARIBBEAN This restaurant is 5 miles (8km) east of Cruz Bay, near the geographical center of the island and close to one of its highest points. It's known for having some of the best views on St. John. A lunch grill on the patio serves burgers and drinks daily from 10am to 4:30pm. In the evening, amid the Victorian decor and lace tablecloths, you can begin with a house-smoked chicken spring roll or velvety carrot soup. After that, move on to one of the saffron-flavored pastas or savory West Indian seafood chowder. Smoked salmon and filet mignon are a bow to the international crowd, and the wild-game specials are more unusual. The well-flavored Dijon mustard and pecan-crusted roast rack of lamb with shallot port reduction is also a good choice. For dessert, there's a changing array of cheesecakes, among other options.

Junction 10, Centerline Rd., Bordeaux Mountain. ✆ 340/776-6611. Reservations recommended. Main courses $22–$36. AE, MC, V. Cash only for lunch. Daily 11am–3pm. Daily 2 nightly seatings, 5:30–6:30pm and 8–9pm. Closed Sun–Mon in summer.

Paradiso ✿✿ CONTEMPORARY/AMERICAN This is the most talked-about restaurant on St. John, other than Asolare (see above), and it's the only one that's air-conditioned. The interior has lots of brass, glowing hardwoods, and nautical antiques, not to mention the most beautiful bar on the island, crafted from mahogany, purpleheart, and angelique.

Try such appetizers as grilled chicken spring rolls with roasted sweet peppers. Roasted garlic Caesar salad with sun-dried tomatoes and Parmesan grizzini is a new twist on this classic dish. But the chefs truly shine in their main dishes, especially pan-roasted sea bass with baby beets and cannelloni, or grilled pork tenderloin with shiitake mushrooms, leeks, and a champagne truffle vinaigrette. Even chicken breast is given new zest and flair, stuffed with prosciutto, Asiago cheese, and basil, and served with garlic mashed potatoes.

Mongoose Junction. ✆ 340/693-8899. Reservations recommended. Main courses $24–$32. AE, MC, V. Daily 5:30–9:30pm. Bar daily 5–10:30pm.

MODERATE

Café Roma ITALIAN This restaurant in the center of Cruz Bay is not a place for great finesse in the kitchen, but it's a longtime favorite, and has pleased a lot of diners who just want a casual meal. To enter, you have to climb a flight of stairs. You might arrive early and have a strawberry colada, then enjoy a standard pasta, veal, seafood, or chicken dish. There are usually 30 to 40 vegetarian items on the menu. The owner claims, with justification, that his pizzas are the best on the island; try the white pizza. Italian wines are sold by the glass or bottle, and you can end the evening with an espresso.

Cruz Bay. ✆ 340/776-6524. Main courses $10–$22. MC, V. Wed–Mon 5–10pm.

La Tapa INTERNATIONAL   This is one of our favorite restaurants in Cruz Bay, where you can sample the *tapas,* Spanish-inspired bite-size morsels of fish, meat, or marinated vegetables, accompanied by pitchers of sangria. There's a tiny bar with no more than five stools, a two-tiered dining room, and lots of original paintings (the establishment doubles as an art gallery for emerging local artists). Menu items are thoughtful and well conceived, and include fast-seared tuna with a Basque-inspired relish of onions, peppers, garlic, and herbs; filet "poivre," a steak soaked with rum, served with a cracked pepper sauce and mashed potatoes; and linguine with shrimp, red peppers, and leeks in peanut sauce. Live jazz is offered on Monday nights.

Centerline Road, across from Scotia Bank, Cruz Bay. ✆ 340/693-7755. Reservations recommended. Tapas from $4; main courses $19–$27. AE, MC, V. Fri–Wed 5:30–10pm.

Mongoose Restaurant/North Shore Deli AMERICAN   There's a hint of New Age California at this popular deli and outdoor restaurant, whose setting is soothing, woodsy, and very tropical. The to-go service at the deli provides one of the best sandwich options on St. John. There's a cluster of wooden tables near the deli, so you can also eat here. Breads are baked fresh every day.

More substantial, and more esoteric, fare is served in the restaurant, where the vegetation of a tropical forest extends up to the deck, and where a high roof and a lack of walls give the impression of eating outdoors. You can always precede or end a meal at the center-stage bar. Perennially popular drinks include rum-and-fruit-based painkillers and a dessert-inspired "chocolate chiquita" (rum, bananas, and chocolate ice cream). The lunch menu includes quesadillas, burgers, grilled chicken, and blackened tuna sandwiches. At dinner, try fresh grilled or sautéed fish, served with a salsa made from local fruits; curried shrimp; blackened snapper with a Caribbean salsa; and lots of vegetarian options as well.

Mongoose Junction. ✆ 340/693-8677. Sandwiches in deli $5–$9. Main courses in restaurant $5–$12 at lunch, $12–$30 at dinner. AE, DISC, MC, V. Deli daily 7am–9pm; Mon–Sat 8:30am–9pm, Sun 10am–9pm.

Morgan's Mango CARIBBEAN   The chefs here roam the Caribbean for tantalizing flavors, which they adapt for their ever-changing menu. The restaurant is easy to spot, with its big canopy, the only protection from the elements. The bar wraps around the main dining room and offers some 30 frozen drinks. Some think the kitchen tries to do too much with the nightly menu, but it does produce some zesty fare—everything from Anegada lobster cakes to spicy Jamaican pickapepper steak. Try flying fish served as an appetizer, followed by Haitian voodoo snapper pressed in Cajun spices, then grilled and served with fresh fruit salsa. Equally delectable is mahi-mahi in Cruzan rum-and-mango sauce. The knockout dessert is the mango-banana pie.

Cruz Bay (across from the National Park dock). ✆ 340/693-8141. Reservations recommended. Main courses $8–$25. AE, MC, V. Daily 5:30–10pm. Bar opens at 5pm.

Shipwreck Landing SEAFOOD/CONTINENTAL   Eight miles (13km) east of Cruz Bay on the road to Salt Pond Beach, Shipwreck Landing offers palms and tropical plants on a veranda overlooking the sea. The intimate bar specializes in tropical frozen drinks. Lunch isn't ignored here, and there's a lot more than sandwiches, salads, and burgers—try pan-seared blackened snapper in Cajun spices, or try conch fritters. The chef shines brighter at night, though, offering a pasta of the day along with such specialties as tantalizing Caribbean blackened shrimp. A lot of the fare is routine, including New York strip steak and fish-and-chips, but the grilled mahi-mahi in lime butter is worth the trip. Entertainment, including jazz and rock, is featured Wednesday and Sunday nights, with no cover.

34 Freeman's Ground, Rte. 107, Coral Bay. © **340/693-5640**. Reservations requested. Main courses $8–$22; lunch from $6–$14. AE, DISC, MC, V. Daily 11am–10pm. Bar daily 11am–11pm.

INEXPENSIVE

Vie's Snack Shack ★ *Finds* WEST INDIAN   Vie's looks like little more than a plywood-sided hut, but its charming and gregarious owner is known as one of the best local chefs on St. John. Her garlic chicken is famous. She also serves conch fritters, johnnycakes, island-style beef pâtés, and coconut and pineapple tarts. Don't leave without a glass of homemade limeade. The place is open most days, but as Vie says, "Some days, we might not be here at all"—so you'd better call before you head out.

East End Rd. (12½ miles/20km east of Cruz Bay). © **340/693-5033**. Main courses $8–$14. No credit cards. Tues–Sat 10am–5pm (but call first!).

HITTING THE BEACH

The best beach, hands down, is **Trunk Bay** ★★, the biggest attraction on St. John. To miss its picture-perfect shoreline of white sand would be like touring Paris and skipping the Eiffel Tower. One of the loveliest beaches in the Caribbean, it offers ideal conditions for diving, snorkeling, swimming, and sailing. The only drawback is the crowds (watch for pickpockets). Beginning snorkelers in particular are attracted to the underwater trail near the shore (see "Sports & Other Outdoor Pursuits," below); you can rent snorkeling gear here. Lifeguards are on duty. Admission is $4 per person for those over age 16. If you're coming from St. Thomas, both taxis and "safari buses" to Trunk Bay meet the ferry from Red Hook when it docks at Cruz Bay.

   Caneel Bay, the stamping ground of the rich and famous, has seven beautiful beaches on its 170 acres (68 hectares), and all are open to the public. **Caneel Bay Beach** is open to everyone and easy to reach from the main entrance of the Caneel Bay resort. A staff member at the gatehouse will provide directions. **Hawksnest Beach** is one of the most beautiful beaches near the Caneel Bay properties. It's not a wide beach, but it is choice. Since it lies near Cruz Bay, where the ferry docks, it is the most overpopulated, especially when cruise ship passengers come over from St. Thomas. Safari buses and taxis from Cruz Bay will take you along Northshore Road.

   The campgrounds of **Cinnamon Bay** have their own beach, where forest rangers sometimes have to remind visitors to put their swim trunks back on. This is our particular favorite, a beautiful strip of white sand with hiking trails, great windsurfing, ruins, and wild donkeys (don't feed or pet them!). Changing rooms and showers are available, and you can rent watersports equipment. Snorkeling is especially popular; you'll often see big schools of purple triggerfish. This beach is best in the morning and at midday, as afternoons are likely to be windy. A marked **nature trail,** with signs identifying the flora, loops through a tropical forest on even turf before leading straight up to Centerline Road.

   Maho Bay Beach is immediately to the east of Cinnamon Bay, and it also borders campgrounds. As you lie on the sand here, you can take in a whole hillside of pitched tents. This is also a popular beach, often with the campers themselves.

Francis Bay Beach and **Watermelon Cay Beach** are just a few more of the beaches you'll encounter traveling eastward along St. John's gently curving coastline. The beach at **Leinster Bay** is another haven for those seeking the solace of a private sunny retreat. You can swim in the bay's shallow water or snorkel over the spectacular and colorful coral reef, perhaps in the company of an occasional turtle or stingray.

The remote **Salt Pond Bay** is known to locals but often missed by visitors. It's on the beautiful coast in the southeast, adjacent to **Coral Bay.** The bay is tranquil, but the beach is somewhat rocky. It's a short walk down the hill from a parking lot (*Beware:* a few cars have recently been broken into). The snorkeling is good, and the bay has some fascinating tidal pools. The Ram Head Trail begins here and, winding for a mile (2km), leads to a belvedere overlooking the bay. Facilities are meager but include an outhouse and a few tattered picnic tables.

If you want to escape the crowds, head for **Lameshur Bay Beach,** along the rugged south coast, west of Salt Pond Bay and accessible only via a bumpy dirt road. The sands are beautiful and the snorkeling is excellent. You can also take a 5-minute stroll down the road past the beach to explore the nearby ruins of an old plantation estate that was destroyed in a slave revolt.

Does St. John have a nude beach? Not officially, but lovely **Solomon Bay Beach** is a contender, although park rangers of late have sometimes asked people to put their swimwear back on. Leave Cruz Bay on Route 20 and turn left at the park service sign, about a ¼ mile (.4km) past the visitor center. Park at the end of a cul-de-sac, then walk along the trail for about 15 minutes. Go early, and you'll practically have the beach to yourself.

SPORTS & OTHER OUTDOOR PURSUITS ★★

St. John offers some of the best snorkeling, scuba diving, swimming, fishing, hiking, sailing, and underwater photography in the Caribbean. The island is known for the Virgin Islands National Park, as well as for its coral-sand beaches, winding mountain roads, hidden coves, and trails that lead past old, bush-covered sugarcane plantations. Just don't visit St. John expecting to play golf.

The most complete line of watersports equipment available, including rentals for windsurfing, snorkeling, kayaking, and sailing, is offered at the **Cinnamon Bay Watersports Center,** on Cinnamon Bay Beach (© **340/776-6330**). One- and two-person sit-on-top kayaks rent for $14 to $20 per hour. You can also sail away in a 12- or 14-foot (4m) Hobie monohull **sailboat,** for $30 to $35 per hour.

BOAT EXCURSIONS You can take half- and full-day boat trips, including a full-day excursion to the Baths at Virgin Gorda, for $95. A snorkel excursion on St. John costs $55 per person. Call **Vacation Vistas and Motor Yachts** (© **340/ 776-6462**) for details. **Cruz Bay Watersports** (© **340/776-6234**), offers trips to the British Virgin Islands (bring your passport) for $90, including food and beverages. British Customs fees are another $15.

FISHING Outfitters located on St. Thomas offer sport-fishing trips here— they'll come over and pick you up. Call the **St. Thomas Sportfishing Center** (© **340/775-7990**) at Red Hook. Count on spending from $400 to $550 per party for a half day of fishing.

HIKING St. John has the most rewarding hiking in the Virgin Islands. The terrain ranges from arid and dry (in the east) to moist and semitropical (in the northwest). The island boasts more than 800 species of plants, 160 species of birds, and more than 20 trails maintained in fine form by the island's crew of park rangers. Much of the land on the island is designated as **Virgin Island's National Park.** Visitors are encouraged to stop by the **Cruz Bay Visitor Center,** where you can pick up the park brochure, which includes a map of the park, and the *Virgin Islands National Park News,* which has the latest information on park activities. It's important to carry a lot of water and wear sunscreen and insect repellent when you hike.

St. John is laced with a wide choice of clearly marked walking paths. At least 20 of these originate from Northshore Road (Route 20) or from the island's main east–west artery, Centerline Road (Route 10). Each is marked at its starting point with a preplanned itinerary; the walks can last anywhere from 10 minutes to 2 hours. Maps are available from the national park headquarters at Cruz Bay.

One of our favorite hikes, the **Annaberg Historic Trail** (identified by the U.S. National Park Service as trail no. 10), requires only about a ½-mile (.8km) stroll. It departs from a clearly marked point along the island's north coast, near the junction of routes 10 and 20. This self-guided tour passes the partially restored ruins of a manor house built during the 1700s. Signs along the way give historical and botanical data. Visiting the ruins costs $4 per person for those over age 16. If you want to prolong your hiking experience, take the **Leinster Bay Trail** (trail no. 11), which begins near the point where trail no. 10 ends. It leads past mangrove swamps and coral inlets rich with plant and marine life; markers identify some of the plants and animals.

Near the beach at **Cinnamon Bay,** there's a marked nature trail, with signs identifying the flora. It's a relatively flat walk through a tropical forest, eventually leading straight up to Centerline Road.

Another series of hikes traversing the more arid eastern section of St. John originates at clearly marked points along the island's **southeastern tip,** off Route 107. Many of the trails wind through the grounds of 18th-century plantations, past ruined schoolhouses, rum distilleries, molasses factories, and great houses, many of which are covered with lush, encroaching vines and trees.

The **National Park Service** (© 340/776-6201) provides a number of ranger-led activities. One of the most popular is the guided 2½-mile (4km) **Reef Bay Hike.** Included is a stop at the only known petroglyphs on the island and a tour of the sugar-mill ruins. A park ranger discusses the area's natural and cultural history along the way. The hike starts at 10am on Monday, Thursday, and Friday, and costs $15 per person. Reservations are required and can be made by phone.

SCUBA DIVING & SNORKELING ★★   Cruz Bay Watersports, P.O. Box 252, Palm Plaza, St. John (© 340/776-6234), is a PADI and NAUI five-star diving center. Certifications can be arranged through a dive master, for $350. Beginner scuba lessons start at $95. Two-tank reef dives with all dive gear cost $85, and wreck dives, night dives, and dive packages are available. In addition, snorkel tours are offered daily.

Divers can ask about scuba packages at **Low Key Watersports,** Wharfside Village (© 800/835-7718 in the U.S., or 340/693-8999). All wreck dives offered are two-tank/two-location dives. One-tank dives cost $80 per person, with night dives going for $70. Snorkel tours are also available at $35 to $75 per person. Parasailing costs $55 per person. The center also rents watersports gear, including masks, fins, snorkels, and dive skins, and arranges day sailing trips, kayaking tours, and deep-sea fishing.

The best place for snorkeling is **Trunk Bay** (see "Hitting the Beach," above). Snorkeling gear can be rented from the Cinnamon Bay Watersports Center (see

---

(Moments Underwater Wonderful

At Trunk Bay, for no charge you can take the **National Park Underwater Trail** (© **340/776-6201**), which stretches for 650 feet (195m) and helps you identify what you see—everything from false coral to colonial anemones. You'll pass lavender sea fans and schools of silversides. Rangers are on hand to provide information.

---

above) for $5, plus a $25 deposit. Two of the best **snorkeling spots** around St. John are **Leinster Bay** ★★ and **Haulover Bay** ★★. Usually uncrowded Leinster Bay offers some of the best snorkeling in the U.S. Virgins. The water is calm, clear, and filled with brilliantly hued tropical fish. Haulover Bay is a favorite among locals. It's often deserted, and the waters are often clearer than in other spots around St. John. The ledges, walls, and nooks here are set very close together, making the bay a lot of fun for anyone with a little bit of experience.

SEA KAYAKING Arawak Expeditions, based in Cruz Bay (© **800/ 238-8687** in the U.S., or 340/693-8312), provides kayaking gear, healthful meals, and experienced guides for full- and half-day outings. Trips cost $75 and $40, respectively. Multiday excursions with camping are also available; call their toll-free number if you'd like to arrange an entire vacation with them. These trips range in price from $995 to $1,295.

WINDSURFING   The windsurfing at Cinnamon Bay is some of the best anywhere, for either the beginner or the expert. The **Cinnamon Bay Watersports Center** (see above) rents high-quality equipment for all levels, even for kids. Boards cost $15 an hour; a 2-hour introductory lesson costs $45.

EXPLORING ST. JOHN

The best way to see St. John quickly, especially if you're on a cruise-ship layover, is to take a 2-hour **taxi tour.** The cost is $35 for one or two passengers, or $15 per person for three or more. Almost any taxi at Cruz Bay will take you on these tours, or you can call the **St. John Taxi Association** (© **340/693-7530**).

Many visitors spend time at **Cruz Bay,** where the ferry docks. This village has interesting bars, restaurants, boutiques, and pastel-painted houses. It's a bit sleepy, but relaxing after the fast pace of St. Thomas.

Most cruise-ship passengers dart through Cruz Bay and head for the island's biggest attraction, **Virgin Islands National Park** ★★ (© **340/776-6201**). The park totals 12,624 acres (5,050 hectares), including submerged lands and water adjacent to St. John, and has more than 20 miles (16km) of hiking trails to explore. See "Sports & Other Outdoor Pursuits," above, for information on trails and organized park activities.

Other major sights on the island include **Trunk Bay** (see "Hitting the Beach," above), one of the world's most beautiful beaches, and **Fort Berg** (also called Fortsberg), at Coral Bay, which served as the base for the soldiers who brutally crushed the 1733 slave revolt. Finally, try to make time for the **Annaberg Ruins** on Leinster Bay Road, where the Danes maintained a thriving plantation and sugar mill after 1718. It's located off Northshore Road, east of Trunk Bay. Admission is $4 for those over age 16. On certain days of the week (dates vary), guided walks of the area are given by park rangers. For information on the **Annaberg Historic Trail,** see "Sports & Other Outdoor Pursuits," above.

SHOPPING ★★

Compared to St. Thomas, St. John's shopping isn't much, but what's here is interesting. The boutiques and shops of Cruz Bay are individualized and quite special. Most of the shops are clustered at **Mongoose Junction,** in a woodsy area beside the roadway, about a 5-minute walk from the ferry dock. We've already recommended restaurants in this complex (see "Dining," earlier in this chapter).

Before you leave the island, you'll want to visit the recently expanded **Wharfside Village,** just a few steps from the ferry-departure point. Here in this complex of courtyards, alleys, and shady patios is a mishmash of all sorts of boutiques, along with some restaurants, fast-food joints, and bars.

Bamboula, Mongoose Junction (© 340/693-8699), has an exotic and very appealing collection of gifts from St. John, the Caribbean, India, Indonesia, and Central Africa. The store also has clothing for both men and women under its own label—hand-batiked soft cottons and rayons made for comfort in a hot climate.

The Canvas Factory, Mongoose Junction (© 340/776-6196), produces its own handmade, rugged, colorful canvas bags, as well as soft-sided luggage and cotton hats.

Clothing Studio, Mongoose Junction (© 340/776-6585), is the Caribbean's oldest hand-painted–clothing studio. Here you can watch talented artists create original designs on fine tropical clothing, including swimwear and daytime and evening clothing, mainly for women and babies, with a few items for men.

Coconut Coast Studios, Frank Bay (© 340/776-6944), is the studio of Elaine Estern, who's especially known for her Caribbean landscapes. It's located 5 minutes from Cruz Bay; walk along the waterfront, bypassing Gallows Point. The outlet also sells calendars, gifts, limited edition prints, and lithographs. From December to March, the studio hosts a free cocktail party Wednesday 5:30 to 7pm to celebrate the setting sun and to view the art for sale.

At the **Donald Schnell Studio,** Mongoose Junction (© 340/776-6420), Mr. Schnell and his assistants have created one of the finest collections of handmade pottery, sculpture, and blown glass in the Caribbean. The staff can be seen working daily. They're known for their rough-textured coral work. Water fountains are a specialty item, as are house signs and coral-pottery dinnerware.

The **Fabric Mill,** Mongoose Junction (© 340/776-6194), features silk-screened and batik fabrics from around the world. Vibrant rugs and bed, bathroom, and table linens can add a Caribbean flair to your home. Whimsical soft sculpture, sarongs, scarves, and handbags are also made here.

Tips The Best Shopping Day

The most fun shopping on the island takes place on **St. John Saturday** ★, a colorful, drum-beating, spice-filled feast for the senses, held on the last Saturday of every month. This daylong event begins early in the morning in the center of town and spills across the park. Vendors hawk handmade items, ranging from jewelry to handcrafts and clothing, and especially food made from local ingredients. One vendor concocts soothing salves from recipes passed on by her ancestors; another designs and makes porcelain earrings; another flavors chicken and burgers with her own wonderful secret hickory barbecue sauce; yet another hollows out and carves gourds from local calabash trees.

R and I Patton Goldsmithing, Mongoose Junction (© **340/776-6548**), is one of the oldest businesses on the island. Three-quarters of the merchandise here is made on St. John. There's a large selection of jewelry in sterling silver, gold, and precious stones. Also featured are the works of goldsmiths from outstanding American studios, as well as Spanish coins.

ST. JOHN AFTER DARK

Bring a good book. When it comes to nightlife, St. John is no St. Thomas, and everybody here seems to want to keep it that way. Most people are content to have a leisurely dinner and then head for bed.

Woody's Seafood Saloon, Cruz Bay (© **340/779-4625**), is the local dive and hangout at Cruz Bay, 50 yards (46m) from the ferry dock. It draws both visitors and a cross-section of island life from ex-pats to villa owners. Michigan-born Woody Mann, the bartender, is often compared to the character of the same name on the sitcom, "Cheers." You can come here to eat or drink. The place is particularly popular during happy hour from 3 to 6pm. It's about the only place on island you can order food at 10pm. Try the blackened fish sandwich. The joint jumps Sunday to Thursday 11am to 1am, Friday and Saturday 11am to 2am.

The **Caneel Bay Bar,** at the Caneel Bay resort (© **340/776-6111**), presents live music nightly from 8 to 10:30pm. The most popular drinks here include the Cool Caneel (local rum with sugar, lime, and anisette) and the trademark of the house, Plantation Punch (lime and orange juice with three different kinds of rum, bitters, and nutmeg).

The two places above are very touristy. If you'd like to drink and gossip with the locals, try **JJ's Texas Coast Café,** Cruz Bay (© **340/776-6908**), a real dive, across the park from the ferry dock. The margaritas here are lethal. Also at Cruz Bay, check out the action at **Fred's** (© **340/776-6363**), across from the Lime Inn. Fred's brings in bands and has dancing on Wednesday, Friday, and Sunday nights. It's just a little hole-in-the-wall and can get crowded fast.

The best sports bar on the island is **Skinny Legs,** Emmaus, Coral Bay, beyond the fire station (© **340/779-4982**). This shack made of tin and wood happens to have the best burgers in St. John. (The chili dogs aren't bad, either.) The yachting crowd likes to hang out here, though you wouldn't know it at first glance—it often seems that the richer they are, the poorer they dress. The bar has a satellite dish, dartboard, and horseshoe pits. Live music is presented on Saturday nights.

Morgan's Mango (© **340/693-8141**), a restaurant, is also one of the hottest watering holes on the island. It's in Cruz Bay, across from the National Park dock. Count yourself lucky if you get in on a crowded night in winter. The place became famous locally when it turned away Harrison Ford, who was vacationing at Caneel Bay. Thursday is Margarita Night.

Index

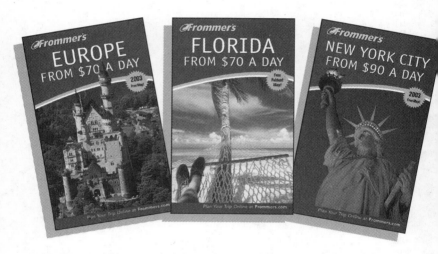

FROMMER'S® COMPLETE TRAVEL GUIDES

Alaska
Alaska Cruises & Ports of Call
Amsterdam
Argentina & Chile
Arizona
Atlanta
Australia
Austria
Bahamas
Barcelona, Madrid & Seville
Beijing
Belgium, Holland & Luxembourg
Bermuda
Boston
Brazil
British Columbia & the Canadian Rockies
Budapest & the Best of Hungary
California
Canada
Cancún, Cozumel & the Yucatán
Cape Cod, Nantucket & Martha's Vineyard
Caribbean
Caribbean Cruises & Ports of Call
Caribbean Ports of Call
Carolinas & Georgia
Chicago
China
Colorado
Costa Rica
Denmark
Denver, Boulder & Colorado Springs
England
Europe
European Cruises & Ports of Call
Florida

France
Germany
Great Britain
Greece
Greek Islands
Hawaii
Hong Kong
Honolulu, Waikiki & Oahu
Ireland
Israel
Italy
Jamaica
Japan
Las Vegas
London
Los Angeles
Maryland & Delaware
Maui
Mexico
Montana & Wyoming
Montréal & Québec City
Munich & the Bavarian Alps
Nashville & Memphis
Nepal
New England
New Mexico
New Orleans
New York City
New Zealand
Northern Italy
Nova Scotia, New Brunswick & Prince Edward Island
Oregon
Paris
Philadelphia & the Amish Country
Portugal
Prague & the Best of the Czech Republic

Provence & the Riviera
Puerto Rico
Rome
San Antonio & Austin
San Diego
San Francisco
Santa Fe, Taos & Albuquerque
Scandinavia
Scotland
Seattle & Portland
Shanghai
Singapore & Malaysia
South Africa
South America
South Florida
South Pacific
Southeast Asia
Spain
Sweden
Switzerland
Texas
Thailand
Tokyo
Toronto
Tuscany & Umbria
USA
Utah
Vancouver & Victoria
Vermont, New Hampshire & Maine
Vienna & the Danube Valley
Virgin Islands
Virginia
Walt Disney World & Orlando
Washington, D.C.
Washington State

FROMMER'S® DOLLAR-A-DAY GUIDES

Australia from $50 a Day
California from $70 a Day
Caribbean from $70 a Day
England from $75 a Day
Europe from $70 a Day

Florida from $70 a Day
Hawaii from $80 a Day
Ireland from $60 a Day
Italy from $70 a Day
London from $85 a Day

New York from $90 a Day
Paris from $80 a Day
San Francisco from $70 a Day
Washington, D.C. from $80 a Day

FROMMER'S® PORTABLE GUIDES

Acapulco, Ixtapa & Zihuatanejo
Amsterdam
Aruba
Australia's Great Barrier Reef
Bahamas
Baja & Los Cabos
Berlin
Boston
California Wine Country
Cancún
Charleston & Savannah
Chicago
Disneyland
Dublin
Florence

Frankfurt
Hawaii: The Big Island
Hong Kong
Houston
Las Vegas
London
Los Angeles
Maine Coast
Maui
Miami
New Orleans
New York City
Paris
Phoenix & Scottsdale

Portland
Puerto Rico
Puerto Vallarta, Manzanillo & Guadalajara
Rio de Janeiro
San Diego
San Francisco
Seattle
Sydney
Tampa & St. Petersburg
Vancouver
Venice
Virgin Islands
Washington, D.C.

FROMMER'S® NATIONAL PARK GUIDES

Banff & Jasper
Family Vacations in the National Parks
Grand Canyon

National Parks of the American West
Rocky Mountain

Yellowstone & Grand Teton
Yosemite & Sequoia/ Kings Canyon
Zion & Bryce Canyon

Frommer's® Memorable Walks

Chicago	New York	San Francisco
London	Paris	

Frommer's® Great Outdoor Guides

Arizona & New Mexico	Northern California	Vermont & New Hampshire
New England	Southern New England	

Suzy Gershman's Born to Shop Guides

Born to Shop: France	Born to Shop: Italy	Born to Shop: New York
Born to Shop: Hong Kong, Shanghai & Beijing	Born to Shop: London	Born to Shop: Paris

Frommer's® Irreverent Guides

Amsterdam	Los Angeles	San Francisco
Boston	Manhattan	Seattle & Portland
Chicago	New Orleans	Vancouver
Las Vegas	Paris	Walt Disney World
London	Rome	Washington, D.C.

Frommer's® Best-Loved Driving Tours

Britain	Germany	Northern Italy
California	Ireland	Scotland
Florida	Italy	Spain
France	New England	Tuscany & Umbria

Hanging Out™ Guides

Hanging Out in England	Hanging Out in France	Hanging Out in Italy
Hanging Out in Europe	Hanging Out in Ireland	Hanging Out in Spain

The Unofficial Guides®

Bed & Breakfasts and Country Inns in:	Southwest & South Central Plains	Mid-Atlantic with Kids
California	U.S.A.	Mini Las Vegas
Great Lakes States	Beyond Disney	Mini-Mickey
Mid-Atlantic	Branson, Missouri	New England and New York with Kids
New England	California with Kids	New Orleans
Northwest	Chicago	New York City
Rockies	Cruises	Paris
Southeast	Disneyland	San Francisco
Southwest	Florida with Kids	Skiing in the West
Best RV & Tent Campgrounds in:	Golf Vacations in the Eastern U.S.	Southeast with Kids
California & the West	Great Smoky & Blue Ridge Region	Walt Disney World
Florida & the Southeast	Inside Disney	Walt Disney World for Grown-ups
Great Lakes States	Hawaii	Walt Disney World with Kids
Mid-Atlantic	Las Vegas	Washington, D.C.
Northeast	London	World's Best Diving Vacations
Northwest & Central Plains		

Special-Interest Titles

Frommer's Adventure Guide to Australia & New Zealand	Frommer's Italy's Best Bed & Breakfasts and Country Inns
Frommer's Adventure Guide to Central America	Frommer's New York City with Kids
Frommer's Adventure Guide to India & Pakistan	Frommer's Ottawa with Kids
Frommer's Adventure Guide to South America	Frommer's Road Atlas Britain
Frommer's Adventure Guide to Southeast Asia	Frommer's Road Atlas Europe
Frommer's Adventure Guide to Southern Africa	Frommer's Road Atlas France
Frommer's Britain's Best Bed & Breakfasts and Country Inns	Frommer's Toronto with Kids
Frommer's Caribbean Hideaways	Frommer's Vancouver with Kids
Frommer's Exploring America by RV	Frommer's Washington, D.C., with Kids
Frommer's Fly Safe, Fly Smart	Israel Past & Present
Frommer's France's Best Bed & Breakfasts and Country Inns	The New York Times' Guide to Unforgettable Weekends
Frommer's Gay & Lesbian Europe	Places Rated Almanac
	Retirement Places Rated

America Online Keyword: Travel
Booked seat 6A, open return.
Rented red 4-wheel drive.
Reserved cabin, no running water.
Discovered space.
h over 700 airlines, 50,000 hotels, 50 rental car companies and
0 cruise and vacation packages, you can create the perfect get-
ay for you. Choose the car, the room, even the ground you walk on.
Travelocity.com
A Sabre Company
Go Virtually Anywhere.
Travelocity,® Travelocity.com® and the Travelocity skyline logo are trademarks and/or servicemarks of Travelocity.com L.P.,

You Need A Vacation.

700 Airlines, 50,000 Hotels, 50 Rental Car Companies, And A Million Ways To Save Money.

Travelocity.com
A Sabre Company
Go Virtually Anywhere.